# JESUS

## An Experiment in Christology

*Dedicated*
    *to all my readers –*
        *known and unknown –*
    *and especially*
    *Bernard Cardinal Alfrink*


*'That you may not grieve as others do
who have no hope' (1 Thess. 4: 13)*

# JESUS
## An Experiment in Christology

*Edward Schillebeeckx*

*Translated by Hubert Hoskins*

CROSSROAD • NEW YORK

1981
The Crossroad Publishing Company
575 Lexington Avenue, New York, NY 10022

The original Dutch version of this book was published under the
title *Jezus, het verhaal van een levende* by Uitgeverij H. Nelissen
B. V., Bloemendaal in 1974

Printed in the United States of America

*Library of Congress Cataloging in Publication Data*
Schillebeeckx, Edward, 1914-
[Jezus. English]
Jesus: an experiment in Christology
Translation of Jezus.
Includes bibliographical references and indexes.
1. Jesus Christ—Person and offices. 2. Jesus Christ—History of
doctrines—Early church, ca. 30-600.
I. Title.
BT202.S33513   1981b      232′.09      81-5440
AACR2
ISBN: 0-8245-0320-1
ISBN: 0-8245-0405-4 (pbk.)

# Foreword

Although I regard this book as a Christian interpretation of Jesus – a Christology – however unconventional it may be, it has not been written to resolve the sometimes very subtle problems that interest the academic theologian. Not that these are unimportant. But the fact is that believers are raising questions about Christ which are not the ones that normally preoccupy academics. I have tried to bridge the gap between academic theology and the concrete needs of the ordinary Christian or, to speak more modestly, I have tried here to shed some light on the nexus of problems presaging that gap and giving rise to the questions that seem most urgent to the ordinary Christian. Even so, this calls for a certain amount of academically disciplined work and theological reflection that takes very seriously the demands of faith as well as of critical thinking.

The book has been written in such a way as one might suppose would put the contents within reach of anybody interested.[1] Some effort may well be needed to follow (in Part Three) the sometimes complicated development of the – initially Jewish – interpretation of Jesus by Christians (from his death up to and including the New Testament). However . . . anyone who fancies reading this or that chapter in the book because it may be of special interest to him is missing the essential point; for the whole thing has been composed so as to enable the reader as it were to share in the process whereby full-fledged Christian belief – including his own – came into being. To pick and choose among the chapters or change the order in which they are read will only rob the book of its inner dynamic.

This book is part only of a more extensive Christological study. The second book examines in particular Pauline and Johannine doctrine, concentrating on the various Christologies of the New Testament itself. The first book, therefore, is a 'Jesus book', not altogether neglecting the Christ; whereas the second is a 'Christ book', with due reference to Jesus of Nazareth.

For the present, it is up to the reader to judge whether this approach is successful or not; and on that score reasoned criticism of any sort is most welcome.

Edward Schillebeeckx, O.P.

[1]Theological jargon has been avoided as much as possible; but it seemed impossible at times to do without it. Therefore definitions of certain technical terms have been provided at the back of the book.

# Contents

# Why this book has been written

We have all seen him, have we not? Day after day, always at the same old pitch, more or less unnoticed by people in a hurry, who still, sometimes with an air of boredom or surprise, sometimes with a friendly nod, will toss him a coin as they go on their way. There he squats in his small corner, alone, the familiar figure of the local crock. So has it ever been. 'And a man lame from birth was being carried, whom they laid daily at that gate of the temple which is called Beautiful to ask alms of those who entered the temple' (Acts 3:2). Came the day when Peter, one of the Nazarene's following, noticed him sitting there. There was some exchange of words between them. The next thing people saw was their neighbourhood cripple fully restored and walking as well as anyone. They 'recognized him as the one who sat for alms at the Beautiful Gate of the temple; and they were filled with wonder and amazement at what had happened to him' (Acts 3:10). Then Peter – so Luke tells us – having first addressed the people, said to the Jewish authorities who had afterwards chosen to concern themselves with the affair: '. . . be it known to you all, and to all the people of Israel, that by the name of Jesus Christ of Nazareth, whom you crucified, whom God raised from the dead, by him this man is standing before you well . . . *And there is salvation in no one else,* for there is no other name under heaven given among men by which we must be saved' (Acts 4:10, 12).[1]

In that – within primitive Christianity – not even very early text of the Acts we can nevertheless hear an echo of early Christianity. When Luke's book of the Acts has been critically dissected, we are still within our rights to detect in this passage some resonance, at least, of the primitive Christian proclamation which Peter – after the execution of Jesus of Nazareth and then only after many misgivings – felt himself permitted, nay, obliged to avow and to address to his fellows in the Jewish faith: that salvation from God is given to us Jews and – this, though, became clear only later on – therewith also to all people, simply and solely in Jesus the Nazarene; which is to say in the language of the New Testament, the crucified-but-risen One. That Petrine profession of belief, which in the end and on the basis of their own experience 'the Twelve' unanimously affirmed – albeit, as Scripture itself emphasizes,

[1]The notes are located at the back of the book.

not without the same kind of initial doubts – actually made history. The Christian churches of today and even those, right up to and including the contemporary Jesus people, outside the churches – though not without the mediating function of the churches down the centuries – who still find an experience of salvation in this Jesus, after the lapse of so much time, are still a living witness among us to Jesus of Nazareth and what he released. Without this historic factor of the Church and its mediating role we today (except for a few specialist historians) would know nothing of one Jesus of Nazareth. Apart from a number of privileged specialists in history, there is nobody, as things stand today, who wants to bear testimony to the quite justifiably rebellious slave, Spartacus, or to that grim critic of the religious culture of his time, John the Baptist. This striking difference, if not absolutely conclusive, is historically of exceptional importance. It is an arresting fact and it makes one think: What goes on here? Why this difference in after-effect between one historical figure and another?

What strikes me especially about the vague echo to be heard here of a primitive Christian catechesis is not that an individual – Jesus of Nazareth – had been (in the firm opinion of his disciples) unjustly put to death. In those harsh times – typical, it might seem, of mankind's whole history – one problematic execution among so many was in no way strange. Such an event – a 'mere incident' in the daily record of the time, which despite Acts 26:26[2] took place in an obscure and remote corner of what was then the *oikoumene* or 'whole inhabited world' – would appear to have attracted little or no attention in those days. Such instances were legion. But what did give Peter – Simon and his fellows – pause for thought was the fact that of all people this one, Jesus of Nazareth, had been done to death by all that passed for, and indeed was, the governing authority. The impression Jesus had made and the notion which Simon and company had formed of him did not square at all with the ultimate fate meted out to him by the governing power: handed over by his co-religionists to the Roman occupier, who sent him to a criminal's death by crucifixion. This it was that simply did not fit in with the impression Jesus had made on many of them as Jews. This is really the sum of what in the Christian tradition has since come to be known as the 'Christological problem'.

## II. THE SITUATION IN OUTLINE

1. However much conditioned in part by historically concrete situations, it is an individual's capacity actually to 'make history' that provides us with a hermeneutic key to the understanding of his identity. Through the movement brought to life by Jesus we are confronted here and now with Jesus of Nazareth. The movement which he set afoot remains the medium for any approach to the historical Jesus event. For me, a believer as well as a thinking person, this fact is one that gives pause for thought; so it is for anyone who reflects without prejudice on what has actually happened in his own intimate history.

This historical process born of Jesus will engage our minds all the more as it becomes clear that, within two or three years after Jesus' death by execution, what have since come to be known as Christological statements of belief had already crystallized, and especially as the historical fact emerges that only three years after Jesus' death a certain Pharisee, Saul by name, became a Christian convert during his travels in pursuit and persecution of Jesus' adherents – near Damascus, which implies that there already existed in Syria at that time a fellowship of Christians.[3] History shows that, within the space of five years or less, the effective rudiments of a new world religion were ready to hand; a quite extraordinary phenomenon indeed.

All the same, this development confronts us with an extremely complex process: a story of people who found salvation, and salvation explicitly of a kind which was 'from God', in Jesus of Nazareth, whom they came to describe – when faced in the context of their expectant hope with this concrete historical manifestation – as 'the Christ, son of God, our Lord'.

Ideas and expectations of salvation and human happiness are invariably projected from within concrete experience and the pondered fact of calamity, pain, misery and alienation – from within negative experiences accumulated through centuries of affliction, with here and there the fleeting promise of a happier lot, fragmentary experiences of well-being in a story, stretching from generation to generation, of hopes unfulfilled, of guilt and evil – the 'Job's problem' of our human history. Hence there eventually emerges an anthropological projection, a vision of what is held to be the true, good and happy mode of human life. This is why man's craving for happiness and well-being, always being submitted to critical judgement yet again and again surviving every critique, inevitably acquires – in diverse forms – the pregnant nuance of 'release from' or 'deliverance out of' and – at the same time – of entering into a 'completely new world'. Thus the negative experiences of mankind contrast with and help to delineate a people's positive notions and expectations of salvation, well-being. From its ideas of what constitutes salvation one can, so to speak, glean the story of a people's sufferings, even when it is no longer possible for us to trace from other sources the precise course those sufferings have taken.

The striking thing about this process of calamitous and also partly benign experiences is that the distinctive ideas a people have about 'salvation' attempt to probe and interpret, not only the depth and un-bounded extent of calamity, suffering, evil and death, endured and enduring, but also their causes, origin and effects. Where salvation is hoped for, it is in the express form of this expectation that evil and suffering are unmasked: in it both are put on exhibition. In the ancient world – but also in the spontaneous experience of every people – there is invariably assigned to each such experience of disaster, thanks to the human, theoretically bottomless and practically irremovable depths of suffering involved, a religious dimension. It is felt instinctively that, whether in theory or in practice, the ill is not to be contained within a merely human reference. And so where men have looked for salvation their hope has received a religious name. Reaching above and beyond themselves, men learned to expect that this good must come 'from God'. They look for mercy and compassion at the very heart of reality, despite every contrary experience.

From a specifically historical viewpoint, for both Jew and Gentile Jesus' time was full to bursting with an assortment of hopes regarding some good thing to come, in the form of a welter of ideas culled from long centuries of fleeting promise and, more especially, of many an expectation unfulfilled. The period of Jewish apocalyptic above all, from the Maccabean struggle (167 BC), the Jewish War (AD 66–70) to Bar Kochba (AD 135), was a 'story of blood and tears',[4] out of which the yearning grew: 'Enough is enough: the world must be changed – positively and radically changed!' In images difficult for us now to feel our way into, these beatific hopes were grandly elaborated upon in apocalyptic visions. Via many and various detours of tradition and through 'international' contact with different trends and currents of thought in those days, divergent expectations of what was to come were run together. A contamination emerged of various kinds of ex-pectation of good, quite separate in their origin: a process historically so complex that it has now become very hard for us to disentangle the several strands of tradition in any detail.

Within the broad range of this general mood of expectancy, containing in Jesus' time the still highly active process of fusing together so many diverse ways of envisaging 'salvation', a living confrontation with Jesus of Nazareth convinced some that 'in no one else is redemption given'. What they experienced as the salvation-in-Jesus, coming from God, those first Christians articulated in pre-established images and concepts of varied origin, with which they themselves strongly concurred. These expectations they now saw fulfilled: in Jesus of Nazareth. For they felt that they were new people. In the New Testament they testified – at any rate after a few generations of Christian living and reflection upon it – to their having recognized salvation-in-Jesus, at the same time consigning to it what had been their ideas and hopes of salvation-to-come. In the gospels, therefore, it is impossible to make a division between their own expectation as such and their joyful acknowledgement of its being fulfilled in Jesus: both strands are more or less inextricably intertwined. The question as to the true nature of man and the discovery of an answer to this in the historical person of Jesus are correlative, at least in the sense that it is not the prior expectations that determine who Jesus is, but the other way round: starting from the peculiar and quite specific historical existence of Jesus, the already given expectations are of course partly assimilated yet at the same time transformed, regauged or corrected. This indicates both a continuity and a discontinuity between the question men were asking about salvation and the historically concrete answer that is Jesus.

For us, therefore, on a first reading of the New Testament there are some major difficulties. We do not live in a cultural-religious tradition that expects a messiah or a mysterious, celestial son of man: nor do we live in expectation of an approaching end of the world. We are confronted in the gospels not just with Jesus of Nazareth but with a portion of ancient religious culture. Jesus is indeed hidden beneath religious ideas belonging to that time, ideas which, if it comes to that, were themselves not altogether alien to him – rather the opposite. Moreover, the original experience of salvation in Jesus gets filled out in the gospels with doctrinal and practical problems of the later Christian congregations which, though initially within the Jewish fraternity (alongside many others), had since then gradually become detached from Judaism and were keeping up a polemic against the synagogues run by the Pharisees, while on the other hand the Jews in their turn formally dissociate themselves from the Christian phenom-

enon in their midst, denounce it and place an interdict upon it as being
no longer something authentically Jewish, and therefore 'outside the
synagogue'.[5] In the gospels Jesus of Nazareth has, so to speak, vanished
into the background of the polemic between 'Israel' and 'Church', a
problem which in that form Jesus had never encountered and perhaps
had never intended. The fact is that the 'phenomenon of Jesus' fractured the hopes of salvation held in common by the Jews and by those
Jews later known as Christians; and because of Jesus' free style of conduct such hopes acquired a discontinuous, no longer traditional meaning. What is more, the Aramaic-speaking Jewish Christians did not
interpret Jesus in the same way as the Hellenistic Jews of the Diaspora,
with their Greek universal humanity and sense of *philanthrôpia*, of
general philanthropy and openness towards the Gentile; and the non-
Jewish Greeks, Syrians, Romans and so forth, who had had absolutely
no part in Israel's hopes of salvation, naturally enough proceeded to
express the salvation they had found in Jesus in quite different categories. Yet despite fundamental differences in the earliest local groups
of Aramaic-speaking Jewish Christians as over against Greek-speaking
congregations of Christianized Jews and, finally, of Christian Gentiles,
they all had at least this in common: that whatever the differences
between them might be, they shared the culture, indeed the Hellenistic
culture, of the ancient world, especially in Galilee (but even in Judea:
in important circles at Jerusalem, with its large number of Greek
synagogues) which, as a practically bilingual country, ringed by the
Greek cities of the Decapolis, was then held by Judea to the south to
be a more or less pagan land out of which no good thing could come.

Whether we take its Jewish or its Hellenistic models of expectation,
that antique culture is strange indeed to us. Our hopes of good-to-
come have a different complexion and focus. Our conceptions of that
good are different too. Quite possibly – if one may venture an *a priori*
opinion – they should be subject to the critique the ancient models
provide; but the latter should perhaps be submitted in their turn to a
modern critique. All ways of envisaging 'salvation' and all hopes
regarding man's 'true mode of existence' are in any case culturally
conditioned. For the Christian, Jesus – whom he encounters in his experience as the final source of salvation – is of course the final criterion
– not the cultural-religious ideas on the subject entertained by Aramaic-
or Greek-speaking Jews and by Greeks who had become Christians.
Still, the salvation those early Christians found in Jesus was couched
in terms of such expectations as were current at that time, however
much transformed, regauged and corrected by the force of Jesus' own

authority and historic impact. So the sheer strangeness, for us, of the New Testament ideas about salvation-to-come can hardly be denied. We do not look for a celestial son of man to appear at any moment as our judge and set up a messianic commonwealth – concerning which we might well enquire anxiously, as people did then, whether Christians already dead will nevertheless have part in it (1 Thess. 4:13–17). We may be rather hasty in our judgement here. One can, after all, wait quite a time for a train that fails to come. But anyone who in this day and age has waited by the track for a scheduled train, not just for hours but for days and weeks – what for us is for centuries – when the train simply fails to materialize, can no longer psychologically maintain or substantiate his 'train-expectancy'. Anyone will conclude soon enough that trains have ceased to run on this particular track. The picture of Christ as it comes to us from the New Testament is in the first instance, therefore, actually weird – not just in the sense of the strange, scandalizing quality inherent in God's peculiar and divine dealings with man that surpass human wisdom; but strange or 'queer' in a purely human, cultural-religious sense. The objection that Jesus Christ is precisely the one who brings our all-too-human conceptions under critical judgement is in itself true; but it is not to the point here. The ancient ideas about salvation, by reason of which the figure of Jesus in the New Testament is on the one hand made historically unrecognizable and, on the other hand, is revealed to the eye of faith in his true identity as the one who brings salvation, do not in themselves place us under any critique, except in so far as, in their own way, they posit the criterion of Jesus as final source of salvation. Anyone who fails to see this distinction is proposing not Jesus Christ but one particular bit of religious culture as the norm of Christian faith – and that ceases to be faith in Jesus of Nazareth, whereas the basic affirmation of the Christian creed is our confession concerning *Jesus*, that is, 'Jesus of Nazareth', that he is 'the Christ, the only-begotten Son, our Lord'. The fully normative factor here is: *'credo in Jesum'*: I believe in the manifestation of this quite concrete person, 'Jesus', who appeared in our history with the historical name 'Jesus of Nazareth'. In him we find final salvation, well-being. This is the fundamental creed of primitive Christianity.

Our pattern of expectation as regards salvation-for-mankind in no way resembles the ancient varieties, centred as they were on a messiah-son of David or a messiah-son of man; and just as foreign to us is the combination of those two originally independent traditions.

That in itself is a principal reason why I have set about writing this book: What does salvation in Jesus, coming to us from God, mean to us now? After all, 'well-being' is a concept which linguistically, and thus in the context of man's experience of reality with social implications, is brought to life and made intelligible only through contrasted negative experiences, conjoined with at least sporadic experiences of what 'makes sense' – whence there arises in hope an anticipation of 'total sense' or 'hale-ness', being whole. Who would ever call pure experience, positive experience 'well-being', except against a contrasting background of very negative experiences already undergone? It has all along been the case that even out of our catastrophic history here in the West a Utopia is in process of growing among us. This concrete experience has been reflected in all sorts of emancipatory movements – movements intended to deliver men from their social alienations, while various scientific techniques (psychotherapeutic release; Gestalt therapy; androgogy, social work, counselling, etc.) have been meant to free people from the loss of personal identity. That apart from Jesus Christ there are a number of factors in our lives which, as a matter of historical truth, do induce well-being and do indeed heal a person or make him whole is something that in our day more than ever before has forced itself on our awareness. This puts the statement – till recently bandied about in some Christian circles without the slightest reserve – that 'all true salvation comes from Jesus Christ alone', in a problematic, thoroughly opaque, at the very least, astounding context of incredibility.

Any critical assessment of our present-day culture reveals that this modern anticipation of future well-being, which especially since the nineteenth century has staked all its hope on science and technology alone, eventually runs amok and leads to alienation in man – simply because its way of conceiving man is so constricted. This narrowed understanding, which has made science and technology, if not the exclusive, at any rate the representative values of our Western culture, has actually wrought fresh disaster, above all in a society that gives virtual priority to economic values and to nothing else. This brings the whole modern concept of what constitutes 'well-being' under critical judgement. Thus the view that all this is alien to the New Testament is grounded not just in a debt owed to that Testament itself but also, and just as essentially, in the defective understanding of ourselves and of reality current among us today. That too calls for a critique. There are sources of well-being and healing in the life of man that go beyond science and technology. This is the new insight achieved by science. In principle, and however paradoxically, it serves to reinstate a variety of gratuitous experiences – even religious ones - as factors in man's well-being.

We must not forget, of course, that this anti-technological insight – in the sense that it relativizes technocracy – is itself partly the result of scientific analysis. It is a scientific insight; and as such it does not in itself serve to validate a different, non-scientific approach to things. What is more, the circles within which this scientific perception of the extra-scientific factors in 'well-being' has emerged are precisely those which are for the most part insistent that such fulfilment is 'self-actualizing', in the sense that while even the religious factor – bringing with it an awareness of gratuitousness and of being centred on other people – is admittedly an essential element in man's well-being, the source and strength of that well-being lie in man himself and in man alone, without any reference to absolute transcendence. There is no place for theology in this view of things. In this perspective, therefore, theology should disappear and could better devote all its energies to the human sciences.

Hence it would seem that (setting aside this last ideological assertion) the religious concept of 'salvation', as over against the New Testament, has really been whittled down in our day: it has had to yield a lot of territory to other, indeed quite visibly effective, 'salvific' agencies. This situation raises the question of what really counts with man as his well-being, at the focal point of all his problems today. For we see that while the possibility of removing various forms of human alienation through science and technology is a very present one, at the same time this desirable possibility only bears on alienations which are basically the outcome of physical, psychosomatic, psychic and social types of conditioning – the absence of liberating or the presence of inhibiting factors likely to condition man's freedom, which in fact expert and active intervention can to a large extent handle successfully. Then the question is whether there is not present in man a more profound alienation, linked with his finiteness and his entanglement with nature (which despite every attempt on man's part to assimilate and humanize it remains fundamentally alien and menacing) – whether, indeed, there is not some alienation through guilt and sin. Man's self-redemption would seem to be limited, after all. And then comes the new problem: whether it is not precisely this range of deeper issues that Jesus of Nazareth in a quite specific way articulates when he speaks of a deliverance which really does liberate man into perfect 'freedom', into an autonomy made possible only in joyful bondage to a transcendent and for that very reason liberating, living God (Gal. 5:1).

That we must look to Jesus Christ alone for every part of what constitutes salvation, as a representative Christian tradition has often asserted, is contradicted anyway by a great many facts of modern experience. This again has confused a lot of Christians, who have been obliged to revise their earlier view of the historic faith on many points. That experience too has been a factor in prompting me to write this book and has helped to settle in what way it should be done.

2. There is more to it than that. In a period when Western society is no longer felt to be the world but just a small, often very pretentious constituent of a larger whole, a larger world of human kind which, furthermore, smarts under the painful impact of Western aspirations and practices, the Christian claim that 'in no one else is there redemption' meets with loud protest. 'Christian imperialism' is a constant and accusing cry – not least on the lips of Western man himself; for often enough he thinks he can only rediscover his own identity by repudiating his own past. With some, the Christian claim is suspect in that it discriminates, as they think, against other non-Christian religions and cultures, or even smacks of Western colonialist one-upmanship and selfish favouritism, subjectively compensated for by an expansive sort of missionizing on a world scale. Even this missionary consciousness has battened upon what was once taken to be the self-evident profession of Christ as the 'Redeemer of the world'. Any current reflection on this from a Christian standpoint, therefore, must include some critical evaluation of the universality of Jesus as a problem, if it is not to stand accused of ideology from the very outset. On the other hand it must not dodge the question of truth here or retreat into accommodation to the modern insistence on pluralism, in so far as this is bound to imply not venturing to go on being oneself and not daring to deviate from the rest.

But suppose that this happens to be the logical outcome of the gospel . . . ?

3. There is something else that our period in particular demonstrates regarding 'Jesus of Nazareth' – even if it is not, historically speaking, altogether novel: it is not just church people who take a serious interest in Jesus of Nazareth.

The gospels tell us what Jesus came to mean to a group of people known eventually as the *ekklesia* of Christ.[6] The early writings of this community, brought together in the New Testament to be read, meditated upon and studied as their book, are still today, for all who are conscious of being included in this 'Christ movement', a source of critical reflection on their life and conduct as Christians.

Yet at the same time being in literature, namely, in that same New Testament, has given Jesus form and substance. He is, as it were, objectivized in it. This puts him in a special way right in the limelight. Thanks to the documents handed down, Jesus is a part of world literature and has become accessible to all. He has become 'common property'; and the New Testament is not just the exclusive book of Christendom. This piece of literature is public property and can be studied from a historical standpoint. The resultant knowledge, verifiable by outsiders, yields a view of Jesus that can also be a touchstone for the pictures that believers have formed of Jesus down the centuries. For the Christian cannot cast aside as being beneath his notice such a generally accessible starting-point for the knowledge of Jesus. The ideas he has as a believer about Christ can learn from it; they must be tested and if necessary revised in the light of it. Thus the fact that Jesus of Nazareth is universally accessible turns out to be of service to the faith of Christians, not in an apologetic context but as a critical confrontation.

The interpretation of Jesus outside the Church is of many different kinds. The Marxist philosopher Roger Garaudy wrote: '*Rendez-le nous*', give Jesus of Nazareth back to us (the non-churchmen, even unbelievers in God); you church people can't keep *him* for yourself. Gandhi said: 'Without needing to be a Christian I can still testify to what this Jesus means in my life.' A lot of humanists too find guidance and inspiration in Jesus of Nazareth (as well as in other sources). In our day it is especially the young people – in the Jesus movement, for instance – who are outside any church and yet find their well-being, inspiration and orientation in Jesus. Jesus is manifestly not the monopoly of the Christian churches. One might say that in many circles he is being 'deconfessionalized'. In India people are asking: What does Jesus mean to me as a Hindu? And elsewhere: What does he mean to me as a Muslim? Behind the Iron Curtain too young people are attracted to 'Jesus of Nazareth'.

Someone who attempts to size up this phenomenon straightaway on the basis of his interpretation of Jesus from within the Church runs the risk of remaining blind to precisely those elements in Jesus which many find so meaningful and inspiring, while church people have ignored them for centuries or have just not seen them. The non-church interpretations of Jesus serve to remind us that Jesus has indeed something to say relevant at a human level, in that he speaks also to the non-

Christian. This raises the question of the close connection between the gospel, the religious aspect and the human. Then too the Church's interpretation of Jesus – in him God's universal mercy has made a personal appearance among us – is perhaps given a highly modern setting. So many people, after all, have ceased to make head or tail of God or of the Christian churches. Church people are themselves guilty in this respect. Yet the very same individuals find their well-being and inspiration in the man Jesus. Via a detour – if such it is – that is to say, Jesus, are they in attaching themselves to him leaving open the question of God and the ecclesiological problem – for the time being or perhaps permanently?[7] Through a divine pedagogy of charitableness (so at least the more flexible sort of believer will interpret the situation) the 'absence of God' is evidently 'compensated for' by the inspiration which Jesus affords to many non-church people. The image which people cannot resist forming of God, even if they acknowledge no such reality, is obviously replaced by many of them with the 'symbol' and the 'myth' of Jesus of Nazareth. For the symbolic and mythical character of 'Jesus' in all interpretations of him – especially outside the churches, and whether 'believing' or otherwise – seems to me the fundamental and most striking thing. In them Jesus becomes an 'a-temporal' model of true humanity. This non-church view of Jesus is unmistakably operative, actually at work in history. Therein lies an opportunity, but also a possible line of retreat: 'Jesus' becomes the answer, that is, the stop-gap, for all our unsolved problems. The Jesus people frequently give this impression; but I get it just as strongly sometimes from orthodox church people. Augustine said it earlier on: '*Christus solutio omnium difficultatum*', Jesus is the answer to every problem. An apt slogan, but a dangerous one! The fact is that for many outside the churches 'Jesus of Nazareth' is made to symbolize transcendence of any sort.

At any rate this encounter with Jesus outside the churches does clearly demonstrate that people as a whole want to keep open the question of authentic transcendence and at least not dismiss 'the sacral' with a categorical 'no'. That this may be a flight from the serious problems with which the reality of God as well as the historico-social reality of the Church confronts us all is not to be gainsaid. Whether (to adopt a modern neo-dogmatic sort of jargon) it is a flight *per se*[8] is open to question. Mankind cannot abandon 'God', for the simple reason (for faith) that God will not abandon man and continues to 'visit' him – by routes which we cannot map in advance. That in a secularized period, of all things, when God is disappearing, the world should be 'sold' on Jesus of Nazareth, whether in a political context or in the dimension of *homo ludens*, the play of what is aimlessly gratuitous – the tomfoolery of 'festivals' – may (no question here of *fatum*, destiny or the law of things, only of a vital chance of freedom, in whatever direction) offer an accepted or rejected prospect of grace and mercy on the part of God, who in Jesus is bent upon our good, whether we stray or no. Here no automatic rules apply. Opportunities of 'saving health' in this contemporary situation are not to be disavowed by the believer in God – I would say: not in spite of but actually because of all the criticism of religion and being sick of the churches and their God.

It is precisely this interpretation of Jesus, going on outside the churches, that constitutes a challenge for the Christian theologian. What have the 'churches of Christ' to say to those outside? What will they have to say after they have first of all listened to what the non-church people have to tell them about Jesus of Nazareth? This too was one of my reasons for writing the book.

4. Inside the churches, too, the traditional and (within a number of Scholastic variants) none the less uniform Christology has fallen apart in our time. There is a nexus of Christological problems there, though it is not separate from what we have already been talking about. Theologically speaking, the problem amounts to this: Can we ascribe to the earthly life of Jesus, to his message and ministry, his 'words and acts', a dogmatic significance, or not? In more everyday language this means: Is 'Christian salvation' vested in the Jesus who lived here on earth, or solely in the crucified-and-risen One? This problem is often clearly formulated as a dilemma.[9] Parallel with the dilemma thus stated, one finds among church-related Christians a number of other mutually contrasted positions: (a) on the one hand a theology of Jesus of Nazareth, experienced as 'saving reality' and interpreted as orientation and inspiration for Christian living in our time; on the other, a Christology that starts from the Easter message (*kerygma*) and celebrates and thematizes the Christ who is present in the ritual worship of the Church; (b) on the one hand a this-worldly Christianity, with a low-profile concern with the Church, which is directly orientated on the message and mode of living of Jesus of Nazareth and is not seldom on the fringe of the churches or outside them altogether; on the other, a Christianity bound up closely with a high-profile style of churchmanship, which draws its life from the *kerygma* of the crucified-and-risen One, 'Head of the Church', present and operative within it today, and

which tends to recoil from social and political engagement 'in Christ's
name'; (c) on the one hand a total emphasis on the man Jesus as inspiration and orientation for working, not uncritically but committedly,
to achieve a better world here on earth, without expressly introducing
any vista of a life eternal or an eschatological encounter with Christ,
sometimes even explicitly rejecting it; on the other hand, a total
emphasis on the God 'Jesus Christ', the Lord exalted to the Father's
side, who is alive and active among us even now, is celebrated in the
liturgy and sheds upon us the Spirit as pledge of an eternal life to come,
which is perpendicular, more or less, to our historical existence in this
world, whereof the form passes away.

Two types of Christianity, based on two types of Christology. In the
one case an explicit allergy to the word 'Christ' (in many a eucharistic
canon of recent times the term is on the way out), in the other an
obvious, sometimes aggressive and un-Christian aversion to the word
'Jesus' (of Nazareth), as though our belief were not in a concrete person
but in a gnostic mystery-cult. There is no point in trying to conceal the
existence of these two types: they are very much with us and are
certainly acted upon: they do not wholly correspond to the contrast
between 'conservative' and 'progressive'. Thus one can set over against
each other on the one hand 'Jesus-followers', who tend to ignore the
fundamental breaking-points in Jesus' life and his totally patient, sub-
missive relationship to his Father, and on the other hand 'disciples of
the Christ', who are in danger of turning him into a myth, in no way
essentially connected with Jesus of Nazareth; and this situation
obviously has important consequences for the understanding of
Scripture, theology and history, and concretely in the pastoral sphere
above all. Contrary positions in Christology not seldom provide the
basis, whether explicitly stated or not, of the current polarization among
Christians.

But before becoming involved in discussion, each would do well to
acknowledge the Christian status of the other. One is a Christian if one
is persuaded that final salvation-from-God is disclosed in the person of
Jesus and that this basic conviction gives rise to the community or
fellowship of grace – even though those who accept this may still
adopt different positions on what the fullness of Jesus Christ entails,
that is, on how to 'fill in' the credal formula: I believe in Jesus (of
Nazareth): the Christ, the only-begotten Son, our Lord; I believe in
Jesus as that definitive saving reality which gives final point and purpose to my life. If one can start from the assumption that the other party
accepts this, then the situation is at any rate one of dialogue among

Christians and, one would hope, of a Christian dialogue.

5. Then there is, confronting the theologian, the (in the 'modern view' admittedly unappealing) question of truth. Having due regard to the intention of faith as well as to the critical and rational posture which our status as human beings demands, the theologian realizes that – whatever the intensity of concrete religious experiences may be, as well as the historical identifications made of 'salvation' and the liberation of man – these intense experiences remain problematical, can never signify for others an invitation that will compel and constrain them, even in freedom, unless it has been reasonably demonstrated that in and through these experiences and identifications of 'salvation', belonging to a particular human community, we really are in contact with the reality to which we human beings in the course of our history have ascribed the name of God, the Creator of all that is and is to be.[10] Much as I may appreciate the significance, the unique importance, of existential experience and religious enthusiasm, I am none the less certain that a God who is encountered simply as '*my* God' and is avowed as such is in my view a non-god, unless it can be reasonably – which is not at all to say mathematically or in a rationally conclusive way – shown that in this person, Jesus of Nazareth, we actually have to do with the One who liberates and yet at the same time – however incomprehensibly – is the final arbiter of meaning, the 'Creator of heaven and earth'. Here if anywhere, in the sphere of religion, pious self-deception is a very real possibility. So religious faith in Jesus of Nazareth, a person appearing within our human history, is problematical for me if the personal relation of this historically localizable individual with the 'Creator of heaven and earth', the universal factor cementing all that lives and moves – the living God – is not clear to us. Enthusiasm for 'Jesus of Nazareth' as an inspiring human being I can appreciate – at the human level, that is quite something in itself! But it entails no binding invitation, can bear no stamp of the universally human, unless it can be shown that 'the Creator', the (monotheistic) God of Jews, Muslims, Christians and so many others, is personally implicated in this Jesus event.

What in this book might appear, therefore, to be apologetic as well as critical is actually prompted by a concern for truth, wherever that may be found to reside – inside or outside the churches. As my study of a Christological belief in Jesus of Nazareth has proceeded, the realization (current even in early Christianity) that such belief contains (like myth) its own justification and certitude has more and more grown upon me: the 'why' of my belief in Jesus as the 'final saving good' is to be justified only in faith (in that sense there is a storm-free zone, immune from criticism); but from the moment I speak of my faith (and I do so as soon as I have it) I have already left this storm-free zone and become vulnerable to the exigencies of critical rationality (in that sense there is no storm-free zone). This is why the book has been written: in deference to the unique and irreducibly original character of believing, of exercising faith, and out of respect for the demands of critical rationality. Each can help protect the other from becoming totalitarian and detrimental to freedom.

6. Lastly there is the painful and unresolved question of the relationship between Christians and Jews. Among others, Christians share the blame for a Western anti-Semitism that made possible the Nazi *Endlösung*. As theologians whose business it is to reflect on the Jewish man, Jesus of Nazareth, we cannot behave as if we knew nothing of the historical relations between Jews and Christians, cannot act as if what a few Jews did to Jesus had not been eclipsed long ago by what we have all done in the course of history to the Jews. Recent Jewish literature about Jesus[11] shows that after centuries of estrangement from him the Jews have become aware through their own 'holocaust' – burnt-offering – at Auschwitz and elsewhere of their solidarity with the 'holocaust' of Jesus of Nazareth. Judaism has no pantheon, but it does have a memorably noble martyrology. Many Jews now recognize that this is where Jesus belongs. As Martin Buber put it: 'From my youth on, I have felt that Jesus was my elder brother. That Christianity has regarded and still does regard him as God and redeemer has always appeared to me a matter of the utmost seriousness which for his sake and for mine I must try to comprehend.'[12]

There is not all that much that a theologian can do to repair these hurtful and dramatically distorted relationships; yet he has his own contribution to make. There is no denying that one of the hermeneutical keys to an understanding of the New Testament is the tussle between 'Israel' and the 'Church';[13] but the historian and the theologian can make out a good case that to a large extent Christianity just took over an internal Jewish critique of Israel and that the early Christian interpretation of Jesus is really a Jewish one. The basic trends in Christianity were touched off by Jews and were firmly established long before non-Jewish, Gentile-Christian influences had started to operate. So an anti-Jewish feeling is quite foreign to the earliest trends in Christianity; which is why I shall keep on emphasizing it, should certain primitive Christian interpretations be nothing but a Christian resumption of pre-Christian, Jewish patterns of thought and action.

III. A CHALLENGE

With all these problems in mind – still accumulating in the course of study – I have written this book as a piece of reflective thinking about Jesus of Nazareth, whom the churches of Christ, to which I belong, confess as final salvation: in Jewish terms, the Christ, Son of God and son of man; in Hellenistic terms, the Son of God in a fully ontological sense.

The intention is not apologetic, although I have no qualms about honest apologetics. That is to say, there is no attempt to legitimate ecclesiastical dogma or to represent it as the only meaningful and possible interpretation of Jesus consonant with reason. I establish that there are other interpretations that dismiss Jesus, others again which inspire and orientate people to good purpose, apart from any Christological confession. Close attention is paid to these interpretations, even though this is not repeatedly being spelled out in so many words. Such a readiness to listen has been part and parcel of the enquiry.

As a believer, I want to look critically into the intelligibility for man of Christological belief in Jesus, especially in its origin. Face to face with the many real problems, my concern is indeed to hold a *fides quaerens intellectum* and an *intellectus quaerens fidem* together: that is, in a like regard for faith and for human reason I want to look for what a Christological belief in Jesus of Nazareth can intelligibly signify for people today.

I said 'intelligibility', in no sense denying thereby that the salvation-in-Jesus deriving from God is a mystery. What the word is meant to convey is a critical posture on the believing theologian's part, which refuses to identify the mystery of God with 'mysteries' – in the sense of 'things incomprehensible' – fabricated by human beings themselves, which have nothing to do with the mystery of God's saving acts in history and are nevertheless often hawked around by some of our brethren, who thus bring the faith into ridicule, as a 'Christian mystery' and unassailable orthodoxy.

That the man Jesus, in the sense of 'a human person', is for me the starting-point of all my reflection I would call a sort of palisade that needs no further proof or justification. It is a truism. There are no ghosts or gods in disguise wandering around in our human history;

J.E.C.–B

only people. What is peculiar, unique, about this person, Jesus – and that may slip from our grasp into depths unfathomable – is what I would seek to discover; for it is a fact that this Jesus of Nazareth succeeded in touching off a religious movement that became a world religion asserting that Jesus is the revelation, in personal form, of God. Thus the question of his ultimate identity governs the whole of this enquiry. My purpose is to look for possible evidences in the picture of Jesus reconstructed by historical criticism, pointers that could direct man's query regarding his 'well-being' to the Christian tender of a reply that refers to a particular saving action of God in this Jesus; and I do so in the same sort of reaction, characteristic of the New Testament, against the pre-canonical *theios anèr* Christologies, against Christology centred in a mundane god, masquerading in human form (after the Greek model), that prompted Paul and Mark, more especially, to inveigh so fiercely against it, because such views misrepresent the authentic import of the true Son of God.

Faith and historical criticism go hand in hand, therefore, on almost every page of this book. It is bound to be so, as we claim to discover salvation in Jesus, a historical human being, manifested in a quite specific period of our history. For then both history and faith have each their own proper competence and angle of approach, while they both nevertheless have to do with one and the same reality: Jesus of Nazareth as a historical phenomenon.

In faith, but yet identifying myself with the doubts concerning the 'Christ of the Church', which in the Netherlands and everywhere else I have been I have heard so sharply expressed all around me, sometimes aggressively, sometimes with regret, among others because they are existentially unable any more to know as once they did, I have set out to search for 'meta-dogmatic' clues – that is, through and beyond ecclesiastical dogma, although aware that this very dogma had driven me to undertake the search – and to pursue them without knowing in advance where this would take me, without even knowing whether this line of attack was not in the end bound to fail, as some of my students contended. Even failures – especially failures, perhaps – make one wiser. There was always that possibility. As the work progressed I could not rid myself of the growing conviction that however exact a historical reconstruction of the so-called 'authentic' Jesus of Nazareth one tries to make, any result with a scientific backing to it can only yield a Jesus image, never the real Jesus of Nazareth. What happens when the historical method is systematically applied in assessing Jesus is, after all, a qualitative change imposed upon the ordinary spontaneous apprehension or recollection of a person from the past. And however well supported historically this scientifically created image may be, the first disciples of Jesus were never confronted with this likeness of him – even though it be wholly relevant to the Jesus who was then living and whom the churches now acknowledge as the Christ. The question of the vital continuity between the faith of the primitive Church and 'Jesus of Nazareth' is something quite different from the question of the continuity between a scientifically based, historical Jesus figure and the aforesaid faith of the primitive Church; different, but in no way extraneous or alien to it.

That this study neither has been nor possibly could be carried out by a process of skipping over what twenty centuries of Christian history have mediated to us of the churches' credal profession and actual conduct, in a period given to hermeneutics need not be said. Of course in writing this book I had an eye to my earlier studies (lectures) on patristic, Carolingian, medieval and post-Tridentine Christologies, although they are not directly discussed here. I confine myself here to a consideration of the 'course taken by the dogma' from the start of primitive Christianity up to the formation of the gospels and the books of the New Testament, a period that brings us closest to Jesus and is still very reticent over the matter of identifying Jesus of Nazareth, in whom followers of Jesus, after his death, found final and definitive salvation. Initially, his death either presented no problem or, where salvation is concerned, was accounted to be 'neutral'. The effect of this incubatory prehistory of the canonical 'New Testament' can be both to liberate and at the same time provide a new focus and perspective for what many feel to be the stultified traditional Christology of our systematized Western theology. The subtitle 'An Experiment in Christology' is still too pretentious and premature, therefore. This book is a prolegomenon. I call it a prolegomenon not because of what is actually said in it, but because of what had been my original intention: to offer a synthetic view of the contemporary problem of 'redemption' and 'emancipation' or man's self-liberation, partly with 'liberation theology' in mind.

Besides sustained reflection, this book is meant to provide constant information, if only because it is not every Christian who can allow himself the luxury enjoyed by someone who has been 'freed' by the community to concern himself with these vital matters, and furthermore, because I must persist in putting it on record that, through a lack of well-grounded information, a lot of people fall into an 'overbearing' style of Christian belief, overbearing and even un-Christian in its absolutist claims, so alien to Jesus and his gospel. Much passes for 'Christian' that for anyone conversant with the New Testament in a spirit of study and prayer turns out to be essentially un-Christian. So I regard this book as an obligation owed to the community, first and foremost the Christian community, but at the same time to all who are interested in man's lot and destiny.

## IV. A NOTE ON EXEGESIS AND THEOLOGY

In the course of more than three years' preliminary exegetical work done on this book I have repeatedly been baffled, sometimes almost to the point of distraction, by a hefty problem: that the fundamental stimulus behind this whole project seemed at times to amount to an impossible enterprise: there is more or less no biblical pericope on the interpretation of which the experts in exegesis do not disagree among themselves – even though one has to admit that over the last ten years there has been an increasing measure of agreement on basic exegetical problems among biblical scholars, both Catholic and Reformed. If the New Testament incorporates the first, constitutive impulse of the movement centred around Jesus in a potent testimony of faith, consciously guided and governed by what had been achieved through God's saving activity in Jesus of Nazareth, then theological reflection of any sort centres inevitably upon understanding this New Testament, where in human language, in words and images, deriving from the social, cultural and religious idioms of the time, Christians expressed their belief in the decisive, God-given salvation-in-Jesus which they had experienced. In those circumstances, to dispense with a scientific approach to the Bible with all the methods of modern literary criticism would simply be to flout what is usually referred to as the 'Word of God' – which in any case only reaches us through the words of religious people. A believing community (which quite properly uses the sacred book for other purposes too, for instance, in liturgical worship), if it would recover precisely what those affirmations of human faith signified at that time, cannot do without literary criticism in its application to the New Testament (in the context of Old Testament, intertestamentary and post-New Testament literature as a whole) – unless it is prepared to ignore a fundamental belief, namely, that the Church itself, whether local congregation or governing authority, lies under the judgement of God and his lordship, being subject to the norm presented by the person and activity of Jesus of Nazareth, whom it acknowledges as the 'Christ, the only-begotten Son, our Lord'.

A thematizing or reflective theologian is not *ipso facto* an expert in exegesis. I am very well aware of that. Yet without the Scriptures the theologian is quite useless. Is he dependent, then, on the specialist exegete? No. But he is, of course, on skilled exegesis; for as in all the sciences, naturally enough, we find among the exegetes a great diversity of opinion. So the theologian cannot make an arbitrary selection from among the views currently available: those, for instance, that would best fit into some dogmatic synthesis of his own! That would be to misunderstand the basic function of Scripture within theology. So what can he do? Although not an exegetical specialist, the theologian should be able to form a judgement as to the value of the exegetical arguments put before him, and more particularly to examine the postulates on the basis of which one expert interprets a Scriptural pericope in one way, another in another way. Non-exegetical presuppositions are often the reason why opinions diverge. Therefore a theologian cannot just give in to his 'preferred exegetes' (even though experience with the works of many authors does often lead spontaneously to the exercise of preference). Where agreement between exegetes of various schools (and by that I also mean explicitly: in various countries) does exist, the theologian will be happy to rely upon it – unless here and there, over a period, questions are raised, first through what is received to begin with as a solitary point of view, later on as a result of other difficulties emerging in a similar context, till suddenly, in the teeth of common exegetical opinion, a commentator presents a quite novel, coherent view. I believe that, having weighed the arguments, a theologian may in certain cases, contrary to the received exegetical opinion, adopt into his dogmatic scheme this new insight – sometimes the resumption of a very old one. (Quite often, as a matter of fact, this 'new' viewpoint eventually turns out to win general approval.) Consensus among the exegetes – if the presuppositions involved be left aside – does not seem to me a proper governing principle for the theologian. After all, the exegetes themselves often work with theological, that is, non-exegetical predilections, on which the theologian is entitled to form a judgement.

Then of course a theologian has to be careful about the kind of 'exegetical slogans' that turn up in theology as in any other discipline: for instance, the one recurrent in exegetical literature since M. Kähler: 'Mark is a Passion-narrative with a lengthy introduction.' The thing is that slogans, while they contain a kernel of truth, usually miss every fine point of detail.

Above all, the theologian will want to object to the practice, so evident among exegetes, of exploiting one particular method alone to sanctify their convictions – the techniques of *Formgeschichte*, for example, or of an exclusive structuralism. As a theologian, he simply cannot commit himself to the results yielded by one exegetical method in isolation (in the confines of which people still arrive at differing opinions – perhaps owing to the very exclusivism of the method, which after all enshrines presuppositions of its own). Even in his day Ernst Troeltsch could say: 'A whole world view lies behind the historico-critical method.'[14] One can see from the literature how national differences in regard to exegesis often have a bearing on problems of 'method and truth', so that a knowledge of these national perspectives affords a greater degree of theological 'independence', without denying some dependence on expert exegesis.

No less disastrous, on the other hand, is the dogmatic choice of a sort of 'common denominator', distilled from the available exegesis; such a procedure is irrelevant to biblical learning and so cannot under-gird a Christian theology. The theologian is therefore obliged to enter upon detailed exegesis; and he cannot trust himself in the first instance to generalizing, 'in the round', exegetical studies (or what is sometimes known as 'biblical theology'). These studies in the round only make sense if they are based on studies made in detail; otherwise they often reflect the theological outlook of the person putting them together rather than the pluralistic yet fundamentally one New Testament interpretation of Jesus; and a personal theological view of that sort is no foundation for a theology that seeks at any rate to be in some degree generally admissible.

In short: doing theology on a really Scriptural basis is indeed a trying and laborious exercise; it is for ever breaking down one's own pre-established 'syntheses' and reconstructing them; expectations are dashed, others are nurtured and increase. The synthesis is itself con-tinually in movement; and so are developed both the capacity to evaluate new exegetical literature and the capacity for synthesis. From time to time people will be able to blame the theologian who works in this way – in other words, ventures 'too much' in the field of exegesis – for committing blunders. Of course! His sole defence then is that without exegesis all your theologizing will be up in the air. Better to err on the proper path than to turn casually, albeit with no blemish or further defect from that moment on, into a false track that can only lead to ideology.

True, there is a distinction to be made between exegesis and systematic theology; but besides exegesis as a purely critical and literary discipline, there is also a theological variety, in which one seeks to discover in Jesus and the earliest witnesses to Christian belief – in other words, in early Christianity – the definitively saving activity of God. It is this that determines the theological character of the exegesis, which is not made theological just by a process of 'updating' to give it a current relevancy (this last is what I call 'systematic theology'). As a matter of fact the separation of biblical exegesis from thematic theology is something relatively recent and was only completed, on a recognized basis, in the seventeenth century. Theological exegesis sets out to discover the theological dimension within the actual historical phenomenon of early Christianity; it is here already that the question of truth arises and not just in the Bible's 'topicality' in relation to us today. To go looking for what is of relevance to the present in the meaning of the New Testament is 'systematic theology', and this presupposes a theological exegesis which examines the New Testament regarding God's conclusive saving activity in the emergence of the Judaeo-Christian religion.

Lastly, the main objection (which is indeed very much on my mind): there is still Christian ecclesiastical tradition, the life of the churches and, for the Catholic, even the magisterium as an ecclesial function, as an authoritative ministry to the church community. Indeed without that Church my quest would never have arisen! But this charisma of the official ministry, in which as in his churches God's Spirit is actively at work, does not operate miraculously, still less through private revelations or instant lines of communication, but rather in a very historical fashion; this official ministry – up to and including the very top – is thus bound to rely on the understanding of Scripture, assisted by exegesis. As it is precisely this assistance from exegetes and theologians that the ministry needs, in view of the ecclesial structure intrinsic to its very nature, there can be no substitute for assistance of this kind. The same thing applies to the Church as a community, the basis of whose living is an experience of Christ. Indeed, for the theologian the living congregation or local church is a 'theological habitat' without which his searching of the Scriptures and his theological reflection have nothing to ground themselves upon. Theology is not the expounding of books. But if people profess to have committed themselves in faith to Jesus, the Christ, and to have found in him inspiration and orientation, with the living community as their setting, then I as a theologian will certainly want to know whom they are talking about: a Jesus selected in accordance with purely contemporary fashion and their actual needs, or Jesus of Nazareth, of whom the great Christian traditions – albeit in many languages and tongues – were meant to glean a very specific and pointed message, which we now, in our own needs, have to pass on in a creative but loyal spirit, first and foremost in living by it ourselves. Neither exegete nor theologian can guarantee through his particular discipline this fidelity and creativity; but within the large number of ecclesiastical and temporal factors which serve in their respective ways to mediate the guidance whereby God holds the Church on its true course as a credible hope for the world, there is a distinctive, indispensable place for exegesis and theology.

I shall conclude this introduction, therefore, with some words of Y. Congar's: '*Je respecte et j'interroge sans cesse la science des exégètes, mais je récuse leur magistère.*'[15]

Finally, I know that a scientific-cum-critical approach (my scientifically disciplined standpoint in this book as a believer) is only one of many possibilities. This relativizes the whole book. Yet even this albeit relative standpoint has its own right to existence and, in the end, an inalienable pastoral value of its own. It is with that pastoral intention – 'translatable', one hopes, by others – that this book has been written, as one of many contributions to what can never be articulated as it should, the life's secret of him whom I acknowledge as Jesus of Nazareth, in whom definitive and final salvation is to be found. That – and not some unbrotherly gesture – is the reason why hardly any theologians, but very many exegetes, are cited in this book.

# Part One

# Questions of Method, Hermeneutics and Criteria

# Jesus of Nazareth, norm and criterion of any interpretation of Jesus

Chapter 1

# Historically grounded access of the believer to Jesus of Nazareth

## §1 The structure of the offer of salvation and the Christian response

Literature on the time of Jesus: A. Alt, *Kleine Schriften zur Geschichte des Volkes Israel*, 3 vols, Munich 1953–9; J. Bonsirven, *Le Judaisme palestinien au temps de Jésus-Christ*, 2 vols, Paris 1934–5; W. Foerster, *Neutestamentliche Zeitgeschichte*, vol. 1, *Das Judentum Palästinas zur Zeit Jesu und der Apostel*, Gütersloh 1964[4]; Ch. Guignebert, *Le Monde juif vers le temps de Jésus*, Paris 1950; A. H. Gunneweg, *Geschichte Israels bis Bar Kochba* (Theol. Wissenschaft, 2), Stuttgart 1972; M. Hengel, *Judentum und Hellenismus* (WUNT, 10), Tübingen 1973[2] (1969); J. Jeremias, *Jerusalem zur Zeit Jesu*, 3 vols, Göttingen 1924, 1929, 1937; M. Lagrange, *Le Judaisme avant Jésus-Christ*, Paris 1931; E. Lohmeyer, *Galiläa und Jerusalem* (FRLANT, 34), Göttingen 1936; E. Lohse, *Umwelt des Neuen Testament*, Göttingen 1971; A. D. Nock, *Essays on Religion and the Ancient World*, 2 vols, Cambridge 1972; B. Reicke, *Neutestamentliche Zeitgeschichte*, Berlin 1965; M. Rostovtzeff, *The Social and Economic History of the Hellenistic World*, New York 1941 (=M. Rostowzew, *Gesellschafts- und Wirtschaftsgeschichte der hellenistischen Welt*, 3 vols, Darmstadt 1955–6); E. Schürer, *Geschichte des Jüdischen Volkes im Zeitalter Jesu Christi*, 3 vols, Leipzig 1909–11[4].

A. THE HUMAN PERSON, FOCUS OF MANIFOLD RELATIONSHIPS

A person forms the focus of an extensive area. Thus one cannot pose the question 'Who is Jesus of Nazareth?' without reference to what has already taken place and to what will happen afterwards. No individual can be understood (a) independently of the course of the past events that have surrounded him, that undergird and confront him and elicit his critical reaction, (b) independently of his relations with those about him, contemporaries who have received from him and in turn have influenced him and touched off specific reactions in him, (c) independently of the effect he has had on subsequent history or of what he might have intended to set in motion by direct action of his own. In other words, an individual human being is the personal focal point of a series of interactive relations to the past, the future and his or her own present.

All this is true of Jesus as well – which is why the starting-point for any Christology or Christian interpretation of Jesus is not simply Jesus of Nazareth, still less the Church's *kerygma* or creed. Rather is it the movement which Jesus himself started in the first century of our era; more particularly because this Jesus is known to us, historically speaking, only via that movement. A historical fact is therefore our most justifiable point of departure; and it is that the gospels tell us what a certain man, Jesus, came to mean for the life of a few groups of people. In other words, the starting-point is the first Christian community – but as a reflection of what Jesus himself was, said and did. To Jesus' offer of salvation certain Jews reacted with an unconditional yes. What that offer was we can infer only indirectly from the reactions and other evidences recorded in the New Testament: through the prism of the Christological response of the earliest Christian communities. Thus they speak of Jesus of Nazareth 'in the language of faith'; but in so doing they are still talking about the actual Jesus of Nazareth, a concrete and historical reality that appealed to it.

This is immediately apparent from the tenor of their language. These Christian congregations put the emphasis not on 'Christ died', but on '. . . died *for our sins*', nay, more 'died for our sins *in accordance with the scriptures*' (1 Cor. 15:3); or again 'died, but was raised' (Rom. 8:34; 1 Cor. 15:3–4). To speak of Jesus in the language of faith is to express what the (indeed) historical Jesus had come to signify for his disciples and how this is anchored in Jesus himself. History and empirical knowledge (information, therefore) are present here – but present as interpreted in the language of faith.

The only knowledge we possess of the Christ event reaches us via the concrete experience of the first local communities of Christians, who were sensible of a new life present in them, which they regarded as a gift of the *Pneuma*, the Spirit; an experience of new life in the embrace of the Spirit, but in remembrance of Jesus. That is why I said that the proto-Christian movement centred around Jesus is the inescapable and historically reliable point of departure. We cannot in isolation ask 'Who was Jesus of Nazareth?' Even a historian, asking himself this question, cannot ignore the actual effect of the man – itself part and parcel of a historical process of tradition or a religious and cultural situation-context – on the one hand upon a group of contemporaries who became his disciples, and on the other hand on those who saw him in a quite different light, while evincing just as extraordinary a reaction – one that was to cost him his life. (It is an established fact of history that Jesus, having been handed over by the Jewish authorities, was put to death by the Roman local government.) So the historian is bound to ask: What manner of man must this have been who could trigger such extreme reactions: on the one hand, unconditional faith and on the other, aggressive disbelief? That the Romans, faced with the possibility of political agitation in an occupied territory, should have him crucified says much about our human record of injustice. That the Jewish authorities should hand him over is only explicable (leaving human passions aside) if from a Jewish viewpoint and by conventional standards Jesus had somehow acted in a fundamentally un-Jewish fashion where religion is concerned (giving himself out to be 'messiah' is not enough to account for this: there were a number of other messianic pretenders in those days, and yet they were not put to death for it). On the other hand there were the disciples, who believed in Jesus, responded unreservedly and positively to him and did so in such a way that after his execution they could not articulate the experience that underlay their response except by reaching out for the most varied, most evocative, most lofty religious ideas and codewords available in the Jewish and Gentile worlds: son of man, eschatological prophet, messiah or christ, 'son of God' (in both its Jewish and its Hellenistic meaning), 'lord' (the Jewish *mar* and Hellenistic *kyrios*), and so forth – evocative titles, some of which were full of meaning for Jewish Christians but were simply unintelligible to Christians from the Gentile world (for instance, son of man; messiah), reason enough for them to disappear from the Greek-speaking churches (son of man, for example) or lose all depth of meaning.

This immediately suggests the relative character of the honorific titles used. The important thing is that on the basis of their communal experiences these believers are obliged to grasp for the loftiest titles provided by their religious and cultural milieu, so as to be able in some degree to express in words their past and present experience with Jesus and arising from him. The Christian experience as the local church's communal response to what Jesus actually does offer is the primary thing; the titles, although not unimportant, are secondary; and there again, even in Scripture they are interchangeable, replaceable by others, and they may die out. The saving experience persists and from time to time calls for an appropriate expression and articulation in new social and historical situations. One might call it a 'disclosure' experience, a discovery event: a source experience (both for the person who had known Jesus directly and for the one who had come to know about him by way of the *memoria Jesu* and the life of the local congregation); that is to say, they have discovered in Jesus something that cannot be pinned down directly, on an empirical basis, but that to any open-minded person confronted with Jesus in a living community is going to present itself as something gratuitous, as *'given* in evidence'.

It is interesting to notice the structure of this community experience, which itself links the 'new life' of the local congregation, present in virtue of the Spirit, with Jesus of Nazareth. *Pneuma* and *anamnesis*, Spirit and recollection of Jesus, are experienced as a single reality. Theologically, this is laid out in the New Testament itself in a number of different ways: if we compare Acts 2 with the Johannine gospel and with the initial (Aramaic) Judaeo-Christian Christology (which it is to some extent possible to distil from the synoptics even now), we see that in Acts 2 the 'event of Pentecost', fifty days after Easter, is an aetiological account of the pneumatic experiences of the Christian congregations over several years. In the Johannine gospel the aetio-logically interpreted outpouring of the Spirit falls on Easter day itself, that is, it is directly associated with the resurrection, so that once again Jesus and Spirit, past recollected and present moment, are intrinsically conjoined; the Johannine gospel thematizes the link between *Pneuma* and *anamnesis* (recollection or remembrance) even more precisely when it makes the Lord say that the Spirit when he comes will bring all things to their remembrance (John 14:26; 15:26; 16:13–14). The local congregation's pneumatic experiences are intrinsically bound up with the *memoria Jesu*. There is an organic connection between the present, the here-and-now of the communal experiences (*Pneuma*), and the Jesus 'past' (recollection).

There is a structure that we find within and even outside the synoptic gospels, only in the Johannine gospel it is more explicitly and deliberately formulated. For the formula 'Do you not remember . . .?' also occurs frequently outside the Johannine gospel (see Mk. 8:18–19 cf. Mt. 16:9; Mk. 14:9 cf. Mt. 26:13; Lk. 24:6–8; Acts 20:35; 2 Pet. 1:12–15; 3:1–2). Lastly, the Church itself affirms in the eucharistic formula that its liturgical celebration is carried out 'in remembrance of Jesus' (Lk. 22:19; 1 Cor. 11:24–25). In other words the Church's *kerygma* is at the same time a recollection of the earthly Jesus, of what he said and did. This whole book should make that clear enough.

So when the Christian congregations reflect upon their own experience, they interpret it in relation both to the Spirit and to Jesus of Nazareth; so much so that these two relations appeared initially to be one: 'The Lord is the *Pneuma*', Paul could still say at an early stage (2 Cor. 3:17). Again, the community articulated its experience of this relationship in (a) stories about Jesus (sayings, stories and parables as a *memoria Jesu*) and in (b) *kerygmata*, hymns and credal declarations, whereby in ways that varied considerably in the different local churches the gist of what Jesus signified for them was couched in the language of faith and thus could be trumpeted abroad.

The experience of the first Christian congregations, inseparably associated with first-hand contact with Jesus and later, through the *memoria Jesu*, with a continuing fellowship with the Lord, is therefore the matrix of the New Testament as a written text. And thanks to that, the earliest Christian congregations, with their experience, are historically accessible to us; they afford, at a historical level, the most reliable access to Jesus of Nazareth. What the historical Jesus has left us is not in the first instance a kind of résumé or bits and pieces of preaching about God's approaching dominion, nor a *kerygma* or string of *verba et facta ipsissima*, that is, a pure record of precisely what he did as a historical individual or a number of directives and wise sayings that can fairly certainly be picked out from the gospels. What he did leave – only through what he was, did and had said, simply through his activities as this particular human being – was a movement, a living fellowship of believers who had become conscious of being the new people of God, the eschatological 'gathering' of God – not a 'sacred remnant' but the firstborn of the gathering together of all Israel, and eventually of all human kind: an eschatological liberation movement for bringing together all people, bringing them together in unity. Universal *shalom*.[1]


## B.    REVELATION AND '*Le Croyable Disponible*'

More or less parallel with the Reformed *kerygma* theology of K. Barth and especially of R. Bultmann, who set up in opposition to the liberal-historical quest for Jesus in the nineteenth century, from around 1910 to 1960 Catholic theology too, reacting against modernism, was dominated by '*Le donné révélé*' (title of a well-known work by A. Gardeil). In so far as this entails a predetermined and as it were positiv-istically interpreted, revealed given, many now regard it with suspicion. The sociology of the cognitive process, and cognate (in particular linguistic) sciences, have given us a more exact insight into the structure of all knowing (to which the knowledge imparted by faith, despite its irreducible character, forms no exception). This makes us realize that actuality, in so far as it is experienced and considered by us – in other words, reality *qua* experience – is inherently coloured and partly con-ditioned by the social (mental and cultural) paraphernalia that we carry with us from the past into the present: the cultural pattern that charges even our inner life.[2] That is why the particular fact of experience that forms the Christian faith is not only dependent on the offer of the reality itself (Jesus of Nazareth) but – as experienced and expressed, for instance, in creeds and statements of belief, in liturgy and theology – at the same time it is inherently coloured and co-determined by the apparatus of the human mind here and now, by what is technically described as the 'cultural situation-context'. This implies that what is reality for faith is set in the midst of history, is itself an intrinsic part of man's history, is itself history and culture. Revelation and the cultural-cum-historical expression of it are not to be had separately. Revelation is always partly given in what P. Ricoeur calls '*le croyable disponible*' of a certain period, that is, the whole formed by generally accepted assump-tions, expectations and ideologies, which none the less (and that is the Christian view) change inwardly in and through the fact that they be-come the 'wave-beat' of revelation. Thus the Christian from the Hellenistic *oikoumene* is in every respect more like other Romans and Greeks than his fellow-Christians in 1973; even so, in an expressly Christian context the 1973 Christian is closer to the Hellenistic Christian than to many of his own contemporaries. Awareness of this fact that every religion, the Christian one included, is conditioned by cultural-cum-historical factors substantially relativizes the absolute character of values as currently apprehended, just as it also mitigates the pressure of the past. On the other hand the gospel makes a proviso with regard to every one of its cultural expressions, in *kerygma*, dogma, creed or theology. It is clear from the primitive Christian use of such honorific titles as son of man, messiah, Christ, Son of God that the Christian faith, in the very appeal it makes to this cultural-religious heritage in which the revelation is articulated, at the same time distances itself from that inheritance. So the Christian's response to the question of Christian identity can never be a total identification with the culture – even the religious culture – which surrounds him and in which he participates; nor indeed can the faith of the Christian be identified completely with even the most official articulations of it, although the mystery of faith which they enshrine is validly and truly expressed in them. Because of this tension between the mystery of faith and its articulation, con-ditioned by the religious culture, there is need not only for a historical approach to dogma and a hermeneutic evaluation of primitive Chris-tianity and its subsequent development, but also for a sociological enquiry that will size up ideologies in a critical spirit. In a new language of faith, identifying Jesus of Nazareth for the believer, the critical reservation about the dominant categories, expectations and ideologies of the day *and* the non-identification with these are bound to appear, therefore, precisely in the appeal to both. In its very expression the reservation is (inevitably, from an anthropological standpoint) essen-tially cultural and formative of culture: formative, therefore, of the Church. Every religious movement is *ipso facto* something inextricably involved in a historical and cultural process. The recurrent question here is: Does it preserve a critical, creative tension *vis-à-vis* this, its own socio-cultural world? This may be ascertained by tracking down the particular Christian variant through which it actually participates in the movements of the whole culture, or else from the absence of such a variant.

We can see this tension present in the earliest belief- and creed-structure of the New Testament. From all the complexes of tradition merging together there, however diverse their origins might be, it becomes evident that the first Christians found salvation in Jesus – salvation that was conclusive and was imparted by God. In the light of this experience they named that saving reality the Christ, the son of man, the Lord, and so forth. Thus they applied certain key concepts already current in their religious culture to Jesus, concepts which were 'vacant', so to speak, and acquired their Christian meaning only when applied to him. In the first instance, therefore, they were expressing their reaction to whatever it was they ended up with of Jesus' person, message and ministry; their actual experiences before and after the death of Jesus were thereby fused together into a single image. All the same, it is an obvious fact that they made use of existing concepts like messiah, son of man, and so forth, which bore their own distinctive meaning – a historical accretion that was not in all respects applicable to Jesus; obvious too that understanding Jesus as they did to be the very essence of final salvation, they deliberately modified these concepts in the very act of applying them to Jesus by filling them out with recollections of his life and death here on earth. It must be said, therefore, that the criterion for the designation or identification of Jesus in the New Testament was not the meaning already attached to the existing titles, but Jesus himself. It is the disciples' way of expressing their conviction that in him they had found their final salvation; and they do it in rather strange conceptual terms so as to put into words the peculiar nature of it.

In this structure of belief there is a pronounced tension. Jesus himself, as an individual human being, was for his part immersed in a developing situation, shifting and uncertain: a very specific historical tradition, namely, that of his people, the Jews, who saw themselves as the 'people of God', servant of and witness to God before the whole world. Jesus, within that tradition (so interpreted), sensed that he was responsible for his own place and particular task in it. But he saw himself confronted with divergent interpretations, already given within his environment, of what this 'people of God' and 'kingdom of God' might signify – an apocalyptic, an eschatological, an ethical, a politico-Zealotic, a Pharisaic interpretation (to mention only the chief ones). Within that diversity Jesus took a very personal stand, although it was in particular his humiliating execution that made his message and his chosen mode of life historically ambiguous. Aside still from any *kerygma* or credal formulation on the side of the Church, all of this is a valid conclusion from careful historical studies of the sources. One must not lose sight, therefore, of the historically contingent framework of Jesus' ministry, when speaking of Jesus in the language of faith as the Messiah or Christ, the son of man, the Lord, the Son of God and so on.

Still less is it permissible to absolutize in a quite unhistorical way the (biblical) articulation of what Jesus said and did in those concrete circumstances by detaching it from the historically coloured speech categories of that time, in which this Jesus event was verbalized: we cannot elevate this linguistic process into 'timeless categories'. Indeed we are warned against that – in the New Testament itself – by the multiplicity of Christological dogmas and diverse formulae for indicating the kingdom of God, redemption and salvation in Christ. For on their side too the earliest congregations reacting to Jesus found themselves in a quite specific cultural and religious context. Not only does the language of the original creeds and *kerygmata* (or declarations of belief) share therefore in the historical ambiguity, but the diversity of these creeds itself (under pressure, none the less, of the historical Jesus-reality) is likewise conditioned in the first instance by what to human understanding are the historical ambiguity, manifold nuances and (rationally speaking) opaque character of this very 'phenomenon of Jesus'; conditioned too by the cultural-religious concepts used by the first Christians, the further development of which was occasioned partly by the concrete activity of Jesus himself.

Hence it may appear that from the outset the hermeneutical problem, or the problem of understanding a Christological belief in Jesus of Nazareth, is centred on a conflict. The problem is, first and foremost, that there exists a critical tension between on the one hand the 'phenomenon of Jesus', his person, message, ministry and death – a richly variegated, extraordinary and distinctive life which, taken as a whole, can be interpreted historically in diverse ways – and on the other, the religious and cultural expectations, aspirations and ideologies present in the culture constituting his environment, with its own pre-established key concepts, employed by other people to express in historically concrete terms what they were confronted with in Jesus, and eventually to record it in the New Testament and in the subsequent history of the Church. Only secondarily is the problem of interpretation in effect the question as to how we can translate what it is in that tension which emerges as a real offer of salvation in Jesus Christ in terms of our contemporary (and critically envisaged) culture. The tension inherent in every credal statement and theology explains the diversity of the numerous Christological responses, in the New Testament itself and in later church history. Thus this pluralism which at rock bottom is 'held together' by Jesus as he lived on earth and was apprehended by other people has a twofold origin: (a) on the one hand the various religious and cultural circumstances and traditions of those who became Christians and (b) on the other, the amazing fascination exerted in all sorts of ways upon his disciples by Jesus' person, life, message and death. Even during Jesus' lifetime this last factor, especially, gave rise to many different sorts of ideas and images which were circulating about him, in which impressions of the milieu in which Jesus operated or particular aspects of his person that fascinated his contemporaries were brought to the fore in a special manner. The tension inherent in this situation was more or less bound to entail that in the course of the Church's history in earlier periods, those derived from the New Testament and from conciliar definitions – which naturally enshrine the tension between the salvation thus offered and its concrete expression in words – should assume an independent status and themselves become as it were the direct object of Christological belief. In this way they may actually obscure the reality of Jesus, calling as it does upon faith to interpret and endow with meaning. Thus there emerges a self-centred, formalized *kerygma* Christology which seems to forget that what is being proclaimed is the resurrection from the dead, not of this, that or the other person among the many crucified at that time but of Jesus alone. Some supporters of a *kerygma* theology would hold it possible to posit as background to the formal Easter *kerygma* equally, in the end, either Barabbas or the 'good murderer', so called, or at any rate John the Baptist. But the *kerygma* is proclaimed only of Jesus; which really means that it must have an intrinsic connection with Jesus as he lived on earth – with his person, message, way of life and death. Anyone who loses sight of that turns the *kerygma* into a myth. In other words, if we ask what is meant by the 'eschatological salvation' given us by the crucified-and-risen One, to give substance and content to this we have to point to Jesus of Nazareth himself, his person and his whole career and course of action up to and including his death.

### C.  THE CONSTANT UNITIVE FACTOR

From this fundamental tension we can see why it is that within the New Testament as it stands there is to be found a motley whole of varying interpretations of Jesus that go back to the first local communities of Christians: the thing is done one way in Mark, differently in Matthew and Luke, differently again in the case of Paul and in the Johannine gospel. Via the gospels and Paul it is possible to reconstruct, with a fair degree of certainty, a number of yet more primitive variations: a Hebrew and Judaeo-Greek Jerusalem Christology, a pre-Pauline Christology, a pre-Marcan, a pre-Johannine one and, finally, the Christology of the Q community, where the Christological confession is often less developed though never totally absent. Of a non-dogmatic representation of Jesus there is no trace anywhere. To look in the synoptic or pre-synoptic material for an undogmatic, as it were totally 'neat' historical core (what indeed is such a thing?) is to hunt a will-o'-the-wisp. Jesus is to be found there only as the subject of confession on the part of Christians. Thus we are always coming up against the Christian movement. The question then arises: What is the constant factor that will create unity within this variegated whole?

There are a number of well-tried solutions, so I shall first of all indicate where the solution cannot lie.

(a) Not in the gospels or in the integral New Testament as such. The canonical writings confront us with diverse Christologies. Attending only to the terms in which they are articulated, I cannot see any place where in this plane a constant unitive factor might be found. Could all these biblical Christologies, taken together, be normative? In a formal sense, of course, and for the Christian the assertion that 'the whole Bible is normative' is a right and proper one – but in itself it gets us nowhere. What are we to do, for instance, with the just as authentically biblical Christology of the son of man, when this initially so important apocalyptic term, first transferred to the Jesus who, though risen, comes as the son of man, disappears in other parts of the New Testament and has not even been adopted, explicitly at any rate, into the Christian creed; whereas it once constituted the entire Christology of certain Graeco-Palestinian, Judaeo-Christian local congregations as far off as Transjordania and Syria? A thoroughly Scriptural orthodoxy does not entail conferring upon Jesus simultaneously all the images and titles available. Formal endorsement of the Bible's authority *in toto* on the part of the exegetes (whether Catholic or Reformed) means in practice only that a particular component or single theme in the Bible is set over the rest, often to accord with an individual's own confessional bent or personal preference, religious and theological. This brings us to a second unsatisfactory solution.

(b) Nor is the constant unitive factor the 'gospel within the gospel', the best of the best in the New Testament. This criterion is very subjective, of course: it usually results in selection determined by confessional allegiance, and again gives rise to pluralism among the Christian exegetes. Moreover, many exponents of *Formgeschichte* often prop up this criterion on the postulate of a single 'primitive *kerygma*' from which, it is supposed, diverse interpretations followed on step by step, while there is good reason to assume that the various *kerygmata* of the 'local churches' subsequently coalesced into the (ecumenical) credal confession of the emerging 'great Church' (see later sections).

(c) For the same reasons it is equally impossible for the most primitive picture of Jesus that we could reconstruct to function as a norm or constant unitive factor. However important the oldest tradition may be (supposing there were not diverse 'oldest pictures of Jesus' in circulation from the very start, as there may well have been), an experience of recognizing-and-recollecting, as first articulated, is not *ipso facto* the richest or most subtle one, although as a delimiting and admonitory factor it is still important to the developing process in which people try to put into words more and more clearly the richness of what has actually been experienced. Later on, the first articulation turns out to have been imperfect, after all, and incomplete, when set over against the impression someone has actually made upon us, which we realize fully only in retrospect. Early and not so early encapsulations of an experience in words often provide a reciprocal critique. Thus in Mark it is fairly evident (especially from a structural analysis) that while he certainly believes in Jesus as the Christ and above all as the Son of God, that is always provided these concepts are made to refer to the 'suffering son of man'. Obviously, a theological critique is already being applied here to partial representations of Jesus.

(d) Nor can Jesus' own self-awareness be a unitive factor or criterion. I mean by self-awareness – as distinct from self-understanding or interpretation – the psychology of Jesus, his inner life and his character. Of this we know very little. Of course we can get to know quite a lot about Jesus' understanding of himself, albeit indirectly, through his proclamation of the kingdom of God, his insistence on 'discipleship', his intercourse with social and religious 'outcasts', his parables confronting the Jews with a decisive choice, and so forth. Jesus' self-understanding in his relation to God and to other people is indeed of capital importance. But the notion of total power and authority or *exousia*, at least as applying to even the earthly Jesus, is clearly an editorial element in Mark. It is only by way of the 'disclosure' experience undergone by disciples that we are able to get at what brought it into being. All along there is an intermediary factor, historically sited, Christian or ecclesiastical.

(e) Again, the very sayings and acts of Jesus ('*ipsissima verba et facta*', so called) are not in the running as a criterion and a unitive factor. Even if historically authentic sayings and actions of Jesus can be distilled from Scripture, they were a matter of choice on the part of local Christian communities which make no mention of other sayings and acts of his. So once again it is only via their interpretative selection that we get anywhere near to Jesus. What is more, even those few sayings and acts said to allow of direct historical access turn up within the gospels in an ecclesiastical context; while the particular context in which Jesus uttered or performed them we cannot usually – and can never fully – recover. Without the situational context of this or that saying (except, up to a point, with parables) one can arrive at many different interpretations; and no one can determine what *the* meaning is. For the same reasons the alleged 'radicalism of Jesus' or the non-Judaizing character of synoptic and earlier traditions cannot be a criterion, either. The traits in question may be based on academic postulates. Someone who starts by accepting various early Christian traditions can actually see in a one-sided emphasis on a single tradition, not so far criticized or corrected by other Jesus traditions, a 'radicalizing' process. In other words they are still purely hypothetical and, it may be, unreliable criteria. The radicalizing may just as well come from certain local churches and not from Jesus.

(f) Lastly, no constant unitive factor is provided by credal statements and homologues in the Bible. How quickly the expression 'son of man' disappears, does it not? It does not turn up in a credal affirmation anywhere. And what is the relevance of Davidic messianism for non-Jewish, Hellenistic Christians? Then again, there is pluralism in these biblical confessions of faith, and development; here it is only with the resurrection that Jesus would seem to be given the status of Christ, Messiah and Lord; there it is the idea of 'adoption' that comes into play. Jesus, having died, held 'in readiness' by God, will presently return as son of man, as a judge armed with authority and power: 'Heaven had to receive him until the time of the restoration of all things', says Acts 3:21;[3] there again we have an incarnation Christology and a pre-existent Christ. In these *credos* and liturgical hymns everything cannot have the same normative value, and certainly not at one and the same time: either one must arraign a bit of Bible or else arrive at an artificial compilation, a kind of sum that as such has nothing to do with the actual Scriptures. It is true, of course, that the meaning of one title eventually gets transferred to other titles, so that in the end they all become elusive and they all try to express everything about Jesus. Then the point is: What precisely does 'everything' mean, in that case? An articulation, in being definitive, is also delimiting; but if all these titles say everything, they run the risk of becoming so many meaningless formalized expressions. Besides the liturgical *credos*, therefore, the pre-synoptic traditions likewise contain transmitted elements of the *memoria Jesu*, especially with regard to his miracles, his message of the approaching rule of God, as well as his conduct and way of life. Are these less prescriptive or constitutive *vis-à-vis* the church community than the formal statements of belief?

From this negative result it is at once evident that a (modern) Christological interpretation of Jesus cannot start from the *kerygma* (or dogma) about Jesus, or indeed from a so-called 'purely historical' Jesus of Nazareth; whereas a historical and critical approach, set within an intention of faith, remains the only proper starting-point. As so far all these sallies have proved to be unsatisfactory, what in the way of a constant unitive factor is left? I would say (and this really is something): the Christian movement itself. In other words a Christian oneness of experience which does indeed take its unity from its pointing to the one figure of Jesus, while none the less being pluriform in its verbal expression or articulation. 'You yourselves', Paul writes to the Christians at Corinth, 'are . . . an open letter from Christ – written not on tablets of stone but on tablets of human hearts' (2 Cor. 3:2–3). By unity of experience I mean not an individual or individualistic religious experience of Jesus, a sort of 'revivalism', but a community experience, in the sense of an ecclesial or collective experience which obliges people to define the ultimate meaning and purport of their lives by reference to Jesus of Nazareth or, to put it in traditional and equally proper terms, which causes people to interpret Jesus' life as the definitive or eschatological activity of God in history for the salvation or deliverance of men and women. The constant factor here is that particular groups of people find final salvation imparted by God in Jesus of Nazareth. In other words, on the basis of and in that experience we see two aspects in the life of Jesus: (a) this life has an effect within the historical situation of the Christian congregations here and now, and (b) has a significance that is crucial for the fundamental option presented by life here on earth and so for the eschatological relation of fellowship with God. Next we see that determining in this way the final and definitive meaning of our own life by reference to Jesus of Nazareth is not something given or appropriated once and for all. It is a decision that a person must take, subject to circumstances, over and over again, and must then continually re-articulate. That is to say, one cannot formalize a *kerygma*, for instance, 'Jesus is the Lord'. One has to make Jesus the prescriptive, determining factor in one's life in accordance with changing situations, cultural, social and ecclesial: and in that context one will proceed to live out, experience and put into words what 'making Jesus the determining factor' really entails at this precise moment. For Christians from a Jewish background the 'words' in question included Lord (*mar*), son of man and messiah; and this had far-reaching consequences for their faith and life. It might be more accurate to say that because they felt these consequences to be meaningful for the life they lived from day to day 'in Jesus', they describe him in that way. To Greek Christians those titles said nothing; but from their cult of Caesar they were familiar with the *'Kyrios'*, so that for them it is not the emperor but Jesus who is the *Kyrios*. That meant a good deal.

Thus the Jesus event lies at the source of the 'local congregation' experience to which we have historical access; and it governs that communal experience. To put it another way: the constant factor is the changing life of the 'assembly of God' or 'assembly (congregation) of Christ', the community-fashioning experience evoked by the impress Jesus makes and, in the Spirit, goes on making upon his followers, people who have experienced final salvation in Jesus of Nazareth. Priority must be conceded to the actual offer that is Jesus; but this is embedded, vested in the assent of faith on the part of the Christian community we experience as being amidst us in our history. We might say: Jesus was such as to engender precisely that typical reaction of faith which was confirmed by the 'local church' sort of experiences.

### D. THE TENSION BETWEEN JESUS AND THE NEW TESTAMENT

What are the implications of all this? First of all, that one cannot in the first instance, I would think, see the revelation of God in Jesus in an infallibly inspired Bible which as a direct Word of God is alleged to be normative for us – and that on a basis of what is (wrongly) described as its literal meaning (which exegetical analysis then often reveals to be very different from what was at first supposed). Revelation is the saving activity of God as both experienced and expressed in words. In that verbalizing process the Old Testament plays an essential role; for Jesus is talked about in the New Testament as the prophet, the son of man, the exalted one, the Lord – all of them notions grounded in the Old Testament or in pre- and non-Christian Judaism of the post-Old Testament period. The New Testament is the Christian interpretation of what had been people's experience with Jesus and was still their experience in the local Christian communities, admittedly in the light of the Old Testament. This Christian exegesis of the Old Testament partly explains the multiplicity of the New Testament interpretations of Jesus, which led to diverse Christologies, a process that was to be continued in patristic theology only up to a point.

The question then arises: Where in that case is the Bible's authority located? To that I want to try and give a two-pronged reply.

On the one hand the New Testament as a document is set within the life of a movement and gives us a close-up of it during the very specific – and extensive – period of its initial crystallization (from the chronologically first piece of writing to the last, a period of about fifty to sixty years). Even this goes to show that the New Testament has no detached, independent authority. It is the deposit of a 'movement' which, albeit within the Old Testament Scriptural tradition, existed before the New Testament writings and carries on as usual after them. The living church community is the normative witnessing instrument that Jesus has given us (see 2 Cor. 3:2–3). Furthermore, it is possible to view the movement centred around Jesus – and the early Jerusalemic and Palestinian congregations did so view it – as a phenomenon inside Judaism itself, even though eschatologically (in line with Old Testament traditions: e.g., Isa. 2:2–5) the pagans were called (by God) to share it (Mt. 8:10–11 and parallels). But the Christian movement goes on developing within contingent, historical circumstances. Thus the witness of the New Testament turns out to be just the deposit of particular communal experiences, during that very period; and this relativizes its authority.

On the other hand there is something irreplaceable, something unique afoot in the New Testament. After all, it gives us the most direct, uniquely practicable and historically most reliable access to the original event, the Christian movement that took its impetus from Jesus of Nazareth. The initial disclosure experience of the first Christians, some of whom had in the meantime already died, is presented freshly in the New Testament via reliable traditions: there are even some happenings on record that are embarrassing for the Christian communities and their leaders and so will not have been constantly in their minds. The first generations of Christians believe that this Jesus (i.e. a historical reality) is the *Christ* (i.e. a 'disclosure', expressed in a Jewish term evocative for them). Their loftiest expectations and Utopias they see realized concretely in Jesus. Neither Jesus nor the earliest 'church community' constitutes the fount and origin of Christianity, but both together as offer and response. No Christianity without Jesus, but equally none without Christians. This source event, the fashioning of the Christian congregation, does indeed have normative value: the primitive Church reflects or mirrors, in its New Testament, the Jesus event in its effect on a group of people. Constantly repeated contact with the primary response to an initial offer in history remains normative, therefore, for its own response. In that sense, as the Church's 'charter' or foundation document, there can be no substitute for the New Testament's authority. If the Catholic interpretation that the Church is the sole living relict of Jesus of Nazareth, and therefore the norm for our understanding of the faith, might be called a splendid intuition (being indirectly corroborated by historical criticism), the Reformation principle of the inalienable normative value of the biblical witnesses finds a like critical confirmation. The two interpretations merge into one: Reformed Christians acknowledge the Bible as the 'book of the Church'[4] and the dogmatic constitution, 'Dei Verbum', of Vatican II recognizes that not even the Church's magisterium is 'lord' over Scripture, but is 'subject' to the revelation of God as articulated by Christians in the Bible.[5] Because the congregation-based experiences deposited in Scripture are the constant factor whereby the whole New Testament is held together in its plural Christologies, the New Testament as a document – and in its totality at that – is to some extent part and parcel of this unitive factor. Thus the interpretative norm provided by Scripture can only be rendered more specific via the method of systematic co-ordination: in that way the biblical text, in so far as it actually mirrors the life of diverse Christian congregations, is the interpretative norm. To that something else must be added. Despite internal tensions the New Testament affords a relatively coherent picture which on the one hand can be taken to be a result of the historical effect of the one Jesus at the source of the somewhat dissonant traditions, and on the other hand to be the expression of an 'ecumenical' desire to marshal the original and diverse Christian traditions into a unity. For us too, therefore, this ecumenical desire for unification, which is noticeable in the synoptics and perhaps even in pre-synoptic traditions, is an indispensable element of the interpretative norm.[6]

At the same time all this implies that the historic process of the Christian response to Jesus is not concluded when the New Testament canon is finally settled. Again and again it stands in the way of a rather exaggerated ascription of authority to the Bible. Even within the New Testament one Christian congregation will present a critique, through the mouth of its evangelist, of the articulation of other congregations: we can see for instance how Matthew and Luke make free with what is after all Mark's material – classified now as 'New Testament material'. No trace of biblicism, then, in the Bible itself; rather the contrary. So how can we make a biblicist appeal to Scripture? Biblicism is unbiblical.

Thus the New Testament – in its normative value, grounded in the experience of the 'churches of Christ' – turns out to be in no sense a depository of eternal, literally unalterable truths that (as regards language and expression) should only be hermeneutically interpreted for our times. Rather is it a differentiated whole of diverse Christological responses to Jesus' offer, a diversity that on the one hand is intrinsically limited by the historical offer itself and so by the *memoria Jesu* and on the other hand is none the less induced by new historical situations. The transition from a Jewish Christianity to a 'Gentile' one produces, for instance, a new Christology, a new 'image' of Jesus inside the Bible itself – yet still within the bounds of the *memoria Jesu*. It is not only that the gift of Christianity is conveyed to the Gentiles; Christianity is itself enriched thereby and thus acquires a new form and aspect, a distinctive and so far unexpressed response (with new problems in its train!). Even in the biblical context the conclusion is plain, therefore: the critical relation to concrete present circumstances is part of the Christological response to Jesus. This relation partly determines the Christology: the 'things remembered of Jesus' remain a governing principle, but then as fertilized by immediate, present issues. Later on, in a concrete situation and starting from his middle Platonic philosophy – generally prevalent in orthodox Christian circles too – Arius made it necessary for the Christian community to use what in origin was actually a semi-gnostic term (*homousia*, consubstantiality) so as faithfully to preserve, having regard to the question posited, the *memoria Jesu*. Over philosophical middle Platonism the Church was illogical (philosophically, Arius was the most consistent); but it was faithful to the community experience gripped by the *anamnesis* of Jesus. Thus the Christian allegiance to him broke through the even for orthodox Christians universally self-evident character of this philosophy.[7] The 'heretics' were not infrequently the most consistent about the concretely given horizon of philosophical understanding, immanent within the system, which all Christians too assumed as their point of departure; but with the 'orthodox' the logical coherence of a philosophical system carried less weight than the *memoria Jesu Christi* as that appears, for example, in the gospels, in liturgical prayer (thus for the Third Person of the Trinity) or in popular devotion (for the *homoousia* of Christ with God) and the praxis (actual conduct) of the local Christian churches, concretely expressed in their way of life. In that way, and at that critical moment in history, they rescued Christianity and at the same time exposed the philosophical falseness of the model currently in use. Subsequently, within a different philosophical horizon or experiential context, 'heretics' who as a matter of history had made a choice of the wrong alternative were able to carry their point when their basically Christian intention came to be detached from the obligatory philosophy of an earlier time. Often enough their heresy was not directly Christological, but rather a question of failing to give the last word to faith and not to philosophy.

What all this means is that the present with its contemporary empirical models (also just a fleeting element in the onward movement of history) has to be the place where we, as Christians, must make our Christological response. Proclamation and theology must always have a time index. The fact that our age yearns for peace and justice, for *shalom*, for liberation of what is unliberated, will rightly – and fundamentally – give our Jesus-image an articulation all its own, but within the bounds set by the 'things remembered of Jesus'. To proclaim him the great political revolutionary is to contradict the *memoria Jesu* (as well as the results of critical study) and is simply projecting our (quite possibly justified) aspirations on to him. But on the other hand, because the constant factor in Christianity is that Christians determine the final or ultimate meaning of their concrete history by reference to Jesus of Nazareth, the new 'exegete' of God and champion of man, the immediate significance of that life, the splendid expectations of our century – the demand for a more just world – rightly help to define our image of Jesus. Did not the first Jewish Christians, even, assimilate their religious and human (messianic) expectations to their Jesus-image? It should not and cannot be otherwise, if the gist of the basic Christological affirmation is God's definitive saving action in our history through and in Jesus, or Jesus as the definitive point of human existence in this world. Unless we do this, we are putting our faith in a purely ideological, abstract or magical *kerygma*: 'Jesus is the Lord.' So it is that the eschatological solidarity and unity of all human beings, of all peoples, must become in the Christian churches of today an exemplary, expansive and active reality in service to the world: 'Church as sacrament, that is, as sign and intermediary, of a profound union with God and of unity between all human beings.'[8]

The things that men experience and expect in these days are one constitutive element, therefore, of our response to 'But whom do you say that I am?'; just as when it came to proclaiming Jewish Christianity to the Gentiles, the Hellenistic situation had a directly hermeneutical function for the question as to what the Christian gospel signified for Gentile Christians. How otherwise was it possible, four centuries after the New Testament had been completed, for yet another dogma – a truth of revelation – to come into being, and to do so in the terms of a post-biblical philosophy (Chalcedon)? Revelation as a real 'public disclosure' is actually accomplished only in the response of faith from within a very concrete situation with its own conceptual horizon and field of questioning. And our questions are other than those of times past.

*Conclusion*: along with the primary reality of the offer constituted by Jesus, in and through Jesus alive in the Church with its living remembrance of Jesus of Nazareth, interpretation from within the current situation is a further constitutive element for what we refer to as God's disclosure of salvation in Jesus Christ. When we take into account the structure that characterizes the 'naming' of Jesus by Christians in the New Testament and the way that structure changes in the light of the continually shifting experience of God's gift of salvation in Jesus, it is clearly in full accord with the gospel for us, with a like experience of salvation, to give new names to Jesus. The basic cultural-religious categories of our period lend themselves equally well to that purpose as those of earlier ages; but then with the same proviso that they are judged to conform to the yardstick of the historical reality that is Jesus himself, for whom 'God's cause' is essentially 'the cause of man' and who is therefore wholly on God's side and wholly on man's side: 'for God' and 'for man'. This saving reality can be assessed from various angles, which is why even in early Christianity some very diverse images of Jesus emerge that seem to us at times to be contradictory. But the way life was envisaged in the ancient East and Asia Minor entailed different standards of reference regarding 'contradiction' and 'non-contradiction' from those which people today have here in the West.[9]

## §2  Jesus of Nazareth, acclaimed as the Christ, object of historico-critical enquiry

*Literature*. Since the discussion between R. Bultmann and E. Käsemann (the 'new Quest' or the post-liberal pursuit of the historical Jesus) it has become impossible to survey the full range of the literature on the subject; which is why only a few studies of real significance are mentioned here.

R. Baumann, *2000 Jahre danach. Eine Bestandsaufnahme zur Sache Jesu*, Stuttgart 1971; Th. Boman, *Die Jesus-Ueberlieferung im Lichte der neueren Volkskunde*, Göttingen 1967; R. Bultmann, 'Das Verhältnis der urchristlichen Christusbotschaft zum historischen Jesus', in *Der historische Jesus und der kerygmatische Christus* (ed. H. Ristow and K.

Matthiae) (Berlin 1960), 233-5 (and the book *in toto*); N. A. Dahl, 'Der historische Jesus als geschichtswissenschaftliches und theologisches Problem', in KuD 1 (1956), 109-37; H. Diem, *Der irdische Jesus und der Christus des Glaubens*, Tübingen 1957; G. Ebeling, 'Die Frage nach dem historischen Jesus und das Problem der Christologie', in ZThK 56 (1959), 14-30; E. Fuchs, *Die Frage nach dem historischen Jesus*, in *Gesammelte Aufsätze*, II, (Tübingen 1960), 143-67; H. Grass, 'Historisch-kritische Forschung und Dogmatik', in *Theologie und Kritik* (Göttingen 1969), 9-27; F. Hahn, W. Lohff, G. Bornkamm, *Die Frage nach dem historischen Jesus und die Eigenart der uns zur Verfügung stehenden Quellen* (Evang. Forum, 2), Göttingen 1962; E. Heitsch, 'Die Aporie des historischen Jesus als Problem theologischer Hermeneutik', in ZThK 53 (1956), 192-210; E. Käsemann, 'Das Problem des historischen Jesus', in *Besinnungen* (I), 187-213; 'Die Anfänge christlicher Theologie', in loc. cit. (II), 82-104; and 'Sackgassen im Streit um den historischen Jesus', in loc. cit. (II), 31-68; L. E. Keck, *A Future for the Historical Jesus*, Nashville-New York 1971; W. G. Kümmel, 'Jesus-forschung seit 1950', in ThR 31 (1965-6), 15-46, 289-315, and: *Das Neue Testament im 20. Jahrhundert. Eine Forschungsbericht* (SBS, 50), Stuttgart 1970; G. Lindeskog, 'Christus-kerygma und Jesustradition', in NovT 5 (1962), 144-56; W. Marxsen, 'Zur Frage nach dem historischen Jesus', in ThZ 87 (1962), 575-88, and 'Jesus, oder das Neue Testament', in *Der Exeget als Theologe* (Gütersloh 1968), 246-64; H. Meyer, 'Die theologische Relevanz der historisch-kritischen Methode', in *Kransbacher Gespräch der lutherischen Bischofskonferenz zur Auseinandersetzung um die Bibel*, Berlin-Hamburg 1967[2]; F. Muszner, 'Der historische Jesus und der Christus des Glaubens', in BZ 1 (1957), 224-52; H. Ott, *Die Frage nach dem historischen Jesus und die Ontologie der Geschichte*, Zürich 1960; James Robinson, *The New Quest of the Historical Jesus*, Naperville, 1959; J. Roloff, *Das Kerygma*, 9-50; S. Schulz, 'Die neue Frage nach dem historischen Jesus', in *Neues Testament und Geschichte* (O. Cullmann, 70th birthday) (Tübingen 1972), 33-42; H. Schürmann, 'Zur aktuellen Situation der Leben-Jesu-Forschung', in GuL 46 (1973), 300-10; G. Strecker, 'Die historische und theologische Problematik der Jesusfrage', in EvTh 29 (1969), 453-76; P. Stuhlmacher, 'Kritische Marginalien zum gegenwärtigen Stand der Frage nach Jesus', in *Fides et Communicatio* (Festschrift for M. Doerne) (Göttingen 1970), 341-61; A. Vögtle, 'Die historische und theologische Tragweite der heutigen Evangelienforschung', in ZKTh 86 (1964), 385-417; *Jésus ou le Christ* (Foi vivante, 130), Paris 1970.

A.  DIVERSE IMAGES OF JESUS AND JESUS THE OBJECT OF HISTORI-
CAL ENQUIRY

Enough has been said to make us realize that every period has its own
way of representing Jesus. That was already the case in the various
phases of primitive Christianity. But the process continued well
beyond that. Just as in the Letter to the Hebrews Jesus was already the
heavenly high priest, for the early Fathers God 'who became man in
order to make man divine' and give him everlasting life, in Byzantium
the 'Christus Victor', Pantocrator and Sun-god, 'Light of Light'; so in
the early and high Middle Ages he became the one who makes satisfaction, who has ransomed us, and at the same time the 'Jesus of the
*via crucis*' and the Christmas manger. Later on, for Luther, he was one
who achieved reconciliation with God in a free and sovereign act that
covers our guilt and invites us to rely unconditionally on God's
favourable verdict; then came the Christ-mystique of the incarnate
Word in French spirituality of the seventeenth century, the veneration
of the 'childhood of Jesus' and of 'Christ, the Sacred Heart'; the Enlightenment saw in him the prototype of human morality, the basis of
true camaraderie. The Romantics felt Jesus to be the model of genuinely human personality; and our twentieth century amid its now fully-
fledged *raison d'état*, proceeded to extol him as Christ the King. Then
after this triumphalism and the experience of two world wars came
Jesus 'our brother', our fellow-man, whose example anticipates what
we have to do, the 'man for others' and the contemporary 'Jesus of
human liberation' (in some quarters even Jesus the combatant and
revolutionary), and so forth. Just as in the course of history men have
given new name after new name to God, as inventive love alone knows
how to do, while on the other hand his name has been soiled and be-
smirched in many different ways, so Christian affection has enabled
each and every period to find its own endearing term for Jesus, though
at the same time his name is for ever being horribly misused: in his
name brothers have been slaughtered, and in ships with the name
'Jesus' emblazoned on their standard black slaves have been stowed
away like cattle destined for the white man's territories. Our 'Jesus-
images' indeed call for the exercise of judgement, indispensable though
they be to our decisive choice of Jesus. This surely applies in the case
of non-believers too: not just belief but unbelief has its own dogmatic
Jesus-image. The Jewish authorities and Pontius Pilate condemned
Jesus because they had formed a certain picture of him for themselves.

Even prior to the Eastertide events there were 'images of Jesus' in a positive and a negative sense. It is only as he is interpreted that a person becomes part and parcel of history.

The question emerging from this potted survey of Jesus-images, however, is whether all these Christological patterns are pure projections of our own, time after time prevailing, incessantly changing interpretation of reality. Once somebody has discovered final salvation in Jesus, it is natural (and proper) that he should project his own expectations and ways of envisaging the 'true being' of man on to Jesus. Correlatively, of course, this means that a real facet in Jesus' life must at least point in that particular direction if we are not to turn Jesus into a mere receptacle for our own predilections, an arbitrary 'cipher' that we are manipulating; in that case, surely, Jesus might very well be left out of it. He becomes indispensable only if and when the really crucial point of our human existence and its proper destiny are actually defined by the historical phenomenon of the real Jesus of Nazareth, and our own projections of truly human being are corrected by that; within that context there is legitimate room for the play of our human projections – always under the corrective and directive criterion of what and who Jesus actually was, in history. Thus the issue of historical truth in the quest for Jesus of Nazareth comes to be of the utmost importance.

## B.   OLD AND NEW, THE CRITICAL APPROACH

The fact of the matter is that in the past the faithful – the Christian community, theologians, the teaching office – have seen all the New Testament traditions about Jesus as directly reflecting historical occurrences. Theology and the responses proper to faith were based on a pre-critical, purely biblicist interpretation of the Jesus event, which ignored, for instance, the different literary genres. Every period inevitably suffers from the limitations of its own historical context – which in no way rule out the possibility of an authentic sort of believing. This only goes to show that Christian belief has a real history and that therefore the faith cannot be settled once and for all, as it were, beyond the reach of history.

In our modern period the historical consciousness with its own critical methods has made a pretty big dent in the pre-critical or biblicist interpretation. Only then did the possibility arise of what one might call a rigid and conservative interpretation of the Bible. Not

J.E.C.–C

before. For as we see, despite a pre-critical consciousness of history the church Fathers, for instance, and the Middle Ages too did not at all insist on what passes now for a conservative biblical interpretation: by way of their allegorical interpretation of what appear to be historical narratives in the Bible they permitted themselves liberties that the most progressive exegete would never concede nowadays. A 'conservative' biblical interpretation, therefore, is only a modern option, that is, a 'no' to the newly arisen challenge constituted by the historico-critical consciousness; in that sense it is a 'modernism', a new thing in the history of biblical interpretation.

On the other hand the historian's critical approach to the Bible is also a new and modern possibility. The ways in which the concrete Jesus of Nazareth had come to be represented by the faithful to some extent fail to tally with the results yielded by the historian's assessment of scientifically assured data. For that reason many people feel that their Christian faith compels them to oppose the critical results of scientifically conducted studies. That sort of thing is always a hopeless and fruitless enterprise, because it is impossible to live with a 'double truth': you cannot deny something as a historian which as a believer you are simultaneously bound to accept. Scientific evidences are not for faith to obstruct, while on their side they may gainsay the notions entertained by faith. Besides a great many established data commanding the general agreement of historians, there are undoubtedly still a lot of uncertainties over detail. But to belittle historical science from the standpoint of faith or to appeal to what is uncertain in the sciences and so to set them aside is unfair and unworthy of the believer. It is enough in itself to disclose a false conception of faith. The fact is, of course, that historically speaking we know much less nowadays about Jesus of Nazareth than our forefathers did, but what we know is scientifically vouched for. Moreover it is still more than enough to position the historical basis of Christianity and enable us to understand better the Christian interpretation of Jesus as such.

Nobody will deny at any rate that especially in the nineteenth century historical and critical study often had an anti-dogmatic or anti-ecclesiastical purpose behind it, and that now that a religious intention usually is the underlying motive, those who seek to popularize these new insights often have too little feeling for the accustomed ways of the faithful and their powers of assimilation. On the other hand one cannot remain silent about the results of criticism – precisely in the best interests of the Christian faith. From new, empirical truth Christian faith has nothing to lose and much to gain.

## C. MODERN HISTORIOGRAPHY AND JESUS OF NAZARETH

From the years 1774 to 1778 onwards the work of Reimarus brought about an appreciable change in the traditional religious 'images of Jesus'. The very idea was so novel that Reimarus did not publish his work. Later on Lessing was to publish, though still with a certain amount of misgiving and therefore 'anonymously', seven fragments of Reimarus' manuscript, to the effect that the historical Jesus, as he really was, presents a quite different picture from that of the Bible and Christian tradition. L. Ranke (1795–1886) formulated the new historical concept which had emerged during that period, namely, that the image people had formed of Louis IX, for instance, or of other celebrated persons in the past, does not tally with the picture we get from a critical study of the historical sources. Thus a distinction was introduced between, for example, the current notion of Alexander the Great and the 'Alexander of history', between Napoleon and the 'Napoleon of history', between the Christian Jesus-image and the historical 'Jesus of Nazareth'. Inevitably the question had become 'the way things really were' (Ranke) – a powerful critical factor in the study of history not previously known in that sense. Unhappily, this starting-point was at the same time given a positivistic interpretation, partly on the model of the so-called exact sciences: it was considered feasible to prise a fact completely away from the interpretation of it by people living at the time, from the course of later tradition and one's own 'mental horizon'. Surrendering thus their own presuppositions in order to submit the historical data to critical analysis on the lines of an exact science, it should be possible, so people thought, to arrive at an 'undogmatized', purely historical Jesus. On closer inspection, however, this Jesus of the historians turned out to be a nineteenth-century projection of ideal notions of humanity: Jesus became a kind of mascot, a symbolic X or cipher on to which nineteenth-century man could project his evolutionist and Utopian optimism; or else Jesus was seen simply as representing the apocalyptic of Palestine in the first century.

Even so, this did uncover a real problem: the 'historical Jesus' would indeed appear to differ in many respects from the Christ of faith. The term 'historical Jesus' is used here to mean that which the methods of historical criticism enable us to retrieve of Jesus of Nazareth, that is, the 'earthly Jesus'. However, the liberal positivism of the nineteenth century tended to identify 'being' and 'being aware of'. For that reason historical reality was taken to coincide with what, on the basis of a science of history, we can know. History became synonymous with the history 'done' by the historians; so that what is 'historical' is whatever has been ascertained by systematic research. That in itself implies a constricted field of vision; for there is a real difference between the 'historical Jesus' and the 'earthly Jesus': what can be reconstructed historically (the 'historical Jesus') does not naturally coincide with the full reality of Jesus, the person who lived when the beginning of the first century was still being called the 'present time'.

It might fairly be said, of course, that this distinction, however real, is for us irrelevant in practice, because what escapes the historical net does in fact vanish into oblivion so far as we are concerned. (With finer meshes or more refined historical methods we can of course catch more in the historian's net; but the yield will never be identical with what the living reality had been: 'what had been going on' at the time.) In the study and writing of history we are dealing only with the historically knowable happening; and although that does not coincide with what actually happened, it is futile to peer 'behind' what is accessible, historically speaking, or to think that from a standpoint of faith we can somehow get access to further *historical* aspects. Faith does not of itself supply any new – and real – facts; it can yield the real significance of facts, which a purely historical assessment fails to discover. Yet the idea that it is only the historical method which gets at the facts often makes an implicit claim to ontological exclusivity. Not only are there events that are accessible to the historian but in fact have not yet been investigated, but furthermore the science of history can never recover everything that really occurred. Less pretentiously, then, we may call 'historical' those events which are ascertainable by use of the historical method. This means that the actual stuff of all historiography is 'abstract', that is, it carves out a part of the real past; it formalizes and provides only images. Thus the historical Jesus, so called, is no less a Jesus-image than the Christ of the believer. This at once relativizes the sharp contrast supposed to exist between the 'Jesus of history' and the 'Jesus of faith'. By way of images, they both derive from the 'earthly Jesus'.

As an epistemological category, that is, *qua* method, historical abstraction is totally justifiable, provided one does not turn it into an ontological category. In this latter case one is isolating oneself in advance from all that may properly be said in non-scientific terms about what the historian has recovered. In other words, to the 'non-historical' (in the sense of what the historian's discipline cannot reach in the past course of events) one still cannot deny reality. Thus in an interpretation from the past allowance may indeed be made there for real 'history' which none the less is no longer accessible to, or is even in principle irrecoverable by, the historian. Thus for the historian it is in principle not possible to ascertain whether 'history' is the locus of God's saving action, whereas this may nevertheless be a reality within the dimension of what really occurs – and for the believer truly is so. Occurrent reality (='the course of historical events') is broader, therefore, than what 'history' (=the job of the historian) is able to recover of it, without the 'interpretation' having to be devalued to something purely subjective and in that sense purely speculative.

In regard to Jesus of Nazareth it means this: that 'historically', that is, in the occurrent reality of his earthly existence, something is present which is in principle inaccessible by way of purely historico-critical methods, the concrete and individual person in himself who (like everyone else) eludes a purely scientific approach. In Jesus' case this 'something', experienced in the encounter with him, was expressed by Christians in images such as son of man, messianic son of David, and so forth. The only question then is whether this concrete articulation is indeed partly determined by the concrete reality that was offered and came to them from Jesus, or derives solely from the socio-cultural context in which these people found themselves. One is bound to ask, therefore, whether their image of Jesus, arising out of their faith, is both the product of the real historical offer constituted by Jesus and (naturally) the result of their tradition – the process within which they interpreted and assented to this concrete offer and deliberately took it to themselves.

In the so-called post-liberal 'New Quest', the renewed historical search for Jesus of Nazareth, it is indeed this last, new type of question that is being asked. Of course, we go in quest of the historical Jesus for the sole reason that we cannot ignore two thousand years of Christendom: the context of our enquiry is the Christianity of the churches today. So we are really enquiring after the historical basis and source of what we have called the 'Christian movement', which still constitutes the distinctive reality of the churches. And we do this because in the passage of time the Christian churches have acquired a fractured relationship to their source. Because of that fracture the initial effect of a historico-critical interpretation of Jesus will be to surprise and even perturb: our Christian identity, shaped but at the same time distorted in the course of history, is endangered by this. Yet the disconcerting experience of surprise is a first and necessary stage in the hermeneutical process that leads from the biblical answer to our answer to the question of who Jesus is. Even in the Bible itself we see operating this sense of surprise regarding pre-canonical traditions in the community. Of course we can never pinpoint the authentic gift of Jesus 'in itself': Jesus' offer to the people of some two thousand years ago is concretely not the same as his – none the less permanent – offer of salvation to people in the twentieth century; after all, our need for deliverance and salvation obtains a historical content in terms of our concrete circumstances. As I said before: if Jesus is God's definitive act of salvation for us now, as he was for the people then, this entails that the relation to the ever new present time must be in part constitutive for the concrete form of his offer. I certainly think that some endeavours on the part of those who represent the so-called 'New Quest' still retain certain liberal vestiges, so that they are really looking for a 'phantom', a sort of Jesus of Nazareth *an sich*. And this seems to me not only a fruitless enterprise, but for theology, for a critique of Church and society and above all for religion itself, one devoid of any prospect.

All the same, the question of whether or not to absorb the historico-critical method is one of life or death for Christianity. If Jesus, for instance, either did not exist (as used not infrequently to be argued) or was something quite other than what faith affirms of him (for example, a *sicarius* or guerrilla, a Zealot or Jewish-nationalist resistance fighter), then the faith or *kerygma* is of course incredible. A radical breach between the knowledge imparted by faith and that imparted by history, of what after all is a single phenomenon, namely, 'Jesus and his first believing disciples', is untenable. Such a dualism leads inevitably to repudiating one of the poles (or at any rate its theological relevance), whether one proceeds, with Kierkegaard and Bultmann, to deny all theological significance to knowledge of the historical Jesus, or with D. F. Strauss dispenses with *kerygma*-centred knowledge, or with H. Braun sets the biblical 'constant factor' in anthropology and the variable one (the diverse *kerygmata*: son of man, Son of God, Messiah, etc.) in Christology (which then in fact becomes superfluous).

If Christian faith is a faith in Jesus of Nazareth, in the sense that our attitude to him definitely settles our choice for or against God, that is to say in biblical terms, if it is a faith in Jesus of Nazareth, confessed as the 'Christ, the only-begotten Son, our Lord', then faith-centred knowledge and confession of the faith are indeed bounded by our knowledge of the historical Jesus; and that knowledge on the other hand is bounded, that is, put in its place or kept within its proper bounds, by faith-directed interpretation.

## D. THEOLOGICAL SIGNIFICANCE OF THE HISTORICAL QUEST FOR JESUS

As over against R. Bultmann, who is by no means sceptical about the possibility of a systematic and historical reconstruction of 'Jesus of Nazareth' but denies the theological relevance of such an enterprise, post-Bultmann exegesis, especially since E. Käsemann, has been right to relativize the distinction between 'Jesus of Nazareth' and the 'Christ of the Church'. This trend has become fairly general. The older *Formgeschichte* looked for the seedbed of the Jesus-tradition solely in the Christian community after Jesus' death, which entailed its putting the main emphasis on the discontinuity between Jesus as a historical figure and the Christ proclaimed by the Church. In recent years, how-ever, exegesis has tended more and more to make room for the social intercourse and fellowship of (the) disciples with Jesus during his earthly life. Within the total picture of the biblical Jesus Christ, there-fore, the continuity between the historical Jesus and the 'Christ pro-claimed' is starting to come into focus more than it had done before, even though opinion as to its concrete form is still sharply divided. This new set of bearings, as it were, have served to show that the New Testament was indeed written in the context of the Church's professed belief that Jesus is the crucified-and-risen One, but that people were also very much aware of the historical tension between the Christian experience of the exalted Christ present in the believing community and the recollection of the life Jesus had lived on earth. The biblical text contains all kinds of signals pointing to that awareness.[10] On that basis it is possible up to a point – quite adequately, at any rate – to mark off what was being recollected of Jesus' life on earth from the process of overlaying it, which stems from the situation obtaining in the primitive Church. And even where this turns out to be in substance impossible, it remains true that for the very sake of the Christian *kerygma* a 'historical' concern with Jesus forms part of the source of the tradition, the deposit of which was found in and even prior to the synoptic gospels. The likely assumption is, therefore, that the Jesus whom the gospels present resembles – not of course in every detail but substantially – the historically 'real thing', in spite of all the Church's updating activities. Thus modern exegesis has abandoned Bultmann's principle that 'the preaching of Jesus belongs to the premises of the theology of the New Testament and forms no part of that theology as such'.[11] The rather abrupt discontinuity which *kerygma* theologians had postulated between the proclaiming Jesus and the Christ proclaimed is being very much relativized at the moment. It is not denied that the four gospels are extensively conditioned by the confessional affirmation, proclamation, catechesis, paraenesis and liturgy of the first Christian congregations, and so are overlaid with the evangelists' own theology; but they are thought none the less to contain sufficient basic information about Jesus and recollections of him, in respect of his message, his attitude to life and his conduct as a whole.

Thus it could be said that the factors serving to touch off the tradition about Jesus lie in the personal fellowship Jesus enjoyed with his disciples during his life, with those, that is, who came under the spell of his person, message and ministry. So the memory of these things, together with their experiences after Jesus' death, forms the matrix out of which, given the initiative of God's saving action (both before and after that death), Christian faith in the risen, that is, personally for ever living, Jesus was born. That acknowledgement and confession of the crucified-and-risen One manifestly embraces the recollected substance of his earthly life: the *kerygma* is itself meant, on the ground of its own self-understanding, to refer back to the past events involving Jesus.

Current exegesis certainly does not accept the extreme interpretation of the Scandinavian school, which uses a concept of tradition that one has to describe as 'Scholastic' and almost technically rabbinical,[12] but is more and more coming to recognize that the recollection of the 'words and acts of Jesus', that is to say, of all that Jesus said, did and went through, is of fundamental significance for the Christology (-ies) in the New Testament, even though the account of it in the gospels is invariably set within the horizon of a particular Christological *kerygma*. In other words, there is a continual interaction between remembering and later experience: detailed reminiscences modify the total picture of Jesus that lives on in the community; and those memories are clarified in the light of the completed life of Jesus. All this enables the disciples to interpret their experiences as the saving activity of God. Thus there would seem to be a correlation between the disciples' self-understanding and their understanding of Jesus, both before and after his death; though it was only after that death, be it noted, on the basis of new experiences setting their recollections in a different light, that they broke through in their own living to the very core of Jesus' ministry. Only then did they come to recognize him as the real and definitive embodiment of salvation, to which they were at last able to give a name: the Christ, the son of man, the Son. When Jesus of Nazareth, in the actual tender of salvation he presents, is the norm and criterion of what believers in Jesus say about him within their own cultural and religious milieu, in other words, when he is the absolute 'Yonder Presence' of the Christ-confessing churches, each and all finding their inspiration and orientation in him, then a view of Jesus based on the approach through historical criticism is of essentially theological importance.

That Jesus is the normative criterion for the Church's proclamation, albeit via the experiences of his disciples before and after his death, is still contested, sometimes fiercely contested, by certain theologians from within the Catholic as well as the Reformed tradition. The reason given for this dissent is that with any such assertion the 'Easter event' ceases to be 'the one point of departure'.[13] We might counter that with the question: how then, assuming one does not want to label it pure ideology, can one manage to arrive at this Easter *kerygma* in the first place? And we might go on to ask why the *kerygma* in the New Testament is what it is only when informed by the recollection of events associated with the life and death of Jesus. The veto on pursuing the quest (via the *kerygma* and the gospels) for Jesus of Nazareth would seem to be based on a prior conviction that salvation in Jesus is bound up exclusively with his resurrection. The question is, though, whether such an exclusive and partial connection accords with the gospels. Why should they, and a tradition regarding Jesus, be necessary if the Easter *kerygma* is the sole and comprehensive ground of salvation?

It seems to me on the other hand that while the present tendency to relativize the distinction between 'Jesus of Nazareth' and the 'Christ of the Church' – in reaction against the heavy stress placed by Bultmann and his successors on the discontinuity – is a right one, it may nevertheless be in danger of falling into another extreme. It is fair enough to make every allowance for the continuity between Jesus' self-understanding and the Church's understanding of Jesus and also to show on historical grounds the continuity between the faith of the disciples before and after Jesus' death; but it is quite another thing to try and validate the Christian faith on that basis. Historical study of Jesus is extremely important, it gives a concrete content to faith; but it can never be a verification of the faith. A historically reconstructed picture of Jesus can never do more than allow for or keep a place for the Christian interpretation; it cannot from its own standpoint make this obligatory. It is possible to interpret Jesus just as reasonably in Jewish, non-Christian or broadly religious terms. In any case a historian as such could not demonstrate that in Jesus some truly saving activity on God's part has occurred. Of salvation *qua* fact there can be no objective confirmation, historically speaking. Whether before or after Jesus' death, it calls for a decisive act of faith based on events centred around Jesus which are certainly identifiable but remain historically ambiguous, so that no one evaluation could command the full force of reason. If through our historical study we discover that Christology after Jesus' death rests fairly and squarely on his life, message and actual conduct, then this points to a real continuity; but it is only an important finding if one starts from the premise of faith that in this Jesus God is indeed at work. That is an act of faith.

However, one can conduct a historical enquiry without presupposing any such thing. Scholars who are also believing Christians usually claim too much regarding the historical Jesus and in fact do so in virtue of their belief, not of their scholarship; even a punctilious historian like G. Bornkamm fails to avoid this in his already somewhat aging study of 'Jesus of Nazareth'. Thus historical research comes to look, in the event, like a sort of justification or duplicating of a Christological interpretation. If one can show that the Christian *kerygma* is in direct line with Jesus' self-understanding as that appears from his whole ministry and from his attitude to the death which in the end he saw to be inevitable, this still proves nothing about the validity of Christian faith. Jesus' sayings and way of life have no absolute, self-warranting validity – except for someone who is a believer. So it is a believer's task in his historical researches to exhibit the life of Jesus as a slanted issue, which historically is then presented in such a way that it invites rejection, that is, repudiation as of something scandalous, or else a decision, taken in faith, to risk commitment to this Jesus. Of course, a question propounds something; it is, after all, slanted, directed. But if one identifies and admits the implication, that is an act of faith or the start of one.

The moment we human beings enquire as to the significance of a historical happening, it reveals itself as complex, ambiguous, susceptible of a many-sided interpretation, whereas as an occurrent phenomenon it has had intrinsically a very specific form: that which it is, and nothing else, thus something of single import (which it is definitively only after a person's – here Jesus' – death). The Christian faith (a particular interpretation of Jesus) takes a decision when faced with this ambivalence (itself continuing all the time open to historical and critical enquiry) and in faith actually repudiates the rightfulness of a non-Christian (for instance, Jewish, secular or atheistic) interpretation of Jesus. The believer will do this on a basis of choosing to trust and thus to affirm the 'single-sense' interpretation, namely, that of Christian faith, as the only true one, that is, as the response (albeit multiform in expression) answering truly to the complex historical reality of Jesus. This interpretative response surmounts the purely historical evidences about Jesus, and yet these last are not outside the option taken up by faith.

The method of historical criticism, applied to Jesus, certainly cannot lay a foundation for faith. But equally its task is not purely negative, that is, a matter of preventing the foundation from crumbling away under our feet (which would be the case if it were demonstrated that Jesus never existed or was a quite different person from what the faith says). That reality is more than what can be recovered by 'objective observation' and scientific analysis is in a positivistic period the presupposition for openness to faith; but on the other hand (and granted our modern historical consciousness) historical enquiry is essential for the access of faith to the authentic gospel. The result of historical investigation is objectively observed material in which the believer sees more, experiences a disclosure. The believer does indeed see God's saving activity realized in Jesus' life, which without the material about Jesus recovered by the historical method would not be possible. This then is the importance of the historical study of Jesus for making up, concretely, the content of faith. Again, the historical approach serves to show that the vital question which Jesus poses for us only acquires its full force – as is the case with every man's life – when his life has run its course to the end, that is, after his death; only then is a definitive verdict possible. Before his death even the disciples acclaim him only as a prophet; honorific titles emerge in the period after his death.

This is why a modern theology or Christology cannot ignore the historical and critical data. To deny this is to fail to take seriously the historical basis of Christianity and to see its constraining power located in a purely formal *kerygma*. That such a *kerygma*-without-Jesus may yet open up new possibilities of existence and can still have a provocative power I would not care to deny. But Christianity does then lose its historical basis and becomes a purely fortuitous phenomenon in the life of man the religious being, liable to vanish out of it as readily as it came. One cannot go on for ever believing in ideas, whether the idea be abstract (D. Strauss's notion of 'God become man' without Jesus) or one given existential content (such as Bultmann's *kerygma*).

In that way Christianity loses its universal purport and forfeits the right
to continue speaking of a final saving activity of God in history: the
world comes to be regulated by an *Ideengeschichte*. Ideas so often let man
down or assume the function of ideologies. I can only believe and put
my trust in persons (even though I am sometimes betrayed by them as
well). That is why for me the Christian faith entails not only the personal living presence of the glorified Jesus, but also a link with his life
on earth; for it is precisely that earthly life that has been acknowledged
and empowered by God through the Resurrection. For me, therefore,
a Christianity or *kerygma* minus the historical Jesus of Nazareth is
ultimately vacuous – not Christianity at all, in fact. If the very heart of
the Christian faith consists of an affirmation, in faith, of God's saving
action in history – and that decisively in the life-history of Jesus of
Nazareth – for the liberation of human beings (in other words, if we
must use the language of faith even when speaking about the historical
Jesus), then the personal history of this Jesus cannot be lost sight of,
nor our speaking of it in the language of faith degenerate into ideology.

Thus Jesus of Nazareth turns out to be, speaking theologically, the
constant anti-pole of the Christ-confessing churches, even though this
Opposite Presence – criterion and norm – can never be grasped *per se*
but only apprehended in the process whereby the Christian churches
let themselves be defined by Jesus. The difficulty about reaching a
scrupulous interpretation of Jesus, therefore, is the orbit within which
it has to be achieved. What I mean is that we are bound to express the
reality of Jesus in our contemporary categories of understanding, given
in advance (which still allows of a critique) and accessible to all; but at
the same time we can recognize what that reality signifies for us only in
and through the use of those categories. In other words, the critical
tension there is between the actual proffer of salvation that Jesus is and
the interpretative response of the believing community is a problem
that bears not only on the New Testament forms of expression but on
ours as well.

# The need is renewed for a post-critical, narrative history

As I was saying, the historian's quest for Jesus is theologically relevant because in its thematic import its aim is to help clarify the continuing 'Opposite Presence' of Jesus of Nazareth, as norm and criterion, *vis-à-vis* the churches and all who consider that salvation is to be found in Jesus.

Yet this scientifically disciplined approach runs into difficulties. To start with, it stands quite outside the 'historical perspective' proper to the Bible. In a pre-critical culture history is experienced in quite a different way. History there is a constant contemporizing, a handing down of stories that live on among human kind. The factuality of history – whether this or that actually occurred in precisely such and such a way – is there of less importance. When Jesus says, 'There was once a man and he had two sons . . .' or 'Somebody lost a sheep or coin . . .', it would not occur to anyone to ask whether this 'really happened'. What matters is the truth of the story itself, that is, whether it 'turns us on', strikes home and makes us the active subject of a new story.[14] The sort of story-telling or narrative history that was usual in antiquity has to do with taking action, with a challenge or appeal or summons to a particular attitude; and in that respect 'true' stories (from a modern viewpoint) have the same function and realistic solidity as fictitious ones.

This affects even ancient historiography proper and the whole approach to literature in the ancient world.[15] Throughout the Graeco-Roman world of the time, people were reared from their youth up in that frame of mind. Everybody knew that one wrote history, not so much for information as to induce in the reader a certain ethical or religious view of things. The Roman historian, Titus Livy (59 BC to AD 17), had given clear-cut expression to this viewpoint as a valid ideal for the writing of history. The nub of it is that one should provide the interpretation one wants to give of particular historical events in-directly, that is, by depicting the characters of the persons involved as the author wishes to interpret them. Thus with what we nowadays hold to be a great deal of 'historical latitude', they give us their view of this or that character without any subsequent interpretative commentary; their view is already 'objectivized' in the characters from the very start: heroes are idealized, 'fictitious' evil actions are attributed to cowards. When for instance the Marcan gospel portrays Jesus' disciples historically as grasping nothing of his message, as timid individuals who when the moment of crisis comes are indifferent and sunk in sleep, turn tail and desert Jesus altogether, it is doing just what other profane historians did in those days. Its view of the apostles prior to Easter is 'objectivized' in the reactions and behaviour it postulates of these disciples in the narrative. In the case of someone like Luke, for example, who takes a different view of the disciples' conduct, they do not behave as in Mark. The reader in those days was not confused by this: he knew that the author meant to make the way he saw and interpreted individuals clear to his reader in a particular character-delineation; and the readers were interested by this particular view of Jesus and the other persons in the biblical story. The way in which the characters behave, the concrete actions the author ascribes to them, are his indirect commentary on the persons in his story. The actions described may then, from a modern historical standpoint, be 'historically true' or (whether or not with a historical core) 'fictitious'; but that is neither here nor there. The actions reflect exactly how the author, with his readers in mind, sees those persons and how they strike him. All the time his aim will be to influence his readers for good and deter them from evil. Anyone who is really held up to be a hero must for that reason have conformed to those high principles it is intended to imprint upon the reader. In the education of the time, when it came to literature, people were trained carefully to understand texts in this way. Even though it was only a primary or secondary stage of education they had received, like any literary man of the period the four evangelists did just the same – and so their readers understood it. Hence the differences in the characters of Jesus, of the Jews and of his disciples, the differences also in their actions, according to whether it is Mark, Matthew, Luke or John telling the story. That is to say, these differences point in the first instance to a divergence of view and interpretation of the Jesus-reality they are meant to convey. It is through the process of making comparisons between them that what (from a modern historian's viewpoint) is 'historically authentic' often emerges; but this 'historical authenticity', so called, is also a pure abstraction, lifted out of a concrete, living whole. This thought-pattern, which applies to the four gospels as elsewhere, at once provides us with an important hermeneutic key to understanding the gospels. Anyone reading the gospels with a keen eye as to how the characters of the people in them are drawn will know how the writer wants to have them interpreted; thus he will know what moral and religious message is meant to be conveyed. So the reader will not be worried about the differences between one gospel-writer and another. It is in a religious context that they are important and also, as it turns out, are actually relevant, given our modern historical discipline, to what from our angle is a more exact 'historical reconstruction'.

This 'narrative innocence', which permeates even the historiography of the ancient world, we no longer have. Since the rise of the 'historical sciences' modern man has been concerned first and foremost with 'true events'; his scientific scholarship sets out to recover the past, as we say, on a value-free basis. We want 'historically warranted' replies to the question about historical truth. Yet the hermeneutic sciences and critical theories have shown how this so-called value-free stance itself serves to conceal another set of positive evaluations that are equally real. The linguists who argue for rehabilitating the narrative 'innocence', as I see it, mistakenly fail to appreciate that in a post-critical period man cannot possibly relapse into an 'initial state of primitiveness' (Kierkegaard). So it has to be a 'second innocence', that is, a style of narration that has been through the 'value-free' neutralizing process of the sciences and the interiorizing of consciousness (reflection) and has acquired the insight that on the one hand there can be a premature resort to the telling of stories (and so it can provide cover for a lot of injustice, lovelessness and real problems); on the other hand that when, after all its analyses and interpretations, reason is no longer able theoretically to express in words what in fact there is still to be said, it is obliged to utter its elusive 'surplus-vested-in-reality' in stories and parables. Thus too an argumentative Christology must end up as a story about Jesus, a narrative Christology, and not as an all-embracing, theoretical 'Christological system'. So that within the intention that goes with the gospel literature, apropos for instance of the miracle-stories about Jesus, the primary question should not be: Did Jesus actually perform these miracles?, but: What is it they signify, what are people wanting to say when they relate or report such miracles of Jesus? Only when this has been made clear comes the secondary question of what it is in Jesus' life that corresponds historically to these miracle-stories. Only in the third place does the question become relevant as to which miracles or signs Jesus did in fact perform. And then it turns out that as a matter of history a number of miracles stand up while other such stories are 'secondary', having often been constructed on Old Testament models after the resurrection. Thus the theological interpretation of Jesus of Nazareth is embodied, on the ancient model of historiography, in Jesus' behaviour during his days here on earth. But this presupposes that Jesus came across to those believers as a person 'who went about doing good', in other words that he was historically of such a character as really did lend itself to this Christological interpretation. The question of the historical Jesus is still basic, therefore, to any responsible construction of a Christology, but then without becoming a positivistic obsession. The historico-critical assessment remains necessary because of Christianity's enormous claim, namely, that it can permissibly affirm that the destiny of man actually depends on the very special history that occurred in Jesus of Nazareth. This cannot be substantiated simply by telling stories the meaning of which is said to lie solely in their practical application. What will do it, though, is the life-story of the man Jesus as a story of God.

*Section Two*

# Criteria for a critical identification of the historical Jesus

## §1 Background against which the historical criteria must be viewed: matrix of the several criteria

Historian and exegete alike agree that in all pre-canonical and New Testament traditions of early Christianity the absolute identification of the earthly Jesus with the Christ proclaimed by the local churches is a basic assumption.[16] One could even call this identity the hermeneutic key to a right understanding of the gospels. This intention of the New Testament, directly relevant for the theologian, is less so of course for the historian, who sees that the recollection enshrined in the New Testament is in any case governed by various *kerygmata* and has been adapted to, 'updated' in, the Church's proclamation and paraenesis, in catechesis, liturgy and so on. I said earlier on that in the New Testament text we find often enough signals of the authors' awareness of the historical distance between Jesus' earthly life and the Church's situation. In other words a kerygmatic intention – one, that is, announcing salvation in Jesus – need in no sense gainsay a historical concern, even though the historical value must be critically tested. What is more, the particular *kerygma* is the motive, the reason for a given tradition about Jesus to emerge. Time and again, therefore, exploration is the primary purpose behind a tradition, that is, the reason why a certain local congregation preserves in its memory and faithfully passes on a particular saying or particular acts of Jesus.[17] For each *kerygma* severally displays a specific historical concern with Jesus of Nazareth. This applies even to the Pauline proclamation of Christ, concentrated on the 'paschal' *kerygma*, which sees in the historical datum of Jesus' death the very core of the true humanity of Jesus, in reaction against a false divinizing of the earthly Jesus. Even if Paul may know little in other respects of Jesus' earthly life, of his message and conduct, it still points to the fact that he intends his *kerygma* to be grounded in a historical Jesus event, perhaps the most profoundly human thing about Jesus' whole life on earth, the fact of his trial and execution. This may be a one-sided view – but concern for a historical foundation for his *kerygma* is none the less evident, for all that. The object of the various testimonies in the New Testament is not an ethereal 'heavenly being', sojourning on earth in human guise, but the concrete person Jesus of Nazareth. This then is the one and only basis for an authentic Christology.

As a matter of history it turns out that there are various groups, namely, a variety of local Christian congregations, differentiated by their cultural past and by sociological factors, which as the carriers of tradition correspond to differing Christological projects derived from pre-canonical and New Testament Jesus traditions.[18] Adapted to this circumstance, the question then becomes: On the basis of which concrete kerygmatic interpretation of Jesus did certain people group together as a local church that made a 'Jesus tradition' possible? The local church is the vehicle of a tradition – which prompts the further question: How was it that these communities, thanks to historical interaction and mutual contact, evaluated, adopted or criticized divergent Christological conceptions, and either handed them on together with their own heritage or rejected them?

Tracing out a precise and specific Christological profession of faith in Jesus, therefore, in fact marks the tracing of one primitive congregation's tradition of belief, that is, of its *kerygma* as well as the distinctive character of its 'historical' concern. Envisaging the gospel tradition or catechetical tradition as secondary, as often happened among the *Formgeschichte* school of exegetes – and that, over against the allegedly primary 'kerygmatic tradition' – is no longer something it is possible to maintain of the primitive Church as a whole. *Kerygma* and a concern with Jesus of Nazareth go hand in hand from the very outset, since it is a fact of history that each of the numerous credal trends to be found in or via the four gospels is paralleled by a historical interest in this or that aspect of the earthly Jesus – even if for each individual kerygmatic or Christological project this entailed a narrowed field of vision: either the miracles of Jesus or his central message or his trial and execution.[19] When we start looking, therefore (in Part Three), for specific and divergent currents of credal material, this will also put us on the track of whatever facet of the life of Jesus this or that local congregation found especially compelling.

If – as is historically the case and is explicable too in terms of social psychology – certain groups of people relate a 'story about Jesus', they do so because in one way or another they have found salvation in Jesus of Nazareth, that is, they all have a '*kerygma*' to propagate, on the basis of which they acclaim Jesus either as Messiah or as the risen One or as the divine miracle-worker or as the sufferer whom God has exalted, and so forth. It becomes their story about Jesus. Recollections of particular words and actions of Jesus are thus handed on because it was salvation that these earliest congregations had somehow found in Jesus. Acknowledgement of salvation in Jesus, therefore, was the matrix of all traditions about him. In that sense a specific 'Christology' lies at the source of, is the driving force behind, every concrete tradition regarding Jesus of Nazareth. So without prejudice to whatever else remains to be said – contrary to what many an exponent of *Formgeschichte* is wont to accept as plainly evident, the presumption must be not against but in favour of, among other things, the primitive Christian traditions enshrining a 'historical' interest in Jesus, taking into account the selectivity peculiar to each tradition, their updating tendencies and the cultural-religious concepts they employ in order to articulate their historical experience of salvation-in-Jesus. That is why I would say, in the first instance, that the burden of proof rests not with someone who is prepared to 'derive' Jesus from certain sayings and acts of his recorded in the New Testament but rather with the person who argues for a 'secondary' interpolation or later process of shaping by the local community;[20] which is not at all meant to imply that the record of Jesus' sayings and actions is a historically exact record of events, but that they do give us a full-length picture of him. Thus even legends may provide a typical, striking and life-size representation of an individual.

In face not of the subsequently emerging but of initially multiform Christological views of Jesus in early Christianity, the technical terms 'secondary' or 'tertiary' tradition, as used by the *Formgeschichte* school, have to be closely defined (which some of them do not fail to do). What after all is 'secondary' (that is, appears later on in the tradition of a particular local church or is plainly the work of an editor – for example, the recognition of the dogmatic significance of Jesus' words and actions, within the Q tradition only emerging in its second, Hellenistic Jewish-Christian phase[21]) may in another local community, say the pre-Marcan, be primary and early.[22] Thus this in the Q tradition most probably somewhat later dogmatic interest has been affected historically by contact with the in this respect older material of the pre-Marcan community's tradition.[23] The fact too that after the gospel of Mark there 'suddenly' turns up in Luke and Matthew a great deal of 'new' material, the Sermon on the Mount or on the Plain, in itself tells us nothing about the 'secondary' character of this tradition, which further-more (although unknown before Mark) might well be thought to exhibit traits in its three beatitudes pre-dating the Easter event. Actually, specific memories come back to us 'as we need them'; they are no less genuine for that! However, the specific recollection in this case will have come in many instances from other Christian congregations which had a distinctive concern of their own with the same Jesus of Nazareth.

From this we may conclude that what is 'primary', 'secondary' or even 'tertiary' for one particular Christian congregation's tradition, within the totality of early Christian traditions, multiform as they were, does not as such have to be described as 'moulded by the church community' or as not 'authentic Jesus'. The attempts of form critics to dissect and separate out tradition from editing still do not enable us to end up with a chronology, genesis or development in the totality of the primitive Christian view of Jesus. Besides the obvious development within a single Christological project or the credal affirmation of one primitive congregation in accordance with its new situation and concrete needs, there is 'development' occurring through the contact of one community's Christological project with that of other local churches. The four gospels, as they lie concretely before us, are not only a Christological interpretation of Jesus, that is, a vision deriving from the experience of salvation-in-Jesus proffered by God, but also a critical adoption of and reaction to previous interpretations of Jesus on the part of other local Christian communities. We can no longer in fact start, as people used to do at one time, from the single *kerygma* of a Jerusalem mother church, as it was called, which only later on branched out in various directions.[24] The facts contradict that. Thus the gospels presuppose an 'interaction', very complex and hard to reconstruct, of divergent Christologies – evolving even within their own orbit of tradition and belonging to a variety of primitive Christian congregations. From the historian's viewpoint we may regard the pre-Marcan, pre-Pauline, pre-Johannine and Aramaic traditions, besides the Graeco-Jewish Jerusalem and, finally, the Palestinian-cum-Trans-jordanian one formed by the Q community, as most probably well established. Each of them would appear to be firmly wedded to particular facets of the life of Jesus that form a basis for their *kerygma*. The later synoptic gospels are an attempt to synthesize the pluriform material of the traditions – and they do so in a way which for twentieth-century Christians indeed presents new possibilities and a Christian freedom, but also sets certain boundaries.

From all this it follows that we can draw no distinction between a 'kerygmatic tradition' and a 'Jesus tradition',[25] between a 'handing on' of Jesus and a 'handing on' of Christ. All early Christian traditions are both 'kerygmatic' and recollection of Jesus of Nazareth, that is to say, they are governed by a quite specific (pluriform) profession of belief regarding Jesus of Nazareth – no one else, nor yet a myth (even though they may speak 'mythically' of Jesus) – and for that very reason they are all at the same time 'Jesus tradition', that is, in the light of a certain faith-directed interpretation of this Jesus they are, after their measure, a true recollection of what the Jesus of history actually was, said and did, even if it was often the case that only one (actual) facet of the life or death of Jesus had been linked up with the *kerygma* proclaimed by the local church in question, and that a 'historical' interest then did not have the same critical importance as in the modern pursuit of history.

A further conclusion follows from what we have been saying. The dissonances and tensions in the gospel material, often explained as reflecting a hiatus between the 'historical Jesus' and the 'kerygmatic Christ', can in fact only be tensions within the post-Easter Christian interpretations of Jesus.[26] Historically speaking, we have to reckon here, first and foremost, with differing early Christian Christologies within the Church and not *per se* with a hiatus between Jesus of Nazareth and the 'Church's Christ' of early Christianity, though it must be admitted that besides the cultural and religious situation of each primitive Christian congregation, the wealth and variety of meaning, the ambivalence, the possibility of an interpretation of the unique figure of Jesus that is 'open' in so many directions, and the complexity of his historical manifestation in what was none the less a quite distinct period in our human history, obviously gave rise to these at the time diverse Christologies.

## §2 Why then the search for criteria relevant to the sifting process ?

In the context of what we have been arguing does it still make sense to go looking for cogent criteria on which to decide what is 'authentic Jesus' or comes directly from Jesus (*verba ipsissima, facta ipsissima* and *intentio ipsissima*)? We could sum up what I have been saying with a proposition of N. A. Dahl's. This veteran scholar in the field of exegesis says that the Jesus tradition in its entirety is 'a thing moulded

by the community' (shaped by the Church), but at the same time just
as entirely a reflex, a reverberation of Jesus' actual career and conduct,
within the post-Easter church(-es) – 'a maximum that contains everything important to our having historical knowledge of Jesus'.[27] After
all, the effect of a faith-directed concern with another human being is
not only 'creative' – tending even to produce legend – but also 're-
tentive', that is, 'keeping in remembrance'. In that sense the master is
recognizable in his disciples. This way of looking at it gives a prior
vote of confidence to the text of the New Testament.

But however well grounded this view may be said to be, in purely
historical terms there are snags attached to it. The basic New Testament affirmation of the absolute identity between Jesus of Nazareth
and the crucified-and-risen One proclaimed by the Church is for the
historian a given fact which he will certainly note; but the affirmation
in itself does not give the historian any guarantee that the continuity
between Jesus and the Church's proclamation of Christ is fact. That
has to be tested in detail. So the historian cannot simply proceed on the
strength of an affirmation about the broad (historical) trustworthiness
of the gospels. Deriving each and every logion and indeed every
Christian truth from the earthly Jesus in person is not a historical but
theological programme of the New Testament, just as the Old Testament traces the Law – the whole and each constituent part – back to
Moses, the inspirer of the entire Jewish legal system. What is more,
not one of the four gospels is the work of eye-witnesses. As they stand,
they are documents of the second and third generation of Christians.
To help us get a good idea of the boundaries as well as the free scope
of a dogmatic Christology, I see a proper place for deploying these
historical criteria in (essaying) a thematic Christology. More especially
because a lot of West European Christologies are grounded in the
Easter event as the point of disjunction between Jesus of Nazareth and
the Christology of the Church, it is also necessary to call upon historical criteria which make it possible to base the thematizing process
on a historically firm foundation and not on the personal views of
theologians. We have to raise the historical issue if we are to feel critically confident of our own Christian faith; otherwise theology will be
blind and authoritarian.

It is only right, therefore, that we should follow H. Braun, J.
Robinson and others in distinguishing between 'authentic matter of
fact' and 'authentic Jesus' (*ipsissima Jesu*).[28] What the Christian churches
or their charismatic prophets declare in the name of the exalted Christ

to their respective congregations may indeed reflect a basic posture adopted by the earthly Jesus, and thus may be 'true in substance', even though the earthly Jesus had uttered never a word on the matter – in that sense they are historically unauthentic. If it were shown that Jesus never said anything to the effect of 'love your enemies', this logion of the New Testament and the Church could still be a faithful and fully rounded representation of Jesus' own preaching. But for anyone pursuing the historical quest for Jesus this logion would indeed be 'unauthentic'. People have often been confused about the *Form-geschichte* terminology; for (at any rate in the case of many who employ that method) there is no intention whatever of denying that what is historically 'unauthentic' may nevertheless capture the deepest real intention of Jesus – only that in a purely historical sense this cannot be demonstrated. And this critical stance does them credit. Even when it is held to be of advantage to Christian faith, it cannot start from the rule *'In dubio pro tradito'* – that would be to betray the basic critical principle. When, for instance, we find in the synoptic material non-apocalpytic conceptions of the *eschaton* on the one hand and, on the other, equally explicit apocalyptic ones (a fact difficult to gainsay), inevitably the question arises: What, historically speaking, was Jesus' own point of view about this? Quite often a somewhat arbitrary decision is made in favour of one or other of these two options and everything that will not fit into it is said to be 'secondary'. And then it is forgotten that they may both be discrepancies between different early Christian traditions and do not in themselves indicate a divergence of outlook between Jesus of Nazareth and the 'primitive Church'. Only when the question of possible discrepancies in and between the various early Christian churches has been settled can we go on to ask about Jesus' own view of the matter. And this becomes necessary as a result.

The sum of what systematic historical enquiry may establish about a person is certainly not the same thing as understanding that person in his irreducible individuality. Over against all the critical results there will always be a residue, a surplus of meaning. A person can only be approached in personal trust or mistrusted in what is a similar attitude of commitment to a decision. Both the opposition of those who were scandalized by this Jesus and the confident trust of those who found in him their salvation witness to a better understanding of Jesus of Nazareth than any 'neat' and neutral account of him which the systematic methods of history might legitimately be able to give. In the end another human being can only be recognized and acknowledged in a 'disclosure' experience, an experience which for one person closes and for another discloses, whether on tried and tested, real grounds or not.

Mention of these 'real grounds' implies not only the importance of the quest for the historical Jesus but the legitimate demand for criteria on the basis of which historically 'authentic Jesus material' can be differentiated from the post-Easter, kerygmatic material superimposed upon it.

Regrettably enough, this search for criteria has for the most part been confined to the champions of *Formgeschichte*, in my view a valid method as form criticism but one which has not sufficiently realized how relative and perhaps 'subordinate' to other methods its significance is. Yet recent years have seen a noticeable change in this respect, if only because this method (which has such assuredly enormous results to its credit) has evidently run into a blind alley, whence 'structural analysis of the Bible' is a (perhaps unintentional) attempt to rescue it. But just as *Formgeschichte* cannot (or will not) lead us to 'Jesus of Nazareth', no more will structuralism. That is by its nature literary; it never goes beyond that, and in fact excludes every extra-literary reference, especially to the historically authentic Jesus of Nazareth, from its purview.

As a theologian concerned with the way that gospel narratives 'bear upon reality', I have kept an eye open for the criteria actually used by exegetes to establish what is 'authentic Jesus' matter; and I have pondered in a theological as well as historical context the arguments between them about reflections on the criteria they employ when sorting out post-Easter interpretation by the Church from 'authentic', that is, pre-Easter recollections in the various local congregations of sayings, acts and intentions of the earthly Jesus in person. In doing so I have taken care to heed the voice of German as well as Anglo-Saxon and Scandinavian exegesis – the French-oriented variety too. For anyone steeping himself in the literature will be particularly struck by these differences – and will feel the socially, culturally and 'nationally' distinctive character of the 'biblical exegesis' to be not so much a 'disturbing' as a relativizing factor.

## §3 The cataloguing of valid, positive criteria

*Literature.* P. Biehl, 'Zur Frage nach dem historischen Jesus', ThR (1957–8), 54–76; M. Black, *An Aramaic Approach to the Gospels and*

*Acts*, Oxford 1967³; G. Bornkamm, *Jesus von Nazareth*, Stuttgart 1963²;
H. Braun, *Jesus*, Stuttgart-Berlin 1969²; R. Bultmann, *Tradition*; F. C.
Burkitt, *The Gospel History and Its Transmission*, London 1906; D. G.
Calvert, 'An examination of the criteria for distinguishing the authentic
words of Jesus', NTS 18 (1971–2), 209–19; C. E. Carlston, 'A positive
criterion of authenticity', BRes 7 (1962), 33–9; H. Conzelmann, s.v.
'Jesus', RGG³, III, 619–53; O. Cullmann, *Heil als Geschichte*, Tübingen
1965; N. A. Dahl, 'Der historische Jesus als geschichtswissenschaft-
liches und theologisches Problem', KuD 1 (1955), 104–32; C. H.
Dodd, *History and the Gospels* (London 1938), 91–101; *The Apostolic
Preaching and its Developments*, London 1944; *Parables of the Kingdom*,
London 1946; E. Fuchs, *Zur Frage nach dem historischen Jesus, Gesammelte
Aufsätze*, 2 vols, Tübingen 1960; R. Fuller, *Critical Introduction to the
New Testament* (London 1966), 94–103; *The Foundations of the New
Testament Christology*, New York 1965 (London-Glasgow 1972²); F. C.
Grant, 'The Authenticity of Jesus' Sayings', *Neutestamentliche Studien*
(for R. Bultmann), BZNW, 21 (Berlin 1957), 137–43; W. Grundmann,
*Die Geschichte Jesu Christi*, Berlin 1956; F. Hahn, 'Hoheitstitel', and
'Methodenprobleme einer Christologie des Neuen Testaments',
Beih. EvTh, 15 (Tübingen 1970), 3–41; B. van Iersel, 'De theologie
en het evangelische detailwerk', Conc 7 (1971), n. 10, 75–84; J.
Jeremias, *Die Abendmahlsworte Jesu*, Göttingen 1967⁴; *Die Verkündigung
Jesu*, Gütersloh 1971; E. Käsemann, *Besinnungen* (passim); L. E. Keck,
*A Future for the Historical Jesus*, Nashville-New York 1971; W.
Kümmel, 'Jesusforschung seit 1950', ThR 31 (1965–6), 15–46; M.
Lehmann, *Synoptische Quellenanalyse und die Frage nach dem historischen
Jesu* (Berlin 1970), 163–205; D. Lührmann, 'Liebet eure Feinde',
ZThK 69 (1972), 412–38; H. K. McArthur, 'Basic issues. A survey of
recent gospel research', *Interpretation* 18 (1964), 39–55; T. W. Manson,
*The Sayings of Jesus as recorded in the Gospels of St Matthew and St Luke*,
London 1949 (1964²); N. Perrin, *Rediscovering the Teaching of Jesus*,
London 1967; R. Pesch, *Jesu ureigene Taten?*, Freiburg 1970; W. Richter,
*Exegese als Literaturwissenschaft. Entwurf einer alttestamentlichen Liter-
aturtheorie und Methodolgie*, Göttingen 1971; J. Robinson, *The New
Quest of the Historical Jesus*, Naperville-London 1959; G. Schille, 'Was
ist ein Logion?', ZNT 61 (1970), 172–82; 'Der Mangel eines kritischen
Geschichtsbildes in der neutestamentlichen Formgeschichte', ThLZ
88 (1963), 491–502; H. Schürmann, *Traditionsgeschichtliche Untersuchungen
zu den synoptischen Evangelien*, (Düsseldorf 1968), 83–110, 111–58; 'Zur
aktuellen Situation der Leben Jesu-Forschung', GuL 46 (1973),
300–10; G. Strecker, *Der Weg der Gerechtigkeit*, Göttingen 1966²; P.

Stuhlmacher, 'Kritische Marginalien zum gegenwärtigen Stand der Frage nach Jesus', *Fides et Communicatio*, Festschrift for M. Doerne (Göttingen 1970), 341–61; W. Trilling, *Fragen zur Geschichtlichkeit Jesu*, Düsseldorf 1966 (*De historiciteit van Jezus*, Bilthoven 1969); *Versuche mehrdimensionaler Schriftauslegung* (ed. H. Harsch and G. Voss), Stuttgart-Munich 1972.


Only within what has been set out under § 1 and § 2 above, in particular the correlation between certain credal accretions and a specific concern with this or that historical facet of Jesus of Nazareth, do I look for concrete criteria on the basis of which such *de facto* correlation can be tested historically in its details. If then with the help of these historical criteria the proposition is soundly demonstrated (I mean the proposition of faith that the New Testament as a whole is a reflex of the earthly Jesus *in* the faith-prompted response of Christians) it follows that besides the exegetical methods known as *Formgeschichte, Redaktiongeschichte* and *Traditionsgeschichte* (these being indispensable aids) the most appropriate method is 'close reading', structural analysis, or in other words the immanent, synchronous approach in line with modern, systematic and critical study of the literature. An immanent analysis of one reflex (for instance, the Marcan gospel *in toto*) will in that case give us a historical insight into Jesus of Nazareth and, along with that, theology. But to open a way to that, and to strengthen confidence that an immanent analysis of the New Testament is the best (though not the sole) approach to Jesus of Nazareth, it is first necessary, by use of historical criteria, to substantiate the proposition that by and large, framed within the acknowledgement of salvation imparted by God in Jesus Christ, the gospels should be seen as an accurate reflex of Jesus of Nazareth.

With that in mind we shall set aside in this survey all 'negative criteria'[29] offering a basis for a positive denial of 'authenticity'. Those negative criteria – a sure pointer, we are told, to the absence of authenticity – are completely unsafe and moreover operate with all kinds of presuppositions which *a priori* isolate Jesus from the Old Testament and Judaic tradition as also from any continuity with the later thinking prompted by the faith of the Church, whereas what we want is to trace the continuity as well as the discontinuity. H. Braun (tilting, apparently, at E. Käsemann) rightly says that the degree of certainty must be greater when we are deciding upon 'what is unauthentic' (secondary texts) than for establishing authenticity.[30] I shall confine myself, therefore, to 'positive criteria' in virtue of which, at least in a combined application of the various criteria, one can legitimately (and with fluctuating certainty) regard a logion or New Testament story as going back to the earthly Jesus.

## A. THE EDITING PROCESS A CRITERION OF HISTORICITY: TRADITIONS INCORPORATED 'WILLY-NILLY'

Of the many criteria employed by exegetes I find the historical study of the editorial process the most valuable one because it resorts least to working with academic hypotheses of various kinds (although even here hypotheses are operative in that no satisfactory solution has so far been found of the 'synoptic problem').

Each of the gospels has its own theological viewpoint, revealed by structural analysis no less than by the disentangling of redaction and tradition. Via their respective eschatological, Christological or ecclesiological perceptions they give away their theological standpoint through the selection they make of stories reporting the sayings and acts of Jesus, as also in the way they order and present the material. Consequently, whenever they hand on material not markedly in accord with their own theological view of things, we may take this to be a sign of deference in face of some revered tradition. It is then reasonable to suppose that we are dealing with traditional matter regarded by them as beyond challenge; matter which whether for historical or theological reasons (the importance of the Church's fidelity to tradition) goes back, as they think, to Jesus.[31] When for instance a gospel reacts against a *theios anèr* Christology – Jesus as the divine miracle-man[32] – and none the less still reports 'miracles' performed by Jesus (e.g. the Q tradition has only two of these), then there is good reason for regarding those miracles as 'authentic'; and in conjunction with other criteria this can yield a historically warrantable certainty. Thus to pick up the trail of authentic historical continuity between Jesus and the Church we have to keep an eye open for those aspects which raise difficulties for the Christological concept of a particular credal trend of thought among early Christian local churches and evangelists and constitute a challenge to the Christian praxis of this or that congregation as well as to the pressure of its cultural assimilation.[33] The fact that traditional matter not even 'intended' for the concept they entertain should stake so strong a claim – even if it does not fit in all that well with the evangelist's purposes so that, though transmitting it, he 'touches it up', somewhat, while not hesitating to drop other strands of tradition (e.g. Matthew or Luke *vis-à-vis* Mark) – is a criterion that points to an authentic tradition concerning Jesus. As Mark sees Jesus' disciples, prior to Easter they are just people full of bewilderment, cowardice and wrong ideas; so when we find in Mark a vein of sympathy in regard to them, there is every chance that this will have arisen straight from actual history; a remark more especially in Luke (whose attitude to the disciples is a more sympathetic one) tending to be critical of them points in a similar direction.

Of course this principle (like all the rest) calls for circumspection. Mark has all the disciples absent from the crucifixion (Mk. 14:50); for Luke they are manifestly present (Lk. 23:49). But Luke needs to have it that way, in view of his notion of 'apostolate': to have been a witness from the time of Jesus' public ministry up to and including his resurrection (Acts 1:21–22), witness, thus, of his death also. This criterion, used by itself, often leaves the question, historically speaking, unresolved. Like all these criteria it has to be used in combination with others.

### B. THE CRITERION OF FORM CRITICISM: THE PRINCIPLE OF DUAL IRREDUCIBILITY

This method, used almost universally by the exponents of *Formgeschichte*[34] to prise what is strictly peculiar to Jesus loose from what belongs to his Jewish contemporaries and the later local churches, is primarily a legacy of Bultmann. But his way of formulating it entailed making a number of pre-emptive decisions ('the specifically eschatological bent of Jesus' preaching' is itself a prejudgement as to what we should look for as being historically distinctive and characteristic of Jesus).[35] The criterion has been gradually refined and then given the stamp of approval by Hans Conzelmann: 'We may accept as authentic what cannot be slotted either into Jewish thinking or into the viewpoints of the later church community'[36] or as O. Cullmann has it: 'if the logion cannot be slotted into the Judaism of the time nor yet into the post-Easter *kerygma*'.[37] The principle has very recently been radicalized by E. Käsemann: 'Only in a few instances are we standing on more or less firm ground: that is, where the tradition, for whatever reason, can be neither inferred from Judaism nor attributed to primitive Christianity.'[38]

There is absolutely no intention of denying, on the basis of this principle, that Jesus took over a great deal of what is in the Old

Testament and in Judaism and that he stands in continuity with post-Easter Christian thinking; only that in such cases of continuity this criterion affords us no historical or critical certainty as to whether the source is Jesus himself or the Jewish-Christian church. In other words it must not be employed as a negative criterion. Used positively, it has a definite if limited value. A saying like 'The law and the prophets were until John [the Baptist]' (Lk. 16:16) was obviously not part and parcel of contemporary Jewish thought but is something quite separate which for Jews would be inconceivable;[39] but it is also possibly an expression formulated not by Jesus but by way of interpretation of a post-Easter Christian idea reflecting in retrospect on the relationship between the Baptist and Jesus, so that the criterion fails here to establish the historical authenticity of this logion. Again, this principle assumes that we know precisely what could be Jewish and what Christian. In deciding that, all sorts of subjective elements are at work, as well as ignorance, sometimes, about the precise situation.

This criterion of the elements in Jesus' message and conduct that have no parallel in either the Judaism of his time or the early Church is in one respect strengthened, that is, where primitive Christianity is really rather embarrassed by certain traditions and yet despite that, and despite a variety of interpretations, does not suppress the facts but passes them on:[40] for instance, Jesus submitting to John's baptism, his being brought to trial and execution, utterances like 'Why do you call me good?' (Mk. 10:18), the fact that the Baptist is presented as the inaugurator of a new era (Mt. 11:12–13) and so on – elements which, it is said, the Church could not possibly have invented. Yet even this argument is subject to all kinds of personal appreciations. For example, 'not even the Son knows of the day' (Mk. 13:32) must on this criterion be authentic, since the Church, it is said, would not have invented Jesus' ignorance on this point. But in many of its traditions the Bible is alien to a line of argument based on Jesus' omniscience and belonging to such a high Christology. Is it not just as likely that when the Parousia failed to materialize, this logion suggested itself to the Church as a way of making Christians realize that as regards the nearness of the end Jesus was not in error? The same is true of the temptations of Jesus, his struggle in Gethsemane, his alleged forsakenness on the cross: it is here that the 'pillar' argument falls down.

Where it does have a certain validity, the 'irreducibility' criterion is still limited in its force. With the American exegete N. Perrin, therefore, we may give the criterion sharper definition by formulating it as follows: a logion, words or acts of Jesus as reported by early Christian communities are more likely to be authentically his, if and when in the earliest stratum we are able to reach, that unique quality and distinctiveness over against the current Judaism and the early Church become apparent.[41] Even this is not completely cogent. Even the earliest local churches could command from the store of their Christianity irreducible elements of their own which stand apart from Judaism as well as from subsequent phases of the early Christian congregations.[42]

Then again, use of the criterion would often seem to be supported on a presupposition about the antithesis between Jesus and contemporary Judaism, whereas other criteria appear to indicate that the general anti-Jewish polemic found in the New Testament is not 'authentic Jesus' at all but reflects a later position adopted by local Christian congregations which *qua* church had broken away from a synagogue[43] bent on persecuting them.

However valuable it may be, within limits, the criterion entails that we can only trace those aspects in which Jesus is unique, being irreducible to Judaism and Christianity; it of course cannot help us to realize how Jesus was rooted in the Old Testament and Judaism or understand the continuity between the Church and Jesus. The result yielded by this criterion is a unique Jesus in a vacuum, minus any intrinsic bond with Judaism and Christianity. It allows no glimpse of how Jesus perhaps epitomizes the profoundest intentions of the Old Testament, how his faith in the creator-God is at the heart and centre of his life, how in his total ascendancy over his contemporaries he was at the same time a man of his age and people, and lastly how the first congregations took hold of the deepest intentions of Jesus himself; it was also in the context of Western European thinking on the radical discontinuity between Jesus and the Christ of the Church that the principle was initially formulated.

Yet it would be naïve to suppose that the exegetes who make use of this criterion do not also realize that it is bound to yield a Jesus 'unique' because isolated. But their purpose is to pursue an insight into a 'critically guaranteed minimum'[44] of Jesus' ascendancy and outreach above and beyond his time. And here any minimum is indeed a gain in understanding. What is more, with every new, critically certified acquisition the assumption is strengthened that the gospels as history are fittingly trustworthy, however much various situations in the Church may have led them to overlay authentic sayings and acts of Jesus and perhaps to create new ones. And then the injunction applies: 'Approximate the maximum of tradition and the critically assured minimum as much as possible to each other, and so gradually approach the historical Jesus.'[45] It is a fact, then, that as a scientifically ascertained minimum increases, this in turn becomes a criterion for evaluating other elements of tradition.

C. TRADITION AS A HISTORICAL CRITERION: THE PRINCIPLE OF THE 'CROSS-SECTION'[46]

There are in the gospels accounts of the sayings and acts of Jesus that appear in divergent and independent literary traditions. What is more, the same logia (whether or not in different traditions) occur in differing 'forms': here in parables, there in catechesis or in liturgical passages or even in a miracle-story. Jesus' dealings with publicans and sinners, with the outcasts of the time, are reported in no less than four independent literary traditions.[47] Burkitt found as many as thirty-one logia that were circulating in both the Marcan and the Q community;[48] whence he concludes that these traditions must go back at least to within ten or fifteen years of Jesus' death. However, S. Schulz has since shown that there are links between the later, Hellenistic-Jewish phase of the Q community and the Marcan material, so that there is no question here of a strict 'cross-section'.[49]

In so far as the principle is based solely on different traditions it is an uncertain one, for the simple reason that the relations between the synoptic gospels have not been resolved and are still a matter of hypothesis. The criterion carries more weight where the same sort of content is to be found in diverse forms (whatever the relationship between them, *qua* tradition, may be); such concordance gives obvious weight to the genuineness of a logion.[50] But equally, it is fatal to make negative use of this criterion; something found in only one tradition can still be an authentic record of Jesus, even if it is found, for instance, only in John (e.g. the historical possibility that as a member of John's entourage Jesus too baptized, John 3:22). Anyway, the 'cross-section' criterion points to the primitive character of a given tradition; and finding the same material in more than one tradition at least indicates a fundamental consistency in primitive Christian tradition. However, used just by itself, the criterion remains problematical, in view of our still considerable ignorance regarding the relation between one early Christian literary tradition and another.

### D.   CONSISTENCY OF CONTENT AS A CRITERION[51]

Both the total view of what emerges on strictly historical grounds as a picture of Jesus on the one hand, and detailed exegesis on the other, are involved in a mutual process of verification.[52] It is the archetype of the already ancient linguistic circle of the constant pendulating action between the parts and the whole – a sensitive and extremely delicate process, but one that belongs to the fundamental condition of our human potentialities in all sorts of areas: the parts illuminate the whole, which itself renders the parts transparent.

This principle does not refer, as Dahl seems to think it does, to the relation between the scientifically guaranteed minimum and the 'bulk of the New Testament tradition'.[53] In the historical quest for Jesus of Nazareth the picture of Jesus afforded by the primitive local churches is precisely what cannot be taken as a criterion, as those kerygmatic interpretations of Jesus were the driving force behind creative tradition.[54] More to the point here is the total picture which as a historical end-result gradually arises out of the detailed analysis and then in turn leads to further analysis in detail; and then the fact that a detail slips or does not slip into the total framework of the picture of Jesus already achieved, historically speaking, and into that of his basic intentions, has a quite definite function. Critically reconstructed details, which bit by bit help to build up a complete picture of the earthly Jesus, are a safer starting-point for further investigation than is *a priori* acceptance of a broad historical reliability, albeit – as with M. Dibelius[55] – that of the earliest layer of tradition. Partly with the help of the consistency-principle S. Schulz has been able to separate a very early Aramaic Christian phase in the theology of the Q community from a more recent, Hellenistic Jewish-Christian phase and thus (despite what in my view are numerous points of contention) has broadly succeeded in laying bare a very early Palestinian Christology.[56]

Moreover, the consistency-principle can in the longer term – namely, as a total and historical picture of Jesus begins to emerge – give rise to various sub-criteria, including the consistency or correlation between Jesus' message and actual conduct;[57] each is a criterion for the other. If it were shown, for instance, that the logion 'He who finds his life will lose it and he who loses his life . . . will find it' (Mt. 10:39= Lk. 17:33, Q) is 'authentic, historical Jesus' (indeed a difficult thing to do on these criteria, because this is a wise proverb commonly met with in Judaism), everything that could be said to contradict this principle in the life of Jesus becomes unauthentic; what is more, we would have a criterion for establishing what value Jesus attached to his death, for example, when he came to realize its inevitability. Yet this at once launches us on a theological interpretation, which must surely find it hard to accommodate psychological inconsistencies between Jesus' teaching and practice, whereas for the historian this possibility remains open all the time. Thus too Jesus' omnipotence is not a historical but theological criterion: it straightaway gives a theological interpretation to the enormous impression Jesus made on his environment.

E.  THE CRITERION OF THE REJECTION OF JESUS' MESSAGE AND PRAXIS: HIS EXECUTION

We might call this the 'execution' criterion; for it is based on the view that the fact of Jesus' trial and execution has a hermeneutical bearing on precisely what it was that he taught and did.[58] His message and conduct must have been of such a nature that they were bound to cause deep offence to (at least) the (conventional) Jewish belief and praxis of the time. This is certainly a historical criterion, but as such it calls only for concentration on the search for elements in what Jesus said and did which gave occasion for it; and it calls for an attendant investigation of what concern the Jewish and Roman authorities might have had with this death. A historical understanding of Jesus' life, message and death is possible only when it is shown why this issued in an execution. It does not of itself imply that everything Jesus said or did from the very start either can or should be seen in this perspective, as for theological purposes the gospels do, because they too were out to find the reason for this execution and so depict Jesus' whole career as a 'way to the cross'.

In and of itself, therefore, this criterion does not serve to discover anything; it only helps to sharpen and concentrate our enquiry.

*Conclusion.* On the basis of these criteria with a positive application we are justified in distinguishing within the Church's recollection of Jesus' earthly life between (a) sayings and actions in his life that turn up in the gospels more or less as they occurred, (b) elements in the life of Jesus already so fused with a current ecclesiastical viewpoint that one can only say of them in general terms that a central core derives from Jesus and hence that historically authentic reminiscences manifestly do have

J.E.C.–D

a part to play in them, and (c) sayings and acts not spoken or performed by the earthly Jesus, in which nevertheless the community, by attributing them to him, gives expression to what the Lord who is alive in its midst concretely signifies for it in the recollection of his life on earth; in other words they serve to show that the earthly Jesus is indeed its norm and criterion. Thus a logion, though not actually spoken by Jesus, may be an utterance of the primitive Church, grounded in Jesus' inspiration and orientation. G. Schille is right when he says: 'It is not form but substance that ties a logion to its point of origin.'[59] The relative though hardly negligible value of the criteria aforementioned lies first and foremost in this: that the modest element of historically authenticated material they yield confirms the theological insight that within a kerygmatic project the gospels really are imbued with a spirit of loyalty, of fidelity to the historical Jesus of Nazareth – which is not to say that they reflect, literally, Jesus' preaching and ministry; this has become for them 'their own way of life', and so their own life-story has penetrated to within the story related of Jesus; the question (already given an ecclesiastical context): 'But who do you say that I am?' (Mk. 8:29; Mt. 16:15; Lk. 9:20) is one that the early Christian communities tried as best they could to answer.

## §4. Frequently employed but invalid criteria

A negative use of the above-mentioned criteria we have dismissed already. Our concern here is with other positive criteria which some exegetes have chosen to employ.

(a) The criterion of the context, whether linguistic or cultural-cum-geographical.

This (in fact illegitimate) criterion has been used in exegesis more especially by T. W. Manson,[60] J. Jeremias[61] and, with greater attention to nuances, by M. Black.[62] Thus J. Jeremias detected in the Greek text of the eucharistic words of institution, as recorded in Mark, no less than twenty Aramaisms, whence he concludes that this text is very 'close to Jesus'; yet he is himself sceptical about the criterion of irreducibility, not infrequently given a negative application: 'It is not the rightness of the critique that has to be demonstrated but its limits.'[63] Of course Jeremias has been able to show that *Abba* (Father) is an 'authentic Jesus' word. For this the linguistic principle was a postulate, though not the decisive factor. But the principle fails signally in every case. On historical grounds it is quite certain (despite some even very recent voices asserting that Jesus was bilingual) that he conveyed his message in Aramaic. But various Aramaisms (Hebraisms) in the New Testament Greek are no proof at all of authenticity (closeness to Jesus), or even, *per se*, of the early origin of a Jesus tradition. Of itself it does not even lead us to an early Aramaic-speaking congregation, but rather to bilingual, Hellenistic-Jewish Christians who (like the Septuagint version of the Old Testament) used a lot of Aramaic constructions in their Greek. In itself, therefore, Jeremias' principle takes us only as far as to some Aramaic-speaking or Hellenistic-Jewish communities of Christians, not (on the strength of this criterion) to Jesus himself. And these people – Greek-speaking Jewish Christians – were the most active element within the very early Church when it came to taking initiatives: from them we get the terms *christianoi, ekklesia* and *euaggelion*; and it was they who acclimatized the apocalyptic expressions 'but I say unto you' and 'truly, truly I say to you' in the New Testament (see below).

Then too Palestinian 'local colour' cannot be a decisive factor, for the same reason. Principally, an 'authentic' parable (one told by Jesus) might subsequently be adapted to other local conditions and thus disclose a non-Palestinian milieu, yet still in substance have its source in Jesus. Conversely, a Palestinian setting is just as likely to be evidence of Aramaic- or Greek-speaking Palestinian Christians.

This criterion does afford contact with this or that circle of Jewish Christians, so helping us to draw a line between what comes out of Jewish-Christian congregations (whether bilingual or not) and what originally transpired in churches composed of Gentile Christians. It certainly goes to show that in essence the contribution made by the latter was smaller than has often been supposed in the past, and that the contribution more especially of the Greek-speaking Jewish Christians was exceptionally large.

(b) Nor indeed has the distinctive character of the parables been adopted as a criterion here, although someone like H. Conzelmann sees them as the most valuable criterion and even as the starting-point for a historical reconstruction, because they serve to reveal the essential message of Jesus.[64] That in the Q community the parables only turn up in the second, Hellenistic-Jewish phase tells us nothing, of course; but for all sorts of reasons we are bound to demonstrate first the authenticity of the parables *vis-à-vis* Jesus, one by one and on the basis of other criteria; then and only then are the parables of proven authenticity a further criterion in their turn. The same thing applies to the love of Jesus, his central message and so on; and that is why I cannot include them among the fundamental starting criteria.

(c) Formulae like 'but I say to you' and 'truly, truly I say to you' are in themselves no guarantee whatever of authenticity, especially because they would themselves appear to be secondary. They are used everywhere in the Hellenistic-Jewish apocalyptic writings and their use in the New Testament gradually increases under the influence of Greek-speaking Jewish Christians, to whose circle it is virtually always restricted.[65] Actually, the special apocalyptic import of 'amen, amen' is that what ensues is not said on the speaker's authority, is not a prophetic utterance nor yet a piece of proverbial or experiential wisdom, but a statement possessing (and requiring) the guarantee of apocalyptic vision and 'divine revelation'; they are the utterances of apocalyptic seers (having the same import as *pistos ho logos*, this saying is true (trustworthy), in Rev. 21:5; 22:6; 3:14; John 4:37, and repeatedly in the Pastoral Letters). Whether this 'seer' is Jesus in person has to be demonstrated piecemeal, case by case.

(d) Finally, though *Abba* is 'authentic Jesus' language, that fact in itself does not enable us to say that the actual logion in which the word occurs is an authentic one (see below).

## §5. Note on the Q hypothesis

*Literature.* P. Hoffmann, *Studien zur Theologie der Logienquelle*, Münster 1972; 'Die Anfänge der Theologie in Logienquelle', *Gestalt und Anspruch des Neuen Testaments* (Würzburg 1969), 134–52; D. Lührmann, *Die Redaktion der Logienquelle*, Neukirchen-Vluyn 1969; S. Schulz, *Q. Die Spruchquelle der Evangelisten*, Zürich 1972, with: *Griechisch-deutsche Synopse der Q-Ueberlieferungen*, Zürich 1972; H. E. Tödt, *Der Menschensohn*, esp. 212–45, 265–7.

Sharp criticism of the way the Q hypothesis is taken for granted and put to use may be found in G. Schille, *Das Vorsynoptische Judenchristentum*, Stuttgart 1970; 'Was ist ein Logion?', ZNW 61 (1970), 172–82; 'Der Mangel eines kritischen Geschichtsbildes in der neutestamentlicher Formgeschichte', ThLZ 88 (1963), 491–502. A critique of the assumptions made about *Formgeschichte* within the Q hypothesis is offered by E. Güttgemanns, *Offene Fragen zur Formgeschichte des Evangeliums*, Munich 1971[2].

See also E. Bammel, 'Das Ende von Q', *Verborum Veritas*, Festschrift f. G. Stählin (Wuppertal 1970), 39–50.

A very different, complex hypothesis has been proposed by P.

Benoit and M.-E. Boismard, *Synopse des quatre évangiles en français*, vol. 2 (Paris 1972), 15–60.

In recent years the Q tradition and Q source have been the object of renewed studies, especially of a synthesizing nature. From these a main outline has clearly emerged and is beginning to find more and more widespread acceptance. As this book, where it has seemed necessary, also utilizes the results of these critical and exegetical researches, it would appear only right to set out briefly what precisely it is that the Q hypothesis entails.

The Q hypothesis is a logical outcome of the synoptic problem. It was hinted at as early as 1794. It follows from the 'Two Sources' theory, namely, that Matthew and Luke made use not only of an obvious main source, the Marcan gospel, but also of a second source or *Quelle* (hence Q). This hypothesis (now virtually a 'scientific fact', despite uncertainties as to the scope of Q's contents) rests on empirically analysable facts. In short: (a) Matthew contains the substance of 600 out of the 661 verses in Mark, and Luke contains the substance of 350 verses from those same (Marcan) verses; (b) although Matthew and Luke often differ in detail from Mark, they seldom tally in their deviations with each other. Had they done so, we would be justified in postulating some degree of mutual literary dependence; thus that would seem to be excluded; (c) everywhere that Matthew and/or Luke diverge from Mark, each of them gives the non-Marcan material a different position and order of sequence in his own gospel. Hence we may infer the priority of Mark over Matthew and Luke, in broad terms at any rate, for each passage has its peculiar history of transmission (thus Mk. 16:9–20 is a much later non-Marcan addition); (d) but certain difficulties remain. In some matters of detail Matthew appears to enjoy priority. The priority of Mark remains a hypothesis, so that the exegete can never proceed on the assumption that it is a fact; it has to be shown to be true in each separate instance; (e) there is, however, another problem. About 200 verses which do not occur in Mark do appear in both Matthew and Luke – often with a striking similarity or even word for word the same, although this material is not inserted by Matthew and Luke at the same places within the Marcan material taken over by them. Thus besides depending on Mark, Luke and Matthew must at least be based on a shared tradition; this is the Q tradition, so called. What is more, the often literal correspondences in this non-Marcan material of Matthew and Luke are so evident that the form in which they know this Q tradition must be a document, that is, the Q source. Hence the 'Two Sources' theory (namely, Mark and Q as sources for Matthew and Luke); (f) there are nevertheless further difficulties. Although an added hypothesis tends to a lesser degree of certainty, quite a lot of exegetes work concretely and effectively with it: namely, that Matthew and Luke also contain material that is peculiar either to Matthew or to Luke and is to be found nowhere else in the synoptists. Thus the existence is postulated of SM (=*Sondergut* or matter peculiar to Matthew) and SL (=*Sondergut* in Luke); whether these are oral traditions or written sources has so far not been determined. Actually, there is no postulate involved in this; the conclusions follow from a literary comparison of three existing documents, Mark, Matthew and Luke (but see further on); (g) then again, it has become clear from analyses undertaken by S. Schulz that an interaction occurred at one stage between Q material and Marcan material, which obliges us to refine somewhat upon the 'Two sources' theory. Again, viewed in a historical perspective, whether of religion or of tradition, the Q tradition is not one uniform whole. Various traditions have been run together in it; it consists of a primary Aramaic phase, next a phase of tradition contributed by Greek-speaking Jewish Christians, and lastly a (possibly Gentile-Christian) phase of editorial activity, although the pluriform whole that results is subsumed within one specific and continuous Christological project.

As we have seen, in the Q tradition nothing is actually postulated. The conclusions follow from the literary comparison of the three existing synoptic gospels. Even so, it is a question whether these literary phenomena might not be accounted for on the basis of a quite different hypothesis. Because there is a 'remainder' not covered by the Q hypothesis, the experts go on looking for other solutions (thus, for instance, the synoptic Institute of the Theological Faculty at Nijmegen). P. Benoit and M.-E. Boismard have also looked in another direction: instead of the 'Two Sources' theory they postulate 'four foundation-documents': a Jewish-Christian gospel-text from Palestine (A), a Gentile-Christian revision of A (called B), an indefinable third document (C), and finally the Q source, so called. What is more, the evangelists are said to have made use of these sources not directly, but via yet other intermediary gospels that relate and refer to one another in various ways. A very complex account of things, which it is difficult to make operational for the work of exegesis.

# *Justification for the structure of this book, as according with the method, hermeneutics and criteriology discussed*

With this section we conclude Part One, in which we have considered method, hermeneutics and criteriology; it serves also to justify the further division of the book into three parts. In the New Testament, after all, we have the testimony of people who found salvation – or grace, mercy and pardon – imparted by God expressly in Jesus of Nazareth; which is why their expectant longings for salvation – critically confronted with the concrete manifestation of Jesus in history – led them to call him 'the Christ, Son of God, our Lord'. Both the proffer of salvation and the Christian response converge within a specific, conjunctural horizon of experience and understanding in the record of the New Testament. A modern Christology, that is, reflection on the New Testament interpretation of Jesus, entails therefore not only a historical and critical study of what the issue posited in Jesus really is (Part Two), but also of the conjunctural horizon of experience within which certain Jews, and then Gentiles, reacted positively to the 'historical phenomenon' of Jesus of Nazareth, whether in terms of their own encounter with Jesus during his earthly life and their experiences subsequent to his death, or of what was handed on to them concerning this Jesus by others (Part Three). It would appear from this that one thing constitutive of a proper, faith-motivated understanding of Jesus Christ is the relation to a present day, ever changing and ever new. This makes it possible to realize why Part Four of the book is so essential.

That teasing apart the delicate web formed by the gracious 'reality on offer' (in Jesus) and the 'assenting response of faith' (on the part of Christians) is not a feasible enterprise becomes clear more especially in Section Three of Part Two: 'The kingdom of God assumes the aspect of Jesus Christ.' It is that subsection of this book which serves to illustrate that however necessary, inescapably necessary, it is to seek a 'picture of Jesus' that will stand up under any historical critique, ultimately no individual can stand revealed in very truth and in the deepest reaches of his unique selfhood through an exclusively scientific, in this case historical and critical, assessment. The two aspects – both the imperative need for a historical critique (along with a critique of the critique, since the critical stance implies its own presuppositions and outlook on the world) and the insight that every human being in his irreducible identity eludes the scientific approach so necessary and indeed valuable in its own right – become evident in Part Two as well as in Part Three, and are consciously taken into account.

In the next two parts of this book, therefore, I shall be intent on searching (in faith and in a critical spirit) for possible signs in the historical Jesus that might direct the human quest for 'salvation' towards what Christian faith proposes as a relevant answer, when it refers us to a specific saving action (identified by Christians) undertaken by God in this Jesus of Nazareth. First and foremost, therefore, we must turn our attention to Jesus' historical manifestation (Part Two), not in the abstract but within the quite specific ongoing tradition in which he and his contemporaries were set – a horizon of experience which we (since Jesus at any rate, and as Christians) now call the 'Old Testament', albeit in its late Jewish or Judaistic context (Part Three). When some degree of illumination has been shed on all this, we shall be in a position to ask ourselves what Jesus of Nazareth might mean for us twentieth-century men and women (Part Four).

# Part Two

# 'The Gospel of Jesus Christ'

# By way of introduction

## Euaggelion or good news

*Literature.* Kl. Berger, 'Zum traditionsgeschichtlichen Hintergrund christologischer Hoheitstitel', NTS 17 (1970-1), 391–425; G. Friedrich, 'Euaggelion', ThWNT II, 718–34; B. van Iersel, *Een begin* (Bilthoven 1973), 22–8; L. E. Keck, 'The introduction to Mark's gospel', NTS 12 (1966), 352–70; W. Marxsen, *Der Evangelist Markus* (Göttingen 1956), 77–101; F. Muszner, ' "Evangelium" und "Mitte des Evangeliums" ', *Gott im Welt* (in honour of Karl Rahner), vol. 1 (Freiburg 1964), 492–514; R. Pesch, 'Anfang des Evangeliums Jesu Christi', *Die Zeit Jesu* (Freiburg 1970), 108–44; J. Roloff, *Das Kerygma*, 215–20; H. Schlier, ' "Euaggelion" im Römerbrief', *Wort Gottes in der Zeit*, Festschrift for K. H. Schelkle (Düsseldorf 1973), 127–42; R. Schnackenburg, 'Das Evangelium im Verständnis des ältesten Evangelisten', *Orientierung an Jesus*, Festschrift for J. Schmid (Freiburg 1973), 309–24; G. Strecker, 'Literarische Ueberlegungen zum Euaggelion-Begriff im Markus-evangelium', *Neues Testament und Geschichte* (Zürich-Tübingen 1972), 91–104; P. Stuhlmacher, *Das paulinische Evangelium*, vol. 1, Göttingen 1968; Th. J. Weeden, *Mark-traditions*, 82–5; U. Wilckens, *Die Missionsreden der Apostelgeschichte*, Neukirchen 1961.

Whereas in the past appeal would have been made primarily to 'the Church', in current Christian usage – both ecclesial and ecumenical – it is now customary to invoke 'the gospel'. This illustrates a change of attitude among Christians. In the four gospels themselves the word 'Church' hardly occurs (and then only in secondary texts), while *euaggelion*, evangel or glad tidings, happy news, or indeed 'to evangelize' (the verbal form) is central to them; it is even the very first phrase in the earliest gospel, its title, as it were: 'The beginning of the gospel of Jesus Christ' (Mk. 1:1). The current reversion to 'the gospel' one can only welcome, therefore. Of course this appeal to 'gospel' as the source of inspiration must not be allowed to become a vague slogan which – though admittedly in justified criticism of the churches' empirical manifestation – replaces the appeal to the Church with one centred on vaguely conceived references to, and highly selective trends within, the gospels. So before we analyse the real meaning of the 'gospel of Jesus Christ', we are right first of all to define more closely the actual concept, *euaggelion*, in the New Testament context.

(1) In Mark's title 'The beginning of the gospel of Jesus Christ', we are straightaway confronted with a grammatical problem. Is the genitive there subjective or objective: glad tidings about Jesus of Nazareth, acknowledged as the Christ, or a gospel, evangel, of Jesus Christ himself? This small philological problem may have far-reaching theological consequences and, in the particular solution accorded to it, deeply colour the interpretation of Jesus or the Christology.

Except for Mk. 1:14 ('gospel of God') and the expression, 'the gospel', used in allusion to it in Mk. 1:15, as also for the title in 1:1 ('gospel of Jesus Christ'), Mark invariably uses '*the* gospel' in an absolute sense, without any addition.[1] With but one exception Matthew, whenever he mentions 'the gospel', for his part always provides a closer definition, principally 'the gospel of the rule of God'.[2] Luke on the other hand appears to avoid the noun 'gospel'; in his book of the gospel it is nowhere to be found – and only twice in Acts (15:7; 20:24); but then he makes all the more frequent use of the verb 'to spread the glad tidings', 'to evangelize' (*euaggelidzesthai*): on ten occasions in the third gospel and fifteen times in the Acts. This somewhat arithmetical exercise is none the less instructive. Apart from those places in the synoptics that rely on Mark, the term 'gospel' never appears, whereas Mark even employs it as a title for his work. In other words, every use of the expression in the gospels derives from the Marcan tradition (or redaction). Paul for his part makes independent and constant use of it (forty-eight times in the authentically Pauline writings; and in twenty-two of those instances standing quite by itself, with no further qualification).[3] Again, in the Q community the use of at any rate the verb 'to evangelize' forms a separate strand within the history of the tradition, even though it is only to be found there in their second, Hellenistic and Jewish Christian phase.[4] This verbal use, in Luke as well as in the Q community, points us to the original setting to which the word belongs, that is, to an initially purely Jewish context linking together the two notions, 'eschatological prophet' and 'preaching the good news to the poor'. It is this complex of tradition that (apropos of the eschatological prophet) we shall be considering later on: Isaiah 61:1–3; 42:1–4; 49:1–2; 51:16; 52:7 and 59:21, texts which were already interconnected in Judaism and elicit a vocabulary comprising, for example, anointing (the Christ tradition), sending forth, holy Spirit, calling and choosing, 'God rules', 'light of the world', the focal point here being 'to bear glad tidings', for it is this very use of the verb by Luke and in the Q community that finds support in the Septuagint version of the messenger-servant tradition in Deutero- and Trito-Isaiah, the glad tidings which the prophetic *christus* or God's anointed one conveys to the poor. 'Gospel' here suggests the prophetic ministry of the messenger who calls upon the people to be converted to God.[5] Starting from that context in the history of Jewish tradition, it seems to me surprising that as a matter of history the word 'evangel' came to be a specifically Christian term – the key word of the movement centred around Jesus, from the moment it started upon its missionary enterprise in Palestine (a mission to all, including Jews of the Diaspora) and, later on, in its mission also to the Gentiles, which none the less entailed applying to the word 'evangel' certain nuances of a different kind (see below). That is why the subsequent Christian development of this Old Testament prophetic term calls for some more precise distinctions to be drawn.

Except for Mk. 1:1 and 1:14–15, Mark consistently puts the word 'gospel' (evangel) into the mouth of Jesus – a not unimportant resolution. As Mark sees it, therefore, the gospel is the glad tidings of Jesus Christ, that is, the glad news which Jesus himself brings to us from God. He also talks about (the Church's) 'proclaiming the gospel' (Mk. 1:14; 13:10; 14:9); that is to say, the *kerygma*, the Church's proclamation, is, according to Mark, the gospel brought by Jesus of Nazareth himself. For some time now exegetes have acknowledged that careful analysis of Mk. 13:10 and 14:9; Mk. 8:35; 10:29 and 13:9–10, and finally of Mk. 1:14 and 1:1 shows that the term 'gospel' is set firmly in a missionary context.[6] With Mark, as also with Paul, mention of the gospel really does imply that Jesus' message is intended for all, Jew and Gentile alike; the gospel has a worldwide, universal significance. This is grounded in the fact that Jesus' suffering, death and resurrection – for Paul virtually the whole essence of the gospel – are for Mark intrinsically bound up with the gospel which Jesus himself conveys: through his person, his ministry, preaching and praxis. Thus 'gospel' includes not only the glad tidings which Jesus himself proclaimed but, at the same time and just as essentially, the Christian message concerning Jesus' suffering and death; it embraces the Christian conviction that Jesus lives; that he is risen again. That in particular the significance of Jesus' death is an essential part of the good news is best illustrated by Mk. 14:9: in remembrance of this woman, who had anointed Jesus' feet at Bethany – interpreted by Mark as the anticipated anointing of a dead person – her deed will be rehearsed wherever the gospel is preached. That she did this to Jesus is what makes her action *qua* gospel unforgettable. What we are saying in effect is that 'gospel' is the story, as transmitted, of Jesus' earthly activity,[7] but also of everything that has to do with his death. The Pauline Easter *kerygma* forms from the Marcan standpoint an essential component or constituent part of the gospel, which no less essentially comprises Jesus' activity throughout his life on earth and, first and foremost, his message. For Mark the gospel is as much the gospel *of* Jesus as it is *about* Jesus as the Christ, the crucified-and-risen One. This notion of 'gospel', continuously operative in all the synoptics, is more comprehensive and more sound, therefore, than the Pauline concept, concentrated as that is on one side of the matter (and determined partly by the nature of Paul's arguments with his opponents).

So the gospel came to be the message, directed to the entire world, of which Jesus is the content: his sayings, his acts, suffering and death, and also the Church's identification of this person, expressed primarily in its affirmation that he has been exalted to the presence of God.[8] (In Part Three this idea finds its confirmation in the theme of the Suffering Servant as elaborated in the prophetic-Solomonic, messianic David tradition.) Indeed the gospel has to do with the Church's (post-Easter) proclamation of Jesus' own message, from which however the person of Jesus, and so also his death and resurrection, are inseparable. For Mark the emphasis falls on the life of Jesus as a *via crucis* that he trod and as something the contemporary Christian is called upon to emulate. Interpretation of the rejection and death of Jesus lies at the very heart of the gospel. For the question is: What might God himself have been about with this rejection and this death? That is partly why Mark calls Jesus' gospel 'the gospel of God' (1:14), primarily because Jesus' message told of the approaching rule of God for the salvation of men, but also because in and through the death of this 'messenger from God' God himself apparently has something to tell us; and so it is an essential element in the gospel *qua* gospel of God. As opposed to Mark, Matthew rightly prefers to speak of 'the gospel of the kingdom of God'. The point here is God's purpose or intention with Jesus. We shall have to take a close look, therefore, as our enquiry proceeds, at the question of the coming of God's rule and how the death of Jesus relates to it. A gospel minus the proclamation of Jesus' death and resurrection is no 'New Testament', any more than the one-sided or exclusive proclamation of the crucified-and-risen One can be described as 'the gospel'. Only the two together constitute the gospel of God, conveyed to us by

Jesus of Nazareth as the Christ. Thus 'The beginning' (Mk. 1:1)[9] – the title of the Marcan gospel – embraces the whole of the book (it makes no sense as a title, otherwise; so the beginning does not only or even primarily refer to the arrival on the scene of John the Baptist): this gospel has its beginning in the appearance of the 'advance messenger', the Baptist, along with the subsequent ministry of Jesus of Nazareth, his message about the imminent rule of God, his travelling here and there, 'doing good' (a sign of the dawning kingdom), his daily inter-course with tax-gatherers and sinners, his parable-stories; but all this meets with resistance and in the end leads to suffering and death; and still, above and beyond that comes God's message: This man is risen. With that the gospel of Mark ends: all that is 'the beginning of the glad tidings of Jesus Christ' (Mk. 1:1), which only now in fact can be heard in full and thereafter proclaimed by the Church as good news, as gospel.[10] What Jesus himself says and does in his earthly ministry is 'the start' of what the Church now proclaims about him. The funda-mental question for us, therefore, is not just: What does Jesus say to us about God?, but together with that: What does God himself say con-cerning Jesus? although this latter question – of Christology – can only be answered via our answer to the former one (and not vice versa).

The term 'gospel', then, illustrates for us in pregnant fashion what was constantly coming out in Part One, the intrinsic connection between the Easter *kerygma* and what had previously been going on during Jesus' earthly days, remembered now in retrospect. Another striking fact, it seems to me, is that the word *euaggelion*, as a technical expression (like the terms *christianoi*, Acts 11:26, and *ekklesia*, in their primitive Christian sense of Christ's 'congregation of Jews and Gentiles'),[11] had its source in the earliest circles of Greek-speaking Jews to become Christians and to missionize Palestine, most probably from among the so-called 'Hellenists', Jewish Christians from Jerusalem who fled in every direction after Stephen's martyrdom, to Egypt (Alexandria) and per-haps above all to West Syria (Antioch, Damascus). It is surely most significant at any rate that the evangelist Philip, one of the Hellenistic Seven (Acts 21:8; see 6:5), set in train the mission to the Samaritans (Acts 8:5, 26–40) and pursued his missionary activity also in other places on the Mediterranean coast among Greek-speaking Jews of the Diaspora, with Caesarea as his centre. It was not among those engaged in the 'mission to the Gentiles', but before then, in circles concerned with a limited mission to Palestine as a whole – and within it more especially to the Diaspora Jews – that the notion of 'gospel' grew up.

In those quarters too (Paul) arose the larger missionary enterprise, aimed at the Gentiles, which turned the gospel into what were indeed glad tidings directed towards all men.

This somewhat lengthy introduction (still too short, however, for the purpose of clarifying all the nuances of the Scriptural concept of 'gospel') seemed to me necessary because in this way the central problem is set before us: Is the nub of the New Testament, and therefore of Jesus' appearing among us, his message, ministry and manner of life and his 'faithfulness unto death', or is it his resurrection – or should one perhaps conclude that this is a false dilemma, and if it is, in what sense? The issue will then be whether faith in Jesus' resurrection does not enshrine an element peculiarly its own, which cannot be dropped without at the same time mutilating the message at the very core and centre of his ministry, leaving behind merely an 'exterior' which of course can orientate and inspire a person's life-style, yet leaves us with only the half of Jesus' real life and message. Are we not bound to say, in fact, that without belief in Jesus as the resurrected, exalted or ever-living One, his ministry and his whole life give occasion rather for gloomy resignation or despair than grounds for hope, since his message was after all rejected and he himself put to death? If one does not follow the New Testament in applying to Jesus the apocalyptic notion 'resurrection from the dead' and accepting the reality which that represents – the Christian tradition having changed radically the apocalyptic substance of the phrase – is Jesus then anything more than one of the immolated messengers of salvation, happiness and deliverance – more a reason for labelling everything 'absurd' than grounds for hope of a better future? One might of course argue that this long line of slaughtered prophets and heralds with a message from God of salvation for mankind, despite all the resistance and rejection they provoked, at least confirms the suspicion that the human race simply will not have this, that it will not resign itself to the endless piling up of injustice and misery; that mankind realizes that good and not evil must have the final word. But if belief in the resurrection is absent from this, is not such a hope the definition of what we call Utopia? And is not that living in hope of some 'final good' a salvation of which we cannot be sure whether it is salvation at all, since we do not know whether salvation is really possible? In that case are we left with anything but a vicious circle? Marcuse's 'huge gamble', supported by a wish-fulfilling Utopian dream, would be the only thing to make mankind's existence at all worth while – as wish and as dream. And even then one is bound to say that we – we who are still alive – may while we live have some prospect before us and so might live upon such a Utopian vision; but what future, then, for those fallen upon evil days? Who will supply with a future those who no longer have any future? Who gives a future to our dead? Or do we include only those who, being alive in our world, may perhaps live to enjoy a happier lot; and do we just forget the rest? Who is really going to call this 'the final good'?

These questions bring us to the fundamental problem: From what and for what has Jesus set us free? What final good has he to offer that we today can find salvation-in-Jesus? What, in other words, what exactly is the 'good tidings, the gospel, of Jesus Christ'?

(2) It should be clear from Part One that to determine what constitutes the salvation that Jesus brings is impossible without taking into account how it relates to us here and now. The material content of what 'good news', salvation and gospel, is concretely for us will change according to our concrete experience of its opposite. Early Christianity and the history of the Christian churches alike show us how mutable the salvation-experienced-in-Jesus is, where descriptions of its substance are concerned. And for us too the story is moving on.

Time and time again, therefore, both the current longing for 'final well-being' and whatever men are faced with in the person of Jesus have together contributed to the process of thematizing a view of salvation which is true to Jesus and yet matters to us as well. In that process it is God's *de facto* tender of salvation in Jesus that will form a critique of our expectations. The question arising here is whether the Christian interpretation of Jesus – the gospel – does not entail precisely those alienating factors which no human, scientific and technical intervention can eliminate. To the 'pagans of today' Christians bring no glad tidings when they inform them that (and how) Jesus was the fulfilment and completion of all the ancient promises to Israel! Of course, study of that fulfilment as a Jewish experience is necessary, because Jesus was manifested concretely, in history: a Jew – therefore sprung from and nurtured in Jewish spirituality. But that study in itself does not issue for us in 'the good news of Jesus Christ'. There are no tidings for modern man in that, any more than if Jesus of Nazareth were to be presented as a kind of exemplar, whether of an existentialist or perhaps a socio-critical modern 'norm for living'. In these instances Jesus himself and the whole question of God that he raises are for us no 'good news'. For what could this news be if, in the very core of our being as men today, our thinking is already existential or socio-critical? Thus we can appeal to Jesus, it would seem, only as the one who confirms, guarantees and blesses the best – which, thank heaven! is still a vital and active reality among us – but then in the same way that the Church in former times used to bless the old crusaders and their weapons of war. Promise and critique of Jesus, computed for and upon what we empirically are (and that today is first and foremost 'critically minded'), form no part of 'the gospel's' agenda. The gospel is then neither news nor heartening, but merely endorses me (us) within either a conservative perspective or a progressive one.

That we Christians are evidently powerless to convey the gospel to men and women today in a spirit of creative fidelity – despite and along with those aspects of it that bear in judgement upon human kind – as glad tidings (except verbally: by authoritarian talk about a gospel and glad tidings that in deference to the authority of the New Testament must be accepted), would certainly appear to be the basic reason why our churches stay empty. Who is still going to listen to what no longer comes across as cheering news – especially when it is backed up with a peremptory appeal to 'the evangel'?

So in this second part we examine first of all what as a matter of history Jesus' message and actual conduct were, as things that issued in his arrest and execution; and then we shall ask how the sum of all this could be experienced as 'salvation' at that time. Only then, in a subsequent part, shall we be able to table the question as to how, even today, we might experience the 'final good' in this ancient Jesus event.

*What Jesus proclaimed and how he lived*

Chapter 1

# Jesus' message of salvation on its way from God

A general notion of the period in which an outstanding individual plays out his role is always important if we are to succeed in locating him and identifying him in his truly human and yet quite distinctive and original character. But, albeit within that general framework, it is primarily quite concrete circumstances, accidental or deliberate encounters, very precise and as it were localized occurrences that serve, in the first instance at any rate, to illustrate and make intelligible the most marked features and public aspect of a person's activity.

However, the earlier life of Jesus, prior to what we can recapture, historically, of his ministry, is almost completely unknown to us. His birth in Bethlehem is a Jewish *theologoumenon*, that is, an interpretative vision and not a historical assertion. That his home was in Nazareth is not altogether certain, but is highly probable. The first historically firm fact about Jesus is that he got himself baptized by John, the son of Zechariah, known as the Baptist. Although we know nothing about how Jesus came in contact with John or of what impelled him to seek out this Baptizer in the Jordan valley – for in contrast with Jesus' own later conduct John does not move around the countryside; he is sought out (Mt. 3:5; Lk. 3:7; Mk. 1:5) – the fact is that John's baptizing of Jesus is the first important historical starting-point for our understanding of him as Jesus of Nazareth.

John the Baptist's religious message, since Jesus gave full assent to the appeal John was making, must have made an extraordinary impression on him; for he did after all have himself baptized. This cannot have been done by him just to 'set an example', as though he were really above it all. John's message about the baptism of repentance must have been a 'disclosure experience' for Jesus, a revelatory event or source experience, an orientation for his own life. To grasp the implications of this act as the initial step in Jesus' own prophetic ministry, the first thing needed, at any rate, is a broad but fairly accurate sketch of the historical and religious background to John's baptismal campaign and his activities.

## §1  Prophetic and apocalyptic penitential movements in Israel

*Literature.* (a) *Conversion and baptismal movements.* O. Betz, 'Die Proselytentaufe der Qumransekte und die Taufe im Neuen Testament', RQumrân 1 (1958), 213–34; H. Braun, 'Die Täufertaufe und die Qumranischen Waschungen', *Theologia Viatorum* 9 (1964), 1–18; ' "Umkehr" in spätjüdisch-häretischer und in Frühchristlicher Sicht', *Gesammelte Studien zum Neuen Testament und seiner Umwelt* (Tübingen 1967²), 70–85; J. Delorme, 'La pratique du baptême dans le judaisme contemporain des origines chrétiennes', LVie n. 26 (1956), 21–59; J. Gnilka, 'Die essenischen Tauchbäder und die Johannestaufe', RQumrân 3 (1961), 185–207; J. Thomas, *Le Mouvement baptiste en Palestine et Syrie*, Gembloux 1935; (b) *Prophetic context.* F. Hahn, *Hoheitstitel*, Anhang, 351–403; M. Hengel, *Judentum und Hellenismus*, Tübingen 1973²; *Charisma und Nachfolge*, Berlin 1968; O. H. Steck, *Gewaltsames Geschick*; H. W. Wolff, 'Das Kerygma des deuteronomistischen Geschichtswerk', ZAW 73 (1961), 171–86; (c) *Apocalyptic context.* J. Bonsirven, *Le Judaisme palestinien au temps de Jésus-Christ*, Paris 1934; S. Frost, *Old Testament Apocalyptic, its Origins and Growth*, London 1952; Kl. Koch, *Ratlos vor der Apokalyptik*, Gütersloh 1970; E. Lohse, *Umwelt des neuen Testaments* (Göttingen 1971), 37–50; 'Apokalyptik und Christologie', ZNW 62 (1971), 48–67; U. B. Müller, *Messias und Menschensohn in jüdischen Apokalypsen und in der Offenbarung des Johannes*, Gütersloh 1972; O. Plöger, *Theokratie und Eschatologie*, Neukirchen (1959), 1962²; J. Schmidt, *Die jüdische Apokalyptik, Die Geschichte ihrer Erforschung von den Anfänge bis zu den Textfunden von Qumran*, Neukirchen 1969; J. Schreiner, *Alttestamentlich-jüdische Apokalyptik*, Munich 1969; G. von Rad, *Theologie des Alten Testaments*, Munich, I ,1957, and II, 1960; D. Rössler, *Gesetz und Geschichte, Untersuchung zur Theologie der jüdischen Apokalyptik und der pharisäischen Orthodoxie* (WMANT, 3), Neukirchen 1960; H. H. Rowley, *The Relevance of Apocalyptic*, London 1952²; Ph. Vielhauer, 'Die Apokalyptik', in E. Hennecke-W. Schneemelcher, *Neutestamentliche Apokryphen*, II (Tübingen 1964³), 405–27, 428–54; W. Zimmerli, *Grundrisz der alttestamentlichen Theologie* (Stuttgart 1972), 199–217.

As a matter of history it is undeniable that the Christian Q community as well as Matthew and Luke understood the role fulfilled by both John the Baptist and Jesus (and also by their own local church) in the light of the already much older Chasidic movements within Judaism that were centred on *metanoia*, repentance or conversion and were eschatologically orientated (Lk. 13:34–35; 6:22; Mt. 11:18–19; see also Lk. 9:58; 11:31–32). From distinctively Jewish but also from profane sources we know that ever since the Maccabean period a number of baptismal movements had been operative in the Jordan valley.[12] John is in line of succession to already traditional revivalist movements that had arisen more especially since the destruction of the First Temple (587 BC), engendering in one new form after another the call to *metanoia*.[13] What fundamentally inspired all this activity was the Deuteronomic movement with its insistent declaration that Israel had killed the prophets and as a people had disobeyed God. In face of this defection the prophets proclaim the necessity for a return to God. The point of departure for this particular development is 2 Kings 17:7–20 (in a piece of Deuteronomic tradition): it ponders the downfall of Israel's northern and southern kingdoms, interpreted as a punishment for the disobedience of God's people. This Deuteronomic view of history had its first (literary) outcome in Neh. 9:26, 30 (and then in Ezra 9:11), passages that link Israel's falling away from God and being subject to his wrath with the theme of the killing of the prophets, imperative demands for *metanoia* or conversion to God. In every unit of Deuteronomic tradition from then on we find this idea.[14] Basic to it is the view of the prophet as one who preaches repentance and conversion and obedience to God's law. Neglect of this prophetic summons incurs the threat of God's annihilating judgement. This view of things became universal in later Old Testament works, including the so-called 'intertestamentary' literature of Judaism: before and during the time of Jesus it inspired all sorts of revivalist movements.

Especially during the period from the Maccabean uprising (167 BC) to the Jewish War that brought the destruction of the Temple in its train (AD 70) and the second Jewish Rebellion led by Bar Kochba (AD 135) this conversion movement acquired a markedly apocalyptic emphasis: before the End Israel is to be confronted just once more with the divine offer of 'grace-for-conversion'; after that it will be too late, for the End is about to happen.[15] It was this prospect that prompted and sustained expectations regarding the 'eschatological prophet', he who at the close of the Age would announce a final opportunity for *metanoia*. An Israel totally fallen away from God and his law is to be summoned by the prophet to return to the 'true law' of God which no laws of men must be allowed to abrogate.

In this line of spirituality, of a quite specific spirituality within Judaism, John the Baptist appears on the scene. By virtue of the already traditional idea of the defection of all Israel and the problem of God's law which that raises, Jesus' own period, seen in the context of Jewish religion, posed three fundamental issues which no one with a message for Israel could avoid.[16]

(a) First there was the vital confrontation with the pagan, foreign, anti-Yahwistic domination successively of Persians, Greeks and Romans. From a Yahwistic standpoint – Israel being exclusively Yahweh's property and heritage - such a state of occupation was also, one might even say mainly, intolerable on religious grounds. Indeed for Jews no meaningful distinction could be drawn here between religious and political factors; nor could anyone who in that spiritually concrete, social and political situation wanted to give a message to Israel avoid taking some sort of a stand on this question.

(b) At the heart of the reformist movements to which we have just been referring was a zealous reverence for the Law. Ever since the resistance to Israel's Hellenization under Antiochus IV the 'zealous of Israel' had intensified their call for fidelity to the Law. Fervent devotion to the Law, to the ancient Jewish traditions (in face of all the pagan, non-Jewish modern innovations) was a prime requirement for those – Pharisees, Essenes and various other groups – who were set on being 'true to Yahweh'. The notion of the 'Holy Remnant' was in its hey-day.[17] Despite an irreligious 'we are the holy remnant' mentality this movement – in the constellation of that time a fairly 'conservative' one – was none the less motivated by a genuinely Jewish and religious impulse, and in particular a zealous commitment to the one and only God, Yahweh, to Jerusalem and to its Temple. All the same, these devotees of Yahweh were by no means united in outlook or agreed on a programme of action. The Greek-speaking Jews of the Diaspora took a view of 'the Law' different from that of the Jerusalem ones, whose tongue was Aramaic.[18] For these Greek-speaking Jews, much inclined as they were to *philanthrōpia*, a universal 'love of humanity', a good deal of what the others were accustomed to call 'the Law' was actually incompatible with the Law proper, that is, with God's decalogue, the

Ten Commandments. In Galilee, as opposed to Jerusalem, this Graeco-Jewish outlook was in fact the 'general thing' (which is why Judea could not expect 'any good' to come out of Galilee, out of Nazareth). That Jesus' disciples were not all that strict about the various ways of washing the hands before meals was not so much something they had taken from Jesus as simply 'Galilean' (in contrast to a Jerusalemic orthodoxy).

(c) Finally, there was 'apocalypticism': views and visions of every sort concerning the 'crisis of the ages', in that sense about the end of the world.[19] All the Jewish groupings – Pharisees, Sadducees, Essenes, Zealots – were to some extent familiar with apocalyptical ideas, although not all could be described as apocalypticists. (Up to the fall of Jerusalem – AD 70 – the Pharisees were keenly opposed to apocalypticism; only after that did they think in apocalyptical terms, albeit from an early stage in an orthodox vein.)

In its historical context apocalypticism is a universal strain in the mental and spiritual outlook of the ancient East. Jewish apocalyptic was only one, if perhaps the most explicit, variant of it. I must linger a while longer over this subject; for it is a fact that after AD 70 the literature of apocalypticism became popular reading-matter more especially among Christians, who saw this Jewish literature as tending to support and nurture what they had come to believe about Christ – a belief which by then had assumed certain settled forms. It was in reaction against such use of the Jewish apocalyptical books by Christians that later on, in the second century, the rabbis attacked this literature – the reason why practically all Hebrew and Aramaic versions of it have disappeared, and only the Greek, Ethiopian and Slavonic versions (read by Christians) have been preserved. The Ethiopian Enoch (an Ethiopian translation of an originally Aramaic book of Enoch) is still regarded by the Ethiopian Church as part and parcel of canonical Old Testament Scripture. The New Testament writings, especially those later than AD 70, show obvious signs of apocalyptic influence.

What is apocalypticism? Who is an apocalypticist? He is one who regards himself not as a prophet but as an interpreter of the ancient prophets. He does not want to be a prophet and so, in order to legitimate his message, makes use of a pseudonym – which automatically means that he can propagate his ideas only in written form: thus he is not a preacher or public speaker. Apocalyptic, therefore, is essentially a literary genre, the expression of a special view of history.

The basic substance of apocalypticism bears the stamp of a long experience of human life, an experience which has ceased to look to man's history for any improvement. Suffering and every kind of misfortune, whether individual or national, are so persistent that one has to postulate at the source of mankind's history a Fall of the first man, which then rolls through history like a snowball (4 Ezra 4:30; Syrian Baruch 23:4). Thus Satan with his entourage obtains power over this world. These evil powers do battle with the pious, those faithful to the Law; the whole purpose of their struggle is eventually to get Jerusalem the holy in their power. It is no longer possible, therefore, to hope for any final good from our human history. All hope is founded on the 'turn of the ages', that is, a sudden intervention on God's part, which just does away altogether with 'this course of events' or 'this aeon' (as the Indian god, Shiva, shatters his perverted world to pieces in order to construct a completely new one upon it) so as to create from the beginning 'a new heaven and earth', a 'second aeon', like the earthly paradise from before the Fall. 'The Most High has created not one aeon, but two' (4 Ezra 7:50).

But just as on the one hand Israel's sin is the cause of present calamity, so on the other hand a turn-about, *metanoia* and religious zeal can hasten the time of salvation (in Zech. 1:3; see Jubilees 23:26–29; Enoch 90:35, 38). In an apocalyptic context expectation of the End and the call to *metanoia* go hand in hand, just as did prophecy and summons to *metanoia* in an earlier situation. (For that reason alone, not every imperative call to *metanoia* should be given an apocalyptic interpretation.)

Apocalyptists are interpreting human history; we are right to speak in this case of a 'theology of history'. They see the course of events in the world in demarcated periods, in clearly defined series which nevertheless, in a veiled fashion, constitute a historical unity. Typical of that is Daniel 2:31–35, where an apocalyptical prophet depicts past history as a statue of terrifying appearance. Admittedly, its head is of pure gold, but its breast and arms are entirely of silver, its belly and loins of bronze, its legs of iron, its feet partly of iron, partly of clay: these are the empires from the neo-Babylonians to Alexander the Great in the age of Hellenism, seen however in a single image, that is, as a single, unified history of rising and vanishing world empires. But then, peering more closely, this visionary or interpreter of history perceives that 'a stone was cut out by no human hand, and it smote the image on its feet of iron and clay, and broke them in pieces; then the iron, the clay, the bronze, the silver and the gold, all together were broken in pieces, and became like the chaff of the summer threshing floors; and the wind carried them away . . .' (Dan. 2:34–35). The text itself then proceeds to expound the meaning of that vision (2:36–45): God will make an end of all those kingdoms and take over command himself: 'The God of heaven will set up a kingdom which shall never be destroyed, nor shall its sovereignty be left to another people' (2:44). Then follows, in typical apocalyptic vein: 'The dream is certain and its interpretation sure' (2:45). Later on, for instance, among the Hellen-istic-Jewish Christians, this becomes: 'Truly, truly I say to you . . .', a typical apocalyptic formula of legitimation. Each time the Parousia, that is, the manifestation in power and might of God's kingly rule, failed to materialize, expectation of the End, instead of being stifled, on the contrary grew more feverish; but each time with fresh nuances, intended to account for the delayed arrival of the Parousia. Typical in this respect is 1 QpHab 7:7–14 (that is, a commentary - *pesher* - on Habakkuk, found in the first cave at Qumrân): 'The final End is taking more time than the prophets predicted, for marvellous are God's mysteries . . . The last days will come according to God's appointed time.' That instead of the actual arrival of this final kingdom there is greater and greater oppression is in its turn given an apocalyptic inter-pretation. For according to later apocalypticism the setting up of God's kingdom is preceded by a period of mounting horrors (4 Ezra 5:4–5), 'eschatological woes': father turns against son, brother against brother, there is no peace left anywhere; flowers and trees wither, women no longer give birth; the old order of things in the world is dying. What-ever still survives is locked in conflict. Finally, the cosmos begins to crack in every joint. But then the pious know that God's kingdom is on its way: God's new world for the zealous of Israel. All sorts of originally astrological numbers: 12 (months), 7 (days), 4 (seasons), with subdivisions as arcane clues (three-and-a-half years is half of 7, etc.; 12 times 7 is 84, etc.) tell the pious when the End is going to come. The final woes themselves, for instance for Daniel, will only last for three-and-a-half years (Dan. 7:25; 12:7), that is, for a brief period. But only God knows the 'length of days'; the course of history is in his hand. The 'Assumption of Moses' (10:1–10) depicts the End, 'when God's dominion over all will be made public', 'then all sadness will be removed – the devil vanquished – "the celestial one" will rise up from his throne; the world begin to quake, mountains tumble down, the sun cease to give light, the moon split in two and grow blood-red and the whole firmament be thrown into chaos; all waters disappear, for the All-Highest has risen up to punish the heathen. Then, Israel, you shall have good fortune . . . and you shall be exalted to the starry heavens. And thence you shall look down and see your enemies below and you shall laugh and give thanks to God, your Creator' (see also Dan. 7:11). Sometimes there appears on the scene of this final act the figure of a messianic judge. Daniel 7:13–14 speaks of 'one like a human being' (in Greek: son of man). As opposed to animals (Dan. 7:4–8), that is, the four great heathen empires, this eschatological governor (Dan. 7:14) has a human form and aspect: this is, on the analogy of Israel's celestial *archon*, Israel herself, the people of the saints of the Most High (Dan. 7:27) that is to rule the world on God's behalf. Israel is the people of the approaching time of salvation (see in Part Three: the son of man). However, in the parable-section of the (Ethiopic) Enoch (chs 37–71) the son of man is set over against the people of God and described as a person: the eschatological judge. The visionary of the Enoch book sees alongside the Ancient of Days 'another, whose countenance was like that of a man, and gracious, it seemed, like that of a holy angel' (46:1), and he hears: 'This is the son of man, who possesses righteousness . . . and who shall reveal all the hidden treasures, for the Lord of spirits has chosen him . . . This son of man, whom you have seen, shall thrust kings and mighty ones out of their place and the strong from their throne' (46:3–4). But although he is a judge, for the pious he is their redeemer, who leads his own on to freedom and is to celebrate the messianic banquet with them (62:13–16): he will reign as a new king of paradise (69:26–29) (see also 2 Baruch 73:1; Ezra 7:33; cf. Rev. 20:11).

After the destruction of the Temple at Jerusalem (AD 70), so far from being stifled, the expectation of the End began to foment and burgeon with new life (only then were 4 Ezra, the Syrian Baruch and the New Testament Apocalypse written and apocalypticism took a hold on the Pharisees, who had previously been its opponents). Apocalypticism may well have been the original reason why the earlier Chasidic movement split up, on the one hand into a Pharisaic school and on the other into the apocalyptic movement proper. When Christians, who already believed in Jesus, risen and glorified, read all this, they must have felt greatly heartened: because for them it all had to do with Jesus Christ. And that they did read it is borne out by a passage quoted from this Enoch-apocalypse in the New Testament itself (Jude 14–15; allusion to Enoch-apocalypse, 1:91).

Many people nowadays see dualism present in the apocalypticism of the two aeons. An ethical dualism – a struggle between good and evil – is unmistakably represented here: it is the warp and woof, the very stuff of all human history. But in contrast to non-Jewish apocalypses, 'this aeon' is, like Satan himself, a thing created by God though admittedly fallen away from him. Again, according to this apocalyptical outlook there is a veiled connection between this mundane course of events and a supra-mundane, a-temporal one in which a host of good and fallen angels is having an effect on our terrestrial history. In particular the 'angel of the peoples' (*archon* or angelic guardian of the nations) exerts a crucial influence at the chief moments of crisis in the history of the nations (see Dan. 10:20–21; Enoch 89:59ff; Rev. 16:14). However, when the last days, that is, the radically new age, begins to dawn, the boundaries between the earthly and the celestial course of events are blurred. Good men now live in company with the angels, they shine like stars in the firmament (Dan. 12:3; Enoch 50:1; 51:4). After the final catastrophe, therefore, there is a new state of affairs: conditions are then reversed: the one who weeps now will laugh then; the poor will be rich, the mighty downcast. The paradisal situation is eschatologically restored; and the pious of non-Israelite nations also share in this 'time of salvation'; they share then in Israel's good fortune or rather in that of the faithful remnant of Israel; for the nation, *qua* nation, is no longer elect, only the devout 'holy remnant'. Daniel 3:10f (also 4 Ezra 4:26ff) makes it clear that God's rule is already operative now, even if it be hidden. With the final Parousia, when God or his chosen one publicly ascends the throne, God's lordship and rule will be visible on earth (Dan. 7:14; Enoch 4:1; see Rev. 11:15); all earthly empires will then be abolished. This exercise of rule by God at the close of the Age is his 'glorious appearing', at which all the structures of society will be changed (a societal critique – directed by Jews at non-Jewish domination – assuredly plays a role here, although this literature is meant primarily to console and encourage men with the idea that, despite every painful experience, God alone is the Lord of history and has the last word). In some apocalypses this final kingdom is still an earthly one, a kind of messianic, this-worldly salvation-history; in other writings the messianic kingdom does not appear and the coming aeon is celestial, supra-mundane from the outset; yet others see the messianic kingdom being realized in a 'new heaven and new earth', a life on earth from which, however, all mundane features have dropped away.

'Apocalypsis', therefore, is the pre-eschatological disclosure of the real background to all terrestrial history, a disclosure which the apocalyptical visionary imparts here and now already in what he writes: he has been allowed to view this background for the benefit of the elect. The eschatological drama is apocalyptically unveiled for the sake of their faith, as though to give them heart to believe that, with God's coming, salvation will be possible. 'Paraenesis' or moral uplift, an ethical orientation, is fundamental therefore to apocalypticism; always the gist of its heartening message is 'Blessed is he who endures to the end' (Dan. 12:12). So apocalypticism is a religious philosophy of life (with an 'apocalyptic' reiteration of a lot of old prophetic ideas) – only one current, however, among many others at that time, though certain ideas were popularized in this way or absorbed into the common way of thinking.

Whatever one may think of apocalypticism, the experience at the bottom of it is existential and realistic, even 'modern': if God is the source of all life, then why so much cruelty, inequality, pain and suffering, unhappiness, misfortune and woe, why so much discord in our nature and our human history? Apocalypticism wrestled with this problem: it looked for a solution in its vision regarding 'this aeon' and the 'coming aeon' or radically new world. The apocalyptic expectation that the 'end of the world' is near is in a modern guise, the Utopian yearning for an end to the course of human suffering, an end to all dire need, oppression, war and wretchedness. Expressed in positive terms, it is the hope of the coming of a 'kingdom of peace', a commonwealth of benefit to all, that seeing how long and above all how obdurate the history of our suffering has been, we can continue to hope from God alone.

Such messianic, apocalyptical expectations are nothing exceptional in human history. Sociologists of religion have turned their attention to a phenomenon occurring periodically among every people, which they have called the 'messianic pattern'.[20] These sociological studies have shown that in extreme situations of social and political *malaise* radical movements of a messianic stamp are a common occurrence at certain critical junctures in the history of most peoples. There are of course tonal variations in the political and social sphere, some even of an interior, mystical nature; the range too may be universal or restricted by nationalism. Even so, these radical messianic movements exhibit a more or less invariable basic pattern. Schematically simplified, the basic messianic pattern looks rather like the following. Socio-political situations of economic and especially of cultural and spiritual debility and loss of identity are always periods in which radical movements presenting a messianic aspect emerge, movements that dream of an imminent, radically new world, because the 'old world' has become utterly intolerable. An ardent longing then ensues: a life liberated and redeemed is about to begin. In such situations of *malaise* fantasy intensifies, Utopian pictures of a totally new world loom ahead: visions of a realm of peace, righteousness, happiness and love such as never was seen. A movement of this sort often crystallizes around a single mediatorial figure whose role is that of a saviour who is expected to make everything come out right.

It is evident to the historian and the sociologist of religion that in fact the radical messianic movements, whether promising an inward or a socio-political liberation, have all failed. Not only did they fail to achieve an earthly paradise or kingdom of peace and righteousness, but the readily appealing experience of a completely new world was always a shortlived dream. Moreover, after an initial conflagration, the mystical or socio-political messianic flame was dimmed – or was violently extinguished. Does that apply also to Jesus of Nazareth?

It would be unhistorical, a misjudgement of Jesus' true humanity, to pass over the fact that the movements centred around John and Jesus made their appearance in this climate. From the historian of religion's standpoint they constitute a particular manifestation within the apocalyptical and eschatological expectancy of Judaism at the time. Uniqueness and originality, transcendence even, do not rule out being conditioned by and rooted in history. On the contrary, 'being the child of his time', a Jew in a Judaic-apocalyptic world reveals in all its particularity the newness of John's and Jesus' message.

But the difficulty raised by an initial approach to Jesus via John the Baptist resides in the fact that, regarding John, we are even more in the dark as to his precise message than in the case of Jesus. The reason is obvious enough. First there is the fact that, except for a few aftereffects that lasted until the third century, John did not touch off any movement centred on himself; so that no people have survived to transmit the authentic tradition of John's charismatic ministry (in contrast with the Jesus movement). Secondly, because we are confronted with the fact that the data available to us about John (reliable enough, no doubt but calling for a careful interpretation) are known to us almost entirely via the Christian understanding of him in the New Testament, orientated from the outset on Jesus – an interpretation less concerned with John's personal career and public ministry than with his role as forerunner of Jesus, and therefore his inferior. Very probably a certain amount of competition gradually ensued, reflected particularly within the Johannine gospel, between John's disciples and those of Jesus (after his death). Even so, a critical process of selecting from the gospels does yield a specific and essentially accurate picture of John's message and conduct, apart from certain points of sharp disagreement among exegetes.[21]

## §2 The message and activity of John the Baptist

*Literature.* J. Becker, *Johannes der Täufer und Jesus von Nazareth*, Neukirchen 1972; H. Braun, 'Entscheidende Motive in den Berichten über die Taufe Jesu von Markus bis Justin', *Gesammelte Studien zum Neuen Testament und seiner Umwelt* (Tübingen 1967²), 168–72; W. Brownlee, 'John the Baptist in the new light of ancient scrolls', in K. Stendahl, *The Scrolls and the New Testament* (New York 1957), 33–53; I. Buse, 'The Marcan account of the baptism of Jesus and Isaiah LXIII', JTS 7 (1956), 74–5; C. Cranfield, 'The baptism of our Lord', ScotJTh 8 (1955), 55–63; J. Daniélou, *Jean-Baptiste*, Paris 1964; G. C. Darton, *St John the Baptist and the Kingdom of Heaven*, London 1961; M. Dibelius, *Die urchristliche Ueberlieferung von Johannes der Täufer*, Göttingen 1911; A. Feuillet, 'Le baptême de Jésus', RB 71 (1964), 321–52; J. Jeremias, 'Der Ursprung der Johannestaufe', ZNW 28 (1929), 312–20; E. Käsemann, 'Zum Thema der urchristlichen Apokalyptik', in *Besinnungen*, II, 105–31; Fr. Lentzen-Deis, *Die Taufe nach den Synoptikern*, Frankfurt 1970; E. Lohmeyer, *Das Urchristentum*, vol. 1, *Johannes der Täufer*, Göttingen 1932; C. McCown, 'The scene of John's ministry', JBL 59 (1940), 113–31; C. Scobie, *John the Baptist*, London 1964; J. Sint, 'Die Eschatologie des Täufers, die Täufergruppen und die Polemik der Evangelien', in K. Schubert, *Vom Messias zum Christum* (Vienna 1964), 55–163; J. Steinmann, *S. Jean Baptiste et la spiritualité du désert*, Paris 1955; W. Trilling, 'Die Täufer-Tradition bei Matthäus', BZ 3 (1959), 271–89; Ph. Vielhauer, *Johannes, der Täufer*, RGG³, III, 804–8; A. Vögtle, *Das öffentliche Wirken Jesu auf dem Hintergrund der Qumranbewegung* (Freiburger Universitätsreden, N.F., H 27), Freiburg 1958; W. Wink, *John the Baptist in the Gospel Tradition*, Cambridge 1968.

John's message and his 'life-style' are closely interrelated.[22] The New Testament enshrines certain memories of his practice of baptizing, his way of dressing and feeding himself, his lack of possessions and the place of his ministry. So when it comes to interpreting his message,

John's 'life-style', as his contemporaries saw and understood it, must provide a hermeneutical key.

John's activity was located 'in the wilderness' (Mt. 11:7 and parallels); that is to say, the role he fulfils is in keeping with the Exodus tradition.[23] The wilderness is the site of the eagerly awaited future, of the eschatological 'new start' and total transformation. This in itself implies a choice of spirituality: not the kind centred on the Temple – a Jerusalem-Zion spirituality (also a focus of expectation in Judaism regarding an eschatological future) – but the wilderness spirituality is what governs the activities of John. In line with this is his ascetic attitude to life: he is destitute, does not work for a living, scorns products like bread and wine (see Lk. 7:33 and parallels) and lives on what the wilderness provides: snails or locusts and honey (Mt. 3:4). He wore camel's-hair with a rough (thus: natural) girdle about him, the typical clothing of a prophet.[24] All this is in itself an 'eschatological demonstration' by someone who knows he is a prophet. That is how he comes across to the later Christians too.[25] John's place and personal appearance are depicted in an eschatological context: this man's living is based wholly on a looking towards the future, which leaves aside what is already given – past and present – for what it is, passes that by in order to live by and for the future alone. The present then can only be filled with *metanoia*, conversion, exodus or leaving behind all that is and journeying towards that future.

What is that future? John does not seem to have proclaimed the kingdom of God.[26] The heart of his message is captured, apparently, in a Q passage: 'He [John] said therefore to the multitudes that came out to be baptized by him: You brood of vipers! Who warned you to flee from the wrath to come? Bear fruits that befit repentance, and do not begin to say to yourselves: We have Abraham as our father; for I tell you, God is able from these stones to raise up children to Abraham. Even now the axe is laid to the root of the trees; every tree therefore that does not bear good fruit is cut down and thrown into the fire' (Lk. 3:7–9 and Mt. 3:7–10, 11–12). John is the penitential preacher prophetically announcing the imminent judgement of God. The future here is God's wrath, his inexorable sentence.[27] The fact that one is a child of Abraham and belongs to the people of God is no guarantee of salvation or exoneration from this judgement. We said earlier on that these are no novel ideas in Israel. It is a traditionally Jewish vision at any rate within the complex of tradition enshrining the Deuteronomic view of events,[28] and not a Christian interpretation of John's preaching. A prophet is in this tradition one who calls to repentance. The Q text faithfully reflects indeed the core of John's message.

Even so, this typically prophetic theme, borrowed from earlier traditions,[29] had little currency in Jesus' days.[30] There was something provocative about John's behaviour, therefore. The term 'brood of vipers' in particular is uncommonly sharp, in that for Jews it is the pagans who are compared with animals ('dogs', see Mk. 7:27; Mt. 15: 26). Here Israel is being called 'pagan'. The divine sentence of annihilation, which according to the ideas, especially the apocalyptic ideas, of the time is to descend upon the heathen, John makes rebound on to the Jewish generation itself; it cannot retreat into the alibi of God's promise to Abraham. 'Bearing fruit' (a Semitic expression for good works that can turn aside God's punishments; see Gen. 1:11–12), doing penance (and to that end getting baptized) can alone ward off calamity. John is no purveyor of an 'evangel' or glad tidings of salvation, he is a prophet of woe, threatening men with the approaching judgement of God. His message and his whole style of life declare this. Again, his critical judgement on the alibi supposedly provided by being a member of God's people is not something new in Israel; it was actually a 'tradition' in Chasidic or pious circles from the Maccabean period onward. Qumrân too, even Pharisees, are familiar with this judgement upon Israel as a whole.[31] The traditional principle of Israel's divine election is not assailed by this – or by John the Baptist who, after all, addressed himself and his message exclusively to Israel, yet denying the automatically guaranteed nature of this election, in line of course with the old prophets. The sharp attack is still something typically Jewish.

A salient feature of this resumption of ancient prophetic traditions on the part of the Baptist is the term 'already' or 'even now': now it is starting to happen (This is part of old prophecy. In conjunction with Mt. 3:10 see especially Isa. 43:19 and 55:6). The axe is already laid to the tree. 'The tree to be cut down' is a typical Isaianic expression for the judgement of God (Isa. 10:33–34; also Dan. 4:11, 14–20).

It is noticeable that in the view of John presented in the New Testament what come across at every point are not specifically apocalyptical but early prophetic motifs. The 'axe', the 'winnow'[32] and the 'fire' – three key-words used in the New Testament to denote John's proclamation of judgement – belong not to apocalyptic but to ancient prophecy. Fire and wrath, in an Old Testament context, are fitting images of God's approaching judgement. That judgement is about to take place.[33] Whoever is not baptized with water – so John proclaims – will suffer the baptism of fire, which is that of the eschatological judgement. The ancient prophets linked this notion of God's judgement at the end of time – a baptism of fire – with three images: the burning up of the chaff after the harvesting,[34] a conflagration in which every withered and barren tree will be consumed[35] and, thirdly, the image of the metal furnace.[36] Of these Old Testament images of the threatening and approaching divine judgement John the Baptist adopts two, along with the accompanying *metanoia* or call to repentance.[37] Remarkably enough, he does not take up the idea of the 'refining fire' (associated with metal smelting); John will hear only of the fire that consumes all. Cosmic ideas of a 'global holocaust' are foreign to him: it is a matter of God's judgement upon man: this too is unapocalyptical. There is nowhere in John's preaching as conveyed by the New Testament any trace of the apocalyptical 'two aeons' doctrine. Only the righteous – those whom John has baptized – are going to survive this conflagration and this tree-felling. Actually, the grim-hearted John does not even give that assurance; explicitly, his message refers only to the trees that are to be cut down! In succession to the majority of Old Testament prophets he is a 'prophet of doom', herald of approaching calamity for every 'unrighteous' person. And the calamity will not even be foreshadowed in pre-eschatological signs and warning events. Here is no apocalypticist speaking but a prophet of the old school.

Yet in respect of the old prophetic tradition John does have something new to contribute: the need for baptism, more specifically, 'the baptism of John'. Immersing oneself in water from motives of *metanoia* had been a known practice in Jewish circles for some time already. But here it is John (in person or with help from his disciples) who baptizes; and this is new. Hence his nickname, 'the Baptizer' (mentioned even by Flavius Josephus), because it was the custom then for one to baptize oneself. Here we have a baptism by John. He 'preaches baptism' (Mk. 1:4; Lk. 3:3; Acts 10:37; 13:24). Baptism is essentially part and parcel of his call to conversion. Apocalypticism may be radical but John is more so; only his baptism yields the possibility (not even the certainty) of escaping God's sentence of annihilation by fire. There speaks a quite explicit prophetic self-awareness. One may wonder whether such a message – uttered in the concrete situation at that time – does not contain a judgement upon Pharisaic, Zealotic and other Jewish expectations current then. Apart from Matthew 3:2 'repenting' is always associated with the baptism of John. John 'baptizes with water for repentance' (Mt. 3:11), in other words the conversion completes the meaning and purpose of the baptismal act. Getting oneself baptized by John, the man sent from God, means letting oneself be

J.E.C.–E

changed by God; for a human being cannot do this of himself. Repentance is understood here as being a free gift from God. In the later Jesus tradition too it is said that the baptism of John is 'from heaven' (Mt. 21:25 and parallels; see below). For this prophet and baptizer the 'one thing necessary' is *metanoia*, 'being converted', repenting and being baptized, a penitential baptism. Everything else is, in view of the approaching judgement, a waste of time, even the Jewish circumcision, albeit a sign of election by God.

There is something of the Second Isaiah in John: think, people of God, no longer of your previous salvation-history, of God's mighty acts in your past; think now only of 'what is to come': the axe is laid to the tree (Isa. 43:18–19). Even the Isaianic 'last chance' this people have thrown away: now comes the verdict pronounced upon their conduct in history. The orientation is typically Jewish still: it has to do with the children of Abraham, whom God can produce, if need be, from the very stones.[38] Without the baptism of *metanoia* Abraham's children are as the heathen.[39] In his originality John is still of the old prophetic school. He stands of course in a new and different period – an apocalyptic one – but he brings to it what was most authentic about Israel's ancient prophets of woe – with a view to salvation.

Yet it is precisely that nuance – 'with a view to salvation' – which raises a question about this Baptizer. Admittedly, John does not disclaim the prospect of salvation which Israel's great prophets until then had always kept open: but nowhere does he enunciate this, according to the New Testament record (which may perhaps be influenced in this regard by the differing impression John, as opposed to Jesus, had made on the latter's disciples).

We have here no[40] (for the time) 'modernist', apocalyptical spokesman, but a man preaching for repentance and motivated by the old prophets of Israel. John's thinking is indeed centred on the future – but it is eschatological, not apocalyptical. No question with him of the peering at the future so typical of apocalyptic, no latter-day wonders, but the raw prophetic voice of doom. He never stops to consider the possibility of salvation for those who escape God's inexorable judgement. That judgement obsesses him: what human being can stand against this measured and objective verdict? John does of course admit a possibility of salvation; if he did not, there would have been no point in his baptizing people. Behind it all is the Old Testament injunction: 'Seek me and live' (Amos 5:4–5). But Amos, the ancient prophet of woe, had already said what the Baptist is saying now: even the remnant of Israel is to perish (Amos 5:18–20; 6:1–14). In this preaching of judgement the prospect of salvation remains 'veiled': it is not, as a theme, enunciated, whereas in Israel's ancient prophecies it was never passed over in total silence.[41] This absence of a promise on John's part of ultimate salvation (see Mk. 3 with a text cited from Isa. 40:3) may be historical but may also be a Christian (Jesus-centred) overlay. Luke 3:5–6 cites the whole Isaianic context, whereby the Baptist goes on to proclaim an 'evangel', a message of joy. The only element that might point to a prospect of salvation is the mention of the 'eschatological *pneuma*' (see Lk. 3:16 and parallels): but this is probably a Christian interpretation of John.[42]

This line of enquiry brings us to a second aspect of John's preaching, as the New Testament sees it: his preaching also refers to 'him who comes', to one mightier than himself. The Q community (Lk. 3:16= Mt. 3:11), Luke and Matthew speak of this; but so also Mk. 1:7 and Acts (Acts 13:25). Indeed the question arises here as to whether the preaching about the 'one who is to come' is a Christian interpolation pointing to John the Baptist as the eschatological prophet, the forerunner of Messiah-Jesus – clearly a problem for Jesus' disciples, who in their transcendently loftier appreciation of their master, Jesus of Nazareth, had none the less to come to terms with the fact that he had been baptized by John. On this point the facts as recalled in the New Testament have been given a Christian colouring, although the Christian interpretation is not meant to negate or cover up the remembered evidences of history. Anyone who for apologetic reasons wanted to do that would have done better to ignore John's baptism of Jesus altogether. Yet none of the early Christian congregations suppress this fact, even if they are set (not without some embarrassment, apparently) on giving it a new, Christian interpretation.

We cannot be quite certain, therefore, whether John himself did proclaim 'the one who is to come'. At any rate there is Christian interpretation of John as forerunner of the (earthly or coming) Jesus. Still, the heralding of the eschatological judge – 'who judges as by fire' – fits perfectly with John's message of judgement. It is an evident fact of history that the coming of Elijah was currently expected among John's circle of disciples; so here we certainly have to do with a (pre-Christian) tradition regarding John.[43] Again the idea of a forerunner of the latter-day mediator (commonly regarded, it is true, as a saviour figure) is not specifically Christian, but Jewish. The interpretation here is Christian, the model for it pre-Christian. The designation of 'the one who is coming' as mightier may itself be the outcome of Christian interpretation of the Baptist. That is why I would argue from the probability that John did himself speak of 'the coming one'.

But who is he, this coming one, in John's own perspective? This cannot be the coming God in person, rather the coming of God's official representative, the eschatological mediator or intermediary, the coming of what in apocalyptical circles is known as the son of man.[44] *Ho erchomenos*, the coming one, was already a popular technical term among the Jews for a coming eschatological figure,[45] but then, in this context, not seen officially as a saviour figure but as a judge, someone coming with winnow and sickle in hand and ready with the fire of judgement now prepared, in which all that is chaff will be destroyed. These are all prophetic images of the final judgement. The one who comes is thus an unmistakably judicial figure. In the Old Testament and in Judaism no one qualifies for this unless it be either God himself (but this is ruled out by the anthropomorphic context 'whose sandals I am not worthy to carry', Mt. 3:11; Lk. 3:16; Acts 13:25; in the New Testament, of course, the 'anthropomorphism' may be prompted just by the Christian identification of 'the coming one' with Jesus himself), or the eschatological messenger from God (about whom people could and constantly did speak in anthropomorphic terms). Only the son of man is in the running as such an eschatological judge figure. Thus we may suppose John himself to have taken over the idea of the son of man, developed earlier on within Judaism, albeit using the vaguer phraseology of 'the coming one'. In that case John will have given a lead for the Christians, later on, to interpret him as forerunner and Jesus as the son of man. It is actually in Dan. 7:11, within the context of Dan. 7:13–14 to which Judaism gave a son-of-man interpretation, that we read of a torrent of fire as the medium for exercising judgement upon the fourth beast.[46] John is prophet, not spokesman for apocalypticism; yet with his appeal to the son of man and agent of fiery judgement he takes over what is in fact an apocalyptical idea, linking the old prophetic notion of judgement with the coming son of man. No Christian innovation, this, but something already provided by Judaism. The sole Christian element is the identification of the coming one with Jesus himself and with that the interpretation of the Baptist as his fore-runner.

By way of the Christian interpretation, therefore, and yet sufficiently well, we can see the broad features of John's preaching of the baptism of *metanoia* as the way of escape from the fiery baptism of judgement. With all this John had only Israel in view, and not the heathen. The 'coming judgement', often treated as Israel's consolation for the coming destruction of the Gentiles, is turned by John the Baptist into a weapon against the people of God, or rather – in view of the individualizing trend of those days – against the Israelites individually: to be a member of God's people, of Israel, is no guarantee of salvation. This proclamation brings out God's unconditional and sovereign transcendence, which is not to be tied down to man's ideas of salvation, not even when they can be to some extent justifiably referred to Yahweh's past saving acts and dealings with his people. The only way to approach God – so John's message runs – is with the fruits of repentance.

After what at that time was felt to be so long an absence of 'prophets', in John there comes to graphic expression, in word and in action, not apocalypticism but, quite distinctly, Israel's age-old prophecy. Amos, as harshly and fiercely as the Baptist, had already declared: 'The day of the Lord . . . is darkness and not light' (Am. 5:18–20). An eschatological hope without right conduct is exposed to the critique of this prophetic tradition. Triumphalist belief in election is given a complete overhaul. Every religious claim on assured salvation and the force of 'Israel's devoted zeal' is critically challenged by this pristinely serious prophet of woe. Nothing will do but *metanoia*, an about-turn, giving one's life a direction quite different from the normal rule. Self-criticism, *metanoia* with an eye to the future, the coming judgement. With John the living God acquires in fact a prophetic aura, wholly non-magical and (to use a modern term) 'non-establishment'. The ideas current at the time regarding divine annihilation of 'God's enemies' – the foes of Israel – and of Israel's final triumph over all her adversaries – the worldwide messianic dominion – are simply knocked to pieces by this grim prophet, John the Baptist. The whole of Israel must be moved once more to confront itself with the living God.

John, living in an apocalyptic age, is essentially not an apocalypticist. He has none of the appropriate features we outlined earlier on: he is a (penitential) preacher, speaks on his own authority without need for legitimation: and except for the idea of 'the coming one' his ideas include none that are typically apocalyptic. The so-called *Naherwartung* or idea of the nearness of the end is itself a prophetic datum (cf. the 'even now' of Mt. 3:10 with the 'now' of Isa. 43:19 and with Isa. 55:6). Concepts and images used by John: conversion, Israel's situation of total calamity, the imminent judgement of God which the unrighteous or unrepentant will not be able to escape, the annihilating judgement-by-fire – all these are Deutero-Isaianic prophetic elements incorporated into apocalyptic; but in themselves they are non-apocalyptical. What John's immediate, historical source of inspiration was eludes us: we are ignorant of John's previous history and background, nor do we know whether he really comes from a priestly family (as Lk. 1:5 intimates). We are bound of course to put on record the striking affinity between John and Deutero-Isaianic ideas. In view of all these evidences one is surely obliged to characterize John's self-understanding as that of a prophetic charismatic in line of succession with the already more ancient Chasidic movement.[47]

The message of judgement and offer of baptism are the hallmark of John's ministry: he is prophet and he is baptizer. What is unique about this is that John does the baptizing himself. The possibility of escape from God's wrath is separated from its connection with the Abrahamic promise to the whole nation and is individualized by a new bond, that is, the baptism of John, engagement with total change, a transformation. Through this baptism God presents a final option of escape from the approaching catastrophe (see Mk. 1:4 and parallels; Lk. 3:8). Implicit therefore in John's whole movement is an unprecedented disavowal of the Jerusalem Temple cult and propitiatory sacrifices. New in John's *metanoia*-preaching, *vis-à-vis* the Deuteronomic and Chasidic tradition in which he stands, is the quite extraordinary mediatorial role ascribed to himself by the prophet: John's baptism is 'necessary to salvation', getting oneself baptized by John bears a (difficult to define but none the less real) relation to one's own destiny at the coming judgement. All this John does and says 'on his own authority'. The narrative that deals with the question of Jesus' competency (Lk. 20:1–8) is important in this respect. This tradition has Jesus responding with a counter-question: 'Was the baptism of John from heaven or from men?' (Lk. 20:4). The Scribes avoid the answer, whereupon Jesus says: 'Neither will I tell you by what authority I do these things' (20:8). The critical method of *Formgeschichte* reveals, from the same story in Mk. 11:27–33, that 11:27–30 (as a source-passage) was at first conjoined with 11:15–16 (the cleansing of the Temple); in the Johannine gospel too the cleansing and the question of Jesus' authority are closely interrelated.[48] Mark 11:28 fits harmoniously on to Mk. 11:18a. The cleansing of the Temple thus acquires the function of leading into the dispute over Jesus' right to act in that way. Thus according to this pericope Jesus takes for granted both his own and John's prophetic authority (see also Mt. 11:13; 16:14). Furthermore, there is in this passage no Christian attempt to represent John simply as forerunner to Jesus. This says much for the authenticity of the scene. Jesus sees an essential correspondence between the baptism of John and his own ministry. As prophets both have full authority. What is more, there is an implicit reference here to the historical fact that, in a sense, Jesus treads in the footsteps of the Baptist. Recognition of John's authority must entail recognition of Jesus' authority; even the Scribes perceive that, so being wise enough not to answer Jesus' question. This is certainly the drift of the argument. Just as John's baptism was a prophetic sign intended to bring about the latter-day repentance and conversion of Israel, so Jesus too sees his line of conduct (in this case the cleansing of the Temple) as such a prophetic sign and summons to complete transformation.

John the Baptist then is a non-messianic figure, no Zealot, either, and a-political in his immediate message: he stands outside Zealotism, outside messianism and outside apocalypticism. His message was a frontal assault on three basic expectations in the Judaism of the time: the eschatological expectation of the destruction of Yahweh's and therefore Israel's foes; Israel's own final victory and worldwide dominion; the guarantee of salvation entailed by the promise to Abraham. All this, past and present, John submits to a complete overhaul; he thinks and lives solely in terms of the future, occupied with God's inexorable and, on a prophetic reading, temporally imminent judgement, from which no one in all Israel can escape. The future for John is God's exclusive potential. Present and past, therefore, lie under the critique of God's future, here denoted by an apocalyptic term 'the coming one' (in virtue of the judgemental perspective, obviously, to be filled out with 'son of man'). Even prior to John the son of man was the linguistic index for God's final judgement. Hence the 'coming person' is himself kept vague (John offers no portrayal in apocalyptic terms of this person). However, this exclusive concentration on the future does affect the present: conversion here and now! That is why we can fairly say that John links up the idea of expecting the end with the demand for orthopraxis. With John eschatology becomes a moral-cum-religious appeal. God's future is conjoined with ethics.[49] The magical, apocalyptical feature of a sudden forceful intervention on God's part is nowhere detectable in John's preaching. One could even say that in the Baptist apocalypticism has been reduced to its purely religious core, with every trace of apocalyptic removed! God stands in radical judgement over against man, who cannot and will not judge himself.[50] John is the prophet who establishes an intrinsic bond between expectation of the future and ethical-religious commitment – yet from an exclusive perspective of judgement, not from the religious perspective of God's graciousness and love. In that, Jesus will be unable to follow John the Baptist.

Lastly, we know regarding the Baptist how he was put to death on the orders of King Herod (one who had the *ius gladii* was empowered to behead); besides the gospels various secular sources mention the event.[51] The interpretations of John's imprisonment and execution are at variance. According to the New Testament version he was arrested because he had accused King Herod of appropriating his brother's wife (Mk. 6:17); and he is said to have been beheaded because Herod gave in to a ruse prearranged with the help of a dancing girl. The Jewish historian Josephus tells us that John baptized and thereby attracted so many people that Herod was afraid John's power over them might incite them to rebellion, for 'they were ready to do whatever he asked'; 'for that reason he caused him to be shut up in the fortress of Macheron'.[52] Historically, this would seem to be a more likely motive; but even so it is not entirely unconnected with what the gospels say. Not only does Mk. 6:20 speak of Herod's fear of John (though perhaps a superstitious fear of a holy man: in Mt. 14:5 on the contrary the fear is fear of the multitude), but on the other hand the historian Josephus (independently of the gospels) also mentions apropos of the Baptist Herod's passion for Herodias, his stepbrother's wife, and his divorce from his previous wife (daughter to King Aretas). In revenge this king inflicts a severe military defeat on Herod,[53] and Josephus comments: 'Many Jews saw in that a much deserved punishment for the murder of John the Baptist.'[54] This popular opinion is presumably the basis of the tradition incorporated in Mark. A hard core of historical fact is: the execution of the Baptist by the tetrarch Herod Antipas. Even John's violent death is to be important later on to Jesus' self-understanding.

## §3   Jesus' first prophetic act: his baptism by John

The preceding section was necessary to help us understand better the extraordinary fact that Jesus got himself baptized by John. This baptism was not just an incidental factor in the life of Jesus. Although the 'baptism of John' did not in itself signify that the person baptized became one of John's disciples, it would seem likely that he did in fact have an entourage of disciples who may have assisted in performing the baptisms (Mk. 2:18; Mt. 11:1-2; Jn. 1:35; 3:22). We are correct, presumably, in believing that Jesus' own earliest disciples, or some of them, came from that quarter (Jn. 1:35-51). Whether Jesus was himself a 'follower of John' and so baptized as one of his assistants, or at any rate carried on some such activity alongside John, as the Johannine gospel says (Jn. 3:22–36; see 4:1–2), it is impossible to determine. That claim belongs to a pre-Johannine tradition in which Jesus is seen as initially a disciple of the Baptist.

The fact of Jesus' baptism in the Jordan, however, is quite certain; and this is a primary hermeneutical key to understanding Jesus – only a primary one, for Jesus cannot be explained simply in terms of the movement headed by John, nor yet apart from the Baptist either. John's preaching spoke to him personally, and he identified personally with John's appeal for conversion. This we must take seriously. If we do not, then this act appears to have been either a kind of exemplary gesture on the part of someone who really knew better (at most an act of public humility, which must however have had something bogus about it) or else (there can be no other alternative in that case) a 'youthful error' by Jesus or even a first flush of religious enthusiasm which turned out later to be not the right and proper thing, so that Jesus afterwards chose a different course.

Anyone prepared to see this step taken by Jesus as a serious and important decision is bound to recognize that for him this baptism must have been a disclosure experience, that is, a source experience that was revelatory. In the absence of sources the historian can neither affirm nor gainsay anything about the life of Jesus prior to his baptism. His undergoing that baptism was not of course his first religious experience. But we know nothing of what he understood about himself up to that moment, except indirectly through what we know about the upbringing of a Jewish youngster at the time.[55] In a historical perspective we have to say, in the first instance, therefore that Jesus was struck by the rightness of John's proclamation and for that reason let himself be baptized by him. Thus he identified with a type of preaching which as we have seen was essentially non-apocalyptical and non-messianic and simply had in view the proper relationship of human beings to the living God and with one another, the doing of God's will. That the gospels incorporate John's message and in particular make no secret of the fact that Jesus was baptized by John, despite the problems this would seem to pose for them after the events of Easter (as being hard to fit into their vision of Jesus as Christ), can only be explained by one overriding reason, the historically based reminiscence of what was for Jesus an important event in his life, namely, an awareness that the Baptist's eschatological preaching of *metanoia* was indeed of crucial significance for the historical public ministry of Jesus himself – for both facts (baptism and public ministry) are clearly bound up together in the New Testament. Being powerless to reach into Jesus' own psychology (for want of material evidence) we must thus look for the point and purpose of this historically quite recognizable connection. Nothing would allow us to see in this step taken by Jesus the first breakthrough of his prophetic self-awareness (or indeed to deny this). About the 'beginnings' of a sense of vocation in Jesus the historian can have nothing to say – only that his public activity as a prophet is in fact quite evidently connected with his baptism in the River Jordan. So it seems to me legitimate to ask, in view of the course taken subsequently by the life of Jesus and of its plainly prophetic character, whether his baptism was not itself his very first public act as a prophet: not simply a way of assenting to the acknowledged earnestness of John's preaching (that is presupposed, of course), but in that very gesture an assertion of his own independent, prophetic role. Instead of seeing in this baptism a first, at any rate explicit breakthrough of Jesus' special calling – as many liberal investigators of Jesus would argue – I venture to propose another solution.

Prophets have a habit of conjoining what they want to say with striking symbolic actions. By way of enacted prophecy Jeremiah carries a yoke on his shoulders to let all Israel know that it was 'held captive'. This yoke is Israel's captivity (Jer. 28:10; 27:2). Hosea marries Gomer, a prostitute – that is, an Israelite girl who had had herself initiated into the fertility rites of the Canaanitic Baal cult – in order to make it publicly known that, despite everything, Yahweh still holds Israel dear (or else to suggest that Israel has so far defected from Yahweh that there remain to be found only girls initiated into paganism) (Hos. 1:1–9). Isaiah stays unmarried and thus declines to set up a family, so as to show Israel how spiritually poor, desolate and barren she is.[56] Of Jesus we are told that not long before he is finally rejected he curses a fig-tree, which by the next day, parched, limp and miserable, is a living image of Israel or of Jerusalem, that will not acknowledge the proffered chance of salvation.

In this light Jesus' baptism in the Jordan, in what is for us its revelatory character, as a fact of history does indeed assume a compact theological quality. It is Jesus' first appearance as a prophet: a symbolic-prophetic action or a prophecy in action, through which he intimates that Israel as a whole does indeed require a change of heart and must return once more to God, as the Baptist demands. As a prophetic act, whereby Jesus submits to 'the baptism of John', his baptism is confirmation of Israel's apostasy, yet at the same time of Israel's repentance and thus of salvation. Fundamentally, this goes a great deal further than what John himself intended with his baptism. Justifiably, albeit in a post-Easter interpretation, the gospels surround John's baptism of Jesus with explanatory visions, setting them within the aura of paschal glory (Mk. 1:2–11; Mt. 3:13–17; Lk. 3:21–22; Jn. 1:29–34). Only within an interpretation that bears on the prophetic character of the event can it be fitted altogether coherently into Jesus' prophetic ministry as a whole. It by no means implies that Jesus' message is the same as John's or that there may subsequently have been a 'rift' between the two; it does entail that Jesus is at one with the central core of John's message of *metanoia*-baptism, and that Jesus sees this 'as being from heaven' (Lk. 20:4). John the Baptist's movement, therefore, is the 'locus' of God's first salvific revelation to us in Jesus. So Mark is right when he sees the Baptist's activity as of a piece with 'the beginning of the gospel of Jesus Christ' (Mk. 1:1); it is not to be separated from Jesus' first appearance in the role of prophet.

The people too were immediately struck by the differences between John and Jesus. A pericope in the New Testament reminds us of this. Whereas John impressed his contemporaries as being a strictly ascetic man, Jesus was felt to be 'an eater and drinker', eating and drinking especially with tax-collectors and sinners (Mk. 2:16). Some played the one prophet off against the other, to avoid having to listen to either. Matthew 11:16–19 and Lk. 7:31–35 (from the Q source) in their parable of the children playing in the market-place[57] give pregnant expression to the obvious difference: '. . . this generation . . . is like children sitting in the market places and calling to their playmates: We piped to you and you did not dance; we wailed, and you did not mourn. For John came neither eating nor drinking, and they say: He has a demon! The Son of man came eating and drinking, and they say: Behold, a glutton and a drunkard, a friend of tax-collectors and sinners!' If John came across to the people as a grim ascetic, in complete harmony with his message of God's approaching and inexorable judgement, as a sort of dirge, therefore, Jesus comes across as a song! This parable, likely in its essentials to have been an authentic parable of Jesus, serves to illustrate the basic difference between the prophet of woe and Jesus, the prophet of salvation. For here again, this conduct on Jesus' part, with its quite different orientation, must have a bearing on that of his message itself.

## §4 The basic impulse behind the message and preaching of Jesus

As with John, the context of Jesus' living and speaking is the future purposed by God; and by virtue of this he, like his precursor, subjects past and present to a prophetic critique. As with John, so for Jesus that future is an exclusive potentiality of God's. All other orientations and projects that do not start from the priority of God's future for man are criticized by Jesus. The coming judgement is also part of Jesus' total message, but its function there is very different from what we find in John's case. And that brings us up against the question of the central core of Jesus' message.

The focus of Jesus' message is a *euaggelion*, that is, in contrast to John, cheering news from God: 'God's lordly rule is at hand.' We find this in no less than five complexes of tradition, word for word: in that of the Q community,[58] in the Marcan tradition,[59] in the source peculiar to Matthew,[60] in that peculiar to Luke[61] and the Johannine tradition[62] and again in the New Testament epistles. The kingdom of God is Jesus' central message, with the emphasis at once on its coming and on its coming close. In other words, 'expectation of the end' here is an expectation of the approaching rule of God. And for Jesus this means the proximity of God's unconditional will to salvation, of reconciling clemency and sufficing graciousness, and along with them opposition to all forms of evil: suffering and sin. This calls for more detailed analysis.

A. GOD'S RULE DIRECTED AT MANKIND: THE KINGDOM OF GOD

*Literature.* J. Becker, *Das Heil Gottes*, Göttingen 1964; J. Blank, *Jesus von Nazareth. Geschichte und Relevanz*, Freiburg 1972; Th. Blatter, *Macht und Herrschaft Gottes*, Freiburg 1962; P. Brunner, 'Elemente einer dogmatischen Lehre von Gottes Reich', in *Die Zeit Jesu* (ed. G. Bornkamm and K. Rahner) (Freiburg 1970), 228–56; Bultmann, *Theologie*, 2–10; H. Conzelmann, *Grundriss*; C. H. Dodd, *The Parables of the Kingdom*, London 1958; H. Flender, *Die Botschaft Jesu von der Herrschaft Gottes*, Munich 1968; M. Hengel, *Die Zeloten*, Leyden-Cologne 1961; J. Héring, *Le Royaume de Dieu et sa venue*, Neuchâtel 1959²; E. Käsemann, 'Eine Apologie der urchristlichen Eschatologie',

*Besinnungen*, I, 135–57; 'Die Anfänge christlicher Theologie', ibid., II, 82–104; 'Zum Thema der urchristlichen Apokalyptik', ibid., II, 105–30; G. Klein, '"Reich Gottes" als biblischer Zentralbegriff', EvTh 30 (1970), 642–70; W. Knörzer, *Reich Gottes, Traum, Hoffnung, Wirklichkeit*, Stuttgart 1970; J. E. Ladd, *Jesus and the Kingdom*, London 1966; E. Lohse, 'Die Gottesherrschaft in den Gleichnissen Jesu', EvTh 18 (1958), 145–57; W. Pannenberg, *Theologie und Reich Gottes*, Gütersloh 1971; N. Perrin, *The Kingdom of God in the Teaching of Jesus*, London 1963; Kl. Schmidt, sub *basileia*, in ThWNT I, 579–93; R. Schnackenburg, *Gottes Herrschaft und Reich*, Freiburg 1967⁴; Ph. Vielhauer, 'Gottesreich und Menschensohn in der Verkündigung Jesu', *Aufsätze*, 55–91; A. Vögtle, *Das Neue Testament und die Zukunft des Kosmos*, Dusseldorf 1972; E. Wolff, on 'Reich Gottes', in RGG³, V, 918–24.

God's 'lordship' or rule and the kingdom of God are two aspects of what the New Testament contains within the single concept *basileia tou Theou*.[63] Mark and Luke speak of the *basileia*, the kingly rule, of God. Peculiar to Matthew is 'the kingdom of heaven', where 'heaven' is the late Jewish abstract way of denoting God. *Basileia tou Theou* is the kingdom of God, the rule of God as Lord, the realm of God. It does not denote some area of sovereignty above and beyond this world, where God is supposed to reside and to reign. What Jesus intends by it is a process, a course of events, whereby God begins to govern or to act as king or Lord, an action, therefore, by which God manifests his being-God in the world of men. Thus God's lordship or dominion is the divine power itself in its saving activity within our history, but at the same time the final, eschatological state of affairs that brings to an end the evil world, dominated by the forces of calamity and woe, and initiates the new world in which God 'appears to full advantage'; 'your kingdom come' (Mt. 6:10). God's rule and the kingdom of God are thus two aspects of one and the same thing. God's dominion points to the dynamic, here-and-now character of God's exercise of control; the kingdom of God refers more to the definitive state of 'final good' to which God's saving activity is directed. Thus present and future are essentially interrelated (in a manner still to be more closely defined): God is the Lord of history and by proxy, as it were, presents salvation to human beings as a gift. This is the gist of the biblical notion, to us rather strange, of the 'kingdom of God'.

God's lordship, therefore, is the exercise of his peculiar and divine function as sovereign Creator: as 'king' he is purveyor of salvation to that which he endowed with life. That this kingdom comes means that God looks to us men and women to make his 'ruling' operational in our world.

Lordship or 'dominion' was a central concept in antiquity, as also was power (i.e. potent authority). For us these ideas have no ready appeal. They sound authoritarian to people who are only now learning how to take advantage of the freedom gained by the French Revolution: '*Nous voulons une humanité sans (Dieu ni) roi*' (J. Ferry). For that reason we may indeed go looking for other words, provided always that the idea of God's sovereign rights as Creator is not dissipated; for such reverence for God's exalted nature is fundamental to Jesus' message and to his ministry. Of course Jesus interpreted this exalted nature of God as an unconditional willing of good towards human beings, an unimpeachable quality of pure love for man. But for Jesus, therefore, God's lordship and exalted nature entail doing God's will. God's lordship is not a function of man's salvation in the sense that God is 'of use' for the salvation of human beings. Jesus is about God's business; and the business of man, the *humanum*, is to search after God 'for God's sake'. In other words, God's lordship is reason enough, in and of itself; the rest is gratuitous. Jesus is the man whose joy and pleasure is God himself. God's lordship is God's mode of being God; and our recognition of that engenders the truly human condition, the salvation of man. For that reason God's lordship, as Jesus understands it, expresses the relation between God and man, in the sense that 'we are each other's happiness'. Ultimately it is the ancient covenant of love, fellowship with God, in which God nevertheless remains the sovereign partner. Thus anyone having anything to do with Jesus is confronted with the God of Jesus. The one thing that Jesus is getting at is that this God is a 'God of human kind'. The Letter to Titus sums it up beautifully: 'There has appeared goodness and the God mindful of humanity' (Tit. 3:4). Jesus presents God as salvation for man. His God is a God who looks after people. Thus God's lordship, by which Jesus lives and which he proclaims, tells us something about God in his relation to man and likewise about man in his relation to God. It is a theological and yet also anthropological reality grounded in experience. A reality indeed, because for Jesus himself God's lordship is not just an idea or theory, but first and foremost an experience of reality. His very life is given decisive shape by his expectation of the kingdom of God in surrender to God's lordship. Jesus is gripped by that lordship, is compelled by it, so that his whole life is on the one hand a 'celebration' of that lordship and on the other it gives a lead in orthopraxis, the right conduct of the kingdom of God. It is what he lived for and what he died for: God's concern as man's concern.

On a superficial view it is an old story that Jesus takes up. Indeed he does – but giving it a new and surprising turn. If we set aside for a moment the nuances attaching to the words 'king' and 'ruling', inherited from the past, the kingly rule of God, as Jesus preaches it and demonstrates it in his own conduct, signifies the radical trustworthiness and commitment of God (the stress here must be on God) to men, that is: God's fidelity to himself and to man, for whom he wills a purposeful future. Dependable, saving power and on our side the certainty of a meaningful future (despite every empirical experience to the contrary) is the heart of Jesus' message of the approaching rule of God; it is after all Jesus' term for what we have come to know as 'grace': the sovereign graciousness of God.

But the nuance which we must always remember and carry over from the old concepts of 'lordly rule' and 'kingdom' or 'kingship' is precisely the critical force stored up in these ancient words. Even for Jesus God's lordship is also a judgement upon our history. This notion of the *basileia* of God implies also the power of the reality that is God to pass judgement on man, culture and society. The message of Jesus, in contrast to John's preaching, really is an 'evangel': heartening news is imparted here, an aspect of God displayed that in the end differs radically from John's one-sided proclamation of God's imminent judgement. Yet neither is the God of Jesus in all his goodness and compassion in any way a kindly granddad, disposed to be not so very critical. Jesus' enthusiasm for God's law as a revelation of his will is authentically Jewish and transcends the Judaism of the time only through his radical zeal for the unimpeachable divine law – but then as God's own law.

The reader will have noticed by now that in this connection there is a sudden and complete dearth of references, the 'critical apparatus' shrinks almost to nothing, at the very moment when it comes to dealing with the heart of Jesus' message, and the most pressing issue is whether with all this we are on 'authentic Jesus' territory or not. The reason is that nowhere does Jesus himself seek to explain the notion of 'God's lordly rule' as such; he presupposes it as a concept familiar to his contemporaries; the concrete content of it emerges from his ministry and activity as a whole, his parables and actual conduct, which we shall be analysing later on and from which what we have just now been saying about the kingdom of God is to be distilled. The whole of the second part, therefore, is designed to justify what has been said here already by way of summary. Even so, this calls for yet further explanation of an exegetical kind.

The account we have given makes the break with the essential core of John's message look so radical that one may well wonder what it was that Jesus had been looking to John for in the first place and, in view of his baptism, had evidently found. We must enquire, therefore, whether in the context of the synoptic tradition there are bits of tradition showing that Jesus, albeit in a modified form of his own, did at any rate continue John's preaching of judgement. Only from that will it become clear what is the drift of Jesus' message of the kingdom of God – more especially whether in this respect he is apocalyptical, champions a 'futurist', on-the-way eschatology or else a here-and-now eschatology, focused on the decision of the present moment – a current and controversial issue in contemporary Christology and eschatology. Exegetes are at complete loggerheads with one another on this subject.

It is irrelevant here to ask whether Jesus' preaching of God's lordship was consciously anti-Zealotic and directed against apocalypticism. It is clear from the New Testament that his conduct and ministry reflect a posture that is never 'anti-' but 'pro-': arising out of a (still to be analysed) personal experience, Jesus' message is positively orientated; and in this positive orientation towards God's universal, saving love it is only 'against' everything which contradicts that essential message. Now there was present in all the sections of Judaism in Jesus' time a tendency directly opposed to the distinctive tenor of his basic message. And on that Jesus launches a frontal attack. It all serves to reveal what he means by this favourite expression, 'kingdom of God'.

The general trend of Judaism at that time, in most of its more lively focal points and conscious groupings, was to go for the formation of 'sects', in conformity with the 'holy remnant' concept of the Daniel literature. The effect of this was to divide people into two classes: whatever they might be called (in apocalyptical terms), 'ourselves, the sons of light' as over against 'the rest as sons of darkness', the latter comprising not only all the heathen but also every Israelite who did not belong to one's own group, that is, to the devout or 'pious ones'.[64] This sectarian tendency led to more and more groups of separatists, each determined to be 'even holier' and each regarding itself as the sole legitimate heir to the true people of God. Hence their names: 'Pharisees' (*perushim*; Aramaic *perishayya*), that is, those separated off from the common people (the *'amè ha' ares*); 'Essenes' (probably from the Aramaic *chasayya*), that is, the zealous or pious ones – a universal aspiration from the time of the Chasidic (sometimes known in academic circles as 'pietistic') movements. These things point to an unmistakable tendency on the part of lay people to assume the obligations of the Levitical priesthood; in other words, a certain clericalizing of lay spirituality ('God's priestly nation'). The settled principle so often applied in these instances was: to love whomever God loves (and chooses) and to hate those he has rejected: 'to hate all the sons of darkness, each according to the measure of their iniquity, in the vengeance of God'.[65] In particular the 'publicans and sinners' were completely beyond the pale: to have any intercourse with them was to make oneself into a sinner. So when we read in Mt. 5:43: 'You have heard that it was said, You shall love your neighbour and hate your enemy' (a text not to be found anywhere in the Old Testament), it would seem that this refers to certain schools of thought current in Jesus' own time. Furthermore the Qumrân Damascus document says that the enfeebled, the lame, blind and deaf cannot join the Essene group; they are shut out of the eschatological 'community of salvation'. Jesus on the other hand, in the parable of the dinner party, makes a deliberate point of seating at the feast just the crippled and the lame, all who are cold-shouldered (Lk. 14:1). All the most active focal points of Judaism at that time were characterized by this ambition to be a 'holy remnant', the pure and true assembly of God. When Jesus therefore calls Israel 'sheep without a shepherd' (Mt. 9:36; Mk. 6:34), he is announcing the bankruptcy of all who are set on gathering together a pure assembly of God through separation and selection and leaving the mass of people to their fate. Instead of standing apart, Jesus goes through the whole country, bringing glad news to all, without exception: he goes looking for the single lost sheep; he is not there to help the healthy (those who think they are 'righteous') but the sick (Mk. 2:17) – and that they all are. Thus he eats and drinks with tax-gatherers and sinners, to bring them also the evidence of God's love for them. What we have here cannot be other than a message and style of conduct that proclaim God's universal love, the true God's lordship, without reservation or remainder. Equally, Jesus will have nothing of the apocalyptic reversal of power-relationships, whereby the poor become top dog and those who are now rich, bottom dog. Jesus sees in the kingdom only an end to all overweening relations based on power, to every repressive domination of one human being over another: it is a kingdom of mutual service (Mk. 10:42–45). We are even warned against 'lording it over things', that is, having riches (Mk. 10:23). Most striking and characteristic of Jesus' living by the future as 'God's potential', crucial

therefore to his understanding of God's lordship, is his utter indiffer-
ence to the sinful past of another person. If it is one of the things that
do come up (as with the adulterous woman), all that Jesus shows is an
extreme reserve. He condemns no one, therefore; his concern is with
the potential, for the future, in the 'now' of the *metanoia*. That kind of
approach resolves all frantic searching for self-identity. Specifically in
the parable of the Prodigal Son (Lk. 15:11–32) we get a complete
picture of Jesus' attitude and his message of God's caring for people
in trouble; at the same time an indictment of those who feel they are
righteous, who insist on getting their due reward. Another typical
feature is that all the *ekklesia* passages in the New Testament are
secondary – which means that they do not derive from Jesus: *qahal*,
synagogue and *ekklesia*, in that period at any rate, were typical names
appropriated by separatist movements dissociating themselves from
'the sinful people'. Jesus desires the salvation of Israel's Twelve
Tribes, that is, of all Israel; and in his mission he restricts himself to
this (Mt. 15:24; 10:5–6). But in that limitation there comes to expression a universality that removes virtually all frontiers. If there was
in fact a personal rift between Jesus and John the Baptist, the reason
for it must have lain here. But it is quite clear, on the other hand, that
John had no wish to form a separate remnant-community; moreover
he nowhere represented the 'seal' of baptism as assuring salvation
against the terrible day of judgement that was approaching. A 'holy
remnant' was of course a threatened implication, though not demonstrably so; the person baptized went back home (what he had still to do
there, and the complications for such a baptized individual, who had to
await the approaching fiery judgement-day, would seem to have lain
beyond John's ken). Feeling oneself to be personally a 'holy remnant'
was a not unlikely possibility. More grave, however, was the fact that
John's whole ministry failed to take account of God's universal compassion; and it was this that, after his baptism by John, Jesus apparently
learnt to recognize as the only true face of God. A substantive break
with the Baptist is hard to deny, therefore.

A Q logion, incorporated into Lk. 16:16=Mt. 11:12–13, may give
us some more help, even though the logion here has been worked into
a different context: 'The law and the prophets were until John; since
then [*apo tote*] the good news of the kingdom of God is preached, and
every one enters it violently' (Lk.). 'From the days of John the
Baptist until now the kingdom of heaven has suffered violence, and
men of violence take it by force. For all the prophets and the law
prophesied until John' (Mt.). This is probably not an authentic saying

of Jesus but a reflection on the Church's part. The Baptist is seen here as a definite caesura: the first period of the divine dispensation runs up to and includes John; then with Jesus a new age begins. In other words, up to and including John there was no presence of God's *basileia*. 'Since then' – *apo tote* (Lk. 16:16b) is, where John is concerned, exclusive.[66] The inclusive aspect is brought out in Matthean theology: only with the entry of Jesus on the scene has the *basileia* become historically present.[67] According to the Q community the Baptist's place is outside the *basileia*; he brings the old course of things to an end. Only with the appearance of Jesus is the kingdom of God assailed by force,[68] but therein it shows itself superior; for the power of the *basileia* is to be detected in Jesus' acts of exorcism and healing and especially in his evangelizing (Lk. 7:18–23=Mt. 11:2–6; likewise apropos of the 'John-and-Jesus' relationship); with all this the old dispensation is ended. In other words the Church, in contrast to John, sees the future – as God's potential – bound up not with John's baptism but with the role and ministry of Jesus of Nazareth. The Christian community may perhaps have seen a bigger gap here than Jesus personally was aware of. The divergence between the inclusive significance of John (in Matthew) and the exclusive (Luke and Q source) *vis-à-vis* the kingdom of God shows how uncertain about it the local Christian congregations were. Remarkable too is the fact that the Q community does indeed describe the Baptist as 'forerunner', but then not of the earthly Jesus but of the eschatological Jesus-son-of-man figure who is on the way.[69] There emerges in the most primitive Christian traditions an increasingly pronounced subordination of John to Jesus. Then again, as was said earlier on, in regard to the question of Jesus' authority Mark enshrines an early, pre-Marcan Jesus tradition in which he is made to respond with a reference to John's prophetic commission: just as the baptism of John is seen by Jesus as the work of God, so as continuer of John's activity Jesus regards his own ministry, though of a different hue, as being God's work as well: he is conscious of being the 'one sent', the man commissioned with God's full authority. Jesus takes up John's call to *metanoia* (Mk. 1:14–15 and parallels) and his ministry likewise aims at the renewal of God's people. They both think exclusively in terms of God's future, but their ways of giving content to it are distinctively and essentially different. But Jesus himself is unaffected by the problem facing the Church, as to whether he or John is 'the greater'. For someone compelled to be about God's business a dispute of that kind is simply (for himself) irrelevant: seek first the kingdom of God, everything else will then fall into place. Jesus' preaching of God's lordship as concentrated upon human kind, that is, of God's concerns as being precisely those of man, did not relate directly to himself as a kind of second subject of his message: in other words, it was not himself that he preached – though it can and must be said of course that in whatever he is most concerned to tell every individual discloses himself – his own identity. Likewise John, though not the subject of his proclamation, associated *metanoia* as a possible means of fending off God's annihilating judgement with his own form of baptism; and without proclaiming himself he showed in that way how very conscious he was of his own quite special prophetic role.

Together with John's message of judgement Jesus evidently takes up John's expectation that the son of man is very soon to come (in judgement). But then it goes without saying that (to understand what was distinctive about Jesus) we have to examine those logia of his which speak of judgement and what (in all historical probability) he had to say about the son of man coming as judge in correlation with, and yet as distinct from, his message of the approaching rule of God.[70] This need is immediately obvious from the fact that the judgement of which Jesus speaks is seen always as lying purely in the future – as the final, eschatological judgement – without ever in the synoptic tradition (as opposed to the Baptist and the later Johannine gospel) being envisaged as now present or on the very threshold – whereas the relationship of the 'present' and 'future' to the approaching rule of God is quite different and not to be settled either with a 'not just now but later on' or with an 'already here and now'. This particular relation calls for much finer distinctions and in any case is very different from John's *Naherwartung* or manner of qualifying the temporal dimension of God's coming judgement. Here the really distinctive thing about Jesus, in contrast to John, appears to its fullest extent. True to John's message of judgement Jesus stripped it, however, in view of his own central message of God's kingdom, of its possibly apocalyptic background and emphasis upon the nearness of the 'latter days'. In such a context, then, Jesus' authentic sayings about the proximity of God's rule not only entail substituting Jesus' notion 'kingdom of God' for John's idea of 'judgement' (in fact there is no 'substitution' here – Jesus also proclaimed a judgement), but imply a totally new message: a *euaggelion*, a term foreign to John. As a query this summary rehearsal is important if we are to find out whether Jesus was actually an apocalypticist or absolutely nothing of the kind; and whether, finally, his essentially non-apocalyptical message none the less went hand-in-hand with what many at the time assumed about the approaching 'end of the world' – which did not in fact occur. According to J. Blank, John connected the expectation of an end 'near at hand' with the idea of judgement and so with the call to conversion, realized in the baptism of repentance, whereas Jesus associates the same *Naherwartung* with the idea of God's lordship or rule and plainly understands this as universal salvation, inclusive of life, happiness and joy for human beings.[71] The question is whether this has been stated with sufficient nuances: in particular, whether the expected nearness of the end, a historically authentic feature of Jesus' teaching which it may be possible to reconstruct, has been made clear enough.

As a matter of fact, the concept of 'God's lordship' and 'the kingdom of God' was not such a central idea in late Judaism as has often been thought.[72] It is noticeable how seldom apocalyptic speaks of the 'anticipated future' under the motif of the kingdom of God.[73] In the Qumrân literature too this concept is nowhere central. Apocalypticism is more concerned with the latter-day transformation or total change from the old to the new aeon what is to follow it. In the later rabbinical matter (which preserves older traditions in a written form) the concept turns up again and again, but as an abstract *theologoumenon* in two standard expressions, 'to take upon one the yoke of the kingdom of God', that is, declare one's allegiance to the one true God, and 'the kingdom of God will be revealed', specifically, at the end of the ages. The rabbis (and Pharisees) focus their lively expectation of 'the end' not so much on the coming of God's rule (lordship) as on that of the messiah.[74] They prefer to speak rather of the *olam ha-ba*,[75] the aeon to come, than of the kingdom of God.

Now there are no texts known to us which suggest that Jesus ever mentioned the 'aeon to come'.[76] The notion of the age to come, with either its transforming renewal of the world or, after the world has been done away with, its radically new creation, is utterly foreign to him. He talks about the coming rule of God: God is Lord and will make this plain to all, and has already set about doing so. To argue that this implies a complete break away from the apocalyptical scheme of things seems to me irrelevant, indeed erroneous.[77] Although the apocalyptic scheme of the two aeons is concerned solely with the enthralling event which will visibly transform the old world into a new one, still this does not entail, even in that context, a dualistic disjunction. Even there the aeon to come or the kingdom of God is already operative, albeit in a clandestine way.[78] For apocalypticism it is not a question of the here-and-now over against a hereafter, but of the old world, in which the divine, celestial process is invisibly on the go, and the new world-aeon in which this celestial course of events will be brought into the open, will become visible on this earth. Of course, this 'bringing into the open' is an unprecedented, radical 'making new' of everything; but no consideration is given to the element of continuity. In Qumrân, particularly, *eschaton* and 'end of the age' did not imply what we moderns understand by 'eschatology'. In definitive terms 'kingdom of God' and 'end of the age' are not the same thing. What in many apocalyptical circles is called 'the end of the age' (or 'last days') we could better describe as pre-eschatological. The 'time of salvation' at the close of the age signifies a glorious, peaceful period 'without end', that is, to which no end is expected. Albeit within an apocalyptical framework, ideas which are simply Jewish, ideas current in apocalyptical as in non-apocalyptical circles also[79] play a distinctive role in all this. Although Jesus is no apocalypticist, we must not look to find him in an opposing role, someone who consciously repudiates apocalypticism. Jesus rejects and opposes only what contravenes God's cause and obedience to God's will; everything else he lets be for what it is – even the payment of tax to the Roman occupying power. None of that directly concerns him; his whole purpose in life is different.

In so far as God's rule is already effective it is discernible only in faith.[80] Jesus' deliberate focus on the future entails no doctrine, no theory about it; only that it will be quite other than the present, with no more precise definition than that. On the one hand the kingdom of God is an eschatological event, still to come (Mk. 14:25; Lk. 22:15–18): the eschatological feast lies in the future; Jesus participates in it with his disciples. This suggests on the other hand that the fellowship at table enjoyed by Jesus and his disciples during his days on earth is a present reality that finds its completion in the kingdom of God. But as regards the nature and manner of that eschatological reunion nothing more is said: is it prior to the death of the disciples? Later on? In what fashion? Jesus has nothing to say on the subject. As A. Vögtle rightly says: on the question whether and how the coming rule of God is to take effect in the existing world, the cosmos, the Jesus tradition affords no ground for saying anything.[81] All that matters to Jesus is people in their relationship to God, and God in his care and concern for people. What he preaches about the coming kingdom of God has to do with the dealings of God with man, his saving acts focused on the future.

Neither in apocalypticism nor yet among the Pharisees and rabbis, therefore, was the theme of the kingdom of God a considerable factor. The one movement in which it flourished greatly was that of the Jewish resistance, the Sicarii as well as the Zealots. It is for the kingdom of God's sake that they demand political liberty and the overthrow of the Roman occupation: God alone is king in Israel. They intend by their militant resistance to hasten the kingdom of God. Here indeed we have the idea of the speedy approach of God's rule. And yet the remarkable thing is that the motif of the approaching kingdom is most vital and influential in the Q community, which (whether or not in express opposition to the nationalist politics of Zealotism) has an explicitly non-violent conception of the approaching kingdom of God.[82] The association of 'approaching kingdom' and 'orthopraxis' (concretely: fidelity to the Law) is typical of the Q community; it is as it were its local community programme (Lk. 6:20–45 and parallels; also Lk. 6:46–49 and parallels).[83] This community (in its Hellenistic-Jewish phase) is already interpreting the activity of the earthly Jesus as a 'latter-day' development preceding the end. In Mt. 11:10 (a Q interpretation of the earlier saying 10:7–9) John the Baptist is the envoy promised in Mal. 3:1, who prepares the way for 'the One who is to come'. But one notices that in the account of the sending forth of the disciples by the earthly Jesus, according to the Q community they are given as the substance of their message 'the rule of God is come upon you' (Lk. 10:9 =Mt. 10:7), in other words, exactly what had already been formulated as the content of Jesus' own message. Although after Easter the Q community gave this message a certain colouring of its own, it does seem to have passed on what was substantially Jesus' own message of the approaching kingdom of God. The peculiar character of this community, especially the intention of its distinctive tradition,[84] guarantees that the message of the 'kingdom of God at hand' really was that of Jesus – even though it remains unclear whether the (apocalyptic) expectation of judgement, so characteristic of the Q community,[85] was equally fundamental in Jesus' preaching.[86] Therefore the continuity between Jesus' preaching and that of the Q community lies primarily not in the *kerygma* but in the eschatology: both proclaim the approaching arrival of God's rule and of the coming son of man, although even the oldest stratum in the Q community identified the son of man, still to come, with the heavenly Jesus, who is to appear at the end of the age, in the latter days, to save his own and to judge the world.[87] Thus in the earliest phase of the Q tradition Jesus was not the One proclaimed; the import of its proclamation is the coming rule of God and the coming judgement, in which Jesus as the son of man will rescue the congregation of his people,[88] as Paul intimates in his earliest letter: We . . . 'wait for his Son from heaven, whom he raised from the dead, Jesus who delivers us from the wrath to come' (1 Thess. 1:10).

That Jesus prophesied the imminent arrival of God's rule is beyond dispute. Was this a mistake on Jesus' part? As in apocalyptical circles, did he have in mind the approaching end of the world? From the interpretations in the New Testament, coloured as they are by the expectations of the early Christians, it is difficult to recover Jesus' own vision of the future. It is after all a fact that belief in his resurrection or at any rate his 'being with God' (see further on) was initially felt to be the starting-signal for the Parousia and 'end of the world'. The enthusiastic expectation of Jesus' coming in glory was after all based precisely on his being alive with God; when Jesus' coming was subsequently 'delayed', that experience made no essential difference, although it did raise problems for a lot of Christians to begin with, as appears from the New Testament. But these Christian expectations of the end cannot be traced back directly to Jesus' preaching. As has been said already, Jesus preaches in the assured conviction of God's rule being at hand; and the 'being at hand' he sees *in* his own ministry (see below); but it nowhere appears from the texts that he identifies this coming, this drawing near, with the end of the world. He confidently proclaimed the speedy coming of God's salvation, and acted accordingly; about his ideas on the *how* of this coming salvation we hear nothing. To speculate about that – in the vein of an expectation of a speedy end of the world or, more properly, of a shortly arriving son of man – is certainly tempting, in my view not even unreasonable, having regard to the spirit of the time; but no historically firm evidence allows us to argue this with any degree of cogency. Jesus' firm belief in salvation, as may still be seen, has a purely religious foundation. We are bound to say also that in the end the nearing prospect of his death was likewise an essential element helping to influence Jesus' notions (or lack thereof) regarding the 'how' of the certain salvation to come; assured of salvation, he abandons himself to God. It may yet become clear later on that even *vis-à-vis* Jesus' own ideas (if any) about how the kingdom of God would come, God remains sovereignly free.

It is plain from the life of Jesus that 'present' and 'future', although distinguished, are essentially bound up together; Jesus proclaims the salvation to come, and at the same time by his conduct he makes it present, thereby at once suggesting a link between his person and the coming lordship of God. What the nature of this link is must gradually emerge from the analyses which follow. What is becoming clear already is this: Jesus makes a connection between the coming of God's rule and *metanoia*, that is, the actual praxis of the kingdom of God. The

Lord's Prayer suggests a fundamental connection between 'your kingdom come' and 'your will be done on earth': carrying out God's will in our mundane history has to do with the coming of God's kingdom, always in that dialectic, typical of Jesus, between 'present' and 'future'; the latter is admittedly always greater than the present but stimulates us in the present to religious and ethical conduct in accord with the kingdom of God. This connection between God's lordship and orthopraxis clearly derives from Jesus: in his 'going about, doing good', in his taking sides with the dispossessed and outcast, which comes out especially in his parables and his associating with sinners (see below). In the practical business of living Jesus provides a concrete view of the kingdom of God; through the premium he set on well-being, on man's wholeness of being – including the physical aspect: acts of healing and expulsion of evil spirits. Where he appears, fear departs, the fear of life as well as the fear of death, he sets people free and restores them to themselves. In particular, he sees attachment to wealth and property, whether little or great and excessive, as being directly opposed to the surrender of the self to God's rule. It imperils the very essence of God's lordship: the unconditional trustworthiness of God (even if his ways are not our ways), which is expressed in the outpouring of salvation on God's part. Orthopraxis, right conduct, is the human manifestation or logical rendering of God's universal saving love, registered in practical human living. It is manifested where love knows no frontiers, no compartmentalizing and sectarian divisions, extending even to enemies, to 'publicans and sinners', that is, to all who in the society of Judaism at the time were shut off from fellowship with their Jewish kin, barred from the table of Pharisee or Essene. Jesus himself sees in such a style of conduct the signs of the coming of God's rule; and in his own conduct above all he can see the sign of that coming. In Jesus, therefore, the coming of God's kingdom is mediated by a human being. Man's caring for his fellow-men is the visible form and aspect in which the coming of God's kingdom is manifested; it is the way that God's lordship takes. In Jesus' conduct of his own life we have not a theoretical but practical and proleptic realization – explorative and forward-reaching – of the 'new world', of the desiderated new praxis of good and true living, worthy of human kind[89] – even though it be within a very concrete historical contingency which in itself we cannot repeat. For that reason the wholly different and better world sought after – namely, the kingdom of God as God's lordship or loving power, charged with concern for humanity – is not something vague and totally indefinable: it has been given a historical likeness in the life and conduct of Jesus, which therefore, for those who trust in him, not only is an inspiration and motive force, but because of its distinctive content, going beyond pure pragmatism, also gives a quite specific orientation to their activity in the world. The effect of all this is at once to turn the apocalyptical link between eschatological hope and a quickly approaching kingdom of peace into an intrinsic bond uniting the eschatological hope and a new mode of conduct in this world, without dropping the idea of an imminent salvation.

Radical conversion, prompted by grace and constituting the visible, historical form in which the coming of God's rule is manifested, has for Jesus at any rate not the apocalyptical (messianic) significance of a 'turn-about' of the ages by an abrupt act on God's part; rather it entails both a new mental outlook and a new way of behaving, based on faith in the approaching rule of God. In its fullness, therefore, Jesus' message of God's lordship and his kingdom is: God's universal love for men as disclosed in and through his actual mode of conduct, consistent with and consequent upon it, and thus as an appeal to us to believe in and hope for this coming salvation and kingdom of peace, 'imparted by God', and likewise faithfully to manifest its coming in a consistent way of living; the praxis of the kingdom of God. This will become evident only from the analytical sections to follow.

B.   THE PRAXIS OF THE KINGDOM OF GOD. JESUS' PARABLES

*Literature.* E. Auerbach, *Mimèsis, Dargestellte Wirklichkeit in der abendländischen Literatur*, Berne 1959[2]; J. Blank, 'Marginalien zur Gleichnisauslegung', *Schriftauslegung in Theorie und Praxis* (Munich 1969), 89–103; E. Biser, *Die Gleichnisse Jesu*, Munich 1965; C. H. Dodd, *The Parables of the Kingdom*, London (1935) 1961[2]; E. Eichholz, *Einführung in die Gleichnisse*, Neukirchen 1963; F. Fiebig, *Altjüdische Gleichnisse und die Gleichnisse Jesu*, Tübingen-Leipzig 1904; *Die Gleichnisse Jesu im Lichte der rabbinischen Gleichnisse des neutestamentlichen Zeitalters*, Tübingen 1912; E. Güttgemanns, *Die linguistisch-didaktische Methodik der Gleichnisse Jesu* (Studia Linguistica Neotestamentica) (Munich 1971), 99–183; R. W. Funk, *Language, Hermeneutic and Word of God* (New York-London 1966), 124–223; J. Jeremias, *Die Gleichnisse Jesu*, Göttingen 1926[6]; A. Jülicher, *Die Gleichnisreden Jesu*, Darmstadt 1963[2]; W. G. Kümmel, 'Noch einmal; Die Gleichnis von der Selbstwachsenden Saat', *Orientierung an Jesus* (Freiburg 1973), 220–37; E. Linnemann, *Gleichnisse Jesu*, Göttingen 1969[5]; E. Lohse, 'Die Gottesherrschaft in den Gleichnissen

Jesu', EvTh 18 (1958), 145–57; N. Perrin, 'The modern interpretation of the parables of Jesus and the problem of hermeneutics', *Interpretation* 25 (1971), 131–48; Et. Trocmé, *Jésus de Nazareth vu par les témoins de sa vie* (Neuchâtel 1971), ch. 6. 'Le Jésus des parables', 94–110; D. O. Via, *The Parables*, Philadelphia 1967; A. Weiser, *Die Knechtsgleichnisse der synoptischen Evangelien*, Munich 1971; theme-issue 'Gleichnisse', EvTh 32 (1972), 413–51.

(a) Speaking in parables

For us modern people, used to the exigencies of the historical sciences, it is often difficult to understand a 'story-telling' culture; in such a culture the deepest mysteries of life are interpreted in stories and parables. An illustration of our inability to understand a narrative culture is the reaction many of us have to the story of Jonah's being lodged for three days 'in the belly of a whale'. The early Fathers of the Church had difficulty with it too; but in our own day the lack of comprehension has sometimes reached laughable proportions. After much systematic research one learned man came to the conclusion that in point of fact the fleeing Jonah went to ground for three days in some sort of private retreat of his, a small café known as 'The Whale'. Obviously we have lost all our 'narrative innocence'! Actually, the tale of a man being swallowed by a large fish is well known to many cultures. It is a story which can be made to express all kinds of profound truths about life. Jonah's prayer (Jon. 2:2–10) serves to show why this folktale – familiar in so many cultures – has been taken up into the Old Testament: God will never abandon his own, however hopeless their situation may be. That is what Jonah's prayer in the belly of the whale, surrounded by the all-engulfing deep – a crazy situation of utter hopelessness and total impasse – is really saying. Such a story can be repeated *ad infinitum*. It neatly enshrines the variety of wisdom accumulated in the course of history by peoples who well know the savage power of the water. But when the Old Testament takes over this age-old, familiar story, a situation of extreme despair is brought within the context of Jonah's very pointed prayer. Thus is a new story born: the story of unconditional trust in Yahweh's nearness and helpfulness when someone is at the end of their wits. Later on this story would be told again; but each retelling is entirely new: Christians cite the Old Testament Jonah story in a completely new context, namely, the death and resurrection of Jesus. A story like this is never-ending. It is continually being retold: the core of it persists and is reinterpreted again and again.

The New Testament too, which tells us the story of Jesus, is set in a 'story-telling culture', not in one like ours that has replaced a narrative innocence with historical disciplines. However, we cannot ignore either. For us modern people the story – including the story of Jesus – is only to be well and truly heard if we arrive at a second primitive stage, a second narrative innocence, that is, when we have passed through the stage of the scientific pursuit of history and criticism and thus can return to a 'story-telling innocence', which itself then recoups its critical power from scholarship and criticism.

Conscious then of the narrative culture of antiquity, we must turn first of all to the gospel texts with the question: What are these gospels really trying to tell us when for instance they report the miracles of Jesus? Only after that can we enquire regarding the hard core of history in these stories. Of course the historical question is not un-important; but it is a constituent part within a wider whole.

Jesus is a parable, and he tells parables. Only parables are able to 'explain' a parable. Why?

The telling of a parable, the way a parable actually takes place, is a marvellous thing. Usually it enshrines a paradox, some startling effect. In a few cases this is the result of us Westerners failing to understand what in the East are the commonplaces in these parables. The parable of the Sower features a farmer who is obviously quite reckless: he scatters his seed not only over the field but also on the rocky ground, in places where the thorns are growing, and even on the pathway. But there is nothing disconcerting about that – it is understandable in terms of oriental custom. It is the effects intended to startle that I am getting at. Those who work for only the one hour get as much pay as those who have toiled right through the day; this shocks not only our social feelings but those of the bystanders who heard the parable at the time. To us the five so-called foolish bridesmaids seem to have the most appeal, whereas the other five, the 'wise ones' who refuse to help the rest, are immediately branded by youngsters hearing the story nowadays as 'rotters' – but so they were then. The fact is, a parable turns around a 'scandalizing' centre, at any rate a core of paradox and novelty. A parable often stands things on their head; it is meant to break through our conventional thinking and being. A parable is meant to start the listener thinking by means of a built-in element of the 'surprising' and the 'alienating' in a common, everyday event. It is not every night that one is hauled out of bed to help a needy stranger in dire straits; and you are not continually losing a sheep or a coin. It never happens at all to a good many of us. And yet in the parable I am confronted with it, here and now. The parable obliges me to go on thinking about it. Parables are 'teasers'. The familiar event is set against an unfamiliar background, and in that way what is commonplace becomes a stimulating challenge. It gives us a jolt.

The idea behind it is to make you consider your own life, your own goings-on, your own world, from a different angle for once. Parables open up new and different potentialities for living, often in contrast with our conventional ways of behaving; they offer a chance to experience things in a new way. Parables can have a strong practical and critical effect that may prompt a renewal of life and society. Although derived from familiar things and happenings in everyday life, by slipping in the scandalous, paradoxical or surprising element they cut right across our spontaneous reactions and behaviour. The Good Samaritan is not just helpful; he does apparently witless things: he walks, lets the wounded man use the animal; he brings him to an inn, comes back the next day, pays for the board and lodging himself and puts all future expenses, if any, on his own bill (Lk. 10:33–35). With a deliberate touch of piquancy, as the story comes to be retold, this helpful fellow is made into a Samaritan, whereas the two clerics (Levite and priest) pass heedlessly by. In the everyday character of the parable there is an element of existential earnestness. Within the concretely human, mundane life of every day it encloses a more profound appeal. Parables point not to another, supranatural world but to a new potentiality within this world of ours: to a real possibility of coming to see life and the world, and to experience them, in a way quite different from the one we are accustomed to. On a conventional view the kind-hearted Samaritan did rather too much of a good thing. And yet that is precisely what the parable-teller is getting at, the astonishing, 'excessive' compassion of the 'good shepherd'.[90] The story sets the new world it discloses in perspective as a concrete possibility in life, even for whoever is listening to the parable now. In the world of Jesus' parables, living and evaluating are not what they are in the world of the ordinary, daily round. With the exception of three parables (the Rich Fool; Dives and Lazarus; the Pharisee and the Publican) they are all 'down to earth'. God does not come into it, directly; and yet anyone who attends to them knows that through these stories he is confronted with God's saving activity in Jesus; this is how God acts, and it is to be seen in the actions of Jesus himself, if, at any rate, you see with a heart ready to be transformed.

The parable remains 'suspended', therefore, so long as the listener has not decided for or against the new possibilities for living opened up in it – and eventually decides for or against Jesus of Nazareth. Shall he, the listener, also enter that new world? He is faced with a choice between two models for living. Is he to accept the new 'logic of grace and of having compassion' which the parables disclose and undergo that radical change in his own life? Or shall he set aside the challenge and return to the life of every day? Jesus and his world in the end become the issue in the parables, which open up a new world, in which only grace and love can dwell, and which places under judgement and seeks to change this history of ours, the course of human suffering that is the outcome of our short-sighted actions. Evidently, therefore, the time-factor in the parable has an a-chronic significance. This does not mean that the story becomes a-temporal or supra-temporal. On the contrary it suggests that what is being narrated always embraces a constitutive relation to my present, here and now; this address to me now is fundamental to telling and listening to the parable. Here are no problems of translation or reinterpretation: I myself, here and at this moment, must come to terms with the parable, must answer the question whether I will acknowledge this new possibility for living as mine. Thus a parable needs no reasoned commentary, no explanation drawn 'from elsewhere', no interpretation. It interprets itself, that is to say, our life, our existence and our actions. What may clarify the meaning of a parable is not argument but, if anything, the telling of a second or third parable – through the recurrently paradoxical effects of shock and 'estrangement' regarding our normal, everyday, conformist behaviour.

## (b) The parables of Jesus

Jesus himself – his person, his stories and his actions – is a parable Therefore the 'shock' effect marks the ongoing sequence of his life. The Marcan gospel saw this very clearly. It brings together (between 2:1 and 3:5) five disconcerting stories, scattered actions of Jesus that oblige those around him to adopt a position towards him; the healing of a paralysed man (whose sin he forgives) (2:1–12) – a meal that Jesus has with tax-collectors, people who gathered in monies and revenues for the Romans (2:13–17) – Jesus' defence of his disciples for not fasting when Jesus is with them (2:18–22) – the justification by Jesus of his disciples' behaviour when they deliberately pluck ears of corn on the sabbath day (2:23–28) – and lastly, by way of climax, how Jesus

himself heals on the sabbath the withered hand of a man in despair
(3:1–5). The leaders' reaction follows at once: 'The Pharisees went out,
and immediately held counsel with the Herodians against him, how to
destroy him' (3:6; see also the context of Mt. 12:14 and Jn. 5:18). The
story which Jesus is in his own person and which will be understood as
such by those who are ready to greet the supporting nearness of God in
Jesus' own mode of conduct (Mt. 13:11) is not understood by many
people. Yet the parable is so provocative that a neutral attitude to it
is impossible. Without openness towards the potential message in the
story, after all, one can see only the incomprehensible conduct of Jesus
(Mk. 4:11–12), scandalous because deviating from the Law (Mk. 6:2–3;
see Mt. 11:6; 15:9). One has to take sides; because the story of Jesus
not only opens up the possibility of a new and different life but subjects
to an annihilating critique our own cherished attitude to life, as it really
is. Out of self-preservation, therefore, some have rejected the Jesus
parable, because for them it was apocryphal and heterodox – a danger
to their own fixed habits. Jesus' execution on the cross is in the end a
natural result of this bafflement in face of the living parable of God.

In the care he shows for man and his record of suffering, for publicans
and sinners, for the poor, the crippled and the blind, for the oppressed
and for people torn apart by 'evil spirits', Jesus is a living parable of
God: that is how God cares for man. In the story of Jesus is told the
story of God. It is God himself who opens up to us in the story that is
the life of Jesus a new world, a different experience of reality and way of
living: thus the New Testament story *about* Jesus forms the response of
the first Christians to the story *of* Jesus himself. That is why all the life-
stories of Jesus live again in the life or the story of the believing fellowship. Thus the Church comes to be a community, sharing a story and a
meal, of people who have opened themselves up to the critical power
of the parable-life of Jesus; so too we today may still attend to and hear
the Jesus story. And now it is we who face the question whether we
dare stake our life upon it.

That the four gospels relate more parables than Jesus ever uttered is
not the main problem. For instance, more than half the parables we find
in Luke are found only there – although Luke himself found them in a
particular tradition. Furthermore the New Testament parables have
been through a process of transmission in which they have acquired
new updatings, especially when the postponement of the Parousia
began to be problematical. Again, about half the parables in Matthew
are not to be found elsewhere in the New Testament. Mark on the
other hand – an older gospel tradition – has only a few parables. The

explanation for this, apparently, is not so much Mark's ignorance of a more extensive parable tradition as his more restricted interest in the genre; and then Mark is more concerned with Jesus' ministry, the instruction of his disciples and way of living than with his parables. The parables seem to him not to be intended for the members of the Christian community. E. Trocmé has shown with some plausibility that the parables belong less to Jesus' general preaching than to the 'table talk' he had with various kinds of people – an interpretation that might also account for the fairly late integration of the parables with the Jesus tradition of the gospels,[91] as well as for the less settled form in which the parables were handed down. The basis of a lot of gospel parables, then, in so far as they are authentic, is something more in the order of Jesus' *Tischreden*, his mealtime conversation; which would also explain why these parables often have to do with meals (of various kinds) and with 'masters' and 'servants'. The parables are not – as a well-meant popular literary genre would have it – the expression of Jesus' own preaching 'to the crowd'; on the contrary they are his refined (perhaps more 'casual') form of forceful conversation, forceful and somewhat ironic, with the on the whole better disposed citizenry who, without 'going after' Jesus, evinced a certain, not necessarily religious, often even doubtful interest in him, and on the strength of that would invite him to supper. There is a good deal to suggest that the memory of Jesus' genuine parables was initially preserved in precisely those circles, whereas the original Jesus tradition would seem to have little to do with parables of Jesus. Yet in the longer term the 'Jesus tradition' was itself confronted with the 'extraneous' tradition of Jesus parables and from then on began, tentatively at first, to become involved with it. This could explain the remarkably complex 'parable' theory of the Marcan gospel (see Mk. 4:10–12): 'for those outside, everything is in parables' (Mk. 4:11b). One does indeed get the impression that Mark was of the opinion that Jesus' disciples knew better and knew more than these parables were saying, and that they were meant 'for outsiders' only. It is not unreasonable to suppose that Mark was trying rather to stop the integration of the parable tradition with the gospel tradition than to stimulate it. Thus when Mark says 'he did not speak to them without a parable, but privately to his own disciples he explained everything' (Mk. 4:34), this runs counter to his whole gospel, in so far as he gives only a few parables and fundamentally is concerned with other matters; in particular with this 'explaining', as he calls it (which for him implies: without what are properly described as 'parables').

All the same it is in those parables that we can perceive Jesus' solidarity both with what is best in the empirical wisdom of late-sapiential Judaism in ethical and religious matters and also the underlying dynamic of the one thing that held him enthralled: God's cause as the cause of man, the lordship of God. In the broadly religious field the 'God of the parables' appears as the almighty one (Lk. 12:20; 17:7–10) who as a tough business-man demands an 'interest yield' from his servants (Mt. 25:14–30 and parallels); but he is also and principally merciful and generous (Lk. 18:10–14; Lk. 18:7), comforting (Lk. 16:19–31), and even perplexingly magnanimous (Mt. 18:23ff; 20:1–16; Lk. 15:20–32); he gives liberal hand-outs (Mt. 25:21, 23), not pay for work done but a gratuity (Mt. 20:15), and in patience and long-suffering he excels (Lk. 13:6–9; Mt. 13:24–30). There we have the God whose lordship is centred upon humanity, the God of Jesus.

Those parables in particular that reflect the core of Jesus' message about God's approaching rule have been worked over a great deal as a result of Jesus' death, belief in the resurrection and the Christian expectation of Jesus' Parousia; but the original tenor can often still be perceived through this perspective added by the Church.

The approach of God's rule is 'like a man going on a journey, when he leaves home and puts his servants in charge, each with his work, and commands the doorkeeper to be on the watch. Watch, therefore – for you do not know when the master of the house will come . . .' (Mk. 13:13–37).[92] We have already seen that in essence Jesus' orientation on the future has to do with the coming of God's rule.[93] That calls for being watchful, on the alert. In Jesus' authentic eschatological parables the theme is always the kingdom of God, the lordship of God, which in Jesus is 'at hand' (Mk. 1:15) and already operative (Lk. 11:20), and yet is 'still to come' (Mt. 6:10 and parallels; Lk. 11:3), the timing of it is unknown (Mk. 13:32) and not to be calculated in advance (Lk. 17:20–21). The insistence on watchfulness points to the fact that the coming of God's kingdom will mean salvation for the watchful, even though they know they are sinners (Lk. 18:9–14) and unworthy (Mt. 8: 8–9, and parallel in Lk.), but judgement for the rest, for the man who takes no action (Mt. 7:24–27, and parallel in Lk.). The link between God's lordship and orthopraxis is brought out more especially in the parables. Of this the parable of the Talents is a typical example (Mt. 25:14–30, parallel in Lk. 19:12–27). The talent entrusted to men is the kingdom of God, admittedly taking us unawares, as pure grace, like the discovery of a treasure (Mt. 13:44) or a costly pearl (Mt. 13:45–46), yet none the less an event demanding of everyone a total conversion,

J.E.C.–F

*metanoia*, for which everything must be sold (Mt. 13:44). The idea of being 'on the job' now, centred on the coming of God's kingdom, turns up again in the story of the Wise and Foolish Virgins (Mt. 25: 1–13; cf. 12:35–40), in connection with the thief (Lk. 12:30–40 and parallel) and the settling of accounts (Lk. 16:1–2; 12:42–48; Mt. 18:23; Lk. 7:41–43). They may be mostly older parables, told in Israel about the judgement to come. But as told by Jesus – who himself raises all sorts of questions through his ministry, considered as a whole – and in the context of his message of God's approaching rule, they are shot through with a new profundity that calls for a disclosure-response. First and foremost because the praxis of the coming kingdom can be carried out here and now: the business of living, *vis-à-vis* what people normally do, has to be turned upside down straightaway (*metanoia*). The parable of the Talents in particular stresses the fact that the kingdom of God is entrusted to us: the third servant is rebuked, not because he has not dared to take risks like the other two but because he has never seized even the one opportunity that was altogether free of risk, and had therefore been really careless with what had been entrusted to him. It might be better to call this story the 'parable of the third servant'. God's lordship demands a corresponding resort to action. Again, the parable of the Watchful Servant (worked up into a Parousia parable) as well as that of the Faithful and Unfaithful Servants (Mt. 24:45–51, parallel in Lk. 12:42–46, 47–48) indicates the need for watchfulness in regard to the coming kingdom of God which may entail either salvation or judgement. Jesus' preaching of judgement would seem from the original tenor of the parables to be the reverse side of his proclamation of God's coming kingdom, which requires men to be actively on the alert, making the most of the goods in pledge entrusted to them. 'Watchfulness now' with an eye to 'the coming then': kingdom of God and orthopraxis.

In particular the parable of the Unimportant Slave is, against the background of Jewish spirituality in Jesus' day, perhaps the most startling – and what is more, in view of its non-Greek style, it belongs to the oldest parable tradition (although occurring only in the source peculiar to Luke) (Lk. 17:7–10). Jewish spirituality in those days was based on obedience to God, with the Law as a norm. It was an objective quantity, so to speak, by which to gauge concretely the prospect of coming to salvation or to judgement. God is after all a righteous God of retribution, which could be measured precisely by the yardstick of fidelity to the Law. An exact knowledge of the Law was naturally a proviso and the basis of any reasonable hope of salvation. The *'amè ha' ares*, the common people, who had no such knowledge of the Law, were because of that very fact badly placed as regards salvation. But anyone who knew the Law and fulfilled it exactly could be assured of salvation; for then God was obligated, by dint of his own righteousness, to give that faithful one salvation.[94] This legalistic notion, on which between the living God and the persons of men an impersonal (albeit 'hypostatized' – thus intensifying the oppressive domination of the impersonal) Law was erected, as an objective yardstick for precise calculation, was the foundation of the whole Judaic idea of merit and reward and assurance of salvation. Now it may be true that, though they were an exception, some rabbis did emphasize the perniciousness of trying to compute salvation; but this was a reaction 'immanent in the system' in this sense: belittling oneself and obeying the Law without an eye to the reward was in some circles the subtlest way to assure oneself of the reward of actual fidelity to the Law. Jesus' parable of the Unimportant Slave – to the benefit, in fact, of the common people – is a frontal attack on this spirituality. That he takes an actual slave as an example of the relation between God and man was nothing scandalous but was normal in those days, particularly in view of the very easy situation of slaves in Israel. The point at issue is the concrete status of a slave, who on the one hand is totally subject to the will of his master, the paterfamilias, but on the other is quite ready for each and every service required of him, and who, notwithstanding all this dedication, has no right whatever to any recompense. That is how we are before God (Lk. 17:10). That the 'law-abiding' and devoted believer can lay no claim to a reward is the shock-effect right through this parable, because it stands the prevailing Judaic ideas on their head. A total readiness to serve God is something taken for granted here, for which however no thanks or reward can be demanded. This may upset our feelings even nowadays. Yet in the terms of the parable this is the supreme personalizing of the individual. The Law is deposed from the hypostatizing which detaches it from God, as an objective yardstick thrust between God and man. The parable puts man back into a direct, personal relationship to God; linked to a personal authority, the individual orientates himself by the substantive meaning of the Law as God's will and not by a merely formal, binding final judgement.[95] Within a personal relationship one does not start counting things up or thinking about thanks and rewards. There is then no question of payment by results, only of gracious clemency, which has a logic of its own with its own affective reward of grace in superfluity. As a result faith's obedient response to God is radicalized in virtue of its personalizing significance, but the formal-cum-juridical observance of the Law, as a basis for calculating the prospects of salvation, is by the same token completely negated; the Law is drawn inside a personal, non-juridical relationship, so being provided with a personal and substantive foundation. This also explains why Jesus, who really did want to uphold the Law as a revelation of God's will (see below), in actual fact – when faced with materially concrete demands and circumstances – sometimes overrode the formal requirements of the Law, even that of keeping the sabbath holy, in what were the real interests of his fellows.

Although this parable is peculiar to Luke, other parables state the same thing in different keys. For me the best example of that is what I would call the parable of 'the elder brother of the lost son' (i.e. the Prodigal Son: Lk. 15:11–32). The father looks with longing for the return and the repentance of his younger son, who is living a fast life on his share of the inheritance. Dire need brings him, at the end of his tether, to repentance. His father is already looking out for him. Not a word is said about what has happened; and there is a grand celebration to mark the return. This is in itself a parable of God's compassion, which is way ahead of any contrite feelings, as other parables make clear (see immediately below): 'For this my son was dead and is alive again' (Lk. 15:24), that is reason enough for plenty of feasting and celebration. But the point of the parable lies as it were in a second parable, interwoven with it. The law-abiding elder son grows jealous and even righteously indignant. He has never had the offer of a party like that, although he had served his father loyally and been at his beck and call. This expresses the Judaic idea, as current at that time, of reward for loyalty to the Law (Lk. 15:29–30), with at the same time an undertone of contempt for the sinner: he never calls the 'lost son' 'my brother', but holds himself aloof; 'now that son of yours has returned' (15:30). The parable transcends all notions of reward for performance and sets fidelity to the Law in the right personal realm: 'Son, you are always with me and all that is mine is yours' (15:31). And with keen perception is added – overturning the aloof attitude of the elder son towards his dissolute brother: 'It was fitting to make merry and be glad, for this your brother was dead, and is alive . . .' (15:32).

The same break with the legalistic notion of payment by results finds expression in the socially scandalizing parable of the Labourers in the Vineyard (Mt. 20:1–16). Here the effect of a 'social shock' is indeed intended. The praxis of the kingdom of God is different. It is not that defaulting on one's social obligations is condoned – that is not the drift of the parable. But measuring out salvation-as-reward against the norm of one's own performance is simply brushed aside. Here again the saying from the other parable applies: 'Son, you are always with me and all that is mine is yours.' Being jealous of someone else's good nature is also condemned; 'Is your eye evil because I am good?' (Mt. 20:15). Not to rejoice in serving 'for the sake of God's kingdom', but – to put it in modern terms – to demand a bigger reward for achievement (because, for instance, one lives a celibate life for the kingdom's sake) and to become angry (because the younger brother, who likewise has offered his life for the cause of the kingdom, gets married) is by this parable held up to ridicule as an attitude directly militating against the praxis of the kingdom of God. Whatever the material verdict on the case, both celibacy as being a claim upon a higher reward and being resentful of the younger brother are attitudes alien to the orthopraxis of the kingdom of God.

Another parable which illuminates another fundamental aspect of this spirituality of Jesus is that of the Unmerciful Servant (Mt. 18:23–35). The man's employer remitted in his favour a debt amounting to a fantastically large sum of money: ten thousand talents, say, something in the region of fifty million guilders;[96] which is why of 'There was once a man [or a certain person]' Matthew makes a king; the sum mentioned is in fact just about the amount of the yearly fiscal revenue in a Roman province at the time, which tax-gatherers had to collect and convey to the king. But not long afterwards the same servant callously insisted that one of his fellows who owed him a small sum should pay it all back. Because the man could not pay at once, he had him put in prison. In its present guise the parable has been updated by the Church, and especially in a Matthean context; but analysis serves to make the original tenor of it fairly plain. The real point is again the lordship of God and *metanoia*, that is, being overcome by the glad tidings of the approaching, indeed already graciously operative, rule of God. The parable is in keeping with other (updated) recollections of Jesus' 'precepts', especially with Mt. 6:12, 14–15, parallels in Lk. 11:4 and Mk. 11:25; see Mt. 19:24–34 (if we set aside Matthean editorializing in Mt. 6:14–15 and Mt. 18:35). God's forgiveness of us precedes and must form the ground and source of our extending forgiveness to others. The parable expresses negatively what is positively expressed in the Lord's Prayer. It puts the emphasis on the charity and mercy shown by the king; 'I forgave you all that debt . . . should not you have had mercy on your fellow-servant, as I had mercy on you?' (Mt. 18:32–33). God's merciful dealing – demonstrated concretely in Jesus' own compassion for the people – must be exemplary for anyone who wishes to enter the kingdom of God. (See Mt. 5:43–48 and parallel in Lk.) The link between the kingdom of God and orthopraxis – *orthôs* here means (acting) in accordance with the kingdom of God – is here concretized in the last element as compassionate dedication to one's fellow-man. For since God's lordship is the universal, compassionate disposition of God towards man, the *metanoia* demanded by the kingdom takes concrete form in empathy with and dedicated commitment to one's fellow human beings; as is said in another place: 'Be merciful even as your Father is merciful' (Lk. 6:36, parallel in Mt. 5:48). Hence also: 'Blessed are the merciful' (Mt. 5:7). The parable of the Good Samaritan mentioned earlier on is just a variant of this praxis of compassion, peculiar to the realm of God's lordship. Thence the further consequences of such praxis of the kingdom – probably primitive Christian insights deriving from the post-Easter experience – become apparent in all their variety: for example, before taking a gift to the altar, the Church requires a man to be first reconciled with his brother (Mt. 5:23–24). Eschatological forgiveness, a gift of the coming lordship of God, is to be exercised by believers, whose own lives are lived within it, towards their fellow-men: that is the praxis, the 'living out', of the kingdom of God. Love for God, demonstrated in love for man, in 'being of service' (Mk. 10:44, parallel in Mt.; Lk. 22:27; Mt. 25:31–46; 7:12, parallel in Lk.; Mt. 23:11; Mk. 9:35 and parallel) is the sign and token of God's lordship, thereby recognizable as breaking through into this world and into our history. When this parable is told by Jesus, who deals mercifully with transgressors (Mt. 11:19, parallel in Lk.), eats with them and so offers salvation and fellowship to publicans and sinners (Mk. 2:15–16 and parallels; Lk. 15:1–10) and promises sinners the kingdom of God (see Lk. 15:2–32; Mt. 21:31) (see in a later section), it becomes clear that the parable also invites us to ask: Who is this Jesus, who in such a fascinating way exemplifies the praxis of God's kingdom in his person and ministry? How can fellowship with Jesus be a 'tender' of salvation on God's part? For as uttered by Jesus, the story suggests that Jesus is himself this parable of God. The parable is a question, left open.

The parable of the Unwilling Marriage-guests (Mt. 22:1–10, 11–14, parallel in Lk. 14:16–24) brings to the fore the aspect of rejection: rejecting the salvation offered with the kingdom of God. The eschatological kingdom is represented as a big party or wedding-feast – something already part of tradition. To a lesser extent in Luke but more especially in Matthew the parable has been overlaid by the situation of the Church after Jesus' death. The core of the original version would seem to be this. Somebody sends his servant to fetch the guests previously invited to the dinner now prepared for them; they refuse to come along and make excuses of one sort or another. The host is deeply offended and gets his servant to invite to the meal, now waiting to be served up, the first people he happens to meet in the street. A simple, everyday 'profane event' (the few who had agreed to come to dinner but at the last moment proffered their excuses are hurriedly re-placed by means of second-in-order invitations) acquires in virtue of its paradoxical and almost unreal exaggeration (the distinguishing mark of the parable), a shock effect calculated to bring us up short and make us think: people straight off the street, without any of the right clothes, are sat down to dinner on this gala occasion. But Jesus' parable has a double bottom. In the context of the parable as related by Jesus, the audience understand the point to be the invitation constituted by the approaching rule of God, which calls for a radical *metanoia*: no excuse whatever will do in this case; everything else must give way to this invitation. Seek first the kingdom of God; then everything else will come right. But there is a further point to the parable: Israel's leaders refuse to accept the coming of God's kingdom in the appearing of Jesus; the *'amè ha' ares*, the common people, not dressed up in the costume of the wages of conformity to the Law, accept the invitation and are let into God's kingdom. Two aspects of Jesus' preaching of God's lordship stand out here: on the one hand the unreservedness with which one is bound to capitulate to God's good tidings, on the other the hope it expresses for 'publicans and sinners': God's salvation is offered to all without exception. (The expulsion of the man in shabby clothes is Matthean and was originally no part of this story; it does correspond to other parables which insist on our making the most of the talent of the kingdom of God. What was salvation becomes in fact for the one who rejects it a judgement.) It is always the same basic elements of Jesus' preaching that in the parables, taken from happen-ings in ordinary 'profane' life, shed light on the message of the coming rule of God. Though they may not all be authentic Jesus-material, in accordance with the applied combination of criteria from Part One, they do give us a full picture of Jesus' central message about the kingdom of God and its *metanoia*. Thus they are really and truly 'from Jesus'. In particular their consistency, the fact that they point repeatedly to three fundamental elements of the graciousness of God's lordship and the demand for a corresponding mode of conduct, yet without any 'right to payment', witnesses to their being 'true to Jesus'.[97]

The idea embedded in these parables actually keeps turning up in many other bits of evidence, each with its own shock-effect: the one who leaves the ninety-nine sheep to fend for themselves in order to go in search of the single lost sheep, because he, the good shepherd, knows each sheep by its pet name (even if Jesus is there picking up already traditional similitudes from Israel's rich heritage) (Lk. 15:4–7 and parallel) – the parable of the Lost Coin (coming from a society where the sheep as a 'unit of exchange' has made way for the coin) (Lk. 15: 8–10)[98] – parables of the hidden treasure, and the at that time universally familiar early Eastern parables regarding 'the pearl' (Mt. 13:45–46).

But towards the end of his life (see a subsequent chapter) the prospect of Israel's rejection of Jesus' message of the coming kingdom comes more and more into the picture. This is apparent also in the parable of the Evil Wine-growers (Mk. 12:1–9, parallels in Mt. 21:33–41; Lk. 20:9–16). Like most others, this parable has been fundamentally revised and updated in view of what had occurred in the meantime: the execution of Jesus. It is difficult (supposing this to be an authentic parable of Jesus) to achieve a pristine reconstruction of Jesus' 'open parable': 'There was once a man', an example taken from Palestine's provision of vineyards with everything appertaining thereto – a common enough matter, which back in Isaiah 5:1–7 had already become an image of God's care for Israel, his vineyard. Every so often the vineyard's owner sends a servant to fetch his master's share of the proceeds; but each time the man is maltreated or killed. In the end the landowner sends his beloved son, hoping that they will have some regard for him. But he is murdered too. The drift of the parable is of course this: whoever has been entrusted with God's vineyard (Israel as God's chosen people) owes it to God to 'show a return'; he must act on the requirements of the property entrusted to him. One who can fail in this is capable of going to any lengths, reaching indeed the peak of wickedness. That is not all, however. The notion of various messengers and then at last of a final messenger, the landowner's actual son, is present in all traditions of this parable. The listener will almost inevitably think of the prophets, sent again and again to Israel by a long-suffering God (the traditional and Deuteronomic idea of Israel's rejecting and even killing God's envoys), and finally be reminded of the latter-day prophet, 'the beloved son'. If this parable, including the elements specified (which are, after all, essential to the unity of the whole, despite possible modifications of detail as between Mark,

Matthew and Luke), derives from Jesus himself (which is hard to ascertain), then it is expressing Jesus' understanding of himself as the latter-day prophet, with the additional prospect, consciously realized, of his coming death. In any event it speaks of an awareness that in its rejection of God's proferred salvation Israel may stop at nothing – a thought not unfamiliar to ancient prophets and thus, among the Jews, pre-Christian.

When we survey this handful of representative parables in the New Testament, we see that in respect of their direct narrative content they reflect secular situations as concretely presented (without any criticism of, for instance, social conditions, but without condoning them, either); those relations, because they are known to all, are used to suggest, through what is well known and familiar, something else, that which is unknown, a new potentiality for living (peculiar to God's kingdom). What they mean Jesus never explains: the listener must supply the meaning himself, or rather, let the parable itself do the interpreting and filling in. Comments like: 'So the last will be first, and the first last' (Mt. 20:16), and 'The master commended the dishonest steward for his prudence' (Lk. 16:8), or 'I tell you, this man went down to his house justified' (Lk. 18:14) and so on, are later editorial conclusions that form no part of the first fresh telling of a parable. Originally, drawing a conclusion is left to the listener. The parable merely opens up the possibility of a new and different kind of living.

But Jesus does not tell parables just like any anonymous popular wise man. They are (or in so far as Jesus simply took over existing parables current as folk-wisdom, they become) part of his whole ministry, characterized by the message of God's coming rule. It is within that whole that the point of each parable must be looked for. Furthermore, very concrete situations in Jesus' life may have given occasion for telling just this particular parable or telling it in that particular way (though the concrete circumstances to which Jesus reacts by telling this or that parable for the most part elude us). A correct structural analysis of the parable (which must indeed come first) misses this. 'Tax-collectors and sinners of all kinds kept coming to him to hear him. The Pharisees and the Scribes grumbled about it' (Lk. 15:1–2; see also Lk. 7:31–35, parallel in Mt. 11:16–19; 20:1–15); thereupon Jesus tells the parable about looking for the single lost sheep and the lost coin (Lk. 15:1–10): again these are fitting occasions to which some parables are obviously a prompt response. Luke suggests this in another context: 'Simon, do you see this woman? I entered your house, you gave me no water for my feet, but she . . .; you gave me no kiss . . .;

you did not anoint my head with oil, but she . . .' (Lk. 7:44–50). There are a lot of secondary elements in that, it is true; but a historical context is certainly suggested. This would be all the more pregnant if it is true that Jesus told parables especially in the course of meals offered him by well-to-do citizens who, though perhaps in two minds about him, were certainly interested, but chary of performing for their guest the ceremonies that current custom demanded at the start of a dinner. But even if we admit our ignorance of the concrete occasion of each separate parable, we do know the context of Jesus' life as a whole, within which they were told. Of course the parables of Jesus in their original tenor, not as yet developed by the New Testament on explicitly Christological lines, remain indeterminate in content and meaning and often, in a literal sense, even secular: they speak directly neither of God nor about Jesus himself. But within the setting of Jesus' message and of his own conduct their real point is clear: it is God's offer of salvation, God's lordship and the inward *metanoia* it demands; clear too that in view of Jesus' own concrete mode of living, his actual behaviour, which is as it were a living illustration of what the parables he tells are all about, they pose the question: Who is this Jesus? For because Jesus is constrained by the coming rule of God and talks about it in parables, while at the same time his life is itself a striking parable of it, we cannot avoid the question: Who is he? Who is this teller of parables in his own person? In this sense Wilder's conclusion regarding the parables is right: 'They should be understood in relation to the speaker (and the occasion).'[99] Although we hardly ever know what concrete occasion led Jesus to tell this or that particular parable, his public activity as a whole does begin to provide us with a notion of who is addressing us here and of what depth-dimension these parables can acquire because of that. The 'living parable' that Jesus is in his own person and the import of his parable-stories confront us with the question whether or not we also wish, venture and are able to see in Jesus' activities a manifestation of God's regard for people. Although on the surface and in their secular content these parables have an obvious theological significance when placed in their Jesus-context, they are not directly Christological; but given the context of Jesus' whole ministry and actual conduct, of which they are an integral part, they are none the less also an expression of Jesus' self-understanding and therefore present us with a 'Christological question': whether or not we will allow goodness, love, mercy and grace to be extended to us by this Jesus and, in accepting that grace, will permit ourselves to be constrained by his unconditional demand for an 'about turn' (*metanoia*) in the conduct of our own lives. If so, then we must go on to ask what this saving relationship to him, as we experience it, implies regarding the person of Jesus himself. In their original setting these parables were doubtless vaguer and more 'open' than they are as they now encounter us in the New Testament, through a couple of generations of Christian tradition whose response to these open parables has already been added and recorded there. For in the New Testament account of these parables the Christological interpretation has already been incorporated into the story itself,[100] following the usage of ancient didactic historiography, which inculcates its own viewpoint and response to the challenge of historical facts in the factual account itself.

Despite their being given a more specific meaning in the New Testament – a process which shut the door, as it were, on these open parables, that is, by turning them into parables with a fixed, single interpretation – they none the less manage to preserve their open, questioning character for us twentieth-century people in a completely new way – just because of the crisis into which Christology or the parables as already pre-interpreted have now entered; so that for us they once more raise the question: 'But you – you who hear these parables – who do you say that I am?' (Mk. 8:29; Mt. 16:15; Lk. 9:20). Is God's mercy in fact manifested in a definitive and decisive way through Jesus of Nazareth? The question cannot be answered by anybody other than the individual who attends to the parables within the whole presented by the 'parabolic life' of Jesus of Nazareth. To the question: 'But you, who do you say that I am?' many church people and theologians are well able to say what answer has been given by Mark and Luke, Augustine, Thomas and Bellarmine, Luther and Calvin, Barth or Bultmann, Pannenberg or Rahner. It is their own answer that we do not hear. Other people or another time cannot answer on our behalf or supply us with the appropriate images, concepts and expressions: that would not be our response to the parable that is the life of Jesus. Guided by the 'recollection of Jesus', in part also by the already numerous responses he has engendered through the centuries, we are now, as we listen, confronted with this 'lived parable'. How do we interpret him? No one else – neither the historical disciplines nor theology nor even the first Christians nor yet the Church's magisterium – can answer that question for us. As we hear the parable the question is put to us: whether we will bet our life on it. There are more than enough pointers present in the gospel narratives to disclose an attendant awareness of the distance between the experience, engendered at the time by Christian faith, of the power of the crucified-and-risen One, present in the Church, and what it was able to recall of association with the historical Jesus during his days on earth. This is extremely important. It is why in the gospels' and the Church's record concerning the parabolic life of Jesus sufficient still comes across of the core of the real story of Jesus himself, the story that 'Jesus of Nazareth' was. In it we may even now get a keen sense of hearing the challenge: 'Who do you say that I am?' (itself already a question framed in an ecclesial context), as a question being put to us.

## C.  ESCHATOLOGICAL REVOLUTION: JESUS' BEATITUDES

The essence of the beatitudes, as they are incorporated in the Sermon on the Mount (Matthew) or the Sermon on the Plain (Luke), in the view of most exegetes has its historical source in Jesus.[101] The Q tradition, which (but for one saying) Luke faithfully reflects (Lk. 6: 20b-21, parallel in Mt. 5:3-4, 6), would seem to belong to the primary stage of this Jesus tradition. The actual genre of beatitudes is Old Testament, late Jewish, Eastern and generally ancient.

This central core of the complex of beatitudes is set in the perspective of the eschatological coming of God's rule and the kingdom of God. It is a prophetic eschatological declaration on the pattern of apocalyptic-cum-dialectical 'blessings'. Strikingly enough, the primary core pronounces no blessing on 'virtuous people': 'Blessed are the poor – for theirs is the kingdom of God. Blessed are they that hunger – for they shall be satisfied. Blessed are they that weep – for they shall laugh' (Lk. 6:20b-21, omitting the twice repeated 'now'); this can fairly be identified as the oldest text of the tradition (in Matthew especially a spiritualizing tendency is already apparent). The eschatological blessing is for the poor, hungry and sorrowful. A characteristic feature is that of the three beatitudes the last two are put into the future tense, the first into the present: the kingdom of God is here already, but the laughing with satisfaction, that still lies in the future. Here we have the typical tension distinctive of Jesus' preaching as a whole: God's lordship is already being realized now, although the consummated kingdom of God has yet to come about; the future has already begun.

The first beatitude makes mention of the poor of society – confirmed by 'those who hunger' and 'those who weep'. Thus the sole point here is the blessing pronounced on the outcast, the individual

with no position in society. Hence too in the Q tradition we are ex-
horted not to pile up worldly possessions (Mt. 6:19, 21, parallel in
Lk. 12:33–34), not to give ourselves over to worldly cares (Mt. 6:25–33,
parallel in Lk. 12:22–31) and are admonished not to serve mammon
(Mt. 6:24, parallel in Lk. 16:13). Here we have the apocalyptic principle
of the reversal of all values: somebody who is poor now will be rich
then. But it is God himself who will reverse these conditions; what is
envisaged is not a directly societal overturning of all existing relations
but an 'eschatological' one. Again, it is not said directly that this
revolution is already coming about in the dimension of our earthly
history, not at any rate in the surface-dimension of our history; for –
even from an apocalyptic standpoint – in a hidden way life on earth
already has its part in the ultimate meaning of history as eschatologically
manifested. Soon God will be king, and right relations among men
will prevail. That is why the message of God's rule is a blessing of the
poor, who now are disinherited. The beatitudes regarding the dispossessed are subject to the assurance that the salvation promised with
the kingdom of God is near. None of this means that for the rest the
Sermon on the Mount is supposed to be a Christian invention. Even
if many parts of it may have developed only after Jesus' death, nurtured in the womb of the local Christian congregations, they can still
be a 'true-to-life' expression of Jesus, especially now that it is increasingly clear that for the Christian Church Jesus of Nazareth was in fact
both criterion and norm of the Jesus tradition (couched however in
terms of the constantly shifting and changing cultural and religious
background and needs of the churches).

The antitheses which follow: 'But woe to you rich . . .' (Mt. 23:25,
23, 6–7a, 27, 4, 29–31, 13, parallels in Lk. 11:39, 42–44, 46–48, 52) are
secondary; in their apocalyptical context, of course, they are the consequence of the eschatological reversal of all values; it is a (sevenfold)
apocalyptical curse. But almost everywhere that Jesus' positively
formulated preaching is given an antithetical and negative expression
in the New Testament it turns out that one is dealing with secondary
texts.

Without having before one the Jewish and late Jewish background
to this noble utterance of benediction, these are indeed disconcerting
texts which we moderns feel to have even a reactionary ring about
them: the poor are having a bad time of it now but – just wait a bit – in
the hereafter they are to be the privileged ones. Apocalyptical circles
even added: and then they will have a good laugh at the deposed and
impoverished rich.[102] Is this Jesus of Nazareth?

Absolutely not. In the first place there is no question here of 'the hereafter', but of God's rule that has come to these poor people here and now. After all, the same Q source (Mt. 22:2-6; Lk. 7:18-23) refers to Isa. 61:1-2 (like Lk. 4:17-21), where the late Jewish tradition mentions the eschatological prophet, anointed by God, who 'brings glad tidings to the poor'. Jesus, the eschatological prophet, is present here and now among the poor and brings them the joyful message now. What is at issue is not a hereafter but God's lordship and rule, beginning to 'come true' in the ministry of Jesus: the eschatological 'about-turn' of things is on the point of happening now. But the one who enters on the scene here is not a Davidic but a prophetic 'anointed' figure, who brings salvation to the poor and so can call them happy and felicitate with them even now.

Matthew (5:3-12) has understood very well the significance of the benediction that he found in his source when he embodies it in a 'noble sermon on the Mount of God': the parallels with Moses who, followed by his nearest companions and after them a great multitude, ascends the mountain of God, where he gets from God the tablets of stone and promulgates the Decalogue to Israel, are obvious: as a new Moses Jesus, 'when he sees this multitude', goes up the mountain and, just as Moses took his closest associates higher up with him, 'his disciples came to him' (Mt. 5:1), and Jesus 'opened his mouth and taught them, saying: blessed are the poor . . .' (Mt. 5:2-3). As Matthew sees it, in the beatitudes Jesus is operating as the leader of the new people of God, to whom a new constitution is being given – not a law but a benediction, a promise of salvation. And this promise is for the poor, the sorrowing and the hungry. An end to their condition is promised here and placed on a constitutional footing.

What does this mean? The fact that Luke simply speaks of 'the poor', whereas Matthew talks about 'the poor in spirit', is not Luke's way of giving this concept a 'social' slant (though throughout his gospel and in the Acts he does indeed show a predilection for the 'poor' in a societal sense), but just an expression of fidelity to the source he is using. He is equally inclined to 'spiritualize'; and had he found 'poor in spirit' in his source, he would have taken it over. Matthew on the other hand does stress the spiritual, as appears from those beatitudes which are absent from Luke and are introduced by him: blessed are the meek, the merciful, the pure in heart, the peace-makers. Thus in the oldest tradition (according to the all but unanimous conviction of the exegetes) one simply had: 'Blessed are you poor.'

This idea has a very long preliminary history, however. Prior to the entry into the Holy Land there were no poor in 'Israel'; and the Exodus brought them to a 'land of milk and honey, a land of plenty', where the poor have no place. But after they had settled down in 'God's country' all sorts of disparities eventually arose among the farming population, as a result of their efforts to accumulate property. To counter this, various 'social laws' were enacted, the most radical being the introduction of the sabbatical year: every seventh year all debts were remitted and slaves set free. In that way every Jew's initial state of equal entitlement under God's covenant could to some extent be restored (Ex. 21:2–6; 23:10–11; Lev. 25:1–7, 18–22; Deut. 15). However, under the monarchy and in the course of urban development nothing could check the growth of social disparity; and so there emerged in Israel the *'amè ha' ares*, the poor people, besides – at the very top – the king, then the army of professional soldiers, officials, the aristocracy in the city, the priests in the Temple and the local notables at the city gates. Much of their own tradition disappeared and a great deal was taken over from the Canaanitic culture – a pragmatically inevitable step. Yet it was precisely in this pragmatism that danger lurked. Their distinctive spirituality became diluted. Against that process the prophets uttered their protest. This prophetic social critique was a call to return, not indeed to a period of pre-urbanization (though it may well give that impression, and one could make 'reactionary' capital out of their critique), but to the pristine experience of Yahweh that went with the good pre-urban times. After all, in their entire social critique Amos, Isaiah and Micah never say what society should be like; they only appeal for a return to the true Yahwism[103] from which people had broken away. Yahweh no longer has any part to play in political decisions (Isa. 31:1–2), the aristocracy and people with official rank enrich themselves at the expense of ordinary folk. That is why the social 'upper crust' is the butt of the prophets' criticism: it is corrupt, uses bribery, pursues 'class justice', and the population are subject to the bondage of debts and rental payments. But all this shows a disregard for Yahweh, the patron and protector of the people. It is because every Israelite is a fully-fledged member of the people of God in this country (Isa. 3:14–15) that the prophets utter their protest: their critique is a religious one. Conduct in Israel is in fact based on *force majeure*; and that is a flouting of the covenant, which certainly has a political and social relevance. The concrete state of affairs is criticized in terms of the notion of God's lordship. Their critique is rooted in their zeal for the cause of God, which must be Israel's cause also. So they pronounce God's judgement: the end and dissolution of the way things are now (Isa. 5:9–10;

Micah 2:4–5, 6–10; 3:12). No proposals for revolutionary action or reform; simple proclamation of God's annihilating judgement. God is going to react is the stance adopted by the prophets. He will not let himself be cornered. In the end a prospect of salvation-from-God does come vaguely into sight (Micah 2:4–5): a new and just redistribution of all possessions – but by God himself. It is God's future alone that is spoken of here. No prophet indicts Israel's institutions, but only their way of concentrating power and their misuse: there is no 'ortho-praxis'. But in their view the future is the work of Yahweh alone. The essence of the prophetic critique is distilled in the 'Exodus' spiritu-ality of Deuteronomy: a return to the way things were before the entry into the Holy Land (Isa. 11:4; Ps. 37:11; 72:2).

What was the situation of the 'common people' in these structures? They were 'the poor', that is, the actual poor of society. But then within the concept a religious implication begins to develop (Isa. 29:19–21; Zeph. 3; Prov. 16:19; Wisdom 2:10–20). After the exile it is the re-patriates in particular who are the 'poor remnant', but now nurtured and stimulated by the old Yahwistic spirituality. The 'renewed people' comes to be synonymous with 'the poor' (Isa. 51:17; 54:13; especially 49:13), sustained by the spiritual genius of the Third Isaiah (Isa. 61:1–3; see 57:15). 'Poor' here (usually coincident with social poverty) refers to the devout and pious individual who in his poverty humbly looks towards God (see also Pss. 25; 34; 37:9–11). The 'poor man' is one who has been hit by misfortune (of whatever kind) and can find his only strength and stay in entrusting himself to God (Isa. 52–53; Ps. 22; Zech. 9:9–10).

Grounded in this age-old tradition, there persisted in the nation the idea that the poor, the hungry and the sorrowful are those who have nothing more to hope from this human history of ours and can only continue to wait expectantly on God, who is the just and righteous One. In Jesus' time, therefore, the 'poor' among the Jews are people who cannot command justice for themselves and so can only trust in the justice of God.

There were, of course, schools of thought (some even religious in character) committed to the view that this 'being unable to stand up for oneself' was a relative matter; they wanted to come to the aid of Israel's God by force of arms: the Sicarii and the Zealots. Although in that respect the time of Jesus was a rather quiet one, between events thirty years previously (Judas the Galilean) and thirty years later (which occasioned the Jewish rebellion against Rome), the fact is that this was not the way Jesus wanted to choose.

So when Jesus said: 'Blessed are the poor, the hungry, the sorrowful', the people understood what he meant. But Jesus did not repeat what they already knew, namely that given the concrete situation, they could not look for help to any earthly court of appeal and that salvation and rescue could come from God alone. Precisely that is the late Jewish notion of 'being poor'; and Jesus is not proclaiming a tautology. What then is he saying?

The eschatological prophet would come, it was said, with glad tidings for the poor. That was a lively part of popular expectation, rooted in older traditions, among many of the poor and oppressed. Jesus' beatitude signifies that it is happening now: that is to say, now this longing and looking for the 'God of help' is to be fulfilled; now promise and expectation are on the very point of being realized. With Jesus the kingdom of God comes upon them. Jesus feels compassion for these poor folk. Against humanity's history of incomprehensible suffering – in so far that our being as men affords no remedy for it – God himself now moves into action. First of all Jesus, through that compassion of his, brings the message 'from God' of God's radical 'no' to the continuing course of man's suffering. The whole point of history, although only the *eschaton* will make this clear, is peace, laughter, total satisfaction: the 'final good' of salvation and happiness. Just as, earlier on, men had tried to articulate the purpose of life and history 'proto-logically', that is, by referring to the proto-history of all things, in Jesus' day they were describing this 'eschatologically', that is, by pointing to the end of the age. Showing mercy is, despite everything, the deepest purpose that God intends to fulfil in history. He wills men to live, wills their salvation, not their misery and death. That Jesus expresses all this in the thought-forms of his time – and so in ways limited and conditioned by the temporal factor – is undeniable. And that for him the End was very near, despite various distinctions that have to be made, can hardly be denied either. To make oneself ready for this rule of God, coming unexpectedly as it would, was the most urgent task, therefore. Indeed Jesus did not preach social revolution, although his eschatological message brings the whole pain-ridden history of mankind radically under God's critical judgement and so calls for an about-turn. This has fundamental consequences for a continuing post-Jesus history – implications which must be made explicit. And yet this is not the profoundest vein in the beatitudes. What they quite unmistakably enshrine is a spiritual affirmation of the ultimate power of powerlessness – of a belief that however much improving the world by our own human resources is necessary (that is to make explicit God's 'no' to our suffering in history), at the deepest level there is a suffering, an impotence which no human being can remove and from which we can be liberated only by virtue of the fact that 'God will rule' for the final good of all men. There is a human impotence which God alone can relieve. That was the basis on which Jesus himself also proceeded. If God wills universal salvation, as Jesus preaches when he puts across the message of God's lordship – if therefore God is love, creative love for man, then even now the poor, the hungry and grief-stricken may rise up in hope, to say: but all the same . . . Laughter, not crying, is the deepest purpose that God wills for man. That means therefore that he does not in any case will suffering. On no account is Jesus prepared to shift suffering and evil on to God. God's essential being is anti-evil, willing good. The later theological distinctions of God's 'positive' and 'permissive' will are differentiations made by theologians wanting to find a theoretical explanation for suffering, like the Greek attempts to describe all forms of evil as a 'non-being' so as not to have to understand it – attempts on the part of people who in fact could not locate evil theoretically to find an escape-hatch. From Jesus' eschatological message we hear only God's radical 'no' to all forms of evil, all forms of poverty and hunger that lead to tears. That is Jesus' message; and it has enormous consequences. That in it God is also refusing to acknowledge the superior strength of evil and so with his own being as God is standing surety for the defeat of evil in all its forms can in no way be turned to reactionary or conservative ends. Jesus gives us on God's behalf only the message that God stands surety for us. And therefore the poor, the suffering and the deprived do indeed have grounds for positive hope. How? Perhaps the rest of the story of Jesus' life, as well as the historical failure of his message and activities, can tell us more about that. In particular his whole conduct should help to determine whether the broad view that has been given of Jesus' message and preaching tallies with reality, more specifically whether Jesus was indeed the prophet of the near approach of God's rule – how he conjoined this message with a course of action intended to change the given situation radically (with all the attendant dangers) – whether and how, inspired by the gracious mandate he received from God, he knew himself to be the saving instrument of God's approaching kingdom, which in the actions he took evidently became present among the people who met and put their trust in him.

Chapter 2

# Jesus' manner of life

## §1  Jesus' caring and abiding presence among people experienced as salvation coming from God

*Introduction*

In the synoptic gospels there are only two places where Jesus speaks to people explicitly of the forgiveness of sins (Mk. 2:1–12 parallels at Mt. 9:2–8; Lk. 5:17–26; and Lk. 7:36–50). But everything points to the fact that in such an explicit form these logia are not authentic sayings of the historical Jesus, that is to say, they are early Christian affirmations on the part of the Church about Jesus, already acknowledged as the Christ. But the ground of this power to forgive sins, of this tender of salvation or fellowship-with-God, which the Christian community ascribes to Jesus after his death, really does lie in the concrete activity of Jesus during his days on earth. Jesus' presence among the people, helping them with his deeds of power, offering or accepting invitations to eat and drink together, not just with his disciples but with the mass of people and especially with outcasts, publicans and sinners, turns out to be an invitation to enter in faith into a companionship with God: the intercourse of Jesus of Nazareth with his fellow-men is an offer of salvation-imparted-by-God; it has to do with the coming rule of God, as proclaimed by him. This we must now examine in its various aspects.

A. THE 'BENEFICENT' REALITY (MK. 7:37) OF GOD'S LORDSHIP, MADE PRESENT IN JESUS' MIGHTY ACTS

*Literature.* J. Blank, 'Zur Christologie auserwählter Wunderberichte', *Schriftauslegung in Theorie und Praxis* (Munich 1969), 104–28; G. Delling, 'Botschaft und Wunder im Wirken Jesu', *Der historische Jesus und der kerygmatische Christus* (Berlin 1961²), 389–402; R. Formesyn, 'Le semeion johannique et le semeion hellénistique', ETL 38 (1962),

856–94; R. Fuller, *Interpreting the Miracles*, London 1966; E. Käsemann, 'Wunder', RGG³VI, 1835–7; K. Kertelge, *Die Wunder Jesu im Markus-evangelium*, Munich 1970; Fr. Lentzen-Deis, 'Die Wunder Jesu', ThPh 43 (1968), 392–402; J. B. Metz, 'Wunder', LThK X², 1263–5; Fr. Muszner, *Die Wunder Jesu*, Munich 1967; K. Niederwimmer, *Jesus* (Göttingen 1968), 32–6; W. A. de Pater, 'Wonder en wetenschap: een taalanalytische benadering', TvT 9 (1969), 11–54; R. Pesch, *Jesu ureigene Taten?* (Quaest. Disp., 52), Freiburg 1970; J. Roloff, *Das Kerygma*, 111–207; G. Schille, *Die urchristliche Wundertradition*, Stuttgart 1967; A. Suhl, *Die Wunder Jesu*, Gütersloh 1968; A. Vögtle, 'Wunder', LThK 10², 1255–61; 'Beweisen oder Zeichen?', *Herderkorrespondenz* 26 (1972), H. 10, 509–14.

(a) Jesus' miracles and the range of understanding

In the so-called missionary homilies edited by Luke but going back to older, proto-Christian traditions, we learn of the first Christians' testimony that Jesus 'went about doing good . . . in the country of the Jews' (Acts 10:38f). This 'doing good' is more specifically defined as healing the sick and driving out devils. This tallies with what the four gospels record about Jesus actively showing pity for the sick and those who by the standards of that time were held to be possessed by 'the demon' or by 'demons', 'the prisoners' whom the eschatological prophet was to set free (Isa. 61:1–2). In ancient categories this recollection of Jesus is often expressed through the term: 'Jesus the thaumaturgist' or 'miracle-worker'; in modern terms, put indeed into the words of Luke in his Acts: Jesus' active commitment in behalf of his fellow-man in distress, Jesus 'who goes about doing good', or as Mark has the people saying: 'He has done all things well; he even makes the deaf hear and the dumb speak' (Mk. 7:37b). Mark after all subsumes pre-gospel, early Christian traditions regarding 'miracles of Jesus' within the concept 'glad tidings of Jesus Christ' (Mk. 1:1). In these wonders, Mark is saying, Jesus makes gladness something real for a lot of people.

For some time now this whole complex of problems clustered around 'the miracles of Jesus' has been dominated in the modern literature on the one hand by apologetic motives which because of miraculous acts that rupture natural law are alleged to prove Jesus' divine mission, on the other hand by a positivistic *a priori* notion which at once expunges everything under the heading of 'gospel miracles' from the New Testament, or at any rate has interpreted them in a 'spiritual sense'.

Fortunately, at least in exegetical circles, this controversy is largely over, thanks to the growing awareness of a prior and more fundamental issue, namely, what are the evangelists really getting at in reporting the wonders performed by Jesus? Only when that question has been answered can we raise the second- or third-order question as to whether Jesus actually did perform miracles and, if so, which ones; in other words whether a historical motive has caused them to be faithfully handed down in the Jesus tradition, in which they are indeed so firmly ensconced.

Even so, the old way of stating the problem has not yet been entirely superseded, though the pendulum may have tended to swing the other way. Just as it used to be argued that Jesus performed acts beyond the limits of every law of nature, so now some would insist, no less apodictically, that Jesus did none of those miracles recounted in the gospels, but that he is in his own person 'the miracle', the miracle of unmerited love and forgiveness; that is what those miraculous legends are meant to bring home to us. Here we have, despite a kernel of truth, the reverse side or counterpart of what once passed for a picture of the historical Jesus. It looked very much like this: a Jesus who cures the blind and deaf, restores the lepers and the lame to health and raises the dead; a Jesus who drives out devils, quells a storm with a word or walks on water as though on solid ground, multiplies loaves so that no one sees it and yet all profit by it, who changes water into wine to oblige some merry wedding-guests, and so forth. Catalogued like that, it is evident on any historical view of tradition that various disparate literary genres in the gospels have really been torn out of their proper ambience, out of the context in which the evangelists themselves meant them to be understood. Then Jesus is indeed turned into a 'miracle-man' in whom we can no longer find any salvation. For even if Jesus had done all this, in a historical and literal sense, what would that signify for us here and now? After all, we no longer see instances of loaves being multiplied among us. For us water – however great our faith in him may be – is just water; and the dead no longer return. In his own day Jesus helped and healed a few; what does that signify for human kind? I remember having read somewhere: What is a remedial worker *now* to make of the miracles Jesus did then? Granted the historical fact that Jesus did feed around five thousand people in a miraculous way, what does that mean for the two-thirds of mankind who go hungry now? We are surely at liberty to conclude that Jesus' contemporaries must have understood by a 'miracle' something other than we do. Even thunder and lightning were 'marvels' of God's nature in those days, whereas on scientific grounds we, as we think, know better.[104] Anyone who recounts miracle-stories is already living in what is plainly a 'transitional world'; he is no longer a primitive for whom everything in fact is 'miraculous' and accounts of individual miracles make nonsense – even though he too recognizes gradations in the world of miracles; but he is not, on the other hand, a member of a secularized, technological welfare state in which there can no longer be any room for 'miracles'. For someone who within the totality of a positively meaningful account of things deliberately recounts miracle-stories as well, the world around him appears as in part rationally intelligible, in part eluding him, yet grounded in basic rules. The telling of marvels and miracles is a genre of human life that is perhaps familiar enough with modern laws of nature but knows that they constitute only a partial view of total reality, seen from one particular angle. Those who report such things would certainly not want to argue that in spite of it all, miracles are still possible in men's lives – for them, whether Jews, Greeks or Romans, that was at the time self-evident; but that this Jesus of all men should be 'doing miracles' everywhere causes astonishment at the identity of this person, whose origin everybody knows. The problem for these people is not the 'miracle'; but being confronted with the 'miracles of Jesus', that is a concrete challenge. That is the spirit in which we have to read the gospels. In Jesus something extraordinary has made its appearance within history, something which his opponents traced back to 'demonic sources', but his followers to an inexpressible closeness to the deepest core of all reality: God. This, for us, is 'what has to be interpreted': the reality that is the historical Jesus, who by his extraordinary conduct succeeded in engendering these two quite extreme, alternative interpretations: 'of God' or 'of the devil'. The fact is that such extreme verdicts are not reached in respect of any old nondescript, 'average person'; they presuppose some sort of 'marvellous phenomenon', perceived and acknowledged as such by all parties. This insight must on any historical reckoning precede any possible theory and argument, if the interpreter of the documents, and in the end the believer too, is not to miss the point of these narratives. To argue that 'modern scholarship' has after all clearly and definitely settled the 'miracle question' may be true (viewing it from one particular angle); but this gets nowhere near the heart of the New Testament problem and, what is more, is based on the false assumption that there is no longer room for an approach to reality which is not that of science. This also fails to ask about the intentions behind the reporting of these miracles in the New Testament, as widely practised in the ancient world, despite essential differences, compared with the New Testament. We must first understand what the New Testament writers' intentions were in reporting miracles before the historical question can assume its equally proper, but also properly located, importance.

## (b) Jesus' wonderful freedom 'to do good' (Mk. 3:4)

The fact is remarkable in itself that the profane Greek word for 'miracle' (*thauma*) does not occur in the gospels; they say only that certain sayings and actions of Jesus aroused a *thaumadzein* among the people, that is, made them feel surprise and amazement. In the gospels certain acts of Jesus are spoken of as being 'signs' (*sèmeia*) and 'mighty acts' (*dunameis*) or simply 'works of the Christ' (*ta erga tou Christou*).[105] This implies that as in former times God was able 'in a marvellous way' to help people who had faith in him, so he is doing that now in Jesus of Nazareth. Whether they are for Jesus or against him, what strikes the people with amazement at his behaviour is interpreted by anyone putting their faith in him as God's saving acts in Jesus of Nazareth. Jesus as it were underwrites God's help to people in distress.

The fact that Jesus' activity was open to a dual interpretation precisely by virtue of what was special and unique about it – 'of God' or 'of the devil' – must be a historical postulate, if we are to be able to understand on the one hand his execution and on the other his being 'hallowed' as Christ. For both these are facts of history and thus presuppose a prior phenomenon, 'wonderful' and at the same time provocative, albeit in human terms also disputable. In other words: both the favourably and unfavourably inclined interpretations of Jesus witness by their own reaction, pro or con, to the surprising quality of Jesus' manifestation. This is in my view the chief important datum in the whole of the 'miracle question', of which we should take most careful note, before the so-called 'real' question about the reason for these miracles in his life can be analysed.

And then it is more than obvious from the New Testament that 'miracles' there are not viewed in the context of our modern understanding or of the question whether or not laws of nature are being abrogated (this view is simply alien to both Old and New Testaments, because there things are what they are through God's ever newly creative, or 'heart-hardening', activity). They have to be viewed within the field of understanding (or interrogation) centred in 'the power of the evil one' as over against 'the power of God'. That is why it is 'expulsions of evil spirits' and healings of the sick (for the Jews illness, in the broadest sense of the word, means 'being in the power of the evil one') that play so central a role in the accounts of Jesus' miraculous acts (in the history of tradition they also form the earliest stage of the pre-canonical miracle tradition). As Jesus pursues his ministry and manifests himself, this in itself is regarded by the evil powers as an act of aggression (Mk. 1:23–24 and parallels; 5:7ff and parallels; 9:20–25). Against the evil and hurtful results produced by these powers Jesus sets only good actions, deeds of beneficence. That is the really striking thing in a human story that for many is above all a story of suffering: suffering under the power of evil. In the struggle between the good power of God and the demonic powers which afflict, torment and seduce people, therefore, Jesus assigns to himself an explicit function. Later on, Christians saw this well enough: as in the beginning at the creation God saw that everything was good, so now it is said of the eschatological prophet: 'He has done all things well' (Mk. 7:37), while Satan, the power of evil, is the one who makes people deaf, blind, leprous and dumb. The power of goodness on the other hand, as manifested in Jesus, delivers a man from all the trials of Satan. That is the ancient way, and the New Testament's way, of understanding what go by the name of Jesus' 'signs and mighty acts'. As for whether natural laws are being broken or respected, nobody has a thought about that, neither Jesus nor his auditors, participating in the event by approving or disapproving of it. The miraculous element that finds expression in Jesus is not a point for his opponents or for his supporters; but what does count is the ultimate interpretation of what both parties alike experience. It is relevant to note that the 'material' of the miracle-stories quite certainly comes from Galilee (north-east Galilee and the environs of the Lake) – the region where Jesus had originally resided and where he stayed to pursue his ministry the longest.[106] The purveyors of this miracle tradition regarding Jesus were initially the circle in which Jesus had been active during his Galilean ministry; thence that tradition came in contact with the other traditions of broader early Christian circles, into which they were integrated, albeit not without certain theological corrections (see Part Three: 'aretalogy').

In the miracle tradition we are confronted with a memory of Jesus of Nazareth as he came across more especially to the ordinary country folk of Galilee, neglected as they were by all religious movements and sectional interests. It is a striking fact that both John the Baptist and Jesus turned to that very same common people and were received by them enthusiastically. In that kind of setting the veneration felt for one who has done so much good naturally expands into a certain legend-making process in which, since power is put to the service of being and doing good, as with Jesus, it is the power that in particular affects the popular imagination. Indeed, from his miracle tradition Mark incorporates elements in which Jesus is depicted near enough as a 'village quack' (Mk. 7:31–37; 8:22–26) and magician (Mk. 5:1–20; 11:12–14, 20-22). In the gospels, though, we still can detect Jesus' attitude of reserve in regard to one-sided misrepresentation; but he takes this risk all the same.

In the Q community, which reports only two miracles of Jesus – an exorcism and an act of healing – in a very matter-of-fact style (and then only in its more recent stage), the theme so strikingly developed in that connection is the *source* of Jesus' astonishing activity, not the miracle itself (Lk. 11:14–23 parallel Mt. 12:22–30; Lk. 7:1–10 parallel Mt. 8: 5–13). In this tradition Jesus himself is saying: If I drive out devils 'with the finger of God' (Lk. 11:20) it must be obvious that God's rule has come upon you. The background here is late Jewish demonology: sickness (in this case a man is blind and dumb) derives from a demon, which is itself called dumb (Lk. 11:14). The expulsion of the dumb demon enables the sick man to speak and see again; and communication is restored. Such acts of exorcism are also to be found among Jesus' Jewish contemporaries (Mt. 12:27; Lk. 11:19). The point of the argument is rather: Why should they ascribe it to God, and Jesus not do so? Thus in the Q community the 'miracle' is in no way regarded as an unparalleled activity on Jesus' part, separating him off from his cultural and religious environment as a whole. And yet this health-imparting activity is given a deeper interpretation: here God's rule is already present. The driving out of demons and healing of the sick point in Jesus to the 'time of salvation' in the latter days, a time now dawning. God himself is active in Jesus ('with the finger of God', that is, in Semitic idiom, 'by God's intervention', Ex. 8:19; Dan. 9:10). This is 'realized' eschatology (in the context, however, of the Church's expectation of Jesus' speedy Parousia). This link between exorcism and the presence ('realization') of God's rule is evidently not something given in advance, either for Christian or for Jew. It presupposes that Jesus is the eschatological prophet.

The second story of a healing in the Q source (Lk. 7:1–10; Mt. 8: 5–13), where the servant or son of a centurion – a pagan – is cured, is a further illustration of this. The fact that it is an act of 'remote' healing is not meant to sensationalize the miracle here. Actually, all cures 'at a distance' in the New Testament have to do with 'pagans'; it is a consequence of the fact that Jews will not enter pagan homes, as the pagan Judaeophile centurion politely explains: 'I am not worthy to have you come under my roof' (Mt. 8:8). The heart of the matter lies in Jesus' *exousia*: he has complete power and authority, as has a centurion over his troops (Mt. 8:9); someone like that need only speak a word, and everybody complies. Thus the centurion acts on the belief that Jesus has only to issue a command and the disease will disappear, in other words, on a belief in the power of Jesus' word. The account of this healing has obviously been included by Q as a paradigm. The Q community is thereby able to present not so much a Christology as a soteriology: salvation in Jesus, imparted by God.[107]

Besides the reporting of these two miracles, it is in Jesus' reply to the question put by the disciples of John (the three pericopes form a single complex of tradition to exactly the same effect and therefore presumably with a similar intention) that the same recent Q community shows how it envisages 'miracles done by Jesus':[108] 'Go and tell John what you hear and see: the blind receive their sight and the lame walk, lepers are cleansed and the deaf hear, and the dead are raised up, and the poor have good news preached to them' (Mt. 11:4–5 parallel Lk. 7:18–23). This passage was for long regarded (in modern exegesis) as 'authentic Jesus material'; but P. Stuhlmacher[109] has fairly cogently demonstrated that it is an early Christian creation on the part of 'Christian prophets'. Matthew speaks in this connection of *ta erga tou Christou*, of Jesus' messianic activities. Even so, those 'works' typify not the messiah of the Davidic dynasty but the messianic 'eschatological prophet' as Judaism had envisaged that figure in the complex of tradition embodied in Isa. 26:19 (the dead are raised); 29:9–10, 18–19 (the blind see); 35:5–6, 8 (likewise the blind see); 42:18 (the deaf hear); 43:8 (the blind see, the deaf hear); 61:1–3 (those that mourn are comforted, to the poor the good news is proclaimed; see also 52:7). The Q logion is a fusion of various Isaianic texts: the miracle-catalogue of the Christ tradition associated with the latter-day prophet. It includes no references to the driving out of devils or to exorcism – nor indeed to lepers being healed or the dead being raised. These last are part of the general prophetic tradition (1 Kings 17:17–24; 2 Kings 4:18–37; 2 Kings 5). Moreover it would seem that Old Testament texts provide a model for the synoptic accounts of reviving the dead (see Mk. 5: 22–43; Lk. 7:11–17). It follows from all this that the distinctive character of miracles reported in the gospels concerning Jesus presupposes that he is to be identified with the 'messianic' eschatological prophet. In the recognition of Jesus as the eschatological prophet it is admittedly difficult to draw the lines before and after his death at all sharply (see Part Three). Nevertheless the secondary elements (healing of lepers and raising of the dead) in the account of Jesus' reply contain very well the principal meaning of this Q logion. Jesus is the eschatological prophet who performs the miracles expected of him (in this complex of tradition). The original form of this passage seems therefore to have been: 'The blind see, the lame walk, and to the poor the good news is proclaimed. Blessed is he who is not scandalized by me.'[110] The 'finger of God' is detectable here.[111] That Jesus is interpreted as the 'eschatological prophet', to whom in this tradition-complex (already interpreted within Judaism) particular miraculous 'acts of power' are attributed, means therefore that in the gospel accounts of those mighty acts we do not in every instance have to see a recollection of specific historical miracles of Jesus, but should see rather a recall of quite specific acts and miracles that justifiably gave occasion for identifying him with the eschatological prophet. Not until that (quite valid) identification had been made was it possible, without raising some fearful problems, to recount the miracles traditionally ascribed to the eschatological prophet as being now, 'very concretely', the acts of Jesus of Nazareth. Thus what is historical and what is 'kerygmatic' in the gospels often form together a tangle of interwoven threads difficult to tease apart. The Q logion and the synoptic logion of Jesus' reply to the question put by the disciples of John are therefore, although secondary, indeed witness on the one hand to the early Christian (pre-Easter?) identification of Jesus with the eschatological prophet (one of the fundamentals of this 'Christological test') and, on the other hand, to a very old miracle tradition regarding Jesus, which helped to make it possible to recognize him as the eschatological prophet. Again, it would appear from the temptation narratives in the Q source (Mt. 4:1–11; Lk. 4:1–13) that Jesus in this tradition refuses to perform 'legitimizing' miracles, without use or benefit to others but to his own advantage. Jesus does the miracles of the charismatic eschatological prophet, and no others. Through his miracles he brings a joyful message to the poor, not just in words but in actual fact. He is the eschatological prophet who brings the tidings of joy: 'Your God reigns' (Isa. 52:7; see 61:1). Even in these Isaianic passages, that the deaf hear and the blind see has a profound metaphorical significance: to be blind is a sign of separation from God; to see is to have access to salvation, and the 'eschatological prophet' is the 'light of the world' (Isa. 42:6–7). Jesus is enlightening and liberating for those who come to meet him. The early Christian tradition of 'miracles of Jesus' must be seen in the first instance, therefore (apart from the likewise important question of the historical authenticity of 'Jesus' miracles'), as evidence of a very ancient tradition that identifies Jesus of Nazareth with the eschatological prophet, as that notion had come down to the Judaism of the time from the 'Isaianic tradition' (Deutero-Isaiah and Trito-Isaiah) and had acquired (see Part Three) an even more pregnant significance in the more recent Jewish 'Solomonic' Wisdom literature. To some extent we are faced here with a 'hermeneutical circle' in which, historically speaking, the very marked activity of Jesus prompts us to recognize him as the 'eschatological prophet', while given that recognition, and bringing in the tradition of the eschatological prophet, people then unhesitatingly ascribe the 'traditionally received' miracles of the eschatological prophet in actual fact – and in very local Galilean guise – to this Jesus of Nazareth (thus identified). To put it crudely: once having acknowledged Jesus on historical grounds as the eschatological prophet, people could also ascribe to him, 'unhistorically', a number of miracles which in (historical) fact he never performed. In the field of literary scholarship this phenomenon is known as epic concentration. (For instance, the heroic deeds of other men were attributed to Charles the Great.) For anyone who keeps this hermeneutical circle in view (and historical facts are the only things to spark this off), the New Testament 'enlargement' of the field of vision (on the basis of already given, earlier complexes of tradition) will present no problem at all – unless to someone for whom religion is a computerized calculation. In that sense R. Pesch's distinction between 'Jesus' historical mighty acts' and their 'kerygmatic implication' is entirely right,[112] although with J. Roloff[113] we should perhaps admit, rather more than Pesch does, reminiscences of historical facts grounded in Jesus' actual life here on earth, because kerygmatic interpretation without any underlying historical fact is quite pointless and opens the door to a purely ideological superstructure, unrelated to the historical phenomenon of Jesus. But within the area of this circle between facts and interpretation, even the miracle-stories that without a directly historical basis in the life of Jesus of Nazareth are told in the gospels take on an eminently theological meaning. Without all this the subsequent resurrection-story would be left high and dry. The condition for any further, more profound interpretation was – and is – the historically grounded, though not apodictically imperative, identification of Jesus with the expected eschatological prophet; in other words, the final criterion even here remains the real, historical Jesus of Nazareth.

So there are indeed purely kerygmatic miracle-stories relating to Jesus, besides the marvellous acts – no doubt, ambivalent – which Jesus did in point of historical fact perform. This explains why there is among the majority of critical exegetes a growing conviction that Jesus carried out historical cures and exorcisms. Thus there is a historically firm basis for affirming, as the New Testament does, that Jesus acted as both healer and exorcist. The gospels make it clear that a salvation which does not manifest itself here and now, in respect of concrete, individual human beings, can have nothing in the way of 'glad tidings' about it. The dawning of God's rule becomes visible on this earth, within our history, through victory over the 'powers of evil'. This it is that the miracles of Jesus exemplify. In the struggle with evil Jesus is totally on the side of God. Jesus is a power of goodness that conquers Satan (Mk. 3:27 and parallels). In this real tender of salvation, actually present in Jesus' life here on earth, a Christological problem emerges in palpable form.

With two borderline cases one can show how on the one hand post-Easter experiences have affected miracle-narratives in the gospels, and how these have sometimes been 'presented' purely as illustrations of the Christian *kerygma*, and how on the other hand miracles have been reported on the grounds of plainly historical recollection.[114]

From a source peculiar to Matthew, Mt. 17:24–27 records a discourse on Temple taxation, to which a miracle has been appended: '. . . not to give offence to them, go to the sea and cast a hook, and take the first fish that comes up and when you open its mouth you will find a shekel; take that and give it to them for me and for yourself' (17:27). This motif from ancient fables was generally familiar at the time (especially in the form of a precious pearl in the mouth of a fish). Obviously, a fabulous motif is being employed here simply to say that should he need it Jesus has everything readily available, because the Father is looking after him. No reader at that time would have taken this passage literally. They understood it rather as a parable designed to illustrate the *kerygma*. This is why it is so difficult to subsume everything that appears in the gospels as 'miraculous' within the general concept of 'miracle-stories'; a whole range of diverse genres comes under that heading; and they do not all arise out of the miracle tradition.

As opposed to the 'non-miracle' of Mt. 17:27 – non-miracle, but parable or illustration of the belief that anyone who seeks first the kingdom of God will have all the rest thrown his way – we have the account of the healing of Peter's fever-stricken mother-in-law (Mk. 1:19–31 and parallels). Various linguistic signals in this story indicate that the passage itself is inviting us to regard the story as in substance a historical incident, even though the model used here is from a literary standpoint that of the miracle-story. It takes place in what is described as the house of Peter and Andrew; and the patient is Peter's mother-in-law. The healing occurs when Jesus happens to drop in, as it were, and so hears about the illness. A very simple miracle, done out of friendship. Obviously, there are remembered biographical details here, embedded in the tradition because of their particular connection with Peter. The homely facts have been preserved, without allegorical language of a poetic sort or the kind of embellishments we get in other cases. And Peter's mother-in-law, up and about again with health restored, at once sets about laying a meal (1:31b). The incident is reported here simply and solely because it happened and has a connection with Peter. Above all, it typifies Jesus. In Lk. 4:38–39 the illness is more grave; and a command is given to the fever as in a case of exorcism. Matthew 8:14–15 on the other hand schematizes the whole scene by confining the characters to Jesus and the ailing mother-in-law; here Jesus sees that she is ill and takes the initiative, without anybody else asking or suggesting a thing. Matthew rounds the whole matter off (along with a summary) by adding a reference to Isa. 53:4: 'He took our infirmities and bore our diseases' (Mt. 8:17), so conjoining the historical reminiscence with a post-Easter interpretation and making its theological implication perfectly clear.

Having taken a first look at Jesus' 'mighty acts' in broad terms – on evidence culled mainly from the Q tradition – we must now examine in more detail how the business of incorporating the miracle-strain from the Jesus tradition into the New Testament gospel tradition has helped to conserve and correct the older strands or has given them a different slant, from a particular theological point of view.

Starting from what within the synoptic context as a whole is a line of approach all its own, the Marcan gospel has geared the material presented to it – or at any rate parts thereof – into what it calls the *euaggelion*. The matter thus incorporated is substantially taken over by Matthew and Luke as well. Apart from this source, Matthew and Luke have only one miracle-story from the Q source (Mt. 8:5–13 = Lk. 7:1–10); and over and above that, Luke takes a number of miracles from a source or tradition peculiar to himself (Lk. 5:1–11; 7:11–17; 13:10–17; 14:1–6; 17:11–19). The material in the Marcan gospel is therefore the chief source of the synoptic tradition in this regard; but the virtually distinct sources and the different tradition that find their outlet in John are enough to show that there were present in early Christianity very wide-ranging miracle traditions relating to Jesus of Nazareth.

This is an arresting fact when we remember that Mk. 8:11–13 illustrates very clearly Jesus' opposition to any demand that he should 'supply signs' or perform miracles (see also Mt. 15:32–39). The source-element there, namely, Mk. 8:12, tallies with a Q logion (Mt. 12:39 and 16:4; Lk 11:29): 'Will this generation be given a sign? . . . It shall not be given.' The miracle refused here is envisaged in the Old Testament sense as *'oth*, that is, a legitimizing sign,[115] distinguished from miracles as 'mighty works' or acts of power (see Mk. 6:2, 5). It is from prophets that legitimizing signs are expected in the form of miracles. That Jesus was asked for a sign implies therefore that he was being asked for his credentials as a prophet – indeed, as the eschatological prophet. According to Mark Jesus refused to give such a miraculous sign. As Mark saw it, therefore, Jesus' actual miracles were good acts of power, corresponding to the need of the moment. The demand for a miracle-sign and its refusal actually follow upon the account of three miracles which Jesus had already performed (Mk. 7:24 – 8:10), thus making all the more evident the radical difference between 'mighty acts' and legitimizing miracle-signs. Mark has Jesus being asked for a 'miracle from heaven', that is, a quite peculiar and specific marvel, whereby God, for his part, would confirm and endorse Jesus' prophetic ministry; then everyone would know for sure that Jesus has been sent by God; then they would believe in him. In Mark's view that is precisely what Jesus declines to do: the earthly Jesus is and remains ambivalent during his lifetime; he must be accepted on trust. Jesus remains himself and will do no miracles 'to order' or as a 'canonical' proof of anything whatever, but solely to help people in dire need (Mk. 1:41; 5:19; 6:34; 8:2; 9:22; 10:47–48). Yet this is also still the best way of showing who he is: simply himself, 'going about doing good'. It in no way involves taking a stand for or against miracles: Mark is here concerned with a Christological issue – with Jesus' real personality and essential nature, just as elsewhere he has Jesus putting an embargo on all (in Mark's view) 'heretical' Christologies. Jesus does not seek to legitimize his mission and ministry; in whatever he does, including his miracles, he is simply himself.

Again in 13:21–23 Mark has Jesus warning us against false prophets who will arise in the last days and perform 'signs and mighty acts'. Here miraculous acts are linked especially with false prophecy, as in Deut. 13:2–4, where in the history of the tradition the term *sèmeia kai terata* pertains to the complex of the legitimation of an envoy from God. Jesus on the other hand is simply good for his fellows, and to that end performs sometimes surprising acts which can be interpreted in more than one way (see Mk. 3:22–30). Thus Mark will never speak of Jesus' salvific acts as *sèmeia kai terata*.[116] Jesus does not seek self-legitimation. He is not worried about his own identity but is himself, in all that he does; his identity is to identify himself with people in distress and fear in order to release them from their self-estrangement and restore them to themselves, so that they are made free again for others and for God.

Where editorial development is concerned, we can distinguish in the Marcan gospel three major groups of miracle-stories:[117] (a) healings and 'demon-expulsions' (Mk. 1 – 3, including the summary passages in 1:32–34 and 3:7–12 and 3:22–27); (b) the major 'mighty acts' recorded in 4:35 – 5:43, of which 6:1–6a provides a concluding interpretation; (c) various miracles in Galilee and its environs, in Mk. 6 – 8. After the digression of Mk. 8:27–30 (Peter's confession of the messiah, and the prospect of suffering) only two miracles, both accomplished with some difficulty, are reported: the cure of a boy possessed (9:14–29) and of a blind man (10:46–52).

In 1:32–34 Mark summarizes, as it were, 'a day's work for Jesus of Nazareth' as follows: he preaches in synagogues (1:21–28) and 'that evening, at sundown, they brought to him all who were sick or possessed with demons. And the whole city was gathered together about the door. And he healed many who were sick with various diseases, and cast out many demons' (1:32–34). Jesus conveys a message – the message of God's lordship and rule – in speech and action. This enshrines a recollection of the impression of potent goodness that Jesus has made on the people, although by now the post-Easter period has ensued, in which Jesus has for some time been venerated as the crucified-but-living One. Even so, one senses very clearly the awareness of the distance between now and then. As yet Mark wants to say no more than that this man, Jesus, during his earthly life was conspicuous among his fellows for his goodness and compassion. What lay behind that, what the source of this astonishing goodness was, is for the present left unsaid. At any rate, in Jesus salvation, a final good, has been encountered as a matter of personal experience. That a divine mystery lies hidden here is for the time being passed over in silence: 'I know who you are, the Holy One of God' (1:24), is the cry of the evil spirits; but on those who were possessed Jesus enjoins silence. For prior to Jesus' suffering and death this secret might be given a one-sided and totally false interpretation. The same embargo applies in Mk. 3:7–12; but in both cases the people cured speak out in spite of it. One thing constantly happening is that Jesus finds himself besieged by crowds of people, first by some from a limited distance around Capernaum in Galilee (1:21, 33), then from other quarters as well, from Judaea and even from pagan districts (Idumaea, Transjordan, Tyre and Sidon; 3:7–8). In the end a large crowd assembles wherever he appears (6:53–56), and he cures each and every disease, out of sheer compassion. One constant feature is that Jesus never himself takes the initiative in performing miracles. Those who come to him for healing he will not disappoint; he is unwilling to attribute to himself the role of healer, but he feels deeply for anyone at all who puts their trust in him (Mk. 5:25–34; Mt. 8:5–13 and parallel). If he notices some doubt on that score he holds back (Mk. 9:14–30 and parallels). To be close to Jesus is to experience a saving good. These acts of his, according to Mark, serve to express 'a new teaching with authority' (1:27). There is no distinction made here between 'sayings' (logia) and acts. Jesus' acts are in themselves 'a gospel'; the glad tidings to the poor consist in their being healed thanks to the presence of Jesus, it being on no occasion said that these people 'believe in him'. They simply come to him with their misery. Here salvation is given to people who in their sense of its opposite, of misery and evil, fulfil the only proper condition for eventually being able to receive the gospel as *glad* tidings. Jesus' being thronged by the people is like the helpless cry of mankind's ongoing calamity. At the same time it represents the hope which, thanks to Jesus, now enters into that sad history; someone who goes about doing nothing but good; a man in whom there is no evil. Although for the time being all this remains highly ambiguous, from Mark's point of view, essentially it reflects the impression Jesus made on so many people during his life on earth. Mark sampled that in the material handed on to him and he respected the purpose behind it and the central theme: the long course of accumulated human suffering, on the look-out for Jesus, who brings deliverance. But at the same time Mark sets an 'eschatological proviso' against the popular rush for salvation. He does so from the very start; but the meaning of it only becomes evident after the caesura in his gospel; Mk. 8:27, Peter's confession of the messiah, a 'triumphalism' which is immediately countered by Jesus and his opening up the prospect of suffering. From then on the report of the people's flocking to Jesus tails off and even ceases altogether. The people, whole towns, reject him. Thenceforward Jesus apparently withdraws from the mass of people and concentrates on

J.E.C.–G

special training for his disciples. The healing that even then follows in Bethsaida, where he is now repudiated (Mk. 8:22–26) (see also 7:31–36), is hard to accomplish, as unbelief encumbers the whole incident; it is also deliberately conducted out of sight of those present (likewise in Mk. 7:33). Jesus withdraws from the crowd and sets about training a central core of disciples.

Besides several general summaries of Jesus' miraculous activity (Mk. 1:32–34; 1:39; 3:7–12; 6:53–56) Mark also has sixteen separate miracle-stories. The very size of Jesus' 'miracle-repertoire' indicates that for Mark Jesus' miracles have a special significance for 'the gospel of Jesus Christ', which they do not have to the same extent in other early Christian traditions (the Q community only speaks of two miracles and then primarily apropos of a discussion arising out of them; Paul's gospel has nothing to say about Jesus' miracles). This would suggest (see above) that for Mark 'the gospel' by its very nature includes a historical recollection of what Jesus said and, more especially, what he did. Mark sets out to portray Jesus as someone who makes people glad, who does indeed bring them a *euaggelion*. In his narrative, therefore, Jesus' miracles have a significance as gospel: Jesus brings well-being, 'saving health', because he is the Son filled with the Spirit (Mk. 1:9–11). That is why Satan retreats where he appears (1:23–28); for where he enters the scene, God's rule, which he proclaims, is close at hand too (1:14–15). That is something the people who flock to him in their misfortune for healing and deliverance do not as yet perceive (and Mark for that matter nowhere attempts to criticize them for it): in Jesus one is faced with the reality of the kingdom of God, which is one of 'well-doing' (see Mk. 7:37). Only after his death, however, will this become completely clear in the experience of the Church, the community to which God's lordship has been revealed.

(c) Jesus' summons to faith in and return to God. Faith and mighty acts

In many places we find within the context of a miracle-narrative the expression 'your faith has saved you' or 'your faith is great, may it happen to you just as you wish'. This is obviously a set formula in the New Testament, whether addressed to the sick person himself (Mk. 5:34; Lk. 8:48; Mt. 9:22; Mk. 10:52; Lk. 18:42; Mt. 20:31; Mt. 9:29; Lk. 7:50; 17:19; Acts 3:16), or to his sponsor-companion (Mt. 8:13); sometimes in the form of an inducement to have faith (Mk. 5:36; Lk. 8:50; Mk. 9:23; Mt. 9:28), sometimes in that of a confirmation of faith already present (Mk. 2:5; Mt. 8:10; Lk. 7:9; Acts 14:9). So it turns out to be a fixed formula, associated with the class of 'healing-stories'. Besides that (and apart from the general use of the term 'believing' or 'having faith') the other thing referred to is the power of faith as over against the lack of it – but then exclusively in connection with the personal attitude of disciples following in the wake of Jesus (Mk. 11:23, parallels Mt. 21:21; Lk. 17:6; Mt. 17:20; lastly in three independent texts). Now the miracles in which 'saving faith' is the most, or next to the most, important issue Jesus does, broadly speaking, with 'outsiders' or with 'disciples' in a wider sense, all who ask him for help. A useful slant on the problems implied here is provided, it seems to me, by the story of the ten cured lepers, one of whom returns to Jesus (according to a peculiarly Lucan tradition; Lk. 17:11–19). The point of the story is that only one, having been cured, comes back to Jesus out of a 'personal change of heart' (in a secondary version this is further sharpened by making that one a Samaritan or semi-pagan, Lk. 17:16, 18). The salient point is that the other nine are also cured, but that the one who makes his way back to Jesus is told: 'Your faith has made you well' (Lk. 17:19). Only one of the ten has got the point of what Jesus has done: in going back to Jesus he has acknowledged that it was Jesus who had afforded him God's help. Nevertheless the others too were 'made well'; thus another form of trust is operative there. This instance is enough to show that the purpose of Jesus' mighty acts is to offer his fellow-man a saving fellowship with God.

Up to a point this is already apparent in Mk. 5:25–34: 'Daughter, your faith has made you well; go in peace, and be healed of your disease' (5:34). The sick woman had been at her wits' end for years, she had tried everything, and it had got worse and worse. Then she heard about Jesus. 'She . . . came up behind him in the crowd and touched his garment' (5:27). A desperate gesture on the part of an ordinary woman full of trust. And 'she was healed'. Faith here is more than a notion of a sort of magical transference of power – although the thing is presented as if some physical energy passed out of Jesus to the woman (5:30). But her faith has made her well, that is, the personal act of resorting to Jesus is the decisive factor here. Within her magical behaviour-pattern she has none the less sought God's help in Jesus.[118]

This narrative is woven into another miracle-story about the small daughter of Jairus, a ruler of the synagogue (Mk. 5:21–24, 35–43). During the 'interruption' caused by the events of the story just mentioned (Mk. 5:25–34) the girl dies. But: 'Do not be afraid, just go on having faith' (Mk. 5:36b); for after the ensuing fatal development they had tried to stop the ruler of the synagogue from pressing matters with Jesus any further. And: the faith with which you came to me, carry on with it, is the eventual reply. The point is: to go on hoping against hope and clinging to Jesus and expecting from him the help of God. 'To persist in having faith' here is not having an overall trust directly in God, but turning here and now to the person of Jesus, who provides assurance of God's help.

In Mk. 9:23 (9:14–29) it is expressly stated that 'all things are possible to him who believes'. First of all the disciples had tried to expel the evil spirit from the sick boy (9:14–18), 'and they were not able', whereupon Jesus says: 'O faithless generation' (9:18–19). However, the boy's father then says: 'I believe, help my unbelief' (9:24). Again, in the healing of the centurion's son or servant (Mt. 8:10b=Lk. 7:9b) the operative factor is the man's own faith in Jesus as one who being empowered by God, has commanding authority even over diseases; likewise with the healing of blind Bartimaeus (Mk. 10:46–52), who in the face of every obstacle to communication with Jesus manages to make personal contact and by that means, namely, by his faith, is made whole (10:52). In Nazareth itself Jesus is unable to carry out any mighty acts of goodness because of the unbelief of the inhabitants (Mk. 6:5–6, although Mt. 13:58 is less insistent that unbelief was universal in Nazareth). This seems to be a secondary account, but is consistent in following through the relationship between miracle and faith. In no way is it suggested that a miracle presupposes faith. The question is not whether the Nazarenes were unconvinced that Jesus really did have the power to work miracles; he was cold-shouldered there because his power was attributed to the demon (see 6:2b–6). In fact the people of Nazareth did believe that Jesus had power to perform miracles. But they were asking for miracles which would make no demand for *metanoia* or imply a call to fellowship with God (see Mt. 4:5–6; Jn. 6: 14–15). The 'faith and miracle' relationship in line with the aims Jesus has in view is encountered here in its starkest form: those 'mighty acts' of his are a constituent part of his mission to Israel, his commission to bring people to faith in God. The point of Jesus' whole ministry is to be the one who brings God's help, who proffers salvation; where this is not recognized his whole mission is misinterpreted, the kingdom of God and the 'works' of that kingdom are misunderstood; it is only in faith that they reach people. Jesus' mission to Israel is a summons to faith.

This is underlined by the faith of a non-Jewish woman (Mt. 15: 21–28, parallel in Mk. 7:24–30). Through Jesus this pagan expects the help of Israel's God. Matthew drives home the point, however, that Jesus' earthly mission is and remains only to the Jews (Mt. 15:23, 24, 26) and is not meant for 'the dogs', that is, the Gentiles; whereupon this heathen woman affirms her faith in Israel's God in a most disarming fashion by saying that 'even the dogs eat the crumbs that fall from their master's table' (15:27). Here (in a secondary text) faith is being expressed in God, the salvation first of Israel but then also of the Gentiles. At this Jesus says: 'Woman, great is your faith.' It is as the one-sent-to-Israel that Jesus acknowledges this faith. The Syro-Phoenician woman has what should be found in Israel: faith in Jesus as God's emissary to Israel. That is faith in Jesus prior to Easter. There is no call for it to be anything more. We shall see in a later chapter that Jesus' earthly mission is that of the 'son of David' to Israel, while only with the resurrection is he revealed by God as 'the universal Christ'. In tune with an early credal recognition of the earthly Jesus as the Solomonic 'son of David', sent exclusively to Israel, is the fact that in a lot of miracle-stories where there is talk of 'faith' and 'marvel' Jesus is deliberately called 'son of David' (Mt. 15:21–28; Mt. 12:23–24; 9:27, 33–34; 20:30; Mk. 10:47–48) in a post-Easter context, of course; but it reflects the historical motive, namely, that they wanted to speak about Jesus' life here on earth without substantially retouching the picture in the light of his exaltation. As son of David Jesus is for Israel, as the fulfilment of Israel's expectations (Mt. 15:22; 21:9, 15).[119] The faith for which in his days on earth Jesus looks to Israel is in the last analysis that people should believe in him as a (latter-day) emissary from God – a confidence in the person of one who would turn Israel back to God. Within that perspective, and only there, Jesus' mighty acts of goodness acquire their proper meaning and purpose. This becomes more obvious in secondary texts where certain trust in the person of Jesus (as it appears more generally from the primary texts) is merely given clearer definition. Whether there is a mention of faith before the miracle (Mk. 2:5; 5:36; 7:29; 9:23; Mt. 8:13; 9:29; 15:28) or after it (Mk. 5:34; Lk. 7:50; 17:19) makes no difference here; for at this point it is not a question of belief on the part of 'followers of Jesus', but of a (first) live encounter with Jesus. This is envisaged as an offer of salvation, of well-being, from God, an incitement to faith.

As distinct from this whole group of texts, therefore, there is another group in which, apropos of the attitude of Jesus' actual disciples, we hear of 'faith' and 'little faith' (*oligopistia*), a notion used a good deal especially by Matthew (Mt. 6:30; 8:26; 14:31; 16:8). These passages presuppose a habitual fellowship with Jesus, grounded in a

faith which yet, prior to his death, is constantly falling short and ending
in failure (Mk. 11:23, parallels in Mt. 21:21; Mt. 17:20; Lk. 17:6; Mk.
4:35–41). Admittedly, the sense of the term 'having faith' is not altered
here, but the words are set 'in a different context of meaning'.[120]
Linguistic signals in the text suggest that any miracles that may be told
with this theme in mind – with the stilling of the storm as a main
example (Mk. 4:35–41) – have a purpose different from that of the
miracles reported out of a historical concern with Jesus of Nazareth.
The fundamental point of the story here is: 'Why are you so afraid? Is
it still possible for you to be without faith?' (Mk. 4:40). The point at
issue is the already given belief of the disciples, which prior to Easter
keeps faltering. They have been such a long time with Jesus and yet
still have not realized that they therefore have nothing to fear, even
though their beloved master sleeps through a storm. The miracle is
not even necessary in that case, from their acquaintance with Jesus
they should have known better. After all, this is not their first contact
with Jesus, as is the case in pretty well all the miracle-stories proper;
concerned here are people who have already formed a bond of fellowship and faith with Jesus. 'Do you not care if we perish?' (Mk. 4:38)
assumes the mutual bond of faith. But then the disciples are blinkered;
hence the (Jewish) term 'you of little faith',[121] that is, not consistently
trusting to their faith-inspired fellowship with their master. In the
disciples at that moment the conduct of the sleeping Jesus creates no
confidence (as opposed to the 'faith and miracle' problem). The
miracle related is the gratuitous 'answer' to the doubt of people who
are in a believing fellowship with Jesus. Genuine faith makes that
miracle superfluous; and that of course is the point of the story (whatever the historical background giving rise to this piece of instruction
may have been). Even so, this pre-Easter faith is still a faithful confidence in Jesus of Nazareth himself, as warranty for the saving nearness of God. Faith means accepting that in Jesus a new fellowship with
God is being proffered, here and now during Jesus' days on earth, as is
clear from Mk. 11:23; Mt. 17:20; Lk. 17:6. If the faith of the disciples,
albeit 'as small as a mustard seed' (Mt. 17:20), is 'faith', then it can
move mountains. This has nothing whatever to do with the miraculous
power to curse a fig-tree or with a strong belief that will work 'wonders'. The wonder here lies much deeper and points to the wonder of
God's grace, in which we can trust at all times. The withered fig-tree
is a prophecy in action: an image of the coming judgement of God
upon Israel or upon Jerusalem. But: 'Have faith in God' (Mk. 11:22);
in face of this approaching judgement the disciples must continue to

rely on God's help; that is the original meaning of this piece of tradition, which Mark has now set in the context of prayer.[122]

Likewise the story of Peter walking over the water towards Jesus and sinking through lack of faith is not placed within the vista of miraculous acts but of Jesus' (and the Church's) appeal against a want of faith on the part of Jesus' disciples, who should know better (Mt. 14:18-32, from a source peculiar to Matthew). Such instances as, in particular, the withered fig-tree and the stilling of the storm are not meant to engender faith (as in the miracle proper), but by virtue of an already present faith-motivated fellowship with Jesus to expose the inconsistency of faithlessness. It is true to form that in the story of the loaves and fishes, despite all the revisions (doublets), according to Mark it is always the doubting disciples who do not know how Jesus will be able to feed such a crowd of people (Mk. 6:37; 8:4).

Those pre-Easter memories of what the habitual fellowship enjoyed, in faith, with Jesus of Nazareth signified – namely, that even the impossible is to be reckoned possible – were later on, after the disciples in their loss of faith had panicked and deserted their master at the time of his arrest, to play a major role in their return to Jesus, as *metanoia*, conversion to the Christ. For it might fairly be called a salient feature that the pre-Easter 'faith' (*pistis* and *pisteuein*), however much it may have to do in all the synoptic texts with an abiding or momentary and passing encounter with the person of Jesus (except for one passage overlaid with a post-Easter interpretation, Mt. 18:6), is never referred to as 'faith *in* Jesus', in the sense of *pisteuein eis*; in a New Testament context this is a post-Easter phenomenon.[123] The task of the earthly Jesus was to arouse an unconditional faith in God, albeit in relation to people who came into transient or continuing contact with him. After Easter the Church, being conscious of the distance between the situation then and its prevailing faith in the exalted Lord, continues despite every attempt at re-presentation to respect this difference in its account of the gospel. This shows the Church reflecting on the significance in its own right of Jesus' earthly life prior to Easter. In contrast to the post-Easter miracles in the Church – comforting signs of the exalted Lord working for the good of those who are already believers – the marvellous and powerful acts of the earthly Jesus are an offer of faith; the synoptic writers, in spite of their post-Easter situation, remain conscious of this distinction. It reveals their historical concern with the proper significance of the earthly Jesus: he proffers to people God's help and fellowship with God. At the same time this historical consideration itself entails a Christological concern: Who is this Jesus, who is able to extend to people the help of God? Who is this man who can arouse people's faith? In his earthly life Jesus shows himself to be the one who, through his very ministry, summons men to faith in God. That is the point and purpose of Jesus' mighty acts.


B.  JESUS' DEALINGS WITH PEOPLE LIBERATE THEM AND MAKE
THEM GLAD: JESUS AS COMPANION (AT TABLE)

*Literature.* G. Braumann, 'Die Schuldner und die Sünderin, Lc. 7: 36–50', NTS 10 (1963–4), 487–93; J. Delobel, 'L'onction par la pécheresse', ETL 42 (1966), 415–75; H. Drexler, 'Die grosse Sünderin Lk. 7:36–50', ZNW 59 (1968), 159–73; R. Feneberg, *Christliche Passafeier und Abendmahl*, Munich 1971; A. Heising, *Die Botschaft der Brotvermehrung*, Stuttgart 1966; O. Hofius, *Jesu Tischgemeinschaft mit dem Sündern*, Stuttgart 1967; B. van Iersel, 'La vocation de Lévi (Mk. 2:13–17; Mt. 9:9–13; Lk. 5:27–32)', *De Jésus aux Évangiles*, II (Gembloux 1967), 212–32; 'Die wunderbare Speisung und das Abendmahl', NovT 7 (1964–5), 167–94; J. Jeremias, 'Zöllner und Sünder', ZNW 30 (1931), 293–300; K. Kertelge, 'Die Vollmacht des Menschensohnes zur Sündenvergebung (Mk. 2:10)', *Orientierung an Jesus* (Freiburg 1973), 205–13; R. Pesch, 'Das Zöllnergastmahl (Mk. 2:15–17)', *Mélanges Bibliques, offertes au R.P.B. Rigaux* (Gembloux 1970), 63–87; 'Lévi-Matthäus (Mk. 2:14; Mt. 9:9; 10:3)', ZNW 59 (1968), 40–56; J. Roloff, *Das Kerygma*, 223–69; L. Schrottroff, 'Das Gleichnis vom verlorenen Sohn', ZThK 68 (1971), 27–52; H. Thyen, *Studien zur Sündenvergebung im Neuen Testament und seinen alttestamentlichen und jüdischen Voraussetzungen*, Göttingen 1970; A. Vögtle, 'Die Einladung zum grossen Gastmahl und zum königlichen Hochzeitsmahl', *Das Evangelium und die Evangelien* (Düsseldorf 1971), 171–218; U. Wilckens, 'Vergebung für die Sünderin (Lk. 7:36–50)', *Orientierung an Jesus*, loc. cit., 394–422.


It has already become apparent from his amazing acts of power in what way the concrete manifestation of Jesus, his presence with and approach to people – whether following him or else remaining 'outsiders' – meant for them both well-being and liberation. It is clear too from Jesus' attitude towards the Law and its Judaic, especially Aramaic, interpretation that in freeing the individual person he gives him back to himself in a joyful commitment to the living God. But because Jesus still feels 'the Law' to be a disclosure of God's will for men, this aspect

of his liberating presence and ministry among people has to be considered and interpreted in the context of his relationship with the Father
as that very attitude to life which makes for man's liberation. The next
stage of enquiry concerns the broad range of dealings Jesus had with
other people in the ordinary affairs of life, in eating and drinking with
his fellows, more especially in his going in search of 'that which is lost'
and his conviviality, shared with outcasts, with tax-gatherers and
sinners.

The best slant on this facet of Jesus' life on earth, it seems to me, is a
particular recollection of the disciples which was embedded firmly in
the primitive Christian tradition at an early stage, under the theme of
the disciples' 'non-fasting' in the living presence of Jesus (Mk. 2:18–22;
with variations in Mt. 9:14–17; Lk. 5:33–39).[124] In point of fact this
uncovers, indirectly, the secret of what the disciples who were Jesus'
followers in his lifetime experienced when they ate and drank in
company with Jesus of Nazareth.

(a) Being sad in Jesus' presence an existential impossibility: his
disciples 'do not fast'

In particular the wording of the narrative in Mk. 2:18–22 is such that –
with the provenance of the passage in mind – from the way it is composed it is still possible to have a vivid impression of what it recalls: the
living presence of Jesus, awakening joy and setting his disciples
free:

18–19a: 'Now John's disciples and the Pharisees were fasting; and
people came and said to him, "Why do John's disciples and
the disciples of the Pharisees fast, but your disciples do not
fast?" And Jesus said to them, "Can the wedding guests fast
while the bridegroom is with them?

19b: As long as they have the bridegroom with them, they cannot
fast.

20: The days will come when the bridegroom is taken away from
them, and then they will fast in that day.

21–22: No one sews a piece of unshrunk cloth on an old garment;
if he does, the patch tears away from it, the new from the old,
and a worse tear is made. And no one puts new wine into old
wineskins; if he does, the wine will burst the skins, and the
wine is lost, and so are the skins; but new wine is for fresh
skins." '

After Easter Christians remember Jesus' reactions to the impression John the Baptist had made on his contemporaries of being a strict ascetic; whereas Jesus gave the impression of being 'an eater and drinker' (Mk. 2:16) and, which was even more shocking, broke the Law by eating and drinking with tax-gatherers and sinners (Mk. 2:16). So as to avoid having to listen to either John or Jesus, people played the one prophet off against the other. The Matthean gospel had a very clear view of the situation. Matthew says: 'It is like children sitting in the market places and calling to their playmates: "We piped to you and you did not dance; we wailed, and you did not mourn." For John came neither eating nor drinking, and they say: "He has a demon"; the Son of man came eating and drinking, and they say: "Behold, a glutton and a drunkard, a friend of tax collectors and sinners!" ' That passage, Mt. 11:16–18, sketches just what the real issue was. It was the freedom exercised by Jesus and his disciples in their whole attitude to life that is being disputed here – not so much the question of fasting or not fasting as something of a casuistical-cum-structural problem for the Church, as so many commentaries would suggest. It goes deeper than that.

To this allegation Jesus' reply is brief and to the point: Friends (or guests) of the bridegroom do not fast while the bridegroom is with them (Mk. 2:19a). Put into our kind of language: at a wedding-party one doesn't abstain, everyone is there to live it up. Of course. Yet Jesus' retort is not so very banal or obvious – for the simple reason that a wedding-party is not what is actually at issue here. Admittedly, his reply is based on the notion of an ordinary experience that everybody takes for granted: one doesn't fast at wedding-parties. There is more to it than that, however.

Nor is this pericope in the gospel meant to give notice of a fundamental break on the part of Jesus with Jewish habits of fasting, whether obligatory or voluntary. Nowhere does Jesus criticize the fact that John's disciples do fast; and indeed it is certain that he set store by the *raison d'être* of the Temple, the sabbath rest, the synagogue and even the Jewish days of fasting (see further on). Actually, Jesus sees in the Law a token of God's goodwill and dealing mercifully with the Jews – for their salvation, but not for their undoing. Here, Jesus declares, is a clear and principal indication of how some people entrench themselves behind the letter of the Law so as to nullify the force of its deepest meaning: to mediate the mercy of God to men. As practised, Law and sabbath have been divorced from their main purpose and turned into an intolerable, crushing burden for the ordinary person. Jesus sees the duties entailed by the Law in the light of a God 'mindful of humanity'. Law should be a manifestation of God's mercy.

Against this background the glad tidings which Jesus is, light up at once: in the light of the Law the concrete person of Jesus appears as a manifestation of God's merciful dealing, at all events for anyone prepared to accept in the life and conduct of Jesus the near and helpful presence of God (Mt. 13:11). The man not prepared for this, the neutral onlooker or the one who believes only in the Law, fails to see that saving presence; instead he sees only the behaviour of Jesus and his followers, deviating from the Law, incomprehensible (Mk. 4:11–12), even exasperating (Mk. 6:2–3; see Mt. 11:6; 15:12).

The question all this raises is: Do you trust, yes or no? It is a matter of deciding for or against Jesus. The person who does give him their trust does so out of a conviction that in Jesus God's own concern for human beings has been manifested. So if this Jesus is present in the flesh among his disciples, for anyone committed in trust to him there can only be reason for gladness. In that case you don't think about fasting. The point, therefore, of the story is: this Jesus, palpable manifestation of God's merciful dealing with man, is present in person here among his disciples. That John the Baptist's disciples should fast, all right, fair enough – say nothing against it. But if Jesus' disciples should fast now, that would be to disregard the concrete situation, namely, the presence of salvation in the actual person of Jesus of Nazareth. The disciples' being together with this Jesus is in essence a festive celebration of good fellowship, a meal prepared by Jesus himself, and a fellowship in which there is salvation. The time that Jesus spent among people who, though perhaps failing as yet to understand him, followed him with enthusiasm and in total commitment is a very special time. So Jesus' presence becomes a living dispensation from fasting and mourning.

It is evident from this that Jesus never takes abstractions or general norms as a basis for living: always he sees a man in his most concrete situation. That is why he was able to surprise other people and take them unawares with his profound humanness. Although his disciples did not always understand precisely what he was getting at, at any rate they were certainly carried away by their master, Jesus – they simply adored him because they knew: in him we are aware of receiving a gift, a present from God to us. When you are so taken up with someone, while his living presence is with you, you are not going to fast and weep and adopt an ascetic role. It is noticeable that this fasting-pericope nowhere says that Jesus himself does not fast; it centres

around something his disciples are taxed with (verse 18). Jesus defends
their conduct and justifies it when he says: What do you expect, they've
a sense of well-being and happiness. That is a clear provocation, and
invitation, to acknowledge or to reject him as a gift from God – but
faced with a provocation like that one is bound to take sides. In this as
in every gospel story the central question is: 'But you, who do you say
that I am?' Whereas John's call to conversion was essentially bound up
with ascetic, penitential practices, the call of Jesus seems to have a
fundamental connection with being a table-companion, eating and
drinking together with Jesus, an activity in which Jesus' disciples
could legitimately feel that the 'latter-day', that is, crucial and definitive,
exercise of God's mercy was already present. To believe in Jesus is to
put one's trust gladly in God; that is no occasion for fasting. As regards
the explicit phraseology used here in the telling, the recollections of all
this have undoubtedly been 'over-exposed' to the Easter experiences,
but they remain historically reliable reminiscences about personal contact with Jesus and how heartening it was.

But after his death Jesus' disciples express their misgiving: Where
do we find ourselves now that he has been taken from us? This is what
Mark is trying to make clear in 2:19b–20. It brings out (what has been
repeatedly mentioned already) Mark's view as distinct from other early
Christian interpretations. Mark's community, recalling and faithfully
passing on these sayings of Jesus after his death, saw itself to be faced
with a serious problem. It realized that now Jesus was dead, convivial
fellowship and companionship with the living Jesus was no longer
possible. What now? Hence the later interpolation of verses 19b and
20; they are a sort of retrospective musing on the part of Mark's community. This Christian group applies the old sayings of Jesus to its own
new situation, created by his absence. It spontaneously corroborates
Jesus' words and says: 'As long as they have the bridegroom with them
they cannot fast. The days will come when the bridegroom is taken
away from them, and then they will fast in that day.' These are no
longer Jesus' own words but the reflection of Christians upon them,
now that Jesus has gone. That is movingly evident from the way in
which the old memories of the disciples' intercourse with Jesus in his
lifetime are spoken of here. These Christians are keenly sensible of the
difference between now and then. The tone of the passage is heart-
rending: when Jesus was still there – it is saying – they could not fast,
they were in no position to do that: because of Jesus' living presence.
The non-fasting of the disciples at that time was in no way a kind of
juridical dispensation from fasting, but a question of being existentially

unable to do otherwise. In these words are revealed something of the enchantment and the power exercised upon them by the living Jesus of Nazareth. The Christian tradition has preserved this memory with the utmost care; for apart from that spell-binding quality Christianity would never have become a fact of history.

But there is also the initial reaction, the reverse side of the coin. For then comes the sober reflection: now, in our situation, this Jesus has been removed from among us. Jesus is dead. Now we may fast, now we may weep – for in biblical terms that is one and the same thing.

The situation is clearly defined in these verses by the contrast: joy and grief – presence and absence. In this passage we are confronted with a community which, although believing in Jesus' resurrection, pending his Parousia now lives in the absence of its Lord – a community which is not filled with joy, like for instance the Pauline churches who believe in the operative presence of the already exalted Jesus Christ (see also Acts 2:46), but which, although assisted by the Spirit, in fasting, sorrowing and suffering is looking forward to the speedy and gladdening return of Jesus.[125] The fact that Jesus had been removed from their midst was not to be ignored. They did indeed long ardently for his return; but meanwhile they felt themselves orphaned, desolate and left to fast in sorrow.

Yet verse 20 here does not point to any rule in the Church about fasting. There is a deeper reason; just as the disciples were unable to fast when Jesus was still with them – how should they – so now they must indeed fast, out of sorrowing: in other words, they cannot eat for sorrowing. That is manifestly the tenor of verses 19b and 20.

And yet – this melancholic reverie is lighted by an element of new and happy hope. For the process of looking back to the fellowship enjoyed with Jesus in the days when he was still alive opens up the prospect of the coming but still pending fellowship with the returning Christ. Strikingly enough, whereas in the preceding, earlier reminiscent text the expressions 'the bridegroom' and 'the wedding-feast' were only images and analogies, now – in the second, retrospective version – they have ceased to be analogical: here Jesus is, speaking Christologically, 'the bridegroom' of the Church. That he is and remains even now (see Mt. 25:1–13; Rev. 22:17; 2 Cor. 11:2; Ephes. 5:21–33), although removed from our history. He is coming back.

The rest of Mark's fasting-pericope[126] is not directly relevant to the present argument. It is important to note, however, that the *de facto* presence of Jesus among us – as regards his contemporaries, during his days on earth; for Christians, as the hope of soon being togethe with the coming Jesus-son of man – means joy and liberation for those permitted to enjoy that presence. The Marcan community does remember that from the time of Jesus' days on earth. Jesus showed himself then to be a man of liberty, a free man, whose sovereign freedom never worked to his own advantage but always to the benefit of others, as an expression of God's free and loving approach to men. That sort of disconcerting freedom of an individual in face of Law and sabbath, and yet having a respect for their real meaning and purpose, which in practice had been wrongly used against God's saving purposes and so against man, instead of serving him and setting him free, was a thorn in the flesh of those unwilling to see in Jesus' manner of life a parable of God's turning towards us with his help – towards us who on personal and social grounds are such very un-free people. Such a human freedom-in-the-service-of-the-other, intended to liberate especially the person who is – in whatever respect – unfree, is incompatible with what the Marcan gospel calls 'the old'. We might say it is incompatible with the accustomed course, officially regarded as 'normal', of the sufferings endured by the 'mass' of humanity, which the leaders of the people neither noticed nor cared about. Indeed, by way of a minor, as it were, marginal incident in the life of Jesus – the fact that his disciples did not fast – Mark manages to portray the new thing that has been manifested in Jesus, in a masterly fashion at once true to Jesus and yet extremely personal. Mark's message is that with Jesus a radically new change has entered our history, a stumbling-block to the man scandalized by him, but the salvation of anyone who commits himself in trust to the mystery of this person, Jesus.

This non-fasting of Jesus' disciples while he was present with them points indirectly to the positive meaning of their fellowship at table with the earthly Jesus; and this is important in the life of Jesus of Nazareth – so much so that it has given rise to the process of 'legend-forming'. Here it is 'the legend' above all that is the surest guarantee of what is being recollected: namely, the day-to-day intercourse of the disciples with Jesus.

(b) Jesus' eating and drinking in fellowship with his own and with 'outcasts', tax-gatherers and sinners, brings freedom and salvation

(i) *The eschatological messenger of God's openness towards sinners*

In no less than four traditions we hear tell of Jesus' having social intercourse and even (what was forbidden among the Jews) sharing a meal with sinners;[127] again, there are many parables that speak of going in

search of what has been lost and, in the end, of God's kingdom being
promised 'to tax-collectors and harlots' (Mt. 21:31b) – obviously
passages in which the Christian community is expressing in realistic
terms what these people had experienced of Jesus' contact with sinners.
The memory of that impression is caught most brilliantly in the story
(albeit overlaid by ecclesial, even liturgical, considerations) found in
Lk. 7:36–50 (from SL) about the 'woman who was a great sinner' –
perhaps an instance where, along with Jesus' telling of a parable, we
have also been given the concrete circumstances that prompted Jesus
to tell it.[128] A Pharisee had invited Jesus to a meal (apparently because
of his fame as a prophet). 'And behold', a woman held officially to be of
ill repute (thought with good reason to be a prostitute) hears that Jesus
is there; she comes up to him, washes his feet 'with her tears', dries
them with her hair and kisses his feet (also anointing them with oil). It
dismays the Pharisee to see how Jesus ventures to let himself be touched
by a sinful woman; such a man cannot be a prophet. It occurs to the
Pharisee that Jesus does not realize he has to do here with a sinful
woman; if he did, he would certainly rebuff her – so he has none of the
prophetic gifts. But the point of the story in Luke is that the Pharisee
'thought to himself', he did not speak out, and that as he was talking
Jesus divined that secret thought of his, and so let it be known *en
passant*, as it were, that of course he knew he was dealing with such a
woman and was prepared none the less to submit to the washing. That
is the point. And then Jesus tells a parable: 'A certain creditor had two
debtors . . .' (Lk. 7:41–43). He forgave both of them their debt, the big
one and the small. 'Now which of them will love him more?' (7:42).
'Therefore, I tell you, her sins, which are many, are forgiven, for she
loved much' (7:47). Only at this point in the Lucan story does it appear
that the woman has fulfilled the duties of the host, who (somewhat
improbably) had neglected them; and she did so unstintingly – being
in that respect like the debtor who had had the biggest debt forgiven
him: thus she loves all the more. This makes the actual host, who had
skimped his duties, the debtor who had the smallest debt remitted. The
Pharisee's attitude here as in the parable of the Pharisee and the
Publican (Lk. 18:9–14) – despite his legally correct aloofness towards
sinners – turns out to be negative, in contrast to the behaviour of the
sinful woman. 'Your faith has saved you' (7:50). 'Faith' here is all at
once made to relate to the 'forgiveness of sins', thus affirming once
again (see above: 'faith and miracles') that faith entails an attitude of
*metanoia* with regard to the (saving) fellowship offered by Jesus. The
woman's display of love and the forgiveness promised by Jesus are to

be understood in the context of the saving fellowship that is brought about in this event. The very presence of Jesus is a proffer of salvation in fellowship which is grasped in faith by the sinful woman. Jesus let the woman carry on, not because he failed to realize that she was a sinner but precisely because she was that: in order to open up a forgiving fellowship for the one who had sinned. It was this that prompted the woman to be so very generous with her service. Exegetes argue fiercely – on confessional lines, even – over whether the woman's faith and love here are a consequence or a condition of Jesus' forgiveness. The account given by Luke is indeed complicated by contamination with another tradition, namely, that of the anointing of Jesus by a woman (Mk. 14:3–9). This anointing is not in the tradition on which Lk. 7:35–50 is based (it does not actually fit in with it). Luke 7:44–46 also appears to be secondary,[129] in view of the introduction of the anointing incident from Mk. 14; Luke himself wants to bring out a contrast between the Pharisee and the sinful woman. But the difference in remission of a (large and small) debt issues (according to the actual gist of the parable) in a greater love on the part of the person to whom the biggest debt is forgiven. The measure of forgiving is the measure of the responsive love, and not vice versa. Everything is forgiven to both, without limit; therefore the greatest sinner has the greatest love. Therein lies the shock administered by the parable (see too the parable of the Labourers in the Vineyard, Mt. 20:14) – and that is said with the Pharisee's proud fidelity to the Law in view. The sinner-woman recognizes the kingdom of God in Jesus: and that is just what the Pharisee does not do. So she has the greater love; for the least in the kingdom of God is greater, even, than a John the Baptist. Letting Jesus turn her to God makes this woman greater than the Pharisee, who is indeed observant of the Law and only to a minor extent in debt to God (see the parable of the elder brother of the Prodigal Son, Lk. 15:12–32, and of the Pharisee and the Publican, Lk. 18:9–14; cf. also the parable of the Two Sons, Mt. 21:28–31). It may fairly be said (on the strength of Jewish parallels) that this narrative belongs within the Christian tradition of a 'conversion story' (and has acquired its *Sitz* in the liturgy of Christian baptism), but as a source of inspiration it goes back in substance to Jesus' care and concern to bring salvation to sinners.

The second passage in which – after Easter – the authority to forgive sins is expressly attributed to Jesus is Mk. 2:10: 'The son of man has authority on earth to forgive sins' (with parallels in Mt. 9:6, 8 and Lk. 5:20–26). Neither in the Danielic tradition of the son of man, which certainly mentions his 'plenary power' (*exousia*), nor in the subsequent Jewish apocalyptic tradition of the son of man is the activity of forgiving sin ever ascribed to him. In Judaism God alone can forgive sins, although according to the Jewish 'threshold-liturgy' the high priest may indeed pronounce somebody 'free of sins', in the sense of adjudging him worthy to take his place in the forefront of the Temple. Forgiving sin is God's exclusive privilege. Even in the Jewish tradition of messianic expectation, while the 'latter-day' messiah may intercede with God on the sinner's behalf, he cannot forgive any sins.[130] To ascribe that sort of authority to a human being is blasphemous (Mk. 2:7; Lk. 5:21; Mt. 9:3). That Jews – which the first Christians were – should after Easter ascribe the power to forgive sins to Jesus cannot be explained, therefore, on the basis of already existing Jewish models (in this respect there are none), but (if it is not to be post-Easter ideology) on that of real facts in the life of the historical Jesus himself: in his liberating intercourse with sinners.

Both for the Jews and for Jewish Christians the remission of sins is an eschatological doing of God. In the oldest, purely eschatological interpretation of Jesus as the coming son of man redemption and the remission of sins still appear to be for some Christians a purely eschatological occurrence. The baptism of John too (according to Mk. 1:4) was not a means of remitting sins, but established a link between this act of *metanoia* and eschatological indemnity against God's wrath (or eschatological deliverance).[131] Again, in the Lord's Prayer from the oldest Q stratum (Lk. 11:1–4; Mt. 6:9–13) the forgiveness of sins is petitioned for as a coming eschatological event.[132] That in itself tells us that there are only two bits of primitive Christian tradition which refer to an explicit forgiving of sins by the earthly Jesus (Mk. 2:10 and Lk. 7:36–50). This indicates that – however early it may be – the explicit recognition of Jesus' authority to be able to forgive sins during his life on earth already presupposes an explicit acknowledgement of the risen Jesus as the coming eschatological son of man (a first, Aramaic Jewish-Christian phase) and furthermore (in a second Greek Jewish-Christian phase) the identification of the earthly Jesus with the coming son of man. Thus in Mk. 2:10 there surfaces an explicit awareness that the eschatological remission of sins by God was already operative in the earthly Jesus himself as the eschatological son of man; in it is made explicit, after Easter, the profoundest meaning of Jesus' historical intercourse with sinners, and then still with a degree of reserve: the son of man has authority to forgive sins. This is a pre-Marcan tradition, in which 'the son of man' has already become a

Christological title,[133] in the oldest stratum with an exclusively eschatological significance, afterwards applied also to the earthly Jesus. To
this Mk. 2:10 (cf. 2:28) already witnesses. That Jesus 'came not to call
the righteous but sinners' (Mk. 2:17) is thus based on historical recollections of Jesus' liberating intercourse with sinful people, the eschatological character of which was expressly recognized later on.

We should notice, however, that except for Mk. 2:10 and 2:18 – the
son of man has authority to forgive sins; and, the son of man is Lord of
the sabbath – the evangelist only starts to use 'son of man' as a title on
his own initiative at Mk. 8:31, the moment Jesus withdraws from the
people to concentrate specifically on training the disciples. This shows
on the one hand that Mark found the term 'son of man' as a Christological title already present (in 2:10 and 2:18) within his tradition, on the
other that for him 'son of man' is a (Christological) title certainly
understood by the disciples, but not by Jesus' opponents (in so far as
this title is applied to the earthly Jesus). In this sense, even in Mk.
2:10, the implication of the 'Jesus-saying' about the son of man's
power to forgive sins, where its meaning in Mark's narrative is concerned, remains concealed from Jesus' opponents. Hidden from the
antagonists of Jesus is God's eschatological power to forgive sins, to
the eye of the believer already visibly operative in the earthly Jesus –
this is what Mk. 2:10 is meant to make clear to us.

This acknowledgement of Jesus' power to forgive sins is explicit on
the Church's part, though appearing in the synoptic gospels in only
two pericopes; and that it is merely translating into the language of the
Church's faith what actually occurred in Jesus' intercourse with sinners
is obvious most of all from Mark's account of a dinner-party for tax-
collectors, attended by Jesus, at the house of the tax-gatherer Levi, son
of Alpheus (Mk. 2:15–17; see Mt. 9:10–13; Lk. 5:29–32). The provenance of Mk. 2:15–17 has this history: starting from the historical
recollection of a quite concrete event in Jesus' earthly life, via a
primary development into an orally transmitted Jesus logion, and an
initial pulling together of these within a grouping of what the exegetes
call 'disputations' of Jesus with his opponents, and via an updating
of this tradition by the Church in the pre-Marcan tradition; finally by
way of Mark's redaction incorporated in his gospel with a quite
specific theological purpose.[134] No need to justify here this complex,
yet plausible and transparently clear process; we are concerned here
only with the result.

The earliest phase of the tradition stems from a historical event. A number of tax-collectors threw a party[135] and Jesus was invited to go (thus he was not himself the host); at the home of Levi, the son of Alpheus (one of the linguistic signals, at any rate in a 'disputation', pointing to a historical reminiscence). This came to the ears of the 'scribes of the Pharisees', in Galilee those suitably empowered to watch that the regulations as to cleanliness were observed, not least in regard to social contact with sinners.[136] So of course they objected to Jesus' behaviour in this instance. The earliest phase of the tradition went more or less as follows: 'And it happened that Jesus was a guest in the house of Levi, son of Alpheus, and a large number of tax-collectors were staying *with him* [*Levi*]' (verse 15). The Pharisaic Scribes who saw him eating with tax-collectors said to us: 'He is eating with sinners' (verse 16); 'Jesus heard of this and said to them: I have not come to call the righteous but sinners' (verse 17ac).[137] We can still hear echoes in that passage of a concrete, historical incident as reported by the disciples, in the tradition through which the memory of it has come down to us. For B. van Iersel, as also for R. Pesch, Mk. 2:17c is an authentic Jesus-saying.[138] 'I have come to call . . .'; 'to call' here implies the task of the servant-messenger who conveys the host's invitation to those he is inviting (see above: the parable of the Reluctant Wedding-guests). Although himself Levi's guest, Jesus sees his own sharing of a meal in company with a lot of tax-collectors in the light of his role as the 'eschatological messenger' of God, that is, as the one who proclaims the near approach of God's lordship and rule and brings to tax-collectors (that is, sinners) on God's behalf the invitation to the great eschatological feast of fellowship with God (Mt. 22:1–14; Lk. 14:16–24). The contrast in Mk. 2:17c is between 'the righteous' (*sadikim*) and 'sinners' – a Jewish contrast (as in a later phase of the very early Christian tradition the Christians come to regard themselves as 'the righteous',[139] so that this logion can hardly have been formed at that subsequent stage of primitive Christianity). The notions coupled together here – 'the righteous' and 'sinners' – do indeed turn up in other layers of the Jesus tradition (Lk. 18:9–13; Lk. 15:7). The *sadikim* or righteous are by no means excluded from the divine invitation brought by the eschatological messenger; what Jesus means is to include those who are excluded by the Pharisees because of the (ritual) cleanness-regulations (no intercourse with sinners). From the viewpoint of official Judaic piety Jesus has 'de-classed' himself by eating with tax-collectors. His self-defence is that it is precisely to sinners, to those beyond the pale, that the invitation to communication must be carried: the sinners must be invited to God's table and his fellowship with human beings, in order to bring them out of their isolation. The sheep that is lost and isolated from the flock must be searched out (Lk. 15:1-8; 19:10; Mt. 9:36; 10:6; 15:24). Jesus, who in his life here on earth has been called to Israel, in order to gather all Israel together under the good shepherd, Israel's God, knows (for that very reason) that he is sent especially to the sinners, the outcasts.

What turns out, therefore, to be the oldest core of what Mk. 2:15-17 is telling us – and it goes back to Jesus himself – is Jesus' special care for sinners, firm in the conviction and knowledge that he has been sent to carry to the outcasts, and to them in particular, the message of restored communication with God and with other human beings: thus in actual fact he is bringing the message of God's coming rule. The very fact that Jesus seeks encounter with them, offering them this fellowship-with-Jesus, breaks through their isolation and gives sinners the chance 'to repent and be converted', the possibility of hearing about the invitation from the kingdom of God, first and foremost in actual fact.[140] The Christian community, therefore, has in no way distorted its picture of his life on earth when it explicitly ascribes 'the authority to forgive sins' to the earthly Jesus (see above).

Mark now slots into this block of disputations (2:1-3, 6) the scene where Levi is called to become a disciple of Jesus (Mk. 2:13-14). Thus Mk. 2:1-3 stands within the Marcan gospel in the magnificent perspective of Jesus' freedom 'to do good' (Mk. 3:4). Jesus' making contact with the sinner, Levi, led to the man's *metanoia*; he turned himself into a disciple of Jesus. (Thus solidarity with sinners is also part of the mandate given to Jesus' disciples.) This solidarity Jesus had with sinners, his contact with sinful people, aimed at opening up communication with God and with men, is indeed a 'being delivered into the hands of sinners'; solidarity of that kind, mingling with sinners, is for their salvation: Jesus means in that way to open up communication; his being delivered into the hands of sinners (Mk. 9:31 with 14:41) is for Mark at the same time the real import of Jesus' death: the 'saving gift' to sinners, so to 'mix with sinners' that in the end he himself goes to the wall. From 3:6 onwards, therefore, this is what Mark declares to be the prospect. Jesus' death becomes the seal set on a life with the conscious calling to invite sinners into fellowship: the eschatological fellowship with God, a foretaste of which may be experienced when we extend forgiveness to our fellow-man (Mk. 11:25; Mt. 6:14-15; 18:21-35).

Although coloured by the gospel narrative, both the story of Jesus' meeting with the 'woman who was a great sinner' and that of his having something to eat with a crowd of tax-collectors derive from facts historically grounded in Jesus' life on earth, so that we catch sight here of a very important facet of that life. Then again, this feature of his life is of a piece with the profoundest intentions of many of his parables as also of his mighty acts, so that we are bound to conclude: in Jesus' earthly career and ministry we are seeing demonstrated the praxis of the kingdom of God which he preached and implemented. In his earthly, historical life the eschatological praxis of the coming rule of God is already coming into view within the dimension of our human history here on earth. More and more insistently the idea presses upon us: in this concrete Jesus-phenomenon, proclamation, praxis and person cannot, it seems, be separated. Jesus identifies himself with God's cause as being man's also.

### (ii) Jesus as host: a copious gift of God

There is yet another aspect which allows us to reach even further into Jesus' dealings with people, with sinners, as friend and fellow. So far we have been concerned with cases where Jesus is someone else's guest, and not himself the host. Where indeed could he – the wandering preacher – play host but under the open sky? However, there is a particular exception to that, the farewell meal (Last Supper), for there 'He broke the bread and passed it round', that is, himself acted as the host, who does the inviting. In these instances where his 'eating with sinners' is not to the fore, what stands out particularly is the sheer abundance of Jesus' gifts, in the reminiscence of early Christian traditions. Although he had not a stone on which to lay his head (Mt. 8:20; Lk. 9:58), he and his disciples, even the listening bystanders, never went short of anything. This works on the imagination and is conducive, of course, to legend-building. But legend itself reveals a core of history without which the legend-forming process is impossible.

It must have made an indelible impression; for not only do all four gospel writers have the story of the 'multiplication of the loaves' (Mk. 6:34–44; parallels Mt. 14:14–21; Lk. 9:11b–17; Mk. 8:1–9; parallels Mt. 15:32–38 with 16:5–12; Jn. 6:1–15), but some even have it in doublets (Mark and Matthew). The fact – already mentioned earlier on – that in the Q tradition Jesus refuses messianic 'manna miracles', whereas here something like a manna miracle is reported none the less (although only the Johannine gospel alludes to it), suggests that within the history of tradition the 'miraculous feeding' belongs less in the miracle tradition than in another corpus with different intentions. This at once gives us, on the basis of the gospel text itself, a main pointer to the interpretation of this story: its basic purpose is not to rehearse a miracle. The very nature of this complex of tradition requires it – and not *a priori* bias, whether modern or not, against miracle.

The first striking thing about the story of the 'fellowship-meal' (in the open air) is the fact that Jesus himself enacts the role of host: he actually blesses and breaks the bread, proffers it and passes it round.[141] This account condenses a basic feature of Jesus' manner of offering fellowship during his days on earth: its focus is a companionship shared at table. The historical recollection of this meal-sharing fellowship between Jesus and his friends, however, is partly overlaid with legend from the post-Easter situation, so that the narrative gives an impression of setting out to relate a 'nature miracle'. The only point we need consider about this is whether the 'touching up' is to be attributed to post-Easter eucharistic observances and other ecclesiological situations, or is owing to the extremely powerful, well-nigh legend-making impact that their fellowship at table with Jesus made on his disciples.[142] H. Lietzmann and E. Lohmeyer have worked out a thesis according to which the eucharist in the primitive Church has a dual origin: on the one hand it is said to be grounded in the memories preserved among the earliest local churches of Palestine of the disciples' daily companionship at table with Jesus; the feeding miracle is in that case a retrospective thematizing of those meals and also the type of the Christians' festive meals after Easter, to which the *anamnesis* of Jesus' death was quite foreign; on the other hand the eucharist proper is said to have arisen in the Hellenistic churches (Lietzmann) or (according to Lohmeyer) already in Palestine (Jerusalem), postulated on the basis of the manifestation-narratives which speak of communal meals taken by the disciples with the risen Lord (Lk. 24:30–31; 24:41–43; Acts 10: 39–41; Jn. 21:10–14).[143] These theses have been repeatedly challenged and very largely also refuted. Even so, they do enshrine a correct intuition, namely, that besides the eucharist (and independently of it) there did exist in the early Church vital recollections of the fellowship at table enjoyed with the earthly Jesus; these same memories have left their traces in accounts of miraculous multiplication of loaves.[144] That this is right appears above all from the analysis of the recurring stories (doublets or variants of the same piece of tradition) (especially Mk. 6: 34–44 and Mk. 8:1–9). In both cases we find a constant structure: (a) conversation with the disciples (6:35–38 and 8:1–5) – (b) preparation for the meal by Jesus (6:39–41 and 8:6–7) – (c) meal and gathering up of the remains (6:42–44 and 8:8–9). The fundamental difference in the two stories lies on the one hand in the dire need of people who have followed Jesus into the wilderness and have had nothing to eat (8:1–9), while in 6:34–38 there is no acute need of any sort and food could easily have been fetched from the village (6:36). But in the former instance Jesus' purpose is to show that he wants to act as host himself and to offer the people a fellowship-meal. The pre-Marcan verse (Mk. 6:34) sets the whole pericope under the Old Testament motif of the good shepherd (Num. 27:17; Ezek. 34:5–8) (though implicitly, since no reference is made to the Old Testament). Jesus has pity on the people, who are leaderless, and himself proceeds to act as the latter-day shepherd sent by God (Ezek. 34:23; Jer. 23:4). The instruction Jesus gives (6:34b) is itself the start of the meal that Jesus now offers to the people as their host – and in a festive context at that. The first story (Mk. 6:30–44) thematizes unambiguously the fellowship-meal proffered by Jesus himself, whereas Mk. 8:1–9 relates the same substance of the tradition in the guise of a 'miracle-story': Jesus comes to the help of people in dire physical need.[145]

Jesus' introductory prayer is the same in both stories; it stays within the terminology of the Jewish 'grace before meals' and so has no 'eucharistic implications' whatever. In Mk. 6:41, as opposed to Mk. 8:7, the blessing of the fishes 'is missing'; this account therefore is older and closer to historical reality (supplementary foods are not blessed separately by Jews).[146] (Mark 8:7 evinces a Hellenistic misunderstanding of Jewish custom and so may imply, in this Hellenistic context, a blessing that procured the 'multiplication' of the fishes. It is logical, therefore, that the Jewish-Christian gospel of Matthew should drop Mark's benediction over the fishes, unintelligible from a Jewish standpoint.) The historical kernel of the story as a whole it is no longer possible to reconstruct, except in broad terms: a meal laid on by Jesus in the open air with a large crowd of hangers-on, with Jesus acting quite explicitly as 'host'. This coming and being together definitely has an eschatological significance: the dawning of the joyous time of plenty, thanks to the presence of Jesus. The story has not in substance been generated out of a post-Easter concern on the part of the Church, but is the outcome of a fascinating historical memory – and that is again confirmed by Mark's interpretation of this 'miraculous multiplication of loaves' (in Mk. 8:14–21). At any rate Mark does not put a eucharistic gloss on the story but interprets it as a lesson aimed at the disciples. The same question arises here as with the stilling of the storm: the disciples are reproached for their lack of faith (Mk. 8:21: 'Do you not yet understand?' The disciples had, after the second feeding miracle, started to squabble over the uneaten loaves). So Mark compares them with the Pharisees and Herodians, who understand Jesus no better. The disciples 'remember' (Mk. 8:18) later on all sorts of details about these disconcerting events, but fail to grasp the point of them: Jesus' proffering of God's salvation.[147]

The focal point of the story, then, is not so much the 'marvel' as the marvellous abundance that comes into play when Jesus offers his fellowship at table. There is no mistaking what is present here; the idea of the 'eschatological abundance' (Amos 9:13).

Besides these stories, we also hear tell in Luke and John of the risen Lord meeting with his disciples at table and communing with them (Lk. 24:28–31; Jn. 21:12–13; cf. Acts 10:41). Yet we have here a pre-Lucan tradition. In Acts 10:41 Luke speaks of 'the risen One eating and drinking with the Twelve' – a circumstance of which we are told nothing at all in the Lucan gospel itself. Luke 24:13–35 refers not to any of the Twelve but to the party walking to Emmaus; and in Lk. 24: 36–43 Jesus does indeed eat – but 'before the eyes' of the disciples (not together with them).

The meal at Emmaus is most instructive in this connection. The Emmaus disciples recognize Jesus in the breaking of bread. Whereas Jesus has been invited as a guest (Lk. 24:29), he himself blesses and breaks the bread: that is, he acts *as host* in the house of two strangers. In so doing he is recognized. In other words, after his death Jesus renews a fellowship at table with his own people; in spite of Jesus' death communal contacts are resumed: on his initiative. (There is nothing in Luke here pointing to reminiscences of a 'Last Supper' tradition.) The passage reminds us rather of Lk. 9:16 and 9:12: Jesus' (purely) mundane fellowship at the mealtable with his friends and followers. Set in a context of historical recollections of that and of what it had meant prior to the events of Easter, the core of the Emmaus story becomes intelligible.

Historical memories of Jesus' earthly life again play an obvious part in Jn. 21:1–14. Here a tradition about a meal shared with the risen Jesus is interwoven with one about catching some fish.[148] If we extricate the second tradition, then 21:12–13 follows upon 21:4–9: in other words, the original story goes like this: after an unsuccessful fishing trip the disciples are making their way back; from their boat they see somebody standing on the shore and watching them; they fail to recognize Jesus. Once on land, they see a small fire burning and a meal ready; Jesus invites them to eat it, and then they recognize him. In other words,

Jesus is again recognized from the fact that he fulfils the role of host, handing out bread and fish to his friends. This story too derives from a 'manifestation' tradition which is pre-Johannine and comes from Galilee, though associated now with a miraculous meal. That is to say, all the stories about Jesus as the host at a meal refer to a tradition emanating from Galilee by the lake. In all variants of this piece of tradition (Jn. 6:1; Mk. 6:45; 8:10) this reference to the Galilean lake is well to the fore; so historical recollections of its origin must be enshrined here. After Easter Jesus resumes in the present the fellowship shared with his disciples prior to his death.

So if this tradition (Lk. 24:28–31; Jn. 21:12–13) bears no relation, no recognizable relation, to that of the 'farewell meal', while the allusions to the stories about the 'feeding miracle' are undeniable, this gives us an even better insight into the latter. J. Roloff has clearly demonstrated, it seems to me, that we are not dealing here with secondary texts, selected (as many scholars believe) from within a post-Easter, specifically eucharistic context, fitted together and projected back on to Jesus' earthly life. The 'miraculous feedings' draw some sort of veil over what happened, whereas the account of eating with Jesus after Easter sets that event in the light of a clear recognition of the Christ, whereby 'the eyes of the disciples were opened' (Lk. 24:31; see Jn. 21:12). The latest forms of meal-sharing in fellowship reveal the meaning and purpose of the similar fellowship shared with Jesus during his life on earth, and at the same time refer back to it. That same reference is thematized in the model-stories of the miraculous feeding by Jesus – the basis for the latter being provided therefore by the historical meal-sharing-in-fellowship enjoyed by the earthly Jesus with his disciples; it had been an essential and characteristic feature of the historical Jesus. This is a datum that in the course of this book will also play an important role when we come to interpret in more detail the 'appearances' of Jesus, as they are called, which after the panic touched off by the disciples' lack of faith serve to restore the broken fellowship and so at last bring out the real point of their companionship with the earthly Jesus.

The gospels eventually highlight one particular instance, when on the eve of his Passion Jesus took bread, blessed and broke it and offered it to his disciples; in other words, a similar meal-sharing, in which Jesus himself acts as host and, face-to-face with his approaching death, nevertheless provides, albeit for the very last time, an occasion of fellowship with his disciples. All this in token of the eschatological superabundant gift. But this historical reminiscence is not to be examined analytically until a subsequent chapter apropos of Jesus' intimations and conviction about his coming death – where within the historical course of the tradition this story really belongs.

To sum up: meal-sharing in fellowship, whether with notorious 'tax-collectors and sinners' or with his friends, casual or close, is a fundamental trait of the historical Jesus. In that way Jesus shows himself to be God's eschatological messenger, conveying the news of God's invitation to all – including especially those officially regarded at the time as outcasts – to attend the peaceful occasion of God's rule; this fellowship at table is itself, as an eating together with Jesus, an offer here and now of eschatological salvation or 'final good'. The instances where Jesus himself acts as host bring home even more forcefully the fact that Jesus himself takes the initiative with this eschatological message, which in the fellowship at table shared with him becomes as it were an enacted prophecy. Once again it serves to demonstrate that Jesus' actual way of living is nothing other than the praxis of the kingdom of God proclaimed by him. It is only through the subsequent effect of this historical praxis on the part of Jesus that the significance of the fellowship-meal among Christians in the primitive Church becomes intelligible. The Christians take over this praxis of Jesus. Acts 2:42–47: 'They devoted themselves ... to the breaking of bread', that is, to the provision of such meals; the concern for widows and orphans (in Luke's time) is a remainder of that. 'They partook of food with glad and generous hearts' (Acts 2:46). Conversions too were celebrated with a meal (Acts 16:34). Thence also the eventual decision to eat in company with uncircumcised Christians, after several clashes on the issue (Acts 11:3; Gal. 2:1–14). The very pronounced interest in fellowship-meals in the early Church is obviously grounded in Jesus' own practice when he was alive on earth.

## C. THE COMMON LIFE AND FELLOWSHIP WITH JESUS, PRIOR TO EASTER, OF DISCIPLES WHO 'GO AFTER HIM'

*Literature.* Kl. Berger, *Gesetzeauslegung*; H. D. Betz, *Nachfolge und Nachahmung Jesu Christi im Neuen Testament* (Beih. EvTh 37), Tübingen 1967; L. Grollenberg, 'Mensen "vangen" (Lc. 5:10): hen redden van de dood', TvT 5 (1965), 330–6; F. Hahn, 'Die Nachfolge Jesu in vorösterlicher Zeit', in F. Hahn, A. Strobel, E. Schweizer, *Die Anfänge der Kirche in Neuen Testament* (Göttingen 1967), 7–36; M. Hengel, *Charisma und Nachfolge*, Berlin 1968; J. Kahmann, 'Het volgen van Christus door zelfverloochening en kruisdragen, volgens Mc. 8:34–38 pls', TvT 1 (1961), 205–26; J. Mánek, 'Fishers of men', NovT 2 (1958), 138–41; K. H. Rengstorf, s.v. *manthanô*, in: ThWNT IV, 392–417, and s.v. *mathètès*, ibid., IV, 417–65; G. Schille, *Die urchristliche Kollegial-mission*, Zürich-Stuttgart 1967; R. Schnackenburg, *Die sittliche Botschaft des Neuen Testament*, Munich 1954; C. Smith, 'Fishers of men', HThR 52 (1959), 187–203; Ans. Schulz, *Nachfolgen und Nachahmen*, Munich 1962; S. Schulz, 'Jesusnachfolge und Gemeinde', in *Q-Quelle*, 404–80.

In what has been said so far in this chapter about Jesus' way of life and conduct we have examined situations of one sort or another which show how his persistent care for and attention to those about him came to be apprehended as salvation imparted by God – a salvation consciously proffered through those encounters by Jesus himself, as the eschatological messenger of God's approaching kingdom. Now what stands out within this variegated whole of (often fleeting) encounters with Jesus is the fact that a very intimate coterie of disciples, along with a somewhat wider circle, were his constant companions – so much so indeed that through this community alone did it prove possible for the experience of salvation in Jesus with God as its source to develop after his death from a soteriological recognition of Jesus into a Christo-logical conversion to Jesus the Christ. We have already seen that the notion of 'little faith' (*oligopistia* = 'lack of faith'), although indicative of periodic failure, nevertheless presupposes an abiding state of commitment to Jesus in faith.

Although scholars in the past have often argued the contrary, they are now coming to see that the earthly Jesus did, prior to his death, appoint disciples as his co-workers and send them out to proclaim, as he did himself, the message of the coming rule of God, as well as to heal the sick and drive out devils. This sending forth of the disciples by Jesus is reported both in Mk. 6:7–13 and in the Q tradition (Lk. 10: 2–12 and parallels), again in Lk. 9:1–6 and in Mt. 9:37–38 with 10: 7–16; but these accounts all stem from no more than two independent forms: namely, the Q tradition (particularly as incorporated in Lk. 10: 2–12; Mt. 9:37–38 and 10:7–16 combine this tradition with Marcan material) and the Marcan tradition (Mk. 6:7–13, which Luke adopts in 9:1–6), whereas for various reasons (not to be enumerated at this point) the Q tradition would seem to be the oldest one.[149] The hard core of this record goes back to the earthly days of Jesus, although it appears to have undergone repeated changes in detail, as a succession of new demands and needs arose for the Church in the post-Easter situation; but the original pre-Easter commissioning continued to function as a criterion and norm. The main evidence for this is that the account given of it is devoid of any Christological content but does employ the pre-Easter terminology of Jesus' message and way of doing things: preaching the coming rule of God, healing the sick and expelling demons. Thus Jesus actually allows his disciples to share his own mission with him. That supposes their vocation to 'go after him' to include imitating Jesus and – since he was an itinerant preacher of no fixed abode – following him wherever he might go (and as will appear later on, following him even on the road to suffering).

The sending out of the disciples in the Q tradition is substantially reproduced in Lk. 10:2–12, parallels at Mt. 9:37–38; 10:7–16 (with Luke staying closer to the Q tradition). From the narrative a clear pattern emerges: (a) the commissioning, (b) the question of paraphernalia, (c) directions as to how the missionaries are to behave in the houses where they take lodgings during the expedition as well as in the places they arrive at.[150] In origin it is an apophthegm, that is, an event in Jesus' life passed on with a kerygmatic intention;[151] actually, this logion functions as a 'missionary instruction' and 'community rule'. In the development of the tradition Lk. 10:2–12 seems always to have formed a single unit – although (according to S. Schulz) this passage is part of the less ancient Graeco-Jewish Christian phase of the Q tradition.[152] Of course the disciples here are being sent on a mission to Israel (not to the Gentiles). But the *de facto* rejection of Jesus' message and person colours the whole narrative (sheep among wolves, Lk. 10:3; shake the dust from your feet, Lk. 10:11; the city which rejects Jesus' emissaries will fare worse than Sodom, Lk. 10:12). It is obvious that for 'equipment' they have 'a state of radical destitution' (Lk. 10:4) – the most elementary needs of even a down-and-out on such a journey are denied them. It is so radical in fact as to be simply 'un-Jewish'; and only the urgent proximity of God's kingdom makes it understandable; through the disciples' preaching, their cures and exorcisms the coming rule of God is already being made present, here and now (Lk. 10:11).

But this being a disciple of Jesus springs from a call on his part; and it is instructive to see how the disciples later on confess to having experienced the compelling force of that call. In his schematized, general account of how the Twelve were called Mark says: '. . . he appointed twelve *to be with him* and *to be sent out to preach* and have *authority to cast out demons*' (Mk. 3:13–15). There had been references already to 'Jesus and his disciples' (3:15), to the call of the first four disciples (1:16–20) and then to the call of Levi, the tax-collector (2:14). A clear distinction is made here between the call of the disciples and the appointing of 'the Twelve' from among them. Particularly interesting is the call and the way in which the New Testament presents it. Along comes Jesus when they are busy at their daily work and says: 'Come, follow me' (Mk. 1:17; 1:20; 2:14). On each occasion they immediately left their work 'and followed him' (1:18; 1:20; 2:14). The parallel with the prophet Elijah's calling of Elisha is a striking one. Elisha was ploughing with a team of twelve oxen when the great prophet Elijah came by. Elijah (summoning him to take over his prophetic role) 'cast his mantle upon him. And he left the oxen and ran after Elijah, and said, "Let me kiss my father and mother, and then I will follow you." And he said to him "Go back again; for what have I done to you?" And he returned from following him and took the yoke of oxen, and slew them, and boiled their flesh with the yokes of the oxen, and gave it to the people, and they ate. Then he arose and went after Elijah, and ministered unto him' (1 Kings 19:19–21). Again, for his part the former herdsman Amos says: 'Yahweh took me from following the flock, and Yahweh said to me: "Go, prophesy to my people Israel"' (Am. 7:15). There can be no excuse whatever for failing to obey such a summons at once; one leaves all behind and follows the one who calls. Anybody who wants to procrastinate is sent away. '. . . a Scribe came up and said to him, "Teacher, I will follow you wherever you go" . . . Another of the disciples said to him, "Lord, let me first go and bury my father." But Jesus said to him, "Follow me, and leave the dead to bury their own dead"' (Mt. 8:19, 21–22; see Lk. 9:57–60). 'Dead buryers of the dead' are people who do not at once get themselves involved with Jesus' message of the kingdom of God and its summons.[153] This call is a matter of life or death. It quite deliberately overrides the claims of a 'good work' (burying the dead), an obligation almost to be set above the fourth commandment (Torah). According to the Pharisaic view of things interring the dead provided exemption from practically every other legal obligation.[154] In the Old Testament we hear of only one prophetic act in which 'for a sign' the prophet neglects to perform the customary ritual in order to bring home to the people that God's judgement is approaching and there is no longer any point in burying the dead (Ezek. 24:15–24), just as Jeremiah for his part will never even marry (Jer. 16:1–4) and forbids taking part in 'lamentations for the dead' (16:5–7), in token of God's coming judgement.[155] Thus Jesus' calling of the disciples is likewise the act of a prophet – and indeed the demand he conjoins with it actually releases a person from one of the strongest of Jewish obligations. Therefore in Jesus' call to 'go after him' we have perhaps the clearest evidence of his role as eschatological prophet of the imminent rule of God. It shatters every frame of the 'master-disciple' relationship, because it is a conclusive, latter-day act on the part of the eschatological prophet; it serves to condense his call to *metanoia* into an eschatological *metanoia* as a disciple of Jesus, a vocation to total commitment, burning all one's boats in the service of the kingdom to come. To associate oneself with Jesus like that is to put oneself unconditionally at the service of the kingdom of God. The situation is a soteriological one; but it does entail a Christological question: whether, that is, one's relation to the coming rule of God is dependent or conditional upon a relationship to Jesus. Of course, considering the whole tenor of the Marcan gospel (up to the avowal of Christological belief beneath the cross), Mk. 8:38 and Mk. 8:34–35 are made less Christologically explicit than even the Q source (Mt. 10:33 and parallel Lk. 12:9; Mt. 10:38 parallel Lk. 14:27). The real issue here is a summons to leave absolutely everything and go along with Jesus, the itinerant preacher who, as opposed to the foxes and the birds who have their holes or nests, has nowhere to lay his head (Mt. 8:20, apropos of a man willing to answer the call). This idea of the call to the imitation of Jesus is a constant theme in the New Testament (Mk. 8:34–38; Lk. 14:16–33 and 9:23–26; Mt. 10:38 and 16:24–27). With his disciples around him, Jesus in the Marcan gospel addresses the crowd as follows: 'If any man would come after me, let him deny himself and take up his cross and follow me. For whoever would save his life will lose it; and whoever loses his life for my sake and the gospel's will save it. For what does it profit a man, to gain the whole world and forfeit his life? . . . For whoever is ashamed of me and of my words in this adulterous and sinful generation, of him will the son of man also be ashamed, when he comes in the glory of his Father with the holy angels' (Mk. 8:34–38, parallels Mt. 16:24–27; Lk. 9:23–26). In another place we read: 'He who loves father or mother more than me is not worthy of me; and he who loves son or daughter more than me is not worthy of me; and he who does not take up his cross and follow me is not worthy of me. He who finds his life will lose it, and he who loses his life for my sake will find it' (Mt. 10:38–39 parallel Lk. 14: 25–27; see Lk. 17:33). The explanation for the 'doublets' in Matthew and Luke is that they incorporate two traditions, the Marcan tradition in the first case, the Q tradition (Mt. 10:37–39 and Lk. 14:27; 17:33) in the second (three separate logia: that of 'following after by taking up one's cross', that of 'losing one's life and gaining it' and that of 'being hated for Jesus' sake'). Obviously, these pericopes were made explicitly Christological in the post-Easter period. The pre-Easter element is the summoning of certain disciples in the service of Jesus' historical proclamation of the kingdom of God (as we shall see).

The summoning by Jesus is evidently envisaged in the gospels in accordance with a stereotyped scheme: (a) Jesus passes by (Mk. 1:16, 19; 2:14); (b) sees somebody (Mk. 1:16, 19; Jn. 1:47); (c) a more detailed account of the man's occupation (Mk. 1:16, 19; 2:14; Lk. 5:2); (d) the call (Mk. 1:17–20; 2:14; Jn. 1:37); (e) 'leaving all' (Mk. 1:18–20; except in Mk. 2:14, but again in Lk. 5:11, 28); (f) the person called goes after Jesus (Mk. 1:18–20; 2:14; Lk. 5:11).[156] Thus it is an obvious case of a literary construction, not of the historically straightforward 'direct reporting' of how a call took place. We are faced with originally self-contained units of tradition, beginning with: 'As he passed by he saw someone' and ending 'he arose and followed him'. Central to this literary unit is the middle section: Jesus calls someone. This call entails surrendering one's occupation, home, family and possessions. As opposed to the sending out of the disciples to instruct others, this fundamental, primary call is an invitation to 'put oneself to school' and learn from Jesus. Matthew 9:13 (in contrast to Mark) has this striking insertion: 'Go and learn . . .', that is, 'learn from me' (see Mt. 11:29; as opposed to Mt. 28:19, where they are to teach others to be the pupil). Jesus' sayings are a *didachè*, an instruction, for the Christian community;[157] Jesus is the instructor of the community.

These 'call' narratives have other implications. In late Judaism conversion to Israel's God – from being a pagan to being a Jew – was an action that resulted in a social break with one's property, home and family – and this had become a traditional commonplace for conversion among Jews of the Diaspora. Being converted meant in practice surrendering all one's possessions, becoming odious, having to leave father and mother, husband or wife, brother and sister, and all one's worldly goods. Hence the *topos* of conversion (even if this social rift was not entailed). The conditions for a conversion, and things that go along with it, are: giving everything away, forsaking family and home, in order to follow after Yahweh, Israel's God. Among Greek-speaking Jews this was associated catechetically with God's command to Abraham to abandon everything and set out for the unknown, the Promised Land (Gen. 12:1–9). This divine command was frequently interpreted in late Judaism as a 'conversionary vision'.[158] The step taken by Jesus' disciples, who leave everything and 'hate' their kith and kin (Lk. 14:26) in order to follow Jesus, is therefore presented – in Graeco-Jewish circles within primitive Christianity – on the model of a conversion,[159] *metanoia*, necessary in view of the approaching rule of God. In other words the traditional (Graeco-) Jewish conversion-pattern is employed in the New Testament to denote the changeover from being a Jew (pagan) to being one who confesses Jesus. To put it another way: to confess Jesus in this way is the *metanoia* which the coming rule of God requires (see Mk. 8:38; Mt. 16:27; Lk. 9:26); for it is on the strength of this that Jesus, as the coming son of man, will judge the individual. According to late, Graeco-Jewish, 'wisdom-oriented' Judaism, the man who gives up everything will get it back 'a hundredfold' here on earth already (also Mk. 10:30), whereas according to the apocalyptical line (Mt. 19:29) this reward is purely eschatological.

That the conversion-model is used here to show that turning to Jesus to follow him is the *metanoia* (complete about-turn) demanded by the coming kingdom of God is clear from a variety of things. We have said already that when the conversion of a Gentile to Israel's God was not in fact accompanied by a social breach, the conversion was still envisaged in accordance with that model. The convert was to give away his property to the poor and, as proof of his readiness for conversion, devote himself to relief of the poor.[160] Typical of the adoption by Christians of this pre-Christian conversion-pattern is the account of a call which in fact did not succeed: the rich young man (Mk. 10:17–31). He had kept the Ten Commandments, and so the Torah, to perfection. What was it he still lacked? Conversion to Jesus, intimated here as both conversion and *metanoia* by the requirement to sell all that the young man possessed and to 'give it to the poor', the condition for 'following Jesus' (Mk. 10:21); that is to say, a readiness to be converted to Jesus is wanting in him, as evidenced by the fact that the 'deeds of conversion' – surrender of possessions and relief of the poor – are things he is not willing to perform. This by no means implies that the yielding up of one's possessions is just a metaphor for a real conversion to Jesus; on the contrary the actual surrender of material goods is the sign and condition of a true conversion. What is radically new in this is not the connection between 'conversion' and 'leaving everything' (these are already given models) but that the activity of following Jesus is qualified as an eschatological *metanoia*, an authentic conversion; the rest – leaving all, and so forth – is not specifically Christian, but the actual expression of the act of being converted (to Jesus). Even the conversion of the pagan proselyte Cornelius to Jesus Christ is described with the same model in view (Acts 10:2, 30–32).

Mark puts the episode of the unsuccessful call of the rich young man after the pericope about accepting the rule of God 'like a child' (Mk. 10:13–16). Becoming like a child is likewise a traditional Jewish formula for 'being converted' to the true God of Israel: going after God, the Father, and becoming his child.[161] The children sent packing by the disciples are 'blessed by Jesus', who pointedly lays hands upon them (Mk. 10:16). This (see also Acts 3:26, as well as here and there in the literature between the Testaments) is the special rite of admission for converts. 'Becoming humble as a child' is the expression used for the eschatological *metanoia* as a conversion to Jesus – for the Christian community after Easter a condition for membership of the eschatological community.

The distinctive thing about following Jesus, therefore, does not lie in abandoning everything in order to achieve a 'master-disciple' relationship, in the sense maintained by A. Schulz,[162] nor yet, as M. Hengel asserts,[163] simply as making one's avowal to Jesus (though in substance this is right enough), but rather in the fact that this avowal is qualified as a religious conversion; that is to say, the salvific scheme of the Jewish Law is thereby declared to be insufficient. The *metanoia* demanded by the coming kingdom of God is a conversion to Jesus – that is the theological relevance of the call 'to go after Jesus'. In that conversion the nevertheless still-to-come rule of God becomes an already present reality.

Whereas Mark sees the total surrender of one's possessions and 'going after Jesus' as the precondition for every conversion to Christianity, Matthew limits these requirements to the Twelve, the basis of the Christian community; in so doing he dismisses any earthly recompense; that is purely eschatological; and the reward is the same for the Twelve as for all who put their faith in Jesus. Moreover, for Matthew the whole pericope provides a foundation for the authority of the Twelve (Mt. 19:28). He is not using it to endorse the *duplex via*, a twofold way to eternal life, on the one hand through keeping the commandments (Mt. 19:17), on the other, for 'the perfect', by selling all and following Jesus (Mt. 19:21); for in Mt. 19:29 those conditions are held to apply to every Christian. Clearly, Mt. 19:29 treats the conversion narrative as applicable to anyone who is becoming a Christian (Lk. 9:23 underlines this general applicability), whereas in Mt. 19:17 the requirement applicable to non-Christians is stated to be a condition for entering into eternal life. One could say: Old Testament here is set over against New Testament, and not a preferential Christian way of life over against a 'common' variety (see Lk. 10:25–37; and in a subsequent exposition of 'the two great commandments', the summary of

J.E.C.–H

the Law). The very thing that keeping just the twofold great commandment – love of God and of one's neighbour – does not encompass
is the 'conversion to Jesus'; this is the 'perfection' of the New Testament as opposed to the Old. It is the condition of membership of the
eschatological community.

In the New Testament the explicit message conveyed by the idea
of 'following Jesus' is that fulfilment of the Law (however necessary
as the command of God; see later) is no longer sufficient for salvation.
What now mediates salvation is one's relation to Jesus; but as the
eschatological messenger Jesus recognizes only the commandments
of God: and he brings no new ones. But the effectiveness of the conversion, the 'about-turn', required and entailed by the coming kingdom
of God, is bound up with the demand that one turn towards Jesus;
prior to Easter, this means acknowledging him as the eschatological
prophet from God, who brings the glad news that 'God shall reign'
(Isa. 61:1–2; 52:7).

Up to a point, this makes it possible to distinguish what is peculiar
to Jesus' way of calling disciples prior to Easter from the explicit
Christology into which it is already incorporated in the New Testament.
Actually, 'to follow (after)' (in the Septuagint *akolouthein*)[164] is used in
Scripture in association with 'going after other gods' or 'following
(after) God' by keeping his commandments (Deut.; 2 Macc. 8:36).
This idea turns up again in 1 Pet. 1:15–16: '. . . as he who called you is
holy, be holy yourselves in all your conduct; since it is written, "You
shall be holy, for I am holy." ' As the eschatological messenger from
God, 'on whom God has set his name' (see Part Three), Jesus is simply
conveying God's message and calling Israel to faith in God; that was
his mission prior to his death (see above: 'Faith and miracle'). Therefore to answer Jesus' call, in acknowledgement of his prophetic
mission, was to show one's faith in God, to put one's faith in the
coming rule of God and undergo the *metanoia* which that required – at
the invitation, that is, of Jesus himself. In other words, the decision to
'follow', prior to Easter, had a soteriological significance but not yet a
consciously Christological one. The Christological issue is of course
implicit: on Jesus' authority *qua* preacher, to be converted to God. In
other words, before Easter there is as yet no question of conversion to
Jesus; this notion entails an explicit Christology. Mark's account of the
calling of the Twelve, therefore (leaving aside, in this context, the
notion of 'Twelve'), is still, as historical reportage, closest to reflecting
the way Jesus actually did call disciples in the pre-Easter situation:
'And he appointed [them] *to be with him and to be sent out to preach and*

*have authority to cast out demons'* (Mk. 3:14–15): Jesus calls on them to 'be his companions' and help him proclaim the coming kingdom of God, made visible as the sick are healed and demons are driven out – as we are told again later on, when they are actually sent out (in the Marcan tradition, Mk. 6:7–13; in the Q tradition, Lk. 10:2–12 parallel Mt. 9: 37–38; 10:16, 9–10a, 11–13, 10b, 7–8, 14–15). This is accurately reflected, indeed, by the idea: 'Follow me and I will make you become fishers of men' (Mk. 1:17; Lk. 5:10). It suggests an Aramaic logion in which the Aramaic term in question can mean both 'fisher' and 'hunter' – and then also 'one who captures alive' (*zôgrein*) (Lk. 5:10), that is, who here rescues from the judgement-to-come and from demonic powers.[165] Service rendered to the kingdom of God is thus one of deliverance, a setting free of one's fellow-men. The disciples play their part in what R. Plesch is rightly wont to call the 'gathering-in campaign' of Jesus.[166] The disciples follow and imitate Jesus here by doing what he does, proclaiming the message of God's kingdom, healing the sick and driving out devils; and this must of course be done within a whole attitude to life on the disciples' part which mirrors the praxis of God's kingdom, as exemplified by Jesus in word, parable and action. After Easter this praxis would be more exactly defined and re-defined to meet the needs and suit the outlook of the first Christian communities in accordance with their own 'community rule' (or subsequently, 'church order') and also to accord with the particular theology of the local church or evangelists. So Mark sees in the 'imitation' of Jesus the missionary commitment of itinerant emissaries ready for martyrdom (Mk. 8: 34–36). On the other hand, Mt. 16:24–28 and Lk. 9:23–27 see it as a matter of conforming to God's will, which Jesus had disclosed. In any event Jesus is for all of them 'the team leader'; that is the recollected fact of history which confronts us through it all.

Of course the decision to accompany, to 'be with', the historical Jesus – so putting oneself at the disposal of the coming kingdom of God – entails a readiness to suffer in the service and for the sake of that kingdom. 'If any man would come after me, let him deny himself and take up his cross and follow me' (Mk. 8:34; see in the Q tradition Mt. 10:38, parallel Lk. 14:27; see Mt. 16:24). Put in the first person like that, it is obviously a piece of post-Easter Christology. In terms of pre-Easter soteriology it means that accompanying Jesus on his mission to proclaim the kingdom of God will meet with opposition and will result in suffering. This logion echoes the old remembered words: 'He who would serve the kingdom of God must deny himself and take up his cross.' The phrase 'take up *his* cross' also occurs in the Q tradition, which has no theology of the cross resembling that of other local churches. 'Carrying one's cross' (not, then, as in a more Pauline vein, 'carrying *my* cross') is therefore far from being, *per se*, a post-Easter reference to Jesus' death on the cross. The expression 'to carry one's cross' was current even in secular Greek,[167] but it is not Semitic. On the other hand, according to M. Hengel, 'to carry one's cross' might have been a phrase in use among the Zealots, because crucifixion was the appropriate death penalty for these resistance fighters; and the picture of crucified people must have been vividly present to the minds of many in Palestine.[168] In any case 'carrying one's cross' is interpreted metaphorically in the Q tradition. It is a summons to be ready to lay down one's life for God's sake, ready for martyrdom. (That this logion of Jesus acquires from Jesus' death on the cross a concrete meaning, in circles where a Passion theology has already been developed, is self-evident.) Thus even in times of persecution God's kingdom must be served unconditionally. That is the very reason why Mark in particular interprets the panic and flight of the disciples when Jesus is arrested as somehow a rupture of their 'going after Jesus' (see later on). This total, unconditional commitment is to be justified eschatologically, like the call itself, that is, for the kingdom of God's sake, or as expressed explicitly in the light of Easter by Mark, 'for my sake and the gospel's' (Mk. 8:35; 10:29).[169] For Mark, 'losing one's life' and taking up one's cross comes about through the proclamation of the gospel, which arouses opposition; and doing exactly that is their way of 'following after' Jesus. As reminding them of Jesus, the disciples at the same time 'enact here and now' what had been accomplished in Jesus' own life. Precisely because the events of Holy Week and Easter, according to Mark, are part and parcel of the *euaggelion* being proclaimed, the preaching of the gospel by Jesus' disciples after Easter is also a following of Jesus 'on his path of suffering'. 'Going-after-Jesus' shatters therefore the pre-established limits of the Jewish, Graeco-Jewish and Greek models for 'following the master'; so that 'going after Jesus' means first and foremost sharing his *lot*, his destiny, with him, as 1 Pet. 2:21–22 was to put it. 'Be you holy, for I [Yahweh] am holy' (1:15–16) and, 'For to this you have been called, because Christ also suffered for you, leaving you an example that you should follow in his steps.'[170] Here is made plain, within the context of the developing tradition, the connection between a 'following after God' and the 'following (imitation) of Christ'. Prior to Easter, fellowship with Jesus – at the meal-table, by turning to him for help and healing, above all by being constantly with him in the service of his message – turns out to be an offer of salvation-on-God's-part; this fellowship has a fundamentally soteriological meaning, of which the Christological implications became explicit only after Jesus' death. Nevertheless – as opposed to the cases where individual passers-by address themselves to Jesus (to receive healing) and at the same time acknowledge him as a prophet sent from God – the more habitual practice on the part of his close disciples of consorting with him, or of 'being his companions' (though often enough still 'with little faith'), is the pre-Easter model of what was reckoned after the Easter events to be simply 'Christian living'. Hence a degree of ambiguity in the New Testament passages on this theme, which sometimes prompt the question whether they are aimed at each and every Christian or just a special group of disciples. In my view, this results from the fact that within the kerygmatic situation of primitive Christianity clearly historical reminiscences are an active ingredient – reminiscences of the special fellowship shared by Jesus with his closest disciples as distinct from the many sympathizers or the many sick people cured by Jesus (one thinks of the ten who were healed, only one of whom returned to him). The close disciples' distinctive 'faith in Jesus', something peculiar to themselves, therefore, is prior to Easter 'in process of becoming', and after Easter will be known as 'Christian faith'. It is this same pre-Easter faith of Jesus' disciples that has become the contributory subject of what is called the 'Jesus tradition'; this faith, the faith of all who went after Jesus in the service of the coming rule of God, the faith in Jesus as the one who enunciates the message of the kingdom of God, provides the continuity between the experience of salvation before Easter and the post-Easter conversion to Jesus as the crucified-and-risen One. Of all the memories of the offer of salvation, as extended in various forms by Jesus during his earthly life, those of the enduring fellowship enjoyed with him by the disciples who 'went after him' are perhaps the most pregnant; this form of the offer, in particular, was to confront them after Jesus' death expressly with the Christological question.

## §2 Man's cause as God's cause: the 'God of Jesus'

A. JESUS AS MAN'S LIBERATOR FROM A CONSTRICTING VIEW OF GOD: JESUS AND THE LAW

*Literature.* Kl. Berger, *Die Gesetzesauslegung Jesu*, I, Neukiechen 1972; J. Blank, 'Zum Problem "ethischer Normen" in Neuen Testament',

*Schriftauslegung in Theorie und Praxis* (Munich 1969), 129–57, and *Jesus von Nazareth* (Freiburg 1972), 112–16, 50–67; H. Braun, *Spätjüdisch-häretischer und frühchristlicher Radikalismus*, I. *Das Spätjudentum*, II, *Die Synoptiker*, Tübingen 1957; F. Gils, 'Le sabbat a été fait pour l'homme et non l'homme pour le sabbat', RB 69 (1962), 506–23; E. Jüngel, *Paulus und Jesus*, Tübingen 1964²; M. Limbeck, *Die Ordnung des Heils. Untersuchungen zum Gesetzesverständnis des Frühjudentums*, Düsseldorf 1971, and *Von der Ohnmacht des Rechts. Zur Gesetzeskritik des Neuen Testaments*, Düsseldorf 1972; J. Roloff, *Das Kerygma*, 51–110; P. Stuhlmacher, *Die Gerechtigkeit Gottes* (FRLANT, 87), Göttingen 1965; S. Schulz, 'Die charismatisch-eschatologische Toraverschärfung', in Schulz, *Q-Quelle*, 94–141.


(a) Difficulty of the exegetical enquiry

Jesus' attitude to the Torah or Jewish Law, filtered as it is through the New Testament, assumes for us a very complicated aspect; so that some regard Jesus as the great revolutionary upstart against the legal establishment, others on the contrary see him as a radical and even a rigorist. Yet we should not lose sight of the fact that Jesus and the earliest generations of Christians saw themselves as a part of Jewry. Parallels of a religio-historical sort become under this condition suspect, therefore. On the other hand, Jesus was condemned and executed. And this shows that there were present in his preaching and conduct aspects at any rate that ran counter to what Judaism or a section of Judaism officially taught in Jesus' time. 'Jewish teaching' was not then as uniform as might be supposed.

For Palestinian Jewry the Torah was first and foremost the Penta-teuch, the so-called five books of Moses; the prophets and the other books of Scripture were commentary on those. Also forming part of this commentary, at least in the Pharisaic tradition (which in this respect contrasted with that of the Sadducees) was the 'fence around the Law', that is, the oral traditions of the fathers, said to be the tradition of Jewish casuistical ethics. In practice, the whole was described as *torah*, law. The underlying idea was in fact that this Torah was the law of God, revelation and proof of God's love, the expression of his saving activity, which was concerned with the final well-being (salvation) of human beings. Anyone, therefore, who impugns the Torah impugns God himself.

The fact is often overlooked that the Greek-speaking Jews of the

Diaspora interpreted the Law in quite a different way from the Aramaic-speaking Jews of Palestine. The former drew a clear distinction between the Torah as the Decalogue, the authentic ordinances of God in creation, and the various 'Mosaic laws' that had been given to the people 'because of the hardness of their heart'. Since they had defected from Yahweh by setting up the golden calf, the post-Sinaitic 'Mosaic laws' are a legal compromise, as it were, merely human ordinances. For this interpretation they would appeal to Ezek. 20:25–26: 'Moreover I gave them statutes that were not good and ordinances by which they could not have life; and I defiled them through their very gifts in making them offer by fire all their first-born, that I might horrify them; I did it that they might know that I am the Lord [Yahweh].' Hence the Graeco-Jewish ideal of the *restitutio principii*: that is, 'it was not so in the beginning'; the aim, therefore, is to restore the pristine order of creation and free it from the subsequent accumulation of 'man-made laws'. In the Wisdom literature this notion of the 'restoration of the original state of things' is a conspicuous feature.[171] Whereas Aramaic Judaism equated the whole Torah with the expression of the ordering of creation, Greek Judaism sharpened the distinction between that ordering (*torah* proper) and the man-made laws in the Mosaic *torah* (as in the matter of the divorce law). The Decalogue is the direct expression of God's will, whereas a lot of those man-made rules on the one hand lay an intolerable burden on people and on the other hand often undermine the will of God and the purpose of the 'divine laws'. Thus Hellenistic Judaism, under the influence of the Wisdom literature, stresses (a) God's creation as the ground of all true commandments as being those of God, (b) primarily too the ethical and socio-ethical (communal) commandments, and (c) uncleanness, not in externals but in a spiritual sense, that is, the worship of false gods. Among these Diaspora Jews, who had a lot of dealings with Gentiles and drew their inspiration, on the whole, from the prophets, many were of a decidedly anti-Levitical persuasion. When large numbers of them, being deeply affected by their religious commitment as Jews, came from the Diaspora to live in Jerusalem, they were disillusioned to find synagogue and Temple there in the religious doldrums: an 'established religion'. In Jerusalem, therefore, prior to the presence of any Christians, there was an internal tension between these Greek-speaking Jews and the 'Levitical Jews'. The former interpreted the Levitical laws as, on an allegorical basis, ethical; and they did not feel bound by the rules prescribed for external cleanness.[172]

In these Graeco-Jewish circles the prophet of the latter days comes to be envisaged as the 'true teacher of the Law', calling the people back to the 'true Law of God', from which the laws of men had seduced them. It is precisely this replacement of God's Law by human laws that is interpreted as Israel's great unfaithfulness and departure from the Law. Here the 'anti-Christ' is set over against the 'Christ'; he is the great opponent of the Law, who leads the nation into apostasy, while the 'anointed one' or the eschatological prophet recalls it to God's true Law, the Decalogue.

The historical background to this twofold interpretation of the Law in Israel takes us back to the time of Antiochus IV Epiphanes, who allowed the Jews their (universal) Decalogue but suspended the other Mosaic laws. To the strictly faithful in Israel his behaviour appeared to be 'anti-God', 'against the Law'.[173] He abolished the sabbath, the sacrificial cult and feast days. His policy was directed 'against the Law and the Temple or holy place'. The more universally inclined, Greek-speaking Jews came to terms with this concrete situation and later on gave it a theoretical basis. Thus the Graeco-Jewish notion of the 'secondary laws' being due to 'hardness of heart' does ultimately come, via a number of different historical routes, from the Deuteronomic tradition; it is a genuine though not universal strain within Judaism. The conflict over the Law is therefore a traditional controversy within Judaism and so pre-dates Christianity. Because of its affinity with the pagan laws of Antiochus IV this Graeco-Jewish conception of the Law was fiercely opposed, especially by the Levitically orthodox Jews of Palestine.

Now it is obvious that the general tenor of Jesus' critical attitude *vis-à-vis* the Law, as couched in the words of the New Testament, has substantially a great deal in common with this Graeco-Jewish inter-pretation of the Law. In other words, Jesus is completely Jewish in this respect and in no way goes beyond what was possible for a Jew at that time. However, there must be a 'but' at this juncture. It is difficult to argue that Jesus the Galilean was brought up with a Graeco-Jewish understanding of the Law. Up to a point, of course, particularly in its towns around the lake and at the sea, Galilee was a kind of Jewish diaspora, a country with a very mixed, even bilingual population; and the purity laws were far from being as fully observed as in Jerusalem orthodoxy. But the synagogues were certainly supervised by 'the Scribes of the Pharisees' (see Mk. 2:16). But if we cannot assume that a Graeco-Jewish way of envisaging the Law was an influence in Jesus' case, the suspicion arises that the New Testament's picture of Jesus' attitude to the Law was revised after Easter – very likely by coteries of

Greek-speaking Jewish Christians. Several times already in the course of this study we have had occasion to notice the great extent to which early Christianity was affected by very active, Greek-speaking Jewish Christians who more or less from the start had been members even of the mother church of Jerusalem. This faces us with the problem: What is historical reminiscence of Jesus' conduct and teaching with respect to the Law, and what is simply participation on the part of an active section of the early Christian Church (the Hellenistic Jews) in the Graeco-Jewish interpretation of the Law? As some sort of check on this, we have by now a fair degree of certainty regarding the insights already obtained into Jesus' preaching and praxis of the kingdom of God. This can now be called in aid as one criterion (see Part One). As we have repeatedly established in the case of earlier themes, on the basis of what we have just been saying we shall have to take account of the fact that two layers have slid along each other – and done so on a basis of historical recollections of Jesus, 'lurking' as it were beneath them, namely an inter-Jewish controversy (e.g. Mk. 7:1, 5, 15) and, after the separation of the Christian communities from the Jewish synagogue, a controversy of the *Church with Israel* (e.g. Mk. 7:2, 3–4, 6–13, 14, 17–19, 20–22).[174] Without going too much into detail, a dip into what has been reliably achieved by exegesis is very necessary here, all the same, although the results so far attained will serve me – 'for theological purposes' as it were - as a guide and as something to work on.

(b) Q traditions and Marcan traditions about 'Jesus and the Law'

In the New Testament, whenever Jesus or his disciples contravene the Law, this is evidently interpreted as one of the factors accounting for Jesus' inevitable progress towards the cross. Such transgressions are recorded as an answer to the question how it could come about that Jesus was crucified. The motive, therefore, is determined by kerygmatic, not historical, considerations. On the other hand it would be wrong to argue that the situation out of which these pericopes were written was merely the concrete practice of the Church regarding the Jewish sabbath – a practice that they wanted to legitimate by an appeal to Jesus. Of course it is impossible to deny that the gospels, written in a period when the Church had completely broken away from Judaism, from the Temple, the Law and the sabbath, had felt the effect of these things; but on analysis it cannot fairly be said that these pericopes about Jesus' attitude to the sabbath are just a projection of the actual practice of the Church back into the life of Jesus. An awareness of the historical distance between Jesus' free stance towards the sabbath and the Church's practice in regard to public worship has left traces within the text itself. The Palestinian local churches continued to observe the sabbath and keep the Law (Mt. 24:20; see Acts 13:3; 14:23); they considered themselves to be a fraternity inside Jewry. In the Pauline churches, on the other hand, people were not interested in keeping the sabbath. But in what were for Paul the areas of his mission (Asia Minor) the Jewish Law and sabbath did have a considerable influence (Col. 2:16-17; Gal. 4:8-11).

The evidence we have to depend upon comes from two traditions: the pre-Marcan tradition and the Q source. Luke, on the other hand, still uses material from his own sources of tradition (Lk. 13:10-17; 14:1-6); but this is secondary in character – quite markedly so. Our starting-point, therefore, is still Mark and the Q tradition.

Although the pre-Marcan complex is very old (Mk. 2:1-3, 6), some of the material from what is perhaps the oldest phase of the Q tradition (thus in its Aramaic period) is, if not older, still less open to the suspicion of having been influenced by the Graeco-Jewish interpretation of the Law.[175] It seems to me the best point of departure, therefore (despite a lesser degree of certainty than S. Schulz would affirm with regard to exclusively Aramaic pericopes throughout the whole).

In these texts we do not find criticism of Israel as such, but of Pharisaic exposition and application of the Law. 'Now you Pharisees cleanse the outside of the cup and of the dish, but inside you are full of extortion and wickedness . . . But woe to you Pharisees, for you tithe mint and rue and every herb, and neglect justice and the love of God; these you ought to have done, without neglecting the others. Woe to you Pharisees for you love the best seat in the synagogues and salutations in the market places. Woe to you for you are like graves which are not seen, and men walk over them without knowing it . . . Woe to you lawyers also; for you load men with burdens hard to bear, and you yourselves do not touch the burdens with one of your fingers. Woe to you; for you build the tombs of the prophets whom your fathers killed. So you are witnesses and consent to the deeds of your fathers; for they killed them and you build their tombs . . . Woe to you lawyers; for you have taken away the key of knowledge; you did not enter yourselves, and you hindered those who were entering': thus the seven 'woes' of the Q community (Lk. 11:39, 42-44, 46-48, 52). They articulate the apocalyptic curse upon the concrete Pharisaic approach to life. What Mark presents in the form of disputations occurs here in that of the 'apocalyptical (that is, definitive) anathema'. As opposed to Matthew (23:26) and Luke (11:41) (both editorializing), the Q community continues to accept the rules prescribed for ceremonial cleanness (doing this, disallowing that); criticism is aimed not at the rules but at the attitude and outlook that govern their observance. Ceremonial conduct and ethical attitude should tally with each other. One could argue that the Law is being given a sharper edge here. A merely outward observance of the rules of purity covers a hidden state of impurity. This criticism of the Pharisees is still a strictly Jewish affair, not a Graeco-Jewish one; and one finds it also among the Essenes (in the Qumrân documents). The plain argument is that a proper concern with one's fellows, or righteousness, and love of God (Lk. 11:42) are the essence of the Law, and that for someone who rides roughshod over these commandments any other sort of conformity to what the Law prescribes is hypocrisy; it makes him 'a grave which is not seen' (it defiles a man to walk across a grave), that is to say, the Pharisees make others unclean.[176] They place heavy burdens on the people (Lk. 11:46), but without lifting a finger themselves. The point of this criticism in no way affects the Law itself, or indeed its stipulations, but the gap separating doctrine and life and the lack of love for others which lies behind it. Lastly, the Pharisees honour the memory of past prophets but will not accept the authority of the prophets living among them. Thus they bar for other people entry into the kingdom of God (Q in Mt.). These Palestinian Christians continue to recognize the regulative authority of the Scribes of the Pharisees, that is, that they are empowered to open up the kingdom of God by a right interpretation of the Law; for keeping the Law means, in a Pharisaic context, 'entering the kingdom of heaven' (it is even the Judaeo-Pharisaic notion of the kingdom of God that is employed here). The Pharisees do not enter this kingdom themselves, and by their behaviour they prevent others from going in. The final criticism by the Q community is aimed at the Pharisees' claim to priority and privilege; in the kingdom of God all are equal (indeed, the Q community's church order is different from that of Jerusalem; its charismatic prophets – not any *presbuteroi* – take the lead).

In these pronouncements of woe Jesus is seen, by implication, as being himself the true teacher of the Law, in contrast to the Pharisees, who fail to keep the Law according to its deepest meaning: love of God and of one's neighbour. For the way they observe the Law the Pharisees are assailed; yet the critique is still a Jewish one.

Even so, in terms of the approaching rule of God, a limit is set to the Mosaic Law; it is subject to an eschatological proviso (Mt. 5:18=

Lk. 16:19). With the arrival of God's rule the Law comes to an end
(Mt. 5:18). Later on it will be said in similar vein: 'The law and the
prophets were until John.' With Jesus the eschatological age sets in;
Jesus comes in place of the Law (Lk. 16:16). But in the thoroughly
eschatological vision of the oldest layer of the Q tradition such a
'realized eschatology' is out of the question.

The strict prohibition of divorce in the Q community (Mt. 5:32=
Lk. 16:18) (leaving out of it the Matthean clause allowing for one
exception), so far as motivation is concerned, is in line with the ideas
on purity in the Levitical tradition (no remarriage with a divorced
person) (whereas Mk. 10:11 puts a Graeco-Jewish emphasis on not
sending the woman away). This prohibition is a clear tightening up of
the Jewish Law.

Lastly, this older stratum of Q contains three stipulations, showing
quite plainly how it would interpret the Law: the need to abandon
completely the principle 'an eye for an eye, a tooth for a tooth' (Lk.
6:29–30=Mt. 5:39–42), love for one's enemy (Mt. 5:44–48=Lk. 6:
27–28, 35b, 32–35a, 36), and finally 'the golden rule' (Mt. 7:12=Lk.
6:31), that is, 'as you wish that men would do to you, do so to them'.
In particular, against the background of the late Jewish sectaries in
Palestine who isolate themselves into 'remnant-communities', regarding the rest as 'non-brothers', the command to 'love one's enemy',[177]
is especially striking. This too might be regarded as an accentuation
of the Law (Lev. 19:18), because the concept of 'neighbour' is enlarged
to include an enemy. It is much to the point that the command to love
one's enemy is associated in the Q community with the promise of the
sonship of God (Mt. 5:45; Lk. 6:35b). As the tradition developed, this
idea came to be connected with the sapiential *theologoumenon*: that the
righteous man, that is, he who stands in a right relation to his fellows,
is a 'son of God'.[178] 'An enemy', in the eyes of the one who sees him
as an enemy, is he who is not righteous and so is in the wrong. Thus
what this command to love calls in question is self-righteousness: to
give up one's own claim to being in the right is said here to be a
demand made by Jesus, a demand 'on God's part' – a demand not to
question God's justice but to doubt one's own; even God 'makes his
sun to rise on the evil and on the good' (again: a sapiential appeal to
God's ordering of creation) (Mt. 5:45); moreoever, tax-collectors and
sinners love those who love them; without love for one's enemy one is
like a 'tax-collector and sinner' (Mt. 5:46–47). The conclusion is: 'Be
merciful [Matthew has 'perfect'], even as your Father is merciful' (Lk.
6:36; see Sirach 4:9–10). Just as God draws no boundaries, a disciple of

Jesus cannot draw any, either: he has no enemy whom he is not enjoined to love. This saying is sanctioned by Jesus' own conduct in consorting, eating and drinking with tax-collectors and sinners; and it is the praxis of the kingdom, the kingdom of God in action. Whether Jesus did or did not utter in person the logion about 'loving one's enemies' is of secondary importance here; the chief thing is that this was his way of life in practice, a result of his proclaiming (even in parables) the approaching rule of God. Seen in that way, it is quite simply 'authentic Jesus', even though the Q community, giving a topical application to the practice and norm of Jesus, may perhaps be reacting here against unrest, discord and tensions in Palestine in the years prior to the Jewish War, and emphasizing some anti-Zealotic point. This insistence on a radical love of neighbour is illustrated by a Graeco-Jewish but also broadly Graeco-Roman, ancient 'golden rule of life': never do to others what you would not wish them to do to you (Mt. 7:12; Lk. 6:31). The ideal demands that we make on others must be the measure of our own behaviour towards them. 'That is the whole Torah': that is what late Graeco-Judaism was already saying.[179]

This gives us a major basic and 'authentic' principle enabling us to assess Jesus' attitude towards the Law: the radicalism of his demand for love of God and love towards all men, even the 'enemy', even tax-collectors and sinners: in other words, Jesus' message of God's rule, centred on the well-being of mankind. *This* is the message by which the Q community knows itself to be inspired; and so these Q pericopes are really a reflex or mirroring of the impression made on his followers by Jesus' public ministry.

The other tradition that confronts us from the pre-Marcan complex (Mk. 2:1 – 3:6), in which some five paradigmatic cases bearing on Jesus' ministry are thematized, may perhaps help us still further.

The first three stories (Mk. 2:1–12; 2:13–17; 2:18–22) have already been discussed in connection with Jesus' forgiving of sins, eating with a party of tax-gatherers, and not making the disciples fast. Whether they also serve to reveal Jesus' attitude to the Law will become clear from the two following stories, in which we hear of Jesus' disciples 'plucking ears of grain on the sabbath' (Mk. 2:23–28) and more especially of Jesus performing a cure on the sabbath (Mk. 3:1–5).

The two pericopes fall within what is known to exegesis as a 'disputation', which has obviously been influenced, therefore, by the post-Easter 'Israel and Church' relationship. The question here is simply whether in its free approach to the sabbath the Christian Church is conscious of being supported by Jesus' own *de facto* conduct, or whether (as many scholars would argue) it is projecting its actual practice back on to Jesus (and then perhaps without finding in the earthly Jesus himself a sufficient occasion and ground for it). In other words: Is the Church here really bringing up to date some authentic leanings on the part of Jesus, or is this just a projection of the Church back into the past, without any continuity with Jesus?

Jesus takes a walk with his disciples through some cornfields on a sabbath day; his disciples – not he – pluck ears of corn as they go along – a usual thing to do (though not on a sabbath). The Pharisees then hold Jesus responsible for the behaviour of those 'who go after him', his disciples. This distinction between Jesus, who does not break the sabbath, and his disciples, who do, can hardly have been motivated by a purely apologetic purpose in the Church; for that would be to lose the whole point of it. On the contrary, what is at issue here is the Jewish relationship between the Master and his disciples: from their behaviour, particularly when Jesus is present, one can correctly deduce what is the teaching of the Master. The crucial point is: Whence does Jesus get the authority to release his disciples from the duties imposed by the Law? Granted that Jesus (like David at an earlier time: 1 Sam. 21:6) does indeed allow the Law to be substantially breached. The point is not so much the general norm, that definite laws must be set aside in an emergency (the Scribes and Pharisees of the time could have gone along quite a way with that), [180] for (a) there is no question here of an emergency (as there was in the case of David and the showbread), but (b) of the parallel between 'David with his men' and 'Jesus with his men': that is, admitting David's exceptional position as a 'servant of God', it was permissible for him to do something for the good of his men which was in fact contrary to the Law; so too Jesus, because of and in his service of the kingdom of God, has complete authority to 'give exemption' from a law made by men. We are faced here with an emissary and envoy of God, who can and must interpret the Law for himself. It is in the end a matter of the authority and status of Jesus as the eschatological prophet 'from God'. The gist of it is faithfully expressed in Mk. 2:27–28: 'The sabbath was made for man, not man for the sabbath.' There has been a lot of discussion about this passage. Some commentators, particularly H. Braun,[181] maintain that man is lord of the sabbath and that the Jewish Christians were subsequently scared of that radical conclusion, therefore restricting this total authority, in a Christological context, to 'the son of man', Jesus. Even Jesus' own conduct they had to justify from Scripture: by an appeal to

1 Sam. 21:1–7 (in Mk. 2:25–26), to Num. 28:9–10 (in Mt. 12:5), or to Hosea 6:6 (in Mt. 12:7), or else they simply dismissed this logion (Mt. and Lk.). Only Mark has the radical logion: 'The sabbath is made for man' (and even then there are a number of variants in the manuscripts, proof of the hesitancy felt by Jewish Christians). H. Braun does admittedly concede that there were, even among the Jews, Scribes who accepted the saying: 'The sabbath is for you, not you for the sabbath'; but they are, he says, 'rare birds' in Judaism and furthermore make no point critical of the sabbath.[182] Jesus' attitude regarding the sabbath he calls downright un-Jewish. Other scholars, on the other hand, especially J. Roloff, who have gone very deeply into this question, have arrived at a contrary interpretation.[183] The meaning of the logion is said to be: 'Because the sabbath is for man, for that very reason the son of man is Lord of the sabbath.' The reasoning of the logion presupposes then, as the accepted basis for discussion, Jewish assent to the principle that the sabbath is for man; from that – with an eye to Jesus, the son of man – certain conclusions are meant to be drawn. Ever since the Maccabean period (see Mekiltha Ex. 31:13–14) the winged words 'the sabbath is for man' had been in circulation; and the argument of Mk. 2:27–28 has to be understood against that background. Behind the sabbath stands God; and even Jesus has no intention of attacking the sabbath in principle. God meant the sabbath to be a gift to man and for man (Deut. 5:12–15; Gen. 2:2–3; Exod. 20:8–11). Actually, the sabbath was introduced into Israel out of social concern and sympathy (to afford rest 'to slaves and cattle'); later on, a theological basis was given to it by the creation story. Judaic casuistry about the sabbath was originally designed to safeguard this divine gift against human wilfulness. But this legal quibbling was the very thing that in the long run betrayed the whole purpose of the sabbath: the sabbath law, intended for rest and relaxation, was perverted by this casuistry into an intolerable burden for the individual. Jesus, who proclaimed the rule of God as centred on humanity and man's well-being, was bound by the very essence of his message to protest against that. Over against the sabbatical decrees of the fathers and the Scribes or lawyers, Mk. 2:28 sets the plenary authority of the son of man. I think that J. Roloff's interpretation points us in the right direction, though with a fundamental proviso. That Jesus opposes his authority to that of the Scribes seems to me more of a post-Easter interpretation (apparent from the use of the term 'son of man' as applied to the earthly Jesus). In so far as historical recollections persist, Jesus is not acting here on his authority as the one empowered 'to grant dispensation' from the Law (even

though in Mark and his tradition that full authority has an obvious part
to play). His claim to authority (prior to Easter) lies elsewhere. What
the passage, as referring to the historical Jesus, articulates, in my
opinion, is Jesus' consciousness of being the 'eschatological prophet'
who was held to be 'the true teacher of the Law'; Jesus carries the law
of the sabbath back to its divine purpose: a gift of God to man, and not
a burden imposed on some people by others who fail to realize the
point of it themselves. His criticism does not apply to the Law as a
revelation of God's will, but to the way the Law is practised. It has
lost all relevance to religion and laid burdens on the people which God
himself does not wish to impose. The total authority with which Jesus
speaks is that of the prophet 'from God', who proclaims the rule of
God (hence: reverence for God's law), centred on the interests of
humanity (hence Jesus' critical view of these laws). Jesus' criticism of
them and his reverence for God's law are essentially bound up together;
it is in complete harmony with his preaching of God's rule and the
praxis of God's kingdom. The passage is soteriological in origin; in
Mark it acquires a Christological point (after Easter rightly enough; but
in itself it makes explicit the soteriology of Jesus' message and way of
doing things. In view of his reserve in testifying to himself – his cause
is after all God's cause – I find it impossible to imagine that Jesus himself could say: 'I [the son of man in the sense of 'I'] am the Lord of
the sabbath'). In his personal identification with God's cause as man's
cause, whence springs his critical approach to the sabbath, there is entailed, it is true, a Christological question – but one that becomes explicit only after Easter.

In the next pericope (Mk. 3:1–5) Jesus himself heals on the sabbath a
man with a 'withered' hand. The story is presented in the Marcan text
as a mutual challenge on the part of some Pharisees and Jesus. They
watched him to see whether he would cure a sick person on a sabbath
day (Mk. 3:2); Jesus for his part challenges them: 'Is it not lawful on
the sabbath rather to do good than to do evil, to save life than to kill?'
(3:4). They say nothing; for, good Pharisees as they are, they must go
along with that. Jesus then heals the hand – angry and at the same time
grieved at 'the hardness of their heart' (3:5). The centre of interest here
is not the miracle but the issue of the sabbath – the life-bringing action of
Jesus is clearly contrasted in the pericope with the 'decision to destroy
him' (3:6): that, according to the thread of the story, is their reply to
the question posed by Jesus (3:4). For Mark the problem is evidently
a Christological one. The original, pre-Easter version of events,

though, is soteriological: the Pharisees must in theory concede that one 'may do good' on the sabbath; but the line of conduct entailed by 'the fence around the Law' in fact prevents the good from being done. Indeed it is permissible from a Pharisaic standpoint to save a life on the sabbath, despite the literal import of the Law. But the case here is that of a shrivelled hand, an already protracted disease, which might equally well have been healed by Jesus on another day, not a sabbath. Jesus' criticism of the sabbath rest of Judaism goes beyond the Jewish casuistry regarding this, that or the other emergency. It relativizes the sabbath laws in a radical way: the sabbath rest is interpreted as a 'time for doing good', not one for 'not being allowed': to help a man in trouble is an action specially suited to the sabbath; for then one is fulfilling the saving will of God, from which the 'sabbath law' has sprung. Here again Jesus acts as the prophet from God, the 'true teacher of the Law'. By his liberating conduct, which is an indictment of prevailing circumstances and conditions of life, Jesus is bringing about what for himself is indeed an explosive situation.

It is evident, of course, that these two cases (within the complex Mk. 2:1 – 3:6), are meant to make a Christological point: where Jesus, the son of man, appears, there occurs an exception as far as the general law is concerned: then one does not fast and the sabbath may be infringed; here is more than the Law. In this sense it is not the question of the interpretation of the Law that provides a perspective for this Marcan narrative; rather, the story is designed to support a Christological conception. Yet that very conception rests partly on historical reminiscences of Jesus of Nazareth, who in word and action was 'the true teacher of the Law' and expounded it according to its proper meaning: the freedom to do good (see Mk. 3:4). What emerges here is in practice a different notion of God: God's rule, with humanity its chief consideration. As the will of God, the Law is radicalized as 'rule' ('dominion'), but at the same time bound up (thus as material law relativized) with the salvation of man. Jesus' critique of the *de facto* observance of sabbath and Law is identical, therefore, with his vision of the living God: the God 'intent on humanity', something on which Jesus' own praxis confers more and more historically substantive content. In a context of their own theological outlook, we find the same thing as the central core in the passages parallel to Mark: Mt. 12:1-8, 9-14; Lk. 6:1-5, 6-11, as also in the peculiarly Lucan tradition in Lk. 13:10-17; 14:1-6 – although the Christology in these pericopes is stated more explicitly than in Mark, who prefers to hint at it, since the Christological confession as such is made only beneath the cross. Out of the gospels, especially out of the 'thematizing' character of these stories – Jesus heals on the sabbath, and in a synagogue at that, a withered hand (Mk. 3:1–5), on the sabbath he cures a crookbacked woman (Lk. 13:10–17), and again on the sabbath a victim of the dropsy (Lk. 14:1–6) – there addresses us a memory of the life of Jesus, who had no time for a formalistic legalism without real content, that is, without real love for God and for neighbour. This practical legalism is accurately pinpointed by Lk. 13:14: 'There are six days on which work ought to be done; come on those days and be healed, and not on the sabbath day.' Over against that we read: 'There is nothing outside a man which by going into him can defile him; but the things which come out of a man are what defile him' (Mk. 7:15; cf. Mt. 23:23–24, 25–28) (nevertheless this is a Graeco-Jewish tradition; it is not from outside but from within that a man is rendered unclean; in other words, the outward rules of purity have no point except as a function of inward, ethical purity. Hence the slogan current among Greek Jews: 'Everything is clean'). Jesus was not against the Law; he radicalized it by bringing into the open its deepest purposes of salvation: a freedom 'to do good'. It meant that all 'man-made laws' are in fact radically relativized in their material content. It meant too that the praxis of the kingdom of God cannot really be 'laid down' in juridical laws (however much the actual business of living may sometimes call for them). It may demand at times that one do more than what the Law lays down; it may however also require one to go against what the Law specifies. At the same time that poses the lofty requirement that we should seek out God's *kairos* or propitious moment in the concrete circumstances of life. This at any rate is the way Jesus approached life. Judged on its own proper import, this implies a more intense emphasis on the Torah, based on a right view of the living God, the coming rule of God – the opposite of what one might call lawless libertinism. It expresses a real philanthropy, but starting from a specific view of who the living God is. Jesus is the exegete, not of the Law but of God; and in being so, he exposes man and provides a new perspective on salvation. When at last, after Easter, this rule of God assumed the concrete features of Jesus Christ, it was logical that people should revise and update the old memories of Jesus, and in place of Jesus' criticism, in the light of God's rule, directed at the practice of the Law, should see in them a historical claim to full authority on Jesus' part; in other words, what was historically the soteriological perspective of Jesus' earthly life was turned into a Christological discussion. The one conjures up the other. (But there is a hidden danger here that Jesus' criticism of the Law might be seen as a privilege belonging only to Christ – not to the Christian.) The Johannine gospel, therefore, *vis-à-vis* the synoptics, enlarges still more on the theme of the sabbath. Of the three healings reported by John, two occur on a sabbath day (Jn. 5:1–47; 9:1–39; see 5:9b and 9:14). Jesus' infringement of the sabbath rest is given an expressly Christological basis. Because of that, his breach of the sabbath rest is represented in even more provocative terms: he not only heals the crippled man on a sabbath, but orders him (as an act of sheer provocation) to pick up his stretcher and carry it himself: a 'gratuitous' breach of the sabbath. Here Jesus is indeed the sovereign and free legislator. His eschatological activity is not to be restricted by any mundane law whatever; for he is the son of the Father, a circumstance which actually fulfils the highest purposes of the Law, and at the same time concludes it: 'Christ is the end of the Law' (Rom. 10:4). The period in which God revealed his will 'through the Law and the prophets' reaches as far as John the Baptist; now it is to be done through the preaching of the gospel of the rule of God (see Lk. 16:16).

## (c) The cleansing of the Temple

There is one last and central piece of evidence that may enable us to determine what Jesus' attitude to the Law really was: the cleansing of the Temple (Mk. 11:15–18, parallels Mt. 21:12–17; Lk. 19:45–48; and Jn. 2:13–22), an extremely difficult gospel pericope which has been interpreted in very diverse ways; even to the extent that (following R. Eisler) S. Brandon has been able to read into the incident a kind of military Zealotic expedition of Jesus and his associates in Jerusalem.[184] An exegetically reliable analysis of the passage is advanced by J. Roloff, in my view to be refined upon from the insights of E. Trocmé. The oldest form of the story is to be found presumably in Mk. 11:15–16, 18a, 28–33.[185] It then becomes clear why early Christianity has handed on this tradition: the event is reported in view of its consequences, namely, Jesus' conflict with the representatives of the Sanhedrin. As a matter of fact, there is in the original block of narrative a seamless joint discernible between Mk. 11:18a and 11:28; that is to say, the question of Jesus' complete authority (which in the final text is left hanging in the air) was originally bound up with the cleansing of the Temple: members of the Sanhedrin ask Jesus by what authority he has done 'these things', that is, the cleansing of the Temple. Thus in the tradition *qua* history, this event is not associated with the solemn entry into Jerusalem. The whole thing points to a prophetic action on Jesus' part;

for the logion at Mk. 11:30 connects Jesus' action here with the prophetic ministry of the Baptist: Jesus postulates that both the baptism
of John and his own public activity (the cleansing) imply prophetic
authority. The argument of the logion is based on a material correspondence between John's and Jesus' ministry: both fall within the
constellation of the message of an eschatological conversion and the
renewal of the people of God. That gives us the angle from which to
view the historical point of the Temple cleansing: it was a prophetic
act, intended by Jesus to engender penitence and the conversion of
Israel, in the 'latter days'. It was in no sense therefore a radical assault
on Temple or cult, still less a solemn and direct 'messianic' proclamation
discarding the Jewish cult in favour of an eschatological universalism
that would open up the Temple to all nations. It has nothing to do, in
fact, with a Temple purification; the scene takes place in the Temple
courtyard, the 'court of the Gentiles', the great enclosure which the
merchants with their wares would take as a short cut (Mk. 11:16). The
actual site of the cult does not come into this – but the sacred character
of the whole Temple complex certainly does. This idea of the holiness
of the Temple is a rigorously Jewish one. But therein lies the point of
Jesus' actions: he is protesting about the gulf between theory and
practice in Judaism – the same complaint he makes about the way the
sabbath is kept. Each time the conflict has to do with the gap between
'orthodoxy' and 'orthopraxis'. Both sabbath and Temple are for Jesus
tokens of God's good and gracious will for Israel; but because of the
way things are done, they have both become divorced from their
proper purpose. It is not the Temple that is under attack here but the
Temple praxis, as it was with the great prophets, for whom the spiritual
quality of the Temple worship lay in the requirement of total obedience
to God 'in deed' (Amos 5:21–25; Jer. 7:3ff). For that matter, Zech.
14:21 too says that at the last day all Jerusalem and the whole Temple
complex will be 'sanctified': 'And every pot in Jerusalem and Judah
shall be sacred to the Lord of hosts, so that all who sacrifice may come
and take of them and boil the flesh of the sacrifice in them. And there
shall no longer be a trader in the house of the Lord of hosts on that
day.'[186] Nothing would make one suspect the presence, over and
above an act of prophecy, of a messianic trait in Jesus' conduct. There
is nothing in the incident that goes beyond the latter-day prophet's
summons to eschatological *metanoia*. Not until after Easter – in the
wake of a total view of Jesus' life – is it possible to interpret the cleansing of the Temple as 'a veiled proclamation of the special authority of
Jesus' (J. Schniewind).[187] The hope of an eschatological renovation of

the Temple is a widespread idea in late Judaism,[188] but it is nowhere associated with the messianic tradition.[189] All this confirms one of the basic propositions of this book: in his life on earth Jesus acts, not in a messianic role but as the eschatological prophet from God – and that, according to one particular Jewish tradition, is equally 'messianic'.

Besides positing the imperative need for absolute sanctification of the Temple, Jesus spoke on other occasions about the Jews' dismantling of it and about its eschatological rebuilding (Mk. 14:58 parallels). This logion, a basically authentic one, when linked up with Jesus' cleansing of the Temple, raises this event above its concrete historical content and significance: the place of encounter with God is not the Temple but Jesus himself. Jesus takes the place of the Temple as the medium of a relationship with God. Later on Matthew is to declare in similar vein: 'Where two or three are gathered in my name, there am I in the midst of them' (Mt. 18:20). What had been present at least as a question implicit in the entire soteriological activity of Jesus is put after Easter into an explicit Christological and even ecclesiological form. Just as the Temple was God's presence on earth, so now Jesus Christ becomes God's presence among us. But in the oldest layer of the account of the Temple cleansing all we have is Jesus' call to an eschatological pro-gramme of conduct in which the gap between theory and practice is closed, and the conflict that this critical exercise has touched off between Jesus and Israel's leaders. For what is clearly historical is that one of the reasons for Jesus' arrest has something to do with this cleansing of the Temple.[190] In this general conflict – the cause of Jesus' journey to the cross – lies therefore the initial purpose of the tradition, that is, the reason why this story was told and retold in the early Church.

In the synoptic tradition the original story (where the echoes of recollected history are strongest) was eventually linked up with pass-ages of Scripture (Isa. 56:7 and Jer. 7:11) (Mk. 11:17). The very fact that these texts were added reveals – being now Scripture for us – the original purpose of the Temple as opposed to what had been made of it in practice: in other words, the gap between orthodoxy and ortho-praxis. The point of relevance is Yahweh's judgement on what was actually going on in the Temple (Jer. 7:11); for God had intended the Temple to be 'a house of prayer (for all peoples)' (see Isa. 56:7). The stress is not really on 'all peoples' but on the 'house of prayer', con-trasted with the 'den of robbers' that men had made of it. The drift of it is not eschatological (in Mark) but concerns God's judgement on false practices. (Only Jn. 4:21–24 interprets the Temple discussion in an eschatological sense.) Thus the whole Marcan pericope would seem to be fairly close to the original meaning of the story. So too in Mt. 21: 12–17, which has actually dropped the 'for all peoples' (because this element was only intelligible in the context of the passage quoted from Isaiah and was not directly applicable to this case – not in Mark, either). It had nothing to do with a plea by Jesus for 'universal salvation', but concerned his indictment of Israel's concrete mode of conduct, although Matthew is to stress the messianic character of Jesus' cleansing of the Temple by conjoining it with the 'messianic entry' into Jerusalem (Mt. 21:10; see also Mt. 21:14 and 11:5) and by reference to Ps. 8:2 in Mt. 21:16. Luke for his part (in 19:45–46) sticks to a brief account of the whole scene: he outlines one element in Jesus' progress towards the cross, without attaching overmuch meaning to it.

Yet it is an arresting fact that John (in 2:13–22) sets the cleansing of the Temple in the early part of his gospel. That rules out any literary dependence on the synoptic tradition: conception and vocabulary are very different. But even in the pre-Johannine tradition the cleansing and the question of Jesus' authority would appear to be closely bound up together (Jn. 2:18), and even more clearly than in the synoptic tradition. What is more, the cleansing is expressly associated in John with the logion about the Temple's being destroyed and built again in three days. John too establishes a connection between that and the decision of the authorities to have Jesus put to death.

The four gospels, then, see a connection between the cleansing of the Temple and the arrest of Jesus. Although it is impossible, on the basis of Jesus' message and conduct and also having regard to the tenor of the gospel story, to distil out of this Temple incident the Zealotic fiction advanced by S. Brandon, one must not on the other hand minimize the political consequences and implications of this behaviour on Jesus' part. The Temple at that time was also a stronghold of the policing authorities; and what happened there was 'hot news' throughout Palestine, certainly on the Jewish feast days, with their influx of people from every part of the country. There is much to be said for the view that in point of historical fact this cleansing of the Temple took place neither at the outset of Jesus' public life (John) nor at its end (synoptics) but somewhere between the two.[191] Jesus' unassuming gesture in cleansing the Temple, to which in fact not a single allusion is made in the account of his Passion and trial, acquired – in view of the situation – an enormous 'political' significance, partly because of the scant popularity of the pro-Roman tradesmen in the Temple courtyard. In the historical situation the cleansing episode may perhaps have served to make Jesus into a popular hero-figure with a people long frustrated and bitterly hostile towards the Temple rulers (who controlled Israel's currency and economy) and the Romans. This would explain the 'messianic' ambience surrounding Jesus, which in the context of his final days it is hard to ignore; and it would give grounds for not assigning the cleansing of the Temple to the very last week of his life and for not interpreting it as the immediate occasion for his arrest. The Johannine gospel, which the exegetes invariably set apart from the rest – at any rate when it comes to historically reliable memories of Jesus' earthly life – would seem nevertheless to have its own 'sources of historical information' (however coloured by theology), specifically, the 'rumours among the people' concerning Jesus of Nazareth. John puts the Temple cleansing at the start of Jesus' public ministry. Historically, that is manifestly wrong; but it does serve to correct the synoptic view. The suddenly more-or-less universal currency, still detectable in the four gospels, given in Palestine to the 'Jesus affair' was most likely connected with the appearance and behaviour of Jesus in the Temple at Jerusalem. This popularity of a man critical of the Temple must have been the first positive reason for political anxiety among the leaders of Israel, the beginning of the fatal outcome of the life of Jesus. To determine the historical facts in more precise detail would seem impossible. But in such an atmosphere of popularity on the one hand and governmental suspicion on the other, various utterances of Jesus (for instance, about the destruction and rebuilding of the Temple) would assume unprecedented and unforeseen proportions (see Mk. 14:56, 59; Mt. 26:60–61, which are clear evidence of rumours circulating about Jesus' sayings; see also Mk. 13:1–2 and Mt. 24:1–2). John is apparently witness, in a particular tradition, to these reports circulating among the people, as he connects the Temple cleansing explicitly with Jesus' words about the Jews' destroying the Temple, while he himself would build it up in no time at all (Jn. 2:19). Clearly in operation here between Jesus' utterances and his arrest is the intermediary filter of 'popular report' concerning somebody who had suddenly become 'national news'. For the one group Jesus eventually became a messianic hope, for the other a dangerous individual. All this would seem to point to a certain period of considerable popularity for Jesus, to which various New Testament data bear testimony: here comes the long awaited son of David! Peter's 'confession of faith' is in that case just an echo of an expectation on the increase in many quarters. This flame of messianism which flared up in connection with Jesus in Palestine, however briefly, would certainly seem to have been the reason for the fateful disquiet of Israel's rulers, who from then on really did keep a watch on Jesus – as the gospels repeatedly suggest. One can also date from that juncture Jesus' assumption of a fatal outcome to his career. From the period of this dubious popularity we can see in Jesus – something still recognizable from the gospels – a certain reticence *vis-à-vis* the people and a concentration on the specific task of training his disciples (see too a later chapter).

The gospels do after all get it right when they establish (though perhaps too directly) a connection between Jesus' arrest and the cleansing of the Temple. What for Jesus is fully in keeping with his message of the praxis of the kingdom of God and his call to Israel to be converted to the true and living God became, considering the concrete situation, in the eyes of an exasperated nation a course of daring and provocative behaviour, which indeed aroused messianic expectations among the people, but among the authorities grave suspicion and hostility. What was in fact – and in conformity with Jesus' life as a whole – a prophetic act on the part of the latter-day messenger from God, intended to stir up in Israel a faith in God – Jesus' attitude to the Law, the sabbath and the Temple – was turned (partly via the prism of popular opinion) into a mortal threat against the official establishment. The *spiritual* threat and indictment that Jesus was, and that should have given occasion for *metanoia*, thus came to nothing.

In answer to the question posed at the start of this section, as to how far Jesus' attitude towards the Law substantially coincides with the view of the Law held by the Greek-speaking Jews, we can now affirm that the outlook of those Jews (in the Hellenistic-cum-Jewish orbit of early Christian tradition) has clearly had an effect on its formulation. Mark contrasts the *entolè*, God's commandment, with *paradosis*, tradition and the precepts of men (7:3, 5 and 7:7 over against 7:8); that is exactly the Hellenistic-Jewish distinction. In a similar perspective the idea of 'hardness of heart' is conjoined with the post-Sinaitic law of the 'certificate of divorce' (Mk. 10:5). This also accounts for the divergent interpretations in early Christianity as between the Levitically orientated Jewish Christians (Mt. 5:32) and the Hellenistic ones (Mk. 10:11 and 1 Cor. 7:10) with regard to the motivation of marital fidelity.[192] We cannot forget, however, that Jesus' own inspiration springs from his vision of the coming rule of God, which prompts him to stand up for the weakest and underprivileged party – in this case the woman.[193] Nowhere does Jesus himself make the (Jewish-Hellenistic) distinction between primary and secondary laws; but he assessed every law on its religious relevance for man and went on to emphasize the inward, ethical attitude to life in all observance of the Law. In effect, this attitude was materially closer to the outlook of the Greek-speaking Jews on the question than to Levitical orthodoxy; but one cannot demonstrate a Graeco-Jewish influence on Jesus' own attitude, nor can it be said that this critical approach to the Law came only from Hellenistic-Jewish circles in early Christianity. Yet the Hellenistic-Jewish Christians made a not inconsiderable contribution to the way Christians formulated Jesus' attitude to the Torah. This should be especially evident from the presentation of the problem that now follows.

(d) The Law as love for God and love for men

The question of the love of God and of one's neighbour, as summing up the Law, is something we meet with in Mk. 12:28–34 (parallel texts Mt. 22:35–40; Lk. 10:25–28) and according to Jn. 13:34–35 in the new commandment, so called, given by Jesus.

Both major commandments, taken separately, are thoroughly Jewish: 'Hear, O Israel: the Lord our God is one Lord; and you shall love the Lord your God with all your heart and with all your soul and with all your might' (Deut. 6:4–5, see 26:16), and: 'You shall not take vengeance or bear any grudge against the sons of your own people, but you shall love your neighbour as yourself: I am the Lord' (Lev. 19:18). Of course, this love of one's neighbour is still confined, here at any rate, to fellow-Israelites, members of the people of God. Subsequently (Lev. 19:34) 'the stranger' is included as a neighbour. Moreover, it seems that 'to love Yahweh' and 'to keep his commandments' were originally synonymous (Deut. 6:4–5 with 6:6; 5:10; 7:9; 10:12; 11:1, 13, 22; 19:9; 30:6; esp. Deut. 6:4–5 with 26:16; 2 Kings 23:25). Not until later, particularly in Graeco-Judaism, did this synonymity become a problem. Hence the Jewish enquiry as to the first and great commandment (which we find also in Mk. 12:28). Hellenism, and so the Greek-speaking Jews, recognized two major commandments: the *eusebeia*, the principal command to worship God, and the *dikaiosunè*, the right relationship with one's fellows, the sum of all the commandments severally.[194] Thus the Greek Jews set two sectors of commandments side by side. The love of neighbour is not a second main commandment here, but an epitome of them all, whereas formerly it had been the love of God that constituted the ground and source of all other obligations, so also of love for one's neighbour: to love God meant keeping the commandments. Thus there emerged the question of 'two great commandments', which meant that the intrinsic relation between love of God and ethics (keeping commandments) became problematical[195] – a result of the effect of the Greek notion of a pair: *eusebeia* (piety) and *dikaiosunè* (ethos). In late Judaism the frequent expression was: God and the Law, rather in line with Deuteronomy. This made the shift to 'love of God' and 'love of neighbour' possible.

'The neighbour' in the Old Testament underwent all sorts of changes of meaning. In the earliest texts it is the compatriot or social peer; later on, the poor or the lowly, less important and socially inferior fellow-countryman, needing protection; finally, all members of the nation are for every Israelite like the 'weak man', entitled to help: all are brothers. According to the final redaction of Deuteronomy, the way one should behave in practice towards the poor is to be extended to all one's fellows within the nation; that is to say, above and beyond all law and justice, love of one's neighbour is a brotherly, protective, loving attitude towards each member of God's people. Then at last what is called for is an inward disposition of love and kindness.[196] For the Wisdom writers and the prophets 'the neighbour' means first and foremost the poor of society. So in Lev. 19:18 we read: you shall love your fellow as yourself; wish a man whatever he wishes for himself; only then can universal peace prevail in Israel (although very early, this outlook was already affected by Hellenistic influences). In the Septuagint the 'neighbour' concept (*ho plèsion*) is subject to a number of refinements. In secular Greek it means the 'person next door', the nearest people around, ultimately the other person you happen to meet. Thus neighbourly love was extended by the Jews of the Diaspora to become universal: it included everybody. 'My neighbour' is each and every person I meet (a consequence of the Diaspora Jews becoming adapted to their Gentile surroundings, and partly of an intensified faith in the God who creates everything and everybody). Affection for the members of a sociologically circumscribed community, on the other hand, comes to be called brotherly love; this kind of love is something maintained within sub-groups (even in the later writings of the New Testament the love of neighbour is gradually displaced by brotherly love, the love of Christians for one another). Eventually, Greek Jews (branded by pagans as 'misanthropes')[197] in the Greek combination of *eusebeia* and *dikaiosunè* replaced the latter with *philanthrôpia*: all social obligations towards the individual 'other person' (not a general 'ideal of humanity').

In the intertestamentary literature, as it is called, the two 'great commandments' (Deut. 6:4–5 and Lev. 19:18) have already been brought together, not so much from Scripture itself but under the influence exerted by the twofold Greek notion: 'Love the Lord and your neighbour', or: 'Love the Lord and each person with your whole heart',[198] where love of neighbour is understood in a universalistic sense: *pas anthrôpos* is the notion stressed here.[199] Thus in the Testaments of the Patriarchs the particularist Jewish standpoint is broken through; indeed there the 'eschatological prophet' is a light for the whole world (albeit coming from Israel). Israel will be the world's instructor.

The amalgamation of two great commandments, therefore, was the work of Greek-speaking Jews; elsewhere, among the Aramaic Jews, we do not find it. That means of course that the problem as stated and formulated in Mk. 12:28 and parallels could as such only have emerged in the admittedly very early Greek-speaking section of the primitive Church; thus a nexus of internal Jewish problems was only there linked up with belief in Jesus Christ.

Again the so-called 'golden rule' (Mt. 7:12) was in origin non-Jewish but assimilated into Judaism through Hellenism.[200] In the Hebrew text of Sir. 34:15 it says (by way of commentary on Lev. 19:18): 'Be friendly towards your friend as towards yourself'; the 'golden rule' is introduced into the Greek text at this point: try to look at the other man's situation with his eyes; put yourself in the other man's place. This rule comes to be regarded as summing up all ethical requirements (as also in Mt. 7:12).

The questions and answers in Mk. 12:28–34, where Deut. 6:4–5 and Lev. 19:18 are conjoined, are therefore neither specifically Christian nor peculiarly 'Jesuanic', as is in fact admitted by the Scribe (Mk. 12:32). The Hellenistic Luke indeed puts the reply into the mouth not of Jesus but of the Scribe, and Jesus simply endorses it (Lk. 10:26–28). In its presentation of the issues Mk. 12:32–33 is Graeco-Jewish. Thus the Scribe is told: 'You are not far from the kingdom of God' (12:34). So what does he still lack? 'After that no one dared to ask him any question' (12:34b). What Mark is secretly getting at here is that what he lacks is belief in Jesus.[201] So the discussion in Mk. 12:34 and parallels does not go back to Jesus or yet to the Old Testament and Hebraic Judaism (a more Hebraic aspect is presented by the triad in Mt. 23:23: *krisis, eleos, pistis*, that is, 'righteousness, mercy and faithfulness', cited there as 'the weightiest matter of the Law', that is, neighbourly love). It falls rather into a Hellenistic-Jewish tradition, in particular, that of its catechesis for proselytes. Keeping the two commandments, that is, standing in a right relation to God (*eusebeia*) and to man (*dikaiosunè*) serves to qualify an individual as *hagios* and *dikaios* (of Jesus, in Acts 3:14; of John the Baptist, in Mk. 6:20; in the Benedictus in Lk. 1:75, where *hosiotès* is synonymous with *eusebeia*; also Lk. 2:25; of the catechumen, Cornelius, in Acts 10:22; also Acts 10:35; yet again in 1 Thess. 2:10; 2:15; 1 Tim. 6:11; Tit. 2:12; 1 Jn. 4:20–21; or in a negative sense, *asebeia* and *adikia*, in Rom. 1:18). In both concepts the love of God and love of neighbour are combined. All passages in this vein go back within the historical development of the tradition to a source in Greek Judaism. It implies too that *qua* obligation 'the Law' is already limited to the Decalogue (invariably cited without a note of criticism, rather as the norm of moral conduct; Mk. 7:10; 10:11–12, 19); Christians do not even feel obliged to give an allegorical explanation of the purity laws. Love of God requires them to fulfil the ethical 'ten commandments of God'. That is how, basing themselves on Graeco-Jewish ideas, they interpret Jesus' critical attitude to the Law.

Mark 12:29–31 takes a hierarchical view of the two main commandments (*prōton-deuteron*); this too is Graeco-Jewish. Matthew 22:39, and also Lk. 10:25–28 (which includes the two 'objects' of love under the single, unrepeated 'you shall love'), treat both commandments as being on a par. Even so, in the rest of the New Testament we find little interest in this question, so that almost every reference is to the love of one's neighbour, and then eventually to brotherly love alone; this is more Hebraic-Jewish (here the two duties are not seen as chief commandments, together summarizing the Law).

All this indicates that the Graeco-Jewish principle of the 'twofold commandment' was no more than relatively widespread in early Christianity (and in the Q tradition it is unknown).[202]

With respect to Jewish Torah-orthodoxy the formula of the 'two great commandments' does indeed have a function for Christians in criticizing the Torah; this twofold commandment is the measure and criterion for assessing and judging each and every law (Mk. 12:28–34; see immediately below). It enabled the Christians, aided by the already existing Graeco-Jewish interpretation of the Law, to reflect accurately with these Graeco-Jewish categories the impression that Jesus' attitude to the Law had made upon them – this all the more readily when after 70 a Hebrew orthodoxy had clearly got control and the conflict with Christianity grew more acute. The point of the story in Mark is: Jesus is here giving authoritative expression to the (in fact Graeco-Jewish) principle of the two great commandments; the intention is a Christological one. A particular (Graeco-) Jewish tradition is put into the mouth of Jesus because 'the nearness of God's kingdom' has to do also with 'right doctrine' (see Mk. 12:34), that is, the doctrine of the Christian community.

Does this pericope simply give thematic structure to a general recollection of Jesus' approach to living, in the sense of God's rule (thus: love of God) centred on human well-being (thus: an insistence on love of one's neighbour)? The Graeco-Jewish great commandments do indeed sum up the praxis of the kingdom of God in its entirety. But does the central core of this logion come from Jesus? The passage quoted from Deut. 6:4–5 in Mk. 12 tallies with neither the Greek nor the Hebrew text of Deuteronomy. It seems plausible, therefore, that the allusion here is to the Jewish prayer-formula of the *Shemah Yisroël*, although no connection is made in it between love of God and love for men. Moreover, in Mk. 12:33b, after the mention of the two great commandments, it says significantly: 'that is much more than all whole burnt offerings and sacrifices'. What does it mean in this context? Evidently a passage critical of the cult: love of God and ethics are much more than all the cultic requirements of the Torah – the very thesis of the Graeco-Jewish literature between the Testaments,[203] at the same time associated with the ancient prophetic critique of the cult (1 Sam. 15:22; Hosea 6:6; but also in the Wisdom literature: Prov. 16:7 and in apocalyptic: Dan. 3:38ff). 'I desire mercy and not sacrifices' (Hosea 6:6 LXX) is for Matthew (9:13; 12:7) already programmatically Christian. Plainly then, the Graeco-Jewish doctrine of the 'two great commandments' is used by Mark on the one hand to encapsulate Jesus' critical attitude to the Law, on the other to vindicate the praxis of the early Church *vis-à-vis* Israel. Thus Mk. 12:29–33 makes a connection between love of God and of neighbour *and* the aloofness from cultic rules (the Temple cult). This points also to the tenets of the 'Stephen' Hellenists within the mother church (see Acts 6:11, 13, 14). At the same time it is saying that, as one concurs with these two great commandments and their power to function as a critique of the cult, one is at the very kernel and centre of Jesus' message of the rule of God (Mk. 12:34).

A comparison of Mark with the parallel passages in Matthew and Luke throws into sharp relief the differences between the three evangelists in their deployment of this pericope. Mark 12:32–34 is missing from Luke and Matthew: that is, they do not have the emphasis on these two great commandments as signifying a critique of the cult; furthermore, the pericope differs in a fairly striking way from Mark's.[204] Mark, it seems, uses a tradition which mentions only the first commandment – the love of God – in the sense of the first question in the catechesis of the Diaspora, where the concern is with the conversion of Gentiles to the one true God. This is linked up in the Marcan gospel with the general Jewish understanding of neighbourly love as a summary of the Law, and thus the Graeco-Jewish twofold notion of the love of God and of one's neighbour is adopted at the same time. Mark's idea in all this is to include mention of the principal commandments drawn out of all that God prescribes for the salvation of men (Mk. 12:28–31). With a view to this he also finds a Scriptural location for the Graeco-Jewish dual commandment (*eusebeia* and *dikaiosunè*). It is all put into the mouth of Jesus, as evidence of his normative authority (without any attempt to hide the fact that these two commandments, as twin commandments, come from elsewhere). Mark 12: 32–34 is a Scribal commentary, therefore, on Mk. 12:28–31: that is, on the basis of these two commandments the cultic and ritual regulations of the Torah have been fundamentally relativized (in that respect agreeably with Matthew's citation from Hosea 6:6). What comes out here is a Greek and late Jewish view of the Law; everything in the Torah not comprehended under the Decalogue commandments and the command to love is a 'precept of men' that can be radically criticized (cf. Mk. 7:10). An internal Jewish, albeit Graeco-Jewish, notion of the Law is deployed against Judaism itself after the separation of Church and synagogue.[205] The Matthean tradition and redaction on the other hand set the question straightaway against the background of the late Jewish conception of *nomos* or law: 'Master, which is the great commandment in the law?' (Mt. 22:36). 'Law' here is the Decalogue, not the Torah as a whole. For Matthew the two great commandments are the foundation principles which undergird and give point to the whole Decalogue (the cult-critique is left out here, because the cult does not even come under this late Jewish *nomos*-concept): 'On these two commandments depend all the Law and the prophets.'[206]

In Matthew the Scribe is really asking about criteria for distinguishing important commandments. That is precisely what Jesus will not go into: the relationship with God and man is the crucial thing in every law; the whole Law depends on that. Elsewhere Matthew says the same of neighbourly love alone (the golden rule) (Mt. 7:12) in a sapiential vein, as first explicitly formulated in the Book of Wisdom 6:18. All other commandments are grounded in the love of one's neighbour, which gives them their point and purpose. The Johannine gospel, being more in line with the Wisdom tradition, even regards the love of neighbour as summing up the Christian way of life – even though concentrated in this case as brotherly love among Christians: 'A new commandment I give to you, that you love one another; even as I have loved you, that you also love one another. By this all men will know that you are my disciples, if you have love for one another' (Jn. 13: 34–35). Here 'love for one another' has already become an ecclesio-logical concept.

With Luke (as with John) the whole nexus of problems centred around the Law in this connection has disappeared; the two main principles are seen within the message of the gospel as 'a way of life' (Lk. 10:25). Then again, the dual commandment is not stressed in any way by having the parable of the Good Samaritan appended to it. Luke is out to explain what the idea of 'a neighbour' signifies, under the inspiration afforded by Jesus (Lk. 10:25–29). Nor are the two great commandments put into the mouth of Jesus; Jesus simply endorses what a Scribe says of his own accord. Luke's real concern is with this parable: only then does Jesus answer the question: 'What shall I do to inherit eternal life?' (Lk. 10:25). What is distinctive of Jesus in the parable does not lie in the doctrine of the two great commandments. Luke intimates that without Jesus we can perfectly well read the one twofold great commandment in the Bible, but now, cutting across that, comes Jesus' teaching: the Good Samaritan, as making concrete that great commandment. Luke turns right around the idea of 'neigh-bour' (from Lev. 19:18 LXX): the neighbour is not so much an object of activity, but the active subject himself makes himself neighbour and helper to the other. The relation between 'neighbours' only comes about when we help and support somebody – when the one person has come 'nigh' to the other. That is the Christian love of neighbour, which is made real as in charity we draw near to a fellow human being: bringing people together in unity, helpful communication, making friends with each other.

With Mark and in Matthew 22 the neighbour is simply 'the other person' (in line with the Septuagint); in Lk. 10:36–37 (and Mt. 5: 43–44) 'neighbour' is understood more in the sapiential (Wisdom) tradition as 'the friend' – but then in a Christian context: the one 'made into a friend' (Q tradition). Again, from Lk. 18:22–30 it seems that for Luke 'the love of one's neighbour' is something to be realized con-cretely in concern for the poor and support of the destitute. Alms-giving is not a commandment in the Decalogue, but a 'command of love' (Lev. 19:18). Turning in repentance to God and helping the help-less – these are held here to be the fundamental commandment. More-over, it is a semi-pagan, the Samaritan, who becomes 'the neighbour'!

Although we do not have in the pericope of the two great commandments historically authentic utterances of Jesus, but a Graeco-Jewish range of questions problematical in certain sectors of early Christianity, the problems stated here are brought within the authentic message of Jesus concerning God's rule and its focus on humanity, and especially of Jesus' practical reverence for the Law on the one hand and his critical view of a legalistic ideology on the other. All this would seem to support the conclusion that Jesus liberates the individual from an oppressive and narrow idea of God, by exposing the ideology as an orthodoxy that stood in a ruptured relationship to orthopraxis, and furthermore, *qua* orthodoxy, had established an ethic as an independent screen between God and man, so that the relevance of the legal obligations to man's salvation had become totally obscured. The repercussion of Jesus' own message of God's rule on human ethics is therefore characterized as a factor of truly human liberation, thanks to his novel and original experience of God.

B.   JESUS' ORIGINAL *ABBA* EXPERIENCE, SOURCE AND SECRET OF HIS BEING, MESSAGE AND MANNER OF LIFE

*Literature.* R. Beauvery, 'Mon Père et votre Père,' in *Refus du père et paternité de Dieu*, LVie, n. 104 (1971), 75–88; A. George, 'Le Père et le Fils dans les Évangiles synoptiques', LVie, n. 29 (1956), 27–40, and 'Jésus, Fils de Dieu dans l'Évangile selon saint Luc', RB 72 (1965), 185–209; P. Giblet, 'Jésus et "le Père" dans le IVe Évangile', *L'Évangile de Jean, Études et problèmes*, RechBibl 3 (Louvain 1958), 111–31; W. Grundmann, *Sohn Gottes*, ZNW 47 (1956), 113–35, and 'Zur Rede Jesu vom Vater im Joh.', ZNW 52 (1961), 214–30; F. Hahn, *Hoheitstitel*, 280–346; B. van Iersel, *Der Sohn*; see also NovTSuppl 3 (1964); J. Jeremias, *Abba. Studien zur neutestamentlichen Theologie und Zeitgeschichte*, Göttingen 1966; and 'Das Gebetsleben Jesu', ZNW 25 (1926), 123–40; T. de Kruyff, *Der Sohn des lebendigen Gottes* (Analecta Biblica, 16), Rome 1962; W. Marchel, *Dieu Père, dans le Nouveau Testament*, Paris 1966, and *Abba, Père, La prière du Christ et des chrétiens* (Analecta Biblica, 19), Rome 1963; A. Mitscherlich, *Auf dem Weg zur Vaterlosen Gesellschaft*, Munich 1970; A. W. Montefiore, 'God as Father in the Synoptic Gospels', NTS 3 (1956–7), 31–46; C. Orrieux, 'La paternité de Dieu dans l'Ancien Testament', LVie, n. 104 (1971), 59–75; J. Pohier, *Au nom du Père*, Paris 1972; P. Pokorný, *Der Gottessohn* (Theol. Stud., 109), Zürich 1971; H. Ringgren, s.v. ab, ThWAT (Stuttgart 1970), I, 1–19; G. Schrenk, s.v. *Patèr*, in ThWNT V, 946–75, 996–1004; R. Schäfer,

*Jesus und der Gottesglaube. Ein christologischer Entwurf*, Tübingen 1970; S. Schulz, 'Das Vaterunser', *Q-Quelle* (84–93), esp. 87–8; A. Vergrote, 'Le Nom du Père et l'écart de la topographie symbolique', *Le Nom de Dieu* (ed. Castelli), Paris-Rome 1969; – s.v. *Huios* (P. Wülfing von Martitz, G. Fohrer, E. Schweizer, E. Lohse, W. Schneemelcher), ThWNT VIII, 334–400.

Even without our willingness to venture on the hopeless enterprise of dissecting the psychology of Jesus (the data needed for that are not available to us), what he said (his message) and what he did (his mode of conduct) are enough to shed light on his self-understanding: his activities spring from his extraordinarily pronounced consciousness of a prophetic role, on which is grounded his message of the approaching rule of God, while in and through his own strangely marvellous ministry he sees clearly that this kingdom is drawing near. The first thing that strikes us is Jesus' Jewish spirituality. Scholars are so often inclined to make much of the Old Testament, whereas Judaism or late Judaism, particularly that of Jesus' own time, is presented in a distorted fashion. As a result, the relation between Jesus and Judaism is itself distorted; one forgets that the Old Testament was not functioning *per se* or in isolation but in the context of late Jewish piety as that had since been developing. One cannot with impunity skip over the time that had elapsed between the great prophets and Jesus. It is clear enough from the Jewish as well as the Christian 'exegesis' of the time how people read the Bible or were nurtured by it via a mental horizon and a perspective on life that had long since been in process of change. They drew their way of living not so much from 'a book' as from traditions: the 'Isaianic tradition' (Isaiah, Deutero- and Trito-Isaiah), Deuteronomic spirituality, the piety of the Wisdom literature, apocalyptic zeal, a Levitical-cum-priestly spirituality and so forth. A verdict of 'pure legalism' as well as the qualification 'apocalyptic fanaticism' gives a false picture of the Judaism in which Jesus lived. It would be quite wrong to ignore Jesus' critical view of real aspects of Jewish piety (we have already seen that his criticisms were subtly tempered and based on implicit assent to Israel's institutions and Law); but Jesus blames his co-religionists not so much for a lack of 'orthodoxy' as an ideological attitude, in which theory and practice drift apart and in particular concern for the ordinary person is lost sight of. But we must not first lay on a thick undercoat of paint to give a dark background in order to depict the figure of Jesus gleaming all the more brilliantly in the front of the picture. What Jesus lived by was the Jewish passion for searching out God's will in everything. His God was Israel's God, the God of the patriarchs and prophets, Israel's God, who lived still in apocalyptic and in the zeal of Pharisee and Essene. Yet at the same time all this enshrined a gravely distorted idea of God because, in its tendency to religious separatism and élitism, late Judaism denied in practice God's universal love.

The distinctive relation of Jesus to God was expressed in the primitive Christian churches more especially by use of the honorific title 'Son of God' and 'the Son'. These were Christian identifications of Jesus of Nazareth after his death. Jesus never spoke of himself as 'the Son' or 'Son of God'; there is no passage in the synoptics pointing in that direction; what is certain is that he referred in a special way to God as *Abba*. To recover something of Jesus' own relationship to God, therefore, we are thrown back on Jesus' message and manner of life and on his prophetic self-understanding, which can also be regarded as a settled fact of history. In other words we have to depend on what at first sight might be called 'indirect' evidence. Actually this fits well with the anthropological insight that, whether for himself or for others, it is only in his actions that a man is finally to be understood.[207] For although Jesus never posited himself (beside the rule of God) as the second subject of his proclamation, in the business that occupied him and with which he identified himself, he also revealed his self-understanding. This is not a blind spot for us within the luminous revelation of his message and praxis. If the rule of God as proclaimed by Jesus assumes a definite form and aspect in his own conduct and way of life, then there is already a detectable relation – albeit one requiring further delimitation – between the actual person of Jesus, his message and his behaviour; and then his person is never entirely separable from his message and ministry. In a post-Easter confessional way of speaking it is possible to affirm *a priori* that Jesus is God's great act of salvation in this world; and on that basis one can go on to interpret what he said and what he did. That is a way of talking about Jesus based on the attempt to identify him and to understand his life as a totality. But our purpose is, along with his disciples, as it were, to follow the way of Jesus from Nazareth right up to his death so as in that way (and again 'as it were') to trace for ourselves how the faith-inspired interpretation of Jesus as the Christ came into being. Secondly, we are looking for traces in the life of Jesus that, for us as for the disciples, could constitute an invitation to assent in faith to what is indeed God's great work of salvation in Jesus of Nazareth. The result is not to 'legitimize' our faith; but it does mean that we can keep a critical watch on the legitimate 'emergence' (or persistence) of distinctively Christian belief.

To go in search of the original and unique centre of someone's religious experience is a highly precarious undertaking. That is true (a) if the person gives direct expression to his private experiences (something which Jesus never does, to judge from the available sources of knowledge about him); for then we have the problem of telling what may be the relationship between the authentic element of experience and its clarifying interpretation, as the two are of course inextricably intertwined, without coinciding in a self-evident or transparent identity; and (b) when somebody does not articulate such experiences directly, but speaks about God and his cause in such a way that by so doing he intimates or discloses his personal religious relationship to God. This is a difficult task, especially in the case of religious experience, because we are then trying to penetrate to the very mystery of a personal being; we are asking after whatever it is with which he identifies his heart, his mind and life, his whole being-as-a-person and which gives his life its synthesis, in other words, after what constitutes him this particular person and provides grounds for this being-a-person. Now the mystery of each person is only accessible to us in his behaviour, which on the other hand is just the inadequate sign of the person manifesting himself in it and at the same time conceals him. It is more than his several actions and yet is disclosed only *in* this activity.[208] This does not stop us from acquiring through these acts a slant on the mystery of the person of another individual human being within the insuperable ambivalence of our history.

Because of all this, even before one starts, it is a risky business to want to deduce from Jesus' very conspicuous (and historically no longer debatable) custom of calling God his *Abba* the distinctive nature of his awareness of being a 'son' and of his religious experience of God. Historians and biblical scholars are admittedly agreed that the absolute use of *Abba* in prayers to God is to be found neither in rabbinical literature nor yet in the official late Jewish literature of devotion.[209] In Jesus' time *Abba* was a familial term denoting one's earthly father; it had formerly been a kind of childish talk, but had been in use among adults for a long time past.[210] Thus that Jesus should say *Abba* to God – apart from the great solemnity, holding God at a distance from men, with which people in Jesus' time used to pray to him[211] – makes no essential difference. We do find in 3 Macc. 6:3, 8 simply *patèr*, in an absolute sense, although it was still exceptional at the time, and evidently a new trend in Greek Judaism around the first century. Palestinian Jewry was very conservative in this respect, particularly in so far as 'fatherhood' evoked 'son' as a correlate. Of course, God was called the Father of the son, the king, in the sense that any legitimacy kingship possessed depended completely on God's authority – and so (under democratizing influences) Israel as a whole was called 'son of God' *vis-à-vis* God the Father; but as against that, Palestinian Jewry showed a great deal of reserve towards pagan conceptions of religious father-son relationships.[212] The Old Testament idea that 'messiah=son of God' was only accepted with reluctance by late Judaism, therefore. Yet the fatherhood of God was accepted more and more generally, however seldom it occurred in the oldest strata of the Old Testament (in contrast to neighbouring religions). Apart from a few cases (which point of course to a new tendency), *Abba* (a secular term, after all, taken from family life) does not occur in Jesus' time in the language of prayer addressed to God. Of Jesus' standing out, in a historico-religious context, purely on the ground of his addressing God as *Abba*, there can be no question, *per se*.[213] Jesus' uniqueness in his relationship to God undoubtedly lies in its unaffected simplicity; and the marks of that in late Judaism, though not absent, were really rare. But we cannot build on it an awareness on Jesus' part of some 'transcendent' sonship and still less a Trinitarian doctrine, as has often happened in the exegetical and theological writings deriving therefrom. For that, more is needed. If we can find it, then in Jesus' unaffected intercourse with God as *Abba* we may justifiably perceive the natural consequences of it; not, however, the other way round.

On a point of exegesis, scholars seem to have established with a justifiable degree of cautious assurance that Jesus' practice of calling God *Abba* – in the Greek gospels cited only once in the Aramaic (Mk. 14:36; later on in the churchly prayer of Christians only twice: Gal. 4:6; Rom. 8:15) – was in fact a persistent habit of his, and that we should supply this same Aramaic word behind the Greek 'the Father', 'Father' or 'my Father' in Mt. 11:25–26; 26:39, 42; Lk. 10:21; 11:2; 22:42; 23:34, 46, besides the explicit reference made in Mk. 14:36 to 'Abba, the Father'.[214] J. Jeremias and B. van Iersel have shown convincingly – in so far as that is possible in a matter of this sort – that *Abba* is one of the most 'authentic' words, one most assuredly used by Jesus.[215] Again, at twelve places in the gospels (not counting the parallel passages) we read that Jesus addresses himself in prayer 'to the Father'.[216] In view of the rarity of an *Abba* prayer at that period, this evidently occurred under the pressure of what was recollected of Jesus' posture towards God in prayer, precisely as *Abba*. It is a clear and characteristic mark of Jesus, without *of itself* implying some kind of theological transcendence. The correlate 'the son', as applied by Jesus to himself, can nowhere be demonstrated (by the critical method) from the New Testament, while the evident distancing of 'my Father and your Father' (Jn. 20:17) is unmistakably post-Easter, Christian theology. Yet this (Johannine) distinction between 'my Father' and 'your Father' rests on a distinction drawn by Jesus himself between *Abba* (my Father) and 'the Father in heaven', using the latter when talking to other people about (their) God.[217] It would be even more wrong to link up this *Abba* concept with the expression 'Truly, I say to you'[218] in order to lend (added) force to the transcendence of Jesus' understanding of himself and his claims.

What we gather in the first instance from the certain knowledge we have of Jesus' praying to God as *Abba* is the unconventional style of Jesus' intercourse with God, its unaffected and natural simplicity, which must have been inscribed on the hearts of the disciples, because this kind of praying to *Abba* at once became generally current in early Christianity. Both the pre-Marcan tradition (Mk. 14:36) and the oldest, Aramaic phase of the Q tradition regarding the 'Our Father' (Lk. 11:1-4; Mt. 6:9-13, where the 'Father' in Luke turns out to be a Q text and 'our Father in heaven' more Matthean) speak in totally different complexes of tradition of 'Abba' (Mk. 'Abba, the Father', *abba hò patèr*; Lk. simply *pater* in the vocative, and absolutely, without the article). That the Christian community ventured, like Jesus, to address God as *Abba* means that they did *not* infer the uniqueness of Jesus' sonship directly from his *Abba* experience (but from other data about Jesus), whereas the Johannine gospel – after a longer period of Christian consciousness of the exclusive uniqueness of Jesus' sonship (John usually refers to Jesus simply as 'the Son') – feels obliged to make a distinction: '*my*' and '*your*' father, in order to underscore the difference in sonship in the two cases. Early texts like Rom. 8:15 and Gal. 4:6, where we find (setting aside Mk. 14:36) the unusual double expression 'Abba, Father' – pointing to a pre-Pauline tradition (possibly, conjoined with the tradition included in Mk. 14:36, from the bilingual Northern, East Palestine, and so too from the bilingual West Syria, Damascus) – and find it, moreover, as a prayer formula used by *Christians*, indicate on the one hand that the first Christians were so taken with this way of praying to God that Jesus had that they adopted it for themselves, but on the other that at that stage of their profession of Christ they did not base Jesus' exclusive sonship on his remarkable

*Abba* experience. The (none the less already current) identification of Jesus as the Son or Son of God must therefore have been drawn from other sources. In short: Jesus' *Abba* consciousness was not the immediate ground for calling him, precisely on that basis, 'the Son'. (In the end that ground – see below – lies in the resurrection, at any rate interpreted as exaltation and 'investment with authority' with the support of Ps. 110, Ps. 2 and Ps. 89, which could only have come about in part through what had been remembered of Jesus' familiar intercourse with God as *Abba* and through the recollection of his eschatological-cum-prophetic mission from God.)

We said in Part One (criteria) that however historically authentic the use of *Abba* by Jesus may be, we cannot deduce directly from that the historical authenticity of the rest of the logion, in which Jesus prays to the Father. Yet it is still important to examine how, according to the New Testament, Jesus prays to God as Father, in other words under what aspect Jesus approaches God as Father.

*Abba* as an ordinary, secular term for one's earthly father for the Jew suggests in particular paternal authority: the father is the one charged with authority, with *exousia*, complete authority, whom the children are in duty bound to obey and treat with piety. The father is also the one available to look after and protect his own, the family, to come to the rescue and to give advice and counsel. He is the focus of the entire family (paternal house), everything revolves around him and through his person forms a community. There is no contending with the father's authority in Judaism. The children must 'gladden' their father (Prov. 15:20; 23:22, 25).[219] Another result was that everything of the father's was also the son's, and vice versa. (These were actually technical formulae within the family: 'What is mine is yours, yours is mine'; see for instance the parable of the elder brother of the Prodigal Son, Lk. 15:11–32). Especially in the Wisdom literature there is considerable emphasis on the son's 'being instructed by' the father (Prov. 1:8; 6:20; 10:1); the son receives 'the teaching of the father' (Prov. 2:1; 3:1; 4:1; 5:1; 7:1). 'Hear, O sons, a father's instruction . . . for I give you good precepts: and do not forsake my teaching' (Prov. 4:1–2). For that reason, 'father' is also applied to Israel's teachers and priests. The fourth commandment in the Decalogue was even interpreted as the duty to comply with the paternal precepts. The relationship of son to father was laid down in law. From the time of one's majority (at thirteen) reverence for the father especially remained operative 'until death' and even beyond, because for a year after his father's death a son had to offer sacrifices on his behalf. To sum up, one can say that in

Jesus' time what the *abba* signified for his son was authority and instruction: the father is the authority and the teacher. Being a son meant 'belonging to'; and one demonstrated this sonship by carrying out father's instructions. Thus the son receives everything from the father. As failure to comply with the father's will is tantamount to rejecting the Torah or Law, this afforded a connection between obeying one's father and obedience to God (Sirach 3:2, 6; 7:27; Prov. 1:7, 8). The son also receives from the father 'missions', tasks which in the name of his father he has to make his own.

If in contrast to the current usage of his day Jesus uses the familial term *Abba* in addressing God, it quite naturally expresses the very core of his religious life exactly as the Christians represented it after his death: 'Not my will, but your will, Father' (Lk. 21:42; Mt. 26:42); for this is the Jewish *Abba* concept. With good reason, as they looked back on Jesus' life, they were able to make him say: 'My food is to do the will of him who sent me' (Jn. 4:34), 'Lo, I have come to do your will' (Hebr. 10:9), 'I seek not my own will but the will of him who sent me' (Jn. 5:30), 'I have come . . . not to do my own will, but the will of him who sent me' (Jn. 6:38). This is simply applying (though in the sapiential context of the Johannine gospel) the familial concept of father and son to the relationship of Jesus towards God, apprehended as *Abba*. These explicit statements are justified by virtue of the characteristic experience and awareness of the Father which the disciples had observed in the religious life of Jesus and which for them reflected the very essence of Jesus' religious genius so clearly that the primitive, bilingual Church in its liturgy addressed the God of Jesus, and thus its God, as *Abba, Pater*.

The 'doing of God's will' was also the kernel of Jewish spirituality. But it involves not so much the idea of 'a father's will' as the ineffable, in Jesus' time unmentionable 'name' of the Most High. If God is to be called 'Father', one must immediately add to that 'Master and Lord of the universe' or something of the sort, for instance, 'Father who art in heaven', as at second remove Matthew frequently does.[220] Jesus' familial expression for God, *Abba*, without any further qualifications suggestive of 'transcendence' ('Lord', 'King', 'in heaven', 'creator of heaven and earth') quite certainly points to a religious experience of deep intimacy with God, in terms of which Jesus would seem to be conscious of a distinction between his experience of God and that of, for instance, his disciples. 'Our Father' never occurs in the gospels on the lips of Jesus; the single text, Mt. 6:9, is (a) clearly Matthean and (b) one where Jesus is teaching his disciples how to pray. But such expressions as 'their Father' (Mt. 13:43) and especially 'your Father'[221] occur constantly; Jesus himself on the other hand says 'my Father' in the gospels (17 times in Matthew; 4 times in Luke; 25 times in John). This linguistic usage in the gospels, consistently maintained, does not point in every case, therefore, to directly and historically authentic sayings of Jesus; it is a kind of literary deposit, strained out of Jesus' earthly ministry and way of speaking.

The most pregnant case of the sapiential 'familial father-concept' turns up in the (wrongly so-called) Johannine logion in the synoptic gospels: 'I thank thee, Father, Lord of heaven and earth, that thou hast hidden these things from the wise and understanding and revealed them to babes; yea, Father, for such was thy gracious will. All things have been delivered to me by my Father; and no one knows the Son except the Father, and no one knows the Father except the Son and anyone to whom the Son chooses to reveal him' (Mt. 11:25–27; Lk. 10:21–22). The distinction between the Jewish father-formula: 'Father, Lord of heaven and earth' (in both Matthew and Luke) and 'Father' (manifestly *Abba*) used absolutely, is very obvious here (even though we cannot attach any peculiar significance to the first, that is, Jewish usage in this pericope). Many have described this pericope as 'Johannine' because it does not fit in, apparently, with the synoptic image of Jesus and tends to evince the highly sapiential Christology of the Johannine gospel. This question will be further considered in connection with the 'Wisdom Christology' and particularly the 'messenger idea' and the 'eschatological prophet' (Part Three). However, the substance is very early; we find it even in the Graeco-Jewish phase of the Q tradition.[222] We shall be explaining in Part Three that the Wisdom Christology divides into a low- and a high-sapiential variety, according to whether the messenger 'from God' is sent by Wisdom or is identified with it. It also appears from this Wisdom tradition that the father-son relation is an element belonging to the tradition-complex of 'revelation' and 'sending the messenger'. This tradition of low-sapiential Christology we find in this Q logion (apothegm), whereas the Johannine gospel is high-sapiential. The sapiential-familial 'father-son' concept is here simply subsumed into the sapiential 'messenger' concept. Two logia must be interwoven here; the prayer-formula and the revelation-logion. In the latter it is first said that Jesus has received *exousia* or full authority from the Father; which is why he is the sole mediator of God's revelation, and the 'little ones' or the Christian (Q) community are the sole recipients of that revelation. That Jesus thanks the Father for this revelation to the elect is given a Christological basis in the second logion; in other words, Mt. 11:27 offers a Christological comment on Mt. 11:25–26. Because people used to pose questions in a religious context and neglected the question of tradition and its history, there has been a great deal of discussion about this pericope; but only situating it within the history of tradition can smooth the way here to a better understanding. The passage is Hellenistic Judaeo-Christian, completely at home in the Old Testament late Jewish, Chasidic heritage,[223] in which the revelation is to those very poor and humble folk whom Jesus also called blessed; and not (that is the assertion of the Q community) to the leaders of Israel who rejected Jesus' message; for them Jesus' latter-day message is not disclosed. They have shut themselves out. But this is included within God's decree. In the second instance it is then given a Christological interpretation in Mt. 11:25–26. The absolute use of 'the Father' and 'the Son' is an exception also in the Q source, but in no way 'Johannine';[224] it is in line with the low-sapiential notion of the messenger as 'being sent by Wisdom', although the tradition of the *exousia*, transferred by God to the son of man (kernel of the Q theology), must surely play some part in Mt. 11:27a. Thus in the Q theology 'the Son' means that Jesus is 'the Son' because the *exousia* is given him from the Father to pass on the 'teaching of the Father' to whomever he chooses: the Son is 'wholly dependent' and at the same time 'wholly free'. Likewise the Son is the sole agent of revelation. 'The Son' in an absolute sense is not late Jewish Palestinian but Greek (-Jewish), and exhibits clear parallels with the 'wisdom' in the Book of Wisdom (6:12 – 9:18; 10:10; 12:1). Within the history of tradition the logion belongs to the distinctive Wisdom Christology of the Graeco-Jewish Q community and so exhibits traits akin to the pre-Johannine milieu (Wisdom and apocalyptic have merged together here). As the eschatological emissary of Wisdom, equipped with full authority, Jesus knows what the Father knows and what he has to convey to men: in him Wisdom dwells, and so he knows the eschatological secrets, the 'mystery of the kingdom [rule] of God' (see Lk. 8:10). In this way the Q community has conjoined its older tradition of the son of man with the (for it more recent) tradition of Graeco-Jewish (*chokma*) wisdom – although still low-sapiential; in other words, here in the Q theology there is as yet no question of identifying Jesus with Wisdom, and thus of his pre-existence.

All this as it stands is post-Easter Christology, yet with recollections of the pre-Easter life of Jesus. In Mk. 6:2–3, after Jesus has been discoursing in the synagogue, comes the question: 'Where did this man get all this? What is the wisdom given to him? What mighty works are wrought by his hands? Is not this the carpenter, the son of Mary and brother of James and Joses and Judas and Simon? . . . And they took offence at him' (see also Mt. 13:54–56, and Jn. 6:42 and 7:27). The logion is meant to give an answer to that question: they do not know Jesus' Father; therefore they cannot properly identify Jesus. For his real *Abba* is God, who has taught him this wisdom. Matthew 11:27 may at one time have formed a unity with Mt. 13:54–56, as the pericope in Jn. 7:27–29 might suggest.[225] Behind these pericopes lies a problem dating from the days of Jesus' life on earth: 'Who is he?', 'Whence this power?', 'Whence this speaking with authroity?' So in essence at any rate (the Graeco-Jewish phrasing is too neat, surely, to be put straight into the mouth of Jesus) Mt. 11:27 may be called an authentic Jesus-saying. Here Jesus himself adopts the Jewish 'messenger' concept, but within and arising out of his *Abba* experience; and this evidently goes deeper than the purely prophetic consciousness. In other words, we can see here that it is not from Jesus' *Abba* experience in itself that conclusions may be drawn, but only from that experience as the soul, source and ground of Jesus' message, praxis and ministry as a whole, which alone serve to illuminate the exceptional and peculiar character of the *Abba* experience (which, as we said before, in a late Jewish context is in itself a strikingly rare phenomenon). By what authority, on what basis is Jesus able to speak of God in this manner? That was the question raised by Jesus' fellow-villagers (Mk. 6:2–3). Jesus' experience and awareness of the Father in prayer was also manifested in what for his listeners was an astonishing way of speaking about God, so much so that some took offence at it. It was not in his use of *Abba* as a way of addressing God that Jesus showed himself to be forsaking late Judaism; but the *Abba* form of address (expressing a religious experience of a special colour), when linked with the substance of Jesus' message, ministry and praxis, began to prompt theological questions. The *Abba* experience would appear to be the source of the peculiar nature of Jesus' message and conduct, which without this religious experience, or apart from it, lose the distinctive meaning and content actually conferred on them by Jesus.

All this goes to show that one of the most reliable facts about the life of Jesus is that he broached the subject of God in and through his message of the coming rule of God; and that what this implied was made plain first and foremost through his authentic parables and the issues they raised: namely, *metanoia* and the praxis of God's kingdom. And then this message was given substantive content by Jesus' actions and way of life; his miracles, his dealings with tax-gatherers and sinners, his offer of salvation from God in fellowship at table with his friends and in his attitude to the Law, sabbath and Temple, and finally in his consorting in fellowship with a more intimate group of disciples. The heart and centre of it all appeared to be the God bent upon humanity. Of this God's rule the whole life of Jesus was a 'celebration' and also 'orthopraxis', that is, a praxis in accord with that kingdom of God. The bond between the two – God's rule and orthopraxis – is so intrinsic that in this praxis itself Jesus recognizes the signs of the coming of God's rule. The living God is the focus of this life.

Against the background of the apocalyptical, Pharisaic, Essene and Zealotic conceptions upheld by current movements which isolated themselves into 'remnant' communities, Jesus' message and praxis of salvation for all Israel without exception, indeed including all that was abandoned and lost – that in particular – are difficult to place in a historico-religious context. For that reason we are bound to enquire whether Jesus' message and praxis do not become intelligible only when we presuppose his special, original religious apprehension of God. For the question is: Whence does Jesus obtain the unconditional assurance of salvation to which his message of God's coming rule as final well-being for men so positively testifies?

In the calamitous and pain-ridden history within which Jesus stood it was impossible to find any grounds or indeed any reason at all which would serve to explain and make sense of the unqualified assurance of salvation that characterized his message. Such a hope, expressed in a proclamation of the coming and already close salvation for men implied in God's rule – now that we have uncovered the unique quality of Jesus' religious life in terms of his (historically exceptional) *Abba* address to God – in Jesus is quite plainly rooted in a personal awareness of contrast: on the one hand the incorrigible, irremediable history of man's suffering, a history of calamity, violence and injustice, of grinding, excruciating and oppressive enslavement; on the other hand Jesus' particular religious awareness of God, his *Abba* experience, his intercourse with God as the benevolent, solicitous 'one who is against evil', who will not admit the supremacy of evil and refuses to allow it the last word. This religious experience of contrast is, after all, what informs his conviction and proclamation of God's liberating rule, which should and can prevail even in this history, as Jesus knows by experience in and from his own praxis. Thus the *Abba* experience of Jesus, although meaningful in itself, is not a self-subsistent religious experience, but is also an experience of God as 'Father', caring for and offering a future to his children, a God, Father, who gives a future to the man who from a mundane viewpoint can be vouchsafed no future at all. Out of his *Abba* experience Jesus is able to bring to a man a message of a hope not inferable from the history of our world, whether in terms of individual or socio-political experiences – although the hope will have to be realized even there. Of such a hopeful potentiality and assurance Jesus came to be explicitly aware on the basis of the originality of his experience of God, fostered in the religious life of the Jewish followers of Yahweh centuries before, but in Jesus concentrated into a characteristic *Abba* experience. The core of what was enunciated in Israel's best moments of its experience of God is somehow in Jesus condensed in an original and personal way: Yahweh is he who is coming, who for the present declines to submit his credentials, but leads Israel towards a future: 'I shall be who I shall be' (Ex. 3:14). To believe in this God is to put one's trust in Someone who takes his identity seriously (hence Torah as a revelation of God's will) and at the same time declines to disclose his identity 'in advance'. Likewise reared in that tradition, Jesus – being in his person a new phenomenon in Israel – apprehends this God as a potency opening up the future, a power of the benevolent, 'anti-evil' one who says no to all that is bad and hurtful to human beings – to the Jew 'creating' means making something good, so that one can see 'that it is good, very good' – and therefore wills good for suffering humanity and its history. Jesus' *Abba* experience is an immediate awareness of God as a power cherishing people and making them free. Against the background of the facts of history the *Abba*, the 'God of Jesus', is the Creator of heaven and earth and is Israel's leader, a God with whom 'everything is possible' (Mk. 10:27). It was to faith in this God that Jesus called men through what he said and did during his days on earth: that was the *raison d'être* of his whole ministry.

That is why trying to delete the special 'relation to God' from the life of Jesus at once destroys his message and the whole point of his way of living; it amounts to denying the historical reality, 'Jesus of Nazareth', and turns him into an 'unhistorical', mythical or symbolic being, a 'non-Jesus'. Then all that remains – in so far as a Jesus trimmed to measure still has power to fascinate – is nothing but the apocalyptical Utopia. For the apocalypticists round and about Jesus were fully confident that from our history – the 'old aeon' – no further good was to be expected. Their hope was centred on the 'over-turn of the ages' (see Part Two, Section One), a sudden act of God radically shattering this present course of things so as to allow a few favoured ones to escape the catastrophe. The purpose of apocalyptic was paraenetic encouragement. Its beatitude was: 'Blessed are those who endure to the end' (Dan. 12:12). Apocalypticism is the threat of an all-consuming judgement on our negative history; it remains within the dialectic of the ongoing course of suffering and wrong that 'calls for vengeance' – and that too will follow. 'The remnant', however, 'the pious ones', live upon the Utopian vision of escaping from that vengeance. Even the Baptist, at bottom no apocalypticist, announces no positive hope, but the certainty of the coming judgement. All this is essentially and fundamentally different from what Jesus is doing: starting from his *Abba* experience, he promises and holds out a positive hope to men and women.

Conclusion and statement of the problem: reality or illusion?

In this chapter we have been examining the fundamental and constitutive elements of Jesus' message and praxis. He proclaimed, 'for God', the approach of salvation for man, he appeared and acted as the eschatological prophet bringing God's 'glad tidings for the poor', news of salvation for all Israel, but for that reason a special cause for rejoicing among the poor, destitute as they were of all prospect of a new and better life. He proclaimed the rule of God, orientated on humanity, a rule that demanded a corresponding practice exemplified in his own life and one that he articulated by speaking in parables and instructive discourses. He identifies himself in person with the cause of God as that also of man (God's rule, which man has to seek first, before everything else), and with the cause of man as God's cause (the kingdom of God as a kingdom of peace and salvation among men). By that he lives, by it he is fulfilled; and it is what he promises to men: human beings are 'people whom God cherishes'. Thus there is positive hope for everyone without exception; and in both casual and constant contact with this Jesus many of his fellows find salvation and healing there and then. In that way many come to a new life; they are enabled to hope once more and renew their lives. For that, Jesus does not even lay down conditions. Whoever comes to him in suffering or distress experiences salvation 'for free'. Salvation and a future are vouchsafed to people without a future.

The source of this message and praxis, demolishing an oppressive notion of God, was his *Abba* experience, without which the picture of the historical Jesus is drastically marred, his message emasculated and his concrete praxis (though still meaningful and inspiring) is robbed of the meaning he himself gave to it.

Over against all this one could say: this very *Abba* experience was the grand illusion of Jesus' life. Such a reaction is certainly possible on our side. But then one is bound to draw from that the inevitable conclusion, namely, that the hope of which Jesus spoke is likewise an illusion. Anyone, therefore, who lives by Jesus and bases his life on him – while dismissing Jesus' *Abba* experience – is in fact wanting to live on a Utopian basis; and all he is actually doing is to pin his own hopes on to an individual who lived two thousand years ago and died for an illusion and a Utopia. In saying this I am in no way denying the historic power and stimulus exerted by Utopias, especially not when they prompt men to a consistent concern with and commitment to their fellows (as was entirely the case with Jesus). What I am saying is that we then have no basis – anywhere – for ever being able to believe in a better world and a definitive 'final good', and that all our expectations of a universal reign of peace are just the Utopian obverse of our negative history of violence, injustice and suffering. No doubt that has a powerful critical function; but it contains no real promise on which a positive hope can be founded.

To find a basis for one's own life in the trustworthiness of Jesus, and ultimately of his *Abba* experience (through which Jesus discovers the ground of his own life in God) is of course an act of faith in Jesus, which is thus – and *ipso facto* - an act attesting faith in God. On purely historical grounds this cannot be verified, since such an *Abba* experience may be disqualified as an illusion. On the other hand for someone who acknowledges and in faith confesses this trustworthiness of Jesus as grounded in truth and reality, the trustworthiness acquires visible contours in the actual life of Jesus of Nazareth; his faith then perceives Jesus' trustworthiness in the material, the biographical data, which the historian can put before him regarding Jesus of Nazareth. This material at any rate confronts us all with the question: Could this person have been right?

Is it in actual fact possible, starting from a deep religious rapport with God, apprehended as Creator of heaven and earth and as a God bent upon the good of humanity, really to say something about man, perhaps even the most important thing that can be said about human beings? For that was indeed what Jesus claimed. Starting from a religious claim – not in some other way - he says something about man and man's final good.

So far this is merely a question. For the story of Jesus' life is not yet finished. His message and his person also were rejected. Jesus was tried and executed, juridically done away with. And this poses more sharply, more bewilderingly, the question: Was his life then something Utopian and an illusion, even the saddest proof of all that positive hope of a better world and a better mankind turns out to be impossible? This we must look at more closely in the next section; and so naturally we must defer for the present the business of identifying who in the final analysis Jesus is.

Section Two

# Kingdom of God, rejection and death of Jesus

*Literature.* H. W. Bartsch, 'Die Passions- und Ostergeschichten bei Matthäus', *Entmythologisierende Auslegung* (Hamburg 1962), 80–92; J. Blinzler, 'Passionsgeschehen und Passionsbericht des Lukas-Evangeliums', BuK 14 (1969), 1–4; P. Borgen, 'John and the Synoptics in the Passion narrative', NTS 5 (1958–9), 246–59; H. Conzelmann, 'Historie und Theologie in den synoptischen Passionsberichten', *Zur Bedeutung des Todes Jesu* (Gütersloh 1967, 1968³), 35–54; and 'Die Mitte der Zeit', 186ff; N. A. Dahl, 'Die Passionsgeschichte bei Matthäus', NTS 2 (1955–6), 17–32; A. Dauer, *Die Passionsgeschichte im Johannes-evangelium*, Munich 1972; G. Delling, *Der Kreuzestod Jesu in der urchrist-lichen Verkündigung*, Berlin 1971; E. Flesseman-van Leer, 'Die Interpretation der Passionsgeschichten vom Alten Testament aus', *Die Bedeutung des Todes Jesu*, l.c., 79–96; A. George, 'Comment Jésus a-t-il perçu sa propre mort?', LVie 20 (1971), 34–59; K. Fischer, 'Der Tod Jesu Heute. Warum muszte Jesus starben?', Or. an Jesus 35 (1971), 196–9; F. Hahn, *Hoheitstitel*, 193–217, and 'Der Prozess Jesu nach dem Joh.-Evangelium', *Evangelisch-Katholischer Kommentar zum NT*, Zürich-Neukirchen 2 (1970), 23–96; M. Horstmann, *Studien zur markinischen Christologie* (Neut. Abh., 6), Münster 1969; J. Jeremias, *Der Opfertod Jesu Christi* (Calwer Hefte, 62), Stuttgart 1963; E. Jüngel, *Tod*, Stutt-gart-Berlin 1971; B. Klappert, *Diskussion um Kreuz und Auferstehung*, Wuppertal 1967²; H. Kessler, *Die theologische Bedeutung des Todes Jesu*, Düsseldorf 1970; X. Léon-Dufour, s.v. *Passion*, in DBS 6 (1960), 1419–92, and 'Mt. et Mc. dans le récit de la passion', Bibl 40 (1959), 684–96; E. Linnemann, *Studien zum Passionsgeschichte* (FRLANT, 102), Göttingen 1970; G. Mainberger, *Jesus starb umsonst*, Freiburg 1970²; N. Perrin, *Rediscovering the Teaching of Jesus*, London 1967; W. Popkes, *Christus Traditus. Eine Untersuchung zum Begriff der Dahingabe im NT*, Zurich-Stuttgart 1967; J. Riedl, 'Die Evangelische Leidensgeschichte und ihre theologische Aussage', BLit 41 (1968), 70–111; J. Roloff, 'Anfänge der soteriologischen Deutung des Todes Jesu (Mk. 10:45

und Lk. 22:27)', NTS 19 (1972-3), 38–64; L. Schenke, *Studien zur Passionsgeschichte des Markus. Tradition und Redaktion im Mk. 14:1-42*, Würzburg 1971; G. Schneider, *Die Passion Jesu nach den drei älteren Evangelien*, Munich 1973; and 'Das Problem einer vorkanonischen Passionserzählung', BZ 16 (1972), 222–44; J. Schreiber, *Die Markuspassion*, Hamburg 1969; E. Schweizer, *Erniedrigung und Erhöhung bei Jesus und seinen Nachfolgen* (AThANT, 28), Zürich 1962²; G. Strecker, 'Die Leidens- und Auferstehungsvoraussagen im Markusevangelium', ZThK 64 (1967), 16–39; H. Schürmann, 'Wie hat Jesus seinen Tod bestanden und verstanden?', *Orientierung an Jesus* (Freiburg 1973) 325–63; V. Taylor, *The Passion Narrative of Saint Luke*, Cambridge 1972; W. Thüsing, *Die Erhöhung und Verherrlichung Jesu im Joh. - Evangelium*, Münster 1970; A. Vanhoye, 'Structure et théologie des récits de la passion dans les évangiles synoptiques', NRTh 99 (1967), 135–63; F. Viering, *Der Kreuzestod Jesu*, Gütersloh 1969; A. Vögtle, 'Jesus', in *Oekumenische Kirchengeschichte*, ed. E. Kottje and B. Möhler (Mainz-Munich 1970), 3–24; B. A. Willems, *Erlösung in Kirche und Welt* (Quaest. Disp. 35), Freiburg 1968; *Das Kreuz Jesu Christi als Grund des Heils*, ed. F. Viering, Gütersloh 1967 (contributions from E. Biser, W. Fürst, J. Göters, W. Kreck, W. Schrage); 'Zur Theologischen Bedeutung des Todes Jesu', *Herderkorrespondenz* 26 (1972), 149–54.

Chapter 1

# The rejection and death of Jesus

## Introduction: the problem

We can construct our view of the death of Jesus on the life which preceded it as well as on the relation of God to his death, as the first Christians, although not unmindful of Jesus' finished life, managed to do in a variety of ways converging as it were in the documents of the New Testament. The first line of approach corresponds to a historical question and so can only be assessed by the methods of historical criticism. The second one presupposes a posture of faith; but even then, the way we are to understand this faith-motivated interpretation, that is, the early Christians' evaluation of Jesus' death as articulated in the language of the New Testament, calls again for historical study and exegesis. In this chapter we shall try to do justice to both sides of this tension between historical reconstruction and interpretation governed by faith.[1]

The outcome to date of historico-exegetical studies on the part of responsible scholars has been the emergence of a consensus, a growing consensus regarding three clearly diverse initiatives in the early Church towards evaluating and coming to understand the death of Jesus. These three traditions we can recognize in the New Testament; with their help it is still possible to reconstruct the initial, independent traditions of Christian interpretation, but without being able in any detail to arrive at a defensible chronology of these three ways of regarding Jesus' death.

## §1   The death of Jesus as interpreted in early Christianity

All the gospels stress the fact that Jesus embraced death of his own free will. One can even see this emphasis on the voluntary aspect gradually increasing. 'Rise, let us be going; see, my betrayer is at hand' (Mk. 14: 42); Jesus forbids his disciples to resist and surrenders himself 'in order that the Scriptures be fulfilled' (Mt. 26:52–56); Jesus comes forward voluntarily, Judas' treacherous kiss is no longer mentioned. Jesus makes his authority felt and declares expressly that he will accept the cup of suffering (Jn. 18:4–11).

For the search for the motive actuating Jesus voluntarily to take upon himself his suffering and death the New Testament offers us three solutions: Jesus died the death of a prophetic martyr; as part of salvation-history Jesus' death is included within God's plan of salvation; and, lastly, his death has a saving efficacy. He brings about reconciliation between God and men, in other words, he is a sacrifice.

### A.   THE ESCHATOLOGICAL PROPHET-MARTYR. CONTRAST-SCHEME

In this (probably earliest) view of things there is felt to be a contrast between the action of the leaders of his co-religionists in killing Jesus and that of God in exalting him. Most relevant to this interpretation are: Acts 4:10 and, already mingled with other strands, Acts 2:22–24; 5:30–31; 10:40; the Christology of the Q community, which nowhere discusses Jesus' death, in so far as it makes any allusion to it, sees it in the line of tradition of Israel's prophets, who have been put to death;[2] and lastly, perhaps also in the tradition peculiar to Luke: Lk. 13:31-33; 11:47-48, 49ff. Although we find this contrast-scheme particularly in Luke (Gospel and Acts), nevertheless it is pre-Lucan and present in independent units of tradition. It is undoubtedly a Jewish viewpoint, but one that played a primary role in the controversy between Jews and Jewish Christians sent among them to convert them. Here the emphasis is put exclusively on God's activity, manifested in the exaltation of Jesus: God declares himself in this rejected prophet. This current of tradition ascribes no salvific implication to the death of Jesus itself.

Yet this interpretation of Jesus' death stands in a very broad tradition that opens up more far-reaching perspectives: the tradition of the martyrdom of the prophet sent by God and the rejection of his message. 'Israel kills its prophets' is something we find in many places within the New Testament.[3] And this view derives from a pre-Christian, Jewish tradition, continued in the later rabbinical writings. Of course the difficulty is that this general utterance about prophets being murdered is not borne out by the facts of history. A lot of prophets did indeed suffer persecution, but only a few were put to death. The first Old Testament passage to mention prophets in general being murdered is Neh. 9:26.[4] It ascribes a violent death to all prophets of the period of the Israelite monarchy. There the reference is to all prophets before the exile: their call to repentance and conversion had been rejected. What gave occasion for it was the disobedience of the whole people of God; it is a defiance of the prophetic message, a murder of the prophets. In the wake of that refusal comes Yahweh's punitive judgement; for now God's patience, which he had shown by constantly raising up new prophets with their summons to repentance, is at an end.[5] In the context of 'salvation-history' this view enshrines an interpretation of Israel's pre-exilic history. The catastrophes of 722 (end of the Northern Kingdom) and of 587 BC (the fall of Jerusalem) are interpreted as God's punishment for Israel's disobeying the message of the prophets. Thus the 'killing the prophets' theme is in effect the same as the conviction of the permanent disobedience of (pre-exilic) Israel as a whole.

Apart from Neh. 9:26 this theme is expressly repeated in the Chronicles, likewise in a penitential prayer, Ezra 9:10-11.[6] But the motif itself is older than the works of the chroniclers and goes back to the Deuteronomic interpretation of history.[7] The point of departure for this development was 2 Kings 17:7-20, which contains some theological reflections on the downfall of the Northern and Southern Kingdoms: Israel had been disobedient, not heeding the admonitions of the prophets. This Deuteronomic theme of Israel's general disregard of the prophets' message was later on represented in the work of the chroniclers in a general statement asserting 'the murder of the prophets'.

Important to our understanding of the 'martyr's death' of the prophet Jesus is that prophets – in this tradition – are defined as propounders of *metanoia* or repentance and of obedience to God's law, the abrogation of which must bring the judgement of God in its train. It is the very heart of John the Baptist's message, in its essence taken up again by Jesus, though in another perspective. It was a view generally current in the literature between the Testaments, although probably less vigorously so in Jesus' time. In apocalyptic this motif was only associated with the eschatological and very last summons to repentance by the prophet of the latter days.

The early Christian tradition which interprets Jesus' death as the destiny of a *metanoia*-prophet – something fully in line with the calamitous course of Israel's history – confirms the idea that, at any rate prior to Easter, Jesus did indeed come across to the disciples as a great prophet. Again, the term 'prophet' in this late Jewish tradition means someone who calls men to maintain the 'true law' of God. For the notion of 'the law' of God, in the sense of laws made by men themselves 'because of the obduracy of Israel', was in some strata of Judaism already the sign of Israel's defection in the last days.[8] Jesus is the latter-day prophet appearing and acting in face of Israel's final disaffection and summoning Israel to a crucial and definitive act of repentance.

Another characteristic thing is that over against the idea of the *christus* or latter-day envoy from God, since the Maccabean period and above all in apocalyptical quarters there had begun to evolve the idea of a figure at the close of the age antagonistic to salvation: the Antichrist. This contestant will bring misery upon Israel, will oppose himself to the law of God (Dan. 7:20; 7:25). In 1 Macc. 1:44–49 especially, his activity is depicted as being 'against the Law'. The abrogation of the Law, of the sabbath, of the cult of sacrifices and the feast days, plays an explicit and major role in the early Christian literature as well.[9] Stephen was stoned because he had spoken blasphemous words against the Mosaic Law and God (Acts 6:11) and against the place, that is, Jerusalem, the Temple with its sacrificial worship (Acts 6:13). This indictment corresponds to that of Dan. 7:20 against the great Accuser. These words uttered against the holy place (see Mt. 26:61 and Jn. 2:19) may have their origin in the (effective) prophetic tirade against the city that will not believe in Jesus. The combination of 'curse upon Jerusalem' and 'speaking against the Law of Moses' corresponds here to a similar combination in Dan. 7:25. We again find the same elements in the complaint against Paul (Acts 21:28).

This will at once suggest to us that for the Jews the confrontation with Jesus' ministry raised the question: Is this Jesus of Nazareth the latter-day prophet, or is he the latter-day pseudo-prophet, the Antichrist (see Mt. 12:24ff)? Of Jesus too we read in the early Christian literature that he has discarded the Law and the Temple (in particular the sabbath and Jewish feast days),[10] obviously the hallmark of the latter-day pseudo-prophet. Already in the Jewish *Liber Antiquitatum*[11] we read of a 'temple made with human hands' in direct association with Israel's defection at Sinai. It appears from Acts 17:24–26 that these sayings are not aimed primarily at Judaism itself; they stem from an already Jewish apologetic-cum-missionary tradition in which is illustrated the transcendence of the God of the Jews above the gods of the heathen, 'made by their own hands'. But the new factor is that the Jewish traditions of Law, sabbath, Temple and feast days had already been disqualified by Greek-speaking Jews of the Diaspora: they saw in these Jewish laws a compromise with the idolatry of the heathen.[12] The idea that the 'secondary laws' were given by Moses because of the 'hardened hearts' of the Jews has come via various channels of tradition from the Deuteronomic spiritual outlook (Ezek. 20:25). From a Hellenistic Jewish standpoint, Moses in Sinai had given these laws to Israel 'because of Israel's stiff neck': Temple, sabbath, feast days, cult of sacrifice, letter of divorce. Now these compromise-laws coincide with the part of the Law abolished by Antiochus IV – an attitude endorsed by the liberalizing Hellenistic Jews as opposed to the others, in particular the Aramaic-speakers. Historically, this would seem to be the outcome of a realistic accommodation to a Persian government in religious matters not, as things turned out, so very hostile. These Diaspora Jews had already spoken of a universal defection of Israel, because it had added the laws of men to God's Decalogue and so had laid on human beings a burden actually inimical to God's will itself, namely the Ten Commandments. These Jews therefore held a return to the 'true law' of God to be necessary.[13] The addition of the secondary laws was attributed in some apocalyptical circles to the work of the great Gainsayer, 'the dragon', who had first caused the angels to defect, then Adam and finally the whole people of God. The prophets who call men back to the 'true law', as it was 'in the beginning', are therefore persecuted. It was the Gainsayer who caused the heart of the people to be hardened, so that they proceeded to set up a golden calf and became disobedient to God's own laws, not 'made by men's hands'.[14]

In the New Testament, then, we are confronted with the adoption by Christians with a Hellenistic-Jewish background of a pre-Christian, Graeco-Jewish tradition, as is particularly evident from Mark 10:[15] there this general view of things is applied to the letter of divorce. We have to bear in mind, therefore, that in the Palestine of Jesus' day there existed two fundamentally different interpretations of the Law. Since the one that deviated from official Judaism was favoured primarily by the Greek-speaking Jews, the synoptic discussion of Christians opposing the Law is in part delimited by this Hellenistic-Jewish view of things, which does not in itself exceed the limits of Judaism as a whole. Of course the viewpoint of these Diaspora Jews was vigorously rejected by the rest because of its affinity with the laws of Antiochus IV. On the strength of the apocalyptical tradition orientated on Daniel 7, it was possible to find a connection between this Hellenistic-Jewish group (with its own Greek synagogues) and the 'great Gainsayer', who led the people astray and egged them on to abandon the Law.

Now it is plain from the controversy in the New Testament that Jesus' opponents regard him as the great Gainsayer, the pseudo-prophet and false teacher of the last days, enticing Israel to defect. Jesus, we hear, is an 'impostor', teacher of falsehood, (Mt. 27:62–64; Jn. 7:12; cf. Test. Levi 16:3; Test. Benjamin 3:3); he 'blasphemes against God' (see Mk. 14:64; Lk. 5:21; 22:65). Moreover, Mt. 27:62–64 discloses that the identifying of Jesus with the teacher of falsehood is not only refuted by a reference to his resurrection, but that the Christians made the argument advanced against him rebound on to Jesus' opponents: they are the impostors, they seduce the people and slander the saints (Mk. 3:28), they have nullified God's law in favour of laws made by men (see Mk. 7:8; 10:1–2); they tempt Jesus himself, just as the Adversary attempts to corrupt the righteous.[16] Here again pre-Christian, Jewish material is worked into a Christian context, namely, on the one hand the contrast between God's law and the laws of men (Mk. 7; see 2 Macc. 7:30), on the other the universal defection from the 'true law' as a sign of the last days.[17] Because of 'the law of the evil wretch (or gainsayer)', men were brought to regard the 'new law' and therefore Jesus' message as the false prophecy of a pseudo-prophet, indeed of the great Gainsayer himself.

In the judgement of this complex of New Testament tradition Jesus was condemned as the (pseudo-) prophet of the last days, the gain-sayer who misleads the people and causes them to apostatize. That is why these Christians see Jesus' death as the martyrdom of the eschato-logical prophet-from-God, while those who have put him to death are themselves disqualified as the great gainsayers and misleaders of the people. In the four gospels the question current in Jesus' lifetime is still made quite apparent: Who is the true emissary from God, who has genuine *exousia* or full authority: Jesus or Israel's leaders, his *de facto* opponents?[18] This conflict is settled with an appeal to Jesus' sayings and miracles in a recognizably Hellenistic-Jewish context. From the basic form (for instance, Mk. 6:1-2, 5, 15) it is possible to gather the gist of it: Jesus is portrayed as the teaching authority in contrast to his opponents, while all secondary interpolations are meant to expose Jesus' opponents as those who gainsay God's true law.

This exposure of Jesus' opponents is closely bound up in the gospels with the traditional idea, also taken over by them, of the prophet's martyrdom. This martyrdom reveals that it is not Jesus but his op-ponents who are the tools of powers opposed to God.[19] These com-plexes of New Testament tradition are obviously based on the idea of the divine sanctioning of Jesus' authority or its endorsement by God, namely, through his martyr's destiny; and on the other hand (in a secondary phase of the same tradition) the Jewish teachers are them-selves pronounced to be the tools of the great Adversary. The syn-optic altercations relating to God's law, therefore, are ultimately not just disputes over doctrine but an expression of the struggle between the latter-day prophet and the anti-divine power.[20] With Paul this tradition is translated into the larger theme of Jesus' fight with 'the powers of this world', the world of evil spirits in the heavenly places, finally with Satan.[21]

The Christian community after Easter understands the liquidation of *de facto* authority in Israel in the light of Jesus' martyrdom not so much as a 'party debate' but as the predicted struggle between the anti-God powers and the latter-day prophet. In this Christian view of things, supported by already available Jewish traditions, his total power and valid authority are confirmed by Jesus' resurrection and exaltation, as also by his earlier miracles. In line with the Deuteronomic tradition of the fate of prophets, interpreted as the inherent con-sequence of Israel's failure to obey God's true law, Christians see the authority of Jesus legitimated. Jesus is *the* authority; whoever denies him is against God.

Of the two already existing Jewish forms of expounding the Law, early Christian traditions incorporated in the New Testament, the traditions of this or that local church – in effect, those of Greek-speaking Jews – have clearly opted in favour of the so-called 'liberal' interpretation: a rigorous interpretation on the one hand of God's will as revealed in the Decalogue, on the other a more free, for the 'man in the street' more amicable, interpretation of the Mosaic laws in so far as they had resulted from a historical compromise, by reason of the Jews' hardness of heart. Those traditions the Christians linked up with the martyrdom of Jesus, for which orthodox Jews were declared to be responsible. Acts 7:51–53 says: 'You stiff-necked people, uncircumcised in heart and ears, you always resist the Holy Spirit. As your fathers did, so do you. Which of the prophets did not your fathers persecute? And they killed those who announced beforehand the coming of the Righteous One . . .'

An early Christian exposition of Jesus' death, relying on already given Jewish categories concerning the martyrdom of the prophets and the 'rising again' of the prophet Elijah, led in view of the accepted and 'Scripturally' proven authority of Jesus to regarding his Jewish opponents as antagonists of God: you killed him, but God gave him his protection, raised him up and exalted him on high.

Departing from the Law, something of which orthodox Jewish circles accused the Jews of the Diaspora, is turned for apologetic purposes in an early Christian tradition into a *Christian* indictment of this official Jewish tradition, which itself appealed to Moses' authority. The apocalyptical cliché about a latter-day defection from the Law is now turned upon *them*. The death of Jesus, which is laid at the door of this 'orthodoxy', is in fact the expression of the 'lost state' of the Jews, showing itself in a false conception of God's 'true Law', which really leads to disobeying God.

This primitive Christian interpretation of Jesus' death implies that, in the eyes of Jews faithful to the Jewish Law, there was a historical ambivalence about Jesus' days on earth and that he was fully vindicated only by his resurrection. It is only because of his martyrdom that his person and ministry can be decisively accounted for within the framework of a traditional, that is, Deuteronomic view of the prophet. Thus in this Jesus tradition committing oneself to Jesus as the coming son of man is crucial to salvation. And the decision, not in and of itself but through the obduracy of those opposed to it, also leads in the end to a social rupture, the secession of Christian Jewry from the Jewish synagogue.[22] The fierce controversies which we can detect so clearly in the four gospels are only understandable and conceivable as arising from the Christian interpretation of Jesus as the latter-day prophet of salvation, put to death but in his resurrection vindicated by God himself: Jesus confessed as the Lord. The memories of early Christian Jewish traditions preserved in the New Testament are in their very acerbity symptomatic of a Christianity in process of breaking away from Judaism.

The reason for the Christian enquiry after what the Law signifies for salvation – heart and centre of Pauline theology – can be understood in its historical context only if we start from an early Christian, Jewish interpretation of Jesus which itself starts from the Deuteronomic conception of Jesus' destiny as a prophet rejected by Israel. This is incontestably a post-Easter interpretation of Jesus; in the light of this Deuteronomic approach to an understanding of him, Jesus of Nazareth is the latter-day prophet, the eschatological 'teacher of the law', who as the final prophet has at the same time become the victim of Israel's defection, in line with the tradition of the 'murder of the classical prophets': the authentic messenger, because of his critical temperament and contentious character, is executed as the bogus prophet and misleader of the people. In this case use has been made of what is indeed invariably the ambivalent and ambiguous implication of every human, historical event so as to ensure Jesus' undoing. So far from being a neutral interpretation of Jesus' death this first motif – a 'contrast-pattern' – is perhaps the interpretation of his death most closely borne out by the concrete facts, when viewed within a lengthy Jewish prophetic tradition.[23]

All this explains why on the one hand Jesus is represented in certain very early Christian traditions as the champion of the 'true Law', whereas with Paul on the other hand the salvific function previously attaching to the Law is now ascribed to Jesus Christ himself – without any fundamental opposition being entailed here between the Jesus tradition and Pauline theology, despite differences of emphasis. Even in the tradition, after all, the latter-day prophet and teacher of the true Law was already the 'light of the world'.[24] This function of the latter-day prophet, which was made much of in some sectors of Jewish tradition, namely, that of being the 'light of the world' – the light, that is, first of Israel but thereby also of the Gentiles – is in fact the source of the early Christian critical enquiry regarding the current relevance of the Law. Within early Christianity the solution to this question yielded a diversified result: (a) the New Testament manifestation-stories are envisaged in a late Jewish genre of Gentile conversions to Judaism ('conversion-visions') as a converting of Jews to Jesus as the

Christ, and (b) again on a Jewish view the latter-day prophet, like the Law, is interpreted as *lumen gentium*, a light to all peoples. From the moment that Jesus is acknowledged in a Christian sense as the latter-day prophet, Jews who have become Christians are confronted with the 'law issue'; the response to that is the central core of the gospel tradition. While for some early Christian traditions (especially the Q community) the eschatological prophet radiates the 'light of the true Law' and faithfully interprets it in judgement upon 'human laws', as Paul sees it the risen Jesus Christ appears and acts in place of the Law as 'light of the world'. Thus in the Pauline view Jesus takes over the salvific function of the Law (Gal. 1:16; 3:2–5; also Mk. 10:17–31). Illumination now comes from the risen Jesus, who replaces circumcision – enlightenment through the Law. The conflict which was bound sooner or later to spring out of the confrontation between the Law and Jesus was in principle entailed by the concept of *lumen gentium*, already the major Jewish honorific title applying to the Law as well as to the prophet of the last days.

As latter-day prophet and true expositor of the Law Jesus is 'the light of the world'. The interpretation of his death as the murdering of God's prophet testifies, therefore, to a view of Jesus' death which, instead of isolating it, sees it in the context of what came before it: his whole prophetic life. One might say that no intrinsic significance is attributed to Jesus' death 'in itself', but that it gives expression to the fact that Jesus' person and ministry and prophetic career is itself the 'light of the world'.

## B. THE DIVINE PLAN OF SALVATION. THE SCHEME OF SALVATION-HISTORY

It was more especially in its catechesis that the Christian community continued to reflect on the meaning of Jesus' death. The place of that death in the scheme of 'salvation-history' would seem to be anchored primarily in the Marcan tradition, actually in its synoptic material dealing with the Passion story. In this complex of tradition the suffering and death of Jesus are interpreted, on a basis of Scripture, as a 'salvific economy', God's plan of salvation. A word that typifies this tradition is the divine δεῖ: it 'had to' happen in this way; the Scriptures acquaint us with God's will concerning the destiny in store for the saviour-figure of the 'latter days'. J. Roloff (following Tödt, Popkes and Hahn) has some grounds for distinguishing within this scheme of salvation-history two sub-traditions: (a) Mk. 8:31a; 9:12b; and Lk. 17:25. The primary form of this tradition is: 'The son of man must suffer many things and so enter into glory.' Constitutive here are the 'much suffering' and the 'being glorified'. In this sub-tradition Jesus is a passive figure standing as it were between two active subjects, on the one hand the Jews, on the other, God; (b) Mk. 9:31a; 14:41c; and Lk. 24:7 (=SL): 'The son of man must be delivered into the hands of the sons of men.' Constitutive for this block of tradition is the Aramaic pun on 'son of man' and 'sons of men', and the kerygmatic key-term 'be handed over' (*paradidonai*). In this sub-group the concept 'son of man' is the *essential* thing (in contrast to the first sub-group). Here Jesus does not stand between two active subjects; the action emanates from God: God himself consigns Jesus to death – which already reveals a more profound theological reflection (though not for that reason of a later date, chronologically speaking).

In the dual form of this framework of interpretation explicit mention of the glorification or resurrection is not fundamental, as opposed to the contrast-scheme; it is in fact omitted, except in a later, albeit already pre-Marcan interpolation (Mk. 8:31). This salvation-history interpretation of Jesus' death also stems from very early church communities in Palestine; it finds its context, however, not in the controversy with the Jews (like the contrast-scheme) but in the churches' own catechesis – although initially it will have been prompted in part by the attempt to resolve and make understandable the aporia of the cross-event. The tenor of this early Christian complex of tradition is precisely reflected in the Emmaus story (Lk. 24:13–32).

The Church, which after the Easter experience confesses Jesus as the messiah, has not only to justify itself, however, *vis-à-vis* the Jews, but for itself as a Jewish-Christian brotherhood it must face up to Scripture, specifically Deut. 21:23: crucifixion is anathema, a divine curse. Paul makes an explicit reference to this Old Testament passage (Gal. 3:13). Also within this interpretative scheme stands the section Mk. 2:1 to 3:6 and 12:13–27 where, from five acts of Jesus, Mark sets out to explain at the historical level how it could come about that Jesus was put to death. Again, the oldest redaction of the synoptic Passion narrative, still traceable in Mark 14 and 15, is meant to shed light on the question: How could things come to such a pass? Thus Jesus' suffering and death are interpreted as an event set in motion by God – one, therefore, in which we can recognize God's activity.

One feature built into this interpretative scheme is an apocalyptic motif – not in the vein of an apocalyptical 'shall be' (that is, an inevitable catastrophe, as in Dan. 2:28 LXX), but in order to put on the dying of Jesus the stamp of a 'latter-day' event. The woes and persecutions suffered by the just are after all among the signs of the close of the Age and stand under the divine governance: Mk. 9:31; 14:21; 15:33, 38. The testimony of Scripture, then, is an illustration of this divine 'must' of Jesus' death. The apocalyptic motif in this case serves only to formulate the latter-day, eschatological relevance of the 'must' of salvation-history. At no stage of the tradition are Jesus' suffering and death reported merely as an atrocious and absurd, more or less unholy and baffling event. The motif of the reportage is the fact (of Jesus' execution) itself, as one that calls for a meaningful interpretation. The Christian insight into the 'must' (in its setting of salvation-history) is precisely what gives rise to the Passion narrative and to formulae like those in Mk. 8:31a and 9:31a.

In the most primitive form of the synoptic Passion narrative, therefore, there is no trace of a soteriological motivation for Jesus' suffering and death; no saving function is as yet ascribed to them as being a propitiation for sin. In the context of this tradition the people appear not as those for whom or for whose benefit Jesus is delivered up, but as those into whose hands he is delivered. Nevertheless in their baleful action they are caught up, although unwittingly (Mk. 14:21), in the saving activity of God. The being delivered 'into the hands of men' (Mk. 9:31) becomes in Mk. 14:41 and Lk. 24:7 'into the hands of sinners'; this looks like a secondary theological generalizing and not a primary accretion to an already soteriological interpretation.

A causal elucidation of Jesus' death in terms of salvation-history is not in itself a soteriologically final account of the matter (as, for instance, in Rom. 4:25). If Jesus' death has a functional place within this interpretative scheme, it can only be this: that this suffering and this death confront the disciples with the decision whether to endorse Jesus' path of suffering as an 'event from God' and be ready to follow suit (Mk. 14:27, 38, 66–72).

Another striking thing is that all allusions to Scripture within this stratum of tradition are restricted to the psalms of the suffering righteous one, who endures persecution but knows himself to be in God's hand.[25] The oldest, pre-Marcan Passion narrative understands Jesus' suffering and death, therefore, not in terms of the resurrection (Mk. 14:28 is Marcan editorializing), or of Isa. 53, at any rate when interpreted as a suffering for other people's sins (Mk. 14:24 and the words of institution, Mk. 14:22–25, come from a different source: the Last Supper tradition). Likewise the son of man Christology stands in a context in which we hear of persecution, martyrdom or suffering of the righteous (see Lk. 12:8–9 and parallels; Mk. 14:62 and parallels; Acts 7:56). In particular the first sub-group of this second interpretative scheme seems to be very closely related to the Old Testament and intertestamentary tradition of the suffering righteous one.

This latter theme has had a complex history.[26] Originally it was applied only to Israel's king, whose enemies lay in wait for him. But the king knows he is a *saddik* or righteous person, because he is saved by Yahweh from lethal hostility;[27] for this the king gives thanks to God.[28] It is not this phase (the suffering or being threatened by enemies) that is a sign of righteousness, but being delivered by God from these dangers. It is the divine righteousness or justification (being released from suffering) that makes the righteousness of the pious person (the king) public.[29] In more recent psalms (individual laments), in which pious (righteous) people are accused and brought to trial or execution, they pray God to 'openly show' their righteousness or fidelity, or they pray to be included within the 'righteousness' of God himself.[30] The judicial aid they seek from Yahweh against their enemies is displayed in the punishment inflicted on the latter,[31] but also in the confirmation God provides of the righteousness of the one who prays.[32] The most recent psalms, particularly after the Exile, speak generally of God coming to the rescue of the pious one under duress.

This theme acquires a peculiar significance in the situation of the prophets, oppressed and misunderstood as they were. The formal subject of the fourth *Ebed* song of the Second Isaiah is not the 'suffering righteous one' but the 'suffering prophet',[33] that is, he suffers on account of the message he brings.[34] Isaiah 53 is apparently already familiar with the given theme of the 'suffering righteous one': the 'suffering servant' is pointedly referred to as the righteous one.[35] Servant, minister and righteous one are interchangeable terms. One may conclude that the more general, already existing motif of the 'suffering righteous one' is applied in a special way (in Isa. 53) to the suffering and rejected prophet.

Nevertheless, it is only in the psalms influenced by the Wisdom literature that the 'suffering (but exalted) righteous one' becomes a fixed formula.[36] The standing expression comes to be: 'Many are the afflictions of the righteous' (Ps. 34:20a), and the assurance: but God will deliver them from it all (Ps. 34:20b).

The Septuagint version seems to have a predilection for the idea of the 'righteous one who must suffer'.[37] Here the idea emerges that the righteous, oppressed by the godless – powerful and rich men – are also the *anawim*, the 'poor';[38] expressions perhaps for Jews of the Diaspora who, because of their fidelity to the Law, find themselves at odds with their environment. All this still has no bearing on a 'martyr theology', which does not emerge, apparently, till later on. Obviously akin to the legends of the martyrs in Daniel and to the 'martyr theology' is the legend of Susanna: Susanna, the innocent woman condemned to death but miraculously rescued by Daniel, is a 'suffering righteous one'.

Even so, it is only in apocalyptic that 'glorification' as a correlative to the 'suffering righteous' concept is given clear expression.[39] But by then belief in the resurrection was already strong. A writing of central importance in the history of the 'suffering righteous' motif is the Book of Wisdom (Wis. 2:12–20; 5:1–7), the necessary inference being that the complete motif, 'suffering much' and 'being glorified', became general only during the first quarter of the first century before Christ, and then within the area of Palestine. Originally, it would seem, according to a study by Lothar Ruppert, that the two parts (Wis. 2: 12–20 and 5:1–7) went together as a sort of diptych.[40] The assumption is that the 'righteous one', violently put to death, who is referred to here (and in whom we may see an updating of Isa. 52:13 – 53:12), conceals what was originally a 'law-observing martyr' (of Pharisaic persuasion or at any rate with a Chasidic affiliation). The enemies who lie in wait for him are evidently Sadducees with liberal ideas, who being hostile to his piety and 'righteousness' (Wis. 2:13, 16) in the end murder him (Wis. 2:20). But this righteous man – after what is probably an interpolation about his resurrection (inserted by the final editor) – is taken up into heavenly glory, where he appears as 'a witness to the guilt of' his oppressors; he does not judge them, but in the light of his being glorified they are obliged to judge themselves (Wis. 5:1–7). Admittedly, this outlook is set by the last editor in a new context (that of the 'poor men' theology – like the Septuagint translation, also a product of Alexandria). It is important in this connection that the diptych in Wisdom is a reinterpretation meant to give topical relevance to the 'suffering servant of God' (Isa. 52:13 – 53:12).

Thus the 'suffering righteous one' and 'martyrdom' (initially two distinct traditions) are eventually conjoined. Evidence of this is the appendix to the Fourth Book of the Maccabees (4 Macc. 18:6b–19) (end of the first century AD). It sees the martyrdom of the seven Maccabean brothers as 'the suffering of righteous men'.[41] The way of the righteous through suffering to glory or to resurrection is already envisaged here as a divine plan of salvation: a divine 'must be', and so – we are explicitly told – 'according to the Scriptures'.[42] We find the idea too in the Ethiopian Enoch (pre-Christian).[43] The theme in it that comes to the fore is that of a 'suffering righteous man's' complaint (heard and answered by God).[44] The oppression and suffering of a righteous person are regarded there as, from a 'this-worldly' standpoint, his 'natural' *modus vivendi*: just because they are faithful to the Law, the pious cannot have an easy time in this world. But in apocalyptic style we are referred to the last judgement (Enoch 104:3): the righteous man's suffering is then interpreted as a promise of eternal glory (Enoch 104:1–2, 4–6). That the pious or righteous are bound to suffer a great deal was, in the period when most of the New Testament documents were written, near enough a 'Jewish dogma'.[45]

In this all too summary survey of the Jewish theme of the 'suffering righteous one' three originally divergent lines of tradition have been finally brought together: (a) the sapiential development, (b) the eschatological development, (c) the apocalyptic tradition. I cite, in paraphrase: inspired by the mortal pains of the Deutero-Isaianic Servant of God (*Ebed*: Isa. 52:13 – 53:12), interpreted as martyrdom or else the 'suffering of the righteous one', the apocalyptical line of development (first as a reflex of the persecution of the Chasidim in the Syrian religious conflict) (Dan. 11:33–35; 12:1–3) results in texts that are an echo of the persecution of the Pharisees under Alexander Jannaeus, that is, in an apocalypticizing tradition, source of the (present) Book of Wisdom (Wis. 2:12–20 and 5:1–7), and finally in the moralizing books of the Ethiopian Enoch, and, via 4 Macc. 18:6b–19, in the view that seeks to assess the 'suffering of the righteous one' as being 'in accordance with the Scriptures'; this ends in the great Apocalypses of Ezra and Baruch, which in the light of the ill-fated Jewish Rebellion (AD 66–72/73) that brought Israel so much suffering interpret that suffering as *passio iusti*, the suffering of the righteous.[46] In the space of about a hundred years, what was first felt to be aporia or the vexation and scandal of the pious-one-under-utmost-duress in the end became, via the theory of zealous dedication to the Law (Ps. 119) and of the Septuagint's 'poor men' theology, a dogma of Judaic piety: the righteous and the pious are bound to suffer, but God will raise them up. Thus the 'suffering of the pious' ends up within a pattern of expectation, in which the righteous man, arraigned, suffering, condemned to destruction, has assurance of salvation and of being ultimately vindicated by God.

It seems to me that these Jewish insights, acquired down the centuries (independently of Jesus of Nazareth), are something it is impossible to dismiss. On the contrary these already existing ideas helped the Jew, now become a Christian, to place in context and understand the life and destiny of the Master he already venerated and worshipped; they were not the cause of that veneration.

There was an obvious growth and development in the Old Testament and the intertestamentary literature of the way men appraised the history of human affliction. To begin with, the pious prayed God that in view of their (as the orthodox saw it, condemnatory) sufferings and failure, he would protect them from such things: 'How long, O Lord?' (Ps. 13:2–3); but by the time of the later psalms the victim can hardly depict his trouble and failure and frustration in sufficient detail (Ps. 22: 7–22). This psalm piles every conceivable type of suffering on to 'the pious ones', who call upon God: they are 'a paradigm' of suffering despite their piety and righteous behaviour. The 'primordial pains' of 'Godforsakenness' oppress these people.[47] Thus 'suffering' becomes a paradigm, an archetype for everyone pious, faithful to the Law, to Yahweh. And this acquires its full relevance only in the Diaspora situation. Yet in spite of the suffering the conviction grows: Yahweh is 'my rock' (deriving probably from the sacred and rocky hill of Zion, Jerusalem, the God of Jerusalem, Mount Zion). The primal image of the 'sufferer' therefore comes to be also that of the man rescued by God. Psalm 18 (=2 Sam. 22) is actually the earliest testimony to this Jewish conviction of the close link between an archetypal 'profoundest suffering' and 'highest exaltation' by Yahweh (Ps. 18:8–20).[48]

Although the Jews made a profound connection between 'suffering' and 'being exalted', in more recent, relatively late psalms the hope of rescue is called in doubt (Ps. 39; Ps. 88). All the same, the hope prevailed. Psalm 119, partly a noisy cry of God-forsaken pain, becomes partly the paradigm of all justness vindicated by God: 'However much oppression and distress afflict me, your commandments are my greatest joy. Close by are those who make plans for their attack, they are far from your law. You, Lord, you are nearby: all your commandments are truth' (Ps. 119:143, 150–51). As a pious person this man is 'the sufferer'; he does not even need God's confirmation of this. The reason for this new outlook is that God's enemies are understood in a different way. The pious man is harassed because of his zeal for the Law. In that respect Ps. 119 is a fundamental link in the chain of development: what had formerly (because of the suffering of the righteous) been an aporia sometimes difficult to place now becomes a sign of election, the hallmark of endorsement by God.

It was mainly when the motif of the suffering righteous one was conjoined with the apocalyptical theology of martyrdom (Dan. 11:33–35;

Wis. 2:12–20) that suffering and deliverance or exaltation came to be closely associated together; so the theology of the suffering of the righteous one, flowering as it did in the literature of apocalyptic, has deep roots in Jewish spirituality. What is new about the late Jewish interpretation is the idea that the righteous man does not just suffer, but does so specifically because of his righteousness and fidelity to the Law (Ps. 119): the just man has to suffer by reason of his 'uprightness' (4 Ezra; Syr. Baruch). It is only in the very much later apocalyptic literature that the 'being glorified' which is spoken of here is permanently linked up with the suffering of the righteous.[49]

Has this Jewish view of suffering anything to do with the early Christian interpretation of Jesus' suffering and death?

Of the theme of a martyrological glorification (in which the *martyr* is glorified) no trace can be found in the primitive form of the pre-Marcan Passion narrative.[50] On the contrary, it is clear from Lk. 23:46 that this evangelist was scandalized by Jesus' being forsaken by God, as that is expressed in Mk. 15:34 and parallels. In that very early Passion story Jesus' role is never exhibited as a heroic one in contrast to the Jewish martyr theology; rather is he the 'passive (suffering) object' of other men's actions. The glorification referred to comes only after Jesus' death; the death itself has nothing of the heroic or intrinsically glorious about it. On the other hand there are present in this early narrative the typical features of the straightforward motif of the 'suffering of a righteous man': the 'to suffer many things' (Mk. 8:31) as well as *paschein* (that is, suffering to the point of death) (in the later texts).[51] Jesus is seen as 'righteous', thus as someone who, *being* righteous, must suffer (Mt. 27:19; Lk. 23:47; also Acts 3:14; 7:52; 22:14). According to some scholars the two epithets 'Holy One' and 'Righteous One' (Acts 3:14) in their pre-Lucan tradition may be not titles but the expression of an ethico-religious verdict on the life of Jesus.[52] Still, with Luke 'the Holy One' is a messianic title (Lk. 1:35), while it is very obvious that Luke employs the phrase 'Jesus, the Just One' (Acts 22:14) solely in connection with the suffering Jesus. Thus Luke is using the old, Jewish notion of the 'suffering righteous one', but in a messianic context (as also in Enoch 38:2 and 53:6 the righteous one is given a messianic interpretation). One layer of early Christian tradition evidently interpreted Jesus' death on the model provided by the theme of the 'suffering of a righteous man'. The allusions to psalms that speak of the suffering of the pious are plain;[53] where Jesus' suffering is predicted there are no references to those psalms but to other

J.E.C.–K

places in the Old Testament.[54] The vague allusions in the Passion narrative to the 'psalms of suffering' interpret Jesus' suffering in a spontaneous and natural way as being 'according to the Scriptures' and so as part of God's plan within the scheme of salvation-history. The whole event of Golgotha is interpreted – or rather envisaged – through the filter of Pss. 22. Again, Ps. 31a nd 69 have been used to help interpret the suffering of Jesus at its true value. Luke 23:46 replaces the offending quotation from Ps. 22:2 with Ps. 31:6; and Mt. 27:34, in response to Mk. 15:23, 36 ('vinegar'), concentrates attention on Ps. 69:22. Thus the spirit of these psalms[55] is partly reproduced in the early Passion narrative: God has indeed vindicated, 'justified',[56] the suffering righteous one. Moreover, these 'psalms of suffering' are also placed in the setting of a song of thanksgiving for deliverance achieved, so that throughout the Passion narrative another evident feature is the prospect of Jesus' definitive deliverance and raising to glory after his death.[57] The Marcan gospel quite plainly understands the course taken by Jesus' life on the basis of a pattern supplied by the motif of 'the suffering but delivered righteous man' in these psalms. Not until this stratum of the early Passion narrative had later on been partly covered over with other explanations of Jesus' suffering did the Johannine gospel (with its penchant for citing passages of reflection) make this 'according to the Scriptures' explicit by means of its introductory formula: 'that the Scripture may be fulfilled' (Jn. 13:18; 19:24, 28).

Then again, the pre-Marcan material would itself appear to contain allusions to the third *Ebed* song (Isa. 50:4–9);[58] and lastly Wis. 2 (itself a reinterpretation of the suffering Servant of God in Isa. 53) has also influenced the account of Jesus' interrogation in Mk. 14:55–65.[59] Mark himself does not set out to show that Jesus suffered 'as a righteous one' but 'as son of man' (see Mk. 8:31; 9:31; 10:33) and 'as son of God' (15:39); but this development is supplied with a point of contact in the dependence of the interrogation episode (Mk. 14:55–64) on the diptych in the Book of Wisdom.[60]

One could say that the primitive form of the Passion story was governed in its conception by the theme of the 'suffering righteous one',[61] but that even in the Marcan redaction and yet more obviously in Matthew and Luke this motif has moved into the background.[62] The Christians of the earliest local churches were apparently able to overcome the embarrassment they continued to feel because of Jesus' execution only by prayerful meditation on the sacred Scriptures – the Old Testament. Hence the many, even merely implicit, allusions to Scripture throughout the (liturgical) Passion narrative, considered by many scholars to be one of the oldest, if not the oldest Christian document. Only the Scriptures could elucidate for them the divine 'must' of this suffering (Lk. 24:26; 24:44–46). The persistence, implicit and allusive, of these Scriptural quotations in the oldest account of the Passion shows that it was not originally apologetic motives that were at work here, but prayerful reflection, bent on overcoming the difficulties they themselves had with this event. This interpretation of Jesus' suffering and death, grounded in prayerful meditation on Scripture – that is, Jesus' suffering is the Scripturally based 'suffering of the righteous one' – might well be called the foundation of the 'salvation-history' scheme of interpretation or the divine δεῖ: ignominious suffering 'must' precede the Easter 'raising to glory'. That there is almost no allusion to Isa. 53 in the earliest stage of the Passion narrative[63] argues that this 'meditation on suffering' had not initially taken into account the salvific implication of Jesus' suffering and death.

## C.   A REDEMPTIVE, ATONING DEATH. SOTERIOLOGICAL SCHEME

By 'soteriological scheme' is meant certain complexes of tradition in which Jesus' death is seen as an atoning death for human beings, as a vicarious propitiatory sacrifice whereby human beings are redeemed. The theme is recognizable by the *hyper* formulae employed: (he) died for us, on account of our sins.

However, the pre-synoptic as well as the pre-Pauline material in which these *hyper* formulae occur is (at any rate at first sight) noticeably sparse. Established (that is, indicative of an already settled tradition) soteriological-cum-Christological formulae can only be recognized with certainty in: Gal. 1:4; Rom. 4:25; 5:8; 8:32; Eph. 5:2; then in the ancient *kerygma* of 1 Cor. 15:3b–5; in the words spoken over the cup in the Marcan tradition of the Last Supper (Mk. 14:24) and as the sole authentically synoptic piece of evidence: the saying about the 'ransom for many' in Mk. 10:45; finally, 1 Pet. 2:21–24, the only early hymn to Christ in which the theme of salvation or redemption is recognizable. Not until a later stage in its development is this soteriological interpretation of Jesus' death to become the governing factor in Paul's Christology, the Letter to the Hebrews and the Deutero-Pauline letters, as also of the Apocalypse and the Johannine gospel. In that sense the theme of redemption is amply represented in the New Testament; but for that very reason the slender basis for it in the oldest layers is all the more striking.[64] A still bigger problem is that later 'testifying' passages of Scripture, which do appeal to Isa. 53, are quite unfamiliar with the idea of vicarious propitiation.[65]

The result of this exegetical situation is that – too hastily, perhaps – the soteriological interpretation of Jesus' death is declared to be a secondary development as compared with a more original interpretation of it, said to be vested either in the contrast-scheme or in the causal interpretation entailed by 'salvation-history'. The secondary development would then be explicable either in terms of the appeal to Isa. 53 or of the then generally widespread Jewish notion of the vicarious propitiation brought about by a martyr's death.

Many scholars have come to see the emergence of the soteriological interpretation of Jesus' death as indeed the outcome of Scriptural testimony: Isa. 53 (the 'servant of God'). But in its earliest elaborations it is difficult to demonstrate any dependence of this motif on Isa. 53; and what is more, it is precisely in these currents of tradition, which explicitly look for proofs in Scripture (the second interpretation scheme), that obvious references to Isa. 53 tend to be avoided (see above). At the moment, therefore, there is a greater consensus among the exegetes about the fact that in Jesus' time the Jews generally did not apply Isa. 53 to a 'suffering messiah' at all. On the other hand one cannot avoid the admission that some elements in the soteriological formula-material, such as 'ransom for many' (Mk. 10:45b), 'he died for our sins' (1 Cor. 15:3b), and 'he was put to death for our trespasses' (Rom. 4:25), are in substance clear echoes of Isa. 53:5. According to J. Roloff there was in an early phase of Palestinian Christianity a rather disjointed use of Isa. 53, one that was as yet outside the main stream of the evolving Scriptural testimony (in relation to Jesus' death) and was still unfamiliar with a theological and systematic use of the *Ebed* songs as a body.[66] In the soteriological formulae the allusions to Isa. 53 are evidently *not* 'proof texts': the idea of the 'divine must' is absent here. But the 'theme' (Isa. 53) had meanwhile become common property for Jews.

1 Cor. 15:3b says: 'Christ died for our sins in accordance with the Scriptures'; this is in no way evidence to the contrary;[67] again in the second clause the resurrection 'in accordance with Scripture' stands disconnectedly beside a broader element of interpretation ('the third day'). The peculiar thing about this credal formula is that it binds together two originally independent strands of tradition: the scheme of interpretation based on 'salvation-history' reveals its presence in the phrase 'in accordance with the Scriptures', whereas the Deutero-Isaianic soteriological interpretation can be heard in 'for our sins'.

The strands of tradition in 1 Cor. 15:3b–5, however early, are not the very first start of the other interpretations of Jesus' death but are themselves the product of a longer process of reflection and merging together of traditions. In itself, at any rate, this says nothing against the antiquity of the independent traditions, including those which offer a soteriological interpretation.[68] It does of course raise the problem of whether Isa. 53 was the reason for interpreting Jesus' death soteriologically. Then again, it seems to me relevant to ask whether the Jews of the time read into those *Ebed* songs what people read into them later on.[69]

Because of the difficulties in demonstrating a link between Isa. 53 and the soteriological interpretation of Jesus' death, others went on to look for a connection with the late Jewish idea of martyrdom as vicarious propitiation.[70] In 2 Macc. 7:37–38 also, the motif of substitution comes to the fore; but only in late Jewish writings after AD 70 do we hear tell of the vicarious nature of the martyr's suffering – more especially in 4 Macc. 6:28–29; 1:11; 17:21; 18:5. In later rabbinical writings, in the midrashes and targums, it was Abraham's sacrifice of Isaac that played a major role; and it is difficult to argue that, however late these documents are in relation to primitive Christianity, the ideas in them came suddenly out of the blue.[71] Even so, where the history of tradition is concerned, the late Jewish theology of the martyr's death, or of the legends associated with rabbinical martyrology, has nothing to do with the soteriological view of Jesus' death, because this martyr motif as such represents a quite different tradition from that articulated in the theme of the 'suffering righteous one'.[72]

As it turns out, therefore, the soteriological formulae form a very old and self-contained complex of tradition, the emergence of which cannot be accounted for either by secondary deduction from other interpretations of Jesus' death or by referring it to Jewish theologies of the martyr's vicarious suffering.[73] All such interpretations come up against difficulties presented by the history of tradition, as well as the absence from the oldest stratum of the *hyper* formulae of any reference to Isa. 53, in spite of material affinities.

This rather negative result where any Jewish antecedent for a soteriological account of the death of Jesus is concerned does of course raise the question whether the motif is not rooted in some memory of Jesus' last days, in which he was himself obliged to come to terms with his approaching violent death. In other words, we must seriously consider whether Mark's reference to the 'ransom for many' (Mk. 14:24) – with its obvious setting in the Church's eucharistic worship – does not have its historical basis in a saying or gesture of Jesus, as even then he interprets for himself his coming death. So, after having examined the early Christian interpretations of Jesus' death, we are once more referred to his earthly life itself, to the 'historical Jesus'. All that we have established so far is that in early Christianity there were three complexes of tradition, existing side by side, in which Jesus' death is variously interpreted, three blocks of tradition all of which appear to be *very* old, but with no very cogent grounds for assigning any chronological order to them.[74]

## §2　The death of Jesus, viewed in the context of his earthly life

### A.　THE REJECTION OF JESUS' MESSAGE AND MODE OF LIFE

In present-day discussion about continuity and discontinuity between Jesus on this earth and Christ in the preaching of the Church there emerges, it seems to me, a fundamental misunderstanding, namely, that the break comes with on one side the death of Jesus and on the other the Church's subsequent preaching of the resurrection. One school would put the whole emphasis on the caesura provided by this datum, others think they should relativize it. What is overlooked here is that while there certainly is a 'breakage-point', it is to be located within the ministry of the historical Jesus, in the resistance to him and the rejection of his message. And the insistent question arising out of this is whether that rejection, as a broad fact of Jesus' earthly life, did not give him occasion in one way or another to interpret his approaching death prior to the event.

　　Time and again exegetes have considered the question of whether Jesus' preaching in Galilee ended in failure, at least in the sense that people did not receive his message.[75]

　　'*But*, blessed is he who takes no offence at me' (Lk. 7:18–23 = Mt. 11:6).[76] Obviously, this passage is not looking back over the whole ministry of Jesus (after his life had finished) but is concerned with a historical recollection of specific facts of Jesus' life and the reactions they evoked: the question whether Jesus is bringing salvation or has within him 'a demon'.[77] We saw earlier on that Jesus rejected both the Aramean-Pharisaic exposition of the Law and the high-handed Sadducees' devotion to the cult. His preaching and praxis struck at the very heart of the Judaic principle of 'performance' in the religious sphere. In particular his solidarity with the 'unclean' and with 'tax-gatherers and sinners' was a thorn in the flesh of pious officialdom – it was contrary to 'the Law'.

If one wants to establish a theology of Jesus of Nazareth which is concerned primarily with his life, message and ministry, then the rift which contact with Jesus engendered within the Jewish community of his day must have a fundamental place in it. After all, even a pre-Easter faith and trust in Jesus had to meet this challenge. Essentially, the question whether Jesus is bringer of good or ill, curse or salvation, is a problem already relevant before Easter. His suffering and death are actually the consequences of a conflict aroused during his life. The problem does not arise only with Jesus' death. After all, he did not die in bed but was put to death.

The Marcan gospel clearly says that Jesus' preaching in Galilee met with initial success.[78] But from Mk. 7 on, the allusions to 'a great crowd of people' diminish, as do the positive reactions.[79] The rule of God was the glad news that Jesus had brought to Galilee; salvation was what was being proclaimed. Yet in the earliest Aramaic layer of the Q tradition the consciousness would seem to be present that the 'Jesus phenomenon' might be rejected: this possibility of 'being offended at him' (Lk. 7:18–23) goes back, apparently, to pre-Easter memories. Thus the possibility of Jesus being rejected is part of the oldest 'Christological package'; it evidently goes back to recollections of failure in Jesus' days on earth. The veiled, ambiguous character of Jesus' historical manifestation – sharing the ambiguity of everything one could call historical – is amplified by Mark; but the Marcan redaction only makes more plain what had already been consciously articulated in the pre-Marcan tradition: a historical opaqueness is cast over Jesus' life. 'The divine' in him, his coming 'from God', is not something given apodictically, with a compelling absence of ambiguity; it calls for a vote of confidence. Mark thematizes the rejection of Jesus' message and ministry as early as the start of his gospel (Mk. 2:1 up to 3:5); and he concludes these first stories with his pregnant interpretation: 'The Pharisees . . . immediately held counsel with the Herodians against him, how to destroy him' (Mk. 3:6). Mark obviously wants to show how it could come about that the revered Master was put to death. Else-where in Mark it is not 'the Pharisees and Herodians' but in particular 'the high priests and Scribes' who contemplate destroying Jesus (Mk. 11:18). But it would seem from the Q tradition that the rejection of Jesus' message extended beyond these schematic categories. From the

'woes' uttered over the towns of Chorazin, Capernaum and Bethsaida
(Lk. 10:13–15 =Mt. 11:20–24) it appears that Jesus' message was
rejected also by whole cities. The asides also, to the effect that a prophet
is without honour in his own country (Mk. 6:4; Mt. 13:57; Lk. 4:24;
Jn. 4:44), as well as the typically Johannine 'Will you also go away?'
(Jn. 6:67), point in much the same direction of historically concrete
experiences of failure. Jesus certainly appears to enjoy popularity so
long as no danger threatens; but in the outcome his preaching of the
great 'about turn' of events as a manifestation of the coming rule of
God has only a limited success.

There are grounds for seeing in this experience of the failure of
Jesus' preaching and proffer of salvation the reason why he decided to
'go up to Jerusalem'. Despite the admittedly heated and persisting
arguments among commentators, one can detect a growing consensus
with regard to a hard core of history in the New Testament record,
according to which Jesus, during his lifetime, sent his disciples out 'to
every town and place' (Lk. 10:1), there to proclaim his message of God's
coming rule (Lk. 10:1, 11; Mt. 10:5b–7; besides Mk. 6:7–13).[80] The
presence of this material in both the Q community and the Marcan
tradition argues for its authenticity. In taking this action Jesus is
evidently facing up to the very imminent approach of God's rule on
the one hand, and on the other the possible definitive rejection of his
message (see Lk. 10:10–12). At the least we are bound to say that this
proclamation of judgement ensuing upon the failure to accept Jesus'
message can hardly be laid purely at the door of the Q community and
have no basis in the latest phase of Jesus' own preaching, after experiences of rejection. That Jesus restricted himself in his message
exclusively to Israel (see also Mt. 15:24) is nowadays less and less
matter for dispute. Apropos of this relatively large-scale dispatch of
disciples to the whole of Israel by Jesus, exegetes are very probably
right in speaking of a 'final offer to Israel on the part of Jesus'.[81] Jesus
here is giving exactly the same commission to the disciples, to do what
he himself is doing; preaching the coming kingdom of God, healing
the sick and driving out devils (Lk. 10:1; Mt. 10:5b–6; Lk. 10:8–11;
Mk. 6:7–13).

After the disciples sent out had returned – apparently full of enthusiasm about their activities – Jesus probably concentrated on training a more intimate group of disciples – the subsequent 'Twelve' (or:
the Twelve already singled out by himself?).[82] This change in apostolic
strategy was apparently the outcome of a growing experience of failure
where his preaching in Galilee was concerned.

The gospels would seem to suggest that Jesus was not himself all that certain of the success which the disciples who had been sent out – two by two – were able to report to their Master concerning their missionary journeys. On their return there is detectable in the gospels an at first gentle but then very plain insistence on Jesus' part that his disciples should have a 'rest' (Mk. 6:30–31), far away from the populace (Mt. 14:22; Mk.6:45). So they all go with Jesus across the lake, but even there, unfortunately, run into a large crowd: 'a flock without shepherds' the gospels muse (Mk. 6:30–44; 8:1–10; Mt. 14:13–21; 15:32–39; and Lk. 9:10–17; Jn. 6:1–15). It is a striking fact that not only do the four gospels feature this story but two of them even have dual accounts of what seems to have followed it: Jesus fed the crowd in miraculous fashion. But especially significant is the comment (Mk. 6:52; 8:17–18, 21): 'They did not understand it.' On the one hand Jesus offers (a meal of) fellowship to sinners; on the other they want to proclaim Jesus king. Jesus' reaction, according to the gospel narrative, is unambiguous: he constrains (as the text has it) his disciples to rest, away from the multitude. A certain 'tendency to isolation', in other words Jesus' determination to keep his more intimate disciples well away from the enthusiasm of these people, would seem to be intimated to us by these New Testament passages. At any rate the Marcan tradition is significant: Jesus is obliged, apparently against the wishes of his disciples, to 'constrain' them (for the time being) to quit the stage, to take the boat back again to the other side – although it was nightfall and a storm was threatening: Jesus himself withdraws 'to a solitary mountain'.[83]

After this incident the focus of Jesus' activity switches apparently from Galilee to Jerusalem – although the connection is difficult to reconstruct, historically speaking. What does become clear is that, according to the gospels, from then on Jesus regards his message as having failed in Galilee and so decides to make for Jerusalem. From that moment on, the gospels begin to make clear allusions to the path of suffering set before Jesus, in other words, to his definitive rejection. This path is described, 'typically', of course, as an 'exodus', a journey to Jerusalem.[84] Whereas in the first phase of his public ministry Jesus travelled around the country proclaiming the approach of God's rule, now he is shown, according to the gospel record, as making 'a journey towards suffering', a journey towards death. This is defined in part, no doubt, by the historical outcome of events; but perhaps also by historical reminiscences of the already admitted fiasco in Galilee.

Although predictions of the Passion in the gospels are certainly not historical reproductions of Jesus' own words, still the question may

be asked whether they are simply *vaticinia ex eventu*, that is, simply projected back from the events of the crucifixion and of Easter. We shall
have to consider whether after the fiasco in Galilee the decision to go
up to Jerusalem did not turn the prospect of a possible violent death
into a potentially concrete experience. In any case Matthew means to
identify, with his *apo tote* – 'from that moment on' (Mt. 16:21) – a
particular moment in time, a moment at which a caesura is clearly
marked out with a 'heretofore'. Of course it is hard to form a historical
judgement as to the chronological exactness of this; the gospels may be
a 'schematic version' of a historically gradual process which in the end
at any rate made Jesus realize that his mission in Galilee had broadly
speaking failed and that, convinced of the rightness and urgency of it
as he was, he should look for a different outcome, with before him the
possibility of total failure.

All of this, though showing clear signs of post-Easter reflection,
none the less has roots in an earlier period: even before Good Friday
Jesus is 'the rejected one' and also feels himself to be so on the basis of
the historically short 'record' of his public career. I believe that F.
Muszner is very perceptive when, apropos of Jesus' decision to leave
Galilee for Jerusalem, he says: 'At first Jesus goes about as the one who
offers the eschatological rule of God; then after the offer is rejected by
Israel he does so as the one who with the rejection of the offer is himself rejected.'[85] Giving historical criticism its full head, the least that
one is bound to say on the score of history is that Jesus of Nazareth,
despite his awareness of a plain lethal threat posed by 'official Jerusalem',
nevertheless deliberately and of set purpose made his way to the city
of Zion. His purpose in so doing is something we must look at more
closely.

B.  JESUS IN FACE OF HIS APPROACHING DEATH

Starting from a one-sided *kerygma* theology, which assigns to the four
gospels a source in the actual life of the Church without an accompanying historical concern (in early times) with recollections of Jesus' own
life, it is indeed problematical to say with confidence anything to the
point about how Jesus understood himself in view of his approaching
death. But in what has been said already we have pointed repeatedly to
unjustified implicit assumptions in this version of *Formgeschichte* as a
method of understanding the New Testament. There are enough
linguistic signals present in the gospels to indicate awareness of the

historical distance between the earthly life of Jesus himself and that of the local Christian churches; so that, along with the proclamation of the Church's Easter *kerygma*, historical recollection of Jesus' days on earth helps to give substance to the four gospels as concretely presented to us.

(a) Gradually increasing certainty of a violent death

One would have to declare Jesus something of a simpleton if it were maintained that he went up from Galilee to Jerusalem in all innocence, without any idea of the deadly opposition he was to encounter there. Every Jew in those days knew that the Romans had the power of crucifixion, Herod Antipas the *ius gladii* – the right to behead someone – and the beheading of John the Baptist must have been vividly present to the mind of Jesus;[86] then lastly, the Sanhedrin was empowered to use stoning (see Stephen's martyrdom). None of this, in itself, is either here or there. It is relevant, though, when the question becomes urgent as to whether Jesus was conscious of doing things, committing actions or proclaiming a message which sooner or later would result in an inevitable collision with one or more of those authorities. When we are dealing with a rational and purposeful individual, and not with an unrealistic, fanatical apocalypticist (even they were anything but fanatical in late Judaism), the consciousness of doing or saying something which could and would cause a fundamental conflict with one of those authorities is at the same time a way of deliberately taking upon oneself responsibility for the legal consequences of such behaviour. So let us link up Jesus' activity with the three centres of power that could possibly impose the death penalty on him.

Jesus was known to have been baptized by John the Baptist; and from the time of his public ministry it was rumoured that he was actually *Johannes redivivus* (Mk. 6:14); furthermore that, in a manner more radical even than the Baptist, he was proclaiming the message of total change in virtue of God's approaching rule, in a way that called for taking sides for or against his person. It would be naïve to suppose that Jesus, having witnessed king Herod Antipas' use of the *ius gladii* in the case of John the Baptist, failed to relate John's ministry to his own. With the Baptist for an example he knew that the sword of Herod was hanging over his head as well. In Mk. 3:6 the 'Herodians', to whom Mark nowhere else refers, are a pointer to a historical reminiscence. In short: such a sane and sensible person as Jesus of Nazareth must have definitely reckoned on possible execution by beheading, like

John the Baptist.

Was the Sanhedrin with its power to inflict death by stoning a threat to Jesus? Apart from Mt. 16:1, 6, 11, 12 and the Gospel of John the Sadducees (strongest party in the Sanhedrin) are not mentioned as opponents of Jesus until the account of the Passion. It is a known fact, on the other hand, that only after the Jewish War (after AD 70) did the Pharisees, who also had a voice in the Sanhedrin, acquire the leading position ascribed to them in the gospels. Evidently, therefore, the New Testament antagonism between Jesus and the Pharisees is up to a point coloured by the later situation of the Church. One may assume that the tension between Jesus and the Sadducees dated from an earlier period than the story of the Passion would suggest. On the other hand, except for Mt. 27:62, the Pharisees are nowhere mentioned in the account of the Passion. Hence one may suspect that the opposition to Jesus came not so much from just one particular group but from the two most important ones at the time: the Pharisees and, especially towards the end, the Sadducees.[87] It is hard to believe that Jesus was so naïve as not to have realized that his words and actions were creating an explosive and for him very dangerous situation, bearing in mind the leaders of the Jewish community at that time.

And then, had Jesus anything to fear directly from the Romans? It was of course by the Romans that he was executed, as the nature of his death – by crucifixion – demonstrates, and so on grounds of possible or alleged Zealotic reactions among the people. Jesus needed least of all to take that possibility into consideration, in view of the tenor of his proclamation, which revealed no interest in the problems of the Roman occupation. There was one particular – that is to say, political – interpretation of messianism, which admirers certainly attributed to him, within the range of possible situations. There were obviously some ex-Zealots among Jesus' disciples ('Simon, the Zealot', Lk. 6:15 and parallels; Acts 1:13); according to some authorities, who associate 'Iscariot' with *sicarius* (dagger-man), Judas is supposed to have belonged to these circles; even 'Boanerges', the sons of thunder, could, it is said, witness to a Zealotic reminiscence.[88] Appearing in Jerusalem with such a following, with at the time – or probably earlier – an incident like the cleansing of the Temple (Mk. 11:15–16 and parallels) and the apparently authentic saying of Jesus about 'demolishing the Temple' (Mk. 14:58 parallel in Mt.; see Jn. 2:19; Mk. 15:29 parallel in Mt. 12:6; Acts 6:14 and Mk. 13:2), coming from someone who proclaims the kingly rule of God over Israel, this may appear, directly or, even more, indirectly, after the complaint registered from the Jewish side with the

Roman authorities, as provocation and would in any case make the always rebellion-conscious occupying power antagonistic towards anyone who aroused the feelings of the people.

As a matter of history it is clear of course that Jesus' death was in continuity with the reaction to his public ministry, especially having in mind the example of John the Baptist, who was also done away with 'for fear of the Romans'. As a final effect Jesus' execution is historically explicable 'from the interplay of various factors, each of which was dangerous enough in itself'.[89] As Jesus was no fanatic – and that is quite certain from what we know about him – then from a particular moment in his career he must have rationally come to terms with the possibility, in the longer term probability and in the end actual certainty of a fatal outcome. This is more or less unanimously agreed nowadays, by exegetes and historians; it is just theologians who are still affected by Bultmann's dictum that we cannot know what Jesus thought about his death and that he may have been steeped in total despair and perplexity because of this surprising turn of events, which had thwarted all his plans. What had been cautiously uttered by Bultmann as a piece of pure speculation has for certain theologians come to be an essential element in their theological thematizing (and thence 'popularized' in some quarters). It smacks more of modish ideology and 'cashing in' than of historical accuracy.

(b) The unavoidable question of Jesus' own interpretation

Granted Jesus' basic attitude towards the will of God, his Father, the obvious question concerns his existential attitude to what he himself perceived to be the threatening possibility, likelihood, and then certainty of being rejected and executed, whether by the sword – because of Herod's royal prerogative (as with John the Baptist before him) – or by stoning – by virtue of the powers assigned to the Sanhedrin (as later on with Stephen) – or by crucifixion – as for many at that time, the Roman penalty for serious criminal acts or rebellion. That someone like Jesus, who was proclaiming the imminent arrival of God's rule, would have failed to ponder, in some way, so probable and to him so clearly recognizable an outcome of his future life, can be ruled out from the start. It would mean that Jesus' end was in flagrant contradiction to what he had himself been saying about having a radical confidence in God, whatever the empirical and historical circumstances might be. And *that* was the kernel both of the message and of the behaviour on Jesus' part which flowed from it; for with all this fulfilled, he could still refer to 'being an unprofitable servant' (Lk. 17:7–10). To lack entirely, or simply to refrain from entertaining, any moral or religious standpoint in regard to approaching death would in this case be not only myopic but must indicate an incomprehensibly divided personality.

Thus the fact of his approaching death was something that Jesus was bound to integrate into his overall surrender to God, but also reconcile with a conviction as to the urgency of his message. 'Not my will but your will be done' (Mk. 14:36c and parallels). Even if this is not a *verbum ipsissimum*, not a historical Jesus-saying, it unmistakably reflects the inner consistency of Jesus' own preaching and personal bearing during his life. But acceptance of God's will and evaluating concretely the point and purpose of what was to happen are not one and the same thing.

There are authentic sayings enough known to us from the life of Jesus that plainly point towards an attitude of 'faithfulness unto death'. Jesus is turning for support to Israel's sapiential experience and wisdom tradition when he says that 'whoever loses his life will save it' (Mk. 8:35 and parallels; see Lk. 17:33 and parallels; 14:26). We can gather from Jesus' sayings and actions that as soon as death came in prospect he not only contemplated that possibility but, existentially speaking, must have lived with it: he was forced by circumstances to give a place to approaching death in his radical confidence in God. What place?

The rejection of his message and the prospect of his personal rejection could hardly have been felt by Jesus to constitute at the human level and in themselves a meaningful event. (The fact of the calamity and the incomprehensible event of Jesus' death have a profound effect on the reactions in the New Testament, especially in the contrast-scheme.) Jesus himself was faced with the concrete task of reconciling the historical eventuality of his violent death with the assurance of his message about the approaching kingdom of God. Did Jesus simply allow the certainty of his death to take possession of him in un-comprehending, though radical trust in God; or did he come to see in this historical situation some sort of divine plan of salvation, that not only in spite of but perhaps through the very failure within history of his message, through his death, his message would be vindicated divinely and in sovereign freedom? In this 'in spite of' or else 'thanks to' is the key to the whole theological problem.

All the gospels or attestations on the part of the first Christians are quite sure that Jesus went to the cross freely and deliberately. What we have here is post-Easter theological reflection 'after the fact', but also perhaps certain historical reminiscences. Filling them out with historical fact is not such an easy business. Still, there are suggestive clues.

(c) A logion of unconditional readiness to serve

We said earlier on that the soteriological interpretation of Jesus' death appears to have only a slender basis in the oldest strata of tradition prior to the gospels. Even so, analysis of a number of *diakonia* texts which feature a logion about Jesus' service and readiness to serve has established that these passages appear to have an intrinsic connection with something that happened at the Last Supper shortly before Jesus' death. Calling for consideration here are Mk. 10:45 and Lk. 22:27 and then, secondarily, Lk. 12:37b and Jn. 13:1–20 – all texts forming part of the Last Supper tradition.

(1) In Mk. 10:45 a clear connection is made between the theme of *diakonein* or service on Jesus' part and that of an expiatory death: 'For the son of man also came not to be served but to serve, and to give his life as a ransom for many.' It is true that this serving is presented here as an ethical paradigm for Jesus' disciples. According to J. Roloff[90] the mention in this context of Jesus' expiatory death is not a Marcan redaction but something already there in the Marcan tradition; Mark has simply accommodated the whole passage (verse 45a and b) at this point in his gospel because of its paraenetic usefulness (as moral exhortation). In view of Lk. 22:24–27 (=SL, and not a Lucan version of the Marcan redaction) it is clear that the two themes did not always go together. The *de facto* combination came about in the Last Supper tradition, for both verse 45b and 45a derive from this tradition: a secondary development of 45a from 45b, or vice versa, is not possible.[91] *Diakonein* originally denoted waiting at table, in secular Greek; but in Hellenistic Jewry this was weakened to cover all kinds of ways of 'providing a service'. In the Hellenistic Jewish-Christian and Pauline Gentile-Christian churches *diakonia* became a specifically Christian and ecclesial concept.[92] The Marcan source itself recognizes the common Greek usage (Mk. 1:13, 31; 15:41) (with elsewhere perhaps a few transitional meanings too). There is an obviously ecclesial connotation in the sole case of Lk. 22:26–27, as a Lucan variant of Mk. 10:43, 45. That is to say, the oldest layers of the synoptic tradition employ the *diakonia* term in its secular sense, while in one particular group of texts, closely interrelated within the historical development of tradition, and in that group alone, a specifically Christian usage is clearly apparent. Roloff

concludes from this that Mk. 10:45 (with its obvious setting in the Last Supper tradition) is the crucial locus within the whole complex, and that from it the process whereby the common Greek usage evolved into the 'service' terminology associated specifically with the Church took its start. In other words, the theological factor which touched off this shift in meaning is to be looked for in an understanding of the 'Lord's Supper' as an act of serving on Jesus' part and a pointed summary of what his mission had signified.[93] The notion of *diakonia*, service(-ability), is the reflection of a very early interpretation of Jesus' death, anchored in the Last Supper tradition.

This is again recognizable in Lk. 22:27: 'For which is the greater, one who sits at table or one who serves? Is it not the one who sits at table? But I am among you as one who serves.' Some of Luke's already given material is overlaid in the context of 22:24–27 with an ecclesiological-cum-ethical exhortation or paraenesis; Jesus' service stands here as a model for those who hold office in the Church, 'the disciples', and a guide for the conduct of the local church leaders when celebrating the supper of the Lord. Here the ecclesial use of 'serving' and 'service' is consummated and complete. J. Roloff disagrees with H. Schürmann in regarding Lk. 22:24–27 not as a Lucan recasting of the Marcan tradition but as SL, a separate, independent tradition, peculiar to Luke. The fact that the earthly Jesus acts as the one who serves at the meal only becomes intelligible to someone aware of the current customs at the meal-table and of the hierarchy maintained so precisely there in Jesus' day. The Aramaic expression: 'I am in your midst', in the present tense, as opposed to the broad retrospect on the whole (and thus already concluded) life of Jesus in Mk. 10:45, points to a very concrete situation, namely, that of 'having a meal', in which Jesus offers to share fellowship with his disciples. There, in the actual meal, Jesus is the servant. This becomes the more stringent, if verse 27 or 27c originally formed part of the earliest pre-Lucan account of the Last Supper, which did not then include verses 24–26, so that verse 27 had a direct connection with the words of institution in verses 15–20: Jesus' act of self-surrender, the shedding of his blood 'for (or in place of) you', is here interpreted as a service that benefits the rest of the company. The Last Supper is seen as a *diakonia* performed on behalf of the disciples. Because of its being related to the Last Supper, 'serving' becomes a technical term in the Church for an ecclesial praxis.[94] What in Luke was suggested by the original conjunction of verse 27 with verses 15–20 is made explicit in Mk. 10:45 by 45b: the self-giving of Jesus 'for many', a brief formula seeming to refer to the words uttered liturgically at the eucharist over bread and wine. In both instances the phrase 'the service of Jesus' echoes the soteriological motif of his death.

(2) With these two passages as background, Lk. 12:37b and Jn. 13:1–20 (the foot-washing), in which the theme of readiness to serve likewise appears, can also be interpreted in a soteriological perspective and at the same time in association with the Last Supper.

'(Blessed are those servants whom the master finds awake, when he comes.) Truly, I say to you, he will gird himself and have them sit at table, and he will come and serve them' (Lk. 12:37b). The whole is a secondary amplification of a Parousia parable used by the Church (Lk. 12:36, 37a). The Lord girds himself, it seems, to wash the feet of the rest, something that takes place before the meal and before the invitation to sit at table. In this passage the heavenly meal 'at the close of the Age', associated with the Parousia of Jesus, is envisaged in terms of a certain action carried out by the earthly Jesus; its effect is to show the identity between the earthly Jesus and the Jesus who is to come 'at the last day'. That action is Jesus' service – his conduct as servant at the feast. Serving, service performed out of love, thus becomes the final stamp set upon the life of Jesus; it is carried over from a historical event to the Lord who is to come. Luke 12:37b presupposes the tradition of the foot-washing. The Johannine foot-washing too (Jn. 13:1–20), as a service performed for the disciples in love, is set in the context of Jesus' last supper with them.

It is fair enough to conclude from these four characteristic passages about the desire of Jesus to serve that the theme of Jesus' serving is firmly rooted in the 'tradition of the meal', although this service motif is already well established in its own right within the pre-Johannine tradition of the account of the foot-washing and also put on record as an ethical model (Jn. 13:15, a *hupodeigma* for the disciples); but even then – in view of verse 1 (the approaching Passover and Jesus' awareness that his hour had come) – the context of the service motif is still the Christian interpretation of the death of Jesus. That death was an act of loving service performed by Jesus for his own, through which they are made a 'new fellowship': a 'new covenant'. That is how it was seen in a very early complex of tradition, already recognizable in 1 Cor. 15:3b as a settled formula, even then: 'he died for our sins'. These passages aptly support what we were saying earlier on about the soteriological interpretative scheme: the tradition of the salvific, redemptive significance of Jesus' death is not a secondary phase of a developing process but was grounded, at a very early stage, in the meaning which early Christian churches descried in the Last Supper of

Jesus with his disciples. In a very old stratum of the Last Supper tradition Jesus' self-giving 'to the point of death' is interpreted as 'an act of loving service'. The Last Supper tradition, therefore, is the oldest starting-point for the Christian interpretation of Jesus' death as a self-giving on Jesus' part that procures salvation.

Again, it is highly probable, historically speaking, that Jesus understood himself to be the latter-day prophet. Thus in his own life he was personally confronted by reason of his approaching death with Israel's rejection of God's last offer of salvation to that people. For Jesus' self-understanding this was the real source of doubt and confusion. And so the question is a justifiable, even pressing one: Did the earthly Jesus himself envisage his death as a 'service performed out of love' and hint at all at this meaning of his death while still living on earth? And if not, how are we to explain the emergence of the soteriological motif in the early Christian Last Supper tradition of such diverse provenance?

(d) The Last Supper: unshaken assurance of salvation when face to face with death

One can hardly maintain that Jesus both willed and sought after his death as the sole possible way of realizing the kingdom of God. There would have been an element of play-acting about his commitment to his message of *metanoia* and the rule of God, if he had thought and known from the very start that salvation would come only in consequence of his death. That death only comes in prospect as a result of his preaching and mode of life, which constituted an offer of salvation, having been rejected. This is not rescinded or nullified by his death. An opposite interpretation would fail to give full value to Jesus' real function of 'pointing the way' by the concrete course of his own life's history; in other words, it disregards the fact of Jesus' 'being truly man' in a historical mode. Furthermore, it would simply formalize the actual significance for salvation of Jesus' death.

What can be said on the strength of the real evidence is that at any rate Jesus did nothing to escape a violent death. On the contrary, despite the growing certainty that his message had, broadly speaking, been rejected, he deliberately made for Jerusalem. But it can hardly be said that to accord with Jesus' self-understanding his message of salvation took its meaning only from his death. The truth is: he died just as he lived, and he lived as he died.

That Jesus had to settle for himself what his attitude to impending death must be follows from his overall attitude to life in confrontation with this new situation. Hence the question whether he kept this final event and the possible meaning he gave to it to himself, remained silent about them, or whether in his very last days, at least within the intimate circle of his disciples, he spoke of them (in one way or another). Only that could make clear in what sense Jesus was able to feel his death to be a service performed out of love.

To the exegete it is evident enough that all allegedly obvious and explicit predictions of the Passion are secondary, that is, have (at least in part) been worded in the light of the actual event of Easter. Yet there is more to it than that. It is hard to believe, bearing in mind the concern he is known to have had for his friends, that even in his last days Jesus would have said nothing at all to his disciples about his approaching violent death. Would he have failed to prepare his disciples in any way for the shock of his death, when he saw himself faced by it with the grave problem of reconciling that death and his message with each other and of coming to terms with them? As a matter of history, therefore, we must take seriously the likelihood that during the final meal with his friends Jesus will have said or done something to ensure that when he was dead his intimate disciples would not fall for good into despair and disillusion. On the other hand any public and patently obvious discussion of it would seem to run counter to the basic tenor of the preaching of Jesus, who never made himself a second subject (next to God or to God's rule) of his preaching: Jesus proclaimed not himself but the coming kingdom of God.

Within these limits, maximal and minimal, the gospel accounts of Jesus' blessing of the bread and cup during the Last Supper, although heavily overlaid by the eucharistic observances which the Church had learned to practise in the meantime, display as their central core certain recollected facts of history.

We were saying in an earlier chapter that Jesus' fellowship at table with, in particular, sinners and 'fringe people' in Israel was an authentic and typical feature of his activity here on earth. Then too the accounts of 'miraculous feedings'[95] play such a role in the gospels that they also make 'eating and drinking with Jesus' a central feature of Jesus' offer of (final) well-being and fellowship, especially when he himself acts as host - as at this last meal. So although it is a separate tradition, we must not see the Last Supper as wholly detached from the many instances during Jesus' earthly life when he made the offer of salvation through the shared meal of fellowship.[96] To put it another way: the Last Supper is itself already set within a broader context of the life of Jesus, by whom salvation imparted by God is tendered under the sign of the fellowship meal. But such fellowship 'in face of approaching death' assumes within this total context a very pregnant significance.

That the Last Supper was actually a Jewish Passover meal is disputable on many different grounds; so that we shall not consider that aspect here. What is beyond dispute is that a farewell meal was offered by Jesus to his disciples in the consciousness of his impending death. Apropos of this problem we find in the gospels two layers: an older and a more recent one.

The less ancient passages turn out to be liturgical formulae current in the Church as a reminder of what Jesus did during this farewell meal. They contain a recognizable Pauline-cum-Lucan tradition (Lk. 22:20a parallel 1 Cor. 11:25) and a Marcan one (Mk. 14:24 parallel Mt. 26:26–28).[97] The Pauline-Lucan tradition might be summarized thus: 'This cup, now proffered, affords a share in the new covenant promised by the prophets, which comes about thanks to my martyrdom.'[98] Within the tradition, 'blood' in this context signifies 'the blood of the martyr'.[99] In the Marcan tradition, on the other hand, the renewing of the covenant comes about by reason of Jesus' death, interpreted in the light of Exod. 24:8 as a cultic sacrifice: 'This is my blood of the covenant.'

That these passages have been influenced by liturgical practice in the Church and so have a post-Easter stamp upon them is clear enough. But in both Luke (22:18) and Mark (14:25) one can detect an older vein, which according to F. Hahn belongs 'to the primeval rock of the tradition',[100] as scholars nowadays almost universally agree: 'Truly I say to you, I shall not drink again of the fruit of the vine until that day when I drink it new in the kingdom of God' (Mk. 14:25). 'From now on I shall not drink of the fruit of the vine until the kingdom of God comes' (Lk. 22:15–18; see 1 Cor. 11:26). The passage contains two elements: (1) on the one hand, a main feature of this meal is the – at any rate – quite emphatic announcement by Jesus of his imminent death, in other words: this meal is a farewell to all such earthly fellowship (it really is the very last cup that Jesus will share with his friends); (2) on the other hand, Jesus offers with it the prospect of fellowship renewed in the kingdom of God. The 'words of institution' mentioned above, in the context of the Church's liturgy, would appear to state these rather more vague pronouncements in a more precise and explicit form. Yet even in the older text we see the effect of the Church's activity subsequent to Easter: it combines two elements which separately form part of the Jesus tradition. The hard centre of historical fact is Jesus' explicitly uttered conviction that this is to be the very last cup he will drink with his disciples in his earthly life; the second element, 'until the day when . . .' is secondary.[101] The emphasis is not on the coming meal but on the 'drinking no more' (*ouketi ou mè*). This is most entitled, historically speaking, to recognition as an intimation of Jesus' own death. The second clause, 'until . . .' has another source: there is mention elsewhere of the eschatological feast or dinner-party; the combination of the utterance about Jesus' suffering and death with the glory-to-be is clearly secondary. A prediction regarding the destiny of the son of man thus becomes at the same time a promise of salvation, apropos of the future fellowship of the disciples with Jesus.

If the second clause is secondary, what salvific relevance is retained by the first clause of this old text? Despite Israel's rejection of the last prophetic offer of salvation made by God, Jesus, face to face with his coming death, continues to offer his disciples the (last) cup: this shows Jesus' unshaken assurance of salvation, so that the addition of the 'until' clause in Mark and Luke, albeit secondary, is simply a way of making explicit the concrete situation. The renewed fellowship-at-table or offer of salvation by Jesus to the disciples, in face of approaching death, still makes perfect sense to Jesus; he has come to proper terms with his death, which he evidently does not feel to be an absurd miscarriage of his mission. Such unassailable religious certainty is surely food for thought. What does it signify, this conviction on Jesus' part that his death will be powerless to obstruct the coming rule of God which he has proclaimed?

Allowing for the diverse interpretations of the eschatological character of Jesus' message, from his preaching and from his whole attitude to life this one thing is certain: Jesus stands open to God's future for man and, on the other hand, his whole life is a service to people, a service of love. 'If anyone would be first, he must be last of all and servant of all' (Mk. 9:35); this and similar comments (Mt. 7:12a parallels; Mk. 12:33; Lk. 6:27–28), the context of which within the tradition, although worked over later by the Church, is grounded in recollection of the Last Supper, clearly reflect Jesus' own fundamental attitude to life. Pro-existence, 'being-as-man for the other' and unconditional obedience to God's will, revealed in the Decalogue and in various situations of man's life, persisted in to the point of death, do indeed evince Jesus' fidelity to his message, which keeps open God's future, gives God the final word and makes Jesus persevere in loving service to people, as a manifestation of God's own benevolence towards them. Even where no salvific implication is ascribed to Jesus' death in the New Testament, it is at any rate seen as the 'martyr's destiny' of the prophet. But this in itself suggests that, even starting from Jesus' attitude to life as a whole, it is difficult to determine anything *a priori* and in detail about the distinctive nature of his death on the cross as an act of loving service. Then too there is the danger that we project our own view of the why and wherefore of Jesus' death into Jesus' approach to life. In view of Jesus' assurance, even in the face of death, of salvation through the approaching rule of God, one cannot simply regard the murder of this innocent man as one case more in the long line of innocent victims of murder. His death would then be a reason for resignation or despair rather than for new hope, which has given birth to the whole Christian Church. For in a purely historical perspective this death by crucifixion is the rejection of Jesus and of his message, and therefore the total failure of his prophetic career. But if Jesus was humiliated by his crucifixion, then this was, even historically, submission to God. 'My God, thou art God. I will praise thee' (Ps. 118:28). An experience of a historical failure and at the same time a passionate faith in God's future for man is for the religious person no contradiction, but a mystery eluding every attempt at theoretical or rational accommodation.

The conclusion would seem to be justified that Jesus felt his death to be (in some way or other) part and parcel of the salvation-offered-by-God, as a historical consequence of his caring and loving service of and solidarity with people. This is the very least – albeit certain – thing about the 'institution narrative' and the account of the Passion that we are bound to hang on to as a historical core. It is of course not permissible to explain the older stratum in the pericope analysed above on the basis of the less ancient liturgical upper stratum; it is really the latter that should be judged in the light of the older text. Yet it is important to notice that even in the oldest stratum Jesus at the Last Supper passes the cup – the last one – to his friends and so continues to offer a saving fellowship with himself, 'in spite of' his approaching death. The link suggested here (and made explicit by Mark) is more one between fellowship with Jesus in the present and the saving, eschatological fellowship with him, which is to come. In other words, the coming of God's rule remains linked to fellowship with Jesus of Nazareth. One can hardly eliminate from these New Testament reports, as a historical suggestion on Jesus' part, the suggestion that fellowship with Jesus is stronger than death. One is bound to say that in fact no certain logion of Jesus is to be found in which Jesus himself might be thought to ascribe a salvific import to his death. Neither the veiled (Mt. 12:39 parallels; Lk. 12:50; 13:32–33; Mk. 10:38–39) nor the open predictions of the Passion (Mk. 8:31 parallel; 9:30–32 parallels; 10:32–34 parallels) contain any allusion to the death as salvation or propitiation. But there is no getting round the historical fact that in the very face of death Jesus offers the cup of fellowship to his disciples; this is a token that he is not just passively allowing death to overcome him but has actively integrated it into his total mission, in other words, that he understands and is undergoing his death as a final and extreme service to the cause of God as the cause of men, and that he has communicated this self-understanding to his intimate disciples under the veiled sign of extending to them the fellowship-at-table shared with his friends. The 'for you' (*hyper* formula), in the sense of Jesus' whole pro-existence, had been the historical intention of his whole ministry, which his very death now substantiates. The crux of the argument – against the background of Jesus' whole approach to life in loyalty to the Father and in service to men – is enshrined, it seems to me, in this, that the entire ministry of Jesus during the period of his public life was not just an assurance or promise of salvation but a concrete tender of salvation then and there. He does not just talk about God and his rule; where he appears he brings salvation and becomes God's rule already realized. The active acceptance of his own death or rejection can only be understood as Jesus' active incorporation of his death into his mission of offering salvation, and not simply and solely as a 'notwithstanding'. This applies with all the greater force because even during his life Jesus' fellowship-at-table shared with sinners was the token of an immediate tender of salvation. Given all this, the fact that it is impossible to find a *verbum ipsissimum* or authentic saying of Jesus that tells us how he regarded and evaluated his death (excepting the first section of Mk. 14:25a; Lk. 22:18a) is really irrelevant. Jesus' whole life is the hermeneusis of his death. The very substance of salvation is sufficiently present in it, which could be and was in fact articulated later on in various ways through faith in him. Although the historico-critical method cannot produce knock-down arguments on this score, still less can it assert categorically that so far as history goes we do not know how Jesus understood his own death.[102] Jesus' understanding of that death as part and parcel of his mission of tendering salvation seems to me, therefore, a fact preceding Easter – and demonstrably so, at least for Jesus' self-understanding in the final days of his life. (This will later on find support in the 'third day' motif.)

This is a very important conclusion; for it means that even prior to Easter Jesus is saying, in effect at any rate, that the 'Jesus affair' is to go ahead. This is not just a vision born of faith and based solely on the disciples' Easter experience; it is his self-understanding that creates the possibility and lays the foundation of the subsequent interpretation by the Christians. There is no gap between Jesus' self-understanding and the Christ proclaimed by the Church. If we ask whether the disciples can be thought to have grasped what Jesus was getting at prior to the whole event of Easter, the answer must be on the negative side. But after the first shock of his dying, the memory of Jesus' life and especially of the Last Supper must have played a vital role in the process of their conversion to faith in Jesus as the Christ, the one imbued to the full with God's Spirit. That Jesus was right in understanding himself thus and was on to the truth when he saw his death as being somehow tied in with his mission to offer salvation cannot of course be legitimated as a fact of history; it can only be dismissed or accepted in faith. But that he did so is a fact of history hard to deny.

## §3   The historical grounds in law for Jesus' execution

Before examining how Jesus came across to his disciples, we would do well to take a look at the 'image' Jesus presented to those who had him put to death. In other words: How did his opponents see him and on what legal grounds did they have Jesus executed?

In our analysis of the 'contrast-scheme' ('you killed him, but God has raised him to life') (this will become clearer still in Part Three), it turned out that the notions of the 'true teacher' and 'prophet from God' as well as of the 'false teacher' and 'pseudo-prophet' had a basic function, more particularly in Judaism. Late Judaism found a guide-rule for getting the measure of 'pseudo-teachers' and corrupters of the people, who assailed the very essence of the Jewish religious spirit, in Deut. 17:12: 'The man who acts presumptuously, by not obeying the priest who stands to minister there before the Lord your God, or the judge, that man shall die.' That is to say, defying the officiating high priest in the exercise of his juridical function, by virtue of which it is his business to pronounce on 'Jewish orthodoxy', is punishable in Israel with death. Showing contempt for Israel's governing authorities, especially when this challenges the Jewish orthodoxy of 'Israel's teachers', is reason in law for a legal execution.

Now it is a fact that in post-New Testament, rabbinical literature[103] this Deuteronomic passage was given a more precise and concrete interpretation, tying the trial and execution of a Jewish 'false teacher' who leads the people astray to a set of clear criteria. After 70, indeed, there grew out of the formerly still pluralistic Jewish doctrine a 'uniform orthodoxy' monitored by Pharisees and rabbis. Even in Jesus' time the Deuteronomic passage played a crucial role; but its jurisprudence was not firmly settled as in the later rabbinics, and so judgement was difficult in practice because of the varying interpretations of the Law. What was possible, valid and legitimate 'on a Jewish view of things' was not then so clearly laid down as in the budding 'rabbinical orthodoxy' of the period after 70. In Jesus' time so much differentiation existed among the 'Jewish parties' that it was difficult, for instance in the Sanhedrin (then under the presidency of the high priest the body empowered to pronounce on any departure from Jewish teaching and orthopraxis), to get a consensus on condemning to death a 'renegade' Jewish teacher – the reason why at that time very many actual or reputed 'false teachers' were exiled or had (voluntarily) left Jerusalem (like the Qumrân Essenes); but rarely was anyone condemned to death as a pseudo-teacher or pseudo-prophet.[104] Antagonism between the parties represented in the Sanhedrin was too great (in Jesus' time) for that.

The fact that Jesus was condemned as a pseudo-teacher (deceiver of the people) on the basis of Deut. 17:12 implies that the leading parties in the Sanhedrin were able to come to a common agreement about Jesus, but maybe on very divergent grounds. In its report of conflicting depositions the Marcan gospel alludes to the fact that there was no unanimity in the Sanhedrin regarding the answer to the question whether the law of Deut. 17:12 was applicable in this case. Apart from the pro-Roman, perhaps rather unprincipled 'Herodians', it is difficult to postulate a lack of principle in the other Sanhedrin parties, divided and disagreeing over Jewish doctrine as they were. On historical grounds it would be wrong to regard the Sanhedrin's enquiry into Jesus' teaching and activities as a kind of 'show trial', with the verdict settled in advance. All parties in the Sanhedrin had of course fundamental objections to Jesus' teaching and public ministry; but the crucial point was whether Jesus came under the law of Deut. 17:12. And no orthodox Jew would play around with that. In this High Court, evidently, there was no common mind about it – a situation which to this day speaks in favour of the Sanhedrin's fair play; the High Court did not immediately give in to pressure from this side or that in the Sanhedrin. For most members of the Sanhedrin, even though they all had fundamental objections to Jesus, or perhaps grudges against him, it was the Law as the revelation of God's will that was still both norm and guideline, not their own arbitrary and subjective predilections. This basic stance was to be apparent again later on, when after Jesus' death a Pharisee, the lawyer Gamaliel, adjured the Sanhedrin: 'Men of Israel, take care what you do with these men [=the apostles] . . . if it is of God, you will not be able to overthrow them. You might even be found opposing God!' (Acts 5:34–39). And he got a vote of agreement on the point. This Jewish cast of mind is something we must in the first instance assume in the Sanhedrin, which nevertheless eventually handed Jesus over to the Romans.

We noted earlier on that 'the Pharisees', who during Jesus' earthly life play a major role in the gospels as his opponents, fade completely into the background in the gospels' account of Jesus' trial and condemnation. In a historical context this is no accident. It goes along with an internal split within the Pharisaic movement, which was completed only after 70, although the first signs of it were already apparent in Jesus' time. A uniform Pharisaic orthodoxy is a Jewish phenomenon from after the year 70. That is why the Pharisees seem to us equivocal. In the gospels they seem on the one hand to be well disposed to Jesus, on the other hand maliciously hostile (and in the New Testament documents later than AD 70 the latter attitude has become a cliché). Perhaps unconsciously, the Marcan gospel is a historically faithful witness to the division that was beginning to occur at the time of Jesus in the 'chakamite' movement of 'interpreters of the Law' between an open, 'liberal' party (in the line of Hillel) and a stricter wing, which only after 70 came to be called simply 'the Pharisees' (*perushim*).[105] From the Jewish standpoint Jesus' teaching and ministry were more in line with the Pharisaic school of Hillel, so that a lot of Pharisees could quite clearly show sympathy with Jesus' activities. All the same, even for the liberalizing notions of the Hillel Pharisees, Jesus really went too far; so much so that he managed to bring upon himself the odium of this not wholly unsympathetic Pharisaic wing. In company with the Hillel Pharisees Jesus saw in the Torah the expression of a right relationship to God and one's fellows; but for Jesus this was an expression of the all-controlling and in every circumstance directly revelatory relation with God; for the open wing of the Pharisees on the other hand the Law – and only the Law – remained the sole means of conciliation with God and other men.[106] What for Jesus was 'illustration' signified for the section of the Pharisees sympathetic towards him an irreplaceable intermediary factor. It had what were actually fundamental objections to Jesus of Nazareth.

The leading Jewish authorities, who had to pass judgement in 'the affair of Jesus', were for the most part thoroughly 'Law-conscious' and by no means people out to 'do for' Jesus – unless Jesus of Nazareth was attacking the heart and centre of Jewish faith in Yahweh. Every party in the Sanhedrin, therefore, had fundamental objections to Jesus; but there was manifestly no common view about the question whether Jesus' message and actions came under the condemnation of Deut. 17:12.

Yet by a majority vote of the Sanhedrin Jesus was 'condemned' (we draw some finer distinctions in a moment). The historical conclusion must be that Jesus was disowned by the Sanhedrin because 'he was silent' before it (Mk. 14:60–61). It was this remaining silent – not what the post-Easter Church put into Jesus' mouth later on (Mk. 14:62) – that gave the Sanhedrin legal grounds for condemning Jesus. Jesus' silence (vouched for, historically, by a variety of very primitive Christian traditions) was a critical posture adopted towards the forum that on the basis of the Law had a competency to judge his teaching and praxis by their Jewish orthodoxy and orthopraxis. Jesus however refused to submit his teaching and praxis to this Jewish court of appeal. He remained silent. This certainly does come under the judgement of Deut. 17:12: if anyone presumes to disobey the officiating high priest or 'judge', 'that man shall die'. In Jesus' keeping silent before the Sanhedrin (as in the presence of Herod and Pilate, though 'corrected' or written up after Easter with a shattering utterance on Jesus' part) his self-understanding finds expression, namely, his knowing himself to have been sent directly by God to summon Israel to faith in God: Jesus refuses to submit his direct 'commissioning by God', his mission, to the Jewish doctrinal authority. The silence of Jesus (in fact a form of diplomatic opposition) before the Sanhedrin seems to me the most salient expression of his self-understanding: just as he will not perform any legitimating miraculous signs, so too he refuses, for this or any other human religious institution, to render an account of his message and his role. Only the God who sends him can call him to account for these things. Jesus knows himself to be obligated solely to God, who has sent him to Israel. This – although in line of descent from ancient prophetism – is what shakes the Judaism of Jesus' time to the core. His remaining silent in face of the institutional and legitimate organ of authority in Israel becomes therefore, according to the Judaic interpretation of Deut. 17:12, the ground valid in Jewish Law for being able to condemn him to death in good (Jewish) conscience. *Contemptus auctoritatis*, holding Israel's highest authority in contempt, seems to me to be the Jewish legal ground for Jesus' condemnation.

Yet an element of doubt remains. Among the members of the

Sanhedrin, each of whom would have his own fundamental objections
to Jesus, there were evidently parties unwilling to condemn Jesus to
death on the basis of Deut. 17:12, as this was not obvious juridically
from the Torah; certain members of the Sanhedrin had what were
apparently fundamental doubts. Was Jesus of Nazareth in fact the
'pseudo-teacher' contemplated by the terms formulated in Deut.
17:12? For many members of the Sanhedrin this was a question of
religious conscience, in spite of their objections to Jesus arising from
their conceptions of Jewish theology. (At any rate the New Testament
preserves a memory, for instance, of the Sanhedrin member, Joseph of
Arimathea, for whom the application of Deut. 17:12 to Jesus was at
least problematical.)

That is not all. Although according to a pre-Marcan tradition (Mk.
14:64) the Sanhedrin 'gave as its verdict that he deserved death', it says
in a later chapter at Mk. 15:1a: 'In the early morning the high priest
with the elders and lawyers, the whole Sanhedrin, came to a decision':
namely, that Jesus was to be handed over to Pilate, the Roman procurator (Mk. 15:1b). This seems to me to reveal the 'Jewish impasse' in
which the Sanhedrin found itself: everybody was against Jesus, but
when it came to legally valid grounds for condemning him, there was
no general agreement. Only at this point does the guilt of the Sanhedrin begin. There was no lack of unanimity about handing Jesus
over to the Romans!

In this second phase of the Sanhedrin's session they did indeed arrive
at a solid consensus: Jesus was to be delivered to Pilate (Mk. 15:1b;
see 15:1a). This decision on their part has often been interpreted on
the basis of the alleged fact that only the Roman occupying power had
the right actually to carry out a Jewish capital sentence. But on a point
of history this has been a much discussed question.[107] Only a few years
previously (perhaps not even that) it had been possible for Herod,
without any sanction from the Romans (albeit not in Jerusalem), to
have John the Baptist beheaded. Everything suggests that (because of
the concrete composition of the Sanhedrin) the doubts nurtured here
were so great that no common mind was reached on the question
whether Deut. 17:12 was applicable to 'the case of Jesus', despite
everybody's objections to him. It argues in favour of this High Council
as a body.

Nevertheless we are also faced with the fact that at a second sitting
(Mk. 15:1b) the Sanhedrin resolves – this time unanimously – 'to
deliver Jesus to the Romans'. This it is that even from a Jewish point
of view constitutes the error and the manifest guilt of the Sanhedrin

in condemning Jesus. Starting from divergent interpretations of the Law, all members of the Sanhedrin had fundamental objections to Jesus of Nazareth; but many of them found in Jesus' teaching and activity no sufficient grounds for subjecting him to the judgement of Deut. 17:12. Because of the fundamental objections that from various standpoints all members of the Sanhedrin had to Jesus, however, they resorted in a second session to a legal shift: owing to the political implications of his public activity let us make over the 'Jesus affair' to the Romans. Let the Romans decide! For very diverse reasons Herodians, Sadducees and Pharisees of very different standpoints – all of them, however, starting from their own fundamental objections to the 'Jesus phenomenon' in Israel – were able to reach a consensus. All parties were agreed that in view of rumours among the people the 'Jesus affair' was potentially dangerous for the Romans. Given the concrete situation (with the execution of John the Baptist still fresh in the memory), so it was. The unhistorical cry of the Jewish populace: 'Crucify him!' (Mk. 15:14) – elaborated in Jn. 19:15b to the (historically inconceivable): 'We have no king but [the Roman] Caesar' – reflects unhistorically, but in the end truthfully enough, a historical state of affairs, namely, that the Jewish Sanhedrin found no adequate juridical grounds for condemning Jesus to death and could reach no common mind on the matter (despite the pressure likely to have been exerted in particular by the Sadducees and Herodians). What they could and did reach was a majority decision to go and hand over (for allegedly political reasons) a compatriot, Jesus of Nazareth, to the Romans – so much hated, as they were, by most of the Sanhedrin themselves!

In that sense Jesus was indeed condemned because he remained true to his prophetic mission 'from God', a mission which he refused to justify to any other authority than God himself. In all this Jesus continued to rely upon the Father who had sent him.

The Father, however, did not intervene. Nowhere indeed did Jesus see any visible aid come from him whose cause he had so much at heart. As a fact of history it can hardly be denied that Jesus was subject to an inner conflict between his consciousness of his mission and the utter silence of the One whom he was accustomed to call his Father. At least in its hard core as an event, the struggle in Gethsemane is not to be cogitated out of existence; and of the 'words of Jesus' from the cross, as reported in the gospels, only his loud cry can be historically warranted. It all puts a severe strain on Jesus' message of the speedily approaching, humanity-orientated rule of God and of a relationship to God not bound by the Law. The question is whether the visible presence of God, to be tested by empirically registrable facts, is the final word, or whether God does not mean to give us his ultimate message through Jesus' ultimate acceptance of his life's destiny and reconciliation to it.

Chapter 2

# Jesus' last prophetic sign: his death as being for others to interpret

In the previous chapter we tried to provide a historical reconstruction of how Jesus' self-understanding was affected by a growing awareness that he could not avoid his approaching death. A great deal, on the other hand, must hang on the (mainly implicit) presuppositions from which one launches into such a critical enquiry. Thus it is clear, for example, that in seeking to recover Jesus' evaluation of his own death H. Schürmann assumes as his point of departure the post-Easter Christian *kerygma* of redemption; he means to demonstrate that in one way or another this dogma articulates what Jesus already understood about himself. I miss in this attempt any critical approach to *kerygma* and dogma. By this I do not at all mean the critique of dogma that an unbeliever or an eclectic person might pursue, but that of a believing Christian who, starting from the 'earthly Jesus', wants to test and check the notions current in the Church and among Christians about the relevance to salvation of Jesus' death, in order to see whether in a Christian soteriology we are tied to concepts like 'ransom', 'propitiation', 'substitution', 'satisfaction' (=reparation) and so forth. In Part One of this book we were constantly pointing out that in its New Testament the early Church is a reflection of the Jesus event as that affected a group of people; it appeared to entail a recurrent tension between, on the one hand, the offer of the reality which Jesus in fact was and, on the other hand, the religious expectations, aspirations, ideas and ideologies used by others to express concretely in words and eventually commit to writing in the New Testament what it was about Jesus that demanded consideration. As a believer, one is bound by whatever Jesus entails, not directly by those articulating concepts. So someone who examines the Jesus event and his self-understanding from a critical standpoint, yet 'in faith', can still see in the exegetically rather vague and meagre result something more than that Jesus had perhaps not yet arrived at the clear articulations of the primitive Christian communities. Then, like the first Christians from out of their background, he may himself reflect as a Christian, out of his own background, on the data provided by this historical reconstruction. The pro-existence or loving service which Jesus' entire life was and (as historical and exegetical analysis would indicate) which manifestly came to a climax in his death, may then have to be expressed for us in an articulation containing different emphases and distinctions from the interpretations in the New Testament, conditioned as they were by already given cultural and religious concepts. The question then becomes pressing as to whether attempts at being too precise may not do more harm than good. Being precise about an event that is a mystery always impoverishes it and so stands on the edge of the precipice of heretical misrepresentation. This is the more true because we are faced here with a violent death. There is no getting away from the fundamental aspect of negativity, particularly inherent in such a death, especially as this actually entails a rejection of Jesus' life *qua* message. This situation calls of course for religious interpretation *or* a verdict of pure non-sense. Was this coming event reconcilable with Jesus' preaching of God's rule and living by it? Or was the kingdom of God to come, notwithstanding the failure of Jesus himself? Can God remain sovereignly free *vis-à-vis* his eschatological messenger, Jesus of Nazareth? Does God's word apply also to him; 'My ways are not your ways' (Isa. 55:8)? Is the kingdom of God God's corrective alternative to all that has been and is being accomplished in our history, even by Jesus? For us the death of Jesus is, after all, a question put to God – to the God whom Jesus proclaimed. That Jesus identified with all oppressed and outcast people is quite obvious from the analysis of his message, preaching, beatitudes and whole way of life. Can we suppose that it was actually God himself who set him through his trial and execution among the oppressed and outcast, thus to make his solidarity with the oppressed a *de facto* identification? Or is such a view not rather a blasphemy, in that it ascribes to God what the course of human wrong and injustice did to Jesus?

But with his death Jesus' story is not yet over. The next thing, therefore, is to examine this sequel.

# The Christian story after Jesus' death; the kingdom of God takes on the appearance of Jesus Christ

Chapter 1

# The disciples scandalized by the arrest and execution of Jesus

*Literature.* Sch. Brown, *Apostasy and Perseverance in the Theology of Luke*, Rome 1969; H. Conzelmann, *Geschichte des Urchristentums* (NTD-Ergänzungsgrehe, 5), Göttingen 1971; A. Dauer, *Passionsgeschichte*, l.c.; M. Hengel, 'Die Ursprünge der christlichen Mission', NTS 18 (1971-2), 15-38; H. Kasting, *Die Anfänge der urchristlichen Mission* (Beih. EvTh, 55), Munich 1969; G. Klein, 'Der Verleugnung des Petrus', ZThK 58 (1961), 285-328, and 'Die Berufung des Petrus', ZNW 58 (1967), 1-44; E. Linnemann, *Studien zur Passionsgeschichte* (Göttingen 1970), 70-108; Ch. Masson, 'Le reniement de Pierre', RHPR 37 (1957), 24-35; G. Schneider, *Verleugnung, Verspottung und Verhör Jesu nach Lk. 22:54-71*, Munich 1969, and *Die Passion Jesu*, l.c. (Munich 1973), 73-82; G. Schille, *Anfänge der Kirche* (Beih. EvTh, 43), Munich 1966, and 'Anfänge der christlichen Mission', KuD 15 (1969), 320-39; Th. J. Weeden, *The Mark-traditions*, 26-51; M. Wilcox, 'The denial-sequence in Mk. 14:26-31, 66-72', NTS 17 (1970-1), 426-36.

## §1 Historicity and superimposed interpretation in the gospels

In Christian homiletics the theme of Peter's denial and the somewhat less pronounced loss of nerve on the part of the disciples as a whole has presented no problem; and in general it has been handled in a moralizing vein only. All the same, I am convinced that in the case of the collapse of the disciples' morale we are not dealing just with an episodic, marginal tale of human frailty, but rather that this event, issuing in the 'conversion' of the disciples after Jesus' death, has also played a vital role in shaping the tradition about the appearances of Jesus, which still bear traces of Jewish conversion-stories for which the 'transforming vision' provides the model.

Historically speaking, however, there are all sorts of difficulties here.[1] In view of these, there are even a few commentators who maintain that Peter's denial of Jesus, in particular, is unhistorical: it is a Christian, post-Easter *theologoumenon*.[2] The question in that case is: What could have been the incipient Church's motive for inventing this fact – so very embarrassing for its mainstays and first ministerial leaders – only to play it down again afterwards? For we can see how, in the four gospels at least, this happening, which they are unwilling to pass over in complete silence, is gradually extenuated. In Mark Jesus rebukes Peter, who cannot even stay awake while Jesus in an agony of prayer is facing up to death (Mk. 14:37–38); but almost at once, in 14:40, comes the half-excuse 'their eyes were very heavy'. Matthew 26:36–46 introduces no change here; but Luke does not mention Jesus' rebuke to Peter; the rebuke is generalized (Lk. 22:46), and the disciples are said to be sleeping 'for sorrow' (22:45). Luke says nothing about the disciples' running away. And then in Jn. 18:8 we read how Jesus himself begs the soldiers to let his disciples go; it contains no reference at all to the disciples falling asleep at the time of Jesus' agony in Gethsemane, or indeed to the agony itself. This tendency to exonerate is very likely a sign of the authentic nature of the tradition about the disciples' turning tail. On the other hand the reputed exonerating tendency may be purely a synoptic delusion. As Mark is deliberately and for thematic reasons exaggerating in this respect (see immediately below), the other evangelists (having lost the thread, perhaps, of Mark's theological thesis or in reaction against these unhistorical exaggerations) may have reduced to its proper proportions the account handed down to them. Again we are bound, in view of the status of the texts, to distinguish between the desertion of Jesus by all the disciples and the story, singled out and emphasized, of a specific act of repudiation by Peter.

The synoptic evangelists' accounts of the disciples' loss of nerve and of Peter's denial are derived mostly from the Marcan tradition or Marcan redaction; even so, both Luke and Matthew draw upon their own

sources;[3] and moreover their view of the disciples is different from
Mark's. Now it is clear from an analysis of Mark's way of characterizing
the people who appear in his version of things that in dealing with the
disciples' bearing prior to Jesus' death he is supporting a theological
position: the disciples understand nothing of Jesus; they are unable to
perceive who he is; there is only incomprehension and misunderstanding and, in the event, total denial and faith discarded.[4] In Mark's
gospel[5] the disciples' bafflement, so far from decreasing, intensifies,
while the mass of people show some understanding. Whereas even non-
Jews recognize Jesus' power to work miracles (Mk. 7:25–30), the
disciples do not (Mk. 4:40; 8:4 and 8:14–21). In Matthew and Luke all
these passages are reduced to juster proportions.[6] Mark makes a great
deal of the fact that Peter and the disciples misunderstand Jesus. Even
Peter's alleged 'profession of faith' at Caesarea Philippi (Mk. 8:27–33:
'You are the messiah') in Mark's view is no such thing, but is a complete misunderstanding of messianism, as appears from the subsequent
verses when Peter disclaims the prospect of suffering and is then called
by Jesus 'a satan' (8:32–33). Jesus forbids all talk of that messianism
(8:30); for Mark it is a heretical *theios anèr* Christology.[7] After this confession (on Peter's part) the conflict between Jesus and the disciples
becomes a general one (9:15–18, 19–23, 23–27). John and other
disciples forbid somebody to cast out devils, simply and solely, it
would seem, because the man did not belong to Jesus' band of followers (9:38 and 9:34–40); they also prevent children from approaching
Jesus (10:13–16). Judas in particular fails to grasp the point of Jesus'
being anointed in Bethany (as an anticipated anointing for burial), in
other words, his act of betrayal lies in his refusal to accept the son of
man as the suffering one. Again in this second series of texts Matthew
and Luke omit what reflects most unfavourably on the disciples in the
Marcan gospel; even here, however, it is sometimes retained, albeit
without the cutting edge it has in Mark.[8] A third phase and series of
texts in Mark introduce the denial by Peter and the apostasy of all the
disciples, along with Judas' decision to betray Jesus (Mk. 14:10ff).
From this moment on (14:10) Mark as good as suggests that the disciples as a whole are little better than Judas. It is precisely the three
men later to become the mainstay of the Jerusalem church – Peter,
James and John – who despite their protestations fall asleep (14:31)
when Jesus is in dire straits (14:32–42). Then comes Judas' act of
betrayal (14:43–52), the flight of all the disciples (14:50) and Peter's
denial of the suffering Jesus (14:66–72). Here Matthew (26:14–16,
36–46, 47–56, 66–75) faithfully reproduces Mark. For his part Luke

waters down Mark's account completely; he calls the betrayal by Judas – and Peter's denial, for that matter – 'the work of Satan' (22:3, 31); they are not fully responsible for what they have done. The disciples even enter into Jesus' agony; for it is from sorrow that they drift into sleep (Lk. 22:40–45); more especially, for Luke there is no question of the disciples' running away; they remain essentially loyal to Jesus (see Lk. 22:28ff).

Much of what Mark says about the disciples' weaknesses can be discovered also in the independent (as regards its literary provenance) gospel of John; but in John the disciples' lack of understanding has nothing to do with their identification of Jesus (Jn. 1:35–51; 2:11; 6:66–67, 68–69; 16:30): there is a continuity about their belief in Jesus;[9] it is the Jews who are unbelieving (Jn. 12:37–40). John does have the disciples deserting Jesus, and the denial by Peter (Jn. 18:2ff, 15–27; 16:32); but they flee with Jesus' express permission (Jn. 16:32). We may fairly conclude from this that, although Mark exaggerates and is caustic about the disciples' attitude because he has a specific purpose in view, he is not simply fantasizing: he takes over already existing tradition-material, but for one reason or another wants to present the behaviour of the apostles in a grim light. He paints the character of the Twelve in a way that reveals his distinctive view of Jesus' disciples. Such a view of them is quite unfamiliar to Paul; and if Mark's picture had been true to history, Paul would not have failed to turn to it for support when he was having trouble with the Christian leaders in Jerusalem (Gal. 2:11–14). Furthermore, and more especially, the pre-Marcan traditions run counter to Mark's view of things.[10] In the source peculiar to Matthew and Luke, which according to a scholarly consensus articulates a very ancient tradition, 'the Twelve' form with Peter a much esteemed body within early Christianity, even with obvious signs of idealizing.[11] It also gives prominence to the idea that it was actually Peter who after Jesus has been arrested attempts 'to go after him' (Lk. 22:32b as an addition to Lk. 22:31–32a, meant to harmonize the two traditions – 22:33–34 and 22:54, 55–67). This does not mean that the tradition on which Mark draws is not itself an old one – only that Mark 'arranges' his material. On the other hand 'the Twelve' are also a highly reputable body in the tradition of the Q community.[12] What emerges particularly clearly from Luke is that he is citing a non-Marcan source which nevertheless – like Mark – has Jesus reprimanding John and James (Lk. 9:51–56); and this goes to show that Luke (in criticism, it is true, of Mark's thematic handling of Jesus' disciples) in no way seeks to remove or tone down the negative echoes of the tradition about them (deriving from the Q source). But whereas in that source Jesus commends the disciples for perceiving what others fail to see (especially Lk. 10:23–24=Mt. 13:16–17), in the Marcan gospel the disciples see nothing whatever (Mk. 4:13; 7:18; 8:17, 21; 9:32).[13]

From this very varied picture which the gospels present of Jesus' close disciples, especially of Peter, we must conclude that there is no uniform tradition indicating what these men actually did at the time of Jesus' arrest. Apart from Mark, all other traditions take a kinder view of the apostles' conduct prior to Easter. Starting from this or that (despite Weeden's thesis, in my view not so far resolved) theological intention, the Marcan gospel makes a point of presenting the behaviour of Jesus' disciples before Easter in the most unfavourable light possible. It is indeed matter for concern that the gospel of Mark (setting aside the pseudo-Marcan tailpiece to his gospel, Mk. 16:9–20), having presented this gloomy picture of the disciples, actually has nothing more to say about these Twelve – except for the appearing of an angel to Mary Magdalene and Salome, who are charged with telling the disciples: 'He is going before you to Galilee, there you will see him, as he told you' (Mk. 16:7: Marcan redaction), whereas the end of Mark's own gospel intimates that this – going to Galilee instead of staying in Jerusalem – is just what the disciples did not do.[14] Nowhere in the authentic Mark do we read of a solemn investiture of the disciples with the status of 'apostle' as in the other gospels.[15]

As regards the behaviour of the disciples, therefore, the Jesus tradition is highly obscure. According to Luke there were standing at a distance (from the scene of the crucifixion), looking on, 'all his acquaintances, and the women who had followed him from Galilee' (Lk. 23:49); Mark on the other hand says nothing about 'the disciples', only about female disciples at the cross (Mk. 15:40–41); for after Jesus had been arrested 'they all [meaning the male disciples] forsook him and fled' (Mk. 14:50). Mark 14:27 speaks of all the disciples of Jesus 'falling away'. The Johannine gospel also refers to a 'flight homewards' (to Galilee) on the disciples' part (Jn. 16:32). Certainly there is a difference between Mk. 14:27–31, where there is no mention of a flight but of 'being scandalized', of 'taking offence' (that is, stumbling in their faith in Jesus) and Mk. 14:43–52 with its clear reference to 'a flight'. It would seem that there is no literary connection between these two blocks of tradition, as there is between Mk. 14:27–31 and 14:54, 66–72, where Peter, according to this tradition, follows at a distance as Jesus is taken away, but in spite of his attempt 'to go after him' nevertheless denies him on three occasions.

The underlying implication of 'being scandalized by someone' or 'taking offence at someone' in the synoptics is the exact opposite of 'believing in someone' (Mk. 6:3 parallel Mt. 13:57; Mt. 26:31, 35 parallel Lk. 7:23). By referring to Zech. 13:7 Mark (14:27b) intimates that the break with Jesus also ruptures completely the bond between his followers: the disciples simply part company. But Matthew makes the passage he quotes from Zechariah refer only to Jesus' arrest, not to what followed upon it, the scattering of the disciples (Mt. 25:56). Peter's 'denying three times' is a literary device for saying that his denial of Jesus is a complete one. In all fairness, therefore, it is difficult to maintain that all the disciples run away, while Peter tries to stay behind.[16] Historically speaking, the hard core of the tradition is that all the disciples somehow or other let Jesus down. The individual disavowal by Peter would appear to be a later literary concretizing of the fact that all the disciples faltered; and it was inspired partly by Peter's subsequent position in early Christianity. Mark 14:31, after Peter's sturdy insistence that 'he at any rate' will not defect, puts added emphasis on 'they all said the same'. The flight of all the disciples would seem to be matter for interest to Mark.[17] Mark 14:50, 51–52 is obviously linked with the Marcan theme of 'the disciples' incomprehension'. He wants to show that Jesus trod his path of suffering 'quite alone', forsaken by everybody. That is his faith-motivated viewpoint; the disciples must have deserted him. Yet again according to Mark this flight of theirs is covered by God's plan of salvation: Mark alone (14:27) cites the 'divine must', by referring to Zech. 13:7 (see Mk. 14:49b and 14:21a, 41b). The account of the flight, according to exegetical experts, is also Marcan in style (Mk. 1:18, 20; 4:36; 8:13; 12:2 and 14:50; beyond those only – in independence of Mark – in Mt. 22:22 and 26:44). For Mark the opposite of following Jesus, of 'going after him', is forsaking and denying Jesus. The disciples' flight is their breach with 'following after Jesus': not one followed him to the end (Mk. 14:51–52). According to Mark the only true disciples of Jesus are those who follow him into the pains of the cross (Mk. 8:31–35). His gospel must be read in that context: that is how he intends it.

Although differing essentially from Mark, Luke endorses this viewpoint. And this is evidently not to be explained by the fact that Luke had more sources of tradition on this subject at his disposal (in particular, SL, the source said to be peculiar to Luke),[18] but by Luke's own working over of the single Marcan source[19] which he reinterprets, in giving another interpretation of Peter's denial *vis-à-vis* the defection of the disciples in general.[20] For Luke will not admit any such defection; he eliminates it from the Marcan account: the disciples do not run away (Mk. 14:50 is dropped by Luke); they even use some swords to defend their master (Lk. 22:50; see 22:38), and – loyal to him, though impotent – they all stand beneath the cross (Lk. 23:49). Mark's prediction of their total loss of faith is simply expunged by Luke, at least in the sense of its being attenuated and at the same time linked with a logion, deriving from a source peculiar to Luke, concerning Jesus' special assistance to Peter – a promise itself weakened, for that matter, by the interpolation 'when you have turned again' (Lk. 22:32). Luke sets out deliberately to defend and justify Peter. As he would have it, Peter does not actually deny Jesus; he tells a white lie. It is a lie, but not a disavowal: 'I have nothing to do with it', that is, I'm staying out of it ('no affair of mine!'). Thus allowing for their respective viewpoints, the difference between Luke and Mark is not as big as a first reading might suggest.

The flight of the disciples is treated in the New Testament primarily from a theological standpoint, as a 'taking offence' at Jesus and a 'falling away' (Mk. 14:27a) and at the same time as providential, 'according to the Scriptures' (14:27b). This was a serious tampering on Mark's part with the material he had to hand: neither the general flight nor its prediction is already given to Mark.[21] What was given was the knowledge that the disciples had not been present as Jesus' sufferings unfolded and so had not 'gone after' him as it behoves 'disciples' to do. By exaggerating as he does, Mark's purpose is to rub in the idea of 'following after, imitating, the suffering Jesus'. Whereas in Luke Peter's denial of Jesus occurs before the interrogation of Jesus and his solemn profession, Mark has the denial taking place after the questioning and affirmation which cost Jesus his life. The avowal by Jesus is contrasted with the denial by Peter, who in that way escapes suffering. Mark quite clearly relates the flight of the disciples to their coming together again after Easter. They have all fallen away (Mk. 14:27a) and Jesus is going 'before the disciples and Peter to Galilee' (Mk. 16:7).

Yet after the mention of this faintheartedness in Mk. 14:29–31 there is inserted a prediction of Peter's denial. Furthermore, exegetes generally are agreed that the pericope of the denial by Peter (Mk. 14:66–72) was originally an independent tradition, before it was fitted into the Passion narrative. Mark is the sole source for all the variants in the tradition of this story; according to G. Schneider's painstaking analysis Lk. 22:54b–61 does not entail a separate source but is a Lucan

redaction of the Marcan material.[22] The fact that Peter's denial is interpolated may mean that Mark did not find Peter's flight in his tradition.
On the contrary, his tradition told him that Peter had followed the
Lord into the court of the high priest – Mark himself modifying this,
however, with the phrase 'at a distance' (Mk. 14:54 is Marcan; see 5:6;
8:3; 11:13; 15:40). Despite his good intentions and his timid attempt
to 'go after Jesus' Peter succumbs. So it is that Mark (14:30–31) can
speak of the disciples as a whole – Peter not excepted – as losing heart
(cf. Mk. 14:29 'they all . . . but not I', says Peter; whereupon Jesus fore-
tells the denial). Luke on the other hand stresses particularly Peter's
attempting to follow Jesus (*akolouthein*, Lk. 22:54b, in the imperfect):
admittedly, Peter does tell a lie, but without repudiating his Jesus. For
Luke, Peter's negative response is not a particular instance of loss of
nerve on the disciples' part (Luke drops Mk. 14:27–28): Peter's faith
in Jesus is not going to flag or fail (Lk. 22:31–32). There is, according
to Luke, no diminution of the disciples' faith: Jesus' sufferings and
death do not mark a lacuna in their faith before and after Easter. At a
glance from Jesus Peter is 'turned again' (Lk. 22:32 and 22:61).[23]
Mark on the other hand emphasizes the fact that Peter's attempt was
not carried through to the end; he wants to drive home the point that
Peter does not, after all, follow his Master into his suffering – not out
of a kind of anti-Petrine bias, but with an eye to the harassment and
persecution of Christians by their Jewish fellow-citizens: then especially it was of vital importance to follow Jesus and not let him
down. So Peter is an incentive example: even 'the man at the top'
has his failings. By dovetailing together prediction and denial Mark
gives to Peter's remembering 'what Jesus had said to him' (Mk.
14:72b) its full theological significance.[24]

The motif of the Christian tradition of the disciples' pusillanimity,
therefore, is embedded in the experience of a concrete frailty, on the
presupposition of faith in Jesus.[25] Later on the disciples feel their
faltering to have been a failure of their faith (*oligopistia*). Therein too
lies the basis for a potential repenting and conversion. Once more to
be going after Jesus. Despite their faintheartedness they know themselves to be – after Jesus' death – in the merciful hand of God. That is
something they have learnt from the words and actions of Jesus.

## §2 The disciples scatter and reassemble: the problem entailed

While Mark found nothing in his tradition about a particular denial of Jesus – on the contrary, the solitary attempt on Peter's part to go after Jesus – he did himself include Peter in the general defection of the disciples, apparently on the strength of the tradition that, apart from the women, not only the disciples but Peter as well failed to be present at the ordeal of Jesus on the cross. There came a moment when Peter gave up his attempt to 'follow after Jesus'. This fact, in itself real enough, is then given by Mark (or on the grounds of some import already attached to it in the tradition) a concrete form (which in itself is more literary composition than a recital of historical fact). That this special interest in Peter's conduct during the events of the Passion ties up with Peter's *de facto* position as leader in the primitive Church has already been said; but the very fact that Peter has this leading position is itself related to his attempt to follow Jesus (remembered by the community), his ceasing to persist with such attempts and also to the multiple tradition that Peter was the first of the (male) disciples to turn to Jesus as the living Lord (see below).

Some time ago M. Dibelius had seen a connection between Peter's denial and the Easter appearances (between Mk. 14:28 and 14:29–31).[26] In this the majority of scholars have not followed him. At all events this positive correlation of the two occurrences is Mark's express intention: the disciples' going their own ways is connected by him with a Scriptural saying: 'I will strike the shepherd and the sheep will be scattered' (Zech. 13:7, in Mk. 14:27). Thus the scattering of the disciples is made part of a divine plan. Corresponding to it is the disciples' reassembling around Jesus: 'But (after I am raised up) I will go before you to Galilee' (Mk. 14:27–28). This tradition would seem therefore to posit an intrinsic link between the disciples' turning tail and breaking up as a group, and the re-grouping after Easter. Again in Jn. 21:15–17 a connection is made, albeit indirectly, between Peter's denial and one of Jesus' post-Easter appearances. It is possible, therefore, despite the arguments advanced against it by E. Linnemann,[27] that in the original link, perceived by Mark, between denial and manifestation (as a conversion-vision; see later on) there lies the motive for the Christian tradition's incorporating the fact of the denial in its proclamation, even if in a later period this relationship may have

faded from the memory of the established local church communities.[28]
The snag with this thesis is of course that within the history of the
tradition the link between the denial and an appearance of Jesus has a
very narrow basis: concretely, Mark's own view of things (Mk. 14:28;
14:29–31 and 16:7; and a vaguer allusion in Jn. 21:15–17). The question
is however whether that basis really is as narrow as at first sight it
would seem to be. If it is true that the appearances of Jesus recorded
in the gospels were initially structured on the model of Jewish conversion-visions, then the tradition of those appearances – one widely
disseminated in the primitive Church – is likewise a basis for this view
of an essential connection between denial and re-grouping (see a later
chapter). Then Mark, who knows nothing of any 'appearances' but on
the other hand makes an explicit connection between the scattering of
the disciples and Jesus' once more going before his disciples into
Galilee (an eschatological reassembling of the disciples), does not have
to be a counter-indication because of his 'isolated' view of things; and
this is more a different expression of what in other traditions is described
as 'appearances'. The Lucan manifestation-stories indicate that the
primitive Church was more variegated than Luke envisages in the
Acts. Not until we can examine the manifestation-stories will the
question raised here be picked up again.

Chapter 2

# 'Why do you seek the living among the dead?' (Lk. 24:5)

Background: local and officially received early Christian traditions

*General literature* (detail-literature passim and later, Part Three). M.
Albertz, 'Zur Formgeschichte der Auferstehungsberichte', ZAW 21
(1922), 259–69; H. W. Bartsch, *Das Auferstehungszeugnis. Sein historisches
und sein theologisches Problem*, Hamburg 1965; P. Benoit, *Passion et résurrection du Seigneur*, Paris 1966; J. Broer, *Die Urgemeinde und das Grab
Jesu*, Munich 1972; H. Cazelles et al., *Le langage de la foi dans l'Écriture
et dans le monde actuel* (Lectio Divina, 72), Paris 1972 (cited *Lectio
Divina*, n. 72); H. Freih. von Campenhausen, *Der Ablauf der Osterereig-*

*nisse und das leere Grab*, Heidelberg 1966; H. Conzelmann, *Die Mitte der Zeit* (Tübingen 1964⁵), 85–6 and 188–92; C. H. Dodd, 'The appearances of the risen Lord', *Studies in the Gospel* (in memory of R. H. Lightfoot) (Oxford 1955), 9–35; J. Delorme, 'Résurrection et tombeau de Jésus: Mc. 16:1–8 dans la tradition évangélique', *La résurrection du Christ et l'exégèse moderne* (Lectio Divina, 50) (Paris 1969), 105–51 (cited *Lectio Divina*, n. 50), and *La résurrection de Jésus dans le langage du Nouveau Testament* (Lectio Divina, 72) (Paris 1972), 101–82 (cited *Lectio Divina*, n. 72); E. Fascher, 'Anastasis, resurrectio, Auferstehung', ZNW 40 (1941), 166–229; R. Fuller, *The Formation of the Resurrection Narratives*, New York-London 1971; A. George, 'Les récits d'apparitions aux onze à partir de Luc 24:36–53', *La résurrection du Christ et l'exégèse moderne* (Lectio Divina, 50) (Paris 1969), 75–104 (cited *Lectio Divina*, n. 50); P. Grelot, 'La résurrection de Jésus et son arrière-plan biblique et juif', *Lectio Divina*, n. 50, 17–54; and 'L'histoire devant la résurrection du Christ', RHS and RAM 48 (1972), 221–50; H. Grasz, *Ostergeschehen und Osterberichte*, Göttingen 1964³ (1956); B. van Iersel, 'Jezus' verrijzenis in het nieuwe testament. Informatie of interpretatie?', Conc 6 (1970), n. 10, 53–65; J. Kremer, *Das älteste Zeugnis von der Auferstehung Christi* (SBS, 17), Stuttgart 1967²; X. Léon-Dufour, *Résurrection de Jésus et message paschal*, Paris 1971; E. Lohse, *Die Auferstehung Jesu Christi in Zeugnis des Lukasevangeliums*, Neukirchen 1961; see also RSR 57 (1969), 599–602; L. Marin, 'Les femmes au tombeau', *Lectio Divina*, n. 50, 39–50, and in C. Cabrol and L. Marin, 'Sémiotique narrative: récits bibliques', *Langages* 6 (1971), 39–50, and 'Du corps au texte', *Esprit* (April 1973), 913–28; W. Marxsen, *Anfangsprobleme der Christologie*, Gütersloh 1960; *Die Auferstehung Jesu als historisches und als theologisches Problem*, Gütersloh 1965², and *Die Auferstehung von Jesus von Nazaret*, Gütersloh 1968; W. Marxsen, U. Wilckens, D. Delling and H. Geyer, *Die Bedeutung der Auferstehungsbotschaft für den Glauben an Jesus Christus*, Gütersloh 1968⁶; F. Muszner, *Die Auferstehung Jesu*, Munich 1969; F. Neyrinck, 'Les femmes au tombeau. Étude de la rédaction matthéenne', NTS 15 (1968–9), 168–90; A. Pelletier, 'Les apparitions du Resuscité en termes de la Septante', Bibl 51 (1970), 76–9; E. Pousset, 'Résurrection de Jésus et message paschal', NRTh 104 (1972), 95–107; B. Rigaux, *Dieu l'a resuscité*, Gembloux 1973; L. Schenke, *Auferstehungsverkündigung und leeres Grab* (SBS, n. 33), Stuttgart 1969²; H. Schlier, *Uber die Auferstehung Jesu Christi*, Einsiedeln 1968; J. Schmitt, *Prédication apostolique*, DBS 8 (1967–8), 251–67; R. Schnackenburg, 'Zur Aussage "Jesus ist (von den Toten) auferstanden"', BZ 13 (1969), 1–17; Ph. Seidensticker, *Die Auferstehung in der Botschaft der Evangelisten*, Stuttgart 1967; G. W. Tropf, 'The first resurrection appearance and the ending of Mark's Gospel', NTS 18 (1971–2), 308–78; A. Vögtle, 'Ekklesiologische Auftragsworte des Auferstanden', *S. Pagina* (Paris-Gembloux 1959), pt. II, 280–94, and 'Das christologische und ekklesiologische Anliegen von Mt. 28:18–20', *Studia Evangelica* II (TU, 87) (Berlin 1964), 266–94; U. Wilckens, 'Der Ursprung der Ueberlieferung der Erscheinungen des Auferstandenen', *Dogma und Denkstrukturen* (Festschrift f. E. Schlink) (Göttingen 1963), 53–95, and *Auferstehung*, Stuttgart-Berlin 1970; Th. J. Weeden, *Marktraditions*, 101–17; special number: 'Lire l'écriture; dire la résurrection', *Esprit* 41 (1973), April, no. 4, 831–935.

The death of Jesus put an end to the common life in fellowship, shared by the earthly Jesus with his disciples – an end reinforced by their leaving him in the lurch. What was it then that after a time gave these same disciples reason to assert that they were once more drawn into a living and present fellowship with Jesus, whom they now proclaimed to be the living one, risen from the dead, either presently operative in the Christian propagandists or soon to return as the son of man? What took place between Jesus' death and the proclamation by the Church?

Nowhere does the New Testament say that the resurrection is itself this event. By way of contrast to the apocryphal writings, especially Ev. Petri 35–45, the resurrection event itself is never related. Not the resurrection but some sort of gracious self-manifestation of the dead Jesus is what leads the disciples, prompted now by faith, to proclaim: 'Jesus is back, he is alive', or 'He is risen'. How do the primitive Christian churches themselves intepret the emergence of their faith in the living or returning crucified One? In other words: What happened to them?

It is only recently that exegetical literature has been able to shed rather more light on this complex matter. We can now be sure that the tradition of the appearances of Jesus to the Twelve[29] was originally independent of the distinctly local Jerusalem tradition in which the local Christians – in keeping with the veneration shown in other ancient burial-places of Jerusalem – had a pious concern with the 'tomb of Jesus' and the other sites connected with his sufferings and death.[30] Since the work done by G. Schille, and in the Netherlands by B. van Iersel, yielded this explanation of the 'sacred tomb' tradition, other scholars have reached a similar conclusion.[31] Christians come to look at and are conducted around various sites at Jerusalem, calculated to remind them of Jesus' journey to the cross. To conclude this pious pilgrimage they would also visit the sacred tomb. They would come to it already committed to faith in the One crucified and risen. Their feelings of religious awe would mount to a climax when, having arrived at the spot, they would hear their guide say: 'And here is the place where they had laid him' (Mk. 16:6c).[32]

Matthew and Luke show an obvious interest in combining the two separate traditions – the sacred tomb and the appearances of Jesus to the Twelve. John in particular makes it very clear that an 'empty tomb', if there were such a thing, could never be proof of the resurrection (Jn. 20:8–9), but at most a token of an already existing faith in the resurrection.

Mark has nothing about appearances of Jesus, not even to the women, as opposed to Matthew, Luke, John and the much later Marcan ending (Mk. 16:9–20). There appears only a 'young man in white', that is, an angel (see 2 Macc. 3:26, 23; also Mk. 9:3; Rev. 7:9, 13), who reminds the women at the 'holy sepulchre' of the 'apostolic *kerygma*': 'He has risen' (Mk. 16:6b). Other evangelists subsequently mention appearances of Jesus to women as well (their names alter, though Mary Magdalene is invariably present). A tradition concerned with an appearance of Jesus to women must therefore have existed. In contrast to Mark on the other hand, other evangelists also involve (male) disciples, especially Peter, in the 'tomb' tradition from Jerusalem (Lk. 24:12; Jn. 20:3–9). Everything points to our having to take Mk. 16:1–8 as our point of departure for the interpretation. J. Delorme rightly says that the silence of the apostolic *kerygma* and catechesis regarding the 'holy sepulchre' tradition need not in any way rule out a local Jerusalem tradition (with other troublesome circumstances as reported in Mk. 16:1–8), a tradition which is not *per se* secondary, therefore, but apparently very old, although associated in the other gospels 'secondarily' with the appearances tradition. Still, the Jerusalem tradition of the 'tomb of Jesus' must be more recent than the tradition of the appearances, but older than the gospel stories about them. The import of the angel's message (Mk. 16:6–7) surely presupposes a vital belief in the apostolic proclamation at Jerusalem, while this gospel story itself assumes the Christian custom of a Jerusalem pilgrimage to the tomb of Jesus. By combining the two originally independent traditions Matthew, Luke and John give the impression that there are two bases for belief in the resurrection: 'the tomb' and the 'appearances', while there was never a mention, originally, of an empty tomb, and the 'holy sepulchre' story presupposes faith in the One crucified and risen – founded, in fact, on the apostolic testimony itself.

Mark had expressly mentioned in his gospel narrative that Jesus had come with his friends from Galilee to Jerusalem. In their company were women who were related to the 'brothers of Jesus' (Mk. 16:1 and 15:47; cf. 6:3) and apparently – later on – enjoyed a certain prestige in the local Christian communities (see Acts 1:14). The Marcan narrative reveals no trace of apologetic (an angel, after all, was not the most suitable medium for that! Again, it is the angel himself who says that Jesus was not there; nowhere in Mark do we read that the women themselves found the tomb empty. And then, it was difficult at that period for women to serve the purposes of apologetic!), but traces certainly of a theological concern. An angel, of course, has a message to convey; and the message of this angel from God is – not an empty tomb but: 'He has risen!' From the evidence as a whole it is quite clear that certain women, likewise 'disciples of Jesus', did as a matter of history play some role in the Christ-confessing community.[33] With J. Delorme and U. Wilckens[34] we can declare that a particular marginal tradition in Jerusalem circles assumed a theological significance in the light of the apostolic faith on the basis of the officially acknowledged appearance of Jesus to Peter and the Eleven. The deepest import of the stories centred around the 'holy sepulchre' lies in the unmistakable Christian concern with the absolute identity between the crucified Jesus of Nazareth and the risen Christ. This for the Marcan account is the really perplexing thing, the Jesus mystery. At the end of the day, the New Testament sees in the tomb what is in our world the 'negative sign' of the new creation, brought about through the eschatological salvific reality of Jesus' resurrection from the dead: 'Death shall be no more' (Rev. 21:4–5). In negative blueprint the tomb is a profoundly human archetypal symbol of that. The other evangelists eagerly adopted a Jerusalem local pilgrimage tradition into their apostolic faith regarding this eschatological newness. In the end it is on this, not on the tomb traditions, that all the emphasis is laid. However, because 'holy sepulchre' and 'appearance of Christ' are in a literary sense fused together in the concrete gospel narratives and as a literary phenomenon the account of the latter entails the former, I am bound to start by examining the traditions about the tomb at Jerusalem, at the same time not forgetting that they are more recent than the tradition of the appearances, which originally were themselves associated only with one particular local community's tradition. More than that: in the development of the tradition it appears that the resurrection *kerygma* was already present even before the traditions about the tomb and appearances had arisen. The Easter faith emerged independently of these two traditions. Therefore the analysis that follows will for the time being give us a rather 'false picture', which will however be corrected in Part Three.

## §1 Traditions centred on the Jerusalem siting of the holy sepulchre

A. MK. 16:1–8: THE APOSTOLIC RESURRECTION *KERYGMA* WITHIN THE CONTEXT OF THE 'HOLY SEPULCHRE'

Underlying this concluding pericope of the original Marcan gospel is a pre-Marcan tradition. Critical exegetes tell us that this tradition was originally independent of the close of the Passion narrative (15:42–47); it is said to consist of 16:2; 16:5–6 and 16:8a.[35] Yet one may well wonder whether this latter piece of tradition was not the very reason for the pre-Marcan tradition of Mk. 15:42–47, the tenor of which would suggest only too clearly that it was conceived on the basis of a resurrection-faith (and thus with an eye to 16:2; 16:5, 6, 8a). With this correction L. Schenke's other arguments seem to me very cogent: (a) 16:1 is Marcan redaction; (b) Mk. 16:7 and therefore 16:8b are Marcan redaction, so that the sequence in this piece of tradition was: 'You seek Jesus the Nazarene, who was crucified. He has risen. He is not here. Look, this is the place where they laid him. The women went out and fled from the tomb, for trembling and astonishment had come upon them.' The Marcan interpolation: 'And they said nothing to anyone, for they were afraid' (16:8b) is then consistent with the other Marcan insert, namely, 16:7: 'But go, tell his disciples and Peter that he is going before you to Galilee; there you will see him, as he told you' (see Mk. 14:28, which is also Marcan redaction).[36]

As the commanding feature of the story is the 'message of the angel' (there is actually no mention of an 'appearance'; he does not arrive or leave; he is 'sitting there'), the style of an 'angelophany' (model of an angelic manifestation) serves to inform the reader that the apostolic faith in the crucified-and-risen One is a revelation by God to the Church community. The narrative evidently presupposes Christian belief in the resurrection. The distinctive thing about this pericope, however, is that in the early Church this apostolic belief was also associated in Jerusalem with Christians' visiting the holy sepulchre, where a religious ceremony then took place and apropos of this visit, in the early morning, the pilgrims were reminded of the apostolic belief in the resurrection. The pericope points to a practice of venerating the tomb of Jesus at Jerusalem. Whether this custom is connected historically with a visit of some women to the tomb after Jesus' death it is no longer possible to ascertain, although there is quite certainly a tradition enshrining the memory of a connection between Jesus' tomb and some women, and at all events with Mary Magdalene. Mark emphasizes the fact that a number of women were witnesses, not so much to Jesus' burial and the detailed circumstances of that as to the site of the tomb (Mk. 15:47; in other words, the Jerusalem church knew where they had laid him). Nowhere in this pericope is there any inference from an empty tomb to the resurrection – the other way round, in fact: 'He has risen, he is not here' (Mk. 16:6b). The tradition of tomb-veneration at Jerusalem does come to be associated with the apostolic belief in the resurrection. But hearing the Christian preaching of this on a visit to Jesus' tomb there has a peculiar religious ambience only possible *in situ*, as it were. The important thing is the explicit reference here to the risen One who had been crucified; this is given further emphasis by appending the epithet 'the Nazarene' to Jesus. The term often has painful overtones:[37] in effect, the Nazarene means the same as 'the one put to death'.[38] Both Acts 4:10 and Mark 16:6 speak of the Nazarene in a context that sets 'cross' over against 'resurrection'.[39] Thus the message of the angel clearly refers to the resurrection of the crucified One. As proclaimed at Jerusalem, particularly at the holy sepulchre, the *kerygma* of the resurrection was bound to appear as a belief in God's rehabilitation of the crucified Nazarene.[40] The Easter message comes 'as from God', it is a revelation by God; that is the whole point of the presence of an angel, or a messenger from God, in a story. 'He has been raised' (the perfect passive is quite deliberate): the resurrection is God's salvific dealing with Jesus. The man crucified is the risen man, and the risen One, he who was crucified: that is the revelation of God, not something to be contrived by men. For a Jewish Christian the place where God speaks and reveals is holy Scripture. Hence in the apostolic creed: 'He was raised . . . in accordance with the Scriptures' (1 Cor. 15:4). The angel says nothing beyond what the Christian community already knows. The community itself, in virtue of God's revealing grace, articulates its faith in the One crucified and risen; and at Jerusalem it does so within a quite special context: 'at the place where they had laid him'. This tomb of Jesus has become the major symbol, the 'memorial' of the One crucified and risen. The

believer is directed away from the tomb to the business of attending to
the resurrection *kerygma*. In that, the first Christians were truly Jewish:
throughout the Old Testament and in Judaism divine revelations are
bound up with sanctuaries or holy places.[41] The resurrection – Mk. 16:
1–8 is suggesting – is a mystery of faith, of which this holy place is the
negative symbol. At Jerusalem – elsewhere it is not possible – the holy
sepulchre is indeed a religious symbol of Christian belief in the resurrection – not an item of apologetic: the tomb is the place where
Christians come to profess their belief in the resurrection. Beyond
Jerusalem, and therefore in the official Christian proclamation, the
story of the holy sepulchre has no function whatever – which is why
both 'credal' declaration and *kerygma* say nothing about 'an empty
tomb'. Mark 16:7 is the first sign of a tradition meant to combine two
traditional strands – the universal belief in the risen (but coming) son
of man *and* the Jerusalem tradition of the tomb of Jesus.[42]

That the vital context of the resurrection narrative in Mark is a tomb
where a liturgical service is conducted is something grounded deep in
human nature. The initial story of the women's going to Jesus' tomb
on Easter morning is an aetiological cult-legend, which is to say that
this story is intended to shed light on the (at least) annual visit of the
Jerusalem church to the tomb in order to honour the risen One there
and to listen to the tale still recognizable in the pre-Marcan tradition
behind Mk. 16:1–8. The cultic celebration at a place of pilgrimage invariably antedates the aetiology – often enough, history cannot even
tell us why men first made a way to this particular place or that.
Structural analysis and semeiotics have done a great deal to help
modern people grasp as meaningful the at first sight largely disconcerting fact of an 'empty tomb' in an already given context of resurrection. The actual analysis shows that the resurrection *kerygma* is presupposed in talking about the tomb; nor has it directly to do with a
Jewish anthropological notion according to which resurrection is
thought of as a kind of 're-animation of a body' (as for instance in the
story of Lazarus). That has nothing to do with the eschatological
character of Jesus' physical resurrection. It is concerned rather with
the human symbolism of the sepulchre, pregnant sign and token of
death, the place where the lack of a person's presence is most plainly
felt, because it is 'the place of death'. The grave is no place for the
living to inhabit! In the Jerusalem story this place is now suddenly
filled with a message from God: 'He is alive! He has been raised!' The
tomb is filled by 'the (gleaming) white of the young man', which con-

centrates attention completely on itself and not on whatever else may or may not be present in this tomb: the place of death becomes the place of God's revelation. The white manifestation annuls, as it were, the presence of what the women had come looking for: a corpse to be embalmed.[43] The angel is there to be listened to. Because Jesus is alive, he is not to be looked for in a sepulchre, the place of death! At no point is the story concerned with a corpse (whether there is or is not one, unless it be in the minds of the women who are seeking not a living but a dead person). That was their fundamental mistake, as Lk. 24:5 will have it: 'One does not seek the living among the dead.' The very character of the sacral place of death – the tomb – as one of enclosure turns out on the women's arrival to be already un-closed: the stone has been rolled away. It sullies the sacrality of death – and this at a moment when the sacral period of the Jewish sabbath is ending and the sun already beginning to rise, the start of the first profane weekday and workday (Mk. 16:1–2). Darkness is becoming light. Even before the women enter, the narrative has itself conducted the reader into the mystery: a new age has dawned. When Mark relates this Jerusalem story the 'first day after the sabbath' has long been the Christian Sunday. The radical change from old to new permeates the whole story, poised in expectation of the fast approaching Parousia. Corresponding to the 'opened' sacral area of the sepulchre is the emptiness of the grave. The closed character of death has made way for the openness of resurrection; in contrast to death resurrection is an open area, not a deathly sacrality. The enclosed sacral area is as it were 'profaned' by the stone that has been rolled away, the empty space is the reverse side of the new plenitude: He has risen! Just because it is difficult to give positive expression to this in so many words, the emptiness of the sepulchre speaks whole volumes. That is the profound, anthropological intention of this Marcan tradition. In this way what is beyond expression – One who was crucified and is alive – becomes utterable and accessible to all; one does not need to be a philosopher or theologian before one can believe in the resurrection (or reject it). The gospels decline to give us an account of the resurrection itself; and so they enable us to consider it, in terms of experience and language, within a story which can be heard and heeded as a message.

## B.  MT. 28:1–10: THE MARCAN ACCOUNT TRANSFERRED INTO A POLEMICAL CONTEXT

As regards the Jerusalem story or the Marcan version of it (on this point) familiar to him, Matthew has no new traditions to adduce. But he shapes the down-to-earth presence of an angel (in the Marcan story) into a magnificent, apocalyptic angelophany; and for him the tomb becomes a polemical issue between Jews and Christians. All this turns it into a quite different account of things.

From the outset the place of Jesus' burial is guarded by soldiers (Mt. 27:62–66); and later on – after they have just missed the event of the resurrection – they are bribed by the Jewish authorities to spread the rumour that Jesus' disciples have stolen the body (28:11–15). The whole thing is conceived by Matthew in those terms because in his narrative his readers have already been informed that Jesus had foretold: 'After three days I will rise again' (Mt. 26:32 and 28:6); thus the official guard is set over the tomb for exactly three days (27:63–64) and the tomb itself sealed and made especially secure (27:65–66). Seen in that way, the purpose of the Matthean story is not to give us historical information; it echoes the controversy that arose between Jews and Christians regarding the 'empty tomb', a discussion in which both sides apparently start from the fact that the tomb is empty (28:15; see Jn. 20:15);[44] their quarrel is only about the interpretation of this datum. Matthew is determined to counter the denial of the Christian message, within a theologically less relevant polemic which had formed around an empty tomb; a polemic based on the Jewish anthropological premise that, for there to be a resurrection, the body must also disappear.[45]

In contrast to Mark, Matthew makes a great deal of the sacral aspects of a spectacular angelic manifestation. Whereas Mark only implies that the man seated in the tomb is an angel, Matthew speaks more directly of 'an angel of the Lord' (28:2), whose 'appearance was like lightning' (28:3), while 'for fear of him the guards trembled' and were paralysed (28:4). The angel is indeed manifested – to the accompaniment of a thunderous earthquake, at that – and it is he who rolls away the stone. The rest of the story is substantially the same, but with small changes of detail which show that the sepulchre here has assumed a different meaning: an empty tomb with an apologetic function. '*He* is not here' is now pointedly placed before 'he has risen' (28:6), although it does not say that the body is no longer there (that is perhaps taken for granted). Moreover, the angel does not bring a revelation from God; he refers to what Jesus had himself predicted prior to his death: his rising again (28:6a with 26:32). The women are instructed to go and tell the disciples: 'He has risen from the dead, and behold, he is going before you to Galilee; there you will see him' (28:7). (Matthew has already couched it in the form of address the women use in speaking to the disciples.)

What is new in Matthew, as opposed to Mark, is the subsequent appearance of Jesus himself to the women on their way back to the disciples. Thus the manifestation of the angel was just a preliminary to that of Jesus, which is in turn secondary to the 'official' appearance of Jesus to the Eleven; in other words the apostolic *kerygma* is given an exclusive emphasis. The substance of Jesus' manifestation consists of an element of grace (Jesus takes the initiative and meets them) and one of *recognition*: 'They came up and took hold of his feet and worshipped him' (28:9), that is, they recognize Jesus as the Christ and as Lord. The message about going to Galilee is here put into the mouth of the manifested Jesus himself (28:10). As the Johannine gospel is an independent literary document but also contains a manifestation of Christ to Mary Magdalene (Jn. 20:11–18), one cannot assert that Mt. 28:9–10 is pure editorializing, without any tradition behind it. Traditions must have existed in Jerusalem regarding not only the holy sepulchre but also a manifestation of Jesus to women.[46] Matthew too intends to make it clear that the appearances and the quality of the witnesses – the Eleven – provide the basis for the Christian faith, and not an empty tomb, which nevertheless has already begun to fulfil an apologetic function within it. The Matthean gospel would seem to be a sustained attempt to combine the local Jerusalem traditions with the apostolic *kerygma*, based on the tradition of 'appearances of Jesus' to the Eleven, from the canonical gospels' viewpoint the only really important one, ecclesially speaking (this being the ultimate standpoint of the gospels themselves); within that context however the Jerusalem traditions have their rightful place. Officially, where the Church is concerned, Jesus' resurrection – according to Matthew predicted by himself – is affirmed on the grounds of his having appeared to the Eleven.

To this the Johannine gospel really adds no new information (as regards the non-official manifestations): the local Jerusalem tradition is conjoined with the official tradition of the appearances to 'the brethren'.

C.   LK. 24:1–12: THE MARCAN NARRATIVE IN A CONTEXT OF THE
(JUDAEO) GREEK 'RAPTURE' MODEL

Despite the literary independence, in a direct sense, of Luke and John,
nevertheless their 'appearance' stories evince similar features, pointing
to a common tradition from a (Hellenistic) Jewish milieu.[47] This
'Hellenism' is especially noticeable in Luke.

That the Lucan motif of the Jesus tomb acquires a completely new
context as over against Mark and Matthew seems to me, in the light of
recent exegetical studies, confirmed beyond a doubt.[48] The distinctive
thing about the motif of the empty tomb in Luke is clear at once from
the fact that in contrast to Mk. 16:6 and Mt. 28:6, in Luke it is for the
first time the women who make sure for themselves that the tomb is
empty (Lk. 24:3). And then, logically enough – within a thesis concerned with confirming that the tomb is empty – Luke has the emptiness of the tomb 'officially' corroborated by Peter (Lk. 24:12 and 24:
3).[49] This has absolutely no apologetic function here (as is often stated)
but follows essentially from the 'rapture' model employed by Luke.
For the failure to find a person or, after his death, his corpse, is typical
of the model in question. If absolutely nothing of an individual (always
a pious, miracle-working or sage individual) remains to be found, then
he has been 'taken up to God' – snatched away. Examples of this in
ancient literature are legion.[50]

Although 'empty tomb' and 'taken up to God' are identical in this
model, this in no way implies that, having established the fact of an
empty tomb, one can immediately conclude that the occupant has been
snatched away – to God. On the contrary, at first there is fear and
astonishment, one begins to suspect the presence of 'the sacral'. Peter
too, who formally pronounces the tomb 'empty', goes away 'amazed
and wondering about what had happened' (Lk. 24:12). The empty
tomb, together with the previous activity of the person in question as
a whole, determines whether or not he has been 'taken up'. The
'rapture' therefore will be just a conviction among disciples or intimate
friends who have lived as companions of the person concerned (before
his death and before his sudden removal); as a rule they are also afforded
manifestations of the subject.

Luke simply takes over the motif of the tomb from the Jerusalem
tradition (Marcan account), but for the benefit of Greek readers he
gives it a quite different function. For him the 'rapture' model is
nothing but an appropriate means for making intelligible to Greeks

the Christian proclamation of resurrection from the dead – which is what he has in view (see Lk. 24:6–7, where he juxtaposes the two terms). In both the Lucan gospel and in the Acts this Graeco-Roman and Hellenistic-Jewish notion is used in many places. So too, at first, Paul envisages those still alive being 'caught up' at the Parousia of Christ (1 Thess. 4:17).[51]

Thus a rapture may be 'corroborated' by the fact of an empty tomb, but also and principally by manifestations of the person 'snatched away' (or of someone representing him). In the 'rapture' theory 'empty tomb' and 'manifestation' go hand in hand: those snatched away are removed, it is true, from 'the world of men' (*ex anthrôpôn*)[52] and 'raised up to God or the gods'; they are divinized (the individual in question is a *divus* and is to be worshipped); but thenceforward they may appear to former companions or disciples. When on the day after his wife Callirhoë had been buried Chaireas goes to the tomb to pay her his last respects and place wreaths at her grave, the stone is already rolled away. On seeing the empty tomb he takes fright but does not dare to go inside. Afterwards, when the tomb is examined, they find nothing.[54] Again, the typically Lucan story of the walkers on the road to Emmaus is couched in a 'rapture' terminology: *aphantos egeneto* (Lk. 24:31); all detail of a resurrection is lacking, while everything reminds one of the 'rapture' model.[55]

Now it is true that some accounts of 'raptures' are older than the gospels; others – relating to cases analogous even in detail - are more recent than the Lucan story. It could be difficult, however, to argue that these somewhat later pagan stories derive from Luke's gospel. In other words, it is not a matter of literary indebtedness, but has to do with the fact that like, for instance, Philostratus, Luke is drawing on the same sort of arsenal of ideas, mythical and legendary, generated by popular piety and generally and widely current at the time; both writers do this with their own radically differing purposes in view. Therefore the real point of Luke's own narrative cannot be explained by a diachronous bringing together of similar kinds of story (obviously suggestive of one model),[56] but only on the basis of a synchronous, structural analysis, whence it should become clear how the empty tomb and the appearances function in the Lucan narrative.

And then it is part and parcel of the classical 'rapture' model that when a manifesting subject takes his farewell he pronounces a blessing or leaves something else as a parting gift.[57] Thus Lk. 24:50–53. The 'adoration (on bended knee)' is also an element of the 'rapture' theory (Lk. 24:52).[58]

The definitive significance of Jesus as son of God had long been given in the Christian tradition; but in order to get his Christian message across to Greeks, Luke clothes the Christian story in concepts which are open to them and which they can understand. Obviously the already given model is not the basis of the Christian interpretation of Jesus; but the interpretation of Christian belief, already an older historical datum, is for this missionary purpose enunciated in terms which do indeed derive from the *theios anèr* theory, but for Luke are evidently just 'his way of dressing it up'. Just as after the event the disciples 'return to the city with great joy' (Lk. 24:52), so also the two Roman pupils, when Romulus has appeared to them and been snatched away, take their journey, as Plutarch says, 'to the city with great joy'.[59] That this 'rapture' model is a dominant feature in the Lucan documents is confirmed in a singular way by the otherwise unintelligible line of argument in Acts 2:25–26. With his Greek readers in mind he lays special emphasis on three facts. The point is driven home in this pericope that the burial-place of David is still known in Jerusalem: 'I may say to you confidently of the patriarch David that he both died and was buried, and his tomb is with us to this day' (Acts 2:29), that is, David has not been 'snatched away'. Thus the words of the psalm quoted cannot be meant for David; they are said with reference to Jesus, the Christ. That is the gist of Luke's line of argument. The resurrection of Jesus and his sitting at God's right hand are evidently contrasted here with the funerary monument of David. Then too Acts 3:19–21, although incorporating a very old tradition, is typically recent, that is, Lucan, in that a very ancient tradition is linked here with the 'rapture' model: 'Heaven must receive him until the time of the restoration of all things.' The notion of the subject's 'being kept with God', in expectation of his eschatological role, is a typical 'rapture' motif.[60] Using the same model, Luke describes in Acts 1:1–11, the 'ascension into heaven' of Jesus, with all the elements of the 'rapture' motifs familiar to Greeks and Hellenistic Jews (cloud; mountain; instruction and exhortation; promise); the 'ascension' of Elijah serves as the concrete model for this (Acts 1:8 and 2 Kings 2:7–10). Acts 1:1–11 is therefore not a doublet of Lk. 24:51. The end of the Lucan gospel and the start of Acts are meant to make Acts 1:2 tie up with Lk. 24:51, but at the same time differentiate sharply between the two works. The Lucan gospel tells us about Jesus' life, from birth to departure; Acts records and relates the missionary activity of the Church between the resurrection and the Parousia, for the proximity of the End is rejected

(Acts 1:6); Jesus is going, but now the Spirit is to carry his work forward (Acts 1:7 and 1:11). Jesus' disciples are not thereby left as orphans; they are baptized 'with the Spirit' (Acts 1:5; see 1:8). Precisely in order to mark this break between earthly fellowship with Jesus and fellowship with the exalted Christ, Luke interpolates the account (in these terms unknown elsewhere in the gospels) of the ascension (Acts 1). And with the same 'rapture' motifs as those he used in his gospel for the scene of the parting (Lk. 24). Luke 24 rounds off Jesus' activity on earth; Acts 1 is the start of his celestial activity through the Spirit.

Then too it is only Luke who has the 'appearances during forty days' (Acts 1:3). This interval is one of the later elements of the 'rapture' scheme.[61] In the apocryphal books this intervening period varies in length. The most conspicuous parallel (more or less of Luke's own time) is a Jewish apocalypse in which Ezra, after having (like Moses) instructed his people (Ex. 24:18), appeared over forty days to commit to writing once more the Law that had been lost (4 Ezra 12 [14]:23, 36, 42, 49). After his death Baruch too instructs his people for forty days; then he is 'taken up' for good (Syr. Ap. Baruch 76:2–4). The 'forty-day period after Easter', therefore, is based on a given model. A 'rapture' always contains a message of mission. The *Imperator*, the Caesar, is the *Kyrios* of the world, say the Romans in the Romulus 'rapture' story – Romulus himself conveys that message to Proclus. Lucan Christians, using a similar model, say 'No! That Lord is Jesus of Nazareth, the Christ, who has been taken up to God.' These parallels should hearten rather than disconcert us. The models are not a starting-point for a mythological interpretation of Jesus; but with the help of models already generally familiar Luke is contrasting Jesus, already acknowledged elsewhere as the actual presence of salvation, with the emperor. It is the same process as when modern Christians speak of Jesus in terms of existential or socio-critical models, as for instance the 'man for others', the contestant and so forth. The question is simply whether, starting from the substance of *our* faith we can preserve a critical tension *vis-à-vis* the cultural categories being used. That Luke is himself conscious of using a model is clear from the fact that when he is summarizing the substance of belief, in Acts 10:40ff and 13:30ff, he no longer speaks of a 'rapture' but only of Jesus' death and resurrection; he has a critical stance towards the model.

Luke, then, deploys the motif of the tomb in a quite different perspective from Mark and Matthew; with him too the resurrection is presupposed; the 'rapture' motif eases the Greek conception of Christian resurrection. Even more than the other evangelists he stresses the 'official' appearances to the Twelve.

## D. FAITH-MOTIVATED EXPERIENCE AND THE LANGUAGE OF AN ESCHATOLOGICAL FAITH

In contrast to Mark both Matthew (28:9–10) and John (20:11–18) have Jesus appearing in person also to women, whereas the apostolic faith (1 Cor. 15:3–8) is grounded not at all on any appearances of Jesus to women. Even so, diverse traditions tell us that Jesus' very first appearance was to Mary Magdalene. Here we can do no more than confirm the existence of a very old tradition, while the historicity of the experience underlying the tradition at this point is something we cannot finally determine. A biblical anthropology establishes a close relation between the status of woman and death: the weeping and mourning, the anointing of the departed, the business of caring for and revisiting the spot where the dead person is buried, all this is entrusted to women. It would seem to be a fact of history that it was women who first spread the report that Jesus was alive, had risen. The gospels show that Jesus had female disciples who – naturally enough, in view of woman's social and cultural status at the time – had functions and responsibilities other than those of male disciples. They had come with Jesus and the rest from Galilee to Jerusalem. They stood close to the cross on which Jesus died (Lk. 23:49). One of them was Mary of Magdala, a small town on the west bank of the Sea of Galilee, near the gay and frivolous capital city of Tiberias where Herod Antipas had his residence. Jesus apparently liberated this young woman and brought her to herself: she broke with her past. But the death of Jesus seemed at first to turn the life she had regained into a problem, until there came to her the loving assurance that this life regained was stronger than death. This Jesus lived.

The assertion that the apostolic 'creed' deliberately passes over in silence this incident involving Mary of Magdala (in view of 1 Cor. 15:3ff) cannot be supported on historical grounds: it derives from a different tradition, not known initially to every local congregation, which the gospels (Matthew; John) have treated with respect and integrated with their report of the 'official' appearances. Actually, the accounts of the latter in the gospels presuppose an already hierarchical Church: only the Twelve, the leaders in the early Christian communities, are afforded 'official' appearances with the status of validity; the women as well as the males on the walk to Emmaus were 'not credited' until the official apostolic testimony was provided; furthermore, they received the subsidiary instruction to inform the Twelve of the event. There is no such thing as an anti-feminist stance here, as P. Schutz would maintain;[62] it is a mode of self-understanding on the part of the Church, aware that its belief is based on apostolic (at that time indeed exclusively male) testimony. But other, as it were, 'lay' experiences within the church community acquire their proper place within the gospel record, which is far from being passed over in the New Testament. On the contrary it is thanks partly to the experiences of these women, as it would seem, that the whole Jesus affair got under way. The very manner in which the Johannine gospel reports this sheds light on the structure of the experiences denoted in the New Testament by the term 'Jesus appearance'. At first Mary thinks that they have 'taken away' the body of Jesus (Jn. 20:11–15). Her recognition that the 'gardener' is Jesus is auditory, not visual; Jesus says 'Mary', and she replies 'Rabboni'. The structuralists call this the 'fatic code', just as when picking up the telephone somebody says 'Hello!'; its only function is to clinch the renewed contact. Then too *rabboni* as a form of address is confined in the gospels to use by intimate disciples. In other words, spiritual contact with Jesus, ruptured by death, has been restored: they can once more address each other in intimate, personal terms, death notwithstanding. Death has not shattered living communication with Jesus: that is, he continues after his death to offer those who are his a fellowship belonging to and constituting life. In this fellowship believers experience Jesus as brought back from the realm of the dead, that is, as the One who lives or the One who has risen again. After his death intercourse, conversation, with him continues – in a very personal sense. Mary Magdalene may have played a part we do not know about in helping to convince the disciples that the new orientation of living which this Jesus has brought about in their lives has not been rendered meaningless by his death – quite the opposite. In these accounts of 'private appearances' – a record of very intimate, personal religious experiences – the community recognizes its own experience.[63] At a particular moment these people's mode of living received a jolt – likewise an intuition – that gave a definitive orientation to their lives. In the radical change they undergo, experienced as something definitive, they apprehend Jesus as the One who lives. A specific here-and-now 'lived' experience is thus given expression in eschatological language.[64] Unless anchored in this source-experience ('disclosure'), the eschatological language is left in the air; from being a very real, 'objective' experience invested with actuality, it becomes objectivizing and abstract and it loses its effect and truth-value. Belief in the resurrection can never be grounded purely in the claims of authority; it presupposes a faith-motivated experience of renewal, of life totally renewed, within which actuality (and not just a subjective conviction) is affirmed in a very fitting way – an experience in which the Church as a whole – people and leaders – recognizes its own *kerygma*, and which is in turn corroborated by the faith of the Church. In itself the Church's preaching of the resurrection is a gracious invitation and sovereign appeal to us to attain to this experience person-ally, each in our own life – in a different way for those on the Emmaus road, different again for Mary Magdalene, different too for Peter and the Eleven. There is not such a big difference between the way we are able, after Jesus' death, to come to faith in the crucified-and-risen One and the way in which the disciples of Jesus arrived at the same faith. Only we suffer from the crude and naïve realism of what 'appearances of Jesus' came to be in the later tradition, through unfamiliarity with the distinctive character of the Jewish-biblical way of speaking. But more of that later on.

## 2 The official apostolic tradition: 'We believe that God raised him from the dead' (1 Thess. 1:10)

### A. 'JESUS MADE HIMSELF SEEN' (1 COR. 15:3–8)

#### (a) A 'unifying formula'

The oldest testimonies regarding Jesus' death and resurrection are to be found in the First Letter of Paul to the Thessalonians: 'We believe: that Jesus died and rose again' (1 Thess. 4:14), and: '(We are waiting for his Son) whom he raised from the dead, Jesus . . .' (1 Thess. 1:10). Here is Paul citing between inverted commas (the Greek *hoti*; I believe *that*) the already traditional *kerygma* of the Church: Jesus' resurrection from the dead is a saving action on God's part, an event that will bring 'deliverance': 'his Son, whom he raised from the dead, Jesus, who de-livers us from the wrath to come' (1 Thess. 1:10). There is no mention here of Jesus appearances; everything centres on the imminent Parousia of Jesus ('We are waiting for his Son . . . who delivers us from the judgement to come').

In a different context, where Paul is taking the identity of belief among the Christian churches as the point of departure for a theological argument, the tradition of Christian belief in the resurrection is conjoined with that of Jesus appearances – actually, with four main elements listed side by side: (a) he died (*apethanen*); (b) he was buried (*etaphē*); (c) he has been raised (*egēgertai*); (d) he has shown himself (*ōphthē*) (1 Cor. 15:3–5). Although the appearances of Jesus are not a conjointly avowed element of the Christian *kerygma* and creed, Paul (or before him, even, the credal confession or catechetical document which he is citing) associates the initiative of what is meant by appearances with the fundamental salvific event of Jesus himself.

'He was dead and buried': this serves to underline not only the factual death of Jesus but in all probability the definitive rejection of Jesus as well.[65] After all, the fact that a member of the Sanhedrin sympathetic towards the Christians, Joseph of Arimathea, is said to have taken it upon himself to give Jesus proper burial according to Jewish custom, is difficult to place, historically speaking; it may be a Christian legend – also known elsewhere, in Qumrân – circulated by pious Christians unable to bear the idea of Jesus' being buried dishonourably.[66] Luke is witness to a different tradition: the same people who had had Jesus put to death 'took him down from the tree and laid him in a tomb' (Acts 13:27–29).[67] The entombment of Jesus is thus the seal, as it were, set on his rejection. Over against that final rejection by men there now stands God's saving action: God raised him up, and the risen One has shown himself to be such. This tallies with the contrast-scheme – an early one: 'You killed him, but God raised him up' (see above).

Jesus 'showed himself' or he appeared. *Ōphthē* is the technical term for this 'paschal event', both in this pre-Pauline tradition and with Luke: Acts 9:17; 13:30–31; Lk. 24:34 (three times, with Luke), and once (though repeated in a similar context four times) in 1 Cor. 15:3–9.[68] The four differentiated instances in 1 Cor. 15 relate to Jesus; what is called the 'appearing', therefore, is obviously not to be characterized as an occurrence deriving merely from human psychology; on the contrary, it is described as an initiative of Jesus himself, as a gracious act of Jesus Christ: God in Christ is party to it.

Paul then gives a list of persons, all of whom are voicing the same resurrection *kerygma*: Jesus has shown himself (1) first to Cephas and the Twelve; (2) afterwards to five hundred brethren; (3) to James and all the apostles; (4) to Paul as the latest of these apostles (1 Cor. 15:3–8).

To understand this passage properly we must first get on the track of what Paul had in mind when he wrote it. It nowhere appears from the context that Paul is seeking to legitimize his apostolic status, as is often argued. The context shows Paul reacting to a false idea of resurrection among the Corinthians. Before engaging in discussion with his opponents he reminds them of the fundamental identity of belief in all Christian churches: 'I would remind you . . . in what terms I preached to you the gospel, which you received, in which you stand' (1 Cor. 15:1), and that is the Easter *kerygma*, the 'One crucified and risen'. 'Whether then it was I or they, so we preach and so you believed' (1 Cor. 15:11). Peter and the Twelve, the five hundred brethren, James, all the apostles and, as being least among them, Paul too, they all proclaim the One crucified and risen (1 Cor. 15:5-8). That is obviously what Paul means by this *ôphthè*: God caused Jesus 'to be seen' by all the people aforementioned; for all these apostles Jesus has become 'epiphanous', that is, they all are proclaiming that the One crucified has risen. Everything that goes by the name of 'apostolic authority' in the early Church testifies to one and the same basic creed: the crucified One has risen. And that, the Corinthians have received in faith. Only they draw from it wrong conclusions, prompted by their enthusiasm, which Paul then goes on to refute (1 Cor. 15:12ff). The identity of belief, therefore, serves the context of the meaning of the epiphany-term *ôphthè* (he appeared); Paul provides a 'unifying formula' at the outset. In this sense *ôphthè* indicates a legitimation-formula, in accordance with the context: the heavenly Jesus is actively at work in his messengers or missionaries. These apostles have been sent by him in person to proclaim this – and no other – faith.

Men have 'killed and buried' Jesus, God has 'raised him and made him epiphanous': this would seem to be the contrast-scheme still evidently lying behind 1 Cor. 15:3-8: all witness to it who have a missionary mandate in the 'great Church'. This, apparently, is the tenor of 1 Cor. 15:3-11. The 'appearances', and thus the *ôphthè* terminology (which plays no part elsewhere in Paul's writings, or in the remaining context of 1 Cor. 15) give clear expression here to the apostolic *kerygma* as 'the universal faith of the Church'. Paul is not listing *witnesses* to the resurrection here – a notion foreign to him. He is providing a list of authorities who all proclaim the same thing, namely, that the crucified One is alive; one and the same evidential ground of faith inspires them all. With this as their starting-point the Christians go on to 'missionize', first in Israel, then beyond it. This historical expansion of Christianity, grounded in a 'unifying formula', is what Paul (in line with his own outlook, albeit on the basis of traditions known to him) is depicting in 1 Cor. 15:3–11.

He speaks first about the faith and the missionary activity of 'Peter and the Twelve'. The five hundred brethren appear to be the oldest kernel of the eschatological 'Church of Christ', the new kingdom of the Twelve Tribes, Israel, won by 'Peter and the Twelve'. Paul is apparently thinking here of what according to him (or his source) was the kernel of the Jerusalem mother church. Then he speaks of the faith and missionary activity of 'James and all the apostles'. 'All the apostles' are not the Twelve again, but 'missionaries' who have spread the Church of Christ outside Jerusalem but as yet within Palestine and its environs, that is, among both Aramaic-speaking and Greek-speaking Jews. Luke has especially in mind here 'the Seven', known as the deacons, who preached the crucified-and-risen One to the Jews of the Diaspora and to Samaria.[69] This second expansion – in which the heavenly Jesus becomes epiphanous – obviously points to missionary activities outside Judea, developments which inaugurated the apostolic mission to Israel as a whole, including the Diaspora. Of this ambitious mission of the Church to Israel James – according to Paul (or his tradition) – was evidently the responsible leader, just as Peter and his followers had taken the lead in the very first proclamation of the faith.[70] To this perhaps traditional view of the expansion of belief in the crucified-and-risen One, Paul now adds his legitimate proclamation to the Gentiles (among others, to the Corinthians who received from him the same faith). Among all those apostolic preachers he is 'the last', that is, the least (because he had previously attacked this faith). With the help of traditional data as well perhaps as his own insights regarding the past of the young Church, Paul sketches the expansion of the one faith in the crucified-and-risen One, as shared by all possessed of apostolic authority in the Church: the primitive Church, the Church in Israel as a whole, and finally the Church among the Gentiles. Luke 24 presents the same (historically as little correct) picture: starting with the Christianization of Jerusalem, the Church of the crucified-and-risen One spreads into Israel as a whole and, beyond that, among the Gentiles. Within the history of tradition there is indeed a link between 1 Cor. 15:3–8 and Lk. 24:34, the oldest kernel of which is: 'The Lord has risen and he appeared to Simon' – itself an amalgam of two traditions: 'He has risen' and 'He appeared to Simon'. In Acts 10:41 and 13:31 we read of appearances in general (10:41), further described in 13:31. It is a striking fact that (although in reverse order) Jn. 21 also has the tradition of a group of disciples, with Peter singled out for mention.

Initially, the new fact of the Jesus appearances was apparently not localized. At any rate Paul does not do so. The localizing intended relates to the area of mission into which the message of the resurrection was being taken. A moment comes when the actual mission in which apostles proclaim the crucified-and-risen One is legitimated, as it were, by what in 'epiphany' circles has come to be called an 'appearing of Jesus': the concrete illustration of their belief in the crucified One's present, here-and-now activity within the missionary activity of the messengers of Jesus. The appearance to 'Peter and the Eleven' would seem, explicitly or implicitly, to be a persisting tradition in all the gospels.[71]

Scholars are for ever arguing about the age of the tradition cited by Paul (1 Cor. 15:4-5; the remainder – 15:6-9 – may be largely his own): from a formula dating from the first years after Jesus' death to one that was more or less worked out by Paul himself, ideas vary between a Jerusalem formula, an Antiochene formula, a formula dating from the forties, from the thirties, or an Antiochene formula based on a Jerusalem recollection, and so forth.[72] The pericope is marked by Semitisms (or, more exactly, Septuagintal features, the language of bilingual Jews), but also by Pauline expressions. However, Semitisms tell us nothing about the age of a tradition (see Part One: 'invalid criteria'), because they were current among Greek-speaking Jews like Paul; and 'Antiochene' does not mean very much, either, as we know that Paul himself played a creative role in the Antiochene church too: so terms like 'Pauline' or 'pre-Pauline' become very ambiguous. Tradition and a Pauline view of things turn out, therefore, to be inextricably mixed up together in 1 Cor. 15:4-9. The list of apostolic authorities summarized by Paul itself presupposes a whole process of development in early Christianity, an evolved theology and even ecclesiology.

If perhaps Paul had particularly in view the beginning of the apostolic mission (in Jerusalem, in all Israel and the Diaspora, and lastly among the Gentiles), the gospels on the other hand speak in the context of an already established 'great Church': here the appearances are a legitimation of the apostolic missionary enterprise of proclaiming the One crucified and risen 'to all peoples', Jew and Gentile. In other words the gospels leave out the phasing in the apostolic mission (and thus in the 'Christ appearances') which Paul evidently still has in mind. In the gospels the appearances reflect the actual missionary practice of the Matthean, Lucan and Johannine local churches with their own theology. The initial recognition of the eschatological presence and epiphany of God in Jesus Christ and thence in the Christian emissaries is then the immediate ground of the apostolic preaching of the crucified-and-risen One to all the world.

(b) Manifestation, preaching and declaration of belief

Theologically speaking, it is well worth while reading the four elements that Paul talks about – he died and was buried, but God raised him up and made him 'epiphanous' – in their proper Pauline context, instead of objectivizing them by lifting them out of it. For in that way something of importance emerges.

In his letter Paul is in conversation with Christians at Corinth. In this discourse, couched in a present form ('I remind you, brethren', 1 Cor. 15:1), there are verbs used in the perfect tense, while the mode of address remains very personal: 'The gospel which I preached to you' (15:1, 2, 3); things common to the Corinthians and to Paul which had happened in the past are brought into the narrative. In this 'I-you' discourse there is suddenly mention of a 'he': another story is thrust into the 'I-you' story, so that three levels intersect one another: Paul addresses the Corinthians – insertion of a biographical story: Paul preached, the Corinthians believed – lastly, the insertion of a story about a third party, Jesus of Nazareth.[73] In that way three biographical stories are intrinsically conjoined: Paul's preaching activity, Corinthians who have been converted, the story of Jesus, who died, was raised to life by God, has revealed himself to official witnesses to Christ. In other words the present of the discourse is that of a life renewed in Christ, both of the Corinthians and of Paul; and what is more, this present has a future.[74] What is said by Paul about Christ and his resurrection cannot be dissociated from the personal character of Paul's speech, in which the Corinthians are involved. The inserted phrase: '(died) for our sins' relates Jesus' death to the present of the Corinthians; Paul also says: Jesus 'appeared also to me'. The appearances are on the one hand a constituent of the basic story (Jesus died but was raised up) and, on the other, at the same time the object of Paul's autobiographical story.[75] Grammatically, the primary story is the object of verbs like evangelize, proclaim – receive and hand on – and believe (1 Cor. 15:1–3, 11). Thus the text itself tells us how we are to understand the primary story: it is a matter of proclaiming Jesus' death, resurrection and manifestation as glad tidings: the announcement of good news and receptive faith form the context in which alone

the primary story in the third person – he died but has risen again – ac-
puires its full significance. The preaching (1 Cor. 15:1) as well as the
accepting belief (15:11) are the operative effect brought about by the
primary story. That is to say, the latter cannot be detached from the
proclaiming and believing; this Jesus story is the *raison d'être* both
of Paul and of the Christians at Corinth; the primary story cannot be
stated in any sort of objectivizing context. To affirm the resurrection
in faith involves the believing person himself in the story thus accepted: to speak of the risen Jesus implies a personal experience which
is interpreted precisely as an initiative on the part of the other, of
Jesus himself.[76]

Jesus is presented as the risen One within a collective – ecclesial –
experience. The source of this talking about Jesus as risen, therefore,
is the experience of a new being or existence. The full meaning of what
Peter and the Eleven experienced becomes evident only in their mission,
in what they do, proclaim, in their actual life and conduct. The fount
and origin of their Christian belief is the permanent and essential
nature of the Christian faith itself. The gospel narratives will make this
clearer still.


B.   'JESUS SHOWED HIMSELF TO PETER AND THE ELEVEN'

The earliest references to Jesus the risen One speak of his death and
resurrection, not about 'appearances'. Neither the Q community nor
the original Marcan gospel refers to Jesus' appearances. In 1 Cor.
15:3–8 there is nothing like an appearance story, but only a list of
official witnesses to Christian belief. Even Matthew has no actual
report of an appearance but fills out Mk. 16:7 with *theologoumena* or
theological insights about the Matthean church's understanding of
itself. Still, Matthew does already mark a transition; one could say
that Matthew presents an account of mission associated with 'the
appearing of Jesus' – not really any account of an appearance: as to the
mode or manner of it he says nothing at all. Only Luke and John contain accounts of appearances in the strict sense: here the tradition of
the actual appearing becomes for the first time an object of reflection.
They begin to talk about the form and manner of these manifestations
– altogether a very recent feature in the gospel tradition as such.

Directly or indirectly, all the gospels refer to the appearance to the
Eleven; Mt. 28:16–20; Lk. 24:36–53; Jn. 20:19–23; also in the new
ending to Mark, which was a later addition. Again, as in 1 Cor. 15:3–4,

so too in Lk. 24:34 the appearance to Peter gets a separate mention, although we are told nothing of real substance about it. Since the Twelve are represented as refusing to credit all other appearances, the evangelists' intention is obvious: it is to present the appearance to Peter and the Eleven as the basis of the Christological *kerygma*. The core of the exegetical result is the official manifestation to Simon Peter and to the Eleven (whether in the presence of others or not, as Lk. 24:33b says); an 'official' appearance which according to Mt. 28:16–20 occurred in Galilee, but according to Lk. 24:36–53 in Jerusalem, while John combines the two traditions: he speaks of appearances in Jerusalem to the Eleven (without Thomas and with him) (Jn. 20:19–23; 20:24–29), and in a later additional chapter appearances in Galilee are mentioned too (Jn. 21:1–15). The appearance 'to Peter and the Eleven' we may describe, therefore, as an apostolic manifestation of Christ, associated in the gospels with the commissioning of the apostles: Mt. 28:19; Lk. 24:48, 49; Jn. 20:22–23 (see also Mt. 28:10; Jn. 20:17; and Mk. 16:15–18).[77]

When we analyse this apostolic manifestation we discover three elements in it:

(a) The initiative for it comes from the risen Jesus himself; the appearance is a salvific action of Jesus in the life of Peter and the Eleven; *ōphthē*, Jesus 'showed himself'; what is normally invisible was made to appear: that the invisible makes itself seen is expressed on lines of human perceiving, the human character of which is at the same time repudiated or corrected (cf. Exod. 33:20–23; Exod. 3:6; Judges 13:23).

(b) An element of acknowledgement, the content of which is provided by the apostolic *kerygma*: (on the third day) the dead man rose (Lk. 24:46, equivalent to the *kerygma* in Acts 2:23–32; 3:15–16; 4:10–11; 5:30–31; 10:39–40; 13:38–41): Jesus is recognized and acknowledged as the Christ, the Lord, as the living Jesus of Nazareth – living beyond his death. The acknowledgement or avowal is expressed in a *proskynesis*, a worshipful prostration: 'When they saw him, they fell down in worship' (Mt. 28:17; by implication also in Jn. 20:17; again: Mt. 28:9–10; see Lk. 24:52).

(c) The element of witness or commitment to mission: on this is grounded the function of the Twelve, filled out each time with the local church's own theology. The principle of apostolic authority – the apostolicity of the Church – is clearly affirmed in the paramount manifestation of Christ to Peter and the Eleven (see Mt. 28:10; Jn. 20:17; in Lk. 24:8 and 24:10 the women on their own initiative report to the Eleven the manifestation of Christ to themselves. The principle

J.E.C.–M

of apostolic authority is already operative). It should be noted that initially the appearances are not reported with any apologetic purpose in view, as a kind of proof of Jesus' resurrection. What is at issue is simply the legitimation of the apostolic missionary mandate, not some confirmation of the resurrection's having taken place. That is why the apostolic 'creed' says nothing about the appearances of Jesus. The resurrection was believed in before there was any question of appearances (see later).

The element of confession (acknowledgement) enshrines the primary, initial experiences of the disciples, of which we are told only that Jesus, after his death, 'made himself seen'; in the element of mission the original experiences of the Twelve are not referred to; what is registered is the meaning, the point, of the Easter event as now understood by the growing Church in the light of its concrete practice and theological reflections. In other words, there are simply appearances; nowhere does the New Testament reproduce 'appearance sayings' of Jesus himself. Interest is drawn not to the primary origin of the community of Christ, but to the essential nature of the Church as grounded in the *kerygma* of the crucified One who has risen. From the differences in the gospel accounts emerge the structure and intention of what is signified by an appearance of Christ.

(Mt. 28:16–20) From this emerges (a) a solemn proclamation of Jesus as *kosmokrator*, ruler of the world, invested with complete power in heaven and on earth (28:18b); (b) a mandating and sending out of the Eleven by the risen One to all nations (28:19); the substance of this mission is to make all nations disciples of Jesus, which entails: baptizing them and instructing them in the words of Jesus (28:19); the reference here is to Christian instruction through baptism, within which the whole Jesus tradition is incorporated; according to Matthew a disciple is therefore someone who has been baptized and keeps Jesus' sayings; (c) lastly, a promise of Jesus' uninterrupted and helping presence and support for this apostolic task (28:20b).

This structure puts us on the track of two facts: on the one hand, to meet its present need the Church put sayings of the earthly Jesus into the mouth of the risen, manifesting Christ; on the other, what the Church as a community in fact does is presented as having its ground in the words of the manifesting Jesus. His solemn proclamation of himself is made up of pre-Matthean logia of Jesus (see Mt. 11:27, from the Q source; with Daniel 7:14 as background); again, the 'missionary' sayings are modelled on the great act of the earthly Jesus in sending out the disciples (cf. Mt. 28:19 with 10:5); in the same way the promise of

Jesus' permanent presence in the Church is based on Jesus-logia: 'Where two or three are gathered together in my name, there am I in the midst of them' (Mt. 18:20; see 1:23). In other words, three logia of Jesus have been combined, in the post-Easter situation, to form the content of what is said to be a Christ manifestation. In Mt. 10:5–6 and 15:24 (see 13:38) the mission was still restricted to Israel; in the account of the appearance it is a mission to the whole world. No longer therefore is the appearance presented as the source and ground of the eschatological community, but as the mandating of the Church for its mission (in respect, here, of the apostolic office). Apart from the affirmation of the gracious initiative of Jesus' self-disclosure after his death, the import of the appearance is as Matthew relates it, a Matthean *theologoumenon*, that is, a theological assertion of the universal and total authority of Christ, which is the basis of the universal mission of the Church to the whole world. The resurrection is the start and the abiding foundation of the Church's life. The Church is founded upon a salvific act of the risen Jesus, but not unrelated to what Jesus said and did in his life here on earth. Except for the fact of a gracious initiative of Jesus after his death nothing is said about the actual manifestation.

(Lk. 24:36–49) Here again we have the core of the apostolic *kerygma*, as formulated by Luke (on the basis of pre-Lucan traditions) in Acts 2:32; 3:15; 5:32; 10:41; 13:31. The pericope, though in a literary sense independent, is akin to Jn. 20:19–23, perhaps on the basis of a piece of tradition embracing the missionary mandate and the gift of the Holy Spirit. Typically Lucan is 24:44–49, where for the 'sending forth' is substituted a commissioning of Peter and the Eleven by the risen One as witnesses and guarantors of the apostolic belief in the resurrection, and where the promise of the gift of the Spirit stands in place of the actual gift. The sending out of the Twelve and the actual giving of the Spirit Luke associates with the event of Pentecost, while for him resurrection and ascension are separated by an interim period of forty days. Thus this Lucan theology entails changes in the substantive meaning of the appearances: the Easter appearance is the bridge between the finish of Jesus' life and task on earth and, via the ascension, the start of the pneumatic missionary task of the Church. The structure of the Christ manifestation in Luke, therefore, is as follows:

(a) First the apostolic *kerygma* is presented (24:44–46), the death and resurrection, but as we hear of them in holy Writ, that is, as they pertain to God's plan of salvation. On the basis of this death and resurrection in their context of salvation-history, the Church proclaims, in the power of Jesus' name, *metanoia* or repentance and the forgiveness of sins (the evident allusion here, as with Matthew, is to the Christian baptism of repentance; see also Jn. 20:23) for all peoples. Of the Twelve it is said: 'You are witnesses of these things' (24:46, 47a).

(b) Then follows, not 'Go, therefore' (as in Matthew), but 'Stay in Jerusalem': the sending forth itself is a gift at Pentecost ('until the Spirit comes', 24:49). The Lucan church has the risen Jesus stating definitively what God's saving plan with Jesus is: Jesus forms a nucleus of followers able during his absence from earth to testify 'to these things', that is, witness to Jesus' place in the divine saving dispensation.[78] By the risen One, now manifested, the Twelve (the Eleven, later supplemented by Matthias, Acts 1:16–26) are in the Lucan account appointed as pillars of the faith (only at Pentecost are they sent out on their mission). As in Acts 1:8, so in Lk. 24:48 the evangelist enunciates in his report of Jesus' appearance the Lucan notion of an apostle:

(c) 'But you shall receive power from the holy Spirit . . . to be my witnesses, starting from Jerusalem, throughout Judea and Samaria and to the end of the earth' (Acts 1:8). The pneumatic witness is the sign and token of the 'age of the Church' between ascension and Parousia, by virtue of the Pentecostal gift of the Spirit. Indeed it is clear from Acts 1:21–22 that according to Luke it is not enough to have been an eye-witness of Jesus' life on earth in order to be an apostle of Jesus Christ; it is also necessary to have been officially appointed a witness to Jesus' resurrection.[79] To be a witness to the resurrection is not being a witness to the mere event of the resurrection (which Luke is not speaking about), but to the resurrection as a salvific event in God's plan of salvation: that is, the Twelve have been appointed witnesses to the saving purposes of God in Jesus Christ.[80] And the mandate of the Twelve within the Church is then placed under the fulfilling of Scripture.

The core of the Lucan manifestation of Christ is thus: (a) the identification of Jesus of Nazareth with the Christ; in other words, the apostolic *kerygma*; (b) the divine legitimation and appointment of the apostles as guarantors of the apostolic faith; (c) the promise of the Spirit to come.

(Jn. 20:19–23) We find within the context of a distinctively Johannine theology the same structural elements; (a) here too, after the element of recognition (20:19–20), there follows (b) the sending out of the disciples:[81] on the basis of the Father's sending of Jesus (Johannine) Jesus now sends his disciples, and (c) to that end he gives them the Spirit (20:21–22); the official ministration of remitting sin (20:23) is mentioned specifically in this connection. In contrast to Mt. 18:18 and 16:19, 'binding and loosing' are here associated rather with Christian baptism (cf. Lk. 24:47). Here *metanoia* is accepting the Christian *kerygma*: turning to God in and through Jesus as the Christ (see Jn. 1:11), for the world's great sin is not 'believing' (Jn. 8:21, 24, 26; 15:22). Here the gift of the Spirit is bound up with the ministry of reconciliation (see also 2 Cor. 5:18). This gift had already been promised beforehand (Jn. 14:26 and 14:17; 15:26–27; 16:7–15). Thus John too fills out the appearance of Christ with a Johannine Christology and ecclesiology.

In the additional chapter, John 21, material from the Galilean tradition of Christ appearances has been incorporated – but accommodated to the spirit of the Johannine gospel, prompted by a special concern with Jesus' beloved disciple (Jn. 21:7; see Jn. 20:8; Jn. 21: 20–23).

(The appended conclusion: Mk. 16:9–20). (As we said earlier on, the original gospel of Mark contains no accounts of appearances.) Mark 16:8–11 has been added on the basis of Jn. 20:1–11, 18; Mk. 16:12–13 on that of Lk. 24:13–35; Mk. 16:14–18, that of Mt. 28:16–20, of Jn. 20:19–23 and especially of Lk. 24:36–49. But this combination has resulted from the Marcan conception of the way from unbelief to belief.[82] From Mark too is drawn the fact that the purpose of the sending forth by the risen Jesus is the preaching of the gospel: to spread the faith and to baptize (Mk. 16:16), and to do what Jesus did: heal the sick and drive out devils, 'while the Lord worked with them and confirmed the message by the signs that attended it' (Mk. 16:20). Here again the constant assistance of the Lord. Although this coda is composed of material from the other three evangelists, it has been edited into a single, coherent whole in the spirit of the Marcan gospel.

From the fourfold account – taken as a whole – of the official, apostolic 'manifestation of Christ' to the Eleven there emerges clearly enough the function of what is referred to as the 'appearing of the risen One': in the acknowledgement of Jesus as the risen Christ, the Church begins to take shape; it legitimates the apostolic mission to the world: to make all and sundry into disciples of Christ (Matthew), as serving the ends of reconciliation (Matthew, John), as proclamation of the gospel (later tailpiece to Mark); or it is the foundation of the apostolic faith (Luke). In all this Jesus himself (Matthew; the later conclusion to Mark) or the Holy Spirit (Luke and John) will assist the Twelve. The actual substance of the official manifestation has been inspired by the apostolic *kerygma* in its differing ecclesiological variants in the local congregations of the primitive Church. The Easter experience – Jesus is the Lord; or the experience of receiving the gift of the Spirit – is the ground of the Church and its mission. The gospels and Paul (1 Cor. 15: 3–8) clearly emphasize the collegiality of the apostolic witness to Christ, apparently under the direction[83] of Simon Peter (1 Cor. 15:3–5; Lk. 24: 34; see Mt. 28:16; Jn. 20:19ff).

Thus the manifestation itself is, as it were, an 'empty' vessel; but the appearing of the risen One is filled with the 'apostolic *kerygma*', which in that way is seen to be a pure disclosure on God's part, whereby the Twelve are consciously empowered to advance the cause of Jesus. The manifestation implies as its heart and centre a specific saving action of God in Christ, enabling the disciples to identify Jesus with the Christ, the Lord, the Son of God, and to know beyond doubt that they have been sent to proclaim this Christ to all the world as the crucified-and-risen One. The element of 'manifestation' points in a 'vertical' way to the apostolic *kerygma* and the praxis or actual conduct of the Church as being characterized by grace and revelation. In the verticality of the manifestation, as the ancient expression for an 'epiphany' or 'disclosure of God', is concentrated the grace, impacted with the saving events of history, of what has for years been occurring (horizontally) in the Matthean, Lucan and Johannine churches: the preaching of the gospel to Jew and pagan, Christian baptism and the ministry of reconciliation, in faith-inspired assurance that in all of this Jesus is at work. The activity of the heavenly Jesus in the Church is expressed in terms of epiphany. The matter or 'substance' of the manifestation is supplied out of the concrete life of the Church as the 'community of Christ'. Worship, adoration, is the answering response to the experience of an act of grace: they see Jesus and they worship him. Structurally, within the story, the 'appearance' is an extrapolation of the grace characterizing it: the saving activity of God in the Church *qua* community, from its very beginnings to what are already the second and third Christian generations, can thus be articulated in the story from the standpoint of faith. Even when after the appearance of Jesus to Peter, Luke, with a little touch of his own, says: 'He has indeed risen' (Lk. 24:34) the other disciples are doubtful; that is, any Christological confession must also be experienced personally by the others, as a sheer 'fact of grace'.

In the appearance narratives, therefore, the doubt itself fulfils a very specific function: Mt. 28:17; Lk. 24:11, 37–41; Jn. 20:9, 25, 27; it is actually not forgotten in the later canonical end to Mark: Mk. 16:11, 13–14. Some have wrongly called this doubt a secondary element.

Matthew, who does not mention the separate appearance to Peter, does however accommodate elsewhere the saying about Peter, the rock.[84] Hence the uneven character of Mt. 28:16: 'Now the eleven disciples went to Galilee, to the mountain to which Jesus had directed them. And when they saw him they fell down and worshipped him; but some doubted.' This doubt (after they have first worshipped him!) may be a vestige of the doubt felt by the disciples after the first appearance to Peter (Lk. 24:34 and 24:38). Nowhere else is there any reference to a doubt after the appearance to the Twelve. The doubt itself is mentioned in too many traditions for us to call it secondary. There are of course theological differences. John does not have the disciples doubting, but 'thematizes' this doubt in his separate story about an appearance to Thomas (Jn. 20:24–29).[85] Again, the nature of the doubt in Matthew is not the same as in the accounts of appearances peculiar to Luke and John 20 and 21. For Matthew the doubt is a question of conversion, that is, whether one is going to acknowledge (the already recognized) Jesus as the risen Christ: the doubt has to do with Jesus 'being viewed Christologically'. In the case of Luke and John on the other hand, whose ideas, at any rate as represented, are affected by features of the 'rapture' theory of the *theios anèr* model, we have doubt on the Greek pattern – doubt, that is, regarding manifestations of one who has been 'snatched away'. That is to say, the doubt here is not as to whether he is the Christ, but whether the one who appears is indeed Jesus of Nazareth. At first they think they are seeing 'a spirit', a spectre or 'shade', not the real Jesus of Nazareth. There fits perfectly into the same 'rapture' model of appearances the detail: 'see – or touch [as to Thomas in John] – my hands and my feet. It is I myself' (Lk. 24:38–39). For Hellenists it is first necessary to establish the presence of the real Jesus (the 'it is I' here in this model has no intended Christological implication). In a Hellenistic context this is given further point by 'the eating of fish' (Lk. 24:40–43). It is this doubt as to the nature of what is being seen that gives rise to the appearance story, the report (neither Paul nor Matthew having accounts of the appearance as such). Only when Jesus has been identified as Jesus can there be any question of 'seeing Christologically', of an acknowledgement of Jesus as the living Christ. The important thing here is of course that – albeit via the model of Hellenistic manifestations – it should fasten attention in a special way on the absolute identity between Jesus of Nazareth and the crucified-and-risen One or the kerygmatic Christ.

Then again, the stress on the disciples' doubting is meant to give extra-special emphasis to the nature of the Christological affirmation of belief as characterized by a divine act of grace. The apostles begin by reacting with hostility to the appearances reported by the women and the Emmaus disciples: they do not believe it. Mark, who makes the disciples' taking offence at the arrest and death of Jesus assume the form of a flight (Mk. 14:50; see 14:40), also has the women fleeing from the tomb without saying a word to anyone about what had happened (Mk. 16:8b). Throughout his gospel what he emphasizes is a human inability to understand the Jesus mystery. Beneath the cross he has a Gentile being the first to acknowledge Jesus as 'son of God' (15:39), that is, the gospel is for all nations (Mk. 13:10; 14:9); Jesus is not only the messiah of the Jews. In the 'women's remaining silent' Mark may be emphasizing the independence of the 'apostolic tradition' *vis-à-vis* the Jerusalem tomb traditions.

The element of acknowledgement – 'seeing Jesus *Christologically*' – finds its most powerful expression in Jn. 20:24–31; after his doubting, Thomas changes his mind and says: 'My Lord and my God' (20:28). *Qua* 'recognitive appearance' a manifestation of Christ is the seeing or recognizing of Jesus as the eschatological presence of God among us.[86]

We may say in conclusion: an analysis, based on systematic study of the literature, of the stories about Jesus 'making himself seen' after his death shows that in them there is enunciated the Christological identification of Jesus of Nazareth, experienced as a sheer act of grace on God's part and as ground and source of the Church's mission. As a primary analysis this must suffice.

C. 'ON THE ROAD PAUL SAW THE LORD' (ACTS 9:27):
   THE DAMASCUS NARRATIVE (ACTS 9; 22, 26)

*Literature* (besides that already mentioned). J. Blank, *Paulus und Jesus*, Münster 1968; Chr. Burchard, *Der dreizehnte Zeuge*, Göttingen 1970; H. Conzelmann, 'Zur Analyse der Bekenntnisformel 1 Cor. 15:3–5', EvTh 25 (1965), 1–11; R. Fuller, *The Formation of the Resurrection Narratives*, New York 1971; B. Gerhardson, *Memory and Manuscript* (ASNT, n. 22), Lund 1961; L. Goppelt, 'Tradition bei Paulus', KuD 4 (1958), 213–33; E. Hirsch, 'Die drei Berichte der Apostelgeschichte und die Bekehrung des Paulus', ZNW 28 (1929), 305–12; H. Kasting, *Die Anfänge der urchristlichen Mission* (Beih, EvTh, n. 55), Munich 1969; G. Lohfink, *La Conversion de saint Paul*, Paris 1967, and: 'Eine alttesta-mentliche Darstellungsform für Gotteserscheinungen in den Damaskusberichten (Apg. 9; 22; 26)', BZ 9 (1965), 246–57; D. Lührmann, *Das Offenbarungsverständnis bei Paulus und in paulinischer Gemeinden*, Neukirchen-Vluyn 1965; D. M. Stanley, 'Paul's Conversion in Acts: Why the three accounts?', CBQ 15 (1953), 315–38; H. Windisch, 'Der Christusepiphanie vor Damaskus (Acts 9; 22 und 26) und ihre religionsgeschichtliche Parallellen', ZNW 31 (1932), 1–23.

It is often said that Paul bases his apostolate on the fact that Jesus, the One crucified and risen, made himself seen also to him. With this in view it is usual to refer to 1 Cor. 9:1; 15:8–11; Gal. 1:15–17: 'last of all, as to one untimely born (*ektrôma*), he appeared also to me'.[87] Before we examine Luke's view of the Damascus affair, therefore, it would be a good thing first to state more precisely how Paul himself regarded it. Earlier on we have provided an interpretation of 1 Cor. 15:3–11; and there this passage turned out not to be set in a context of apostolic legitimation based on appearances of Jesus. The same applies to 1 Cor. 9:1: 'Am I not free? Am I not an apostle? Have I not seen Jesus our Lord? Are you not my workmanship in the Lord?' Evidently four relatively separate questions, though the second is usually taken as providing a basis for the third. On what grounds, however – if we read the passage, not with the gospels as background but in its Pauline context? The typical epiphany-term *ôphthè* – (which is non-Pauline, anyway) – is absent here (what we do have is *heoraka*, I have seen). After all, it is not certain that Gal. 1:15–17: 'when he was pleased to reveal his son to me' (reading here: 'to reveal his son *in* me') bears directly on Paul's Damascus experience. In other words, nowhere in Paul's own writings does it appear that he grounds his apostolate on his Damascus experience as a 'seeing of Jesus'. He is 'by calling an apostle' (Rom. 1:1), 'set apart and called from the womb' (Gal. 1:15) and eventually, with the Church's legitimation through the laying on of hands, sent forth by the leaders of the congregation at Antioch (Acts 13:1–3). No doubt Paul sees his conversion to Jesus Christ directly as a divine way of bringing the gospel 'to all nations' (Gal. 1:13–16); but there is no mention in this context of a 'manifestation'; and though he did not consult with those who had been apostles longer than he (Gal. 1:16–17), nevertheless he was initiated into Christianity by Christians at Antioch. This he feels to have been 'a gracious favour of the Lord'; and he sees in it his independence *vis-à-vis* the other apostles at Jerusalem, who had not laid hands upon him, although he preaches the same belief in the crucified-and-risen One (1 Cor. 15:11). 'To have seen Jesus Christ' (1 Cor. 9:1) implies the same faith as that proclaimed by all the apostles; but it can hardly be said that at any rate for Paul (as distinct from Luke) the 'Jesus appearance' to Paul is the actual mandate for his apostolate. It does signify the identity of belief prevailing among all the apostles.

But how does Luke interpret the tradition of Paul's Damascus experience? In the Acts, Luke recounts this all of three times: in Acts 9, Acts 22 and 26. Structural analysis of this, based on the principles of 'the semeiotics of narration'[88] allows us to settle the import of what Luke intended by a 'Christ appearance' more exactly than has until now been the case. For according to the rules of the systematic study of literature, a text will contain linguistic signals that show us how the passage itself requires to be understood. To this end the three Damascus stories are all the more important because the differences, transformations and shifts between them show how 'manipulable' is the thing called 'an appearance of Jesus'. The second and third accounts are in point of fact a way of discussing, and thus interpreting, the first Damascus narrative (in other words, meta-language). Thus the Scriptural text is self-interpreting. That is what serves to reveal the 'matrix' of the vision. Actually, Acts 22 and 26 do not refer to the Damascus event itself but – in the context supplied by the Acts – to the Damascus story already related there (Acts 9).

The story of Paul in the Acts is about the great mission among the Gentiles, achieved by Paul but needing to be interpreted as a glorious manifestation of God's mercy, graciousness and absolute initiative. One notices that thanks to the vision of Ananias (Acts 9:15) – which in the story as recounted is not told to Paul – the reader knows from the start that the first story (of Paul's conversion to Christianity, Acts 9) already contains the germ of what is then fully disclosed in Acts 26: there the 'conversion-vision' makes way for a 'missionary' one. Between the three Damascus stories the text is filled out, as it proceeds, with Paul's constant changes of residence: he travels, is for ever 'on the road'. Thus in a topographical sense we see the bare vision of Ananias being filled in with a dynamic and local content. The journeying is determined partly by Paul's opponents: the Jews, who turn the former persecutor, Saul, into the persecuted Paul, and want to kill him. In making these journeys Paul is also fleeing from town to town; but because of that very circumstance 'his gospel' gets carried here, there and everywhere. Conflict has an essential role to play in the process: of this too Ananias says nothing (in the narrative) to Paul; it becomes clear to him only in the course of his concrete experience of his new way of life. Apostolic journeys (escapes), persecution and imprisonment form in the structure of the narrative a nexus of events into which the triple account of the Damascus vision is incorporated. One characteristic feature is that the three accounts have a different audience on each occasion. Thus the report itself becomes the Pauline gospel in action, it is the conveying of the Message to yet another group of people. It presents in diagram,[89] as it were, the unlimited character of the grace implied in the 'Gentile mission'.

To make the aim of the following analysis more intelligible, it would seem right for me to say at the outset that in view of its structure the threefold account of the 'manifestation' is meant to express in words the character, as an act of grace, of what unfolds in Paul's life as historical events. God's salvific activity in Paul's undertakings is represented – in advance (Acts 9), in middle course (Acts 22) and towards the end of Paul's life history (Acts 26) – in a purely 'vertical scheme' (a vision). But as placed in a vertical dimension ('grace *per se*') the substance of the manifestation is remarkably 'vacant' or at least extremely meagre; it has to be filled in from the subsequent account of the concrete, historical (horizontal) series of events in the life of Paul itself. From the first report of a manifestation (Acts 9) and the transformations, omissions and condensations provided in Acts 22 and 26, it is clear that the account as a whole is meant to show that we, the readers, are to interpret 'the vision' as a way of expressing the δεῖ of salvation-history, the 'divine must' or scheme of salvation. It is about God's purposive graciousness, manifested in Paul's concrete, apostolic life, not beside or above and beyond it. Paul's life as it actually was, his journeyings and conflicts, must be understood in the process of their occurrence as a divine epiphany through Jesus Christ, as the disclosure of God's saving plan which, as experienced and articulated 'in faith', is as it were 'formalized' (apocalyptically and) vertically in an appearance-vision. In the account of that vision grace, God's initiative in all this, is so to speak extrapolated, represented within the model of an (isolated) vertical event. The extrapolation is evident from the 'vacant' character of the manifestation to the extent that it is not 'filled in' elsewhere (Paul's own life). (The same applied to the attempts in Matthew, Luke and John to fill in the Christ manifestation.)

The three accounts are laid out in parallel columns at this juncture (see pages 364–67), so that the adjustments, omissions and concentrations may become clear.

| Story I: Acts 9 | | Story II: Acts 22 | | Story III: Acts 26 | |
|---|---|---|---|---|---|
| 1–2 | Paul: persecutor of the disciples of 'the Way' | | Paul's Hebraic speech at Jerusalem | | Paul's speech to Agrippa I, a strict Pharisee, persecuted the name of J. of Naz. |
| 3–8 | *Paul's vision –* On the way to Damascus | 1–5 | I, a strict Jew, persecuted 'the Way' | 9–11 | |
| 3 | – light from heaven on Paul | 6–10 | Close to Damascus – at noon | 12–18 | Towards Damascus |
| | | 6 | – a fierce light from heaven upon me | 13 | – at midday – light from heaven, fiercer than sun, – on me and my companions |
| 7 | – He falls down – A voice: 'Saul, why do you persecute Me?' – Companions: hear voice, see nobody | 7 | – I fall, hear a voice: 'Saul, why do you persecute Me?' | 14 | – We fell to the ground. A voice in Hebrew said to me: 'Saul, why do you persecute Me? It hurts you to kick against the goads' |
| | | 8 | – 'Who are you, Lord?' – 'J. of Naz., whom you are persecuting.' | 15 | – 'Who are you, Lord?' – 'Jesus, whom you are persecuting' |
| | | 9 | Companions: hear no voice and yet do see the light | | |
| | | 10 | Paul: 'What must I do, Lord?' 'Rise; go into Damascus; there they will tell you everything you have to do' | 16 | 'But rise . . . For I appeared to you for this purpose: |
| 6 | 'Rise and enter the city, and you will be told what you are to do.' | | | | |
| 8 | Paul is blind(ed); they have to bring him into the town | 11 | I could not see because of the brightness of that light; was led into the town | | |
| 9 | For three days Paul neither eats nor drinks | | | | |

| | | | |
|---|---|---|---|
| 10–16 | *Vision of Ananias:* | | |
| 10 | Jesus appears to a disciple called Ananias, at Damascus: 'Ananias!' – 'Lord!' 'Go to the street called Straight and enquire in the house of Judas for Saul of Tarsus; for behold, he is praying.' | | |
| | *Vision of Paul:* | | |
| 12 | (Simultaneously with vv. 10–16). While praying Paul has a vision: sees a man enter and lay hands on him to restore his sight. | 12 | A certain Ananias, a man law-abiding and of good reputation |
| 13–14 | – Ananias protests: . . . that persecutor of Christians! | | |
| 15 | The Lord gave an order: 'Go, for this man is a chosen instrument of mine to carry [confess] my Name before the Gentiles and kings and the sons of Israel. I will show him how much he must suffer for the sake of my Name.' | | |
| 17 | So Ananias made his way to that house, laid hands on Paul, saying: 'Brother Saul, the Lord Jesus who appeared to you on the way here has | 12 | came to visit me, and said: |

| Story I: Acts 9 (continued) | Story II: Acts 22 (continued) | Story III: Acts 26 (continued) |
| --- | --- | --- |
| sent me that you may see again and be filled with the Holy Spirit.' | 'Brother Saul, receive your sight.' | |
| 18 Immediately the scales fell from his eyes; he saw again, | 14 Immediately, I saw him standing there. Ananias says to Paul 'The God of our Fathers appointed you to know his will, to see the Just One and to hear a voice from his mouth; for | |
| | 15 you will be a witness for him to all men of what you have seen and heard.' | |
| and he was at once baptized | 16 – 'Now why do you wait? Rise and be baptized, and wash away your sins, calling on his Name.' | 16 (substance of Jesus' words in Damascus vision) 'I have appeared to you for this purpose, to appoint you to serve and bear witness to the things in which you have seen me and to those in which I will appear to you, deliver- |
| 19 He ate. | (Paul at Jerusalem) praying in the Temple, a trance: 18 'I saw him there,' he said (to me): 'Make haste and get quickly out of Jerusalem, because they will not accept your testimony about me.' | |

| | | |
|---|---|---|
| 17 | ing you from the people and from the Gentiles – to whom I send you to open their eyes, | |
| 18 | (a) that they may turn from darkness to light and from the power of Satan to God, and (b) that they may receive forgiveness of sins and a place among those who are sanctified by faith in me' – (the sermon proceeds) | |
| 23 | 'The Christ must suffer, so that, by being the first to rise from the dead, he would proclaim Light both to the people and to the Gentiles.' | |

| | | |
|---|---|---|
| 19–20 | Paul protests: condones the behaviour of people he had after all persecuted. | |
| 21 | Jesus says: 'Depart; for I will send you far away to the Gentiles.' | |

In an initial sermon by Paul at Damascus:

| | |
|---|---|
| 20 | 'Jesus is the Son of God' |
| 22 | 'Jesus is the Christ' |

Barnabas' report delivered at Jerusalem:

| | |
|---|---|
| 27 | 'On the road Paul had seen the Lord' |

*Between chs 22 and 26*

23:11: 'The following night the Lord stood by him and said: Take courage, for as you have testified about me at Jerusalem, so you must bear witness also at Rome.'

(a) Acts 9: the conversion vision

In this first story three aspects stand out:

(1) The meaning of the vision is not disclosed to Paul. The vision – under the already traditional Hellenistic-Jewish commonplace of 'experience of light' as a conversion-model – is so far 'empty' even for Paul himself: Saul must set out for Damascus without knowing why; there he will meet with somebody. That is all (9:6). But Ananias too has a vision relating to Paul. At first his position in the narrative is that of opponent to Saul the persecutor (9:13–14); and this gives added impact to Paul's conversion and calling as a 'work of grace'. God cuts short Ananias' resistance with a command: 'Go, for this man is a chosen instrument of mine to carry my Name before the Gentiles and kings and the sons of Israel; for I will show him how much he must suffer for the sake of my Name' (9:15–16). That is what Ananias does not impart to Paul; it is meant for the reader; at this point in the story Paul is not himself aware of the significance of his future career as a Christian. Yet the fact that Paul allows the whole chain of events to take him over and does not set himself against it means that he accepts what is happening. And so he fasts for three days and is contrite.

(2) Another peculiar feature of the story is the simultaneous vision of Ananias and of Paul (9:10–11 and 9:12): as Ananias is being instructed to go to Paul in the street called Straight at Damascus, the Lord says: 'for behold, he is praying' (9:11b); at the same moment Paul at prayer sees in a vision 'a man named Ananias come in and lay his hands on him so that he might regain his sight' (9:12). This is then repeated (9:17–18). What Paul actually experiences is, because of its character as grace, extrapolated in advance as a 'vision'. Through the synchronous nature of the two visions (a Graeco-Jewish traditional model), arranged by the Lord, we are given to understand that the (presumably historical) occurrence of a meeting between Paul and Ananias[90] is an aspect of salvation-history. Thus the structure itself reveals the importance of what took place between men at the time of Paul's conversion.

(3) In the vision Jesus addresses Paul personally: 'Saul, why do you persecute me?' (9:4), as Jesus had said 'Mary', and she, 'Rabboni'. But here things are different: Jesus presents himself as one whom Paul certainly does know, that is, as the Jesus persecuted by Paul. The real Jesus, however, is unknown to Paul, who for that reason asks: 'Who are you, Lord?' (9:5). Paul does not yet know Jesus as the Christ. So Jesus Christ holds the initiative in Paul's conversion, that is, in his

recognition of Jesus as the Son and the Christ, as Paul will immediately afterwards be proclaiming (9:20 and 9:22).

The central core of the conversion vision is 'thin', therefore, but also full of light-symbols: light, blinding. The blinding light which completely surrounds Paul tells him at once that he has been blinded in his persecution of Jesus. He must be contrite, that is, 'fast for three days' (9:9). In Old and New Testaments 'the third day' (see later on) is always the decisive day of the fundamental change and the crucial event;[91] on the third day Paul's decision 'to be converted 'is definitive. Ananias' part in this process is to cure Paul of his blindness. He goes to Paul to restore his sight and to impart the Spirit (9:17-18). With the laying on of hands 'his sight was restored and he was at once baptized. And he ate' (9:18-19). His state of blindness removed, he sees Jesus as the Christ (Christological confession) and then there is no further obstacle to his being baptized (see Acts 8:35-36). Paul turns to Jesus as the Christ; and this is a pure act of grace on God's part. Acts 9 is a conversion vision, not a missionary one. 'Carrying my Name before the world' (*bastadzein*) means not 'to carry forth' but to conduct or carry oneself as one who confesses Christ, even in suffering;[92] before Gentiles, kings (see Acts 4:27) and Jews (Acts 21) Paul is to confess Christ. According to the vision of Ananias not disclosed to Paul, Paul is 'a vessel of election' (chosen instrument), that is, elected, called to suffer. Suffering, according to Luke, is an aspect of grace (Acts 5:41; see Lk. 8:13; Acts 14:22): that is, Paul the persecutor now becomes the persecuted confessor of Christ.

Acts 9, as an account of conversion, derives from a local Damascus tradition; because of this attachment to a common source this first part of the Damascus story remains more or less unaltered in the three accounts. In itself this first manifestation story has nothing to do with 'Easter appearances' like those to Peter and the Eleven. Paul, who at first rejects (persecutes) Jesus, now accepts him. In Jerusalem Barnabas speaks up for Paul: 'He declared to them how on the road he [Paul] had seen the Lord, who spoke to him' (9:27). Luke is intimating here that the Damascus vision was indeed 'a seeing of the Lord' – even though Paul did not *see* Jesus, had only heard a voice. Thus in a Christ manifestation it is not necessary for one actually to see Jesus, in a visual sense.

(b) Acts 22

After Acts 9 Paul disappears for a while from Luke's narrative; but from chapter 13 he is the principal figure in the Acts. In the report he gives of these events Luke proceeds to fill out the vision of Ananias (unknown to Paul), who had already seen Paul as the persecuted confessor of Christ and as one destined to undergo much suffering (9:16). After his first bout of activity (9:20–31), in which Paul 'proclaims Jesus', that is (see Acts 17:3; 18:5, 28), proclaims him as the Christ (9:22) – or Jesus in his eschatological function – and as 'Son of God' (9:20), that is, as the risen One who sits at God's right hand (see Lk. 22:69), certain Jews are already plotting to kill him (Acts 9:23). The alternation is obvious: the persecutor, Saul, is now the persecuted Paul. When he comes to Jerusalem as a convert, even the Jewish Christians do not trust him (9:26). The 'Hellenists' in particular want to murder him (9:29).

Between the first and second Damascus stories Paul is on tour, preaching as he goes (Acts 13 to 21). The leading group in the Antiochene church (13:1) decide to commission Barnabas and Paul by the laying on of hands, with prayer and fasting, and to send them out (13:3). This dispatch, authorized by the Church, of Barnabas and Paul as 'apostles', in the sense here of 'missionaries', is also a special salvific action on God's part; from this point on, a divine scheme begins to be implemented; for with that in view Luke again introduces the activity of the Holy Spirit 'in a vertical dimension'. 'Set apart for me Barnabas and Saul for the work to which I have called them' (13:2). This 'vertical' factor was already accommodated in the Church's practice of commissioning by the liturgical laying on of hands; but Luke again gives extra point in a vision to the reason for this laying on of hands in its context of salvation-history. It marks the beginning of Paul's journey along the path of suffering as one who confesses Christ, but not yet the start of his mission to the Gentiles. On the contrary, according to Luke, Paul goes about everywhere preaching salvation 'in the synagogues of the Jews' (13:5; 13:14; 17:1–2; 17:10). He himself says: 'Brethren, sons of the family of Abraham, and those among you who fear God [God-fearers=proselytes of Judaism, see 9:43], to us has been sent the message of this salvation' (13:26). 'For those who live in Jerusalem and their rulers . . . did not recognize Him' (13:27). Nevertheless, opposition to Paul intensifies (13:45; 13:50; 14:2–5; 14:19; 17:13; 18:6ff, 21, 22). It is precisely this opposition that in Luke's view impels Paul towards the Gentiles. That this was a gradual process is clear from three elements in Luke's account: (1) In 13:46 Luke has Paul saying to the Jews: 'It was necessary that the Word of God should be spoken first to you. But since you thrust it from you . . . we turn from now on to the Gentiles.' That 'first to the Jews' tallies with Paul's own theology (Rom. 1:16–17; Rom. 9 to 11; see Rom. 11:26). From this moment on, allusion in the Acts to 'the conversion of the Gentiles' becomes more and more frequent (13:47, 48); and in his report of his first missionary journey, made to the church at Antioch, Paul is already talking with enthusiasm (Acts 14:27) about 'how he had opened a door of faith to the Gentiles'; (2) Much later, while preaching at Corinth, Paul meets again with opposition from Jews, and following on that again says: 'I am innocent. From now on I will go to the Gentiles' (18:6); (3) We hear this scheme for a third time in 28:23–28, near the close of the Acts: 'The Gentiles, they will listen.' Thus the repetition discloses an exemplary pattern: according to Luke Paul begins each time with his message first to the Jews, but because of their opposition he is forced to go to the Gentiles. Yet in 21:19 his apostolate is described as 'Paul's ministry among the Gentiles'. Luke, then, sees the Pauline gospel as directed from the very start 'to all men' (17:30), all nations, that is, to Jew as well as to Gentile, not simply to Gentile. Should the Jews – in this case those of the Diaspora – not accept it, there remain, alas, only the Gentiles. According to Luke, Paul is the 'apostle of the Gentiles' only because of the Jews' self-exclusion (whereas Paul, with for his part less than complete historical accuracy – see further on – sees his mission from the outset as a specific task among the Gentiles). Since Paul spent about fourteen years working at the instance of the Antiochene church in the Roman province of Syria and Cilicia (with Cyprus and the border territories of Asia Minor), it is likely, as a matter of history, that Paul probably did not initially envisage his worldwide apostolic mission. The Council of Jerusalem's decree and the dispute at Antioch (the setting apart of Barnabas) were the occasion for it: 'We should go to the Gentiles and they to the circumcised' (Gal. 2:9). Hence Paul's consciousness of being 'an apostle to the Gentiles' (Rom. 11:13).

In the middle of this narrative comes chapter 22, in which Paul himself now relates his Damascus experience, at any rate in Luke's account.

Paul is arrested in Jerusalem (21:27–38) and the commandant of the barracks is drawn into it. Accused of making propaganda against the nation, the Law and the Temple and of taking Gentiles into the Temple (21:28), from the Temple steps Paul addresses the inhabitants of

Jerusalem in a sort of speech for the defence, in which he emphasizes that he is a Jewish devotee (of God and the Law), admittedly born in Tarsus but nurtured from boyhood 'here in Jerusalem'. Luke has Paul speaking in Hebrew (21:40 and 22:2). Now (although himself formulating this second story) Luke can have Paul in person recounting his Damascus vision, for meanwhile it has already been 'filled in' with the events of Paul's own career. In view of Paul's own experiences Ananias' vision is no longer necessary; as a result of his own experiences Paul is now fully cognizant of God's purposes with himself, as a persecuted, suffering confessor of Christ. This part of the vision (from Acts 9) drops out, therefore.

The first part of the vision remains more or less unchanged. Jesus is now referred to as 'the Nazarene', that is, the suffering and crucified One. The cure takes place without mention of the laying on of hands; Ananias now acts on his own responsibility, he explains what is going on (22:14). Paul himself has become more active in the proceedings: 'What shall I do, Lord?' (22:10). He was on his way to Damascus, persecuting the notorious Greek-speaking Jewish Christians on the strength of his strict notions of the Law, which from the Pharisaic viewpoint included not only the Decalogue but the 'laws of the forefathers' (22:3-5). As after his conversion Paul found himself up against the Hebrew-speaking Jews in particular, he addressed the people in Hebrew. The 'Jewish (Hebrew) – Gentile (Greek)' contrast is in view here. In lieu of the missing Ananias vision (from Acts 9) Paul now learns from Ananias (no longer: that he has come in Jesus' name to cure him of his 'blindness'; but) that he has been chosen 'to see the Just One and to hear a voice from his mouth'; he is to witness to what he has seen and heard (22:14-15). The 'Just One' is the Lord (Acts 22: 13-14 with 9:17), the exalted 'suffering and crucified just one'. The seeing and hearing are the ground of his valid testimony concerning Jesus to all people, Jews and Gentiles. The seeing relates to the actual Damascus vision, in 22:6-8; and 'hearing a voice from his mouth' (22:14) refers to the voice in 22:17: what we have here is an interpretation of the Damascus experience as such (not a 'seeing of Jesus' which is to occur in a vision later on). This interpretation goes beyond both 22:6-11 and 9:3-9. In typically Lucan terms regarding the apostolate (see Acts 1:21-22) it is the definition of an apostle in the strict sense that is suggested here. The point and purpose of the manifestation vision are already inflected: Paul's *de facto* apostolic ministry – substantially in the sense of the apostolate of the Twelve – is now (because the first account of the vision has acquired a different function) seen as a gift, commission and salvific dispensation of God in Christ; it is not a self-appointed, 'private' enterprise. Here the Damascus vision becomes the divine, gracious legitimation and ground of Paul's own apostolate to all people, Jew and Gentile. The actual historical state of affairs, therefore, through the importation into the story of the vertical but transformed 'vision dimension', is envisaged in its character of a divine ordering and salvific initiative on God's part. Ananias uses the technical Lucan term for 'apostolic election': *pro-echeirisato se*, God 'has appointed you to . . .'. Yet the narrative still ends with Paul's baptism. Structurally, this is important. In this second account the light-element is reinforced: 'a fierce light from heaven' (22:6), it is also 'about noon' (22:6); Paul's companions do not hear the voice this time, but now they too see the light (22:9). Then again, we are not told that Paul was blind for three days, only: 'I could not see because of the brightness of that light' (22:11). The emphatically spiritual meaning of his blindness in the first story (conversion vision) – his being blind *vis-à-vis* Jesus – now becomes a physical privation, while the spiritual meaning of light and illumination is deepened. In other words it is still a conversion vision, but one used to provide a ground for Paul's apostolic mission to all peoples; it is a vision recounted by someone who has come to experience Jesus as 'the light of the Gentiles'. 'Light of Israel and of the Gentiles' is a technical term taken from Hellenistic-Jewish accounts of Gentile conversion to Judaism. The Law is indeed a 'light of the world'.[93] Paul, who sees the Law as replaced by Christ, now encounters Jesus the Christ as Light of Israel and of Gentiles. In Luke's time (see Lk. 2:32; Acts 13:47; see also Jn. 1:9; 3:19–21; 8:12; Mt. 4:14ff) Jesus (and the apostles) are described as the light of the Gentiles (with reference to Isa. 49:6).[94] 'Therefore we turn from now on to the Gentiles. For so the Lord has commanded us, saying: "I have set you to be a light for the Gentiles" ' – thus Luke, in Acts 13:46–47. This now has its consequences for the second presentation of the Damascus vision. By way of the shifting significance of the light-element, in Acts 22 Luke has already linked up the 'conversion vision' (Acts 9) with the 'missionary vision' or call to be an apostle (Acts 26); Acts 22 marks the transition between the two.

(c) Acts 26

Before moving on to the third account of the Damascus event in Acts 26, Luke has Jesus appearing to Paul on two occasions – but then in a quite different sense: namely, in a 'rapture' or a 'being carried away in the spirit' (which implies something entirely different from the *óphthè* of the gospel) (Jesus makes himself seen, discloses himself). In the same address to the people of Jerusalem Paul says: 'When I had returned to Jerusalem and was praying in the Temple, I fell into a trance and saw him saying to me: "Make haste and get quickly out of Jerusalem, because they will not accept your testimony about me"' (22:17–18). But now Paul appears in an opposing role; for he finds the mistrust felt for himself as the one-time persecutor understandable (22:19–20). Luke is saying that Paul's decision to stay away from Jerusalem was not a high-handed or anti-Jewish resolution on his part, but was divinely legitimated; God's salvific ordering of affairs (hence the vision) is operative in this; for there follows at once the command of Christ: 'Depart; for I will send you far away to the Gentiles' (22:21). Paul must go to the non-Jews. This is a new element; so far Paul has been preaching among Jews and non-Jews, to all men. This vision adumbrates Paul's great missionary journeys; the Gentiles converted up to then had apparently been proselytes within Judaism. There must of course be a tradition lying behind 22:17–21, since Luke would certainly not invent so substantial a manifestation.[95]

In Acts 23:11 there is yet another report of a 'Jesus vision'. Paul, arrested in Jerusalem, has won his case in the Sanhedrin by playing off Pharisees and Sadducees against each other on the issue of the resurrection; but in the barracks' prison he is presented during the night with a manifestation: 'The Lord stood by him and said: "Take courage, for as you have testified about me at Jerusalem, so you must bear witness also at Rome"' (23:11). As a prisoner, but also a Roman citizen, Paul will indeed lodge an appeal with the emperor at Rome (25:11b). Had he not done so, Luke tells us, he would have been released: 'This man could have been set free if he had not appealed to Caesar' (26:32), says King Agrippa II to the governor, Festus. Luke evidently wants to emphasize that this decision was none of Paul's doing but that he was destined to proclaim the gospel even in Rome, in accordance with God's scheme of salvation. (The Acts concludes with Paul actually preaching in Rome.) The tradition of this Pauline vision, analogous with a Scriptural proof, is again meant to underline the character of a historical event as belonging to 'salvation-history'.

Then, for a third time, comes the Damascus story (Acts 26). Paul is being kept prisoner at Caesarea. King Agrippa and the governor, Festus, interest themselves in his case; so that Paul has an opportunity to make Ananias' vision (9:15) come true: the gospel is brought before 'kings'. The third story is cast in the form of a 'speech by Paul addressed to King Agrippa'. The Damascus story is this time filled out with the whole life of Paul (Acts 13 to 26). The conversion vision fades completely into the background; and Paul's baptism is not even mentioned. The conversion is reduced to what is a constant factor in the three stories: 'Saul, why do you persecute me?' To that is appended an adage: 'It hurts you to kick against the goads' (26:14-15). In this account the Jesus-persecutor, Paul, is called through the vision of Christ to become Christ's apostle to the Gentiles. Ananias vanishes completely from the story; in the end it ceases to be about Paul's conversion. His baptism drops out of the story; but in its place there has come the 'baptism of the Gentiles', although this is only suggested by a further intensification of the light-element: 'a light from heaven, brighter than the sun', 'at midday' (26:13), it shines not only around Paul but around all his companions; this time they all prostrate themselves (26:14); but Paul alone hears a voice speaking to him 'in the Hebrew language' (26:14). Now what this Hebrew-speaking voice says is important structurally; for it is nothing less than Paul's 'gospel for the non-Hebrews', the Gentiles. The manifesting Jesus now himself declares to what purpose 'he has made himself seen'; here at last appears the Easter term *ôphthè*. Nor in this third story is anything more said about Paul's being blind or blinded, as in 9:17, 27 and 22:14. Jesus appears to Paul 'for this purpose, to appoint you to serve and bear witness to the things in which you have seen me and to those in which I will appear to you' (26:16). The 'will appear' is a reference to the Jesus visions of 22:17-18 and 23:11 (Paul in his letters says nothing about them himself). Being appointed *hupèretès* (a servant) and *martur* (a witness) no longer refers to a conversion vision but to one containing a 'call'. By using these technical terms Luke is suggesting the notion of the Twelve, *qua* apostles, which is characteristically his own (see Lk. 1:2: eye-witnesses and ministers of the word) – a company, however, to which Paul does not belong. Acts 26:16b expresses the core of the Lucan idea: by virtue of being elected by the risen One himself, Paul, like the Twelve, acquires a mission of his own (Lk. 24:48; Acts 1:8, 22; 2:32; 3:15; 5:32; 10:39, 41; 13:31; 22:15; 26:16). The new fellowship with Jesus from his baptism to his ascension (Acts 1:21-22) is not sufficient; for the authentic apostolate a special election by the risen One is needed (a vision in which the call and the missionary mandate are given); being a witness to the risen One is the constitutive element of Luke's notion of an apostle. Thus Paul has what is essential for an apostle, without however belonging to the 'body corporate' of the Twelve.

Christ has 'removed' Paul, that is, has delivered him from dangers posed by Jew and Gentile (26:17);[96] this refers to Christ's support and succour in all Paul's activity throughout his life. According to this third Damascus story he is sent 'to open the Gentiles' eyes'; the blindness or blinding that has to be cured is no longer Paul's but that of the Gentiles: (a) 'that they may turn from darkness to light and from the power of Satan to God', and (b) 'that they may receive forgiveness of sins and a place among those who are sanctified by faith in me' (26:17–18). Preaching (opening eyes) (see Lk. 9:3), faith (turning around), and baptism (forgiveness of sins and incorporation in the 'fellowship of saints') are the three technical terms of the conversion, not now of Paul but of the Gentiles. 'Turning from darkness to light and from the power of Satan to God' is a Hellenistic-Jewish cliché associated with the conversion of Gentiles to Judaism;[97] it indicates conversion to the monotheism of Israel's God. Again, the expression 'place among those who are sanctified' is Hellenistic-Jewish; it was adopted by the second generation of Christians to denote incorporation into the Church as the congregation of God.[98]

The import of the vision is now focused in the Christological affirmation that Jesus of Nazareth is 'the light of the people and of the Gentiles' (26:23); the Christian meaning of baptism is also explained: it is an action signifying an ethico-religious reversal, but at the same time a 'light-vision' which mediates knowledge of God and of Jesus Christ whom he has sent, and incorporates the convert into the *ekklesia* from among Jews and Gentiles. The Damascus vision is eventually filled out with the Lucan church's theology of baptism.

In the first story it had become clear to Ananias in a vision that Paul had been chosen 'to suffer many things'; in the third story there is a principal reversal of roles, and Luke has Paul saying: I have said 'nothing but . . . that the Christ must suffer and that, by being the first to rise from the dead, he would proclaim light both to the people [Israel] and to the Gentiles' (26:23). Paul's whole life has been simply an 'imitation' of the suffering Jesus – so says Luke; partly through his own living and suffering he has proclaimed the crucified-and-risen One as the light of all peoples.

From the three stories taken together Luke's argument emerges: in actual fact, as well as chronologically, Paul's mission to the Gentiles is to be seen as distinct from his conversion and initial calling. Luke puts the emphasis on a Church of Jews and Gentiles, not on a 'Church (composed) of Gentiles'. But this calling is frustrated because the Jews of the Diaspora spurn Paul's preaching; hence the *de facto* necessity for his turning to the Gentiles (13:44-48; 18:5-7; 28:23-28). The mission to the Gentiles is, according to Luke, Paul's personal cause;[99] thus there emerged a Church of Gentiles without any Jews.

Acts 26:12-18, then, is constructed quite differently from Acts 9 and 22; what is being reported here is really an 'Easter appearance' of Christ, in the same sense as the formal, official appearances of Christ to Peter and the Eleven. Acts 9 comes from a local Damascus tradition with some Lucan redactions in it; there no 'Easter appearance' was envisaged, only an *optasia*, a vision; Acts 26 is elaborating a different tradition, which suggests that in this case Luke was presented with an already extant, authentic Pauline tradition: here Paul's Damascus vision is an 'Easter appearance', theologically grounded in and legitimated by Paul's mission as an apostle to the Gentiles; it is an ecclesial 'vision of a calling', like that of Peter and the Eleven. That is what Paul himself apprehended it to be, to judge from the evidence of his letters (1 Cor. 15:3-5), whereas for Luke Paul was called to be an apostle to all, Jew and Gentile alike; that he became 'the apostle of the Gentiles' was a historic turning-point in his life, a transformation for which the Jews were responsible. Contrary, in some degree, to his own viewpoint, Luke presents in Acts 26 (because of his being tied to an already existing tradition) a picture of the authentic apostle Paul.[100] Luke is drawing here on a tradition which offers a different interpretation of the Damascus event from the one supplying the substance of Acts 9.[101] Paul is indeed a convert; yet he himself sees his Damascus experience not as the occasion for his conversion but (albeit many years afterwards) as his appointment (by the risen One) to be the apostle of the Gentiles (see 1 Cor. 15:3-5). The tradition behind Acts 9 is less ancient than that lying behind Acts 26; it assumes a hagiographical concern with the person of the great apostle, a Church subject to the authority of the suffering apostle Paul and now looking back over the completed course of his life.[102] In the post-Pauline period reports are circulating in Damascus about Paul's conversion; in 1 Tim. 1:12ff that event becomes the paradigm of the pardoning of a sinner.[103] Luke, then, has adopted two differing traditions and worked them into the text of the Acts with considerable literary as well as theological expertise.

When Paul eventually ends up in Rome, he preaches the gospel there too: 'Let it be known to you then that this salvation of God has been sent to the Gentiles; they will listen' (28:28). The Hellenist Christian, Luke, has been writing throughout his narrative with this verse in prospect; and in the process he has sketched in the topography – endorsed by the divine sanctioning, calling and salvific dispensation (visions) – of Paul's propagation of the message of God's rule, given its concrete aspect in Jesus, the crucified-and-risen One.

Paul himself, in Gal. 1:15–16, sees his career as a 'dispensation of grace': '. . . when he who had set me apart before I was born, and had called me through his grace, was pleased to reveal his Son to me, in order that I might preach him among the Gentiles . . .' (Gal. 1:15–16). In Paul's own words, he felt his calling to the apostolate of the Christological confession to be a 'merciful act' or revelation of God. Is this self-understanding on Paul's part (who clearly distinguishes his understanding of a Christological 'seeing of Jesus' from various kinds of visions, 'sightings' and revelations 'in a state of rapture' or trance; see 2 Cor. 12:1–4) not essentially what Luke reports, where the grace-dimension of what took place is expressed in a vision? For in all the variants within the three accounts there is one, often forgotten, fundamentally constant datum: the purpose of what occurs is invariably concealed from Paul's companions;[104] a Jesus appearance is not the object of neutral observation; it is a faith-motivated experience in response to an eschatological disclosure, expressed in a Christological affirmation of Jesus as the risen One, that is, disclosure of and faith in Jesus in his eschatological, Christological significance. This was again the sole essence of all other Christ manifestations, which have subsequently been filled out either with the theology of the communities represented by Matthew, Luke and John or with the concrete career of the apostle Paul himself. At Jerusalem Barnabas describes the Damascus event as Paul's 'seeing of Jesus' (Acts 9:27), although Paul did not see Jesus visually at all; and this seeing Paul himself equates with the official Christ appearances to Peter and the Twelve (1 Cor. 15:3–5). The 'seeing of Jesus' is a Christological seeing: an understanding of Jesus – made possible by grace alone – an understanding of him as the Christ, in a personal experience that serves to orientate the whole life of the one who undergoes it; but this experience is not called an 'official' manifestation of Christ unless and until it constitutes the basis of an apostolic mission.

It is very plain that in the Acts an 'Easter' missionary vision has developed out of a conversion vision (Acts 9 and 22). To begin to see the Christ in Jesus indeed calls for conversion and illumination. The next question is whether the tradition of the appearance of Christ to Simon and the Eleven did not undergo in the course of the first few Christian generations the same sort of development, growth and structuring that we detect in the Acts in a comparison between Acts 9, Acts 22 and 26.

Chapter 3

# The Easter experience: being converted, on Jesus' initiative, to Jesus as the Christ – salvation found conclusively in Jesus

*Literature* as in this part (Part Two, Section Three, ch. 1: 'The disciples scandalized by the arrest and death of Jesus'). Further: J. Blank, 'Nieuwtestamentische Petrus-typologie en Petrus-ambt', Conc 9 (1973), n. 3, 40–52; K. Carroll, 'Thou art Peter', NovT 6 (1963), 268–76; H. Conzelmann, 'Zur Analyse der Bekenntnisformel 1 Kor. 15:3–5', EvTh 25 (1965), 1- 11; O. Cullmann, *Petrus, Jünger, Apostel, Martyrer*, Zürich-Stuttgart 1960²; J. Dupont, 'Le nom d'apôtres a-t-il été donné aux Douze par Jésus?', OrSyr 1 (1956), 278–80, also (same title): Louvain 1956, and 'La révélation du Fils de Dieu en faveur de Pierre (Mt. 16:17) et de Paul (Gal. 1:16)', RSR 52 (1964), 411–20; R. Fuller, ' "Thou art Peter" pericope and the Easter appearances', *McCormick Quarterly* 20 (1967), 309–15; F. Gils, 'Pierre et la foi au Christ ressuscité', ETL 38 (1962), 5–43; G. Klein, 'Die Berufung des Petrus', ZNW 58 (1967), 1–44; R. Pesch, 'De plaats en betekenis van Petrus in de kerk van het nieuwe testament', Conc 7 (1971), n. 4, 19–29; J. Roloff, *Apostolat, Verkündigung, Kirche*, Gütersloh 1965; W. Trilling, 'Zum Petrusamt im Neuen Testament', ThQ 151 (1971), 110–33; A. Vögtle, 'Messiasbekenntnis und Petrusverheissung', BZ 1 (1957), 252–72 and 2 (1958), 85–103.

## §1 An account of some converts. A Jewish conversion model?

The question raised earlier on but so far left unanswered was: What brought the disciples who had left Jesus in the lurch at the time of his arrest and crucifixion together again – and together now in the name of Jesus, acknowledged as the Christ, Son of God, the Lord? We posited as a working hypothesis that there was a connection between the scattering of the disciples and their 'Easter experience', so called, as the reason for their coming together again. In other words, did not the Easter manifestation of Christ derive from what we might call a Christian 'conversion vision'?

Both the outcome and the starting-point are important here. On the one hand, the group of intimate disciples disintegrates because they have betrayed the very thing that keeps them together, the person of Jesus of Nazareth; on the other hand, reassembled in Jesus' name they proclaim, a while after Jesus' death, that this same Jesus has risen. What occurred in the period between on the one hand their Master's suffering and dying and the disciples' panic-stricken loss of nerve and, on the other, the moment when they were heard boldly and confidently proclaiming that Jesus was to return to judge the world or had risen from the dead? For even the historian must face the problem involved here: something must surely have happened to make this transformation at any rate psychologically intelligible.

The primary and immediate reply to this cannot be: the reality of the resurrection itself. The resurrection in its eschatological 'eventuality' is after all nowhere recounted in the New Testament; nor of course could it be, because it no longer forms part of our mundane, human history; it is, *qua* reality, meta-empirical and meta-historical: 'eschatological'. On the other hand, a resurrection about which nothing is said is an event of which nobody knows anything, for us, naturally, 'nonexistent'. Opening up the subject of a meta-historical resurrection, as in fact is done in the New Testament, presupposes of course experiential events which are interpreted as saving acts of God in Christ. It presupposes a particular experience and an interpretation of it. The question then becomes: What, after Jesus' death, were the concrete, experienced events which induced the disciples to proclaim with such a degree of challenge and cogent witness that Jesus of Nazareth was actually alive: the coming or risen One? If it cannot be the resurrection itself, or the empty tomb (even if this be a historical fact, theologically it could yield no proof of a resurrection. A 'vanished corpse' is not in itself a resurrection, and an actual bodily resurrection does not require as its outcome a vanished corpse), nor yet 'appearances', taken to be real, which within the history of tradition already presuppose belief in the resurrection – then, what?

Anyone who has at first taken offence at Jesus and subsequently proclaims him to be the only bringer of salvation has of necessity undergone a 'conversion process'. As a first reply to the question: What actually took place between the two historical events – Jesus' death and the apostles' preaching – we are therefore bound to say at once: the conversion of the disciples, who 'notwithstanding' Jesus' scandalizing death came together again – and did so in the name of this same Jesus, through the recognition of their paucity of faith. It is a process of conversion that lies between the two historically accessible elements. Only then can we go on to ask about the circumstances making such a conversion possible and more especially about what the essential requirements would be for such a thing. A straight exegesis of the 'empty tomb' and of the 'appearance stories' by-passes, it seems to me, this primary and fundamental question of the conversion or re-assembly of the disciples. That is why as the 'first section' of this chapter we have tabled the problem posed by the outrage felt by the disciples and the question of their coming together again. The central core of what took place is indeed lodged in the biblical accounts of the Christ appearances, but overlaid by later experiences of what was after all an already established Church, from within which the four gospels and the Acts were written. Can the threefold Damascus story – in which the 'Christ manifestation' to Paul is depicted initially as a 'conversion vision' and then as a 'missionary' one – perhaps provide a model for understanding a similar development in the tradition of the official appearances of Christ to the Twelve? Admittedly, there is a fundamental difference: the disciples had not been persecutors of Jesus – quite the opposite; they had of course fallen short in their 'going after Jesus'; but in the New Testament this would seem to be the essential demand put to Christians. Thus they are in need of conversion: to resume the task of 'being a disciple' and 'imitating Jesus'. But the first condition for that is the experience of having received forgiveness from Jesus – a quite specific experience of grace and mercy, the result of which was that they were received back into a present fellowship with Jesus and confessed him to be their definitive salvation, which was not at an end with his death and through which they were brought together again and restored to fellowship with him and each other.

In some modern attempts to make the manifestation experience intelligible, people have seen in the Christ appearances a sort of condensation of various pneumatic experiences within the primitive local congregations. What is basically wrong with that, however, is that one is then postulating what has to be demonstrated. In fact one is presupposing the existence of the 'gathered congregation' (in which the pneumatic experiences occur), whereas the very thing the appearance traditions in the gospels are meant to signify marks the point from which the bringing together of the scattered disciples begins, in other words the very earliest event constitutive of the Church (albeit still, to begin with, as a fraternity within the Jewish religion). The reassembly of the disciples is precisely what has to be explained. Appearance stories and accounts of the empty tomb assume the fact of the reassembled community and its Christological *kerygma*.

We must therefore look in the direction of the 'conversion process' of the disciples. Fundamentally, 'conversion' entails a relationship (a) to him whom the disciples had let down: Jesus of Nazareth, and (b) to him to whom they return: Jesus as the Christ.

The disciples (perhaps in panic) fell short in their task of 'being a disciple' or 'going after Jesus': at what was for him the very worst moment they left him in the lurch, and then especially were they 'of little faith' – something against which Jesus had repeatedly warned them. Yet their relationship to Jesus of Nazareth, whom they had deserted, enshrines also their recollection of his whole ministry, of his message of the coming rule of God, a God mindful of human kind, who wills only the well-being and not the destruction of men; of his admonitions regarding lack of faith; but they had also come to know the 'God of Jesus' as a God of unconditional mercy and forgiveness; he had helped so many people simply because they came to him in distress; they remembered Jesus' eating and drinking in fellowship with sinners, that is, his proffering salvation to sinners in particular. And then finally there was their recollection of the quite special temper prevailing at the farewell meal – memories of what Jesus had said at the time, however vague. These remembered aspects of their life shared in fellowship with Jesus and of Jesus' whole line of conduct are essential elements in the process of conversion undergone by these men who did indeed fail, but had not in the end lost their faith in Jesus. They had been thrown off balance rather than been deliberately disloyal.

On the other hand the relationship they have with the one to whom they have returned is quite new. They deserted a Jesus marked down for death; they return to a fellowship in the here and now with that same Jesus, acknowledging him now as the returning Judge or the crucified-and-risen One. It is this second relationship that connects with what lies at the source of the appearance traditions in the gospels. What, historically speaking, occurred that was experienced by the disciples as a pure act of grace on God's part and through which they arrived at the Christological confession of the crucified One, risen or coming?

In Part Three it will appear that on the basis of Isa. 42:6-7, 16; 49:6, 8-9; 50:10; 51:4-6; 62:1 with 49:6 the latter-day prophet was characterized in Judaism as 'the light of the world', just as the Law itself was 'the light of all nations'; then too it will appear from Part Three that the identification of Jesus with the eschatological emissary from God was the bridge between 'Jesus of Nazareth' and the Christ proclaimed by the Church. Now this idea of the eschatological prophet (with the whole range of meaning which it evokes in Judaism) also had a part to play in the emergence of the appearance traditions. In the Jewish conversion stories the conversion of a Gentile to the Jewish Law is often called an illumination and is represented by what has become the classic model of a 'conversion vision': the individual concerned is suddenly confronted with a brilliant light and hears a voice (Acts 9; Paul's Damascus vision has evidently been constructed with this model in view). From Isa. 29:9-10, 18; 35:5; 42:18-21; 43:8 a recurrent theme within Judaism emerges, in which 'not seeing' or a state of blindness becomes a symbol for culpably cutting oneself off from the revelation of God; 'seeing' on the other hand symbolizes a person's entry into the salvation proferred by God (see also Deut. 29:4; Isa. 6:9; 42:6-7; 56:10; 59:10; Jer. 5:21). Mark 4:12 is referring to Isa. 6:9-10, when it says 'so that they may indeed see but not perceive, and may indeed hear but not understand; lest they should turn again and be forgiven'. More particularly in Hellenistic Judaism there arose a generally accepted cliché – occasioned by Isa. 42:6-7 – which represents a Gentile's conversion to Judaism as a 'seeing' or an 'enlightenment' of one who was previously blind.[105] In many places in the New Testament the symbolism of light, and thus of seeing, is associated with conversion (Rom. 13:12; Eph. 5:8-14; 1 Pet. 2:9-12; Heb. 6:4; 10:32). In Acts 26:17-18 there are clear traces of 'Isaianic' influence (Isa. 42:7); Paul's conversion is conceived of on the light-model of a conversion vision. Although Christian baptism and conversion or illumination frequently coincide (later on, baptism will itself be described as a *phôtismos*, an illumination), the two terms are not *per se* identical. 'You are the light of the world' (Mt. 5:14; Lk. 8:16) was applied initially to the eschatological prophet (Isa. 42:6–7; 49:6, 8–9; 51:4–6; 62:1 with 49:6; also Sirach 48:10b), in Judaism to the Torah.[106] Elsewhere, the term 'light of the Gentiles' or 'of the world' (first for the Jews, but because of that for all pagans) occurs repeatedly.[107] Then too it is applied both to Jesus (Jn. 1:9; 3:19–21; 8:12) and to the apostles of Christ (Acts 13:47; 26:23; Mt. 5:14; Lk. 8:16). This way of looking at it is also an obvious influence on 'light' texts as in 1 Thess. 5:1–6 and 1 Pet. 2:9–12 (in other words, on Christian catechesis). In view of this already existing Jewish tradition of conversion by way of illumination (frequently pictured in a light-vision), the notion – or the possibility – is already here that the marvellous occurrence of a conversion, not now to the revelation of God in the Law but to the revelation of God in Jesus, has been expressed in the model of a conversion vision, which in essence signifies a 'disclosure of God', epiphany and thus 'enlightenment'. Acts 9, Luke's version of the story of Paul's conversion, is the obvious example of this. Even the 'baptismal vision' in the interpretative traditions about Jesus' baptism in the Jordan stands (where the model employed is concerned) within a similar complex of tradition; and Jesus appears there as 'light of the world' and latter-day prophet: an epiphany of Jesus as son of God.

What happens in the Christian resurrection vision (the Easter appearances) is a conversion to Jesus as the Christ, who now comes as the light of the world.[108] Just as the 'enlightenment' of the Law justifies someone (see Gal. 1:14; 3:2ff), so the disciples are justified by the illumination of the risen One. In the 'manifestation' or the 'vision' the gracious gift of conversion to Jesus *as* the Christ (thanks to an enlightening revelation of God) is effected and expressed. It is Jesus himself who enlightens, who discloses himself as the risen Christ in and through the grace of conversion: he is the enlightening Christ; he 'makes himself seen'.

Now it is a striking fact that in the New Testament appearance stories (outside the Acts) there is nowhere any mention of 'light'; and that might be taken to run counter to the interpretation proposed. Yet it is equally striking that the accounts of appearances in the four gospels exhibit the commonplace of (a) a 'sending forth into the world' (thus 'light of the world') and (b) referring explicitly or more allusively to Christian baptism (forgiveness of sins) – the Jewish conversion model is clearly recognizable in all this. It must be said too that of the original 'epiphany' character of the appearances in the gospels (independently of all 'illumination' or 'enlightenment' phenomena) only the identification persists: Jesus is the one who is alive. (I shall come back to this in Part Two.)

## §2  Jesus' disciples reassembled on the historic initiative of Peter

Commitment to Jesus was conceived of in the early Church as a 'conversion'.[109] This conversion to Jesus is frequently represented on the lines of the Jewish conversion vision, which in the early Church gradually becomes an 'appearance' accompanied by the motif of a 'commissioning' or 'sending forth'. Can we, via these latter appearances in the gospels, still envisage something of the primary source, the 'conversion vision', so called, of Simon and the Twelve?

The events lying at the source of the earliest testifying to the faith on the part of Peter and his associates have evidently been overlaid in the course taken by the most primitive Christian traditions by updating interpretations from Matthean theology (Mt. 28:9–10 and 16:20), Lucan theology (Lk. 24:13–35, 44–53), Johannine theology (especially Jn. 20:17–18; 20:21b and even 20:24–31), and by Paul's personal experiences. They already contain the central core of a reflexive ecclesiology. The matrix account of the appearances is no longer recoverable out of the sifting of tradition and redaction. The appearance stories in the gospels are no longer telling us about the initial conversion to Jesus as the risen One but about the ground and source of the one faith of the by then established Church of Christ. The existence of this Christ-confessing Church is presupposed. In the gospel account the apostles have already come together *before* the appearances, apparently in expectation of things to come. John has evidently seen the problem; and so he says that the disciples were together behind lock and bolt (Jn. 20:19) 'for fear of the Jews'. Even the appearance to Simon, clearly an important one in the New Testament, gets only a bald mention (Lk. 24:34), while the dynamic thrust of the narrative is focused on the manifestation to the Eleven as a group: to all assembled together. This serves to make it very clear that only the communal, 'ecclesial' Christological confession of the crucified-and-risen One is the sole valid norm of the apostolic faith.

Thus the way the Christ appearances are presented in the New Testament gives us no direct historical information as to how the

J.E.C.–N

disciples, who were at first scattered after Jesus' death,[110] were gathered together again in the name of their deceased Master – and in such a manner that this reassembling called the Christ movement into lively being. What these reports of appearances do plainly have a bearing upon is the grounding and legitimation of the Church's mission to the whole world. Such accounts in the gospels reflect the Church's self-understanding: the local congregations of Christ see themselves as grounded upon, and sent into the world in the power of, their faith in the risen and living Jesus.

Although the product of already established churches, at the same time there is operative in these gospel narratives the recollection of something that happened, a historical occurrence that provided a basis for disciples of Jesus to come together again after his death, in the name of Jesus as the Christ, the definitive 'final good'. This memory still at work behind the gospel stories I shall try to retrieve, although the result of the investigation, because of the difficulty of sifting tradition and redaction down to their primary source, will only permit of probable and reasonable hypotheses, albeit founded on discernible signals in the gospel texts.

How and on what bases of experience and recollection the disciples after Jesus' death reassemble around the none-the-less deceased Jesus is therefore a question calculated to send us back to the point at which the disciples – not yet a 'congregation of Christ' – constituted themselves a Christ community (even if initially within Judaism).[111]

In pursuing this enquiry we must suppose it more than very likely that upon his arrest and at his death Jesus' intimate disciples failed in one way or another to stand by him. We must also take into account the fact that so long as Jesus was still living on earth it was altogether impossible to make any essential and constitutive connection of his person – not just one or more of his actions – with the coming of God's rule. So long as Jesus was living in human history, which is *ipso facto* contingent, God's saving revelation in him was after all 'un-finished' – still in process of coming to be. At that stage, therefore, 'Christology' was out of the question; for a 'Christological confession' is a (faith-motivated) statement about the totality of Jesus' life, not about a salvific power thought to be due to particular sayings or actions on his part; for that was certainly 'self-evident' to his disciples, even prior to his death. If one accepts the actual historicity of God's revelation in Jesus and sees how the faith of Jesus' disciples responded to this temporal event – Jesus' whole ministry – one realizes that the disciples had an incredible enthusiasm for their Master – and that, in their fundamental relationship to God – and yet had not come to recognize that he was in his person of constitutive, all-decisive significance for the dawning of the kingdom of God. Now the whole point of a Christological affirmation lies – if words still bear their proper meaning – in the acknowledgement of that constitutive significance. The reason why, prior to Jesus' death, an implicit 'Christological confession' (in a full Christological sense) was impossible is, in my view, the genuine historicity – here again any kind of docetism is out of place – of Jesus' self-understanding and of his message, which gradually made him rise to the inevitability of a violent death. The Christian disclosure experience, ground, source and release of a truly Christological confession of Jesus, presupposes the totality of his life, up to and including its being ended by his execution. From a theological standpoint too, only this completed life is God's revelation in Jesus of Nazareth. Only with Jesus' death is his life-story – in so far as his 'person' is concerned – at an end; only then can our account of Jesus begin.

Of course the disciples felt the violent end of their Master's life as a tremendous shock and so, understandably enough, fell because of their 'little faith' into a state of panic; but they did not in consequence of these last events undergo a total lapse of faith. Apart from Mark, who (for reasons in my view not yet satisfactorily explained) is keenly critical of the conduct of the Twelve prior to Jesus' death, the panicky defection of the disciples, their deserting of Jesus, is nowhere represented in the gospels as a total breach, in the sense of a loss of faith. It was *oligopistia* – a 'being of little faith' (see above). These disciples did of course come to realize – in a process of repentance and conversion which it is no longer possible to reconstruct on a historical basis – something about their experience of disclosure that had taken them by storm: their 'recognition' and 'acknowledgement' of Jesus in the totality of his life. This is what I call the 'Easter experience', which could be expressed in a variety of ways: the crucified One is the coming Judge (a *maranatha* Christology); the crucified One as miracle-worker is actively present in his disciples; the crucified One has risen. And then we may indeed say: at that juncture there dawns the experience of their really seeing Jesus at last – the basis of what is being made explicit in the Easter appearances: Jesus 'makes himself seen' (*ôphthè*); not till after his death does he become 'epiphanous', that is, transparent; it is through faith that we grasp who he is. This acknowledging on the disciples' part is at the same time a recollective and yet new seeing of Jesus – of Jesus of Nazareth; not of someone different, nor yet a myth. Jesus as they had encountered him remains the sole criterion for their recollections as well as for their new experiences after his death.

Historically speaking, it is likely (and accepted more or less universally by scholars at the moment) that - apart from the appearances to women, who in that antique, primarily Jewish culture could not provide any 'legitimate' testimony – the first manifestation of Jesus (protophany) was to Simon Peter (1 Cor. 15:5; Lk. 24:34; and, indirectly, Mk. 16:7),[112] that Peter was the first to experience what is called in the New Testament the 'seeing of Jesus' after his death. This is correlative with the Marcan tradition (or more probably redaction) which in the context of the shock and dismay felt by the disciples generally attributes to Simon alone an individual denial of Jesus – something which in the Marcan redaction is interpreted in terms of 'salvation-history', that is, as a 'divine must' or salvific design, in that Mark quotes at this point a passage of Scripture and puts it directly into the mouth of Jesus (Mk. 14:27; see the connection made by Mark between Mk. 14:27 and 14:28 with Mk. 16:7).

Then there are strong indications (noticed by many exegetes) that the name 'Kepha(s)', Peter or rock, acquired by Simon, has a link with his prime position in the Christ appearances. Apropos of this first 'official-cum-hierarchical' appearance Luke simply calls Peter 'Simon': 'he . . . has appeared to Simon' (Lk. 24:34); elsewhere he usually speaks of 'Peter'. Moreover, B. Gerhardson has shown[113] (with the backing of many other commentators) that it is 'extremely probable' that Mt. 16: 17–19 stems from a (now lost) tradition which tells of the first appearance of Jesus, specifically, to Peter. With some admittedly fundamental corrections A. Vögtle[114] too sees Mt. 16:18–19 as a fragment which originally formed part of an account of a Peter-protophany (although A. Vögtle denies that a Christological confession by Peter was associated with this account of the official 'first appearance' to Peter). An important point is that A. Vögtle also recognizes that the Jesus logion in Matthew: 'You are Peter (rock)' is the initial introduction of the name Peter for Simon; and that this name was certainly not given to Simon by the earthly Jesus.[115] The linking up of the designation 'rock' and Peter's protophany therefore is now held by many scholars to be the best hypothesis.[116] The pre-Pauline use of Peter instead of Simon points, within this short period after Jesus' death, to an already established tradition.

Notwithstanding this central position of Peter, partly in connection with the first appearance of Jesus to Simon, the gospels refer to the Petrine 'protophany' only in close association with the appearance of Christ to the Eleven (Lk. 24:34 with 24:36; 1 Cor. 15:3–5).

There is yet another noticeable feature found in the Acts that might be of importance in this context. In Acts 1:4 is written *sunalidzomenos*, often translated as 'while he was eating with them' (that is, after his resurrection). But at about the same time the Jewish author Josephus employs the same word once in the middle sense 'to gather (themselves) together', and once in the active 'to gather (bring) together'.[117] Luke may be reflecting a tradition here which says that after his death Jesus, the Lord, reassembled his disciples and commanded them 'not to leave Jerusalem but wait for the promise of the Father [the Spirit] . . . (John baptized with water but you shall be baptized with the holy Spirit before many days)' (Acts 1:4–5). The Lucan theology in this is evident enough; but it articulates a tradition that ascribes the initiative for the reassembly to the risen Jesus himself – as the 'grace-aspect' of what in point of historical fact occurred.

All these things give us reasonable grounds for postulating that after Jesus' death Peter was the first (male) disciple to reach the point of 'conversion' and to resume 'following after Jesus', and then other disciples as well, on Peter's initiative. Peter is therefore the first Christian confessor to arrive at a Christological affirmation; by virtue of his conversion he takes the initiative in assembling a (or the) 'band of Twelve' (whether it was by then called that or not; see immediately below). This is how he becomes the rock of the primal core of the Christian community, 'the Twelve' who acknowledged Jesus as the coming or risen 'crucified One', that is, the community of the latter days, of the final aeon, the new kingdom of the Twelve Tribes, the gathered 'Church of Christ' (Rom. 16:16) or 'Church of God' (1 Cor. 1:2; 10:32; etc.). This, we may suppose, is the hard historical centre of the process that brought about the reassembling of Jesus' disciples as the congregation of Christ. Very probably Peter was not himself the founder of 'the Twelve' – rather, the group of twelve was already in existence before Easter (how otherwise could Judas Iscariot be called 'one of the Twelve', and – more particularly – how can we explain the technical term 'the Eleven'?). It would seem, rather, that the pre-Easter action of Jesus in sending the disciples out on their mission served to constitute the group of the Twelve. It was then a consequence of Jesus' protophany that Peter had the credit for reassembling this Twelve.[118] An echo or recollection of this historical event I find in Lk. 22:32: 'Simon, Simon . . . when you have turned again [*epistrepsas*: converted], strengthen your brethren' (in this complex, Lk. 22:31–33, the use of 'Simon' is a striking feature). Thus a link is forged here between Peter's denial, his conversion and initiative in bringing the disciples together again; in constituting them disciples of Christ. Yet Peter's act of conversion is not something detached from that of the Twelve: belief in the resurrection presupposes a process of reciprocal communication among the Twelve. Hence the testimony of Scripture to their 'at first doubting'.

## §3  The experience of grace as forgiveness

It should have become clear, now that we have examined the structure of the appearance stories, that they point to an event set within a context of salvation-history, and that, like the appeal to Scripture, the 'vision' model is a means of articulating an event engendered by grace, a divine, salvific initiative – a grace manifesting itself in historical events and human experiences. In other words, the reporting of what occurred in the guise of appearances indicates that the process whereby Peter and his friends were brought together again after their dispersal was felt by them to be an act of sheer grace on God's part, as (set in a different context) appears from the gospels. 'Blessed are you, Simon Bar-Jona, for flesh and blood has not revealed this to you, but my Father who is in heaven' (Mt. 16:17). At the same time the fact that this conversion is presented in the form of an appearance vision serves to underline the divine endorsement of the Christological affirmation. Christianity arises out of the message and total career of Jesus, up to and including his death and, along with that, out of a *renewed* offer on God's part, after Jesus' death, of salvation through the heavenly Jesus, which meant that the disciples' return to Jesus became a return to the living, crucified One.[119]

In which concrete historical events this 'grace and favour' or renewed offer of salvation in Jesus has been manifested the New Testament nowhere explicitly states; it only speaks of the character of this event as one of amazing grace. The objective, sovereignly free initiative of Jesus that led them on to a Christological faith – an initiative independent of any belief on the part of Peter and his companions – is a gracious act of Christ, which as regards their 'enlightenment' is of course revelation – not a construct of men's minds, but revelation within a disclosure experience, in this case given verbal embodiment later on in the 'appearances' model. What it signifies is no model but a living reality. Understood thus, the ground of Christian belief is indubitably Jesus of Nazareth in his earthly proffer of salvation, renewed after his death, now experienced and enunciated by Peter and the Twelve. It means too that this same Jesus is acknowledged by God: the man put to death by his fellows was vindicated when he appealed to God. This is brought out more especially in the formulae stating that God caused Jesus to rise from the dead.[120] How did the disciples come to be convinced, on the premise of this absolute priority of grace, that Jesus was the risen One?

In the theology of the New Testament there is a recognizable association of 'resurrection' with 'forgiveness of sins'. It is specifically on the 'Easter day' that the Johannine gospel concludes a Jesus appearance with the words: 'If you forgive the sins of any, they are forgiven; if you retain the sins of any, they are retained' (Jn. 20:22–23). The 'ministry of reconciliation' (2 Cor. 5:18) is mentioned along with Christian baptism in all the accounts of official appearances (Lk. 24:47; Mt. 28:19; Jn. 20:23). The forgiveness of sins is a gracious Easter gift. After their Easter experiences the disciples preach 'the forgiveness of sins' (Lk. 24:47; Acts 26). Paul says: 'If Christ has not been raised . . . you are still in your sins' (1 Cor. 15:17–18); elsewhere: 'Jesus was . . . raised for our justification' (Rom. 4:25b). The forgiving of sin is associated with the name of Jesus (Acts 5:31; 10:43; 26:18).[121]

The question is then whether we should not invert those kerygmatic utterances – when it comes to the process in which the disciples were converted. May it not be that Simon Peter – and indeed the Twelve – arrived via their concrete experience of forgiveness after Jesus' death, encountered as grace and discussed among themselves (as they remembered Jesus' sayings about, among other things, the gracious God) at the 'evidence for belief': the Lord is alive? He renews for them the offer of salvation; this they experience in their own conversion; he must therefore be alive. In their experience here and now of 'returning to Jesus', in the renewal of their own life they encounter in the present the grace of Jesus' forgiving; in doing so they experience Jesus as the one who is alive. A dead man does not proffer forgiveness. A present fellowship with Jesus is thus restored.

The experience of having their cowardice and want of faith forgiven them, an experience further illuminated by what they were able to remember of the general tenor of Jesus' life on earth, thus became the matrix in which faith in Jesus as the risen One was brought to birth. They all of a sudden 'saw' it. This seeing may have been the outcome of a lengthier process of maturation, one primary and important element of which was enough to make Peter take action and bring the disciples together again. About this initial element there was obviously a collective exchange of ideas – 'they doubted' – until a consensus emerged. Even the oldest, pre-Pauline credal formulae are the result of an already protracted theological reflection and not the instant articulation of the original experience. In the experience of forgiveness as a gift of grace – the renewed offer of saving fellowship by the cruci-fied One – lies the venture of faith, which is not, after all, an obligatory conclusion from this, that or the other premise. It is the individual's experience of new being that imparts to faith the assurance that Jesus is alive or is the coming judge of the world.

## §4   A critical question: ambiguity of the term ‘Easter experience’

The question is whether we are to identify the Easter experience in all the early Christian traditions with the tradition of the resurrection *kerygma*; for the historical development of tradition presents certain problems here.

First of all we must draw a distinction – even if an inadequate one – between ‘Easter experience’ and the articulation factor in this ‘ex-periential event’, the resort to language, which is at the same time an interpretation within a given horizon of understanding. The term ‘experiential event’ is used advisedly in order to exclude a purely ‘subjective’ experience. To put it another way: after his death Jesus himself stands at the source of what we are calling the ‘Easter ex-perience’ of the disciples; at all events what we meet with here is an experience of grace. But *qua* human experience it is self-cognizant and spontaneously allied with a particular expression of itself. This (non-reflexive) expression is an intrinsic aspect of the experience itself – and for that very reason the distinction intended cannot be pressed all the way home and so is not an adequate one. Pure experiencing does not exist; to however minimal an extent it is articulated and in that respect interpreted. Thus the experience can never be detached from its lin-guistic context,[122] any more than from its conjunctural intellective horizon (for this see Part Four). Experiences are brought to expression not only via a ‘language filter’ but also within given models of com-prehension. What is more, in a more advanced phase there is *post hoc* reflection on the original experience plus its pre-reflexive element of interpretation. Such reflection is not a foreign, extraneous element, but it ‘extends’ the experience along with its interpretation, even though various divagations from the initial experience may now appear. The original experience is however clarified and completed by a right and proper exercise of reflection.

So in speaking of an 'Easter experience' one cannot isolate a pre-linguistic phase from the interpretative element (e.g. 'resurrection'). The question is simply whether 'resurrection' was the primary element of articulation, or whether there were other bits of interpretation that may possibly be older than the Christian resurrection idea.[123] The question we are considering is quite different, therefore, from that posed by W. Marxsen[124], who also distinguishes between 'experience' and 'the thing as interpreted', but traces the Easter experience itself back to a specific experience of the historical, earthly Jesus; in other words, there is then an immediate danger of the term 'Easter experience' becoming itself a piece of interpretation – faith interpreting the earthly life of the Jesus who died. In one sense this seems to me fair enough: after Jesus' death there begins the Christological interpretation. Thus the Easter experience with its interpretative element is already part and parcel of the 'Christology' *qua* interpretation of the historical or earthly Jesus of Nazareth. If the exegetes and theologians who start from the death of Jesus as the point of disjunction (and so not from men's rejection of him as the real break) want to convince me in this regard, they must first show me why, when John the Baptist had been beheaded, his movement was able simply to continue on Jewish ground – as if that death entailed no break at all. Did the Jewish mentality change within a year or two (that is, with the death of Jesus) so fundamentally that people suddenly began to think that Jesus' death set a big question-mark against his entire ministry here on earth? The whole of Judaic literature between the Testaments and the movement inspired by John (after his death by execution) radically contradicts that point of view. True, in a Pauline (or pre-Pauline?) context and in the heat of controversy between Jew and Jewish Christian an appeal is made to Deut. 21:23: 'Cursed be everyone who hangs on a tree' (see Gal. 3:13); but to what extent was this polemical point representative of early Christianity? This is all the more pertinent because since the mass crucifixions under the Roman occupation, for the rabbis 'crucifixion' had come to stand rather for the Jews' loyalty to Yahweh. That is not at all to deny the historical fiasco of Jesus.

If we are not to regard Jesus' death on the cross as in itself a final parting of the ways within a Jewish and Judaic context, are we then obliged to see the 'Easter experience' itself as a Christian interpretation of the earthly, that is, pre-Easter Jesus? My reply to that is: up to a point, yes; up to a point (and on balance), no! The question is, surely, whether the Christian interpretation, after Jesus' death, rests solely on experiences with the earthly Jesus or whether it is not partly undergirded by new experiences after his death. This is the crucial point, it seems to me. And I mean, not experiences of an 'empty tomb' or of 'appearances' (themselves already an interpretation of the resurrection faith), but experiences such as I have already enumerated: the 'conversion process' undergone by the disciples, their 'encounter with grace' after Jesus' death. That the New Testament bases itself on specific experiences after Jesus' death (however they might be interpreted) seems to me, on the strength of the foregoing analysis, undeniable. As opposed to W. Marxsen I would proceed from the 'Easter experience' as reality, real experience and experience of reality, which none the less carries within it an element of articulation. And now to tackle this last point: that is, granted the 'Easter experience', was the resurrection idea the oldest and original interpretative factor, or were there other interpretations?

Ph. Seidensticker may have relied excessively on the work of E. Schweizer,[125] which had got little or no support from the exegetes, yet Schweizer's intuition seems to have been correct in this case. By renewing this study, centred particularly on the historical development of the tradition, L. Ruppert and G. Nickelsburg succeeded in presenting a view based on some nicer distinctions[126] and – although independently of the 'resurrection' issue – Kl. Berger in a recent study has pointed in a similar direction.[127] The milieu in which the Judaic-cum-sapiential notion of the 'humbled and exalted suffering prophet' (with the martyr's death) was widespread is quite clearly that of the Graeco-Palestinian Jews – which says nothing for or against a very great antiquity for it within the primitive Church (see Part Three).

But then there is another pressing distinction. Even before there was any talk in the Old Testament of resurrection, there was a vaguely articulated belief in God as Lord over life and death: Yahweh is a 'God of the living'.[128] Later this became: God has the power to make dead people alive again. This faith in the living God in relation to the dead could still be expressed in diverse ways: either by resurrection or (more in the Greek mode) by the fact that God calls to himself 'souls' lingering in Hades or the underworld. For it is not the case that on the Greek view of things souls after death are 'with God': for the Greeks too the individual is indeed dead, and the soul is in the realm of the dead ('Hades' being the Greek counterpart of the Jewish 'Sheol'); but then God is thought to have the power to retrieve souls from the realm of the dead.[129] For the Aramaic-speaking Jew the whole (corporeal) human being, albeit in a shadowy kind of existence, is in the realm of the dead; being rescued from it by God is therefore (though it was only a century or so before Christ that a complete differentiation crept into the Semitic notion of Sheol) described as 'resurrection'. Apart from the difference in anthropology, both Greek- and Aramaic-speaking Jews were talking about the same thing: God's power to bring a dead person to life, even though a Greek-speaking Jew would feel less tied to the concept of 'resurrection'. The latter then came to be envisaged, especially in apocalyptic Jewish circles, in a very 'materialistic' way: a return to life on earth with the same body and even, so the rabbis say, with the same clothing.[130] Later apocalyptic actually introduces the remarkable idea of a 'progressive resurrection'.[131] The central core of the Jewish belief in resurrection, therefore, goes beyond the apocalyptic form given to it; it amounts to a faith in God, who is able to fetch the dead out of the realm of the dead, and so make them alive again. This is not as such a specifically apocalyptic conception. In fact the idea is also to be found in the non-apocalyptic (probably Pharisaical) 'Psalmi Salomonis' (3:12); and in late Jewish literature, assumption or 'taking up into heaven' without any 'resurrection' is very common (see Part Three).

That this Jewish notion – God's power to bring the dead from the realm of the dead, that is, to bring them alive – is the conceptual ambit within which the Christians after Jesus' death speak of the living Jesus, is not to be doubted. Even so, this new state of Jesus' being is envisaged in a totally non-apocalyptic way. In the first place the Jewish conception of the resurrection is eschatological and (for the faithful) collective; that even before the end of the Age an individual might experience the eschatological resurrection – for that there is no Jewish precedent whatever; it even falls outside the scheme of apocalyptic. What Jewish literature does recognize is non-eschatological resurrections of particular individuals, who return to this world from the realm of the dead (although they may then have a specific mission *vis-à-vis* the coming 'last days'). In the New Testament too we catch echoes of this Jewish idea: some indeed suppose that the earthly Jesus is none other than John the Baptist, risen from the dead (Mk. 6:14; Lk. 9:7-9). Thus it is clear enough from the New Testament as a whole that the Christian idea of resurrection differs radically from this notion of 'coming back alive into our world' (see later). What we have here is the eschatological resurrection, but fulfilled non-apocalyptically in a single person; that is to say, for Christians it means that the eschatological 'final Age' has already started: Jesus is the 'first of those fallen asleep', soon will come 'the new heaven and new earth'.

Now what is apparently the earliest creed expresses belief in the Jesus who is to return as judge of the world and (for the Church) bringer of salvation, without any explicit mention of his resurrection. At this point we tend tacitly to postulate the resurrection, for instance, in the Q tradition.[132] The question is whether this can be said to be justifiable. From an examination, still to follow, of four ancient credal strands, it should become apparent that only the various Easter Christologies make Jesus' resurrection explicitly an object of Christian proclamation; in the three other early Christian creeds the resurrection is at any rate not an object of *kerygma*. That is broadly admitted by a good many scholars, but with the proviso: the resurrection is of course presupposed; yet not a single argument is ever advanced for this; it is simply postulated (apparently on the strength of the resurrection *kerygma* present everywhere in the New Testament, which is indeed the unitive factor of the canonical New Testament). But it is another question whether for some Jewish Christians the resurrection was not a 'second thought', which proved the best way to make explicit an earlier spontaneous experience, without their initially having done so. This process alone was the condition making it possible to constitute the resurrection an object of *kerygma*.[133]

What we can say however is that early Christian local churches did nevertheless all have an experience of Easter, that is, knew the reality which other churches explicitly referred to as 'resurrection'. Thus for the Q community the crucified One is the saviour, and judge of the world, soon to return but even now actively present in the preaching of the Christian prophets; in other words, for them Jesus has evidently been 'taken up to God'. How? This is nowhere dwelt upon. Their Easter experience is the 'enthusiastic' one of the Lord actively present in their community, and soon to come: a *maranatha* experience. They do not ponder the question whether Jesus has been brought from the realm of the dead by way of a resurrection, a 'rapture' or (on the Greek model) by God. He is in any case 'with God'. Something like that would be true of other local communities. That is the very reason why we must examine their *kerygma*, which does not explicitly take the resurrection as its object, in order to discover whether the 'Easter Christology' did not become the governing and canonical *kerygma* precisely because it so aptly articulated a reality which in the kerygmatic scheme of other early Christian communities was given only implicitly in their *kerygma*. For this and other reasons it will become clear, nevertheless, that the *reality* denoted by 'Easter experience' is independent both of the traditions centred around the Jerusalem tomb and of that of the appearances (which in my view already presuppose the Easter faith), while each and every Easter experience, in whatever guise, really is the faith-motivated experience and confession of the power of God that has brought the crucified One to life again. To this enquiry in particular Part Three, which now follows, will be devoted.

# Part Three

# Christian interpretation of the Crucified-and-Risen One

# *The gospels as general hermeneusis of the risen Jesus*

## *Introduction*

The New Testament hermeneusis of Jesus' resurrection must be looked for not only, nor yet perhaps primarily, in what it says in explanation of 'raising from the dead', 'risen on the third day', 'exalted' and so forth, but in its accounts of Jesus' message, his ministry, his 'mighty works', his dealings with people and with sinners, his manner of living and dying. The idea of Jesus' resurrection was not suggested to the Christians directly by apocalyptic, but by his earthly career and ministry, based on his identification with the cause of God. The apocalyptic resurrection idea was only one of the resources available in this connection – one moreover which (as may appear later on) the historical impact of Jesus of Nazareth served to transform from within into a specifically Christian concept.

Thus we end up in a remarkable hermeneutical circle: Jesus' living and dying on earth suggested to Christians, in virtue of their experiences after Jesus' death, the idea of the resurrection or of the coming Parousia of Jesus, while on the basis of their faith in the risen or coming crucified One they relate the story of Jesus in the gospels; in other words, these gospel stories of Jesus are themselves a hermeneusis of Jesus' Parousia and resurrection, while belief in the Parousia or in the resurrection was engendered by things remembered of the historical Jesus. The 'matter to be interpreted' – Jesus of Nazareth – came eventually to be interpreted in and through the faith-inspired affirmation of his resurrection (Parousia), while that resurrection or Parousia is in its turn the 'object of interpretation' which is then interpreted through the gospel narratives as remembrances of Jesus' earthly life, as also in the light of his resurrection or coming Parousia. Jesus' life as a whole illuminates its constituent parts and these evoke the total picture – all this within the traditions of Jewish experience with their peculiar ideas, expectations and conceptual images. That is why it is so difficult to sift from the gospels, in any detail, precise historical recollections of the earthly Jesus from the post-Easter 're-living' of them in the light of the Easter experience. Actually, complete success in that respect is not even what is required. Access to the life-story of the disciples is through the story of Jesus; they really did 'go after' Jesus, and in the trail that is their historical legacy, above all in the New Testament, we are able to follow exactly the trail of Jesus' own life and the course it took. Jesus himself left no collection of homilies behind him, no writings, still less a diary. He knew nothing of the convulsive quest of people for self-identity; he was an utterly free person, his living rooted in the sovereignly free God whom he called his *Abba*. In one of his flashes of wit A. Loisy remarked: Jesus preached the coming kingdom of God – and what came was the Church! It would be more true to say: heedless of self, concerned only for his fellows, Jesus proclaimed the coming kingdom of God, and that kingdom did come, in the guise of the crucified-and-risen One. Jesus may, within the Father's governance, have forgotten himself, but God 'remembers' the historical Jesus and of this divine remembrance resurrection and Parousia are the end result: God himself identifies the kingdom of God with Jesus of Nazareth, the crucified One. Whatever Jesus' concrete notions in his preaching of the imminent kingdom of God may have been, he was not deceived in his proclamation. The kingdom proclaimed did indeed come: in the living One who was crucified. The selfless proclaimer becomes thus the One proclaimed, the centre of the Christian affirmation of belief. That Jesus Christ is himself the 'firstborn' and the initiator of the kingdom of God was felt so intensely by the first Christians that they did indeed at first think that our mundane history was over and done with, in its present mode: the dominion of Christ was about to be inaugurated. Hence the problem of the relationship between these eschatological events and our earthly history, an issue hardly touched on in the New Testament, but one which would inevitably become urgent in the longer term. This simply goes to show that the Christian affirmation is no 'system' but a fundamental, living experience of encounter with Jesus of Nazareth, an experiential encounter the import and relevance of which were bound to be realized in ever new and changing circumstances, in thoroughly creative yet obedient fidelity to what God's saving actions have accomplished in Jesus.

Chapter 1

# The early Christian movement centred around Jesus: divergent 'reflexes' of the one Jesus of Nazareth

## §1 Taking stock of early Christian credal trends

*Introduction: the historical and theological bearing of these initial credal models*

Pre-Pauline, pre-Marcan, pre-Johannine local traditions, as well as those of the Q community have all – reinterpreted or conjoined, and thus corrected in both their kerygmatic and their corresponding historical bias – been merged in the four gospels under the canonical vision, present and prevailing in them, of the One crucified and risen. From those traditions we can discover even now that there were in circulation all kinds of pre-canonical independent Christological interpretations of Jesus, each having evident points of contact with particular facets of Jesus' life on earth, albeit on a selective basis for each local community. The historical continuity between each distinctive *kerygma* and particular aspects of the earthly Jesus is a striking fact about all such primitive Christian 'creeds'. Equally striking, however, is their perspectival view of Jesus, in other words the one-sidedness of these pre-canonical interpretations of Jesus. Despite that, however, it turns out that in each and every case, allowing for the particular *kerygma* and the religious milieu supplying them with the specific language in which to speak of him, Jesus of Nazareth himself was the criterion and norm. The merging of these divergent traditions in the four gospels is therefore, via the essential focus of the diverse Christological projects on special facets of Jesus' earthly career, at the same time also an accretion of historical information about Jesus. No cue for a credal proposition without a specific recollection of the earthly Jesus; no pointing to a historical fact about Jesus of Nazareth without some *kerygma*. Belief and history go hand in hand, because human beings, standing within history, are simply bound to play an interpertative role; and to proffer any definitive explanation is always a question of trust and faith.

## §2 Primitive Christian creeds and their historical foundation in Jesus

The question of God only has meaning for us human beings in so far as, being a human question, it speaks to our humanity; that is, if we then come to realize that the whole issue of man is in the end the issue of God himself. The human and the religious, although not fully identical, affect each other very closely indeed. The historically accessible human being, Jesus, becomes a new and more profound question for us as soon as, and because, he is the one with something crucial and definitive to say about God. In Jesus the issue is raised as to who or what God is. No doubt the Christian tradition has let go almost everything to do with Jesus that does not bear directly on the 'Jesus business',[1] that is, the cause of man as the cause of God, formulated in the New Testament as the lordship or rule of God and the kingdom of God.

The study of modern exegesis helps us to recognize diverse early Christian credal strands, each of which perpetuates certain facets of Jesus' life on earth. I do not have in mind, in referring to these credal accretions, giving an analysis of Christ's honorific titles within the local early Christian communities. Although those titles may originally have typified particular credal trends, they turn up eventually in them all; only then do they acquire their properly interchangeable meaning. Nor is there any point in settling a chronology of these credal declarations in the early Church (unless it be incidentally, where this is a likely historical conjecture). Yet this enquiry is a requisite stage on the way to getting at the appeal which Jesus of Nazareth makes to Israel and thus also to ourselves. Again, we are not to see these various tendencies as departures from the 'one gospel'; they existed before the gospels and are to be distilled from them. The canon of the creed did not come till much later; and even then its norm continues to be the historical Jesus of Nazareth.[2]

A. *MARANATHA* OR PAROUSIA CHRISTOLOGY: JESUS, THE ONE
WHO BRINGS THE APPROACHING SALVATION, LORD OF THE FUTURE
AND JUDGE OF THE WORLD

*Literature.* H. R. Balz, *Methodische Probleme der neutestamentlichen Christologie*, Neukirchen 1967; Kl. Berger, 'Zum traditions-geschichtlichen Hintergrund christologischer Hoheitstitel', NTS 17 (1970–1), 391–425; M. Black, 'The Christological use of the Old Testament in the New Testament', NTS 18 (1971–2), 1–14; J. Blinzler et al., *Jesus in den Evangelien* (SBS, 45), Stuttgart 1970; R. Casey, 'The earliest Christologies', JTS 9 (1958), 253–77; H. Conzelmann, *Grundriss*, and 'Randbemerkungen zum "Lage" in Neuen Testament', EvTh 22 (1962), 225–33; Cullmann, *Christologie*, 200–44; J. Daniélou, *Théologie du Judéo-Christianisme*, Tournai 1958, and *Études d'exégèse judéochrétienne*, Paris 1966; R. Edwards, 'An approach to a Christology of Q', JRel 51 (1971), 247–69; J. Ernst, *Anfänge der Christologie* (SBS, 57), Stuttgart 1972; W. Foerster, s.v., *Kurios*, ThWNT III, 1081–95; R. Fuller, *Critical Introduction to the New Testament*, London 1966, and *The Foundations of the New Testament Christology*, New York 1965 (1972²); J. Gnilka, *Jesus Christus nach frühen Zeugnissen des Glaubens*, Munich 1970; F. Hahn, *Hoheitstitel*, 67–125; E. Haechen, 'Die frühe Christologie', ZThK 63 (1966), 145–59; P. Hoffmann, *Q-Studien*, and 'Die Anfänge der Theologie in Logienquelle', *Gestalt und anspruch des Neuen Testaments* (Würzburg 1969), 134–52; J. Jeremias, 'Die älteste Schicht der Menschensohn-Logien', ZNW 58 (1967), 159–72; E. Käsemann, *Besinnungen*, I, 135–57; II, 82–104; II, 105–30; L. E. Keck, 'Mark 3:7–12 and Mark's Christology', JBL 84 (1965), 341–58; H. Koester, in Robinson-Koester, *Trajectories*, 158–204 and 205–31; W. Kramer, *Christos, Kyrios, Gottessohn*, Zürich-Stuttgart 1963; Lührmann, *Q-Redaktion*, and 'Erwägungen zur Geschichte des Urchristentums', EvTh 32 (1972), 452–67; W. Marxsen, *Der Evangelist Markus*, Göttingen 1959²; E. Meyer, *Ursprung und Anfänge des Christentums*, 3 vols, Stuttgart-Berlin 1921 and 1923; N. Perrin, 'The Christology of Mark', JRel 51 (1971), 173–87; J. A. Robinson, 'The most primitive Christology of all?', JTS 7 (1956), 177–89; G. Schille, *Das vorsynoptische Juden-christentum*, Berlin 1970; J. Schneider, 'Der Beitrag der Urgemeinde zur Jesus Überlieferung im Lichte der neuesten Forschung', TLZ 87 (1962), 40–412; S. Schulz, 'Maranatha und Kyrios Jèsous', ZNW 53 (1962), 125–44, and *Q-Quelle*; H.-E. Tödt, *Der Menschensohn*; W. Thüsing, 'Erhöhungsvorstellung und Parusieerwartung in der ältesten nachösterlichen Christologie', BZ (1967), 95–108 and 205–22, and 12 (1968), 54–80 and 223–40 (whence passages are quoted here; now also in book form: Stuttgart 1969); Ph. Vielhauer, in *Aufsätze*, 55–91, 92–140 and 147–67; Weeden, *Mark-traditions; Aux origines de l'Église* (RechBibl, 7), Bruges 1965.

## (a) The essential gist and purpose of this creed

In view of the primary identification of Jesus with the eschatological prophet, the *maranatha* Christology is very likely to have been the oldest credal affirmation, although difficult to reconstruct in its oldest form. It was not in the Old Testament but in the so-called inter-testamentary literature and thus in Jesus' time that the messiah was seen as the bringer of eschatological salvation.[3] H. Koester sees the sociological setting of this creed in apocalyptic circles in Jerusalem, the place where the coming messiah was expected.[4] S. Schulz, however, sees this apocalyptical propensity just as much in the Palestinian Q communities which, although akin to the kerygmatic set-up at Jerusalem, nevertheless differ from it.[5] Then again, allowing for what are in my view a number of points in his book open to fundamental criticism, Th. J. Weeden has shown in a remarkable study that even the Marcan gospel contains the same fundamental credal traits, albeit within the distinctively Marcan Christology of the 'suffering son of man'.[6] I shall first synthesize the main features of this Parousia *kerygma* common to the Q and Marcan communities in order then to analyse the essential differences in the Q community's tradition on the one hand and on the other hand in the pre-Marcan tradition and Marcan redaction.

This eschatological creed derives in the first instance from the prophetic and apocalyptic logia tradition in the primitive Church,[7] although it is uncertain which honorific title, if any, was originally connected with this eschatological credal bias; F. Hahn and Ph. Vielhauer are completely at loggerheads over this.[8] But the appropriate Christological titles are a poor guide to exploring what have been called primitive Christian credal strands, because through contact between the various local congregations they turn up in more or less all the traditions and become the expression, in each case, of a distinctive creed.

This first credal pattern in the primitive Church found its expression in apocalyptic and prophetic logia. These local congregations turned to an already existing Jewish apocalyptic belief in order to interpret Jesus after his death as the coming decisive figure of the 'final future' which was thought to be close at hand. Christological belief in Jesus means, according to this creed, believing this Jesus of Nazareth to be the Lord who will come in the last days to bring salvation (grace, mercy) and judgement. (In the New Testament, as also in our classic declaration of belief, this initially single affirmation becomes a component of a more amply developed and articulated creed: 'Thence he shall come to judge the living and the dead.') This eschatological creed looks forward to what is to come and what exists already as a heavenly reality: the judge of the world, Jesus, already exalted yet still to come; in the practice of the cult this reality is anticipated (*maranatha* – the Lord is coming – in the liturgy; see 1 Cor. 16:22; Rev. 22:20; Didache 10:6). We find an echo of this eschatological-apocalyptic creed in Paul, where he is in fact reflecting pre-Pauline tradition: 'For the *Maran* [the Lord] himself will descend from heaven with a cry of command, with the archangel's call, and with the sound of the trumpet of God. And the dead in Christ will arise first; then we who are alive, who are left, shall be caught up together with them in the clouds to meet the Lord in the air' (1 Thess. 4:16–17); the motif of the resurrection of the dead, and the 'rapture' or assumption of those still alive, is here the imminent coming of Jesus as Lord, that is, adjudicator of mercy and judgement (for Paul himself this creed is contained already in the proclamation of Jesus' resurrection); or even: we . . . 'wait for his Son from heaven, whom he raised from the dead, Jesus who delivers us from the wrath to come' (1 Thess. 1:10).

Two titles of Jesus are set originally in a similar religio-historical, apocalyptic context: *Mar* or *Maran* (the Lord or *Kyrios* of the Jerusalem and Palestinian congregations) and son of man.

'Lord', *Mar* or *Maran*, is in origin evidently associated with this eschatological creed; above all, this title is connected with the Aramaic I Enoch 1:9, which is in fact cited with express reference to Enoch in Jude 14; 'Behold, the Lord is coming with his holy myriads, to execute judgement on all, and to convict all the ungodly . . .';[9] 'The Lord is coming' is in Aramaic, *Maran atha*, and most probably implied originally a sort of anathema: 'The Lord is coming to judge.'[10] This ancient 'Lord Christology' is at the same time (though not primarily) connected with Ps. 110:1, which is cited independently in Mk. 12:36; Acts (frequently); Phil. 2:7–10 (a very old, pre-Pauline tradition – the earliest mention, as some think, of a *Maran* Christology); Rom. 10:5–10 and 14:9ff.[11]

'Son of man' too suggests the same apocalyptic circles, and so the bringer of salvation who is coming. The term is manifestly present in an apocalyptic perspective in Mk. 13:26; but it is still possible, in my view, that 'son of man' in the apocalyptic sense becomes part of the tradition only when there is a word-for-word citation of Dan. 7:13.[12] In the earliest, Aramaic phase of the Q community the term 'son of man' occurs in the sense of the son of man's function as the coming judge (Lk. 12:8-9),[13] whereas the coming Parousia or appearing of the son of man emerges only in the later phase of Q (Lk. 17:23-24).[14] What the earliest phase is meant to convey is the identity between the heavenly exalted Jesus and the son of man (not at this stage an identification of the *earthly* Jesus with the son of man); and this identification in Q is grounded not in appearances of Jesus nor yet in Jesus' own proclamation of a coming son of man, rather in the 'enthusiastic' eschatological pneuma-experience of the original prophetic and apocalyptic local congregations.[15] A Parousia *kerygma* without a resurrection (see later).

However much a special meaning of Lord (*Maran*) and son of man may be associated with this first creed, even so these titles are not typical features of it. 'Son of man', although characteristic of this eschatological-apocalyptic Christology, is not a credal term, not even in this tradition. It never has been; and it is absent from all ancient credal formulae.

As is the case with every kind of early Christian creed, the structure of this one points to a correlation between this Christian *kerygma* and a typical aspect of Jesus himself. Which aspect of the earthly Jesus of Nazareth did these communities take as the historical point of departure for their *kerygma*? What, in other words, was the motif, the principal element of their tradition? Or what did they see in the earthly Jesus? The answer is clear enough: Jesus' own proclamation and tidings of the imminent rule of God. Quite deliberately, these communities put themselves in continuity with Jesus' historical message of the kingdom of God as 'near at hand'.[16] According to this creed the community, as it 'goes after Jesus', means to do what Jesus did: announce the proximity of the kingdom of God. It does so, however, in an awareness of the historical distance between Jesus' earthly days and its own proclamation; for the proclamation of the coming kingdom of God is something it updates in proclaiming the imminent, latter-day Parousia of Jesus, in such a way at any rate that the 'coming of God's rule' and the 'coming of Jesus – son of man', the judge of the world, still to some extent stand side by side, yet manifestly not without some, albeit unthematized, intrinsic connection.

This type of creed assumes the identification of Jesus with the son of man, whether it be primarily of the earthly Jesus with the Jesus returning eschatologically as the son of man (as in the Marcan tradition and redaction; see below), or primarily of the heavenly Jesus with the coming son of man-cum-judge of the world (the earliest phase, that is, of the Q community; see below). At the same time this entails, within the 'ecclesial' continuity with Jesus' own proclamation here on earth, the presence of a discontinuous element: Jesus' person as the eschatological judge of the world, in other words, his Parousia, itself now becomes the object of proclamation. Jesus' historical message is taken over by the Church and passed on – but in the awareness that the person of Jesus has become impacted with his own message, whereas it was not himself that Jesus proclaimed but the coming rule of God; that however, being men's salvation, was 'his cause'. This these congregations understood. Jesus' selfless annunciation of the imminent rule of God was 'personalized' by them. Within this credal strand the Easter experience is not thematized; it knows nothing of any appearance traditions. Not only is the resurrection not proclaimed; it is nowhere mentioned in the Q tradition.

In certain early Christian communities, then, Jesus is identified with the eschatological 'salvific figure', as currently encountered in the post-Old Testament, non-Christian, Jewish apocalyptic of those days. These local churches find salvation in Jesus as the world's judge who is about to come, dispensing both mercy and judgement. In this identification we see on the one hand a continuity with the historical 'given' of God's rule, on the other hand a process of articulating the 'identification' of Jesus with an already existing Jewish religious key notion of the period: the eschatological bringer of salvation.

But there is also a second important factor of historical and substantial continuity between Jesus' message of the nearby kingdom of God and the Church's proclamation of Jesus' Parousia, namely, the sending out of the disciples by the pre-Easter Jesus to Israel as a whole, a mission which, by all the criteria of what authentically represents him, derives essentially from the earthly Jesus, especially since in the Q tradition this possesses no recognizably Christological content and the disciples are charged more with passing on Jesus' own message, as well as healing the sick and driving out devils.[17] 'Following after Jesus' here consists in handing on his message of the near approach of God's rule for man's salvation. The general principle here becomes the truth:

via the reflex of Jesus in the local churches we do indeed reach the historical Jesus. In his disciples we may detect the Master.

After that brief sketch of a very ancient, early Christian attempt at proposing a creed – the *kerygma* of belief in Jesus' speedy return as eschatological deliverer, saviour and judge of the world – I am in a position to account for the two subsidiary strands within it.

## (b) The creed in the tradition of the Q community

The kerygmatic scheme or ecclesial proclamation of this community has its original roots (during, that is, its primary, very early, Aramaic phase[18]) not in a formal concern with the earthly ministry of Jesus as a whole, but with his message of the approaching and now close at hand rule of God.

The Lord's Prayer, from this earliest phase of the Q tradition, is obviously and in all its parts a straight *Maranatha* Christology: '*Abba*, hallowed be your name, your kingdom come, give us each day bread for today; forgive us our sins, for we also forgive the sin committed against us; and lead us not into temptation'[19] – a prayer unknown in the Marcan material, in the Pauline and Johannine traditions. This Q community prays for the coming of God's rule and pleads to be kept safe in, or else preserved from, the *peirasmos*, the tribulations and trials of the end of the Age. There is no sign at all here of any 'delaying of the Parousia' – the oldest layer of Q is unique in that respect; all other pre-canonical traditions that we can recover, as well as the synoptics, show symptoms of a 'postponement' of the Parousia. For oneself one prays only for the barest necessities, for whatever is absolutely necessary just before the Parousia happens: physical sustenance for one day, as long as the Parousia is still pending (Luke himself makes it 'from one day to the next'); then too debts recoverable against other people are remitted because with the prospect of an imminent Parousia they have no further point. Finally, the community prays that when the eschatological woes descend they will not apostatize, a prayer too (not unknown in the Jewish tradition)[20] that the elect, in this case the Christians, be spared the ordeals and be carried up straightaway into the kingdom of God.

The oldest Q material contains both the idea of the proximity of the kingdom of God (Lk. 6:20b) and that of the imminent arrival of the latter-day son of man (Lk. 12:8–9). Although the notions of *basileia* (lordship or rule and kingdom of God) and 'son of man' belong in Jewish thought to separate complexes of tradition, they are nevertheless conjoined in Q: the son of man brings the *basileia*.[21]

In the oldest Q tradition the earthly Jesus is the eschatological prophet; it is only the heavenly Jesus who is identified with the coming son of man. But this does of course presuppose Jesus' being 'with God', while not making it directly an object of *kerygma*. The heavenly Jesus, presently operative in the Christian prophets, is proclaimed as the coming eschatological saviour, and yet as judge of those who will not accept the community's message regarding the coming Jesus-son of man. Crucial here are the Q passages Lk. 12:8–9=Mt. 10:32–33: 'And I tell you, everyone who acknowledges me before men, the son of man also will acknowledge before the angels of God' (Lk. 12:8). First of all there is an identity here between 'me' and 'the son of man': it is a question of a distinction in function of the same person. But the identification relates the heavenly Jesus with the son of man.[22] The point is, therefore, that the stance we adopt towards the exalted son of man, announced by the Church as being 'on the way', is decisive in respect of our final salvation or condemnation at the 'last judgement'. The heavenly Jesus is the eschatological bringer of salvation; but for anyone not accepting the Church's message about Jesus he is their judge.[23] This is of course an 'implicit Christology'; but in this oldest phase of Q it applies not to Jesus in his earthly existence (Jesus of Nazareth is the eschatological prophet), but to the heavenly Jesus, present and operative in his eschatological community; in other words, Jesus is already exercising his lordship 'at the right hand of God'. Yet this exalted state is still not the same as the exaltation of the *Kyrios* in pre-Pauline and Pauline or even synoptic theology;[24] it is seen as a very brief interlude or prelude to the rapid arrival of the kingdom of God. The early Q tradition, therefore, contains no *kerygma* of Jesus' being presently enthroned in heaven,[25] but of his coming Parousia. The celestial action of Jesus, here and now, results in the outpouring of the Spirit, the prophetic activity of the Church; that is the source of assurance regarding his (imminent) coming. It is the 'Easter experience' of this community. The proclamation, through Christian prophecy in and by the Church, is in itself the dawning of God's kingdom. In other words, the eschatological community, being grounded in the heavenly Jesus, is itself the dawning of the final kingdom.

As for the suffering and death of Jesus, these have no significant place in the theology or the *kerygma* represented by this particular type of credal affirmation. They are the lot of every prophet, but especially of the eschatological prophet.[26] In its earliest phase this 'Church of the latter days' is still a religious movement within Jewry and the synagogue. Nowhere can one detect an anti-Jewish polemic, only a religious critique of the Pharisees; and that was also feasible within Judaism. An anti-Pharisaic stance was equally prevalent in Qumrân circles and Baptist movements.[27]

The oldest Q tradition reveals a community which, being full of hope and enthusiasm for the coming Parousia, went to great lengths in renouncing possessions, a community in which the poor, the hungry and the sorrowful were held to be blessed, because in view of the apocalyptic transformation that would reverse every condition and relationship they would soon be rejoicing; a community in which men paid no heed to earthly cares but, putting such concerns out of mind, trusted unconditionally in God's providential nearness to them; a community which drew out and emphasized the place of the Decalogue within the Law, and in which divorce was not permitted, people were asked to love their enemies and surrender the principle of 'eye for eye, tooth for tooth', accepting as a golden rule: 'As you wish that men would do to you, do so to them' (Mt. 7:12=Lk. 6:31). Since it was rooted in an apocalyptic eschatology it was a-political, although all un-social behaviour was deplored (Mk. 11:42=Mt. 23:23; Mt. 23:27= Lk. 11:44; Mt. 23:13=Lk. 11:52; all anti-Pharisaic). The Q community was a withdrawn one, waiting as it was upon God, as upon the approach of the heavenly Jesus.[28] The only Christological title occurring in this primary phase of Q is 'the son of man' (Lk. 12:8–9) in the sense of the heavenly Jesus, the coming world-judge of the last days. The (messianic) Christ-title does not appear anywhere in the Q tradition.

It was only in a later, albeit still pre-New Testament, phase of this community, when Greek-speaking Jewish Christians had taken charge of it, that (without any loss of what we have just been describing) essentially new elements were added to this eschatological Christology, thanks to the distinctive contribution of Greek-speaking Jews, besides the notion of the 'deferment' of the Parousia and the reciprocal contacts between Marcan material and Q material. The most strikingly new factor that now emerges is a dogmatic concern with every facet of the earthly Jesus, the enlargement of the anti-Pharisaic critique into a general judgement upon Israel as a whole (the Q community has got separated from the synagogue-connection and has become 'church') and the gathering in to the Church of tax-collectors and sinners.

This increasing concern with the earthly Jesus not only shows the influence of Marcan material but serves a Christological purpose: a polemic aimed at a *theios anèr* Christology (more about that later on), at any rate in the sense of a theological posture that demands sensational miracles for reasons of self-advantage and legitimation. In the Q tradition this theology is most clearly exhibited in the temptation stories (Mt. 4:1–11=Lk. 4:1–13; cf. Mk. 1:12–13). In this narrative we have a Jewish, Scriptural and polemical interpretation of what the title 'Son of God' implies for the Q community. It is interpreted as a contention or dispute between 'the Jesus' (*ho Jèsous*) and 'the devil' (Mt. 4:1). Here for the first time in the Q community the notion of the 'Son of God' is transferred to the earthly Jesus. The temptations are not meant to be specifically messianic ones. The first and second temptations (according to the more correct sequence in Matthew) are a reaction against the Hellenistic-Jewish, Galilean idea that miracles prove somebody to be a son of God; the third temptation (on a mythical mountain) is more apocalyptic in nature: the narrative at this point is a Christological reaction to a worldwide dominion exercised by a messianic king – understood here in a political sense. In other words, the Q Christology rejects both a *theios anèr* Christology and the Zealotic-messianic liberation movement bent on world-domination by Israel.[29] These temptation stories intimate that the earthly Jesus is the 'Son of God' – not however in virtue of miracles and a show of worldly power but of his trust in God and obedient conformity to God's will as revealed in the Law (the Q community, ever faithful to the Law, is stranger to any controversy or dispute in that field). According to Q, any other interpretation of this Christological title is 'of the devil'. The Law itself legitimates the claim to sonship of God. The Son of God is the obedient One, faithful to the Law. The title 'Son of God', as well as the 'divine miracle-man' Christology or the epiphany Christology of a *deus praesens*, a god clothed in human form, comes from the pre-Marcan tradition with which this Q community now makes contact and against which it reacts. The complete absence of the messianic Christ-title in the Q community obviously betokens a reaction against a 'power' Christology which asks for miracles without any good or benefit accruing to other human beings.

In the question put by John's disciples to Jesus, whether he is 'the One to come' (that is, the coming 'judge by fire', and thus the son of man), clearly the suggestion is that the earthly Jesus also is now to be identified with the son of man (Mt. 11:2–6=Lk. 7:18–23). Not just the heavenly but also the earthly Jesus is the son of man coming in judgement, not simply an eschatological prophet, as had previously been said.[30] Jesus' own career or public ministry is itself a latter-day event, and the eschatological community is not the very first sign of the kingdom's dawning. Via the reflex of their communal pneumatic experiences they get a better idea of the truly eschatological character of the earthly Jesus. Now it is not only the heavenly Jesus but (through the impact of the Marcan tradition) the earthly Jesus as well who re-inforces their hope of the coming Parousia; after all, Jesus answers the disciples of John by saying: 'Look at what I am doing.' In that way he points to the near approach of God's rule in his own ministry, es-pecially in his 'good tidings for the poor' (Isa. 29:18–19; 35:5; 61:1). Jesus' reply in Q is totally un-messianic, if one takes 'messianic' to refer to one particular Jewish tradition centred on the Davidic dynasty; but it is Jewish and messianic in a sense which we shall be examining later on. Jesus is invoking in these passages the functions of the latter-day prophet (the Isaianic texts in their late Jewish interpretation): the rule of God is already present for those who accept his message and are not scandalized by it. One's attitude to the earthly Jesus is decisive here and now in the matter of final salvation or final undoing (Mt. 11:6=Lk. 7:23). Thus the Q community finds already against the Jews who have rejected Jesus.

To the extent, however, that this later trend in the Q community is a reflection upon Jesus' death, it sees in it the lot of all the prophets of Israel; they are rejected by the people of God (Mt. 23:34–36=Lk. 11: 49–51; and Mt. 23:37–39=Lk. 13:34). Therefore a salvific function attaches to the words and acts of the earthly Jesus, not to his death. The deliverer, for one who comprehends Jesus' sayings and actions, is none other than the coming son of man. But that depends on one's attitude here and now to Jesus.

The second phase of Q is concerned with two miracles of Jesus (Mt. 12:22–30=Lk. 11:14–23; Mt. 8:5–13=Lk. 7:1–10). What these miracles are meant to express is, on the one hand, the rejection of a false Christ-ology and, on the other, opposition to Jews who accuse Jesus of being in league with the devil. These are no epiphany miracles – the title 'Son of God' does not occur in them – but signs of dawning salvation and the kingdom of God. The *basileia* is coming and yet is already present, not just in the prophetic message of the community but before that in the earthly Jesus; in Jesus it has already reached people (*ephthasèn eph' hèmas hè basileia tou theou*, Mt. 12:28b): the eschatology adopted here is one 'in process of realization'. Thus for Q Jesus of Nazareth is indeed 'an eschatological phenomenon'.[31] In face of this Jesus no neutral stance is possible (Mt. 12:30=Lk. 11:23) (although the perspective provided by Q is still wholly restricted to Israel. Again, it is characteristic that even in the synoptic tradition Jesus' 'miracles *in absentia*' [Mt. 8:5–13=Lk. 7:1–10; and Mk. 7:24ff] concern only Gentiles; the point at issue is not the sensational aspect of such a miracle, but the Jewish background to these traditions; the pagan centurion knows that a Jew will not come beneath the roof of a Gentile, so he asks for a 're-mote control' miracle; Jesus' latter-day, eschatological activity is directed exclusively to Israel).

In Q the problem entailed by the failure of the constantly awaited Parousia to arrive is discussed primarily in parables (Mt. 24:43–44= Lk. 12:39–40; Mt. 24:45–51=Lk. 12:42b–46; Mt. 25:14–30=Lk. 19: 12–27; Mt. 13:31–32=Lk. 13:18–19; Mt. 13:33=Lk. 13:20–21), but also in the Q apocalypse (Mt. 24:26–28, 37–41=Lk. 17:23–24, 26–27, 30, 34–35, 37). Because the Parousia 'tarries' attention is centred on being watchful; and people are cautioned against premature identifica-tions. The Parousia will be public and plain to everyone; but it is not to be recognized from signs and omens; it will happen 'all of a sudden'.

In this phase of Q the person of the earthly Jesus is already identified with the (coming) son of man, in an entirely non-apocalyptic use of the term (the parable of the children at play in the market-place; Mt. 11:16–19=Lk. 7:31–35): the son of man-Jesus of Nazareth is a friend of tax-collectors and sinners, the kingdom of universal peace is beginning; his earthly life lies already in the shadow of the dawning *basileia*; rejecting or accepting Jesus has an eschatological relevance.

Moreover, the earthly Jesus is now also called 'the Son' (Mt. 11:27= Lk. 10:22). (Mt. 11:25–27=Lk. 10:21–22 is of course a much disputed Q text – though not, in my view, with any good reason.)[32] The Son here is the intermediary who reveals God's eschatological secrets to the 'little ones', that is, the members of the community (in keeping with the sapiential tradition which crops up here and is especially typical of the Q community in its later phase). The wise ones, Israel's Scribes and Israel's leaders, shut themselves off from the revelation by Jesus and so forfeit their last chance of salvation. Jesus is 'the Son' because the Father has given him the eschatological 'total authority' (*exousia*); and so even in his life on earth he is son of man, invested with complete power. Here too the *exousia* has still to come, and yet already is. In this one can detect the primary influence of another credal strand: namely, the Wisdom Christology (see below).

Besides son of man, Son of God and the Son, 'Lord' (*Kyrios*) also now makes its appearance in the Q tradition (Mt. 24:42, 45–46, 48, 50 and 7:21, 22 parallels) – and does so invariably in an apocalyptic context. As regards the earthly Jesus, the title 'Lord' is uttered only in the pericope of the centurion of Capernaum, a Gentile (Mt. 8:5–13 = Lk. 7:1–10). It could be translated as 'sir'; and yet there is a deeper intention: *Kyrie* amounts to addressing Jesus as 'wonder-working deliverer'[33] and, having regard to the tenor of the whole pericope, as someone with complete power and authority, such as this centurion or officer also enjoyed in his own sphere. In the parable of the Faithful and Unfaithful Servants (Mt. 24:45–51=Lk. 12:42b, 46) we again hear mention of 'the Lord' (Mt. 24:50); but allowing for the nature of the story as straightforward parable, 'the Lord' can only mean the master of these slaves, without any immediately Christological implication. Different again is the meaning of 'the Lord' (Mt. 25:20, 22, 24, 25) in the parable of the Talents (Mt. 25:14–30=Lk. 19:12–27), which in Q is evidently a Parousia parable: Jesus is away, gone abroad, the disciples have stayed behind. There is reference here, although in veiled terms, to crucifixion, but without any kerygmatic motives in view. 'After a long time' (the Parousia is delayed) the Lord returns. In these verses 'the Lord', *Kyrios*, obviously signifies Jesus as the son of man of the last days. He is the son of man-*Kyrios* who at the close of the Age will ask us to account for what we have done with the talents we have received. Thus the eschatological mode of existence of this Q community, as it awaits the Lord's coming, is an actively busy existence in a moral and religious sense, rock-hard as in the world of business. After all, even the term *Kyrios* is advanced in a critical context (Lk. 6:46 =Mt. 7:21): 'Why do you call me "Lord, Lord", and not do what I tell you?'; here in the Q context *Kyrios* has an eschatological significance, it expresses the *maranatha* Christology which calls for performance, not for non-activity. Doing, orthopraxis, is so important in this layer of Q that it may be responsible (in keeping with Graeco-Judaism) for the 'doctrine of the two ways', on the one hand that of apocalyptic revelation, on the other the way of the moral code (the Decalogue), to which the *Didachè* explicitly refers.[34]

*Conclusion*: the Q version is a form of a very widely disseminated early Christian *kerygma*. It has no explicit resurrection *kerygma*, although one might say that, in its idea of the heavenly Jesus being operatively present in the Christian prophets, it possesses an equivalent of what other early Christian traditions call the resurrection. On contact with this latter tradition, therefore, it was able to recognize itself in it and integrate this resurrection *kerygma* into its proclamation of the Parousia. Parallel to this, and eventually affecting and being affected by it, we find another, perhaps equally ancient version of this type of creed: in the Marcan tradition.

## (c) The Lord of the future in Mark's Christology

The Marcan gospel presents both the earthly 'suffering son of man' and the son of man who will come in power and glory only at the Parousia. It is a striking fact – but also a hermeneutical key to the understanding of this gospel – that Mark has Jesus enjoining silence in face of certain acknowledgements of the Christ, all of which pointedly suggest a 'power' Christology, yet never where the one acknowledged is the real Jesus of Mark: that is, (a) the Jesus-son of man who is suffering in his earthly life, (b) is absent in the brief period of the eschatological community, but (c) is soon to come.[35] It is not the 'son of man', indeed only used by Jesus in the Marcan gospel,[36] of which mention is forbidden, but rather all those Christological affirmations which suggest a 'power' Christology: Mk. 3:11–12; 5–7; 1:25; 1:34; and also healings that might be wrongly understood in a similar perspective: 1:44; 5:43; 7:36 and 8:26; in other words, unorthodox Christology is not to be mentioned. That is the so-called 'messianic secret' in Mark, which is thus less a secret than a veto on what Mark considers to be a false Christology: 'Son of God', a title often employed in terms enshrining *theios anèr* ideas, Mark is quite willing to accept, on condition however that by it is understood the suffering son of man[37] and not therefore any 'power' Christology. In this Mark is at the same time honouring the drift of his older tradition, which calls the earthly Jesus the hidden 'Son of God', who only through suffering and death and the legitimation consequent upon them is to be recognized as the true Son of God. Set within this perspective the peculiarly Marcan scheme for an eschatological Christology becomes clear.

Because Mark's gospel, in contrast to the tradition of the Q community, does not assume, in the (for it equally fleeting) period between the death and Parousia of Jesus, an operative presence of the heavenly Jesus who is now living with God, its Christology depends solely on the one hand upon the memory of Jesus' days on earth and on the other upon the hopeful expectation that the son of man is about to come. As regards the latter it is at one with the Q tradition, whereas on the former point the Marcan material has affected the Christology of (what S. Schulz and D. Lührmann regard as) the second, Hellenistic-Jewish phase of the Q community. Thus the dogmatic difference between Marcan gospel and Q tradition (as well as the consequences flowing from it) lies in the fact that while for the latter resurrection and exaltation are identical, Mark transfers the exaltation to and identifies it with the mighty Parousia of the Lord, although that too many are to expect

J.E.C.–O

within their lifetime (Mk. 9:1). But on this very point Mark's community is noticeably disheartened: Jesus has so far not come! In his absence there is of course the present gift of the Spirit (see Mk. 13:11); but the Spirit and Jesus are in no way identical (see 3:28–29). Jesus, though risen and destined later, as son of man, to judge the world by its acceptance or rejection of Jesus of Nazareth, is meanwhile concealed and kept in readiness in heaven, to await his exaltation and coming in power.

The Lord's absence: 'The days will come when the bridegroom is taken away from them, and then they will fast in that day' (Mk. 2:20) (that is, will grieve over his absence, although the disciples will be strengthened by God's eschatological Spirit and their hope of the speedy arrival of Jesus-son of man), is on the one hand symbolized polemically by the conspicuous absence of any account of appearances in the authentic Mark (Mk. 16:9–20 is post-Marcan and, although canonical, quite obviously a later attempt to synthesize diverse local church traditions and to integrate the by then baffling, 'archaic' Christology of Mark with the vision of unity in faith entertained by the Church at large). If the assertion is correct that in associating exaltation with Parousia (thus not with resurrection) Mark does not see the celestial Jesus as presently operative, but affirms the complete absence of Jesus from his sorrowing and suffering Church, it then becomes possible to understand his not accepting the tradition of the Jesus appearances: 'appearing' is what Jesus will do at the Parousia, not before.

We can take it that Mark's purpose is to place at the centre the central *kerygma* of the eschatological coming of Jesus-son of man, the Parousia – an event which by then had already been awaited for more than a generation – so as to counter a sense of discouragement and a tendency to make the resurrection itself – for Mark the basis, ground and premise of the Parousia-expectation – the object of proclamation instead of the Parousia. He wants to ground the faith of Christians in Jesus of Nazareth as the Christ who came to suffer and be rejected and is soon to come in power, as Son of God and son of man. In this time of fasting for the Church Jesus is absent; no more will he drink the wine with his disciples until 'that day' when they are reunited (14:25). Between the two manifestations of the selfsame Jesus of Nazareth: his being manifested on earth in preaching and conduct, in suffering and rejection, and his eschatological appearing 'in power and glory', stands 'the tomb'. This local congregation looks to the words and actions of Jesus and to the whole course of his life and ministry on earth in anticipation of his coming in power. The crucified One is the coming son of man. Thus Mark shares something of the Pauline Christological concept and something of the Q community's eschatological *kerygma*, but his own *kerygma* is vested in the intrinsic connection between the earthly Jesus (especially in his suffering) and the Parousia (8:27 – 9:8; 10:32–40). For him the coming of the kingdom of God and that of Jesus-son of man 'in power' (Parousia) coincide (9:1 with 13:26–27; see 14:25); and so meanwhile the Church is 'orphaned', though comforted by the gift of the Spirit of God.

Therefore the resurrection, which Mark presupposes in his *kerygma* of the Parousia (16:6; 8:31; 9:31; 10:34), is not in itself an exaltation in glory or investing with power, but something on which to found expectation of the Parousia. For Mark the exaltation is invariably bound up with the Parousia, which is on the point of arriving and yet cannot be calculated in advance (8:38; 9:2–8; 10:37; 13:26; 14:62). The key passages in support of this interpretation are: 2:18–20; 14:61–62; 13:24–27, and the connection between 14:28 and 16:7, of great importance to anyone who does not read them having in mind what Matthew, Luke or John says about it subsequently, but just as they stand in Mark and are read by the members of Mark's community, who evidently have no tradition in which appearances of Jesus are acknowledged, but one in which the focal point of attention is Jesus' Parousia. Having regard to these actual premises, 14:28 and 16:7 could, even taken as they stand, refer as much to the Parousia as to the appearances. Usually, however, appearances are read into this context because of other traditions (Matthew, Luke, John and the later ending added to Mark); yet in a structural analysis of the Marcan gospel they can be better understood as a direct reference to the eschatological Parousia of Jesus-son of man.[38] This interpretation depends partly on how one interprets 13:24–27 and 14:62.

Daniel 7:13 (Septuagint) speaks of an *ascensus*, an exaltation of the son of man, not of a 'descent'. So too in Mk. 13:26. Mark describes, in 13:14–27, a 'heavenly scenario': the enthronement of Jesus as son of man in power, as an eschatological event. As in other and older creeds that we find in the New Testament (Phil. 2:10–11; 1 Pet. 3:19, 22; Col. 1:15–20) so here we are told that Jesus is to be glorified after the hosts of heaven or the spiritual powers have been conquered and made subject to Jesus. In 13:25 Mark portrays in apocalyptic terms Jesus' victory over these powers, who then themselves see the full enthronement of the son of man.[39] The whole action (in contrast, for instance, to Mt. 24:30, where the seeing is related to terrestrial beings) takes place in celestial spheres between Jesus and heavenly powers; the earthly action was drawn to a close in Mk. 13:24a, and not until 13:27 is there any further mention of people; after that comes the gathering together of Jesus' followers by the angels. Only then is the union between Jesus and his disciples restored. Matthew and Luke turn Mark's exaltation of the son of man into a 'descent' of the son of man exalted already from the time of his resurrection (Mt. 24:29–31; Lk. 21:25–28). But not Mark himself!

Mark 14:62, therefore, should be explained in terms consistent with this. It is noticeable that 14:62: 'I am [he]; and you will see the Son of man sitting at the right hand of Power and coming with the clouds of heaven' conjoins the 'standing' son of man of Dan. 7:13 (see also Acts 7:55–56) with the 'seated' Lord of Ps. 110:1. This combined quotation is typical of a credal trend which associates the exaltation of Jesus not with the resurrection but with the Parousia.[40] (Again in Acts 7:55–56 there is an implicit link via the combination of 'standing' and 'at my right hand'.) Psalm 110:1 is usually associated in the New Testament with Jesus' resurrection, which is at the same time envisaged as exaltation (Rom. 8:34; Col. 3:1; Eph. 1:20; 1 Pet. 3:22; Heb. 1:3; 8:1; 10:12; 12:2), whereas Dan. 7:13 is usually linked with the Parousia. According to H. E. Tödt they cannot both together serve to denote the exaltation:[41] the 'sitting at the right hand' can (in an Old Testament context) only occur after exaltation and inauguration; the resurrection is then an 'ascending up' to God's right hand. Indeed Ps. 110 (in its Greek version, Ps. 109) exhibits this difference: the Son of David sits at God's right hand till all enemies have been made subject to him. Only prior to the judgement does one (in a Jewish context) stand upright (the Jesus-son of man, the world's judge, 'stands up'). Throughout the New Testament, therefore, there is this apparent 'tension': resurrection as a 'sitting at God's right hand' (Mk. 14:62 parallels; 16:19 [pseudo-Mk.]; Acts 2:34–35; Eph. 1:20; Col. 3:1; Heb. 1:3, 13; 8:1; 12:2) and, on the other hand, the 'subjugation of all the powers' (not until the Parousia) (1 Cor. 15:23 and 25; Heb. 10:13). Paul is himself evidence of the divergent viewpoints about this in early Christian tradition; even in his case tradition and (Pauline) redaction do not tally (cf. 1 Cor. 15:25, referring to the future, with 15:27: 'it has already happened').

A (later) early Christian interpretation uses Dan. 7:13 as an expression of the Parousia by reversing the motion and making it a 'descending' or 'coming down'.[42] In Mk. 13:26 and 14:62b the combination 'resurrection-exaltation' is altered to 'exaltation-Parousia'; not as though 14:62b is appending a later interpretation to 14:62a; the two are framed from the start to constitute a single verse (14:62).[43] In 14:62b it is Mark's intention to depict an exaltation (ascension), not a descent, of the son of man; but he marks it out as a latter-day event.[44] The deliverance is an eschatological event (13:13), although due to occur in the near future.

Couple exaltation with resurrection, and you are bound in consequence to accept the celestial operation of the Christ present in the Church. Anyone who, like Mark, links exaltation with Parousia will not be prepared to acknowledge the celestial but operative presence of Jesus in the Church.[45] And Mark was evidently not the only person in the primitive Church to think like that, as witness Acts 3:20, 21a and the story of the bridesmaids in Mt. 25:1–13; Phil. 2:10–11; Col. 1:15–20 and 1 Pet. 3:19–22.[46] For these Christians the Lord has indeed been 'removed' from among them (Mk. 2:20). This would account for the impatience and dejection in Mark's community.

Mark is clearly campaigning against various forms of (a premature) 'power' Christology, *vis-à-vis* both the earthly Jesus and the exalted, heavenly Jesus, risen but not yet invested with power. Thus he has Jesus reacting vehemently against the 'confession of Peter', so called, because in Mark Peter obviously understands this confession of the messiah in terms of a 'power' Christology, in which the 'epiphany' of Jesus is prematurely disclosed and laid open to misinterpretation; this becomes apparent from the reactions to the first prediction of suffering that immediately follow (Mk. 8:27–28, 31–33). Peter is a Satan! For Mark Jesus of Nazareth is the son of man, suffering in his earthly life, absent now, but later at the Parousia coming in power, Christ and Son. It is characteristic that in contrast to the messianic 'power-centred' confession of Peter, the Marcan gospel has a pagan centurion, symbol of authority and *exousia*, who being in charge of the execution has followed the whole course of events at close hand ('he saw and believed'), asserting that this suffering Jesus is truly 'a son of God' (15:39); for it was not until after Jesus' ignominious suffering and death that the danger was removed of attaching to Jesus as 'Son of God' a false significance based on a 'power' Christology. Mark countenances no Christ-mystique, except the Jesus-mystique of following after the earthly, suffering Jesus, who puts all his trust in the coming of God's rule. In contrast to Paul, with whom he shares some common features of a *theologia crucis*, he is chary of pneumatic experiences of the risen Lord. Mark's is the gospel of 'Jesus' absence', and above all the gospel of the earthly Jesus recollected and the expectation, in hope, of the coming heavenly son of man, an expectant awaiting of his exaltation, which is to usher in the eschatological kingdom, the rule of God. He has an anti-triumphalist Christology and puts at the centre the rejected Jesus of Nazareth. Since Jesus' departure we find ourselves living in a rather drab but necessary interim period (13:9–13) in which Christian faith will be severely tested. But anyone who accepts this Christology will be saved (13:10–13). This is Mark's *theologia negativa*.

Of course, a degree of uncertainty still attaches to this Marcan interpretation. The idea of 'exaltation' turns out to be ambiguous and elusive in the New Testament; 'sitting at God's right hand' *can* imply a rule exercised here and now (and in many New Testament passages actually does so); but in a pronounced *maranatha* Christology only 'standing' marks the start of the eschatological victor's activity: only then are all enemies (including death) overcome. That is what Mark has in mind, whereas he has nothing to say at any rate about an interim activity of the heavenly Christ (that is how I would want to refine upon Weeden's thesis).

The original Mark, corrected by way of the later canonical ending to the gospel (16:9–20) and so integrated into the official Church, strikes a note still helpful to us twentieth-century Christians if and when we turn our minds to its Christological scheme as well as this integration into the biblical canon.

Within the New Testament as a whole Mark sounds a fairly solitary note. But we may well ask ourselves whether we do not detect here – right in the New Testament – an echo of possibly the oldest Palestinian Christology (with a different feel to it from the appearances Christology and the prophetic-charismatic 'enthusiasm' of some primitive Christian communities, for instance, the Q tradition). In Mark Palestinian Christian traditions are proffered which are concerned on the one hand with the whole earthly ministry of Jesus, on the other with his eschatological functions as saviour and judge. The Pauline theology of the Church as the 'body of the Lord', locus of the celestial activity of the exalted Jesus, has strongly affected the canonical image of Jesus – although we may not be in a rush to discover the Pauline notion of the Church as the 'body of Christ' in the Synoptic Gospels; but in the Marcan gospel there is not the slightest opening for it.

Though differing essentially on fundamental points, the two eschatological communities – the tradition of the Q community and the gospel of Mark – nevertheless agree in their basic creed, that Jesus, as the coming son of man, is the Lord of the future. They both represent a *maranatha* Christology: eschatologically speaking, Jesus brings a salvation that is on the way. The forgiveness of sins lies 'in the future'. Again, in their focusing on the earthly Jesus of Nazareth (and on every aspect of his whole ministry) the Marcan gospel and the second phase of the Q community (albeit under the influence of Marcan material) are fundamentally at one, even though what was intended in the tradition of the Marcan material did not match that of the Q community, which drew its life from the Lord present and operative in the Church,[47] while the Marcan tradition and Mark looked to the 'earthly Jesus'.

This purely eschatological creed subsequently made its influence felt, for example, in the Apocalypse of Asia Minor (the canonical Apocalypse) (and also in the later Montanist movements).

*In conclusion* let us repeat: this creed (of the Marcan and Q communities) sees its continuity with the earthly Jesus of Nazareth in his message of the near-at-hand kingdom of God and the rapidly approaching rule of God. Jesus' death marks no break in this; it is the first phase, the start, of the eschatological woes. The message of the historical Jesus, which the Marcan and Q communities faithfully hand down, is in that way simply linked with their Christian *kerygma* of the imminent coming of Jesus-son of man, a creed (in the Marcan tradition) developed on the basis of Jesus' resurrection (which is not in itself, however, the central core or object of this type of creed); in the Q community the Parousia *kerygma* relies more on the charismatic-prophetic experiences of those Christians who see in them the hand of the one whom God is holding in readiness, the son of man coming as judge. The difference between the two communities lies in the fact that the Marcan congregation, which would appear (in all historical probability) not to acclaim any immediate salvific activity of the risen Christ prior to the Parousia, puts its faith in the ministry of the earthly Jesus *in toto*, and not just in his eschatological message of judgement and of mercy near at hand, as in the earliest phase of the Q tradition, which is therefore interested only in Jesus' preaching (logia) and hardly at all in his miracles. A historical concern with every facet of the life of Jesus of Nazareth, therefore, really follows from the Marcan (or pre-Marcan) *kerygma* itself, just as concern with the historical message of the earthly Jesus (the rule of God) follows from the Q *kerygma* (which in a later phase, under the influence of the Marcan material, enlarged its historical concern with the earthly Jesus).

B. *THEIOS ANÈR* CHRISTOLOGY (?): JESUS THE DIVINE MIRACLE-
MAN. CHRISTOLOGY OF THE SOLOMONIC SON OF DAVID

*Literature*. F. C. Baur, 'Apollonius von Tyana und Christus', *Drei
Abhandlungen zur Geschichte der alten Philosophie und ihres Verhältnisses
zum Christentum* (ed. E. Zeller), Hildesheim 1966[2]; H. D. Betz, *Lukian
von Samosata und das Neue Testament, Religions-geschichtliche und paränetische
Parallellen* (TU, 76), Berlin 1961; L. Bieler, *Theios anèr. Das Bild des
'göttlichen Menschen' in Spätantike und Frühchristentum*, Vienna 1967[2]; G.
Friedrich, 'Lk. 9:51 und die Entrückungs-christologie des Lukas',
*Orientierung an Jesus* (Freiburg 1973), 48–77; H. Koester, *Trajectories*,
187–93 and 216–19; G. Lohfink, *Die Himmelfahrt Jesu*, Munich 1971;
G. Petzke, *Die Tradition über Apollonius von Tyana und das Neue Testament*,
Leyden 1970; J. Roloff, *Das Kerygma*, especially 182–202.

There is an extensive secular Graeco-Roman literature about people
in whom 'divine strength' has become visible (strength, *virtus* or *areté*,
that is, virtuousness, good quality and energy; hence this literature is
known as 'aretalogy') – a genre that within Christian circles in the early
Church also appropriated 'the life of Jesus' and was kept going later
on in the *acta martyrum* and *acta sanctorum*.

This *theios anèr* doctrine comes from Hellenism but strongly influenced the Hellenistic Jews of the Diaspora who later became
Christians. Apollonius of Tyana, great rulers like Alexander the Great
and the emperor Augustus were regarded as 'divine prodigies'; they
are described as 'sons of God', *divus* Augustus, the divine emperor.
They are in reality celestial beings who, clothed in terrestrial form,
appear in our world, performing such deeds of virtue (often by renouncing all pleasure, meat and wine and sexuality) and strength
(*aretè*; they are exorcists and cure the sick, sometimes even raise the
dead) that they are evident 'epiphanies' of God: the divine is made
visible in their mundane, but marvellous, appearing. They are preter-
natural, therefore, often virgin, born of God himself (that is to say:
they are divine). At death they are 'snatched away', removed 'from the
world of men' and 'admitted among' the divine beings; and after that
they frequently appear to their intimate acquaintance and admirers.
The lives of such heroes are recorded for purposes of propaganda, so
that people will follow and imitate the hero in question; it is a
literature of edification – thus a summary reflection of the Graeco-

Roman, Hellenistic-oriental *theios anèr* ambience.

Greek-speaking Jews, nurtured on these ideas, were given every occasion, when they heard the message about Jesus of Nazareth and became Christians, to interpret Jesus within the framework of the Hellenistic pattern of the 'divine miracle-man'. (However, it is only provisionally that I employ the term 'Christology' of the 'divine miracle-man'; later on – under sapiential messianism – it may well appear that the latter is a more appropriate terminology, better supported by the history of the tradition. That is why I have qualified the title of this particular 'credal strand' with a question-mark. Even so, the influence of the *theios anèr* idea on it remains, in my view, real enough – the reason why, despite my reservations, the title has been retained.)

On the one hand the New Testament here and there scolds people who abominate marriage and the use of certain foods (1 Tim. 4:3), on the other we see in Paul[48] and in the gospels[49] passages that are clearly contending against *theios anèr* conceptions among Christians. The sources used by Mark and John respectively for their own gospels are very likely *theios anèr* Christologies, 'miracle traditions', though not the same ones in both cases.[50] In this aretalogical interpretation Jesus is seen as 'a divine miracle-man', demonstrating his divine character by acts of power. John 20:30–31 is probably the last part of John's 'source-book of signs': 'Now Jesus did many other signs in the presence of the disciples, which are not written in this book; but these are written that you may believe that Jesus is the Christ, the Son of God, and that believing you may have life in his name.' The *vitae* of all prodigious men of God end in more or less the same way; for instance, the miracle stories told of Judas Maccabaeus: 'Now the rest of the acts of Judas, and his wars and the brave deeds that he did, and his greatness, have not been recorded, for they were very many' (1 Macc. 9:22; see also Ecclesiasticus 43:27). Aretalogies or the lives of heroes are recorded for purposes of propaganda. Thus the accounts of the extraordinary events associated with the hero being extolled are, as it were, the distinctive creed of this interpretation of Jesus, irrespective of which honorific titles are then applied to Jesus, although in the profane literature 'Son of God' is the most fitting title for the divine, virtuous and mighty prodigy whose life is being described. But neither Paul, who will not know Christ 'after the flesh', that is, from the viewpoint of this aretalogical model (2 Cor. 5:16 and 11:4), nor Mark, John or Luke will accept, at any rate without some kerygmatic correction, the *theios anèr* Christology. For Paul this means preaching 'another Jesus' (2 Cor. 11:4). Luke's Christology too (in Gospel and in Acts) is substantially not a *theios anèr* one;[51] and Mark invariably follows up the (allegedly 'God-epiphanous') miracles of Jesus with a disconcerting lack of comprehension on the disciples' part; what is more, he has the disciples failing in their attempt to heal the sick (Mk. 9:14–29):[52] a Christian veto on a theology of Christ as the divine miracle-man.

Although it is uncanonical, there clearly did exist, in the oldest strata of primitive Christianity and in some circles consisting of Greek-speaking, Jewish Christians, a *theios anèr* Christology. A good deal of evidence points to a Galilean Christology based on a 'miracle tradition' and 'calling' traditions (Mt. 28:16ff; see Mk. 3:13ff; 9:2ff; Jn. 21: 2–13; also Mk. 14:28 and 16:7–8). There was a pre-Pauline, pre-Marcan and pre-Johannine Christological aretalogy; too many data in the New Testament point in that direction to make it possible to deny the fact. It proclaims that a divine power was operative in Jesus of Nazareth and consequently in those who followed him: through faith in him his admirers too acquire the same power to exorcize, perform cures and so forth. Although divested of a *theios anèr* Christology, Luke often uses *theios anèr* concepts so as to help Greeks to 'empathize' with the gospel.[53] Thus after his gospel as the story of Jesus' mighty deeds, his Acts are indeed the record of the 'mighty deeds' of his followers, the apostles. Nevertheless, even in its Lucan redaction, Acts 2:22 reveals typical features of an aretalogical Christology: 'Jesus of Nazareth, a man attested to you by God with mighty works and wonders and signs which God did through him in your midst . . .' His infancy narrative too is aretalogical in conception, even though his theological purpose with it is to show that Jesus of Nazareth is truly the Son of God, not just at the resurrection, not just at his baptism in Jordan, but from his very birth. Luke's notion of Jesus' virgin birth ('therefore the child to be born will be called holy, the Son of God', Lk. 1:35) only becomes intelligible within a Christology which knows nothing of (or denies) the ancient tradition of the pre-existent Christ-Wisdom, and on the other hand calls Jesus Son of God from the outset (and not just at baptism or resurrection).

It is quite obvious, however, that even this (never canonically sanctioned) aretalogical vein of belief affirms a historical and theological continuity between Jesus and Church. Historical criteria serve to establish it as a fact that Jesus performed a number of miracles, but as signs of the coming kingdom of God (Mt. 11:5; Mk. 3:24ff; Lk. 11:20), not as proof of his divine power; miracles are evidence of an eschatological event, illustrations of Jesus' eschatological proclamation.[54]

Confronted with them, we are called to enter the kingdom of God. Miracles are a praxis of the kingdom of God. Although interpreted in a one-sided way, the credal strain represented by Christological aretalogy is grounded all the same in a historical datum in the life of Jesus of Nazareth. After all, this creed too proves in its non-canonicity the first Christians' concern to know their *kerygma* to be founded on real facts concerning the historical Jesus. The general correlation-principle, that in the disciples (here miracle-workers) one can recognize the Master (Jesus as miracle-worker), continues to apply here: the community is a reflection of Jesus; the 'imitation' of Jesus lays bare an aspect of the historical Jesus.

In view of the frequent, explicit and implicit criticism in the New Testament of this aretalogical creed, this interpretation of Jesus would seem to have been a virulent factor in early Church congregations, especially because its missionary propaganda is an essential part of aretalogy. The miracle stories and accounts of the calling and sending out of disciples seem to cohere in a particular complex of traditional material, pointing to Galilee. No *maranatha* Christology here; on the contrary, the disciples already receive salvation from Jesus here and now. Even the resurrection *kerygma* would seem to have been unheard of here, to begin with. It is a (very ancient) Christology, entirely centred on the earthly Jesus, in whom salvation is actually given; but the interest in this case fastens on God's activity and how it becomes epiphanous in Jesus' historical ministry. Perhaps one should speak not so much of a *theios anèr* Christology as of a prophetic-sapiential messianism, in which certain traits of the divine miracle-man are present (see later). Here again the death of Jesus constitutes no break. In the miracle-working disciples the divine power of Jesus persists and continues to operate.

The tradition of Jesus' 'appearances' would also seem to have arisen within this credal model. The *ôphthè* term – 'he made himself seen' – is in itself something coming from the 'epiphany' tradition. It is not Pauline and occurs in Paul only in the context of a quotation (1 Cor. 15:3–8). The 'epiphany' Christology is essentially linked with the Galilean tradition which hands on Jesus' miracles and exorcisms: God visibly acts in this person. On the other hand, after his death the divine miracle-man (the eschatological Solomon-prophet) turns out to be at work in his trusted friends (see Lk. 10:16; Mt. 10:40; 28:20b). The association of the tradition of the (messianic) divine miracle-man with that of Jesus' resurrection yields the theme of 'appearances', that is, a theologoumenon in which Christians from an 'epiphany' tradition assimilated the resurrection *kerygma* from other local Christian communities, incorporating and articulating it in their own 'epiphany' theology: the 'epiphanizing' of the crucified-and-risen One, who even after his death is operatively present here and now in his followers. This current presence is in 'epiphany' terms thematized in 'appearances'; and this explains why belief in the resurrection could already be present before there was any talk of appearances. It also explains why the 'appearances' are essentially bound up with the dispatch of missionary followers and why they point so persistently to a Galilean provenance, the place to which the traditions about miracles, calling or 'sending out' also point. Hence we may perhaps understand the tendency of the New Testament to speak of 'apostolic appearances': that is, manifestations to 'Peter and the Eleven'.

In 2 Cor. 3:1 Paul talks about emissaries carrying letters of commendation – in which apparently their 'miraculous acts' in imitation of Jesus were attested by one or another local congregation. They emulate Jesus in his mighty acts, as opposed to which Paul says that he follows after Jesus 'in weakness', through his suffering; with a mixture of irony and sarcasm, Paul replies to his opponents: you are strong, I am weak (1 Cor. 4:10; 2 Cor. 4:7); and in a fit of exuberance, for which he apologizes, he goes on to list his heroic achievements: a life of hardship, suffering, persecution (2 Cor. 6:4–10; 12:12; 1 Cor. 4:11–13). These emissaries preach not Christ but themselves, says Paul (2 Cor. 4:5). He sees through the one-sidedness of this Christological scheme (2 Cor. 4:7–12; 6:4–10; 11:23–33). The absence of orthopraxis, right conduct, in Paul's opponents tells against the orthodoxy of their Christology. When later on this form of creed was 'christened' and incorporated into the canonical creed, it lost its independent existence, although via the Marcan and Johannine gospels it would continue to make an impact. [55] Comparison of the Q theology (only two miracles of Jesus) with the four gospels, and of the gospels with one another, reveals the tendency to magnify the miraculous element in Jesus' life or to project miracle stories well known from other (secular) sources on to Jesus of Nazareth, in whom an amazing kind of liberation or emancipation was indeed manifest. The apocryphal gospels and many *Acta apostolorum* show to what extent a propagandizing and moralizing *theios anèr* literature strayed away from Jesus of Nazareth as its norm and criterion when it stepped beyond the limits of the canonical New Testament.

Even this Christology, just because of its aberration, still has something to teach us, as also has the canonical reaction to it: the New

Testament is totally set against an unreal divinizing of the historical person and refuses to abandon contact with the real criterion, Jesus of Nazareth. And in the ministry of Jesus startling phenomena are not to be denied.

C. 'WISDOM' CHRISTOLOGIES: JESUS, THE SERVANT, BRINGER AND TEACHER OF WISDOM: JESUS, PRE-EXISTENT, INCARNATE, HUMBLED YET EXALTED WISDOM

*Literature.* Kl. Berger, 'Zum traditionsgeschichtlichen Hintergrund der christologischen Hoheitstitel', NTS 17 (1970–1), 391–425; F. Christ, *Jesus Sophia. Die Sophia-Christologie bei den Synoptikern*, Zürich 1970; M. Hengel, *Judentum und Hellenismus*, Tübingen 1973[2]; A. Feuillet, *Le Christ la sagesse de Dieu d'après les épîtres pauliniennes*, Paris 1966, and 'Jésus et la sagesse divine d'après les Évangiles synoptiques', RB 62 (1955), 161–96; H. Koester, *Trajectories*, 193–8 and 219–23; C. Larcher, *Études sur le livre de la Sagesse*, Paris 1969; R. Martin, *Carmen Christi*, New York 1967; J. T. Sanders, *The New Testament Christological Hymns*, Cambridge 1971; S. Schulz, *Q-Quelle* (passim); J. Suggs, *Wisdom, Christology and Law in Matthew's Gospel*, New York 1970; Kl. Wengst, *Christologische Formeln und Lieder des Urchristentums*, Gütersloh 1972; U. Wilckens, *Weisheit und Torheit* (BHTh, 26), Tübingen 1959.

Set formulae and hymns, adopted into the New Testament, as well as various passages in the gospels taken over from the Q tradition, reveal a close connection between Jesus and Wisdom.

In the more recent collection of Proverbs from the early Hellenistic period we find that both wisdom and foolishness are to some extent personified. Wisdom is a 'mythically' pre-existent, heavenly being (Prov. 8:22–31), she is as it were the playful darling of God (also Job 28). According to Job 28 this wisdom is hidden with God and inaccessible to human beings, except it be to the one to whom God reveals her. In a historical combination of Apocalyptic with Wisdom, Wisdom comes down to earth, where she is a stranger unacknowledged and rejected, who then returns to heaven. Yet at the same time she is the teacher of men (Prov. 9:1ff) as mediatrix of divine revelation. Early sapiential, Greek and oriental ideas and apocalyptic here begin to merge. In this period we see throughout the East, but also in Greece, the rise in speculation about heavenly 'intermediaries' between God and man. A relationship with God comes about through intermediary beings of a mythical kind. This hypostatized Wisdom was associated in particular with the doctrine of creation (Prov. 3:19; Job 38 – 42; Ps. 104:24; 136:5 etc.).

That there is a certain connection between this and Greek aretalogy (see above) can hardly be denied (see Ecclesiasticus 24:3–7; 1:1–20; 24:5–6; with obvious allusions to Eastern religiosity). Logos, Wisdom and Law are identified as the power permeating and holding together the whole of creation. Although universal, this Wisdom is attainable only by a few chosen individuals, the elect.

Alongside that, from the Maccabean period onwards there emerges another concept of wisdom, specifically in the pietistic circles of the 'Chasidim', a Jewish coterie of pious religionists, out of which grew later on both the Pharisaic party and the Essenes. From these circles came also the book of Daniel. The Chasidim or pious ones formed a penitential movement with a very definite apocalyptic view of human history. 'The wise' here are the righteous ones (Dan. 11:33, 35; 12:3, 10). The Chasidic wisdom is based on a direct revelation from God: wisdom, insight into the 'last things' (*eschata*), is a result of revelation on the part of heavenly Wisdom (esp. Dan. 2:20–23; 1 Enoch). Here prophecy, Wisdom and Apocalyptic are combined. To sum up: the Chasidic idea of wisdom contains three layers, so to speak: (a) only the righteous person is wise (Dan. 12:10); the wise man is one who acquires true knowledge of the Law and practises it; (b) to these wise and trusty keepers of the Law are imparted, in the testing circumstances of the 'last days', divine disclosures which enable them to understand the eschatological event; (c) complete wisdom is an eschatological gift of the time of salvation. This Chasidic notion of wisdom conflicted quite sharply with the hypostatizing speculations of Hellenistic Wisdom ('Greek Wisdom'). That then is a brief survey of the cultural and religious key concepts, used in this (third) early Christian type of creed to give a Christological meaning to Jesus of Nazareth.

In the later phase of the Q community Jesus is associated with a pre-existent Wisdom; the latter sends her messengers, the prophets, but also the eschatological prophet, without Jesus ever being identified with pre-existent Wisdom – a circumspect Wisdom Christology.[56] Jesus, the earthly son of man, is the Son known only by the Father because the Father has given him all authority and power, so that in him the heavenly Wisdom has come to dwell; he appears and acts as the eschatological emissary of a pre-existent Wisdom. Formulae that suggest a 'sending forth' are a typical feature of this Wisdom Christology. The Matthean gospel goes further and identifies Jesus with Wisdom; eventually, in the apocryphal Gospel of Thomas, Jesus identifies himself with this Wisdom.

But apart from these logia the sapiential myth of a pre-existent Wisdom is applied to Jesus, particularly in very ancient hymns that we find in the New Testament, in the poetic form of a *drômenon* or cosmic drama in different acts: pre-existence, condescension (coming down to earth), return and exaltation of Wisdom. The oldest of these hymns are: Phil. 2:6–11 (deprived to some extent of its mythical character by Paul when he interpolates a mention of Jesus' death), still more decidedly the Johannine prologue, Hebr. 1:3–4 and Col. 1:15–20. (Set in a quite different perspective are 1 Tim. 3:16 and 1 Pet. 3:18–22.) In these (especially in view of Phil. 2:6–11) the model of the pre-existence, incarnation, humbling and exaltation, in other words, the *descensus-ascensus* model (*katabasis* and *anabasis*) is applied to Jesus Christ very early on in the primitive Christian churches.[57] To speak of 'contingent factors' foreign to Christianity is not accurate. The fact is that in the second half of the first century three currents (Judaism, Christianity and 'pre-gnosis') were finding literary embodiment at more or less the same time; and they were making use of almost the same cultural and religious ideas. There was a 'spirit of the age', universally disseminated, and a similar cast of thought in which they all shared. The question is only how and to what extent, in assimilating already given, social and cultural thought patterns, the Christians managed to discriminate on the basis of the norm and sole criterion: Jesus of Nazareth; and so what was the Christian variant in their accommodation to the *Zeitgeist*.

The close approximation of the *theios anèr* Christology (deriving as it does from a similar mixed source) is clear enough, even though in the incarnation of the *deus praesens* it is more the aspect of 'condescension' that is emphasized in this case. That is why they have been dealt with separately. Yet under another key term, namely, Solomonic-Davidic messianism, we are bound to see them as a single early Christian movement in line with a Jewish tradition in which the 'divine miracle-man' has already coalesced with the sapiential messianism of the suffering wise and righteous one (see further on). The Wisdom Christology was subsequently to get bogged down in gnostic speculations, while on the other hand it was also to inspire the universalistic Logos Christology of the Church Fathers. It seems to have been widely diffused in diverse early Christian traditions and even to have appeared in diverse forms, although the favourite form, apparently, was the hymn. Even so, it would seem to be a Christology nurtured above all in 'sophisticated' Graeco-Jewish circles.

The question is: What is the historical Jesus event that is correlative with this creed? What is the continuity, of history and content, such as we have found in the case of the other types of creed? Jesus quite clearly made use of 'Wisdom' sayings and proverbs. In that sense it is historically legitimate to see Jesus as a teacher of wisdom. The continuity is shown in the way the disciples emulate Jesus: just as Jesus is a mystagogue initiating people into God's secrets, so too are the apostles mystagogues. In essence, what it implies is a belief that Jesus has a connection with God and presents the question of God: he tells us about the Father – indeed an important, even central, thing in the life of the earthly Jesus. For the emphasis in the *katabasis* model falls, after all, on this: salvation in Jesus, but from God. The continuity between Jesus of Nazareth and this Wisdom Christology, for anyone looking through and beyond the mythical model, is really considerable, but its alien character as a vantage-point is for us equally real. We see the canonical Scriptures reserving their position on this; on the one hand the New Testament does cite these hymns, but then they are worked over and set within the gospels' canonical creed. We see too, in Paul especially, a degree of hostility towards the practical consequences of this model, which threatens to degenerate into a 'scholastic' kind of mystery doctrine meant only for initiates who 'care nothing for the common herd' (see 1 Cor. 1 – 4, where Paul is inveighing against 'the wisdom of the Greeks').

D. 'EASTER' CHRISTOLOGIES: JESUS, THE CRUCIFIED-AND-RISEN ONE

*Literature.* See Part Two, in the chapters about death and resurrection.

It is wrong to call this credal model 'Pauline'. Paul refers to the creed regarding the crucified-and-risen One as 'the gospel' (1 Cor. 15:1ff); death and resurrection are not in this case presupposed as a basis for proclaiming the Parousia, but are themselves the object of proclamation, albeit in the context, for Paul, of his expectation of an imminent Parousia. Paul represents only one subsidiary strand within the 'paschal' or Easter Christology. The distinction becomes clear if we set his ideas about baptism over against those of the Deutero-Pauline letters. Resurrection and Christian baptism are interrelated and complementary in the Pauline tradition. But in Paul's view baptism enables us to share in the death of Jesus, not immediately in his resurrection: 'We were buried therefore with him by baptism into death, so that as Christ was raised from the dead by the glory of the Father, we too might walk in newness of life [or: 'we too shall walk in newness . . .']' (Rom. 6:4–11). Paul speaks of a shared dying; but the shared resurrection, 'being raised with him', is a strictly eschatological event. In the Deutero-Pauline context, on the other hand, Christians have been raised already by virtue of their baptism: 'God . . . raised us up with him, and made us sit with him in the heavenly places in Christ Jesus' (Eph. 2:4–7). What we have here is clearly a different view of the relation between Jesus' resurrection and Christian baptism, a viewpoint against which Paul is evidently reacting in 1 Cor. 15. Thus both before and after Paul there was an 'enthusiastic' interpretation of baptism, based on Jesus' resurrection and appearances. The Corinthians are not denying Jesus' resurrection in 1 Cor. 15:12; they have received the faith and are established in it (1 Cor. 15:1–7; 15:11). Christ is risen already. They do believe, however, that Christians have not only died with Christ through baptism but are already raised with him; they are already enthroned in heaven. They embrace a realized eschatology: through baptism they are already raised, and so there is no longer any resurrection to come (15:12): that is now behind them. Here we have a genuine resurrection Christology to which Paul opposes a 'paschal', Easter and Parousia Christology, although on the basis of Jesus' resurrection. There was a pre-Pauline tradition in which the Parousia no longer had any place, because everything had been accomplished and completed in Jesus' resurrection itself, and through his baptism the Christian participated in it – a resurrection *kerygma* minus a Parousia (a realized and purely presential eschatology). Ephesians 2:6: God . . . 'raised us up with him and made us sit with him in the heavenly places' comes from an old baptismal hymn in which baptism is itself taken to be resurrection: 'Therefore it is said: Awake, O sleeper, and arise from the dead, and Christ shall give you light' (Eph. 5:14). 'He has delivered us from the dominion of darkness and transferred us to the kingdom of his beloved Son' (Col. 1:13). Paul himself does not recognize this resurrection *kerygma* (see Rom. 6 and 1 Cor. 15), which would appear to be pre-Pauline, in view of the ancient fragments of these baptismal hymns and Paul's reaction to certain ideas at Corinth. We have also seen Mark reacting against this self-contained tradition of resurrection and appearances which exclude the Parousia. A 'pre-sential (realized) eschatology' is not the terminal point of a long evolutionary process; it is one of the many very early Christian eschatologies, even prior to Paul. 'The resurrection is past already' (2 Tim. 2:18), that is, in Christian baptism; and for that reason there is no resurrection yet to come: '. . . when he raised him from the dead and made him sit at his right hand in the heavenly places, far above all rule and authority and power and dominion, and above every name that is named, not only in this age but also in that which is to come; and he has put all things under his feet and has made him the head over all things for the church, which is his body, the fullness of him who fills all in all' (Eph. 1:20–23). This too seems to be a hymnic fragment from the same tradition, which sees the subjugation of all the powers to Jesus as already an accomplished fact, in contrast to the Marcan gospel (Mark 13) and to Paul, for whom death is 'the last enemy' (1 Cor. 15:26, fairly obviously pointing to some disparity here between tradition and redaction).

As against that, Paul presents us with another form of Easter Christology that insists on the futurity of the Parousia and the general resurrection to come, and in particular promotes the atoning death of Jesus to a central place in the *kerygma*. Paul's own Christology finds its sharpest expression in 1 Cor. 15, in that there he places several diverse bits of tradition within a peculiarly Pauline perspective. He wishes to stress the identity and continuity embodied in the apostolic preaching: they all proclaim the crucified-and-risen One: 'Whether then it was I or they, so we preach and so you believed' (1 Cor. 15:11). In 1 Cor. 15, Paul is combining the Parousia *kerygma* or *maranatha* Christology with an explicit Easter Christology, so negating the pre-Pauline baptismal *kerygma* of 'being raised together with Christ'. In that way two pre-Pauline traditions acquire a peculiarly Pauline cachet: the basis of the Parousia Christology – namely, the resurrection – is thereby exposed (not yet declared explicitly in the Q tradition, though plainly enough in the pre-Marcan one), and the 'enthusiastic' resurrection *kerygma* is integrated with the Parousia Christology and thus once again 'eschato-logically' stretched (from 'now already' to 'not yet'). To assume, from a chronological standpoint, that the New Testament has gradually 'demythologized' a mythical-cum-eschatological orientation and so transformed it into a purely presential eschatology is to overlook the initially pluriform traditions of the early Christians. The 'enthusiasm' that goes with a presential eschatology is, after all, as old as can be, in certain Christian milieux; and it is precisely against this that other local

Christian communities react, on the basis of other Christological schemes.

The 'paschal' or Easter creed on the one hand stresses the saving merit and atoning, reconciling character of Jesus' death 'for our salvation', on the other hand the salvific import of the resurrection as expressing God's victory over all the powers of iniquity, especially over 'the last enemy', death: for the Christian, however, this lies in the future. The two oldest credal formulations of this we are able to reconstruct from 1 Thess. 4:14; Rom. 4:17; 1 Pet. 3:18 and Rom. 14:9 (and other pre-Pauline formulae). On the one hand 'God raised Jesus (from the dead)', on the other 'Jesus, who died and was raised' (see Rom. 4:25; 8:34; 1 Cor. 15:4; Gal. 1:1; 1 Thess. 1:10; Acts 2:24).[58] As the significance of Jesus' death and resurrection has been examined already in some detail, this brief reference to them must suffice here.

Typically, the term Christ, messiah, hardly ever used in the other kinds of creed, is the most commonly used title in connection with the 'paschal' creed. The point of that is clear enough: this man, namely, the crucified One, is messiah.[59] Here too, among Greek-speaking Jewish Christians, appears the name 'Jesus Christ' or 'Christ Jesus', its purpose being to point to and drive home the significance of Jesus, suffering, death and resurrection. To this credal tradition also belongs the title son of David (Rom. 1:3-4; 2 Tim. 2:8).[60] The connection made between 'Christ' and 'son of David' and suffering and death is out of context where the Davidic dynasty is concerned, and yet on the other hand is not specifically Christian; it is a pre-established Jewish idea in a particular prophetic and sapiential tradition (see later).

Here again there is a continuity of history and substance between Jesus of Nazareth and the Easter *kerygma*. It is a historical fact that (around the year 30) Jesus was put to death by the Roman occupying power. The angle from which, according to this creed, the earthly Jesus is the norm and criterion of Christian belief is supplied by his historical suffering and death. The most profoundly human thing about man – the matter of his suffering and death – is here made the starting-point for a Christological project. Better than in the second and third types of creed, it is Jesus' truly human mode of existence that is safeguarded by the Easter or paschal creed; and it is Paul in particular who shows himself passionately opposed to an aretalogical and sapiential conception of the earthly Jesus as a disguised *deus praesens*.

What alone justifies appealing to other actions and sayings of Jesus, according to this creed, is that this illustrates the context of Jesus' suffering and death. The dangerous thing about this creed, of course, is that it comes near to disregarding all the other aspects, in other words what is legitimate in the other credal patterns, and the different focus of historical concern with Jesus of Nazareth found in them. Nor may one call this type of creed expressive of the Easter Christology in itself canonical. What is true is that this Easter *kerygma* is essential to a canonical Christology. But in the actual canonical writings the four pre-canonical credal strands are included in a sort of synthetic coalescence both of their kerygmatic programme and of the special historical concern which that implies with particular facets of Jesus of Nazareth. Taken together they are canonical, whereas an isolated Easter Christology is in fact un-canonical, as would be a theology of Jesus of Nazareth without the Easter *kerygma*. That is why an examination of these four strains of creed – in which we were looking first and foremost and all the time for the underlying historical *memoria Jesu* (on the working hypothesis that the Christian community is a reflex of the earthly Jesus) – was so important. It seemed to me the only way in.

Then again, the 'paschal', Easter creed is not uniform and must not be identified with Pauline theology. For Paul (and even before him, in the pre-Pauline congregations) this creed goes hand in hand with the proclamation of the present powers of the risen Christ as *Kyrios*, thus with a cult of the risen Lord, of whom the Church is 'the body'. We heard earlier on that though the *kerygma* of the crucified One is equally fundamental to the Marcan gospel as to Paul, the resurrection is put in a different theological position; and then too Mark is firmly opposed, it would seem, to an ecclesiological notion of the Church as 'the body of Christ'; for him it is the latter-day community under the eschatological guidance of the Spirit of God in the absence of the coming Christ. What is more, there are subtle differences in the Easter Christology of each of the four evangelists.

In the post-New Testament period the 'Easter *kerygma*' of the gospels gradually developed into a credal affirmation which as the *regula fidei* itself in the end became a norm. The gospels came to be accounted authoritative utterances, no longer on the criterion of Jesus of Nazareth but with, as criterion, the creed of the Church. Later still, with the Council of Nicea, there came a break with pre-Nicene Christological pluralism: one particular strand in the New Testament, namely, the Johannine, came to be the criterion on the basis of which the Christian's (Christological) orthodoxy was assessed, whereas before it had been only one of many Christological options.

*

*Conclusion.* There was, as it turned out, no creed or *kerygma* in primitive Christianity that did not at the same time take a particular historical aspect of Jesus' earthly life as ground, starting-point and criterion of its interpretation of the faith. Underlying each of these creeds is a historically warranted facet of the life of Jesus. The running together in the canonical gospels of these diverse credal strands, each with its appropriate historical concern with Jesus of Nazareth, is therefore not just a merging of various interpretations of Jesus; it also brings together a lot of information about Jesus' life on earth culled from various local church traditions. Of course this information has no built-in historical guarantee (thus the historical criteria proposed earlier on still have their function to fulfil). What it does show is that different Christian congregations, each in its own way and basing itself on its own creed, cultivated a particular *memoria Jesu* and became a channel of authentic Jesus tradition. Because of its *kerygma*, which left the significance of the risen Jesus, living in heaven, at any rate completely overshadowed, the Marcan tradition held within its purview only the historical Jesus and the hopeful expectation of his speedy coming in glory: this tradition has the broadest possible interest, therefore, in Jesus' earthly life, his whole ministry, all his doings, his sayings, his suffering and death. Actually, the oldest stratum of the Q community also passed on certain logia of Jesus; but its dogmatic interest in all aspects of the earthly Jesus arose only later on, partly under the influence of the Marcan material. Furthermore, there is every reason to assume (within the complex problem of the synoptic question) that Matthew and Luke not only made liberal use of Mark's gospel but also of the material provided by the Q communities, and that they both in addition used their own independent traditions or sources. John, standing in a quite different tradition (where it is difficult, if we stick to our given historical criteria, to ascertain the value of the historical *memoria Jesu*), may in virtue of his theological view of the connection between *Pneuma* and *anamnesis* or memory (Jn. 14:26; 15:26; 16:13–14) include just as many historical recollections of detail concerning Jesus without our being able to apply the historian's checks to it.

All in all, we are led to conclude that the New Testament, not in spite of its diverse kerygmatic projects but because of them, gives us substantial information about Jesus of Nazareth, at least as reliably as any other serious secular book whatever of that period. But it is intellectually irresponsible simply to assume this in advance. Once problems have been raised, one cannot shrug them off with some authoritarian, fideistic reply. Within the totality of tradition, so sketchily depicted, with such a variegated and manifold range of meaning and interpretation, we are none the less able to confront ourselves with the vital question with which the earthly Jesus presents us.

What does emerge from these outline sketches of early Christian Christologies is that they all respond in faith to the immediate, permanent and definitive significance of Jesus. Although prompted and vitalized in every case by Jesus of Nazareth, the immediate experiential ground of the Christian affirmation of Jesus' present and continuing significance would appear to vary: the focal point of each and every type of creed is the definitive importance, here and now, of Jesus in person, not just of his message or of his resurrection – because the person of Jesus is the coming judge of the world, who brings salvation or judgement; because the person of Jesus is a divine prodigy to be 'imitated', operatively present in his followers; because his person is itself for us an 'account of God'; because he alone can cause us to participate in his resurrection. Although Jesus' historical message about the coming kingdom of God is of abiding value, there is no single instance, either pre-canonical or in the New Testament, of an attempt to implement the task of carrying forward this good news without linking it intrinsically with the person of Jesus. The heart of Christianity is not just the abiding message of Jesus and its definitive relevance, but the persisting eschatological relevance of his person itself. That is the real Christological unity in these four credal models.

Then too the four distinct credal strands have served to demonstrate concretely what was said more abstractly in Part One, where our concern was with method and hermeneutics: finding definitive meaning and purpose, or salvation, in somebody, as that is experienced and articulated, is inevitably going to be expressed in certain key concepts, anthropological viewpoints and expectations that have stirred and inspired people in a particular era: that, under the pressure of the earthly Jesus, has produced by the four credal models we have been discussing.

# First identification of the person, a link between the earthly Jesus and the very early Christian creeds

## The problem presented

One would have to call it a happy coincidence indeed if on the basis of certain aspects of Jesus' earthly life the early Church had succeeded in arriving at four fundamental models for a creed which later on, albeit with some reciprocal correction, blended naturally together to form the Jesus image of the gospels and the whole New Testament. Presumably the gospels would then have succeeded in producing out of a number of separate bits and pieces – rather like a solved jigsaw puzzle – one coherent, congruous figure. What happened in fact was something different. Starting with certain data about the life of Jesus, before being in a position to formulate their creed, these local congregations first got as far as identifying the person of Jesus, and only then could this recognition and naming of the person of Jesus (albeit in each case seen in profile against a particular facet of Jesus' life) become the source of the divergent varieties of creed. What is more, this process of identifying a person was originally the same in each local community, in other words, it stands at the source of all four credal strands; which is the very reason why they cohere and were able to coalesce in the gospels recognized by the Church. This accrediting Jesus with a designation, therefore, is the link between the earthly Jesus and the creed of the churches, between Jesus proclaiming and Christ proclaimed. For the fact that the four credal models were able to merge in the canonical gospels presupposes (except perhaps for someone who sees primitive Christianity in ideological terms as a syncretism formed of many different currents) not only a reference, common to all the creeds, to the one Jesus of Nazareth as norm and criterion, but also that the same sort of basic inspiration, precisely the same identification of the person, must have preceded the four fundamental perspectives of belief. It would not otherwise have been possible for the local congregations eventually to see themselves reflected (even though sometimes it was not without quarrels and contention) in the creeds of other early Christian churches. Now the one fundamental source of inspiration common to all the credal models is their acknowledgement, from the outset, of salvation in the very person of Jesus: their identification of Jesus with the latter-day prophet – the basic creed of all Christianity. If then it can be shown (partly on the basis of the 'historical criteria' specified) that the identification of the person of Jesus with the eschatological prophet of God's 'season of mercy' is most likely – though perhaps only as a *question* (lying constantly upon the hearts, or sometimes even the lips, of his life's companions: 'Is he the coming One?') – a pre-Easter datum, then an 'implicit Christology' is indeed something from before Easter; although we cannot then understand the post-Easter explicit Christology of early Christianity in so high a Christological sense as for instance the Nicene tradition was to do in a legitimate but not inevitable direction. The modern problem, raised since D. Strauss and F. Bauer, M. Kähler and R. Bultmann – that of the historical Jesus and the kerygmatic Christ – must then be stated in reverse: the identification of the person of Jesus of Nazareth, already under way prior to Easter, can then show us what exactly it was that very early Christianity understood by the affirmation: he is the Christ, the son of man, the Son of God, the Lord. Now we often behave as if we knew only too well the meaning given to these words in the New Testament and the early Church; and we go on to enquire whether these titles really fit the earthly Jesus whom we are supposed to reconstruct *a priori*, 'in an objectively historical spirit'. Using our working hypothesis – that for the first Christians the historical Jesus is both norm and criterion of all confession, homology, catechesis and paraenesis – we have to set aside our hastily assumed and precise knowledge of what these confessional notions imply, and enquire how the identification of Jesus' person as eschatological prophet really does give us an insight into what the local Christian congregations meant or were even bound to mean by these confessional utterances of theirs. This is not to deny the validity of later developments of dogma in the context of newly framed questions or of a different philosophical understanding of reality; but it is to assign a great deal of weight to the very first identification of Jesus' person, an avowal for which the concrete, historical Jesus phenomenon provides an immediate norm, whereas later problems may belong purely to 'the history of ideas' – aporias arising out of the stock of concepts by then pre-selected.

## §1   Ready-to-hand Jewish models of latter-day salvific figures

A. THE LATTER-DAY PROPHET, THE ONE 'FILLED WITH GOD'S SPIRIT', WHO BRINGS THE GLAD NEWS OF SALVATION TO THE OPPRESSED: 'GOD RULES FROM NOW ON'

*Literature.* J. Becker, *Johannes der Täufer und Jesus von Nazareth* (Neukirchen-Vluyn 1972), 44–53; Kl. Berger, 'Zum traditions-geschichtlichen Hintergrund der christologischen Hoheitstitel', NTS 17 (1970–1), 391–425; and 'Die königlichen Messias-traditionen des Neuen Testaments', NTS 20 (1973–4), 1–45; J. Coppens, 'Les origines du messianisme', in *L'Attente du Messie* (RechBibl) (Bruges 1954), 31–8; 'La relève du messianisme royale', ETL 47 (1971), 117–43; 'Le messianisme israélite. La relève prophétique', ibid., 47 (1971), 321–39; within that: 'Le Serviteur de Yahwé figure prophétique de l'avenir', ETL 47 (1971), 329–35; 'La mission du serviteur de Yahwé et son statut eschatologique', ETL 48 (1972), 343–71; 'Le prophète eschatologique. L'annonce de sa venue. Les relectures', ibid., 49 (1973), 5–35; Cullmann, *Christologie*, 11–49; R. Fuller, *Foundations*, 46–9, 67, 125–9, 167–73; F. Gils, *Jésus prophète d'après les évangiles synoptiques*, Louvain 1957; J. Giblet, 'Prophétisme et attente d'un messie prophète dans l'Ancien Testament', *L'Attente du Messie* (RechBibl) (Paris-Bruges 1954), 85–130; F. Hahn, *Hoheitstitel*, Appendix: 'Der eschatologische Prophet', 351–404; E. Haechen, 'Die frühe Christologie', ZThK 63 (1966), 145–59; M. Hengel, *Die Zeloten*, Leyden-Cologne 1961; W. de Jong, *Studies in the Jewish background of the New Testament*, Assen 1969; Kl. Koch, *Ratlos vor der Apokalyptik*, Gütersloh 1970; R. Meyer, s.v. *prophètes*, in ThWNT VI, 813–28; A. Néher, *L'Essence du prophétisme*, Paris 1955; O. Plöger, *Theokratie und Eschatologie*, Neukirchen 1962²; J. Scharbert, *Heilsmittler im Alten Testament und im Alten Orient* (Quaest. Disp. 23–4), Freiburg 1963; O. H. Steck, *Gewaltsames Geschick*; G. M. Styler, 'Stages in Christology in the Synoptic Gospels', NTS 10 (1963–4), 398–409; H. M. Teeple, *The Mosaic Eschatological Prophet* (JBL-Monogr. Ser., 10), Philadelphia 1957; S. van der Woude, *Die Messianischen Vorstellungen der Gemeinde von Qumrân*, Assen 1957. Finally: Strack-Billerbeck, II, 479ff, and IV-2, 764–98.

To begin with, only the king was anointed in Israel: for that reason he was *mashiach*, messiah or 'Yahweh's anointed one'.[61] In that capacity he was 'the man after God's heart' (1 Sam. 13:14), the one 'equipped with God's strength' (1 Sam. 2:10; Ps. 21:2). This tradition was afterwards incorporated into the main religious tradition of Israel as the locus of God's salvific activity (2 Sam. 7:4–17). In this stratum of tradition Israel's king, as the anointed one, is called 'son of God'. The king's commissioning was accompanied by the formula: 'I will be to you a Father, and you shall be to me a Son' (Ps. 89; 2 Sam. 7:4–17). Christ and Son of God are the official names of the kings of Israel. Later on this royal christ tradition is sealed by a covenant of God with the Davidic dynasty (2 Sam. 23:1–7; Ps. 2 and Ps. 110). Because the messiah or king is the representative of Yahweh, ruler of the world, Israel's Davidic-messianic christ tradition eventually took on certain universal features (Ps. 2:7–12). Little by little the king became such a predominant figure that he drew to himself all other marks of function: the Davidic king or christ also acquired priestly and prophetic traits.

The result was that after the fall of the kingdom and with the beginning of the exile, first the high priests,[62] then the priests as well[63] and finally the prophets[64] were installed in their office by anointing (for according to the original meaning of Deut. 18:15–19 prophetism had also become an office and an institution in Israel). The anointed high priest, particularly, came in his turn to adopt an air of royalty: he was 'the anointed prince' (Dan. 9:25). His christ-function was to guard the laws of Yahweh,[65] to be a teacher in Israel, in total dedication to the cause of God. The anointed prophet, for his part, is first and foremost 'the man of the Spirit';[66] 'to anoint' signifies here 'passing on to someone the prophetic spirit'.

Via this christ-concept of anointing, what were originally quite distinct functions – king, priest and prophet – showed a tendency to merge into one another. Because the (originally) regal unction and the institution of kingship had succeeded to the judges in Israel, the anointing of the king drew to itself the charismatic aspect of the judges, who had been moved by the Spirit. 'Yahweh was with them'; and God's Spirit rested upon them.[67] When Samuel anointed the king, he said that God was with the king and that he must himself be turned towards God – and this, 'in order to deliver Israel'.[68] Thus 'christ' came to imply 'God with us' and 'the man near to God', that is, the prototype of the pious venerator of God: the heart of the christ is 'wholly with Yahweh' (1 Kings 11:14), 'walking before Yahweh with integrity of heart and uprightness' (1 Kings 9:4). For that reason the christ or king is a 'deliverer': mediator between God and the people. That is how an anointed king should be, say the Deuteronomic chroniclers, being disenchanted as they were with the actual behaviour of these kingly anointed ones. They therefore show a tendency to harmonize the Davidic christ with Mosaic traits in the ideal image of the royal christ. They depict Moses as the 'suffering servant', 'humbler than every child of man'.[69] The end-point of this development was the figure of christ or messiah as 'the one filled with God's Spirit;[70] a christ-idea that could be applied to kingly as well as priestly and prophetic figures. Two 'messianic' trends were to spring from this: on the one hand a dynastic-cum-Davidic messianism (the Davidic christ), on the other, a prophetic messianism (in a yet later tradition fused with non-dynastic features of 'the son of David'): the prophetic christ. In this last case, especially, 'messiah' means simply the prophet filled with God's Spirit (Zech. 7:12; Neh. 9:30); christ and *Pneuma*-possession are synonymous.

Only in later Judaism, however, did this christ-figure assume an eschatological significance. Before that, people had already swung away from looking back to the idealized past – which as a concrete reality caused so much disillusion; they now looked to a better and hopeful future. Just before, during and after the exile we see the first signs of hope centred on a coming saviour-figure. This subsequently took many different forms. Some were in line of descent from a Davidic messianism (Isa. 11:1-2), others from prophetism, out of which, at a still later stage, the expectation of a coming 'eschatological prophet' was to grow. For this last line a number of Trito- and Deutero-Isaianic passages are important; fundamentally, they illustrate the Judaism of Jesus' day and the New Testament. The main passages are these:

'Behold my *servant*, whom I uphold,
my *chosen*, in whom my soul delights;
*I have put my Spirit upon him,*
he will bring forth justice to the nations.
. . . a bruised reed he will not break,
and a dimly burning wick he will not quench;
he will faithfully bring forth *justice.*
. . . I am the Lord, I have called you in righteousness . . .
*as a light to the nations*' (Isa. 42:1-6).

'Listen to me, O coastlands,
and hearken, you peoples from afar.
The Lord called me from the womb,
*from the body of my mother he named my name.*

He made my mouth like a sharp sword,
in the shadow of his hand he hid me;
he made me a polished arrow,
in his quiver he hid me away.
And he said to me: *you are my servant,*
Israel, *in whom I will be glorified*' (Isa. 49:1–3).

'How beautiful upon the mountains
are the feet of him who brings good tidings,
*who publishes peace, who brings good tidings of good,*
*who publishes salvation,*
who says to Zion, "*Your God reigns*" ' (Isa. 52:7).

'This is my covenant with you, says the Lord: my spirit which is
upon you, and my words which I have put in your mouth, shall
not depart out of my mouth, or out of the mouth of your children,
or out of the mouth of your children's children, says the Lord, from
this time forth and for evermore' (Isa. 59:21f).

'*The Spirit of the Lord God is upon me,*
because the Lord has *anointed* me,
to bring *good tidings to the afflicted*;
he has sent me to bind up the brokenhearted,
to proclaim liberty to the captives,
and the opening of the prison to them that are bound,
to proclaim the year of the Lord's favour,
and the day of vengeance of our God;
to comfort all who mourn . . .' (Isa. 61:1–2).

In the Judaism of Jesus' time and in the New Testament the passages
cited here come together in the form of an anthology, as it were. They
provided a basis for what the Jewish apocalyptic literature calls the
christ, as an eschatological figure. For he is 'anointed' (Isa. 61:1–2),
that is, God's Spirit rests upon him (ibid. and Isa. 59:21). In Isaiah 42,
which subsequently came to be read in a similar perspective, people
detected certain Mosaic features of this prophetic christ: he is the great
teacher of righteousness – that is, in a Judaic sense: the true interpreter of the Law as a revelation of God's will. They associated this
with Deut. 18:9–22: a coming 'prophet like Moses'. This christ bears
none of the marks of dynastic-Davidic messianism: he has been
anointed, commissioned by God and sent as his prophet to bring good

news (Isa. 52:7 and 61:1–2): of God's approaching rule (Isa. 52:7) on the one hand – but that also entails Zion's deliverance, salvation and release for the wretched and the sorrowful, as well as judgement on all the iniquitous (Isa. 61:1–2), a judgement uttered with a tongue 'like a sharp sword' (Isa. 49:1–3). Where this prophetic christ appears, there come peace, justice and liberation. It is a coming, prophetic christ-figure with, in addition, certain priestly traits (see Isa. 61:6), not a ruler-messiah. In this complex of tradition later Judaism sees emerging a christ-figure bringing a gospel, the glad tidings of God's rule and of men's salvation and liberation. It is actually not improbable that in Jesus' day there existed anthologies, *testimonia*, in which similar texts are brought together, just as in cave 4 at Qumrân selections have been found of biblical (Old Testament) texts which have furnished the idea of a dual messiah: a priestly messiah and a kingly Davidic one (see later on).

But between these texts and later Jewish apocalyptic exegesis lies a whole period that brought with it a fundamental change in Jewish spirituality. For a time after the Exile there was a certain amount of prophetic activity (1 Ezra 5:1–2; 1 Macc. 9:54); even so, the absence of prophets in Israel was frequently lamented.[71] The rabbinism of a later period was to regard Haggai, Zechariah and the anonymous Malachi as the last of the prophets.[72] But this disappearance of the prophets points to something else, a different outlook on prophetism. From being a prophetic movement Israel now becomes, in Judaism, a religion of the sacred book. Scribes, experts in Scripture, take over what had been the prophets' task: to interpret God's will from the signs of the times. Now begins the period of hermeneusis (*haggada* and *halakha*) of biblical texts. 'And [Ezra] read from the book, from the law of God, clearly; and . . . gave the sense, so that the people understood the reading' (Neh. 8:8).[73] God's will and message are discovered no longer through living prophets but through the hermeneutics of sacred texts, now seen as coming straight from heaven, 'out of the blue'. What had once been prophetism is now found to be deposited in divinely inspired texts, which the Greek-speaking Jews envisage as 'the dictates of God'. Thus 1 Macc. 9:27 can say: 'since the time that prophets ceased to appear'. A further consequence of this revolution in spirituality was that even the major prophets were subordinate to the 'books of Moses'; they were simply a reminder of God's Torah.[74] After the fall of Jerusalem (in AD 70) even rabbis were to say that 'since the destruction of the Temple the prophetic gift is given over to fools'.[75] In a world dominated by lawyers and theologians there is no longer a place for

prophets. Nor for a prophetic messianism. A prophet superior to
Moses is a blasphemy, as a tradition interpolated later on into Deut.
34:10 suggests: 'There has not arisen a prophet since in Israel like
Moses.' It is not till after the Exile and the disappearance of the
prophets that Moses becomes the major authority: in Judaism. He
then becomes the ideal type: king, legislator, priest and prophet, all at
once; and the Greek-speaking Jews of the Diaspora, familiar with the
*theios anèr* model, present Moses as the divine prodigy: 'He was subsumed into the divine, so that he became akin to God, and truly godlike,' says Philo[76] – this apropos of an Exodus tradition that speaks of
Moses being caught up to God.

It is at once apparent that a 'non-Scribal', charismatic and truly
prophetic kind of public activity, like that of John the Baptist and
Jesus of Nazareth who revived and repeated what had most power-
fully impelled the great prophets,[77] would in the eyes of the official
establishment and its representatives be a threat and would be viewed
as provocation.

All the same there was, apart from a legalistic sort of biblical exegesis,
also a charismatic interpretation of the prophetic books.[78] And it was
thus that prophetism continued, albeit in an apocalyptic perspective,
in keeping with the spirit of the times. Daniel – and a good deal of
non-canonical literature – is evidence of that. That the spirit of God
was a gift of the last days has been said already;[79] but Joel puts it very
forcefully: in those days the whole of Israel will be a nation of prophets
(3:1–5). More particularly in circles which began to entertain the conviction that the end of the world was at hand, possession of the
*pneuma* was seen as the start of the last days. Hence alongside official
Judaism there flourished all sorts of popular movements, nurtured on
the old prophetic texts as channelled through apocalyptic exegesis. It
was in these quarters that the idea began to prevail of coming eschatological saviour-figures, whose form is not always very clear. For under
the Hasmonean dynasty the functions of king and high priest became
united in a single person (though not, even then, a 'son of David') –
and that, in a provisional context (while awaiting a better prophetic
resolution) (1 Macc. 14:25–49). In that way the christ-concept of 'the
anointed one' begins to be in the air.

Because people were disenchanted with the Hasmonean dynasty,
which brought a kind of prosperity but ignored the lot of the nation,
it was in various popular movements that the longing was awakened
for a mighty intervention by God. Under the Roman occupation this
grew into a universal feeling of certainty, supported by the apoca-

lyptic spirit of the times. God was about to send a great prophet.

Davidic-messianic expectations of an approaching saviour-figure were on the increase (see below); there were expectations too of the latter-day christ-prophet, which charismatic exegesis helped to encourage. For in these circles people could only recognize the 'time of salvation', only identify the messiah – whether royal or prophetic – on a basis of Scriptural texts interpreted as prophecy. Prophetic exegesis and latter-day saviour-figure were tied up together: the prophetic exegete read temporal events in the light of the sacred books and thus identified the coming christ. (So too did the first Jewish Christians.) According to the Jewish historiographer (Flavius) Josephus, a prophet during the Jewish War foretold by this means, on the basis of certain passages in Daniel, the exact week in which God would intervene to bring about deliverance; and, says Josephus, when they stormed the Temple in AD 70, the Romans found 6000 Jews inside it, awaiting God's arrival.[80] Acts 5:35–39 alludes to the same kind of christ-identifications; and the gospels are full of reminiscence regarding these prophetic or Davidic christ-expectations of 'the one to come'.[81] These popular hopes were also given a literary, élite expression in many varieties of Jewish apocalyptic literature both before and after the time of Jesus Christ. Climactic points in this process were the middle of the 'fifties before Christ and also the later years of the first century; after 70 (the fall of Jerusalem) came a new flowering of apocalyptic (the period, that is, in which almost certainly Mark but also all the gospels were written, along with many other New Testament documents).[82] In this literary apocalyptic, eschatological saviour-mediators do not hold a central place (sometimes they are not even there); what is central is the radical transformation of the old into a new world. In this intermediary figures are often secondary. The expositor of the ancient prophets is the apocalyptic author himself; he is a 'revealer': he unveils for initiates secrets about the future received from God. He is a charismatic expounder of the Bible with no authority of his own; and so he records his visions and prophecies, his exposition of the Bible (eschatological exegesis), in the name of the great men of the past: Moses, Daniel, Ezra, Enoch, Elijah and so forth; for of what stands written about them in the sacred books they provide an 'exegesis', which is thus no interpretation of theirs; it is just an eschatological hermeneusis of what these ancient books contain. That is why this sort of apocalyptic exegesis is essentially pseudonymous. Most of all it likes to pick out biblical figures said to have been 'carried up', that is, taken before or after their death to be with God (particularly Enoch and Elijah, but also Moses). Malachi (itself an anonymous collection) had already written: 'Behold, I send my messenger to prepare the way before me . . . Behold, he is coming, says the Lord . . . Behold I will send you Elijah the prophet before the great and terrible day of the Lord comes' (3:1; 4:5; also Ecclesiasticus [Sirach] 48:10–11). Here in an Old Testament passage Elijah *redivivus* is declared to be the prophet of the last days. A charismatic interpretation of Deut. 18:15–18 promises the appearance also of a latter-day 'prophet like Moses' (thus Elijah and Moses are the companions of Jesus in the transfiguration narrative). In this literature, then, there is a whole crop of eschatological saviour-figures of various kinds, with the people favouring above all the idea of the coming Elijah or, more vaguely, 'the one to come'.

In Judaism eschatological prophets are individuals to whom God has allotted a special task in the latter days, either as the forerunner of the actual eschatological saviour-figure or as the mighty and solitary figure destined to come to the fore in this time preceding the End. One can point to, in all, five variants.

(a) The eschatological prophet-cum-miracle-worker. 'Miracle' in this context serves to legitimize the prophetic mission and to prove that the time of salvation is about to dawn. This type includes mainly (more or less) Zealotic, anti-Roman propagandists. Rehearsing the marvellous events of the Exodus is typical of these eschatological prophets: the manna miracle is repeated, also the parting of the river Jordan[83] and the Isaianic marvels from the Exodus tradition (Isa. 40: 4–5). Such a one was Theudas under the Roman procurator Cuspius Fadus (AD 44–6) (see Acts 5:36); he undertook to repeat the Jordan miracle.[84] Again under the procurator Felix there was an Egypto-Jewish eschatological wonder-working prophet who predicted that the walls of Jerusalem would be demolished,[85] just as Jericho had fallen long before (Josh. 6); also under Festus an eschatological prophet led his followers into the wilderness, promising miracles and deliverance from misery of every kind.[86]

(b) The eschatological, salvific figure of Elijah *redivivus*, already foreshadowed by Malachi (3:1 with 3:23–24), whose task was to restore the Twelve Tribes (Ecclesiasticus 48:10; see Isa. 49:6), was not the forerunner of the messianic eschatological figure, but was directly preparing a way for God. Yet even in the pre-Christian period the eschatological Elijah had become associated with the great political expectations of the nation and so was turned already into a precursor of the messiah. When therefore Christians identified John the Baptist with the forerunner of Jesus as the Christ, they were using an already existing model (e.g., in Qumrân).

(c) The messianic latter-day prophet. This is a mutual contamination between two complexes, each with a different history of tradition behind it, namely Davidic messianism and 'eschatological prophet', primarily dynastic and 'non-messianic'. At a secondary stage the two traditions have come together.[87] This category embraces all sorts of pretender-messiahs, associating the latter-day prophet with the idea of dominion.

(d) There is also the latter-day 'prophet like Moses', especially in Qumrân,[88] with explicit reference, even, to Deut. 18:15–18. This too was originally an independent, non-messianic prophet-figure; but eventually he too came to be linked, apparently as a forerunner, with the latter-day messiah(s). The 'prophet like Moses' of the last days was to complete the giving of the Law and validly interpret it. The Samaritans and Essenes, who both nurtured – although independently – the idea of the eschatological Moses-prophet, must have drawn on shared earlier traditions. One thing of importance here is the connection between Law and eschatological prophet, the teacher and true expositor of the Law.

(e) Finally, and in the period after Christ, there is the eschatological Moses *redivivus*. This relates not to an eschatological interpretation of Deut. 18:15–18, but to the 'rapture' of Moses himself, to Moses carried off to live with God and returning at the close of the Age; only this idea is not pre-Christian (even the New Testament passages – Mk. 9:2ff; Rev. 11:2ff – cannot be interpreted in the sense of an eschatological Moses *redivivus*); it is of a later rabbinical complexion.

*Conclusion.* As precursor of the messianic saviour-figure or of the coming of God's rule at the close of the Age Judaism has, therefore, two types of latter-day prophet: the messenger of the 'day of God', that is, the judgement (Mal. 3:1), quickly identified with the Elijah *redivivus* (Mal. 3:23, 24), and 'a prophet like Moses' (Judaic exegesis of Deut. 18: 15–18); but in such fashion that the difference of substance between the two types is sometimes blurred. In the story of the transfiguration Jesus appears flanked by the eschatological Moses and Elijah, which suggests that their respective functions and significance within Judaism did not wholly coincide. Moses is a genuine lawgiver, whereas (in Judaism) the prophet is more teacher and interpreter of the Law. However, the distinction between the eschatological prophet and the messiah of the Davidic dynasty is sharply drawn and maintained, even though that prophet could also be called, in a religious sense, 'messianic': christ, the one anointed with God's Spirit, and ultimately even 'son of David'.

J.E.C.–P

## B.   THE LATTER-DAY MESSIANIC SON OF DAVID

*Literature.* (See above, under 'eschatological prophet'). Further: Kl. Berger, 'Die königlichen Messiastraditionen des Neuen Testaments', NTS 20 (1973–4), 1–45; J. Blank, *Paulus und Jesus* (Munich 1968), 250–5; M. Chevallier, *L'Esprit et le Messie dans le bas Judaisme et le Nouveau Testament,* Paris 1958; H. Conzelmann, *Grundriss,* 91–4 and 149–50; J. Coppens, *Le Messianisme royal. Ses origines. Son développement. Son accomplissement* (Lectio Divina, 54), Paris 1969; O. Cullmann, *Christologie,* 111–37; D. Duling, 'The promises to David and their entrance into Christianity', NTS 20 (1973–4), 55–77; J. Fitzmyer, 'De Zoon van David-traditie en Mt. 22:41–6 parr', Conc 2 (1966), n. 10, 74–87; P. Grelot, *Le Messie dans les apocryphes de l'Ancien Testament,* RechBibl (Louvain 1962), 24–8; F. Hahn, *Hoheitstitel,* 242–79; R. Koch, 'Der Gottesgeist und der Messias', Bibl 27 (1946), 241–68 and 376–403; K. Kuhn, 'Die Beiden Messias Aaron und Israels', NTS 1 (1954–5), 168–79; U. B. Müller, *Messias und Menschensohn in jüdischen Apokalypsen und in der Offenbarung des Johannes,* Gütersloh 1972; G. Schneider, 'Die Davidssohnfrage (Mk. 12:35–37)', Bibl 53 (1972), 65–90, and 'Zur Vorgeschichte des christologischen Prädikats "Sohn Davids"', TrThZ 80 (1971), 247–53; D. Scholem, *The Messianic Idea in Judaism,* New York 1971; K. Schubert, *Vom Messias zum Christum,* Vienna 1964; J. Starcky, 'Les quatre étapes de messianisme à Qumrân', RB 70 (1963), 481–505; W. C. van Unnik, 'Jesus the Christ', NTS 8 (1961–2), 101–16, and 'Dominus vobiscum', *New Testament Essays* in memory of T. W. Manson, ed. A. Higgins (Manchester 1959), 270–88; *L'Attente du Messie,* Paris-Bruges 1954; G. Voss, *Die Christologie der lukanischen Schriften in Grundzügen* (Studia Neotestamentica, Studia 2), Paris-Bruges 1965.

(a)  National-cum-dynastic 'Davidic messianism'

As the notion of creation grew more profound, especially in Deutero-Isaiah, 'when Yahweh opened up the whole world to Israel, as it were, and showed his power over the nations',[89] the belief was engendered that 'God himself is going to rule' (Ps. 47; 93; 95 – 99; 22:29; Mal. 1:14). This universal, kingly rule Yahweh exercises through Israel (Isa. 43: 15; 44:6). But a viceregent – Israel's own king, of course – is to reign on earth in his stead. In the end this kingdom comes to be of an eschatological character, belonging to 'the close of the Age' (Isa.

24:23; 33:22; Zech. 14:9, 16; Obadiah 21). So we find (in fairly late texts) that people are more and more on the look out for an eschatological Davidic world-ruler. This expectation arose after the Exile in Judah, where under Persian domination a new community had been formed. Hope of a coming king at the close of the Age, one who will apply God's rule on earth, emerged therefore at a time when eschatological ideas were in the air, and in circles which being inclined to favour a Davidic king hoped that the coming messiah would hail from the deposed dynasty of David. Old Testament passages where this messianic expectation is enunciated are as follows: Isa. 9:1–6; 11:1–10 (from the stem of Jesse or from the Davidic dynasty); 16:5 – Jer. 23: 5–6 (33:15–16) (a scion of the house of David); Ezek. 17:22–24 (a twig of the topmost shoots) – Mic. 5:1–3 (Bethlehem as city of the family or house of David); Hagg. 2:20–23 (Zerubbabel is the expected messiah), so also in Zech. 6:9–15 – when Zerubbabel became king and Joshua high priest there arose the prospect of a divided messianic office: a royal and a high-priestly messiah: Zech. 4 – finally, Zech. 9: 9–10 (triumphal entry of the king-messiah into Jerusalem). These are the strict, Old Testament messianic promises regarding the coming 'son of David'. (In Qumrân and in the New Testament Isa. 7:14, the 'Emmanuel', is also interpreted from this standpoint; but the original allusion was to a threat of disaster.)

All this goes to show that the Davidic-messianic expectation is not a central belief in the Old Testament and moreover is limited to certain circles. Almost all the aforementioned texts come from the post-Exilic period of the fifth and fourth centuries before Christ. There is nowhere any mention of this Davidic saviour-figure, 'the messiah'; it is as king, of course, that he is anointed; 'the anointed one' is a synonym for the (reigning) king; thus the Persian king, Cyrus, too is simply 'the anointed one' (that is, the king) (Isa. 45:1). In other words, the messiah, as a latter-day salvific figure belonging to the Davidic dynasty, is unknown in the Old Testament. Later on – see above (when priests and prophets were also anointed) – the term 'anointed one' came to express a very intimate relationship of an (anointed) individual with God. When in due course the title 'messiah' is used to denote the coming, eschatological Davidic saviour-figure, this too therefore signifies, in virtue of the Old Testament idea of anointing (christ), a salvific figure standing in a very special relation to Yahweh.

The prophets Haggai and Zechariah thought that King Zerubbabel, King Joachim's uncle living in Jerusalem, would be this king-messiah. But when nothing came of that, there was more circumspect talk of an offshoot of the tree of Jesse, of a descendant of the old Bethlehem line of the ancient dynasty of David.

Not until after the Maccabean rebellion did 'the messiah' of the eschatological period in Israel become, in late Judaism, a very specific expectation about the future. In the Hellenistic period most people felt no need at all of a Davidic king; and what is more, many groups in Israel were not in the least eschatologically minded; the religion was a settled, established thing. Only in eschatological groups was there a lively and ardent looking with expectancy to the future – but without any messianic interest. Even the forward-looking Essenes had at first no messianic expectations. It was among the Pharisees that a 'royal' messianism emerged, as the 'Psalms of Solomon' illustrate (Ps. Sol. 17 – 18); they hoped for the messiah, an eschatological salvific figure of the house of David, who would deliver Israel. The idea could only have arisen in circles which still had an interest in restoring the Jewish royal house of David – as is clear from the allusions to the Old Testament in the Psalms of Solomon[90] – and had at the same time an eschatological outlook. The effect of the concrete situation – Palestine was being governed by the 'unlawful' line of Hasmonean kings – was to revive old hopes and aspirations. Handing on the messianic tradition was essentially a matter for the Scribes; but at critical moments in history this could generate the impulse to apply it to the current situation. The first indication that some were looking expectantly for 'the messiah' is in the Psalms of Solomon. This longing was engendered by the conflict between the Hasmonean high priests and the Pharisees. The latter, who represented the old Chasidic school of thought, could not accept Jonathan, who had been unlawfully installed as high priest. Under John Hyrcanus (134–104 BC) the conflict with the Pharisees was intensified. He had united in his person Israel's three major sources or centres of authority: prophet, high priest and king. Then when Aristobulus I assumed the royal diadem and the high priest Alexander Jannai (103–76) put the title of 'king' on Israel's coinage, it was too much for the Pharisees: this was blasphemy: a high priest was not permitted to be king. Not the tribe of Levi but that of Judah alone had a right to kingship. It was a circumstance against which Ps. Sol. 17:5–6 utters a fierce protest; Ps. Sol. 17:7–8 goes on to give a picture of God's imminent judgement, linking with it the hopeful expectation of the messiah as Israel's king, the one who is to bring final deliverance. Thus the messianic movement had its origins in the abuse of power and the infringement of Jewish Law during the Hasmonean period.[91] This explains why the first traces of messianism among the Qumrân

Essenes, who were also opposed to the Hasmonean high priest but withdrew into the wilderness, as well as in the Testamentum Levi 17 and 18, evince an eschatological priestly messianism in reaction to the Hasmonean priest-king. Eschatological Davidic messianism turns out to be an expectation which on the one hand is reacting against the degradation of the high-priestly office and so stands for a priestly messianism; on the other hand it is reacting also against the degeneration of the kingship, and so centres its hope upon a final messiah of the royal Davidic line. The first strain is evidently apocalyptic, focused on the future, the second more of a restorative movement. Therefore the eschatology at the back of these two messianic schools of thought is differently orientated in each case.[92] Both seem to have run a similar course and to have emerged in a similar period (Ps. Sol. and Test. Levi both presuppose the conquest of Jerusalem by Pompey – and therefore the events of the year 63 BC). The Qumrân Essenes put the emphasis on a high-priestly messianism, the Pharisees on the royal variety. In the same period that saw the rise of messianism, there was also, besides an emphasis on the Chasidic notion of the approaching kingdom of God (Dan. 3:45; 4:31; 5:27, etc.), a breakthrough on the part of the resurrection-idea.

Among the Qumrân Essenes the dual character of messianism developed in a quite distinctive fashion. New members at Qumrân apparently brought Pharisaic ideas with them to the Essene community; and the Pharisees had embraced the Davidic type of messianic expectation. In 4QTestimonia from Qumrân there is mention in this period of a coming prophet and also of two messiahs, the high-priestly Aaron-messiah and the royal Israel-messiah, both of whom exegesis 'extracted' from Deut. 18:15–18 (prophet), from Num. 24: 15–17 (star of Jacob: Israel-messiah) and Deut. 33:8–11 (blessing of Levi: the Aaron-messiah),[93] without any actual presence at least of the name 'messiah' in that context. A similar passage in 1QS 9:11 does indeed refer explicitly to two messiahs and one eschatological prophet. The high-priestly 'last' messiah is placed above the king-messiah here (in view of the anti-Hasmonean attitude of these Essenes and the Levitical origin of their grand master). It remains an open question whether these two messianic functions could or could not be carried out by one person. Again, in the Pharisaically orientated Testamentum XII Patriarcharum (at the end of John Hyrcanus' reign) we hear tell of a twofold messiah-figure – from Levi and Judah.[94] An obvious tendency appears to merge Pharisaic Davidic messianism with the high-priestly sort – a purpose fully achieved in Qumrân at the start of the

Roman occupation. The dual messiah-figure disappears: the sole coming messiah is the deliverer of Aaron and of Israel, alongside the eschatological prophet faithful to the Law, who is perhaps identified with the returning Teacher of Righteousness.[95] Rather later, in 4 QarP, the eschatological prophet is identified with the Elijah-to-come of Mal. 3:23, who becomes the forerunner of the one messiah. The situation after 63 is, therefore, that (partly under Pharisaic influence) the Essenes look for a single messiah, with the eschatological prophet, faithful keeper of the Law, as his precursor.

When the Essenes, after a period of absence from Qumrân owing to an earthquake and to the fact that they had not been persecuted under Herod the Great, returned after his death to Qumrân during the troubled years of rebellion under Archelaus and the Roman procurators, certain anti-Roman, more or less Zealotic elements went with them. This was when the Scroll of War was written, in which military Davidic messianism came to a head. 4QFlorilegium[96] alludes to the coming messianic son of David together with the Law-fulfilling last prophet, while the functions of the royal messiah now take precedence over the high-priestly messianic functions (although the messiah is still a priest-king).

Such then were the Qumrânic expectations, which contained nothing about a coming son of man. The parable-book of Enoch 37 right up to 71, the major evidence for the son-of-man expectation, was unknown in Qumrân; and nowhere in the Qumrân literature (in the opinion of the experts) do we find a clear allusion to the son of man. The culminating point – and situation of the Essene messianic expectation in Jesus' day – was a looking out in hope for a Davidic king(-priest) messiah, 'engendered by God', with allusions to Ps. 2 and Ps. 110. References also to Dan. 7:13–14 (a 'celestial figure') and to Isa. 9:5 and 7:14 (the Emmanuel – according to the Greek – born of a virgin) might suggest that, when all is said and done, a virgin birth of a messiah descending out of heaven was perhaps already a pre-Christian, Jewish concept, associated with Davidic messianism.[97] The traditions respectively of the messiah and of the son of man had some mutual influence. In Qumrân, however, there is no hint of either the son of man or the messiah as the 'suffering servant of Yahweh'.

The revival of the royal messianism of the son of David, and the more or less central position accorded to it in Jesus' time, was the work of the Pharisees (who influenced Qumrân) as well as of, in particular, the nationalist resistance fighters, the Sicarii and the Zealots.[98] For the Zealots God alone was leader of Israel, and she was his possession.

Hence an occupation was against God himself. The pith, therefore, of the Jewish resistance lay in the religious conviction about God's absolute and supreme rule over Israel and grew from the very heart of Jewish belief. So paying tax to a Roman emperor was felt to be impious. That was the universal Jewish conviction; the pragmatic question was: What to do in such circumstances? The official leaders of the nation and their entourage: Herodians and the aristocratic Sadducees opted for far-reaching collaboration; the democratic Pharisees were more in favour of moral resistance within an outward obedience that could at least preserve what was essential, the Jewish Law. The 'wilderness people' withheld all, even outward, co-operation, but fled into the desert in order to set up there, in a community of their own, an ideal order and to lead a 'life like the angels', in anticipation of the coming kingdom;[99] they knew very well that through their prayer and Bible study (eschatological exegesis), waiting for God's intervention from above, they were provoking God to action. That is why – in addition to practical and tactical reasons – they chose the wilderness, the country of the Exodus, Israel's period of well-being without a king, on the way, under God's sole leadership, towards the Promised Land. That was the position of the Essenes, to which the Qumrân group belonged. In AD 70 and 72/73 the latter was completely eradicated (the survivors having then committed suicide).[100] Other radicals chose the way of subversive military resistance (though moved by the same sort of religio-Jewish inspiration): the Sicarii and the Zealots, the former prompted partly by social and economic hardships, the latter acting from sheer zeal for the Temple of God, now controlled by an upstart priesthood. They were fortified in their struggle by their belief in resurrection. In between all these factions lay the great mass of people, affected by all kinds of influences, passive and yet stirred by obscure feelings of expectancy and hope. They applauded the activists when successful but disowned the resistance fighters when things went wrong. The Zealots and the Sicarii were driven on by the same basic impulses that were felt by the general run of people: the restoration of Israel in a kingdom independent of the foreigner, properly Jewish and faithful to the Law. Of this popular expectation traces can also be found in the New Testament (Mt. 19:28; Lk. 22:28; 24:21; Rev. 1:6, etc.).[101]

The Zealots' expectations of a Davidic messiah reached a climax in the Jewish War (66–70) and later on in the rebellion led by Bar Kochba (AD 135). Part of what lay behind the Jewish War was charismatic exegesis of the Bible, according to various secular sources that refer to an oracular utterance allegedly telling of 'a coming, Jewish world ruler'.[102] This suggests that the expectation among the Jews of a Jewish world ruler, due very soon to arrive, was universal at the time. Josephus himself refers to 'a star out of Jacob' (Num. 24:17ff), indeed something of which Zealotic circles were well aware; but M. Hengel[103] thinks Num. 24:15–19 to be more likely, as saying: 'This is the oracle of Balaam – of the one allowed to see secret things. I see him, but not now. I behold him, but not nigh; a star shall come forth out of Jacob, and a sceptre shall rise out of Israel [ . . . ]. Israel shall deploy power. And the one who comes out of Jacob shall have dominion' (Num. 24:17, 19, 21). Numbers 24, taken with Dan. 7:13–14, prompted the Zealots' recognition that the days were fulfilled and the messiah could be identified.

## (b) Prophetic-cum-sapiential 'Davidic messianism'

It is clear even from the Qumrân literature that in later times the initial conflict centred around the Hasmonean king-priest had ceased to be the key issue; that was now a concern with *theologoumena* and their own sort of eschatological-messianic expectations. In the traditions sustained and handed on by historically-minded circles prophetic and late-sapiential strands merged together; and so there arose a quite new messianism of 'the son of David'. The son of David in the Old Testament is (apart from Absalom) first and foremost King Solomon. Already in Pharisaic circles, which had produced the so-called Psalmi Salomonis, the eschatological son of David was endowed with the character-traits of Solomon the wise, whose seamier aspects had been suppressed as early as in 2 Chron. 1:1–9, 31. It is also remarkable that the whole of the Wisdom literature was passed down under the name of Solomon. 'Wisdom' is Solomon, the son of David. According to 1 Kings 4:29 Solomon received from God 'wisdom and understanding beyond measure, and largeness of mind like the sand on the seashore'. He possessed not only an enormous knowledge of nature (4:33), but according to the Book of Wisdom (7:20b) also 'the powers of spirits and the reasonings of men'; he had 'the distinguishing of spirits', and in the Testamentum Salomonis lordship over demons is ascribed to the son of David (3:4; 15:3). Expelling demons and performing exorcisms are said by the Jewish historian Josephus[104] to be the characteristic activity of Solomon, the son of David. In such Graeco-Jewish quarters the son of David was celebrated thus as the great miracle-worker and exorcist, the mighty and wise king, initiated into the divine knowledge. Every demon, therefore, knew the name of Solomon, son of David. The expression 'King Solomon, son of David, have mercy on me' was current in those circles.[105] Solomon is son of David, prophet, miracle-worker; and this comes out in the context of his authority over demons. In the Old Testament Ps. 72 the figure of the true king is obviously blended with this Solomonic image: a pacific king who brings *shalom* and to whom every power on earth is subject. A broad Jewish tradition connects the title 'son of David' with cures and exorcisms: he is the true king, filled with wisdom, exorcist, prophet, in short, son of God. For the time being the mystery of his person remains hidden from other men.

The question raised by this temporary concealment is a 'from whence?'. Has this son of David the *pneuma* of God or of Beëlzebub? Apocalyptically – how else indeed? – history is seen as a battle between good and evil powers. Both kinds work miracles: God's anointed as well as his 'gainsayer' or opponent. In this same relatively closed tradition the question of legitimation is fundamental. The criterion for the dividing of spirits is whether or not miracles are performed 'out of wisdom' or simply to private advantage. Wisdom is bound up with authority or *exousia*, the authority of whoever has sent the 'wise one': the clean or the unclean *pneuma*. Obviously the prophetic tradition is here blended with that of the son of David. The messiah-miracle-worker is therefore 'put to the test': 'If the righteous man is God's son' (Wis. 2:18), then God will help him and save him from the hand of his enemies. The son of David and 'king of the Jews' is he who shares God's dominion; and this becomes clear from his total authority over demons and all the elements.[106] This was anticipated in the late Jewish conception of Moses: Moses was king of the whole nation because he had full authority to do miracles, whereas the elements of the demonic world obeyed him, indeed he is 'the God and king of all peoples'.[107] In the Wisdom literature, after all, 'the wise man' possesses 'the whole world'. All this occurs within a tradition in which the priestly and royal messiah gets levelled out and the emphasis comes to be placed on the Deutero-Isaianic anointed prophet.[108] What is stressed in the national, dynastic type of Davidic messianism is the judgement which is to destroy Israel's enemies. But the task of passing judgement itself belongs to this prophet-messiah; for because his authority has been ignored by his opponents, the End will reveal how wrong they were; the martyr's death suffered by the messianic prophet will prove to be charge, testimony and verdict on his opponents.[109] The messianic prophet *is* thus the coming judge; later on he will exercise this judgemental function of a king. And then as prophet of wisdom he is described as 'Son of God', *doulos* (slave), Servant of God, and *pais Theou* (child of God): in the prophetic-sapiential tradition these three titles are synonymous (see Wis. 2:13, 16d, 18 and 9:4b, 5a). As a recipient of God's wisdom this prophet, who eschatologically is to exercise the function of the royal judge, is called God's Beloved, *agapètos*; for the heavens have opened above him: he has received God's wisdom and revelation, God's Spirit.

This messiah is to manifest himself only in Jerusalem:[110] just as Simon the Maccabee, after conquering the city (of Gezer), showed mercy, made gentleness the order of the day, cleared all the houses of idols and entered the city amid songs of praise and thanksgiving, jubilation and the waving of palm branches (1 Macc. 13:46–48a and 13:50–51).

In Wis. 2:19 it says explicitly that only through suffering will the wise One enter into his *basileia* or kingship. Only after his rescue by God will it be possible to acclaim him with the words: this is truly a son of God (Wis. 2:18), in other words, the 'last end of the righteous' (Wis. 2:16c) will vindicate the righteous or wise One (Wis. 5:1ff; 18: 13).[111] In this Book of Wisdom a great many originally independent traditions have been merged and synthesized under the notion: the imparting of God's wisdom to his messenger, the messiah, the son of God. In the process Israel's kingly messianism was clearly altered, and profoundly altered, by the Hellenistic conception of a king, now re-interpreted by Greek-speaking Jews against a background of the more properly Jewish, prophetic and sapiential traditions.

Within the complexes of sapiential tradition it is still possible to recognize, along with Kl. Berger, a dual *basileia* concept:[112] (a) God's rule will be realized through knowledge of God and radical change (see Lk. 17:20–21), and (b) the righteous man after his death will obtain a royal crown. The wise man is king and owns the universe,[113] and on the other hand: the martyr is a child of God, who acquires after his death a heavenly crown.[114]

In this Jewish tradition there is a prominent conception in which the messiah is a non-political, latter-day saviour-figure, so that it would be wrong to insist that only the politico-national messiah is typically Jewish.[115] This prophetic-sapiential strand does afford, partly on the basis of the Deutero-Isaianic 'latter-day christ', messiah or anointed one (whom we call non-'Isaianic' yet none the less 'son of David'), a Jewish reinterpretation of the older royal messianism of Israel.

*Conclusion.* In the 'Davidic messianism' of the Jewish period in which Jesus lived two strands are clearly present: (a) a political and national messianism, centred on the Davidic dynasty, which however among the Pharisees exhibits mainly spiritual traits and is orientated differently among them than among the Zealots, differently even than in Qumrân, and (b) a non-political Davidic messianism, merged both with the Deutero-Isaianic eschatological, anointed prophet and with the sapiential elaboration of the older Deuteronomistic 'messenger' idea; this 'Davidic messianism' had universal features. In both cases the Davidic messiah was called 'son of God', but in the second, prophetic-sapiential strand a chief place is given to the son, servant or child, the one initiated into wisdom and the knowledge of God by his father.

C. THE SON OF MAN

*Literature.* (a) General surveys of the exegetical discussions: G. Haufe, 'Das Menschensohn-Problem in der gegenwärtigen wissenschaftlichen Diskussion', EvTh 26 (1966), 130–41; I. H. Marshall, 'The synoptic Son of Man Sayings in recent discussion', NTS 12 (1965–6), 327–51, and 'The Son of Man in contemporary debate', EvQ 42 (1970), 67–87; R. Maddox, 'Methodenfragen in der Menschensohnforschung', EvTh 32 (1972), 143–60. (b) *Monografieën*: H. R. Balz, *Methodische Probleme der neutestamentlichen Christologie* (Neukirchen 1967), 61–112; F. H. Borsch, *The Son of Man in myth and history*, London 1967; and *The Christian and Gnostic Son of Man*, London 1970; R. Bultmann, *Tradition*; C. Colpe, 'Huios tou anthrôpou', ThWNT 8 (1967), 403–81; J. Coppens and L. Dequeker, 'Le fils de l'homme et les saints du Très-Haut en Daniel, dans les apocryphes et dans le nouveau testament', Anal. Lov. Bibl. Orient. III, 23, Bruges 1961; H. Conzelmann, *Grundriss*, 151–6; O. Cullmann, *Christologie*, 138–98; F. Hahn, *Hoheitstitel*, 13–53; M. D. Hooker, *The Son of Man in Mark*, London 1967; R. Leivestad, 'Exit the apocalyptic Son of Man?', NTS 18 (1971–2), 243–67; W. Marxsen, *Anfangsprobleme*, 20–34; U. Müller, *Messias und Menschensohn in jüdischen Apokalypsen und in der Offenbarung des Johannes* (Studien zum NT), Gütersloh 1972; N. Perrin, 'The Christology of Mark. A study in methodology', JRel 51 (1971), 173–87, and the studies preparatory to it: 'The Son of Man in ancient Judaism and primitive Christianity', BRes 11 (1968), 1–12; 'The Son of Man in the Synoptic Tradition', ibid., 13 (1968), 1–23; 'The creative use of the Son of Man traditions by Mark', UnSQR 23 (1967–8), 357–65, and 'Mark 14:62: End-product of a Christian *pesher*-tradition', NTS 12 (1965–6), 150–5; and L. E. Keck, 'Mark 3:7–12 and Mark's Christology', JBL 84

(1965), 341–58; Th. Preiss, 'Le Fils de l'homme', *Études théologiques et religieuses* 26 (1951), 3–76; E. Schweizer, 'Der Menschensohn', ZNW 50 (1959), 185–209; E. Sjöberg, *Der verborgene Menschensohn in den Evangelien*, Lund 1955; H. M. Teeple, 'The origin of the Son of Man', JBL 84 (1965), 213–50; H. H. Tödt, *Der Menschensohn*; Ph. Vielhauer, in *Aufsätze*, 55–91 and 92–140.

(1) Perhaps no New Testament concept has been so much discussed without any agreement being reached as that of the son of man. The discussion concerns both the religious and historical background to the pre-Christian notion of the son of man and the question of whether Jesus used the term himself, either with reference to himself or to denote a third person.

First of all, 'son of man' comes from quite another complex of tradition and originally had nothing to do with messianism. If the messiah is the latter-day king of Israel, an earthly being belonging to the Davidic dynasty, then he will destroy all Israel's enemies and so usher in the time of salvation for Israel. In this messianic tradition that time is not so much 'the End', but within human history it is the actualization of a peace without end. The son of man, on the other hand, is a heavenly figure who in a pure, justicial act is to pass sentence on the godless. This view of things presupposes that our history does indeed have an end. The guarantee of belonging to the eschatological community of the saved is here not so much being part of the national people of Israel, but simply the final verdict of the judge who as a criterion for his verdict will judge the individual by his loyalty to the Law. Thus the idea of the son of man is embedded in a non-messianic complex of traditions and only later comes to be associated with messianic ones, so that eventually one could speak of the 'messianic son of man'. Two contradictory notions (an earthly figure – a celestial one) were ultimately reconciled in that way.

Although Dan. 7:13–14 does not actually mention a son of man (except in the Greek Septuagintal version), even so this passage is fundamental to the prehistory of the idea. Into the chaos of interpretations at least the new study by Ulrich Müller[116] has introduced a degree of order and clarity. Daniel 7 has to be read in the apocalyptic perspective of a dual – that is, earthly and heavenly – history. Celestial history forms the background to our earthly kind (see Part Two). Each people or nation has an 'angelic custodian', a heavenly *archon*, an angel in whom the nation is as it were represented and who is also its heavenly guardian, protector and 'leader'. Together these *archons* constitute the council of God (see Job 1:6ff; 2:1; 1 Kings 22:19); they stand before God's throne, ready for each and every service (see also Ps. 103:19ff). In Deut. 32:7–8 God determines the frontiers of the nations – and does so in correlation with the number of *elohim*, sons of God or angels. So too Israel has its national angelic guardian (in Daniel as also in the Qumrân literature it is more particularly Michael; see likewise the Christian Book of Revelation). Mundane history now runs parallel with the exemplary celestial sort. So if at the close of the Age God puts power into the hands of the saints of Israel, that is, the pious among the people of God, then corresponding to – and anticipating – that, is the heavenly transfer of power over all the angels of the nations to the 'angel of Israel', who (as angels often are represented) in the pictorial language of apocalyptic looks 'like a human being' (Dan. 7:13). Thus the apocalyptic vision of the exaltation of Israel's angel in heaven explains the events to come on earth, during which the fourth and grimmest beast (the regime of Antiochus IV Epiphanes in the Maccabean period) will be destroyed and the pious of Israel will take over control of the world. Again in Dan. 10:20–21 the angel Gabriel does battle with the *archon* of Persia and Greece; when with Michael's help he has defeated Persia he has to turn against Greece (Dan. 10:20, 21b): celestial visions that foretell the earthly events related in Dan. 11. In 7:13–14, then, Daniel is permitted in a vision to catch a glimpse of celestial history (transfer of all remaining power to Israel's national angel) and so is able to glance at what is due to happen in mundane history in the 'latter days': the exaltation of the saints of the Most High, that is, the devout of Israel, the eschatological remnant. In that sense the son of man is the heavenly, symbolic aspect of (pious) Israel.

In this very plausible hypothesis we have no further need to go looking for other mythologies, whether of old Iranian, Babylonian or Egyptian provenance – the 'primordial man' (F. H. Borsch) – or for myths originating on the home soil of Palestine, from ancient Ugarit (C. Colpe) (although what Müller appears to deny is undeniable: namely, that the current idea of the heavenly archon of a nation itself has older roots). The apocalyptic book, Assumptio Moysis (10:1), refers to God's dominion over all things and the 'filling of the hands of the chief angel'. Here, obviously, is something of the prehistory of the later 'son of man' idea.

In 1 Enoch (that is, the Ethiopian Book of Enoch, in substance dating from about 50 BC) the heavenly figure 'like a man' (Daniel) has grown into the apocalyptic son of man – but in a phase not yet completed, in that the ideas are still uncertain, tentative, and the concept 'son of man' is constantly alternating with the chosen, righteous and holy one;[117] these last concepts are more central, even, than the son of man. It seems to have been at a later stage that the son of man concept was worked into the text.[118] We may assume that 'God's elect' and 'the righteous one' in 1 Enoch only became 'son of man' under the influence of Dan. 7:13–14. At first the eschatological figure in 1 Enoch is called 'the elect' (Enoch 40:5; 45:3), 'the elect of righteousness and faithfulness' (39:6), with the main emphasis on election. Here what again comes to the fore is the complex of tradition fairly often encountered already. Enoch 48:3–4 speaks of the 'light of the nations' (Isa. 42:6), while in Isa. 42:1 we have 'my chosen (one)' (see also Isa. 49:1–3). From the womb God has named the name of this chosen one, indeed, from the beginning of the creation (Enoch 48:3). At this point the chosen one is to be linked up with the Deutero-Isaianic tradition-complex (Isa. 42 and 49). In apocalyptic he came to be associated with the End, the latter days: the eschatological salvific figure.

The 'son of man', then, makes his entrance in Enoch 46. Just as the chosen one derives via an apocalyptical exegesis from Deutero-Isaiah, so via a similar kind of speculative exegesis the son of man goes back to Dan. 7. Fundamental in this case is the vision in Enoch 46, to which the expression 'this son of man' is a constant back-reference, whereas there is never a mention of *this* chosen one and *this* righteous one. In other words, 'this son of man' unmistakably bears the signature of the anonymous apocalypticist. With the introduction in chapter 46 of the 'son of man' figure, a new name of God is brought in as well: a grey-beard or one advanced in years ('an ancient of days') (see also Dan. 7:9) (Enoch 47:3; 48:2; 71:10). Along with the very aged one appears 'someone else whose form looks like that of a man' (Enoch 46:1). But the Enoch book means to identify the mysterious, Danielic celestial figure (actually in a different sense from Daniel): a form like that of a man with a countenance charming like that of an angel. Hence the question: 'Who is this son of man, and whence comes he and why is he companion to the ancient of days' (Enoch 46:2)? The Enoch book intends to make this manifestly clear. The answer connects the vision of Enoch with Enoch 37:6–7, where we read of 'the elect of justice and of faith', and 'in the days of the chosen one shall justice and faithfulness prevail'. Hence Enoch 46:3: 'This is the son of man, who possesses justice and in whom righteousness dwells.' It identifies this son of man with the 'elect of justice'; so that 'the son of man', it would appear, is a later meaning or interpretation of the already familiar 'chosen one'. The vision then proceeds to define the function of this son of man (Enoch 46:4): he has an eschatological significance *vis-à-vis* kings, the mighty and the strong. Previously we had been told of the judicial function of the elect one in regard to the godless (Enoch 45:3, 6). Thus Enoch 46:3, 6 combines in a unitive image what had before been said in a diffuse way about the chosen one who is to live amid his eschatological community. The son of man is a judge for the godless but a salvific figure for the righteous. Only later, in the appendix (Enoch 71), does 'the son of man' become the sole title for the (eschatological) figure of the judge, for the title 'the chosen one' was afterwards to disappear in these apocalyptic circles. Nevertheless, there is as yet nothing said in Enoch about 'having dominion over every nation', because all that is godless is condemned and will be destroyed. It is only the eschatological, holy community that survives – prime evidence that messianism has not so far affected this notion of the son of man in Enoch. An already existing tradition regarding the (Deutero-Isaianic) chosen one is conjoined in the Enoch book by the apocalypticist with the Danielic figure, and so 'the chosen one' becomes identified with it. Only subsequently, therefore, is the 'son of man' concept applied to that of the chosen and the righteous one. As a result of the identification the son of man, instead of being a symbol of Israel in heavenly guise, is now envisaged as a quite specific, elect and eschatological individual person.

An essential role in all this was played by the ancient oriental idea of pre-existence, as extended and elaborated in apocalyptic thinking. According to the apocalyptic scheme of correlation, the primal image of everything earthly pre-exists in heaven. There everything is already 'prepared' from the creation of the world (Enoch 9:6); in particular all that pertains to eschatological salvation lies stored up in heaven: thus the New Jerusalem will descend from heaven to earth (Rev. 21:2; 4 Ezra 7:26; Syrian Baruch 4). The difference with the early Eastern conception is that the idea of co-existence has disappeared. The empirical Israel no longer corresponds to the heavenly Israel. What will come from heaven to earth at the close of the Age, therefore, is the pre-existent, primal image itself (see Rev. 21:10ff). The eschatological son of man too is pre-existent (Enoch 48:3ff; 62:7); for he of course is one of the principal components of what constitutes eschatological salvation, a hidden secret, made ready in heaven. The apocalypticist sees events to come on earth because he has been allowed a glimpse of the course of events in heaven. There the visionary sees the eschatological community already prepared, with the son of man in its midst

(Enoch 39:3ff). But from Enoch 48 onwards the son of man within this vision is 'dogmatized': before all other created things he was created. Not until now, in this eschatological hour (48:2), is this pre-existent son of man revealed to the saints.

At a later stage a commentator edited into the Enoch book an alien, messianic strand of tradition (Enoch 48:10 and 52:4); it speaks of 'the rule or lordship of his messiah [anointed one], that the latter may be strong and mighty upon earth' (52:4). Here the son of man is identified with the national messianic son of David. The messianic reinterpretation is even more striking in Enoch 56:5–8 and 57 (again in the second part of the Enoch book, according to the experts, the messiah in Enoch 90:37–39 is a later interpolation): a plainly Davidic-messianic tradition; which indicates that contamination has occurred here and there between the tradition of a national, Davidic messianism and that of the universal, eschatological son of man-cum-world judge. It is Davidic messianism, coming apparently from the Pharisaic Psalmi Salomonis (17:22–25, 26–31), that in the later apocalypse of 4 Ezra (13:5–11, 12–13) forms a much firmer unitive bond with the son of man tradition, whereas in the Enoch book it is a so far not yet harmonized coming together of two originally independent traditions.

Lastly, a further development of the 'son of man' concept (not in a much later stage, therefore) is to be found in Enoch 71, in which Enoch is himself identified with the son of man. The Enoch 'caught up to be with God' (Enoch 70:1–4 and 71:1–4) is elevated to be son of man. If before he had been the apocalyptic seer (Enoch 37 – 69), he himself is now accorded the status of son of man (Enoch 71:5–17). The difficulty arises that this is a later addition by way of apocalyptic commentary on the already given tradition of the Enoch book. The problem posed is: How can this commentary on the one hand accept the pre-existent son of man (as presented in the source being used) and on the other speak simultaneously of the earthly Enoch being appointed son of man? What has struck the new author in the son of man is the apocalyptic figure of the judge (not his pre-existence), and to this Enoch the function of the latter-day judge is accorded; for that reason the pre-existence idea has again to be expunged. The account of the son of man's enthronement reminds one of Ps. 2:7 and 110:4 (Enoch 71:14), with which is conjoined a promise (Ps. 2:8; 89:29–30) of a new covenant with God, a covenant of peace (Enoch 71:15). This covenant applies to the son of man and to all his coming righteous ones (71:16), with a view to the world to come. The son of man, then, is the eschatological mediator of peace, if only at least for the just. This covenant of God with the son of man is the ground of pious men's hopeful expectation. So Enoch 71 in fact reinterprets the Enoch tradition: Enoch is himself the eschatological judge of the wicked and the eschatological deliverer of the just. This entails dropping the pre-existence idea.[119]

We are to notice that although messianism in the strict sense is absent from the earlier apocalypses (allowing for the later interpolations in the Enoch book), Davidic messianism acquires a salient function within the son of man tradition of the more recent apocalypses (of after AD 70; specifically, 4 Ezra and the Syrian Baruch). The absence of messianism in early apocalyptic is accounted for by the Danielic figure 'on the clouds'; in other words, this figure 'like a man' is seen as a heavenly being. Daniel expects the crucial turn of temporal events to come only from God (Dan. 2:34; 8:25; 11:33–35). There is no place in this vision for a mediating messiah who at the same time is of earthly origin. The same thing applies to the Assumptio Moysis 10. Here there is room only for a son of man, that is, a celestial figure who is to be judge. Originally, therefore, the apocalyptic son of man stands over against the more Pharisaic expectation of a Davidic messiah. The former contemplates a completely new future; the latter a restoration of the (idealized) period of David. A focus on the future contrasts here with recall of the past. Sheer newness with a restoration movement.[120] The former (apocalypticists) talk of a 'sacred remnant' of Israel (see Dan. 12:1–3), the Pharisees believe on the contrary in God's compassion and mercy and so contemplate a total restoration and purification of the whole of Israel; to this end God sends the messiah: 'And he shall cleanse Jerusalem in holiness as at the beginning' (Ps. Sal. 17:30; see 17:21–30 and 18:5). The figure of the coming judge was bound therefore to vary, depending either on the radically negative assessment of past and present (among the apocalypticists) or on a more positive outlook on Israel's past and present despite her frailties (Pharisees). The latter-day figure envisaged by the Pharisees is a redeemer and saviour, therefore. The figure of apocalyptic eschatology on the other hand is first of all the judge of the godless, of a lapsed Israel.

Only in the later (post-Christian) apocalypses is the Pharisaic expectation of a human latter-day messiah-king reconciled with that of the son of man (4 Ezra; Syrian Baruch); but even there the messianic character of the son of man was never central. In apocalyptic too the messiah-figure is really a 'foreign body'. Indeed these 'later apocalypses' have ceased to be pure apocalyptic; the orthodoxy of the rabbinate has already begun to show itself in them.[121] The purpose of these books is to console and hearten after the bitter affliction of the fall of Jerusalem and the destruction of the Temple (AD 70). It is rather the son of man idea that gets pushed back. The 'heavenly manifestation' makes way for a human appearing on earth of the eschatological judge. The messiah here becomes the destroyer of all the nations and the salvation of Israel (4 Ezra 13:26). The messiah has affected the son of man tradition, and that tradition in turn colours the messiah concept; for instance, the idea of a 'pre-existent messiah' in 4 Ezra.[122] The task allotted to the latter-day messiah-son of man is interpreted in a purely Jewish and national sense: he gathers together all the Israelites 'scattered abroad'. To that end the peoples from every quarter of the world will go up, in the last days, to Jerusalem in order to fetch back to the Holy Land the Jews at present living in their countries as a 'gift-offering', that all Israel may again be one (4 Ezra 13; obviously influenced by the messiah concept in the Psalmi Salomonis 17:26–31). The procession of the nations to Jerusalem implies no eschatological universalism but is seen as a function of the final coming together of the whole of Israel. At no stage, therefore, does Jewish messianism attain to real universalism. The final liberation is not a deliverance of the world from bondage to sin but a freeing of Jews from the sinful nations round about. The late apocalypses know nothing of a 'redemption of mankind'. The world was and continues to be created for the sake of Israel. The existential question for this later apocalypticism is: 'As the world has been created for our sake, why is it, then, that this world, our world, is not under our control?' (4 Ezra 6:59). Redemption therefore signifies Israel's deliverance from her enemies, who keep from her the world she should possess. The messiah's annihilation of all Israel's enemies is part of the eschatological condition for the final deliverance of Israel. Not until this has taken place (4 Ezra 13:26) can the messiah devote himself fully to his holy remnant, the eschatological community. Yet in a positive light the event is seen as a restoration of the old created order: a restoration of the original paradise. The kingdom of God, the complete 'new heaven and earth', follows only in the wake of this messianic kingdom of peace (4 Ezra 7:30–31).

These later apocalypses have a noticeable tendency to make all the beings intermediate between God and man (an almost inevitable cast of thought throughout the East in the preceding periods) more and more plainly Jewish and expressly subordinate to the God who in the last days operates alone (see particularly 4 Ezra 6:6b, 10b; *'ut et finis sit per Me et non per alium'*). Only God can rebuild, restore. The contamination between the son of man tradition and the messiah tradition is already surmounted in 4 Ezra 13 in the direction of purifying the messiah idea by separating it out from the son of man tradition. The apocalypticists, responsible for upholding the son of man tradition, in the end are the ones to relegate the 'heavenly son of man', opting instead for an earthly, human, messianic son of David. (Some have seen in this an anti-Christian bias; others a purely internal Jewish controversy.) 'Apocalyptic' comes back in its final stage to the Pharisaic messiah-figure of the Psalmi Salomonis, originally quite alien to it. This later apocalyptic has rightly been described as the start of rabbinical ortho-doxy. But the obvious reaction detectable in these apocalypses (dating from after AD 70) shows too that the idea of 'the son of man' must have been more widespread at the time than the literary records that sur-vive would enable us to verify. The echo in the New Testament of a general, popular expectation of 'the one to come' could be understood, therefore, depending on the sectional interest concerned, either in a Davidic-messianic sense or in the apocalyptic perspective of the son of man. Against the background of these originally independent but subsequently converging complexes of tradition, 'the man in the street' simply inferred one thing in particular: that there is in Israel 'one who is to come'. And on this figure the burden of all the people's expectations was laid, in a period like that of Jesus when the ordinary people were faced with great difficulties, religious as well as social and economic, and were going through a time of crisis.

(2) What has this apparently adventitious idea of the son of man, determined in part by a variety of previous events and circumstances, to do with Jesus of Nazareth? It is a fact that in the New Testament, especially in the four gospels, Jesus of Nazareth (called by a number of different names) speaks of himself as 'the son of man'. Since R. Bult-mann it has become clear that this occurs in three categories, each with its distinct motif: (a) logia in which the son of man-Jesus is a coming, eschatological judge; (b) logia in which Jesus is referred to as the suffering, dying but risen son of man, and (c) logia in which the whole earthly career of Jesus is ascribed to an active subject called Jesus-son of man. The point at issue among the exegetes is simply whether the use of the term 'son of man' can be laid at the door solely of the Christian community (in particular N. Perrin, H. Teeple, H. Conzel-mann. Ph. Vielhauer) or whether Jesus himself employed it. Of those who would have it that Jesus himself talked about the son of man, the one group (in particular, Bultmann, Hahn and Tödt) hold that he spoke only of the eschatological judge – and then not as identified with

himself (first motif-category); the other group maintain that talk of the suffering son of man is 'authentic Jesus' talk (E. Schweizer; also with certain finer distinctions, M. D. Hooker); for others again – in line more with the third motif – 'son of man' is not an eschatological title but a Hebrew (Aramaic) equivalent of 'I' (thus, with some reservations in detail, R. Leivestad, C. Colpe, J. Jeremias). Lastly, F. Borsch in his new study attributes all the motif-categories in which the son of man is mentioned, at least essentially to Jesus (an Anglo-Saxon tendency, becoming more generally evident in the more recent writings of M. Hooker, F. Borsch and I. Marshall; with a similar inclination among several exegetes with a German orientation; for instance, R. Maddox). The whole question has become technically so complex, it seems, that even some of the specialists in the subject have declared any further effort to investigate it pointless. The dogmatist must therefore look beyond it. As an inexpert commentator in this special field he can shed no light upon it. He can however point out the assumptions underlying this bewildering chaos of exegetical opinions. Moreover the last five years have perforce led in any case to some degree of agreement regarding the history and prehistory of the 'son of man' concept, at least where its essence is concerned. And then it turns out that the differing presuppositions go some way towards explaining the diversity in the biblical exegesis. And then too it would seem that people simply overlook a synchronous 'close reading' of the son of man concept, as concretely presented to us in the redaction of the four gospels, and so are left with the jumbled pieces of a jigsaw puzzle, raising again the question how the puzzle might be once more pieced together as a well-fitting whole. What has to be done first, it seems to me, is to examine on its own (synchronous) form what is set concretely before us, namely, the end result of a (clearly present in the background) jigsaw puzzle, before going on to look for the separate bits and pieces that precede it. Even a child when playing with a jigsaw puzzle first gets the final picture firmly imprinted in its mind, then takes all the pieces apart, with a view to facilitating the subsequent process of reconstruction. The dismantling certainly brings its reward; for the investigator it is just about the most exciting stage; but the real satisfaction comes only when we are able to see the total picture.

All this goes to show that between Daniel and the New Testament, through contamination of the messiah tradition with that of the son of man, the term 'son of man' was indeed given a messianic interpretation in Judaism and therefore became a title; so that it is difficult to accept the radical conception of R. Leivestad.[123] In Qumrân circles too, where the son of man idea seems not to flourish, the messianic expectation current there is supported by reference not only to Pss. 2 and 110 but also to Dan. 7:13–14; and this suggests that the Danielic 'heavenly figure' has also coloured the messiah concept: thus the messiah becomes Daniel's 'one sent by the Most High'. That is why the 'messianic son of man' idea belongs to pre-Christian Judaism.[124]

Few commentators doubt that 'son of man' is used in the New Testament in a titular sense,[125] and furthermore is identified with Jesus Christ, that is, Jesus of Nazareth, the exalted Jesus-son of man, 'coming' to judge the living and the dead. Yet this calls for a nicer distinction; for in the synoptics mention of the son of man is attributed only to Jesus (with an exception – outside the gospels – in Acts 7:56, where before his martyrdom Stephen says that he sees the son of man standing by God's throne; and of Rev. 1:13 and 14:14, where it is employed in a broadly apocalyptic sense). Except in Acts nobody else calls Jesus the son of man; nor does anyone speak of him in the third person as of the son of man. Nowhere in the synoptics do we find a declaration in the vein of J. Ernst, who has the New Testament saying: 'Jesus is the son of man.'[126] In other words, that Jesus is the son of man is something assumed right through Christianity, but nowhere made into a *kerygma* of the Church or a message proclaimed. The title never comes into any Christological confession; and it gradually vanishes from use among the Christian congregations, just as outside the gospels the term 'kingdom of God' is thrust into the background and more or less disappears. After all, both 'kingdom of God' and 'son of man' have for Christians taken on the concrete guise of Jesus Christ: the suffering but exalted son of man. Besides, it was a term which could not have had a ready meaning for Gentile Christians. Finally, one notices that after AD 70, in the later apocalyptic of Judaism too, the term 'son of man' moved into the background (see above). I wonder whether by any chance certain causes as yet unexamined but rooted in a common situation underlie this parallel development.

Although a small, radical minority among critical exegetes ascribe all use of the term 'son of man' in the New Testament to the Christian communities and none to the earthly Jesus himself[127], still critical commentators like Bultmann, Tödt and Hahn[128] admit that in one particular usage of 'the son of man' (first motif-group) this concept was used by the historical Jesus himself, not in reference to himself but to the eschatological figure of the coming world judge; Jesus did not identify himself with this figure. The reasons why such an identification on the part of Jesus himself would have been psychologically difficult to entertain have been examined principally by H. M. Teeple (who denies any use of 'son of man' to Jesus) and by E. Gräszer.[129]

We must of course concede H. Conzelmann's point that indeed the New Testament use of 'son of man' is most often secondary[130] and that every use of it is set in the context of an identification of Jesus with the son of man, already made by the Church. One may wonder, however, more especially with certain Anglo-Saxon scholars, whether all these son of man passages, coloured as they are by the Church's identification, cannot nevertheless also be supported by a life of their own in sayings of Jesus of Nazareth, and that the thing most probably common to the three motif-groups is: the relation to God's eschatological mercy, rule (lordship) and judgement. Of that relation Jesus, in and through his own public ministry, is evidently conscious: it is the heart and centre of his self-understanding, as this is unveiled in his message and his conduct both towards God (the Law or disclosed will of God) and towards people. Thus it is Jesus himself who provides the basis for the possible interpretation which would see the judgement passed by the son of man – the one coming in the 'last days' – as being already accomplished in Jesus' prophetic ministry, but also in his suffering and death.

Against that background Anglo-Saxon exegetes adopt a fairly sceptical stance towards in particular certain German colleagues for allowing a possibly authentic link with Jesus only to the first of the three motif-groups aforementioned: the son of man as eschatological world judge.[131] They emphasize that a contrary movement can be detected in the gospels. There is, after all, no leaning in them towards intensifying the title 'son of man', but rather to keep it under restraint and give it a 'new' interpretation. Although the son of man is frequently referred to, none of the four gospels seeks to advance an explicit 'son of man Christology'; quite the reverse: a tradition not all that easily lending itself to a distinctive Christological project, yet persistent (because apparently going back to Jesus), obliges all the evangelists not to pass over the term 'son of man' in total silence. The fact that during his life on earth Jesus appears to have spoken only too plainly of 'the son of man' – and that in connection with his own task and destiny – would seem to be too deeply rooted in the Jesus tradition to justify our removing this kind of discourse in a quite arbitrary way from the record. Jesus was himself expecting a coming son of man as judge. The 'cross-section' criterion, here as anywhere, is certainly compelling. There is, then, in the English-language exegetical literature a clear trend towards regarding the 'three motif-groups' in which a son of man is mentioned as being both completely coloured by an ecclesiastical overlay and at the same time as basically 'authentic Jesus',[132] yet with a significance evidently common to all and tending to support the assertion that the 'son of man' is the eschatological judge and 'lord of the world' sent from God.

At this point, however, we have to take into account another tradition: that of the suffering righteous one and/or suffering prophet. For the very reason that the son of man was a vague and elusive idea to begin with, it lent itself easily to being contaminated with all sorts of other bodies of tradition. The tradition of the suffering righteous one, with its ultimate prospect of exaltation, was perhaps not yet associated in pre-Christian times with that of the son of man; but the Jesus affair gave occasion for bringing these traditions together with that of the son of man. If Jesus did speak of 'the son of man' – and on a critical view this is a probability hard to gainsay – the question arises as to what his listeners must have understood by it, either from Jesus' own explanation (but nowhere has this been recorded) or from the meaning presupposed and already attaching to the idea: and this is quite certainly the (messianic) 'apocalyptic salvific figure' or judge of the world, sent from God – with by way of detail from another tradition: via exaltation after suffering. By Jesus' time, because of the contamination of originally quite independent traditions, even this shade of meaning was no longer extraneous to the at bottom equally 'celestial' notion of 'son of man'.[133]

What confirms Jesus' own use of the term 'the son of man' is a logion about John the Baptist, who as herald of God's approaching wrath – according to Mk. 1:7; Mt. 3:11; Lk. 3:16; Acts 13:25 – speaks of 'the one to come' (with, perhaps, a Christian overlay: 'the mightier one to come'), who will come to judge with fire: evidently the image of the eschatological world judge, the son of man. Likewise in Dan. 7 we find the context of the 'judgement' and of the 'stream of fire' as the means employed to 'judge' the fourth beast (Dan. 7:11). The son of man is in this context a being sent by heaven, about whom (in contrast to God) Judaism does indeed speak anthropomorphically ('I am not worthy to untie the shoestrings of this coming One'). The 'mightier one' whom John expects is the apocalyptic son of man (by the Baptist's followers identified with Elijah to come) – identified not by John but by the Christian congregations with Jesus, thus (in the Christian context) making the Baptist at the same time the forerunner of Jesus.[134]

There is nothing to be said against – and a great deal in favour of –

making a historical connection of John's preaching of repentance in face of the coming judgement with this talk of 'the one to come', the 'apocalyptical son of man' already familiar to Judaism, and so for not describing this as a post-Easter creation on the part of the Church. As a former recipient of John's baptism Jesus was familiar with this preaching of the coming son of man; he himself extends it in line with his own message. With John, Jesus was expecting the speedy arrival of the son of man.[135] 'You will not have gone through all the towns of Israel before the Son of man comes' (Mt. 10:23); and Jesus clearly saw his own activity in relation to this coming son of man (Mk. 8:38; Lk. 12:8).

Yet the identification of Jesus with the son of man presupposes the Easter experience. And only that experience makes possible the Christological project in which Jesus of Nazareth, in his ministry, in his suffering, death, resurrection/exaltation and coming Parousia, comes to be seen in a single synthesis as 'the son of man' – although this threefold identification did not happen, it seems, all at once, nor in the same way in all the early local churches.

## §2 The Christian 'first option' from among the existing Jewish models of latter-day salvific figures

### A. EARLY CHRISTIANITY AS A JEWISH INTERPRETATION OF JESUS

It is no part of our purpose to suggest that Jesus' disciples found in the Judaism of their time the prototype, as it were, of what they had encountered in and with Jesus – as though Jesus of Nazareth were just a historical illustration of an idea already 'realized' in the history of post-exilic Jewry. For it very soon appeared that all the existing models were bound to break down if and when they were applied to Jesus.

On the other hand giving a person an identification is not something done in a single moment; it is a matter of maturation, of expectations and surmise, of first tentative identifications later on corrected, of recognition, sharpening of the contours, until Jesus does indeed 'appear' in his true form and aspect. The exposition that now follows is meant to show that the 'eschatological prophet' was an essential stage in the growing, early Christian recognition of Jesus of Nazareth in his true identity – a stage moreover that called into being a primary identification of the person which at once enables us to understand the oldest, pre-canonical credal models.

Setting aside the cleansing of the Temple and the account (coloured by the Church's intentions) of the 'triumphal entry into Jerusalem', the public career of Jesus in no way tallied with the activity expected of a royal, Davidic messiah. There was no real ground, therefore (apart from the resurrection), for using the Davidic saviour figure to help identify Jesus. Only when the interpretative experience of Jesus as the risen One had taken place was it possible to adduce Pss. 2 and 110 and 2 Sam. 7, already given a messianic interpretation by some Jews, in order to represent the resurrection as an exaltation and investing with power, thus interpreting Jesus eschatologically as a Davidic messiah. But this was in itself a second reflection, only made possible by a process of thinking in which Jesus' person had already been identified in the first instance. For that first personal identification 'the son of man' was not considered, either, because this term suggested a being coming down out of heaven; and that above all was difficult to identify with an earthly Jesus whose parents were known. Apart from the 'eschatological prophet', who took on some features of the *ebed Yahweh* or the 'servant of God'[136] (which as a 'collective Israel' was not immediately taken into account), no other models of the means of eschatological salvation were available to Jesus' disciples.

Without wishing to deny the influence of the other two traditions of eschatological salvific figures, therefore, we are bound on analytical grounds to say that at primary source all four credal models start from the fundamental interpretation of the life of Jesus under the model of the 'messianic', that is, Spirit-filled, religious 'latter-day prophet'. Because of what they had experienced in their intercourse with Jesus during his time on earth, the choice of the very first followers of Jesus, later to become Christians, fell upon the Jewish model of the eschatological prophet, with which they were familiar. In that model they recognized a full reflection of Jesus – exactly as he had appeared to them in daily intercourse. To put it baldly: if the model had not already existed, the impression that Jesus had made on them in his whole ministry would have obliged them to invent it.

This implies that there was not, originally, any question of a contrast between a Jewish and a Christian messianism, but rather of a deliberate choice (arising from the peculiar import and character of Jesus' earthly ministry as it had actually come to pass) between two already given Jewish models: a choice was made in favour of the messianism of the latter-day prophet, the anointed final prophet of the glad tidings from God – although partly because of the already existing contamination

of Davidic and prophetic messianism, and especially thanks to the
resurrection, the Davidic-messianic tradition also played an unmistakable role in some early Christian communities and thus in the
gospels. Yet even here the Davidic messiah is transformed by the
fundamental decision to opt for the messianic prophet, the one filled
with God's Spirit, who brings the joyful news of God's approaching
graciousness and mercy. The very first Christians who supplied the
initial thrust to the early Christian traditions and so decided fundamentally in which direction they would tend to move were not Greeks,
but Aramaic- and Greek-speaking Jews; *that* we should not forget. In
the Christian notion of the messiah is enshrined a Jewish and Christian
reaction to one particular Jewish conception of the messiah, as expressed primarily in the Zealotic messianism of Israel's resistance
fighters. Certain Jews and all Christians were here imposing a veto on
an interpretation of the 'rule of God' which was obviously not in
keeping with Yahwism and with Israel's ancient idea of God's lordship. In this regard the first Christians felt themselves to be simply
Jews who went up to the Temple as all pious Jews would do.

The identification of Jesus with the 'messianic' latter-day prophet
had large-scale consequences. For in the Judaism of the time this concept evoked a whole range of meanings: christ, the anointed one, but
also *Maran* or Lord (*Kyrios*), Wisdom and mediator of God's revelation, son of God, teacher of the Law, and so forth. Not only was this
'christological model' – I mean: all the terms centred around 'christ' as
the anointed prophet – ready to hand in the Judaism of the time; it was
also already personalized in it: Enoch, Moses, Elijah, Samuel were
already being interpreted 'christologically' in Judaism, as in 4 Ezra
(though written after Jesus Christ) Ezra too is given a 'christological'
interpretation; but then again the Aramaic Enoch (written substantially half a century before Jesus) provides a similar 'christology' of
Enoch. To the Jews they are all known as *christus, kyrios,* son of God.
Fodder enough for the historians of religion – but what a crucial
difference with Jesus! What is in their case a literary process within the
developing course of tradition – all this apocalyptic literature is essentially pseudonymous; all these models are merely applied to figures
from the dim and distant past – for the first Christians became a means
of articulating their assessment of a very recently deceased historical
person on his own merit and importance: all this is being said of Jesus
of Nazareth at a moment when many friends and companions of Jesus
are still living. This has nothing to do, therefore, with the peculiar
tenor of all that Jewish apocalyptic literature; it disrupts all existing

frameworks and in comparison with the parallel literature of the time is simply unfamiliar within a Jewish context, and non-apocalyptic. Furthermore, there is no need even to think in terms of literary dependence, but simply of a shared participation in the spirit of the age and a similar cast of thought. Starting from the common 'charismatic exegesis' of texts in the sacred books, this provides the horizon of understanding within which the Christians were able to interpret Jesus of Nazareth 'according to the Scriptures'. The use of what has come to be known to Christians as the 'Old Testament' is fundamental to their interpretation of Jesus of Nazareth – but controlled by the weighty import, criterion and norm of Jesus' historical ministry and career. What are the reliable evidences for this?

## B.  JESUS, ENVISAGED AS THE LATTER-DAY PROPHET

The New Testament clearly shows that in his lifetime Jesus of Nazareth had made on many people the impression of being 'a prophet' – something by then already rare – just as John the Baptist too is treated as an exception. According to the people Jesus is 'one of the prophets' – a Semitism for: he is a prophet (Mk. 6:15; 8:27-28). This Marcan tradition is confirmed (criterion of the cross-section) by the peculiarly Lucan tradition (Lk. 7:39) and by the additional passages (as compared with Mark) in Mt. 21:11, 46; see also Lk. 9:7-9; Jn. 6:14-15 and 1:21. Likewise in Lk. 24:19 the party walking to Emmaus show that in Jesus' lifetime they had acknowledged him as a prophet. That the people, and more especially his own disciples, judged Jesus to be a prophet was certainly the case prior to the events of Easter.

Yet another circumstance appears to be a recollection of Jesus' life on earth. The question of the bond between Jesus and the Spirit of God – a connection that characterized the prophet – was one of the first problems presented by Jesus' public role. It was clear from the start that there was something extraordinary about Jesus. People said of him: 'He is beside himself' (Mk. 3:21). This gave rise to a diversity of opinion: either he is a man possessed by the devil (Mk. 3:22; Mt. 12:24; Lk. 11:15; Jn. 7:20; 8:48; 9:16) or one possessed by God's Spirit – a prophet (Lk. 7:18-23 parallels; 11:14-23 parallels; see also: Jn. 8:48-50, 52 and 10:20-21). For those who trusted him he was filled with the Spirit (Lk. 11:14-23=Mt. 12:22-30 from the Q source; also Mt. 11:13-20; cf. Jn. 6:14; 8:48-50, 52 and 10:20-21). This question of the spirit of the devil or the spirit of God – in other words, did Jesus have the prophetic spirit? – seems, to judge from these independent literary traditions, to reflect quite definitely a recollection of Jesus' days here on earth.[137]

There are also passages which, though already touched up by the Church, none the less point to an expectant hope, prior to Easter, that Jesus is the eschatological prophet: a *propheta redivivus*, either Elijah or the deceased but resuscitated John the Baptist, or even (Matthew adds) Jeremiah (Lk. 9:8 as against Mk. 6:15; Lk. 9:19 as against Mk. 8:28; Mt. 16:14; Jn. 6:14–15). In other words, with Luke, the Marcan 'a prophet' becomes 'one of the old prophets' (Lk. 9:19), an expression for the eschatological prophet, or in other words, 'a great prophet' (Lk. 7:16). Luke has the party on the road to Emmaus acknowledging Jesus not simply as a prophet but as the eschatological prophet 'who was the one to redeem Israel' (also Mt. 16:14 as compared with Mk. 8:28). It is particularly striking that Lk. 4:16–21 starts off the public ministry of Jesus with a sermon in the synagogue in which Jesus expounds Isa. 61:1–2 (interpreted in his day as the great annunciation of the eschatological christ-prophet) as beginning here and now to be fulfilled. According to Luke Jesus represents himself to be the latter-day prophet ushering in God's time of mercy. Plainly a post-Easter reflection. But Mark too is aware that Jesus is thought to be the eschatological prophet: is he the revivified John the Baptist or Elijah (Mk. 6:14–15; 8:28)? It is difficult to argue that this is solely a post-Easter appreciation, as in the same primitive Christian tradition John the Baptist is himself already being interpreted as Elias *redivivus* (Mk. 9:13). Luke too, who elsewhere depicts Jesus as the final prophet, in 7:25–27 identifies John the Baptist with the latter-day Elijah-prophet, and in so doing reflects a post-Easter controversy between John's disciples and those of Jesus, with these latter declaring Jesus greater than John and so 'more than a prophet' (Lk. 7:26b). In the historical development of tradition, therefore, Mk. 6:14 and 8:28 enshrine authentic reminiscences of the notion which even before Easter had been formed (interrogatively, at least) regarding Jesus: at any rate the expectant hope that Jesus is the eschatological prophet (without implying as yet a 'Christology', unless – see below – applying the 'eschatological prophet' idea to Jesus must in itself be called a ' Christological identification'). Relevant perhaps to a 'messianic' interpretation of Jesus as eschatological prophet is Jn. 6:14: 'This is indeed the prophet who is to come into the world!' (except for the Johannine 'into the world' this verse would seem to contain historical memories). Jesus saw ideas about a Davidic messiah behind that popular reaction (Jn.

6:15); and 'he withdrew'.

In Mk. 6:4 parallels and Lk. 13:33 Jesus himself compares his destiny with that of a prophet (in line with the Q tradition: Lk. 11:49–52); the implicit suggestion here is that Jesus envisages his life in prophetic categories, in this case, in so far as they include rejection and martyrdom. Bultmann himself concedes the historical character of Jesus' prophetic self-understanding (on the basis more particularly of Lk. 12:49; Mk. 2:17; Mt. 15:24),[138] especially in his prophetic, nay, more-than-prophetic siding with humble and lowly people and the socially and religiously 'disinherited'. There again, bearing in mind Isa. 11:4, 6; Isa. 42:1–4 and 61:1–2, are displayed evident traits of the great and last prophet. According also to O. Cullmann[139] Jesus admittedly never identifies himself with the eschatological prophet; but he does nevertheless interpret his mission and course of action in terms of latter-day prophecy. Post-Easter theology about the historical fact of Jesus' baptism in the Jordan (Mk. 1:10–11; Mt. 3:16–17; Lk. 3:21–22 and Jn. 1:32) is dealing, as further examination will show, with the recognition of Jesus as the eschatological prophet, in whom however (because of the contamination of various originally independent traditions in the Old Testament) a royal and priestly messianism are also merged; Jesus is 'the one filled with God's Spirit', the fulfilment of all the great promises of the Old Testament: Isa. 11:2 as well as 42:1–2; Isa. 61:1 (see Acts 10 and Lk. 4) and Ps. 2:7. That is how the synoptic and Johannine interpretations of Jesus' baptism see it. In Acts 3:11–26 and 7:37 Jesus expressly fulfils the expectation concerning the latter-day 'prophet like Moses' (Deut. 18:15). (In that way Christian prophets explained Jesus' life in the light of Old Testament texts.) 2 Peter 1:16–21 alludes to this by then Christian practice of prophetic exposition, in a Jewish-charismatic vein, of the Old Testament (in keeping also with intertestamentary exegesis). Thus Paul could say: Jesus is 'the anointed one in whom God's promises have become yes and amen' (2 Cor. 1:20): the latter-day prophet, filled with God's Spirit, foreshadowed in Isa. 61, has been made concretely manifest in Jesus of Nazareth. It could be argued that according to this primitive Christian interpretation what is being officially and solemnly proclaimed at Jesus' baptism in Jordan in the very presence of the 'old testament' (concluded by John the Baptist) is his office as messianic 'eschatological prophet'. The Q community contains logia in which Jesus sees his mission in line of succession to the prophets (Mt. 23:29–30 and 23:34–36, 37 parallels) and often in relation to the eschatological judgement; quite certainly, therefore, for the Q community the earthly Jesus is the eschatological prophet, but without any messianism associated with the house of David; the title 'Christ' has no place at all in this Q tradition; and in view of the three temptation-stories about Jesus (see above) this cannot be just an accident. It implies the repudiation of dynastic-Davidic messianism centred around a ruler-figure.

Luke and Matthew trace this 'being filled with the Spirit' back to Jesus' birth (infancy gospels). For a man is a prophet 'from his mother's womb' (Jer. 1:5; Isa. 49:1-3; Ps. 110); Paul is in the same tradition when he says about his own election as an apostle that his calling was 'from his mother's womb', despite his late conversion at Damascus (Gal. 1:15). (This idea is part of one complex of tradition.) Because the prophet in this tradition is 'God with us', Matthew too starts his gospel by identifying Jesus with the prophetic 'being with us' of God (Mt. 1:23). Various independent traditions in the primitive Church call Jesus simply 'the prophet', with a more or less declared option on the 'eschatological prophet'.

The Johannine gospel is very obviously constructed on the prophetic Moses-model: Jesus is the new Moses, the eschatological 'prophet like Moses', and one yet greater than he (Jn. 1:17). John 1:16-18 is formulated with an eye to the account of the covenant at Sinai (Ex. 33 – 34): Moses has to lead the people to the Promised Land (Ex. 33:1-12; 34:34), for which purpose he asks for God's continuing presence (33:15, 16; 34:9 and 40:34): Jn. 1:14 (*eskènôsen*); then Moses asks: 'Show me thy glory' (Ex. 33:18): Jn. 1:14b ('We have beheld his glory'); then comes: 'No one sees God but he dies' (Ex. 33:20): Jn. 1:18 ('No one has ever seen God'). Yet Yahweh reveals his name to Moses: 'Yahweh . . . full of grace and truth' (Ex. 34:6): Jn. 1:17 ('For the law was given through Moses; grace and truth came through Jesus Christ'); God then undertakes to go with his people (Ex. 34:9-10) and gives Moses the tablets of stone containing the Law (34:28): Jn. 1:17 ('The Law was given by Moses . . .'). This parallel with Moses is sustained throughout the Johannine gospel: Moses' calling (Ex. 3) and Jesus' calling after the baptism in Jordan (Jn. 1:29-34; see 8:32-36); then come the enactments of Moses' marvellous power, with the Nile waters being turned red with blood: Jesus' miracle at Cana (Jn. 2:1-11). Moses celebrates the first Passover feast (Ex. 11 – 12): Jesus goes to Jerusalem for the Passover and – there and then, according to John – carries out the cleansing of the Temple (Jn. 2:13-16); next, Moses with his people passes through the Red Sea (Ex. 14): in Jn. 3:1-5 Jesus talks to Nicodemus about the need 'to be born of water and spirit'. When the people had run out of bread and water and were also plagued with poisonous snakes, Moses made a bronze serpent, raised it and set it up on a pole, and everybody bitten by a snake who gazed up at the bronze image stayed alive (Num. 21:4–9): 'And as Moses lifted up the serpent in the wilderness, so must the Son of man be lifted up' (Jn. 3:14). After the crossing of the Red Sea Moses and the people of God discover a water-spring (Ex. 15:22–25): in Jn. 4 at the 'spring of living water' Jesus is heard conversing with a Samaritan woman. In Ex. 16 we hear tell of the miraculous manna: in Jn. 6 of the feeding of the five thousand and (cf. Ex. 17:1–7) also Jesus' discourse on the manna from heaven. John 10 and 11 contain various allusions to Moses' successor, Joshua, who actually led God's people into the Promised Land. Structurally the Johannine gospel is formed on a view of Jesus as the eschatological Moses-prophet, leading people into the kingdom of God. One might of course infer that within a late-sapiential context (third credal model) John is presenting a theology of Jesus the eschatological prophet *qua* Moses, who himself leads the people into the Promised Land: 'in the bosom of the Father' (Jn. 1:18), the kingdom of God.

All the gospels preserve the memory of the first identification of Jesus' person, suggested by his own life: Jesus is the prophet of the approaching – and in and through his public ministry already manifested – final kingdom of God. It seems to me wrong, therefore, that in many exegetical surveys of Jesus' titles that of 'Jesus as prophet' is often brought in at the end, is usually put low down on the list[140] and furthermore is regarded as somehow defective or inadequate.[141] One may well ask whether there is not some failure here to appreciate the prophetic self-understanding of Jesus, particularly as he is dismissive towards 'house of David' messianism and speaks about the son of man as of the coming world judge; in other words, whether one is not simply evacuating Jesus' self-understanding of all content or even filling the vacuum with later Christological insights. As a result, the matrix of all the other honorific titles and credal strands is entirely overlooked.

That the link between the earthly Jesus and the kerygmatic Christ is the recognition, common to all credal strands, of the earthly Jesus as the eschatological prophet (who does, it is true, surpass all expectations) and that this identification (at least as question and surmise) was most likely made prior to Easter, has enormous consequences. It points to a considerable continuity between the impression that Jesus made during his earthly days and the apparently 'advanced Christology' of the Church's *kerygmata* or affirmations of belief after his death. For from the history of tradition it is still possible to show that all these *kerygmata* are in the Judaism of the time already supplied along with the title 'eschatological prophet'. In other words: whoever acknowledges Jesus as the eschatological prophet of the nearness of God's kingdom, viewed from the standpoint of the developing tradition, has broached a store of synonyms or at any rate associations in which there figure prominently such titles as the Christ, the *Kyrios*, the Son of God. This we must now discuss in more precise detail.

## C.   JESUS, THE LATTER-DAY MESSENGER FROM GOD, SOURCE OF THE EARLIEST CREDAL STRANDS AND MAIN SOURCE OF THE VERY EARLIEST CHRISTIAN USE OF THE TITLES CHRIST, THE LORD, THE SON

(a) A premise at one time often stated but even more frequently challenged[142] is that there were already circulating in Jesus' day *testimonia*, that is, anthologies of Old Testament Scripture, in which on the pattern of the 'eschatological exegesis' common at the time, proof-texts from the Scriptures were collected, in which the contemporary interpreters of Jewish apocalyptic saw 'prophecies' concerning events of the 'last days' and certain salvific individuals who were supposed to play a specific part in them. This *pesher* hermeneusis (midrashic exegesis) of the Scriptures, deposited in summaries, had long been recognized as dating from the second, third and fourth centuries; and the specialist scholars also conceded that these were simply a codified version of older, even very ancient traditions – like the rabbinical writings of the second century after Christ. But finds from the Qumrân caves have now served to show that such eschatological-exegetical *testimonia* are in fact of a much older date;[143] scrolls of them have even been found (though in a damaged state), written in Aramaic as it must have been spoken more or less in the time of Jesus. Particularly in Qumrân (and that means at the latest prior to 70 and 72/73, when at the time of the fall of Jerusalem the Qumrân community was exterminated after having secured the safety of its library) they made intensive use for their theology of such 'anthologies' (if a lot of them were not actually the work of the Qumrân community itself). They would seem, as appears from similar references to the Old Testament in the New Testament and the proof-texts (identical though differently interpreted) cited there in regard to the events of the last days, to have been known and used among a wider circle. But quite apart from whether New Testament writers knew and made use of such 'anthologies', these indicate a general use in that period for the purpose of interpreting, in the light of Scripture, contemporary events (more or less universally held to signify the end of the Age).[144] The New Testament procedure of using Scripture as so many pieces of evidence for interpreting the Jesus event is not simply and solely 'anti-Jewish polemic', nor yet a specifically Christian kind of exegesis, but a practice current in the Judaism of the time.

The basic assumption of this exegesis, as presented to us in these *testimonia*, was that Scripture had an arcane, that is, an eschatological meaning. Charismatic exegesis could unveil that meaning, thereby giving people a picture of the end of the Age, so shedding light on what was currently taking place. Such exegesis is carried out by combining Scriptural passages from different traditions, often by way of Hebrew texts already 'updated' through the Greek version known as the Septuagint, and on the strength of similar-sounding words; so that by switching certain letters around, if need be, one can obtain quite different combinations from those intended by the original text. The *sensus scripturisticus* thus acquired (Paul's letters are a clear, albeit traditionally Jewish example of this) can then be applied to contemporary events in which that biblical meaning was seen as being fulfilled.[145] It was a general method of exegesis in those days, applied in a fairly austere way by the Pharisaical rabbis and much more freely in Qumrân and among other apocalyptic groups in Palestine; it was the method used for the Septuagint itself, by Philo in particular, and for the later Targums as we know them, which are however only carrying forward a longer tradition. (Patristics and the whole further development of Christian exegesis have drawn from this source what is known as the *sensus plenior* of the Scriptures, at the same time applying this procedure to the writings of the New Testament.)

It is against this background that we must set the Jewish 'christ tradition' of the coming eschatological prophet, whom the first Christians identified on the strength of the tradition with Jesus of Nazareth. Not starting from this already given model but from what had in point of historical fact been manifested to them in Jesus, they took hold of that model as best reflecting or reproducing the impression that Jesus had made upon them. The model fully and accurately represented the concrete person of Jesus: he was that christ.

In the anthologies found at Qumrân – 4Qtest and 4Qflor (that is to say: the *testimonia* and *florilegia* found in the fourth cave at Qumrân, or anthologies of Scriptural texts thus compiled and eschatologically interpreted) – we have an inventory of latter-day, salvific figures: on the one hand the eschatological 'prophet like Moses', with reference to Deut. 18:15–19 (not Deut. 18 as expounded in modern exegesis, which sees in it the institutionalizing of the 'prophetic college' in Israel, but taking it as a prophecy about a latter-day prophet). This Qumrân exegesis is done by combining and reading together Deut. 18:15–19; 5:28–29; 33:8–11 and Num. 24:15–17. Along with that, again by way of combining a number of different Scriptural passages, there emerges a messianic oracle concerning two messiahs: a Davidic messiah and a 'high-priestly' one who interprets God's Law (partly apropos of the controversy that had arisen since the Hasmonean ascendancy, as to whether the two functions in Israel might not be united in a single person).[146] For the notion of 'two messiahs' (besides the aforementioned eschatological prophet) the most crucial passage was Zech. 4:3, 11–14. These two, the royal and the priestly messiah, are from the Qumrânic standpoint the messiah of Israel and the messiah of Aaron; but in the Testamentum Levi, the messiah from Judah and the messiah from Levi. For this Moses and Aaron, Israel's great leaders, supply the model; but that in different traditions they are readily interchanged with other salvific figures of the past – especially Elijah and Enoch – points to the process of literary development. In circles envisaging only one eschatological salvific figure it is normally Elijah, in other words, the latter-day prophet (under the weight of Scripture itself: Mal. 3:1 with 3:23–24). Of all this hair-splitting exegesis in the end only this last – the eschatological Elijah figure – got through to broad sectors of the people (and even Malachi itself may well be witness to and echo of a popular expectation in process of formation).

At any rate all these things in the period of Jewish apocalypticism give us an idea of how Israel's sacred books were used to give point to events at the time and still to come. This Jewish exegesis became that of the first Christians as well. (How could those Jewish Christians have done otherwise?)

In many – for us most difficult – passages of his letters Paul is an obvious exemplar of such 'charismatic exegesis'; it is less striking but no less real and (in a rather deceptive way) widespread in the Acts and the gospels. An understanding of the process should convince us that the Old Testament is not in fact the source of the interpretation of current events, but that the view already held of such events (provided by the weighty impact of the events themselves) – an insight not easy to express in so many words – is precisely articulated and successfully formulated thanks to the range of concepts supplied by the sacred books. Again, in view of the given Jewish thought-pattern, a peculiar interpretation (for instance: this Jesus is the 'christ') can only acquire full validity if the promised 'christ figure' (of the Old Testament) can 'exegetically' be shown to have its fulfilment in Jesus. In other words, this Jewish hermeneutic interprets contemporary events in the light of the Bible, which supplies the range of articulation and vocabulary for putting effectively into words the 'interpretation of actual facts' (the understanding of a current or coming event), that is, for formulating it in concepts immediately intelligible to those who stand within this tradition (even though it is often by this time just a literary tradition – yet for the practitioners of pious spirituality still very much a vital part of their lives). After so many centuries such a process seems wholly strange to us because, given our past – steeped as it is in Western philosophy – we at once conclude from it things which this Jewish biblical hermeneusis of Jesus of Nazareth never really intended or indeed could have intended. The process itself, however, we can certainly empathize with in a social and psychological context. That this hermeneusis should have become the foundation of the whole Christian Christology, while at the time the same key ideas were applied just as ingenuously to, for example, Moses, Elijah and in particular the 'son of man Enoch', is therefore (even granting a possible literary dependence) not in the least disquieting. (It is much to the point that the Christian Trinitarian interpretation of the living God is the result or implication of a refusal on the part of Christians to identify Jesus absolutely, without distinctions, with the living God.) These already given models are no cause for anxiety. On the contrary, Moses, Elijah, Enoch or the 'coming son of man Ezra' are envisaged in the literature of the time as literary figures, pseudonyms, admittedly, for real persons from a misty past, but concrete fictions for expressing how the contemporary state of affairs was to be understood. They are 'literary categories', confined in fact to the élite circle of religious intellectuals. The only idea encompassed by the man in the street about this was that there was 'a One to come'; and given his historical and social situation, he had every reason to hope for a liberator and deliverer! That came to be his spontaneous personal expectation, to which 'the people' referred to in the New Testament still bear a clear witness. Over against that, in the early Christian tradition and its credal models, all these familiar literary motifs are adopted in order to express in an intelligible way a contemporary human phenomenon: that of a man who had only just recently died. If anyone had so wished, he could have carried out a critical investigation of the whole thing. An identification of this sort is completely unknown in the entire range of this Jewish, non-Christian literature. It was literature – simply that; not a campaign or a movement. Seeking to divinize Moses, Enoch or Ezra, figures from the remote past, was recognized by all and sundry as a literary procedure – or even as an edifying and exemplary bit of anthropology – and that is what everyone understood it to be. The anointed 'Enoch-christ' no more gives rise to an Enoch movement than a 'christ-Ezra' does to an Ezra movement, even though the same messianic name is attached to both of them. In other words, a literary model will not of itself engender any movement. From Jesus there did arise a Christ movement. And that is a fundamental difference. And so to this Jesus, in whom many found salvation particularized in history, it was possible to apply familiar literary models without misgiving (in order, that is, to be understood by people at that time) – provided always that Jesus had indeed made himself known through his message as well as by word and action to be the real 'prophet of the last days'. For individual claimants to a messianic role, leaders of resistance movements against Rome, were common enough during that period, before and after Jesus. Applying the method of form criticism to the New Testament forces us to recognize that the impression Jesus made on those about him (though not at first thoroughly grasped in all its consequences) of being no 'messianic' resistance fighter but the messenger and prophet of a deeper liberation (in which the very idea of 'occupation' ceases to make any point) was already a matter of experience before Easter, at least as a question and a vaguely formulated expectation. After his death, when his life could be considered as a whole, people went on to draw consequences from the phenomenon manifested in this latter-day prophet. Here is Christological interpretation of Jesus, present implicitly even in the pre-Easter surmise that the prophet of God's 'final day' had now appeared. This invites us, not so much to look for highly developed Christological elements in the lifetime of Jesus of Nazareth but, contrariwise, starting from the historical experience of Jesus as prophet of the nearby kingdom of God (I had almost, though wrongly, said: to enable us to grasp the latent Christological implications of the post-Easter Christological confession of Jesus. Wrongly, of course, and yet it was not a bad thing to put it like that!) – starting thus from the impression the earthly Jesus made on his loyal followers, to understand better the theological drift of the Church's *kerygma* and of the first credal formulations. Jesus of Nazareth is, after all, the norm and criterion of Christian belief. So too, for me as a Christian, is Chalcedon: but under the compelling norm of the same Jesus Christ, whom this council – within a framework of specific and specifically Greek philosophical enquiry, proper to its time though strange to us – likewise took to be the norm and criterion of its dogmatic definitions, because the Christians (church leaders) who uttered these things were also confronted in their time with the question: how are we to formulate our experience that decisive and definitive salvation from God comes solely from Jesus Christ, 'true man', without surrendering what is equally precious to us all, our Jewish Christian heritage of strict monotheism, and slipping into the acknowledgement of a 'second God' alongside the living God?

(b) Starting then from Jesus of Nazareth identified as the eschatological prophet, there emerges into view the first version to be formulated of New Testament Christology and of its four credal models, as well as the early use (prior to any influence of Gentile Christian churches) of the affirmation that Jesus of Nazareth 'is the Christ, the only-begotten Son, our Lord'. This is not to deny in any way that in the later version of the New Testament, where the voice we hear is that of Christians who had been not only non-Jewish but actually pagan (Hellenistic Syrians, or whatever), Hellenistic patterns of thought had a part to play. It *is* saying, however, that for decades the very earliest Christianity was kept going solely by Jews, Aramaic-speaking Jews and Greek-speaking Jews of the Diaspora; and that the fundamental features of the Christological interpretation of Jesus had already been formed before ever a single Gentile Christian could have contributed anything from that quarter. That 'Hellenism' did actually have a very early influence, via the Greek-speaking Jews, and that these Diaspora Jews were the most active, even, in primitive Christianity is hard to deny, in the wake of the literature of the last ten years. But those Jews, once gone out of the Diaspora to Jerusalem, moved by that deep Jewish spirituality centred in the religious cult of Zion (in Jerusalem they had several Greek synagogues), were inspired by the ancient faith of Israel – and not uncritically when it came to the subsequently 'established religion' of Jewry. What they contributed (albeit in Greek models) was 'more Jewish' than the official religion. In spite of and even in their many Hellenistic trains of thought they were devoted heart and soul to the (anti-Gentile) spirituality of the Bible (they were the Greek translation or version of the most authentic 'Israel').

In order thus to grasp the early Christian credal models at source, as well as to understand what follows from the earliest (pre- or post-Easter) identification of Jesus with the eschatological prophet of the rule of God for men's salvation, we first of all have to consider the broad range of meaning which for a Jew of that period, in Jerusalem as well as more especially perhaps in the Diaspora, the eschatological prophet of grace and judgement was naturally bound to evoke. Other ideas, Jewish and non-Jewish, have broadened the purport of this original meaning, deepened it or perhaps distorted it; yet for that very reason the study of the original Christian impulse is (not the only vehicle of salvation, it is true, but) extremely important, because it permits us to test this earliest as well as the later Christian interpretation of Jesus by the sole criterion: Jesus of Nazareth. For once an interpretation has been given, it is a sociological fact that it can go on to lead a life of its own; and then the further history of that interpretation *may* become a pure history of 'ideas', divorced from the reality it is meant to be about: the Nazarene. This typically human process no one – and in particular no Christian – should lose sight of.

Basic to the early Christian interpretation of Jesus as the eschatological 'messenger from God' is a Deuteronomic text (see Deut. 18:15) from Exodus, which played an important role in the Judaistic exegesis with which the first Christians were at home. 'Behold, I send my *messenger* [*aggelos*, angel] *before you, to guard you on the way and to bring you to the place which I have prepared. Give heed to him and hearken to his voice, do not rebel against him, for he will not pardon your transgression; for my name is in him. But if you hearken attentively to his voice* and *do all that I say*, then I will be an enemy to your enemies and *an adversary to your adversaries. My messenger shall go before you*' (Ex. 23:20–23; see 33:2).[147] We are not concerned here with an exposition of the passage based on modern exegesis, but with the Jewish tradition that grew out of it and was flourishing in Jesus' time, in that way providing the Christological interpretation of Jesus as the eschatological messenger with the set of ideas from which its Christology was born. It is often said that it is the intention of the New Testament to interpret Jesus 'according to the Scriptures' (for us the Old Testament) and not according to the Jewish literature between the Testaments. In a formal sense that is right; but in virtue of the principles and practice of Scriptural exposition in those days ('charismatic' and prophetic exegesis) the distinction is hardly a relevant one, because it was hard to differentiate, in any way that mattered, between 'Scripture' and 'Scriptural interpretation' at the time.[148] (Medieval theologians too describe both the Bible and the patristic theological exegesis of the Bible as simply *Sacra pagina*.) What functions in the New Testament is not an 'objective' Bible but Scrip-

ture in the current mode of exegesis, that is, in line with that of intertestamentary literature (which is therefore a positive aid to understanding the New Testament). The whole range of meaning attached
to the notion of a 'latter-day prophet' in Jesus' time is indeed important,
therefore, to a proper comprehension of it. So then, when in the New
Testament we come across concepts such as (full) authority, Christ,
Lord, Son of God, etc., the main principle of interpretation must surely
be: to which complex of tradition does the use of these terms, in this
context or in that, actually belong? After that, we can consider to what
extent other traditions, whether of the New Testament or stemming
from late Judaism, have been amalgamated with it.

The Deuteronomistic messenger idea cited above – which also runs
through the passages from the Second and Third Isaiah quoted earlier
on – sees in the prophet, the messenger from God, 'something of God'
who sent him: God's name is set upon the envoy. In synagogue
circles within the Diaspora (the Septuagint version) God's name,
*Adonai*, is called *Kyrios*, Lord. Thus the name *Kyrios* is conferred on the
messenger sent by God. For that reason Jesus is called 'the Lord',
*Kyrios*, or in the Aramaic *Maran* (basis of the first credal strand in both
the Q community and in Mark). As is shown by the old formula in the
Greek gospels, *Maran atha* (incorporated into the liturgy), the kyrial
interpretation derives not from Hellenistic religions but from a Palestinian setting.[149] Within the history of tradition the *Kyrios* name of Jesus
is located first of all in the messenger-concept of Deuteronomistic
Judaism. On the prophetic envoy of God, God's name – *Kyrios ho
theos* – is set. Anyone therefore who acknowledges God's messenger in
effect confesses God; whoever rejects him commits sin – and this sin,
says Mk. 3:28–29, is unforgivable[150] ('for he will not pardon your
transgression', Ex. 23:21). This continues to operate, obviously enough,
in Matthew and Luke: 'So everyone who acknowledges me before men,
I also will acknowledge before my Father who is in heaven; but whoever denies me before men, I also will deny before my Father who is in
heaven' (thus the Matthean version, Mt. 10:32–33=Lk. 12:8–9);
hence: 'Blessed is he who takes no offence at me' (Mt. 11:6=Lk. 7:23).
Both series of texts come from the messenger tradition of the Q source.
But not only Mark and the Q community (in independent texts, Lk.
12:8–9 parallels) – John too, in his own way, says exactly the same
thing: 'He who rejects me and does not receive my sayings has a judge;
the word that I have spoken will be his judge on the last day' (Jn. 12:
48).[151] These sentiments – whether 'authentic Jesus material' or not –
in the consciousness of a prophet, and certainly of one who knows

himself to be the prophet of God's nearby kingdom (and that awareness no exegete would deny to Jesus) are contained explicitly, as it
were, in the Deuteronomistic and Judaic notion, then current, of a
'messenger from God'. It implies a prophetic identification with the
cause of God, with God himself: God's name, the Lord, is set upon
him. Mark 3:28 equates God's name, set upon the Christ-messenger,
the anointed prophet, with *Pneuma*, the Spirit (while it is actually Mark
who distinguishes so sharply between Jesus and the Spirit). Rejecting
the earthly Jesus, therefore, is in Mk. 3:28–29 (as opposed to Mt. 12:32
and Lk. 12:10) an unforgivable sin in itself. Understandably enough,
if Jesus is seen as the latter-day prophet, that is, the messenger of God's
final offer of grace and mercy. Thus the attitude taken towards this
messenger has an eschatological relevance; it is a definitive decision
for or against God, who has sent him. Accepting or rejecting Jesus
settles the question of final well-being (salvation) or final calamity.
The New Testament idea of *exousia* or the 'plenary power' of Jesus
(whether prior to Easter or after it is matter for dispute among exegetes)
takes its original meaning from the Deuteronomistic tradition of the
(eschatological) messenger from God. The idea has of course been
given another dimension by the resurrection event, which extends this
authority of Jesus to include the final judgement: he is the son of man
(who is also) judge of the world (the first type of creed in its two subsidiary strands, in Mark and the Q community). So then, on the strength
of the resurrection, Jesus is also the 'Lord of the future'. And this
last idea was further elaborated by an appeal to other traditions: Ps. 2;
Ps. 110:1; Dan. 7:13–14, whereby the resurrection/exaltation gives an
eschatological depth to the latter-day concept of 'Lord', which in any
case attached to Jesus because of his mission as the eschatological
messenger from God. This messenger idea was to be carried through
within the Christian community in the 'messengers of Jesus Christ': 'I
say to you, he who receives anyone whom I send receives me; and he
who receives me receives him who sent me' (Jn. 13:20); this utterance
is in a vein similar to the idea of an 'apostle' in 2 Cor. In his own person
the messenger must 'stand down' in order to make possible his identification with the cause of God – for the apostles the 'cause of Christ' –
entrusted to him (2 Cor. 4:5). Again, the Johannine gospel as a whole
becomes intelligible on the basis of an admittedly highly sapiential
interpretation of the eschatological prophet from God. For the
Deuteronomistic messenger idea had by Jesus' time (and already
before then) been in contact with the more recent Wisdom literature.
The messenger of God is a 'messenger of Wisdom', sent by it or, in

highly sapiential circles, identified with the Wisdom which was itself already hypostatized and existed with God 'before all creation'. Thus in this tradition prophets were identified with archangels, with the 'Logos of God', with the 'Wisdom of God', or with patriarchs like Moses and Abraham, who dwell with God. Enoch is identified with the Wisdom of God (or 'Wisdom with God') as well as with the celestial being called 'son of man'.[152] As was said earlier on (regarding the third credal model), Wisdom is God's mediator or intermediary in creation. John's 'sending' formulae and his conception of Jesus as the Word of God, the Logos, instrument of creation, become understandable when we note how the tradition of the eschatological prophet comes to be merged with the more recent Judaic Wisdom tradition; just as in the Graeco-Jewish phase of the Q community the messenger idea is worked out in an at any rate broadly sapiential context. In Judaic exegesis the source-text of the messenger tradition – the *aggelos*, angel or messenger of Ex. 23:20 – is already identified with the prophet Elijah, who will return as the eschatological prophet. Wisdom, who pitches her tent among men (see Jn. 1:14; *eskènôsen*), is in the literature of the period mainly the Torah, Jacob or simply 'the eschatological prophet'.[153] In other words, by way of a terrestrial form in which Wisdom has come to lodge, the relationship to God is settled – a view which evidently governs the synoptic characterization of Jesus too. God has set his Name upon the messenger, his own Name; so that the identification of Jesus with Wisdom serves to express the validity of his message and public activity as the eschatological prophet. 'Yet for us there is one God, the Father, from whom are all things and for whom we exist, and one Lord, Jesus Christ, through whom are all things and through whom we exist' (1 Cor. 8:6): that Pauline passage is not bound in this perspective to mean what it would come to signify in a post-biblical, philosophical context, but rather in the import (in its own way close to reality) of the sapiential interpretation of the envoy sent by God (see also Jn. 1:3–10); what takes place here is an unprecedented revelatory event, divinely endorsed and so bearing the stamp of full prophetic authority.

By virtue of this messenger concept the prophet is addressed not only as 'master' and 'teacher' (Mk. 10:17–18; in Jn. 3:2: 'a teacher come from God'; Mk. 7:28; 11:3; 14:14; Jn. 13:13, 16; Lk. 9:54 and 10:1), but also as 'Lord'. This last has often been explained either in the sense of the form of address, 'Sir', or in that of what is known as the 'highly Christological' *Kyrios* title (as already enhanced, on the basis of the resurrection, in the Pauline writings). Yet this *kyrie* form of address turns up even in the Q source in messenger contexts, for instance, where it is dealing with Jesus the prophetic miracle-worker (Lk. 10:17; Mk. 9:38; cf. 1 Cor. 12:1-3; James 2:1 with 2:7). With Paul this 'Lord' concept – even when he very occasionally appeals to a logion of Jesus of Nazareth ('to the married I give charge, not I but the Lord', 1 Cor. 7:10, and: 'Now concerning the unmarried I have no command of the Lord', 1 Cor. 7:25) – has no doubt already been 'consolidated' by his understanding of the resurrection/exaltation; but on the other hand he continues in line with the messenger tradition to distinguish clearly between 'one God, the Father' and 'one Lord, Jesus Christ' (1 Cor. 8:6); these are pronouncements about a messenger come from God. When the centurion, in asking Jesus for help, addresses him as 'Lord', the Q community is making him use (so far irrespective of the resurrection) the typical form of address applied to a 'messenger from God the Lord', the messenger on whom God's name, 'Lord', is set and who may also be addressed, therefore, as 'Lord'. A striking case for the *kyrios* conception of the prophetic teacher as God's envoy is the saying (so difficult to understand outside this context): 'Good Master, what must I do . . .? Jesus said to him: Why do you call me good? No one is good but God alone' (Mk. 10:17-18). This passage reflects precisely the reaction of the messenger tradition of Deuteronomistic Judaism. The messenger's authority, his teaching and goodness have their source in God who sent him, not in himself. Does not John present the same reaction on Jesus' part when, albeit admittedly in a highly sapiential sense, he none the less says: 'The Father is greater than I' (Jn. 14:28)? And when after an effective speech and miracle by Barnabas and Paul an enthusiastic crowd, already well acquainted with the *theios anèr* concept, exclaimed: 'The gods have come down to us in the likeness of men' (Acts 14:11; also 28:6), do not Paul and Barnabas – messengers of Jesus the Lord – do the same as Jesus, by repudiating this non-prophetic identification with God and saying 'that they are but men', although with a message that speaks of their being sent from God (Acts 14:14-15)? Leaving aside all the differences, what the refusal to let himself be called 'good' (Jesus) or a 'divine miracle-man' (Paul and Barnabas) does in both instances is to clarify on both sides the proper notion of 'the messenger', at the same time serving to discountenance all the *theios anèr* tendencies which for the monotheistic Jew were an anti-Yahwistic abomination.[154]

That in a perspective of the messenger tradition God as Lord is indeed manifested in the messenger is a view common to all the apocalyptic literature.[155] This Jewish epiphany of God has a quite different basis from the Hellenistic *epiphaneia* of God in human beings. The connection between the eschatological 'messenger from God' and his *Kyrios* name again plainly appears in the Christological hymn of Phil. 2:9–11, which purely and simply expresses the messenger tradition of Deuteronomistic Judaism, albeit linked with and set within the thought-pattern of the Wisdom tradition (in which at that period the old messenger idea found exactly its proper context, as witness the 'messenger of Wisdom' in the Q community and the synoptics): 'Therefore God has highly exalted him and bestowed on him the name which is above every name, that at the name of Jesus every knee should bow, in heaven and on earth and under the earth, and every tongue confess that Jesus Christ is Lord, to the glory of God the Father.' The name of God, the Lord – that is (as a Graeco-Jewish periphrasis for the tetragram), 'the name above every name' – is set upon Jesus, assigned to him as a messenger who has been sent by God, goes into a strange land and then, his task accomplished, lays it again before the feet of God. Thus in the apocalyptic literature Enoch and Moses, likewise both envoys whom God has taken up, receive the name of God himself: they are called 'the Lord'. Enoch even acquires the seventy – all seventy – names of God;[156] and to him lordship is given, power and authority over every created thing. We find in this same literature the name given to Moses as 'Lord of all the prophets', which is to say that all the prophets received their teaching from him; and this is applied to the same effect in Rev. 11:8b, in connection with Jesus Christ. That God's own name should be conferred on the prophet of God, more especially on the eschatological messenger, is quite conceivable, therefore, in a Jewish context; it goes back to an Old Testament tradition, put by the Greek-speaking Jews of Jesus' time into a late sapiential setting. In no way does it clash with the Jews' strictly monotheistic way of thinking. It is in those very circles within the early Jewish Christian community that Jesus is first called *Mara* (or *Maran*), *Kyrios* – and not against a background of Hellenistic religions.

This prophetic identification of the eschatological messenger with the name of God himself, the Lord, lies behind the emergence and growth of the four types of creed (obviously enough in the case of the first three; whether that is true also of the Easter Christology should become clear later on).

Even more important is the fact that the 'christ' title (not in the Davidic sense) also belongs essentially within the tradition of the eschatological prophet. For he is the one (see Isa. 61:1–2) anointed with God's Spirit, messiah, with a non-royal, non-Davidic connotation (and in that sense 'non-messianic'; but to speak thus is to misjudge a particular Jewish messianic tradition and so contrast Christian messianism wrongly with the multiplicity of Jewish messianism). Because of the teaching function of priest as well as of prophet the concepts of 'the prophetic' and 'the priestly' have already been amalgamated with this non-Davidic messianism of the last prophet. In Jesus, therefore, this prophet-messiah is at the same time the true interpreter of God's Torah, the true 'servant of Yahweh', even: the new lawgiver, the new Moses.

In view of the recollections – in the earliest stages of Christianity surely for the most part still capable of being checked and corrected – of the actual career and public ministry of Jesus of Nazareth,[157] of which within the context of credal affirmation the New Testament is a broadly reliable echo, it becomes obvious that the original Jewish Christian naming of Jesus as the Christ, messiah, could have had nothing to do with the particular messianic expectation of a primarily national-cum-political restoration of Israel. The only element in Jesus' life that might point in that direction is the (not so far satisfactorily resolved, precise significance of the) 'cleansing of the Temple' by Jesus (see earlier on). Considering the historical weight of evidence regarding Jesus' *de facto* behaviour, the Davidic-messianic interpretation was not in the running as a real interpretation of Jesus (although it was to play a not inconsiderable role in an interpretation of Jesus' resurrection in the sense of exaltation – but this assumes a preceding interpretation of Jesus as eschatological prophet). In opting originally against a dynastic-Davidic messianism the first Christians (actually themselves Jewish) were being in no way anti-Jewish; they were merely taking up other (likewise Jewish) messianic models. John gives us to understand even more clearly that in the early Christian tradition they were not putting up a Christian notion of the messiah against a Jewish one, but that under the pressure of the historical phenomenon of Jesus the Christians chose from among the many Jewish christ models available that of the eschatological prophet: the messianic prophet (Jn. 1:25, 41): the anointed One (*masiiach*) and the bringer of good news (an evangel) in Isa. 61 and 52 (with associated complexes of tradition).[158]

That the Christ title has a central position in the New Testament appears not only from the statistics regarding the use of the term (readily accessible with the help of R. Morgenthaler),[159] but chiefly and with greater theological precision from Jesus' dual name: this prophet is called 'Jesus Christ'. A salient expression in Matthew is: 'Jesus who is called Christ' (*Jèsous ho legomenos Christos*) (Mt. 1:16; 27:17) and 'Simon who is called Peter' (*Simon ho legomenos Petros*) (Mt. 4:18; 10:2). Elsewhere it says 'Jesus Christ' and 'Simon Peter', as well as simply 'Christ' and 'Peter'. Just as Peter is for Simon, so is Christ for Jesus a 'proper name', a theological sobriquet: the eschatological function they exercise is annexed to the personal names Simon and Jesus. This does not in the least indicate a demoting of 'Christ', a name that was to recede before the more evocative and incisive name 'the Lord'; but it does suggest a name of office,[160] added to the personal name (a custom of the time). The three pillars of the primitive Church, John, James and Peter (also the witnesses in the transfiguration story with its recognizably eschatological purpose), are the only people in the synoptic account of the calling of the Twelve to have an eschatological name added to their own: James Boanerges and John Boanerges, that is, 'son of thunder': by receiving that name they are both appointed to be heralds of the eschatological judgement (a fundamental *kerygma* of the Jerusalem congregation of which, along with Peter, they are the mainstay). Such namings are based on a calling and commissioning. Thus for the naming of Jesus as the Christ Acts 2:36 envisages a divine installation: 'Let all the house of Israel therefore know assuredly that God has made him both Lord and Christ, this Jesus whom you crucified.' In the tradition recalled here, Jesus gets that name in and through the resurrection, seen as an anointing (*chrisma*) (cf. Acts 4:27). However, in Acts 10:38 this anointing with the Spirit is associated with Jesus' baptism in the Jordan (as in the synoptics). On each occasion the anointing as Christ is inspired by Isa. 61:1–2. Luke 4:18 refers expressly to it. In Lk. 2:26 this anointing (as Christ) is also linked with Jesus' birth, wholly in line with the complex of tradition about the prophetic messenger, the one filled with the Spirit, who has been called 'from his mother's womb' (Isa. 49:1–3).

These Lucan passages show that the name 'messiah' or 'christ' (in many interrelated units of primitive Christian tradition) is connected not with the tradition of national and political messianism but with the Jewish tradition of the christ figure of the eschatological prophet, the man anointed with God's Spirit, servant of Yahweh, standing in a close relationship with God.

Going along with this one 'anointed with the Holy Spirit' (Isa. 61:1; see 52:7), interpreted in Judaism as the eschatological prophet, identified by the Christians with Jesus, are all sorts of ideas important to primitive Christianity: evangel, bringing of glad tidings, anointing, calling and election, rule of God, apostle, the 'Spirit of God who rests on . . .', covenant (testament), *and*: light of the Gentiles and ultimate peace (Isa. 61:1–3; 42:1ff; 49:1–2; 51:16; 52:7; 59:21). In particular the conjoining of Christ with gospel (Evangel) in the New Testament is grounded in this tradition of the eschatological prophet.[161] The latter-day prophet who 'brings the good news', the gospel (Isa. 61:1–2), is also referred to in this complex of prophetic tradition as the 'light of the world' (Isa. 42:6–7, 16; 49:6; 50:10; 51:4–6). Final prophet, evangel, and universal perspective (light of the world) are already linked in this Jewish tradition before Christian times. With the early Christian writings identifying Jesus with the Christ, as the eschatological prophet 'filled with the Spirit', the problem of a mission among the Gentiles is actually, in principle, already posed; likewise the Pauline question about the end of the Law. For in Judaism the Law had itself come to be called the 'light of the Gentiles',[162] whereas the (Greek-speaking) Jewish Christians in particular (as Jews already open to the Gentiles) now called Jesus, the Christ, the 'light of the Gentiles' in his own person.

In the late Jewish tradition the anointed one of Isa. 61:1–2 was often closely linked with an image of Samuel, who as a model came to have priestly traits in the Levitical tradition: Samuel is referred to as the 'christ' as well as *lumen gentium*.[163] His appearing among the people of God is portrayed almost as a theophany, more or less in the same way as Luke (who of course drew his inspiration from it) describes the birth of Jesus as the Christ.[164] For Luke (in his gospel as well as in Acts) the Christ title evidently lies within the 'christ Samuel' strand of tradition (though mixed in with Davidic-messianic traditions too); and all this before we get to Lk. 2:11: 'I bring you good news of a great joy' . . . 'for to you is born this day in the city of David a Saviour, who is Christ the Lord'. Furthermore, in this Jewish christ tradition the figure of Samuel was in its turn blended with the coming Elijah figure.[165] O. Steck and Kl. Berger rightly concluded from this that the milieu which nurtured and transmitted this priestly-prophetic christ tradition was a group of instructors in the Law and synagogue, who represented the legacy of the prophetic and Levitical tradition,[166] faithful upholders of the Deuteronomistic 'messenger' concept.

So the old royal messianism, associated in part with one of the two messianic strands already outlined in Zech. 4:3, 11–14, was in some circles retracted in favour of the prophetic-messianic and priestly-prophetic 'messianic' line of the Judaic christ tradition. Priest and prophet-teacher then become a single figure, so that the latter-day prophet and the high priest of the last days are seen as one. In this complex of tradition the christ idea points to a priestly conception of the latter-day prophet (elaborated in particular by the Letter to the Hebrews). The priestly-prophetic unction – 'chrisma' – referred to here is seen as an anointing by the Spirit in conjunction with revelation, instruction and that gracious gift of faith which is insight into what has been revealed. It is an idea transferred in both the Johannine (1 Jn. 2:20, 22, 27; Jn. 14:26)[167] and the Pauline view of things (2 Cor. 1:21–23; Eph. 1:13) to the Christian's anointing with the insight of faith; the notion of the Christians 'being enlightened' on their becoming Christian (or at their baptism) has undoubtedly been influenced by this Jewish christ tradition. Conversion to Christianity is envisaged, on the Jewish model of the conversion of a Gentile to the Jewish Torah, as an anointing – that is, surrender and acceptance of a doctrinal tradition – an anointing which is described as an illumination of mind and spirit and is frequently represented under the image of a vision, by analogy with visions of 'being called'.[168] In the Jewish christ tradition and in the priestly interpretation of the latter-day prophet, 'being anointed' means being instructed in God's mysteries and will, 'being put to school'.

So when Jesus is called the Christ, in line with this tradition, he is obviously being interpreted as the latter-day prophet who possesses 'the true doctrine', the one anointed by the Spirit, who speaks in a true and definitive way of God, and speaks therefore as the true interpreter of God's law and thus of what it must mean to be man.[169] Anointing by the Spirit of God in other words 'being Christ', indicates the divine origin of the wisdom this prophet divulges. There is no need at all, therefore, for us to think in terms of various esoteric, gnostic influences when John makes Jesus say: 'For I have given them the words which thou gavest me, and they have received them and know in truth that I came from thee; and they have believed that thou didst send me' (Jn. 17:8), or: 'The words that I say to you I do not speak on my own authority; but the Father who dwells in me does his works' (14:10), 'for I have not spoken on my own authority; the Father who sent me has himself given me commandment what to say and what to speak' (12:49): these are all ideas from the old Jewish 'messenger' tradition, albeit within a more recent, intensely sapiential framework. Paul's use of the Christ title in a 'good news' context is also in line with the tradition of the Deuteronomistic 'messenger', interpreted in the sense of the Trito-Isaianic passages, expounded in the Judaism of the time as the 'arrival' of the eschatological prophet who brings the good tidings (Isa. 61:1–2; 52:7) of God's rule (Isa. 52:7) and on whom God's Spirit rests, so putting God's words into his mouth for ever, under a covenant of God to eternity (Isa. 59:21). The priestly, latter-day prophet, the

Christ, brings to men sound and proper doctrine concerning the one true God and thus has true things to say also of man. *That* the Christians saw realized in Jesus of Nazareth.

A passage typical of this is Mt. 11:2: 'Now when John heard in prison about the deeds of the Christ, he sent word by his disciples and said to him, "Are you he who is to come or shall we look for another?" ' The deeds of the anointed One, spoken of in the Jewish tradition, are then included in Jesus' reply via the reference to Isa. 61:1–2 and Isa. 35:5–6, already associated in Judaism with the latter-day prophet who 'proclaims good news to the poor' and 'makes the blind to see and the lame walk'. All the strands of the latter-day prophet come together in this 'Christ', Jesus of Nazareth. In that Marcan passage the Christ title is set unmistakably in the tradition of the priestly-prophetic eschatological prophet (see also Mt. 26:28; Col. 2:8, 20–21; 1 Cor. 4:15).

That is not all. The sayings about the Parousia contain no reference to the Christ title, whereas it does occur to a noticeable extent in utterances about Jesus' death and resurrection.[170] This tallies with the Deuteronomistic tradition of the 'messenger' concept (prior to Chronicles)[171] which subsequently (see Neh. 9:26; Wis. 2:19 and the whole complex 2 to 7; Ezra 9:10–11; Zech. 1:4–6; 7:7, 12) became linked with the idea of the messenger 'from God' being rejected and of his fate as a prophet-martyr: prophets are done to death, is the theme of this Jewish tradition. The Apocalypse – evidently recalling the tradition of two latter-day prophets – assigns a dramatic end to their lives: 'because these two prophets had been a torment (to those that dwell on the earth)' (Rev. 11:3–10). The New Testament is constantly alluding to this tradition.[172] Prophets are killed because as men who preach repentance and demand conversion they press home the Law of God. That prophets are destined to martyrdom was a commonplace in Jesus' time – a received *theologoumenon* in religious circles.

That Jesus is called Christ in the New Testament – explicitly in passages that speak of his death – confirms the idea that he came over to the disciples as a prophet, in fact as the latter-day prophet who recalls the back-sliding people of God to God's 'true Law', summoning them to *metanoia* and conversion, but that he succumbed to this prophetic mission of his. The motive of Jesus' execution lies therefore in the fact that Israel's leaders saw in him the anti-'christ', the pseudo-prophet of the end of the Age, the Gainsayer who leads the people astray and into apostasy.[173] This enables us to understand the early Christians' insistence on the Christ title in connection with Jesus' death: this man, Jesus of Nazareth, the crucified One, he alone is the true Christ, the anointed one of the 'last days': the true messenger of God, empowered with full authority from God, the true magisterium. In this context the martyr's death serves to corroborate Jesus' message and prophetic authority: it confirms the identification of the person of Jesus as the Christ, rejected, it is true, but the real eschatological prophet. 'You stiff-necked people . . . you always resist the Holy Spirit. As your fathers did, so do you. Which of the prophets did not your fathers persecute? And they killed those who announced before-hand the coming of the Righteous One' (Acts 7:51–53) (see 1 Pet. 1:10–11; Lk. 24:25–26; Acts 26:22–23). Here again, the death of the messianic christ figure is a pre-Christian, Jewish idea, and certainly not, to begin with, a Christian 'anti-Jewish' conception of messianism. In this Jewish and Christian tradition Jesus is called the Christ because as the eschatological prophet he raises the question of God and, inter-preting human ethics as obedient conformity to God's will, in so doing proffers an accurate and true interpretation of our human mode of being; that is why he too was removed from the scene. For that reason even the Easter Christology (the fourth credal strand) was originally grounded in and justified by the Christians' identifying the person of Jesus with the eschatological prophet.

Thus it was the salvific character of their experience with the earthly Jesus which eventually convinced these Jews that in Jesus specifically their expectations of a christ were being fulfilled. The public ministry of Jesus – whatever facet of it were taken as a starting-point – was of a kind that for Jews open in heart and mind to what was manifested in him was bound to prompt thoughts of the eschatological prophet. Jesus it was who spoke aright of God and of man and, in a concrete fashion, acted accordingly. In him alone true conversion to the living God is given and a right relationship to other people delineated. Paul saw this very clearly: Jesus mediates to us the 'true knowledge of God' (2 Cor. 2:14), thanks to his being filled with the Spirit of God (see Rom. 8:9; Phil. 1:19; also 1 Pet. 1:11). Although in doubt and question-ing, this was the ground of the disciples' confidence in Jesus of Nazareth even before Easter. An explicit recognition that Jesus was the latter-day prophet of God's fast approaching kingdom and rule later on became fruitful soil for the further growth of an elaborated Chris-tology in the earliest Christian generations.

This, in conclusion. We said earlier on that the title 'the Son' had already appeared in the incipiently Christological tradition of the Q community – and does so in a complex which obviously fits in with 'the messenger of wisdom' (Mt. 11:27=Lk. 10:22; in the context of

Mt. 11:25–27=Lk. 10:21–22). There Jesus is 'the Son' who reveals God's eschatological secrets to 'the little ones'. That is now conjoined with Jesus' complete authority as the messenger from God. This situation, historically confirmed, faces us with the question of whether the 'father-son' relationship in the New Testament coheres with the 'messenger' concept, at any rate in its sapiential version. That would now appear to be the case. It is noticeable on the one hand that at places where God is called Father Jesus for his part is described as *Kyrios*, which may in itself suggest the notion of the prophetic 'Lord', whereas on the other hand where Jesus is called 'Christ', God is himself described as 'the Lord'.[174] This is no coincidence, but points to a cohesive relation of tradition-complexes. We find a similar use of terms in pre-Christian statements about Enoch and post-Christian ones about Ezra.[175] In late Jewish literature concerned with the 'messenger' concept and influenced particularly by the Wisdom tradition God, as the one who sends the messenger, is called Father: as source of the message and teaching which the messenger, his son, conveys to men (see the Q passage mentioned a moment ago). In this Wisdom tradition the father-son relationship – the envoy *vis-à-vis* God – even acquires a touch of intimacy.[176] Especially in Wis. 2:13, 16d and 18, also in 9:4b, 5a, it seems that *pais* (*puer*, child), *doulos* or servant, and *huios* or son of God are synonyms: God is the Father of the sage, of the wise one who shares in the paternal purpose of instruction; the initiate is 'the beloved'. The *abba* form of address is fairly inserted, therefore, into this sapiential tradition; it gives expression to the true knowledge of God and the right relationship to God. The final prophet is son of God because, initiated into God's wisdom, he speaks of and for God to men; and that he is able to do on the basis of his being 'christ', being anointed by the Spirit – 'Spirit of sonship' (Rom. 8:15; Gal. 3:26; 4:7). 'For the law was given through Moses; grace and truth came through Jesus Christ. No one has ever seen God; the only Son, who is in the bosom of the Father, he has made him known' (Jn. 1:18):[177] in a highly sapiential affirmation John is reflecting here the prophetic tradition of the father-son relationship, applied Christologically to Jesus, the Christ, 'embraced within the bosom of the Father';[178] he is the true 'exegete of God' (*ekeinos exegèsato*). He is the final messenger from God: the Son. His intimate fellowship with God who sent him – 'I am not alone, for the Father is with me' (Jn. 16:32) – is the source and ground, not to say the guarantee of his message, of his expounding of God's law, and of all his words and actions. In full accord with that we have: 'Call no man your father on earth, for you have one Father, who is in heaven' (Mt.

23:9) – the same sort of messenger-reaction as in the logion; 'Why do you call me good?' The idea of the messenger in Ex. 23:20: 'Give heed to him' and 'obey his word and do what I say to you' evidently operates throughout the New Testament: 'This is my beloved Son; listen to him' (Mk. 9:7, in a context where the eschatological Moses and Elijah figures also appear). In the Judaic messenger-tradition the title 'Son of God' is used not of the Davidic but of the prophetic messiah. Anyone therefore who takes Jesus to be 'just a human being' like all the rest – 'Is not this the carpenter, the son of Mary and brother of James and Joses and Judas and Simon?' (Mk. 6:3), or: 'Is not this Jesus the son of Joseph, whose father and mother we know?' (Jn. 6:42) – has according to the New Testament not understood him; such a one has yet to be converted; for Jesus is the eschatological envoy from God, and to reject him is to reject the one whom God has sent, the Son, and so it is to blaspheme against God (Mk. 3:28–29). In those passages; 'Is not this the carpenter . . .?' we can still hear the questions that Jesus evoked during his life on earth: is he not perhaps the latter-day prophet, for anyone who sees more deeply, beyond the mere asseverations of men? 'For I have given them the words which thou gavest me, and they have received them and know in truth that I came from thee; and they have believed that thou didst send me' (Jn. 17:8); 'All that the Father has is mine' (Jn. 16:15b): these (along with many other things uttered by John) are ways of expressing the identification of Jesus with the Christ, the Son of the messenger tradition, blended with the more recent Wisdom traditions: Jesus, the eschatological prophet of God's time of mercy.

## D. THE CHRISTIAN INTERPRETATION, PROPHETIC-CUM-SAPIENTIAL, OF JESUS AS THE 'MESSIANIC SON OF DAVID', AND REJECTION OF THE DYNASTIC MESSIANISM OF THE HOUSE OF DAVID

That Ps. 110:1 fulfils a main function in the interpretation of Jesus after his death is undeniable. This psalm expresses the fact on the one hand that Jesus was exalted 'at the right hand of God' and on the other that the 'subjection of all the powers' had *not yet* been accomplished (according to the Greek version of Psalm 109): 'Sit at my right hand till (*heos an thō* . . .) I make your enemies your footstool.' (This text was employed especially in Graeco-Jewish Christian circles to articulate both the 'already' and the 'not yet' of salvation.) (Thus Mk. 12:36 is obviously citing the Greek Psalm 109.) Even before the liturgical separation in the mother church of Jerusalem between Aramaic-speaking and Greek-speaking Jewish Christians – apropos of the affair centring around the 'Stephen' party or the Graeco-Palestinian Jews – Jesus had already been acknowledged in both quarters as 'Jesus, our Lord' – which is why in the bilingual Greek-speaking circle of the Jerusalem Jews, after they had been harassed by the Jewish authorities in Jerusalem, the *maranatha* had been taken with them to the places to which these Christian Graeco-Palestinians had fled. Even before Saul's conversion to Christianity (three or four years after Jesus' death) Jesus was being venerated as 'Lord'. So this has nothing to do with specifically Gentile-Greek influence. It was these same Graeco-Palestinian, Jewish Christians whose part in developing a Christological interpretation of Jesus was so important. For the future of Christianity, therefore, the decisive role was played not by Paul's Hellenistic congregations, as is often said, but by the Greek-speaking Jews who had fled from Jerusalem (with their Jerusalem Christian legacy) to Syria (Damascus and Antioch). These Jewish Christians supplied a Christian interpretation of Jesus on the basis of which – primarily through Paul's theology – a Torah-free Christianity was proclaimed. Very likely not without the conciliating action of Simon Peter, who championed a middle position *vis-à-vis* the Aramaic- and Greek-speaking Jewish Christians (see the Council of Jerusalem). What is clear is that especially in Greek-speaking Jewish circles 'messiah' and 'son of man' were being used interchangeably even before Christianity.[179] In this regard Christians would emphasize the fact that the Jesus handed over to the Romans and crucified is the true messiah. For them 'Christology' and 'Scriptural demonstration' (in dependence on the earthly Jesus) were one and the same thing. That is why 2 Sam. 2:7 and Ps. 2 as well as Ps. 8 and Ps. 110 play for them a fundamental role in the Christian interpretation of Jesus; and in face of Jewish objections the Jewish Christians utilized in particular Ps. 22 and bits and pieces from Isa. 53. All this may categorically be described as pre-Pauline, not just in the sense of literary activity prior to Paul but also as indicating the substance of what Jewish Christians had achieved already before Paul's conversion.[180]

In our analysis of Jesus' self-understanding, which was articulated in his prophetic message concerning the approach of God's rule and in the conduct of his own life, there nowhere appeared any element pointing in the direction of a dynastic-Davidic messianism. All the evidence suggests a Jesus who is the eschatological prophet and thus the prophetic messiah: the one filled with God's Spirit, the latter-day messenger or envoy of God (Isa. 52:7; 61:1).

In early Christianity Ps. 110:1 none the less became the *locus classicus*, the 'Scriptural proof', of Jesus' resurrection and/or exaltation.[181] This use of Scripture belongs initially within a Christian interpretation in which, on the grounds of his resurrection and/or exaltation, Jesus is appointed or acknowledged as 'Christ', the Messiah.

In the pre-Marcan tradition (still recoverable from Mk. 12:35-37, specifically Mk. 12:35b-37a) the idea is deliberately refuted – with the aid of Ps. 110 – that the coming messiah should be of Davidic descent. As Jesus taught in the Temple he said: 'How can the scribes say that the Christ is the son of David? David himself, inspired by the Holy Spirit, declared, "The Lord said to my Lord, Sit thou at my right hand, till I put thy enemies under thy feet" [Ps. 110:1]. David himself calls him Lord; so how is he his son?' (Mk. 12:35-37). The commentators do argue, it is true, over the interpretation of this passage.[182] But a thesis previously advocated by a lot of exegetes is now once more accepted, with supporting argument, by both Chr. Burger and G. Schneider.[183] Davidic descent is not seen here as an absolute requirement for being messiah. Thus at any rate to begin with, Ps. 110 provided the Christians with an argument on the one hand for contesting Jesus' Davidic origin and on the other to justify their calling him messiah (and even son of David).

The import of Mk. 12:35b-37a seems originally to have been a discussion about the coming messiah. Some people, more especially the Pharisees (see Psalmi Salomonis 17:21-25), were interested primarily in the origin of the messiah in the Davidic dynasty; others entertained a Davidic messianism free of any genealogical concern. Then if the Christians were faced with the objection that the son of David comes from Judah (Bethlehem) and cannot be a Galilean or a Nazarene, they were able (in accordance with a particular Jewish tradition) to argue rightly against it. That was not all. In Jesus' time the Jews did not give Ps. 110 a messianic interpretation;[184] and so it provided the Christians with a ready argument against a genealogical origin of the son of David. David himself, in a prophecy, had called the coming messiah 'the Lord', *Kyrios* (see especially the Septuagint, Ps. 109:1); that is to say, David's prophecy confirms the Christian affirmation that Jesus is 'the Lord'. (Again in Acts 2:32-36 Jesus-messiah's 'being Lord' is evidenced by an appeal to Ps. 110.) Thus there is every reason to suppose that the pre-Marcan tradition understood the pericope (Mk. 12: 35b-37a) in a negative sense: Jesus is not descended from the dynastic line of David (Mark is therefore still unaware of any Christian tradition that has Jesus being born as a dynastic-Davidic messiah at Bethlehem in

Judah. This last is a positive answer to what was probably the same line of enquiry.) The negative answer was not meant directly as a Christian repudiation of the national-cum-political messiah, but as a reaction to the fact that Jesus' origin was known; he was known not to be of the house of David. The Johannine gospel too knows nothing of Jesus' birth in Bethlehem. In his gospel the birth of the dynastic son of David in Bethlehem is adduced precisely as a counter-argument against the messianic status of Jesus (Jn. 7:41–42: these verses indeed say a great deal!). The fact that still in the later Epistle of Barnabas (12:10–11) Ps. 110:1 specifically serves as offering Scriptural grounds for denying that the (Jesus-) messiah must be of dynastic-Davidic origin points to a particular tradition in which Christians felt sure that Jesus was not of the Davidic 'royal blood'. 'Son of David' in this tradition has not a historical but a theological significance (a *theologoumenon*). The pre-synoptic tradition, therefore, makes a rather negative response on the matter of Jesus' Davidic descent (and this would seem to tally with the facts of history).

Mark himself, however, puts the tradition given to him in a quite new setting; perhaps he did not even know any more (in contrast with his tradition) that according to the Pharisaic view 'son of David' implied descent from the royal dynasty. At any rate Jesus is for him the messianic son of David, as a *theologoumenon* from the Jewish tradition (see Mk. 10:47, 48). Yet Jesus is more than that: he is the Lord, and Son of God. The question is, then, what Mark understood by it, when he calls Jesus truly David's son. In other words: with which tradition is he in contact? It is clear from what has been said already that when the title 'son of David' is applied to Jesus, this does not derive from remembered facts or genealogical trees, whether of Joseph's family or of Mary's.

In Greek-speaking Jewish Christian circles the term 'messianism' sounded a different note; and they took a different direction too. Certainly, Davidic messianism was their starting-point; but they gave it a prophetic, Levitical and sapiential interpretation in which 'the son of David' had itself already become a *theologoumenon*. That is why they could as readily speak of Jesus the son of David as of the prophetic figure 'anointed with the Spirit'. Thus although Mark's source is in that sense negative, he interprets it in a more or less positive way (albeit without any thought behind it of genealogical descent): Jesus is the messianic son of David. No more do Matthew and Luke find in their own traditions, separate from Mark, anything about Jesus as the dynastic-Davidic messiah; they are completely dependent on Mark whom, as editors, they adapt still further to Davidic messianism. In the Marcan gospel, then, the earthly Jesus is indeed seen as the son of David, but construed as 'the miracle-worker' (Mk. 10:46–52). Jesus' entry into Jerusalem (Mk. 11:1–11) is also explained by Mark as the messianic son of David's advance on the city. The fact that the messianic son of David is already linked with 'the miracle-worker' in Mark (10:47–48) becomes even more a conspicuous feature in Matthew. Here Jesus as 'messianic son of David' is simply 'miracle-worker': it is precisely in a context of healings and exorcisms that he is addressed with 'Son of David, have mercy on me' (Mt. 9:27; 15:22; 20:30, 31; 21:9; 21:15; 12:23; Lk. 18:38–39). A second memorable feature comes out after Peter's confession of the messiah in the Marcan gospel (8:29), where he opposes himself to the prospect of the son of man's suffering. As a result Jesus calls him a Satan. Many commentators regard these two messianic traits as specifically Christian, a break with Jewish messianism.[185] But it is these two features of the New Testament messiah concept – the messiah, the son of David, is a miracle-worker and exorcist, and he must suffer, – which point within the history of tradition to the Jewish prophetic and sapiential concept of the messianic son of David (see above). In other words: in the choice between two Jewish schools of 'Davidic messianism' early, perhaps mainly Galilean, Christianity was unable on a basis of what was recollected of Jesus' life on earth to opt for an interpretation of him grounded in the dynastic-Davidic, national and political idea of the messiah; nor did it project a Christian messianic concept of its own, but appealed rather to the prophetic-sapiential notion of the messianic son of David (see above). A number of different facts should make this evident enough.

The son of David as miracle-worker and exorcist is simply unknown in dynastic-Davidic messianism. Since in the synoptic tradition it is as miracle-worker and exorcist that Jesus is addressed with 'Son of David, have mercy on me', the New Testament obviously fits well with 'Solomonic' Wisdom messianism. In particular there is the stress, typical of the New Testament, on the fact that it is the One crucified who is Christ, the messiah. A radical switch from the Jewish national-cum-dynastic David concept to the Christian notion of the 'suffering messiah' within the short period of the very earliest Christianity is simply inconceivable; for that, Jewish postulations had to be already in existence. We saw earlier on (prompted especially by a comparison of studies by L. Ruppert, G. Nickelsburg Jr and Kl. Berger, working quite independently) that the idea of a wise but 'suffering messiah', even a suffering (though not dynastic) son of David, was a familiar Jewish idea among the Graeco-Palestinian Jews. On a basis of the so far moderate case presented by Mark, it is clear for the Matthean gospel that the import of the 'Davidic messiah', applied by early Christianity to Jesus, points in the direction of the Deutero-Isaianic 'christ' tradition, as it was blended with the Solomonic 'son of David': miracle-worker and exorcist. 'Something greater than Solomon is here' (Mt. 12: 42). Matthew typifies *ta erga tou Christou* (Mt. 11:2), that is, the messianic activity of Jesus, by referring to instances of the expulsion of demons: the blind see, the lame walk. And people ask: 'Is he not the son of David?' or say: 'He is from Beelzebub.' These summarized 'works of the messiah', considered within the history of tradition, have nothing to do with the expected arrival and activity of the dynastic son of David. Jesus is the messiah because he cures the blind and the lame, etc., not in spite of it! (This 'in spite of' applies only to one particular Jewish tradition'.) Christianity has obviously taken over (for the purpose of interpreting Jesus) the Jewish tradition in which the prophetic and sapiential messenger tradition had been combined with that of the messianic son of David. Adopting the appellation of 'the servant' (*pais*, attendant, serving-man, 'child' or 'son') in Mt. 12:18–21 evidently comes from this prophetic-sapiential tradition, in Isa. 42:1–4. Mark 3:11 speaks in a similar context of the 'son of God'. This current of Jewish tradition is not endorsed in the New Testament without justification: someone greater than Jonah is here – an eschatological prophet; greater than Solomon, the eschatological king of the royal and sapiential tradition (Mt. 12:41–42). The connection between healings, exorcisms and the 'proclamation of the gospel' makes no sense at all in terms of the older dynastic-Davidic messianism, but certainly does on the basis of the Deutero-Isaianic latter-day 'christ-prophet', who has taken on the characteristics of the Solomonic son of David.

The concept of 'gospel' presented by the synoptic writers can be fully understood only in terms of the Deutero-Isaianic messiah-prophet within the Deuteronomistic tradition of the messenger idea. Jesus, who works miracles, cures sick people and drives out devils, refuses to perform legitimating miracles (see Part Two). In the gospels only Jesus' resurrection is God's legitimation. Jesus refuses to provide any advance legitimation: (a) In the temptation narratives he will not perform any 'pointless' wonders that do nobody any good; but for a lot of people this renders his ministry ambiguous – for people perform miracles who are filled with unclean as well as clean *pneumata* or 'spirits'.

Jesus declines to perform miracles in order to advantage himself – even to ratify the fact that 'his spirit' is the *Pneuma* of God; of this the temptations in the wilderness are a plastic illustration. 'If you are the Son of God' (Lk. 4:9; Mt. 4:3, 6) is clearly a reminiscence of Wis. 2:18. (b) Even at his crucifixion Jesus refuses to perform miracles that would legitimate his claims: 'He saved others; he cannot save himself' (Mt. 27:42; Lk. 23:35, 37, 39). Here the Satanic temptations in the wilderness as it were return; but Jesus refuses to entertain them. That is the 'Messiah's secret'. Only after death will God justify him in the resurrection. Now is the time of *peirasmos*, of testing: refusing to employ divine powers to personal advantage. (c) Jesus repudiates Peter who while acknowledging the messiah looks to be provided with sensational supporting evidence, as the voice of Satan. God's prophet 'bears witness'; he is to be believed on the strength of his actions, his wisdom and the content of his message; he performs miracles and exorcisms when others in dire distress ask for them, not to legitimate his own mission. That entails testing, suffering, even martyrdom. Only the one who sends, God, will produce the legitimating proof: by his resurrection from the dead, or by his death in itself (which is a 'raising up', first phase of the eschatological set of events). Being 'messiah' implies, therefore, suffering and martyrdom, because the prophet declines to legitimate himself to his own advantage (Mk. 15:29–30, 31–32). Jesus was in fact condemned as the 'Adversary', the pseudo-prophet who cannot vindicate himself (Mt. 26:68). (d) Even before the crucifixion, at the session of the High Council, Jesus refuses to reply (Lk. 22:67d; 20:18; Jn. 10:24–25; see Greek Jer. 38:14–15; 38:45; 41:28). The Christian community understood well enough this complex of tradition regarding the prophet who suffers but is legitimated by God: it follows up this refusal on Jesus' part to speak with his ominous warning of the judgement to come (Mk. 14:62b). If anyone fails to acknowledge God's true representative, that rejection will, eschatologically speaking, be held in evidence against them; the one rejected is the judge, therefore. Of course the question is: Who blasphemes against God: Jesus or his present judges? (Mk. 14:63–64). Who has the Spirit of God? Jesus, who refuses to justify himself, is indeed condemned here and now; but in virtue of his martyrdom the one condemned is the eschatological witness, prosecutor and judge (Mk. 14:62); the 'hereafter' of Mt. 26:64 makes it clear that the Christians have already identified the person of Jesus with the son of man-judge.

All this points to one complex of tradition: the idea of 'the messenger', the prophet – the eschatological prophet with certain features of the prophetic-sapiential son of David: Jesus of Nazareth, of whom it was remembered that he went about doing good to others, healed the sick, drove out devils, but also refused to perform any legitimating action in his own interest – as though 'the freedom to do good' were not in itself sufficient legitimation.

Another thing to notice is that the latter-day Solomon, 'the son of David', is to demolish the Temple. This logion has been transmitted quite by itself, without a mention, even, of any rebuilding. Here we have the tradition of the 'potentially destructive power' (of the prophetic imprecation), while the logion about rebuilding likewise comes from the Solomon tradition;[186] the plenary powers of the prophet are already associated in this tradition with the power of the Solomonic son of David to construct 'within a short period of time'[187] a completely new Temple. This, deriving from Jewish models, is the 'kingly messianism' of the New Testament.

The meaning of 'Jesus' entry into Jerusalem' (Mk. 11: 1–10 parallels) – the subject of much exegetical discussion – also becomes intelligible when viewed in the context of this particular messianic tradition. That this was the procession of Jesus with his companions – entering the gates of Jerusalem as pilgrims, praying and exulting in expectation of the coming rule of God – would seem to be on historical grounds a fair assumption.[188] But that the Christian account of it was originally non-messianic remains to be shown. The only question is: Which messianism did the Christians have in mind here? We know from the Jewish historian Josephus[189] that a Zealotic messiah wanted to enter Jerusalem from the Mount of Olives with an armed force in order to establish the rule of God there. Christians portray Jesus' messianic entry into Jerusalem on a colt, the foal of an ass, as that of the 'meek messiah', in other words, the prophetic-sapiential son of David. 'The coming one' – *ho erchomenos* – is greeted with cheers:[190] that is, not a kingdom of God yet to come, yet to be established, but the appearing of Jesus in Jerusalem – especially in the Temple (for that is the whole point) – is the coming here and now of the wise king-messiah Jesus, destined to institute there 'the kingdom of our father David' (Mk. 11:10).[191] In this (Jewish) tradition the king-messiah is 'the meek one' (Wisdom), who refuses to anticipate God's anger (see Lk. 9:54); he restricts himself to imparting Wisdom from God and the summons to *metanoia*. The meek and gentle messiah is not a Christian 'topsy-turvy' version of the Jewish idea of the messiah but a reaching out, under the pressure of the reality that was Jesus, for a different, equally Jewish, messianic conception. Being instructed by Jesus as the messenger of Wisdom entails for the hearer: 'learning meekness from him' (Mt. 11:29-30).

Kl. Berger even ventures (and speaking independently, though not in messianic terms, L. Ruppert says much the same thing) to see Wis. 2 and Wis. 5 as the foundation or model of the genus, 'evangel'.[192] 'Evangel', 'gospel', in the New Testament is conceived out of the prophetic-sapiential struggle to legitimate the 'sonship of God' as the status of the one who presents himself through his conduct and activity as the (latter-day) prophet: it comes out in the temptation narrative, in Jesus' acts of power, in various disputations and teaching discourses, in his intercourse with tax-gatherers and sinners, his cleansing of the Temple, in his trial, on the cross. The gospel response is: Jesus refuses to justify himself in his own interest; he is condemned as a 'false' prophet and through a diplomatic deployment of the term 'king of the Jews' is handed over to the Romans. Only through the resurrection does God vindicate his envoy – after his suffering and death. The connection of this Deutero-Isaianic, sapientially interpreted 'prophet of God' and 'anointed one' with Davidic messianism is made by way of the tradition of Solomon as 'son of David', the one initiated into God's Wisdom (Wis. 7). Not until afterwards, and in the second place, are Pss. 2 and 110 used as proof-texts. This Davidic-messianic, prophetic tradition, then, confirms what has already been said: the notion of an eschatological 'messianic prophet' (in that sense: the son of David) is the link between 'Jesus of Nazareth' and the 'kerygmatic Christ'. Jesus is the 'anointed' or messianic revelation of God.

All this is supported by Rom. 1:3-4b, where within a pre-existence theology of his own Paul incorporates an older catechesis or credal declaration. In this letter to the Christians of Rome Paul cites an earlier creed[193] that goes back to Graeco-Jewish Christians. Incorrectly in fact, a binary Christology – a 'two-stage Christology' – has usually (more or less as a consensus among exegetes) been read in at this point: the earthly 'Davidic messiah' and his 'eschatological messianic status'. It has generally been assumed among the commentators that what is interposed between 'gospel of the Son of God' and the concluding 'Jesus Christ our Lord' (both Pauline editorializing) is a pre-Pauline formula that had undergone some development prior to Paul. At least three stages of that earlier development are to some extent ascertainable. (a) In the very oldest phase of this tradition the credal statement went more or less as follows: 'who was of the seed of David – and because of the awakening from the dead has shown himself the Son of God'. (b) In a later phase, that was elaborated as follows: in his life on earth Jesus was 'of the seed of David according to the flesh, but he showed himself the Son of God according to the spirit of holiness (*kata pneuma hagiosunès*) by reason of (and from the moment of) his resurrection from the dead'. This too seems to be pre-Pauline. (c) Lastly, the Pauline version which we read in Rom. 1:3–4b, within a pre-existence Christology: through his resurrection Jesus, the Son of God who became 'son of David', has been exalted as 'Son of God in power'.

In its earliest phase this passage turns out to lie within the prophetic-sapiential tradition; that is to say, Jesus is 'of the seed of David', he is a Jewish man and belonged to Israel as the people of the promise[194] – in another place it says: 'according to the flesh Jesus is of the race of the patriarchs' (Rom. 9:5), that is, he is a true Jew – but through the resurrection it has become clear that he is truly 'Son of God'.[195] In his days on earth as a Jew Jesus was the Son of God already, but he had refused to legitimize his mission to his own advantage in any way. His earthly life remained ambiguous, therefore; only through the resurrection did God afford the proof that this man, this Jew, was and is indeed 'the Son of God'. The duality present here refers not to a 'two-stage' Christology but to something else, explained in the second phase of the credal confession on 'sapiential' lines. The exegetes certainly disagree on the question of whether 'according to the flesh' and 'according to the Spirit' is Pauline or pre-Pauline.[196] True, Paul is familiar in his letters with the contrast between 'flesh' (*sarx*) and 'spirit' (*pneuma*) (Gal. 4:29; Rom. 8:4ff), but – according to H. Schlier[197] – the expression *pneuma hagiosunès* is clearly non-Pauline (thus: pre-Pauline). This term is apparently the Greek rendering of the Hebrew for 'exaltedness', 'holiness', and especially of 'power and glory'. 'The Spirit of holiness' (Rom. 1:4) would then signify: Yahweh's holy exaltedness and power as an intrinsic feature of his *doxa* (glory). 'According to the flesh', that is, from the human point of view, it is obvious that Jesus made his appearance as a Jewish man, but on a 'pneumatic viewpoint' grounded in revelation it is clear that over and above that – something demonstrated by his resurrection – he is the 'Son of God': for that reason he has the universal significance that makes him Christ also for the Gentiles. 'According to the flesh' and 'according to the Spirit' are not meant here to express Jesus' two different modes of being, but they point to the domain 'outside wisdom' on the one hand and on the other, 'inside wisdom'; this is a Jewish-sapiential polarity. In this confession Christians are seeking to express their belief on the lines of a particular scheme: that of the 'hidden status' and 'disclosed status' of the Son of God – a scheme that was to structure the whole gospel of

Mark (the so-called 'messianic secret'): in his earthly life Jesus already is the Son of God, but this only becomes apparent after his suffering and death, with the (legitimating) resurrection. That legitimation and its public promulgation cannot be anticipated. I would think it hard to detect in this early text a reaction to a baptismal 'adoption Christology' – in this sense that the latter would argue for Jesus' having become 'Son of God' at his baptism in Jordan; in that case the oldest stratum of this credal formula would supposedly see Jesus 'constituted' the Son of God only from the moment (and at the same time, by reason) of his resurrection.[198] This would not seem to tally with the complex of tradition underlying it nor with Mark's view (Mk. 12:35–37) conjoined with Mk. 1:11; 9:7 and 15:39; although a son of David (Marcan redaction of 12:35–37), Jesus is already 'adopted' as 'Son of God' at his baptism (Mk. 1:11), proclaimed at the transfiguration (Mk. 9:7) and acclaimed by all after his death (Mk. 15:39). Whether Mark had before him the ritual of the king's enthronement is neither here nor there; it is impossible to overlook the three salient 'phases' in his gospel. For Mark also, therefore, Jesus during his days on earth is indeed the son of David; but he is more: on the basis of his suffering and death, only with the resurrection does it appear (at any rate, appear fully) that he was and is 'the Lord of David': Son of God.

Thus a very ancient Christology is founded upon the idea of the legitimation of the (latter-day) messenger from God, whose earthly life remains ambiguous for anyone who asks for knockdown proofs of legitimation, but who nevertheless yields his secret in the context of a specific, Jewish conception of the Son of God, as it emerges particularly in the Book of Wisdom from ch. 2 to ch. 7 (a basic theme to be found in all sorts of variations: for instance, Isa. 52 – 53; 1 Enoch 62 – 63 and 46; 2 Macc. 9; 1 Macc. 6; Assumption of Moses 10; 2 Baruch 49 – 51, etc.): only through suffering and death, the lot of the prophet as martyr, is the *basileia* to be entered (Wis. 2:19); therefore the resurrection is the public inauguration of Jesus as the true king. Jesus' manner of life on earth is the time of mortification and testing. Even though 'son of David' (albeit not this but only 'man of the Jews' is written here) be supposed a mark of honour, in any case it points here to the earthly mortification. Salvation only begins fully when the king, at first 'disguised', is publicly vindicated. The initially concealed identity of Jesus of Nazareth, therefore, is not just a (literary) move on the part of Mark but an almost universal datum in early Christianity, present in this pre-Pauline tradition as well as in the pre-Marcan tradition and in the Q community; it is the key to the conceptual frame of New Testament Christology as a whole. H. Flender[199] is right, it seems to me, to find in Rom. 1:3–4, in miniature, the structure of the Marcan gospel; but then that structure will have to be interpreted in a different way and in any case not on the lines of a 'two-stage' Christology. The suggestions put forward by L. Ruppert, who assigns Wis. 2 to 5 a central function in the gospels (in which Wis. 2 and 5 – on the suffering and exalted one – come to be seen as a Jewish 'updating' of the *Ebed Yahweh* of the 'Isaianic' tradition), also the prophetic-sapiential conception of the king, as interpreted by Kl. Berger, and finally the recent analyses of intertestamentary material by G. Nickelsburg,[200] all point to the conclusion that the ideas (from a longer tradition) concentrated in Wis. 2 to 5 have served as a model for the genus 'gospel' – something which came about (see Part Two) within a Graeco-Jewish environment: what we have in the gospels is a struggle or contest over the legitimation of the 'Sonship of God': in Jesus' miracles, in his 'temptations in the wilderness', in his disputations and teaching discourses. And all this culminates in suffering and death. Only after his deliverance – with his resurrection from the dead – can it be said that he really is the 'Son of God' (Wis. 2:18). He is not appointed, not *constituted* 'Son of God' at the resurrection, but not until then did it appear (or, for the Marcan gospel, from that moment on we have the firm ground and assurance that it will appear at the Parousia). Therefore the judgement given against Jesus' opponents is already accomplished at the resurrection (while for Mark this judgement goes along rather with the Parousia).

Luke for his part combines the two Davidic-messianic traditions. But first and foremost he means to set these traditions within God's whole plan of salvation. This comes out very well in Acts 13:16–41, where Luke presents an 'apostolic sermon' in a Diaspora synagogue – at Antioch – and so for obvious reasons puts it into the mouth of Paul (although the whole thing is Luke's own composition, based on his own Christological design). His purpose is to relate what has occurred with and through Jesus of Nazareth to God's saving activity in Israel down the centuries; of that the Jesus event is the eschatological fulfilment. The people being addressed in this sermon are Jews and 'God-fearers', that is, Gentile affiliates or sympathizers (Acts 13:16, 26). It treats of the 'God of Israel' (13:17), of the fathers (13:17), specifically of Abraham, Isaac and Jacob. It reminds them of three great salvific acts on God's part: the choosing or election of Israel, God's 'increasing' of Israel in Egypt and lastly the Exodus (13:17). Then came the wandering through the wilderness and the occupation of the Promised Land (13:18–20). The way leading to Christ is depicted as a lengthy course of preparation by Israel's God. The period of the Judges and in particular of King David is recalled as well (13:20–22). God has been in control of Israel's entire history: Jesus is the messianic son of David (13:23). Just as God testifies to King David (13:22 *marturèsas*) by 'raising him up' (*egeirô* 13:22; not in the sense of 'resurrection' but in the Old Testament sense of 'calling' and making him perform the role of a prophet), so also Israel's God testifies to Jesus: this is 'the man after God's heart, who in everything will do God's will' (see 13:22b). Jesus is 'Israel's deliverer' (13:23), that is, 'messiah'. This again serves to join the history of Jesus to the whole salvation-history of Israel: in Jesus the Christ the God of Israel fulfils the ancient promises to Israel (13:32–33); or to put it round the other way: the God who has acted in Jesus is none other than the God of Abraham, Isaac and Jacob. Israel and Jesus are mutually inseparable. Yet there is a breach, specifically in the rejection of Jesus by 'those who live in Jerusalem and their rulers' (13:27). But God continues to bear testimony to this Jesus by raising him from the dead (13:30–31). Thus the resurrection becomes the fulfilment of the ancient promises (13:32–33).

Because of the so-called 'apostolic addresses' (Acts 2:14–39; 3:12–26; 4:9–12; 5:30–32; 10:34–43; 13:16–38), and on the basis in particular of Acts 2:22–36, it has usually been held (even up to the present time) that Luke is reflecting here a very ancient Christology which sees Jesus as being appointed as 'Christ the Lord' only by virtue of his resurrection and from that moment (Acts 2:36). People saw in those passages a very old early Christian homiletic scheme with a dual structure, the two parts of which had originally formed separate and independent traditions and had subsequently been merged together; on the one hand an interpretation in which Jesus was regarded as the messianic son of David, sent to Israel, on the other the crucified-and-risen One as the 'redeemer of the world'.[201] But U. Wilckens has with good reason argued that Luke himself arranged these 'apostolic sermons' as a single composition, making use – within the distinctively Lucan Christology – of what the tradition was saying already about Jesus Christ. So what has been called 'very old' turns out in fact to be a late – Lucan – Christology. People found this early Christology (which certainly does appear elsewhere in the New Testament) mainly in Acts 2:36; 'Let all the house of Israel therefore know assuredly that God has made him both Lord and Christ, this Jesus whom you crucified.' But the 'therefore' (meant for the reader) is clearly intended

as the conclusion of the entire homily (2:14–35): God has predestined
Jesus to be Lord and Christ. This he has brought about in the whole
life-history of this Jesus: in his mighty acts, miracles and signs (2:12);
through his being rejected and put to death 'according to the plan and
foreknowledge of God' (2:23); in that God raised him from the dead
(2:24); by seating Jesus at his right hand (2:25) – by way of resurrection
(2:32) and exaltation (2:33) and the sending of the Spirit (2:33) (which
is conjoined with his exaltation) (2:33, 34): by all this God has made
him 'Lord and Christ', Luke says in conclusion (2:36). What Luke gives
us here is not bits and pieces of two originally divergent interpretations
of Jesus, but a single coherent, personal view of Jesus, preordained to
be Lord and Christ in the context of 'salvation-history', and of the
plan of salvation executed by God himself in the concrete history of
Jesus. Luke sets out to show that God was all the time 'with this
anointed one' (Acts 10:37–39). 'God was with him' from the beginning
(2:22; 10:38); yes, from birth he is the 'Son of God' (Lk. 1:32, 35; 3:22;
4:3; 8:28; 9:35; 22:70).

It is noticeable that in other passages in Acts Jesus is referred to not
so much as 'the messiah' as 'Jesus Messiah', Jesus Christ. These
passages occur in a (broadly speaking) liturgical context (preaching;
baptism; exorcism): 2:38; 3:6; 4:10; 10:36, 48; 15:26; 16:18. All other
passages in which 'messiah' or 'christ' is explicitly taken to mean 'the
one anointed with God's Spirit' (the so-called apostolic proclamation
to the Jews) have been composed by Luke himself and set within a
context of missionary preaching to the Jews (including Greek-speaking
Jews). Their tenor is: Messiah is this very Jesus of Nazareth, that is, the
crucified One (2:36; 3:18, 20; 4:26; 5:42; 8:5; 9:22; 18:5, 28).

In doing this Luke invariably stresses the relationship between Jesus
and the Holy Spirit, and between the exalted Jesus and the outpouring
of the promised Spirit (Acts 2:33). Jesus lives because he is 'indwelt by'
another, the Holy Spirit. That is why in his life on earth power goes
hand in hand in him with goodness (2:22 and 10:38), the sign of God's
being 'with him' (2:22; 3:14; 10:38): God is at work in Jesus. In the
second phase, of death and resurrection, the bond between Jesus and
God appears even more explicitly; Jesus is a possession of God: 'your
holy one', 'your servant (serving-man or 'child')', 'his messiah', 'my
son' (see 2:27; 3:14; 4:27; 13:35; 3:13; 3:26; 4:27; 4:30; 3:18; 13:33).
Whereas outside of Luke the usual reference is to 'the Christ', Luke
talks about 'the Christ of God' (Acts 3:18; Lk. 9:20, 23, 35; see Acts 4:
26–27). It serves to emphasize the saving activity of God in and
through Jesus. He is the 'Christ of the Lord' (Lk. 2:26). Jesus' being

rejected by men is counterbalanced by his belonging to God, which cannot be shattered even by death. Finally, Jesus appears in his glorified state endowed with transcendent new gifts that bring him into relationship with all, Jew and Gentile alike: he is 'the Lord of all' (2:36; 10:36), 'judge of the living and the dead' (10:42), 'Saviour' (5:31; 13:23), given by God to the world as its definitive deliverer (3:20; 4:12; 10:43; 13:38).

On the other hand Luke is also aware of the dynastic variety of Davidic messianism. This tradition comes out especially in Lk. 1, where Jesus comes 'of the house of David', evidently in a historicizing sense. How could Luke connect this up with the actual life and lot of Jesus of Nazareth? Precisely by means of the non-dynastic, prophetic-sapiential 'son of David': a prophet who has been rejected appears, eschatologically, *ipso facto* as witness for the prosecution (or as judge); thus he has the function of a royal judge. Furthermore, according to Judaeo-Greek Wisdom ideas a prophet's role as martyr issues in an eventual king-like ascendancy (see above). The synthesis is easily detectable in Lk. 22:29–30: 'As my Father appointed a kingdom for me, so do I appoint for you that you may eat and drink at my table in my kingdom, and sit on thrones, judging the twelve tribes of Israel'; here the 'universal world-rule' of the sapiential martyr tradition is linked with the national-cum-Davidic governance of Israel's twelve tribes. That Davidic and prophetic messianism had already been run together Luke shows clearly enough in Acts 2:29–30: here David is himself both king and prophet. Luke never says that Jesus is set on David's throne (Acts 13:32–37); he uses Ps. 2:7 only to show that he is the 'Son of God'. Jesus is 'Son of God' because the *Pneuma* of the Father is in him (Acts 2:33). Jesus' sitting as king at God's right hand is not associated by Luke with Israel. In no sense, therefore, according to Luke, is the exaltation of Jesus the fulfilment of the promise of David's throne in Lk. 1:32–33. Thus in Luke a dynastic-Davidic messianism is completely at odds with the prophetic-sapiential messianism of the son of David general in the New Testament, which also governs his Christology: for him 'son of God', 'child' (*pais*) and 'messiah' (christ) are synonymous, as everywhere else in this sapiential corpus of tradition (see Acts 4:26–27 and Lk. 3:22; Lk. 4:9; 22:69–71).

*Conclusion.* The 'messianism' of the New Testament reminds us of three pre-canonical currents: Jesus was not, to begin with, held to be the dynastic-Davidic messiah; rather was this interpretation rejected; in certain, in particular Greek-speaking, Jewish Christian congregations

J.E.C.–R

(in which the 'messiah' concept was subsumed within other prophetic-sapiential eschatological ideas of salvation) Jesus was indeed seen as the Davidic-messianic, latter-day salvific figure, yet in a non-national and universal sense. The dynastic 'David' Christology is therefore not a great deal of use in helping us understand better the Christian interpretation of Jesus' exaltation. In line with the Old Testament Jesus appears and acts as a Jew – in the theological capacity of 'son of David' – only in behalf of Israel's expectations of final salvation within the prospect limited by such expectations in the Old Testament. His earthly career is a Jewish 'inside event', but in the plane of Jewish eschatological expectations: he is the eschatological prophet with (sapiential) Davidic-messianic attributes, and the *eschaton* will see all nations being led by God to Zion. To that end Jesus was baptized, anointed with the Holy Spirit. Only through his resurrection, exaltation and investment with power does it become apparent that he is the 'Lord of all' (Acts 10): that is 'the message concerning the Son of God' (Rom. 1:1–3a), 'the glad tidings of Jesus Messiah, Son of God' (Mk. 1:1). Jesus 'as son of David' would seem to be a *theologoumenon* in certain early Christian circles, without further implication for an updated Christology. Dynastic-Davidic messianism, it is true, with its own 'lord', 'son' and 'christ' tradition, profoundly affected the first identification of Jesus with the latter-day, definitive 'messianic' prophet (even by way of pre-Christian contaminations of these originally divergent traditions). But dynastic-Davidic messianism, with its somewhat triumphal traits, was applied to the risen Jesus only in order to construe the resurrection as exaltation. The dynastic-Davidic 'christ' tradition could not in itself provide any terms of experience to justify proclaiming the deceased Jesus to be, in spite of everything, 'the risen One'. Without already existing Jewish models it was out of the question for a triumphalist, Jewish messiah concept to be re-shaped within a few years by the Christians into the notion of a suffering messiah. What is more, Jesus' earthly career contradicted the 'christ' idea of dynastic-Davidic messianism. But there was a model of the 'suffering messiah' even within Jewry itself. Only this prophetic 'messianism' (the latter-day prophet, wise and filled with God's Spirit), since it was already combined with the sapiential 'suffering and righteous one' and the 'wise man put to the test', was able (in face of the actual turn of events in Jesus' life) to supply the ground and potential condition for experiencing Jesus, after his death, as indeed the risen messiah. '*Makaridzei eschata dikaiôn*' (Wis. 2:16c): the fact that the righteous one is glorified and comes to be king is an 'eschatological event'. Then and only then, at a secondary stage, could the Easter experience be elaborated upon still further with passages like 2 Sam. 7; Pss. 2:7 and 110:1, as well as with the son of man tradition as it had grown in Judaism from the Greek Dan. 7:13–14 – although we are still left, in my view, with the question as to whether the next step was from the recognition of Jesus as the eschatological Christ prophet to the exaltation Christology or *Kyrios* Christology of 2 Sam. 7; Pss. 2 and 110, or (chronologically, that is) first to a son of man Christology (Dan. 7:13–14), which would then itself have been a bridge to the 'king' Christology, as it was first called. This uncertainty goes along with the complete absence of any agreement among scholars regarding the New Testament 'son of man'. A chronology open to reconstruction may well be out of the question here, because (starting from the messenger idea) the two subsequent elaborations of the identification of Jesus with the prophetic christ could have had a parallel origin in different primitive congregations and after that – at a pre-canonical stage – have encountered each other, only then to coalesce within the New Testament. For the tenor and purpose of this 'try at a Christology', this problem seems to me in any case secondary. Fundamental to it was the identification of Jesus' person with the messianic prophet of the latter-day gospel of God's approaching rule, as a link between the historical Jesus and the kerygmatic Christ. Whence it appears that at the root of the divergent traditions merged together in the New Testament and as the matrix of its plural Christologies there is a basic vision with a fundamentally single identity. In spite of the not inconsiderable distinctions Jesus 'comes across' everywhere in the early Christian traditions in the selfsame way. The unity turns out to be more universal and profound than the pluralism. This, as I see it, is of decisive importance; it confirms the initial working hypothesis: broadly speaking, the New Testament is a true to life (faith-motivated) reflection or mirroring of the historical role enacted by Jesus of Nazareth.

# Direct hermeneusis of the resurrection in the New Testament

*Literature*. Besides the literature mentioned in Part Two in connection with Jesus' appearances, see especially: L. Bakker, 'Geloven in de verrijzenis', *Bijdragen* 28 (1967), 294–320; H. R. Balz, *Methodische Probleme der neutestamentlichen Christologie*, Neukirchen – Vluyn 1967; I. Berten, *Histoire, révélation et foi*, Brussels-Paris 1969; C. Bussmann, 'Themen der paulinischen Missionspredigt auf dem Hintergrund der spätjüdisch-hellenistischen Missionsliteratur' (Europäische Hochschulschriften, 33–3) (Berne 1971), 84–108; H. Conzelmann and P. Althaus, 'Auferstehung', RGG³ I, 694–701; O. Cullmann, *Christologie*; and *Heil als Geschichte*, Tübingen 1965, Chr. Duquoc, *Christologie*, vol. 2, *Le Messie*, Paris 1972; H. Elert, 'Die Krise der Osterglaubens', *Hochland* 60 (1967–8), 305–18; A. Grabner-Haider, 'Auferstehungsleiblichkeit. Biblische Bemerkungen', StdZ 93 (1968), 217–22, and 'Leibliche Auferstehung', *Diakonia* 3 (1968), 121–2; H. Grasz, *Ostergeschehen und Osterbericht*, Göttingen 1964³; W. Grossouw, *La glorification du Christ dans le quatrième évangile* (RechBibl), Bruges 131–45; E. Jüngel, *Unterwegs zur Sache*, Munich 1972; G. Kegel, *Auferstehung Jesu, Auferstehung der Toten*, Gütersloh 1970; W. Kramer, *Christos, Kyrios, Gottessohn* (AThANT, 44), Zürich-Stuttgart 1963; J. Kremer, *Das älteste Zeugnis von der Auferstehung Christi*, Stuttgart 1966; G. W. Lampe and D. M. McKinnon, *The Resurrection: a Dialogue*, London 1966; X. Léon-Dufour, *Résurrection de Jésus et message pascal*, Paris 1971; G. Lohfink, 'Die Auferstehung Jesu und die historische kritik', BuL 9 (1968), 37–57; W. Marxsen, *Die Auferstehung Jesu als historisches und theologisches Problem*, Gütersloh 1967⁵, and *Die Auferstehung der Jesu von Nazareth*, Gütersloh 1968; Br. O. McDermott, *The Personal Unity of Jesus and God according to W. Pannenberg*, St Ottilien 1973; A. Moore, *The Parousia in the New Testament* (NovTSuppl, 13), Leyden 1966; Fr. Muszner, *Die Auferstehung Jesu*, Munich 1969; W. Pannenberg, *Grundzüge der Christologie*, Gütersloh (1964) 1969³; 'Die Offenbarung Gottes in Jesus von

Nazareth', *Neuland in der Theologie*, pt. 3, *Theologie als Geschichte*, Zürich-Stuttgart 1957, 135–69 and 285–351, and 'Dogmatische Erwägungen zur Auferstehung Jesu', KuD 14 (1968), 105–18; R. Pesch, 'Heilszukunft und Zukunft des Heils', *Gestalt und Anspruch des Neuen Testaments*, ed. G. Schreiner (Würzburg 1969), 313–29; N. Pittenger, *Christology reconsidered*, London 1970; K. Rahner and W. Thüsing, *Christologie, systematisch und exegetisch*, Freiburg 1972; K. H. Rengstorf, *Die Auferstehung Jesu*, Witten 1960[4]; B. Rigaux, *Dieu l'a ressuscité*, Gembloux 1973; J. M. Robinson, *Kerygma und historischer Jesus*, Stuttgart 1967[2]; J. Rohde, *Die Redaktionsgeschichtliche Methode* (Hamburg 1966), especially 44–194; H. Schlier, *Ueber die Auferstehung Jesu Christi*, Einsiedeln 1968; H. R. Schlette, *Epiphanie als Geschichte*, Munich 1966; J. Sint, 'Die Auferstehung Jesu in der Verkündigung der Urgemeinde', ZThTH 84 (1962), 129–51; H. Schwantes, *Schöpfung der Endzeit. Ein Beitrag zum Verständnis der Auferweckung bei Paulus*, Stuttgart 1963; W. Thüsing, *Erhöhungsvorstellung und Parusieerwartung der ältesten nachösterlichen Christologie*, BZ 11 (1967), 95–108 and 205–22, and 12 (1968), 54–80 and 223–40 (now also in book form: SBS 42, Stuttgart 1969); Rob. C. Ware, 'De interpretatie van de verrijzenis: een zaak van leven en dood', TvT 9 (1969), 55–78; H. Weber, *Die Lehre von der Auferstehung in den Haupttraktaten der scholastischen Theologie* (Freib. Theol. Stud., 91), Freiburg 1973; U. Wilckens, *Auferstehung. Das biblische Auferstehungszeugnis historisch untersucht und erklärt*, Berlin-Stuttgart 1970; J. H. Wilson, 'The Corinthians who say there is no resurrection of the dead', ZNW 59 (1968), 90–107. Works by further authors: W. Marxsen, U. Wilckens, G. Delling, H. Geyer, *Die Bedeutung der Auferstehungsbotschaft für den Glauben an Jesus Christus*, Gütersloh 1966 (cit. *Auferstehungsbotschaft*); *Christ, faith, history*; B. Klappert (ed.), *Diskussion um Kreuz und Auferstehung*, Wuppertal 1967[2].

# Chapter 1

# 'Raised from the dead'

As opposed to some apocryphal books the gospels have nothing to say about the resurrection event as such; they speak of the dead Jesus only via experiences associated with their own standpoint of belief, divining in them the hand of the living Lord. In trying to express this in so many words the disciples reached for concepts familiar to them: exaltation; the 'assumption' of the righteous one into heaven; resurrection and so forth.

## §1  Late Jewish ideas about life after death

Jewish belief in life after death was by no means uniform in Jesus' day. What is more, the particular contrast, accepted more or less unanimously since O. Cullmann, between the Jewish resurrection and Judaeo-Greek immortality turns out to be far from corresponding to the historically documented evidence;[1] nor is it justifiable on historical grounds to regard the resurrection as self-evidently an explicitly held apocalyptic conviction.

According to the Book of Wisdom (Wis. 1 – 6) the righteous or wise one does not actually die (Wis. 5:15; 1:15; 1:4–14). The unrighteous man or sinner dies; his death is 'unto death' (1:12; 5:9–14), whereas that of the righteous is 'unto life' (1:15; 5:15). This view of things is held in the context of a conviction that God will vindicate the righteous who are persecuted for religious reasons (2:12–20; 4:18c to 5:14). The wise or righteous man 'taken up to God' will then be judge or prosecutor of those who persecuted him; they anticipate their own sentence (4:18c – 5:14).[2] All this echoes ancient 'wisdom stories' in which the righteous, having been persecuted, eventually obtain a high position at the royal court and are appointed judge over their former persecutors (a typical example would be Joseph in Egypt). Later on the wise man comes to be the one who obeys God's law and suffers persecution on that account. Then God assumes the role of the avenger; and the persecuted individual is taken up into the court of heaven, where he is allotted *ad hoc* (that is, *vis-à-vis* his persecutors) the function of a judge; then follows the acclamation. All are constrained to confess: 'Truly, this was a righteous man' (a 'son of God'). This is the context of, in particular, Wis. 2:12–20 and 5:1–7: the suffering righteous man is 'taken up into heaven' and vindicated in the celestial court of judgement: just to see the righteous one exalted is in itself a punishment for the malefactors (Wis. 5:1–2 and 5:3–8). Seeing the exalted one in the ranks of the 'sons of God' (2:13, 16, 18), the celestial court of angels, causes his former enemies to acclaim the royal dignity to which he has attained. In this Solomonic-sapiential literature, therefore, the exaltation of the suffering righteous one means promoting him to the status of a king; the suffering and persecuted righteous one will judge the peoples and nations (3:7–8; 4:16). The idea is, of course, that the one now exalted passes only an *ad hoc* judgement; not the universal judgement – that is not in question here – but the judgement of the righteous one upon his persecutors.

In this respect Wis. 1 – 6 has been influenced by Isa. 52 – 53 (the suffering *Ebed Yahweh*). In both, the righteous one who suffers is *pais Kyriou* (the child of the Lord).[3] The parallel construction is very obvious (Wis. 5:1a and Isa. 52:13; Wis. 5:1bc and Isa. 52:15; Wis. 5:3–8 and Isa. 53:1–6). The *Ebed* too hopes that he will be vindicated by God (Isa. 50:7–9) – and vindicated in a juridical, legal fashion, because his suffering and death were apparently the result of a juridical process (Isa. 53:8). The exaltation of the *Ebed* prophet (Isa. 52:13 and 53:12) is, although less explicit, a royal elevation as (a kind of) grand vizier. Here too this elevation entails a judgement on previous persecutors (Isa. 53:1–6); they realize that their judgement was at fault. Here again elevation and acclamation bring the scene to an end.

In both accounts resurrection is never mentioned, only 'being taken up into heaven' after death. Sin leads to death (Wis. 1:12); the righteous man is 'immortal' (1:15). Life and death (see the discussion in Wis. 2:1–5) are regarded by the godless as a mundane issue; after death there is no reward or punishment; it all happens here on earth (2:6–11). But then, however (in the light of the wise one or servant of God) they are obliged to alter their findings (4:20 – 5:14; especially 5:9–14): there is life after death, but sinners have no part in it. According to the Book of Wisdom, therefore, 'immortality' is a condition of the righteous: their requital, vindication and elevation. Conversely, their persecutors, despite the earthly success of their juridical conspiracy against them, are punished after their death.[4]

A similar thematic pattern or scheme as in Isa. 52 – 53 and Wis. 4:20ff (as revealed by form criticism) is present in Enoch 62 – 63: the righteous one[5] (here referred to as the son of man) is raised to the (*ad hoc*) status of heavenly judge. Both Wisdom and Enoch are interpretations of the Deutero-Isaianic *Ebed Yahweh*. In Enoch the righteous one or son of man is not a suffering or persecuted individual, it is true; the connection consists in the fact that what all three cases ultimately present is a 'celestial figure', enacting the role of judge. If it comes to that, the 'son of man' in Dan. 7 (as was said earlier on) is also the heavenly *archon* or guardian angel of the now suffering Israel, so that the discrepancy between 'suffering' and 'son of man' even in this Danielic tradition is not so great as is commonly supposed. Again, the installation of this *archon* in heaven is a celestial pre-figuration of the 'lifting up' of Israel; Israel's enemies will be punished. In other words, for the form critic Dan. 7 has the same theme as one finds in Enoch, Wisdom and the *Ebed Yahweh* songs. The Deutero-Isaianic tradition of the 'exaltation' and that of the heavenly figure, the son of man, have been merged together.

Between the *Ebed Yahweh* and the period of persecution under Antiochus IV, the persecution of Israel's religious leaders prompted an interpretation of Isa. 52–53 in which are thematized the lifting up after death of the persecuted and the punishment of their tormentors. This gave rise to a tradition with a stock passage, the basis of which is the *Ebed* song (also taken partly from material in Isa. 13 and 14).[6] Every time the reference is to being taken up to heaven, not to resurrection.

This becomes a general theme (that is, separate from the idea of persecution) in the Assumptio Moysis 10 and in Enoch 104: all the righteous are taken up into heaven where they shine as stars in the firmament,[7] without any mention in this case of being installed in a specific office carrying authority with it. After their death the righteous are in heaven.

In Dan. 12:1–3 the same theme is expressed by using the concept of 'resurrection', for some Jews to eternal life, for others to eternal ignominy. This is the oldest evidence for belief in the resurrection in Israel. At the close of the Ages Michael, Israel's *archon* or guardian angel, will 'stand up', apparently in the midst of a juridical and heavenly court of angels: a sitting with an accuser ('satan') and a spokesman for the defence. In this court Michael represents Israel's righteous ones in their conflict with the Seleucid king (Dan. 10:13–21). The real business is the final struggle between Michael and Lucifer (the celestial *archon* behind the anti-Israelite Antiochus) in the form of a divine judgement. For this, that is, so that they may be judged, the dead are aroused. Those whose death was unjust are brought back to life, because it was taken from them wrongly: *their* resurrection is an act of divine justice. Daniel 12:2a is an obvious reminiscence of Isa. 26:19: the context is Israel's national restoration which was represented in Isaiah under the image of 'resurrection from the dead'. The many pious ones or Chasidim who had fallen victim to the persecution did however constitute in these circles a theological problem: they died because of their obedience to the Torah (1 Macc. 1:50, 60–61, 62–63; 2 Macc. 6 – 7). Piety was the cause of their death, whereas the Hellenizing Jews, who were the disobedient ones, had remained alive. According to Jewish notions of reward and retribution this was a problem. Resurrection and punishment, then, were the only possible answer to this vital problem; and the answer was given in terms borrowed from Isa. 26. But for Daniel, as opposed to Isaiah, resurrection is not in itself a salvific event, but simply the means of presenting the dead – good and bad – as living subjects for God's judgement: rewarding and punishing Jews in accordance with their behaviour during the persecution. Resurrection here is wholly preparatory to the judgement, and not in itself an event that brings salvation; furthermore, this is not the general resurrection but simply a resurrection *ad hoc*; the judgement itself is the restoration of Israel, in which those resurrected to life are to take part. Daniel 12:3 identifies the 'wise' with 'servants' (*Ebed* in the plural) (see Isa. 52:13 with Dan. 12:3). The 'resurrection' is a taking up into heaven (Dan. 12:3).

The Book of Jubilees 23:27–31 reflects upon the same events as Daniel; the solution is on the same lines as the somewhat later Daniel, but there is no question of resurrection: while the bones of the righteous rest in the earth, their souls are taken up into heaven. The only thing spoken of here is a 'rising' of the soul: Enoch 102 – 104 also speaks of a 'resurrection' of the souls of the righteous, but in a wider context; unmerited suffering (not so much death as such), even when it is not in the cause of God, calls for some requital, namely, that the souls of these righteous ones be taken up into heaven. At death the souls of the righteous go to Sheol (Enoch 102:5), and at the judgement they are taken up to heaven; the unrighteous, on the other hand, stay in Sheol. In 4 Macc. the death of the righteous is simply a passage to 'immortality' (4 Macc. 7:3; 9:22; 14:5–6; 16:13; 17:12), 'eternal life' (15:3), or an immediate assumption into heaven (9:22; 13:17; 16:25; 17:18–19). In Qumrân too the resurrection would appear to be unknown; there is talk of eternal life, which however is already a present reality here on earth.[8] When 'immortality' is mentioned, it does not mean any sort of natural immortality, as an attribute of the human spirit (nor yet in the Book of Wisdom): it has to do with God's rewarding the righteous. Only if and when God's Spirit resides in a man is he 'immortal' (Wis. 1:4–7). There is no intrinsic link between 'soul' and 'immortality', as there is between 'fellowship with God' and 'immortality' or assumption into heaven. Thus the Greek concept of immortality is completely assimilated among these Greek-speaking Jews to the Jewish outlook: it is a matter of 'life' or 'death', in a Jewish sense, not of a 'philosophical' deathlessness.

Then too there is sometimes a reference in late Jewish literature to an interim stage (Enoch 22; 4 Ezra 7): the righteous are already 'in paradise' before the close of the Ages; in this period the earlier 'shadowy existence' in Sheol is really an 'outdated' scheme.

Again, physical resurrection is mentioned in 2 Macc. 7 as a form of divine reparation for death by martyrdom (more in line with the *Ebed* tradition than that of Dan. 12:1–3). In 2 Baruch 49 – 51 the dead are to rise in the condition of their former body, so that the living may see it is the dead who have been resurrected. Only when recognition has followed will the judgement take place (50:4); the righteous will shine as stars in the firmament. The Testamentum Judae also refers to a bodily resurrection. In the Psalmi Salomonis (middle of the first century BC), which most probably come from Pharisaic circles, God's judgement is a central theme: reward and punishment (Ps. Sal. 2:3–18; 8:7–26; 2:22–31; 3:13–15), that is, 'life' or 'destruction' (*apôleia*). Psalmi Salomonis 3 is plainly concerned with the issue of 'just recompense' after death: eternal life or eternal death. In this case eternal life is not bound up with the problem of unmerited suffering or death: it is a matter of God's rewarding a life of piety. For sinners their death is definitive, without any further (eschatological or renewed) confirmation. There is in these psalms no explicit mention of a resurrection of the body or indeed of the soul: they endorse the categories of eternal life, whereas the death of sinners means death – simply that. We have so far examined four categories whereby Judaism tries to express the notion of post-terrestrial life: being taken up to heaven (without any further specification), resurrection of the body, removal of the soul from Sheol, eternal life.

4 Ezra 7:32 (first century AD) also speaks of the release of the dead from Sheol in a universal sense (universal resurrection), so that all may be judged: rewarded with paradise or with Gehenna (7:33–37). Oracula

Sybyllina 4 tells of a world conflagration; everything will be destroyed, people and things; then God will cause all human beings to rise from the dead in their former state, whereupon follows the general judgement; sinners return 'beneath the earth' (Gehenna), the good live happily 'upon the earth' (the same universal resurrection is to be found in Testamentum Benjamin 10). In other words the two datable Jewish testimonies concerning a general resurrection come from the end of the first century AD.[9]

We may conclude this survey thus: in Jesus' time no uniform ideas existed about life after death – a problem to which Israel had begun to pay attention no more than a century or two before Christ. Although there had been for a century past a gradual tendency to express the assumption into heaven of the persecuted, and then of all pious and righteous Jews, in terms of 'bodily resurrection', nevertheless all kinds of other ideas were in circulation: either of the soul's assumption into heaven (in the case of the righteous) or of 'eternal life' (filled out more specifically, maybe, with 'bodily resurrection' or with an assumption of the soul into heaven, whether straight after death or from Sheol). What was after all still an exceptional resurrection was initially associated with God's recompensing those faithful to the Law who had been unjustly put to death during the Antiochene persecution; then with all and sundry who have suffered without due cause; and finally with each and every pious and righteous life as such. In this last form the prospect was eventually opened up of a general resurrection, which even then was not so much a salvific event in its own right, but rather the indispensable condition for ensuring that everyone could appear at the judgement.[10] In New Testament times the general resurrection would seem to have been more especially a dogma of the Pharisees; although they were not nearly so representative prior to AD 70 as they were after the Jewish War. We can assume, therefore, that particularly after AD 70 the physical resurrection was fairly widespread as an aspect of popular Jewish belief. Before that, there was certainly the expectation that specific individuals would be resurrected, who then return to earth (see Mk. 6:14) in order to carry out a particular salvific task; but these are not instances of an 'eschatological' resurrection.

## §2 God raised him 'from the dead'

The difference between the New Testament and late Jewish ideas of resurrection is immediately obvious. Jesus' resurrection is a saving event *per se*, not a condition for appearing alive before God's throne in order to be judged. His resurrection itself is interpreted directly as the 'amen' of God upon the person of Jesus. Even in the older, non-apocalyptic books of the Old Testament we hear of a resurrection that is a salvific event, but then in a spiritual sense (the 'resurrection of the people of Israel', Isa. 26:19; 25:8). The idea of Jesus' bodily resurrection is more akin to that than to the apocalyptic, neutral concept of resurrection. 'Resurrection' is God's eschatological, saving activity, accomplished in Jesus.

And then we should keep in mind a terminological distinction. The late Jewish general resurrection is technically known as a 'resurrection *of* the dead' (*anastasis nekrōn*); the resurrection of Jesus on the other hand is almost invariably referred to as being '*from* the dead' (*ek nekrōn*).[11] Yet this raises several problems. Excepting the Apocalypse, James, Jude and 2 Peter (see also Rom. 1:4), the resurrection of Jesus is always in the New Testament said to be a 'rising *from* the dead', whereas this formula is scarcely heard of outside the New Testament literature.[12] The Septuagint usually speaks of arising 'from death' (*ek thanatou*).[13] But the formula 'from the dead' is not unknown even in the Old Testament.[14] In the New Testament, it is true, a verbal expression is used in connection with 'from the dead' almost exclusively apropos of Jesus' resurrection, whereas the general resurrection is regularly described as *anastasis nekrōn*, resurrection of the dead.[15] Yet it is worth noting that according to Bauer's lexicon the term *anastasis nekrōn* (resurrection of the dead) was derived, as a substantive, from the verbal phrase *anastènai ek nekrōn* (to rise *from* the dead). According to G. Kegel[16] the separate formula – 'he is risen', and so forth – are therefore older than the formula, 'risen from the dead'; this last phrase is said to have been formed in controversy with the Jews who pointed to the death of Jesus. Then again, it goes without saying that terms like 'rising', 'raising up' – familiar words from everyday vocabulary – have a multiple significance, so that additions are needed to make clear what is meant: 'awakened from the dead' or 'having died and risen', or in other words: 'having died *but* having risen'.

Nevertheless the verbal use (to arise) with 'from the dead' and the substantive use resurrection *of* the dead, disclose a peculiarity of the New Testament; for the substantive, '*the* resurrection', is in any case seldom used in connection with Jesus.[17] Therefore the remarkably frequent use in the New Testament of *ek nekrōn* – *from* the dead – is not itself the distinctive thing about the New Testament, it seems to me, but merely the consequence of what is indeed distinctive: the well-nigh exclusive verbal expression used in speaking of Jesus' resurrection, with its suggestion of activity, of a dynamic factor. What is typical is the marked avoidance of the substantive in connection with Jesus' resurrection. The saving activity of God in raising Jesus from the dead does not lend itself easily to substantification. This points to the profession of Christian belief not so much in 'the resurrection' of Jesus Christ but in the fact that Jesus is risen or, more accurately, that God caused him to rise from the dead. The constant use in speech of *'from* the dead' is then the (more in the nature of a grammatical) consequence of that.

But more important than this grammatical dissection is the proven point that all the early texts say it is God who raised Jesus from the dead.[18] The emphasis is on God's saving action in Jesus of Nazareth.

There are of course passages in which we read that 'Jesus himself rises from the dead'.[19] Very often the meaning is still: Jesus has risen (from the dead) through the power of him who raised him up. In part, this formula would seem to be the normal result of a grammatical construction: 'Jesus died, was buried, was raised (i.e. rose).' Whenever, that is, death and resurrection have the same subject, it is an obvious point of grammar that no change of subject will occur (except in the contrast: 'You killed him but God [has] awakened him'). The separate affirmation of the resurrection by itself is probably earlier (1 Thess. 1:10) and then it always runs: 'God [has] awakened him', or: 'He has been awakened (raised)'. On the other hand we must bear in mind that it is the son of man tradition that tells us Jesus himself rises, apparently in his own strength (Mk. 8:31: *anastènai*; 9:31 and 10:34: *anastèsetai*; here, evidently, the terminology employed is that of 'rising up', and not of 'being awakened [raised]'). So it would appear that there existed a tradition in early Christianity – the son of man tradition – which speaks quite clearly of Jesus' arising. This tradition comes right to the fore only in Jn. 10:17–18, where it is on his own authority that Jesus 'takes his life again'; somewhat later this is put with considerable emphasis by Ignatius of Antioch,[20] and the formula became a classical one in Christianity from the second century onwards. In early Christianity up to and including the New Testament, however, the emphasis was broadly on God's saving action in raising Jesus from the dead. *Ho egeiras* – 'God, who awakens to life' – therefore became for the Christians as it were a divine attribute,[21] that is, a way of extolling God.

§3   'The third day rose again according to the Scriptures':
the resurrection of Jesus as an eschatological, conclusive event

*Literature.* J. Blank, *Paulus und Jesus* (Munich 1968), 133–97; J.
Dupont, 'Ressuscité "le troisième jour"', Bibl 40 (1959), 742–61; F.
Hahn, *Hoheitstitel*, 197–211; K. Lehmann, *Auferweckt am dritten Tag
nach der Schrift*, Freiburg 1968; F. Mildenberger, 'Auferstanden am
dritten Tag nach den Schriften', EvTh 23 (1963), 265–80; F. Nötscher,
'Zur Auferstehung nach drei Tagen', Bibl 35 (1954), 313–19; H. Tödt,
*Der Menschensohn*, l.c., 167–72; N. Walker, 'After three days', NovT 4
(1960), 261–2; J. Wijngaards, 'Death and resurrection in covenantal
context', VT 17 (1967), 226–39.

The term 'Scriptural proof'[22] does not represent exactly what the
first Christians felt and experienced when they described the salvation
encountered in and through Jesus as being 'according to the Scriptures'.
Scripture for them was really and truly the book of God's magnificent
acts and promises, the expression of his will and plan of salvation. To
begin with, this Scripture was not what it was to become later on – the
Old Testament; it was their living Scripture, in the light of which the
first Christians 'read' or interpreted new historical events and experiences. The ordinary run of faithful Jews were in no sense expert in
the Scriptures; but their lives were governed above all by the psalms
and by the writings that were always being read out and expounded in
their services at the synagogue. In the earliest commemoration of their
Master's Passion, still recognizable behind Mark's Passion narrative,
we can see how the first Christians identified with the meditative prayer
of the psalmists who, however great their humiliation, continued to
put their trust in God. At first those Christians did not know what to
make of Jesus' suffering and death; so great however was their faith in
God that they had more confidence in him than in all that the concrete
and painful facts of history so manifestly shouted aloud. The insight
provided by their faith may have needed time; in the end they knew:
through their official authorities men might give judgement against
this righteous one; but he cannot be forsaken by God. That was the
spiritual tenor of their Scriptures. Against the background of that
spirituality, on the basis of which Jesus himself had lived, they tried to

assign a place to the events centring around Jesus. Jesus was a Jew; and his close friends and disciples also thought as faithful Jews would think. It was as Jews that they were to interpret Jesus. Both the unique element in what they had experienced in Jesus and the experiential confines of the Jewish religion, within which they articulated their experiences, comprised for them a single course of tradition, in which their present seen in the light of their Jewish past and their past understood in the light of Jesus the Jew constituted one happening. Thus the new thing that had been accomplished in Jesus was made intelligible and capable of expression in Old Testament and Judaistic categories of belief, the deposit of the Jewish encounter with God's will down the centuries, expressed in their sacred writings.

In the credal affirmation 'He is risen' the determining factor is what they recollected of Jesus' days on earth and their experience of the grace and mercy encountered through conversion; but almost equally important for putting this reality into words is the whole tradition of religious experience within Jewry. Despite and because of the fact that what was utterly new about Jesus of Nazareth could not be pigeon-holed, it was possible for them to make sense of Jesus' newness only with models of experience familiar to Jewish religion and tested over centuries.

The salvific character of the resurrection in a non-apocalyptic, New Testament sense is further reinforced by the addition of 'the third day (rose)', and then of 'the third day according to the Scriptures'. The combination of the third day with the Scriptures (1 Cor. 15:4b) is again present in an obvious reflection in Mt. 12:40 (the three days of Jonah: Jon. 2:1), more vaguely in Lk. 24:46, and conjoined with a Temple-logion also in Jn. 2:22; minus the reference to Scripture but, as in 1 Cor. 15:4b, again in a credal context in Acts 10:40. Apart from the two statements affirming resurrection on the third day (1 Cor. 15:4b; Acts 10:40) there are sixteen places where the three-day scheme is firmly linked to one or other of three blocks of tradition: the Temple-logion, predictions of the Passion, and the prediction of a consummation: the third day I will rise again; on the third day rebuild the Temple; the third day reach a final completion.[23]

That within the history of tradition a link emerged between the 'after three days' of the tradition enshrining the 'predictions of the Passion' and the 'on the third day' of the resurrection tradition is immediately apparent from the fact that Luke and Matthew change 'after three days' into '(on) the third day' (Mt. 16:21; 17:23; 20:19; Lk. 9:22; 18:33; see Lk. 24:7, 46). Thus the phrase 'on the third day' eventually prevailed.

It is at once obvious that outside the credal formulae and these

accounts of prediction the 'third day' motif is totally absent from the
Easter and appearance narratives of the gospels. What these say in
each case is: 'on the first day of the week'.[24] That day refers not to the
third day after Good Friday but to the 'day after the sabbath',[25] and so
has nothing to do with the 'three day' motif. What we do find in Luke
and John is the historicizing tendency designed to show that Christ
manifests his presence particularly on that (Jewish) first day of the
week – what has since emerged as 'the Christian Sunday'. But even
with Luke (and Mark) the rising on the third day is not made to relate
directly to the chronological events of the Easter story; the expression
occurs only when the earlier predictions on the part of Jesus are being
cited (Lk. 24:7 and 24:46) (Lk. 24:21 may have a more general meaning;
see below). Thus within the diverse complexes of tradition there is a
clear distinction between the 'first day of the week' (Easter and appearance narratives) and the 'third day' (credal formulae and predictions).

The 'third day' formula antedates Paul: 'He was raised on the third
day in accordance with the Scriptures' (1 Cor. 15:4b) is a quotation on
Paul's part. F. Hahn, who can still extract a historical dating from
this,[26] has argued that this formula breaks down into various, originally independent, component formulae: 'He has been raised according
to the Scriptures' and 'He was raised on the third day'. As a result of
the amalgamation, 'the third day' became in the end part of the
Scriptural proof-text; and so it became necessary to look for an Old
Testament locus which mentions a resurrection on the third day. And
that raised a number of problems.[27] Yet some of the evidence – even
for the complete formula (albeit emerging out of what were originally
two variants) – points to local Palestinian congregations or, if the
formula be held to have arisen in Antioch, then still to a very early stage
of the Antiochene tradition. We have said already that in the formula
of 1 Cor. 15:4b both pre-Pauline and Pauline features are to be detected.[28]

A perspective of major significance is provided for us by the Jewish
notion that a dead person is well and truly dead only 'after three days'.
Rising on the third day could then imply that Jesus had risen not after
a seeming death but after he had really died; in other words, 'on the
third day' has the same function as the expression: 'he was dead and
buried'.[29] Yet it does not occur to people to ask why it is only on the
third day that certainty is possible. This points to the fact that 'the
third day' or 'after three days' has to the Jewish way of thinking a

very special significance, even in ordinary, day-to-day living. Indeed the third day amounts to the same thing as the 'decisive day', the critical day on which something definitive is concluded or on which something quite new begins. So also with death: after three days it is finally certain whether all hope is to be abandoned or whether a new and decisive turn of events is on the way (Jn. 11:17–39). For three days men seek for the lost Jesus; the third day brings with it the happy outcome (Lk. 2:46). Paul fasts for three days; then the *metanoia*, his conversion, is definitive and he has himself baptized (Acts 9:9).[30] The third day, then, is the decisive day, the crucial turning-point or definitive conclusion of a matter.[31]

That is not all. The third day as the critical, decisive day is used without any chronological qualification at no less than thirty places in the Old Testament simply to indicate the day of important salvific events or of sudden, overwhelming calamity.[32] 'On the third day' Joseph releases his brothers from prison (Gen. 42:18); after three days of active waiting, it is on the third that God makes a covenant with his people (Ex. 19:11, 16); on the third day David hears the news of the death of Saul and Jonathan (2 Sam. 1:2); on the third day is accomplished the division of the kingdom into Israel and Judah (1 Kings 12:12); on the third day King Hezekiah gives thanks to God after an illness he had supposed to be mortal (2 Kings 20:5, 8); Esther begins her noble task of delivering Israel on the third day (Esther 5:1); on the third day Yahweh gives new life to his people and raises them up (Hos. 6:2–3).

After three days of more or less troublesome, burdensome, deadly experiences the third day brings deliverance: that is the basic implication of the 'three day' motif. What in the end it is all about is the certitude of the decisive V-day. The third day is not, therefore, a focal point of time but of salvation. That Jesus rises from the dead on the third day is meant in primitive Christianity to signify: God leaves his righteous one in dire extremity for three days only; after the painful shock of his death comes the conclusive news: the Lord is alive. Not death but God has the final word; that is, 'the third day' belongs to God. The resurrection of Christ does indeed introduce a radically new turn of events into the temporal existence of the disciples; it ushers in the day of salvation. An expression in temporal terms – the third day – is most suited to the purpose of suggesting all this. Through God's saving action in Jesus and at a given moment in our history – 'the third day' – and in the renewal, for the disciples, of their existence the eschatological deliverance has indeed been brought in,[33] but 'after three days', that is, after the peak of Jesus' need and utmost distress: his Passion and death. As contrasted with the V-day, 'three days' indicates brevity, the 'short term'. Despite the hopeless position of Abraham, faced with the duty of sacrificing Isaac, despite the lost and desperate situation of Jonah (in the belly of the whale), despite the total humiliation and defeat of the people of Israel, each time, 'on the third day', God brings salvation and deliverance out of dire calamity. But Isaac was not sacrificed, Jonah did not perish, and the nation was in due time delivered. Only Jesus 'was not spared' (see Rom. 8:32); yet his deliverance came: albeit after his death: 'the third day he rose again'.

Thus Hosea 6:2–3 is an apt, though by no means the sole, Scriptural reference: 'After two days he will revive us; on the third day he will raise us up, that we may live before him'; on the morning of 'the third day' the making of the covenant is celebrated and renewed (Hosea 6: 2–3). Against this Scriptural reference it may of course be objected that nowhere in any reflection of the New Testament does it appear that the third day is understood in the sense of the Hosean passage (which in fact is nowhere cited).

What do serve to confirm all this, however, are the targums and midrashes which speak of the universal 'resurrection on the third day' and actually include a reference to Hosea 6:2–3. Now these Jewish commentaries are of course of very recent date (2nd and 3rd centuries AD); but like the rabbinics they derive from much older traditions.[34] That these Jewish commentaries on Scripture, which – as opposed to the use of Scripture in the New Testament – are not arguing from what has already been realized in Jesus Christ yet do interpret past events (as recorded in Scripture) with the coming general 'resurrection on the third day' in prospect,[35] shows that we are not to regard the New Testament's exposition of Scripture as providing evidence *pour les besoins de la cause*. In virtue of its own experiences, read in the light of its sacred books, Israel has itself succeeded in encompassing the idea of the 'resurrection on the third day' in the future. So, likewise on the basis of their own specific experiences, that is, as bound up with the Jesus event, the first Christians came to be convinced of a resurrection on the third day – but then as personally already realized in Jesus of Nazareth.

Thus although the idea of 'resurrection on the third day' is also a Jewish one, and by the time of Jesus perhaps already a familiar one, what is new about the Christian view is that this third day is not going to happen 'three days after the world's end' (thus the targums), but has already been brought about in Jesus, the Christ. Furthermore, the combination of the third day with 'according to the Scriptures' implies that Jesus' resurrection is not only a fundamental and unique salvific event, but is being expressly proclaimed as the definitive and eschatological saving fact. If the Jewish idea of the 'resurrection on the third day' was already something familiar in Jesus' time, the Christian affirmation 'the third day rose again' signifies that this third day, the V-day, has already been realized, at any rate in Jesus Christ, as the basis for our eschatological resurrection. The resurrection of Jesus is then hailed as the great turning-point of all times, in accordance with God's plan of salvation ('according to the Scriptures').

*Conclusion*: When Christians affirm that Jesus was raised from the dead on the third day, they are affirming that God's rule has assumed the aspect of the crucified-and-risen One, Jesus of Nazareth.

There is more to it than that. In some logia, the core of which many critics and exegetes attribute to Jesus, Jesus himself speaks of the 'third day' or V-day, at any rate without relating this explicitly to his death or to a possible resurrection; that is, he speaks of a dire situation or event ('three days'), but at the same time expressing his sense that – somehow – 'the third day' is in God's hand. He mentions this in connection with the sly fox, Herod (Lk. 13:31–33), with the demolition and rebuilding of the Temple (Mk. 14:58; Mt. 26:61). Many scholars, following Bultmann,[36] now consider Mk. 14:58 in particular to be an authentic Jesus-saying. In every tribulation Jesus is aware, according to these logia, that he can rely upon God's 'third day'. The authenticity of this logion would also explain, in my view, why the 'third day' motif does not occur in the gospels' Easter, tomb and appearance traditions and appears only in the complexes of tradition dealing with Jesus' predictions, as well as in the credal formulae. Noteworthy, therefore, is John's comment on the Temple-logion: 'When therefore he was raised from the dead, his disciples remembered that he had said this; and they believed the Scripture and the word which Jesus had spoken' (Jn. 2:22). The third day is a Scriptural term and a Jesus term. If the term 'the third day' (not attached specifically to death or resurrection) was used by Jesus, this was an expression of Jesus' self-understanding: an awareness of having to go through the deepest distress, but in the firm conviction of knowing that he was in God's mighty hand, come what may. For whatever might happen, the 'third day' is in God's power. Then Jesus knew he was the suffering prophet who, one way or another, would be vindicated by God. Jesus reckoned on his life's being renewed – before, in or after his death:[37] with a 'consummation on the third day' (Lk. 13:32). God will leave his own in distress for no longer than 'three days'; in other words, the suffering of the righteous, their failure, may be severe; but the God of salvation will have the last word. Compared with that, the suffering is short-lived: a mere 'three days', and so transient. The 'three day' motif fits perfectly, therefore, into the tradition-complex of the 'suffering righteous one'. Mark 8:31 speaks of 'suffering many things' and of 'after three days rising again'; here Mark has taken over a kerygmatic formula; for 'after three days' ('three days later') does not tally with his 'chronology' of the Passion narrative. The model here is Ps. 34:19: '*Pollai hai thlipseis tôn dikaiôn*': many are the afflictions of the righteous (see also 4 Macc. 18:15); but they are rescued from them by the living God: 'but the Lord delivers him out of them all' (Ps. 34:19; see Wis. 2:13–20 and 5:1–7). Perhaps as Jesus became aware of his suffering and violent death, this was a catalyst for his self-understanding.[38]

For all these reasons the seemingly banal expression 'on the third day (rose again)' is charged with immense salvific implications. It tells us nothing about a chronological dating of the resurrection *qua* event (as, for instance, three days after Good Friday) or even of the 'Easter appearances'; but it suggests everything about the eschatological, definitive, saving action of God *vis-à-vis* the crucified Jesus; his resurrection is an eschatological reality that breaks through the apocalyptic concept of resurrection. The third day, the day of salvation, is already a living reality and unfolds within our history, which continues on its accustomed way (with no apocalyptic transformation of the temporal course of events), a radical newness and a future charged with hope.

# Resurrection, exaltation, the sending of the Spirit. The Parousia

The resurrection and exaltation or empowering of Jesus are central New Testament concepts. But what is the relation between resurrection and exaltation?

Here we take up again a question from Part Two (Section Three, chapter 3, §4): the ambiguity of the term 'Easter experience'. It became clear from the summary already presented of late Jewish ideas about life after death that no uniform expectations on this matter existed in Jesus' time. Belief in life after death as a divine reward for the righteous was general, it is true; but on the other hand a premature and above all violent death was often interpreted as a punishment on God's part. 'Eternal life' could moreover be expressed in divergent categories: hence resurrection was only one among several possibilities.

In many primitive Christian traditions Jesus' resurrection is directly associated with his exaltation and being invested by God with power. The exaltation of Jesus has a hermeneutical function *vis-à-vis* the resurrection, which it serves essentially to differentiate from, say, the resurrection occurring in the story of Jairus, of Elijah and so forth. In many primitive traditions Jesus' resurrection is his investiture as Lord and Christ, as 'Son of God in power' (Rom. 1:4). It goes along with his 'being seated at the right hand of God' (Rom. 8:34; Col. 3:1) or 'having received authority', subsequently elucidated by reference to Ps. 110:1 and Ps. 2:7. The resurrection is Jesus' solemn enthronement as the coming son of man (although that is never explicitly stated), as Lord, Messiah, Son of God: that is the gist of a very early Christian interpretation. It is evident from a large number of traditions and complexes of tradition: in Mt. 28:18b–20 it is clearly the One manifested as risen who is already the exalted One, to whom all power is given. Other passages refer to resurrection, while implying exaltation in so doing (1 Thess. 1:9–10; Rom. 14:9; 1 Cor. 15:3–8). Sometimes exaltation is mentioned just by itself, but then with the resurrection taken as understood or entailed (Mt. 28:18b; Eph. 4:8–10; Phil. 2:6–11;

1 Tim. 3:16; Hebr. 1:3, 5; 2:9; 5:5; 12:2); an intrinsic result of the resurrection is Jesus' sitting at God's right hand or his regency over the world (Rom. 8:34; Col. 3:1). There are also passages where resurrection and exaltation are mentioned side by side, yet even then as two facets of a single reality.[39] Broadly speaking – and making provisional allowance for other positions in the New Testament – we may say that in the New Testament affirmation, resurrection, exaltation and 'being invested with power' denote one and the same undivided reality, where resurrection is the *terminus a quo* and exaltation the *terminus ad quem* of the selfsame event.[40]

It does strike one, however, that whereas the resurrection terminology is fairly constant in the New Testament, ways of talking about the exaltation shift and fluctuate. Not only Luke but Mark as well has ideas of his own about this; and we find a variety of set formulae which do not conform to the New Testament classical model.

We mentioned earlier on that a characteristic of Luke's own interpretation is the distinction he makes between resurrection and exaltation, between Easter and ascension. The distinction is an important one principally because Luke connects the sending of the Spirit, not with the risen Jesus but quite expressly with his exaltation alone (Acts 1:2, 9–10; see Lk. 24:50–53). Here for the first time the resurrection is illustrated from Ps. 16:10 (arising from the world of the dead), whereas Ps. 110:1 is shifted on so that it functions as a proof-text for the exaltation 'to God's right hand' (Acts 2:31 and 2:33–35). Thus according to Luke it is only with the exaltation of Jesus that the Church's proclamation of repentance and salvation can begin (Acts 5:31b); for what is presupposed is the gift of the Spirit, which only the exalted One is able to impart (Acts 2:33). For Luke the exaltation brings to an end the period of Jesus' earthly life and marks the beginning of the Church, thanks to the sending of the Spirit (see Acts 2:33; 5:31; 3:20). The 'short time' between exaltation (ascension) and the outpouring of the Spirit (Whitsun) is filled by an expectation, waiting for the Spirit (Lk 24:49; Acts 1:8; 1:4). Even when Luke mentions resurrection and exaltation in the same breath (Acts 2:32–33; 5:30–31), for him there is a distinction between them; and just as he invariably stresses the fact that it was God who raised Jesus, he likewise puts the emphasis on God's saving action in exalting Jesus (Lk. 9:51; Acts 1:2, 11, 22).[41] The risen Jesus promises the Spirit (Lk. 24:49; Acts 1:5), but only the exalted Jesus can actually impart it (Acts 2:33). We might say that, for Luke, Jesus and God are intrinsically linked together by the Spirit. His is a *Pneuma* Christology, not adoptionist but 'subordinationist': as the one filled with God's Spirit he is Son of God – from birth (Lk. 1:32, 35), at his baptism (3:22), at his exaltation (Acts 2:33). In Jesus Christ we encounter directly not the Father but the gift of the Spirit, which the Father imparts to Jesus.

John on the other hand sees the Father-Son relationship as a direct one, while likewise associating the gift of the Spirit – the Paraclete – with Jesus' exaltation: 'the Counsellor, the Holy Spirit, whom the Father will send in my name' (Jn. 14:26), 'and I will pray the Father and he will give you another Counsellor, to be with you for ever, even the Spirit . . .' (Jn. 14:16–17). In late Jewish tradition too the messiah can indeed pray for the Spirit, but not give it himself.[42] The Spirit can only come when Jesus has been glorified (Jn. 7:39); 'It is to your advantage that I go away, for if I do not go away, the Counsellor will not come to you; but if I go, I will send him to you' (16:7). As with Luke, sending of the Spirit and exaltation belong together here. John, who more often tends to display affinities with Luke where tradition is concerned, has at any rate a very minimal diachronic scheme: there is a brief period between 'resurrection' and 'going to the Father' (Jn. 20:17: here Jesus, after his resurrection, is still on his way to the Father); yet when he appears 'that same day' to the disciples he is already exalted; for he then imparts the Holy Spirit (Jn. 20:19–23; the scheme of the ascension into heaven is plainly operative here).

Certain ancient hymns to Christ (Phil. 2:6–11 and 1 Tim. 3:16) appear to pass over the resurrection, acknowledging only the exaltation. 'He who, though he was [*hyparchōn*=being and abiding] in the form of God did not count equality with God a thing to be grasped, but emptied himself, taking the form of a servant, being born in the likeness of men. And being found in human form he humbled himself and became obedient unto death, even death on a cross. Therefore God has highly exalted him and bestowed on him the name which is above every name, that at the name of Jesus every knee should bow, in heaven and on earth and under the earth, and every tongue confess that Jesus Christ is Lord, to the glory of God the Father' (Phil. 2:6–11). Obviously, what we have here is the *katabasis-anabasis* scheme: a descent of the pre-existent Christ, a terrestrial condition of 'abasement' and, finally, post-existence.[43] In this pericope, a liturgical hymn to Christ, the resurrection is not mentioned. It features the model of abasement (Phil. 2:6–8) and exaltation (2:9–11). Death is relativized *a priori* by the idea of pre-existence; death is indeed the lowest point of the descent, but this point of deadlock is already absorbed by the pre-existence; passing through death, Jesus then returns 'from the inside of it', as it were, to his former elevated condition. In this model, resurrection is simply not required. Thus too in 1 Tim. 3:16: 'Great indeed, we confess, is the mystery of our religion: He was manifested in the flesh, vindicated in the Spirit, seen by angels, preached among the nations, believed on in the world, taken up in glory' (1 Tim. 3:16). The opposites in this hymn are obvious enough: flesh-spirit; angels-nations; world-glory, while the whole is again enveloped by the polarity: flesh-glory. The 'low and high' scheme structures the verse both internally and as a unit; and the verse is itself embraced in its totality by the tension of 'mystery' and 'revelation'. The mystery hidden for ages in God is revealed in the flesh of the man Jesus, who died; but in the celestial action-at-law between God and World Jesus is vindicated: 'justified', so that the one indicted emerges from this trial gloriously (*dikaioun*: see also Lk. 7:29; Rom. 3:4, which cites Ps. 50:6 in the Septuagintal translation: *nikân*, that is, emerging triumphant, as victor in the battle).[44] Yet this model, 'existing in the flesh' and 'existing in heaven', is used (albeit in cited passages) in the same letters that also present the resurrection model (Phil. 3:10–11, 21; 2 Tim. 2:8); but these letters are themselves not as old as the quotations in them.

The fact that mention is made here of pre-existence would not, in the first instance, seem to indicate that the passages in question are of any great age. Even so, they cannot be described as secondary formulations of belief, in the sense of being inferred or derived from the resurrection model. For, setting aside the idea of pre-existence, the 'high-low-high' model is a very old one in its own right; and the sapiential model of pre-existence is itself very old. This particular scheme, 'humiliation-exaltation', is classical in Old Testament and Judaistic literature.[45] The allusions to Deutero-Isaianic traditions in that hymn to Christ are obvious: that every knee should bow and every tongue confess recalls Isa. 45:23; furthermore, in the Aquila version of Isa. 52:13 we find not *pais* (*puer*, child) but *doulos* (and in the Septuagint *douleuonta*) in the same context: Isa. 53:11. He 'emptied himself' is a vague allusion to the Greek Isa. 49:4;[46] 'he humbled himself' (Phil. 2:8) reminds us of Isa. 53:8, while 'was made in the likeness of men' refers to Isa. 53:3; and then lastly, 'unto death' (Phil. 2:8b) takes up Isa. 53:8 and Isa. 53:12. Again, Isa. 49:7 speaks of 'the Lord' (*Kyrios*) and of 'my Name' (Isa. 45:4). If L. Cerfaux saw a very close affinity of this hymn to Christ (Phil. 2:6–11) with the 'Greek Isaiah', J. Sanders was able to make even more significant the similarities with the Hebrew text, above all with Isa. 53.[47] 'He emptied himself' (Phil. 2:7) – nowhere to be found in the Greek Isaiah – is an exact rendering of the Hebrew (Isa. 53:12), so that the hymn to Christ was inspired by Isa. 52:13 – 53:12 (see the *Ebed* servant term in Isa. 52:13).

Yet it should not be forgotten that these Old Testament ideas had undergone changes in the thought of late Judaism, which provides the immediate background for the earliest Christian reflection. In the hymn (Phil. 2:6–8) the Old Testament and primitive Christian idea of the exemplary 'suffering and exalted righteous one' is applied solely to the pre-existent Christ. It would also seem likely that the Deutero-Isaianic exalted and suffering righteous one in pre-Christian Judaism was already identified with the apocalyptic son of man;[48] at all events, the exalted 'suffering and righteous one' acquires the juridical function of the son of man.[49]

But whatever the contribution of apocalyptic Jewish ideas may have been, the crucial factor is what was remembered from Jesus' life here on earth: 'Whoever exalts himself shall be humbled', and the least are to be the greatest in God's kingdom.[50] The suffering righteous man knows that he can depend on God, even if he sees no concrete result (Mk. 14:25 parallels). This scheme of humiliation and exaltation does not of itself and at first sight have to take cognizance of the resurrection (or to deny it).[51] In the oldest strata of the early Christian son of man tradition there is no explicit reference to resurrection, but there is reference to Jesus' being exalted to the presence of God and to his coming Parousia. This is a Jewish theme which occurs in a number of different variants, whether with the category of the resurrection or with that of the assumption of the soul into heaven either immediately after death or after a stay in Sheol, or with the category of 'eternal life' with God. So when we hear tell of Jesus' exalted dwelling with God, without any mention of the resurrection at all (as in the Q tradition), there is no ground whatever for simply postulating the resurrection; after all, the same thing can be envisaged in terms of other categories. A broad late Jewish tradition finds it easy to envisage the exaltation of the suffering righteous one to God's presence without the idea of resurrection; and both Q and the aforementioned hymns to Christ are clearly in line with this broad late Jewish tradition. In other words, once reflection about life after death had assumed a concrete form in Israel, resurrection (Dan. 12:1–3) was one possible solution, but by no means the only one (see above). Although silence regarding the resurrection is no proof that people do not actually have it in mind, we must not presuppose the resurrection idea *per se*. Indeed it is noticeable that Pss. 2 and 110 (exaltation minus the resurrection idea) were applied to Christ earlier than Ps. 16 (which talks about 'deliverance' from the

realm of the dead, specifically just by Luke: Acts 2:25–28; 13:33–37).
In the four credal strands analysed earlier on, the *maranatha* Christology,
the Christology of the exaltation of the prophetic-sapiential, Solomonic
son of David (or less accurately: the *theios anèr* Christology), as well as
the Wisdom Christologies, become intelligible within a tradition which
envisages exaltation without resurrection – traditions which moreover
have no need at all of an empty tomb or appearances in order nevertheless to acclaim the crucified One as the royal Lord, exalted to be with
God. What one can say is that both with the Jews and with the Jewish
Christians the general belief in life after death (for the righteous)
began more and more to assume the form of belief in physical resurrection (a trend quite evident in late Jewish literature); and this gradual
ascendancy of the resurrection idea over other ways of conceiving of
the actual form of an 'assumption into heaven' took place also in
Christian circles during the first few generations. But with or without
resurrection, in no way does the affirmation of belief in Jesus' being
taken up into heaven depend on a possible empty tomb or on appearances; both these last presuppose belief in Jesus' assumption into
heaven after his death, whether after a sojourn in the realm of the dead
or 'from off the cross'. In a Jewish context all the models were to hand;
and in any case each of them entailed the notion of Jesus' actually and
truly 'living with God'. It was only when people began to see that the
deliverance of Jesus was also a conquest of death itself, and in every
local Christian congregation began to reflect on the salvific implication
of Jesus' death that the idea of resurrection forced itself upon all the
early Christian communities everywhere as the best way of articulating
the fact of Jesus' being 'alive to God'.

This course of events explains too why there were fluctuations in the
attempt to define more precisely the relation between resurrection and
exaltation. Not until the resurrection idea had come to be canonical,
as it were, for all the local Christian churches, could differing interpretations appear regarding the relation between resurrection and
exaltation, both of which had initially expressed what was 'in substance' the same idea (of 'life with God'). When the resurrection idea
was imported and made explicit in congregations that at first had
spoken only of a 'taking up (exaltation) into heaven' – or vice versa –
that could indeed raise problems: Were the two things identical or
distinct? The evidence of Scripture, here based on Ps. 110 (exaltation)
and there on Ps. 16:10 (a rescue out of Sheol), would have had a lot to
do with this.

If Th. J. Weeden's study of Mark – on this point, at any rate – is correct (and his arguments seem persuasive enough to me),[52] even Mark was still linking the exaltation, not with the resurrection but with the Parousia (Mk. 8:38; 9:2–8; 10:37; 13:26; 14:62, to be understood in the light of 13:14–27; 14:62 and 13:26) (see above under *Maranatha* Christology). For Mark the resurrection provides grounds for expecting the Parousia, for the confirmation of Jesus' status as the (soon to come) son of man. But the inauguration of Jesus' immediate lordship is not coincidental with the resurrection (or, as in Luke, with the ascent to heaven) but with the Parousia (Mk. 13:26 and 14:62b).[53] Thus in this ancient Christology the resurrection is seen, not primarily as God's correcting the scandal of the cross but as the ground of the approaching Parousia, as ushering in the eschatological universal arising from the dead and as the event confirming Jesus' message of the coming rule of God;[54] the present (risen Jesus) *is* already the coming of the future (the Parousia; God's rule). Thus the coming of God's rule gradually comes to be interpreted in Christological terms. The risen One or (for some others) the exalted One is also the One soon to come: the *eschaton* is about to happen. That was the original Easter experience. Resurrection and Parousia, although distinct, were closely adjoining. Nor in the Q community do the Twelve form the foundation of the Church, but with Jesus they are the eschatological judges of the latter days already dawning (Mt. 19:28=Lk. 22:28–30).[55] The Easter experience was initially an experience of Jesus as the One about to come; it was assuring men of the imminent Parousia, confirming God's coming rule, the substance of Jesus' preaching. So resurrection and Parousia were originally not antithetical; the dawning of God's rule was at first bound up with the Parousia.[56] To this early, primitive Christian notion Mark's gospel continues to testify in a later period. That the resurrection as itself exaltation came to be central (which is how I would resolve the renowned argument between F. Hahn and Ph. Vielhauer), is a sign of a later (though still very early) stage, in which the 'quasi-identity' between resurrection and Parousia had been loosened up and (in quarters where Jesus' assumption into heaven had always been interpreted as resurrection) Ps. 110:1 was used to bring together resurrection and exaltation.[57] But originally the resurrection was the start of a succession of eschatological events that were to have their climax in the Parousia. On this view God will justify his way of doing things not with the resurrection but at the Parousia, which is to vindicate Jesus and his disciples.

So then the assumption into heaven or resurrection was widely regarded in early Christian circles as the prior condition for the approaching deliverance of believers, thanks to the redemptive activity of the coming Christ.[58] Redemption was felt to be an eschatological event that would be to the benefit of anyone confessing Jesus as the Christ living with God or as risen but 'soon to come'. Within this, there were still two strands or schools of thought: during this brief period of waiting for the coming Christ the Q community saw itself as permeated by the pneumatic activity of the risen and already exalted Lord; Mark on the other hand would have it that in the interim God's eschatological, pneumatic gifts were what gave its life to the Christian Church – in the absence, however, of the risen but not as yet exalted Lord. Finally, the 'forty-day' period of the risen but not as yet ascended or exalted Lord is the concluding episode of Jesus' earthly life. With Jesus' exaltation there occurs more or less immediately the sending of the Spirit by the One exalted, the beginning of the Church's life. Luke is therefore reacting against a way of interpreting resurrection and exaltation solely as providing the basis for an imminent Parousia,[59] which is nevertheless not discounted (Acts 1:11). Without excluding a futurist eschatology, Luke stresses the 'realized' one, the redeemed life of Christians within the Church. What is both eschatological and future in Mk. 10:26 is by him changed into something present here and now (Lk. 18:26); Lk. 9:24 simply cancels out Mk. 13:20. For Luke salvation lies in membership of the Church.

Paul for his part has a quite different way of understanding this. His idea of Christian salvation embraces a fundamental tension between present and future, whatever the intrinsic connection between them might be. At Corinth Paul was confronted with Christians who considered they had already been resurrected, thanks to their mystical union with Christ.[60] 'In a spirit of enthusiasm' they had resolved the tension between present and future in favour of the present, whence Paul takes them to be denying their as yet pending bodily resurrection still to come (1 Cor. 15:12). For him, that meant salvation itself was at stake: if the futurity of salvation be denied (by its being 'dissolved' in a presential experience), the very essence of it has been misunderstood. These Christians at Corinth, then, were not denying the resurrection of Jesus but were equating their present condition, so to speak, with that of Jesus; so that for them the 'final good' of their coming resurrection was quite superfluous. How does Paul put his case here? First he refers them to the creed with its *memoria Jesu*, that is, the things remembered about Jesus that were reported and passed on in the local congregations

– and then not just 'memories' but recollections, forming and inform-
ing the existence of the Church, of what Jesus' offer to men had actually
been. But the thrust of his argument goes beyond that: 'If Christ has not
been raised, your faith is futile and you are still in your sins' (1 Cor.
15:17). The argument runs: if for Christians there is no bodily resurrection to come, then neither did Jesus Christ rise from the dead (the
very substance of their creed); but then their faith has nothing to support it; and so these Christians, instead of being 'already risen', are still
in their sins, and for believers who have already died no hope can
remain (1 Cor. 15:18). Thus if the resurrection has come about already
in those who believe, all has been in vain. Paul is reacting against a one-
sided 'presential eschatology' that would turn salvation into a fleeting,
enthusiastic illusion. For Paul, Jesus' resurrection is the ground of the
'latter-day' or ultimate resurrection of believers (at this point he does
not have in mind a universal resurrection); between these there is a
*tagma*, a before and after (1 Cor. 15:23). For Paul (as opposed to the
Deutero-Pauline writings) the resurrection of believers is in no way a
thing to be anticipated: death is 'the last enemy' (1 Cor. 15:28; see 15:
24–28). Thus there is a distinction between on the one hand Jesus'
resurrection and sending of the Spirit and, on the other, the future
salvation of believers, which is vested in the eschatological resurrection. The Pauline letters proper, despite their explicit thematizing of
Jesus' resurrection (in contrast to the Q traditions and the Marcan
traditions), stand none the less within the same kind of purely eschatological perspective as these last. We 'were saved in hope' (Rom. 8:24).
It is fair to say, therefore, that Paul too does not acknowledge an 'interim regime'. Jesus as Lord does of course command the power of
final salvation, the *Pneuma*, who is to renew us bodily (1 Cor. 15:29–34).
In this way Paul succeeds in inverting the final apocalyptic expectations:
eschatology is grounded in Christology and not (as for instance is
argued by G. Fohrer[61]) vice versa. Paul reckons here first of all with the
early occurrence of the Parousia and bodily resurrection (1 Cor.
15:51).[62] As in the gospel of Mark, the concluding advice to Christians
is to 'be steadfast' (1 Cor. 15:58). The time-span between Jesus' resurrection and his Parousia (the bodily resurrection of believers) is in
Paul's view occupied by the worldwide mission to the Gentiles; for not
until the full number of Gentiles, as determined by God, has been 'made
up' will Israel's definitive deliverance come with the Parousia (Rom.
11:25–27; see 13:11, as opposed to 1 Thess. 5:2). In saying this Paul is
turning the traditional Jewish idea of things upside down; for according to that, Israel's eschatological redemption and world ascendancy

will see all nations making their way to Zion; then and only then will Israel's deliverance assume a universal significance. According to Paul, Israel will be saved only when all nations acknowledge the Christ; for him, evidently, the Christian mission to Jewry is in the meantime a vain enterprise. That is why he gives urgent priority, for Israel's sake, to the mission among the Gentiles, the Christian 'world mission' as the great event falling between resurrection and Parousia.

It is imperative, therefore, to find some answer to the question already raised earlier on: was Jesus, who proclaimed the imminent arrival of God's rule, mistaken? People often try to skirt around the problem by arguing that Jesus did not speak of the definitive salvation to be imparted by God as being 'near at hand' in a temporal sense, but of an ontological 'nearness' of the God of salvation. Yet this distinction is nowhere to be found in the New Testament. Jesus did in fact speak of the rapidly approaching Parousia of *God*, possibly in terms of the coming son of man. The temporal-cum-linear aspect is something we cannot eliminate from his message; and it would be false hermeneusis to claim that the temporal aspect is a historically variable 'way of putting it', at the same time advancing the 'ontological proximity' as what was meant to be the real heart of the message. That, moreover, would neutralize one of the things which induced the first Christians to proclaim Jesus as the risen One. We have seen that Jesus announced the imminent arrival of salvation from God and that this confidence of his did not wane when he came face to face with death; also that – not comprehending it, perhaps, but as a heartfelt conviction – he integrated this death into his proffer of salvation, the point and purpose of his whole life. So when he died, the disciples were faced with the issue: this man was wrong – the kingdom of God has not come; or else, he was right. But in that case the Parousia of God which he proclaimed has indeed occurred, that is, in the resurrection of Jesus; and then this resurrection becomes the ground of the coming Parousia of Jesus – son of man. The Christian conviction that in his *Abba* experience Jesus was not mistaken was one of the elements, therefore, inducing the Christians to identify God's coming rule, as proclaimed by Jesus, with the crucified-and-risen One in person: in him the kingdom of God has come. That was the fundamental intuition to which the first Christians were giving expression when they proclaimed that Jesus had risen from the dead. The kingdom of God which he proclaimed had come, just as he had said: in the One crucified and risen. (This will be further explored in Part Four.) It has to be said, of course, that initially the

Christians interpreted Jesus' resurrection as the start of his immediately subsequent Parousia; this generation would live to see the great event. They were living already 'at the end of the times' (1 Pet. 1:20; 2 Pet. 3:3; Jude 18; also 2 Tim. 3:1; Mk. 9:1). The earliest phase of the Q community is the sole witness to a period in which there is no indication at all, as yet, that Jesus' Parousia might be 'delayed'. All other traditions, as we know them, are already confronted with the new situation: the non-arrival of Jesus' glorious appearing (Mk. 13:32; Mt. 24:36; Mk. 13:30; Mt. 10:23; Mt. 25:1-13; Lk. 12:38; Mt. 24:25-41; Lk. 12:42-46). Although this 'tarrying' did result in a crisis of a sort, fundamentally what Jesus' resurrection supplied was the irrevocable guarantee of the coming Parousia; so that for the Christians nothing essential was altered by this circumstance; it simply made plainer and more obvious the tension between 'already' and 'not yet', between a presential and a futurist eschatology.

*Conclusion.* The New Testament hermeneusis of Jesus' resurrection – under the stimulus of what had taken place with Jesus and, after his death, had befallen the disciples – shattered the apocalyptic view of resurrection. Although history goes on much as before, God's definitive saving action has been accomplished in Jesus of Nazareth, the crucified-and-risen One. Jesus, who had announced the imminent rule of God, had not, despite the contradiction of his rejection and death, been wrong. With him, who during his life had identified himself with God's cause, the coming rule of God, God has now identified himself by raising him from the dead; Jesus Christ is himself that rule of God. Unintentionally, therefore, though Jesus preached not himself but the rule and lordship of God, it was 'himself' that he had proclaimed: the Proclaimer is the One proclaimed.

This has ushered in the 'eschatological times', whose characteristic mark is experience of the eschatological gift: God's Spirit, referred to (with the likely exception of the Marcan gospel) as the 'Spirit of Jesus' (Acts 2:33; 10:44ff; 19:5-6; Rom. 8:9; Phil. 1:19; Gal. 4:6). And Jesus' Spirit is the Spirit of God himself (1 Cor. 2:12; see 1 Cor. 3:16; 6:11; 7:40; 12:3). The eschatological period was reckoned to start with the sending of the Spirit (Joel 3:1ff; Ezek. 36 – 37) and go hand in hand with the forgiveness of sins and the new law, written in the hearts of the faithful (Jer. 31:31ff). And: 'Where the Spirit of the Lord is, there is freedom' (2 Cor. 3:17). People had encountered this freedom in the very life of the earthly Jesus; it was a human freedom, rooted in a dedicated commitment to God's absolute freedom. The 'liberty of the children of God' (Rom. 8:21) was the distinctive thing, then, about early Christianity, which had disengaged itself from the Law. The basic creed or article of faith maintained by the first Christians was: Jesus of Nazareth is the Christ, that is, the one totally filled with God's eschatological Spirit. He is the latter-day and definitive revelation of God and in being so is at the same time the paradigm of an 'eschatological humanity'.

# From a 'theology of Jesus' to a Christology

Chapter 1

# Theology 'to the power of two'

The gospels relate how, starting from his *Abba* experience, as contrasted with the course of our human suffering, Jesus both announced and offered to people, in word and action, 'salvation from God' and a real future. Confronted with the historical rejection of Jesus' message and eventually of his person, the first Christians were moved by the renewal of their own lives after the death of their master, and recalling the fellowship they had enjoyed with him during his life on earth, to confess this Jesus as the crucified-and-risen One, in whom they had experience of definitive and final salvation; in him God himself has brought about redemption, salvation and liberation. Using the religious and cultural key concepts already available to them, and in virtue of this salvific function, they called Jesus the Christ, Son of God, their Lord.

With all this we are still within the 'theology' of Jesus of Nazareth: that is to say, within the area of reflection upon what Jesus himself had to say about the coming rule of God as salvation, liberation and redemption for man; that is, within the discourse of Jesus concerning God, which was clothed in flesh and blood by his own public ministry, mode of living and death: 'For the kingdom of God does not consist in talk but in power' (1 Cor. 4:20). Living contact with this person who proclaimed the kingdom of God was experienced as God-given salvation. This yielded, as the outcome of a primarily theological, faith-motivated reflection, the credal affirmation: God himself, the God of salvation-history, has acted decisively in Jesus for the salvation of men: 'It is God who through Jesus reconciled us to himself' (2 Cor. 5:18). In that sense all the honorific titles of Jesus, including 'Son of God', are in

J.E.C.—S

the first instance functional, are elements within salvation-history – even in the late sapiential Johannine gospel with its pre-existence idea. As a matter of fact, in the line of traditions within which John stands, the Torah too was pre-existent, with God prior to all creation, although no Jew would have regarded the pre-existent Torah of the Wisdom tradition as a sort of 'second divine person' – not even John in respect to his 'pre-existent logos', which he identifies with Jesus of Nazareth and calls Son rather than 'logos'.

However, logos, Torah, even *pneuma*, as hypostatized entities, were really abstract concepts, *theologoumena*. Of course, they are a living, concrete reality as an expression, for example, of God's will (the Torah); after all, God is himself Torah. But the Mosaic Law, which flourished among the Jewish people and on which the Jews had a lien, as it were, in their sacred books, in other words which had tabernacled among the Jews, is not however the 'transcendent God'. Jesus' period abounded in 'intermediaries' between God and man just because God was thought of as lifted up, transcendent and therefore unapproachable, and his immanence could only be envisaged by means of an intermediary link of all sorts of celestial beings – angels and actually higher up still: hypostatized entities such as 'law', 'logos', 'wisdom'. These served to articulate the transcendent God's turning towards the world (of men), while people still trembled before his un-approachable, 'secluded' transcendence. In no other way could people throughout the East at that time conceive of the real immanence of the transcendent God – least of all in more 'sophisticated' circles. The result was that one's relationship to God was essentially determined by the attitude one adopted to, for instance, the pre-existent Torah, the pre-existent sabbath, the pre-existent latter-day prophet; that is to say, from one's attitude to mundane, visible things – 'indwelt' by these pre-existent, exemplary namesakes or identified with them – one's relation-ship to God was decided.

This is why in Judaism prophetic figures were identified with wisdom and the logos, or with archangels. Thus Moses and Jacob were identified with the pre-existent mediator of creation. Enoch and the son of man are also identified with a pre-existent wisdom (1 Enoch 41:9; 42:1–3; 48:7; 51:3). We mentioned earlier on that this is a sapiential extension of the Deuteronomic tradition of the 'angel' and the 'messen-ger': 'do not rebel against him, for he will not pardon your trans-gression; for My Name is in him' (Ex. 23:21). Wisdom, taking up her abode among men, comes to be identified, now with the Law or the sabbath, now with Jacob or with the latter-day prophet: the attitude one adopts to these intermediaries decides the issue of salvation as proffered by God (cf. Mk. 8:38 and Lk. 10:6). These identifications serve to legitimate their message and do so by way of a claim to 'unique transcendence', that is, as mediating the transcendent God. It is from this identification with pre-existent beings that their authority, their sole authority to mediate in the matter of salvation between God and man, takes its warrant. This is true from the viewpoint of both an early and a late, more advanced sapiential scheme.

The thing to bear in mind, then, is that this scheme of ideas (which in late Judaism served to underwrite the divine authority of an earthly being) is applied by Christians to a quite concrete historical person, Jesus of Nazareth. That is something radically new and in a religious context unprecedented – at any rate if we leave aside the ascription of divine status to the Roman emperors (associated not with any religious interest but with 'reasons of state'). Intertestamentary literature, before and after Jesus, does admittedly speak of the pre-existent Enoch or Ezra, who after their life on earth are taken up to God and exalted. They are called son of man, son of God and Lord of the universe; and all the peculiar names of God are assigned to them. But though once historical beings in a remote and hazy past, they were now in fact abstract *theologoumena*. On the one hand this only goes to show that in the first instance the honorific titles given to Jesus in the New Testament are understood to be functional, in a context of salvation-history; on the other hand, however, that in the historical life of Jesus certain things had become apparent – an obvious authority deriving from God – which invited people to apply this already existing model of understanding and interpretation – which, *qua* model, implies nothing more or less than that we are faced here with an earthly manifestation in and through which a personal relationship to God is decided.

Since the idea of using these existing models is to throw light on a function, more precisely, the crucial, salvific function, of Jesus – salvation in Jesus imparted by God – we cannot in the end dodge the question: Who then is this Jesus in himself, if all this is supposed to have happened in and through him 'as from God'? Particularly among Graeco-Jewish Christians, and more so later on among Christians with a background of pagan Hellenism (which enquires not only about what has happened in somebody but what and who that person really is), the question of *ousia* or 'essential being', in the spirit in which one may speak of 'identification of the person' in an ontological sense, was bound to arise. Indeed the Aramaic and Graeco-Jewish Christians, within their own ontology, were least of all able to avoid this question.

For them this became a profounder question: What does the individual person, Jesus, who talks in this way about God, his *Abba*, mean for God himself? A primary insight into the initial, peculiar nature of the 'God of Jesus', the *Abba*, raises the question of the 'Jesus of God', that is, how does this Jesus pertain to God himself: '*my* son', '*my* servant', 'my holy one' and so forth. This 'possessive relationship' of God towards Jesus – corroborated here, there and everywhere in the New Testament – was sooner or later bound to lead on to more pregnant questions, to a second stage of reflection. Who is this Jesus, who to this degree is the 'exclusive possession' of God? It was above all their belief in the crucified-and-risen One – evidencing for the first Christians this exclusive title and possession on God's part – that compelled a further reflection. For Jesus was not an 'organ of salvation', in the sense in which Moses with his staff had struck water from the dry rock. That definitive salvation from God had been encountered in the man Jesus, and not in some celestial being or other, for Jews would quite certainly point to God's act of election, 'gratis and for nothing'; it expresses God's pure pleasure. Jesus for his part – such was their express impression – had not falsified or betrayed this election of his, but in love and loyalty to Yahweh had lived and moved among people, caring for them, until he was broken by it. From a religious standpoint and within the framework of a particular pattern of thought, that says everything. Yet in its attempts to determine the moment at which God's choice was concretely and effectively accomplished in the man Jesus we see within the New Testament some very subtle and delicate changes, pointing to a persisting process of reflection, all the time refining, correcting and deepening the first one. It turns out that identification of the person can be intensified without ever coming up against a conclusive 'delimitation'. This further reflection does not actually reveal any completely new insights; yet neither is it meant simply as a 'meta-language', that is, as a way of discoursing about 'faith-motivated discourse about Jesus', in a linguistic-analytical sense. It does not have to do (however necessary the analysis of it may be) with talk about the very act of identifying (the act of faith as such), but about the self identified: a deepening, in faith, of understanding of a Jesus already interpreted and identified. And then all that has already been said about Jesus of Nazareth can be reformulated from another standpoint, namely, from that of God's saving initiative. Of course, there are no new and different roads to revelation provided here – a sort of private access – that would let us know just how God sees Jesus. It is only via the 'theology of Jesus of Nazareth', in his words and his actions, that we are able to find out what God himself is disclosing about this Jesus. But this second concern is orientated differently from the first. We might fairly refer – using a term, at any rate, from modern linguistic analysis – to 'second-order assertions', without thereby implying 'second-class' affirmations of belief. This distinction is an important one, and more fundamental than what is usually referred to as 'the hierarchy of truths' in matters of faith, or rather, it gives us an objective criterion (outside all personal, subjective, theological predilections) for obtaining a real hierarchy in the whole of the revelation of God in Jesus Christ. If we should affirm our belief that in Jesus God saves human beings ('first-order assertion'), how then are we to understand Jesus himself, in whom God's definitive saving action has become a reality ('second-order assertion')? One is already a Christian in entertaining the former conviction, even though at the level of 'second-order' affirmations a whole range of nicer distinctions and definitions may exist. A primary and fundamental Christian orthodoxy is to be gauged from 'first-order' asseverations above all. The history of Christological dogmas, therefore, would seem to lie in the plane of 'second-order' affirmations, albeit with the purpose of, and real concern for, bearing out the 'first-order' affirmations. In a second phase of reflection the quest must be for a fitting answer to the question of how it is possible that whoever is brought in contact with Jesus is confronted with God's definitive saving activity. In the answer to this, reflection on our part has a major role to play. In other words 'Christology' is more relative than a 'theology' of Jesus, although by no means unimportant, if only for the proper understanding of that 'theology'. Whereas in his message Jesus is not concerned about his own identity – that would appear to lie in his identifying himself with God's cause as the cause of man, and with the salvation and wholeness of man as the concern of God – Christology concentrates on precisely Jesus' own identity. In the first instance this took place within the New Testament, where God's rule assumed the very aspect of Jesus and became identified with the claim that Jesus the Christ 'was Lord'. An explicit Christology is meant to give yet greater depth to that primary, faith-orientated interpretation of Jesus: Jesus, implicated as subject and person in his message and praxis, becomes in that respect 'thematized'. When person and message are essentially conjoined in Jesus, as has appeared from the analysis, what then does this signify for the actual person of Jesus? It is a legitimate question.

It was out of this enquiry, already under way in the New Testament, that the early Church was eventually to give birth to the Nicene dogma of Jesus' 'co-essential being' with the Father, with later on, as a counter-balance to that in Chalcedon, the nature of Jesus as co-essential with the humanity of us all: 'one and the same person' – Jesus Christ – is 'true God' and 'true man', not in a hybrid blending, but *asunchutôs* and *atreptôs*, that is, without merging and without loss of peculiar sub-stance and significance, and at the same time *adiairetôs* and *achôristôs*, that is, indissolubly one. The historical growth of this dogma is familiar enough (or can be read up in many places elsewhere). Within the design of this book I am only concerned to explain how and why people wanted to reach a more exact identification of the person of Jesus, comment on the inevitability of these questions and also on the limits and hazards of every theoretical answer to them; then on the difficulties which such ancient attempts at precision have raised for people of a different cultural background, and the new task with which all this faces us now. To avoid keeping the immediately following line of argument wholly abstract, here is in advance a short summary of a few fundamental data from this developing process of interpretation, which resulted in the Christological dogma of Chalcedon, the chief aim being to show that while it was inevitable that the questions should be raised, there was nothing necessary about the conceptual terms or limits within which an answer was looked for.

Chapter 2

# Growing reflection within the traditions of the New Testament

It is impossible to establish a chronological thread in this reflection as it grew within early Christianity. We have pointed out time and again in this study that a 'secondary' element in one particular early Christian community is not *per se* a late creation of that community, but may have been a very old element in another one, only later, after reciprocal contact between the various local church traditions, being integrated into the Jesus tradition of other churches, who were able to recognize and acknowledge their Jesus in it. (Some more exact chronological pin-pointing is of course possible.) In view of the already ample analysis given in Part Two and Part Three, we can keep the following survey brief.

Nowhere in the course of examining the New Testament have we detected Jesus calling himself the Son of God; what we have pointed to is Jesus' extraordinary – and in the context of the history of religion very striking – way of addressing God as *Abba*, and to the fact that this Father experience of his was the source and soul of his message and conduct. There, however, the focus lay not in Jesus himself but in the Father. The question certainly does present itself as to who Jesus himself is within this intimate relationship to God the Father. Even though dodging this question were of small consequence, it is illogical or is blinking the facts to do so – unless the prior historical data have long ago been thrust aside.

We can still trace in the New Testament the vestiges of the diverse solutions to this question provided by early Christianity.

(a) In line with the Deuteronomistic messenger idea a very old tradition calls Jesus 'the Son', as the one who perfectly observes the commandments of God the Father and faithfully passes on to his own people the Fatherly precepts. He is 'the Son' as God's eschatological messenger.

(b) In the oldest Jesus tradition the title 'Jesus the son of David' is unknown: the Q tradition, in which the 'messiah' title does not occur, actually seems to controvert the Davidic-messianic status of Jesus. Again the pre-Marcan tradition (which lies behind Mk. 12:35–37) rejects the dynastic-Davidic messianism for Jesus with an appeal to Ps. 110. But in Greek-speaking, Jewish Christian local churches the title of messianic son of David is assigned to Jesus – and that, as appears from Mark, in the Jewish, prophetic-sapiential sense of 'miracle-worker' and exorcist. In the pre-Pauline tradition, worked over by Paul, the earthly Jesus is a son of David, a Jewish man; but this points rather to the descent into humiliation of the pre-existent Son of God, who only through the resurrection becomes Son of God in power, and Lord. For Luke on the other hand (gospel and Acts) the son of David is the Son of God. Out of this grows the idea that in his life on earth Jesus is sent exclusively to Israel: as messianic son of David, fulfiller of Israel's promises, he is sent for the regathering together of Israel.[1] Even in the Qumrân literature the title 'son of God' was applied to the messianic son of David on the basis of 2 Sam. 7:14 and Ps. 2.[2] But this title is surmounted in the resurrection, whereby Jesus is simply 'the Son of God' for all men.

(c) From our examination of the *Maranatha* Christology it became clear that the risen Jesus was identified with the one who at the close of the Age would come to judge the world. Here Jesus is the universal Lord of the eschatological future. In this it is most likely that two distinct strands are to be detected. Although themselves already the eschatological Church (so that the last days are held to have started already), some local congregations regard Jesus as the risen son of man, destined to be the world's judge but not as yet solemnly invested with these full eschatological powers; for others the risen Jesus is at the same time the exalted Son of Man, operative here and now in his eschatological (Q) community. In both cases, however, not only the risen but the earthly Jesus too is called 'Son of God' (for a diversity of reasons).

(d) In Luke's so-called missionary sermons, spoken by Peter and Paul, the two earlier interpretations of Jesus are conjoined in a single view: during his earthly life Jesus was the messianic son of David, sent to Israel, but with his resurrection it is made publicly obvious that God has predestined him to be universal Christ, Lord and Son of God (in particular Acts 2:36; 5:30–31; and the pre-Pauline layers of Rom. 1:3–4).[3] Here the disclosure of Jesus' 'sonship' is associated with his resurrection, to which is applied (see Acts 4:25–26; 13:33) the 'you are my son' of the royal psalms (Ps. 2:7 and 2 Sam. 7:14). 'Resurrection' here has the richly full sense of: risen from the dead, exalted to be with God, filled with the Spirit and sender of the Spirit, and soon to come in glory. In other words, Davidic messianism acquires from the resurrection a quite new significance: the One crucified and risen is the 'Christ' (messiah). And so the messianic sonship of Jesus comes to be bound up with his death and resurrection.

(e) In the baptismal traditions, incorporated in the gospels into the Christology of each of the four evangelists, God's proclamation about Jesus being his Son is conspicuously linked with his baptism by John (Mk. 1:10–11; Mt. 3:16–17; Lk. 3:21–22; Jn. 1:32): 'Thou art my beloved Son; with thee I am well pleased.' The divine voice from heaven which says this comes in fact from the Bible as the word of God, for example, in Ps. 2:7 and Isa. 42:1. The Spirit conferred on Jesus is the eschatological gift. Psalm 2:7, used elsewhere to denote Jesus' being exalted at his resurrection (Acts 13:33), is here employed to make it clear how even at his baptism Jesus 'is the Son' and is filled with God's Spirit (God is with him, he is with God). From the moment of his baptism Jesus is the Son, the 'messiah', 'servant of God', the 'eschatological prophet' who is to be listened to (Deut. 18:15). In other words, this is the truth of God regarding Jesus: it is how God sees him and will have him. Although the main emphasis in all this falls on his appointment as eschatological prophet, the messianic and royal anointing is very much present too. To put it another way: from his baptism Jesus is the one filled, eschatologically, with God's Spirit: God is with him, just as in Isa. 63 – 64 the coming of God, after the crossing of the Red Sea, is described as the heavens being opened and God's Spirit descending therefrom. In Jesus, after his coming out of the waters of the Jordan, this is now fulfilled. So Jesus' being 'fulfilled' with the Spirit brings to pass Isa. 11:2; 42:1-2; 61:1; Ps. 2:7: he it is who completes all the promises to Israel. That is why no passage of Scripture cited in these baptismal traditions can be accurately located; they are allusions to fundamental promises in the Old Testament, in which bits and pieces from recognizable texts are 'adjusted' and synthesized on a basis of what men and women had experienced of the life event of Jesus – replies to the Church's questions: How could Jesus let himself be baptized? Was he a sinner, then? And is he therefore subordinate to John the Baptist? A 'Son of God' Christology lies behind this interpretative viewpoint. The whole public ministry of the earthly Jesus is explained in these baptismal traditions in terms of his fully possessing the eschatological gift of the Spirit. But the traditions here do not in any way suggest that Jesus' baptism should be regarded as his calling; on the contrary, the models employed and the style point rather to an 'interpretative vision':[4] Jesus' baptism is interpreted as the start of the saving activity of God in his 'beloved Son', who, being filled with the Spirit, has been sent to Israel: by getting himself baptized Jesus accepts that God is at work in John the Baptist; and at the same time he himself performs (according to the interpretation already mentioned) his first prophetic act. Thus the vision functions as an element of a faith-motivated interpretation of a historical process; in the account given and word spoken is articulated what had been transmitted in the living tradition concerning the historical effect of what took place at the Jordan. Whoever comes in contact with this baptized Jesus is faced with salvation or rejection. The New Testament has no interest in what went on in the mind of Jesus at the time, psychologically speaking; it interprets Jesus' later history with this event as its point of departure. Here again, 'Son of God' is a functional appellation in a context of salvation-history: Jesus' being sent for the salvation of the people of God, that is, he is 'God's Son' for Israel.

(f) The 'today' of Ps. 2:7: 'You are my son, today I have begotten you', has already been applied to the resurrection and afterwards to

Jesus' baptism by John; lastly, it is applied to the 'today' of Jesus' conception or birth. At first sight it is not so evident that Ps. 2:7 has anything to do with the Matthean or Lucan account of the Virgin Birth; yet this verse of the psalm – starting perhaps from its prior application to what took place at the river Jordan – forms the background to the tradition of the Virgin Birth as the 'today' of God's appointment of Jesus as 'his Son' for Israel.

In the first place Mt. 1:18–20 and Lk. 1:26–38 are the only two places in the New Testament referring to a 'virgin birth'. Recent exegetical studies have made it clear that elsewhere, in other early Christian communities, this was unknown (or actually refuted) and there is no question of 'historical information' here, for instance, information acquired via Mary's private family tradition, as is often said. What we have here is a theological reflection, not a supply of new informative data, as the New Testament texts themselves show quite clearly.[5] Moreover all the roots of the already existing tradition common to Matthew and Luke point to a Graeco-Jewish milieu as its source; it is an early, and yet relatively recent, tradition in early Christianity, indeed one that was and remained confined to certain local congregations. It turns out that the tradition on which Luke and Matthew draw did not originally make any direct mention of an explicitly 'fatherless' birth but emphasized the (soteriological) fact that the human existence of Jesus as the one who brings salvation is entirely the work of the Spirit of God, not just from the moment of his resurrection or his baptism by John: Jesus' conception or birth must also be understood with a Godward reference as a being filled by the Spirit. Gradually and to an increasing extent this point was further elaborated in a biological-material sense. In the apocryphal proto-gospel of James (second century)[6] a midwife confirms, on empirical, palpable grounds, that Mary remained a virgin (one reason among others why this document was 'apocryphal'). But though less inclined to stress the historical and material aspect in his infancy narrative, it is clear from the plain import of the grammatical phrase, in Greek *gennaô ek* (the man being regarded in antiquity as the sole generative principle), that Matthew actually has the Holy Spirit operating by analogy with the principle of male generation. Luke on the other hand avoids any analogy with this masculine principle; he speaks not, like Matthew, of 'begetting' (*to gennèthen*, in the first aorist passive: that is, 'what is begotten by . . .'), but of *to gennômenon* (in the present passive), that is, 'what is born', namely, 'the child' (so that everything is viewed from the mother's standpoint; the man's role is 'disregarded'). Thus Matthew is at an already advanced stage of an originally still reserved tradition which in the apocryphal writings issues in an empirically ascertainable biological virginity or fatherless birth. The original tradition is more reticent in this respect; and from the fact that in both Matthew and Luke there is talk of an angel making known the Virgin Birth it is sufficiently obvious (in view of this Scriptural stylistic method; cf. the appearing of an angel in the tomb at Jerusalem) that the aim of this tradition is not to impart any empirically apprehensible truth or secret information about the family history, but a truth of revelation. It is dealing with a Christological interpretation, imparted by God, concerning Jesus: this Jesus is holy and Son of God from the very first moment of his human existence: 'because he is truly born of Mary by the power of God's Spirit', 'therefore (*dio kai*) he will be called holy, the Son of God' (Lk. 1:35). It is not the case, however, that Luke needs the Greek postulate of a virgin birth so as to be able to find grounds for the sonship of Jesus 'from his conception';[7] form criticism has shown that belief in Jesus' Virgin Birth in certain local churches is for Luke and Matthew an already given fact. But where does this Christian tradition come from? It is clear from Matthew that the appeal to (the Greek) Isa. 7:14 (where in connection with the Emmanuel prophecy there may be explicit reference to 'a virgin', in contrast to the Hebrew text) is a 'reflection-citation', that is, a Scriptural proof applied in retrospect to an already available Christian tradition of a Virgin Birth of Jesus. In Lk. 1:26–33, however, the passage from Isaiah is completely interwoven with the story – in such a way that the narrative has been built on Isa. 7:14 (clear enough in 1:26–31).

The problem is, however, that the 'birth from a virgin' in Isa. 7:14 is in no way associated with the 'Spirit of God', whereas that is the whole point of the interpretation in the gospel. But if the link between Jesus' birth and the Holy Spirit is a divine revelation (an angelic message), then it follows that the 'today' of Ps. 2:7, by virtue of the resurrection first linked up with the sonship of Jesus and his being filled with the Holy Spirit (Acts 13:33), then because of this same connection between 'sonship' and 'power of the Holy Spirit' linked up with John's baptism of Jesus, is finally applied in a further faith-inspired reflection to Jesus' conception and birth as a human being (Matthew and Luke).[8] What was first, as a result of the Easter experience, associated with Jesus' resurrection – his being the Son and being completely filled with the Spirit – is on subsequent reflection shifted to Jesus' baptism by John, and on further reflection affirmed as the reality of the emergence and actual constitution of his being as man. That is to say: Jesus owes his human existence *in toto*, his very being as man, to the Holy Spirit (Lk. 1:35): this is the Christological tenor of the whole infancy gospel, although with Luke and still more expressly with Matthew it assumes a historical form – one that is indeed concrete, albeit not empirically ascertainable, but to be approached and evaluated only within a context of faith – in a Virgin Birth. The connection already perceived between Jesus Christ and his being filled with the Spirit (resurrection; baptism in the Jordan), always conjoined with Ps. 2:7, is eventually applied to a specific early Christian tradition which, starting from the (Greek) late Jewish interpretation of Isa. 7:14, already spoke of the Virgin Birth of the messiah Jesus.[9]

Even here we have to do with a functional sonship, one that is a factor of salvation-history, not yet with a 'Christology of being (substance)', in the Greek sense; rather with a 'being (existence)' Christology in a Jewish sense: the end and purpose of Jesus' entire life from start to finish is to proffer salvation on God's behalf; this indeed is the ground of *proskynèsis*, that is, latreutic adoration of, or cultic worship directed to, Jesus (Mt. 2:11).[10]

(g) Again, Jesus' sonship is related with his heavenly pre-existence, at any rate as conceived of in a high sapiential sense, which – compared with the Nicene dogma – even in the Johannine gospel belongs more to a low Christology,[11] implying a hypostasis in a late Jewish sense. Here the accent is on the Son's 'dwelling among us' (Jn. 1:14; 1 Jn. 4:2–3; 2 Jn. 7). Such pre-existence points to God's counsel or transcendent ages-old wisdom concerning the historical role of Jesus as mediator between God and man. Thus this Wisdom Christology, with a late sapiential ambience, is already to be found in very old, pre-Pauline hymns; it does not represent at all a later phase of theological reflection in the New Testament – yet another reason for seeing the late Jewish sapiential model of interpretation in it. John, despite the living unity between the Son and the Father, who is greater than the one he has sent (Jn. 14:28; 17), stresses the obedient subjection of the Son to the Father: Jesus has obtained everything from the Father for the salvation of many (Jn. 3:35; 5:12–23; see 6:40; 10:38; 14:10, 12; cf. 1 Jn. 2:22–25; 5:12; 2 Jn. 9). Paul for his part, being opposed both to the *theios anèr* Christology of a *deus praesens* clothed in human form and also to Wisdom Christologies of a speculative kind, nevertheless accepts a pre-existence which in my view entails even more plainly than does the Johannine gospel an explicit incarnation Christology (Gal. 4:4; Rom. 8:3; 1 Cor. 2:7 and 8:6; Phil. 2:6ff; which in no way contradicts the Son's 'subjection' to the Father, 1 Cor. 15:23–28).

\*

Thus three major divergent – and at a pre-canonical stage even competitive – interpretations of Jesus' sonship come together in the New Testament; and in so doing – in the process of integration within the gospels – these three theological reflections undergo an inward change of their original meaning: (1) Jesus is 'Son of God' as 'messiah ben David', as son of David (his mission to Israel) and as 'son of Abraham' (his mission to all peoples) (Matthean genealogy); (2) Jesus is in a special way Son of God by virtue of the resurrection – by virtue of the sending of the Spirit at his baptism by John – and of the gift of the Spirit in his conception and birth; (3) Jesus is Son of God in a pre-existent way. All these Christological assertions are functional, in a context of salvation-history; but from a Jewish Christian standpoint this entails defining the being of Jesus, more especially because the appellation 'Son', 'Christ', 'Lord' is each time given by God (his voice in Scripture, particularly Ps. 2:7) (or by his angel or messenger); in other words it is an interpretation of Jesus seen from God's standpoint, that is, one prompted by a response of faith towards God: Jesus is to be regarded thus within God's plan of salvation. It is the Jewish ontology that speaks here, in which the name is given and the being determined by God himself. Within this ontology the alternative question whether Jesus is the Son because he has been sent by God for the people's salvation, or whether he has been sent because he is the Son, is nonsensical. There is no problem, therefore, about saying: 'God sent his Son in order to . . .' (Gal. 4:4–5; Rom. 8:3–4; Jn. 3:17; 1 Jn. 4:9). Both a late sapiential Christology and an explicit incarnation Christology in the New Testament assume a 'salvation-history' ontology; not a Greek but a Jewish ontology of being. Thus Paul is able to take Jesus' sonship for granted and at the same time describe Jesus as 'Son of God in power' (Rom. 1:3–4) only with and after his resurrection: a Jewish being-ontology allows of this by definition; the 'son' concept is a dynamic one, cognizant of history and of salvation-history. After much and varied reflection in the light of the apostles' Easter experience the whole life's work, and eventually Jesus' very existence as a man, comes to be understood as an existence and activity (coming) 'from God'. Jesus is from God and for his fellow-men, he is God's gift to all people: this is the New Testament's final view, and as it were definition, of Jesus of Nazareth. And again: salvation in Jesus coming from God (the title I had at first intended to give this book – but which requires the book to be read, perhaps, before it can itself be understood). Human pro-existence (or shared humanity), but proceeding from God and to the praise of God. To that end Jesus is filled with

God's Spirit and his very existence as a man is wholly the work of God's Spirit. Whatever new name (or names) we can and may think up for Jesus, those two aspects will have to be in them, if we still want to be talking about the Jesus of the gospels, and thus, having regard to the conspicuous fidelity of the gospels to the norm and criterion of the earthly Jesus, about the historical Jesus of Nazareth – him and none other.

# Reflection in the early Church of the post-New Testament period: Christological dogma

Because Christians were constantly being obliged to explain and defend their Christian profession and their own identity to others who attacked what they were saying: first Aramaic and Greek Jews, then pagans, finally fellow-Christians who deviated from what had meanwhile come to be recognized within Christian circles as a universal 'apostolic faith', they found themselves being forced again and again to draw finer and yet finer, more closely defined distinctions – a vital and inevitable rule with each and every conviction concerning life! But besides this apologetic motive, compelling them to renewed reflection, there is (though connected with the first) another stimulus prompting them to do it: their own belief gave them reason to ponder (although this never happened apart from the action and reaction of the environment in which they were living; and that, before very long, was the Gentile environment, with a world of thought and notions of God all its own).

For a time the Christians had to find and draw their lines of demarcation, that is, formulate more sharply their own profession of belief concerning Christ in face of objections from their co-religionists, the Jews. In the New Testament what in particular emerges against the common Jewish background is the definition of the confession of Christ, while in the meantime there had appeared 'church', 'the Church'; and the Jewish Christian 'eschatological brotherhood' had separated off from the synagogue. In the post-New Testament period this led to a new and spirited controversy with the Jews and after that more especially with the pagans. Jews attacked both the Christology and ecclesiology of the Christians: on the one hand the Christian affirmation of the divinity of a human being, which they took as casting an aspersion upon Jewish monotheism, on the other the Christian contention that the Church is 'the true Israel'.

Originally Jews themselves, the last thing the Christians intended with their creed was to support a 'ditheism', a kind of 'two gods scheme': Yahweh and the Lord Jesus. And so these Jewish Christians were faced with the question of how their strict Jewish monotheism could be reconciled with their Christian *proskynèsis*, that is, with their adoration of Jesus as the Lord, Christ and Son, a veneration that must be described as quite certainly latreutic, meaning: a celebration in acknowledgement of Jesus' divinity. This Christian belief and, above all, this growing Christian praxis indeed gave them, as true-bred and truly religious Jews, cause to think; and furthermore they were forced by the objections of their non-Christian compatriots to do so. On the other hand the objections voiced by the Gentiles (with all their elitist, Greek philosophical tradition behind them) were sharper and more penetrating and, especially for Christians coming from the Greek 'pagan world', dangerously alluring. Origen later on showed with razor-edged sharpness how a Greek like Celsus would argue against Christianity: 'If these people [the Christians] know no other God than the One, then they might have a valid argument . . . But in fact they offer public worship [divine worship] to this man who recently appeared, and that is not consistent with their own monotheism.'[12] In other words the veneration of Christ is opposed to the Christian confession of the one true God; that is exposed as an inherent contradiction. Either the Christians are guilty of offering divine worship to a man – of whom everyone knows that he was still living among us not so very long ago – and in that case they forsake what was even for Greeks at that time the only intelligible form of transcendent monotheism; or else theory and practice are in total contradiction for the Christians. These Greeks who had long before abandoned the *theios anèr* theology as a myth and were emphasizing God's transcendence and unapproachable majesty, saw in the Christ creed something that impugned God's inaccessible exaltedness. These cutting objections[13] at first compelled the Christians to adopt all sorts of complicated defensive constructions. Either they would proceed in their theory to attenuate the divinity of Jesus – acknowledged in their public prayer – and this gave rise to what has been known historically as 'dynamic monarchianism', that is to say, there is but one *Archè*, a universal 'Cause', namely, God (monotheism in terms of *archè*); Jesus on the other hand is a person equipped with the special *dunamis* or power of this God (Theodotus of Byzantium; Paul of Samosata, who consequently reacted against the practice of praying *to* Jesus instead of to God the Father, *per Jesum Christum*). Or else they were obliged to deny the distinction between Jesus and the Father; and this occasioned what is known as 'modalist monarchianism', that is, Jesus as the son of God is an alternative mode of being of the Father himself (Noëtus). This latter view went down better with the Christians, who saw in it a theological justification for their devotion to Christ. So these two Christological strands resulted from the conflict between Christian belief and Greek thinking, a conflict that worked itself out partly within the ways of thinking of Greeks who were also Christians. Celsus' objection led Origen to accept two distinct existences in God – Father and Son – both none the less one through unanimity of will. To the objection that this is a conception of God unworthy of God's majesty – Origen is himself Greek and feels in his very bones the force of these objections – he tries to preserve God's transcendence by saying that of course the (Greek) *Deus immutabilis*, the unchanging God, is not affected by the psychological experiences in Jesus' humanity – in soul or body.[14] In itself this is a purely apologetic argument, only intelligible within the range of questions available and of the objections actually proposed. Subsequently, however, this questioning, within the frame of which the answer had its function, became detached in the further course of its development; and Origen's reply became an autonomous 'Christological affirmation', which took on a life of its own and from which yet further conclusions were deduced.

There is more to it than that. As intellectuals these Greeks, understandably enough, wanted to make the Christian affirmation of belief intelligible to Greek minds. They thought they could find a shared basis for dialogue between Christians and Greeks in a belief in the one true God. Just as Israel's God, Yahweh, was the common basis on which Jews and Jewish Christians were able to carry on their controversy, so now the philosophical notion of God of the Greeks was held to be the common ground for discussion between Christians and (Hellenistic) pagans. The Pythagoreans, Plato, Aristotle and the Stoics were allies of Christianity, of that monotheism which the Christians too professed. Intense criticism has been levelled – especially in our own day – at this patristic attempt to express the original Christian inspiration within the terms of a 'Greek intellectual horizon'. But – admitting the Christian correction made to that – this critique of Greek patristics is ill founded and hardly to be described as scientific. To set the biblical way of thinking over against the Greek one is in some circles fashionable, more or less a 'must'; but structuralist depth-analyses of the Hebrew and Greek languages have exposed many of the allegedly typical and fundamental differences as ideology, a prejudice without responsible argumentation. No one is going to deny that it would be a hard job to bring the Old Testament's prophetic idea of God into line with the Greeks' dispassionate *Deus immutabilis*, who creates the world as a *fait accompli*, with no further concern and personal love for men and women: the well-nigh mathematical point, alpha and omega of all that exists, turned in self-sufficiently upon himself (God as *noèsis noèseôs*). With all this, the Greek vision of life has been reduced to a pure abstraction, quite alien to a living Hellenism.

The Greek ideal of *paideia* or upbringing was to attain to true humanity and freedom. *Paideia* signifies 'lore of release'.[15] For the Greeks it was truth, not success, that was crucial to true humanity. We are therefore bound to look for criteria, for norm and paradigm, by which humanity and freedom may be gauged. In the search for these Hellenism exhibits two emphases: the Dionysian and the Apollonian. The older Greek religious sensibility (and poetry) struggle to bridge the chasm between 'God' and man: 'Seek not to become as Zeus' (Pindar), for God and man are 'of different stock', stood in contrast to what later on in his Prometheus-myth Aeschylos was to call the *suggeneia*, the affinity between God and man, what for the Stoics was to become: 'We are of God's lineage' (Aratos; see Acts 17:28). In other words, Hellenism swung between two ideals; 'Man is the measure of all things' (Protagoras), and: 'God is the measure of all things' (Plato). On the one hand recognizing the limits of man's mode of being, not requiring too much of man; on the other, not ascribing any jealousy to God, man may exceed himself. These two currents in Greek life and thought came together: man may become similar in form to God; this formal similarity is true humanity, liberation and freedom.

In looking for a normative idea or image for the nurture of man, however, the Greeks had difficulty, to begin with, in finding the primary notion that was to show man the way, in our mundane world of experience *per se*: it was the domain of fleeting occurrences (*panta rhei*). The *phusis* (nature) or the being (*ousia*) of things must lie elsewhere. Greek (and especially Platonic) thought found this model in 'the world of the divine', a transcendent reality on which, in its deepest, essential being, this sublunary world has been modelled. The goal and purpose of the nurture or release of the human mind, therefore, was *mimèsis*, the imitation of this normative, divine paradigm. In that way we may come to participate in the divine, and man is set free from all that is unworthy of him: liberated freedom is the goal of all *paideia*. Coming to resemble God is the humanizing process: it is truly to become man. The tarnished 'image of God' is restored through man's conformity to the example of the divine paradigm. 'The imitation of

God' ('deification' they called it later on) is therefore an ethical duty intended to realize both a right relationship between one human being and others (*dikaiosune* or righteousness) and to God (*eusebèia* or piety). Thus the process of divinizing man, of making him as God, is a humanizing task: the free human being in a justly ordered *polis* or state-community, a mirroring of the divine world.

This release or deliverance of human kind entails a hard struggle, in which man cannot free himself. He is a prisoner in the cave. 'Philosophers' sent by God are necessary: that is, 'wise educators' or 'political liberators' who, advantaged by their knowledge of the primal image, are able to point people the right way to true humanity or resemblance to God. Therefore deliverance (salvation) means following the directions and incentives to be found in nature, in history, in the example of wise men. It is obtained through 'revelation' of true knowledge. That is why Hellenism has often been accused of being a one-sided intellectualism – and in a certain sense justly so. Yet our interpretation is often at fault here; for the Greek *nous* (faculty of intelligence) embraces intellect and will – which is why the Roman Cicero invariably translates *nous* as *ratio et voluntas*.[16] Greek knowledge is *aretè*, best quality, thoroughness, theory and practice taken together. It has to do not with a neutral kind of knowing but with a knowledge within the process of progressive liberation achieved by *paideia*; as an effective means, true knowledge opens up *values* to which in his deepest being as *imago Dei* man directs his longing. Thus knowledge is a vivifying power. For the individual Greek 'remission', in the sense of pardon, is not so much an 'inward grace' but a direction indicator outside him in nature and history; by means of external stimuli the inner *imago Dei*, dulled and lulled by ignorance and sinfulness, is re-energized and roused so that it becomes itself again and can take advantage of its intrinsic power to act.

This magnificent notion of *paideia* was later taken up, but also radically altered, by the Stoics and in the 'popular philosophy' of Hellenism as a whole. For meanwhile Aristotle had produced a thorough critique of Platonic dualism and had set the 'ideas' in our experiential world. According to the Stoics the paradigm of true humanity is to be found in the world, in the divine Logos who interpenetrates the whole world of man and matter from within and resides in each one of us. Therefore the rule of God is realized in 'living according to nature', in accordance with reason, with the Logos. Nature and history are a single splendid 'epiphany' of the Logos, which is meant to nurture and train man into true humanity. In 'sages' and 'political saviours' this noble pedagogy of the Logos is condensed and climaxed. 'Being made natural', 'being made human' and being made godlike are one and the same thing. In that way the *imago Dei* in man is released and man becomes truly man, truly human. Notwithstanding his ideal of the 'imitation of God' the Greek never quite forgot his very oldest Homeric and Pindaric tradition: the *condition humaine*. It is a remarkable fact that the Roman Stoics render the Greek ideal of *paideia* (training to be godlike) simply and solely by the word *humanitas*.

The Greek fathers of the Church lived as Christians within this Greek system of culture. Just as at any earlier time Jews who had found final salvation in Jesus had expressed this within their own range of cultural and religious concepts, as God's salvific action in their Jewish history and the perspective, opened up by it, on eschatological saviour figures (latter-day prophet, messianic son of David, son of man), so in the patristic writings (from the Apostolic Fathers and Apologists onwards) the Greek Christians proceeded to express the salvation they had found in Jesus in the terminology of the Greek *paideia* notion: *paideia Christou* (1 Clem. 21:8). God's pedagogy of salvation via nature and history acquired its highest concentration in Jesus Christ: he is simultaneously paradigm and imitation, he is the 'primal image' in which the tarnished *imago Dei*, man, is at the same time restored.[17] The progressive pedagogic process of man's liberation, set going by the unfolding course of nature and history, comes to its climax in Jesus Christ: Jesus is the educator and teacher who brings the 'true knowledge', 'so that through our imitation of what he did and obedience to his sayings we might have fellowship with him', says Irenaeus (adv. Haer. V, 1:1). By this means man is snatched from death, from transitoriness and the power of sin and taken up into living fellowship with God. Thus there arose (especially among the Alexandrians and Cappadocians) the saying: If Christ be not God, he would be unable, in exchange for the human nature which he receives from us, to transform our fallen nature into a divine one; or: God became man so that man should be deified.[18] Thus patristics adopted the *paideia* notion of Hellenism, at the same time enriching it in a Christian perspective and christianizing it thanks to its personalist conception of God and therefore its emphasis on God's freedom.

Starting from the salvation brought by Jesus, patristic thought sets out to define more accurately the person of the one who brings it. Within this conjunctural range of questioning (for this idea see Part Four) the intention of the Councils of Nicea, Ephesus, Constantinople and Chalcedon was really to secure the basic 'first-order' confession of belief (decisive salvation in Jesus given by God) at the second stage of reflection – 'second-order' affirmations. In line with the Greek way of framing questions in terms of *ousia* and *phusis* they wanted to underwrite the saving pedagogy of God in Christ: on the one hand God and God alone is the only source of total salvation for man, of release and liberation; on the other, the locus where this release and salvation become reality is the historical human being within the eventualizing cosmos. So Jesus has to be simultaneously *idea-paradeigma* and *eikôn-mimèma*: both primal image and supreme realization of 'imitation' through his consistent living-out of the *imago Dei*: at one and the same time 'God' and 'man'. In short: 'one and the same' (Chalcedon) must stand wholly 'on God's side' (otherwise he is not a 'paradigm'); in Greek *ousia* terms this implies 'consubstantial with the Father', that is, 'true God'; on the other, he has to stand wholly 'on man's side' (as the supremely successful *eikôn* of humanity, in which he is a paradigm for us), that is, 'true man'. The Hellenistic identity between 'divinizing' and 'humanizing' was made concrete in the one person of Jesus Christ. There, transposed into Greek *ousia* terms, we have the fundamental inspiration of the whole New Testament: 'salvation in Jesus' but 'as coming from God', 'in behalf of God'. Within the not indispensable but historically given intellectual horizon supplied by the Greek *paideia* notion the gospels' message is here accurately conveyed. The New Testament 'first-order' affirmation (salvation in Jesus, imparted by God), which has always guided and governed Christological thinking through the centuries when the dogma was being formed, could only be reinforced (once the structure had emerged in which the ultimate question concerns the *ousia* of all that is: What ultimately is Jesus?) by a 'second-order' affirmation that would preserve its accuracy and meaning, embodied in the gospels; and would do as Chalcedon eventually did: by at the same time correcting the one-sided leanings of Nicea (one-sided through a failure to define what had nevertheless been presupposed).

It is a revelation to study what, amid all the highly philosophical subtleties of these Greek minds, which were also Christian, in the end governed their conciliar conclusion. Not indeed their philosophy, but the Church's tradition of 'devotion to Christ'. Actually, the heretical alternatives started from the same principle: salvation in the man Jesus given by God; after all, they too were believing Christians. Like 'the orthodox' they maintained – as Greeks of the middle Platonic school – the notion that God's transcendence is so exalted and 'wholly other' that his contact with the world of men – in creation and re-demption – could only come about through an 'intervening being', the demi-urge, or Logos of what takes place outside of God. In the end, under the pressure of professing their Christian faith, the 'orthodox' broke through this philosophy and dropped middle Platonism,[19] whereas their opponents clung to the logical consequences of it. That this ultimate repudiation by the Church of middle Platonism, this de-Hellenizing, was actually prompted by the demands of Christian belief can be shown with some precision. This does not mean that arguments from Scripture were a decisive factor; both parties found their cherished arguments in various places in Scripture, which lent itself to all sorts of manipulation. Their Scriptural proofs seem to have been purely illustrative.[20] The main argument, admittedly, was not the official liturgical form of devotion (which was to be decisive regarding the later dogma of the Holy Spirit), since in the period before Nicea the liturgy had addressed prayers only to the Father, albeit 'through Christ our Lord'; it was in fact the devotion to Christ as practised by many of the faithful, who had adopted the habit of 'praying to Jesus', and not just 'in and through Jesus' to the Father, as did the official liturgy. Because of this the bishops at Nicea were prepared to surrender the supposed logic of their middle Platonism; what is more, they were brought to see that middle Platonic views were philosophically un-tenable; and so, unlike Arius, they could not allow the logic of this philosophy, immanent in the system, to have the last word. This, at one time their own, philosophy they now rejected. Salvation in Jesus given by God, in the faithful practice of praying to Jesus, was inter-preted by them in the perspective of Jesus' true divinity. The fathers of the Council gave more weight to this devotional practice among Christians than to philosophical thinking; and because of that the Church was able to break with the middle Platonism which for two centuries had governed the thinking of the theologians.[21] However much the *ousia* philsophy may have provided the intellectual horizon within which Christological dogma was able to take definitive shape, we must not underestimate the crucial factor of the Christ mystique as a living reality of prayer among Christians (even though a recent practice prior to the Nicene dogma).[22] In Jesus God stands personally on our side of life, that after all is the gist of the Nicene dogma which affirms, does it not, the self-subsistent co-being of the human being, Jesus, with the Father. The Council of Chalcedon, intending thereby to stress the true humanity of Jesus, says at the same time that this human being is set wholly on God's side. Thus Nicea emphasizes 'salvation coming from God' (albeit made explicit in Jesus); Chalcedon on the other hand, salvation in Jesus (but as in behalf of God). So the focus of both declarations lies in the one undivided 'Jesus Christ'. The Graeco-Christian idea of God, then, comes to expression in the familiar patristic notion of God which breaks through the Hellenistic one and grafts it into the ancient Jewish Christian tradition: *Theos pros hèmas*, that is: He is a God of human beings, turned towards us in Jesus Christ. I have no trouble at all with any of this, seen from within a Greek intellectual outlook and the questions posed by it at that time: it is straight gospel; but . . . within a nexus of philosophical problems which is no longer in all respects entirely ours and indeed presents us nowadays with certain difficulties.

Although originally inspired by Greek patristics, Latin patristic theology elaborated the Greek Christological insights – release or redemption is the restoring of the 'image of God' through *paideia* – on the basis of an Afro-Roman horizon of experience and understanding. And in many respects this differed radically from the Greek experience of life and conception of history. For the Latins it had less to do with a noble view of history than with the actual conduct of individual and socio-political life. The Greek view of life, centred on orthopraxis governed by the norm of 'nature' or 'the Logos', stood as a model for the Roman design for living. The Roman Stoic thinkers (Cicero and Seneca) found in the Greek Stoa a thematizing of their own specifically Latin, Punic-Roman sense of justice. What for the Greeks was the *paideia* idea was for them the ordering of justice, integrated into the 'ordered cosmos', the expression of a 'divine justice'.[23] 'Divine justice' takes the place of the Greek *paideia* or divine salvific pedagogy. Thus their reflection is given a markedly anthropological emphasis. Instead of the Greek 'paradigm' and its illustrations come the categories of legal order, its abrogation and restoration; in other words, not an ontology of the cosmological-cum-pedagogical arrangement of 'primal image' and 'representation', but the ontological relation between a pure system of justice and its historical abrogation. Every breach of this order calls for a sanction and reparation so as to restore the relationships thus infringed. Even more than Greek Christianity, therefore, Latin patristics was to stress the contribution of man's freedom in the process of release. From the Latin viewpoint the honour of the human subject was at stake. A deliverance that descended on man from outside, as alms are tossed to a beggar, conflicts with the Roman sense of justice; the beggar must stand on his own feet. Later on Anselm was to give sharp expression to this Roman feeling for justice when he has the Son saying to the sinner: 'Take me, and save yourself.'[24] It is this insistence on justice, ensuring that the proper value of human freedom is not overridden by God's omnipotence, which Anselm sees as the highest expression of God's mercifulness, whereby of his goodness he not only gives salvation and forgiveness to man, but in and through this free gift declines to injure or reduce man's freedom and dignity: man will be allowed to save himself. This is the distinctive Latin view of the salvation which is 'of God'. To this end Jesus, our fellow-man, is given to us. In certain of its modern evaluations this Western doctrine of 'satisfaction' – thematized in particular by Anselm, but germinally much older – has been caricatured in such a way as to misinterpret the deepest intention of Anselm and of Western sensibilities. Essentially, Anselm's concern as a Christian is with the 'good name' of God; but in his satisfaction doctrine he is concerned primarily with that of man, the *dignitas humanitatis* (a slogan current in the emerging humanism of Anselm's time):[25] man does credit to God by putting himself to rights. 'Making satisfaction' means in this case restoring the order of things where it had been disrupted, namely, in man himself. Thus Anselm was able to envisage redemption as a judicial action in which God and man are involved. In contrast to Greek patristic thought with its metaphysical-cosmological, universal, divine pedagogy of salvation (in which, ultimately, 'grace is everything') the Latins put human subjectivity at the centre. Therefore redemption, deliverance, must be an event worthy of man and so authentic – not an overwhelming gesture of divine omnipotence. In this doctrine there is already apparent something of what in our field of vision today we see as the question of deliverance and emancipation, a problem in fact which could only arise within Western culture.

Just as in Greek patristics Jesus is identified in terms of both elements of redemption: 'paradigm' and *mimèma*, primal image and imitation, so too Latin patristics identifies the person of Jesus in terms of the salvation procured: *'totus in suis, totus in nostris'* (*Tomus ad Flavianum*, Leo the Great): only God can procure salvation; and he can only do it without violating man's freedom. In and through the freedom of man divine salvation is procured. Both are realized in Jesus as the 'God-man'. From the vantage-point of their juridical outlook, therefore, the Latins had no difficulty at all with the dogma of Chalcedon: it had preserved human freedom and dignity intact. From a Roman viewpoint God's honour and man's could never be in conflict. Anselm's doctrine of satisfaction is a doctrine about God's dealing with man in utmost mercy; it does not mean 'making satisfaction to God' to the very last penny. According to Anselm God only takes pleasure in the man who freely raises himself out of his tarnished state; for this, God provides the condition and the strength in Jesus Christ. So the satisfaction doctrine really introduces a new element into the whole story of man's liberation: the *dignitas humana* and its freedom, not in any way denied by Greek patristic theology but never given there the emphasis it acquired in the feeling for freedom peculiar to the West. Redemption, release, although the gratuitous gift of God, must take place within the grand history of man's self-liberation. Rooted in the peculiar experience and mental outlook of the Latin West, this has been its distinctive contribution to articulating the decisive and definitive salvation found in Jesus of Nazareth, the Christ.

For us patristic Christology (if we pass over an unjustifiable interpretation of Greek as well as Western Christology) only becomes really problematical the moment that the (in fact non-dogmatic) neo-Chalcedonian tradition begins to speak of an *anhypostasis*: that is, the man Jesus is no human person (something the dogma of Chalcedon had never said; that dogma speaks only of 'one person'), but solely a divine person with a 'human' and a 'divine nature'.[26] This at least intimated that something was lacking in Jesus of a completely authentic humanity. It made the 'consubstantiality' of Jesus, his 'being co-essential with' the Father (in an almost monophysite fashion) seem over-exposed, and his being truly man under-exposed. Jesus is thus lifted, as it were, above and beyond our humanity, and his 'shared humanness' – a man like us, except in the matter of sin – would seem to be ontologically constricted. This was bound to evoke a reaction.

The Middle Ages, to which only bits and pieces of these patristic conciliar documents were available, were in fact obliged to conduct all over again – in their own way – the struggle that had marked the whole development of patristic Christology, with more or less the same pitfalls and almost the same twofold result: on the one hand tending towards the *unio secundum hypostasin* (hypostatic union; one person, who is Logos, God and man), on the other towards the *homo assumptus* doctrine. They have – at any rate for the school of Bonaventura and of Thomas – this advantage over the neo-Chalcedonian position, that in their doctrine – a highly abstract affair, it is true – 'being-a-person' was narrowed to the single totality of the person, in other words, that someone cannot be simultaneously two persons. That is why Thomas

Aquinas was able to say that by very reason of his divine sonship within
the Trinity Jesus Christ is 'personally God (the Son)' as well as
'personally man'.[27] According to medieval ideas – though raising
questions for us – that is the point of Thomas's refusal to deny in
Christ any part of what makes up the definition of our human mode of
being. Cajetanus, his subtle disciple, was to put it - for the time – even
more daringly: 'this (human) being means – also in the case of Jesus –
simply: this human person'.[28] But for the purpose of this book it seems
to me unnecessary, even if instructive, to examine further the Christological discussions of the Middle Ages and what later issued from them
in the way of Scotist and Thomist interpretations of Jesus (up as far as
modern Christology between the two world wars); for this further
course of things, each time new doubts and objections arise, tries for
better or worse to settle them within the beaten track and the given
model; no new model emerges.

Conclusion of Part Three: the problem stated

Parts Two and Three may not unfairly have given rise to the impression
that the New Testament presents a 'Christology from beneath'; that
is, itself sets out from the encounter with and recollection of Jesus of
Nazareth, the prophet of the near approach of God's rule and the praxis
of the kingdom of God, who turns our human way of living upside
down and thus is able to touch off some explosive situations; Jesus, who
goes into opposition only when people's ideas or conduct conflict with
this practice of the kingdom of God. The New Testament recognizes
in Jesus the eschatological messenger of joy, who after his death was
vindicated by God.

At the same time we have been given to see that the New Testament
and later interpretations of Jesus are each one of them set within a very
specific horizon of experience and understanding; that as such these
are historically contingent and not in themselves the necessary context
in which Christological belief in Jesus must be thought out.

That is not all. From the Council of Nicea onwards one particular
Christological model – the Johannine – has been developed as a norm
within very narrow limits and one direction; and in fact only this
tradition has made history in the Christian churches. For that reason
the course of history has never done justice to the possibilities inherent
in the synoptic model; its peculiar dynamic was checked and halted and
the model relegated to the 'forgotten truths' of Christianity. Although
our own time is not connected therefore with this or that pre-Nicene

Christology by means of a continuous tradition, nevertheless there are factors present in our experience of cultural and social life which put pertinent questions to the Nicene Christology and its historical dominance, and so open up perspectives offering a view of possibilities before Nicea.

To return to what at the time was a crossroads in order to take the other, alternative route – as it then was – is hermeneutically and historically impossible, even apart from the queries about dogma that such an attempt at restoration would entail. We cannot undo the history that has already taken place. We can however seek to discover why at the parting of the ways on the eve of Nicea this Council chose the one way, did not take the alternative road and, having regard to the situation, could not do so. It may become clear in the process how – willy-nilly but as a matter of hard fact – Christological perspectives got pushed into the background by the emphasis on what was Johannine. In the long run the one-sided choice led to objections and misgivings which, the path once taken, have proved difficult to resolve. For that very reason it calls for a new and critical recall of pre-Nicene trends that will help to cancel out not the old choice but its one-sided emphasis and its silence regarding complementary but essential aspects. In that way a renewal of Christology will become possible within a new range of experience and new categories of understanding, in which definitive and final salvation in Jesus, imparted by God, is still encountered and still expressed.

I do not even think that the theologian needs to find new models, or simply on his own initiative (in a formal sense *qua* theologian) ever can do so. His job – a serious and responsible one at that – is to gather together elements which may lead to a new, authentic 'disclosure' experience or source experience. For without this disclosure or discovery experience, finding a possible new model, it seems to me, must be a rather dissociated and pointless Christological chore – whereas a real source experience (one that sees an unfathomable depth disclosed in historically observable data) in being experienced evokes for itself models of its own. In this theology can assist, can help to lay open a possible way, partly by showing how from long ago up to today Christians have attained to such a source experience with regard to Jesus of Nazareth; just as the theologian too – but then formally as a believer (among believers) – may himself come to a 'disclosure' and perhaps be able to make it meaningful and accessible to others. In the concluding Part Four I can only offer a prolegomenon to such an enterprise.

# Part Four

# Who do we say that he is?

# *The present Christological crisis and its presuppositions*

## Introduction

We said in Part One that our relation to 'the present ever new' must be one of the factors that determine how we put into words the substance or content of belief in Jesus as the Christ. This insight has far-reaching consequences. In fact if Christianity really does have universal significance, we are faced with a paradox: on the one hand Christianity will then transcend every historical definition of what one may call the essence of the Christian faith; on the other, this essence will only be found in specific historical embodiments of it. Identifying the essence of Christianity exclusively with one historical form and manifestation of it or with one particular definition of Christian belief then becomes impossible. That is the unavoidable consequence of the 'universal significance' of Jesus Christ.

It follows that Christianity only stays alive and real if each successive period, from out of its relationship to Jesus Christ, declares anew for Jesus of Nazareth. Then it is impossible to determine 'first' the essence of the Christian faith in order subsequently – 'in the second instance', as it were – to interpret it as accommodated to our own time. Anyone who, with the Christian churches, affirms the universal significance of belief in Jesus must have the humility loyally to shoulder, along with that, the difficulties accruing to it – or else must surrender the claim to universality. Only those two possibilities are genuine and consistent. To accept the universality while at the same time denying the hermeneutical problem – thereby positing one exclusive definition, *ne varietur*, of essential Christianity – is neither an accessible road nor an authentic possibility; it *is* to disregard and evacuate of all substance the true universality of the Christian faith.

All the same, we cannot make of Christianity just what we fancy. Within the variable, shifting dimensions of history an authentic

Christianity, true to Jesus' message, life and death, must be realized and must be articulated. A mere appeal to the practical conduct of life or 'orthopraxis', as being praxis of the kingdom of God, affords no solution here; for the essential nature of God's rule, as that has drawn near to us in Jesus, is the very thing at issue. Orthopraxis, a right course of action, is only feasible through a grasp of the point at issue. Of course we shall never be able to put into words in an absolute way the absolute as manifested in Jesus Christ. Others after us will have to take the thing over, learn to express what it means within an expanded experience of history and bring it to pass within the still open future. We can only speak from our situation and standpoint in this year of grace, though of course with our eye upon an anticipated future. After us the story will go on, but as the story of Jesus of Nazareth, the definitive meaning of which will only become apparent 'eschatologic-ally'. Meanwhile some provisional verifications are of course possible.

Chapter 1

# A conjunctural horizon of ideas and non-synchronous rhythm in the complex transformation of a culture

It is often said that we live in a period of radical intellectual and cultural upheaval. The limits of our world and of our comprehension have suffered a sea change. Quite so. Yet we are well advised to try mapping out and qualifying, especially qualifying, this transformation (even if the whole of our experience and our thinking is implicated in it); for every cultural shift, however radical, is still in a certain respect fairly relative. After all, we are able to grasp ideas and images of the world and of man that strike us as being out of date, just as we can also under-stand foreign languages and alien cultures; thus at the human level fundamental communication is possible between what are for people (or human cultures) on both sides the strangest of symbols, traces and expressions of man's life (see below in this Part). A strange vista of thinking, interpretation and experience is never wholly strange to us. What are the conditions making this possible?

In particular, French writers on culture[1] have realized that even when there is quite an appreciable change in the culture, nothing like a synchronous development occurs in every sector of it at the same pace and rhythm of acceleration. Of course all sectors of man's life share in this process of cultural change – thought, society, the economy, politics, art, fashion and so on – but they do not all share the same rhythm. Within the one historical process there are discernible at least three planes, which are not however adjacent or parallel but enfold and inter-penetrate one another, and together constitute the one history of human kind. There is 'fact-constituted history' or 'ephemeral history', with its brief and rapidly expiring rhythm: the events of every day come and go; there is 'conjunctural history', which is more expansive, has a more profound reach and is more comprehensive, but then at a much slower tempo or rate of change; in other words, a cultural conjuncture lasts for a long time; lastly there is 'structural history', with a time-span of centuries, almost bordering on the central point between what moves and what does not, although not standing outside of history. 'Structural history', around which the histories constituted by 'conjuncture' and by 'facts' circle like concentric orbs about a slow-moving axis, appears between these two as a kind of invariable: a turning but stationary top, around which everything revolves fast or not so fast. Other analysts of culture have shown that, even after a successful political and social revolution, eighty per cent of the old, rejected structures 'recur' in one way or another. Actually, in the third plane the process of change is extremely cumbersome and slow; basic structures survive even the most radical of revolutions. The earlier hypothesis of a convergent and synchronous development in all the elements of a culture, with a sudden switch in the mental or material cultural pattern, turns out therefore to be wrong – a 'myth'.

Understanding this can be of help to us with the problem in hand. For what is true of culture as a whole applies also to sub-sectors and cultural vectors, as also to 'human thinking' (and so to thinking motivated by religious belief). Here again we can recognize the same three intrinsically interconnected but non-synchronous segments. In man's evolving intellective life (and religious life) there are circling round an all but stationary depth-element which we have called structural the somewhat faster-moving circle of conjuncturally con-ditioned thinking and, on the outermost rim of these concentric circles, the fleeting thoughts of every passing day, with their often 'modish' aspects. Now what has been called the 'epochal horizon of the intellect',[2] or thinking done within the bounds of 'interpretative

J.E.C.–T

models' (with the mark of a particular period upon them)[3] or a horizon of 'current' experience – all this I would put in the second plane of 'history'; in other words, the particular horizon of experience and intellection, conditioned by the spirit of the age, belongs to 'conjunctural history': this is more deeply and firmly based than is day-to-day thinking and experience, with their fleeting character; a given intellective horizon, therefore, persists through a whole period. Even so, it is less stable, 'more superficial', than the 'in depth' structural elements of reflection on human experience. A cultural transformation, whether in the experiential horizon or the models of intellection, takes place within all but stationary, persisting structures of man's thinking. We must remember that even in that sector these three planes of non-simultaneity are not parallel nor separately procurable but criss-crossing one another: together they form just a single history of thinking. We do not mean to say that in addition to changing concepts in man's thinking there are also lastingly valid concepts which can be supposed to survive intact every more or less fundamental shift in the experiential or world horizon. We do mean that the basic structure of human thinking asserts itself in the conjuncturally conditioned ideas and in the changing horizon of man's understanding and experience. (Aristotle made an attempt to catalogue, as it were, or register these 'root ideas' of man's thinking. But he did not recognize the distinction between the 'structural' and the 'conjunctural' aspect of our thinking; and so his attempt is for us obsolete. Certainly, it is a start.) On this sort of basis it is none the less possible for us (living as we do in a different historical or conjunctural horizon of the intellect) to understand, for instance, biblical ways of thought, or the horizon within which the Council of Chalcedon succeeded in formulating its definition of a dogma. Both the structural and (at that time) conjunctural elements of (religious) thinking are operative factors in this. For somebody living within a different conjunctural horizon, therefore – setting aside the theological import of a dogmatic definition – on the one hand Chalcedon certainly has something meaningful to say, while on the other it may irritate and alienate. The reason for this is the dialectical tension between the conjunctural and structural aspects of the thinking; it is this tension in particular that makes each history ambivalent – a constant imperative to engage in interpretation, which itself stands within the ambiguity of history. This history with its ambiguity is surmounted, but not annulled, by our 'time-consciousness', by means of which we do in some measure transcend the 'lived' temporality, not, it is true, in a *conscience survolante* but still in an 'openness' to the Mystery which encompasses all 'history'.[4]

Having once set the periodically changing, conjunctural (or historical) intellective horizon within the concrete and complicated whole
of what we call 'human history' (thus up to a point relativizing the so-
called 'epochal jerks' in our history and at least reducing them to right
proportions), we can and should then recognize also the seriousness
and depth of a spiritual change in a culture; for the consequences of
such a shift in the limits and range of experience and understanding for
the life of (Christian) faith call for a state of preparedness and give a
mandate for a new interpretation of it.

More clearly, perhaps, than in earlier times modern man has come to
realize not only that he looks at reality through a 'language filter', but
that all supposedly direct dealings with the world and with people,
with reality, always come about via conjuncturally conditioned models
of thinking and interpretation. It is with our thinking as it is with the
physical sciences – at first sight a curious comparison for most of us
who are laymen in that discipline and so expect from it little insight
into life's affairs! I have in mind, however, an example familiar to us all:
the Copernican revolution. Before Copernicus (or, more precisely,
before his period; for long before him doubts had existed) everyone
supposed that the universe revolved around the earth; that is, everybody thought spontaneously with the old Ptolemaic interpretative
model. They did not even know that it was 'a model', because they
actually saw the sun rise up and go down again. For man in the ancient
world and the Middle Ages this did not look like a 'filter' through
which he contemplated the reality: it was the reality of direct experience. And we still go on, even after Copernicus, talking like that
– and in the field within which our ordinary, day-to-day speech is
exercised, rightly so. Out of a different way of evaluating the same
reality, namely a scientific one, we now talk about it, just as correctly
(but no less from a conditioned angle of vision, not alone sacrosanct or
uniquely meaningful), yet quite differently. We can put on various
spectacles – and often do so without knowing it – when we look at
reality. What is more, each period of culture would appear to have its
own pair, which a preceding period did not possess; they see things as
their predecessors did not. The 'reading-models', the filters and
'viewing-models' are different. Suppose we think spontaneously in the
Ptolemaic model of interpretation. New experiential data are then interpreted within that model. For a long time the model does well enough;
and then even natural science, operating within that one model, can

progress steadily without rift or crisis, and can keep on giving new pieces of evidence their place within the received model. There is a 'homogeneous development', as it were. But at a certain moment (and this was noticed even prior to Copernicus) it is established that some empirical data do not fit into the model: there is a remainder of facts which cannot be accommodated. When such a surplus becomes too big, a crisis occurs: then the model itself is called in question and science proceeds to reflect upon it until a new interpretative model is found that can explain (at least most of) the surplus. When it is postulated that the earth moves around the sun (and not vice versa) – the Copernican model – a lot of facts inexplicable within the old model suddenly become clear: they find their place. Within such a new model science heads once more for a longer spell of quiet, homogeneous development in which, within the model, new data are investigated and given their place – although in the long term recalcitrant facts are again established (and noted), till after a time an excessively large tally of unplaceable facts is built up once more, and people are forced to look out for a new model.

This holds good in distinctive and highly analogous ways for all areas of human culture, including religious thinking, that is, reflection on God's saving activity as experienced by human beings and brought to expression in the language of faith. In this expression – which takes place in an already given language – our understanding of man and the world plays an inevitable part. This experiential horizon is socially and historically, that is, conjuncturally conditioned; it shares in the historical character of the whole life of man. With Th. Kuhn (who is admittedly talking only about 'exact sciences') we can register a dual form of progress in our human cogitation: (a) a homogeneous, mostly continuous development within one and the same intellective model, in which new experiences are successively interpreted and located – this is an 'evolutive' progress; (b) progress through a fundamental change in the (conjunctural) horizon of experience or the 'intellective model', whereby all meaning already attained has to be 'translated' anew; this process entails something of a 'revolution' (albeit in a relative sense, because prior to the 'revolution' there is always a pre-revolutionary situation, in which for some time past the model had actually ceased to work. Every sharp change in an intellective and empirical horizon still has its own history!). Besides long periods of quiet, homogeneous progress, every so often history exhibits more fundamental jerks: a transition from one historical or conjunctural intellective horizon to another. When a new model has been found, it takes time for this to be accepted by everybody as new evidence (n.b. because of their specialized nature some models remain within the sphere of interest of experts and specialists). For a while old and new culture models will co-exist; the respective champions of the two models often come into conflict; there is even polarization at times: two groups of people, though contemporaries, live in mutually 'alien' worlds, they cease to understand each other. For the result – especially of a marked cultural change (involving models, experience, interpretation and various transactions) – goes deep and reaches wide. As Wittgenstein says (though in a somewhat different context): 'What were ducks before the revolution are rabbits afterwards.' What for instance in the old model of physics was (and still is) a solid, easy chair appears in the new atom-model as a kind of empty space with atoms and molecules whirling and dancing about inside it. An 'outsider', hearing about this for the first time, will either shake his head in disbelief – or angry protest – over such a new-fangled aberration, since the chair's solidity seems perfectly obvious – or never dare sit on a chair with a quiet mind again!

So via a (deliberate) detour we have managed to get as far as a fairly full outline of the situation in which we find ourselves regarding matters of belief, as a result of the radical change in models, whether of experience or interpretation, in which a fresh but loyal attempt is being made to enunciate the old faith. Christology and Trinity, redemption, grace and original sin, Church and sacraments, prayer and 'the last things' (eschatology): it all seems no longer to be what we all used to take for granted. Indeed: what were 'ducks', and still are so for many of the faithful, others are now calling 'rabbits'; and not a few people feel that they are being led up the garden path.

When our ways of understanding reality, our models, our whole intellectual and spiritual equipment, begin to shift and alter, the way we think about the faith as a whole will be different too.[4a] That in this process of re-thinking the faith mistakes will be made goes without saying – how could it be otherwise? But these are the humanly unavoidable by-products of what are authentically Christian attempts to prevent the faith from becoming a historical relic and to make it a living reality, here and now. That in such a period of drastic change there should be enthusiasts who see the past as just a prehistorical epoch and think that only now are we arriving at true and genuine insight – people with a feeling of radical liberation and with an eye only for the new as such – is likewise a fairly normal secondary phenomenon in all such periods of radical change. We should never judge the revolution as a whole by uncritical elements it contains; if we do, then such periods soon begin to look like the coming of the apocalyptic beast, when the love of many grows cold: the eve of the eschatological end. This 'model' too we know from history; and it will keep coming back. Those who (for whatever reasons) fail to understand what is really going on will – true to that apocalyptic model – utter their reproaches; for they have a fixed impression that the faith is being – the charitable among them would say involuntarily, but others systematically – eaten away from within.

It is undeniably true that within certain limited areas it is still possible to live, act and think to very good purpose in what are already obsolete models. Navigation, for instance, has always been able, quite successfully, to work with the old Ptolemaic thought-model. But air- and space-travel cannot. The point is that only a new model will help forward science as well as the faith, and open up the future to them. If we had gone on talking about a table or a chair on the old physical model, flights to the moon would not have been possible. And yet we can still remain sitting in a solid chair without misgiving. The same applies to the Christian faith. I do not begrudge any believer the right to describe and live out his belief in accordance with old models of experience, culture and ideas. But this attitude isolates the Church's faith from any future and divests it of any real missionary power to carry conviction with contemporaries for whom the gospel is – here and now – intended. Obviously, the new models will in turn be replaced by others (just as the Copernican model has already for the most part been superseded). The question is not whether we know better than the faithful of earlier times. The question is what, in view of the new models of thought and experience, we must do, here and now, to preserve a living faith which in this age and because of its truth has relevance for man, his community and society. What Christian, for example, still knows what 'the son of man' is? – a concept which once formed the basic outlook of an early Christian generation. Are we therefore non-Christian or less Christian? In that way the problem is at any rate clearly put.

Chapter 2

# The break with tradition since the Enlightenment

## §1 The Lessing question against a background of the Enlightenment[5]

'Accidental, historical truths can never become evidence for necessary truths of reason';[6] 'a broad, common-or-garden ditch' yawns between the two:[7] thus Gotthold Ephraim Lessing. This utterance of his has often been interpreted as in line with the philosophy of B. Leibniz and Chr. Wolff, in relation therefore to their distinction between *vérités de fait* and *vérités nécessaires*, which last – the 'truths of reason' – were alone relevant in the Enlightenment to a truly human, emancipated life. For the Enlightenment 'experience' had nothing like the importance attaching to innate 'truths of reason'. However much a child of his time, Lessing took a different view of this polarity. For him what mattered was the antithesis between 'truths from the past', concerning which we can be historically informed, and 'truths lived out' here and now, something that we are now going through ourselves. The point at issue is not the shifting terrain of our experience over against the Enlightened terrain of immutable, rationally evident truths; but it is a contrast within the sector of what we call 'factive experience': on the one hand of facts handed down from the past – which we may scrutinize for their historical accuracy (although the result of this enquiry is somewhat relative and problematical, Lessing takes no exception to that) – on the other, of here-and-now events, lived out by the self, which possess an intrinsic evidential function. Here Lessing is standing on the ground of the original, that is, anti-traditional Enlightenment. What is 'lived out by myself' has an intrinsic evidential value that no 'historical truth' can give me. Jesus may have performed all sorts of miracles – this can even be tested and confirmed, on good grounds, by historical studies – but the question is: What does this mean for me, who myself, here and now, no longer experience any miracles? For the period of the Enlightenment has no experience of miracles. Historically verified miracles of Jesus do nothing for me, say nothing to me, any more. 'I have not experienced, not lived them.' Bits of historical information about past miracles are still not in themselves miracles. For Lessing, therefore, historical criticism of the Bible or updating hermeneutics are superfluous, of no service to man's Reason and of no relevance to current experiences. Historically contingent truths are in fact contingent in that all positive religions can fulfil a useful function with respect to Reason – they 'put Reason on the right track'. Yet above and beyond this auxiliary function, no historical religion which has come to us through being handed down has any significance in its own right. Thus Lessing stresses 'rational experiential evidence' or 'immediate experiential evidence'. In that sense he reinterprets the Enlightenment's distinction between 'contingent truths' and 'necessary truths of reason'. What according to God's providential, pedagogic design were necessary truths 'in the past', become now, for the developed intellect which apprehends for itself the intrinsic evidence of what 'religion' is, 'contingent truth'. So what Jesus proclaimed and taught then, as being suited to his own time, did attain its purpose, which was to put man's Reason on the right track. And all that human Reason has itself set going along this track and has set in motion is 'the product of Jesus' miracles; they are prophecies fulfilled'.[8] The negation of the significance here and now of historical truths corresponds according to Lessing to the recognition of a developing historical process, for this is seen as a 'revelation', in the sense of education of mankind by God, an education having as its goal a rationally perceived 'intrinsic truth'. 'Particular revelation' is in Lessing's view a thrust in one particular direction, an impulse that was necessary in the infancy or childhood of the human race as of the individual, and indirectly mediated knowledge of the evident truth of reason at which man had been able to arrive – though by many a circuitous route – in his own strength. What divine revelation, understood as a kind of nurture, offers us in the concrete history of human beings is and was already 'formed' in our human mode of being itself; the divine pedagogy of revelation only gives man more swiftly and easily what he could have found in and for himself on the basis of the rationality principle.

What had once, in view of the state of man's reason, been necessary, Enlightened reason now made unnecessary, contingent and finally superfluous. To the modern Enlightened status of Reason neither Jesus' miracles nor Jesus himself are any longer necessary. An interpretation of the Bible that will be up to date is therefore declared to be superfluous, without prejudice however to the historical, thus the past relevance of the Bible – having regard to the situation of Reason at the time. For the Reason of the Enlightenment the Bible is *passé*. For the New Testament Lessing dare not say this as clearly and openly as for the Old; certainly it was his personal conviction, which he found ways and means of expressing, because he judged his age not yet ready for such a radical critique of Bible and dogma. For the present, then, we are not yet able to do without Jesus and the New Testament. (Lessing himself can, of course; but his contemporaries – orthodox or, as they were then called, 'neologists' – not yet; this is why Lessing vacillates in his public pronouncements.) The in his origins 'Christian Lessing' is at times – to judge from his letters – worried as to whether he is not trying to force God's pedagogy along at too fast a pace. He is aware of God's long-suffering with man – God has to pursue many devious ways with him. He sometimes wonders quite frankly whether he is not forcing God's providential, controlling hand with his premature, Enlightened ideas. But that God is leading people towards this Enlightenment and intends to make every religion not based on intrinsic, rational and experiential evidence superfluous, is for him a fact beyond dispute. Lessing really wants a total emancipation of Reason from the biblical Christian tradition. 'Intrinsic experiential evidence', Reason, is the final criterion. Each religion of particular revelation must be made to serve the emancipated, moral and religious human ideal of 'intrinsic truth' – instead of impeding it; in being serviceable like that a revealed religion gets its meaning and purpose within history. The fundamental message in all this is what Immanuel Kant was to express as: 'Religion within the boundaries of pure Reason'.[9] Here of course human reason becomes (despite the idea of a 'divine pedagogy') unhistorical, self-subsistent and isolated from its historical-empirical tradition. This a-temporality of Reason coincides, moreover, with the contemporaneous moment of a particular phase of culture: the present, today, is as it were an *eschaton*, *the* time of truth.

## §2 Modern 'Christological' trends in the wake of the Enlightenment

I want at this point not indeed to analyse the positive and much to be welcomed 'critical impulse' which the Enlightenment brought into our Western way of thinking for its own sake, but only to ask how the historically conditioned partiality or bias of the effect of this critical impulse has influenced certain sectors of contemporary Christological thinking, sometimes unconsciously, often in conscious association with this critical phase of human thought. In doing so I shall give expression to a trend which I have nowhere ever read set out in so many words but of which the broad prospect became especially clear to me in North America in the course of many conversations with theologians of many different denominational backgrounds – certain fundamental trends I can also see here and there on the home front (still least of all, however, among Dutch theologians).

According to this trend Jesus inspired, served as a catalyst for and animated religious values; and he is at the same time an example of religious experience. Jesus was indeed one who mediated new religious values and even a religiously original experience. But, the argument runs, this historical mediation must not itself be universalized. The values he inspired do of course bear fruit in subsequent history; and so we can ascribe to Jesus a universal, even definitive, importance. Just because the religious values touched off by Jesus then go forward in history, believers inspired by him will constantly be creating new images of Jesus out of earlier material. It has always happened like that in history. After all (so my reconstruction of the argument runs): how many ways of envisaging Moses and David do we not find in the diverse strata of the Old Testament? The story, the religious story of mankind in its concreteness, is always on the move. We do right in this connection to remember the great religious figures who went before us, especially the great inspirer of the religious traditions associated with the name of Jesus of Nazareth.

Nevertheless these new images of Jesus (allowing for our need as human beings) are on this view insignificant and, to say the truth, superfluous. They are really expressions of completely new religious experiences. But because Jesus was the great devotee and champion of 'things religious', religious people still remember him with gratitude in their own new experiences, as the one who went before them. That is precisely why we project our own new experiences of God back on to Jesus: in that way a new 'Jesus image' emerges. Yet this says nothing whatever about Jesus of Nazareth himself, only something about our own new experiences – just as there was projected on to Moses as a prototype, as it were, as he had been the ancient leader and initiator of the Jewish people, anything of good which emerged in that people later on. And indeed an anthropological model would seem to be in use here, whereby on the basis of earlier historical material new experiences are transferred back to the initiator of the movement or of a particular fillip given to the tradition. Literature is full of such 'updatings' (or 'epic concentrations'), which turn out (on this view) to be no such thing, but pure novelty, though within a course of events in which 'religiousness' and its articulation are nothing new; the religious story had begun long before.

More especially in a history still possessing an ingenuous spirit of reportage, the picking up of ancient stories (actually to give verbal expression to a completely new experience) is an everyday occurrence. It means putting together what is a whole new story based on a new experience, although the composition involves older material which had served to express analogous experiences.

From this viewpoint the new Jesus images are purely mythical conceptions, the real, non-mythical content of which is nothing other than our own historically new religious experience (with Jesus still seen of course as exemplar and animator at the time). The stated belief that Jesus affirmed a uniquely original relation to God and to other men is preserved up to a point in this conception, but – the case goes – it entails a refusal to absolutize the person of Jesus himself; in other words, Jesus is the historical mediation of a unique religious experience, without our being able to speak of a universal mediation. What has been mediated, therefore, is itself (on this showing) not irreducibly bound up with the person of Jesus as mediator of religious values and experiences.

The upshot of all this is that one of the tasks of theology must be to examine the relationship between the various forms of religious expression (in the non-Western and Western religions) as well as the central core of religious experience. Christian theology would then be the study of how the Christian message is the expression in one form of the religious experience of man. From top to bottom indeed it is all Enlightenment, *Aufklärung*, which along with the critical impulses of the spirit of that age at the same time incorporated certain unconsidered assumptions.

## §3 Acknowledged and unacknowledged presuppositions

The thematizing argument set out above starts from all kinds of assumptions, partly acknowledged and partly not. It starts for instance from the admitted premise that historical statements are always open and reversible, and so can offer nothing to go upon. The consequence of that is plain: affirming a universal significance for Jesus of Nazareth is regarded *per se* as a pre-critical way of postulating the problem; it is by definition an extra-cultural utterance – and that runs counter to the fundamental pluralism of human culture. In other words this premise resolves in advance the question of a possibly unique universality of Jesus of Nazareth, giving a negative answer before an enquiry has even begun. Just putting the question is thrust aside as a pseudo-problem. But because our place is *de facto* within a specific, namely, a Christian, tradition, having accepted this *a priori* negative solution, the next thing is to try and give a considered explanation of what the Christian claim to universality could have meant in a pre-critical age. The basic assertion in this negative view of the matter amounts to this: because we all – including Jesus – are historical beings, no one in our history can be given an absolute status. A historical person may indeed reveal absolute value; but this absoluteness must not be transferred to the historical intermediary himself; this is the actual presupposition of the historical Enlightenment. It follows that there is no essential link between the person of Jesus and the religious message of absolute values which he conveyed. The heart of what the Christian *kerygma* affirms is thus denied: the fundamental connection between Jesus' person and his message of God's approaching rule.

Taking into account the many parallels in world literature of 'eponymous' tendencies (or 'epic concentrations'), whereby experiences undergone by people or groups of people historically located are 'prototypically' projected on to key figures from the past (for example, the tribal ancestor: Jacob, Abraham, Cain, Adam), we must accept that an anthropological structure is at work in them; but recognizing such a structure resolves nothing, *a priori*, where the question of reality is concerned. This very human thing merely points to structures of human consciousness which in themselves can provide neither a positive nor a negative solution to the question of truth and reality. At the same time this structuring does show us that if a transcendent reality is truly given in Jesus, it is not a bogus, mystifying transcendence but one that will manifest itself via our normal structures of human consciousness. Whether a transcendent universality is given in Jesus must in any case be either confirmed or denied on other grounds. Thus the 'Christological' tendency previously mentioned stands within an intellective horizon in which, according to the Enlightenment, human Reason is supposed to be able to set *a priori* limits to meaningful possibilities. Certainly, we in the twentieth century can no longer devise a Christology on pre-critical lines. The question is, though, whether this narrow rationality-principle of the Enlightenment does not itself call for criticism.

Moreover, this type of 'new Christology' contains a second form of rationalism and apriorism, regarding the assertion that all historical knowledge is radically reversible. That the findings of every historical enquiry always remain open to revision, refinement and correction no historian is going to deny. That therefore no historical judgement whatever can be described as permanent and must be purely and simply a 'probable hypothesis' seems to me a glaring falsehood. Nevertheless it is on the rightness of this premise that (according to what its defenders themselves have to say) the whole of the 'Christological' movement mentioned above is built. What is unjustifiable about this premise is its facile identification of 'objectivity' with a kind of 'omniscience'; and as that is in no way given, every form of historical objectivity is denied.[10] People lose sight of the fact that the historian can do with having sufficient safeguards for what he gives out as a historical conclusion. Of course diverse, complementary views of the past are possible; but they do not necessarily or for that reason have to contradict each other. That the so-called 'biographical lives' of Jesus of Nazareth in the nineteenth century not only differed but actually contradict each other does not in the least mean that all historical knowledge of Jesus is uncertain in principle.

The underlying assumption there is right enough (though false conclusions have been drawn from it): namely, that there is always a theoretical possibility that in making historical statements we could be mistaken. That is right, if we allow of a distinction: (a) having sufficient guarantees for laying claim to a stated historical conclusion, that is to say, for reasonably discounting the 'theoretical possibility' that one may always be mistaken; (b) knowing that things in the past were thus or thus.[11] This last can indeed be falsified, whereas the historian can nevertheless have, here and now, sufficient, rationally justifiable guarantees for making a historical judgement. To contend that because of the standing 'theoretical possibility' of a correction still to come (for instance, through the discovery of new sources or documents) our historical judgements are false now, or at any rate can have no claim to a proper historical certainty, betrays an unwarranted rationalism in the field of history. The arguments adduced merely indicate that our historical knowledge is never unhistorical or supra-historical and itself forms a part of the historical process in the quest for truth. Affirming or denying an event in the past is something we never do on the basis of 'evidence' but on that of specific arguments which permit the affirmation or negation. If somebody adduces grounds for denying X, for instance, that is not to say that in reality X did not occur; only that we have no grounds on which to corroborate it. (Therefore the search for a 'storm-free area' for faith – that is, independently of the proper degree of permanent uncertainty of the historical result – is equally unjustified.)

No actual error is entailed by the ever-present logical and theoretical possibility of error in every historical judgement. In the context of a non-rationalistic understanding of human life as a whole the historian can have good enough reasons for ceasing to concern himself concretely with this abstract and theoretical possibility. There are innumerable instances in which we both could and should ignore this theoretical possibility, if our life as human beings is to remain viable. The conclusion would seem to be justified, therefore: it is wrong to maintain that the Christian faith can find no ground in historical data, merely because of the fact that a judgement about a past event is itself historical. It is wrong – for the same reasons – to contend that judgements concerning or involving faith must be completely detached from historical judgements (as many *kerygma* theologians since Bultmann – but also P. Tillich – would argue).

The same Christological movement contains a third rationalistic *a priori*. We heard tell of the core of religious experience, which the theologian is supposed to verify from the various forms of religious expression: in Christianity, Buddhism, Islam and so on. But who is to decide what 'the core' of religious experience is? What is to be one's criterion? One's own religion?

'Religious experience' as such seems to me to be a pure abstraction, first extrapolated in the Enlightenment from various empirically given religions that had become accessible at the time. In making this abstraction these students of religion have themselves become 'founders' as it were of a new religion, more specifically, a 'universal religiosity' as that emerged – a kind of chemical precipitate – in the abstract world of deism. It is the product of an unhistorical way of thinking; thus the historical and cultural context of a religion, its very history, is covered over and whittled away behind a merely abstract and theoretical universality without flesh and blood and, as history has witnessed, without any power of attraction at all: this deistic 'abstraction' was shortlived.

I do not mean to deny in any way that a useful attempt might be made, 'starting from the configuration of personal existence', to define what religion is 'as a system of symbols which functions by bringing about potent, insistent and enduring states of mind and motivations in people, by putting into words a scheme for a universal order of existence and surrounding this scheme or project with such an aura of factuality that those states of mind and motivations seem to be real in a unique way'.[12] That sort of definition of religion is quite a different thing from isolating a core in the religious experiences of all religions in such a way that the core is then absolutized and the historical character of those religions is reduced to an object of barter.

## §4 Universality through historically particular mediation

Although the critical impulse of the Enlightenment with regard to the traditions handed down to us must be described as a permanent gain, we cannot help pointing out the poverty of a critical attitude pursued in a rationalistic vein. The anti-historical posture of enlightened and enlightening Reason is at the moment coming under more and more general attack.[13] It was the Enlightenment's narrow principle of rationality that was so uncritical. On that basis the Enlightenment went on to talk about an ideal universal humanity, the *humanum*, without any historical, particular and real mediation. Its 'sound Reason' was an abstraction, divorced from or lifted above history. Such an ideal of human kind serves every purpose but that of humanity. Since the Enlightenment, after many sorts of untoward experiences, our age has come to see that mankind does not have at its beck and call this *humanum*; what is truly worthy of man is not something we all know and have within our power. It is 'outstanding'; a sought essence of humanity. We have rightly come to speak of *homo absconditus* (E. Bloch). A general concept of humanity is always in itself ambiguous; it needs a critical point of reference, a criterion; and this is in fact given in the record of our human suffering, which since the Enlightenment has not been all that much alleviated, unless we are to identify humanity with the welfare of a consumer society based on science and technology.

The Enlightenment saw every distinction between human beings as having sprung simply and solely from particular institutions of a historically random character. In the name of a natural, as it were, precultural brotherhood it demanded the abolition of all frontiers and at the same time the 'ethical unification' or unified ideals of excellence that must apply in identical measure to all human beings. There is something magnificent about this vision, rarified though it be: a fraternalism of such generous proportions becomes unreal and meaningless. Romanticism was to express it so: '*Seid umschlungen, Millionen*' (Schiller) and Beethoven's Ninth sounded the same note: '*Alle Menschen werden*

*Brüder'*. But with a universal brotherhood which is aimed unrealistically at all alike and insists on the 'impartial' exercise of love for human kind one in fact reaches nobody – certainly not the outcast! Now sociologists are facing the problem of whether in principle small groups, cells, 'ground-level communities' are not the necessary and indeed the only means of effectively influencing the whole, for the good of all.

Also for the Marxism that came out of the Enlightenment, the distinction between human beings was a fact of history, that is, the infidelity of history to nature; the self-alienation of man. But Marxism believes in the conquest of this historical alienation through a return to 'pure nature', in a purposeful struggle: via the limited brotherhood of the Socialist Party to a universal brotherhood.[14] In contrast to the Enlightenment, what has already become evident here is the sound principle of universality through a historically particular intermediary.

For its part, the Christology of the 'death of God' theologians sees in the rejection or disregard of 'divine transcendence' the necessary condition for constructing a universal fraternal community. It is Jesus the Christ who will deliver us from God's man-alienating transcendence. Instead of launching into an attack on these theologians as people who undermine the Christian faith, we would do better to examine what it is in theological theories of redemption as actually proposed that has had such a man-alienating effect as to enable a lot of people to find in a denial of divine transcendence an experience of real liberation! In a post-medieval theory of Christian redemption as 'penal substitution' (offering a thoroughly false interpretation of Anselm's doctrine of satisfaction), man really was condemned by God's 'transcendent righteousness' to blind submission and barren culpability: God demands the sacrifice of an innocent Jesus in order to release mankind from its guilt in the sight of God. It is just what the aeroplane hijackers do nowadays with their innocent hostages in order to expose at the bar of world opinion the guilt of society as a whole.

Here again a critique of the ideology is called for in terms of our fractured relationship to the Enlightenment. It is fractured primarily because we have come to realize the critical importance of traditions and institutions from the past, as opposed to the attitude taken towards them by the Enlightenment. The 'critical recollection of the past' has a humanizing importance which the Enlightenment failed to notice.

We have also to reckon with the fact that the Christian affirmation – namely, that the 'God of Jesus' is a God of all men and that this is evident precisely from the person, message and conduct of Jesus – specifically implies that this was manifested expressly through a member of one of the most persecuted peoples in the world: the Jew, Jesus of Nazareth. Just because he sensed the deepest inspiration of prophetic Yahwism in such a radical way, Jesus was able to explode the system of Judaism, identifying himself with the outcast, the poor, the deprived, sinners: with each and every person in need. Although in behalf of a real universality, that speaks of an unmistakable bias in Jesus' exercise of love with a view to God's universal rule. In discriminative, even biased particularity, a universal value and reality of life can of course be revealed as uniting all human beings – though for an only too human, as it were, 'possessive' outlook this may well entail a real 'stumbling-block'. Jesus' practice of deliberately keeping company with sinners and others who were officially beyond the pale, thus extending to them the offer of salvation, was to give offence to the official representatives of the nation – it was an explosive sort of conduct.

The New Testament understands this very well; one can still sense in it the tension that goes along with a 'universality via particularizing'. On the one hand 'the brother' is for Jesus simply 'the neighbour', that is, the particular individual whom one meets and who is in distress: the little or the least.[15] Above and beyond all boundaries, those who require help simply because of their need are 'brothers of Jesus'. Thus the brotherhood is grounded in the fact of the long course of human suffering, which has to be surmounted and which summons us to universal solidarity. 'The neighbour' is the one who concerns himself with the plight of the very first person he finds in distress; for the sufferer, the distressed person, is brother to Jesus. Straightaway this gives to the real, universal brotherhood a historically particular reference: Jesus of Nazareth – without its thereby losing anything of its own concretely historical reference to these particular people in need. On the other hand, in that same New Testament the members of the small, peculiar, specifically 'Christian community', as distinct from non-Christians, are in a special way called 'brothers' (fellow-Christians) (even in the synoptics, but especially by Paul and in the Johannine gospel). That is to say: the restricted, well-defined brotherhood of the Christian community is at the service of a universal brotherhood. Thus the universal brotherhood is effectively mediated by a historically particular, limited brotherhood. Therein lies the profound importance of the performative utterance of the Second Vatican Council, when it declared that 'the Church is a sacrament, that is, an effectual and operatively mediating sign of the unity of mankind'.[16] Both theologically and sociologically this would appear to be a justifiably performative statement, calling upon Christians actually to live out their Christian brotherhood as serving the project of universal brotherhood among all people, and as a way of life anticipating in miniature what on a larger scale must be the goal of all human endeavour. It at once becomes clear that the distinctive identity of Jesus must be found in his identification with all men – and that, of course, in the context of his identification with the cause of God: God's rule as salvation for all people and as the universal *shalom* or kingdom of God. For that reason the rationalistic, *a priori* assumption that universal salvation thanks to a historically mediatorial particularity (itself concretely the object of discrimination by others), namely, Jesus the Jew, is below the dignity of man, impossible and pre-critical, is hard to maintain as a critical proposition; it is unhistorical and uncritical. For within the intention of the Christian creed the historical particularity and even partiality have not the Christian interest in view but that of other people. We must not fall below the level of the Enlightenment; but neither can we put up with the restrictions and specific, patently unjustifiable rationalistic assumptions of the historical Enlightenment: our current relationship to the Enlightenment is a ruptured one. Thus we cannot re-adopt into the present the whole Enlightenment (any more than the larger past). We should update and implement its critical impulse while setting a veto on its uncritical presuppositions.

# A 'universal intellective horizon' not amenable to theorizing

Chapter 1

# Unique universality of a particular human being in history

## §1 The notion of 'human transcendence'

*Literature.* As regards an 'upward from below' Christology, only a selection from the abundant literature is possible; here we cite in particular works which look for Jesus' transcendence in his humanity itself, whether in a Christological sense or in a reductive one (H. Braun; P. van Buren), and also a number of reactions to that. T. van Bavel, 'God absorbeert niet: de christologie van Schoonenberg', TvT 11 (1971), 383–411, and 'Verrijzenis: grondslag of object van het geloof in Christus', TvT 13 (1973), 133–44; H. Berkhof, 'Schoonenberg en Pannenberg: de tweesprong van de huidige christologie', TvT 11 (1971), 413–22; H. Braun, *Jesus*, Berlin 1969², chs 12 and 13; P. van Buren, *The Secular Meaning of the Gospel*, New York 1963, and *Theological Explorations*, New York 1963; P. Colin, 'Le caractère sacré de la personne de Jésus-Christ. Approche philosophique', RSR 57 (1969), 519–42; Chr. Duquoc, *Christologie, II. Le Messie*, Paris 1972; G. Ebeling, *Wort und Glaube*, Tübingen 1967³, 203–54; G. Galot, *Vers une nouvelle théologie*, Paris 1971 (this book is based however on a completely mistaken interpretation of the authors dealt with, and so does not make the grade as a piece of scholarship); N. Greinacher, K. Lang and P. Scheuermann (eds), *In Sachen Synode* (Düsseldorf 1970), 150–69; A. Hulsbosch, 'Jezus Christus, gekend als mens, beleden als Zoon Gods', TvT 6 (1966), 250–72, and 'Christus, de scheppende wijsheid van God', TvT 11 (1971), 66–76; H. I. Iwand, *Die Gegenwart des Kommenden*,

Göttingen 1955; E. Jüngel, *Unterwegs zur Sache*, Munich 1972; Ph. Kaiser, *Die Gottmenschliche Einigung in Christus als Problem der spekulativen Theologie seit der Scholastik*, Munich 1968; W. Kasper, *Einführung in den Glauben* (Mainz 1972), 43–56, and 'Die Sache Jesu: Recht und Grenzen eines Interpretationsversuchs', *Herderkorrespondenz* 26 (1972), 185–9; L. E. Keck, *A Future for the Historical Jesus*, Nashville-New York 1971; A. Kolb, *Menschwerdung und Evolution*, Grasz 1970; H. Küng, *Menschwerdung Gottes*, Freiburg-i.-Br. 1970; H. M. Kuitert, *Om en Om. Een bundel theologie en geloofsbezinning*, Kampen 1972; R. Michiels, *Een mens om nooit te vergeten*, Antwerp-Utrecht; J. Moltmann, *Theologie der Hoffnung*, Munich 1968, and *Der gekreuzigte Gott*, Munich 1972; G. Muschalek, 'Gott in Jesus. Dogmatische ueberlegungen zur heutigen Fremdheit des menschgewordenen Sohn Gottes', ZKTh 94 (1972), 145–57; W. Pannenberg, especially *Grundzüge der Christologie*, Gütersloh 1969³ (1964), and *Grundfragen systematischer Theologie*, Göttingen 1967; K. Rahner, 'Die zwei Grundtypen der Christologie', *Schriften zur Theologie*, vol. 10 (Einsiedeln 1972), 227–38 (and passim in *Schriften z. Theologie*); K. Rahner and W. Thüsing, *Christologie – systematisch und exegetisch* (Quaestiones Disputatae, 55), Freiburg-i.-Br. 1972; J. Ratzinger, *Einführung in das Christentum* (Munich 1968), 168–221; Kl. Reinhardt, 'Die Einzigartigkeit der Person Jesu Christi', IKZ (1973), 206–24, and 'Die menschliche Transzendenz', Fr.ThZ 80 (1971), 273–89; John A. Robinson, 'Need Jesus have been perfect?' *Christ, Faith, History*, 39–52, and 'A reply to Mr Sykes', ibid., 73–5; E. Schillebeeckx, 'Persoonlijke openbaringsgestalte van de Vader', TvT 6 (1966), 274–88, and 'Crisis van de geloofstaal als hermeneutisch probleem', Conc 9 (1973, n. 5), 33–47; 'Ons heil: Jezus' leven of Christus de verrezene?', TvT 13 (1973), 145–66; T. M. Schoof, *Aggiornamento*, Baarn 1968; P. Schoonenberg, 'Christus zonder tweeheid', TvT 6 (1966), 289–306; 'Jezus Christus vandaag dezelfde', *Geloof bij kenterend getij* (Roermond-Maaseik, undated), 163–84; 'Het avontuur der christologie', TvT 12 (1972), 307–22; 'De zoekende christologie van A. Hulsbosch', TvT 13 (1973), 261–87; *Hij is een God van mensen*, Den Bosch 1969; H. Schürmann, 'Der proexistente Christus – die Mitte des Glaubens von morgen?', *Diakonia* 3 (1972), 147–60; S. W. Sykes, 'The theology of the humanity of Christ?', *Christ, Faith, History*, 53–72; D. Sölle, *Stellvertretung*, Stuttgart 1965; D. Wiederkehr, 'Entwurf einer systematischen Christologie', *Mysterium Salutis*, III–1 (Einsiedeln 1970), 478–645.

*

In their search for the focus where a unique universality in Jesus Christ can be found, many theologians in recent years have set this transcendence within the dimensions of Jesus' humanity: Jesus is then seen either as the summit of the general relation of creature to Creator, or as 'eschatological man' or last Adam, or else as the 'new man', the presence of the One to come, and so on. A. Hulsbosch in particular has expressed the principle sharply and logically: 'The divine nature of Jesus is only of significance in the saving mystery in so far as it changes and uplifts the human nature. In so far as it does this we have a new mode of "being human" . . . The divine nature is irrelevant except in so far as it uplifts the human nature; in so far as it does not do this, it has no significance for us; but in so far as it *does*, we have to do with something really human. If we say: besides being man Jesus is also God, then the "also God" is no business of ours, because it is not translated into the human reality of salvation.'[17] What that so strikingly expresses is an attempt to set the whole salvific reality that Jesus is in the sector of his humanity; in other words, if there is a unique universality in Jesus, then it must lie in Jesus' actual being-as-man, not behind or above it. The form of God's revelation is the man Jesus. Thus God's being-God will be disclosed in Jesus' being-as-man. The mystery of Jesus, which faith affirms of him, must therefore be given *in* the man Jesus as such. Here the human is indeed the measure (I do not say norm and criterion) in which the divine appears, for God is nowhere accessible but in his created manifestations. If Jesus Christ is God the Son, then we know this only from the manner of his 'being human'; and it must arise clearly out of his human existence; so that he must 'be human' in a completely unique way.[18] If that were not the case, there would be no access at all from the man Jesus to the Father. P. Schoonenberg too expressed this very clearly: 'That human transcendence can never be fully objectivized . . . God brings to pass in Christ what it essentially is to be human, and so it is impossible to say in his case precisely what is a reality in Him and in others not . . . We cannot point to anything divine in Jesus that is not realized in and from what is human.'[19]

Of course that at once raises the problem of what is meant by 'human transcendence', for 'being human' of itself implies constantly transcending or surpassing oneself. To this a Sartrian philosophy would reply that such anthropological self-transcendence is not the expression of a plethora or surplus but of a deep-seated defect, of a hole in our existence that can never be filled. Of itself it tells us nothing about the possible point of human life. For the present, then, human transcendence in Jesus must signify that in his life it expresses the discovery of an unconditional ground in God, whence the concrete life of the man Jesus becomes comprehensible. And then the question is: in what respect does this transcendent grounding of his human life manifest itself in the man Jesus.

Speaking about Jesus' 'transcendental humanity' *vis-à-vis* other human beings immediately raises the question as to a relative or absolute transcendence, one gradated in quality or quintessential. Hulsbosch had at first talked just of 'a difference of degree and not of kind',[20] but said at the same time 'that in his human consciousness Jesus commands an experience of God essentially different from that of other human beings', which 'means to say that he differs from other people in his essential being'.[21] This shows the struggle for the right terminology, regarding which Schoonenberg comments: 'The terms "relative" and "qualitative" do express very well the fact that the transcendence of Jesus Christ falls within our being-as-man, but they threaten to make him into a fortuitous climax instead of God's ultimate revelation. This last is brought out by talk of an "absolute" and "essential" difference between Christ and ourselves, but these terms threaten to place him outside our humanity.'[22] Schoonenberg goes on to formulate his own view of the matter: 'One could say that the Christ is a climactic point of sanctification, not of being-as-man; but his sanctification is being-as-man in its height and depth. It would seem better not to use the opposites mentioned above and to look for another term such as "eschatological", "definitive", "ultimate". These set Christ within our history; and our very use of them says something about the substance of his human transcendence. We might say that in him the fullness of what it is to be man is realized, just because the fullness of the Godhead dwells in him.'[23] The fullness of 'being-human' is not understood in a mythical or Graeco-patristic sense, nor in an annulment of Jesus' own individuality; but 'in the forms of his kinship to ourselves lies the transcendent fullness of his being-as-man': man-for-others. Later on this is corrected: the expression 'Jesus is the man-for-others' is a partial one.[24]

In all this one can find obvious tendencies to seek the point of contact required by the profession of Jesus' universality in his manner of being-man, even if Jesus' human transcendence can only be apprehended and evaluated in faith. This is in no way a contradiction. Human life would not be viable without faith in one another; a thing can be authentically human and yet accessible only to faith and trust.

Still, the idea of 'human transcendence' is not so straightforward as might appear. It seems to assume that we know precisely what 'human-ness' is, so that starting from that we can come to realize what tran-scendental humanness is. However, the Anglo-Saxon argument between S. Sykes and J. Robinson goes to show that in so doing we are working with a good many unfamiliar elements. There is a tendency to break down the declaration of Chalcedon as follows: 'Jesus is true God', that is a faith-utterance; 'He is true man' is then said to be not a faith-utterance but an ordinary human statement. This use of various language games is also to be found in the creed: for instance, 'that he suffered, was dead, buried and is risen'; suffering, death and burial are historically apprehensible events and lie in a different plane from resurrection. This is true, so far as it goes; but notice the context: that Jesus died is a historically accessible truth and as such cannot be a direct object of faith; but 'died for our sins' – that is an object of faith. Faith is concerned also with the point or purpose of a historically retrievable fact. Something of the same occurs in the affirmation: Jesus is truly man. Is this (a) a purely historical pronouncement? (b) Is it not at the same time, albeit seen from a different angle, an affirmation of faith? (c) Is it an *a priori* assumption of any human history, unless the contrary be demonstrated? In short, is it right to say we know that Jesus is truly man, but believe that (in a manner to be more closely and carefully defined) he is truly God?[25]

We take it for granted of all historiography that it has to do with people and with human behaviour; that in the course of his account the historian will come upon ghosts and spirits or supra-human beings, or whatever, will call for proof; normally he starts from the postulate of *human* behaviour, even if the people in question may possibly speak either of ghosts and spirits or of God, angels and devils. This implies a certain prior understanding of what man's mode of being is and what is possible to man. But it is now becoming clearer and clearer that con-cepts like humanity, freedom, justice and so on are empty formulae in the name of which, whether as ideas on the historical or the political front, very disparate and contradictory things have been justified. We must either leave these concepts on one side (which would seem quite impossible) or constantly be justifying and explaining their use.

Yet this has its limits. Can the historian exclude, *a priori*, from his notion of what is 'humanly possible' the report of people who say that their master, Jesus Christ, has risen again? What is humanly possible? S. Sykes makes a relevant distinction here between 'aspective humanity' and 'empirical humanity'.[26] What after all is the basis of our con-fidence that we are dealing with a real human being? Several aspects of this are obvious: that he has been born of parents belonging to the human race (setting aside possible cases of parthenogenesis – in which case the baby is a girl, according to modern genetics), and that he has the appearance of a human being. Thus we know from history that Jesus looked and behaved like a human being. That is 'aspective humanity'.

But in addition our notion of 'being human' is the product of a whole series of generalizations regarding 'what is normal'; the sum total of this is 'empirical humanity': a picture of 'being human' based on innumerable examples of human beings known to us in various phases of their lives.

As to Jesus' 'aspective humanity' there can be no doubt. But what of his 'empirical humanity'? The Church fathers provide us with a good instance of the misgivings felt by Christians on this score. It is difficult for them to admit that Jesus could have felt real hunger and thirst, was ignorant or made mistakes and so forth. The possibility that Jesus might have shared certain false presuppositions of his own time has for centuries been a bone of contention among Christians. In particular Jesus' sinlessness posed a problem about his humanity:[27] was he *per se* unable to sin, because he is the Son of God; or was he indeed able to sin, but in fact (when it came to the point) never did so?[28] All this points to diverse views of Jesus' being-as-man. These are theological utterances. And then pre-Nicene theology battled over the question of whether Jesus had assumed the 'fallen nature' of man or the 'unspoilt nature' which (it is said) existed before the Fall. Although Pope Leo I had written in his celebrated *Tomus ad Flavium* that Jesus Christ is *totus in suis, totus in nostris*, that is, completely one with God and completely one with men, nevertheless he was thinking of an 'unspoilt nature' in Christ. Thus from the standpoint of an incarnation theology S. Sykes poses the pertinent question whether in this situation we are able to define *a priori* the substance of Jesus' being-as-man. Is God's salvific activity to be descried in historical phenomena? And if God acts in a special way in Jesus for the salvation of men, in a manner not observable elsewhere, what does all that entail for Jesus' mode of being human?

The problem of finding a locality for the focus in which God's special saving activity in Jesus is manifest to the eye of the believer is inescapable; and for that reason consideration of Jesus' humanity is not simply a matter of asking purely historical questions. There is always a tendency in both orthodox and heterodox circles, so called, to prescribe for God how we would like to see salvation in Jesus incarnate. It must strike us that the more theology insists on the humanity of Jesus, the more need it has to qualify that humanity in some special way: fullness of being-as-man, the new man, the definitive and eschatological man, primal image of all humanity, and so on. It seems difficult to show how Jesus' humanity – a human being as we are, save in respect of sin – differs from our own. What is clear is that our idea of 'being human' cannot be a norm and criterion for forming a view of Jesus. His concrete being-as-man is perhaps the norm and criterion for our conception of it; and it is just those elements in the man Jesus that give us reasons for being preoccupied with him in a Christological sense. *A priori* and in the first instance I do indeed start from the notion that the man Jesus, who appeared within our history, is a human person – what else should he be? But what 'human person' ultimately signifies in the case of Jesus is something which for the time being, while conducting the enquiry, I have to leave open. Jesus' concrete, human-cum-personal mode of being will have to be filled in on the basis of his life, death and resurrection; and that process might well serve to correct my *a priori* concept of 'human person'. Jesus might well instruct us as to what 'being human' really means, teach us in other words that it is not our idea of 'humanity' that is the measure for assessing Jesus, but that his humanity is the measure by which we ought to judge ourselves. Perhaps he is the God-given revelation of what 'being human' really implies and in and through that very fact there is disclosed what it means to 'be God'. Impotently questing, in a history constituted by human suffering, for meaning, for well-being and a truly liberated and free humanity, when confronted with the message of the religions and more especially with Jesus' message of God's humanely orientated rule, we should at least start by being open and ready to listen to that message: to see whether it may provide a prospect where satisfying prospects are nowhere else provided. The question is whether *our* idea of 'normal humanity' can still be allowed to function as a criterion. But if Jesus is 'true man', while the Christian faith asserts of him that he is the revelation in personal form of the Father – the living God – then we are indeed bound to recognize the consequences of God's saving presence within the measure and finite compass of Jesus' humanity. In Jesus we see what man is capable of when he is wholly 'of God' and wholly 'of men' – when he experiences the 'interest of humanity' as above all else the 'interest of God'. And then it appears too that man only attains his completion in the risk inherent in the appearance of every historical particularity, limitation and contingency. Chr. Duquoc seems to have felt the same thing on the basis of different data:[29] an

'absolute ideality', with no consideration of the concrete historical
contingency and limitation in it, cannot become a foundation for
Christology. So we need not go on to compare Jesus of Nazareth with
our idea of 'humanity', but must simply try, through the New Testament, to discover how Jesus concretely lived out his being-as-man and
how, for those who accepted him on trust, it became clear that people
were able to encounter him in their experience as the saviour of all
men.

However ambivalent and contingent Jesus' being-as-man may have
been, there must have been grounds in his historical humanity (where
else?) for interpreting him – at any rate after his death as the rounding
off of his life – as was done in the New Testament. Without this historical foundation, such an interpretation on the part of his trusted
followers after his death would be mere ideology and mystification. To
go looking for these historical grounds is to be open to the real
ambivalence of what was manifested in Jesus as well as to the possibility that a historical study of this Jew, the man Jesus of Nazareth,
will reveal him as a complex and problematical figure – and in such a
way that, alongside other possible interpretations, that of Christian
faith will appear as a rationally meaningful possibility, properly
grounded in Jesus' history, even if for the historian it is neither the sole
possibility nor a totally unambiguous one. For a worthy, rationally and
morally supportable option for living this is more than adequate – no
other movement or view of life anywhere can lay claim to stronger
assurances of accountably real possibilities regarding the future. Under
these conditions the Christian interpretation of history and a way of
living in conformity with it are neither ideology nor mystification.

## §2 Unique universality: the universal appeal of what is 'proper to man'

### A. THE PROBLEM STATED

That a reality should have universal significance means that it has a
determinative effect on every person in settling the ultimate purpose
of his life, in other words that his end in life is settled by a fundamental
and – having regard to our freedom – freely accepted reference to this
universally valuable thing. It is a reality that imparts universal meaning;
but you yourself have to 'go along with it', if it is in fact going to exert

its purposive effect. In other words the universal meaning which may possibly appear in this thing or that, has no concrete consistency, if we personally do not recognize it as an appeal directed to our understanding consciousness. Through a personal motivation, what is of universal value can have a fascinating effect all its own: thus we ourselves decide the meaning and end of our lives in a condition of dependence on what actually appears to be of universal value.

The problem now confronting us is: Can such a unique universality be present and be recognized in one historical person, Jesus of Nazareth? To put it another way: Does this man, Jesus of Nazareth, confessed by his followers at the time as the Christ, Son of God and Lord, still have importance for us today, in such manner that we too can find in him definitive and conclusive salvation? The underlying problem is bound up with the question of how a particular event in history can have a universal significance for all human beings, and therefore for us now. If this is even possible, it would seem to require a historical intermediary.

Finding the meaning of one's life in a constitutive reference to Jesus of Nazareth naturally presents itself as a religious position, that is, it is a way of determining the total meaning of life. Now 'religious' says something about the relation of man to the totality and so ultimately to the living God; it also says something about God in his relation to man. A religious utterance, in other words, always entails both anthropological and theological discourse: it is a way of speaking about man and about God all at once. This automatically implies that a religious utterance can only have a universal significance with a bearing on all human beings, if it can be at any rate to a degree sensibly verified, that is, if it can be made clear that the believer's affirmation of God's universal love for men – a directly non-empirical reality – opens up at the same time the true humanity of man, which can be both pointed to and experienced.

The question of the unique universality of Jesus therefore encompasses two interrelated poles: on the one hand, an unveiling of the true face of God; and on the other a disclosure of the true being of man – the former being mediated through the latter. The one true and living God is made a shadow and an abstraction, universally unattainable, unless at the same time the true aspect of being-as-man is elevated in the religious reality and what is said about it. Only respect for this fundamental structure of religious discourse can give a claim to universality a certain 'intrinsic evidential value' which distinguishes it from an ideological pretension.

But then the best way into the distinctive nature of Jesus of Nazareth, in his significance for all, it seems to me, is indeed not to approach him either from a given idea of what 'being God' means or from a preconception of what 'being man' – and thus being-a-human-person – really entails. It will not do to fit together two models or two concepts – 'being man' and 'being God' – so as to arrive in that way at a conceivable (or inconceivable) 'amalgam' of a God-man, at the abstractly perhaps conceivable model of a 'God made man', for which Jesus of Nazareth might then have been a historical occasion. Going to Jesus in order to find in him salvation is to approach him in a state of ignorance, or better, of 'open knowledge', of what 'being man' properly means, and likewise of what 'being God' means, perhaps in order to learn from him the real content of both – and *that* precisely through their interrelation as manifested in Jesus. Of course we have definite conceptions of man as also of God, just as the Jews had when they encountered Jesus. Jesus himself stood within the tradition of the peculiar Yahwistic Jewish experience of God. This already given understanding is in no sense disavowed. But we are asked to be open to Jesus' own interpretative experience of the God-reality which he manifests in his 'being man'.

Of course, the question about the unique and universal significance of Jesus is one that can only be answered in terms of belief, whether we say yes to it or no. Therefore the relevance of a positive reply is essentially theological; it cannot be simply historical. On the other hand faith-utterances must have a basis in the history of Jesus; were the opposite the case, they would have a disjunctive, thus an ideological relation to the real state of affairs. So from the historical reality that was Jesus something must have issued which people could, should and in the end were compelled by their faith to express, and rightly express, in those faith-utterances. There must have been something in the historical situation to indicate that anyone who sees Jesus has actually seen the Father. Had the gap between these two planes been too great, Christianity would never have stood a chance.[30] On the other hand the faith-motivated affirmation is always vulnerable in face of the historian's conclusions. To put it another way: the unique universality of Jesus cannot be historically demonstrated either by starting from Jesus of Nazareth simply or from a systematic comparison between the various world religions. What we have is an affirmation of Christian faith which claims however to be an assent to reality – although the claim to reality is in itself also an act of faith.

Yet if we give our assent, albeit in the language of faith, to some reality – that is, something which is not as such constituted by me (the believing agent) but on the contrary commands my assent and constitutes it an act of faith – then this historical reality must itself offer the basis for what is being said when the faith-language is used and at the same time give substance to it. The opposite of this would entail an ideological claim. The only way, therefore, in which the affirmation of Christian belief can be shown to have credibility is twofold: (a) on the one hand by means of the historical study of Jesus' baptism, his words and actions, life and death and of finding out what they may possibly signify, and (b) on the other hand by showing how the Christian claim to universality is substantiated in the true humanness of 'being human', as that confronts us in Jesus of Nazareth. Although the concept 'true humanness' does not refer to a fact or datum open to complete rationalization, but in its concrete implication of substance itself entails a specific option and viewpoint, we are entitled to say that the Christian claim to universality will have to prove itself in the phenomenon of 'being human' as that actually transpires. What is ultimately at issue is the intrinsic relationship between Jesus of Nazareth and the kingdom of God and the final good and happiness of human beings. To put it in modern terms: the point at issue is the transcendent form of manifestation assumed by what sociologists call the 'significant alternates'.

That a fitting approach to Jesus of Nazareth entails a critique of our given ideas and ways of envisaging God and man does not mean that any prior understanding is totally unnecessary as an intermediary factor. All modern attempts – K. Rahner, W. Pannenberg, J. Moltmann, P. Tillich, etc. – to arrive at a meaningful Christology, that is, to achieve an intelligible thematic presentation of the universal significance of what is none the less a particular event in history, take the path of 'mediation': that is to say, they look for an intermediary factor between the 'once-only' Jesus of history and his universal significance, expressed in ancient terms as Christ, the Lord, and Son of God. Nevertheless all these mediation theologies entail the presupposition that, theoretically, human reason should be able to thematize a universal horizon of understanding and action. In many of these Christological systems human reason is as it were 'extrapolated' from its social, cultural, economic, historical structures, and is in danger of becoming an unhistorical type of reason. We have already said that Jesus becomes indispensable only if the really decisive purpose and end of our human existence is in fact determined by the historical phenomenon of the real Jesus of Nazareth, this serving to correct our own human expectations and projections of 'being human'; only within this focus and this normative function, therefore, is there a legitimate place for our human projection of what may be expected and hoped for to play its part.

### B.   THE *HUMANUM* THAT WE SEEK

Any enquiry about the vital significance for all human beings of a particular individual among them immediately calls for a distinction to be drawn between (a) people who – in whatever way – are confronted in history with the movement centred around Jesus, and (b) those who have never heard of Jesus or have heard something about him, but in such socially or personally conditioned circumstances that there can be no question of a real confrontation. The real problem is with the first of these two articles. If that can be given a solution which makes sense, all the data are available (in a missiological perspective) for dealing with the second one as well.

That each human being is a fellow human being, receiving and giving within the larger whole of various expanding circles which ultimately embrace the entire human race; that ultimately, therefore, each individual can only be understood within the whole, as having a personally unique and inalienable importance in it, would be hard to deny as an anthropological truth. The human visage which we ourselves never see and which is evidently there to be looked at by others and to substantiate our openness to the other person, plainly symbolizes our fundamental dependence on and orientation towards the other.

For Christology this is in itself a relevant fact; but it is, as such, a universally human structure and not a peculiar attribute of Jesus of Nazareth. 'Being human for the other' is a task as it were sketched into the structure of our 'human constitution' – which is not to say that we actually make a good job of it. The question of concretely bringing about this 'being human for the other' remains important, therefore, in connection with Jesus of Nazareth; but it becomes relevant for Christology only if this personally unique, particular realization is of such a nature that it becomes a point of reference for the total meaning or ultimately determinative meaning of every human life. That is why Jesus' being human for the other is an important presupposition and a precondition for making sense of any more exact qualification of his Christological uniqueness.

An explanation too which for an insight into the Christological significance of Jesus would look exclusively towards the fact that Jesus put into words and practised profoundly and universally human and yet simple 'things of life', accessible to all, in such wise that they will continue to challenge and summon all people of goodwill in the search for true humanity, is right enough; what is being asserted can be pointed to in history and is accepted even by non-Christians. It is likewise an essential presupposition and precondition for making meaningful and intelligible the Christological or universal importance of Jesus implied by the credal statements of the Church. Yet more of the world's religious literature of or about 'founders' of existing religions can fairly make a similar claim. A call to authentic humanity, indeed every good action, of course has a universal significance (taking into account the inevitable pluralism and the meaning, situated in society and history, in which the 'authentically human' has to be realized here and now). That 'everything of worth in man may be not just discriminating where other people are concerned, but actually binding'[31] is a truth which we often no longer dare utter aloud for fear of being different from others. The question here is whether such a universal appeal to humanity, as manifested in the peculiar being of Jesus, reflects the full historical reality of Jesus. If it is intended solely to denote Jesus' peculiar being, the problem presents itself as to whether that is not the very way to misconstrue the deepest originality and distinctiveness of Jesus of Nazareth. After all, it appeared from our examination of Jesus' message regarding God's rule and from his actual conduct that the 'cause of Jesus' was certainly the cause of man – but as that of God. In other words, we do not get at what was truly distinctive about Jesus if we ignore what was closest to his heart: the God mindful of humanity. Jesus' relationship to God, therefore, is an essential part of the argument.

## C.  THE HUMAN AND THE RELIGIOUS

That in general terms (leaving Jesus aside) the religious relationship to God is an essential element in the possibilities of truly human living can no longer, it is true, lay claim to universal agreement among human beings; but it can nevertheless be shown, in a context of cultural history and psychology, to have meaning, without prejudice to a non-theistic humanism. For that matter, religion might in the first place be defined and interpreted – leaving aside for now its proper contents – as a way of denoting an inalienable attribute of being-as-man which – if and when neutralized or supplanted – turns up in disguise, for instance, in modern 'absolutist' myths (such as Progress, Happy Land, New Future, with their own representative saints and rituals).[32] The disregard for religion shown by a one-track, for example, purely technical-cum-rational culture, constitutes a real danger because it contains within itself a fatal and therefore inadmissible impoverishment of man, as not only 'humanistic psychology' but also critics of society like J. Habermas and L. Kolakowski have demonstrated.[33] Although psychology and critical sociology cannot, it is true, pronounce on the reality-value of religious convictions, they can confirm, in parallel with its repudiation on other grounds, an impoverishment of perception – in more areas than just that of the religious. The result is a reduction of people and things to the status of objects; they become vacuous, neutral, useful but valueless. Human emotions cease to be forms of communication with the world, they become self-enclosed, inner 'states' of the person. They are de-naturized; and at the same time the world is left without a soul.[34]

That religion has its own language and terminology – the language of faith, so called – goes without saying. Up to now we have said only that the religious relationship to the transcendent, all-embracing reality really does have, because of its humanity, a universal significance. More than that: we might say that via this humanity the relation of God himself to man is the ultimate basis of a feasible universality which calls all men and concerns all men. The immediate basis of the universality of the religious lies in our being-as-man itself, but ultimately, and in an ontological sense primarily, in the reality of God as 'maker of all things and all men'; in other words in the monotheism that acknowledges God's creative and saving nearness. Put in another way: the deepest justification and foundation for the universality of a religion lies in what the religious person confesses to be the reality of the universal love of God for men, or in the affirmation that the cause of man coincides at every point with the cause of God. That religion, then, is really universal which does indeed acknowledge the universal love for men of the one creative, near-at-hand God.

But the message of the vital necessity of a religious relation to God is a universal claim on the part of all (monotheistic) religions; in itself, therefore, not peculiar to Jesus of Nazareth and the movement centred around him. In its general aspect, then, the religious relation to God (and to the real totality) cannot be called specifically Christian. The religious gives us the reason for ultimacy and totality, for the transcending of the self in love; it has to do with the acceptance of a total purpose and so with the exercise of trust in reality as ultimately benevolent – in reality as compassion (as Tibetan religions have it). This, expressed in many human modulations, would appear to be the affirmation of all religious experiences as a dimension of truly human existence.

This dimension is experienced and verbalized, however, within the concrete history of peoples and races with the aid of various and differently coloured 'disclosure' or discovery experiences inside the structure of this or that culture. Hence the existence of different religions, each in its own way bent on sorting out the record of sense and inanity, of the search that enquires after salvation, happiness and liberation and man's experience of guilt and suffering.

The original and peculiar quality of Jesus of Nazareth cannot possibly be reduced, at any rate within the meaning of the Christian creed, to this general problem of religious monotheism or to the problem of God and experience of God. That would be to treat Jesus as no more than a cipher of God's universal saving activity in the history of all people, or as one of the many prophets of the religious relation to God. If there is in Jesus, who undeniably came to the Jews with a religious message, if there is present in him an original and peculiar something, it must be sought in the unique character of that religious message and the conduct, the way of living, that went with it, in other words in the distinctiveness of Jesus' experience of God as source and soul of his message and ministry. Having in mind what we were saying earlier on, we are therefore faced with the fundamental question whether God's universal love for men has come to us in and through a human, personal, historically particular figure called Jesus of Nazareth. Thus what it comes to in the end is the Christian modulation of the universal religious theme of God's saving nearness.

It follows, of course, that the peculiar element in the Christian religion implies no exclusivism *vis-à-vis* other religions; it refers to a distinctively Christian factor within the thematic presentation, in a universal religious context, of God's (universal) saving nearness, which in their own way the majority of religions propose. But only when the Christian distinctiveness and identity are to some extent localized will it be possible to frame the question about the relationship of Christianity to the other religions to any good purpose. On that score

J.E.C.–U

a hermeneutical problem immediately presents itself. The identity – and thus the original distinguishing mark – of Jesus and his 'movement', the Church, cannot be encapsulated in some immutable, eternal essence. For if Jesus does have a universal significance, for us here and now, the relation of that to our present must enter into our description of Jesus' original identity; and then this, our account of that identity, is at the same time the interpretative act of faith in which I acknowledge Jesus as the universal and unique person. Even so, it is not I who constitute him the universal and unique one; rather I give myself in assent to this Jesus who thus reveals himself to me. So the process of defining the unique universality of Jesus lies in the very act of constructing a contemporary Christology; that is nothing else but the interpretation of Jesus of Nazareth affirmed as the Christ and as God's proffer of salvation to all.

If then 'being religious' means directly experiencing and articulating the relationship of man to the Transcendent and therefore of the Absolute to man, we may say that in its intrinsic momentum each and every experience of God, however much conditioned by social and historical factors, tends to become a 'universal religion of human kind'. Yet we see that this is not how many religions have felt themselves to be: lacking any missionary or missionizing consciousness, they leave each people to its own religion. Indeed there are religions that are essentially clannish or tribal or see themselves as tied up with one particular culture. Rome and Greece never imposed their Olympic gods on the territories they occupied, except when the emperor was himself deified, as a divine *raison d'état*; but that was more of a state-ideology, witnessing rather to universal imperialism than to a universal religious sense. Though not without a degree of tension, in many non-Christian religions there is a stronger intrinsic bond between religion and culture - which puts a counter-active brake on the dynamic tendency to become a religion of mankind. Therefore a universal religion, valid for all people, will, whenever inculturation in diverse cultures takes place, nevertheless be bound in principle to maintain a certain reserve – in the sense of transcendence – towards each culture, even towards its own cultural articulations, and yet at the same time (although in historical contingency) uplift and illuminate true cultural humaneness.

We should not overlook the fact that of its own nature and substance a religion can be universal even if its founder or actual inspirer - for instance, John the Baptist and Jesus of Nazareth – did not directly address themselves with their message to mankind as a whole, or did not even have the explicit intention of founding a new world religion. A religion which affirms that God is the salvation of all, without discrimination of any sort, is of its nature intensely universalist, even when in the first instance – as for example in the case of Jesus – the universality is proclaimed only within the context of Israel. This goes to show that on the score of universality the historical mediation is essential. Yet we should not shrug off too quickly, on theological grounds, what is implied in the historically certain fact that Jesus confined his message to his own people, the house of Israel, even if there are also present in Jesus' preaching and ministry elements which enabled him as a Jew to break out of the particularism of Israel's religion, encountered in its Judaic form.

It yet must be said that Jesus' life and death form part of our concrete human history; this Jesus event is therefore linked with what came before and what followed upon it and from it. Reason enough for it to be the object of a historically illuminating study. Within this whole we can even ascribe to the Jesus event on historical grounds a unique importance in relation to later events, namely, the rise of Christianity and the Christian churches. Without Jesus no Christianity. But this kind of importance is always relative, that is, relative to the Church. Mohammed too has a historically unique importance for the rise of Islam.[35] But a historically unique significance of this sort is essentially relative. When, however, we talk of the significance of Jesus for human history as a whole, then we are no longer speaking 'in a historical plane'; for having significance for the whole of history includes the future as well – and so it lies beyond the bounds of any historiography.

*Conclusion.* From this initial exploration we may fairly conclude that whatever stands out as 'specifically Christian' must be of such a character that it both unites all human beings and binds them together in freedom – in such a way that in the human the truly religious will to some extent begin to be obvious. In other words: (a) the universal meaning of Jesus only becomes matter for discussion when it is substantiated in and by the universal phenomenon of our being-as-man; (b) if the Christian affirmation of Jesus' universal significance is not ideological but is an assent to reality, something in the record of Jesus must point in that direction; the subject to which this universality is ascribed is, after all, a man from within our history, Jesus of Nazareth. In other words, in the historical man Jesus there must be present some ground or reason for our being able to acknowledge him in that way.

For if a historical truth be grounded exclusively in a dogmatic or theological statement, it ceases to be a historical truth; (c) finally, if the universal significance of Jesus has to substantiate itself via the universal phenomenon of 'humaneness' or 'humanity', the problem inevitably arises of a universal horizon of understanding (not so far open to theoretical construction) having to precede any possible credal affirmation that Jesus is the Lord of all, in whom all can find final salvation. And that at once presents a new objection, a new problem of whether any description of a 'prior understanding' is feasible on a rational basis. Can the question of a definitive purpose and point to human life be rationally objectivized?

Chapter 2

# The history of human suffering in the search for meaning and liberation

## §1    The problem of 'universal history'

The concept of 'universal history' is often employed as an essential mediatory factor in a Christological synthesis. But this notion is itself at bottom a religious and theological one. Yet having once recognized its religious origin, we can also more accurately define what it signifies in a rational context.

Both the historian and the philosopher use the category 'universal history' – but with a very special connotation. For universal history *per se* is not a reality but a conceptual postulate, *une idée de raison*. For the historian it is a premise or presupposition, that is, a prior conclusion in the strict sense, which it is not his business as a historian to examine further. In this context the concept is simply saying that the historian's job is to trace significant connections. He should not and cannot proceed on the assumption that people, groups of people and cultures form hermetically sealed units; he starts from the implicit assumption that despite every difficulty and imperfection, communication is always possible. The universal intellective horizon of historical interpretation, therefore, expressed in very general but real terms, is in every case human existence as the potentiality for reciprocal communication. Looked at in that way, 'the oneness of human history' is presupposed by any purposive historical study.

But from a philosophical standpoint this presupposition on the historian's part must be critically examined. P. Ricoeur has helped considerably if indirectly to clarify this problem in distinguishing two extreme demarcating types in the current philosophy of history.[36] (a) On the one hand the so-called 'Hegelian type' or unitary system (identity-based thinking): here the divergent philosophies *in toto* are a single philosophy of which particular concrete, historical philosophies are only (component) elements. To understand then means to understand the totality (*'Das Wahre ist das Ganze'*). Where history has occurred, we assume *a priori* that this symbol of humanity is something we too can comprehend, can understand; it can be linked up with the broad spectrum of humanity; this is the prior understanding of all historical study, the 'prior conclusion' of the historian. (b) On the other hand the pluralistic type: each philosophical system has to be understood in its wholly distinctive character as a separate philosophy and not as an element in a 'universal spirit of intellection' (thus no '-isms'!).

We must declare, however, that both types come up against an impassable frontier. If the Hegelian type were to realize its ideal, it would end by resolving history into a system; in that case there no longer is any real history. But even with Hegel himself this cherished unitary system is never attained. If on the other hand the pluralistic type were to carry the day completely, history would likewise be resolved in a multiplicity of mutually inaccessible, unrelated and dispersed particularities, in other words, in a schizophrenic universe or a sum of supra-temporal, separate and adjacent essences. But this type also can never succeed in realizing its own intention and at most must be content with typological approximations (for example: Spinoza is a 'pantheist'). Thus both the unitary system and the utterly independent essence annihilate living history. Both 'logic' (logos) and 'pure facticity' are the end of all real history. (It is something to be noted, therefore, that a system of 'universal history' – hermeneutic key to the understanding of Christianity – also, in essence, postulates 'the end of history': thus, in particular, W. Pannenberg.)[37] Even so, these two readings, or interpretative approaches to history, correspond to two requirements and expectations and, in the end, two models of truth.[38] From the first estimation of history, where we are meant to understand it by way of the totality, what is looked for is 'the emergence of a meaning' in history; for rationality will produce significant and coherent relations in it. The other side of this rationality principle, however, is that there will be a considerable remainder which slips between the meshes of the rational system – a sort of 'historical scrap'. But: *'ce déchet est justement l'histoire'*.[39] There is, in point of fact, unmeaningful history; there is non-sense in our history: violence, lust for power, coveting at the expense of others, enslavement and oppression – there is Auschwitz, and goodness knows what else in the private sphere and in our own personal life. All of that does indeed fall outside the 'logos' which the historian looks for in history – so much the worse for the varieties of concrete historical experience! What is forgotten here, however, is this: not only is the real inanity present in our history left on one side and not taken into account, but *a priori* the real possibility of 'a different meaning' in history is ignored.[40] So in recent years a type of historiography has emerged which we might call an 'anti-history' in that it concentrates on the study of just this 'historical scrap' as its object.[41]

Anyone, then, open to the 'sense' and 'non-sense' that are manifested to us in history cannot be 'Hegelian'; both possibilities – the meaning discovered (by dispensing with a lot of reality) by the Hegelians and the possible 'different meaning' (which would take into account all the 'non-sense') – have an equal claim and are not reducible to a unitary system. To say that a particular philosophy (for instance, that of Aristotle, Kant or Spinoza) is just an element of 'a universal mind' is a forcible encroachment on the peculiar distinctiveness of each thinker, whatever his socio-historical situation.

Between the Charybdis of insistence upon totality and the Scylla of reverence for what is historically particular and unique there lies only one possible, significant perspective: the imperative need for communication; dialogue instead of totality, and so a ban on any pretension to reduce 'the other' to a constituent part of my 'total discourse'. The place, therefore, where truth may possibly be found is human-being-as-possibility-of-communication.[42]

This possibility of two readings of history which – carried through to the end – result in absurdity, that is, in the elimination of all true history, none the less discloses a dual aspect of history itself: each (example of) history is a manifestation of meaning (it lends itself to the establishing of some significant interconnections) and also the manifestation of unfathomable, irreducible particularity, to which thinking on the identity principle gives no access. Without being able to maintain the totality principle we must allow that whatever is articulated by human beings must form one cohesive whole, accessible to others. This is why we are right to speak, in the singular, of 'history'. The system, as an unattainable, borderline possibility of the understanding of history, shows us that our plural history is 'potentially one';[43] to refine on that: the question of universal meaning, *qua* question, is given inevitably (arising not just out of human thinking but out of historical reality as such). On the other hand we are really confronted with histories (in the plural): of people, groups, races, cultures. Moreover, we are just as aware of this pluralism as of the potential unity. It follows that the reality which occurs as history reveals itself both as a potential unity and as a plurality of events that cannot be eliminated. In other words, the question of the universal meaning of history *qua* question (extracted and elucidated from history by man's reason) is both insuperable and insoluble. It is this very fact that shows us the nature of history as history: it is the field of ambiguity; which is to say: history is real, contingent, human history only in so far as it is neither absolutely one nor absolutely plural. The real history of human beings occurs where sense and non-sense lie side by side and one upon the other, are commingled where there is joy and suffering, laughter and lamentation, in short: finitude. Human history is ambiguous, with flashes of light and clouds of impenetrable darkness, a realm of knowing and unknowing. The co-existing of meaning and unmeaning in this history – and so history itself – is not capable of complete rationalization; the 'reason for' history is not accessible to theory. History is 'the realm of the inexact',[44] and therefore amenable only to inexact methods. The end of history, regarded as its boundary and termination, does not show us the point of history, but that our question as to its meaning is as inevitable as it is beyond rational solution.

If history presents itself concretely as a tangle of meaning and unmeaning, the question arises: What will it amount to in the end: sense or non-sense? And how? Or is it a story without limits, indeterminately open for ever and ever? Or does this uncertainty face us with the question: Should we not change and make a different history? At any rate this latter is a sensible resolution to begin with: let us try and make history with more meaning to it! The question is, though: Can we do that? Can we overcome every form of evil, of suffering? Even cope with all kinds of natural disaster? Conquer even death itself? . . . So that a new question would seem to be justified: Does human history not confront us, perhaps, with a theological problem – the problem of creation, salvation and covenant, so that, although not amenable to theorizing, absolute confidence in the *point* of history, entrusted and given in pledge to us despite everything (the real possibility of a universal and single meaning), can only be endorsed with God as starting-point, in commitment to the Mystery? Resistance to all forms of evil and suffering, in whatever guise they appear among us, is then the precondition for (if not actually the hidden reverse side of) an authentic faith in God and sincere confession of Christ. But at the same time the historical manifestation of Jesus, in whom, Christians would claim, the promise of a possible total meaning is concretely given, shows us that this ardent and aggressive yet non-violent opposition to all forms of evil, just because it conflicts with the self-interest of powerful people or groups of people, itself arouses violent opposition; in the end the one who proclaimed the glad tidings of goodwill to all and of universal peace was himself done away with. This obviously says something to us about the resistance to any theoreticizing explanation of Christian redemption or deliverance through Jesus' suffering and death.

It follows that Christian faith in God prohibits all premature attempts, whether theoretical or practical, to fix a totality of meaning, every unitary system and every totalitarian programme of action that pretends to be able to put into effect the meaning and purpose of history. The meaning of which Christianity speaks in that connection, rooted as it is in Jesus of Nazareth, is both the promise of total meaning, by reason of which the Christian does not identify what has already been achieved with the promised eschatological meaning nor feels discouraged by failures and even disasters, and a prophetic or critical source of authoritative judgement upon all anticipatory attempts to realize the totality (in the world or in the Church).

All this raises the question of the relationship between history *qua* suffering and history *qua* salvation. One part of our history – the segment occupied by the life and death of Jesus – cannot possibly determine history as a totality, unless this life (up to and including the death) does in some sense concentrate in itself the total meaning of history, as being itself an eschatological event, even though history continues on its way.

## §2   The question of an ultimate meaning and of the universal horizon of understanding resistant to theorizing

Particular experience of meaning, it has been argued, is logically only possible on grounds of a question about total meaning inevitably implied in it because of the logical implication of a potential total meaning. Thus the meaning of each historical event becomes definitive and only fully evident in the context of the universal, final meaning of history as a whole – should that in fact be given. What is implied in particular experiences of meaning is only the *question* about universal meaning. This logical implication does not, however, say that 'universal history' must or will in reality signify a definitive, positive meaning, and thus a 'final good' or salvation. Logos and facticity stand related in an irresolvable tension, and for us history remains ambiguous: we cannot on a rational and theoretical basis reach out in advance for a universal total meaning. Since the historical process of coming-to-be has not been concluded, every particular experience of meaning is subject to a fundamental doubt which neither philosophy nor science can resolve.

Now the question of universal meaning, implied in all partial meaning experiences as well as in expostulatory contrast experiences within the same history, is confronted with the phenomenon of 'religions'. In the religious way of encountering reality there is clearly and explicitly thematized and affirmed 'in faith' a definite, universal, final meaning – the *eschaton* of history. Thus Christianity speaks of Jesus Christ as the ultimate 'point' of all history. That is a profession of faith. The question then is whether human reason is open, on a critical and rational basis, to the understanding of this divine revelation – and in such a way that, for its part, faith cannot entrench itself in a trouble-free zone and declare itself immune from critical thinking.

Elsewhere, in an essay not as yet developed further, it is true, I have argued that what for religious faith is a conviction and a thesis functions in theological thinking as a 'hypothesis', which then in one way or another is tested on the material of our human experiences.[45] This means that the at least implicit question about total meaning which appears from the analysis of particular meaning experiences in our history, is not the same thing as the Christian affirmation of total meaning in Jesus Christ. It is an open question, because the implication of a total meaning does not shed light on any registrable, specific form in which that meaning becomes reality and is not simply a logical implication. Reflecting upon it the theologian, hypothetically at first, identifies the Christian confession of belief as the response confirming the logically implied final meaning as a specific reality: as a specific answer to the question about universal meaning. From the standpoint of systematic theology, or theology as a scientific discipline, this identification is in the first instance provisional and hypothetical. The theologian must verify (or disallow) the hypothesis from the concrete data provided by man's experience of history.[46] Only so can the theologian as 'scientific investigator' rebut the charge of reasoning inside a closed 'hermeneutical circle' which presupposes what still has to be critically tested. For nothing is taken for granted here: as in every scientific discipline, one simply works with a hypothesis which is going to be tested. Naturally, this testing will be quite different from the verification of hypotheses and theories in the physical sciences; it is not direct and will never be apodictically compelling; yet a real testability must still be possible, if theology wants to be able to make meaningful, non-ideological pronouncements and so be described as a scientific discipline. There must exist a method of ascertaining whether the hypothesis finds support in our experience and whether in so doing it opens up everybody's future.

Whether some salvific activity on God's part does indeed take place in Jesus of Nazareth must up to a point be a matter of actual experience and be expressible in faith-language. For if, according to Christian belief, God is the ultimate all-determining reality (for the time being still 'broadly speaking', that is: allowing for the substantial limitation, as for instance almighty love displaying itself in 'weakness'), then in this view of reality there is no earthly thing within the whole that can be fully understood without its reference to God; then God opens a deeper understanding of all reality. From this it follows that the theologian's 'hypothesis' (the thesis of faith) must be capable in one or another (not apodictic but very significant) way of being tested by and finding support in the reality of man, his world and society, in short, in our historical experience.

I long ago realized that this entails a clear break with the 'implicit intuition' of the meaning-totality maintained by classical philosophy like that of D. de Petter, L. Lavelle and the French *philosophes de l'Esprit*. Within this tradition (not without a real grounding in Thomas Aquinas' view of reality) the participation of the total meaning in every particular experience of meaning was brilliantly analysed. This implicit participation of the total meaning in each individual meaning experience Thomas was able casually to endorse – rightly so, at the time – in a medieval (-patristic) society, where a single (Christian) destiny for the life of man – the beatific vision of God – was a self-evident social truth with (from a sociological viewpoint) appropriate plausibility-structures. Now, in our society where divergent ideologies and outlooks on life compete in the 'common market' of world history, that is certainly not the case! Therefore the participation idea, as it is called, has to be replaced by the idea of anticipation of a total meaning amid a history still in the making. The result is that each specific or identifying, anticipative total meaning (whether that of the *eschaton* of Christian faith or that of the classless society of the future or J. Habermas's ideal anticipation of a non-coercive communication in an ideally democratic society) can only present itself to the forum of critical reason (in the first instance) as a 'hypothesis', of which the cognitive value – and so the value as reality or truth – will have to 'appear' from its being tested on the material of our human experiences in history. Those experiences will allow or disallow the identifying anticipation of total meaning (the Christian one, the Marxist one or that of the critical society-theory, etc.) before the forum of critical reflection, in an at any rate rationally meaningful if not rationally compelling way (as is the case in the physical sciences; but they have no patented rights in what constitutes a 'scientific approach'). In saying this I do realize that the scientific standpoint is only one of many human potentialities and strengths, and not at all uniquely effectual – even relatively. But it is an inalienable right of man's critical reason; and therefore no faith can without loss of credibility try to dodge it by appealing to the pseudo-argument that God and religion belong to a plane of our human existence that is above or beyond science. In their very nature they really are so; and one cannot define the heart of a religion in terms of its functional importance to man and his society. No direct verification is possible, therefore; but indirectly it is – that is, in respect of the definitive significance of faith in God for human experience: that is to say, religion is then tested on its own implications (and though indirectly, therefore, yet in no sense 'extrinsically'). Being able to demonstrate the personal, socio-political, secular, historical relevance of the Christian faith (within a critical stance towards society and culture) thus becomes an indirect test of religious, faith-motivated utterances.

So the question of the universal significance of Jesus of Nazareth finds its proper context within the universal horizon of understanding which, although in itself resistant to theorizing, is included (as a logical implication) in negative contrast experiences and in particular experiences of meaning – therefore within the horizon of the question, forced upon us by our history itself, as to the ultimate sense or non-sense of our human history and as to the nature of that sense or non-sense. That is our question because the process of our history evokes it in our consciousness, a process which is, after all, a variegated, pluralistic record with a potential unity (whatever concrete verbal expression one may choose to give to this fundamental thematic structure of our life; for many approaches are possible here to what reveals itself as the problem of human existence). Of special importance, it seems to me, is the fact with which we are continually being confronted, that of unaccommodated and innocent suffering, in short, the story of mankind's suffering in those shadowy patches of it for which no rational or theoretical place is any longer to be found. Mankind's suffering and the problem of evil go hand in hand with our history as a permanently thriving parasitical 'epiphenomenon' of our localized freedom. Both philosophy and theology stand bereft of counsel and of speech, faced with this complex totality of evil and of human suffering, brought about by nature, by persons and by structures. There is too much innocent and senseless suffering to rationalize the calamity in the field of ethics, hermeneutics or ontology. And history testifies to man's inability to achieve the longed-for dream of an inviolate human society, free from suffering.

The salvation that Jesus offered was dismissed, moreover, because of our praxis, the age-old yet ever new praxis of man and society, which sweeps away whatever or whoever does not fit into the pattern of things. The offer of religious salvation is – paradoxically enough – the condition of its potential rejection. Only thus was that rejection made manifest in its religious implication and only thus did it acquire an ethical depth that cannot be plumbed or measured. We rightly speak of a demonic strain in our history which, despite amelioration here and there, appears over and over again: a fundamental human impotence dogs our best intentions and achievements. The hard facts of history do not in themselves offer any guarantee or hope that ultimate *shalom* and reconciliation are possible. We humans are good at making our history on this earth go wrong or allowing it to do so. *Shalom*, universal meaning and reconciliation can therefore only be articulated, given our negative contrast experiences, in parables and eschatological symbols, in images of promise and admonition, finally of God's kingdom or God's rule, of forgiveness and *metanoia*. The rejection of proffered salvation is not theoretically explicable, because evil in all its depth is in the last analysis not amenable to understanding and eludes every theory; it will not fit into any system of ontological unity or identity-philosophy; and the only adequate response is via a practical exercise of resistance to evil, not a theory about it. Believing in a universal meaning to history therefore cannot be thematized in a 'universal history', philosophically interpreted; it only validates itself in a course of action that tries to overcome evil and suffering in the strength of the religious affirmation that things can be otherwise. Evil and suffering are the dark stain upon our history to which no one can offer a solution and which we cannot reconcile with a theodicy or ever wipe away with a social critique and the praxis resulting from it (however necessary they may be). How then is it possible to thematize the 'universal meaning' of history, in which evil and suffering are such massive components, on a basis of reason and theoretical hermeneusis?

Contrast experience, however, especially in recollection of man's actual history of accumulated suffering, has a critical cognitive value and force of its own,[47] which are not reducible to a purposive *Herrschaftwissen* (the form of knowledge proper to science and technology) or to the diverse forms of contemplative, aesthetic and ludic 'goal-less' knowledge. The peculiar cognitive value of the contrast experience of suffering grounded in iniquity is critical: *vis-à-vis* all forms of inopportunely contemplative as well as exclusively scientific-cum-technical knowledge. It is critical *vis-à-vis* a purely contemplative total perception and every theoretical unitary system, because they have already accomplished universal reconciliation; but it is critical too *vis-à-vis* the world-manipulating knowledge of science and technology in so far as they postulate man only as the controlling subject and pass over the ethical priority to which the suffering among us have a right.

The cognitive value peculiar to suffering is not only critical in regard to both positive forms of human knowing; dialectically it can also form the link between the two, contemplative and actively controlling, potentialities for knowledge of the human psyche. I am even convinced that only the passive contrast experience (with its implicit ethical demand) is able to establish an intrinsic bond between the two, because it alone possesses characteristics of both forms of knowledge. For on the one hand experiences of suffering befall man, even though this form of 'lived' experience is a negative happening, not at all the same as in the equally 'lived through' but positive joyousness of contemplative, ludic and aesthetic experiences. And on the other hand, precisely with respect to contrast experience or critical negativity, the suffering experienced lays the bridge over to a possible praxis, intended to remove both the suffering and its causes. By virtue of this intrinsic affinity, albeit in critical negativity, with both the contemplative and the nature-regulating kind of knowledge, I would call the peculiar cognitive force of the suffering practical-cum-critical, that is, a critical faculty which touches off a new praxis, which opens up and indeed is meant to bring about a better future (even though it remains a question whether this will succeed).

All this means that – given our *condition humaine* and our concrete social culture – it is only through the ethical critique of the history of mankind's accumulated suffering that in a paradoxical yet real fashion contemplation and action can be intrinsically connected with a possible realization of meaning. As a contrast experience, after all, man's experience of suffering presupposes an implicit craving for happiness, a craving for well-being or 'making whole'; and as unjust suffering it implies at least a vague consciousness of what in a positive sense human integrity or wholeness should entail. In other words, *qua* contrast experience it implies indirectly an awareness of a positive call of and to the *humanum*. Anyone who examines contrast experiences, from which new and imperative tasks are engendered, for the conditions making them possible, can confirm that such negative experiences include a positive, if so far unarticulated, feeling for value, at the same time releasing it and compelling its expression in the conscience, which begins to protest. The absence of what pertains to being is indirectly apprehended in the negative experience, and so we are able to spot what has to be done here and now, hazily still, and yet unmistakably. In that sense activity designed to overcome suffering is only possible by virtue of an at least implicit or confused anticipation of a possible universal meaning yet to come.

In contrast to the goal-directed knowledge of science and technology and also to the 'goal-less' knowledge of contemplation (which does not point beyond itself but is its own end and purpose), the peculiar cognitive value of the passive contrast experience is a knowledge which demands a future and opens it up. Besides the concepts 'goal' and 'goal-less', already used ('goal-less' here meaning 'having a point in and of itself'), the idea of 'future' now comes into our quest for a universal pre-understanding within which the question about Jesus can have a comprehensible answer. The long course of human suffering yet possesses a critical cognitive force that calls out for a praxis that will open up 'future'. Passive (suffering) contrast experiences are therefore the negative and dialectical coming to consciousness of a desiderium, a longing, and of a question about meaning 'on its way' and real freedom, wholeness and happiness to come.

Within this as yet unfinished human history of suffering in quest of meaning, liberation and final good, Jesus of Nazareth presented himself, with a message and praxis of salvation, as a fellow human being who nevertheless through his new approach to the conduct of life and his innocent suffering and dying on the cross gave us a new reading of our old history that is a source also of renewal. Its effect is to reveal that the factor mediating between the historical person, Jesus, and his significance for us now is in concrete terms the practice of Christian living within our continuing human history. Apart from the churches' solidarity with the sufferer, whoever or whatever that may be, their gospel becomes impossible to believe and understand. A 'universal horizon of understanding', therefore, is a question of man's liberated freedom, and so of a course of action in practice, of *de facto* liberation. This does not tell us what in point of substance real freedom and humanity are. The universal horizon within which question and answer concerning Jesus of Nazareth become generally accessible to all is the very concrete question of the *humanum* – a question to which no answer can be given – still less anticipated – with any absolute theory or doctrine (not even that of Christianity); for it is only to be answered by way of searching, and to a large extent empirical, initiatives. But whether man will succeed with this is nowhere inscribed in our history.

What place has Jesus of Nazareth in this whole history of human suffering in quest of meaning, liberation and salvation? It will already have become apparent from what has been said that Jesus' universal significance cannot be affirmed unmediated or by some abstractly objectivizing argument, apart from the continuing, concrete effects of Jesus' history. Those effects are vested more especially in a historically locatable practice of Christian living, offering both hope and freedom. What is more, we must not only ask about the universal 'pre-understanding', given to all and sundry as human beings, of what has been expressed in Jesus, but also stress that the Church as vehicle of the Jesus tradition must itself listen intently to the world if it is to get across to people its message of the gospel. The issue here is not simply what there is present in mankind by way of universal pre-understanding, so that everyone might be able to attend to the message of Jesus as something of concern to them at the deepest level; but equally, on the part of the churches of Christ, their deferring to the world's right to be 'world' and their listening to what the world itself has to say and is itself already doing for the well-being and happiness of men. Then, perhaps, 'the world' may have the freedom to listen to what the Christian gospel has to say to it. The concrete question with which mankind in history confronts the gospel now is: What do Jesus' message and praxis have to contribute to the overall effort to liberate humanity in the full sense of the term?

Human freedom is not a purely interior affair. It is a bodily, outward-turning freedom, which comes into its own only in an encounter of truly free persons within social provisions and structures that make freedom possible. Of ourselves we are just a potentiality for freedom and the freedom is still vacuous, if it has no content; it is through culture that freedom gives creative content to the vacuum. But no single form or degree of culture can fill it completely. Freedom concretely realized is a freedom constantly interiorized; that is to say, interior freedom depends on the encounter with free persons within social structures that give it room and protect it. The social dimension is an essential component of our inwardly free act, it helps to constitute experience of ourselves and of the world. 'Liberated freedom' thus surmounts the dualistic division between the inward and the outward. There is a constitutive relation between personal identity and collective consensus or recognition, between interior freedom and the social structures which make us free.

Liberation or 'salvation', then, is the conquest of all human, personal and social forms of alienation: salvation is the 'being in wholeness' of man, of his life and his history. Individual and society stand towards each other in an irreducibly dialectical tension. And the 'vacuum' of our freedom is never totally filled by culture. There always remains a 'balance', an openness. On the one hand we cannot say that society is the transcendental, all-embracing horizon of reality; if we do, we fail to appreciate the unimpeachable character of the human person, who is not simply a product of the social process. Nor on the other hand is personal interiority with its necessary privacy and intimacy a transcendental and all-embracing horizon, either. It follows that the alienation in man's life cannot be completely overcome in the personal or the social plane; 'liberated freedom' or true well-being transcends both person and society. There is human hurt for which no social or political cure exists; in the best of social structures men may still disintegrate in alienation; optimal structures do not automatically turn human beings into good, fully grown, humane people. Nature can be humanized and yet remain largely and ineluctably alien to man (we have only to think of death); and in the end there is our inescapable finitude, which can be a source of trust in God, but also of loneliness and anguish. That a mundane factor should be lord and master of man's total well-being, therefore, is the beginning of tyranny.

That is why whatever might ultimately close up the rift, the dichotomy in our existence, can only emerge out of an operative reality that embraces person and society, that is, the sum total of things, without doing violence to it.[48] In that way the possibility is opened up of linking the question of salvation and liberation with the question of God; the question of salvation imparted by God. Only an absolute freedom that is at the same time creative love would seem capable of bringing about universal reconciliation; which leads us to the proposition or question as to whether the recognition, in practice, of the 'being God' of God is not also the recognition of the humanness of man. This brings us to the heart of Jesus' message: God's rule or lordship, intent upon humanity. Despite the historical failure of this message Jesus bore witness to the indestructible certainty he felt regarding the salvation given by God, to a certainty which in his case was grounded in an exceptional *Abba* experience. For us it entails a promise from God that the salvation and 'making whole' of man is possible and that there is ultimately a point, a meaning, to human life. So faith in Jesus makes it possible to affirm together the two theoretically irreconcilable aspects in our human history: evil-and-suffering and salvation or a final good, enabling, allowing and obliging us none the less, in a way that is grounded in Jesus, to give the last word to well-being and goodness, because the Father is greater than all our suffering and grief and greater than our inability to experience the deepest reality as in the end a trustworthy gift.

# Jesus, parable of God and paradigm of humanity

## Chapter 1

## God's saving action in history

### §1 Historical discourse and speaking in the language of faith

A lot of people have trouble with expressions such as: God acts in history. Is this mythological talk? That is to say: Is it actually saying something, albeit in mythological language, not about God but about man, so that the substance of the reality to which it refers can be better and more fittingly expressed, in an age of critical awareness, in purely human categories? Or are we really and truly saying something here about God himself, even if it be in inadequate, merely evocative and suggestive human language (at a comprehensible level described as 'analogous')?

Our talk about God is never single in meaning, at most 'analogous', that is, a kind of indirect speech: with the world and our being-as-man as point of departure we are saying something about God himself, but with concepts and expressions really to be tested only against our mundane reality. After all, God does not act in history as men conduct their affairs in it. According to our modern varieties of experience our history, set in a context of natural history, is made by men; and it is not, as the ancients used to think, the plaything of supramundane good or evil spirits. Within a cosmic nature which to a great extent remains alien to them, (persistently surviving) human beings – I do not say 'mankind', which is an abstraction and cannot be an active subject – are themselves the active subjects of history. To speak about history *qua* history is therefore something different from speaking in faith-language about what is nevertheless the same history. If we then say that God acts in history we are not talking 'history-language' but religious language. Even so, the history discussed in faith-language is the same history of which the historiographer speaks. Faith-language has a function quite distinct from historical discourse, with a logic of its own. In both cases we are talking about our history, made by human beings. Somebody talking about it as a historian does not work in that respect with a concept of God; for him it would be, if anything, just an expression of convictions held by the people he is studying.

It follows at once that God's acting in history is not some 'interventionist activity', the outcome of which the historian should be able to measure and verify. God's activity is of course divine activity, that is, absolute, transcendent, creative. But this so far transcendent activity cannot be described as his acting in history, as this absolute initiative of God could not be at the same time immanent in our history without losing its transcendence; in other words the immanence is not a link in the totality of mundane historical factors of which history is constituted, and yet is none the less a reality. Thus it is an activity which cannot be counted in with what history already is as the activity of free persons. Yet in speaking of it we are saying, in faith-language, something about God himself and not just something about, for instance, man's attitude to God: for example, about the love or obedience man shows towards him; we are also affirming God to be such that he evokes love and merits man's adoration. If God is indeed the 'Wholly Other' without a recognizable immanence in our world, then we would revere him best by saying nothing about him. The very fact that God the Wholly Other is Creator means that he is also the Ultimate-Intimate One, the One Wholly near at hand. All this implies that in one way or another God's transcendent, creative activity will come to expression in our world; otherwise there would be no ground, no occasion even, for justifying our talk of God's acting in our history – not even in an evocative and analogous way. The transcending act which God is would be a thing we could not so much as speak of – not even in faith-language – were it not to manifest itself in the interior traffic of our world. Speaking in faith-language about God acting in history, therefore, has an experiential basis – albeit one that only faith can interpret – in our human situation within the world and history. For our speaking about God's transcendence has no ground other than our own contingency; religious language draws its material from our experience of contingency as 'disclosure', in which deeper perspectives are opened up.

Yet since for the believer in God the world and history do actually constitute the field of God's activity, evocatively communicated to us, then religious discourse (or faith-language) and scientific discourse, however mutually distinct, really must have something to do with each other; they are both talking about the same reality: our world and our history. If, for instance, scientific discourse and historical discourse are true, then living nature and our history must intrinsically be such that they are a real basis for, and give content or substance to, the account of things proffered by the physical scientist and the historian. But then it is equally the case that this same world and history are intrinsically such as to be the basis for, and give substance to, faith-language and the theological account of things. In other words there must be traces in history itself sufficient to permit and enable us to speak justifiably in the language of faith about a saving activity of God in history.[49]

To speak in faith-language implies that the human relevance of what is said in 'secular' and scientific language regarding nature and history has at the same time a religious relevance, is ultimately relevant for God and our relationship to him. The religious language of faith adds nothing new, no 'new information', to what the non-religious language has already said (where would it get any such new information from?), but it does articulate and thematize the non-divine or contingent character of the reality already made discussable; it sees in it as in a shadow the passing presence of the creating God – as with Moses of old, who did not see God, only 'his back', when he had already passed on his way.

## §2  The revelation or action of God in salvation-history as experienced and enunciated in the language of faith

A.  THE CREATIVE ACTIVITY OF GOD IN OUR WORLD: 'HUMAN PERSON' AND 'BEING OF GOD'

The person who believes in God will speak of man as 'having been created' by God; by which he means to say that at the deepest level man derives his whole existence and activity from the creator-God. He is as it were 'first' of God and only in that and through that, himself; his existence and life are 'grounded' in God: his whole life is undergirded by the inexhaustible freedom of God, who in a transcendent fashion literally gives man to himself. If it then appears from a 'secular' manner of speaking that the human individual is a person, this, expressed in faith-language, signifies that he is a person through the transcending, active immanence of God. Through transcendence God is immanent: that is to say, all that man enjoys of positivity is genuinely of himself – yet as derived from God. Although really separate and distinct from God, the human person cannot at bottom be contrasted to God. The ground of the distinction between God and man (creature) therefore cannot lie on God's side, only on that of man, and then not even in what he is positively, but only in the fact that he does not have this positive human existence in and of himself; in other words, the ground of the real distinction between God and man is vested in man's finitude. It is that in fact which serves to distinguish all creatures from God, even in regard to their positive being. We therefore cannot lump God and man together as two beings standing next each other or vying with each other. Nevertheless God falls outside the proper description and definition of what it is to be man, while man himself derives purely from God. Thus 'being-as-man' is a quite specific, substantive description of a way of 'being of God'. By 'being of God' man is himself.

Both 'aspects' – being oneself and being of God – are not partial but total 'views' of one and the same reality, so that the one adds nothing new to what the other already is. That is why we cannot speak in this connection of 'two components' or of 'two natures': a 'human person' and a 'being of God'. A degree of tension, however, a dialectic of an 'aspectual' sort, is undeniable. We can contemplate things – including man – in themselves, that is, in their own order of secular reality, as it were, without taking into account their constitutive 'being of God'; but it is precisely in this peculiar and independent quality of theirs (approachable in its own right) that for faith-language (which affirms their constitutive derivation from God) they are 'of and by God'. Their peculiar selfhood and their creatureliness are not two part-aspects or two components that together might be supposed to form a whole. No more are they to be lumped together. For faith-language, therefore, the creature is actually more of God than of itself, because it draws its self-being from God's transcendence. In other words, the creature, man, is not identical with his deepest reality; there is in him a 'credit factor', an inner reality (which he himself is) that points to the transcendently creating but through immanence indwelling God. For that very reason the reality in which we live and which we ourselves are is an inexhaustible mystery: the Mystery itself of God overflowing into his creatures. In their fashion, therefore, profane language and scientific language are speaking about a reality which they too are never able adequately to explain. However restricted the object of their study might be, they are drawing upon what is inexhaustible.

Naturally, therefore, we are bound to speak about these two total 'aspects' of the single reality within which we are set in two different languages; for the way of approach – although on both sides given only in perception on man's part – divides off where for some there occurs in this perception a 'disclosure', and we perceive in the distinctively secular character of man and world a breach and a depth-dimension in which we apprehend the traces of their 'being of God'. This creatureliness or 'being of God' is brought to expression in the language of faith; the 'being themselves' of things, on the other hand, can be discussed from many different angles of vision: in the discourse of psychology and sociology, of the physical sciences and of history, and so forth. This also entails that the deepest mystery of things, and more especially of man, cannot be articulated in terms of the exact sciences; it eludes them, while at the same time making this scientific way of speaking possible. The ultimate problem of man's salvation, his final good, lies therefore in a plane beyond that of science – however much may be done – and it is a great deal – at the scientific and thus at the technical level for the liberation of man, in so far as he is alienated from himself by physical, psychic and social conditioning factors.

So for the believer, who affirms the creative and living God, every created thing, according to its own measure and definition, is a constitutive reference to God. For human beings this means that the dimension of their very being makes them open to a conscious, mutual presence between God and man – even if of a very peculiar kind. For this 'being of God' which attends man and all his works because it is the very ground and source of his own being-as-man is at the same time the root and breeding-place of all religious awareness, at least as a constitutive question as to what could give a ground and a meaning to his own problematical 'just being'; it also provides a basis for the core of that order of reality and experience which presents itself in our history as 'religions'.

Independently of this interior reference to God in the heart of our existence we can also reflect on the human person and come to realize that the individual human being only becomes a person through self-giving to his fellows in a world which he has to humanize. For seeing this, a sense of religion is not *per se* necessary. Being a man for others, therefore, may be the revealing definition of an individual human being who – aside from those people who believe in God – stands within history. The other has need of me in order to be himself and achieve identity as a person. The notion that people can be a 'burden' or a 'blessing' to one another is indeed a cultural thing which man can discover. In faith-language the believer in God will express the same thing – and more. The moment the other person appeals to my caring commitment to him – somebody for whom I could and should work and who signifies for me an invitation to caring and dedication – all this likewise manifests the sovereignly free call of the Creator, making himself known in our human world. The believer in God will interpret this, on the basis of what for him is reality, as a summons to communion also with God, experienced in the (ambivalent) forms of our very localized common humanity and responsible concern with our human history. Admittedly, this love and care have a historical and geographical situation but are none the less unlimited; they have more intimate as well as wider and in the end distant horizons which open up, as it were, more and more. This is how being human in concern for the other, the release of human love, via my delimited and yet boundlessly open situation (especially in modern circumstances) becomes virtually unlimited and universal. In it the believer catches a glimpse of the universal, creative love of the one God who, in and through human beings, means to bring about liberation, for their salvation and final good.

Yet in all this it must not be forgotten that the creature, concretely man, not only reveals but at the same time veils God. That is to say: God's transcendence through immanence, and with respect to man (as a personal being) through overwhelming immanence, has a referential character. Please understand me: I am not saying at all that God's transcendence as such stands over against his own immanence in the world (history and human beings) – that is indeed an unthinkable idea; but we are bound to say that God's immanence only permits us a non-divine, creaturely view, in profile, of his transcendence, which after all is not constituted by his immanence in the creature. To affirm that it is would in my view be the definition of pantheism or panentheism. True, it is not so easy to provide a satisfactory definition of pantheism as contrasted with not only the Christian idea of creation but all sorts of tenets born of a monistic, a-cosmic and pan-cosmic religiosity. Furthermore, as L. Lavelle has already pointed out, even for (Christian) theism there is always a risk of pantheism.[50] Pantheism is not defined by its powerful emphasis on the unity between God and his creatures; expressions such as *sumus aliquid Dei* or *sumus Dei* – we are 'of God' – can have a Christian as well as a pantheistic implication; and what is more, many forms of authentic pantheism accept both God's activity in creation and a term distinct from it: the creature. What is specifically peculiar to pantheism is its denial of the gratuity or radical quality of 'grace' in being creaturely, so that (tacitly or explicitly) it asserts that God intrinsically needs created things in order to complete the very definition of the 'being-God' of God. Such a pantheistic conception of God rules out in principle the possibility of a sovereignly free self-yielding of God to his creatures, to man, in that the need for self-completion then makes impossible any free and abounding self-communication on God's part. A self-giving of God is then a term without meaning or content. Moreover, history is deprived of the meaning it may have for God's freedom.

If therefore God does not derive his peculiar selfhood or being-God (meaning, for us, his transcendence) from his actually superabundant immanence in created things – which do not restrict or truncate God's transcendence but manifest his presence only in a confined, creaturely, non-divine measure – then this does indeed imply that being-as-man, in its very disclosure of its 'being of God', at the same time actually veils the 'being-God'. And thereby it acquires a referential character, indicating what God's transcendence (God himself) is in and of itself, since it is not constituted by his immanent presence in our history; for that immanence is more of a free gift. To put it pictorially: the creature – world, history, man – is the presence of and the area in which God is '*qua* gift'; God himself is the presence of and area in which God is 'in the nature of the case', in and through his absolutely free being-as-God itself. To deny this, it seems to me, would entail a restriction and reduction of God's transcendence. For that very reason our human world can only permit of a mediated immediacy[51] between God and man. Not as if a dual notion of transcendence were thereby created: God's intrinsic peculiarity and his transcendence through interiority; but that we get only a limited perspective on the transcending God via his immanence and traces in this world, in history and in man, in our fellow-men. Indeed only a 'seeing the back of God', as the Old Testament puts it. Not however because God has already 'gone by' but because he is always 'before' man in history: he is God 'before us'. For historical, still future-making men, God's transcendence through interiority is indeed essentially something that points towards the future: he goes before us towards a future, his future in us. 'Being secure in God', then, is assurance of a future, is hope and confidence, not resting in the present.

However much it is created things, and they alone, that mediate God's presence to us, yet they are not God, not even in their cosmic or historical totality. When therefore we consider God, it can only be from within the perspective provided by the non-divine, that is, by precisely what does not make God God: the creaturely world. This is an insight we must never forget when the question is raised as to the unique character of the revelation of God that has occurred in Jesus.

It follows, of course, from what we have just been saying that the humanly peculiar and universal unicity of Jesus of Nazareth – as confessed by the Christian churches – ought to become apparent from the peculiarity and unicity of his relationship to his fellow-man, as a way of living in practice imbued with a peculiar and unique relationship to the living God – and that within the restricted, very contingent, ambivalent limits of a restricted, earthly course of events. Any question of a 'supra-historical' and absolute ideality is ruled out from the start. Jesus is *the* 'significantly other' one among us.

## B. GOD'S SAVING ACTIVITY IN HISTORY

The ground of any justifiable, albeit evocative and analogous, talk about God's activity in our world is his (through immanence) transcendent activity in creation: our world and its actual history. However, there may be present in our world good grounds for introducing into our talk about God's activity in the world differentiations, in virtue of which (without shifting these on to God himself) we go on to describe the living reality of God in different ways. After all, the ultimate ground and source of this world, even in its differentiations, is still the living reality of God.

All continuity notwithstanding, an unmistakable distinction would appear to emerge, for instance, between man and animal. In man a surprising novelty discloses itself, something specifically human – a degree of discontinuity with all other creatures. Anyone who believes in the creator-God and so would speak of these things in faith-language can and may justifiably speak, although in evocative and analogous language, of a 'special activity' of God directed towards man as a whole, and therefore of a special, overflowing immanence of the transcendent God – an immanence, that is, which (in view of human consciousness) really can become 'presence': conciliation, the question of encounter, calling, disclosing oneself as present, 'revelation'. By virtue of for instance the distinction between the inner processes of nature and human history (despite their being essentially interwoven) the believer in God has justification and reason for speaking of God's special activity in human history.

In his history man's concern is with his well-being and happiness, with the sought-after *humanum*. Starting from that, the believer in God is entitled to describe God's activity in history as God's salvific activity in history. This latter activity too is transcendent, is not 'intervention' in the 'normal' course of events. Like any properly divine activity it is 'creative', sovereignly free, transcendent and therefore none the less immanent in our history; it is this 'secular history', so called, but in its 'total' aspect of 'being of God'. Only in a 'disclosure' experience, therefore, will it be possible for faith-language to articulate it in terms of its experienceable and recognizable expressions in that history. It must be possible, then, to discover in our history 'traces' of God's saving presence passing on its way, if there is to be a basis for speaking of his salvific activity in history. Just as the discontinuity we experience between man and animal causes us, in using faith-language, to speak in differing terms about God's dealing with man and with the animals, so – every form of continuity conceded – a human experience of discontinuity must be the sole reason enabling us to speak with justification of a special saving activity of God in history. Such universal activity on the part of the creative God, co-extensive with the whole of human history, the believer in God is able and entitled to call (in the language of faith) a 'special saving activity' only if within that history 'discontinuous' phenomena do indeed occur here and there, phenomena which are nevertheless the work of man himself. Here again there is no question of non-transcendent, and thus intervening, salvific acts of God. All this implies that only in an 'indirect revelation' does God manifest and make himself known to human beings as active in salvation-history. Through the intermediary or agency of the liberating conduct of men in quest of salvation-from-God, God reveals himself 'indirectly' in history as salvation for men. It is more especially in surprising, 'discontinuous' historical events, experiences and interpretations that God's saving initiative is shown. If God's saving action is both a 'here-and-now' and a divine reality, it will be possible to find in our history 'signs' of God's liberating concern with man – signs which must be noted, seen and interpreted, because in themselves they are, like every historical phenomenon, ambiguous, ambivalent and calling for interpretation. It is only in the interpretation, only as experienced and verbalized by human beings, that they come to be recognized as signs of God's salvific activity in a history that is nevertheless made by men.

### C. THE DEFINITIVE SAVING ACTS OF GOD IN HISTORY

Should there be a definitive and decisive saving action of God in our history, then it will be achieved in experienceable, historical events, interpreted and enunciated in the language of faith. If Jesus of Nazareth is declared to be the eschatological, definitive, saving action of God, this must be something available to religious experience and discussion in faith-language, with as its starting-point the earthly, historical phenomenon of Jesus. Then within all the continuity of our normal human history there will nevertheless be made visible in Jesus a striking 'discontinuity', an overwhelming immanence of God, which can be experienced and, in faith-language, expounded as the historically operative sign in which God's definitive salvific action for the salvation of all men is concentrated. Then in Jesus a decisive sign of definitive salvation must have appeared within our history. Then we indeed have to do with a human story in which 'the story of God' has itself been brought to expression.

It means that in the human life of Jesus the ultimate point of man's existence has been expressed in word and action – and that, in a normative and exemplary sense. Here again the manifestation of God is only 'revealed' in the interpretative act of faith, in that, therefore, of those who understand and accept Jesus as definitive for their understanding of themselves and of reality. Revelation then issues in the response of faith: yes, indeed! This is how a truly human existence has to be lived. The eschatological presence of God in Jesus and man's ultimate comprehension of reality are correlative.

What this amounts to is that we have to speak about Jesus Christ in historical terms as well as in faith-language, while both languages are dealing with one and the same reality, without our being able to lump together and treat as one these two total aspects of Jesus' life – he is fully man and in so being is the decisive historical manifestation of God's definitive salvific activity – in as it were a 'third language' (which would encompass the other two within a unitive language), although it is through faith alone that we can experience in the historical person of Jesus the definitive salvific activity in its transcendence. Both languages retain their own logic (as Chalcedon so rightly said 'without confusion'), but they are both talking about the one Jesus of Nazareth. Of 'one and the same person', the man Jesus of Nazareth, it is then said that he is true historical man and yet precisely, in being that, is also the definitive saving action of God. How these two total 'aspects' are ultimately to be viewed is the Christological problem.

Chapter 2

# The Christological problem

## §1 Definitive salvation in Jesus as coming from God

### A. GOD'S MESSAGE IN JESUS

From a historical standpoint it is impossible to determine whether a human being bound by time and history has a universal significance, universal and definitive for all human beings. But signs and traces of this, calling for some identification and interpretation on the part of others, must be given, of course, within our human compass of understanding if what is said about Jesus' unique universality is not to be ideological. Jesus of Nazareth must at least have been manifest in history as being, in respect of man's definitive salvation or final good, a catalysing question – an invitation. Christians have interpreted that question and invitation in a very specific way: they have found the definitive promise of salvation and liberation imparted by God in Jesus and so have had reason enough to commend him to others, and thus to witness to Jesus Christ. This has been going on right up to the present day; so that we too are confronted now with the possibility of the catalysing question and invitation that Jesus is; but . . . in an entirely new situation: for us Jesus raises the issue of God in an age which in most if not all sectors of its life appears to do without God. The issue that arises out of Jesus cannot be the assertion, whether justifiable or not, that Jesus is the historical embodiment of an existential message or critique of society. For such a message we of the twentieth century have less and less need to look back to someone who lived in the first century of our era – whyever should we? The historical Jesus was a person who still faces us with the question whether the reality of God is not the most important thing in the life of man, a question which, given a positive answer, demands of us a radical *metanoia*: a re-orientating of our own lives. That is why the question which Jesus continues to put to us is in the first instance fundamentally dis-orientating.

In a modern situation particularly we do well to recognize the dis-tinction between Jesus of Nazareth as being this catalysing question and invitation, and the Christological answer given by the Christian churches to the question. This is also, it seems to me, a consequence of the new pastoral situation in which we are living: namely, that (besides ourselves acknowledging and celebrating the salvation found to be imparted by God in Jesus) we contrive in our proclamation (as well as in Christology) to present Jesus as first and foremost a question catalysing what are the problems of our most deeply human, personal and social life. The earthly Jesus was precisely, in fact, someone who in specific, historically very localized circumstances raised the issue of taking a stand for him or against him. Jesus himself never directly answers the question of who he is. His personal identity is as it were woven into his message, way of life and death. Therefore the question raised for us by his message, ministry and death can only be fully answered by making a response to the person of Jesus. Like every other historical occurrence the earthly Jesus did after all share in the ambiguity of history, needing to be interpreted and identified.

In Jesus we are confronted with someone who out of his personal *Abba* experience makes us an assured promise of a 'future with and from God' and in his ministry actually proffers it. Apart from the reality of this very original *Abba* experience his message is an illusion, a vacuous myth. To put one's trust in Jesus is to ground oneself in what was named as the ground of Jesus' experience: the Father. It entails recognizing the authentic non-illusory reality of Jesus' *Abba* experience. This recognition is alone possible in an act of believing trust which, although not deriving from rational motives, can yet adduce sufficient rational motives for us to describe such believing trust as humanly and morally not unjustified. The 'historical Jesus' allows of the Christian response as an interpretation which because of the ambiguity of everything historical is never necessary but is ration-ally and morally justified, recognizable in the historical phenomenon, but in itself going beyond rational motives without excluding them.

The startling thing – in our modern situation – about the consequence of Jesus' conduct, his message and its historical miscarriage in his death is that it requires a thorough overhaul of the current idea of total emancipation through self-liberation. His death by execution, which failed to shake his confidence in the coming rule of God, centred as it was in the interests of humanity – he continued, when faced with his approaching death, to proffer salvation on God's behalf – constitutes for us the challenging message that historical failures are not the last word – that even in radical fiascos we may continue to trust in God. Jesus' message is essentially aimed at being a message about God and from God, a message which in the successes and failures of his life as well as in the historical fiasco on the cross he maintained to the end, as sealing the authenticity of his life and message. This life of Jesus calls us to a *metanoia*, to this effect: whatever may happen, go on trusting in God; then will be realized – how? 'I know not', just look at the cross! – a liberation, salvation for men, eschatologically completed. This is the challenging message of Jesus, which on the one hand leaves room for and encourages the process of man's liberation and emancipation, on the other surmounts it in an unshakeable confidence in a total salvation that only God can give and that is a transcendent, since divine, answer to the finite character of our being-as-man, a finitude under the index and exponent of which every emancipation and critical praxis must stand. Because of his finitude (the metaphysical fissure in his nature) man is a being whose well-being, wholeness and fulfilment are dependent on the grace and mercy of his Creator. His realization, in faith, of being accepted by God in Jesus Christ marks proleptically the victory of grace, even in the historical, no longer accommodatable discomfiture of man's finite autonomy.

Even when dying, Jesus has no desperate concern with his own identity and thus with self-preservation, but is taken up with the matter of God's rule which, although receding as his eyes grow dim, will most surely come. Thus Jesus' message, bearing the signature of his death, calls upon us to revise our self-understanding, by speaking of God who silently reveals himself in Jesus' historically helpless failure on the cross. God has man's interest at heart, but in a world which itself does not always appear to do so; for that reason God's love for man in Jesus takes on a colouring which we ourselves have mixed. In his love for man, however, God surmounts all our mixing and making without doing violence to our own finite autonomy. It says something that it was a Jewish thinker and philosopher, E. Lévinas,[52] who could speak of the irresistible power of the 'defenceless other one' who goes on trusting. But from that it would appear that although interrelated, ethics and religion cannot be simply identical.

Why – so it might be argued – not look for the same sort of inspiration from other figures in world history? There could be some hard and long discussion about that; but the question ignores a very concrete datum already to hand: namely, that Jesus has appeared in our concrete history, can no longer be spirited out of it, so that the recollection of this thing will always be an irremovable historical challenge. The response to this challenge with a Christian identification has grounds enough, therefore, to continue to recommend this trust in Jesus and to witness to it, not just 'in words' but primarily through a concrete 'lived' witness in which the praxis of God's kingdom as proclaimed by Jesus tries to take on flesh and blood. 'The message' without the practice of it in real life will in modern circumstances simply not work any more. In that case it becomes ideological propaganda, not a challenge or an inviting testimony. That is why – even a 'new' – theological Christology will be inefficient in its witness if it is not a theological reflex of what is actually made visible in the life of the churches by way of praxis of the kingdom of God, of Christian ortho-praxis – in prayer and care for other people. Only then will a deeper reflection upon Jesus' identity be productive.

It could be said – and is indeed the obscure as well as lucid feeling of not a few among us: Is 'human life' not living on illusion and . . . dying in illusions? I would say: Indeed! that is an alternative possibility. Only I do not see it as the Christian alternative, and believe that in face of the historical fiasco of Jesus of Nazareth not history, but the benevolent One opposed to evil – God – has the last word. This the early Christians try to express with their credal affirmation of Jesus' resurrection. That wording may be subjected to criticism – and rightly so. However, what I as a Christian believer will not give up is *this*: for anyone who believes in a 'God of creation and covenant' the historical failure of Jesus of Nazareth cannot possibly be the final word. On this score is not the 'Christian response' of the New Testament something profoundly human and full of real meaning – even rationally, if not rationalistically, cogent – 'that you may not grieve as others do who have no hope' (1 Thess. 4:13)? Human history – with its successes, failures, illusions and disillusions – is surmounted by the living God. That is the heart of the Christian message.

B.   SALVATION IN JESUS OR IN THE CRUCIFIED-AND-RISEN ONE?

It is true that man's life in history is concluded by death in a definitive way and so is then able to be seen as a fixed, rounded totality; but death itself does not constitute this whole. Although it is only after death, therefore, that a final judgement can be given on somebody's life, we cannot assign to death an exclusive, all-determining importance. So long as Jesus was living in our contingent, unfinished human history, for those who had already been able to experience in him something of God's saving revelation that revelation was incomplete, therefore, and still in process of coming to be. So 'Christology' is fundamentally a declaration, made in faith, about the totality of Jesus' life. The Christian 'disclosure' experience therefore presupposes the life of Jesus as a whole. Only with Jesus' death, the conclusion of his earthly life, can our account of Jesus begin – even though our Jesus story or our recognition of Christ will also be a way of identifying Jesus of Nazareth – no myth or gnosis.

Jesus' message, his way of living his life and in the end his very person were in fact rejected. In a straight historical sense Jesus failed in his life's project. If therefore his message and conduct, however essential, cannot be the final word, at any rate they can be for us a ground of real hope. It is precisely to this question that the gospel responds with faith in Jesus' resurrection.

It becomes apparent more particularly from the missionary sermons, so called, in the Acts (see Part Three) that there is a connection between Jesus and the Spirit (Acts 10:34–43; 2:22–36; 4:26–27; 3:12–26; 13:16–41). In those sermons Luke elucidates for his Greek readers the meaning of 'christ', anointed, that is, the one filled with God's Spirit: 'God was with him' (Acts 2:22; 3:14; 10:38); Christ himself is 'God's' (1 Cor. 3:23). Jesus belongs to God: 'your holy one', 'your servant', 'his messiah', 'my son' (Acts 2:27; 3:14; 4:27; 13:35; 3:13; 3:26; 4:30; 3:18; 13:33). The rejection of Jesus by people is counterbalanced by Jesus' belonging to God. Believing in the earthly Jesus means (in these missionary addresses) recognizing him to be God's eschatological prophet of and for Israel, the final messenger 'from God', filled with God's Spirit, proclaiming the rule of God to be near at hand and turning it into word and action. Believing in the *risen* Jesus is to acknowledge him in his universal saving importance to all people. These two phases are contained, on the one hand by Jesus' belonging to God in a peculiar sense, on the other by God's fidelity to this Jesus. The resurrection, as the action of God in and with Jesus, therefore not only endorses Jesus' message and praxis, it also reveals his person to be inseparably linked with God and with the message itself. In Jesus' death and resurrection men's total rejection of God's offer of salvation and the persisting offer of it extended in the risen Jesus meet each other. The One crucified and risen is God's victory over what on man's side was a rejection of God's offer of definitive salvation in Jesus. Through the resurrection God actually breaks that rejection of definitive salvation. God gives definitive salvation thus in Jesus Christ, a future to him who neither has nor really deserves to have any future. He loved us even 'while we were yet sinners' (Rom. 5:8). In the risen Jesus God shows himself to be the power of anti-evil, of unconditional goodness that in sovereign fashion refuses to recognize, and breaks, the overweening power of evil. In his acutest need, in suffering and crucifixion, true to his prophetic mission and message, Jesus yields his personal secret, the mystery of his person: his inviolable link with God, while the Father too gives up his secret concerning Jesus: the permanent commitment of the Father to Jesus. Jesus' life, his cross and resurrection in the power of the Spirit thereby reveal the depth of the Father-Son relationship, and indeed raise the problem of the Trinitarian God.

With the mission of Jesus to Israel, God fulfils the promise of the old covenant, thus saying 'yes' to creation and covenant. Only when Israel has rejected God's definitive offer of salvation in Jesus does God bring about in and through the resurrection of Jesus a 'new creation'. So at one and the same time Jesus of Nazareth is the completion of the Old Testament, and in him as the rejected yet risen One the New Testament has started. Despite all the continuity between our real human history and the new creation on the basis of Jesus' resurrection there is, because of the rejection of Jesus as the completer of creation and covenant, a discontinuity that no human activity can bridge. This is intrinsically conjoined with continuity thanks to the new, unexpected salvific action of God which surmounts all the failure associated with the rejected and crucified fulfiller of creation and covenant and confirms the One rejected in his function of universal saviour. Of this surmounting, Jesus' integration of his own rejection and death into his real proffer of salvation (the point of his whole life) within our history is the intra-historical index: 'It was God who reconciled us to himself in Jesus Christ' (2 Cor. 5:19).

Because Jesus' belonging to him whom he called *Abba* is confirmed

J.E.C.–X

by God in the resurrection, that resurrection is at the same time God's endorsement of Jesus' message and way of conducting himself, his praxis. It means too that the 'contents' of the eschatological liberation expressed in faith-language with the category 'resurrection from the dead' has to be filled in from the historical ministry of Jesus, therefore from his sayings and actions which are 'endorsed' by it. The dilemma: salvation in Jesus of Nazareth or salvation in the crucified-and-risen One, is therefore a false dilemma, since in the second term God's 'ratification' of 'Jesus of Nazareth' is affirmed, while the first term gives concrete substance to what God is ratifying. To put it another way: 'crucified-and-risen One' without the concrete Jesus of Nazareth is a myth or a gnostic mystery, while the 'historical Jesus', despite his surprising message and conduct, without what Christians call the resurrection would have been one more failure, slipping into place in the succession of innocent victims in our history of human suffering – a fleeting hope which each time seems to confirm the surmise that a lot of people do not *take* this, but at the same time the Utopian character of which is felt, in view of the peculiar nature and force of gravity exerted by our own history.

Thus there is no gap between 'Jesus of Nazareth' and the 'crucified-and-risen One'. Because of the life which preceded it, the death of Jesus does face us, it is true, with a fundamental question about God, with as sole alternatives: either that we have to say that God – that is, the God of the rule of God proclaimed by Jesus – was an illusion on Jesus' part (and for his followers a disillusion); or that we are obliged by this rejection and death of Jesus radically to revise our understanding of God, our own ideas of God and our understanding of history and to discard them as invalid, in that the proper nature of God is validly manifested only in the life and death of this Jesus, and through it a new perspective on the future is opened up. God, of whom Jesus spoke as being utterly reliable, is either a tragic farce or we are invited to commit ourselves to this God of Jesus, both in his preaching and in his historical failure. Faith in Jesus can only take the form of this affirmation of belief in God.

Within a context of Christian faith, the rift or gap does not lie in Jesus' death – this, after all, he felt to be part and parcel of his being sent to proffer salvation, and experienced as a historical consequence of his caring, loving service of people (this is the very least -- but then also certain – thing we have to hold on to as the 'historically hard' core of the Last Supper tradition). The break does lie in the rejection of his message and praxis, which ended in the rejection of his person. That is why God's act of endorsement in the resurrection bears upon the very person of Jesus inherent in his message and conduct. Both the rejection and God's 'amen' to the person of Jesus ratify the specific character of the Jesus event, in which both person and project – thus person, message and praxis – form an indissoluble unity. For the Christian affirmation of belief, therefore, God's rule could assume the aspect of Jesus Christ; and it was possible to speak of the 'Lord Jesus Christ' as a concrete synonym for the rule of God proclaimed by Jesus.

When we talk about God's 'amen' to Jesus' person, message and praxis, we have to bear in mind, of course, that this too is an affirmation of faith – not a ratification or legitimation in the customary human sense. The resurrection confirms that God was constantly with Jesus throughout his life – right up to the human dereliction of his death on the cross, the moment also of God's own silence. One faith-motivated conviction – the resurrection – cannot serve to legitimate another, namely, that of God's saving activity in Jesus of Nazareth. The real legitimation, evident to all, remains thus totally eschatological (this is the point of the Parousia). For that reason our faith in the resurrection is itself still a prophecy and a promise for this world – *qua* prophecy unsheltered and unprotected, defenceless and vulnerable. And so the life of the Christian is not visibly 'justified' by the facts of history. But a person believing in Jesus' resurrection is surely freed by this belief from any compulsive urge to self-justification and from any insistence that God should take man and his world, here and now, under his protection and should ratify them. The servant is not greater than his Lord. Just as Jesus did, the Christian takes the risk of entrusting himself and the vindication of his living to God; he is prepared to receive that vindication where Jesus did: beyond death. And so, reconciled to God's way of doing things, he is reconciled also with himself, with others, with history, in which he tries nevertheless to achieve emancipation and justice. For that very reason he is able to throw himself without fierce resentment or aggressiveness into the business of turning this world into a fairer and happier one, without alienation. Yet no more than Jesus can the Christian present any legitimating credentials unless it be through his putting into practice the kingdom of God, concretely, in this human history of ours.

C. THE INTRINSIC SIGNIFICANCE OF JESUS' RESURRECTION FOR SALVATION

The resurrection of Jesus has often functioned in many theological traditions as the great miracle, accomplished in Jesus by God, of course, yet without any relation to ourselves. It has been envisaged as something empirical and objectivized, as though, given the empty tomb and the appearances, it should really be obvious to believer and unbeliever alike, even if not with mathematical certainty, that Jesus rose. In modern Protestant and, less distinctly, in some Catholic publications on the other hand, there is a more or less undeniable tendency to identify Jesus' resurrection with the renewed life and Easter (Christian) faith of the disciples after the death of their Master. The disciples then hand on 'the things of Jesus', basing themselves on this Easter renewal of their lives. However, these writers (in particular R. Bultmann and W. Marxsen) leave us guessing as to whether Jesus has risen in person and whether, living now beyond death and present among us in a new way, it is he himself who brings about for the apostles this renewal of their lives – in his strength.

Before we start criticizing this school of thought for what is indeed, in my view, its error and for what it fails to say, we ought to ask whether in what it does assert it does not capture an aspect of truth (traditionally rather neglected). These theologians have, I think, caught sight of an aspect not seldom ignored in traditional teaching about the resurrection. Rightly, in my view, they have been reacting against a sort of empiricist objectivism in which, apart from the act of faith – and so without any faith experience – people were supposedly able to see the resurrected Jesus. The question is, however, whether although rightly stressing the apostles' experience, with its ground in their faith, they in their turn have not ignored what happened to Jesus himself and thus too what occurred to enable the disciples' Easter experience to arise: the risen Jesus himself (even if socio-cultural, socio-psychological interpretations, from their own angle, are also relevant, the Christian interpretation – from its angle and from the standpoint of reason – likewise calls for similar consideration. Whyever not?). At any rate some exegetical theologians give the impression that resurrection and belief in the resurrection are one and the same thing; in other words, that the resurrection was achieved not in the person of Jesus but only in the believing disciples, as it were. 'Resurrection' is then more a symbolic expression of the renewal of life for the disciples, albeit empowered by the inspiration they drew from the earthly Jesus. It is not clear whether that is exactly what these authors mean. What is certain is that (contrary, perhaps, to their truest intentions) a popularized version has developed in which that is unmistakably intended, defended and sometimes even promulgated from the pulpit. But this interpretation seems to me foreign both to the New Testament and to the major Christian traditions. I dissociate myself from it completely.

From our earlier analysis of what actually lies behind the accounts of the appearances, it did indeed become clear that the resurrection *kerygma* preceded the completed accounts of 'appearances of Jesus', but that on the other hand the New Testament suggests an undeniably intrinsic connection between Jesus' resurrection and the Christian, faith-inspired experiences at Easter, expressed in the model of 'appearances'. The Easter experience I have described as a 'conversion process', not simply in the sense of being 'very sorry' that in one way or another Jesus' disciples had let him down (this aspect of their conversion had obviously begun prior to Jesus' death, at any rate if we are to allow historical value to Mk. 14:72c and Lk. 22:62), but – granting that – as the major transformation, whereby after the death of Jesus his disciples acknowledge and confess him as the Christ – a conversion process, that is, whereby they became 'Christian' in the strict sense of the word. It is evident from that analysis of the Easter experience that the objective cannot be separated from the subjective aspect of the apostolic belief in the resurrection. Apart from the faith-motivated experience it is not possible to speak meaningfully about Jesus' resurrection. It would be like talking about 'colours' to somebody blind from birth. Without being identical with it, the resurrection of Jesus – that is, what happened to him, personally, after his death – is inseparable from the Easter experience, or faith-motivated experience, of the disciples: that is to say, from their conversion process, in which they perceive the work of the Spirit of Christ (see above, for example, p. 383ff). Apart from this experience of Christian faith the disciples had no organ that could afford them a sight of Jesus' resurrection. But besides this subjective aspect it is equally apparent that (according to Christian conviction) no Easter experience of renewed life was possible without the personal resurrection of Jesus – in the sense that Jesus' personal-cum-bodily resurrection (in keeping with a logical and ontological priority; a chronological priority is not to the point here) 'precedes' any faith-motivated experience. That Jesus is risen, in his own person, therefore entails not only that he has been raised from the dead by the Father (what after all would this 'in itself' signify for us?), but also – and just as essentially – that in the dimension of our history God gives him a community (Church, as was to be said later on); at the same time it means that the Jesus exalted to be with the Father is with us, in an altogether new way. It is precisely from this indissoluble link between the personal resurrection of Jesus and the Christian experience of Jesus' Easter presence in their midst that the intrinsically salvific implication of Jesus' resurrection becomes directly evident to the disciples – the significance of his resurrection, that is, for us. The earlier and (of set purpose) ample analyses of what is meant in the New Testament by 'appearances of Jesus' have served to show that in and through the very experience of Jesus' renewed presence and the renewed offer of salvation (after his death) the disciples were enabled to arrive at the settled conviction that Jesus had risen. Of its very nature, therefore, Jesus' resurrection is at the same time the sending of the Spirit, and thus intrinsically bound up with the experience of Christian faith or of Easter – the work of Christ's Spirit, not through any 'hocus pocus' but in human, secular, historical ways accessible, what is more, when viewed from a particular angle, to human analysis. So from our preceding analysis it appears that Jesus' resurrection is at one and the same time the sending of the Spirit and the founding of the Church: the fellowship of the risen One with his people on earth. That is why I insisted so strongly earlier on in this passage that belief in the resurrection is not 'pure interpretation' of the earthly Jesus on the part of Christians, but that this Christological interpretation must involve new (faith-motivated) experiences after Jesus' death. The Easter experience lies in the experience of an event: namely, the reassembling of the disciples, not merely in the name of Jesus (although we fail to give sufficient value, in a Jewish context, to that), but in the power of the risen Christ himself: 'Where two or three are gathered together in his name, Jesus is in the midst of them'; this New Testament text is in my view perhaps the purest, most adequate reflection of the Easter experience. Jesus' resurrection and the reassembly of his disciples – in fact: the coming into being of the Church (aside from any shredding off from the Jewish people of God), and this on the basis of the apostles' experience after Jesus' death – are two real facets of just one grand salvific event: from the Father's side Jesus is present in a new way with his disciples on earth. Therefore one cannot speak of Jesus' personal resurrection without speaking at the same time of his saving presence in our midst as experienced here and now and articulated in belief in the resurrection: Easter experience, renewal of life and reassembling or 'being the Church'. Precisely in and through the (faith-motivated) Easter experience and the experienced renewal of life (expressed in the New Testament in the model of 'appearances') there is articulated what happened to Jesus himself: He is alive! The experience of that reality and the reality of the experience, as I said, are here inseparable. To affirm this has nothing to do, therefore, with the idea that Jesus has risen only 'in the *kerygma*' or 'in our experience as believers', whereas he himself lingers still 'in the realm of the dead'. Such an interpretation I would repudiate.

Consequently we have to get beyond empiricism as well as fideism. On that score I 'interiorize' no more than the New Testament does in its report of the appearances, which – however we are to explain them – at any rate point to the subjective, interiorizing, experiential aspect as a correlate of Jesus' personal resurrection. Making every allowance for the admittedly special, 'once only' character of the very first – and for our faith likewise determinative – Easter experience and faith experience of the apostles, who had after all known Jesus prior to his death (a circumstance that gave them a unique privilege – 'election', to use the proper faith-language for it), I would want to 'generalize' the structure at least of what is signified by 'appearances of Jesus' (namely, the intrinsic relation between the risen Jesus and the faith-motivated experience of the community of God or the Church): the origin of Christianity also points to the abiding nature of this. Despite the unrepeatable and peculiar status of the first apostles, who had known Jesus before his death, the way the apostles then found reason for 'becoming Christians' does not differ so very much in fundamentals from our way now. So for all Christians the affirmation of their belief that God has raised Jesus from the dead may fairly describe an immediate experience of reality, and not a secondary interpretation or ideological construction, detachable from the experiential situation. Again: it is in the Easter experience as apprehended by faith that what happened to Jesus himself finds expression, to the salvation of all. This was true for the apostles; but it applies – if our belief is not to be a mere matter of convention – just as much to present-day Christians (thanks to the intermediary function of the living community of the Church). All this becomes clear from the idea of revelation that we examined earlier on. Revelation is God's saving action in history, as experienced and expressed in faith-language by God's faithful people, on a basis of the 'primary stories' which, for a Christian, start with the historical reality of Jesus of Nazareth (though not excluding such religious 'accounts' in a general human context).

When we take a systematic look back at the exegetical analyses, yet another problem arises. It is sometimes said, apropos of this, that resurrection is just the reverse side of death, that is, the salvific aspect of Jesus' death. I would not wish to accept that, either. I stressed (earlier on) the negativity of death, including that of Jesus' death, considered simply as the death of a human being. Obviously, the negativity of death was a thing that Jesus filled inwardly with his *Abba* experience and therein with his love for people, his prophetic loving service 'unto death'. As it were from outside the inherently negative nature of death, Jesus' death was given a positive 'content', imbued as he was with his positive spirit of service – as servant of the cause of man as the cause of God. In bearing it Jesus was able to give point to what was pointless – death, and even to gear it into his immediate proffer of salvation. But unmeaning death itself is not thereby annulled or annihilated. Therefore Jesus' resurrection must be more than simply 'the publicizing of what has taken place in the death of Jesus', as some would argue. It is precisely as the triumph that corrects the negativity even of Jesus' death that the resurrection of Jesus (on God's side) is naturally an event both new and different from Jesus' suffering and death, even in their salvific dimensions. Thus Jesus' resurrection is also essentially an exaltation, a completely new mode of existence, and not only the perpetuation, for eternity, of his person, message and way of living. In the end the human being gets his final identity only from God, even if it be on the basis of his fellowship in this earthly life with God, but through death and through God's victory over death and over all that is negative in the history of our human suffering.

That is why the Christian believer can with good reason say – starting from the view of Jesus' death provided for him by the resurrection (and not otherwise!) - that through the dying of Jesus death itself has been stripped of the power to separate us from God. For in every religious, especially *Jewish* religious understanding of life (the intellective horizon of the Christian interpretation of Jesus), death (in and of itself) is not only a separation from this earthly scene, a parting from one's nearest and dearest, but the end of everything and thus (for the faithful believer in God) at its very centre a parting from God: the end of a living relatedness with God and in that and because of that the end of all that we share of humanity and creaturely being with others. But Jesus' resurrection, by way of a new life and exalted existence, shows that his death at any rate could not part him from his life's fellowship with God, his *Abba*. In Christ, then, death has acquired an entirely new significance: in his death God refuses to part with Jesus, and death is defeated. And in that way for us also a new life is opened up on the other side of death: life's relatedness to God cannot be impaired by suffering and death for anyone who, like Jesus, goes on trusting in God.

Before we set out to look for the deepest foundations of this surprising Jesus event, which would seem to provide a meaningful answer to the thorny question presented by the record of our human suffering in quest of purpose and liberation, we can sum up the New Testament data concerning the 'resurrection' and 'manifestation' of Jesus from a systematic theological standpoint, as follows: Jesus' resurrection, acknowledged and confessed in and through the apostolic conversion or Easter experience, is (a) God's legitimation, ratifying and sanctifying of Jesus' person, message and life of service 'unto death'; (b) it is also exaltation and new creation, that is to say, God's corrective triumph over the negativity of death and man's history of suffering, in which Jesus participated; in other words, there is life after death; (c) the resurrection is at the same time the sending of the Spirit and, in being that, the founding of the Church, a living fellowship, now renewed, of the personal, living Jesus Christ with his people on earth. But a Christian can only speak about these three most fundamental aspects of Jesus' resurrection out of his faith-motivated experiences – 'churchly' (that is, also collective) experiences – and never outside or apart from such faith-imbued experience.

That brings us to the following conclusion. The heart of the whole New Testament, as regards Jesus' resurrection and appearances, amounts to this: the conviction on the part of the Christian Church (it is human beings, after all, Christians, who assert that Jesus has risen, and the assertion of human beings that this is a matter of God's revelation does not alter the fact that this is an assertion by people, who are asserting that all this is undergirded by God's grace; we must not minimize the problems presented by it all), the conviction that Jesus has risen (the import of the Christian proclamation), is an assurance of faith that comes from God alone. As to the way in which the divine source of that assurance took a historical form (for there can be no question of any supernatural 'hocus pocus') discussion on exegetical grounds could be endless. But anyone who accepts the origin of this apostolic conviction as rooted in divine grace (and the New Testament affirmation of that divine origin was constantly stressed, earlier on, in the course of examining the 'Jesus appearances') stands on Christian ground. He cannot be dismissed as heretical; and then he can only be judged and, if necessary, criticized for his way of presenting the matter on a basis of historico-critical and anthropological arguments – but then as a brother in the same Christian faith.

## §2 Necessity, problematic character and limits of a theoretical-cum-Christological identification of the person

The response whereby Christians acknowledge Jesus of Nazareth as the decisive and definitive salvation imparted by God and thus recognize and confess in Jesus' human story the 'story of God', cannot be reduced via exegesis to a sort of conclusion to a far-reaching analysis of New Testament passages (however much that may be necessary to finding out about the true record of Jesus). For it is in this very Jesus, as well in his arcane as in his revelatory mediation, that the mediated nearness of God's compassion is more condensed than anywhere else. For nowhere was the veiling mediation so improbably great: it was even possible to send Jesus to his death in the name of orthodox religious sentiment. Yet nowhere is God's direct and gratuitous nearness in him so palpably present for anyone who encounters him openly and places himself under his *metanoia*: church traditions dare to call him 'true God'. The assessment of a person *qua* person cannot be a matter of scientific and theoretical analysis. And yet anybody willing to venture on it can – even now – listen to the Jesus story in such a way as to recognize in it the parable of God himself and so too the paradigm of the human character of our being-as-men: a new, unprecedented possibility of existence, thanks to the God whose concern is with man. But it is part and parcel of the plot, the intrigue of the Jesus story, that his startling freedom should serve to scandalize somebody who takes offence at him (Lk. 7:23) and at the same time become salvation (as a liberating freedom) for anyone venturing to commit himself to the fascinating mystery of Jesus' life-story.

For that reason it is indeed a question whether an excessive amount of theoretical hair-splitting with respect to who Jesus Christ is might not hinder rather than help. Drawing nice, theoretical distinctions about the divine event, overwhelming Jesus as it does and determining the purpose and the heart of all his living, impoverishes that event and so stands on the edge of the abyss of heretical, one-sided distortion. This is all the more true because in this case a violent death is involved. And however much we are bound to argue (on the basis, be it said, of a critically justifiable exegesis) that with his approaching death in prospect Jesus integrated it into his surrender to God and his offer of salvation to men – the core of his whole life – the negativity of this death on the other hand, especially when viewed as rejection, cannot just be rationalized out of existence. Salvation and the record of human suffering, especially the course of undeserved, unjust suffering, cannot be brought together or reconciled in any theoretical or rational way. On the one hand salvation-history, salvific history, is accomplished in the actual life of Jesus; this fact is not removed by his death nor suspended by it; on the other hand, as a rejection, Jesus' suffering and death, in historical terms, can only be described as a calamity; the negativity of them is undeniable. So a theoretical – in the sense of rationally transparent – reconciliation of the two is impossible. This tallies with the earlier analysis in which we maintained that there can be no theoretical basis for rationalizing the universal horizon of understanding. We are bound to say therefore that there is only one possible way out: to contemplate salvation as imparted by God 'in the non-identity of' Jesus' history of suffering and death.[53] This really places the suffering outside God and leaves it inside the mundane sphere of legitimacy proper to the *condition humaine* and human freedom; it intimates that in this non-divine situation of suffering and dying Jesus none the less continues to identify himself with the cause of God, without contaminating God himself by his own suffering. In and over against Jesus God evidently remains sovereignly free: 'My ways are not your ways' (Isa. 55:8); something that applies to every child of man. But as his death approaches it is precisely with this incomprehensible thing that, struggling yet in willing commitment, Jesus identifies himself in surrender, just as in Jesus' resurrection God for his part identifies the kingdom of God with Jesus. It is in the non-divine circumstance of innocent suffering and death, and so in what is ultimately opaque, that Jesus 'underwent' and preserved his personal identification with the coming rule of God. Thus the definitive and supreme revelation of God took place in a silent but none the less extremely intimate nearness of God to the suffering and dying Jesus, who in that way reached the lowest depths of the human condition, and at the same time lived through his inviolable affinity to God. That is what no theory can effectively reduce to a rationally sound system. Here the only deposition to be made is that of faith. It is here that *our* story begins.

Realizing this, should make us more cautious about trying to reach a more exact theoretical definition of the soteriological import of Jesus' death. We are confronted here with a salvation beyond any further thematizing, which presents itself as purpose and principle for living. This reticence goes back to the attempt at providing a theoretically over-precise account of Jesus' personal identity. Obviously, Jesus is altogether on God's side and at the same time completely on man's side: in radical solidarity with God and his sovereignly free being-as-God, but also in total solidarity with people. In fact this is the very definition of God's rule, having man as its central concern, but: lived out by Jesus in the radical alienation of innocent suffering and death, that which is 'non-divine'. This makes the cross by definition not an 'event between God and God',[54] but on the contrary the index of what is to be opposed as the 'anti-divine' in our human history, which in Jesus has nevertheless been overcome from within through his affinity with God. This belonging to God in an 'anti-godly' situation serves to effect our salvation. Jesus would not admit any competition between God's honour and loftiness and man's happiness and final well-being. But anyone who can give a more exact theoretical account of all this, as both a definition of God and a definition of what being-as-man is, leaves us unpersuaded: their accuracy eludes us. The same reservation governs the following attempt at a more detailed discussion, conducted of course at the level of 'second-order' pronouncements, where the element of human reflection is considerably bigger and where the result must be measured by its importance and relevance for the salvation God imparts to man as well as by its 'doxological' significance, that is, the degree to which such reflection pays prayerful homage to God.

## §3 In search of the grounds of Jesus' *Abba* experience, the heart of his message, life and death: the secret of his life disclosed

It became apparent from the detailed discussion in Part Two that what Jesus had to say about God as man's salvation springs directly from his personal experience of God, of the reality which in his own, for the time extraordinary, way he referred to as *Abba*, a concept borrowed from the Jewish family life of the period. We may fairly go on to ask, in particular, what is the ultimate ground of this awareness on Jesus' part, uniquely rooted thus in God, brought to expression in an *Abba* experience that could be the source of his assured proclamation of God's coming rule and at the same time the 'power-house' of a way of living and course of conduct anticipating the praxis of the kingdom of God.

We said earlier on that the status as reality and the empirical value of a religious experience is rooted in the creaturely condition of our finite being-as-man, in other words, in the given reality of a distinctively human, finite autonomy, as supported from within by God's creative activity. This finite 'being oneself' is in the end more 'of God' than 'of oneself', and thus a trace of God's reality at the very heart of our existence.

The Christological question then becomes: Can this fundamental, creaturely status, this 'being of God' – common to all human beings and at the same time differentiated according to each individual's own localized and personal profile – be sufficient ground also in Jesus for elucidating his private, certainly highly profiled *Abba* experience? Or does this source-experience of God transcend the gravitational pull of this universal status of the creature? As a Christological question, of course, this presupposes the believer's acknowledging definitive salvation in Jesus, coming from God: apart from that, after all, a Christological question has no point. Of course, the commitment to faith in definitive salvation imparted by God in and through Jesus may already be the implicit response to a Christological question; but in that case the job is to distil this implicit Christology from it.

This 'being in, of and through God' – definition of the creaturely status of a human person (see above) – we might, generally speaking, have some grounds for calling an *enhypostasis*, the incorporation or adoption of the human person *into* the 'person' (*hypostasis*) of God.[55] We must realize that we are then using a theological terminology in a very unhistorical way and so in a confusing way. And though human language is very elastic, the fact that it is historically limited has to be reckoned with. On the other hand an arresting non-historical use of a given terminology may through its initial impact help to fasten our attention on an aspect which normally escapes it because the thing is so familiar to us. For if the creative presence of God in man – man's lingering in God, as Eastern theology prefers to call it – is God himself, and therefore his 'person' (*hypostasis*), then a created human person's 'being of and in God' really is an *enhypostasis*; the one is the other. If in his being God is pure *hypostasis* (however he might be further defined), then 'being a creature' is naturally a 'hypostatic union'. But this is saying no more or less than that things and people are created by God and that man in particular can become aware of God's indwelling. We do better therefore to leave aside use of the 'hypostatic union' terminology in this context; it says nothing new and, in view of its historical application, it can only cause confusion, as so often with an unhistorical use of a very precisely defined terminology.[56]

However much it may be 'of God' and 'itself' for that very reason, a creature is none the less by definition 'not-God', a secular reality, called by its own creatureliness to see itself precisely not as 'God', and moreover to treat nothing outside God as God. Belief in creation is essentially a radical critique of every ideological idolatry out of a jealous reverence for God's unique transcendence. Hence in the first instance the reaction of, for example, the Jewish as well as the Muslim religion to Christian worship, in regard to the person, Jesus Christ, is immediately understandable; it arises from the jealous zeal, shared by Jews, Muslims and Christians alike, for the monotheistic confession of the One God. To begin with at least, this reaction deserves to be met with Christian sympathy; for Christians too the Yahwistic monotheism in which and from which Jesus himself lived is the basic affirmation of their creed. It is against this background of Jewish monotheism that Jesus' own *Abba* experience should be interpreted.

Especially because, within the spectrum of creatureliness, 'being-as-man', by the measure appropriate to human existence, is an 'open form of being', difficult to mark off inside specific – albeit generally creaturely – boundaries (as is the case with other creatures despite certain crossing or overstepping even here),[57] in Jesus' case we shall have to reckon *a priori* with the nature of man as 'sited' yet open freedom, not admitting of any predetermination by Nature. The potentialities and concrete modalities of a certain individual's 'being of God' therefore cannot possibly be restricted *a priori* through some claim on our part to know the limits of 'being-as-man'. Even if we were able to define, approximately, the extent and boundaries of whatever contains the situating and conditioning of the human, physical, psychic and social condition of our freedom, we cannot possibly predict in advance – within those conditioning factors – what human freedom is capable of, all the more so if it is aware of being grounded in the absolute freedom of God. What for instance a person, building his life on the living God, can draw from that by way of indestructible assurance as regards ultimate possibilities 'coming from God' and what sort of explosive historical forces could thus be released, no 'speculative anthropology' is going to be able to inform me. The historical power peculiar to the religious awareness of the *Deus, intimior intimo meo*, that is, of the creative God who in and via our human history takes absolute initiatives in a manner that transcends through immanence or through a wholly intimate nearness, cannot be measured or comprehended by any kind of non-religious approach. Therefore these potentialities of the 'religious consciousness', which cannot be circumscribed in advance, should make us chary of looking for the ground of Jesus' original *Abba* experience in anything other than his creaturely status as a human being.

Within this religious relationship Jesus transfers the epicentre of his life to God, the Father. But this does not mean that he finds his centre outside himself. That 'spatial' notion is misleading, once the subject of trust in God realizes that this 'outside' – 'greater than I' (see Jn. 14:28) – is actually *intimior intimo meo*, that is, constitutes Jesus' being-as-man in his deepest subsistence as himself. The human being aware of his creatureliness apprehends himself to be pure gift of God. Because of the totally unprecedented depth of Jesus' experience (of himself as gift of God, the Father) the faith of the Church – as of the Christian *oikoumene* – identifying with him, proceeded to call Jesus 'the Son', thereby specifying Jesus' creaturely relation to God. What in non-religious language is called – and rightly called – a human person in the language of Christian faith is called Son of God, by virtue of the constitutive relation of this human being to the Father.

From this it should be clear that, because a human being grounds himself in and upon God, on the basis of his acknowledged creature-liness, this can never result in the loss of any aspect of his 'being human'. As in the language of faith, which tries to 'put reality into words', 'grounding' the self in God is a source of real and surprising humanity, the highest experience of God will be for our humanity an unlooked-for 'revelation of man'. If we start from the authentic meaning of what is signified by creatureliness (despite all debasing and intrusive deformation to which, owing to the complications of our human finitude, 'the highest in man' is invariably prone) the supreme union of a man with God (in and of itself) can never result in loss to his own being-as-man, since it is God's creative activity that constitutes man in his (albeit finite yet) proper autonomy and full humanity. What is more, however intimately this union with God is displayed in a historical human being, we can never speak of two components: humanity *and* divinity, only of two total 'aspects': a real humanity in which 'being of God', in this case 'being of the Father', is realized.

Thus it would be misleading to say that Jesus who in himself is a human person 'is taken up' into the Logos, in that way deepening and completing his being a human person. What is wrong about this is that two language-games in which it becomes possible to speak of

Jesus – as of each and every human being – have been muddled up together. Jesus is first posited – naturally within one particular language-game – as already in himself constituted a 'human person' in order then – in a second instance, actually in faith-language – to justify talk of his being assumed into the Logos. Talking like that at the first as well as the second level of language is all right; the only misleading thing is the ingenuous combination of the two; for then Jesus would seem to be 'postulated' in advance as in himself already constituted a human person, so that 'after that' this person is (in faith-language) 'incorporated into the Logos'. It should be evident from what was said previously that for the religious language which none the less recognizes and approves the distinctive character of non-religious language, this being-a-person, already 'given' as something separate from his 'being of the Father', is nowhere ever postulated. It is of course a legitimate result of the inevitable 'two-language' evaluation of one and the same reality, which because of its self-subsistence and its 'being of the Father', lends itself to this twofold assessment. We have no over-arching, unitive language capable of expressing the two total aspects together at one go. But then in accordance with the logic proper to faith-language this 'being a human person', in Jesus' case, can no more be presupposed from the constitutive relation to the Father, into which he is incorporated. That relation postulates this 'being a person' in his peculiar personal identity as Jesus. Speaking in the humanly 'secular' language-game we shall of course call Jesus a 'human person' – apart from a human-cum-personal mode of being, nobody is 'a human being'. In faith-language we say that the man Jesus is this person *qua* human being, thanks to his constitutive relation to the Father, just as – at his own level – every human being *qua* human being is this person, thanks to his essential relation to the creator-God. For Jesus this implies that his relation to the Father makes him in his humanity Son of God. In the same analogous fashion we call every human being a person; but in faith-language we say, without denying the previous affirmation (on the contrary designating it the ground of this 'being a person'), that precisely this 'being a person' is entirely 'of God'. Jesus *qua* human being is this person through being, by virtue of that very thing, 'the Son of the Father' and, in the nature of the case, without any loss of humanity, but on the contrary, through the confirmation, deepening and completion of all that positive human perfection, thus *a fortiori*, a human-cum-personal mode of being, entails. *Anhypostasis*, as privation or loss of the human person, must therefore be denied, of course, in Jesus; yet this negation of any loss is not, after all, in itself a positive definition of what precisely is entailed in Jesus' human-cum-personal mode of being in his relation to the Father.

The presence model, which applies to each and every creature (especially and formally to a human person), holds good of Jesus too, of course; but in and of itself, having regard to its universal character and possible modalities, it cannot help to define more closely the peculiar character of the presence of God the Father in Jesus, at any rate as long as the ground of that presence is not specified. It is not a question of a divine presence with and in a human being who is supposedly 'first' constituted a person in himself by God's creative act and then, as it were, in the second instance, 'incorporated into the Logos'. The question is therefore: Is the general creative, constitutive act of God the ground of Jesus' conscious or mystical 'connectedness' with the Father, owing to his being completely filled with the Holy Spirit? Or is this creative constituting act, to the extent that at the same time the man Jesus is constituted by it Son of the Father, the ground of Jesus' 'being a person' and consequently of his mystical union with the Father?

The patristic and indeed the whole Christian tradition has always attempted to define the actual person of Jesus in terms of the purport of the salvation brought by him. Because the salvation is 'imparted by God', the one who brought it was himself called divine, and thence it was concluded that Jesus is a divine person. The governing principle, that there is at any rate a significant, intrinsic and real link between the person of Jesus and the salvation brought by him on God's behalf, would seem to me to be right; it is plainly suggested by the gospels, which see Jesus Christ as the eschatological, salvific gift of God. But then the definitive or eschatological character of the salvation that he brought must in the end have something to tell us about the actual person of the bringer, and not the Greek presuppositions of this patristic principle.

In view of all this, there does indeed come a point where Christology reaches a fork in the road: to choose the route of the Unitarians or that of the Trinitarians. It may be that a Unitarian Christology has not always been sufficiently understood (even though it seems to me to offer no solution at all!). For although a great deal has been written about the triune God, everything said about the Trinity is constantly alternating between a 'modalism' more or less devoid of content and a 'tri-theism' that says only too much, while the attempts to dodge this Scylla and Charybdis lapse into more or less rarified, insubstantial, purely verbal distinctions.[58] This comes, however, of considering the

Trinity in separation from the Christological interpretation of Jesus, whereas the immediate post-biblical doctrine of the Trinity is clearly presented as a way of making explicit the Christ-mystery. This last conclusion in itself entails that we should not interpret Jesus with the Trinity as our starting-point, but vice versa: only if we start with Jesus is God's unity in its fullness (not so much a *unitas trinitatis* but a *trinitas unitatis*) to some extent accessible to us. Only in the light of Jesus' life, death and resurrection can we know that the Trinity is the divine mode of God's perfect unity of being. Only on the basis of Jesus of Nazareth, his *Abba* experience – source and soul of his message, ministry and death – and his resurrection, is it possible to say anything meaningful about Father, Son and Spirit. For what matters in the *Abba* experience of Jesus is that this unique turning of Jesus to the Father in absolute priority is 'preceded' and inwardly supported by the unique turning of the Father himself to Jesus. Now early Christian tradition calls this self-communication of the Father – ground and source of Jesus' peculiar *Abba* experience – 'the Word'. This implies that the Word of God is the undergirding ground of the whole Jesus phenomenon.

In his humanity Jesus is so intimately 'of the Father' that by virtue of this very intimacy he is 'Son of God'. This implies that the centre of Jesus' being-as-man was vested not in himself but in God the Father – something borne out also by the historical evidence about Jesus; the centre, support, *hypostasis*, in the sense of what confers steadfastness, was his relationship to the Father with whose cause he identified himself. As this human being Jesus is constitutively 'allo-centric': orientated upon the Father and on the 'salvation coming from God' for men; hence the profile and the face that he alone presents. This is what identifies Jesus of Nazareth. His autonomy as Jesus of Nazareth is his constitutive total relation to the One whom he calls 'Father', the God whose special concern is with humanity. This is his *Abba* experience, soul, source and ground of his going out and his coming in, his living and dying.

Where does this experience come from? Every experience of a human person, granted all its originality, stands at the same time in a tradition of social experience and is never a simple drawing upon some interior plenitude without any mediatory factors. Jesus' human self-consciousness, like that of every human being, was a consciousness in and of the concrete world of living encounter in which he was set – this, for Jesus, was the Jewish practice of piety, bred and fed by the synagogue, in a family where it was a father's duty to initiate the boys into God's revelation, the Law. Experience of the creator-God, the Lord of history, was partly nurtured in Jesus by the living tradition in which he stood; the living hand of God was apprehended in nature and in the world of men. This creaturely consciousness, the living centre of which is the fact of God's lordship, is already noticeable in Jesus' basic message of God's rule. In contrast, however, to John the Baptist and the traditional prophetic legacy, he proclaims not God's eschatological judgement (although he does not suppress that) but God's approaching definitive salvation for man, with a determination that did not falter in face of death. Either this man lived in an illusion – as some are able to say because after his death history went on its customary way – or we put our trust in him, partly on the strength of his career as a whole and the manner of his dying, a trust which is only possible in the form of an affirmation of God, namely, that God vindicates him. This latter, specifically Christian solution implies in the final instance the affirmation: the salvation that is coming is this man Jesus himself, the crucified-and-risen One. There really is no middle way: Jesus' message of approaching salvation is either an illusion or, 'if it is of God' (Acts 5:35–39), it is true, that is, a reality to be found nowhere else than in the risen Jesus himself. To identify the coming kingdom of God with Jesus Christ is then – unless one maintains the illusion thesis – the sole appropriate response to Jesus' positive offer of salvation. Yet that identification cannot be based simply on the creaturely status of Jesus, sufficient indeed to foster the message of God's rule and, in an experience at odds with what was happening at the time, to give birth to a prophetic consciousness – but not to a God-given salvation identified with the person of Jesus himself.

Such an identification is made, of course, by Christians; in itself it would appear to say nothing directly about the private *Abba* experience of Jesus himself, unless we give credit to that experience: Jesus proclaims God's eschatological coming to be 'at hand'; God himself identifies this coming with the crucified-and-risen One, acknowledged by Christians in faith: Jesus is the eschatological salvation. In a formally structuralist view of Scripture, E. Haulotte had a very pertinent intuition, it seems to me, when he wrote: '*Tout se passe comme si le propre de cet être (Jésus) était d'être dit par d'autres*',[59] Jesus' being is of such a kind that it has to be identified by others. This must be the case, if Jesus' death is essentially part and parcel of God's message in Jesus and if the resurrection (only apprehensible in an identifying faith on the part of those trusting in Jesus) forms therefore an essential part of the salvific message that comes from God. (Thus Christian tradition is right when it declares that the apostolic witness is fundamental to the 'constitutive revelation' in Jesus Christ.)

We said before that every creature evinces, despite its unity, a duality of an aspectual kind: completely 'itself' and in being so completely 'of God'. This duality of total aspects we also find in Jesus – and in a special way. Of course, in Jesus the divine is disclosed only in a creaturely, human way, which we might call in this case a 'human transcendence' or a 'transcending humanity': eschatological humanity. But every revealed manifestation of God, including that in Jesus' transcending humanity, is always infinitely inadequate to God's divine transcendence. Consequently, the man Jesus, the personal revelation of God, at the same time veils him. There is in Jesus' humanity, therefore, not only a manifestation of God, but along with that some inward reference to the infinite divine transcendence, ground of what is manifested in Jesus' human transcendence. Thus we must never lose sight of the revealing and veiling – thus referential – character of Jesus' human transcendence or eminence. In other words Jesus' human transcendence itself, by virtue of its intrinsically referential character, calls for a deeper grounding of his *Abba* experience in its uniqueness and distinctiveness.

If we start from Jesus, it is quite obvious that Jesus prays to the Father; in other words he stands in an interpersonal relationship to the Father; he speaks of 'my Father'. *Vis-à-vis* the Father, Jesus is most certainly to be called a 'person'. Although we have no historically assured evidence, derived from Jesus himself, about the New Testament promise that Jesus will impart the Holy Spirit, yet all the gospels speak in every one of their traditions about the Christian experience of the eschatological gift of the Spirit, the 'other paraclete', and do so in connection with God's coming rule as proclaimed by Jesus and their identification, in faith, of Jesus with this kingdom of God which the eschatological sending of the Spirit by Jesus brings with it. As over against the Holy Spirit too – albeit not in the same way as with the Father – Jesus is a person. It means that through and in the person of the man Jesus, God is manifest to us as an interpersonal relation between the Father, Jesus Christ and the Holy Spirit. Starting therefore from the person of Jesus, it is although analogously and evocatively nevertheless on good grounds that we also refer to the Father as person and to the Holy Spirit as person; and through this 'over against' of Jesus *vis-à-vis* the Father, as also the Holy Spirit, Jesus reveals to us 'three persons' in God: Father, Jesus Christ, *Pneuma*. Any distinction between a Trinity arising within the 'economy of salvation' and one that is 'intratrinitarian' is meaningless, therefore, as regards the cognitive structure of an (in a Jesus context) analogous way of speaking that is conscious of the finite character of its discourse but also of the well-grounded nature (Jesus himself) of its cognitive intentionality. Thomas has rightly said: these human notions purport to denote a reality in God but are not as such applicable to God;[60] they hold good of the reality that is God himself, but the divine mode of their doing so eludes us. In Jesus and on that basis, at any rate, in a human fashion and so in a state of 'human alienation', something is made clear to us of this applicability to the divine. It is Jesus' own being-as-man (and nothing else) that reveals God to us as a Trinity.

All this leaves 'the person' of Jesus still somewhat blurred. It has been said: because of Jesus we know that God is 'tri-personal': Father, Jesus Christ, Holy Spirit. As it is through Jesus that God is revealed to us in his intrinsic plenitude, unknown to us from creation, in its articulation this nomenclature is of course 'anthropomorphic', yet in a manner that goes beyond sheer anthropomorphism. It is evident from Jesus' *Abba* experience, because of the stress laid on doing the will of the Father, that the intended correlate of 'Father' is obviously 'the Son'. Thus the plenitude or trinity of God's absolute unity revealed through Jesus is: Father, Son, Holy Spirit. As a revelation of God therefore, Jesus does not constitute that in God which corresponds to the 'Son of God', the Father and the Spirit. The man Jesus is indeed the ground that enables us to denote the intratrinitarian reality by our human concept of a 'person', because the man Jesus is identified with the intratrinitarian reality called, in the context provided by the man Jesus, Son of God – which is why it is as man that he is able to reveal the Trinitarian unity and also why, taking as our starting-point Jesus as identified with the Son, we may legitimately speak of three divine persons (even though we start from the man Jesus and therefore with a notion of 'the human person').

Here we run straight into the difficulties. The gospels do not speak of 'persons' in God any more than do the first great (Christological) councils; and when we talk about persons, the whole philosophical and semantic history of the 'person' concept looms before us. What is a 'divine person', since we are having to speak about God, albeit analogously, in terms of the concept of 'human person', and that is one of the most argued-over concepts in the entire history of philosophical reflection? More especially, does the fact that Jesus is Son of God exclude his being a human person? What in other words is the positive implication of denying Jesus' human *anhypostasis*? The two questions are closely interconnected.

It is not a question one can solve with a wave of the hand by appealing to the common-sense idea of a 'person'; for it is just that which serves to conceal all the problems. Linguistic analysis, in so far as it takes 'ordinary language' as its point of departure, has been intensively concerned with the person concept; but though the writings of P. F. Strawson, S. Hampshire and G. Ryle have managed to shed some light on it, they have not cleared up the problem. Worth remarking upon is Strawson's attempt – in his 'descriptive metaphysic', starting from everyday language – to uncover the foundations and basic structures of our human conceptual system.[61] As Aristotle had once done, he looks for 'fundamental categories' and generally valid *universalia* in the human thinking of us all: 'a massive central core of human thinking which had no history';[62] and that massive core consists of certain basic concepts: 'There are categories and concepts which, in their most fundamental character, change not at all' (l. c.). Apropos of what I was saying earlier on, what we are dealing with here is the plane of 'structural history', the more or less immutable central core in the history of human thinking. It is there that the person concept belongs. According to Strawson's analysis it is given within the structure of this concept that a subject, a person, cannot posit himself without at the same time affirming the other, the co-person. Without affirmation of the other I can have no idea of what I myself, *qua* person, am.[63] In other words, being a person entails interpersonality. This would lead us to assume that if God is personal (it makes no sense here to entertain an infrapersonal notion of God), he is bound to be in one way or another 'interpersonal' as well; to put it more accurately (in terms of the Christian credal affirmation): that (the) Trinity is the plenitude of God's personal, absolute unity of being, and that God is therefore, without any becoming (in the sense of growing towards or into his own definition), none the less eternal youth and intrinsic dynamic Life, not an impassive self-contemplator. Although each time within a different conjunctural horizon of understanding, we do indeed find this basic concept of the human person wherever people have reflected on 'being-as-person'. Even for medieval theologians, not given to thematizing intersubjectivity, part of the condition for being able to define the person is the *divisum ab alio*, in other words, the 'other person'. In patristics it was the same.[64] I conclude: the modern concept of the person, so called, differs from, for instance, that of the Council of Chalcedon not structurally but more 'superficially', that is, conjuncturally. It is precisely the structural elements that provide the opening for giving a very dynamic content to the person concept – the definition itself of all that is dynamic! Thus W. Pannenberg, in his *Grundzüge der Christologie*, was able to avoid a lot of difficulties by in fact speaking only about the structural elements of the concept and 'wisely' saying nothing about the primarily modern conjunctural aspect, namely, about the person as conscious centre of action with his or her own irreducible consciousness and freedom. Thomas Aquinas was not afraid of tackling this problem, but had to infer the consequence: 'The (three divine) persons are not formally distinct as persons but as in origin antithetical relations' (see above); he was apparently forced to that conclusion because there is in God only a single consciousness and a single freedom, the one consciousness and the one freedom of the three divine persons. One may question whether this unity is really a counter-indication, since even love among human beings talks in terms of 'a single thought' and 'a single desire'. What would be the divine mode of this in God? The absolutely single freedom and absolutely single thinking, to us unimaginable, of the three Persons. A plenitude of unity, not a solitary and excessive fixity. In other words Thomas too falls back on the structural elements of the person concept: what is essentially relational in the reality of the person, being orientated on fellow-persons, whereas (in God) the ground of this orientation is the single divine nature or the single divine freedom. The 'person' concept is in this view enough to fulfil what (because of a reaction against a rigidified idea of 'person') Process Theology still holds to be necessary (as a 'consequent nature' in God) in order to preserve the dynamic of God's being – or Palamism requires (namely, the distinction between God's 'nature' – *ousia* – and God's 'energies') in order to save the same dynamic in the divine nature. Both are propitious reactions to an un-Christian *Deus immutabilis*.

This relational aspect (remarkable as it may seem) is more amenable to our general human understanding than having to decide what that 'I' (which is orientated on another) is in itself. (Child psychologists have ascertained that even babies first discover 'the other' and only then the world and themselves.) It may be that we really become a 'person' only when we are unconcerned with our own identity and, in losing ourself, identify ourself with the other.

Characteristic of the dual aspect in the person concept are the two definitions that governed medieval theology: on the one hand the definition of Boëthius,[65] on the other that of Richard of St Victor.[66] Boëthius (trying deliberately to give both Chalcedon and neo-

Chalcedonism a wide berth) does tell us of what nature a person is, namely, a concrete substance or nature capable of consciousness and freedom, but does not say how a person arrives at being a person. He ignores, Richard says, the source relationship, the relation to the person by whom one is made to be a person; Boëthius passes over the *unde habeat esse*. The result is, as deacon Rusticus had observed before him, that according to Boëthius' definition of 'person' the man Jesus must really be called a 'human person', while on the other hand his definition fails to apply to the Trinity,[67] in other words, Boëthius' person concept would seem to be theologically quite useless, whether the context is Christology or Trinity. In consequence of this, it was through early Scholasticism that the idea of totality made its entry into the Western concept of a 'person': nobody can be simultaneously 'two persons', for that would make each of them a part of one undivided whole – which contradicts the essence of the person concept. Actually, because of his concretely human, formally spiritual nature Jesus would have to be called just a human person, says Rusticus,[68] but because he forms an indivisible unity with the Word, in this one case that cannot be said: only 'the single whole' is a person. Thus we can accept the human-cum-personalistic character of Jesus' being-as-man and starting from the *enhypostasis* ascribe to him a more or less nominal *anhypostasis*, since nothing is lost to Jesus of his real being-as-man. These were extremely subtle, knife-edge discussions – people tried to achieve a balance between the demands of philosophical anthropology and what seemed to them to be the requirement of faith, based on dogma. Strikingly enough, Thomas who particularly in his anthropology makes use of Boëthius' definition of the person, in his doctrine of the Trinity actually revises it with Richard's definition (the interrelational concept of a person) and with Rusticus' notion of totality.[69] It is these three elements of the person concept that we come across in the 'linguistic analysis' of today.

At the time of the Enlightenment there arose a new dispute centred around the person concept. In the battle over atheism in 1798, J. G. Fichte said that God could not be thought of as 'person' without inner contradiction. For Fichte the concept of 'person' essentially entailed finitude. For 'person' necessarily calls for a partner, a *vis-à-vis* over against what is other – something or someone else. To put it another way: along with the 'I' concept there necessarily goes the 'not I', the 'you' and the 'that' (*Du und Es*). An 'I' that is said to be everything, all, and finds itself without any 'opposite' is sheer nonsense. Being-a-person is therefore essentially delimited and finite. Thus God is no person.

Hegel reacts against this argument of Fichte's (one of the foundations of Feuerbach's atheism). He concedes that 'person' implies an 'opposite', but not *per se* 'outside itself', as a delimiting of one's own 'I'. On the contrary, it belongs to the essential being of the person so to be involved with an opposite that this 'I' 'exteriorizes' itself in an opposite, in order thus to recover itself in the other thing (other being), either in the thing which the 'I' composes or recognizes or in the 'Thou' with whom the 'I' is conjoined in love and friendship. A person discovers himself in the other to the degree that he has surrendered and yielded himself to the other. So it is in personal living that the opposition or contrast to the other – finitude itself, therefore – is cancelled out and overcome. Person *qua* person, that is, the very nature of being-a-person, entails infinity. Thus God, the Trinity, is the supreme and unique realization of personal being. It does not prevent there being finite persons too; but then of course this is a restriction of personal being. The human person is *qua* person delimited by and marked off from another human person; he is delimited by the other. That is to say, the human person can only in part overcome being contrasted with the other; no human being can identify himself totally with another. Thus the human being is 'a person' in an attenuated, alienated sense, not in the full sense of the word.

In this Hegelian concept of 'person' there is present a great deal – even if in a different intellectual atmosphere – of the turbulent battle over the person dating both from the patristic period and from the twelfth and thirteenth centuries, and then also much inspiration derived from the Christian confession of a Trinity. The modern phenomenology of the person very largely tallies with this Hegelian concept. Being-as-oneself but through a giving to the other, in whom one recovers oneself – completely or in some degree of alienation – is therefore the current, modern concept of the person too. It coincides with what we might call the structural elements of the concept.

If we now take as our starting-point not this modern concept of the person but simply what has been manifested concretely in the life, death and resurrection of Jesus, it is remarkable how these real evidences of Jesus lend themselves to being interpreted, and successfully interpreted, within the structural elements of the person concept.

The given factor is, after all: definitive salvation-coming-from-God in Jesus of Nazareth, the crucified-and-risen One. 'It is God who delivers us in Jesus Christ' (see 2 Cor. 5:19). God saves, but in and through the man Jesus, his message, life and death. The question then is: Is it possible for Jesus of Nazareth, within the limits of a human and personal mode of being, to 'live out' the essential nature of a 'divine person', that is, to be himself in radical self-giving to the other – which within the divine would entail no element of alienation or limitation? Is such a divine self-giving to be experienced even within the limitation of a human mode of being-as-person, that is, in radical self-giving to and identification with the Father and with the others, fellow-men, and even with those who reject and cast him out? The human limitation within which God's redeeming salvation in Jesus is accomplished then becomes the field in which that radical self-giving of God in the alienation of human life and death is made a historical reality. Then the notion or, to be more accurate, the reality of a human and personal mode of being is the very thing needed to make the depth of the redemptive self-giving of God comprehensible, while yet not imputing suffering, death and alienation to God but leaving them where they in fact belong, in the mundane reality of human existence. In that way limitation, human alienation and death are finally overcome and the finite is released: man's humanity is freed into acceptance of finitude and so too of his 'being of God'. Upon all that is done 'for love's sake' in our human world there rests God's eschatological promise. Salvation in Jesus is salvation given by God – and yet is historically mediated among us through our concrete history: it is a making whole, whereby limitation and alienation, impotence and even death, are finally overcome: the finite itself – for that is what we are – is redeemed: in Jesus the humanity of man is freed for a redeemed and redemptive acceptance: that 'through grace' alone we are enabled and allowed to realize our proper being-as-promise (which we are the one for the other), and that we may experience the call to love which surmounts each of us, severally and together, person and society, in the redemptive experience of an absolute assurance that transcends us all and yet is in no respect alien to our being-as-man: the living God.

Saying all this, we say nothing new, nothing that from an examination of the gospels we did not already know; it is only an account, now rendered explicitly Trinitarian, of the Christ-mystery which according to Christian credence is the redemptive revelation of the mystery of God as the Trinitarian plenitude of absolute unity: God as essential gift in the necessary existence of absolute freedom. Thus the true face of God is shown to us in the humanity of Jesus. We said earlier on that Jesus' unique turning to the Father in absolute priority is 'preceded' and supported by the absolute turning of the Father to Jesus: and that this self-communication of the Father is precisely what early Christian tradition calls 'the Word'. Deeper than the *Abba* experience, therefore, and its ground, is the Word of God, the self-communication of the Father. This signifies some such thing as a 'hypostatic identification' without *anhypostasis*: this man, Jesus, within the human confines of a (psychologically and ontologically) personal-cum-human mode of being, is identically the Son, that is, the 'Second Person' of the Trinitarian plenitude of divine unity, 'the Second Person' coming to human self-consciousness and shared humanity in Jesus. An identity between two finite modes of personal being (two persons 'in one') is indeed an inner contradiction; but an identity of a finite personal-cum-human mode of being and a divine, infinite (and thus analogous) mode of 'being person' is no contradiction, since the ground of the distinction between the creature and God lies not in the perfection of the creature but in its finitude, while all that is positive in it is yet totally 'derived' from God. Creature and God can never be added the one to the other. The constitutive relation to God resides already in the core of each creature as being and person. Thus, thanks to the hypostatic identification of that in God which because of Jesus we call 'Son of God' with Jesus' personal-cum-human mode of being, the man Jesus is a constitutive (filial) relation to the Father, a relation that in the dynamic process of Jesus' human life grows into a deepening, mutual *enhypostasis*, with the resurrection as its climactic point. In this respect Jesus stands over against the Father and the Spirit; not however over against the Son of God. In him the one divine consciousness and absolute freedom, as 'filially' experienced within the Godhead (in complete union with the Father), is in alienation rendered man, as a humanly conscious centre of action and human (situated) freedom. In that sense we are bound to say that Jesus' being-as-person in no way lies outside his being-as-man; yet in the end we cannot (without all sorts of qualifications) describe him as simply and solely a 'human person', for then there would indeed appear an inconceivable 'over against' between the man Jesus and the Son of God – a theory consistently argued – along these lines – and defended, following Deodatus de Basly, by Léon Seiller.[70] What we might well say is that the Word itself became a 'human person' without there being any 'opposite' between this man Jesus and the Son of God. But this seems to me impossible apart from what is falteringly expressed or signified by 'hypostatic identification' (I prefer this term to *unio hypostatica*). This very fact (to be assessed only from a starting-point in Jesus) intimates to us that in Jesus' human life the Father is 'person' in a different way from the Son – perhaps the reason why Eastern Christology and Trinitarian doctrine in particular call the Father 'the fount of the Godhead'. When having begun with Jesus we eventually arrive at the Trinity, we are in a position at last the better to understand Jesus in the context of the Trinity itself: bearing in mind that this is, after all, theology 'to the power of three'!

What follows from all this for me is that God does not become 'Trinitarian' only when Jesus Christ becomes a man; I find the very idea inconceivable. Equally, what is clear to me is that our calling the Trinity three divine persons is possible only on the basis of the man Jesus and that only then does this have any real meaning. Our actual human history, in which Jesus participates, also signifies something for the very life of God. He is not 'impassible': that much, surely, the Bible teaches us. Seen in that light 'Process Philosophy'[71] with its distinction between 'existential non-dependence' and 'actual depend-ence' in God is on the trail of something real, although the term 'con-sequent nature' is an unhappy one in this connection. The distinction seems to me not to be needed, either, by anyone wanting to assert the dynamic of God's eternally youthful being, an eternal attribute in which pure, absolute freedom entails no contingency. In God there is no 'natural necessity' at all, and no 'necessary nature': he is in his very being pure and absolute freedom, which also implies fidelity to himself and his creation. Concepts such as 'nature' and 'person' are of them-selves inadequate terms for enabling us to comprehend God's absolute freedom. What is in God freedom without contingency-or-becoming, when viewed from our side of things, is pure contingency. We would do better, therefore, in view of the *de facto* givenness of our history and of Jesus, to say that on the one hand God would be no God without creatures and Jesus of Nazareth, on the other hand that we and Jesus also (viewed in a 'we' context) could have *not* been. This tension, it seems to me, affords a sounder perspective on the divine, essential being of God and the creaturely character of our whole history than the distinctions (circuitously influenced by Hegel) of 'Process Philosophy', which for that matter also attempts in some degree to put into words a mystery, without however envisaging the 'unvarying-ness' of God (a sounder notion than 'invariability') sufficiently in conjunction with the eternal dynamic of the nature of absolute freedom, which – in our faltering human discourse – is an eternal 'newness' without growth or what in a mundane context we call variability. To adduce distinctions in God just because of the inadequate way in which we talk about him seems to me a perilous undertaking.

Jesus of Nazareth, the crucified-and-risen One, is the Son of God in the fashion of an actual and contingent human being: within the dimension of being proper to a genuine and uncurtailed historical human nature he brings to us – through his person, preaching, way of life and death – the vital message of the unrestricted self-giving which God is in himself and is also willing to be for us human beings. Having regard to the contingent, non-necessary fact of our history – and the Jesus event in it – God would yet be no God without this historical happening. Therefore this history, our history (which of itself did not have to be), is nevertheless the only realistic way for us to speak meaningfully about the essential being of God. Through his historical self-giving, accepted by the Father, Jesus has shown us who God is: a *Deus humanissimus*. How the man Jesus can be for us at the same time the form and aspect of a present divine 'person', the Son, transcending our future through an overwhelming immanence, is in my view, despite the non-contradiction that we recognize and the fact that Jesus of Nazareth's living of it has made sense of it, a mystery theoretically unfathomable beyond this point. *Anagkè stènai*: sometimes it is high time – and tide! – for keeping silent in reverence and adoration, and for critical recollection of the great tradition of *theologia negativa*. After all that we do know of him, in the end we do not know who God is.

This book – I did after all describe it as a prolegomenon – does call of course for a substantial complement in what I would envisage as a reflection on what 'grace' is: an exposition, that is, dealing within a modern horizon of understanding and procedure with the problem of deliverance (redemption) and emancipation – the current problem of our history as the history of liberation. So there may still be a sequel to this book.

Chapter 3

# Theoretical Christology, story, and praxis of the kingdom of God

The approaching salvation-imparted-by-God which Jesus preached and for which he lived and met his death, the rule of God centred on and concerned with humanity, proves in the end to be the person of Jesus Christ himself, the eschatological man, Jesus of Nazareth, who is exalted to the presence of God and of his plenitude sends us the

Spirit of God, to open up 'communication' among human beings. Thus Jesus of Nazareth reveals in his own person the eschatological face of all humanity and in so doing discloses the Trinitarian fullness of God's unity of being, as in its essence and in absolute freedom a gift to man. Jesus' being-as-man is 'God translated' for us. His pro-existence as man is the sacrament among us of the pro-existence or self-giving of God's own being. In Jesus God has willed in his Son, and 'in fashion as a man', to be God for us. The unique universality lies, therefore, in Jesus' eschatological humanity, sacrament of God's universal love for human beings. In forgetfulness of self Jesus identified himself completely with God's cause as man's cause. God has identified himself with this identification of Jesus; that is, Jesus is the firstborn of the kingdom of God. The cause of God as the cause of man is personified in the very person of Jesus Christ. In any place this is the sole heart and centre of what goes by the name of 'Christianity'. It also affirms Jesus' role as universal mediator. He is the firstborn and 'the leader' of a new mankind in that he has lived out proleptically in his own experience the praxis of the kingdom of God and because that praxis has been endorsed by God. Jesus brought no new total system, therefore, in which everything is made comprehensible and finds its significant place. Both before and after Jesus every theoretical total system remains an ideology; our history as men continues to be completely open. But the praxis of the eschatological kingdom is actually made possible in this world, in our history. History itself stands under a promise that summons men to prayer and action – but a philosophy or theology of history remains impossible, theoretically inadequate and open. Thus what befell Jesus can still happen to many people: murder done to innocence. Even to those with faith in Christ the prophet Micah's admonition applies: 'Yet they lean upon the Lord and say: Is not the Lord in the midst of us? No evil shall come upon us' (Micah 3:11). But it may well come upon us, as upon Jesus; and then our confidence in God will be hard put to it indeed. The salvation in Jesus proffered by God can never be reduced to a theoretically conclusive system. 'Blessed is he who is not offended in me.'

Although this explicitly Christological account of Jesus of Nazareth (the one who proclaims the rule of God, setting man's conduct under judgement, and leads the way in the praxis of the kingdom of God) turns out to be intrinsically necessary (in the light of Jesus and the figure he presents), it can give rise to some dangerous secondary phenomena. The process of Christologizing Jesus of Nazareth may indeed 'freeze' or neutralize his message and praxis but lose sight of him and leave us with only a celestial cult mystery: the great Ikon Christ, shunted so far off in a Godward direction (God himself having already been edged out of this world of men) that he too, Jesus Christ, ceases to have any critical impact on the life of the world. To contend for the divinity of Jesus in a world of which God has long since taken his leave may well be a battle lost before it has begun. It also fails to grasp the deepest intention of God's plan of salvation, namely, God's resolve to encounter us 'in fashion as a man', so that – indeed – we might eventually be enabled to find him. If we mean to honour God's saving purposes we shall submit to the judgement of the man Jesus; only then will we acquire an outlook upon the living God. This will require us to forbear – even in catechesis. To put it starkly: whereas God is bent on showing himself in human form, we on our side slip past this human aspect as quickly as we can in order to admire a 'divine Ikon' from which every trait of the critical prophet has been smoothed away. Thus we 'neutralize' the critical impact of God himself and run the risk simply of adding a new ideology to those which mankind already possesses in such plenty: that is to say, Christology itself! I fear at times that with the keen edge of our credal utterances about Jesus we dull the critical vision of his prophecy, having as it does real consequences for our society and politics. A one-sided apotheosis of Jesus that restricts him exclusively to the divine side actually has the effect of removing from our history a nuisance-figure who would challenge our self-indulgence, and the dangerous memory of some provocative and vital prophesying – is also a way of silencing Jesus the prophet! As against this Christology the words apply: 'Why do you call me "Lord, Lord", and not do what I tell you? . . . Depart from me, all you workers of iniquity' (Lk. 6:46 and 13:27). It is only right that straightaway after this Christological section – as theology to the second and even the third power – this should be stated in so many words.

Jesus' unique universal significance, which (according to what the Christian faith affirms) touches all human beings in the matter of their destiny and its determination, is at the same time, however, historically mediated: through his eschatological assembly of believers, the 'Church of Christ'. The intermediary linking the historical with the universal significance of Jesus is the historical mission of the Church in the world. That is the memorable and also perilous implication expressed in what the New Testament calls 'Jesus' appearances'. The universality of Jesus Christ, the 'catholicity' of his Church, and the missionary, witnessing enterprise (especially through the praxis of the kingdom of

God) of the Christian churches are so many facets of one and the same, historically always mediated, faith-motivated reality: a work of service, carried out by us in faith, as we are led by the Spirit of Christ. Thus it is in the power of Jesus' Spirit that the Church mediates the manner in which God is concerned with all human beings. In other words: concretely, the unique universality of Jesus is a historical task and mandate for the Christian, 'that they know thee, the only true God, and Jesus Christ whom thou hast sent' (Jn. 17:3), thanks to the Church's 'praxis of the kingdom of God'. Such a definition of the nature of the Church is at the same time a performative kind of discourse, not simply a descriptive account of its concrete formal manifestation – though this nature goes on finding expression 'here, there and anywhere', for instance, in the anonymous yet active concern of so many 'ordinary Christians' – lay people as well as the junior and senior clergy. The 'anonymous Christian' is to be found primarily within the churches. Across the frontiers of the denominations 'Christians' discover one another there. This is why the ecumenical and institutional recognition of 'one Christian faith' is a primary and pressing stipulation – recognizing oneself in a differently constituted but real Christianity. And then – remembering the plural yet fundamentally one Christianity of the 'New Testament' – I think that we cultivate and cherish divisions where to judge from the New Testament they are no longer tenable.

There is yet another aspect, however, which may become clear in the light of the eschatological man Jesus, the Son of God. For us the future is not a still outstanding hope unless and until we have ourselves settled accounts with the past. A future is opened to us only as we become reconciled to the past. Our deliverance is not just the prospect of a new future, it is that only through the conquest of past history by way of reconciliation with one's own past. Deliverance, redemption, consists in so being reconciled to one's own past that confidence in the future is again made possible. The latter is not possible without the former. 'Being justified', as a piece of religious discourse, implies being reconciled to the ways of God and so to history, to one's own past, one's own life and death, and confidence in the future. All of this is the consequence of what Jesus calls *metanoia* as a result of the coming rule of God. *Metanoia* entails having done with the past and going to meet the future in confidence – a future which none the less remains open, does not exclude risk and cannot be theoretically 'sealed off' from every threat. The churches of Christ are the areas in which the unique universality of Jesus is potentially to be experienced, or in which it is obscured, so that even the world vanishes in the fog.

Why, in the end, anyone should put their trust in a given person is a mystery. One can adduce various factors having to do with psychology, biography, sociology, cultural history and the family; they are relevant, of course, within each of these limited levels of explanation. But they leave intact the mystery of the person, of every person, and can never explain the trust motivated by faith. No more is an appeal to God's grace envisaged as an explanation. To speak of God's work of grace is to speak in the language of religious affirmation about the human mystery of trusting in someone. Any human being anywhere lives on the basis of 'models', and nobody can ever supply rationally cogent grounds for the confidence he has in someone else. Yet to be able to trust a person and not make relying on his trustworthiness a totally rash decision one must first have substantial information about his life, career and death. That is why I put so much into Parts One, Two and Three. It also serves to induce us to sort out what as Christians we believe. Having sight of any purposeful life, *a fortiori* of the person of Jesus of Nazareth, leads to *metanoia*, to taking a new look at one's living and to discovering, though as Christians we may live indifferently well, what a rare event among Christians, even, is the consistent praxis of the kingdom of God. 'News of Jesus', in the event the *euaggelion*, raises the question of how in fact we live; the effect of it is first to disorientate, then to liberate.

Christology often becomes a matter of system and systematization, for which Jesus of Nazareth, teller of parables, champion of men, one who went about doing good and was at the same time mystic and exegete of God, merely provides the occasion. To say this is not to exhort to silence or put a stop to continuous reflection; on the contrary. It is meant simply to give expression to the proper diffidence with which a mystery of love and solidarity on the part of a fellow human being filled by God's Spirit ought to be approached; and also to invite us to combine the theoretical theology with stories (neither too soon nor yet too late) and more especially with orthopraxis, that is, the 'practice' of the kingdom of God, without which every theory and every story loses its credibility – certainly in a world calling in its impotence for justice and liberation. Then and only then will theory, story and parable – hand in hand with the praxis of the kingdom of God – be for this world an invitation to make a reply, in real freedom and on its own behalf, to the question: 'But you – you who read this – whom do you say that I – Jesus of Nazareth – am?'

At the start of this book I repeated the story from the Acts (4:10–12)

J.E.C.–Y

about the lame man who was cured when he heard from Peter the 'story of Jesus'. M. Buber too recognizes the potential of the story in the telling, when he has a rabbi relate the following: 'My grandfather was paralysed. One day he was asked to tell about something that happened with his teacher – the great Baalschem. Then he told how the saintly Baalschem used to leap about and dance while he was at his prayers. As he went on with the story my grandfather stood up; he was so carried away that he had to show how the master had done it, and started to caper about and dance. From that moment on he was cured. That is how stories should be told.'[72]

Should this book be a warrantable introduction to the recovery of 'a kind of believing that really tells',[73] to practical and critical effect, because its basis is the abiding and appealing presence in the world of the kingdom of God and the praxis that goes with it, then I count myself a happy man. If that is not so, then for my part the book can be marked down for sale in any 'curio' shop tomorrow.

# Notes

The notes are numbered consecutively within each Section.

*Why this book has been written* (pp. 17–40)

1. *'must* be saved'; in New Testament usage this 'must' signifies: the living God has provided for this, it is his divine plan for men's salvation. Hence the rendering: 'according to God's plan of salvation'.
2. 'For this was not done in a corner' (Acts 26: 26).
3. M. Hengel, 'Christologie und neutestamentliche Chronologie, in *Neues Testament und Geschichte* (O. Cullmann on his 70th birthday) (Zürich-Tübingen 1972), 43–67.
4. M. Hengel, *Judentum und Hellenismus* (Tübingen 1973²), 354.
5. See the interpolation in the twelfth petition of the Jewish prayer of 'Eighteen Supplications': 'May the Nazarenes and heretics perish instantly. May they be expunged from the book of life and not be recorded among the righteous' (see K. G. Kuhn, *Achtzehngebet und Vaterunser und der Reim* [WUNT, 1] (Tübingen 1950), 18–21).
6. Rom. 16: 16, or: '*ekklesia* of God' (1 Cor: 1: 2; 10: 32; 16: 22; 15: 9, etc.).
7. See H. Bourgeois, 'Visages de Jésus et manifestation de Dieu', in LVie, n. 112 (1973) (71–84), 82.
8. H. van Zoelen, 'Jezus van Nazareth: persoonsverheerlijking als symptoom', in *Dwang, dwaling en bedrog* (Baarn 1971), 52–67.
9. We have a typical example of this dilemma in the contrast between two articles, on the one hand by G. Fohrer, 'Das Alte Testament und das Thema "Christologie" ', in EvTh 30 (1970), 281–98, on the other by G. Klein, ' "Reich Gottes" als biblischer Zentralbegriff', ib., 642–70.
10. See also W. Pannenberg, *Das Glaubensbekenntnis ausgelegt und verantwortet vor den Fragen der Gegenwart* (Hamburg 1972), 44.
11. See e.g. Schalom Asch, *Der Nazarener* (Amsterdam 1950); M. Brod, *Der Meister* (Gütersloh 1951); M. Buber, *Zwei Glaubensweisen* (Zürich 1950); and *Der Jude und sein Judentum* (Cologne 1963); Joel Carmichael, *Leben und Tod des Jesus von Nazareth* (Munich 1966); Schalom ben Chorin, *Bruder Jesus* (Munich 1967); Haim Cohen, *Trial and Death of Jesus* (Tel Aviv 1968); W. P. Eckert, *Judenhasz, Schuld der Christen?* (Essen 1966); David Flusser, *Jesus* (Hamburg-Reinbeck 1968); J. Isaac, *Jésus et Israel* (Paris 1970); Ascher Finkel, *The Teacher of Nazareth* (Leyden 1964); Aharon Kabak, *The Narrow Path* (Jerusalem 1968); J. Klausner, *Jesus von Nazareth* (Jerusalem 1952); Pinehas E. Lapide, *Jesus in Israel* (Gladbeck 1970); S. Schwartz, *La Réhabilitation juive de Jésus* (Martizay 1969); see also Morris Goldstein, *Jesus in the Jewish Tradition* (New York 1950), and Frank Andermann, *Das grosze Gesicht* (Munich 1971).
12. M. Buber, *Zwei Glaubensweisen*, foreword.
13. Kl. Berger, *Die Gesetzesauslegung Jesu* (thesis of the book).

14. See E. Troeltsch, 'Ueber historische und dogmatische Methode in der Theologie', in *Gesammelte Schriften*, vol. 2 (Tübingen 1922²) (Aalen 1962), 729-53.
15. Y. Congar, *Vraie et fausse réforme dans l'Église* (Paris 1950, 498-9)

PART ONE (pp. 41-104)

1. This brief summary is borne out in the course of the book as a whole.
2. See P. Berger and Th. Luckmann, *The Social Construction of Reality* (New York 1966); B. Lee Woolf, *Sprache, Denken, Wirklichkeit* (Hamburg 1968⁴) (from the English, 1956).
3. Although this text in Acts has in part been influenced by the 'rapture'-model which Luke employs (and in the New Testament this is a recent thing) (see in a later chapter), the idea itself (of the *assumptio*-model) is much older. Apart from the ending added later on (Mk. 16: 9-20) the Marcan gospel supports the view of Jesus as risen, *appointed* but not yet *inaugurated* as son of man, who is to *appear* only at the close of the Age (see Th. J. Weeden, *Mark-Traditions in Conflict* (Philadelphia 1971)) (see later). Luke himself is here 'Christianizing' a speculation, familiar to the Baptist's followers, concerning Elijah (see Part Three, Section Two, n. 41).
4. e.g., W. Marxsen, *Das Neue Testament als Buch der Kirche* (Gütersloh 1966), and *Der Streit um die Bibel* (Gladbeck 1965).
5. Dogmatic Constitution 'Dei Verbum', no. 10.
6. This I see expressed in the fact that pre-synoptic, single-item formulae, deriving from diverse local church traditions, coalesce in the New Testament into more complex formulations of belief; this is evidently the result of synthetic critique, tending towards a unitive picture of Jesus within the universal Church.
7. See especially Fr. Ricken, 'Das Homoousis von Nikaia als Krisis des altchristlichen Platonismus', in *Zur Frühgeschichte der Christologie* (Quaest. Disp., 51) (Freiburg 1970), 74-99.
8. Dogmatic Constitution 'Lumen Gentium', no. 1.
9. See W. S. Haas, *The Destiny of Mind, East and West* (London 1965) (= *Oestliches und westliches Denken* (Hamburg 1957)), and H. Frankfort, *Kingship and the Gods*, (Chicago 1948), VII-VIII. The ground of 'oriental tolerance' lies in its outlook, according to which totally divergent 'systems' can none the less articulate a similar basic intuition. Eventually the 'participation idea', so called, came from the East into Western philosophy, but with another, 'un-Eastern' meaning. It is easier for orientals than for westerners to detect a profounder *unity* in divergent systems. One fact in the Church's history – the creation of a 'canon' of New Testament writings – expresses this intuition of unity without giving it a concrete name. But this much was clear: the subject of which all these plural interpretations speak is the one Jesus of Nazareth.
10. Of the recent literature see especially J. Roloff, *Das Kerygma*; Th. Boman, *Die Jesusüberlieferung im Lichte der neueren Volkskunde* (Göttingen

1967); J. Robinson-H. Koester, *Trajectories*; D. Lührmann, 'Erwägungen zur Geschichte des Urchristentums', in EvTh 32 (1972), 452–67; U. Wilckens, 'Jesusüberlieferung und Christus-kerygma', in *Theologia Viatorum* 10 (1966), 311–39; N. A. Dahl, 'Der historische Jesus als geschichtswissenschaftliches und theologisches Problem', in KuD 1 (1955), 104–32; Schulz, *Q-Quelle*; A. Vögtle, *Das Evangelium und die Evangelien* (Düsseldorf 1971), and 'Jesus von Nazareth', in *Oekumenische Kirchengeschichte* (ed. E. Kottje and B. Möhler) (Mainz-Munich 1970), 3–24; Leander E. Keck, *A Future for the Historical Jesus* (Nashville-New York 1971); also: E. Güttgemanns, *Offene Fragen zur Formgeschichte des Evangeliums* (Munich 1971[2]). (See further on in the detailed analysis.) 11. German text; 'Die Verkündigung Jesu gehört zu den Voraussetzungen der Theologie des Neuen Testaments und ist nicht ein Teil dieser selbst' (*Theologie*, 1).

12. e.g., B. Gerhardson, *Memory and Manuscript* (Uppsala 1961); *Tradition and Transmission in Early Christianity* (Coniectanea Neotestamentica, 20) (Lund 1964).

13. Thus, for example, N. Schmithals, 'Kein Streit um des Kaisers Bart', in *Evangelische Kommentare* 3 (1970), 78–82 and 416–18; G. Strecker, 'Die historische und theologische Problematik der Jesusfrage', in EvTh 29 (1969), 453–76, in particular 469.

14. See: R. Koselleck and W. Stempel (eds.), *Geschichten und Geschichte* (Munich 1972); H. Weinrich, *Literatur für Leser* (Stuttgart 1972), and 'Narratieve theologie', in Conc 9 (1973), n. 5, 48–57; K. Stierle, 'L'histoire comme exemple, l'exemple comme histoire', in *Poétique* 10 (1972), 176–98; Alb. B. Lord, *Der Sänger erzählt* (Göttingen 1965); see also 'Leven met verhalen', in *Schrift*, n. 26 (1973), 41–76.

15. See H. Marrou, *Histoire de l'éducation dans l'Antiquité* (Paris 1948), and more recently, with emphasis on historical reliability: A. W. Mosely, 'Historical reporting in the ancient world', in NTS 12 (1965–6), 10–26. This insight is made to yield results in exegesis by, among others, Th. J. Weeden, *Marktraditions*; J. A. Baird, *Audience Criticism and the Historical Jesus* (Philadelphia 1969), and J. L. Martyn, *History and Theology in the Fourth Gospel* (New York 1969).

16. Thus e.g., N. Perrin, *Rediscovering the Teaching of Jesus* (London 1967), 245; H. Bartsch, *Jesus, Prophet und Messias* (Frankfurt 1970), 11, 17–20 and 39–40; P. Stuhlmacher, 'Kritische Marginalien zum gegenwärtigen Stand der Frage nach Jesus', in *Fides et Communicatio* (Festschrift for M. Doerne) (Göttingen 1970), 341–61; J. Blank, *Jesus von Nazareth* (Freiburg 1972), 78; W. Kümmel, *Die Theologie des Neuen Testaments nach seinen Hauptzeugen* (Göttingen 1969), 23; Roloff, *Das Kerygma* (the whole book); A. Vögtle, 'Das Evangelium', l.c., 16–30; H. Schlier, 'Die Anfänge des christologischen Credo', in *Zur Frühgeschichte der Christologie* (Freiburg 1970), 13–58.

17. See Roloff, *Das Kerygma*, 70.

18. D. Lührmann, 'Erwägungen zur Geschichte der Urchristentums', l.c., 452–67, and 'Liebet eure Feinde', in ZThK 69 (1972) (412–38), 435–6; J. M. Robinson and H. Koester, *Trajectories* (likewise one of the theses of this book);

also G. Schille, *Anfänge der Kirche* (Munich 1966); 'Prolegomena zur Jesus-frage', in ThLZ 93 (1968), 481–8; 'Was ist ein Logion?', in ZNW 61 (1970), 172–82, and *Das vorsynoptische Judenchristentum* (Stuttgart 1970).

19. The different facets have been dissected in a fascinating way by E. Trocmé, *Jésus de Nazareth vu par les témoins de sa vie* (Neuchâtel 1971), although some of his views are problematical.

20. D. Lührmann, 'Liebet eure Feinde', l.c., 434–5.

21. Schulz, *Q-Quelle*, 55–176 as over against 177–480; see 481–9.

22. See G. Schille, 'Prolegomena zur Jesusfrage', in ThLZ, l.c., 485–6; H. Grasz, *Theologie und Kritik* (Göttingen 1969), 9–27.

23. Schulz, *Q-Quelle*, 241.

24. Rightly reacting to that are the works, cited here, by E. Güttgemanns, *Offene Fragen*; D. Lührmann, 'Erwägungen', l.c., and 'Liebet eure Feinde', l.c., and G. Schille.

25. As opposed to the current twofold division; 'Life of Jesus-tradition' and '*Kerygma*-tradition' (maintained by Schulz, *Q-Quelle*, 31, with many others), Th. Boman, 'Die Jesus-überlieferung', l.c., 29–61, esp. 42–4, tries to resolve the problem by calling the twofold 'kerygmatic tradition' and 'Jesus tradition', both of them, 'tradition concerning Jesus', two forms of Jesus traditions. But in fact there is no more a purely kerygmatic tradition without reference to Jesus of Nazareth than there is reference to Jesus without *kerygma*. Even James Robinson's distinction (Robinson-Koester, *Trajectories*, 20–70) between *kerygma* and history is not given within the New Testament itself.

26. G. Schille, 'Was ist ein Logion?', l.c., 172–82.

27. N. A. Dahl, 'Der historische Jesus als geschichtswissenschaftliches und theologisches Problem', in KuD 1 (1955), 104–32.

28. H. Braun, *Jesus. Der Mann aus Nazareth und seine Zeit* (Berlin 1969[2]), 33–4; J. Robinson, *The New Quest of the Historical Jesus* (Naperville 1959), 99.

29. As, for instance, those logia are not authentic sayings of Jesus, which reflect the teaching of the early Church; tally with the doctrine of contemporary Judaism or the Old Testament; presuppose a situation inconceivable in Jesus' time; contradict other logia; turn out, when the gospels are compared one with another, to be a further development.

30. H. Braun, 'Jesus', l.c., 35–7.

31. D. G. Calvert, 'An Examination', 219; Helmut Koester's thinking tends in a similar direction in J. Robinson-H. Koester, *Trajectories*, 209.

32. See Part Three.

33. Koester, in Robinson-Koester, *Trajectories*, 209.

34. 'Criterion of distinctiveness', 'criterion of dissimilarity', 'Ausgrenzungs-kriterium', 'Kriterium der doppelten Abgrenzung', 'critère du distinctif spécifique'. Thus esp.: R. Fuller, *Critical Introduction*, 96–7, and 'The clue to Jesus' self-understanding' (Studia Evang., III–2) (Berlin 1964), 58–66; E. Käsemann, *Besinnungen*, I, 205; H. Conzelmann, in RGG III[3], 623; N. Perrin, *Rediscovering*, 39; M. Lehmann, *Quellenanalyse*, 163–205, for this criterion in

particular: 178–86; O. Cullmann, *Heil als Geschichte*, 169; W. Kümmel, in ThR, 15–46.

35. R. Bultmann: 'Where opposition to the morality and piety of Judaism and the specifically eschatological tone, which constitute what is characteristic of Jesus' preaching, are expressed, and where on the other hand there are no specifically Christian features, it is easiest to conclude that here is an authentic parable of Jesus' (*Tradition*, 222). For the 'eschatological frame', see: Bultmann, *Theologie*, 110–13.

36. RGG III³, 623.

37. Cullmann, *Heil als Geschichte*, 169.

38. E. Käsemann, *Besinnungen*, I, 206ff.

39. See W. Trilling, *Fragen zur Geschichtlichkeit Jesu*, 46–50.

40. Käsemann, *Besinnungen*, I, 205. P. W. Schmiedel in particular called this the 'pillar argument' – 'foundation-pillars for a truly scientific life of Jesus' (!) – in *Biblical Encyclopaedia* 1901, vol. 2 (1761–1898), 1847, cited by M. Lehmann, *Quellenanalyse*, 174–5.

41. N. Perrin, *Rediscovering*, l.c., 38–9.

42. M. Lehmann, *Quellenanalyse*, 185; O. Cullmann, *Heil als Geschichte*, 154; W. Marxsen, *Anfangsprobleme der Christologie* (Gütersloh 1964²), 15.

43. Berger, *Gesetzesauslegung*, 2 and 11–31 (thesis of the whole book); Schulz, *Q-Quelle*, 485–6. Moreover, a certain anti-Pharisaic attitude would appear to be given already with Jesus' Galilean origin. See W. Bauer, 'Jesus, der Galiläer', in *Aufsätze und kleine Schriften* (ed. G. Strecker) (Tübingen 1967) (91–108), 100. See also L. E. Elliott-Binns, *Galilean Christianity* (London 1956). The Lake of Gennesareth was a centre of intense communication between Jewish and Greek-speaking people (M. Hengel, *Judentum und Hellenismus*, 191–8). The attitude to the Law was not the same there as in Jerusalem, where Galilee was looked upon as a 'semi-pagan' country.

44. Dahl, 'Der historische Jesus', l.c., 119.

45. Dahl, l.c., 120; see also M. Lehmann, *Quellenanalyse*, l.c., 185.

46. Known also as the 'criterion of multiple attestation'. See especially F. C. Burkitt, *The Gospel History*, 147–68; also C. H. Dodd, *History and the Gospel*, 91–101, applied by him in particular to the parables: *Parables of the Kingdom*, 24; H. K. McArthur, *Basic Issues*, 39–55; N. Perrin, *Rediscovering the teaching of Jesus*, l.c., 45.

47. Marcan tradition: Mk. 2: 17 pls Q tradition: Lk. 15: 4–10 pls SL (=Luke's own tradition or source): Lk. 7: 36–47; 15: 11–32; 19: 1–10; SM (=Matthew's own source or, perhaps, the evolved Q tradition): Mt. 10: 6.

48. Burkitt, *The Gospel History*, 147–8.

49. S. Schulz, *Q-Quelle*, 241 and 371.

50. D. Calvert, 'An Examination', 217.

51. R. Fuller, *Critical Introduction*, 95 and 98; C. E. Carlston, in BRes, 33–4. (Actually, Carlston confines his argument to the parables; they are said to be authentic only if they are associated with Jesus' eschatological insistence on *metanoia*.) See B. van Iersel, in Conc 7 (1971), n. 10, 75–84.

52. B. van Iersel, l.c., 75.

53. N. A. Dahl, *Der historische Jesus*, 120; see Lehmann, *Quellenanalyse*, 185.

54. M. Lehmann, *Quellenanalyse*, 196–7.

55. 'Discussion as to whether an individual logion is "authentic" is often pointless, because the reasons for and against are indecisive. Generally speaking, the historian is well advised to look at the tradition as a whole and not build too much on a particular logion when it deviates from the rest of the traditions' (M. Dibelius, *Jesus* (Berlin 1966[4]), 21).

56. S. Schulz, *Q-Quelle*, 55–176.

57. E. Jüngel, *Paulus und Jesus* (Tübingen 1964[2]), 4.

58. Especially K. Niederwimmer, *Jesus* (Göttingen 1968), 26 and 31: 'Tatsächlich musz ja die Hinrichtung Jesu als Schlüssel zum Gesamtverständnis dienen' – 'The fact is, of course, that Jesus' execution must serve as key to an understanding of the whole' (31). Also N. A. Dahl, *Der historische Jesus*, 121.

59. G. Schille, 'Was ist ein Logion?', 172–82.

60. *Sayings of Jesus*, 18ff.

61. The tenor of all J. Jeremias' works; see especially *Die Abendmahlsworte Jesu* (Göttingen (1949), 1967[4]); sub *pascha*, in ThWNT V, 895–903, and *paschô*, V, 903–23; *Abba, Studien zur neutestamentlichen Theologie und Zeitgeschichte* (Göttingen 1966).

62. *An Aramaic Approach* (gist of the book as a whole).

63. Kasemann, in *Besinnungen*, I, 203.

64. RGG III[3], 643. Many exegetes support him in this. M. Lehmann even calls it the 'communis opinio' (*Quellenanalyse*, 186).

65. See especially Berger, *Amen-Worte*, and his criticism in this regard (152–63) of V. Hasler, *Amen. Redaktionsgeschichtliche Untersuchung zur Einleitungsformel der Herrenworte 'Wahrlich ich sage euch'* (Zürich 1969).


PART TWO, *Section One (pp. 115–271)*

1. Mk. 8: 35; 10: 29; 13: 10 and 14: 9 (Mk. 16: 15 is a later addition, although so far as the use of the term is concerned, completely in line with Mark). See also the actual context of the pericope on the anointing at Bethany: J. Roloff, *Das Kerygma*, 210–15, to some extent disagreeing with that: R. Pesch, 'Die Salbung Jesu in Bethanien', in *Orientierung an Jesus*, 267–85.

2. Mt. 4: 23; 9: 35; 24: 14.

3. See Schlier, 'Euaggelion', l.c., 127; and P. Stuhlmacher, *Das paulinische Evangelium*, 56–108.

4. Schulz, *Q-Quelle*, 199.

5. See in a similar context of the history of tradition: Gal. 1: 7 with 1: 1; Rom. 4: 24; 1 Pet. 1: 19–21.

6. U. Wilckens, *Die Missionsreden der Apostelgeschichte* (Neukirchen 1963[2]), 69–70; Schnackenburg, 'Das Evangelium', l.c., 311, is therefore correct in rendering (contrary to Marxsen) not: the gospel *about* Jesus, but *of* Jesus; likewise Roloff, *Das Kerygma*, 215–20. Yet (contrary to Schnackenburg's

assertion) 'gospel' (evangel) did not initially signify a mission to Jews *and* Gentiles (see further on).

7. Roloff, *Das Kerygma*, 210–15.

8. Schnackenburg, 'Das Evangelium', l.c., 317; Roloff, *Das Kerygma*, 217–18.

9. B. van Iersel, *Een begin*, l.c., 28.

10. Schnackenburg, 'Das Evangelium', l.c., 323.

11. See W. Schrage, *'Ekklesia'* and *'Synagoge'*, in ZThK 60 (1963), 178–202.

12. See above, literature under (a) 'conversion-movements'.

13. Literature under (b) 'prophetic context'.

14. Jer. 25: 4a, 5–6; 26: 5; 29: 19; 35: 15; 44: 4; Zech. 1: 4–6; 7: 7, 12; 2 Chron. 36: 14–16.

15. Steck, *Gewaltsames Geschick*, 184–9 and 196–225; Berger, *Gesetzesauslegung*, 15.

16. J. Blank, *Jesus von Nazareth*, 95ff.

17. A. Vögtle, *Das öffentliche Wirken Jesu auf den Hintergrund der Qumrân-Bewegung* (Freiburger Universitätsreden, 27) (Freiburg 1958), 5–19; M. Hengel, *Judentum und Hellenismus*, 563.

18. Berger, *Gesetzesauslegung* (argument of the book as a whole).

19. See above literature under (c) 'apocalyptical context'.

20. Especially H. Desroche, *Sociologies religieuses* (Paris 1968); *Dictionnaire des messies, messianismes et millénarismes de l'ère chrétienne* (Paris 1968), 1–40; *Sociologie de l'espérance* (Paris 1973).

21. I refer repeatedly to H. Marrou, and A. W. Mosely, who has examined the trustworthiness of ancient historical writings (Part One, Section One, footnote 15).

22. In the exegetical literature this aspect has been examined in particular by J. Becker, *Joh. der Täufer*, l.c., 16–26.

23. Isa. 40: 3–4; 41: 18–19; 43: 19–20; 48: 20–21; 49: 10–11; 51: 10–11; Hosea 2: 14; 12: 10. See: ThWNT II, 655–6.

24. See 2 Kings 1: 7–8 (the typical leather girdle of Elijah); Zech. 13: 4 (a hairy mantle as the mark of a prophet).

25. Mt. 11: 9 pls Mk. 6: 15 pls 11: 32 pls Lk. 1: 76; Jn. 1: 21–25.

26. On one occasion, in Mt. 3: 2, there is mention of John's proclamation of God's rule; clearly a Matthean redaction intended to harmonize John's message with that of Jesus.

27. Mk. 1: 1–8 presents (as is frequent enough; see Hoffmann, *Q-Studien*, 14; Schulz, *Q-Quelle*, 370, n. 317) a shortened version of Q material. Starting from his concern with Christian baptism, he puts more emphasis on John's baptismal activity than on his preaching of judgement. On 'generation of vipers' see Foerster, in ThWNT II, 815.

28. Sirach (Ecclesiast.) 36; Psalmi Salomonis 8: 17; also O. Steck, *Gewaltsames Geschick*, 188–9 and 286, n. 1.

29. Ezek. 33: 24; Amos 4: 1; Isa. 1: 10–23; 54: 3–4; 57: 3; see Mt. 12: 34 and the secondary Mt. 23: 22.

30. Lohmeyer, *Joh. der Täufer*, 58–9 and 129–41.

31. See Strack-Billerbeck, I, 392–6; Steck, *Gewaltsames Geschick*, 286, n. 1;

188–99; C. Westermann, *Grundformen prophetischer Rede* (Beih. EvTh, 31) (Tübingen 1964²). Israel stands self-accused of murdering the prophets (1 Kings 19: 10; Neh. 9: 26); the New Testament (Mt. 5: 12; 23: 31–32, 34, 37; Acts 7: 52; James 5: 10; Hebr. 11: 36–37; 1 Thess. 2: 15–16) concurs thus with a Jewish critique.

32. See Isa. 30: 24; 41: 15–16; Jer. 15: 7; 51: 33; Micah 4: 12–14; Joel 3: 13.

33. Amos 8: 2; Isa. 40: 3–5.

34. Isa. 5: 24; 10: 17; 47: 14; Nahum 1: 10; Obad. 18; Mal. 3: 19.

35. Isa. 10: 18–19; Jer. 21: 14; 22: 7; Ezek. 21: 2–3; Zech. 11: 1–2.

36. Isa. 1: 24–25.

37. Mk. 1: 4 p Mt. 3: 2, 8 pl Acts 13: 24; 19: 4.

38. A play perhaps on the Hebrew words for 'child' (son=*ben*) and 'stone' (*'eben*). A similar kind of word-play occurs in the image of the 'rejected (corner-) stone' (Mk. 12: 10 with Ps. 118: 22; Lk. 20: 18 with Isa. 8: 14).

39. See as far back as Amos 9: 7–10; Jer. 7: 1–15.

40. E. Käsemann calls John simply an apocalypticist: *Besinnungen*, II, 99, 108–10.

41. J. Behm and E. Würthwein, *metanoia*, in ThWNT IV, 972–94; H. Wolff, 'Das Thema "Umkehr" in der alttestamentlichen prophetie', in *Gesammelte Studien zum Alten Testament* (Th. B. 22) (Munich 1964); H. Braun, '"Umkehr" im spätjüdischhäretischer und in frühchristlicher Sicht', in *Gesammelte Studien zum NT und seiner Umwelt* (Tübingen 1967²), 70–85.

42. J. Becker, *Joh. der Täufer*, 22–6; Schulz, *Q-Quelle*, 370. This seems to me by no means certain. The ancient prophets talk not just about being cleansed from guilt by *water* in the latter days (Isa. 4: 4; Ezek. 36: 25–26; 47: 1–12; Zech. 13: 1) but also about the *pouring out* (like water) of the Spirit (Zech. 12: 10–12; 13: 1–6; Joel 3: 1–2). See P. Reymond, 'L'eau, sa vie et sa signification dans l'ancien testament', in VTS 6 (1958), 233–8; see also J. Gnilka, l.c., in RQum 3 (1961), 196–7.

43. Bultmann, *Tradition*, 123, considers it to be a (pre-Christian) John tradition; also Dibelius, *Joh. der Täufer*, 53–7. It is called a Christian tradition by: Hoffmann, *Q-Studien*, 20; Lührmann, *Q-Redaktion*, 31; Schulz, *Q-Quelle*, 371–2; V. Hasler, *Amen*, 55. See immediately below under note 44.

44. J. Becker, *Joh. der Täufer*, 34–7; U. Müller, *Messias und Menschensohn in jüdischen Apokalypsen und in der Offenbarung des Johannes* (Gütersloh 1972), 36–60; J. Schneider, in ThWNT II, 664–72. That the New Testament identifies 'the one who is to come', of whom John speaks, with Jesus is obvious. In the oldest layer of the Q source, however, he is identified not with the earthly Jesus but with the coming Jesus-son of man figure, living with God; Schulz, *Q-Quelle*, 377. One is struck by the fact that speculations regarding the coming Elijah (based on Mal. 3: 23–24) were current among the followers of John the Baptist (U. Wilckens, *Die Missionsreden der Apostelgeschichte* (Neukirchen 1963²), 153–6), which confirms the assumption that John himself spoke of 'the one who is coming'.

45. See Mt. 3: 11; 11: 2–6; Lk. 7: 18–23; cf. Mk. 1: 7; Lk. 3: 16; Jn. 1: 15, 21.

46. Becker, *Joh. der Täufer*, 36. Again, there are references to the call to

repentance in the son of man tradition (Eth. Enoch 50).

47. Becker, ibid., 56–61.

48. Roloff, *Das Kerygma*, 90–3. Thus the oldest form of the pre-Marcan account is: Mk. 11: 15–16, 18a, 28–33.

49. J. Blank, *Jesus von Nazareth*, 102.

50. ibid., 102.

51. Josephus, *Antiquitates*, 18: 5, 2.

52. ibid.

53. See J. Gnilka, 'Das Martyrium Johannes' des Täufers'(Mk. 6: 17–29), in *Orientierung an Jesus* (78–92), 84–5 and especially 90–1. The story of the banquet at which a dancing-girl was put up to asking for the head of John was a later interpolation; viewed within the history of tradition, it turns out to reflect certain well-known, popular legends.

54. *Antiquitates*, 18: 5, 2.

55. A (rather mediocre but) suggestive outline of this was provided by R. Aron, *Les Années obscures de Jésus* (Paris 1960).

56. See G. Fohrer, *Die symbolische Handlugen der Propheten* (Basle-Zürich 1953).

57. According to Lührmann, *Q-Redaktion*, 29, in essence one of Jesus' own parables; see Roloff, *Das Kerygma*, 228–9; Schulz, *Q-Quelle*, 379–86.

58. Lk. 6: 20 and Mt. 5: 3; Lk. 7: 28 and Mt. 11: 11; Lk. 10: 9 and Mt. 10: 7; Lk. 11: 20 and Mt. 12: 28, Lk. 13: 18, 20 and Mt. 13: 31, 33; Lk. 13: 28 and Mt. 8: 11; Lk. 16: 16 and Mt. 11: 12.

59. Mk. 1: 15; 4: 11; 4: 26; 9: 1, 47; 10: 14; 12: 34; 14: 25; 15: 43; etc.

60. Mt. 3: 2; 4: 17; 5: 19-20; 19: 24; 21: 31; 21: 43.

61. Lk. 4: 43; 9: 2, 11, 60, 62; 14: 15; 16: 16; 17: 20; 19: 11; 22: 16, 18.

62. Jn. 3: 3 and 5.

63. See e.g., A. Vögtle, *Das Neue Testament*, l.c., 144–66.

64. The tendency, current throughout Jewry at the time, to form sectarian remnants, has been examined in particular by A. Vögtle, *Das öffentliche Wirken Jesu auf den Hintergrund der Qumranbewegung*, l.c., 5–19; J. Jeremias, 'Der Gedanke des "Heiligen Restes" im Spätjudentum und in der Verkündigung Jesu', in *Abba* (Göttingen 1966), 121–31; see on the distinctive character of these groups: E. Lohse, *Umwelt des Neuen Testaments* (Göttingen 1971), 51–85.

65. Thus in Qumrân: 1 QS 1: 4 and 1: 10.

66. Thus E. Käsemann, *Besinnungen*, II, 210, who at every point sticks to an inclusive interpretation. How this is possible if John himself is unfamiliar with any proclamation of the kingdom of God remains unexplained.

67. J. Becker, *Joh. der Täufer*, l.c., 87–8.

68. Attempts to read into this ideas of a Zealotic state have proved to be groundless. See sub *biadzesthai*, in ThWNT I, 608–13; this verb is always associated with the *enemies* of God's kingdom. Also Schulz, *Q-Quelle*, 265, n. 622. Not Luke but the Matthean text is primary here: 'the kingdom . . . has suffered violence'. The battle against God's *basileia*, and thus against the Christian messengers, begins with the activities of Jesus of Nazareth, in whom this kingdom has come. The parables about the growth of God's kingdom show that nothing can impede that growth.

69. P. Hoffmann, 'Die Anfänge der Theologie in Logienquelle', in *Gestalt und Anspruch des Neuen Testaments*, 142; Schulz, *Q-Quelle*, 196.

70. Of the many studies of John the most convincing is the account given by J. Becker, *Joh. der Täufer*, 76.

71. *Jesus von Nazareth*, 104.

72. See G. Klein, ' "Reich Gottes" als biblischer Zentralbegriff', in EvTh 30 (1970), 642–70; A. Vögtle, *Das Neue Testament*, 144.

73. Dan. 2: 44 (4: 31 and 6: 27 are not eschatological); Oracula Sibyllina 3: 767; Assumptio Moysis 10: 1ff.

74. Vögtle, *Das Neue Testament*, 144.

75. Strack-Billerbeck, I, 252, 477, 829.

76. Mt. 12: 32; here 'nor in the age (aeon) to come' means simply 'never' (see Mk. 3: 29). 'Sons of this world' (Lk. 16: 8; 20: 34) does indeed sound apocalyptical and Qumrânic, but means in an ordinary Jewish context 'we earthly people'. There is of course Mk. 10: 29–30: 'now in this time (*kairos*) . . . and in the age (aeon) to come'; setting aside the (at least) dubious authenticity, where Jesus is concerned, of this saying, what we have here is not any teaching about the future but a paraenesis, an exhortation to forsake everything. At issue here is the eschatological relevance of the present. The hundredfold 'compensation' is something that belongs to Hellenistic Judaism; see Berger, *Gesetzesauslegung*, 404–17.

77. Thus e.g., R. Schnackenburg, *Gottes Herrschaft*, 249–62; A. Vögtle, *Das Neue Testament*, 145–8; J. Becker, *Das Heil Gottes, Heils- und Sündenbegriff in den Qumrântexten und in Neuen Testament* (SUNT, 3) (Göttingen 1964), 206.

78. Dan. 3: 33; 4 Ezra 5: 26ff; Rev. 1: 9.

79. See e.g. Fr. Muszner, 'In den letzten tagen' (Apg. 2, 17a), in BZ 5 (1961) 263–5; this we already find in Gen. 49: 1; Num. 24: 14; Mic. 4: 1; Isa. 2: 2; Jer. 23: 20; Dan. 10: 14.

80. H. Riesenfeld, sub *paratèrèsis*, in ThWNT VIII, 150.

81. A. Vögtle, *Das Neue Testament*, l.c., 150. Only Mt. 19: 28 has the obviously eschatological-cum-futuristic '*paliggenesia*', as well as the '*sunteleia tou aiônos*' (Mt. 13: 39, 40, 49; 24: 3; 28: 20), the end (or the final re-creation) of this aeon; in the New Testament this is typically Matthean; it would appear to be an apocalyptical term from the Septuagintal version of Daniel (12: 13b; 9: 27; see Hebr. 9: 26). Vögtle, ibid., 151–66. Without doubt Mk. 9: 1 in particular (some of Jesus' contemporaries will still be alive when the rule of God is established in power) is secondary. See C. Colpe, sub *huios tou anthrôpou*, in ThWNT VIII, 459; Berger, *Amen-Worte*, 62–70.

82. K. Schubert, 'Die Entwicklung der eschatologischen Naherwartung im Frühjudentum', in *Vom Messias zu Christus* (ed. K. Schubert) (Vienna-Freiburg 1964), 1–54; P. Hoffmann, 'Die Anfänge', l.c., 134–52; M. Hengel, *Die Zeloten*, 385–6.

83. H. Schürmann, 'Die Warnung des Lk. vor der Falschlehre in der "Predigt am Berge" ', in BZ 10 (1966), 59–81.

84. See Tödt, *Menschensohn*, 212ff; also Lührmann, *Q-Redaktion*, 96.

85. The main thesis of Lührmann's *Q-Redaktion*, see especially 94.

86. The commentators are totally disagreed on this point. See the state of the discussion (at any rate up to 1964) as presented by W. G. Kümmel, 'Die Naherwartung in der Verkündigung Jesu', in *Zeit und Geschichte* (Dankesgabe and R. Bultmann) (Tübingen 1964), 31–46. Since 1964 see in particular: R. Pesch, *Naherwartungen. Tradition und Redaktion in Mk. 13* (Düsseldorf 1968) (with a variety of literature); J. Bornkamm, 'Die Verzögerung der Parusie', in *Geschichte und Glaube* (*Gesammelte Aufsätze* – Collected Essays, III–1) (Munich 1968), 46–55; E. Gräszer, *Die Naherwartung Jesu* (Stuttgart 1973). The question at issue is whether, where Jesus is concerned, early Christianity exhibits 're-apocalypticizing' tendencies – which for instance Lührmann, *Q-Redaktion*, 94, simply takes to be a fact. This presupposes, of course, that proclamation of the final judgement or of coming salvation is 'in essence' apocalyptical. In this enquiry everything depends on how we define the essential character of 'apocalyptic'. Furthermore, the exegetes fail to attach enough weight to the 'sociology of expectation of the end'. And then, as it seems to me, there is such a thing as a prophetic expectation of the end, which is indeed *represented* in temporal terms of 'nearness', and is even intended in that sense, without entitling us to give this expectation of 'it's on the point of happening now' a precise chronological interpretation. An over-complicated anthropology *and* religious impulse come into play here.

87. Lührmann, *Q-Redaktion*, 97; Schulz, *Q-Quelle*, 165–75; U. Wilckens, *Jesus-überlieferung*, 336–7.

88. See Lührmann, *Q-Redaktion*, 97.

89. R. Pesch, *Von der 'Praxis des Himmels'. Kritische Elemente im Neuen Testament* (Grasz 1971).

90. In Hebrew *re'*, fellow being, sounds more or less the same as *ro'*, shepherd; so that this parable may perhaps be a story about the good shepherd, as a mortifying example of what is elsewhere described as a 'flock without shepherds'.

91. See e.g., Lk. 10: 38–42; Jn. 12: 1–8; Lk. 7: 36–50; 11: 37–52; 14: 1–6; Mk. 2: 16 pl Lk. 19: 1–10; see E. Trocmé, *Jésus*, 103–4.

92. See J. Dupont, *La parabole du maître qui rentre dans la nuit* (Mk. 13: 34–36), in *Mélanges Bibliques* (en hommage à R.P.B. Rigaux) (Gembloux 1970), 89–116.

93. The object of Jesus' looking forward to a 'coming event' has to do in the synoptic gospels with: (a) the coming rule of God (Mt. 6: 10, pl Lk. 11: 3; Mt. 10: 7, pl Lk. 10: 9, 11; – Mk. 9: 1 pls Mt. 16: 28; Lk. 9: 27; Mk. 1: 15, pl Mt. 4: 17; – Lk. 17: 20; 21: 31; 22: 18); – (b) the son of man (Mt. 10: 32–33, pl Lk. 12: 8–9; Lk. 17: 24, 26, 30; Mt. 24: 44, pl Lk. 12: 40; – Mk. 8: 38, pl Mt. 16: 27, Lk. 9: 26; Mk. 13: 26 pls Mt. 24: 30, Lk. 21: 27; Mk. 14: 62, pl Mt. 26: 64; – Mt. 10: 23; 16: 28; 25: 31; – Lk. 18: 8); – (c) the coming one (Mt. 23: 39, pl Lk. 13: 35; see also Mt. 11: 3, pl Lk. 7: 19; Mk. 11: 9–10, pls Mt. 21: 9; Lk. 19: 30); – (d) then 'the Day' or 'the days of the son of man' (Lk. 17: 24, 26, 30; Mt. 10: 15, pl Lk. 10: 12; – Mk. 13: 30, pl Mt. 24: 36; – Mt. 25: 13; – Lk. 17: 22; 21: 34–35; 23: 29; – (e) the judgement (Mt. 11: 23, pl Lk. 10: 14). – In the preaching of Jesus the coming rule of God predominates over

all else; the judgement is as it were the negative obverse of it or the catastrophe for whoever does not accept the offer of eschatological salvation. A subsidiary element is the 'coming son of man' as the eschatological world-judge, providing in his person a thematization of 'the judgement'. Thus being alert, on the watch for the coming event, I would interpret (in the context of Jesus' own times) always in this sense: be on the lookout, because the rule or kingdom of God, which may be a judgement for anyone who turns down the *metanoia*, is about to come. Primitive Christianity already interprets many parables with the Parousia of Jesus-son of man explicitly in view.

94. See W. Pesch, *Der Lohngedanke in der Lehre Jesu verglichen mit der religiösen Lohnlehre des Spätjudentum*, (Munich 1955).

95. A Weiser, *Die Knechtsgleichnisse*, 116.

96. Weiser, l.c., 78.

97. Dan. O. Via, *The Parables*, 192.

98. H. Weinrich, 'Narratieve theologie', in Conc 9 (1973), n. 5 (48–57), 49.

99. Amos Wilder, *The Language of the Gospel* (New York-Evanston 1964), 94.

100. See, e.g., quite plainly in Mt. 22: 1–14, pl Lk. 14: 16–24; Mt. 25: 14–30; Lk. 19: 11–27; Mt. 13: 36–43; especially Mk. 12: 1–2, pl Mt. 21: 33–46; Lk. 20: 9–19.

101. *Literature*. J. Dupont, *Les Béatitudes* (Louvain 1969²) (1954), and: *Béatitudes égyptiennes*, in Bibl. 47 (1966), 185–222; S. Légasse, 'Les pauvres en Esprit et les "volontaires" de Qumran', in NTS 8 (1967–8), 336–45; W. Nauck, *Freude im Leiden*, in ZNW 46 (1955), 68–80; E. Schweizer, 'Formgeschichtliches zu den Seligpreisungen Jesu', in NTS 19 (1972–3), 121–6; A. Gelin, 'Heureux les pauvres', in *Grands thèmes bibliques* (Paris 1966), 79–83; P. Hoffmann, 'Selig sind die Armen', in BuL 10 (1969), 111–22.

102. Schulz, *Q-Quelle*, 76–84.

103. See O. H. Steck, 'Prophetische Kritik der Gesellschaft', in *Christentum und Gesellschaft* (Göttingen 1969), 46–62; F. L. Hoszfeld, 'Prophet und Politik in Israel', in BuK 1971, 39–43; J. Schreiner, 'Prophetische Kritik um Israels Institutionen', in *Die Kirche im Wandel der Gesellschaft* (Würzburg 1970), 15–29; H. Donner, *Israel unter den Völkern* (Leyden 1964); H. W. Wolff, *Die Stunde des Amos* (Munich 1969).

104. Thus – and rightly so – Niederwimmer, *Jesus*, 32.

105. The word-pair '*sèmeia kai terata*' comes from the Deuteronomic view of the prophets: Deut. 6: 22; 7: 19; 13: 2–3; 26: 8; Ex. 7: 3; Jer. 32: 20–21; Isa. 8: 18; 20: 3; Ps. 78: 43; Neh. 9: 10. See Rengstorf in ThWNT VII, 209. 219. In NT: Acts 4: 30; 5: 12; 14: 3; 15: 12; Rom. 15: 19; 2 Cor. 12: 12; 2 Thess. 2: 9; – Acts 2: 19, 22, 43; 6: 8; 7: 36. Elsewhere: '*sèmeia kai dunameis*' (Acts 8: 13; Rom. 15: 19). '*Sèmeion*' only: Acts 4: 16–22; 8: 6; Rev. 13: 13–14. In very broad terms: '*teras*' refers to the astonishing aspect of an incomprehensible event; '*sèmeion*' points in an event to God; '*dunameis*' (Gal. 3: 5; Acts 2: 22) are 'mighty works' or acts of power. All three appear together in Hebr. 2: 4.

106. R. Pesch, *Jesu Ureigene Taten?*, 19–20; E. Trocmé, *Jésus de Nazareth*, 117–

18, followed by his pupil K. Tagawa, *Miracles et évangile* (Paris 1966), 48 ('récits provinciaux et folkloriques').

107. A. P. Polag, 'Zu den Stufen der Christologie in Q' (Studia Evangelica, IV-1) (Berlin 1968), 72–4; Schulz, *Q-Quelle*, 203–13; 236–46; G. Delling, 'Botschaft und Wunder', l.c., 393; cf. Blank, *Schriftauslegung*, 121ff; R. Pesch, *Jesu Ureigene Taten?*, 36–44.

108. J. Blank, *Schriftauslegung*, 124–8; R. Pesch, *Jesu Ureigene Taten?*, 36–44; Schulz, *Q-Quelle*, 190–203.

109. *Das paulinische Evangelium*, I. *Vorgeschichte* (Tübingen 1968), 223–4.

110. J. Blank, *Schriftauslegung*, 125.

111. R. Pesch, *Jesus Ureigene Taten?*, 152, n. 138; Muszner, *Auferstehung*, 51; Polag, *Stufen der Christologie*, 72–4; Schulz, *Q-Quelle*, 203–13.

112. R. Pesch, *Jesu Ureigene Taten?*, 143.

113. Roloff, *Das Kerygma*, 111–207.

114. Roloff, *Das Kerygma*, 115–19.

115. K. Rengstorf, in ThWNT VII, 217–18.

116. Only in Acts 2: 22 are the terms '*sèmeia kai terata*' applied to Jesus' wonderful acts of goodness, in a context of mission, where his miracles do indeed function as legitimizing proof of his divine mission. See: K. Kertelge, *Die Wunder Jesu*, 29.

117. Kertelge, *Die Wunder Jesu*, 49.

118. Roloff, *Das Kerygma*, 154.

119. G. Strecker, *Der Weg der Gerechtigkeit. Untersuchung zur Theologie des Mathäus* (FRLANTO, 82) (Göttingen 1966), 118–19; Roloff, *Das Kerygma*, 113–34.

120. Roloff, l.c., 164.

121. Strack-Billerbeck, I, 438–9.

122. Roloff, *Das Kerygma*, 168.

123. l.c., 172.

124. This pericope is undoubtedly interpreted by the commentators in a variety of ways, according to whether they see the whole New Testament as determined by post-Easter situations within the Church or whether they accept a concern with history in the early Christian traditions (albeit within a kerygmatic situation). See H. J. Ebeling, 'Die Fastenfrage Mk. 2: 18–22', in ThStKr 108 (1937–38), 387ff; R. Bultmann, *Tradition*, 13–14; E. Lohmeyer, *Das Evangelium des Markus* (Göttingen 1967), ch. 1; A. Kee, 'The question about fasting', in NovT 11 (1969), 161–73; G. Braumann, 'An jenem Tag, Mc. 2: 20', in NovT 6 (1963), 264–7. Personally I find J. Roloff's line of argument in particular (in so far as this question admits of any such possibility) makes convincing sense, in *Das Kerygma*, 223–37. The case is quite otherwise, e.g., with G. Schille, *Das vorsynoptische Judenchristentum* (Berlin 1970), 43–6, and 'Was ist ein Logion?', in ZNT 61 (1970), 177–82.

125. See Weeden, *Mark-traditions* (thesis of the book). Cf. Roloff, *Das Kerygma*, 233, n. 107. See also Acts 1: 11; Phil. 1: 23; Jn. 16: 16–24.

126. The whole composition of Mk. (2: 18–22) presents (a) a stereotype line-up of the Pharisees' disciples (with those of John), (b) adds (from the tradi-

tion, or as a piece of Marcan redaction) two new images (2: 21–22) and (c) sets the whole of 2: 18–22 in the context of a larger group of 'startling postures' on the part of Jesus (2: 1 to 3: 5), concluding with: 'they . . . sought to get rid of Jesus' (3: 6).

127. Marcan tradition: Mk. 2: 15–17, pl Lk. 15: 2; Q tradition: Lk. 15: 4–10, pl Mt.; SL (source or tradition peculiar to Luke): Lk. 7: 36–47; 15: 11–32; 19: 1–10; SM (source or tradition peculiar to Matthew): Mt. 20: 1–15. See also Lk. 11: 19, pl. Then too the Johannine tradition: Jn: 4: 7–42.

128. Thus J. Jeremias, *Die Gleichnisse Jesu* (Göttingen 1965⁷), 126–7. The revision for liturgical purposes by the church is discussed from his own standpoint by U. Wilckens, 'Vergebung für die Sünderin', in *Orientierung an Jesus* (Freiburg 1973), 394–424, who also accepts a historical basis, 404. A survey of the exegetical positions up to 1966 is provided by J. Delobel, 'L'onction par la pécheresse', in ETL 42 (1966), 415–75.

129. Thus Wilckens, l.c., 399; also Roloff, *Das Kerygma*, 162, n. 204, who moreover thinks it unlikely that a law-abiding Pharisee would have ignored his obligations as a host.

130. Strack-Billerbeck, I, 495.

131. R. Schnackenburg, *Gottes Herrschaft und Reich*, 59.

132. Schulz, *Q-Quelle*, 91–2.

133. Tödt, *Menschensohn*, 265–7; Hahn, *Hoheitstitel*, 46; Kertelge, in *Orientierung an Jesus*, l.c., 211.

134. This pericope has been analysed with unusual thoroughness in two studies: B. van Iersel, 'La vocation de Lévi', l.c. (1967) and R. Pesch, 'Das Zöllnergastmahl' (1970), l.c. The primary difference (along with the consequences of it) between the two studies lies in the fact that van Iersel sees Mk. 2: 15 as a Marcan redaction (225–6), Pesch on the other hand as pre-Marcan tradition.

135. Tax-gatherers of the period worked in groups, collecting dues and rents; historically, therefore, their sharing dinner together is quite plausible.

136. A unique expression in Mark, which is again pointing to concrete historical circumstances. 'Scribes of the Pharisees' are to be sought mainly in Galilee, where they superintended the synagogues and the laws regarding purity, with respect, for instance, to 'sinners'.

137. R. Pesch, l.c., 73.

138. The ἦλθον-formula (in the first person: 'I have come in order to') – in contrast to the ἦλθεν-form ('he has come to') – does not *per se* indicate a retrospective look at the total life of Jesus after his death, but renders a Hebrew word meaning: 'to intend, to will, be instructed to': or 'I must', 'I have to . . .'; the Semitism is reinforced by the 'dialectical negation': '. . . come not for the righteous but for sinners' (R. Pesch, l.c., 79; B. van Iersel, l.c., 223–4). See also M. Black, in *The Expository Times*, 81 (1970), 115–18; see in opposite vein Käsemann, in *Besinnungen*, II, 82–104.

139. Mt. 10: 41; 13: 43, 49; Lk. 14: 14; Rom. 2: 13; Jam. 5: 16; 1 Jn. 3: 7.

140. This ancient tradition has been 'updated' in a later but still pre-Marcan one. For Christians tax-collectors were not sinners; furthermore, there had

arisen in the Church the problem of meal-sharing between Jewish Christians and uncircumcised Gentile Christians (R. Pesch, l.c., 82, and B. van Iersel, l.c., 218–19). For Christians then 'sinners' means primarily 'pagans' (Mt. 5: 47: cf. Mk. 14: 41, pl Lk. 6: 32ff; esp. Gal. 2: 15). Meal-sharing between Jewish and Gentile Christians had become a problem (Acts 11: 1–3). Because of that the formula acquired another meaning: 'tax-collectors (=sinners) and sinners (=pagans)'; in the spirit of Jesus who ate with sinners (tax-collectors) it was possible to appeal to *him* in the matter of meal-sharing with 'pagans' (sinners) (van Iersel, l.c., 219, n. 16; R. Pesch, l.c., 82–4). Again: in the process of editing the pre-Marcan collection of disputatious sayings (2: 1–3, 6) the one 'about the physician' was interpolated (Mk. 2: 17b): 'those who are well have no need of a physician, but those who are sick' (*kakôs echontes*). The image of the doctor is conjured up naturally by the fact that within this assembled whole Jesus emerges as saviour of the sick and of sinners (Mk. 2: 1–12).

141. Blessing and breaking the bread and offering it to the company is, according to Jewish custom, the privilege of the 'head of table', the host. See Strack-Billerbeck, IV, 614.

142. A survey of the diverse exegetical interpretations is provided by A. Heising, *Brotvermehrung*, l.c., 56–9, n. 71 (literature there 6–7).

143. H. Lietzmann, *Messe und Herrenmahl. Eine Studie zur Geschichte der Liturgie* (Bonn 1926); E. Lohmeyer, 'Vom urchristlichen Abendmahl', in ThR 9 (1937), 168–227, 273–311; 10 (1938), 81–99. See R. Feneberg, *Christliche Passafeier*, l.c., 45–59.

144. In particular, Roloff, *Das Kerygma*, l.c., 241.

145. Roloff, l.c., 243.

146. Strack-Billerbeck, IV, 614.

147. A separate analysis of Mt., Lk. and Jn. is unnecessary for the purpose of this chapter. Suffice it to say that Matthew introduces no substantial changes, but makes the 'miraculous feeding' refer from first to last to the disciples; the people disappear into the background. John especially gives added depth to the story: the people see in Jesus the 'divine miracle-man' who satisfies physical needs in a marvellous way; they want to make him king. They have not understood 'the sign': Jesus' concern was with the bread of eternal life – and that is faith in Jesus as the one sent by God. What matters is the Giver, not just the gift. But even here Jesus declines to see any reference to the 'manna-miracle'. Jesus is himself God's latter-day gift to the people. Thus from Jn. 6: 51c–58 on what clearly emerges is a eucharistic perspective.

148. Roloff, *Das Kerygma*, 259.

149. See F. Hahn, *Das Verständnis der Mission im Neuen Testament* (WMANT, 13) (Neukirchen-Vluyn 1963), 33–6; J. Roloff, *Apostolat, Verkündigung. Kirche* (Gütersloh 1965), 150ff; M. Hengel, *Nachfolge*, 82–5; F. W. Beare, 'Mission of the disciples and the mission charge: Mt. 10 and parallels', in JBL 89 (1970), 1–13; Schulz, *Q-Quelle* (404–19), 408; Hoffmann, *Q-Studien*, 229–70; Lührmann, *Q-Redaktion*, 59–60.

150. Hahn, *Mission*, 34; Lührmann, *Q-Redaktion*, 59; Hoffmann, *Q-Studien*, 264; Schulz, *Q-Quelle*, 408.

151. I have so far avoided this technical exegetical word. Bultmann borrowed it from the history of Greek literature (Bultmann, *Tradition*, 8–72, especially 8–9). 'Apophthegmata' are brief anecdotes in the synoptic tradition, having at their centre a logion of Jesus; thus the sole purpose of the story is to provide a framework for the logion (which was often transmitted on its own). Bultmann divides them into (a) disputations and (b) biographical anecdotes. B. van Iersel offers the following definition: 'Dans leur forme la plus pure, les apothegmes sont des péricopes réduites à une extension minime au cours de la transmission orale' ('La vocation de Lévi', 217).

152. The criterion in this case is that an authoritative voice is allowed not only to the exalted to but the earthly Jesus too (Schulz, *Q-Quelle*, 409). Whether the sending out of the disciples is a creation of the Church, projecting its own mission back on to Jesus' earthly life (as Schulz, *Q-Quelle*, 510 argues) is another matter; and this objection applies to his whole book, which puts too little store by the integration of traditions from other local churches into that of the Q community. What is a 'second phase' in the Q community, therefore, is by no means *a priori* a 'recent' tradition within early Christianity as a whole (see Part One, Criteria).

153. M. Hengel, *Nachfolge*, 3–16, especially 8.

154. Strack-Billerbeck, I, 487ff; IV, 560.

155. Hengel, l.c., 13.

156. Van Iersel, 'La vocation de Lévi', 216; Schille, *Kollegialmission*, 28–30.

157. l.c., 227.

158. Berger, *Gesetzesauslegung*, 425. The Graeco-Jewish conversion-model becomes particularly clear in the conversion of the heathen Asenath to Judaism, in the religious novel: *Joseph and Asenath*; also in 4 Ezra 13: 54–6. It contains all the elements: forsaking everything, being hated, leaving and losing family, home and possessions, etc.

159. It is noteworthy that Schulz has sufficient grounds for locating the logia about 'following' within the Graeco-Jewish phase of the Q community; S. Schulz, *Q-Quelle*, 430–3; 444–6, 446–9.

160. Thus the point here is not poverty as an 'ideal'; relinquishing everything is a once-for-all act, a consequence of the conversion, which entailed a break with one's former social relationships. True, a general disparagement of earthly possessions comes to be associated later on with this conversion-model (Test. Job 15: 8; 4: 6; *Joseph and Asenath*, p. 55, 14; Wis. 5: 8; Mk. 10: 25). For Luke poverty is an ideal. If the current humanistic Greek ideal of a perfect friendship through the sharing of goods may be an *ideal* in such circles, Christians actually *realize* it; this is Luke's view (see Berger, *Gesetzesauslegung*, 456). – See M. Philonenko, *Joseph et Asénath* (Leyden 1968), with edited text (old edition, P. Batiffol [Studia Patrist., 1] (Berlin 1889)). The non-Christian character of this work is now (contrary to earlier doubts) more and more accepted (G. Kilpatrick; Ch. Burchard; J. Jeremias; M. Philonenko, etc.).

161. Berger, l.c., 428, and in *Amen-Worte*, 41–6.

162. A. Schulz, *Nachfolgen*, 63, 131.

163. M. Hengel, *Nachfolge* (the thesis of this whole study).

164. See, e.g., Hosea 2: 5 (7); Ezek. 29: 16; 13: 3; Ps. 16: 4.

165. See M. Hengel, *Nachfolge*, 85–7; cf. L. Grollenberg, *Mensen vangen* (as 'rescuing from death'), 330–6.

166. R. Pesch, *Jesu Ureigene Taten?*, 154.

167. Schulz, *Q-Quelle*, 432; see H. Braun, *Radikalismus*, II, 104–5.

168. Hengel, *Nachfolge*, 64.

169. R. Schnackenburg, 'Das "Evangelium" im Verständnis des ältesten Evangelisten', in *Orientierung an Jesus* (Freiburg 1973), 309–23, 316–18.

170. After the healing of blind Bartimaeus Mk. 10: 52 says: 'He was at once able to see and he went along with him (*ekolouthhei*) on his way', that is, for Mark: going after Jesus on his way to the passion (his going up to Jerusalem).

171. *Ap'archès*, '*ab initio*', see Wis. 6: 22; 9: 8; 14: 12; 24: 14; Ecclus. 15: 14; 16: 26; 24: 9; 39: 25; Prov. 8: 23; Eccles. 3: 11.

172. Berger, *Gesetzesauslegung*, 15, and 474–7.

173. See 1 Macc. 1: 44–49; Dan. 7: 20; 7: 25. See 2 Macc. 7: 30.

174. Berger, *Gesetzesauslegung*, 477.

175. Lk. 11: 39, 42–44, 46–48, 52=Mt. 23: 25, 23, 6–7a, 27, 4, 29–31, 13; Mt. 5: 18=Lk. 16: 17; Mt. 5: 32=Lk. 16: 18; Mt. 5: 39–42=Lk. 6: 29–30; Mt. 5: 44–48=Lk. 6: 27–28, 32–36; Mt. 7: 12=Lk. 6: 31. See Schulz, *Q-Quelle*, 94–141.

176. 'Invisible tomb' and 'whitewashed tomb': both expressions become intelligible in the light of late Jewish rules for purification. Just before the Passover feast polluted graves were whitened with a limewash so that no one would 'unwittingly' continue to walk over them and thus become 'unclean' (Num. 19: 16).

177. See especially D. Lührmann, 'Liebet eure Feinde', in ZThK 69 (1972), 412–38, and Ch. Burchard, 'Das doppelte Liebesgebot in der frühen christlichen Ueberlieferung', in *Der Ruf Jesu und die Antwort der Gemeinde* (Festschrift: J. Jeremias) (Göttingen-Zürich 1970), 39–62, and W. Bauer, 'Das Gebot der Feindesliebe und die alten Christen', in *Aufsätze und kleine Schriften* (Tübingen 1967), 235–52; G. Bornkamm, 'Das Doppelgebot der Liebe', in *Neutestamentliche Studien* (for R. Bultmann) (Berlin 1957), 85–93. See also D. Nestlé, *Eleutheria*, I (Tübingen 1967).

178. Lührmann, 'Liebet eure Feinde', 432; S. Schulz, *Q-Quelle*, 135.

179. Strack-Billerbeck, I, 460.

180. E. Lohse, sub *sabbaton*, in ThWNT VII, 14–15.

181. H. Braun, *Jesus* (Stuttgart-Berlin 1969²), 72–85 and 86–95. See also Tödt, *Der Menschensohn*, 121–3.

182. l.c., 81.

183. Roloff, *Das Kerygma*, 58–62.

184. *Literature.* H. W. Bartsch, *Jesus. Prophet und Messias aus Galiläa* (Frankfort 1970), and 'Theologie und Geschichte in der Ueberlieferung vom Leben

Jesu', in EvTh 32 (1972), 128–42; M. Hengel, *Die Zeloten*, 346–7; S. G. F. Brandon, *Jesus and the Zealots*, 238–64 (passim); V. Eppstein, 'The historicity of the Gospel account of the Cleansing of the Temple', in ZNW 55 (1964), 42–58; Roloff, *Das Kerygma*, l.c., 89–110; C. Roth, 'The Cleansing of the Temple and Zechariah 14: 21', in NovT 4 (1960), 174–81; E. Trocmé, 'L'expulsion des marchands du temple', NTS 15 (1968–9), 1–22, and *Vie de Jésus de Nazareth vu par ses témoins* (Neuchâtel 1971), 127–36.

185. Roloff, l.c., 93.

186. Hahn, *Hoheitstitel*, 172; Roloff, l.c., 96.

187. J. Schniewind, *Das Evangelium nach Markus* (Göttingen 1949⁵), 150; Roloff, *Das Kerygma*, 97.

188. Ezek. 40–48; Hag. 2: 9; Zech. 14: 8; Ethiop. Enoch 90: 28–38; 91: 13; Jubilees 1: 17, 27, 29.

189. Excepting *Oracula Sibyllina* 5, 420ff, Strack-Billerbeck, I, 1005; see Roloff, l.c., 96, n. 154.

190. H. W. Bartsch, *Jesus*, l.c., 43–59.

191. E. Trocmé, l.c., 1–2, and *Vie de Jésus de Nazareth*, 129.

192. Berger, *Gesetzesauslegung*, 557–69.

193. See B. van Iersel, 'Heeft Jezus in Mc. 10: 2–12 de onontbindbaarheid van het huwelijk uitgesproken?', in *(On)ontbindbaarheid van het huwelijk* (Annalen van het Thijmgenootschap 58, 1970, n. 1) (Hilversum 1970) (11–22), especially 18.

194. Berger, *Gesetzesauslegung*, 165–6.

195. l.c., 63–208.

196. l.c., 81–91.

197. Berger, *Gesetzesauslegung*, 153.

198. Testamentum Issachar, 5: 2 and 7: 6; Test. Gad, 5: 3; Test. Benjamin 3: 3; 3: 4; 4: 4. Berger, l.c., 126–7.

199. Test. Zabulon 7: 2; 8: 1; 5: 1; 6: 4; Test. Benjamin 4: 2; Test. Issachar 7: 5; 7: 6.

200. A. Dihle, *Die Goldene Regel* (Göttingen 1962), 117–25.

201. Cf. Psalms of Solomon 6, 17–20; here too being near to God and entering the *basileia* are associated with keeping the Law.

202. Clearly enough, within the Q text of the eschatological 'woes' Lk. 11: 42 has: 'justice (a right attitude to one's fellow men) and the love of God', in other words, the Graeco-Jewish dual notion; but this is Lucan editorializing; the parallel passage in Mt. 23: 23b mentions as 'the weightier matters of the law': '*krisis, eleos, pistis*' that is, 'justice, mercy and faith (fullness)', actually Hebraic-Jewish terms for one's whole relationship to other people (love of one's neighbour), which again in Mt. 7: 12 is the quintessence of the Law. This, it would seem, reproduces the actual text of Q. Luke does not understand this Hebraic triad and substitutes for it the Graeco-Jewish twofold idea (love of God and a right way of relating to man).

203. Berger, *Gesetzesauslegung*, 192–202.

204. Certain words unusual for Matthew (e.g. '*nomikos*') point to a tradition common to Matthew and Luke – not, however, the Q tradition, but

one parallel to the pre-Marcan tradition, where the twofold commandment is already present. In contrast to Mark, there is no reference to Scripture. All this goes to show that Mk. 12: 32–34 is more or less secondary *vis-à-vis* an older tradition-phase on which Luke and Matthew evidently depend.

205. Berger, *Gesetzesauslegung*, 506–7.

206. *'Kremasthai'* (hang upon, be derivative from) means here something like 'depend for their existence', just as conclusions are derived from premises; they are the foundation-principles of moral and religious life; 'Law and prophets' are 'inferable' from them but do not render the other obligations superfluous.

207. See for instance G. Gusdorf, *La Connaissance de soi* (Paris 1948): 'My very being, my personal existence, remains, prior to and outside of the world, an incomprehensible void, a form without any matter. I am accessible to myself only through and in this world, which turns me from nothing into something' (513) (transl.); P. Ricoeur, 'Existence et herméneutique', in *Le conflit des interprétations* (Paris 1969), 7–30; F. J. Buytendijk, *Het kennen van de innerlijkheid* (Utrecht 1947).

208. Gusdorf has (in general terms) given sharp expression to the dialectic in our knowledge of other persons: 'The crucial element in man becomes apparent (. . .) in that he rebuts every identification, every equation. Find a formula and you have contained the reality of a thing, its consistency. We are given to wanting this or that definitive determination – and then, whenever it turns up, to rejecting it . . . A *thing* appears to us in total exteriority, the exterior is all. But the outside of a man takes its whole significance from his inside. In itself it is never enough. It points to a *personal surreality* of which it is *always an incomplete sign*. The only value of any formula given in this circumstance is as a reference. Yet a human being is nothing apart from the formulae in which he is enfleshed . . .' (l.c., 293). (Transl.)

209. J. Jeremias, *Abba*, 163; Kittel, in ThWNT I, 4–5; Marchel, *Abba, Père*, 115; Schulz, *Q-Quelle*, 87, etc.

210. Indeed (like all father- and mother-words) *ab* had its origin in babytalk, as following Köhler in ZAW 55 (1937), 169ff, H. Ringgren maintains in the recent Old Testament lexicon (l.c., col. 1). The Aramaic *abi* had fallen out of use and been replaced by *abba*, in the senses of 'the father', 'father', 'my father'. That *abba* signified 'dad', in a diminutive and affective sense ('daddy', 'Vati'), is affirmed in particular by J. Jeremias (*Abba*, 59–60 and 163) and subsequently adopted by many others: Conzelmann, *Grundriss*, 122; Kittel, in ThWNT I, 4–5; Schrenk, in ThWNT V, 985; Marchel, *Abba, Père*, 115; but later on retracted by J. Jeremias (*The Central Message of the New Testament* (London 1965), 21); further study of the Aramaic tongue and its history led him to see that (as in many languages) this 'childish' character of *abba*-daddy had vanished long before and that in Jesus' time *abba* was the ordinary, familiar form of address by adults to their father too.

211. See Strack-Billerbeck, IV–1, 208–49.

212. E. Schweizer, sub *Huios*, in ThWNT VIII, 357, and P. Pokorný, *Gottessohn*, 22–5.

213. Conzelmann, *Grundriss*, 122; Schulz, *Q-Quelle*, 88.

214. B. van Iersel, *Der Sohn*, 100–3; W. Marchel, *Abba, Père*, 130–8.

215. J. Jeremias, *Abba*, 59 and 163; van Iersel, *Der Sohn*, 103.

216. (a) in the thanksgiving for God's revelation to 'the little ones' (Mt. 11: 25–26; Lk. 10: 21; cf. Jn. 11: 41); (b) in Gethsemane (Mk. 14: 36; Mt. 26: 39; 26: 42; Lk. 22: 42); (c) on the cross (Lk. 23: 34; 23: 46); (d) in the Johannine high-priestly prayer (Jn. 17: 1, 5, 11, 21, 24, 25). See W. Marchel, *Abba*, 132–8.

217. See G. Schrenk, in ThWNT V, 987; van Iersel, *Der Sohn*, 108.

218. As, following J. Jeremias, *Abba*, 148–50, do Käsemann, in *Besinnungen*, I, 209 and M. Hengel, *Nachfolge und Charisma*, 77. Both V. Hasler, *Amen. Redaktionsgeschichtliche Untersuchung zur Einleitungsformel der Herrenworte 'Wahrlich, ich sage euch'* (Zürich 1969), and Berger, *Amen-Worte*, have shown that 'truly, truly I say to you' is in apocalyptical circles an expression typical of people (visionaries) who do *not* speak on their own authority but have to legitimate that authority. Now this is not something that characterizes Jesus. To the extent that the 'truly I say to you' utterances become more plentiful in the synoptics they are secondary: they appear to come from an apocalyptical, Graeco-Jewish Christian milieu and to remain more or less restricted to it.

219. J. Pedersen, *Israel. Its Life and Culture* (London 1926–40).

220. Van Iersel, *Der Sohn*, l.c., 96–103, 106–9; Strack-Billerbeck, II, 49–50.

221. Mt. 6: 8, 15; 10: 20, 29; 23: 9; 5: 16, 45, 48; 6: 1, 14, 18, 32; 7: 11; Lk. 6: 36; 11: 13; 12: 30, 32; Mk. 11: 25.

222. Schulz, *Q-Quelle*, 213–28.

223. Schulz, *Q-Quelle*, 217, n. 280, n. 284. See also S. Légasse, 'La révélation aux nèpioi', in RB 67 (1960), 321–48.

224. Already van Iersel, *Der Sohn*, 151; now also Schulz, *Q-Quelle*, 220–2, and especially Kl. Berger, 'Zum traditions-geschichtlichen Hintergrund christologischer Hoheitstitel', in NTS 17 (1970–1) (391–425), 422–4. See also Hoffmann, *Q-Studien*, 88–90. J. Jeremias, *Abba*, 47–54, sees in the passage simply the ordinary *abba* concept, with the Father instructing the Son. At all events this is certainly the essential meaning, although when incorporated in diverse complexes of tradition it presents differing perspectives.

225. Van Iersel, *Der Sohn*, 154–61; he regards Mt. 11: 27 therefore as authentically belonging to the historical Jesus.

PART TWO, *Section Two (pp. 272–319)*

1. Thus we examine first the post-Easter reflections on Jesus' rejection and death in the New Testament; only after that the pre-Easter way of envisaging this rejection and death. Theological consideration of the whole – our understanding here and now of this Jesus event – will come only in Parts Three and Four.

2. Schulz, *Q-Quelle*, 265–7; 343; 433; 486; see Hahn, *Hoheitstitel*, 382.

3. Mt. 5: 11–12 par. Lk. 6: 22–23; Mt. 23: 29–36 par. Lk. 11: 47–51; Lk. 13: 31–33 and 13: 34–35 par. Mt. 23: 37–39; Lk. 11: 49ff.

4. Steck, *Gewaltsames Geschick*, 60–80.

5. ibid., 62–3.

6. The same idea is still at work in Jer. 25: 4a, 5–6; 26: 5; 29: 19; 35: 15; 44: 4; themselves all occurring in a Deuteronomic complex of tradition. Also Zech. 1: 4–6; 7: 7, 12; 2 Chron. 36: 14–16.

7. Steck, ibid., 64–7.

8. Berger, *Gesetzesauslegung*, 15.

9. ibid., 18.

10. Acta Philippi, 15, p. 8. Also Justin, *Dial.* 18: 2.

11. Pseudo-Philo, *Liber Antiquitatum*, 22, 5.

12. Berger, *Gesetzesauslegung*, 19.

13. Berger, *Gesetzesauslegung*, 21.

14. ibid., 21.

15. In particular, Mk. 10: 5. See also H. Braun, *Spätjüdisch-häretischer und frühchristlicher Radikalismus*, II, 108–14; Berger, *Gesetzesauslegung*, 508–75.

16. Mk. 8: 11; 10: 2; 12: 15; Mt. 16: 1; 19: 3; 22: 18, 35; Jn. 6: 6; 8: 6; see Wis. 2: 24.

17. Especially: the Coptic Peter-apocalypse, c. 1; Acta Philippi, 141 (pp. 82, 24–6), in which other traditions have been incorporated.

18. It has been established above that the issue of total authority goes along with the cleansing of the Temple; see Roloff, *Das Kerygma*, 91–8.

19. Berger, *Gesetzesauslegung*, 24.

20. Cf. Apocalypse of Elijah, p. 163 (Berger, l.c., 24–5).

21. Source of the interpretation of the doctrine of redemption as victory over the evil spirits. See G. Aulén, *Christus Victor* (Les religions, 4), Paris 1949.

22. Berger, *Gesetzesauslegung*, 26.

23. A typical prefiguring of this interpretation of Jesus' death in connection with Israel's failure to keep God's true law can be found in a Christian interpolation into the earlier Testament of Levi, 16: 2-4; see Berger, *Gesetzesauslegung*, 26.

24. See Isa. 42: 6–7, 16; 49: 6, 8–9, 10; 51: 4–6; 62: 1 with 49: 6; Sirach 48: 10b; Paralip. Jer. 6: 9. 12; passages which are in part read together in *Joseph and Asenath*, p. 46: 18–19; in Pseudo-Philo, *Liber Antiquitatum* 51: 4–6; Test. Levi 14: 3–4; Test. Zabulon, 9: 8; – in the New Testament: Acts 1: 8b; Lk. 2: 32; Jn. 1: 9; 3: 19–21; 8: 12, and – applied to Jesus' apostles – in Acts 13: 47; Mt. 5: 14.

25. Ps. 22: 2; Mk. 15: 34; Mt. 27: 46; Ps. 22: 8; Mk. 15: 29; Mt. 27: 39; Ps. 22: 9; Mt. 27: 43; Ps. 22: 19; Mk. 15: 24; Mt. 27: 35; Lk. 23: 34; Jn. 19: 24; Ps. 41; Mk. 14: 18; Ps. 42; Mk. 14: 34; Ps. 69; Mk. 15: 23, 26. See also J. Delorme, in *Lectio Divina*. n. 72, 137; A. George, in LVie 101 (1971), 34–9; E. Schweizer, *Erniedrigung*, 59–62; L. Ruppert, *Jesus, als der leidende Gerechte?* (SBS, 59) (Stuttgart 1972), 48–52.

26. H. Dechent, 'Der "Gerechte" – eine Bezeichnung für den Messias', in ThStKr 100 (1927–8), 439–43; L. Ruppert, *Jesus, als der leidende Gerechte?*, l.c., and *Der leidende Gerechte. Eine motivgeschichtliche Untersuchung zum Alten Testament*

*und zwischentestamentlichen Judentum* (Forschung zur Bibel, 5) (Würzburg 1972), and *Der leidende Gerechte und seine Feinde* (Würzburg 1973); H. J. Kraus, *Klagerlieder* (Neukirchen 1960); E. Flesseman-van Leer, in H. Conzelmann, *et al.*, *Zur Bedeutung des Todes Jesu*, 79–96; G. Nickelsburg, *Resurrection, Immortality and eternal life in intertestamental Judaism* (Harvard, Cambridge 1972), 49–143.

27. Ps. 18: (21) 25 (verse 21 looks to be an accretion to the Deuteronomically orientated verses 22–24; verse 25 picks up verse 21).

28. Ps. 18=2 Sam. 22.

29. Cf. Ps. 143: 1, 11; 5: 9; 31: 2; 71: 2; 119: 40, where people pray for God's righteous aid.

30. Ps. 5; Ps. 7; Ps. 17; Ps. 31; Ps. 25; Ps. 71; Ps. 119; Ps. 143.

31. Ps. 7: 7–9a, 10b; 17: 13–14; 35: 24–26.

32. Ps. 7: 4–10; 35: 23–28.

33. Isa. 52: 13–53: 12; see L. Ruppert, *Jesus* (SBS, 59), 19.

34. See Isa. 50: 4–9 (third *Ebed* song). See also Habb. 1: 4, 13 and 2: 4.

35. Isa. 53: 11.

36. Ps. 34 and 37.

37. L. Ruppert, *Jesus*, l.c., 21. See especially Ps. 9: 29 LXX: '*meta plousion*'.

38. Prov. 19: 22; 28: 28.

39. Ruppert, *Jesus*, 23.

40. ibid.

41. ibid., 24.

42. 4 Macc. 18: 15 cites Ps. 34: 20a.

43. Ruppert, *Jesus*, 24–5. We explained earlier on how in the book of Enoch 'the righteous one' was identified in a later phase with the son of man (see Part Three).

44. Eth. Enoch 103: 5c, 6, 9b, c,–15; 104: 3.

45. Ezra-apocalypse, 7: 79, 89, 96; 8: 27, 56, 58, and (Syrian) Baruchapocalypse 15: 7–8; 52: 6–7; see Ruppert, *Jesus*, 25–6 and Nickelsburg, *Resurrection*, 109–43.

46. Ruppert, *Jesus*, 25–6; Nickelsburg, *Resurrection*, 84–5 and 138–40.

47. Thus an exact formulation of Ruppert, *Jesus*, 31 and 41.

48. See also Ps. 30; 31; 40: 2–12; Isa. 38: 10–20; Jonah 2: 3–10; Sirach (Ecclesiasticus) 51: 1–12. Then in a very late psalm: Ps. 34: 20.

49. Thus Ruppert, *Jesus*, 43–4, in argument with E. Schweizer, *Erniedrigung*, 21–33. See also Balz, *Methodische Probleme*, 44–5.

50. Luke on the other hand depicts the story of the Passion in what are clearly martyrological colours, and also as the suffering of the *prophet* (Lk. 11: 49–51; 13: 33; 24: 19). Jesus dies not with a loud cry but in an almost triumphant prayer of surrender to God's will (Lk. 23: 46), the centurion praises God (23: 47) and the multitude beat their breasts (23: 48).

51. Lk. 22: 15; 24: 26, 46; Acts 1: 3; 3: 18; 17: 3; Hebr. 2: 18; 9: 26; 13: 12; 1 Pet. 2: 21–23; 4: 1.

52. U. Wilckens, *Missionsreden*, 170; L. Ruppert, *Jesus*, 47–8.

53. See sub note 25. J. Gnilka, 'Die Verhandlungen vor dem Synhedrion und vor Pilatus nach Mk. 14: 53–15: 5', in *Evangelisch-katholischer Kommentar*

*zum NT.*, H. 2 (Neukirchen-Zürich 1970), (5–21) 11–12, sees even the scenes of Jesus' trial itself as full of allusions to the psalms of the 'suffering righteous one': Ps. 37: 14, 16; Ps. 38: 9–10 (Jesus keeps silent); Ps. 108: 2–3 (accusations made by enemies); investigation of what motivates the trial and execution: Ps. 36: 22; 53: 5; see also 37: 13; 62: 10; 69: 2–3; 85: 14; false witnesses: Ps. 26: 12; 34: 11 (each time from the Septuagint).

54. Mk. 14: 27 par. Zech. 13: 7; Mt. 27: 10; Zech. 11: 12–13; Lk. 22: 37: Isa. 53: 12.

55. Ps. 22: 23ff; Ps. 31: 20–25; Ps. 69: 31–35; Ps. 41.

56. E. Flesseman-van Leer, in H. Conzelmann *et al.*, *Zur Bedeutung des Todes Jesu*, 93.

57. L. Ruppert, *Jesus*, 51.

58. Isa. 50: 6; Mk. 14: 65 and 15: 19.

59. The *'pais Theou'* (Wis. 2: 18; Isa. 52: 13 LXX) is interpreted as *'huios Theou'* in Wis. 2: 13. Mk. 14: 61–62 speaks of the 'Son of the Most High'. In fact Jesus is here represented as the suffering servant of God in Deutero-Isaiah. See the discussion: J. Jeremias, *pais theou*, in ThWNT V, 709–13; Cullmann, *Christologie*, 59–68; H. W. Wolff, *Jesaja 53 im Urchristentum* (Berlin 1950²), 55–71; B. van Iersel, *Der Sohn*, 60ff; U. Wilckens, *Die Missionsreden der Apostelgeschichte*, l.c., 163–8. Even before Luke, the son of Ps. 2: 7 has been merged with the *'pais'* of Isa. 42: 1. (Cf. Mk. 1: 11 parr., and Mk. 9: 7 parr.). In Acts 4 Luke employs both titles interchangeably. *'Per Jesum Puerum tuum'* is particularly evident in liturgy (Acts 4: 30; Didache 9: 2–3; 10: 2–3; 1 Clem. 59: 2–4). Within the New Testament, excepting Mt. 12: 18, the *'puer'*-Christology is characteristic of Luke. That Jesus was himself conscious of being the Deutero-Isaianic suffering *Ebed* is dismissed by critical exegetes; W. Popkes, *Christus traditus* (Zürich 1967), 172–3; F. Hahn, *Hoheitstitel*, 64–6. Mk. 14: 62: 'you will *see* (*opsesthe*) the son of man sitting...'; also in Wis. 5: 2a *seeing* the exalted righteous one, after his death, will in itself be a condemnation of his murderers. The fact of seeing the exalted one is a silent testimony against them, intimating to them indirectly that they have already been condemned (Wis. 5: 3–7). See Nickelsburg, *Resurrection*, 49–92 (see Part Three).

60. Ruppert, *Jesus*, 53ff. I leave aside here Ruppert's disputed hypothesis as to whether this Wisdom-diptych originally existed in Hebrew. At all events, if the influence of Isa. 53 *via* the re-interpretation of Wis. 2: 12–20 and 5: 1–7 on the Marcan material has been proven (and it very likely has), the latter would seem to have been shaped partly by Greek-speaking Jewish Christians; for in these allusions (as with allusions to the Psalms) the Book of Wisdom is already assumed to be 'Scripture'.

61. It is a striking fact that *'ho dikaios'* (the righteous one, with the nuance: 'vindicated by God') occurs seven times, six of them in connection with suffering: Lk. 23: 47; Acts 3: 14; 7: 52; Mt. 27: 19; 1 Pet. 3: 18; 1 Jn. 2: 1.

62. This tallies with G. Schille's hypothesis, which finds more and more support in respect of his contention that the primitive local churches held (annual) services to commemorate Jesus' suffering and death, and prayer-

fully meditated upon this event in the light of Scripture (see above), in ZThK 52 (1955), 161–205. The precise chronological sequence of the Passion story (Mark) would therefore presumably have been settled on liturgical, not historiographical, grounds.

63. Roloff, 'Soteriologische Deutung des Todes Jesu', l.c., 42–3; also Ruppert, *Jesus*, 59–60; E. Schweizer, *Erniedrigung*, 72–3.

64. J. Roloff, 'Soteriologische Deutung', 43.

65. Mk. 14: 61a; Mt. 8: 17; Acts 8: 32–33. There is one exception: the '*hyper hèmōn*' of 1 Pet. 2: 21–24; but the context here is a hymn, composed with Deutero-Isaianic motifs, not a Scriptural proof.

66. l.c., 44.

67. Thus Hahn, *Hoheitstitel*, 197–211, and Roloff, l.c., 45.

68. Thus Roloff, l.c., 45–6.

69. G. Fohrer, 'Das Alte Testament und das Thema "Christologie"', in EvTh 30 (1970) (281–98), 286–91, has shown that in these *Ebed* songs there is no question of suffering vicariously on behalf of others but of paying the penalty of one's own *unknown* sins.

70. Thus H. Kessler, *Die theologische Bedeutung des Todes Jesu* (Düsseldorf 1971²), 232–5.

71. See below in Part Three: 'The third day rose.'

72. Ruppert, *Jesus*, 40–1. A martyr as such did not need to be 'a righteous one' (see 2 Macc. 7: 32), and just by dying as a martyr he could make reparation for his own sins and those of others; see E. Lohse, *Martyrer und Gottesknecht* (Göttingen 1963²), 29–32; Ruppert, *Jesus*, 74, n. 6.

73. Roloff, l.c., 50.

74. H. Schürmann, in *Orientierung an Jesus*, 357.

75. See e.g., C. H. Dodd, *The Founder of Christianity* (London 1971), 119–36; Fr. Muszner, 'Gab es eine "Galiläische Krise"?', in *Orientierung an Jesus*, l.c., 238–52. Cf. S. Schulz, *Q-Quelle*, 364, n. 275, apropos of what is in essence the Q text of Mt. 11: 21–24=Lk. 10: 13–15.

76. *Kai* (=and) here signifies a contrast: i.e., 'but'.

77. Lk. 11: 14–23; Mt. 12: 22–23; cf. the Marcan tradition: Mk. 3: 2; Jn. 7: 11; 8: 48 and 10: 20. See A. Polag, *Zu den Stufen der Christologie in Q* (Studia Evangelica, IV-1) (Berlin 1968), 72–4. (I have not been able to obtain his detailed typescript about this.)

78. Mk. 1: 33–34, 38; 2: 1b, 12b; 2: 13; 3: 7–11, 20; 4: 1; 5: 21, 24; 6: 6b, 12b; 6: 33–34, 44, 55–56.

79. Again in Mk. 7: 37; 8: 1, 4; 9: 14, 15; 10: 1b; 10: 46 and 11: 8–10–18b.

80. See especially H. Schürmann, *Traditionsgeschichtliche Untersuchungen zu den synoptischen Evangelien* (Düsseldorf 1968), 137–49; J. Roloff, *Apostolat, Verkündigung, Kirche* (Gütersloh 1965), 151; M. Hengel, *Die Ursprünge der christlichen Mission*, in NTS 18 (1971–2), 15–38.

81. Muszner, in *Orientierung an Jesus*, 243 and 249–50.

82. Dodd, *The Founder*, 130ff; Muszner, in *Orientierung an Jesus*, 247ff.

83. Dodd, *The Founder*, 134, inspired at this point, of course, in particular by the Johannine gospel.

84. H. Conzelmann, *Die Mitte der Zeit* (Tübingen 1960³), 67; G. Friedrich, 'Lk. 9: 51 und die Entrückungschristologie', in *Orientierung an Jesus*, esp. 70–4.
85. l.c., 249–50.
86. Some historians maintain that this *'ius gladii'* of the Jewish authorities was not recognized by the Roman occupying power: thus J. Blinzler, *Der Prozeß Jesu. Das jüdische und das römische Gerichtsverfahren gegen Jesus Christus* (Regensburg 1960³), 163–74; see below under note 107.
87. H. Schürmann, in *Orientierung an Jesus*, 335–6.
88. O. Cullmann, *Jesus und die Revolutionären seiner (Zeit* Tübingen 1970).
89. Schürmann, l.c., 337.
90. J. Roloff, 'Soteriologische Deutung des Todes Jesu', 51.
91. Roloff, l.c., 50–5. Cf. W. Popkes, *Christus traditus*, 169–74; Hahn, *Hoheitstitel*, 57–9.
92. Rom. 11: 13; 12: 7; 15: 31; 2 Cor. 3: 7ff; 4: 1; 5: 18; also Acts 1: 17–25; 6: 1–4; 11: 29; 12: 25; 19: 22; 20: 24; 21: 19.
93. The $\tilde{\eta}\lambda\theta o\nu$ – formula ('I am come in order that . . .') does not point *per se* to a retrospective evaluation of Jesus' entire ministry, as opposed to the $\tilde{\eta}\lambda\theta\epsilon\nu$ – formula (see note 138 in the previous Section).
94. Roloff, l.c., 58–9.
95. Mk. 6: 34–44 par. Mt. 14: 21; Lk. 9: 11b–17; Mk. 8: 1–9 par. Mt. 15: 32–38; Jn. 6: 1–15.
96. Roloff, *Das Kerygma*, 237–69; see also 'Heil als Gemeinschaft', in *Gottesdienst und Oeffentlichkeit* (eds P. Cornehl-H. Bahr) (Hamburg 1970), 88–117; and 'Soteriologische Deutung des Todes Jesu', 62.
97. See Schürmann, *Der Einsetzungsbericht Lk. 22: 19–20* (Münster 1970²); 'Wie hat Jesus seinen Tod bestanden und verstanden?', in *Orientierung an Jesus*, l.c., 354–8; *Jesu Abendmahlshandlung als Zeichen für die Welt* (Leipzig 1970), and 'Das Weiterleben der Sache Jesu in nachösterlichen Herrenmahl', in BZ16 (1972), 1–23; H. Kessler, *Die theologische Bedeutung des Todes Jesu*, 277.
98. Schürmann, in *Orientierung an Jesus*, 344.
99. Schürmann, *Jesu Abendmahlshandlung*, 89.
100. In EvTh 27 (1967), 340–1.
101. See Berger, *Amen-Worte*, 54–8. Matthew in his gospel retains Mark's 'amen, amen'; 'amen' here is secondary, therefore, after Matthew and Luke had already known the Marcan text without 'amen, amen'. Mark adds 'amen' wherever an explicit reference to the coming glory or the coming aeon has been inserted.
102. Thus e.g., W. Marxsen, *Erwägungen*, 165; likewise, it seems to me, the exegetically unjustifiable, minimalizing tendency of H. Kessler, *Die theologische Bedeutung des Todes Jesu*, 232–5.
103. The meaning of Deut. 17: 12 has been trenchantly examined (from a historical standpoint) by J. Bowker, *Jesus and the Pharisees*, Cambridge 1973, 46–52; see id., *The Targums and Rabbinic Literature* (Cambridge 1969).
104. J. Bowker, *Jesus*, 42.
105. In the study first referred to under note 103 Bowker, using texts from outside the New Testament, has analysed the ambiguous meaning of the

name 'Pharisee' and shown convincingly that it is Mark's gospel which (unconsciously, perhaps, but accurately enough) reflects the transitional and still unsettled meaning of 'Pharisee' in Jesus' time; *Jesus and the Pharisees*, l.c., 1–46.

106. 'Where Jesus evidently saw in Torah an exemplification of God's intention to be in a real and covenanted relationship with men, the *Chakamim* saw in the exemplification of Torah in the details of men's lives the only possible way to the reality of that relationship' (J. Bowker, l.c., 52). '*Chakamim*' (sages, wise ones) is what the later rabbis called their predecessors in the 'interpretation of the Law'; only an offshoot, namely, the '*perushim*', are to become the later 'true Pharisees', criticized just as keenly by the rabbis as by the Christian gospels.

107. See the discussion of this in E. Bammel (ed.), *The Trial of Jesus* (London 1970), the study by D. Catchpole, 'The problem of the historicity of the Sanhedrin trial', 47–65.

PART TWO, *Section Three* (*pp.* 320–97)

1. See specified literature: especially the discussion between E. Linnemann and G. Klein.
2. Thus e.g., R. Bultmann, *Tradition*, 301; especially G. Klein, 'Verleugnung' (argument of the whole article). This again raises the problem of whether the disciples did or did not flee *to Galilee*. They *did* flee to Galilee, thus: Bultmann, Käsemann, Grasz, Finegan, Vögtle, Seidensticker, etc.; they did *not* flee to Galilee, thus: Marxsen, Weisz, Holtzmann, Michaelis, Lohmeyer, Bertram, Taylor, Thüsing, Schenke, Weeden, etc. The former hypothesis seems to me the more likely, because of very ancient traditions indicating Galilee and only thence finding their way also into the Jerusalem traditions.
3. e.g., Mt. 13: 13; 13: 16–17; 13: 51; 10: 40–41; 12: 49–50; Lk. 5: 1–11; 6: 20.
4. According to Weeden, *Mark-traditions*, 138–68, the gospel of Mark is a frontal attack on 'the Twelve'; the same thing is said in a quite different connection by L. Schenke, *Auferstehungsverkündigung*, 21–2 and 51; see also J. Schreiber, 'Die Christologie des Markus-evangeliums', in ZThK 58 (1961) (154–83), 178–9; Mark shows some inclination to pass judgement on the Twelve for staying in Jerusalem instead – as the Marcan gospel would have it – of going at Jesus' behest to Galilee, the place of Jesus' message, exorcisms and healings. Mark's criticism is apparently applied to the 'church of Jerusalem', which seems to have been opposed to the 'Hellenistic' – in the sense of 'Galilean' – mission. Mk. 16: 8 is unmistakably critical of 'the Twelve'. This criticism in Mark is undeniable; the question is only how it should be interpreted. And Weeden's thesis of Mark's 'vendetta' against the Twelve goes too far, in my view. His thesis is extremely interesting but seems to me to founder on some unresolved difficulties in the text. How is Weeden to explain the fact that, as Mark himself mentions, Peter after having denied Jesus 'broke down and wept' (Mk. 14: 72d)? Then too how can he explain

that – despite the women's having said nothing (Mk. 16: 8) – according to Mark's own account the disciples *already knew* (had heard from Jesus) that he, Jesus, would 'go before [them] to Galilee' (Mk. 14: 28)? Weeden alas! does not engage in a structural analysis of the Marcan gospel.

5. Mk. 1: 37; 4: 10, 13, 38–41; 5: 31; 6: 37, 51–52; 7: 17; 8: 4, 14–21.

6. Mk. 1: 37–38; 4: 13 and 6: 37 Matthew omits; Mk. 4: 38–41: in Mt. 8: 25 the disciples do show understanding; Mk. 6: 51–52 as against Mt. 14: 33. All insinuations about the disciples' lack of comprehension (in Mk. 6: 51–52; 7: 17–18; 8: 4, 14, 21) are eliminated in Luke, who also omits Mk. 6: 45–48, 26 in its entirety.

7. See also: Mk. 9: 31–33, 35; 10: 35–45; 10: 42 and 10: 43–44; 10: 23–31 and 10: 23–28; 8: 34–35 and 10: 21–22.

8. e.g., Mk. 8: 32–33 and Mt. 16: 22ff and Mt. 16: 17; Matthew also retains Mk. 10: 23–31, but qualifies: Mt. 19: 28. Mt. 17: 15ff conserves Mk. 9: 17ff; Mt. 26: 8 and Mk. 14: 4; – Luke frequently qualifies (Mk. 10: 14 with Lk. 18: 16; Mk. 10: 23–31 with Lk. 18: 24–30), but none the less keeps a good deal from Mark here, yet placing the course of events within God's providential plan. Luke apparently has access to new tradition-material in a similar pejorative vein regarding John and James's lack of understanding (Lk. 9: 51–55; see 10: 23–24 and 19: 39–40).

9. There is indeed a failure to understand Jesus' teaching: Jn. 11: 7–16; 12: 16; 13: 6–8; 14: 4–9; 16: 16–18; but they had no need to grasp everything before Jesus' death (Jn. 16: 12–13, 25). The resurrection will remove all misapprehension (Jn. 2: 22; 12: 16; 13: 7), through the power of the 'Paraclete' (14: 16–17; 16: 7 in association with 14: 25–26): then the disciples will be, along with Jesus, one with the Father (17: 6–26).

10. See Weeden, *Mark-traditions*, 42.

11. Mt. 16: 17–19 and Lk. 22: 31–32.

12. Mt. 5: 1–12=Lk. 6: 20–23; Mt. 13: 16–17=Lk. 10: 23–24; Mt. 19: 28= Lk. 22: 30. See Schulz, *Q-Quelle*, 335.

13. But even Mark, when overstating things, obviously means to keep within bounds: 4: 11 (unless this is meant ironically).

14. This, it seems to me, is the 'strong point' in Weeden's none the less dubious final solution, see *Mark-traditions*, 44. Of Jesus' disciples there is no further mention: either at the crucifixion (Mk. 15: 22–41), or at the burial of Jesus (15: 42–47), or at the 'holy tomb' (16: 1–8), unless it be – in this last case – to drive home the point that they have not done what Jesus wanted done. I do not find Weeden's 'point' here satisfactorily resolved anywhere in the exegetical literature. Yet it seems to me important.

15. Thus Mt. 28: 16–20; Lk. 24: 36–49; Jn. 20: 19–23; Acts 1: 8. Mark says nothing about all this, so that the consensus – on the increase during the last few years – that Mk. 16: 8 is indeed the 'intended' ending to Mark's gospel has in my opinion theological presuppositions in Mark's view of 'the Twelve' – even though Weeden's solution to this problem seems to me too radical, having regard to the posture of Mark's own text in the gospel. One thing is clear: Mark wants nothing to do with a tradition of 'Jesus' appear-

ances' to the Twelve.

16. Etta Linnemann's line of argument seems to me to the point (*Passions-geschichte*, l.c., 92–3).

17. G. Schneider, *Die Passion Jesu*, 46–7, accepting the historical core of the single denial by Peter (74).

18. The position held by Bultmann, Grundmann, Rengstorf and other commentators.

19. Thus Schürmann, Blinzler, Dupont, Linnemann and especially Schneider, who has made an exact analysis of this detail and considers a Marcan derivation for the denial-pericope (with a peculiarly Lucan redaction) to be very likely indeed.

20. E. Linnemann, *Passionsgeschichte*, 93–5.

21. G. Schneider, *Die Passion Jesu*, 75.

22. G. Schneider, *Verleugnung*, l.c., 73–95.

23. Brown, *Apostasy*, 70–1; Schneider, *Passion Jesu*, 81–2.

24. Cf. 1 Cor. 7: 10; 9: 14; 1 Thess. 4: 15–16; Acts 20: 35, etc. Especially M. Wilcox, *Denial-sequence*, 426–36.

25. Linnemann, *Passionsgeschichte*, 103.

26. *Die Formgeschichte des Evangeliums* (Tübingen 1961[4]), 216.

27. *Passionsgeschichte*, 82.

28. Although, unfortunately, H. Conzelmann provides no evidence or reference whatever in his book (admittedly meant as a general introduction), *Geschichte des Urchristentums* (Göttingen 1971), still he baldly asserts in it: 'That Jesus appeared (first) to Simon Peter Cephas is confirmed by Lk. 24: 34. On this appearance depends Peter's prominent position in the first years of the Church. It stands out from the background that before the death of Jesus he denied his master' (27). In other words he too makes a connection between appearance and denial. See also J. Jeremias, *Der Opfertod Jesu Christi* (Calwer-Hefte, 62) (Stuttgart 1963).

29. The gospels present the following traditions: (a) *Mt.*: an appearance of Jesus to women as they return from the tomb (28: 9–10) and an appearance to the Eleven 'on the mountain' in Galilee (28: 16–20); (b) *Lk.*: an appearance to the Emmaus-disciples (24: 13–35) and an appearance to the Eleven with others present (24: 36–53); (c) *Jn.*: an appearance to Mary Magdalene (20: 14–18), an appearance to the disciples in the presence of Thomas (20: 19–23), an appearance to Thomas with the disciples in the background (20: 24–29), finally in the additional closing chapter: Galilean appearance to seven disciples during a fishing trip (Jn. 21); (d) the later Marcan ending: brings together three appearances from other gospels: to Mary Magdalene (Jn.), to those on the way to Emmaus (Lk.) and to the Eleven (Mt.; Lk.) (Mk. 16: 9–20). Thus the appearance to the Eleven (or 'the Twelve', 1 Cor. 15: 3–5) is a constant factor in all the traditions.

30. B. van Iersel, l.c., in Conc 6 (1971), n. 10, 53–65, bases his argument primarily on the typical expression '*hic est locus ubi*', later (from the fourth century) a technical expression in Christian pilgrim literature. Yet it remains hypothetical whether the expression already had this meaning for Mark (it

does not occur, according to van Iersel himself, in classical Greek literature or in rabbinical writings). See also J. Delorme, in *Lectio Divina*, n. 50, 123–5.

31. Furthermore: we nowhere find in the New Testament the expression 'the empty tomb'. See B. van Iersel, in Conc, l.c., 57–60; G. Schille, 'Das Leiden des Herrn', in ZThK 52 (1955), 161–205; J. Delorme, in *Lectio Divina*, n. 50, especially 123–8; L. Schenke, *Auferstehungsverkündigung*, 93–103; and 63–83.

32. This formula (later on, at any rate) is a technical term with 'guides' at the places where martyrs were venerated (van Iersel, l.c., footnote 2; Delorme, in *Lectio Divina*, n. 50, 123–9). Again, the detailed specifications as to time ('on the first day of the week – very early – when the sun had risen', Mk. 16: 2) in a text not intended as a historiographical record likewise point to a cultic and liturgical context; see in particular G. Schille, 'Das Leiden des Herrn', l.c. (taken over by J. Delorme and L. Schenke). According to Schille the origin of the Passion-narrative lies in an (annual) celebration at Jerusalem, with three major elements: (a) an *anamnesis* of the farewell evening; (b) a liturgy of Jesus' Passion and death at the hours of the Jewish prayer (see Mk. 15: 2–41); (c) a liturgy early on Easter morning with a visit (later a solemn procession) to the sacred tomb (see Mk. 15: 42 and 16: 1–8) (Schille, l.c., 182–3). Out of this the Easter festival eventually grew (J. Delorme, l.c., 129). Even so, some important commentators trace the tradition of 'the tomb' back to a very early tradition of an actual confirmation that the tomb was empty (thus i.a.: L. Cerfaux, J. Jeremias, E. Lohse, J. Héring, J. Weisz, J. Dupont, K. Rengstorf, J. Blank). But these exegetes are defending the *antiquity* of the tomb tradition against a number of interpretations according to which that tradition is said to be very late. The antiquity of this tradition is now more generally accepted than heretofore. The new problem is whether we have a tradition of an 'empty tomb' or a tradition of the 'holy tomb' (in other words, a cultic tradition).

33. See: Acts 1: 14; Mk. 15: 40–41; Jn. 21: 24; Lk. 1: 1–4; Lk. 2: 19; 2: 51; 8: 1–3; 10: 38–42; 24: 10. Th. Boman, *Die Jesusüberlieferung*, 123–37, even feels compelled to recognize an explicit 'women tradition' in many passages of the Lucan gospel (and actually identifies this with the peculiarly Lucan source). It is indeed noticeable that in the pro-feminist Luke (is this simply Hellenistic?) the feminine viewpoint (especially in the infancy narrative as contrasted with Matthew's) is very marked.

34. U. Wilckens, in W. Marxsen *et al.*, *Die Bedeutung der Auferstehungs-botschaft*, 48 and 61; Delorme, in *Lectio Divina*, n. 50, 123–45.

35. L. Schenke, *Auferstehungsverkündigung*, 20–9; Weeden, *Mark-traditions*, 101–17 (himself referring otherwise to L. Schenke).

36. It looks as though according to Mark the disciples did *not* go to Galilee and that Mark is criticizing this very fact (Schenke, *Auferstehungsverkündigung*, 49–52, footnote 71). According to Delorme, on the other hand (in *Lectio Divina*, n. 50, 131), Mk. 16: 7 has been added to link the local Jerusalem tradition with the appearances to the Twelve (in Matthew and Luke this is clear, in any case). But in Part Three (second sub-strand of the *maranatha-*

Christology) it will emerge that it is anything but certain that Mark is referring to appearances and not to the Parousia. Mark does of course see the flight of the women (16: 8) as parallel with that of the disciples (14: 50; see 14: 41): that is, the failure of them all to comprehend the Jesus mystery (see 8: 22; 9: 10, 32). The resurrection is not something thought up by men, but the amazing activity of God.

37. Mk. 1: 24 par. Lk.; Mk. 14: 67 par. Mt.; Acts 6: 14, see also Acts 22: 8; 26: 9; 24: 5 and Mt. 2: 23.

38. According to Jn. 19: 19 also written on the cross was the inscription 'Jesus the Nazarene'; for Jews in particular Jesus is 'the Nazarene' (Acts 2: 23–24, 26).

39. Also in the so-called Petrine speeches or sermons: Acts 2: 23–24; 3: 15; 4: 10; 5: 30; 10: 40.

40. J. Delorme, *Lectio Divina*, n. 50, 120–1; Schenke, l.c., 75.

41. J. Jeremias, *Heiligengräber in Jesu Umwelt* (Göttingen 1958); on popular pilgrimages: 138–43.

42. That in Mk. 16: 8 the women *say nothing* about what has taken place is variously explained by the commentators in accordance with their overall interpretation of Mark, and depending especially on their interpretation of Mk. 16: 7b as relating either to the Parousia or the Galilean appearances.

43. L. Marin, 'Les femmes au tombeau', in C. Cabrol and L. Marin, *Sémiotique narrative: récits bibliques*, in *Langages* 6 (1971) (39–50), 44, and 'Du corps au texte', in *Esprit* (April 1973), 913–28; J. Delorme, in *Lectio Divina*, n. 50, 105–51.

44. H. van Campenhausen, *Der Ablauf der Osterereignisse und das leere Grab*, 50–1; J. Kremer, *Die Osterbotschaft der vier Evangelien* (Stuttgart 1968[2]), 28–31; F. Muszner, *Die Auferstehung Jesu* (Munich 1969), 128–33; H. Grasz, *Ostergeschehen und Osterberichte*, 23–32.

45. An eschatological, bodily resurrection, theologically speaking, has nothing to do, however, with a corpse.

46. F. Neyrinck, 'Les femmes au tombeau, Étude de la rédaction matthéenne', in NTS 15 (1968–9), 168–90.

47. A. George, in *Lectio Divina*, n. 50, 75–104.

48. Especially G. Friedrich, 'Lukas 9: 51 und die Entrückungs-Christologie des Lukas', in *Orientierung an Jesus*, l.c., 48–77, and 'Die Auferweckung Jesu, eine Tat Gottes oder ein Interpretament der Jünger', in KuD 17 (1971), 170–9; G. Lohfink, *Die Himmelfahrt Jesu* (Munich 1971); G. Strecker, 'Entrückung', in RAC, V, 461–76.

49. This is Lucan editorializing: G. Schneider, *Die Passion Jesu nach den drei älteren Evangelien* (Munich 1973), 151–3.

50. A 'translation' or 'rapture', sudden removal (to be distinguished from, in particular, the ancient, classical Greek 'journey of a soul' in celestial spheres) (Lohfink, *Himmelfahrt*, 34ff) was known from of old in Egypt, Babylonia, in the Greek and Roman world, among the Jews of earlier times and the Judaic period. The two classic instances in the Old Testament itself are those of Enoch and Elijah. See Gen. 5: 24; 2 Kings 2: 9–11; 1 Macc. 2: 58;

Ps. 49: 16. Also Deut. 34: 5–6, where it says that nobody knows 'the grave of Moses'. See Hebr. 11: 5; Rev. 11: 12; even 1 Thess. 1: 9–10. The technical terms for a 'rapture' are: *aphanismos, harpagè, metastasis*; in Hebrew *laqach*; in the Septuagintal translation: *metatithèmi* (Gen. 5: 24) or *analambanein* (2 Kings 2: 9–10).

51. The rapture can occur as well before as after death. That is why Br. O. McDermott's argument is not to the point (*The Personal Unity of Jesus and God according to W. Pannenberg* (St Ottilien 1973), 259).

52. Notice the essential difference in expression between the New Testament terminology 'ex tôn nekrôn' (removed from the *dead*) and the rapture-terminology 'ex tôn anthrôpôn': radically removed from our *world of human beings*, so that not even a corpse is left; thus: pertaining completely to the divine sphere (*theios anèr* theory; see Part Three).

53. See especially Philostratus, *Vita Apollonii* VIII, 5, 10, 11.

54. Chariton, *De Chaerea et Callirhoë*, III – a widely disseminated ancient novel, cited by Friedrich, in KuD, 177; Lohfink, *Himmelfahrt*, 47.

55. That the party on the way to Emmaus recognize Jesus in the breaking of the bread signifies: Jesus, who was himself the *guest* of his two hosts, never-theless acts as the host himself: *he* breaks the bread in the home of strangers. That is: he once more affords the disciples fellowship-with-him (see Part Two, Section One).

56. Cicero, Livy and Plutarch still use the model themselves, at the same time revealing that they no longer believe in what popular credulity stills sees as being 'for real'. In other words for them a break, a process of demythol-ogizing, has already taken place: they are conscious of the distinction between what is really intended (namely, that Romulus be venerated as the Quirinus-god of Rome) and the model (empty tomb, appearances). See Lohfink, *Himmelfahrt*, 49–50.

57. Slavonic Enoch 64: 4; 57: 2; Gen. 27: 4; Tob. 10: 11; Jubilees 22: 10ff; 2 Kings 2: 9 (Elijah).

58. As opposed to Mark and Matthew, Luke avoids the term '*proskynesis*' (prostrate adoration) as worship of the earthly Jesus; he reserves this term for the risen Jesus, taken up to God and now (after a series of appearances) definitely removed from the scene (Lk. 24, 52).

59. Friedrich, in *Orientierung an Jesus*, l.c., 61.

60. Sir. (Eccles.) 48: 9; 4 Ezra 6: 26; Syr. Apoc. Baruch 13: 3; 25: 1; 76: 2; 'you (Ezra) will be snatched away from men and will thenceforth sojourn with my son and companions, until the times are at an end' (4 Ezra, 14: 9). See F. Hahn, *Hoheitstitel*, 184–6; Lohfink, *Himmelfahrt*, 224, also 'Christologie und Geschichtsbild in Apg. 3: 19–21', in BZ 13 (1969) (223–41), 231–9; G. Haufe, 'Entrückung und eschatologische Funktion im Spätjudentum', in ZRGG 13 (1961), 105–13; U. Müller, *Messias und Menschensohn in jüdischen Apokalypsen und in der Offenbarung des Johannes* (Gütersloh 1972), 150–4. See below Part III, Section Two, note 41.

61. Syr. Apoc. Baruch 76: 4; 4 Ezra 12 (14): 23, 36, 42, 44, 45.

62. P. Schutz, 'Jesus liebte auch die Frauen', in *Die Zeit*, n. 17, 20 April 1973.

J.E.C.–Z

63. J. Schmitt, 'La résurrection de Jésus; des formules kérygmatiques aux récits évangéliques', in *Parole de Dieu et Sacerdoce* (Mélanges Mgr. Weber) (Paris 1962), 93–105; E. Pousset, 'La résurrection', in NRTh 91 (1969) (1009–44), 1020–1.

64. G. Wagner, *La Résurrection, signe du monde nouveau* (Paris 1970), 79–86; J. Delorme, in *Lectio Divina*, n. 72, 158.

65. See U. Wilckens, *Missionsreden*, 135.

66. J. Delorme, in *Lectio Divina*, n. 50, 118, n. 40.

67. This does not in itself necessarily run counter to the other tradition; Joseph of Arimathea was after all a member of the Sanhedrin. But the gospels differ regarding him: for Mark he is 'a respected member of the Sanhedrin' and 'living in expectation of the kingdom of God' (15: 43); in Matthew he is already 'a disciple' (27: 57); for Luke a Hellenized and goodly fellow (Lk. 23: 50); for John a 'secret disciple' (Jn. 19: 38), hardly distinguishable from the Nicodemus-figure (Jn. 3: 2).

68. Lk. 24: 34; Acts 13: 31; 9: 17; 26: 16; 1 Tim. 3: 16 and four times in 1 Cor. 15: 5–8. It is remarkable too that only in this pre-Pauline passage does Paul use the word in association with 'appearances'. The term comes from the Hebrew (niphal-form of *ra'ah*), meaning 'he showed himself (let himself be seen)' as well as 'he is seen'. See L. Koehler-W. Baumgartner, *Lexicon in V.T. libros* (Leyden 1958), 865; H. Grasz, *Ostergeschehen und Osterberichte*, 186–9 (the word '*ôphthè*' in itself settles nothing; it does however underline Jesus' own initiative). See especially A. Pelletier, 'Les apparitions du Ressuscité', l.c., 76–9; 'He showed himself' or '*God* made him epiphanous' is preferred, as appears also, for instance, from the Septuagint: *ôphthè ho Theos tōi Abram* (Gen. 12: 7); see other Old Testament theophanies (Gen. 18: 1–2; Num. 12: 5; Josh. 5: 13) or angelophanies (Judges 13; Ex. 3: 2; 6: 3; Gen. 12: 7). '*Ôphthè*' is also frequently used in Genesis for revelations, even when no visual element at all is present (Gen. 12: 7; 17: 1; 22: 14; 26: 2, 24; 35: 9; 48: 3 with 35: 11), or when the visual elements are minimal (Judges 13: 3; 2 Chron. 3: 1; 1 Chron. 21: 16; Judges 6: 11–12, 21). '*Ôphthè*' with the dative expresses God's initiative; it contrasts with '*ephanè* 'and '*phainesthai*', which rather suggests a vision (Mt. 1: 20; 2: 13, 19). The terminology comes quite clearly, via the Septuagint, from the Old Testament theophanies (a self-disclosure on God's part). Use of another word might evoke the idea of the reanimation of a corpse. This danger is already there in Acts 1: 3 (*Ièsous . . . parestèsen heauton dzōnta*), but we nowhere read what Josephus says later on: '*Ièsous . . . ephanè autois palin dzōn*' (*Antiquities*, 20, 64). Cf. J. Delorme, in *Lectio Divina*, n. 72, 143–4; Léon-Dufour, in *Lectio Divina*, n. 50, 167; R. Fuller, *Resurrection narratives*, 30; G. Delling, in W. Marxsen *et al.*, *Die Bedeutung der Auferstehungsbotschaft*, 72; H. Braun, in ThLZ 77 (1952), 533–6.

69. In Rom. 16: 7 Paul mentions Andronicus and Junias – two Greek names – as apostles, that is, missionaries who proclaim Christ to (Greek-speaking) *Jews* 'as far as in Phoenicia, Cyprus and Antioch' (see Acts 11: 19b). See H. van Campenhausen, *Der urchristliche Apostelbegriff*, in *Studia Theologica* 1 (1948) 96ff; G. Klein, *Die zwölf Apostel* (FRLANT, 59) (Göttingen 1961), 39–43.

70. See Gal. 1: 19; 2: 9, 12; also Mt. 10: 23; Rom. 10: 21. After his conversion Paul visits only Peter and also James (Gal. 1: 19); moreover, in the best manuscripts James comes before Peter in Gal. 2: 9. According to Gal. 2: 12 *James* sends messengers to inspect the missionary area of Antioch.

71. Besides 1 Cor. 15: 3–5; Lk. 24: 34 (see 24: 12); Jn. 21: 15–17. Mk. 16: 7 refers (very probably: see later) to the Parousia, but by the later ending to Mark (16: 9–20) has been attached to the appearances. Only Matthew seems to be unfamiliar with the special mention of Peter in this connection, but elsewhere he has highlighted the '*kefa*' function.

72. B. van Iersel, *St. Paul et la prédication de l'église primitive* (An. Bibl. 17–18) (Rome 1963), I, 433–41; K. Lehmann, *Am dritten Tag*, 87–115; Ph. Seidensticker, 'Das Antiochenische Glaubensbekenntnis 1 Kor. 15: 3–7 im Lichte seiner Traditionsgeschichte', in ThGl 57 (1967), 286–323; Hahn, *Hoheitstitel*, 197–8; H. Conzelmann, *Grundriss*, 84–5, and 'Zur Analyse der Bekenntnisformel 1 Kor. 15: 3b–5', in EvTh 25 (1965), 1–11; J. Jeremias, 'Zur Ursprache von 1 Kor. 15: 3b–5', in ZNW 57 (1966), 211–15; H. Grasz, *Ostergeschehen und Osterberichte*, 94–106; U. Wilckens, *Die Missionsreden der Apostelgeschichte* (Neukirchen 1963²), 73–81; B. Klappert, 'Zur Frage des semitischen oder griechischen Urtextes von 1 Kor. 15: 3–5', in NTS 13 (1966–7), 168–73; Käsemann, in *Besinnungen I*, 225; E. Lohse, *Die Auferstehung Jesu Christi*, 10; G. Schille, *Die urchristliche Kollegialmission* (Zürich 1967), and *Die Anfänge der Kirche* (Munich 1966; H. W. Bartsch, 'Die Argumentation des Paulus in 1 Kor. 15: 3–11', in ZNW 55 (1964), 261–74; J. Kremer, *Das älteste Zeugnis*, l.c.

73. J. Delorme, in *Lectio Divina*, n. 72, 107–13.

74. 1 Cor. 15: 23–28; 15: 19, 30–32, 58; 15: 20–22, 42–53.

75. Delorme, in *Lectio Divina*, n. 72, 110–11.

76. Although in a complicated form the same kind of structural analysis is possible in the case of Acts 2: 22–23; 3: 13–15; 4: 10; 5: 30, and all New Testament passages referring to Jesus' death 'for our sins' and his resuscitation by God.

77. The distinction between official and private appearances has been a classic one since the study by M. Albertz, 'Zur Formgeschichte der Auferstehungsberichte', in ZAW 21 (1922), 259–69.

78. Chr. Burchard, *Der dreizehnte Zeuge* (Göttingen 1970), 130–5; U. Wilckens, *Die Missionsreden der Apostelgeschichte* (Neukirchen 1963²), 148.

79. In Acts 10: 39 an exception appears to be made to this: his whole life from his baptism is apparently sufficient here; so also in this discourse: 10: 34–43; but that life is seen there as a prelude to death and resurrection.

80. 'It is written' (Lk. 24: 46) is identical with 'necessary to salvation-history' (24: 26).

81. Since John is unfamiliar with the idea of 'the Eleven', and the notion of 'the Twelve' is hardly known to him (only in Jn. 6: 67–71 and here: Jn. 20: 24), he speaks of 'the disciples'.

82. See B. van Iersel, *Een begin*, 96–7; R. Fuller, *Resurrection narratives*, 156.

83. See A. Vögtle, 'Ekklesiologische aufträge', l.c. (Sacra Pagina, II, 280–94),

now also in *Das Evangelium und die Evangelien* (Düsseldorf 1971), 243–52; see also, op. cit., 137–70.

84. According to A. Vögtle there lurks behind Mt. 16: 17–19 a historical recollection of the first appearance of Jesus to Peter, in 'Zum Problem der Herkunft von Mt. 16: 17–19', in *Orientierung an Jesus* (372–93), especially 377–83.

85. It seems to me no coincidence that only Thomas, in whose name the East Syrian Church (Edessa) according to its tradition considers itself to have been founded, has doubts about the risen One. East Syria became the cradle of a Christology minus a resurrection *kerygma*, out of which subsequently the Gospel of Thomas, and later still the Acts of Thomas, were to grow.

86. Does not signify, therefore: Jesus is God *tout court*; see Jn. 5: 18; 8: 58; 10: 30; 10: 33; 12: 45; 14: 9; 17: 11. See R. Fuller, *Resurrection narratives*, 143–4.

87. '*Ektrôma*' is a medical term; it means: someone who by means of surgical intervention has been born of a dying mother, who was therefore never seen by the new-born child. But Paul calls himself an 'eye-witness' (therein lies the point of the expression).

88. See R. Barthes, 'Introduction à l'analyse structurale des récits', in *Communications* 8 (1966), 1–28; 'L'écriture de l'évènement', in l.c., 12 (1968), 108–13; and *Analyse structurale et exégèse biblique* (Neuchâtel 1971); T. van Dijk, *Moderne literatuur-theorie* (Amsterdam 1971); F. Maatje, *Literatuurwetenschap* (Utrecht 1971²); R. Barthes *et al.*, *Exégèse et herméneutique* (Paris 1971); C. Cabrol and L. Marin, *Sémiotique narrative: récits bibliques*, in *Langages* 6 (1971), n. 22 (in its entirety); H. Weinrich, *Literatur für Leser* (Stuttgart 1971).

89. R. Barthes, 'L'analyse structurale du récit à propos d'Actes X–XI', in *Exégèse et herméneutique* (Paris 1971), 202–3.

90. In his letters Paul nowhere alludes to this Ananias.

91. 2 Kings 2: 17; 2 Chron. 20: 25; Ex. 15: 22; 2 Macc. 13: 12; Lk. 2: 46; 24: 21; Mk. 8: 2; Mt. 15: 32.

92. With Luke '*bastadzein*' usually has the secondary meaning of 'dragging along with' (Lk. 7: 14; 10: 4; 11: 27; 14: 27; 22: 10; Acts 3: 2; 15: 10; 21: 35; it belongs to the terminology of martyrdom. See Burchard, *Der dreizehnte Zeuge*, 100–1.

93. As latter-day prophet and teacher of the law Jesus is 'light of the world'. See Isa. 42: 6–7, 16; 49: 6, 8–9; 50: 10; 51: 4–6; 62: 1 with 49: 6; Sirach 48: 10b; Acts 1: 8b; Lk. 2: 32; Jn. 1: 8, 9; 3: 19–21; 8: 12. Also Paralip. Jer. 6: 9, 12; *Joseph and Asenath*, p. 46; especially pseudo-Philo, *Liber Antiquitatum* 51: 4–6; Test. Levi 14: 3–4; Test. Zabulon 9: 8; Test. Benjamin 10: 2. For the apostles: Acts 13: 47; Mt. 5: 14. See also Kl. Berger, *Gesetzesauslegung*, 27.

94. In the oldest liturgies the idea of the 'light of the Gentiles' also comes to be associated with Christian baptism, which is itself described as 'illumination'.

95. According to H. Conzelmann we have here a rival variant of the Damascus-event (*Die Apostelgeschichte* (Tübingen 1963), 126). According to Chr. Burchard, *Der dreizehnte Zeuge*, 161–8, it refers to another incident,

localized in Jerusalem; it is *there* that Paul is called to be an apostle *of the Gentiles*. This is in any case non-Pauline; Paul is aware from the very start of being called to the Gentiles. This tradition does of course concede *that* Paul is the apostle of the Gentiles.

96. See Acts 7: 10–34; 12: 11; 23: 27; 26: 17; Gal, 1: 4.

97. See 1 Thess. 1: 9; Col. 1: 13; 1 Pet. 2: 9.

98. See also Acts 20: 32; cf. Eph. 1: 18; Col. 1: 12.

99. Chr. Burchard, *Der dreizehnte Zeuge*, 166–7.

100. Cf. Acts 26: 10–11 with Gal. 1: 12–13; Acts 26: 6 with Gal. 1: 14; Acts 26: 7 with Gal. 1: 16; Acts 26: 18 with Gal. 1: 16.

101. Furthermore Acts 26 is in the so-called 'we-sections' of the Acts.

102. See Burchard, l.c., 126–7.

103. The notion of the suffering apostle (Acts 9: 15–16) is post-Pauline (Col. 1: 24; Eph. 3: 1, 13; 2 Tim. 3: 11–12).

104. R. Fuller, *Resurrection narratives*, 46, rightly emphasizes this.

105. Wis. 18: 4 ('the imperishable light of the law which was to be given to the world'); Test. Levi 18: 3, 9; 1 QH 4: 27.

106. Test. Levi 14: 3; 18: 3, 9; Test. Benjamin 10: 2; 1 QH 4: 27; cf. Jn. 1: 8; Mt. 5: 3.

107. Paral. Jer. 6: 9, 12; *Joseph and Asenath*, p. 46: 18–19; 47: 1–2; pseudo-Philo, *Liber Antiquitatum biblicarum*, 51: 4–6; Test. Zabulon, 51: 4–6. In the New Testament: Acts 1: 8b; Lk. 2: 32; Jn. 1: 9; 3: 19–21; 8: 12. See W. Nauck, *Die Tradition und der Charakter des ersten Johannesbrief* (Tübingen 1957); Roloff, *Das Kerygma*, 119–21; Lk. Berger, *Gesetzesauslegung*, 27–8.

108. Berger, *Gesetzesauslegung*, 27, rightly says that the function of the latter-day prophet as '*lumen gentium*' within Judaism is the key to a series of so far unelucidated central issues in early Christianity. His much heralded study on this subject is unfortunately not yet available.

109. All the Jewish *topoi* of a Gentile's conversion to the Jewish Law were taken over by Christianity. The convert starts by giving alms, even by giving away all his possessions, but he will recover them a hundredfold: Berger, *Gesetzesauslegung*, 29–30.

110. The sources are imprecise about the disciples having fled to Galilee and having afterwards returned to Jerusalem. (It therefore remains historically arguable that the 'Galilean appearances' are the earliest; certainly, the appearance traditions refer to a Galilean origin.) It is another thing, however, to see 'the Twelve' as having already been brought together (awaiting, as it were, news of 'appearances') *before* their experience of what the New Testament calls 'Christ appearances'! See the argument about this: Hahn, *Hoheitstitel*, 205–6; H. Grasz, *Ostergeschehen*, 128–9; H. Conzelmann, 'Zur analyse der Bekenntnisformel', l.c., 8, n. 49; K. Lehmann, *Am dritten Tag*, 162.

111. Despite all sorts of fortuitous circumstances which helped to bring about the rift between Christianity and Jewry, the primitive Christian identification of Jesus with the '*lumen gentium*', in place of the Law as the 'light of the world', was *germinally* a breach with Judaic Jewry, and in essence therefore the founding of the '*ecclesia Christi*' as an *ecclesia* of Jews *and* Gentiles.

112. H. Conzelmann, *Geschichte des Urchristentums*, 27–8; Delorme, in *Lectio Divina*, n. 72, 114; Fuller, *Resurrection narratives*, 57–8.

113. *Memory and Manuscript* (Uppsala 1961), 266–71.

114. 'Zum Problem der Herkunft von Mt. 16: 17–19', in *Orientierung an Jesus*, l.c., 372–93.

115. l.c., 382.

116. See the literature above.

117. Josephus, *De bello Judaico*, 3, 162; and *Antiquitates* 8, 105. Apropos of an exposition of the fellowship-meal in the post-Easter period I was struck by this footnote in J. Roloff, *Das Kerygma*, 255, n. 191.

118. Thus – and rightly – M. Hengel, 'Die Ursprünge der christlichen Mission', l.c., 33–4; J. Roloff, *Apostolat, Verkündigung, Kirche* (Gütersloh 1965), 138ff.

119. We are not to see in this any kind of 'rationalism', intended somehow to demythologize the appearances of Christ. It has become clear, not from rationalism but from the actual intentions of Scripture, as shown by the structure of the appearances, that there are always intermediary historical factors in occurrences of divine grace. The appearances form no exception to this scheme of grace. And then, what would a straight appearance of Jesus in the flesh prove? Only *believers* see the one who appears; a faith-motivated interpretation enters into the very heart of the event. Christ appearances are not like the 'manifestations' of St Nicholas. Faith is emasculated if we insist on grounding it in pseudo-empiricism, thereby raising all sorts of false problems: whether, for instance, this 'Christological mode of seeing' was a sensory seeing of Jesus, whether it was 'objective' or 'subjective' seeing, a 'manifestation' or a 'vision', and things of that sort. To the New Testament all such questions are alien. I do not understand Pannenberg's lengthy exposition of this (*Grundzüge*, 93–103) nor the further discussion by his not even average cross-section of critics (Br. O. McDermott, *The Personal Unity of Jesus and God according to W. Pannenberg* (St Ottilien), 262–9). Although I regard my hypothesis as justifiable, I realize that it constitutes a break with a centuries-old hermeneutical tradition. That is why I give it here '*salvo meliori iudicio*' (*and* cogent counter-arguments). The appearances as such are, after all, not an *object* of Christian faith.

120. 1 Thess. 1: 10; Rom. 10: 9; Acts 3: 15; 4: 10; 5: 30; 10: 40; 13: 30, 37; Rom. 4: 24; 2 Cor. 4: 14; Col. 2: 12; 1 Pet. 1: 21; etc. See further on.

121. Another tradition links the forgiveness of sin with Jesus' death (1 Cor. 15: 3).

122. See, e.g., the discussion between N. Schreurs, 'Naar de basis van ons spreken over God: de weg van L. Gilkey', in TvT 11 (1971) (275–92), especially 289 and L. Gilkey, 'Ervaring en interpretatie van de religieuse dimensie: een reactie', ibid., 293–302. And P. Ricoeur, *De l'interprétation* (Paris 1965), dealing with the same nexus of problems.

123. Thus, e.g., Ph. Seidensticker, *Die Auferstehung Jesu in der Botschaft der Evangelisten* (Stuttgart 1967). According to this author experience of Jesus as the humiliated yet exalted servant is the earliest expression of the Easter faith.

124. W. Marxsen, *Die Auferstehung Jesu als historisches und theologisches Problem* (Gütersloh 1964), with slight corrections in *Die Auferstehung Jesu von Nazareth* (Gütersloh 1968).

125. *Erniedrigung und Erhöhung bei Jesu und seinen Nachfolgern* (AThANT, 28) (Zürich 1962²) (1955).

126. L. Ruppert, *Der leidende Gerechte. Eine motivgeschichtliche Untersuchung zum Alten Testament und zwischentestamentlichen Judentum* (Würzburg 1972), and the brief summary: *Jesus, als der leidende Gerechte?* (SBS, 59) (Stuttgart 1972); also G. Nickelsburg, *Resurrection*, l.c.

127. Kl. Berger, 'Die königlichen Messiastraditionen des Neuen Testaments', in NTS 20 (1973–4), 1–45.

128. See literature in Part Three, Section Two, note 1.

129. e.g., Plato, *Symposium*, 179c: '*ex Haidou aneinai palin tèn psuchèn*'.

130. Strack-Billerbeck, III, 475; even with the same physical blemishes that one had had; l.c., IV, 1175–6.

131. Syrian Baruch 51.

132. Likewise (after Hahn, Tödt, Fuller, *et al.*) also S. Schulz in his major study of Q, *Q-Quelle*, e.g., 74.

133. Although not entirely unconnected with it, this problem is not the same as F. Hahn's (*Hoheitstitel*, 112–32), according to whom the 'exaltation' formulae are of a later date in early Christianity, presupposing as they do the delay or postponement of the Parousia. This is rightly contested, not only by Ph. Vielhauer, in *Aufsätze*, 164 and 173–5, but also by W. Thüsing, 'Erhöhungsvorstellung und Parusieerwartung in der ältesten nachösterlichen Christologie', in BZ 11 (1967), especially 216–19, and 12 (1968), especially 226–8; and G. Lohfink, *Die Himmelfahrt Jesu* (Munich 1971), 80–98; see 96, n. 42 (see Part Three).

PART THREE, *Section One* (*pp.* 399–515)

1. J. Blank, *Jesus von Nazareth* (Freiburg 1972), 13–14.

2. The problem of the canon is not dealt with here. See D. K. Aland, 'Das Problem das neutestamentlichen Kanons', in NZSTh 4 (1962), 220–42; E. Käsemann, in *Besinnungen*, I, 214–23, and (ed.) *Das Neue Testament als Kanon* (Göttingen 1970); J. Frank, *Der Sinn der Kanonbildung* (Freiburg 1971); K. H. Ohlig, *Die theologische Begründung des neutestamentlichen Kanons in der alten Kirche* (Düsseldorf 1972).

3. Between 400 BC and about AD 70/71 there emerge expectations regarding all sorts of 'latter-day prophets' and latter-day salvific figures, including the expectation – now separate, now quite clearly interconnected – of a latter-day prophet and a latter-day messiah; as well as – independently, to begin with, of any messianology – the expectation of a 'prophet like Moses'. Echoes of a popular expectation of 'the coming One' abound therefore in the New Testament: Jn. 6: 14–15; 1: 15, 21; Mt. 3: 11; 11: 3; Lk. 3: 16; 7: 19, 20b (see the detailed analyses that follow).

4. *Trajectories*, 215.

5. Schulz, *Q-Quelle*, 166–7.
6. Th. J. Weeden, *Mark-traditions*; see below on this.
7. Käsemann, in *Besinnungen*, II, 105–30; II, 31–68; II, 82–104; I, 187–213.
8. Hahn, *Hoheitstitel*, 13–53; Vielhauer, in *Aufsätze*, 145–6, and 92–140.
9. See M. Black, 'The Christological use', 6–11.
10. Black, ib., 11; C. F. Moule, 'A reconsideration of the context of Mara-natha', in NTS 6 (1960), 307–8; cf. S. Schulz, *Maranatha*, l.c., 125–44.
11. C. H. Dodd, *According to the Scriptures: the sub-structure of New Testament Theology* (London 1950), 35.
12. See further on, at: The son of man.
13. Schulz, *Q-Quelle*, 71.
14. ibid., 71, aimed at Hahn, *Hoheitstitel*, 32–3.
15. Thus Schulz, *Q-Quelle*, 73. Yet uncertainties persist, on account of the arguments advanced by H. M. Teeple, 'The origin of the Son of Man Christ-ology', in JBL 84 (1965), 213–50 (see further on).
16. Koester, in Robinson-Koester, *Trajectories*, 215.
17. Mk. 6: 6b–13, and substantially from the Q source: Mt. 9: 37–38; 10: 16, 9–10a, 11–13, 10b–7–8, 14–15=Lk. 10: 2–12. See M. Hengel, *Nachfolge und Charisma* (Berlin 1968), 82–9; F. Hahn, *Das Verständnis der Mission im Neuen Testament* (Neukirchen-Vluyn 1963); J. Roloff, *Apostolat, Verkündigung, Kirche* (Gütersloh 1965); F. Beare, 'The mission of the disciples and the mission charge: Mt. 10 and parallels', in JBL 89 (1970), 1–13; Schulz, *Q-Quelle*, 404–10.
18. See Schulz, *Q-Quelle*, 55–176.
19. Lk. 11: 1–4=Mt. 6: 9–13; see Schulz, *Q-Quelle*, 84–93.
20. See Dan. 12: 10; Apoc. 3: 10.
21. See J. Becker, *Johannes der Täufer und Jesus von Nazareth* (Neukirchen-Vluyn 1972), 100ff; Schulz, *Q-Quelle*, 71; Vielhauer, in *Aufsätze*, 80–7.
22. This differs fundamentally from Mk. 8: 38 (see Mt. 16: 27 and Lk. 9: 26), even though Q material also seems to underlie Mk. 8: 38. See Schulz, *Q-Quelle*, 66–76; Lührmann, *Q-Redaktion*, 51; Hahn, *Hoheitstitel*, 33.
23. Thus the basic thesis of Lührmann's book, *Q-Redaktion*; also Schulz, *Q-Quelle*, 66–76.
24. Schulz, *Q-Quelle*, 74; Tödt, *Menschensohn*, 259–60.
25. Thus H. R. Balz, *Methodische Probleme der neutestamentlichen Christologie* (Neukirchen 1967), 186.
26. The Q community adopts 'a non-Passion Christology': R. Edwards, 'An Approach to a Christology of Q', in JRel 51 (1971) (247–69), 253–9; also Tödt, *Menschensohn*, 238–57; Fr. Muszner, *Jesus in den Evangelien* (SBS, 45) (Stuttgart 1970), 38–49; Lührmann, *Q-Redaktion*, 94–5 and 103; Schulz, *Q-Quelle*, 486, and passim; all this as against W. Kümmel, *Einleitung in das Neue Testament* (Heidelberg, 1963[12]), 39.
27. Schulz, *Q-Quelle*, 94 and 99.
28. Thus Schulz, *Q-Quelle*, 55–176, after an analysis of the passages regarded as the oldest, Aramaic-Jewish layer in Q: Mt. 10: 32–33=Lk. 12: 8–9; Mt. 5: 3–4, 6=Lk. 6: 20b–21; Mt. 6: 9–13=Lk. 11: 1–4; Mt. 23: 25, 23, 6–7a, 27, 4, 29–31, 13=Lk. 11: 39, 42–44, 46–48, 52; Mt. 5: 18=Lk. 16: 17; Mt. 5: 32=

Lk. 16: 18; Mt. 5: 39–42=Lk. 6: 29–30; Mt. 5: 44–48=Lk. 6: 27–28, 35b, 32–35a, 36; Mt. 7: 12=Lk. 6: 31; Mt. 6: 19–22=Lk. 12: 33–34; Mt. 7: 1–5= Lk. 6: 37–38, 41–42; Mt. 6: 25–33=Lk. 12: 22–31; Mt. 10: 28–31=Lk. 12: 4–7; Mt. 7: 7–11=Lk. 11: 9–13. For a similar conclusion, though argued in less detail, see H. Koester, in Robinson-Koester, *Trajectories*, 211–16, see also 168–75; Hahn, *Hoheitstitel*, 32–39; R. Fuller, *Critical introduction*, 102–3, and *Foundations*, 130–1; D. E. Nineham, *The New Testament Gospels* (Harmondsworth 1965), 34–7; Tödt, *Menschensohn*, 265–7, 212–45; A. Vögtle, 'Jesus', in E. Kottje-B. Möller (eds), *Oekumenische Kirchengeschichte* (Mainz-Munich, 1970), 3–24. This lines up an impressive array of specialists (despite the differences of detail found among them).

29. Schulz, *Q-Quelle*, 177–89. Cf. P. Hoffmann, 'Die Versuchungsgeschichte in der Logienquelle', in BZ 13 (1969), 207–23; see J. Dupont, 'L'origine du récit des tentations de Jésus au désert', in RB 73 (1966), 30–76; B. van Iersel, 'Jezus, duivel en demonen. Notities bij Mt. 4: 1–11 en Mk. 5: 1–20', in *Engelen en duivels* (Annalen van het Thijmgenootschap 55, afl. 3) (Hilversum 1968), 5–22; A. Feuillet, 'Le récit lucanien de la tentation', in Bibl 40 (1959), 613–31.

30. ibid., 195; Hoffmann, *Q-Studien*, 198–215; Tödt, *Menschensohn*, 234.

31. The term is Schulz's, *Q-Quelle*, 212.

32. Schulz, *Q-Quelle*, 215ff; Hoffmann, *Q-Studien*, 77–8; B. van Iersel, *Der Sohn*, 151ff.

33. Tödt, *Menschensohn*, 83 and 241; Schulz, *Q-Quelle*, 242.

34. J. B. Audet, *La Didaché* (Paris 1958), 252–7; P. Stuhlmacher, in EvTh 28 (1968), 178–9; Berger, *Gesetzesauslegung*, e.g., 458–60, passim.

35. Although certain of his detailed assertions are hard to accept, it seems to me that Weeden's basic view in *Mark-traditions* – viz. Mark's postulate of 'the absence' of Jesus between death and Parousia – is, exegetically speaking, at any rate highly probable.

36. Mk. 8: 31–32, 38; 9: 12, 31; 10: 33; 13: 26; 14: 62.

37. See N. Perrin, 'The Christology of Mark. A study in methodology', in JRel 51 (1971), 173–87; 'The Son of Man in the Synoptic tradition', BRes 13 (1968), 1–23; 'The creative use of the Son of Man traditions by Mark', in UnSQR 23 (1967–8), 357–65; finally 'Mark 14: 62: End-product of a Christian pesher-tradition', in NTS 12 (1965–6), 150–5; and L. E. Keck, 'Mark 3: 7–12 and Mark's Christology', in JBL 84 (1965), 341–58.

38. Thus, earlier on already, W. Marxsen, *Der Evangelist Markus* (Göttingen 1959²), also Weeden, *Mark-traditions*, 111–17, and 45–51.

39. Weeden, ibid., 129–30.

40. Hahn, *Hoheitstitel*, 128–9, 181–3, 288–9; see also 177 and 282; and Weeden, ibid., 126–9.

41. Tödt, *Menschensohn*, 33–7.

42. Weeden, ibid., 126–31.

43. R. Fuller, *Foundations*, 145–6; 152 and 175; Hahn, *Hoheitstitel*, 181–3 and 39.

44. Weeden, ibid., 128–9.

45. W. Thüsing, 'Erhöhungsvorstellung und Parusieerwartung in der ältesten nachösterlichen Christologie', in BZ 11 (1967), 95–108 and 205–22; 12 (1968), 54–80 and 223–40 (now also in book form: SBS 42, (Stuttgart 1969)), denied this, because the Spirit's presence in the community is a gift of the heavenly Jesus. But it is very much a question whether this gift of the Spirit, in which Mark does indeed concur, actually stands, *within the Marcan gospel*, in a direct and intrinsic connection with the risen Jesus himself: nothing points in that direction, rather to the contrary (e.g., Mk. 3: 28–29; cf. Mk. 13: 11 with Lk. 21: 15). Even the Didache says: 'you shall not judge a prophet speaking in the Spirit' (17: 27). This articulates a theology which acknowledges the Spirit as primate over the son of man. See R. Scroggs, 'The exhaltation of the Spirit by some early Christians', in JBL (1965), 359–73.

46. See R. Fuller, *Foundations*, l.c., 145ff and 185–6; Hahn, *Hoheitstitel*, 126–32 and 184–5.

47. Whether the Letter of James is a late, re-judaizing document or a very primitive one (perhaps the earliest in the New Testament) which is in line with this very old (possibly oldest) credal strand I leave an open question. There are arguments for an early dating (see Elliot-Binns, *Galilean Christianity*, l.c., 45–8 and Th. Boman, *Die Jesus-Ueberlieferung*, l.c., 197), but also several passages in James that would appear to contradict that. We know little, however, about the course of the tradition (later corrections or interpolations) affecting these texts.

48. H. D. Betz, 'Eine Christus-Aretalogie bei Poulus (2 Cor. 12: 7–10)', in ZThK 66 (1969), 288–305; H. W. Kuhn, 'Der irdisches Jesus bei Paulus als traditionsgeschichtliches und theologisches Problem', ibid., 67 (1970), 308–18; cf. Th. Boman, *Die Jesus-Ueberlieferung*, l.c., 184–207.

49. Th. Weeden, *Mark-traditions*, 138–58; Hahn, *Hoheitstitel*, 292–7; Roloff, *Das Kerygma*, especially 182, n. 265, in reaction to G. Georgi, *Die Gegner des Paulus im 2. Korintherbrief* (Neukirchen 1964).

50. See Weeden for the Marcan gospel and Robinson, in Robinson-Koester, *Trajectories*, regarding John's *'sèmeia'*-source ('The Johannine Trajectory'), 232–68.

51. Roloff, *Das Kerygma*, 188–205.

52. See also R. Pesch, *Jesu Ureigene Taten?* (Freiburg 1970).

53. See later the 'sacred tomb' according to the Lucan version.

54. See later in the chapter on Jesus' 'mighty works'.

55. Koester, in Robinson-Koester, *Trajectories*, 190–1.

56. Mt. 11: 25–27=Lk. 10: 21–22 (see Wis. 6–10). Also Mt. 23: 34–36= Lk. 11: 49–51; Mt. 9: 37–38, 10, 7–16=Lk. 10: 2–12.

57. See also S. van Tilborg, ' "Neerdaling" en incarnatie', in TvT 13 (1973), 20–33, although his suggestion that with the departure of Jesus the incarnation is 'at an end' seems to me insufficiently established in a Johannine context.

58. See G. Kegel, *Auferstehung Jesu. Auferstehung der Toten* (Gütersloh 1970), 12–20; also Koester, in Robinson-Koester, *Trajectories*, 198–204 and 223–9. And further literature in the later chapters on death and resurrection.

59. H. Schlier, 'Die Anfänge des christologischen Credo', in *Zur Frühgeschichte der Christologie* (Freiburg 1970), 13–58.

60. See C. Burger, *Jesus als Davidssohn. Eine traditionsgeschichtliche Untersuchung* (Göttingen 1970); J. Ernst, *Anfänge der Christologie* (SBS, 57) (Stuttgart 1972), 39–42. 'Son of David', used of Jesus, is a *theologoumenon* without a meaning subject to historical checks (see further on in this Part).

61. 1 Sam. 10: 1; 16: 13; 2 Sam. 19: 10; 1 Kings 1: 39; 2 Kings 11: 12; 23: 30.

62. This anointing is then projected back into the past or is antedated: Ex. 29: 30, 40; 28: 41; Levi. 2: 7, 8.

63. Ex. 30: 30; 28: 41; 40: 15; Lev. 7: 36; 10: 7; Num. 3: 3.

64. 1 Kings 19: 16; Ps. 105: 15.

65. 2 Kings 17: 26; Jer. 5: 4; 8: 7.

66. Hosea 9: 7; Isa. 48: 16; Ezek. 2: 2; 11: 5.

67. Judges 6: 16; 3: 10; 6: 34; 11: 29; 13: 25; 14: 1, 19; 15: 14; 1 Sam. 11: 6; 1 Sam. 10; 1 Sam. 16: 13.

68. 1 Sam. 10: 1, 6, 9.

69. Deut. 1: 36–37; 4: 21–22; 34: 5; Num. 12: 1–2.

70. See especially the (cited) work by M. Chevallier with some finer points from W. van Unnik.

71. This complaint is voiced already in an older source: 1 Sam. 3: 1.

72. J. Bonsirven, *Le judaisme palestinien*, vol. I, XXVI-XXX.

73. R. Le Déaut, *Les études targumiques*, in ETL 44 (1968) (5–34), 5.

74. Strack-Billerbeck, I, 601.

75. J. Gibler, *Messie prophète*, 98.

76. '*Transmutatur in divinum, ita ut fiat Deo cognatus, vereque divinus*' (*Quaest. in Exodum*, II, 29). See Josephus, *Antiquitates*, 2: 201–4, 233, 331; 4: 326, who describes Moses explicitly as a '*theios anèr*'. See J. Giblet, *Messie prophète*, 101, and J. Jeremias, sub *Moyses*, in ThWNT 4, 852–3.

77. See G. von Rad, *Die Botschaft der Propheten* (Munich 1967).

78. M. Hengel, *Die Zeloten* (Leyden-Cologne 1961), 240–2; J. Giblet, *Messie prophète*, 122.

79. Isa. 32: 15; 44: 3; Ezek. 11: 19; 36: 26–27.

80. *De bello Judaico* 6: 285–6, cited in M. Hengel, *Die Zeloten*, 249. Apoc. 11: 1–2 could very well be an allusion to this prophecy.

81. Mt. 3: 11; 11: 3, 9, 14; Lk. 3: 16; 7: 19, 20b; Jn. 1: 15, 21, especially 6: 14–15.

82. As compared with these two climaxes, more than half a century before, and somewhat less than a half-century after, Jesus, his own time was rather a quiet one where the literature of apocalyptic is concerned. We should not push the feverish outburst of apocalypticism after the fall of Jerusalem (with its obvious influence on a great part of the New Testament) back into Jesus' own lifetime.

83. Syrian Apoc. Baruch 29: 4–8; 4 Ezra 13: 43–44.

84. Josephus, *Antiquitatum Judaicarum libri* (=*Antiquitates*) 20: 97–8.

85. Josephus, *De bello Judaico*, 2: 26ff; *Antiquitates*, 20: 169–70.

86. *Antiquitates*, 20: 188.

87. F. Hahn, *Hoheitstitel*, 353–4; Kl. Berger, 'Die königlichen Messias-traditionen', 1–45.
88. ibid., 366ff.
89. Th. C. Vriezen, *Hoofdlijnen der theologie van het Oude Testament* (Wageningen 1966³).
90. 2 Sam. 7: 12–16→Ps. Sal. 17: 4; Ps. 2: 9→Ps. Sal. 17: 22–24; Ps. 110: 5–6→Ps. Sal. 17: 22; Isa. 11: 1–9→Ps. Sal. 17: 23a, 23–28; Mic. 5: 4→Ps. Sal. 17: 40, etc.
91. Müller, *Messias*, 72–80.
92. ibid., 79–80.
93. P. Grelot, *Le Messie dans les apocryphes*, l.c., 24–8.
94. According to Starcky, *Quatre étapes*, 490–1, the dual messiah-figure is a compromise between the actual situation (a non-Davidic, Hasmonean king) and the '*de iure*' principle (the prophetic promises to Judah). Again in Jubilees 31: 9–20 (from Chasidic circles) we hear tell of a Levi- and a Judah-messiah.
95. QD 19: 10–11; 20: 1; 12: 23; 14: 19; also 7: 18–21; 19: 35–20, 1; see Starcky, *Quatre étapes*, l.c., 495. 497.
96. Pub. in JBL 77 (1958), 350–4.
97. 4 Q Mess ar: see Starcky, ibid., 502–4.
98. M. Hengel, *Die Zeloten*, l.c.; S. Brandon, *Jesus and the Zealots* (Manchester 1967), with: '*Jesus and the Zealots?*: A correction', in NTS 17 (1970), 453. More detailed discussion: G. Baumbach, 'Zeloten und Sikarier', in ThLZ 90 (1965), 727–40, and 'Die Zeloten', in BuL 41 (1968), 2–19; C. Daniel, 'Esséniens, zélotes et sicaires et leur mention par paronymie dans le Nouveau Testament', in *Numen* 13 (1966), 88–105; M. Maccoby, 'Jesus and Barabbas', in NTS 16 (1969), 55–60; M. Smith, 'Zealots and Sicarii. Their origins and relation', in HThR 1 (1971), 1–20; H. P. Kingdom, 'The origins of the Zealots', in NTS 19 (1972–3), 74–81.
99. S. van der Woude, *Qumrân*, l.c., 218.
100. See Y. Yadin, *Masada. Der letzte Kamf um die Festung des Herodes* (Hamburg 1967). Of the Qumrân Essenes who escaped some later became Christians. With a terminology possibly derived from Qumrân the Christians too were called, in some Christian circles, 'followers of the Way' (see Acts 9: 2; 18: 25–26; 19: 9, 23; 22: 4; 24: 14 and 22).
101. Here we must utter a warning, however, about modern eschatological misconceptions – not only in general (see J. Carmignac, 'Les dangers de l'eschatologie', in NTS 17 [1970–71] 365–90), but also in particular. That Jews and Christians at that time lived in expectation of being the last generation does not imply 'the end of the world' in the modern sense of the phrase. 'Eschatological' at that time, especially when associated with messianism, did, it is true, imply something transcendent but still within this world, albeit in a completely new order. Even in the New Testament various pointers are present to very peculiar interpretations *vis-à-vis* modern Christian ones. A typical feature is that many Christians expected the rule of God, as promised by Jesus Christ, for those still living ('this generation'; one generation was then equivalent to a period of fifty years): Mt. 10: 23; Mk. 9: 1; Acts 1: 6;

1 Thess. 4: 15–17; and so they were afraid that those already dead would have no part in it (1 Thess. 4: 13–18).

102. Josephus, *De bello Judaico*, 6, 212–313; Tacitus, *Historiae*, 5: 13; Suetonius, *Vespasianus*, 4: 5; see M. Hengel, *Die Zeloten*, l.c., 245.

103. *Antiquitates*, 10: 210; 4: 114 and 4: 116–17.

104. *Antiquitates*, 8: 44–49; *Test. Salomonis*, 16: 3. See Kl. Berger, *Die königlichen Messiastraditionen*, 7, n. 29.

105. *Test. Salomonis*, 20: 1.

106. Berger, l.c., 22.

107. *Vita Moysis*, 1: 158; Berger, l.c., 23, n. 89.

108. *Jubilees*, 31: 15; *Joseph and Asenath*, 22; *Test. Levi*, 18: 1, 3. See Apoc. 11: 3ff.

109. L. Ruppert, *Jesus, als der leidende Gerechte?* (SBS, 59) (Stuttgart 1972), 54–6.

110. 4 Ezra 13: 55; 5 Ezra 2: 40, 42, 47. Cf. Lk. 19: 11; Rom. 11: 26–27. Berger, l.c., 31.

111. Also Philo, *Prob. liber*, 117; *Test. Dan.*, 5: 13.

112. Kl. Berger, l.c., 36–7.

113. Prov. 8: 15; 4: 8–9; *Test. Levi*, 13: 9.

114. 2 Macc. 7: 34. See Apoc. (Rev.) 21: 7; Rom. 8: 17; 2 Tim. 2: 11.

115. Thus F. Hahn, *Hoheitstitel*, 264, n. 6.

116. In what is for a theologian the very difficult choice to be made amid this chaos of opinions, after some hesitation I lean towards the study by Ulrich Müller (1972). A degree of hesitation remains, on the one hand because of the very powerful arguments adduced by H. M. Teeple, who sees in the New Testament idea of the son of man a Hellenistic-Jewish Christian contribution (possibly from Syria, whence comes also the book of Enoch). The sole use of son of man not put into the mouth of Jesus – outside the Revelation – is, strikingly enough, by the Jerusalem 'Hellenist' deacon, Stephen, whose supporters fled principally to Syria (Acts 7: 56); and on the other hand because of the critical arguments of Bultmann, Hahn, Tödt and Colpe, who have made a plausible case for the sole use of the term 'son of man' by Jesus himself.

117. 1 Enoch 39 to 62, while 'son of man' is restricted to three sections only: En. 64–68; 60–63; 69–71; see Maddox, *Methodenfrage*, 149; Müller, 38 and 42.

118. H. Conzelmann, *Grundriss*, 152–3; Müller, *Messias*, 38–47; L. Ruppert, *Jesus, als der leidende Gerechte?* (SBS, 59) (Stuttgart 1972), 70–1.

119. Müller, *Messias*, l.c., 47–60.

120. The absence of any form of messianism in early apocalyptic is bound up with the rise of the Chasidic movement, springing from the Maccabean struggle with its principle of the 'holy war'; this last theme comes out of a completely non-messianic complex of tradition; see Müller, *Messias*, 61–72.

121. Müller, *Messias*, 84–5.

122. ibid., 147–53.

123. Leivestad, 'Apocalyptic Son?', (thesis of the whole article).

124. Thus Tödt, *Menschensohn*, 52–3; Colpe, in ThWNT VIII, 433; P.

Hoffmann, *Q-Studien*, 143–4; Hahn, *Hoheitstitel*, 16–19; Cullmann, *Christologie*, 157–8; Müller, *Messias*, 107–56.
125. Except, notably, R. Leivestad.
126. J. Ernst, *Anfänge*, 49.
127. Vielhauer, in *Aufsätze*, 118ff; Conzelmann, *Grundriss*, 151–6; Teeple, *Son of Man*, 237–50.
128. Bultmann, *Theologie*, 35–9, and *Tradition*, 145–6; Tödt, *Menschensohn*, 131ff and 250ff; Hahn, *Hoheitstitel*, 23–32 and 32–42.
129. Teeple, *Son of Man*, 220–2; E. Gräszer, *Naherwartung*, 122–4.
130. According to Conzelmann three groups are left (see Bultmann, *Theologie*, 31–3) that might have a claim to being authentic utterances of Jesus: (a) the son of man must suffer many things (typical Marcan tradition: Mk. 8: 31; 9: 31; 10: 33–34; 14: 21; see 14: 41); he calls this group (along with the redactional Mk. 9: 9, 12) a Christian post-Easter reflection, not 'authentic Jesus-matter'; (b) centred on the activities of Jesus in his earthly life: seeking what is lost; as opposed to animals the son of man has no stone on which to lay his head, etc. (in Mark, in Q and in Luke: Mk. 2: 28; 8: 20 par. Lk. 9: 58; Lk. 7: 33–34 par. Mt. 11: 18–19; Lk. 11: 30 Q, Mt. 12: 40; Mk. 10: 45 par. Mt. 20: 28; Mt. 12: 32 par. Lk. 12: 10; Lk. 19: 10); the possibly authentic' instances among these (according to Conzelmann) are: Mt. 11: 18–19 par. Lk. 7: 33–34; also Lk. 11: 30 Q; general verdict is: post-Easter communal reflection; (c) finally: the coming son of man (in Mark – in Q – and in the source peculiar to Mark; and always in the third person: Mk. 13: 26 par. Mk. 14: 62; 10: 23; Mt. 16: 27; Lk. 17: 22ff; Lk. 17: 22; and lastly the central passage: Mk. 8: 38, and in Q: Lk. 1͞2: 8–9=Mt. 10: 32–33): all these (according to Conzelmann) assume situations relating to the Christian Church; also in the last Q passage, where the distinction between 'Jesus' and 'son of man' is not given, but points to two periods of activity by one and the same person: this logion too identifies Jesus with the son of man, as the context of the 'ecclesial *homology*' (Lk. 12: 8) in fact confirms (thus Conzelmann, *Grundriss*, 152–5; see also in RGG³, III, 630–2).
131. Maddox, *Methodenfrage*, 154.
132. M. Hooker, *Son of Man*, 7; F. Borsch, *The Son of Man*, 314; I. Marshall, *Son of Man Debate*, 66–87; Maddox, *Methodenfrage*, 155.
133. L. Ruppert, *Jesus, als der leidende Gerechte?* l.c., 64–71. Again, the passage in Daniel which speaks of somebody 'like a man' – Israel's celestial *archon* (see U. Müller, *Messias*, l.c., 19–30) – is set in the context of a presently suffering Israel very soon to be exalted. In other words: from the very outset the notion 'son of man' stands partly in the context of the theme of the exaltation of the suffering righteous one; see G. Nickelsburg, *Resurrection, immortality and eternal life in intertestamental Judaism*, (Harvard, Cambridge 1972), 76–8.
134. J. Becker, *Joh. der Täufer*, l.c., 27–38.
135. E. Gräszer, *Naherwartung*, l.c., 92, and his more ample study: *Das Problem der Parusieverzögerung in den synoptische Evangelien und in der Apostelgeschichte* (BZNW, 22) (Berlin (1957), 1960²) (cf. O. Cullmann's critique of

this, 'Parusieverzögerung und Urchristentum', in *Vorträge und Aufsätze 1925–1962* [ed. K. Fröhlich] (Tübingen-Zürich 1966), 427–44).

136. See the articles by J. Coppens, 'Le messianisme israélite. La relève prophétique', l.c., and 'La mission du Serviteur de Yahwé', l.c.; also J. Coppens, 'Nieuw licht over de Ebed-Jahweh-liederen', (Analecta Lovaniensia Biblica et Orientalia, Ser. 2, fasc. 15) (Louvain-Paris 1950), 3–16.

137. See A. Polag, *Zu den Stufen der Christologie in Q* (Studia Evang., IV-1) (Berlin 1968), 72–4, who sees pre-Easter material there. According to Schulz, *Q-Quelle*, 203–12, they come to the fore only in the second Q phase, but influenced by the independent (actually older) Marcan tradition (Mk. 3: 22).

138. R. Bultmann, *Theologie*, 35–9.

139. O. Cullmann, *Christologie*, 37; also R. Fuller, *Foundations*, l.c., 46–9.

140. Thus still in the recent little work by J. Ernst, *Anfänge der Christologie* (Stuttgart 1972), 53–4.

141. Cullmann, *Christologie*, 46; J. Blank, *Jesus von Nazareth*, devotes only a few lines – understandably so, given the design of his assemblage of individual articles – to Jesus as the eschatological prophet (79–80), but says none the less: 'Jesus carried out the function of the eschatological prophet' (80); H. W. Bartsch, *Jesus, Prophet und Messias aus Galiläa* (Frankfurt 1970), looks only for the precise reasons for Jesus' arrest and execution.

142. J. P. Audet, 'L'hypothèse des Testimonia', in RB 70 (1963), 381–405.

143. G. R. Driver, *The Judean Scrolls* (Oxford 1965); J. Fitzmyer, 'The use of explicit Old Testament quotations in Qumrân literature and the New Testament', in NTS 7 (1960–1), 297–333, and '4 Q Test and the New Testament', in ThSt 18 (1967), 513–22; J. de Waard, *A comparative study of the Old Testament text in the Dead Sea Scrolls and the New Testament* (Leyden 1965); especially R. Le Déaut, 'La présentation targumique du sacrifice d'Isaac et la sotériologie paulinienne', (Analecta Biblica, 17–18) (Rome 1963), vol. 2, 563–74; 'Les études targumiques', in ETL 44 (1968), 5–34; *Introduction à la littérature targumique* (Rome 1966), and 'Tradition juive ancienne et exégèse chrétienne', in RHPR 51 (1971), 31–51. See i.c.: G. Vermès, *The Dead Sea Scrolls in English* (Harmondsworth 1962).

144. Expectation of the world's end was a fitful but powerful phenomenon at that time (rather like the end of the world by means of hydrogen bombs and pollution of the environment in our time). To that certain great events contributed: the tyranny of Nero; the struggle centred around Galba, Otto, Vitellius and Vespasian; rebellion in Gaul (a. 68), in Germania (a. 69), in Judea (a. 66–70); earthquakes in Laodicea (a. 60), in Pompeii (a. 63); the eruption of Vesuvius (a. 79), etc. Also previously: ever since the Maccabean period (with the first flowering of apocalyptic) expectation of the end of the world had been growing, as with the Essenes – 1QpHab 2: 5 and 9: 6 and CD 4: 4 and 6: 11 – and with the Pharisees (Ps. Sal.; Josephus, *Antiquitates*, 17: 43ff). For Jews the divinizing emperor-cult in particular was intolerable, the beginning of 'the end'.

145. See M. Hengel, *Die Zeloten*, 240–2; J. Giblet, *Messie prophète*, 122.

146. Vermès, l.c., 244, Fitzmyer, in ThSt 513ff.

147. All the passages italicized are those which have been applied in the gospels literally to Jesus as the 'messenger from God' and in that way discover their first Christological implications.

148. Giblet, *Messie prophète*, 122–3.

149. According to Hahn, *Hoheitstitel*, 349 the *kyrios*-title is an amalgam of the Aramean '*mar*'-Christology, the Hellenistic *kyrios*-cult and the '*Kyrios ho Theos*' usage of the Jewish synagogue; this last title is obviously a term from the Greek synagogue (W. Kramer, *Christos, Kyrios Gottessohn* [AThANT, 44] (Zürich 1963), 157). The only question is what originally gave occasion for further assimilations.

150. Berger, *Amen-Worte*, 36–40.

151. Is not this exactly the same 'Jesus logion' as in the synoptics? Almost without exception the study of Jesus is wrongly restricted to the synoptics; why, since all the gospels are 'theology' as well as being at the same time recollection of Jesus' earthly life? Although the entire Johannine gospel is highly sapiential (this is not yet the same as what is later known as 'evincing a high Christology', where the synoptics are said to be marked by a 'low Christology'), it is in fact just an elaboration of the theme of the 'messenger of Wisdom', identified with the Wisdom of God, who sent him as a messenger.

152. Enoch, 41: 9; 42: 1–3; 48: 7; 51: 3; see Berger, *Zum traditionsgeschichtlichen Hintergrund*, l.c., 411.

153. Syr. Ap. Baruch, 3: 38–4: 1; cited by Berger, ibid., 412, footnote 2.

154. At the same time this makes it evident that the 'criterion of irreducibility' employed for this text is insufficient to establish as an authentic Jesus-saying the words: 'Why do you call me good?' The utterance fits in completely with the reactions of the 'messenger from God' in this complex of tradition – though there is a greater chance that the messenger himself (in this case, Jesus) said it than that the Church should so emphatically have put it into the mouth of Jesus.

155. Dan. 5: 1, 13; Testamentum Levi 2: 11; Test. Zabulon 9: 8; *Oracula Sibyllina*, 8: 318; see Berger, *Zum traditionsgeschichtlichen Hintergrund*, 419.

156. Berger: for Enoch, l.c., 414–15; for Moses: 416.

157. Th. Boman, *Die Jesus-Ueberlieferung*, 62–7.

158. See P. Stuhlmacher, *Das paulinische Evangelium*, 148–51.

159. R. Morgenthaler, *Statistik des neutestamentlichen Wortschatzes* (Zürich 1958), and: *Statistische Synopse* (Zürich 1971).

160. Berger, *Zum traditionsgeschichtlichen Hintergrund*, 391–2.

161. Stuhlmacher, ibid., 148–51; Berger, ibid., 393.

162. Berger, *Gesetzesauslegung*, 27–8.

163. Berger, *Zum traditionsgeschichtlichen Hintergrund*, 394.

164. R. Laurentin, *Structure et théologie de Luc, I-II* (Paris 1957).

165. The Samuelian christ-figure; in Ps.-Philo, *Liber Antiquitatum*, 59.

166. Steck, *Gewaltsames Geschick*, 196–212; Berger, *Zum traditionsgeschichtlichen Hintergrund*, 394.

167. See I. de la Potterie, 'L'onction du chrétien par la foi', in Bibl 40 (1959), 12–69; J. Ysebaert, *Greek Baptismal Terminology* (Nijmegen 1962); Berger,

*Zum traditionsgeschichtlichen Hintergrund*, l.c., 395–6.

168. Berger, *Gesetzesauslegung*, 27–8.

169. Berger, *Zum traditionsgeschichtlichen Hintergrund*, 396.

170. W. Kramer, *Christos*, l.c., 139.

171. Steck, *Gewaltsames Geschick*, 64–77.

172. Mt. 5: 11–12 par. Lk. 6: 22–23; Mt. 23: 29–36 par. Lk. 11: 47–51; Lk. 13: 31–33, 34–35 par. Mt. 23: 37–39; Lk. 11: 49ff. See later; on the death of Jesus.

173. See further on (significance of the death of Jesus). The eschatological pseudo-prophet or 'anti-Christ' was also a commonplace in the Judaism of Jesus' time. (Especially Apoc. Eliae).

174. 1 Thess. 1: 1, 3; Gal. 1: 1, 3; Rom. 1: 4; 15: 6; Phil. 1: 2; 2: 11; 1 Cor. 1: 9; 8: 6; Col. 1: 3; Eph. 1: 3; 1 Pet. 1: 3; 1 Thess. 1: 1–2; 1 Tim. 1: 2; 2 Tim. 1: 2; Philem. 3.

175. Berger, *Zum traditionsgeschichtlichen Hintergrund*, 422.

176. In the Test. Levi 17: 2–3 it is the high priest's privilege 'to address God as father': '*Lalèsei Theôi bōs Patri*'; see also in the renowned Graeco-Jewish romance of conversion, *Joseph and Asenath*, 12–13; cited in Berger, *Zum traditionsgeschichtlichen Hintergrund*, 423, n. 3.

177. Into the bosom of the Father, or of the fathers (e.g., 'into Abraham's bosom') (Lk. 16: 22) are *taken up* those who keep the commandments of the fathers and their teachings, and have faithfully handed them on. What it says in the Greek is: *eis ton kolpon*; after his death, as pre-existent Wisdom-and-messenger, Jesus is received (back) into the Father's bosom. The variant 'the only-begotten *Son*' is to be preferred to 'the only-begotten God'.

178. M. E. Boismard, ' "Dans le sein du Père" (Jo. 1: 18)', in RB59 (1952) 23–39.

179. See Ethiop. Enoch 48: 10; 52: 4; 4 Ezra 13: 1–13, 25; Strack-Billerbeck, I, 485–6 and 956–7, in which a messianic interpretation of Dan. 7: 13 comes into view. See Ph. Vielhauer, in *Aufsätze*, 175ff; Balz, *Methodische Probleme*, 48ff: especially U. Müller, *Messias und Menschensohn in jüdischen apokalypsen*, 107–53.

180. M. Hengel, 'Christologie und neutestamentliche Chronologie', in *Neues Testament und Geschichte* (Zürich-Tübingen 1972) (43–68), 46 and 62.

181. e.g.: 1 Cor. 15: 25; Rom. 8: 34 (cf. Col. 3: 1 and 1 Pet. 3: 22); Eph. 1: 20; Hebr. 1: 13; 1: 3; 8: 1; 10: 12–13; 12: 3; Mk. 16: 19 (in additional ending). In the synoptic tradition Ps. 110 is cited on the one hand in the question about the son of David (Mk. 12: 35–37 par. Mt. 21: 41–45; Lk. 20: 41–44) and, on the other, in the Passion narrative (son of man tradition) (Mk. 14: 62 par. Mt. 26: 64; Lk. 22: 69). Finally Acts 2: 34 and (implicitly) 5: 31 and Rev. 3: 21.

182. Two interpretations are current: (a) Jesus knew himself to be the Davidic messiah; (b) messianic-Davidic status, as applied to Jesus, is a piece of the Church's theology (Bultmann, *Tradition*, 146; Hahn, *Hoheitstitel*, 114). So far as the implication of Mk. 12: 35–37 is concerned, it has been expounded in three ways: (a) Jesus intends with this question (Ps. 110: 1) to silence his

opponents; (b) the question expects a positive answer: Jesus is indeed the messianic son of David (J. Jeremias and many others); (c) Mk. 12: 27 is a rhetorical question, to which a negative reply is expected: as David himself refers to the messiah as his Lord, then the messiah cannot be a son of David (W. Wrede; R. Gagg; M. Goguel; E. Haenchen and many others). A good survey of the exegetical state of affairs is provided by G. Schneider, 'Die Davidssohnfrage (Mk. 12: 35–37)', in Bibl 53 (1972) (65–90), 65–87.

183. Chr. Burger, *Jesus als Davidssohn* (Göttingen 1970), 52–9; G. Schneider, *Die Davidssohnfrage*, l.c., 83 and 89, n. 1.

184. See Strack-Billerbeck, IV, 452–65. See also Hahn, *Hoheitstitel*, 127, n. 1.

185. Thus e.g., Hahn, *Hoheitstitel*, 262; Ph. Vielhauer, in *Aufsätze*, 185; Chr. Burger, *Der Davidssohn*, 44.

186. Berger, 'Die königliche Messiastraditionen', 9.

187. l.c., 21.

188. On this issue F. Hahn, *Hoheitstitel*, 87–8 and 264 and Chr. Burger, *Der Davidssohn*, 46–52, are in my view certainly right.

189. *De bello Judaico*, 2: 261–8 (see above).

190. G. Schneider, *Die Davidssohnfrage*, l.c., 65–90; Kl. Berger, l.c., 31.

191. This is not at all 'unJewish', as Chr. Burger, *Der Davidssohn*, 50 and Hahn, *Hoheitstitel*, 264, maintain, but prophetic-sapiential, Graeco-Jewish; Kl. Berger, l.c., 31, n. 118, and G. Schneider, *Die Davidssohnfrage*, l.c., 88.

192. Berger, l.c., 33, n. 128.

193. *Literature*. H. Schlier, 'Zu Rom. 1: 3–4', in *Neues Testament und Geschichte* (O. Cullmann zum 70. Geburtstag) (Zürich-Tübingen 1972), 207–18; van Iersel, *Der Sohn*, 71–5; H. Flender, *Die Botschaft Jesu*, 19–22; H. W. Bartsch, 'Zur vorpaulinischen Bekenntnisformel im Eingang des Römerbriefes', in ThZ 23 (1967), 329–39; E. Linnemann, 'Tradition und Interpretation in Rom. 1: 3–4', in EvTh 31 (1971), 264–75; Chr. Burger, *Jesus als Davidssohn*, 25–35; Hahn, *Hoheitstitel*, 251–8; Kl. Berger, 'Die königlichen Messiastraditionen', l.c., 17.

194. 'Of the seed of David' does not of itself carry any messianic implication; it is not (as is commonly assumed) another version of 'son of David'. The term means simply: a Jewish male. See, for instance: 'He who keeps the Law is *of the seed of David*' (Ethiop. Apoc. Ezra; Kl. Berger, l.c., 17, n. 62). See Gal. 3: 16.

195. *'Horidzein'* not only has the meaning of 'being appointed' (as it is usually translated) but also of 'being legitimated', 'showing oneself as': then (with the resurrection) it becomes evident what Jesus *is*. This meaning occurs in contexts such as Rom. 1: 3–4. See Berger, l.c., 17.

196. According to Bultmann, *Theologie*, 52–3, this antithesis is an instance of Pauline editorializing; according to many other commentators it is actually pre-Pauline.

197. Schlier, l.c., in *Neues Testament und Geschichte*, 211–12.

198. The Jewish formula *'anastasis nekrôn'*, with the New Testament *'ek'* (see further on), points to a very ancient tradition.

199. H. Flender, *Die Botschaft Jesu*, l.c., 19–20.

200. Kl. Berger, 'Die königlichen Messiastraditionen', 33, n. 128; L. Ruppert, *Jesus, als der leidende Gerechte?* (the book's thesis); G. Nickelsburg, *Resurrection, Immortality and Eternal Life in Intertestamental Judaism* (Harvard, Cambridge 1972), especially 49–143.

201. See U. Wilckens, *Die Missionsreden der Apostelgeschichte* (Neukirchen 1963[2]); J. Dupont, *Études sur les Actes des Apôtres* (Paris 1962); D. Delling, 'Israels Geschichte und Jesusgeschehen nach Acta', in *Neues Testament und Geschichte* (Tübingen 1972), 189–98; H. Flender, *Die Botschaft Jesu*, l.c., 19–22; Chr. Burger, *Jesus als Davidssohn*, l.c., 137–45; Hahn, *Hoheitstitel*, 242–79.

PART THREE, *Section Two* (*pp.* 516–44)

1. O. Cullmann, *Immortalité de l'âme ou résurrection des morts?* (Neuchâtel-Paris 1956). For late Jewish ideas about life after death see in particular: H. Bardtke, 'Der Erweckungsgedanke in der exilischnachexilischen Literatur des Alten Testaments', in *Von Ugarit nach Qumran* (Festschrift for O. Eissfeldt) (Berlin 1961), 9–24; G. Friedrich, 'Die Auferweckung Jesu, eine Tat Gottes oder ein Interpretament der Jünger', in KuD 17 (1971), 170–9; M. Hengel, *Judentum und Hellenismus* (Tübingen 1973[2]), especially 357–69; P. Hoffmann, *Die Toten in Christus* (Münster 1966); R. Martin-Achard, *De la mort à la résurrection d'après l'Ancien Testament* (Neuchâtel-Paris 1956); G. Nickelsburg, *Resurrection, Immortality and Eternal Life* (Harvard, Cambridge 1972); J. Nelis, 'Het geloof in de verrijzenis in het oude testament', in TvT 10 (1970), 362–81; J. van der Ploeg, 'The belief in immortality in the writings of Qumrân', in *Bibliotheca Orientalis* 18 (1961), 118–24; K. Schubert, 'Die Entwicklung der Auferstehunglehre von der nachexilischen bis zur frührabbinischen Zeit', in BZ 6 (1962), 177–214; Strack-Billerbeck, IV, 1166–98; and II, 265–9; Kr. Stendahl (ed.), *Immortality and Resurrection* (New York 1965); P. Volz, *Die Eschatologie des jüdischen Gemeinde im neutestamentlichen Zeitalter* (Tübingen 1934).

2. L. Ruppert, *Jesus, als der leidende Gerechte?*, 54–5 and 69; Kl. Berger, 'Die königlichen Messiastraditionen des Neuen Testaments', in NTS 20 (1973–4), 1–45; G. Nickelsburg, *Resurrection*, l.c., 48–70.

3. According to Ruppert Wisdom is an 'updated' version or elaboration of Isa. 52–53; see also Nickelsburg, l.c., 62–6. Both works (Ruppert and Nickelsburg) were written independently of each other.

4. Nickelsburg, *Resurrection*, 68.

5. Nickelsburg, l.c., 70–8.

6. Nickelsburg, l.c., 81–2.

7. For this see in particular M. Hengel, *Judentum und Hellenismus* (Tübingen 1973[2]), 358–9; Nickelsburg, l.c., 82–7.

8. Especially Nickelsburg, l.c., 144–69.

9. Nickelsburg, l.c., 143.

10. Dan. 12: 2; Ethiop. Enoch 50: 1; 62: 15, 22 and 37–71; 4 Ezra 7: 29ff; Syr. Apoc. Baruch 30: 1–5; 50: 2–51: 3.

11. B. van Iersel, in Conc 6 (1970), n. 10, 53–65; P. Hoffmann, *Die Toten in Christus*, 180–5.

12. Even so, in the new edition of Bauer's *Wörterbuch* several instances are mentioned, 138–9.

13. Sir. 48: 5; Est. 4: 8; Job 5: 20; Prov. 10: 2; 23: 14, etc.

14. Judges 16: 14, 20; Gen. 28: 16; Deut. 18: 5. See Hahn, *Hoheitstitel*, 204; Delorme, in *Lectio Divina*, n. 72, 114–119, 124–125; C. Perrot, 'La descente du Christ aux enfers dans le Nouveau Testament', in LVie 87 (1968), 5–29; E. Fascher, 'Anastasis, Resurrectio, Auferstehung', in ZNW 40 (1941), 166–229; H. Oepke, in ThWNT, I, 368–72; II, 332–7; R. Schnackenburg, 'Zur Aussageweise "Jesus (von den Toten) auferstanden"', in BZ 13 (1969), 10–11; U. Wilckens, *Die Missionsreden*, l.c., 137–45; H. Braun, 'Zur Terminologie der Acta von der Auferstehung', in ThLZ 77 (1952), 533–6.

15. '*Egeirein ek nekrôn*': only of Jesus in the New Testament (Rom. 4: 24; 8: 11; 10: 9; Gal. 1: 1; 1 Thess. 1: 10; see Eph. 1: 20; Col. 1: 12); '*Egeiresthai ek nekrôn*': likewise only for Jesus (Rom. 6: 4, 9; 7: 4; 8: 34; 1 Cor. 15: 12, 20; (*anagein ek nekrôn* was already an old Septuagintal formula: 1 Cor. 2: 26; 28: 8, 11; Tob. 13: 2; Wis. 16: 13; Ps. 29: 3); '*anastasis nekrôn*', generally used in the New Testament for the universal resurrection, is applied once to Christ (Rom. 1: 4), whereas the general resurrection of the dead is twice called '*anastasis hè ek nekrôn*' (Lk. 20: 35 and Acts 4: 2). See Hoffmann, l.c., 182; Delorme, in *Lectio Divina*, n. 72, 114, n. 10; Wilckens, *Die Missionsreden*, 137–45. According to the admittedly plausible thesis of G. Kegel, *Auferstehung Jesu. Auferstehung der Toten* (Gütersloh 1970), the New Testament spoke initially of Jesus' resurrection *within* the horizon set by the Jewish expectation of the general resurrection, whereas later on (Luke's gospel and Acts mark the volte-face) the relationship is switched round the other way: starting from Jesus' resurrection the attempt is made to render the general resurrection intelligible to Greeks. The core of this fundamental change seems to me difficult to disclaim for the New Testament.

16. G. Kegel, *Auferstehung Jesus*, 24.

17. '*Anastasis nekrôn*' (Rom. 1: 4); '*anastasis*' (Phil. 3: 10), '*exanastasis*' (Phil. 3: 11), and '*egersis*' (Mt. 27: 53).

18. The '*egeirein*': Rom. 10: 9 (a pre-Pauline confession); Acts 3: 15; 4: 10; 5: 30; 10: 40; 13: 30, 37 (all places where traditional *kerygma* is discernible); 1 Thess. 1: 10; Rom. 4: 24; 1 Cor. 6: 14; 1 Cor. 15: 15; 2 Cor. 4: 4; 1 Pet. 1: 21; with '*anistanai*': Acts 2: 24, 32; 13: 34. Also 1 Thess. 4: 14 should be translated thus (not: 'risen', but 'raised', 'resuscitated'). God's action can be expressed, therefore, in the passive. 'Jesus has been raised' (that is, by God): Mk. 14: 28 par. Mt. 28: 7; Mk. 16: 6, 14; Mt. 16: 21 and Lk. 9: 22; Mt. 17: 23; 20: 19; 27: 63–64; Lk. 24: 34; Jn. 2: 22; 21: 14; Rom. 4: 25; 6: 4, 9; 7: 4; 8: 34; 1 Cor. 15: 4; 15: 12–13, 14, 16, 17, 20; 2 Cor. 5: 15; 2 Tim. 2: 8. The passive form is not to be found in Acts, which has a clear preference for the active form: God caused him to rise (*egeirein*), even so that '*anistanai*', as focused on Jesus (and coming from the tradition), is understood by Luke nevertheless as a 'raising up', not as a 'rising' (cf. Lk. 24: 7 and 24: 34; Acts 10: 41 with 10: 40; Acts 17: 3 with 17: 1; especially Acts 13: 23 and 13: 34 with 13: 30 and 13: 37).

19. Mk. 16: 6; Mt. 27: 64; 28: 6, 7; Lk. 24: 6, 34; Rom. 4: 25; 6: 4; 1 Cor. 15:

3–5; Rom. 6: 9; 7: 4; 8: 34; Jn. 21: 14.

20. *Anestèsen heauton* (Ignatius, *ad Smyrn.* 2).

21. Rom. 4: 24; 8: 11; 2 Cor. 4: 14; Gal. 1: 1; Eph. 1: 20; Col. 2: 12; 1 Pet. 1: 21. In the second blessing of the Jewish prayer '*Schmone Esre*' too there is a eulogy 'to God who makes the dead alive' (*mechayye hammatim*); it is a prayer which from the time of Gamaliel II the Jews were obliged to pray three times a day; based on older traditions, this second blessing was formulated only around AD 100 and in all likelihood it does not expressly refer to resurrection from the dead but to the Old Testament asseveration: 'with God everything is possible'.

22. See e.g., C. H. Dodd, *According to the Scriptures* (London 1961); E. Flesseman-van Leer, in *Zur Bedeutung des Todes Jesu*, l.c., 79–96; E. Fuchs, *Hermeneutik* (Bad Cannstadt 1958²), 21–210; P. Grelot, *Sens chrétien de l'Ancien Testament* (Paris 1962); A. Suhl, *Die Funktion der alttestamentlichen Zitate und Anspielungen im Mk.-Evangelium* (Gütersloh 1965); C. Westermann, 'Die Prophetenzitate in den neutestamentlichen Reden von der Zukunft', in EvTh 27 (1967), 307–17.

23. Mk. 8: 31; 9: 31; 10: 34; 14: 58; 15: 29; Mt. 16: 21; 17: 23; 20: 19; 12: 38–42; 26: 61; 27: 40; Lk. 9: 22; 18: 33; 11: 29–32; 13: 31–33; Jn. 18: 19.

24. Mk. 16: 2; Mt. 18: 1ff; Lk. 24: 1; Jn. 20: 1, 19. Or again: 'eight days later', the next first weekday (Lk. 24: 30–31; Jn. 20: 26).

25. Strack-Billerbeck, I, 1052–4.

26. *Hoheitstitel*, 197–211, 210.

27. Furthermore, the gospels are fairly discordant: 'after three days', 'within three days', 'after three days and three nights', 'the third day'. On a purely chronological basis this indeed entails different days. See Mt. 16: 21; 17: 23; 20: 19; Lk. 9: 22; 18: 33; Mk. 8: 31; 9: 31; 10: 34; 14: 58; 15: 29; Lk. 9: 22; 18: 33; 24: 7, (21), 46; Mt. 12: 40; see Lk. 11: 29–32; Mk. 8: 11–12; Mt. 12: 38–41; Mk. 14: 58; Mt. 26: 61; Mk. 15: 29; Mt. 27: 40; Jn. 2: 13–22. These variations would seem to relate to problems of the Septuagintal translation of the Hebrew text (see Gen. 42: 17ff; Ex. 19: 11–16; Esther 4: 16–5: 1; Hosea 6: 2 LXX).

28. See Part Two, Section Three, note 71.

29. Thus Kegel, *Auferstehung Jesu*, 27.

30. See also Mk. 8: 2; Mt. 15: 32; Lk. 24: 21; Ex. 15: 22; 2 Kings 2: 17; 2 Chron. 20: 25; Jonah 3: 3, etc.

31. To say nothing of yet other meanings of 'after three days', specifically for an uncommonly brief period, for which we should really use an immensely longer one. The Temple, which had taken forty-six years to build, Jesus will destroy in three days (in a minimum of time) and build it again (Jn. 2: 13–22). See also Josh. 1: 11; 2 Macc. 5: 14; Hosea 6: 2.

32. See *Biblisch-Historisches Handwörterbuch* (eds. B. Reicke and L. Rost) (Göttingen 1962), I (W. Schmauch).

33. The third day had nothing to do, therefore, with 'three days after Good Friday', on which the 'triduum paschale' is based. In the liturgy this historicizing is right and meaningful, but it should not lead us to forget the

deeper salvific import of the decisive turning-point.

34. In cave XI at Qumrân was found a Job-targum in Palestinian Aramaic, 'more or less in the language which Jesus spoke' (A. S. van der Woude, 'Das Hiobtargum aus Qumrân, Höhle XI', in VTS 1963 [322–31], 329). Thence arises the tendency among exegetes to assume rather more extensively the existence of written targums in Jesus' time. Now in those targums and midrashes there is extant a 'theology of the third day', especially apropos of the sacrifice of Abraham. See in particular R. le Déaut, 'La nuit paschale. Essai sur la signification de la pâque juive à partir du Targum d'Exode XII' 42 (Anal. Bibl., 22) (Rome 1963); and 'La présentation targumique du sacrifice d'Isaac et la sotériologie paulinienne', (Anal. Bibl., 17–18) (Rome 1963), II, 563–74. We are more and more coming to see clear affinities between certain Pauline and synoptic ideas and the Jewish targums, not least in connection with ideas about redemption.

35. In the midrash Rabbah on Gen. 22: 4 all events taking place 'on the third day' are brought together (H. Freedman – M. Simon, *Midrash Rabba*, I, (London 1939), 491); including the eschatological resurrection with reference to Hosea 6: 2 (Septuagint).

36. *Tradition*, 19; W. Popkes, *Christus Traditus*, 232; C. Colpe, in ThWNT VIII, 447–8.

37. L. Ruppert, *Jesus, als der leidende Gerechte?*, 63–4 and 75; K. Lehmann, *Am dritten Tag*, 236.

38. According to Ruppert, l.c., 71, this way of envisaging suffering (his Passion) must have been the matrix of Jesus' self-understanding as the 'suffering *son of man*'. I am not at all convinced about that; it says in precise detail what Jesus (none the less sure that God has the final word) leaves open, in reliance on God's future.

39. 1 Pet. 1: 21; Rom. 8: 34; Eph. 1: 19–21; 1 Pet. 3: 21–22; and Rom. 1: 4, where the '*ek*' implies 'by virtue of', as well as 'from the moment of', the resurrection. Resurrection and 'being Lord' are then completely identical (Rom. 10: 9). Paul himself associates the title '*Kyrios*' with the resurrection (2 Cor. 4: 14; Rom. 1: 4; 4: 24, etc.). The resurrection *is* the exaltation.

40. Lohfink, *Himmelfahrt*, 81–98. In 1 Pet. 1: 20–21; 3: 18–19, 21–22 resurrection and exaltation (in the setting of an emerging 'cosmic Christology') are placed side by side, without their unity being entirely obvious: '*thanatōtheis, dzōöpoiètheis, poreutheis*'; this relates not to the 'rapture' model, but to the ancient model of the 'celestial journey'; the risen one makes a journey to heaven and in so doing traverses all the celestial spheres (*katabasis-anabasis* model).

41. 'Heaven must receive him until the time of the restoration (*apokatastasis*) of all things' (Acts 3: 21) has to be assessed on its own. Jesus has been taken up to God and is being held ready in heaven in expectation of the final events; only then will God 'send' him to bring refreshment to the faithful. There is no allusion whatever here to what is known as 'perhaps the oldest Christology'. Along with others U. Wilckens, *Die Missionsreden*, l.c., 153–6, has shown convincingly that here Luke has adopted a piece of tradition from a

late Jewish speculation about Elijah (current in circles connected with John
the Baptist) and has Christianized it (as he had done elsewhere: Zechariah's
'Benedictus' in the infancy narrative). The terminology is peculiar to these
Elijah-speculations; see Mal. 3: 23–24 (see also Mk. 12: 12). See also Cullmann, *Christologie*, 22–8; Strack-Billerbeck, IV, 764ff; 792ff; 787–9; Sirach
(Ecclesiasticus 48: 10 LXX. See above: Part Two, Section Three, note
60 (works by G. Haufe and U. Müller).

42. In late Judaism also the Messiah can pray for God's Spirit, but not give
it (E. Schweizer, in ThWNT VI, 382; see also Strack-Billerbeck, I, 495).

43. See Part Three, above: 'Wisdom' Christologies.

44. See Schrenk, in ThWNT II, 218; E. Schweizer, *Erniedrigung*, 164, n.
273; Delorme, in *Lectio Divina*, n. 72, 135.

45. *On this point*, at any rate, E. Schweizer, *Erniedrigung*, 21–52 – as L. Ruppert, *Jesus, als der leidende Gerechte?*, 26–8, has shown – is undoubtedly right. See
also Delorme, in *Lectio Divina*, n. 72, 136–9. See 1 Sam. 2: 4–9; Ps. 27: 2, 5;
75: 8–11; Job 5: 11–16; Isa. 52: 13–53, where the reference is in fact not to
the suffering but to the exalted servant of God (52: 13); Wis. 2: 12–20 and
5: 1–7.

46. L. Cerfaux, 'L'hymne au Christ-Serviteur de Dieu', in *Miscellanea historica*
(in honorem A. de Meyer) (Louvain 1946), vol. 1, 117–30; J. T. Sanders, *The
New Testament Christological Hymns* (Cambridge 1971), 59.

47. J. Sanders, *Christological Hymns*, 60.

48. See above: Part Three, Section One, at 'the son of man' and Part Three,
Section Two, §1. Also E. Schweizer, *Erniedrigung*, 30; L. Ruppert, *Jesus,
als der leidende Gerechte?*, 70; and recently: G. Nickelsburg, *Resurrection*, 77–8.

49. J. Sanders, *Christological Hymns*, 62. See especially Wis. 2: 12–20 with
5: 1–7.

50. Mt. 23: 12; Lk. 14: 11; 18: 14; Jas. 1: 12; 4: 10; 1 Pet. 4: 13–14; 5: 6–10.

51. Berger, *Amen-Worte*, 56. Hahn, *Hoheitstitel*, 130, and G. Lohfink,
*Himmelfahrt*, 96, n. 42, and 'Die Auferstehung und die historische Kritik', in
BuL 9 (1968) 37–53, rightly deny that the exaltation-motif must be older than
that of the resurrection. It would be wrong to infer from that, however, that
the exaltation-motif derived from the resurrection one. Both are very old
(Marxsen, *Die Auferstehung von Jesus von Nazareth*, 147ff). That it is secon-
dary, i.e., deduced from the resurrection (thus: Schulz, *Q-Quelle*, 74;
Vielhauer, in *Aufsätze*, 173–5) is by no means proven. See also U. Wilckens,
*Auferstehung*, 132–44 and G. Bertram, sub *Erhöhung*, in RAC VI, 22–43; W.
Thüsing, *Erhöhungsvorstellung*, l.c. (1967), 216–19 and (1968), 226–8; and Tödt,
*Menschensohn*, 228–57. Vielhauer is certainly correct when he argues that the
traditions which include the appearances identify resurrection and exalta-
tion. What is more, Weeden has shown that the original Marcan gospel,
which knows nothing of Jesus appearances, links the exaltation to the
Parousia and not to the resurrection. Yet the idea of exaltation in no way presupposes, as Hahn asserts (*Hoheitstitel*, 113–15 and 126–32), a delayed
Parousia (rightly against this, Vielhauer, in *Aufsätze*, 164).

52. See above in this Part, first credal model. Weeden, *Mark-traditions*, 126ff.

53. Echoes of a similar idea are to be found in Acts 3: 20, 21a; Mt. 25: 1–13; Phil. 2: 10–11; Col. 1: 15–20 and 1 Pet. 3: 19, 22. See also R. Fuller, *Foundations*, 145ff and 185–6; G. Schille, *Anfänge*, 125ff.

54. Thüsing, *Erhöhungsvorstellung* (article), 228.

55. Recollections of this near enough 'quasi-identity' between resurrection and Parousia are to be found in a few remarkable texts: 'There are some standing here who will not taste death before they see the kingdom of God come with power' (Mk. 9: 1; Lk. 9: 27). So too Jn. 21: 18–23; 1 Thess. 4: 15.

56. Schulz, *Q-Quelle*, 75.

57. That it is not the eschatologically 'coming One', but the son of man already enthroned in heaven which constitutes the oldest motif, as Balz maintains in *Methodische Probleme*, 106, therefore seems to me unjustifiable.

58. e.g., 1 Thess. 1: 10; 5: 9; Rom. 5: 9–10; 10: 9, 13; 1 Cor. 3: 15; 5: 5; 1 Pet. 1: 5; Mk. 13: 1, 3, 20 par. Mt. 10: 22; Mk. 16: 16.

59. Lk. 1: 69, 71, 77; 19: 9, and Acts 13: 26; 16: 17; Lk. 8: 12, 36–50; 19: 10, and Acts 2: 47; 11: 14; 14: 9; 15: 1, 11; 16: 30–31.

60. J. H. Wilson, 'The Corinthians who say There is no resurrection of the dead', in ZNW 59 (1968), 90–107; R. Pesch, 'Heilszukunft und Zukunft des Heils', in *Gestalt und Anspruch des Neuen Testaments* (ed. G. Schreiner) (Würzburg 1969), 313–29; H. A. Wilcke, *Das Problem eines messianischen Zwischenreiches bei Paulus* (Zürich 1967), 60–2; G. Kegel, *Auferstehung Jesu*, 38–47.

61. G. Fohrer, 'Das Alte Testament und des Thema "Christologie" ', in EvTh 30 (1970), 281–98.

62. For those still living Paul no longer speaks of their being 'caught up' to meet Jesus, as in 1 Thess. 4: 17, but of a 'transformation' of the body (1 Cor. 15: 51). The resurrection is not something apocalyptical, but a salvific event in itself; a resurrection-in-glory.

PART THREE, *Section Three and Section Four* (*pp.* 545–71)

1. See above in this Part Three.

2. e.g., W. Grundmann, 'Die Frage nach der Gottessohnschaft des Messias im Lichte von Qumrân', in *Bibel und Qumrân* (Festschrift for H. Bardtke) (Berlin 1968), 86–111; P. Pokorný, *Der Gottessohn* (Zürich 1971), 23.

3. See above.

4. Fr. Lentzen-Deis, *Die Taufe Jesu nach den Synoptikern* (Frankfurt 1970), 288.

5. *Literature. Jungfrauenbeburt. Gestern und heute* (eds. H. Borsch and J. Hasenfuss) (Essen 1969); R. E. Brown, 'The problem of the virginal conception of Jesus', in ThS 33 (1972), 3–34; G. Delling, sub *parthenos*, in ThWNT V, 824–35; A. George, 'Jésus Fils de Dieu dans l'évangile selon saint Luc', in RB 72 (1965), 185–209, and 'Le parallèle entre Jean-Baptiste et Jésus en Lc. 1–2', in *Mélanges Bibliques* (hommage au R. P. B. Rigaux) (Gembloux 1970), 147–71; F. Neyrinck, 'Maria bewaarde al de woorden in haar hart (Lc. 2: 19, 51)', in CollBrugGand 5 (1959), 433–66; W. Pannenberg, *Das Glaubenbekenntnis* (Hamburg 1972), 78–85; R. Pesch, 'Eine alttestamentliche

Ausführungsformel im Mt.-Evangelium', in BZ 10 (1966), 220–45 and 11 (1967), 79–97, and 'Der Gottessohn in matthäischen Evangelienprolog (Mt. 1–2)', in Bibl 48 (1967), 345–420; J. Riedl, *Die Vorgeschichte Jesu* (Stuttgart 1968); G. Schneider, 'Jesu geistgewirkte Empfängnis (Lk. 1: 34–35)', in ThPQ 119 (1971), 105–16; H. Schürmann, 'Aufbau, Eingenart und Geschichtswert der Vorgeschichte von Lk. 1–2', in BuK 21 (1966), 106–11; A. Vögtle, 'Das Schickal des Messiaskindes. Zur Auslegung und Theologie von Mt. 2', in BuL 6 (1965), 249–67; *Messias und Gottessohn* (Düsseldorf 1971), and 'Offene Fragen zur Lukanischen Geburts-und Kindheitsgeschichte', in BuL 11 (1970); now in *Das Evangelium und die Evangelien* (Düsseldorf 1971), 43–56; see also 57–102.

6. Especially 19: 1–3 (Hennecke, I, 277–90).

7. Pannenberg's line of argument, l.c. 78–85, ignores completely what Form criticism has shown to be the tradition of the Virgin Birth *inherited by Luke*; where Scripture is concerned his conclusion is correct, but not his reasoning.

8. G. Schneider, *Jesu Empfängnis*, l.c., 113–14.

9. In particular, Philo, *De Cherubim*, 40–52. See also above (Part Three, messianic son of David), where we say that in late Judaism too the idea of a virgin birth of the messiah was probably already current among Greek-speaking Jews.

10. R. Pesch, *Der Gottessohn*, l.c., 414.

11. See above in this Part Three.

11b. I have been unable on this occasion to consult the study by R. G. Hammerton-Kelly, *Pre-existence, Wisdom and the Son of Man* (Cambridge 1973), which apparently defends the *ontological* dimension of the Jewish pre-existence.

12. Origen, *Contra Celsum*, 1: 26 and 8: 12; 4: 3.

13. For the significance of Greek thought in patristics see P. de Labriolle, *La réaction païenne. Étude sur la polémique anti-chrétienne du Ie au VIe siècle* (Paris 1942[2]); M. Wiles, *The Making of Christian Doctrine* (Cambridge 1967); G. L. Prestige, *God in Patristic Thought* (London 1956), and *Fathers and heretics* (London 1968); J. Lebreton, *Histoire du dogme de la trinité*, 2 vols (Paris 1927); Ph. Merlan, *Greek Philosophy from Plato to Plotinus* (Cambridge 1967); J. E. Pollard, *Johannine Christology and the Early Church* (Cambridge 1970); J. Daniélou, *Théologie du judéo-christianisme* (Paris 1958), and *Message évangélique et culture hellénistique aux IIe et IIIe siècles* (Tournai 1961); W. Pannenberg, 'Die Aufnahme des philosophischen Gottesbegriffes als dogmatisches Problem der frühchristlichen Theologie', in *Grundfragen systematischer Theologie* (Göttingen 1967), 296–346; W. Bauer, *Rechtgläubigkeit und Ketzerei im ältesten Christentum* (Tübingen 1963[2]).

14. Origen, *Contra Celsum*, 4: 5; 4: 14–15.

15. See especially W. Jäger, *Paideia*, 3 vols (Berlin 1934, 1944 and 1947); M. Pohlenz, *Der hellenistische Mensch* (Göttingen 1947), and *Die Stoa* (Göttingen 1964[3]); D. Nestlé, *Eleutheria*, I (Tübingen 1967); A. Festugière, *L'Idéal religieux des Grecs et l'évangile* (Paris 1932[2]); *L'Enfant d'Agrigente* (Paris

1950²), and his standard work *La Révélation d'Hermès Trismégiste*, 4 vols (Paris 1944–54); see also H. Marrou, *Histoire de l'éducation dans l'antiquité* (Paris 1948), and U. v. Wilamowitz-Moellendorf, *Der Glaube der Hellenen*, 3 vols (Darmstadt 1959³).

16. P. Stockmeier, *Glaube und Religion in der frühen Kirche* (Freiburg 1972), 137, n. 17. Also Festugière, *L'Idéal religieux*, 56.

17. *Fundamental literature.* W. Jäger, *Das frühe Christentum und die griechische Bildung* (Berlin 1963); H. Niederstraszer, *Kerygma und Paideia* (Stuttgart 1967); S. Otto, '*Natura*' *und* '*dispositio*' (Munich 1960); G. Greshake, *Gnade als konkrete Freiheit. Eine Untersuchung zur Gnadenlehre des Pelagius* (Mainz 1972); P. Stockmeier, 'Glaube und Paideia', in ThQ 147 (1967), 432–52, and *Glaube und Religion in der frühen Kirche* (Freiburg 1973); A. Heitmann, *Imitatio Dei* (Rome 1940); P. Schwanz, *Imago Dei* (Halle 1970); M. Lot-Borodine, *La déification de l'homme selon les doctrines des Pères Grecs* (Paris 1970); J. Meyendorff, *Le Christ dans la théologie byzantine* (Paris 1969). Finally, the by now outdated but still informative book J. Gross, *La divinisation du chrétien d'après les Pères Grecs* (Paris 1938).

18. e.g., Cyril of Alexandria, *Thesaurus*, Ass. 1; Irenaeus, *Adv. Haer.* 5, pref.; Athanasius, *De incarnatione*, 54, etc. This patristic principle is based on two Greek premises: (a) the reprieve or pardon is envisaged as a '*theopoièsis*', in the sense of '*homoiôsis Theou*', and (b) '*quod non est assumptum, non est sanatum*', that which has not been subsumed within Jesus' human nature is also not redeemed. This last principle in particular is based on the Greek realism of the '*universalia*': in the '*natura humana*' of Jesus all human beings are included *qua* physical reality, almost (something we can hardly 'experience' now). Fundamentally, therefore, all human beings are already redeemed through the contact of the human nature with the divine nature in Christ. It has more to do with 'human nature' than with the human individual. Yet albeit with the aid of this Greek model, the Greek Fathers do intend to express the biblical idea of the 'vicarious' action of Jesus. The deifying on a basis of Jesus' being-as-man is still something Greek: that is, a coming through *knowledge* to the invisible Father, as Athanasius makes explicit in the celebrated adage (*De incarnatione*, 54): in the man Jesus the 'divine paradigm' becomes *visible* in a human, imitable form. In other words, Christ is an 'exemplar'; his life was a living-in-advance of what we have to 'imitate'. From an anthropological standpoint this does indeed serve to 'demythologize' the 'divinizing process'. It is in fact a 'humanizing' on a divine model: sanctity.

19. Fr. Ricken, 'Das Homoousios von Nikaia als Krisis des altchristlichen Platonismus', in H. Schlier *et al.*, *Zur Frühgeschichte der Christologie* (Quaest. Disp., 51) (Freiburg 1970), 74–99; see also H.-J. Vogt, 'Politische Erfahrung als Quelle des Gottesbildes bei Kaiser Konstantin d. Gr.', in *Dogma und Politik* (Mainz 1973), 35–61.

20. Wiles, *The Making*, l.c., 41–61.

21. Ricken, *Das Homoousios*, l.c., seems to me right in the end result, but wrong in attributing this 'breakthrough' of middle Platonism purely to

'theological cogitation'. This breakthrough in thinking was at the same time a reflecting upon a concrete experience of piety and devotion; see Wiles, *The Making*, l.c., 62–93; J. Lebreton, 'Le désaccord de la foi populaire et de la théologie savante dans l'église chrétienne du IIIe siècle', in RHE 19 (1923), 481–506 and 20 (1924), 5–37. Discrepancy between the Church's teaching and the belief of its members is as old as the Church itself.

22. A similar instance occurred with the definition of the Roman Catholic dogma of Mary's immaculate conception. Against all the resistance put up by the theologians this piece of popular piety persisted until under the pressure it exerted Scotus found a theological concept capable of reconciling it with the theological affirmation of *universal* sinfulness (namely, salvation 'by prevention' or indemnification from sin). Only then did academic theology kowtow.

23. See A. Schindler, 'Gnade und Freiheit. Zum Vergleich zwischen den griechischen und lateinischen Kirchenvätern', in ZThK 62 (1965), 178–95; N. Brox, 'Soteria und Salus', in EvTh 33 (1973), 253–79; J. Plagnieux, *Heil und Heiland. Dogmengeschichtliche Texte und Studien* (Paris 1969); R. Haubst, 'Anselms Satisfaktionslehre einst und heute', in TrThZ 80 (1971), 88–109; Greshake, *Gnade als konkrete Freiheit*, 193–274.

24. *Cur Deus homo?*, II, 20. Elsewhere: *'Oportet ut, si idem genus (humanum) resurgit post casum, per se resurgat'* (l.c., II, 8). The Latin way of seeing redemption as a restoration of the contravened legal order had a twofold consequence: (a) on the one hand it sharpened the distinction between 'justification' and 'sanctification' to a greater extent than did the more dynamic Greek-patristic idea of redemption, based on a progressive process of liberation; and (b) it sharpened also the distinction between 'objective' and 'subjective redemption': in and through Jesus Christ the order of law and justice is indeed restored; but the individual freedom of each person, thanks to the merits of Jesus, must now be squared with the concrete 'I' and 'put things in good order'. Nor must any person's individual freedom be overridden by the saving work of Christ: each one must, in the power of Jesus' merits, stand on his own feet and 'introduce' himself into the just order of things.

25. See M. D. Chenu, *La théologie au douzième siècle* (Paris 1957). In Greek patristics Jesus' humanity was much more an *'organon'* or *'instrumentum Deitatis'*; God was the active subject. Without denying that, Western soteriology puts the stress on man as the active centre of instrumentality in the redemptive process.

26. See the well-known survey in A. Grillmeier and H. Bacht, *Das Konzil von Chalkedon*, 3 vols (Würzburg 1951–4) (1959², 1962³); also J. Liébaert, *Handbuch der Dogmengeschichte*, III-1a (Freiburg 1965); P. Smulders, 'Dogmengeschichtliche und lehramtliche Entfaltung der Christologie', in *Mysterium Salutis* (eds J. Feiner and M. Löhrer) vol. III-1, (Einsiedeln 1970), 389–476.

27. 'Verbum caro factum est, i.e. homo, quasi (=ita ut) ipsum Verbum *personaliter* sit *homo*' (*Q.D. de unione Verbi Incarnati*, a.l.). St Augustine said: 'Nec sic assumptus est ut prius creatus post assumeretur, sed ut ipsa assump-

tione crearetur' (*Contra sermonem Arianorum*, 8, 6: 'ipsa assumptione creatur'). 28. 'Hypostasis enim Verbi Dei in quantum est hic homo, per naturam humanam hanc constituitur . . . Quod est dicere personam Verbi constitui in hoc quod est esse *personam humanam*; hic enim homo *personam humanam* significat' (Cajetanus, *In III partem Summae Theologiae*, q. 2, a. 5, n. II, ed. Leonina, p. 35 A-B). These niceties, then, are meant on the one hand to deny 'two persons' in Jesus and on the other to affirm as well the reality of Jesus' human personalism, albeit by virtue of the divine person *and on the basis of* his humanity (human nature). Actually Cajetanus no more than Scotus wants to speak of any deprivation of human being; both accept the human personalism of Jesus; they differ only on the definition of what precisely constitutes a person a person. Thomas had said: 'non minuit sed auget' (*Summa Theologiae*, III, q. 2, a. 5, ad 1).

PART FOUR (*pp.* 573–674)

1. See e.g., F. Braudel, *Écrits sur l'histoire* (Paris 1969); F. Furet, 'Histoire quantitative et la construction du fait historique', in *Annales d'Economie, Société et Civilisation* (1971) (Jan. – Feb.); P. Chaunu, 'L'histoire sérielle. Bilan et perspectives', in *Revue Historique* (1970) (April – June).
2. This terminology frequently used, for instance, by K. Rahner and J.-B. Metz has been analysed by B. Welte, 'Die Lehrformel von Nikaia und die Abendländische Metaphysik', in *Zur Frühgeschichte der Christologie* (Quaest. Disp., 51) (Freiburg 1970), 100–17; see also E. Schillebeeckx, 'Het onfeilbare ambt in de kerk', in Conc 9 (1973), n. 3 (86–107), especially 91–8; G. Vass, 'On the historical structure of Christian truth', in *The Heythrop Journal* 9 (1968), 129–42 and 274–89.
3. See especially Thomas S. Kuhn, *Die Struktur wissenschaftlicher Revolutionen* (Theorie, 2) (Frankfurt 1967) (from the English, 1962).
4. Schillebeeckx, *Geloofsverstaan: interpretatie en kritiek* (Bloemendaal 1972), 37–9.
4a. Newly published analyses of the 'epochal intellective horizon': B. Welte, 'Die Krisis der dogmatischen Christusaussagen', in *Die Frage nach Jesu* (ed. A. Paus) (Graz-Cologne 1973), 151–80, and N. Lash, *Change in Focus* (London 1973).
5. See e.g., K. Aner, *Die Theologie der Lessingzeit* (Hildesheim 1964²) (Tübingen 1929); W. Lepenies and H. Nolte, *Kritik der Anthropologie* (Reihe Hanser, 61) (Munich 1971); O. Macquard, 'Wie irrational kann Geschichtsphilosophie sein?', in PhJ 79 (1972), 241–53; W. Oelmüller, *Was ist heute Aufklärung?* (Düsseldorf 1972); W. Oelmüller (ed.), *Fortschritt wohin?* (Düsseldorf 1972); M. Riedel, *Rehabilitierung der praktischen Philosophie, I. Geschichte, Probleme, Aufgaben* (Freiburg i. Br. 1972); D. Schellong, 'Lessings Frage an die Theologie', in EvTh 30 (1970), 418–32; H. Scholz, 'Zufällige Geschichts- und notwendige Vernunftwahrheiten', in *Harnack-Ehrung. Beiträge zur Kirchengeschichte* (Leipzig 1921), 377–93; R. Schwarz, 'Lessings "Spinozismus" ' in

ZThK 65 (1968), 271–90; R. Slenczka, *Geschichtlichkeit und Personsein Jesu Christi* (Göttingen 1967).

6. 'Zufällige Geschichtswahrheiten können der Beweis von notwendigen Vernunftwahrheiten nie werden' (*Lessings Werke*, ed. J. Pedersen and W. von Olshausen (Berlin-Leipzig 1924), vol. 23, 47).

7. Lessing, ibid., vol. 23, 49.

8. l.c., 49ff.

9. *Kants Werke* (ed. W. Weischedel) (Darmstadt 1956–64), vol. 7 (title).

10. See P. Carnley, 'The poverty of historical scepticism', in *Christ, Faith, History*, 165–90.

11. Thus, rightly, P. Carnley, l.c., 171ff.

12. C. Geertz, 'Religion as a cultural system', cited by W. Dupré, 'Wat is religie?', in *Toekomst van de religie: Religie van de toekomst?* (Bruges-Utrecht 1972), 17.

13. See literature under note 5, especially W. Oelmüller; in addition N. Luhmann, *Soziologische Aufklärung* (Cologne-Opladen 1970), 85; see also J. Habermas, *Erkenntnis und Interesse* (Frankfurt 1968), 344.

14. K. Löwith, *Weltgeschichte und Heilsgeschichte* (Stuttgart 1953³), 38–54.

15. Mt. 10: 42; 11: 11; 18: 6–10. See ThWNT IV, 650–61. In the gospels the meanest and the least are themselves already identified with the Christians. See e.g., Berger, *Amen-Worte*, 41, p. 38, and 41–6.

16. *Lumen Gentium*, n. 1.

17. In TvT 6 (1966), 255–6.

18. Schoonenberg speaks of 'human transcendence' and of 'transcendent humanity' in *Geloof bij kenterend getij*, 180–1 and 177–8; see Schillebeeckx, in TvT 6 (1966), 276–7.

19. l.c., 188–98.

20. TvT 6 (1966), 255.

21. l.c., 270.

22. *Geloof bij kenterend getij*, 179–80.

23. l.c., 180. The same in TvT 12 (1972), 313–14.

24. TvT 12 (1972), 318.

25. Thus the problem as sharply stated by S. W. Sykes, 'Theology of the humanity of Christ', in *Christ, Faith, History*, 53–72.

26. l.c., 54–5.

27. See J. A. T. Robinson, in *Christ, Faith, History*, 39–52; and then Th. Lorenzmeier, 'Wider das Dogma von der Sündlosigkeit Jesu', in EvTh 31 (1971), 452–71; H. Gollwitzer, 'Zur Frage der Sündlosigkeit Jesu', in EvTh 31 (1971), 496–506; Pannenberg, *Grundzüge*, 368–78; A. Durand, 'La liberté du Christ dans son rapport à l'impeccabilité', in NRTh (1948), 811–22.

28. Thus J. Robinson: 'He was fallible, but when the sticking point came *he did not fail*', in *Christ, Faith, History*, 75.

29. Chr. Duquoc, *Christologie*, II. *Le Messie*, 350–1.

30. J. Robinson, in *Christ, Faith, History*, 48.

31. Thus, rightly, P. Schoonenberg, in *Geloof bij kenterend getij*, l.c., 178.

32. See W. Dupré, 'Wat is religie?', in *Toekomst van de religie: Religie van de*

*toekomst* (Bruges-Utrecht 1972) (9–27); this H. Fortmann has also demonstrated in his numerous works; see P. A. van Gennip, *Het verminkte midden* (Bilthoven 1972).

33. According to J. Habermas failure to keep the great religious traditions in remembrance almost inevitably leads to a decay or collapse 'of the fundamental strata of assured identity' *'der fundamentalen Schichten der Identitätssicherung'* (*Philosophisch-politische Profile* (Frankfurt 1971), 35); in similar vein L. Kolakowski, 'Der Anspruch auf die selbstverschuldete Unmündigkeit', in *Vom Sinn der Tradition* (Munich 1970), 1–18.

34. See also J. Weima, *Wat willen we met de toekomst doen?* (Bilthoven 1972); E. Schillebeeckx, 'Naar een "definitieve toekomst": belofte en menselijke bemiddeling', in *Toekomst van de religie: Religie van de toekomst*, l.c., (37–55).

35. In *Christ, Faith, History*, 31–2.

36. P. Ricoeur, *Histoire et vérité* (Paris 1955), ed. 3, undated, 66–80; 'Histoire de la philosophie et historicité'.

37. See the discussion between I. Berten and W. Pannenberg, in I. Berten, *Histoire, révélation et foi* (Brussels 1969), 107–8.

38. Ricoeur, l.c., 69.

39. l.c.

40. 'Une autre façon d'avoir du sens' (Ricoeur, l.c., 70–1).

41. e.g., F. Fanon, *Damnés de la terre* (Paris 1968); R. Jaulin, *La paix blanche* (Paris 1970); N. Wachtel, *La vision des vaincus: les Indiens du Pérou devant la conquête espagnole 1536–1570* (Paris 1967).

42. Emm. Lévinas, 'La philosophie et l'idée de l'infini', in RMM 62 (1957), 241–53; 'Liberté de commandement', in RMM 58 (1953), 264–73.

43. Ricoeur, l.c., 77.

44. l.c., 79.

45. See *Geloofsverstaan: interpretatie en kritiek* (Theol. Peilingen, n. 5) (Bloemendaal 1972), 211–16, especially 214.

46. What in particular brought me to state explicitly the implications of my own essay was an article by W. Pannenberg, 'The nature of a theological statement', in *Zygon* 7 (1972), 6–19.

47. E. Schillebeeckx, 'Naar een "definitieve toekomst": belofte en menselijke bemiddeling', in *Toekomst van de religie: Religie van de toekomst?* (Bruges 1972), especially 48–53; and the well-known memoria-articles by J. B. Metz, in particular 'Toekomst vanuit de herinnering aan het lijden', in Con 8 (1972), n. 6, 5–21.

48. Sharply formulated by W. Kasper, *Einführung in den Glauben* (Mainz 1972), in these terms: '. . . eine Grösze . . . welche das Ganze umgreift und eint, ohne es zu vergewaltigen' (110).

49. See Peter R. Baelz, 'A deliberate mistake?', in *Christ, Faith, History*, 13–34; cf. Sch. Ogden, *The Reality of God and other essays* (London 1957), ch. 6, 164–87.

50. L. Lavelle, 'La voie étroite', in TPh 13 (1951) (42–61), 54.

51. E. Schillebeeckx, 'Stilte gevuld met parabels', in *Politiek of mystiek?* (Bruges-Utrecht 1973), 69–81.

52. E. Lévinas, *Totalité et Infini* (The Hague 1961); see also *Het menselijk gelaat* (Utrecht 1969).

53. An apt expression on the part of J. B. Metz, 'Erlösung und Emanzipation', in StdZ (1973) (171–84), 182.

54. J. Moltmann, *Der gekreuzigte Gott* (Munich 1972).

55. Thus P. Schoonenberg, in TvT 12 (1972), 313–14.

56. In a historical context it is not just a matter of a 'unio *in* hypostasi' but also – and formally – of a 'unio *secundum* hypostasin', that is to say, as Thomas so well expresses the tradition: 'unio in persona secundum rationem personae' (*Q.D. de unione Verbi Incarnati*, a.l. ad 8), that is, so that the divine person does really exercise the function of the man Jesus *qua* person.

57. Thomas actually calls this openness a 'capacitas ad unionem hypostaticam' (*Summa Theologiae*, III, q. 6, a. 4, ad 3).

58. We see Thomas wrestling with this problem: formally, according to him, the divine persons are not at all distinct *as* persons, but as 'relationes', that is, in origin antithetical relations (*Q.D. de potentia*, q. 9, a. 4); elsewhere he says: 'distinctio divinarum hypostasum est *minina distinctio realis quae possit esse*' (*In I Sent.* d. 26, q. 2, a. 2, ad 2; *De potentia*, q. 9, a. 5, ad 2; *Contra Gentiles*, IV, 14; *Summa Theologiae*, I, q. 40, a. 2, ad 3). Thomas obviously wants to secure monotheism against any form of tritheism.

59. E. Haulotte, 'Lisibilité des "Ecritures" ', in *Langages* 6 (1971), 103.

60. For Thomas the 'res significata' and the 'res concepta' are never sufficient; but the act of *signifying* extends beyond the comprehensible element of the concept. See E. Schillebeeckx, 'Het niet-begrippelijk kenmoment in onze Godskennis volgens Thomas van Aquino', in *Openbaring en Theologie* (Theologische Peilingen, n. 1) (Bilthoven 1966²), especially 207–13 and 215–32. Let it be said that Thomas knows nothing of the implications of what we moderns call the 'father-symbol' and 'symbol-theory' in general.

61. P. F. Strawson, *Individuals. An essay in descriptive metaphysics* (London 1959).

62. l.c., 10.

63. On the concept of 'person': l.c., especially 87–116.

64. See e.g., Fr. Erdin, *Das Wort Hypostasis. Seine bedeutungsgeschichtliche Entwicklung in der altchristlichen Literatur bis zum Abschlusz der trinitarischen Auseinandersetzungen* (Freiburg 1939); G. Kretschmar, *Studien zur frühchristlichen Trinitätstheologie* (Tübingen 1956); A. Malet, *Personne et amour dans la théologie trinitaire de saint Thomas d'Aquin* (Paris 1956); J. Schneider, *Die Lehre vom Dreieinigen Gott in der Schule des Petrus Lombardus* (Munich 1961); J. Jolivet, *Godescale d'Orbais et la Trinité. La méthode de la théologie à l'époque carolingienne* (Paris 1958); M. Bergeron, *La structure du concept latin de personne* (Ottawa-Paris 1932); M. Marshall, 'Boëthius' definition of person and medieval understanding of the Roman theatre', in *Speculum* 25 (1950), 471–82; I. Backes, *Die Christologie des hl. Thomas von Aquin und die Griechischen Kirchenväter* (Paderborn 1931); V. Schurr, *Die Trinitätslehre des Boëthius im Lichte der skytischen Kontroversen* (Paderborn 1935), especially 108–232.

65. *Opuscula sacra*, tract. 5, *Opusculum contra Eutychen et Nestorium*, 2: 'Reperta

personae est igitur definitio: persona est naturae rationalis individua substantia' (PL 64, 1343).

66. *De trinitate*, 4: 'intellectualis naturae incommunicabilis existentia' (PL 196, especially 944-5).

67. *Contra acephalos disputatio* (PL 67, 1195-6; 1238-41).

68. l.c. (PL 67, 1239).

69. In particular *Quaest. Disp. de potentia*, q. 9, a. 4. The three characteristics of 'being a person': (a) 'substantia completa', (b) 'per se subsistens', (c) 'separatim ab aliis' (see especially *In III Sent.* d. 5, q. 1, a. 3). What it amounts to for Thomas is a threefold incommunicability (see also: *Summa Theologiae*, III, q. 2, a. 2c and ad 1, ad 2, ad 3; I, 29, a. 4).

70. L. Seiller, *L'Activité humaine du Christ selon Duns Scot* (Paris 1944).

71. 'Process philosophy' is based on principles enunciated by two American philosophers (of religion): Alfred N. Whitehead and Charles Hartshorne. See especially A. Whitehead, *Process and Reality* (New York 1929); *Religion in the Making* (New York 1926); Ch. Hartshorne, *The Divine Reality. A social conception of God* (New Haven 1964²) (1948); see also the celebratory collection: *Process and Divinity. The Hartshorne Festschrift* (W. Reese and E. Freeman eds) (La Salle (Illinois) 1964); further: Eul. R. Baltazar, *God within Process* (New York-London 1970). Theologians who have elaborated a 'process theology' are, in particular: Norman Pittenger, *Process Thought and Christian Faith* (New York-London 1968); *Christology Reconsidered* (London 1970), and *'The Last Things' in a Process Perspective* (London 1970) (in which is elaborated a completely intramundane eschatology), and to some extent Sch. Ogden, *The Reality of God and other essays* (London 1967³) (1963).

72. M. Buber, *Werke*, vol. 3 (Munich 1963), 71.

73. K. Derksen, 'Vertellend geloven', in *Reliëf* 41 (1973), 230-44. See literature: Part One, Section One, note 14.

# Technical Information

## A. EXPLANATION OF SOME TECHNICAL AND UNFAMILIAR TERMS

*Note*. – This list contains just a few technical terms presently used in exegesis, theology or general literary studies, not dealt with – or insufficiently dealt with – elsewhere. Not included are notions (like 'son of man', 'apocalypticism') expressly and amply examined in the book itself. What the list does include, for the reader's convenience, are technical or unfamiliar terms which are explained on their first appearance in the book but then recur throughout it without any further explanation being given. For some concepts which among exegetes are taken for granted (for instance, *Formgeschichte*, semiotic analysis) a lengthier account was called for in this vocabulary because trying to explain them within the text of the book would obscure the drift of the narrative unnecessarily, while on the other hand one cannot assume that they are well known.

Aeon: 738
Aporia: 738
Anamnesis: 738
An-hypostasis (see: Hypostasis).
Apocryphal: 738
Aretalogy: 739
Articulation (of belief): 740
Canonical: 740
Chasidism, Chasidic: 740
Christological: 740
Cipher (chiffre): 741
Commonplace (see: Topical/topos).
Deutero- and Trito-Isaianic: 741
Deuteronomistic: 741
Disclosure and disclosure experience: 742
En-hypostasis (see: Hypostasis).
Epiphany (and epiphanous): 742
Eschatological: 742
Etiological story: 743
Experiential (and intellective) horizon: 743
Form Criticism (see: *Formgeschichte*).
*Formgeschichte*: 744
Gnosis (gnostic and gnosticism): 744

Hermeneusis and hermeneutics: 745
Homology: 745
Hypostasis: 745
Intellective horizon (see: Experiential).
Interpretation, matter for (= interpretandum) and interpretation (= interpretament): 746
Intertestamentary literature (see: Apocryphal).
Kerygma(tic): 746
Kyrial: 747
Linguistic signals: 747
Memoria Jesu (see: Anamnesis).
Metanoia: 747
Ontological: 747
Orthopraxis: 747
Paradigm: 747
Paraenesis (paraenetic): 748
Performative utterance: 748
Pre-existence and pro-existence: 748
Prolegomenon: 749
Pseudepigrapha (see: Apocryphal).
*Redaktionsgeschichte*: 749

### Aeon

From the Greek *aiôn*: a time, life-time, period of time; hence: the world's (allotted) span, as that of the whole of mundane history; finally, also: eternity. In this book the word occurs only in a context of apocalypticism: 'old' and 'new aeon'. The 'old aeon' is the period of our history seen as a history marked by suffering; the 'new aeon' is the time of universal well-being free from misery and iniquity; this is understood as a post-mundane perpetuity, but also and more especially as an indefinite period of well-being on earth after the sudden intervention of God, who will bring about 'the transformation of the ages' (see also: → Eschatological).

### Aporia

From the Greek *aporia* (*a-poros* means 'no exit', 'no thoroughfare': in fact, a blind alley, a dead end). We may resolve a difficulty, arising out of a particular way of posing a problem, in such a way that a further difficulty emerges, and within the framework of the problems thus formulated we eventually argue ourselves to a standstill; that is, from within the system itself there is no longer a way out. We are then obliged to formulate, articulate the original problem quite differently, in order to escape from the *aporia*.

### Anamnesis

From the Greek for: 'recollection', 'memory' (*anamnèsis*). This strange word is used in this book only when a 'recollection of Jesus' (*memoria Jesu*) does not have a purely historical reference but *qua* historical concern is subsumed within an experience, prompted by and affirming faith, of the risen and living Lord.

### Apocryphal

*Apokruphon* means 'concealed'. The official (early) Church called those writings apocryphal which for the public Church were not 'officially' or 'openly' acknowledged but were, so to speak, 'hidden': that is, had no importance as setting a standard for faith and on that account were not incorporated in the canonical holy scriptures, in spite of their religious (Jewish or Christian) content. In particular we speak of apocryphal 'gospels' (e.g., Gospel of Thomas, Gospel of Peter, etc.), 'Acts of the apostles' (e.g.,

*Acta Thomae*, etc.), and then also Jewish or Christian apocalypses which are not canonical, unlike our four gospels, (Luke's) 'Acts of the Apostles' and the Apocalypse or New Testament 'Book of Revelation'. As regards the Old Testament, Catholics and Protestants clearly differ in official appreciation of certain books, specifically, the Book of Wisdom, the first two books of Maccabees, Sirach (Ecclesiasticus), Baruch, Tobit, Judith and, lastly, some Greek fragments in Esther and Daniel. Since the sixteenth century these parts of the Bible have been referred to by Catholics as 'deutero-canonical' books (canonical but secondary), because they have not been regarded by all Christian churches from the beginning as canonical; principally they were books revered by Greek-speaking Jews, but not held by Hebrew- or Aramaic-speaking Jews to belong to the Jewish canon. Catholics also regard these books as canonical, whereas Protestants call them apocryphal. 'Apocryphal' describes those particular parts of the Bible, called by Catholics canonical, which are regarded by Protestants as non-canonical (and thus uninspired), while the latter give the name of 'pseudepigrapha' to those (Jewish or Christian) works which Catholics call 'apocrypha' (see further: Intertestamentary literature). Hence the shifting meaning of the term 'apocryphal', according to whether it is used by Catholics or Protestants, because the latter also regard the Catholic, so-called 'deutero-canonical' books as 'pseudepigrapha', that is, as apocryphal: falling outside the 'canonical Bible'. Hence, too, a certain confessional difference in what we call 'intertestamentary literature', that is, the extra-canonical literature, of Jewish or even of Christian inspiration, of the period as it were 'between' (or concomitant with) the canonical, recent 'Old Testament' and the 'New Testament' literature. After a certain hesitation regarding the canonicity of some Christian literature (the Letter to the Hebrews, 2 Peter, 2 John, 3 John, James, Jude and the Book of Revelation), this New Testament literature is now generally accepted as canonical by Protestants also (along with the Catholics). In 'purely critical' study of the ancient Jewish and Christian literature we make no distinction between canonical books regarded by the Jewish and Christian faiths as 'inspired by God' and the contemporary 'uninspired' Jewish and Christian literature.

*Aretalogy*

This is fully dealt with in the text. In brief compass, therefore: the Greek word *aretè* means virtue, wisdom and heroic valour, strength. 'Aretalogy' is a sort of pagan equivalent of Christian hagiography and the lives of the martyrs, in which are celebrated – usually with a degree of exaggeration – with reverence and enthusiasm the admirable lives of wise or brave individuals. Aretalogy, then, is a literary genre in which the lives of these people are described to edify the rest of us. Their relevance for us is expressed through their final 'elevation' (exaltation) to be among the gods (from whom they came) and because in the literary genre of 'manifestations' (after their death) they are enabled in person to explain the essential significance of their lives.

*Articulation (of belief)*

'Articulation' is the result of a → thematizing: that is to say, it is the explicit expression, in a properly considered formulation, of what to begin with was substantially given in a (faith-motivated) experience, albeit to some extent so far not articulated or enunciated. At the same time, however, there enters into the idea of 'articulating' something the Latin word *artus*, that is, 'joint'. Hence the medieval expression *articulus fidei* or article of faith, in the sense of a cardinal (*cardo:* hinge) junctural element. Bringing a faith-motivated experience to articulation *qua* belief entails formulating a given matter of belief in such a way as to illuminate its relevance and affinity to the message at the heart of the gospel.

*Canonical*

*Kanôn* (Greek) means 'guiding principle, norm'; hence: canonical, that which sets the standard, in the sense of a norm and criterion. In this book it is used only for what is the norm, criterion, guiding principle for the authenticity or proper direction of the Christian faith: namely, the canonical writings of the Old and New Testaments. Those early Christian documents are canonical which were acknowledged by the Christian churches as the official expression of their common faith and were officially endorsed as such by the church leaders; as such they are to be distinguished from Jewish and early Christian literature of the same period, from apocryphal and heretical literature. 'Pre-canonical' means (apropos of the New Testament): the Christian interpretations of Jesus which were in circulation (orally or perhaps in writing) even before the canonical writings of the New Testament had seen the light of day; thence it was that those canonical writings drew their material, handing on, correcting and synthesizing these traditions, especially in the context of faith in Jesus' death and resurrection.

*Chasidism, Chasidic*

We mean by this not the similarly named medieval Jewish school of spirituality but a particular form and expression of piety in the course taken by ancient Judaism from the time of the Maccabean struggle against the imposition of Greek culture on Jewish life. 'Chasidim' (= pious ones) in the technical sense emerged from an amalgam of diverse, already existing heterogeneous groups that occurred in the period after the Book of Sirach; they form an eschatologically orientated, 'radical change' movement, inspired by the Deuteronomistic view of history and sapiential ideas. In the middle of the second century BC the Chasidic movement disintegrated, giving rise then to both Essenes and Pharisees. 'Chasidism' was a lively tradition in Jesus' time.

*Christological*

This means, in the book: identifying Jesus of Nazareth as someone who on behalf of God brings definitive and decisive salvation to men. Further to expatiate upon and develop this identification, by thematizing it, and through examining its implications, is thus 'to be doing Christology'. Christology therefore is a reflection, at one remove and in a context of faith, on the historical phenomenon of Jesus of Nazareth.

## Cipher (*chiffre*)

This term owes its use here to German and French philosophy, with as its original and basic meaning: 'the key to a cryptogram'. The German philosopher, Karl Jaspers, used it in this sense to express the manner in which the transcendent may be to some extent directly apprehensible *within* metaphysical experience which itself, however, cannot be objectivized: what becomes visible in it cannot be more closely defined; we can only 'point' to it in evocative language. In connection with it (but then – except once – in a more or less adverse sense) 'cipher' is used in this book as a *blank* cipher, a kind of blank sheet which anyone can fill in as he pleases: an unknown X, the content of which one can determine for oneself on the basis of one's own wishes and desires without definitive influence from the thing to be named. 'Cipher' (chiffre) then is associated with *pure* projection.

## Deutero-Isaianic; Trito-Isaianic

In contrast to the older parts of the Old Testament book, Isaiah, which commemorate and reflect (Isa. 1–39) the prophetic activity of the great prophet Isaiah (*c.* 765–700 BC), the chapters Isa. 40 up to and including 55 are most likely by an unknown prophet from the end of the Exile (the 'second' or Deutero-Isaiah), and the chapters Isa. 56 to 66 a prophetic collection which at any rate in substance comes from the period after the Exile (the 'third' or Trito-Isaiah).

## Deuteronomistic

'Deuteronomic' means: relating to the Book of Deuteronomy, the fifth of the so called 'five books' (the Pentateuch). 'Deuteronomistic' on the other hand implies the peculiar spirituality of those units of tradition which (as distinct from the Yahwistic, Elohist and priestly traditions) are to be found in the Book of Deuteronomy, as well as in Joshua, Judges, Samuel and the Kings and have also influenced various pieces of tradition in later Jewish literature. The end of the Northern kingdom and more especially of the Southern kingdom (in 587) marks the beginning of the Deuteronomistic interpretation of history. God cherishes his people; but if they are disloyal, the curse of which Deuteronomy speaks will be visited upon them. Those who conveyed this tradition were the Levites from the countryside of the Northern kingdom, who after the fall of that kingdom came (with their 'collections') to Jerusalem, living there in a state of conflict with the Jerusalem priests; there, however, they became the 'theological force' of which the inspiration was distilled and deposited in the 'Deuteronomistic tradition': 'Deuteronomistic' refers to the 'second edition' of the Book of Deuteronomy (in the period of Josiah's restoration). In it the Deuteronomistic interpretation of history is completed from an insight into the Babylonian exile and from sapiential ideas. The → Chasidic movement in particular was inspired by this Deuteronomistic idea of history.

### Disclosure and disclosure experience

The language of faith or talking in religious terms is grounded in an experience of a special sort. That contains an empirical basis: the things we experience are accessible to all, but in them some experience (whether suddenly or gradually) a deeper dimension which in itself is not to be objectivized and yet really does disclose itself through this empirical (or historical) datum of experience: there is more to the phenomenon, or more within it, than what constitutes public experience or is simply empirical or just flatly descriptive. Someone's friendly glance can suddenly open up for us a whole new world. That is a 'disclosure' which is not purely subjective. Thus in registrable facts a deeper reality unfolds, through which the person who undergoes this disclosure experience at the same time comes to himself. That is why a 'disclosure' experience is not an objectivizing perception while it none the less springs from an objective appeal; furthermore, it has a catalysing effect, whereby the 'disclosure' claims the whole person undergoing it (self-disclosure). What is revealed in this way cannot be pinpointed in objectivizing language, but can only be verbalized in some evocative fashion; for that reason we employ not *descriptive* language but an evocative 'language of faith' so as in some measure to render the substance and meaning of the experience open and comprehensible to others, as an invitation to share experience of the same thing. This is not to deny that there may also be false, illusory disclosure experiences.

### Epiphany (epiphaneia); epiphanous

In this book 'epiphany' – being made public – is always used for God's becoming visible ('epiphanous' or transparent) in the man Jesus: in his acts (e.g., his miracles), in his death, in the life of the Christian community, in what we call 'Jesus' appearances', etc. 'Epiphany' points to the visible presence, here and now, of God in the activity and ministry of the man Jesus. 'Epiphany Christology' speaks in 'revelational terms' about the salvation imparted by God and manifest in Jesus.

### Eschatological

According to Van Dale: 'doctrine concerning the last things', that is: 'everything taught about the lot of human beings after death'. This definition is certainly basic but, theologically speaking, inadequate. *Eschata* means 'last things, extremities'; everything that has to do with the ultimate, deepest but therefore final meaning of human life is called 'eschatological'; therefore not just the *post-mundane* but also whatever concerns the *definitive* meaning of life as well as the 'last days', the end of the age – and indeed as the time of salvation (leaving open the question of whether this is 'the end of history' or is a historically indeterminate, extensive time of well-being). The context must each time provide the intended nuance, although the emphasis always lies on the aspect of 'what is definitely decisive', what will become publicly evident only 'in the end' and after death, but is already at issue in the present and is being decided in it.

## Etiological story

'Etiological' comes from Greek discourse (logos) regarding the *aitia* (cause, ground) of things. 'Ground', like *arché*, has to do with 'beginning' (= principle) as well as with 'beginning' (= start), especially on the ancient (classical) presupposition that the inception ('in the beginning') as it were reveals the *essential being* of things; in each case, therefore, 'a beginning' operates as a model for *universal* experiences of humanity. Thus an 'etiological story' is not meant to provide a reconstruction of facts or events in their historically precise order of occurrence in the past; its purpose is rather to afford an insight into the nature and internal structure of particular experiences in the present.

## Experiential (and intellective) horizon

Just as in everyday language we speak of a 'horizon' beyond which we cannot see anything, but within which we become aware of visible things, so we speak – in what is admittedly a figurative and yet very real sort of language – about a horizon *within which* we *experience* and, by interpreting, *understand* things (persons, affairs, events) – and in such a way that we are unable to look over and beyond this horizon, can experience and understand nothing outside it. In fact this experiential and intellective horizon embraces the whole historical course of events within which we stand and which has made us what we are as creatures orientated notwithstanding towards the future. Our horizon of experience is therefore historical and social. But (according to a certain philosophical and, more especially, Christian insight) it is backed by a more profound (ontological) experiential horizon which spans the dimension of time (present, past and future). Thanks to this depth-element our experiential horizon is not 'closed' but 'open', ultimately open to the point of the mystery of God; nothing of what we call reality falls completely outside it. In our day-to-day experiences and in our ordinary thinking the historical and social (even ontological) horizon of our experience goes unnoticed, but at an unconscious level it certainly comes into play, colouring all our judgements and utterances. Even this horizon, however, may to a certain albeit limited extent be thematized (also hermeneutically). (See for a more detailed specification: Part Four of this book, pp. 576–8.)

## Formgeschichte

This (literally: Form-history) is a method used in particular by German exegetes. It starts from the postulate (which by now can fairly be called a scientific fact) that the gospels are formed out of small, already existing but separate units (broadly speaking, the pericopes in our gospels): an account of a miracle, of a saying of Jesus and so forth. These have already – at a pre-canonical stage – been combined according to certain genres, listed as logia or sayings of Jesus, stories, miracles, paradigms, etc. An important point here is that the gospels, in assembling and passing on these traditions, do so with a particular interest in view – that of confessing the Christ (thus representing from within the interest of the Church). In the first instance, therefore, the gospels are expressions of the Church's faith in Jesus, confessed as the Christ. The older practitioners of this *Formgeschichte* method argued with some prejudice that the Church was itself the *ground* out of which these pericopes directly grew (that is, they have their *Sitz im Leben* in catechetic, liturgical, apologetic and other needs of the Church itself); thus they are creations of the Church. This partial approach quite rightly came up against a lot of opposition, because the result was to reduce the bond connecting Christian belief (*kerygma*) with the historical reality of Jesus of Nazareth to a very flimsy thread; thus the historical grounding of the Christian faith in Jesus of Nazareth became problematical. So the more recent exponents of *Formgeschichte* without denying the *Sitz im Leben* of the pericopes-tradition within the Church, have emphasized more the fact that within this updating and accommodation on the Church's part the (ancient-) historical concern with the earthly Jesus is clearly operative and that on the basis of linguistic signals in the text itself it is possible to point to the evangelists' awareness of the distance between 'recollection of Jesus' and 'updating' or contemporary adaptation by the Church. With the aid of *Formgeschichte* our aim is, among other things, to penetrate to the earliest layer of the pre-canonical tradition, in order thus to open the way to Jesus of Nazareth. Because the exponents of *Formgeschichte* often draw from it conclusions as to the *chronology* of diverse traditions, where these are often confronted with serious objections, Anglo-Saxon scholars in particular prefer to speak of 'Form-criticism' rather than of 'Form-history'. See also: *Redaktionsgeschichte* and *Traditionsgeschichte*.

### Gnosis *(gnostic and gnosticism)*

*Gnôsis* (Greek) means 'knowledge'. Gnosis or gnosticism in the second century AD was a philosophico-religious movement of an eclectic sort, but still within a clearly religious-cum-philosophical approach to life. The basic idea was that man has within him, specifically within his soul, a divine spark which has slipped down into matter and on being released must re-ascend into its divine source. This deliverance or ascent comes about through a messenger (having the semblance of a human being), who mediates divine knowledge. A central place is attributed to knowledge, therefore, as the means of salvation – knowledge in the form of a special revelatory knowledge, imparted via tradition and initiation. Knowledge is salvation. When we say in this book that Christianity is not a gnosis, this means that the Christian faith must not be reduced to a doctrine or simply to 'orthodoxy'. Since gnosis arose from a general trend towards interiorization and ascetic religious sensibility, towards a 'flight from the world', we do right to speak also of a 'pre-gnosis'. This pre-gnosis is something neither purely within Judaism nor purely internal to Christianity nor yet an oriental version of Christianity, but a general phenomenon, typical of late antiquity, in which the whole culture was involved. Mainly because there is some sort of connection between late Jewish wisdom literature and the genuine gnosticism of a later time, there is no end to the discussion about whether gnostic ideas are or are not present in the New Testament, according to whether one derives gnosticism from Judaism, regards it as an oriental syncretism or a Hellenistic philosophy of life, or as a heretical movement within Christianity in the second century. Historians nowadays are more and more inclined to talk about a universal gnostic proclivity (pre-gnosis) of the entire culture with the rise of Christianity. The French and the Anglo-Saxons draw a distinction, therefore, between 'gnosis' and 'gnosticism', both of which however they characterize as 'gnostic'. Others speak of 'pre-gnosis' and 'gnosis', insisting that the former should not be read too much in the light of the latter, which updates and accommodates older material to second-century gnosticism. Many ideas from apocalypticism and Platonism recur in gnosticism, in which they then, and only then, acquire their really gnostic import. Concepts in themselves (e.g., *plêroma*) do not as such tell us anything about what if anything their 'gnostic' meaning might be.

### Hermeneutics (*hermeneusis, hermeneutic*)

Hermeneusis is 'explanation'; hermeneutics is 'the science of explanation', which examines the prior factors necessary to achieving a hermeneusis or explanation (for instance, understanding of the Bible). This study is necessary because of the ever-growing experiential and intellective horizon of our experiences, our thinking and our ways of verbally expressing these. See also: Updating.

### Homology

This means: credal affirmation, confession of belief; *homologein*, 'to confess' (belief), is not materially to be differentiated from *pistis*, faith. We confess with the lips, we believe with the heart (Rom. 10:9–10). A homology or affirmation of belief occurs either in the form of an acclamation (Jesus the Lord!) or in that of a confessional declaration of faith, centred upon God's action in Jesus (e.g., Gal. 8:11; 2 Cor. 4:14; 1 Thess. 4:14).

### Hypostasis (*hypostasizing; an-hypostasis and en-hypostasis*)

*Hypostasis* is the Greek word for 'that which supports and props up' or, in a figurative sense, for 'something substantial' (substantial nourishment; a substantial reading). In a philosophical usage it acquired the meaning of a 'person' as a complete, independent, self-subsistent existence.

'To hypostasize' therefore is to ascribe or confer independent or substantive existence, in this sense: that of a merely functional characterization of something or somebody we make what is an entity in itself.

Further to this, in Christology we speak of *an-hypostasis* and *en-hypostasis*. An-hypostasis (*an* = 'non-', or 'not') indicates a condition from which 'being-a-human-person' is absent; it is implied that Jesus does indeed have a human nature and (in that sense) is a human being, but that his being-*qua*-person is constituted by the divine person, with the result that Christ is not a human person. This at any rate suggests that Christ is not a human being 'complete and unabridged'.

En-hypostasis (*en* = 'in') signifies (on the presumption of *an*-hypostasis) that the human non-personal nature is nevertheless personalized by the divine person. The an-hypostasis is in that case the consequence of the en-hypostasis in the divine Word. In current Christology an attempt is made (in diverse ways) to explain the en-hypostasis without an-hypostasis: that is, Jesus suffers no deprivation of human *personal* being and yet is one with the Son of God.

### *Interpretation, matter for (= interpretandum), and interpretation (= interpretament)*

An interpretandum is 'what has to be interpreted' – thus what is only rendered intelligible in an interpretation. This latter (the interpretation) may also be described as the 'interpretament'. But sometimes the term 'interpretament' is used in the sense of 'a mere interpretament'; then it signifies not an interpretation (e.g., faith in the resurrection) of one and the same interpretandum envisaged by all (e.g., the reality of Jesus' resurrection), but of a quite other interpretandum (e.g., Jesus' earthly life and death). In the one case belief in the resurrection is the interpretative understanding of an in itself inaccessible, post-Easter real event, in the latter case, on the other hand, it is an interpretative understanding of the pre-Easter event of Jesus' life and death.

### *Kerygma (kerygmatic)*

*Kerygma* means literally the message which a herald proclaims at the top of his voice. A 'kerygmatic' utterance about Jesus of Nazareth is a Christological pronouncement in which Jesus is confessed and proclaimed as the one in whom is experienced salvation, final good of a decisive and definitive kind. The word *kerygma* (see also: *Formgeschichte*) has acquired a favourable or pejorative resonance in theology, according to whether this confession of Christ on the Church's part (*kerygma*) is or is not considered to be grounded in the reality of the earthly Jesus. The standpoint occupied by the author in this book is that the Christ-*kerygma* is a faith-motivated profession and proclamatory interpretation (by the community of faith) of what actually did occur in the earthly Jesus (his person, his message and mode of life), while a *kerygma* which in no single respect could draw substance and support from the earthly Jesus is more of an ideology and should be described as a mystification or, if it comes to that, a theologoumenon. Here *kerygma* theologians are so called because their point of departure is the Church's credal affirmation of Christ, so that they either deny the theological significance of the earthly Jesus or minimize it.

## Kyrial

Adjective from *Kyrios*, the Lord; literally thus: 'Lord-ly'; it refers to Jesus' 'being the Lord', to his exaltation and saving power.

## Linguistic signals

This is a term from semiotic, structural textual analysis. It means that, embedded within the text itself, there are tokens and signals, signposts, telling the reader how the text requires to be understood. They make it clear to us that we are to understand a given text as, for example, poetic and non-historical, or as a novel, a didactic exercise in moralizing, a historical narrative or a religious interpretation of human experiences, and so forth.

## Metanoia

This means repentance and conversion in the sense of making a right-about turn. In a context of faith in God it entails radical self-criticism. *Metanoia* is the consequence and implication of the coming of God's kingdom.

## Ontological

This is discourse or speech about (*logos*) what something – a person, matter, event – is according to its proper and real being (*on, ontos*). In this book the (otherwise exceptional) use of this word is applied in the sense of what is expressing something about the actuality with which I am presented, in accordance with its real nature or being, not constituted by me and yet effectively limiting me.

## Orthopraxis

Literally 'right action'. The constant meaning of orthopraxis in this book is action or conduct consonant with the standard or 'directives' of the kingdom of God (criteria and directives examined in this book).

## Paradigm

From the Greek *para-* and *deigma*: that is, a (prior) example as opposed to a reproduction or copy; something exemplary, therefore. Particularly in Greek philosophy the word acquired a special meaning: the terrestrial is only a reflection of the true reality, present in the celestial spheres; and so the latter is the 'paradigm', primal image, norm and criterion in accordance with which our earthly life should be formed. When Jesus is called the paradigm of true humanity, this means that Jesus has lived out in advance, before us, what we have to bring about, in creative fidelity and in circumstances different from those he himself knew. In that, therefore, he is our norm, criterion, orientation and inspiration. It does not however imply that the complete significance of Jesus for us is exhausted by his paradigmatic character.

### Paraenesis (paraenetic)

From the Greek *parainesis*. It is an exegetical concept, denoting in biblical pericopes that literary genre which includes various admonitions, encouragement, comfort, or the call to a certain kind of conduct answering to the demands of God's lordship. Thus paraenesis has to do with ethical guidelines, which in the New Testament articulate what at that time were the consequences for human behaviour of faith in Christ. So it is common in paraenesis for an already existing ethic – not itself biblical but applicable in a biblical setting – to be adopted and integrated *in Christo*. Such norms have in themselves no permanent validity, therefore.

### Performative utterance

This is a term from linguistic analysis. Its function is to make the point that language is not always *descriptive* speech. There are utterances which in no sense describe anything, but for instance are meant to excite emotions, prescribe a rule of behaviour or influence a person's conduct. This is known as performative speech. One illustrative example of it is the promises undertaken at a marriage ceremony: they are an utterance that *effects* what it *signifies*. Promises, the sacramental word, statements like 'I hereby declare the meeting open', are forms of 'performative utterance'. This so far very general theory has subsequently taken on all sorts of (necessary) distinctions apropos of the 'truth value' of the performative speech – a matter of nicer distinction than was envisaged at first.

### Pre-existence and pro-existence

'Pre-existence' (from: *prae-existentia*) has been from early times in classical Christology the technical term for affirming 'the being from eternity' of Christ as the Son of God: in regard to his being-as-God Christ already existed, prior to his conception and birth, *qua* Son of God. The Second Person of the Trinity became a human being in time (incarnational Christology).

'Pro-existence' on the other hand is a modern neologism, derived primarily from phenomenology. It means 'existing for the other', being-human-for-the-other. It might be rendered as 'shared humanity', being open and ready to serve one's fellow man.

### Prolegomenon

From the Greek *pro-legein* (to say something beforehand). What has to be said at the outset – thus before one gets to one's real subject – is called a 'prolegomenon'. Now in that my ultimate aim is to write a soteriology, that is, to consider what 'Christian redemption' really means, especially in relation to the modern emancipatory liberation movements and to other forms of achieving health and wholeness for man, this whole book could be regarded as a prolegomenon thereto. In a wider sense (quite apart from any further intentions) I call this book, as a finished article, a prolegomenon because what it deals with is not what is usually described as the whole of Christology, but just its foundations.

## *Redaktionsgeschichte*

This exegetical method in fact represents an even more recent branch of *Formgeschichte*. It sets out, by sorting and separating 'tradition' and 'redaction' (with the help of *Formgeschichte* here), to track down what was the conception, *in toto*, of each redactor (evangelist). After all, the evangelists are not just compilers, bringing together transmitted material and editing it into a single whole; on the contrary, they are also creative authors, each with their own very specific theological vision, *into which* they integrate the pericopes, or collections of pericopes, which they have inherited. Through this editorial process the older traditions acquire new perspectives. The evangelist's theological outlook stands in (at times) critical relation to the theology of the Christian community, the local church to which he belonged. This method of *Redaktionsgeschichte* gives us a better insight into what is distinctive about the Christologies of, respectively, Mark, Matthew, Luke and John.

## *Sapiential*

Literally: 'concerning wisdom'. In this book the term is used of the Jewish wisdom literature, which went through a long course of 'pre-history' and is associated mostly with the name of Solomon. This folk wisdom and 'art of living' as found in Israel (not without an affinity with ancient Eastern, more especially Egyptian and Mesopotamian wisdom) later on came in contact with Greek popular wisdom (primarily in Alexandria, where a great many Jews of the Diaspora lived), and even before Jesus' time had also linked up with Israel's prophetic traditions, so that we can fairly speak of a late Judaistic, prophetic-sapiential tradition. This again coalesces with apocalyptic. The late Judaistic, sapiential tradition, albeit in a Hellenistic atmosphere, was often a truer reflection of Israel's Yahwistic piety than was the established mode of religion at Jerusalem in the time of Jesus.

## *Semiotics (and structural textual analysis)*

'Semiotics' is a specific new branch among the methods used in the systematic study of literature. It is used primarily for the task of elucidating 'mythical stories' and the New Testament narrative. It has links on the one hand with the broader, anthropological structuralism of Cl. Lévi-Strauss, on the other with the reviving concern with 'story-telling cultures' and 'narrative history'.

Semiotics is still a discipline in process of formation, mostly still at the stage of hypothesis, without any obvious cohesion (there are divergent 'semiotics'), and still questing for a theory of its own. Its champions even hold the fact of a non-uniform semiotics to be in some sense necessary to the 'semiotics of the story'. *Sèmeion* is a 'sign'; so we can describe semiotics as a 'theory of signs', but in a very special sense; it is something like a 'psychoanalysis' of texts, in this sense that it refuses to take the superficial, immediately obvious signification of a text as being its real or original meaning. Despite being in a formative stage, the semiotics of the biblical record (especially in France) already has considerable results to its credit, so that the exegete cannot simply ignore it. Semiotics starts from the text as a 'whole' laid concretely before us; its method is, wherever possible, immanent and 'synchronous', confined to the one text, without any 'diachronous' or historical concern, at any rate in the first instance, and so with no interest in the prehistory of a text (which was the fundamental interest of *Formgeschichte*). Semiotics proceeds on the principle that before all other possible, and perhaps still valid, ways of assessing the biblical text, we should first examine the elements within the text ('within the text' means primarily 'intra-textual', that is, within for instance the Marcan gospel taken as a whole, and then 'extra-textual' would mean 'between a number of texts', for example, comparing Mark's with Matthew's; or comparing the New Testament with the apocryphal literature). The semiotic model concentrates on the semantic level (that is, the substance or content of the story) and its narrative structure (the formal structuring of that content in the story). That is the reason for talking about 'structural analysis' (and why semiotics is a particular form of what is known more broadly as 'structuralism'). The narrative structure is inspected for 'guiding rules', codes enabling us to 'de-code' the text. One of the basic principles of this semiotics is that one must not reduce the text to the level of the 'significatum', that is, the reality – whether economic, historical or even kerygmatic and so forth – which is supposed to underlie it. The purpose of semiotics is not to discover something beneath or behind the texts, but to grasp the meaning or point of the texts themselves: their 'sense'. 'Sense', in the structural analysis of the 'semiotics of the story', comprises all types of correlation inside and outside *this* text; thus every feature in a story which refers to another element in the story is sense-disclosing (semiotics as actually practised does not concern itself with the *niveau des signifiés* – what is signified – but with the *niveau des signifiants* – that which does the signifying). Thus the point of it is not to be caught by looking up the meaning of the word employed in a dictionary, but by tracing the correlations in which it functions within the story. Essential to this is the so-called 'anagogic code', that is to say: the text, and nothing else, must itself yield up its sense, and in this process the oppositions – in particular 'semantic axes', such as high-low, light-darkness, death-life, heavy-light, father-son, etc. – have a very pronounced function. So the analysis starts with a certain, rather arbitrary delimitation of a 'narrative-unit' (isotopy) (e.g., the Passion story) and proceeds by way of dissecting its narrative structure. Here deduction plays a major role, on the basis of what is called the 'narrational competence' of mankind; from a large number of texts of story-telling literature we distil a general model of this human capacity to narrate. On that basis some semiologists at any rate distinguish principally four elements in a story: the poetic, the emotive, the conative and the referential. In fact, however, most of them analyse mainly the poetic elements (and indeed in so doing arrive at some suggestive insights) and beyond that they totally neglect the referential elements. For it is undeniable that in the biblical narrative there are to be found (thus within the text *qua* text) linguistic signals with an undoubtedly referential code – one, that is, pointing beyond the text – (which therefore calls for a hermeneutical and not just a structural understanding of the story). Thus the structural and deductive understanding of the Bible leads to a 'transformation' of the biblical text (that is, something that has already been said or recounted one says for oneself yet again); for semiotics knows no 'original' story; each account is *ipso facto* a transformation. (*L'objet n'est pas décrit par la lecture mais se ré-écrit grâce à elle*'. C. Cabrol, a celebrated French semiologist.) My view is that we are justified in saying that a semiotic analysis of the text should precede other ways of elucidating or understanding it via *Formgeschichte*, *Redaktionsgeschichte* and, finally, hermeneutics.

### Soteriology

*Sôtèria* means salvation (well-being) or redemption (release). Soteriology is the doctrine of redemption: the view we take of men's salvation, redemption or deliverance.

### Synoptists (and synoptic)

The meaning here is: 'to be read together'. The three evangelists – Mark, Matthew and Luke – should so to speak be 'read together' and compared the one with the other, because each in his own way presents what is largely the same transmitted material about Jesus (see in the book: the Q tradition). Although the situation in regard to the Johannine gospel is somewhat different, so that it is set over against the synoptic gospels, there is now a slight tendency to break down the 'synoptic gospels' idea and, albeit on distinctive terms, to draw the Johannine gospel into association with them. In this book we use 'synoptic' in the classical sense (of the first three gospels).

### Thematizing

Making explicit, that is, revealing, reflecting and uttering that which is implicitly, actually and as a rule tacitly accepted as given along with our experience. In other words, making something the *theme* of our enquiry and giving it a theoretical formulation is known as 'thematizing'. (Originally the term came from the 'phenomenological' method of Heidegger and more especially of Husserl.)

*Theologoumenon*

In broad terms a 'theologoumenon' means an interpretation having (no more than) a theological value. But this unfamiliar word is used only when it is meant to imply that a theological interpretation (a) is to be distinguished from a commonly recognized interpretation, normative for faith, and (b) is also distinguishable from a historically verifiable affirmation. Thus the locating of Jesus' birth 'in Bethlehem' is not on the one hand an article of faith, nor on the other a historically verifiable fact. It was not historical reminiscences but theological exegesis of Old Testament texts (with an originally quite different drift) that gave occasion for speaking of 'Bethlehem' in connection with Jesus' birth. Whether Jesus was born in Bethlehem or in Nazareth does not affect the Christian faith; it is a 'theologoumenon'. In a theologoumenon, however, this or that article of faith is often thematized.

*Topical, 'topica', topos*

In the art of rhetoric we hear tell of 'topica', that is, 'the skill of finding and marshalling data for an oration or disquisition of a broadly contemplative kind; the teaching of commonplaces or topoi' (Van Dale). In this book 'topos' or 'topica' is used in the sense of 'commonplace', a 'model', in which specific characteristics keep on recurring.

*Traditionsgeschichte*

This term refers to the historical investigation of particular units of tradition, an enquiry which likewise presupposes *Formgeschichte* and *Redaktionsgeschichte*. The Old Testament is no monolithic block; all sorts of 'spiritual strands' are present in it, as for instance the priestly-Levitical, the earlier and later sapiential tradition, the apocalyptical, Chasidic, Deuteronomistic and so on. Very specific milieux are often the vehicles of units of tradition with a definite orientation (though in the long run there is contamination of all these originally independent traditions). The business of examining the background, in the tradition, of the history of biblical concepts like 'messenger', 'wisdom', 'Christ', 'Lord', 'Son', etc. (synchronously as well as diachronously, that is, within a single gospel as well as within the whole New Testament and pre-canonical prehistory and its Old Testament roots) is known as *Traditionsgeschichte*. Placing a biblical concept correctly within the precise unit of tradition where it belongs helps to define more accurately the meaning of these biblical concepts and to mark it off from other meanings which a similar concept has in other units of tradition (with which nevertheless it has later on often been amalgamated), because that is how we can track down the intention peculiar to a tradition, the motive for passing on a given tradition. *Traditionsgeschichte* is also important for the process whereby the New Testament itself came into being: it determines whether a logion of Jesus has been transmitted in the context of the liturgy (e.g., in the 'Last Supper' tradition) or in catechesis or paraenesis, in the miracle tradition, etc. Being integrated in this or that unit of tradition also affects the meaning-content of a biblical concept. In this book we have actually put great store by discovering or following the historical background of tradition as it concerns the Jewish models and key terms relevant to Christology – although doubt very often still hangs over the results of such an enquiry because of the inextricable fusion of so many initially very clear-cut units of tradition.

## Updating (*i.e. contemporary application*)

This is a term in hermeneutics: a particular (e.g., biblical) way of speaking, formulated within a Jewish, Greek or ancient → experiential horizon, is articulated in a new way within our altered, contemporary experience of life and the world – 'updated' – so that what was formerly intended to be its meaning may also come across today. Updating (the task of bringing up to date) amounts therefore to interpretation; but because the old utterance is itself already an interpretation, we might also speak of 're-interpretation' or 'modernizing interpretation'. In it there appears what the past has to say to us here and now. On the other hand 'updating' can also and equally mean putting the gospel message into operation in the present day, having regard to completely new experiences which are in themselves foreign to the Bible. What such updating demands therefore is an interpretation which is *creative* and yet *true to Jesus*.

## Zealots and sicarii or 'brigands'

Older even than the party of the Pharisees and Essenes, there was in ancient Israel a *tradition* of Zealots – more especially in priestly circles. Like Yahweh, 'the jealous God' (Ex. 20:5;34:14), they too were jealous, jealous for Israel, Yahweh's exclusive possession; every occupation of their land by foreign powers was an 'abomination to Yahweh', and so they were passionately bent on Israel's liberation and were even ready to resort to armed resistance. For this reason the religious motive had at the same time essentially political implications. An example of this (conducive to emulation) was Phinehas, son of the priest Eleazar, son of Aaron the priest (fragment of priestly tradition in Num. 25:10–11; Num. 31:6–54). Again during the Maccabean rebellion Mattathias repeatedly calls himself or other combatants 'sticklers for God and the Law': 'Zealots' (see 1 Macc. 2:23–68; 2 Macc. 4:2). The Book of Wisdom describes this spiritual fervour thus: 'The Lord will take his zeal (*quana; zelus*) as his whole armour, and will arm all creation to repel his enemies' (Wis. 5:17). At the time of the Jewish War (AD 66–70/73) there is reference (on the part of the historian Josephus) to 'Zealots', led, among others, by a man who gave himself a new second name, Phinehas – an obvious allusion to the spiritual dedication of the old priestly resistance fighter. Zealots in the New Testament period, therefore, are likely to be found among the Temple priests, who on the one hand came to be opposed to Rome because of the 'defilement of the Temple' and, on the other, to the late-Zadokitic Jewish high priests in Jerusalem who contravened the Law and collaborated with the Romans: they 'were zealous' during that Jewish rebellion for the sanctity of the Temple and the priesthood, in opposition to the Romans. Distinct from these priest-Zealots there were also all kinds of groups which Josephus calls 'brigands' or, using a Roman term, *sicarii* (dagger-wearers). However, Josephus fails to see clearly enough that the *sicarii* too were not simply bands of plundering robbers (which certainly did exist in the wilderness) but (non-priestly) resistance fighters with – like the Zealots – the same sort of religious 'zeal for Yahweh' and against the Romans (perhaps, especially in Galilee, with social motives as well). Then too there flourished in these groups a strongly messianic expectation (a real Jew will once more become king in Yahweh's name); some of these 'gang-leaders' presented themselves as messianic claimants (and were crucified as resistance fighters; others were slaughtered in the course of battle). During the Jewish War these resistance fighters seem to have aligned themselves with the priestly Zealots, thus frequently operating together; but various conflicts led to cross-sections being divided, so that in the heat of the struggle the clear distinction between Zealots and *sicarii* was to some extent obscured. Both groups were actuated by a similar archaic ideology; but they did not really form a single movement. Both Judas the Galilean, who in AD 6 rejected and refused to pay the Roman tax imposed by Quirinius and set out to stop this 'abomination to Yahweh' by way of subversive activities, and also the resistance fighters of, for example, Massada during the Jewish War, are called by Josephus 'brigands' and *sicarii*. That according to the evangelists Jesus was crucified 'between two thieves' is most probably an intimation that these were no ordinary bandits but a pair of resistance fighters (also in view of the historically doubtful story of the resistance fighter 'Jesus Barabbas', who is supposed to have been released).

## B. ABBREVIATIONS

Here follow abbreviations for works repeatedly cited (throughout every section of the book). Other abbreviated *titles* in the *Notes* refer – by means of the covering word in each title – to works mentioned within a like section, at the head of it (the section, chapter or paragraph) in the text itself, or else have been cited in full in a note within the three immediately preceding pages.

| | |
|---|---|
| Berger, *Gesetzesauslegung* | = Kl. Berger, *Die Gesetzesauslegung Jesu. Ihr historischer Hintergrund im Judentum und im Alten Testament*, vol. 1, *Markus und Parallelen* (WMANT, 40), Neukirchen-Vluyn 1972. |
| Berger, *Amen-Worte* | = Lk. Berger, *Die Amen-Worte Jesu. Eine Versuchung zum Problem der legitimation in apokalyptischer Rede* (BZNW, 39), Berlin 1970. |
| Bultmann, *Tradition* | = R. Bultmann, *Die Geschichte der synoptischen Tradition* (FRLANT, N.F. 12), Göttingen |

1970[8] (with supplement).

| | |
|---|---|
| Bultmann, *Theologie* | = R. Bultmann, *Theologie des Neuen Testaments*, Tübingen 1965[5] (I quote from 1958[3]). |
| Conzelmann, *Grundriss* | = H. Conzelmann, *Grundriss der Theologie des Neuen Testaments*, Munich 1968[2]. |
| *Christ, Faith, History* | = *Christ, Faith and History* (ed. by S. Sykes and J. P. Clayton), *Cambridge Studies in Christology*, Cambridge 1972. |
| Cullmann, *Christologie* | = O. Cullmann, *Die Christologie des Neuen Testaments*, Tübingen 1965[3]. |
| Hahn, *Hoheitstitel* | = F. Hahn, *Christologische Hoheitstitel. Ihre Geschichte im frühen Christentum* (FRLANT, 83), Göttingen 1963. |
| Hoffmann, *Q-Studien* | = P. Hoffmann, *Studien zur Theologie der Logienquelle* (Neut. Abh., N.F. 8), Münster 1972. |
| Van Iersel, *Der Sohn* | = B. van Iersel, '*Der Sohn*' *in den synoptischen Jesusworten*, Leyden 1961. |
| Käsemann, *Besinnungen* | = E. Käsemann, *Exegetische Versuche und Besinnungen*, 2 vols, Göttingen 1965[4] (1960) (collected articles). |
| Lührmann, *Q-Redaktion* | = D. Lührmann, *Die Redaktion der Logienquelle* (WMANT, 33), Neukirchen-Vluyn 1969. |
| Robinson-Koester, *Trajectories* | = J. M. Robinson and H. Koester, *Trajectories through early Christianity*, Philadelphia 1971. |
| Roloff, *Das Kerygma* | = J. Roloff, *Das Kerygma und der irdische Jesus*, Göttingen 1970. |
| Schulz, *Q-Quelle* | = S. Schulz, *Q. Die Spruch-Quelle der Evangelisten*, Zürich 1972. |
| Steck, *Gewaltsames Geschick* | = O. H. Steck, *Israel und das gewaltsames Geschick der Propheten* (WMANT, 23), Neukirchen-Vluyn 1967. |
| Strack-Billerbeck | = P. Billerbeck and H. L. Strack, *Kommentar zum Neuen Testament aus Talmud und Midrasch*, 4 vols and two supplementary parts (ed. J. Jeremias with K. Adolph), Munich I–IV, 1965; V, 1956; VI, 1961. |
| Tödt, *Der Menschensohn* | = H.-E. Tödt, *Der Menschensohn in der synoptischen Ueberlieferung*, Gütersloh 1963[2] (1959). |
| Vielhauer, *Aufsätze* | = Ph. Vielhauer, *Aufsätze zum Neuen Testament* (Theologische Bücherei, 31), Munich 1965 (collected articles). |

Weeden, *Mark-traditions*     = Th. J. Weeden, *The Mark-traditions in Conflict*, Philadelphia 1971.

## C. PSEUDEPIGRAPHA (or non-canonical, intertestamentary literature)

J. Becker, *Untersuchungen zur Entstehungsgeschichte der zwölf Patriarchen* (AGSU, 8), Leyden-Cologne 1970.

P. Bogaert, *L'Apocalypse syriaque de Baruch I–II* (Sources chrétiennes, 144), Paris 1969.

R. H. Charles (ed.), *The Greek Versions of the Testaments of the Twelve Patriarchs*, Oxford 1908 (= Darmstadt 1960).

R. H. Charles, *The Book of Enoch*, Oxford 1912.

C. Clemen (ed.), *Assumptio Moysis* (Kleine Texte, 10), Berlin 1904.

J. Flemming and L. Radermacker, *Das Buch Henoch* (GCS, 5), Leipzig 1901.

O. von Gebhardt (ed.), *Psalmoi Salomonis* (TU, XIII–2), Leipzig 1895.

J. Geffcken (ed.), *Die Oracula Sibyllina* (GCS, 8), Leipzig 1902.

M. Hadas, *The Third and Fourth books of Maccabees* (JAL, 12), New York 1953.

E. Hennecke and W. Schneemelcher, *Neutestamentliche Apokryphen*, 2 vols, Tübingen 1964[3].

E. Kautsch (ed.), *Die Apokryphen und Pseudepigraphen des Alten Testaments*, 2 vols, Tübingen 1900 (or Darmstadt 1962).

G. Kish (ed.), Ps.-Philo, *Liber Antiquitatum Biblicarum*, Notre-Dame 1949.

K. Kuhn, *Konkordanz zu den Qumran-Texten*, Göttingen 1960.

G. Vermès, *The Dead Sea Scrolls in English*, Harmondsworth 1962.

B. Violet, *Esra-Apokalypse* (GCS, 18/32), 2 vols, Leipzig 1910, 1924.

## D. SIGLA EMPLOYED (periodicals, dictionaries, series)

| | |
|---|---|
| AGSU | = Archiven zur Geschichte des Spätjudentums und Urchristentums (Leyden-Cologne) |
| ASNT | = Acta Seminariorum Novi Testamenti (of Uppsala) (Lund) |
| AThANT | = Abhandlungen zur Theologie des Alten und Neuen Testaments (Basle-Zürich) |
| BHTh | = Beiträge zur historischen Theologie (Tübingen) |
| Bibl | = Biblica (Rome) |
| BLit | = Bibel und Liturgie (Vienna) |
| BRes | = Biblical Research (Chicago) |
| BuK | = Bibel und Kirche (Stuttgart) |
| BuL | = Bibel und Leben (Düsseldorf) |
| BZ | = Biblische Zeitschrift (Freiburg i. Br.) |
| BZNW | = Beiheft zur 'Zeitschrift für die neutestamentliche Wissenschaft', see ZNW |
| CBQ | = The Catholic Biblical Quarterly (Washington) |
| CollBrugGand | = Collationes Brugenses et Gandavenses (Ghent; Bruges) |

| | | |
|---|---|---|
| Conc | = | Concilium (international theological journal) |
| DBS | = | Dictionnaire de la Bible. Supplément (Paris) |
| EvQ | = | The Evangelical Quarterly (London) |
| EvTh | = | Evangelische Theologie (Munich) |
| ETL | = | Ephemerides Theologicae Lovanienses (Louvain; Gembloux) |
| FRLANT | = | Forschungen zur Religion und Literatur des Alten und Neuen Testaments (Göttingen) |
| GCS | = | Die Griechischen Christlichen Schriftsteller der ersten drei Jahrhunderte (Leipzig) |
| Gul | = | Geist und Leben (Grasz-Würzburg) |
| HThR | = | The Harvard Theological Review (Cambridge, Mass.) |
| IKZ | = | Internationale Katholische Zeitschrift (Frankfurt) |
| Interpretation | = | Interpretation (Richmond, USA) |
| JAL | = | Jewish Apocryphal Literature (New York) |
| JBL | = | Journal of Biblical Literature (Boston) |
| JRel | = | The Journal of Religion (Chicago) |
| JTS | = | The Journal of Theological Studies (London) |
| KuD | = | Kerygma und Dogma (Göttingen) |
| LThK² | = | Lexikon für Theologie und Kirche (Freiburg i.Br.; 2nd ed.) |
| LVie | = | Lumière et Vie (Lyons) |
| Neut. Abh. | = | Neutestamentliche Abhandlungen (Münster) |
| NovT | = | Novum Testamentum (Leyden) |
| NovTSuppl | = | Supplements to NovT |
| NRTh | = | Nouvelle Revue Théologique (Louvain-Tournai) |
| NTD | = | Das Neue Testament Deutsch (Göttingen) |
| NTS | = | New Testament Studies (Cambridge and Washington) |
| NZSTh | = | Neue Zeitschrift für systematische Theologie und Religionsphilosophie (Berlin) |
| OrSyr | = | L'Orient Syrien (Paris) |
| PhJ | = | Philosophisches Jahrbuch der Görres-Gesellschaft (Fulda) |
| RAC | = | Reallexikon für Antike und Christentum (Stuttgart) |
| RB | = | Revue Biblique (Paris-Jerusalem) |
| RechBibl | = | Recherches Bibliques (Bruges) |
| RGG³ | = | Die Religion in Geschichte und Gegenwart (Tübingen, 3rd ed.) |
| RHE | = | Revue d'Histoire ecclésiastique (Louvain) |
| RHPR | = | Revue d'Histoire et de Philosophie religieuse (Strasbourg) |
| RMM | = | Revue de Métaphysique et de Morale (Paris) |
| RQumrân | = | Revue de Qumrân (Paris) |
| RSPT | = | Revue des Sciences philosophiques et théologiques (Paris) |
| RSR | = | Recherches de Science Religieuse (Paris) |
| SBS | = | Stuttgarter Bibel-Studien (Stuttgart) |
| ScotJTh | = | The Scottish Journal of Theology (Edinburgh) |
| StdZ | = | Stimmen der Zeit (Freiburg i.Br.) |
| TCR | = | The Clergy Review |
| ThGl | = | Theologie und Glaube (Paderborn) |

| | | |
|---|---|---|
| ThLZ | = | Theologische Literaturzeitung (Leipzig) |
| ThPQ | = | Theologisch-praktische Quartalschrift (Linz) |
| ThPh | = | Theologie und Philosophie (Freiburg i.Br.) |
| ThQ | = | Theologische Quartalschrift (Tübingen-Stuttgart) |
| ThR | = | Theologische Rundschau (Tübingen) |
| ThS | = | Theological Studies (Woodstock) |
| ThSt | = | Theologische Studien (Utrecht) |
| ThStKr | = | Theologische Studien und Kritiken (Hamburg) |
| ThWAT | = | Theologisches Wörterbuch zum Alten Testament (Stuttgart) |
| ThWNT | = | Theologisches Wörterbuch zum Neuen Testament (Stuttgart) |
| ThZ | = | Theologische Zeitschrift (Basle) |
| TPh | = | Tijdschrift voor Filosofie (Louvain) |
| TrThZ | = | Trierer Theologische Zeitschrift (Trier) |
| TvT | = | Tijdschrift voor Theologie (Nijmegen-Bruges) |
| TU | = | Texte und Untersuchungen zur Geschichte der altchristlichen Literatur (Leipzig-Berlin) |
| UnSQR | = | Union Seminary Quarterly Review (New York) |
| VT | = | Vetus Testamentum (Leyden) |
| VTS | = | Supplements to VT |
| WMANT | = | Wissenschaftliche Monographien zum Alten und Neuen Testament (Neukirchen-Vluyn) |
| WUNT | = | Wissenschaftliche Untersuchungen zum Neuen Testament (Tübingen) |
| ZAW | = | Zeitschrift für die alttestamentliche Wissenschaft (Berlin) |
| ZKTh | = | Zeitschrift für katholische Theologie (Innsbruck) |
| ZNW | = | Zeitschrift für die neutestamentliche Wissenschaft und die Kunde der älteren Kirche (Gieszen) |
| ZRGG | = | Zeitschrift für Religions- und Geistesgeschichte (Marburg) |
| ZThK | = | Zeitschrift für Theologie und Kirche (Tübingen) |
| Zygon | = | Zygon. Journal of religion and science (Chicago) |

## E. BIBLIOGRAPHICAL INDEX OF SUBJECTS

*Note.* The relevant literature is mentioned in the text itself at the start of each section, chapter or paragraph. More detailed literature is also given in the footnotes.

## F. INDEX OF AUTHORS

*Note.* – The references are to the pages in this book where the author in question is mentioned or discussed. Only 'contemporary' authors have been listed. When it comes to *Festschriften* (symposia, etc.), this index includes the authors cited from them (but not the name of the author to whom the Festschrift was dedicated, who in most cases has been included on other grounds). In the case of footnotes (from p. 551) the reference is first to the page, then the note.